The Mind of the Master Class

History and Faith in the Southern Slaveholders' Worldview

The Mind of the Master Class tells of America's greatest historical tragedy. It presents the slaveholders as men and women, a great many of whom were intelligent, honorable, and pious. It asks how people who were admirable in so many ways could have presided over a social system that proved itself an enormity and inflicted horrors on their slaves. The South had formidable proslavery intellectuals who participated fully in transatlantic debates and boldly challenged an ascendant capitalist ("free-labor") society. Blending classical and Christian traditions, they forged a moral and political philosophy designed to sustain conservative principles in history, political economy, social theory, and theology while translating them into political action. Even those who judge their way of life most harshly have much to learn from the probing moral and political reflections on their times – and ours – beginning with the virtues and failings of their own society and culture.

Elizabeth Fox-Genovese is Eléonore Raoul Professor of the Humanities at Emory University, where she was founding director of Women's Studies. She serves on the Governing Council of the National Endowment for the Humanities (2002–2008). In 2003 President George W. Bush honored her with a National Humanities Medal, and the Fellowship of Catholic Scholars honored her with its Cardinal Wright Award. Among her books are: *The Origins of Physiocracy: Economic Revolution and Social Order in Eighteenth-Century France*; *Within the Plantation Household: Black and White Women of the Old South*; and *Feminism without Illusions: A Critique of Individualism*.

Eugene D. Genovese, a retired professor of history, has written, among other books, *Roll, Jordan, Roll: The World the Slaves Made*; *The Slaveholders' Dilemma: Southern Conservative Thought, 1820–1860*; and *A Consuming Fire: The Fall of the Confederacy in the Mind of the White Christian South*.

Fox-Genovese and Genovese serve on the editorial boards of a number of scholarly journals and are co-authors of *Fruits of Merchant Capital: Slavery and Bourgeois Property in the Rise and Expansion of Capitalism*. In 2004 The Intercollegiate Studies Institute presented them jointly with its Gerhard Niemeyer Award for Distinguished Contributions to Scholarship in the Liberal Arts.

Publication of this book has been aided by the generosity of
the Earhart Foundation, the L. J. and Mary C. Skaggs Foundation,
and the Watson–Brown Foundation, Inc.

The Mind of the Master Class

History and Faith in the
Southern Slaveholders' Worldview

ELIZABETH FOX-GENOVESE
EUGENE D. GENOVESE

CAMBRIDGE
UNIVERSITY PRESS

F 213 .F69 2005
BLT1008

CAMBRIDGE UNIVERSITY PRESS
Cambridge, New York, Melbourne, Madrid, Cape Town, Singapore, São Paulo

Cambridge University Press
40 West 20th Street, New York, NY 10011-4211, USA

www.cambridge.org
Information on this title: www.cambridge.org/9780521850650

© Elizabeth Fox-Genovese and Eugene D. Genovese 2005

This publication is in copyright. Subject to statutory exception
and to the provisions of relevant collective licensing agreements,
no reproduction of any part may take place without
the written permission of Cambridge University Press.

First published 2005

Printed in the United States of America

A catalog record for this publication is available from the British Library.

Library of Congress Cataloging in Publication data
Fox-Genovese, Elizabeth, 1941–
The mind of the master class : history and faith in the Southern slaveholders' worldview /
Elizabeth Fox-Genovese, Eugene D. Genovese.
p.   cm.
Includes bibliographical references and index.
ISBN 0-521-85065-7 – ISBN 0-521-61562-3 (pbk.)
1. Slaveholders – Southern States – Social life and customs. 2. Slaveholders – Religious
life – Southern States. 3. Slaveholders – Southern States – Intellectual life. 4.
Slavery – Southern States – Justification. 5. Slavery – Moral and ethical aspects – Southern
States – History. 6. Slavery – Political aspects – Southern States – History. 7. Southern
States – Social life and customs – 1775–1865. 8. Southern States – Religious life and
customs. 9. Southern States – Intellectual life. 10. Southern States – History – Philosophy.
I. Genovese, Eugene D., 1930– II. Title.

F213.F69   2005
306.3′62′0975 – dc22   2005047136

ISBN-13   978-0-521-85065-0 hardback
ISBN-10   0-521-85065-7 hardback

ISBN-13   978-0-521-61562-4 paperback
ISBN-10   0-521-61562-3 paperback

Cambridge University Press has no responsibility for
the persistence or accuracy of URLs for external or
third-party Internet Web sites referred to in this publication
and does not guarantee that any content on such
Web sites is, or will remain, accurate or appropriate.

For Msgr. Richard Lopez,
Catholic Archdiocese of Atlanta

A token of our love and of our appreciation for the immeasurable and
inexpressible difference he has made in our lives

The necessity of rejecting and destroying some things that are beautiful is the deepest curse of existence.

—George Santayana

Contents

Preface

In writing of what Yankees call "the Civil War," what red-blooded Southrons call "the War of Northern Aggression," and what we prefer to call "the War for Southern Independence," we here refer simply to "the War." For Southerners – liberal and conservative, black and white – and for no few Northerners as well, there was, after all, only one war that really mattered. In a few cases, however, we have used "War for Southern Independence" to avoid ambiguity.

Many articles, pamphlets, and books of the period were published anonymously. Where we have identified the author, the name appears in brackets; a question mark indicates that we consider the author in brackets probable. All words in italics were emphasized in the original sources quoted. We use *"sic"* only in rare cases in which it seems indispensable. Thomas Jefferson, John C. Calhoun, and numerous other Southerners and Northerners often misspelled words, omitted apostrophes in possessive nouns, and lapsed from the King's (Queen's) English. We have retained the original punctuation – for example, dashes for commas – except in a few cases. Nineteenth-century Americans used commas freely, and we have dropped some to ensure clarity of meaning.

A few technical terms are defined as follows. *Arminianism*: Man's free will and the resistibility of God's grace. *Arianism*: An ancient doctrine that affirmed the second-order deity of Jesus, attributing to Jesus the Son a nature different from (and inferior to) that of the Father. *Socinianism* (sixteenth century): Jesus a human being with a divine mission – a moral teacher. *Pelagianism*: Denies the doctrine of original sin and proclaims free will; sees Jesus as a moral teacher not as God; sees humanity as intrinsically good; insists that Scripture must conform to reason and that faith is theoretical, whereas moral action is of supreme importance – men can earn salvation by leading good lives and avoiding sin.

We have used some postbellum materials as legitimate sources for the antebellum period. Personal reminiscences written after the War (as well as writings on political theory, theology, and other subjects) must be used with the utmost care, as we have done our best to do. The War compelled drastic revisions in people's thinking, so that thoughts expressed in the 1870s were often far removed from what the authors had thought before the War. We accept postbellum views only to the extent that they clearly represent the essentials of the author's antebellum thought. Thus we accept much of, say, Robert Louis Dabney's *Systematic Theology* (1871) as consistent with his long-held views.

Other materials, which some readers might expect us to have used, we have used little or not at all. Poetry enjoyed a privileged place among Southerners' favorite genres. Men as well as women read – and wrote – large amounts of poetry, not always discriminating between the good and the bad. According to an apocryphal but nonetheless famous anecdote, John C. Calhoun forswore writing poetry when he found himself beginning a poem with, "Whereas ...." Not all aspiring poets were that self-critical, although most erred on the side of flowery sentiment rather than the side of political discourse. Notwithstanding the aspersions cast by hostile Northerners, who harbored their own share of amateur poets, educated Southerners recognized and admired superior poetic talent. Many were steeped in the ancient poets, in Shakespeare and Milton, and in later British and French poets, as well as in the German Romantics, the French Symbolists, and others, including such Northerners as Longfellow. Southerners may not instinctively have seen recent and contemporary poetry as a source of information. But if this explanation is plausible, it is also puzzling. For they held their own most talented poets in high regard, and those poets, notably Henry Timrod, devoted some of their most celebrated work precisely to historical and political questions. In any case, we do take some notice of the impact of Dante, Tasso, Goethe, and a few others on southern historical, philosophical, and religious thought.

Specialists may wish more detailed analyses of certain large themes, which we expect to provide in volumes now in draft. Most notably, we here discuss only briefly the southern slaveholders' critique of capitalism ("free-labor societies") and their projection of a world in which some form of personal servitude would be the ordinary and proper condition of all labor regardless of race. We shall in a more appropriate place treat at length the rise and development of this unique proslavery ideology – unique in that it appeared in no other modern slave society – and demonstrate its widespread acceptance by the clergy as well as secular proslavery theorists and political leaders, including leaders of the yeomanry.

In awe, we thank Jeannette Hopkins, a great editor, for her extraordinary efforts – the more extraordinary since we know she did not always enjoy our interpretations, not to mention our biases.

For helping us to collect materials and for checking references and quotations we are indebted to Laura Crawley, Mary Margaret Johnston-Miller, Christopher Luse, and John Merriman. Alex Shulman's skills kept us sane through assorted computer problems. Peter Carmichael generously shared with us material he culled from southern college publications.

Over many years we presented papers at professional meetings and published articles the substance of which has been woven into this book. A long list of colleagues criticized those papers and helped us to hone our analyses and correct errors. We could not possibly name them all here but want them to know that their efforts have not been forgotten. A number of colleagues read late drafts of this book: Robert Calhoon, Forrest McDonald, David Moltke-Hansen, and Mark

Noll. Others read substantial sections: Thomas Burns, James Oscar Farmer, Louis A. Ferleger, William W. Freehling, Donald Kagan, David Konstan, D. G. Hart, E. Brooks Holifield, Bo Morgan, Robert L. Paquette, Paul Rahe, Jeffrey Burton Russell, and Edwin Yamauchi. We do not want to think about the messes we would be in were it not for the painstaking criticism and insights of all of these critics. We received Michael O'Brien's learned two-volume *Conjectures of Order* after this book was in the hands of our publisher and thus too late to take it into account. Having learned a great deal from Dr. O'Brien's work and from our many discussions – and friendly arguments – over the years, we are very much in his debt.

This volume enjoyed the support of grants from the National Endowment for the Humanities, The National Humanities Center in North Carolina, the Earhart Foundation, the Rockefeller Foundation, and the Guggenheim Foundation. We have also benefited more richly than we can ever acknowledge from the gracious assistance of libraries and librarians throughout the South.

Several portions of this book appeared in preliminary form as articles or pamphlets, and we thank the publishers for granting permission to use the material freely. An early and briefer version of the chapters on the French Revolution and subsequent revolutions appeared as "Political Virtue and the Lessons of the French Revolution: The View from the Slaveholding South," in *Virtue, Corruption, and Self-Interest: Political Values in the Eighteenth Century,* ed. Richard K. Matthews (Lehigh, PA: Lehigh University Press, 1994). For a preliminary version of the chapter on the response to the Middle Ages see "The Southern Slaveholders' View of the Middle Ages," in Bernard Rosenthal and Paul E. Szarmach, eds., *Medievalism in American Culture* (Binghamton, NY: Medieval and Renaissance Texts & Studies, 1989), and a brief version of the chapters on the response to the Middle Ages appeared as "The Chivalric Tradition in the Old South," *Sewanee Review* (2000). Certain sections of chapters appeared in *Southern Cultures*: "Olmsted's Cracker Preacher" (1998), "The Dulcet Tones of Christian Disputation in the Democratic Upcountry" (2002), and "King Solomon's Dilemma – And the Confederacy" (2004); also see "The Gracchi and Their Mother in the Mind of American Slaveholders," *Journal of The Historical Society* (2002). We have, with permission, lifted freely from our articles, *"Slavery Ordained of God": The Southern Slaveholders' View of Biblical History and Modern Politics* (Fortenbaugh Lecture, Gettysburg College, 1985); "The Religious Ideals of Southern Slave Society," *Georgia Historical Quarterly* (1986); "Western Civilization through Slaveholding Eyes: The Social and Historical Thought of Thomas Roderick Dew" (Andrew Mellon Lecture, Tulane University, 1986); "The Divine Sanction of Social Order: Religious Foundations of the Southern Slaveholders' Worldview," *Journal of the American Academy of Religion* (1987); "The Social Thought of the Antebellum Southern Theologians," in W. B. Moore, Jr., and J. F. Tripp, eds., *Looking South: Chapters in the Story of an American Region* (Westport, CT: Greenwood Press, 1989).

Abbreviations

JMM	*Jefferson Monument Magazine*
JPH	*Journal of Presbyterian History*
JSH	*Journal of Southern History*
LCL	Loeb Classical Library (Cambridge, MA, many editions)
LSU	Louisiana State University
MMQR	*Methodist Magazine and Quarterly Review* [also *Methodist Quarterly Review*]
QRMECS	*Quarterly Review of the Methodist Episcopal Church, South*
RM	*Russell's Magazine*
SBN	*The South in the Building of the Nation*, ed. J. A. Chandler, 12 vols. (Richmond, VA, 1909)
SLC	*Southern Lady's Companion*
SLJ	*Southern Literary Journal*
SLM	*Southern Literary Messenger*
SPR	*Southern Presbyterian Review*
SQR	*Southern Quarterly Review*
SR	*Southern Review*
SRCR	*Southern Repertory and College Review* [Emory and Henry College]
SWMR	*Southern and Western Magazine and Review*
TCWVQ	*The Tennessee Civil War Veterans Questionnaires*, ed. Coleen Morse Elliott and Louise Armstrong Moxley, 5 vols. (Easley, SC, 1985)
TSW	*Complete Works of the Reverend Thomas Smyth, D.D.*, ed. J. William Flinn, 10 vols. (Columbia, SC, 1908)
UNC-NCC	University of North Carolina – North Carolina Collection
UNC-SHC	University of North Carolina – Southern Historical Collection
USC	University of South Carolina
UVA	University of Virginia
VLM	*Virginia Literary Museum and Journal of Belles Lettres, Arts, &c.*
VUM	*Virginia University Magazine*
WMQ	*William and Mary Quarterly*

Prologue

> Wherever the main purpose of speech is flattery, there the word becomes corrupted and necessarily so. And instead of genuine communication, there will exist something for which domination is too benign a term; more appropriately we should speak of tyranny, of despotism.
>
> —Josef Pieper[1]

This book is about white Southerners, and it is not about their "whiteness" – whatever that term may mean. It explores the ways in which they reflected on the world they lived in and on the bearing of history and Christian faith on their lives as masters in a slaveholding society. We take the ground that the Lower South and large parts of the Upper constituted not merely a society that accepted slavery as part of its social order but a genuine slave society – that is, a society based upon slave labor. Accordingly, we strive to avoid two errors: the one that has these white Southerners with nothing much on their minds except slavery, the other that denies the pervasive influence of slavery on their widespread interests. We recognize that slaveholders, big and small, generally concentrated their thoughts on religion or politics or literature or mundane matters without fretting over the implications for their lives as slaveholders, and certainly without thinking that they had to defend their ownership of slaves at every turn. But we insist that, whether readily apparent or not, the master–slave relation permeated the lives and thought of all who lived in the society it dominated.

Most of those who figure most prominently in these pages owned slaves, some in large numbers; many more had a direct or indirect interest in slaveholding through family connections or professional and business arrangements. During the first half of the nineteenth century, as today, the richer the family, the better their children's chances of receiving a good education and enjoying the leisure to express thoughts, whether for publication or privately in letters, diaries, and journals. Since slaves produced the crops that afforded the primary source of wealth, the more slaves a family owned, the more highly educated its members were likely to be and the greater their leisure to read and think and write.

---

[1] Joseph Pieper, *Abuse of Language – Abuse of Power,* tr. Lothar Krauth (San Francisco, 1992 [1974]), 30.

The southern states were rural and, by every significant measure, decisively more so than the northern states. They had fewer urban centers, and a much smaller proportion of their population lived in them. Yet more telling was that the number and size of urban centers were growing less rapidly in the South than in the North. While cities and towns were setting the tone and driving the development of northern society, the countryside continued to set the tone for southern towns and cities and to control their development. The South contained fewer miles of railroad in proportion to its size, and its railroads overwhelmingly connected areas of rich agricultural production with centers of export – rather than binding centers of industrial production and centers of population into an ever denser web. The North was also spawning vastly more industrial production than the South. Few historians have denied the rural nature of southern society: some have attributed the distinctive features of southern society exclusively to its persisting rural character, and some have insisted that southern rural society was essentially capitalist. At the margins, these arguments merge, primarily because they both seek to demonstrate that the South should not be viewed as a slave society different in quality, not just in level of economic development, from the North.[2]

Ruling classes enjoy disproportionate opportunities to shape the values and worldview of their societies, although none ever does so completely or unilaterally. Southern slaveholders prized the literate culture of Western Civilization, claiming it as their own. Many were, in fact, deeply conversant with it; others, through lack of interest or time, were less so. But even the most learned and broadly read straddled the worlds of literate and oral culture, remaining hostage in myriad ways to the sensibilities of those – slave and free – less fortunate than they. Our culture's categorical condemnation of slavery has made it easy for ideologues to demonize the slaveholders, even dismissing them, with breathtaking absurdity, as premature Nazis. Yet those who do so fail to recognize that such demonization of the slaveholders trivializes the slaves and nonslaveholding whites by reducing them to objects and implicitly denying their substantial contributions to southern culture.

Today, almost everyone views slavery as an enormity and abolition as a moral and political imperative. Yet as recently as two or three hundred years ago, the overwhelming majority of civilized, decent people would not have agreed: Indeed, they would have found such notions surprising. Before the eighteenth century, and especially before the dramatic revolutions with which it closed, most Europeans would have viewed the principle of free labor as surprising, if not alarming. Slavery, like other forms of unfree labor, had existed throughout history. Neither Judaism, nor Christianity, nor Islam, nor other religions condemned it at the time. The current recognition of the horror and intolerability of slavery represents a rare example of unambiguous moral progress, although whether what is now recognized as wrong

[2] For elaboration of our views on these matters see Elizabeth Fox-Genovese, *Within the Plantation Household: Black and White Women of the Old South* (Chapel Hill, NC, 1988), ch. 1; also, Elizabeth Fox-Genovese and Eugene D. Genovese, *Fruits of Merchant Capital: Slavery and Bourgeois Property in the Rise and Development of Capitalism* (New York, 1983).

was always wrong – wrong in all circumstances and contexts – is a more complex issue than generally acknowledged.

Unsympathetic readers have been known to conclude that our respect for the southern slaveholders means that we agree with their defense of slavery. Other readers, including many who understand that respect for southern slaveholders does not depend upon approbation of slavery, may nonetheless think we view "traditional" societies, including southern slave society, as superior to modern capitalist societies. We do not, although the question transcends the necessity for and desirability of emancipation. The question is especially complex because the slaveholders embraced many features of modernity and progress. Their slaveholding society was enmeshed in the tentacles of the expanding capitalism from which it was born. Similarly, their slaveholding culture and intellectual life were inextricably tied to the most advanced intellectual and philosophical developments of the day. Southerners frequently argued against the more radical implications of modern ideas, but they never refused to engage them.

The tension between tradition and modernity in southern thought invites confusion. For example, many southern intellectuals did condemn capitalism for its wanton disregard of the networks of mutual responsibility that bind the sexes, social classes, members of families, and societies. In this respect, they effectively conflated capitalist social relations with the rise of an increasingly radical bourgeois individualism. But they also acknowledged their own adherence to and respect for many of the principles of individualism, notably its emphasis on individual conscience and moral responsibility. The problem, as they saw it, was to know when and how to call a halt to the seemingly self-revolutionizing momentum of fundamentally beneficial, but potentially destructive, developments. Their attitude toward the Middle Ages makes it impossible to claim that they saw previous epochs as superior to their own. But they did worry that the excesses of their own epoch might prove their undoing, and they did believe that slavery – with all of its wrongs, which many southern intellectuals sorrowfully acknowledged – could provide a hedge against capitalism's most destructive forces, especially its erosion of binding human relations.

Throughout this book, we do our best to distinguish our attitudes from those of the people we are writing about. We never argue that capitalist societies are inferior to traditional societies, much less to southern slaveholding society. We have scant patience with the romanticization of what Karl Marx derisively called "rural idiocy." We have tried to understand the mind-set of people who feared that the advantages of capitalism and individualism were threatening to extract too high a price. Unlike many of the Southerners we write about, we do not believe that capitalism and individualism have been worse than other systems and ideologies; but, like those Southerners, we do believe that they leave much more to be desired than generally admitted.

The ultimate horror of slavery lay not in the extent of its physical abuse but in the extent and depth of the enforced subordination. Some masters did brutally and irresponsibly overwork and abuse their slaves, although possibly nowhere near as many as contemporary detractors routinely claimed. Still, countless masters, often letting their tempers get the better of them, recklessly unleashed a power that could corrupt even those who sincerely strove to behave decently. Fits of temper and acts of cruelty should come as no surprise: What human being with comparable power might not do the same? "Aristotle," C. S. Lewis recalled, "said that some people were only fit to be slaves. I do not contradict him. But I reject slavery because I see no men fit to be masters."[3]

The slaveholding South was born of the very revolutions that declared slavery the antithesis of freedom and an enormity; simultaneously, it was heir to a world that took unfree labor, including slavery, for granted. The transatlantic revolutionary movement of 1789–1848 proposed a new understanding of freedom as the freedom of the individual, but slaveholders, slaves, and nonslaveholding whites all descended from cultures that viewed family, clan, and community as more important than the individual. That is, they viewed the group as the main source of the individual's standing and sense of self. And they were originally rooted in oral cultures that typically rely heavily on the clichés and formulas that members of literate cultures self-consciously seek to avoid. Walter J. Ong, the distinguished literary scholar, noted that the formulas "are necessary for history" because they facilitate the preservation of knowledge, which is then available when needed. Oral cultures depend heavily upon recall and recognition and consequently favor verbosity, repetition, standardization of themes, and narrative, which wraps the knowledge to be preserved and transmitted in tales and songs easy to remember.[4]

Oral cultures establish clear heroes and villains, avoiding difficult cases of moral ambiguity. In these ways and others, they contrast markedly with the literate culture of recent centuries. Modern literate cultures have enthusiastically promoted habits of analysis and irony over those of participation and mimesis, and modern narratives have turned inward, favoring subjectivity over the shared values of the group. The modern narrative tends to present the writer as at odds "with society's presuppositions and values" rather than as united to them. The point is to highlight the antagonism between the goals of the society and those of the individual, who exposes the falsity and hypocrisy of society's codes and values. Postmodern culture has extended this attitude toward the individual's conflict with society to emphasize the individual's conflict with authority – both natural and divine – and especially with history, viewed as a reservoir of oppression and a fetter upon the individual's infinite possibilities for self-invention.[5] North and South shared a commitment to freedom, but the years between the Missouri crisis of 1819–20 and the beginning of the War for Southern Independence resounded with bitter quarrels over its meaning. Few Southerners credited an idea of freedom that included slave emancipation, and even fewer had any use for the emerging campaign for the rights of women. The defense of slavery doubtless propelled Southerners' interest in history, but it neither

---

[3] "Equality," in C. S. Lewis, *Present Concerns* (New York, 1986).
[4] Walter J. Ong, *Interfaces of the Word: Studies in the Evolution of Consciousness and Culture* (Ithaca, NY, 1977), 103.
[5] Ibid., 111.

began nor exhausted it. From the beginnings of settlement, they had demonstrated sensitivity to the historical dimension of their experience and to the balance between the old and new.

Throughout this book, we use "Southerners" to refer to the white people of the South, our primary subject here. We see no point in cluttering sentence after sentence with an unnecessary adjective. Millions of blacks were no less "Southerners" than those whites were. We trust our readers to know as much and to know that we know. Having written elsewhere about the lives and culture of the slaves of the South, we are acutely aware of the deep antagonisms that set them against their masters and their enslavement. Other antagonisms divided slaveholders from nonslaveholders and nonslaveholders from slaves. The South was riddled with tensions and conflicts of interest that set social groups against one another, and always at the forefront were the intersecting lines of slave versus free and black versus white. Although the importance of the antagonisms ought not to be minimized, a narrow focus on them obscures the many cultural assumptions shared by white Southerners of different classes and, within narrower limits, by blacks as well. Members of a rural society, all Southerners preserved inherited traditions derived from their respective societies of origin, and they were more likely than not to agree on general principles that emphasized family, tradition, and inherited concepts of authority, honor, courage, and duty.

Permit us to anticipate two criticisms. First, we do not disguise – and never have disguised – our respect for the slaveholders who constituted the hegemonic master class of the Old South. Nor do we disguise our admiration for much in their character and achievements. We see no point in arguing with those who maintain that any expression of respect and admiration for slaveholders prettifies slavery, slighting its cruelties and abominations, and absolves white slaveholders from collective and personal responsibility for their crimes against black people. The late I. F. Stone was once asked how he, a prominent spokesman for the radical Left with unimpeachable credentials as a lifelong warrior against racism and social injustice, could admire a slaveholder like Thomas Jefferson. If we recall correctly, he replied, "Because history is tragedy, not melodrama."

Second, readers may quarrel with our broad use of "Southerners." Since only a small minority of Southerners owned slaves and since nonslaveholders, to say nothing of slaves, could think for themselves, do we not conflate the master class with the whole of the white southern population? No. Only a nitwit would argue that nonslaveholders let slaveholders – and elite planters at that – do their thinking for them. We speak of the master class as "hegemonic," a term that implies deep social chasms and acute social struggles but also a measure of agreement. Ruling classes, especially in democratic societies in which most white men had ready access to firearms, cannot unilaterally impose their will on others. Even under conditions of a pronounced uneven balance of forces, a ruling class – in order to survive – must to some degree respond to the mores and expectations of those it dominates.

With large exceptions, especially in the Upper South, planters, middling and small slaveholders, and nonslaveholders shared a broadly conservative worldview, however widely they diverged on political and religious specifics. Agreement on some essentials grew the more easily because virtually all members of southern society shared a fundamental attachment to independent rural households anchored in absolute private property. That slaves could not hope to realize the dream goes without saying, but they, too, continued to nourish it; with emancipation, the majority of freedmen chose it over any alternative, even if potentially more lucrative. Thus, when we write of "Southerners," we seek to capture a discernibly wide majority view on the issues under discussion.

The social and intellectual elite of the master class did shape the culture to a considerable degree, and we endeavor to show not the presumed ways in which they forced themselves on the classes below them but rather the extent to which they brought their vision and aspirations into harmony with those they sought to lead. If we draw heavily on the ideas and work of ministers, let it be remembered that they carried principal responsibility for the education of the boys and girls of all classes. Hence, a good many of the books by clergymen as well as laymen that we cite frequently were, in fact, polished versions of college lectures given over many years; they were part of the education of the thousands of young people, not all of them from the elite, who shaped southern politics and ideology: Thomas Roderick Dew on history and political economy; Thomas Cooper and George Tucker on political economy; Nathaniel Beverley Tucker on political theory; Jasper Adams, R. H. Rivers, and William A. Smith on moral philosophy; John Leadley Dagg, Robert Lewis Dabney, and James Henley Thornwell on theology and social questions.

Here, we explore the views of an educated elite, supplemented by those of "ordinary" slaveholding readers. We pay little attention to the ways in which the views of the elite intersected with and were informed by the traditions of others; we assume that influence ran in various directions, reinforcing the ways in which literate Southerners read historical texts. To take but one example, the Roman comedies, beloved of the slaveholding elite, were infused with elements of oral culture, as were the *Iliad* and Shakespeare's plays, among many of their favorites. Were there world enough and time – although there never is – it would be possible to suggest, if not demonstrate, distinct resonances between the oral cultures and traditions that informed the Southerners' favorite works of literature and those that informed the oral culture of African-American slaves and nonslaveholders. Any such exploration would have to begin with the Bible, which emerged from the dawn of literacy and continued to provide a living bridge between oral and literate cultures in the South. But there was more. Gifted novelist and folklorist Zora Neale Hurston underscored the common elements of white and black southern culture, calling the South as a whole "the purest English section of the United States":

What is actually the truth is, that the South, up until the 1930s was a relic of England.... and you find the retention of old English beliefs and customs, songs and ballads and Elizabethan figures of speech. They go for the simile and especially the metaphor. As in the bloom of Elizabethan literature, they love speech for the sake of speech. This is common to white and black. The invective is practiced as a folk art from earliest childhood. You have observed that when a southern Senator or Representative gets the floor, no Yankee can stand up to him so far as compelling language goes .... They did not get it from the Negroes. The Africans coming to America got it from them. If it were African, then why is it not in evidence among all Negroes in the western world? No, the agrarian system stabilized in the South by slavery slowed down change ... and so the tendency to colorful language that characterized Shakespeare and his contemporaries and made possible the beautiful and poetic language of the King James Bible got left over to an extent in the rural South.[6]

Hurston's genius with words captures the centrality of history to Southerners' worldview as well as to their attempts to understand immediate problems and the ultimate prospects for their society. A lot of the past did get "left over" among all elements of southern society, and the abiding presence of the past in the regional culture reinforced and informed Southerners' reading of history. Neither naïve nor uncritical in their admiration for aspects of previous civilizations, they searched the past for a template for what it meant to be human: nobility, honor, courage, piety, loyalty, faithfulness, generosity, and a capacity to survive both victory and defeat with grace whether in public matters or private. And they took for granted that these qualities were compatible with power over others. Thus, as the young wife of a Methodist minister, Fanny Webb Bumpas prayed, "Lord help me to govern my family and my servants aright."

Two traditions preeminently influenced southern thinking on these questions: classical culture and Christianity. From the Greeks and Romans, Southerners, like countless others, drew a profound sense of cyclical time: That which has been will recur; the archetypal forms of human character, the havoc wreaked by human passions, and the configuration of events would all reappear with regularity. Empires rise, decay internally, and fall to superior eternal foes. From Christianity, Southerners drew a vision of time's linearity – of progress toward a better world. Christianity held out the possibility that their society might break the cycle, avoiding decadence and destruction. Living through what struck all concerned as an age of momentous change, Southerners turned to history for instruction in the great affairs of individuals and nations: what changes and what remains the same? In an age of rapid change, how much could people rely on constants of human nature? Is moral progress possible or is humanity bound by the same temptations and character flaws that have permeated all past and present societies? And most pressing, how could the children of revolution, which they knew themselves to be, defend slavery as an omnipresent and justified feature of history? If the dethroning and execution of monarchs, which Southerners overwhelmingly applauded, should be welcomed in the name of "the rights of man and the citizen," then how could the historical precedents for slavery remain immune?

In the end, Southerners were asking, "What is history about? What is it for?" In what measure are human beings the children, grandchildren, and great-grandchildren of those who have gone before and in what measure denizens of a "brave new

---

[6] Zora Neale Hurston to Burroughs Mitchell, Oct. 2, 1947, Charles Scribner's Sons Archives, Author's File 3, Department of Rare Books and Special Collections, Princeton University Libraries, quoted by Hazel V. Carby, "Foreword," in Zora Neale Hurston, *Seraph on the Suwanee* (New York, 1991), vii–xvi.

world"? The accelerating technological changes of the nineteenth century seemed to push all history into a uniform penumbra, but Southerners refused to accept the argument that those changes irrevocably changed the reigning principles of Western culture. They fought, as best they could, to control material progress rather than to become its plaything. However unpalatable the solutions they proposed, the questions they asked remain as compelling now as they were then.

PART ONE

CRADLED IN THE STORMS OF REVOLUTION

Indeed, it may be said, without fear of contradiction, that the leading ideas connected with the progress of the human race have been cradled in the storms of revolutions.
—Bishop R. H. Wilmer of Alabama*

* R. H. Wilmer, *Future Good – The Explanation of Present Reverses: A Sermon Preached at Mobile and Sundry Other Points in the State of Alabama during the Spring of 1864* (Charlotte, NC, 1864) – a spirited defense of secession aimed at fellow Episcopalians.

I

"That Terrible Tragedy"

"... that terrible tragedy, the French Revolution ...."

—James Henry Hammond

On February 1, 1836, James Henry Hammond – freshman congressman from South Carolina – intervened in a rancorous debate in the House of Representatives over antislavery petitions to condemn abolitionism as evidence of an ascendant radicalism that threatened the foundations of social order. The destructive principles initiated by "that terrible tragedy, the French Revolution" were now spreading across Europe and the northern states of the American Union. Slavery, he proclaimed, provided the last bulwark against catastrophe: "Sir, I do firmly believe that domestic slavery regulated as ours is produces the highest toned, the purest, best organization of society that has ever existed on the face of the earth." Radicalism, spreading westward from New England, was undermining the constitutional and political framework of the Republic. Waxing philosophical while mincing no words, Hammond credited southern slavery with ensuring the fragile republican compromise between society and the individual.[1]

For Hammond, a large planter who had edited a pro-nullification newspaper, and for his proslavery countrymen and countrywomen, slavery guaranteed the protection of property rights necessary for the preservation of an ordered and civilized society. In a frequently repeated southern theory, slavery unified capital and labor and thus forestalled class struggle, considered the most dangerous and corrosive of sociopolitical antagonisms. The theory had wide appeal, but it mired slavery's proponents in tension between commitment to social hierarchy and commitment to

---

[1] "Speech on the Justice of Receiving Petitions for the Abolition of Slavery in the District of Columbia," in [Clyde N. Wilson], ed., *Selections from the Letters and Speeches of James H. Hammond* (Spartanburg, SC, 1978), 15–50. Some of the broad themes are sensitively explored in Thomas Horne, "Bourgeois Virtue: Property and Moral Philosophy in America, 1750–1800," *History of Political Thought,* 4 (1983), 317–40.

a material progress that required free labor and industrialization and opened the road to Jacobinism.[2]

During the years before and immediately after the American Revolution, party divided Americans more than section. Within sections, people differed over the appropriate character and sway of the federal government. Divergent attitudes toward slavery were significant but not fundamental. Federalists and Jeffersonian Republicans each had proslavery and antislavery factions. Party antagonisms pitted advocates of commercial expansion against advocates of rural stability as well as advocates of a strong federal government against advocates of greater decentralization. At bottom lay deep differences over the proper relation of the individual to society.[3]

Responses to the onset of the French Revolution proceeded under a cloud of domestic and foreign-policy rivalries. Southern Republicans combined joy at the overthrow of aristocracy with a pro-French policy largely derived from hatred of Britain and opposition to Jay's Treaty. Virginia Federalists – John Marshall, George Washington, Patrick Henry, Light-Horse Harry Lee – became ever more lavish in their adulation of England as they observed the Terror and then Bonaparte. Republicans charged Federalists with anti-French bias, but many pro-French Republicans remained more conservative than appearances suggested. By 1801 important Republicans, too – John Breckenridge of Kentucky and William Crawford and John Clark of Georgia – grew disenchanted with revolutionary France. Conservatives dwelt on the unpleasantness in France in order to discredit American Democrats. The War of 1812 brought another Jeffersonian embrace of France, but it did not last. Public opinion, notably in the Carolinas, loved France less than it hated Britain. Even before the French Revolution, George Washington warned that American hatred of England was leading to unwise adherence to France – a warning implicitly reiterated in his Farewell Address – but much pro-French feeling in the South flowed from practical considerations and misunderstandings. Republicans, hostile to the pro-British Federalists' policy of consolidating power in a strong central government, turned to France in blithe disregard of their Parisian heroes' ultra-consolidationism. Chafing under British economic policies, some southern merchants placed their hopes on direct trade with France. Spokesmen recalled the Bourbon support of America but preferred to dwell on other matters. Had not the revered Lafayette himself become a revolutionary? Had not the moderates of the Gironde, their radical opponents (the Mountain), the five-man Directory, and the great Napoleon Bonaparte emerged in turn to defy the power and insolence of Great Britain?[4]

[2] "Republican" then referred to the Jeffersonian party and should not be confused with the antislavery party that emerged in the 1850s. For an elaboration of this problem in southern thought see Eugene D. Genovese, *The Slaveholders' Dilemma: Freedom and Progress in Southern Conservative Thought, 1820–1860* (Columbia, SC, 1991), esp. ch. 3.

[3] See esp. James Roger Sharp, *American Politics in the Early Republic: The New Nation in Crisis* (New Haven, CT, 1993).

[4] Albert J. Beveridge, *The Life of John Marshall*, 4 vols. (Boston, 1916), 2:ch. 1; on Henry and Lee, see M. E. Bradford, *Against the Barbarians, and Other Reflections on Familiar Themes* (Columbia,

Admiration for France swept America during the 1780s, and French support for the American Revolution earned the Bourbons wild popularity. Portraits of Louis XVI and Marie Antoinette hung in the congressional meeting hall in Philadelphia. Pro-French plays flooded Charleston theaters in the 1790s; Federalists sometimes disrupted them but could not get their own plays produced. Artisans and the gentry rallied to the new cause. As late as 1810, students at the College of South Carolina were singing French songs and quoting Tom Paine on the beauties of the Revolution. Planters, mechanics, and merchants – ardent patriots during the American Revolution – turned to revolutionary France to carry the banner of freedom in the Old World. In Charleston, citizens from the "best families" joined the two Jacobin clubs. In 1793 Charlestonians honored the French National Assembly with a two-day celebration; the governor, judges, and other luminaries carried the French tricolor through the streets, and in the towns of the interior (the upcountry) great celebrations greeted Bastille Day. At the opening of a French theater in 1794, the *South Carolina State Gazette* proclaimed the cause of France "the cause of all nations." Years later, Charles Fraser, Charleston's foremost artist, would remember 1794 as the year "when Sansculottes and their principles had great ascendancy in Charleston – when the tri-colored cockade of France was the great badge of honour, and *Ça Ira!* and the Marseillaise hymn the most popular airs – and 'Vive la republique Francaise!' the universal shout."[5]

During the wave of Francomania, as firm a Federalist as Robert Goodloe Harper, who served as a congressman from South Carolina and then as a senator from Maryland, accepted the Revolution and even swallowed its Jacobins. The pendulum

MO, 1992), 83–99, 114–27. James C. Klotter, *The Breckenridges of Kentucky, 1760–1981* (Frankfort, KY, 1986), ch. 2; Chase C. Mooney, *William H. Crawford, 1772–1834* (Lexington, KY, 1974), 4–5; Matthew Spalding, *A Sacred Union of Citizens: George Washington's Farewell Address and the American Character* (Lanham, MD, 1996), 116, 143; Hugh A. Garland, *The Life of John Randolph of Roanoke,* 2 vols. (New York, 1969 [1859]), 2:113, 116; Robert McColley, *Slavery and Jeffersonian Virginia* (Urbana, IL, 1964), 4, 50–53; Henry H. Simms, *Life of John Taylor: The Story of a Brilliant Leader in the Early Virginia State Rights School* (Richmond, VA, 1932), 126. In Worthington Chauncey Ford, ed., *Writings of John Quincy Adams,* 7 vols. (New York, 1913–17), see J. Q. Adams to John Adams, Apr. 30, 1810 (3:425–7), J. Q. Adams to Abigail Adams, Mar. 30, 1814 (5:26), J. Q. Adams to Louisa Catherine Adams, Oct. 7, 1814 (5:153–5), J. Q. Adams to John Adams, Apr. 24, 1815 (5:308–9). See also Supplementary References: "Responses to the French Revolution."

[5] Charles Fraser, *Reminiscences of Charleston* (Charleston, SC, 1969 [1854]), 35–6, 43; Edward McCrady, *The History of South Carolina in the Revolution, 1775–1780* (New York, 1902), 253; John Harold Wolfe, *Jeffersonian Democracy in South Carolina* (Chapel Hill, NC, 1940), 78; Charles S. Watson, *Antebellum Charleston Dramatists* (University, AL, 1976), 33–4; Eola Willis, *The Charleston Stage in the XVIIIth Century: With Social Settings of the Times* (Columbia, SC, 1924), 236; Rachel N. Klein, *Unification of a Slave State: The Rise of the Planter Class in the South Carolina Backcountry, 1760–1808* (Chapel Hill, NC, 1990), ch. 7; Daniel Walker Hollis, *University of South Carolina,* 2 vols. (Columbia, SC, 1951), 1:53. See also George C. Rogers, Jr., *Charleston in the Age of the Pinckneys* (Columbia, SC, 1980), 53; Rogers, *Evolution of a Federalist: William Loughton Smith of Charleston, 1758–1812* (Columbia, SC, 1962); Joseph W. Cox, *Champion of Southern Federalism: Robert Goodloe Harper of South Carolina* (Port Washington, NY, 1972), 30. Charleston housed the largest and most active of America's six radical clubs: Michael L. Kennedy, "A French Jacobin Club in Charleston, South Carolina, 1792–1795," *South Carolina Historical Magazine,* 91 (1990), 4–22.

swung from enthusiasm for Louis XVI and Marie Antoinette to enthusiasm for their executioners, but in time the Bourbons looked better. As early as 1789, Pierce Butler of South Carolina, a member of the Constitutional Convention, and other conservative planters applauded the Revolution but expressed dismay at its bloodletting. Conservative South Carolinians had second thoughts, their spirits dampened by the black revolution in Saint Domingue, rechristened Haiti. In Orangeburg in 1799 the supporters toasted John Rutledge, "Our representative in Congress – may he long continue to wear the odium of the Jacobins, the most distinguished and incontestable proof of merit and true patriotism." In 1800 Federalists cited Saint Domingue as a reason to reject Jefferson's doctrines and pleas for eventual emancipation. If equality is the natural condition of man, scoffed the prominent planter and civic leader, Henry William DeSaussure, then slaveholders must instantly free their slaves. Mary Legaré presented a standard to the members of the Federalist Club of Charleston as she fumed that France, that "nation of atheists," had designs on the United States.[6]

In June 1793, James Madison had assured Jefferson that American public opinion continued to support the French Revolution; by September, he and Jefferson agreed that Citizen Genet, the French representative who rashly intervened in American politics, was undermining his own cause. Shortly after, they judged Genet's successor, Pierre Adet, as even worse. By 1798, Madison wrote Jefferson in disgust about Robespierre's "bloody reign," while Jefferson bled for the white refugees from Saint Domingue. James Monroe, who had risked his political career in defense of France, finally repudiated the Terror. Disdaining "the violence and cruelty" of the radicals of the Mountain, he welcomed the downfall of Robespierre in the coup of Thermidor while fearful that a victory for the anti-French allies would crush the spirit of liberty in Europe. In Charleston the Pennsylvania-born Dr. David Ramsay, a prominent physician and historian, doggedly supported France until the late 1790s, when he finally lost patience. For Monroe and Ramsay the world was going awry.[7]

---

[6] Lewright B. Sikes, *The Public Life of Pierce Butler, South Carolina Statesman* (Washington, DC, 1979), 65; Cox, *Champion of South Carolina Federalism*, 31, 43; Charleston *City Gazette*, Jan. 5 (Mary Legaré) and July 12, 1799; Wolfe, *Jeffersonian Democracy in South Carolina*, 121, 127, 150; David Duncan Wallace, *The History of South Carolina*, 4 vols. (New York, 1934), 2:ch. 70. Pro-French feeling in South Carolina also reflected concern with the struggle against the British in Florida. It waned in 1794 with the Terror; see John C. Meleney, *The Public Life of Aedanus Burke: Revolutionary Republican in Post-Revolutionary South Carolina* (Columbia, SC, 1989), 215–16. Refugees from Saint Domingue constituted a numerically important portion of the total immigrant population: George Tucker, *Progress of the United States in Population and Wealth in Fifty Years* (New York, 1964 [1855]), 20.

[7] See the letters in James Morton Smith, ed., *The Republic of Letters: The Correspondence between Thomas Jefferson and James Madison, 1776–1826*, 3 vols. (New York, 1995): Madison to Jefferson, June 17, 1793 (2:785); Jefferson to Madison, Sept. 1 and 2, 1793, and Madison to Jefferson, Sept. 2, 1793 (2:813); Madison to Jefferson, Feb. 18, 1798 (2:1021); and the Editor's Note (2:941–2). For Jefferson on the refugees from Saint Domingue see George Tucker, *The Life of Thomas Jefferson*, 2 vols. (London, 1837), 1:445–6; Stuart Gerry Brown, *Autobiography of James Monroe* (Syracuse, NY, 1959), 10, 58–61, 67–9, 156–7; Harry Ammon, *James Monroe: The Quest for National Unity* (New York, 1971), 131–2; Arthur H. Shaffer, *To Be an American: David Ramsay and the Making of*

Southern Republicans and Federalists were using the French Revolution as a prism through which to interpret the political implications of the American Revolution. Republicans linked Federalists' aristocratic leanings with pro-British sympathies. Federalists and some Republicans feared that American republicanism would deteriorate into a French-style democracy. John Taylor of Caroline (Caroline County, Virginia), supporting western Virginia's petition for a more democratic election system, blistered the Alien and Sedition Acts as tyrannical. George Keith Taylor, a Virginia Federalist and brother-in-law of John Marshall, replied that the Constitution guaranteed the states' protection against invasion and that the Alien and Sedition Acts protected the South against French-incited slave revolts. Taylor acknowledged that the French Revolution had espoused good abstract principles but "turned out to be a foolish and mischievous speculation; what then can be expected from making republicans of negro slaves, and conquerors of ignorant, infuriated barbarians?"[8]

Unlike the American Revolution, the French sought to transform society thoroughly. It toppled a venerable, decaying monarchy and jettisoned a legally privileged nobility, an established church, and a residually feudal property system. For a brief period, it even abolished the calendar, the monetary system, and the system of weights and measures. Revolutionaries crowed that they had wiped the historical slate clean. As republicans, slaveholders welcomed the overthrow of the monarchy and the demise of the aristocracy, but as substantial propertyholders, they treasured social order and had no use for social leveling. The southern love affair with France and its great Revolution receded painfully and with remorse.[9]

The prevalence of the Girondists over Lafayette and the liberal monarchists aroused mixed feelings among slaveholders; the victory of the radical Montagnards over the Girondists worried them; the August–September massacres and the ensuing Terror frightened them; and the emergence of the revolutionary black republic of Haiti froze their blood. Southern slave society looked better and better. The

---

the American Consciousness (Columbia, SC, 1991), 108, 153, 202; Robert L. Brunhouse, ed., "David Ramsay, 1794–1815: Selections from His Writings," *Transactions of the American Philosophical Society*, n.s., 55, pt. 4 (1965), 21–2, 148. In the South as well as the North, the reaction against the XYZ Affair cost the Francophiles dearly: see e.g. E. Merton Coulter, *Abraham Baldwin: Patriot, Educator, and Founding Father* (Arlington, VA, 1987), 174–6. For the vicissitudes of pro-French politics in Virginia see esp. Charles Henry Ambler, *Sectionalism in Virginia from 1776 to 1861* (Chicago, 1910), 64, 75–9, 153–4.

8 Richard R. Beeman, *The Old Dominion and New Nation* (Lexington, KY, 1972), 157, 170; Simms, *John Taylor*, 66–7, 76–9, quote at 79; John Taylor, *Arator: Being a Series of Agricultural Essays, Practical and Political: In Sixty-Four Numbers* (Indianapolis, IN, 1977 [1818]), 177. Shortly before Napoleon sold Louisiana to the United States, feelings were rising against perceived French intrigues: see William Barry Grove to John Steele, June 7, 1799, and Feb. 25, 1803, in H. M. Wagstaff, ed., *The Papers of John Steele*, 2 vols. (Raleigh, NC, 1924), 1:169, 365–6, quote at 169.

9 For parallel reactions in the North see Charles Downer Hazen, *Contemporary American Opinion of the French Revolution* (Gloucester, MA, 1964), esp. 171–2, 253–5; Henry F. May, *The Enlightenment in America* (New York, 1976), 195–6, 218–25; and Richard C. Rohrs, "American Critics of the French Revolution of 1848," *JER*, 14 (1994), 360–77, which compares the reaction to the Revolution of 1789 to the revolutions of 1830 and 1848.

rise of a southern slaveholding Cotton Kingdom accompanied the triumph of an evangelical Protestantism that espoused conservative social and political principles. The French Revolution's radicalism and the Enlightenment's materialist philosophies and utopian visions appeared ever less plausible as embodiments of liberty and political virtue.[10]

The decline of the Federalist party after 1800 hardly spelled the collapse of southern conservatism. If anything, conservative principles infused Jeffersonian thought and politics. *Minerva*, the most openly Federalist paper in North Carolina before 1800, became *Minerva; or Anti-Jacobin*. Early in the nineteenth century, Parson Weems of Maryland, itinerant democratic bookseller and publisher of an expurgated version of Tom Paine's *Age of Reason*, assaulted *sans-culottes* egalitarianism. For Weems, equality meant equal dignity but in appropriate station: Some must direct, others obey. Weems epitomized a popular southern inclination to preserve liberal democratic thought without succumbing to its radical implications.[11]

The anti-Jacobin temper suffused Fourth of July orations that celebrated the ideals of the Declaration of Independence. In Mississippi in 1819, William B. Griffith, a prominent lawyer, delivered a paean to democracy and a ritual denunciation of aristocracy while condemning the French Revolution's "abominable cruelty, such unheard of atrocities, that human nature revolts at the recital." Thomas Cooper, a radical who supported the emancipationist movement in England and became a friend of Jefferson, turned conservative well before he became president of South Carolina College in 1820. A Deist, he remained a materialist and an intellectual but not a political radical. Others rejected the materialism of the French Enlightenment as subversive of social order.[12]

From the vantage point of 1824, a friend wrote Virginia's ex-senator and future governor William Branch Giles of their generation's youthful folly, recalling that in 1789 Virginians, "inflated with the spirit of French liberty," had predicated their political principles on "the metaphysics of Locke" and "the sophistry of Sir Thomas More." Experience and age convinced Virginians that "every innovation or change was not an improvement – that the pigeon hole constitutions of Abbé Sièyes were a flimsy shield against the sword of Buonaparte – that the recipes of Paine and Goodwin [William A. Godwin], aided by the arithmetical

---

[10] The wilder the hopes unleashed by the French Revolution, the more pronounced the reaction. The blood of August provoked a frenzy of disillusionment: see M. H. Abrams, *Natural Supernaturalism: Tradition and Revolution in Romantic Literature* (New York, 1971), 381–3. Even pro-French Southerners were appalled by the slaughter of the Swiss Guards on August 10: see e.g. William C. Somerville, *Letters from Paris on the Causes and Consequences of the French Revolution* (Baltimore, 1822), 10.

[11] David Hackett Fischer, *The Revolution of American Conservatism: The Federalist Party in the Era of Jeffersonian Democracy* (New York, 1965), 138; Lewis Gaston Leery, *The Book-Peddling Parson: An Account of the Life and Works of Mason Locke Weems, Patriot, Pitchman, Author, and Purveyor of Morality to the Citizenry of the Early United States of America* (Chapel Hill, NC, 1984), 21–2, 29.

[12] For Griffith's text see James D. Lynch, *The Bench and Bar of Mississippi* (New York, 1881), 113–26; quote at 116; for Cooper see Dumas Malone, *The Public Life of Thomas Cooper, 1783–1839* (New Haven, CT, 1926).

calculation of newfangled statesmen, could not govern the world" and that "the millennium had not yet arrived." In 1848 William Hutson of South Carolina, a formidable Presbyterian polemicist, had Reason and Intelligence triumph in the Reign of Terror: "The sickly cast of French political philosophy is to us even more dreadful than the contemplation of its bloody history; for it speaks of a dark future, yet unread."[13]

Responding to the Revolution's detractors in 1820, William Somerville, a Virginian resident in Paris, feared that Americans might consider excesses inherent in risings against tyranny. Pre-revolutionary France, he said, wallowed in "puerile debaucheries and pusillanimous intrigues." The Old Régime split France between "rioters in wealth and hewers of wood and drawers of water. Hence the spirit of liberty became converted into the rage for equality, and this overthrew everything." Peasants mistook "equality for freedom and rapine for justice," and Frenchmen "prated as much about liberty as if they really possessed it." The Jacobins, those "bloodhounds of human butchery," and the "Ultra-monarchists" were of a piece – mass murderers.[14]

A thoughtful critique of the French Revolution emerged during Virginia's constitutional convention of 1829–30. John Randolph of Roanoke and other conservatives compared American suffrage reformers to Jacobins and stressed the frailty of men and fragility of institutions. Philip Nicholas, an experienced diplomat, called the early leaders of the French Revolution "virtuous, enlightened men" who, unfortunately, proved to be philosophers and theorists rather than statesmen: "They raised a storm, which they had not the power to direct, and of which they became the victims." The Revolution threw up "dissolute and depraved" men with nothing to lose, who to acquire wealth and power pretended to patriotism, recruited desperate men, and enlisted Parisian mobs to push revolutionary principles "to an extreme, which those who commenced the work of reformation never contemplated." Thomas Roderick Dew, president of The College of William and Mary and a leading proslavery theorist, feared the French radicals' skill in opening politics to the masses. He referred to "the Paris mob, one of the worst in the world" and spoke of the "power and infamous notoriety" of the Jacobin clubs of Paris.[15]

---

[13] William Halyburton to William Branch Giles, May 25, 1824, quoted in Richard Beale Davis, *Intellectual Life in Jefferson's Virginia, 1790–1830* (Chapel Hill, NC, 1964), 387; William Hutson, "History of the Girondists," *SPR*, 2 (1848), 389, 395. The bombastic Robert Charlton of Georgia captured the general attitude of southern commentators when he referred to the Reign of Terror as a time in which "man changed, not only into a fiend, but into an insane and inconsistent demon": Charlton, *The Romance of Life: A Historical Lecture, Delivered before the Georgia Historical Society* (Savannah, GA, 1845), 7. Sièyes was a leading intellectual of the Revolution, William A. Godwin a widely read anarchist political theorist.

[14] Somerville, *Letters from Paris*, 140, quotes at 108, 173, 129, 182, and 78 (bloodhounds), 154 (ultramonarchists), 174. When Southerners spoke of "Jacobins," they almost invariably meant Montagnards.

[15] Nicholas in *Proceedings and Debates of the Virginia State Convention, of 1829–1830* (Richmond, VA, 1830), 367–8; Thomas Roderick Dew, *Digest of the Laws, Customs, Manners, and Institutions of the Ancient and Modern Nations* (New York, 1884 [1852]), 590, 594. R. S. Gladney of Mississippi also acknowledged the leaders of the French Revolution as intellectually outstanding philosophers

American divines maintained that religious revival saved the United States from atheism and anarchy during the first decade of the nineteenth century. They exaggerated French influence in America but – by raising the specter of godless anarchy – defined their own crusade to win souls to Christ as a conservative and stabilizing political force. Their appeals found a ready audience among slaveholders prone to nightmares of a Haiti on their own shores. The defense of the French Revolution shrank dramatically after 1800, as antirevolutionary literature inundated both North and South. Not even heightened anti-British sentiment during the War of 1812 reversed the trend.[16]

In the post-1800 climate, conservatives embraced the American Revolution while sternly criticizing the French. Edmund Burke proved invaluable to the mercurial John Randolph, as he moved from being Jefferson's floor leader in Congress to dubbing him "St. Thomas of Cantingbury." Randolph had shrugged off Burke's *Reflections on the Revolution in France* and declared the French Revolution to be of noble impulse. He dated letters according to the revolutionary calendar; addressed friends as "Citizen"; and named his favorite horses "Jacobin" and "Sans-Culotte." In 1800 he pronounced himself a Jacobin and *Ami des Noirs*, but in 1814, having re-read Burke, he found "sublime truths" and wrote to Harmanus Bleeker, a New York poltroon: "It has been an intellectual banquet of the richest viands. What a man!" And later, "What a treasure, what a mine of eloquence, sagacity, and political wisdom!"[17]

In 1817, Madison questioned Jefferson's notion that each generation must renew its compact with the polity and leaned toward Burke's view of society as "a partnership not only between those who are living, but between those who are living, those who are dead, and those who are to be born." A slaveholder who considered slavery a great evil, Madison wrestled with the interlocking issues of republicanism, slavery, and tyranny. Uncomfortable with slavery's challenge to republicanism, unwilling to follow Jefferson into the labyrinth of scientific racism, and distressed by the proliferation of free blacks in Virginia, Madison looked to gradual emancipation and colonization. The next generation of southern leaders had to look elsewhere for a way out. In 1833 Hugh Legaré captured a new mood when he referred to *Reflections on the Revolution in France* as "incomparable both for thought and eloquence." Censure of the radical turn in the French Revolution mounted during the 1840s. Bishop Christopher Gadsden, longtime rector of St. John's Episcopal Church in Charleston, recalled the "terrible atrocities and miseries" of Jacobin rule.

and statesmen who, destitute of religion and morality, became monsters: Gladney, "Moral Philosophy," SPR, 9 (1855), 116.

[16] For a succinct review, which needs some qualification for the South, see Perry Miller, *The Life of the Mind in America from the Revolution to the Civil War* (New York, 1965), esp. 3–5. For the reaction in the South Carolina lowcountry see George C. Rogers, Jr., *The History of Georgetown County, South Carolina* (Columbia, SC, 1970), 183; for the upcountry, see Klein, *Unification of a Slave State*.

[17] Robert Dawidoff, *The Education of John Randolph* (New York, 1979), 217–18; William Cabell Bruce, *John Randolph of Roanoke, 1773–1833*, 2 vols. (New York, 1970 [1922]), 1:140, 239, 2:675; K. Shorey, ed., *Collected Letters of John Randolph of Roanoke to Dr. John Brockenbrough, 1812–1833* (New Brunswick, NJ, 1988), xvii. See also Supplementary References: "Burke."

Former Congressman James B. Reynolds of Tennessee, from the vantage point of 1848, labeled the Revolution of 1789 "abominable."[18]

The popularity of British and French histories and biographies of the French Revolution and Napoleon – Thomas Carlyle, Jules Michelet, Louis Adolphe Thiers, Edgar Mignet, and Alphonse de Lamartine – reflected the shift in the American South. Dew recommended Mignet and Thiers as the most reliable of French historians, Mignet for "the most condensed, most philosophical and beautiful narrative of the progress of events," while Thiers provided "one of the most copious and expanded" of histories. Without philosophizing, Thiers enabled readers "to gather the philosophy of the revolution more accurately from his work than any other historian." But W. C. Rives, a leader of Virginia's Whigs, rebuked Thiers, Mignet, and Thomas Babington Macaulay for a fatalistic view of the onset of the Terror, thereby excusing it. To Mitchell King, Charleston's esteemed merchant-planter, the "very able but thoroughly jacobinical" Michelet expressed unwarranted zeal for an implicitly anti-Christian French Revolution: "The impulses of the masses, the voice of God – man is his own God. Thoroughly destructive."[19]

Sir Archibald Alison, staunch Tory and admirer of Castlereagh and Wellington, published a multivolume *History of Europe* (1833–1842), which rapidly went through ten editions and provided the first extended account of the French Revolution in English. Notwithstanding its pro-monarchist and antislavery biases, it became popular in the South. Francis Lieber, liberal political theorist at the College of South Carolina, accused Alison of ignorance and distortions of American history, and A. B. Meek, Alabama's historian and man of letters, scorned him for having "strutted forth in pompous tomes" to revile democracy. A contributor to *Southern Quarterly Review* condescendingly referred to Sir Walter Scott as "an honest hater of French and Frenchmen" but snarled at Alison as a peddler of "all the commonplace prejudices of the Tory party." Dew dismissed Alison's account of the French Revolution, as well as Scott's, as superficial. Alison "most signally failed" to link cause and effect, and, defying the facts, he made the Revolution out to be "one great unmixed crime." Among English historians, Dew said, only Carlyle did justice to the Revolution. Carlyle won accolades from both radicals and

---

[18] Drew R. McCoy, *The Last of the Fathers: James Madison and the Republican Legacy* (Cambridge, MA, 1989), 59; Christopher Gadsden, *The Times, Morally Considered* (Charleston, SC, 1843), 11; James B. Reynolds to John C. Calhoun, July 25, 1848, in *JCCP*, 25:626. Winfield Scott, campaigning for the presidential nomination, strove to avoid the equally dangerous labels of "Federalist" and "Jacobin": Timothy D. Johnson, *Winfield Scott: The Quest for Military Glory* (Lawrence, KS, 1998), 144.

[19] Dew, *Digest*, 573, 656–7; W. C. Rives, *Discourse on the Use and Importance of History, Illustrated by a Comparison of the American and French Revolutions* (Richmond, VA, 1847), 38; Mitchell King Diary, Sept. 25, 1854, at USC. The influential George Bancroft judged "magnificent" Thiers's *Consulate and Empire* and *Napoleon*: George Bancroft to Elizabeth Davis Bancroft, Jan. 9, 1848, in M. A. DeWolfe, *The Life and Letters of George Bancroft*, 2 vols. (New York, 1908), 2:82. Simms was among those who admired Michelet. The libraries of lowcountry planters had Lamartine's *Histoire des Girondins*, and Thiers's *Consulate et l'Empire* (among other works): see e.g. Rosalie Roos to Ulrika Roos, Dec. 2, 1853, in Rosalie Roos, *Travels in America, 1851–1855*, tr. Carl L. Anderson (Carbondale, IL, 1982), 99. See also Supplementary References: "Michelet and Thiers."

Tories: from the one for his contempt for the ancien régime and sympathy for the Revolution; from the other for his exposé of the Revolution's disastrous course.[20]

Southern Literary Messenger judged Alison's *History of Europe* fair-minded, published excerpts, and recommended it as a "beautiful history," "charming," and "elegantly written and valuable." A long unsigned review in two parts endorsed Alison's view that enormities awaited those who indulged in radical assaults on venerable institutions, including slavery; who open the way to violent insurrection of the laboring classes at home and in the colonies; and who think irreligious ruling classes can maintain power solely through force. Jesse B. Ferguson, pastor of the First Christian Church of Nashville, M. R. H. Garnett and James Holcombe, luminaries of the Virginia bar, and Representative J. L. M. Curry of Alabama cited the antislavery Alison to argue that the emancipated blacks of the West Indies had proven miserably incapable of sustained labor and self-rule. Robert Reid Howison drew upon *History of Europe* for his own history of Virginia. Alison was "an English historian proverbial for his distrust for democracy" and a lover of the British Crown, but Howison warmed to his suggestion of an America destined to carry British civilization forward.[21]

Old affections die hard. The slaveholders' affection for movements to overthrow Old World monarchies proved no exception. Neither support for the Revolution nor contempt for the Old Régime ever wholly evaporated. The Revolution was a great popular uprising against tyranny, Henry Lee of Virginia said in the 1830s, its excesses "incidental atrocities." Treated like brutes, the great mass of Frenchmen

[20] For Alison see James Westfall Thompson, *History of Historical Writing* (Gloucester, MA, 1967 [1942]), 2:281–2, 292–3, 297, and for the reception of Carlyle's history by radicals and Tories see 2:302. Francis Lieber, *On Civil Liberty and Self-Government*, 3rd ed., rev., ed. Theodore D. Woolsey (Philadelphia, 1874 [1853]), 104–5; A. B. Meek, *Americanism in Literature: An Oration before the Phi Kappa and Demosthenian Societies of the University of Georgia* (Tuscaloosa, AL, 1844), 17. "Napoleon Bonaparte and Sir Hudson Lowe," *SQR*, n.s., 10 (1854), 101; Dew, *Digest*, 573. Professor A. B. Stark hailed Carlyle's *French Revolution* for its "marvelous intensity of feeling, lurid vividness of portraiture, and astonishing depth of earnestness," declaring it "by far the most satisfactory picture and exposition of that fearful drama": "Thomas Carlyle," *QRMECS*, 15 (1861), 191. William Gilmore Simms rejected its politics but granted its richness and value: *Magnolia*, 2 (1843), 269.

　　Speaking at Erskine College in 1844, Benjamin Perry described Alison's *History of Europe* as "charming": Stephen Meats and Edwin T. Arnold, eds., *The Writings of Benjamin F. Perry*, 3 vols. (Spartanburg, SC, 1980), 1:325. George Frederick Holmes associated himself with Alison's fear of a new Dark Age: [Holmes], "Revival of the Black Arts," *MMQR*, 4th ser., 6 (1854), 202. For those outside the elite who read Alison's six-volume *History of Europe* and other works, see Columbus Morrison Journal, 1845 (Tuscaloosa, AL), at UNC-SHC; Haigh Diary, 1840s, at UNC-SHC.

[21] "Alison's History of Europe," *SLM*, 9 (1843), 136–44, 281–96; *SQR*, 5 (1844), 259, 532; also, *SLM*, 9 (1843); 22 (1856), 479; 26 (1858), 475. J. B. Ferguson, *Address on the History, Authority, and Influence of Slavery* (Nashville, TN, 1850), 9; [M. R. H. Garnett], *The Union, Past and Future: How It Works, and How to Save It*, 4th ed. (Charleston, SC, 1850), 22; James P. Holcombe, "Is Slavery Consistent with Natural Law?" *SLM*, 27 (1858), 411–12; J. L. M. Curry, *Congressional Globe*, 35th Cong., 1st Sess. (Feb. 25, 1853), 819–20; *A History of Virginia from Its Discovery and Settlement by Europeans to the Present Time*, 2 vols. (Philadelphia, 1846), 1:21, 2:19–20; *DBR*, 24 (1858), 608. For Alison as an authority on the French Revolution see "B. H. B." [of LaGrange, GA], "The Consulate," *QRMECS*, 2 (1848), 142. For James White see Supplementary References: "White and Abbott."

became brutal and "maddened." Professor George Tucker of the University of Virginia defended the French Revolution with a Burkean twist. He told the Virginia Historical and Philosophical Society that the oppression, injustice, and absurdities of the monarchy, together with the chasm between its institutions and a changing society, brought on the Revolution and its attendant excesses and vicious irrationality. In his impressive biography of Jefferson, Tucker wrote that revolutions had long "decided the political destiny of nations – have given freedom to people, or have transferred them from one set of rulers to another; yet customs, manners, habits, and ways of thinking remained unchanged." Rigid institutions resist self-reformation, but the diffusion of knowledge and prosperity sway the actions of civilized men more than physical force; sooner or later they compel a salutary redistribution of political power in accordance with the shift in "moral power." In the French Revolution, "The desire of reform soon became the love of innovation, until a prurient thirst for novelty, seeking gratification in everything, from the highest to the lowest concerns of life subverted all that seemed most stable by time, habit, or affection."[22]

A. B. Meek, impatient with Tucker's shadings, in a speech at the University of Georgia berated the Old Régime, staunchly defended the Revolution, and regretted that Sir Walter Scott had "prostituted his fine genius to the miserable task of framing a distorted argument in defence of the aristocratic principle." Sheer horrors had driven the French people into a Revolution, and it was no savage uprising. Why, even Robespierre was not the criminal portrayed in biased histories; his extreme measures answered aristocratic excesses. In 1850 William Henry Trescot of South Carolina, diplomat and historian devoted to slavery and secession, took a different view. After paying tribute to Louis XVI for aiding America and supporting reforms at home, Trescot got down to business. The French Revolution shattered European institutional and ideological foundations and split American public opinion into warring camps, opening the way for anti-British demagogues. The despicable principles of the French Revolution became confused with the noble principles of the American Revolution. In two outstanding books on American diplomacy, Trescot tried to curb hatred of Britain. Rives and John Reuben Thompson, editor of *Southern Literary Messenger,* recalled centuries-long oppression in appraising the evil fruits of the Revolution, including exacerbation of class conflict.[23]

As republicans, slaveholders or no, Southerners considered the French Revolution a new day of freedom. "The sufferings of the people," an Alabamian concluded in

---

[22] Henry Lee, *The Life of Napoleon Bonaparte, Down to the Peace of Tolentino and the Close of His First Campaign in Italy* (London, 1837), 24–6, quotes at 25, 24; George Tucker, "A Discourse on the Progress and Influence of Philosophy," *SLM,* 1 (1835), 412; Tucker, *Thomas Jefferson,* 1:250–3. See also the defense of the Revolution for having introduced education to the French populace: "C. C.", "Education of the People," *VLM,* 1 (1829), 249–53.

[23] Meek, *Americanism in Literature,* 17–18; William Henry Trescot, *The Diplomacy of the Revolution: An Historical Study* (New York, 1852), esp. 24, 115–28, 138–9; Trescot, *The Diplomatic History of the Washington and Adams Administrations, 1789–1801* (Boston, 1857), esp. 277, 281; [John R. Thompson?], "Failure of Free Society," *SLM,* 21 (1855), 141; Rives, *Use and Importance of History,* 38. The same Southerners who applauded Meek probably also applauded Henry Stuart Foote when he blamed Robespierre, Marat, and Danton for a centralization of power that ended in butchery and despotism: Foote, *Texas and the Texans; Or the Advance of the Anglo-Americans to the South-West,* 2 vols. (Austin, TX, 1935 [1841]), 2:39–40, 300.

1861, "bathed France in blood and cost Louis XVI his head." Defending slavery and social order, Thomas Cobb of Georgia, a firmly conservative legal scholar, found the horrors of the Revolution almost excusable in light of the Old Régime's severity. The Presbyterian Reverend John B. Adger of Columbia, South Carolina, blamed profligate nobles, rapacious courtiers, and a disputatious and vicious clergy, who together "had sapped the foundations of social order." Those who should have bolstered authority abused it and goaded "able and eloquent writers" to undermine "all the ancient establishments both of Church and State" and to labor "to introduce, as they hoped, a better condition of affairs." Acknowledging the revolutionaries' deep grievances, Adger nonetheless condemned the Revolution as the embodiment of nihilistic challenge to divine and human authority. Authority must reform itself or risk catastrophe.[24]

As Southerners perceived a rise in infidelity in France's revolutionary barbarism, their anger overwhelmed acknowledgment of provocation. The Reverend W. A. Cave, rector of St. John's Episcopal Church in Tallahassee, identified Red Republican doctrines as at the root of northern theology as well as political theory. Knowledge without virtue is pernicious, Episcopal Bishop J. H. Otey of Tennessee preached in Richmond: "It is precisely the principle which was preached by sceptics of the last century, and was in truth the fruitful parent of that direful progeny of evils which the world witnessed in the excesses and horrors of the French Revolution."[25]

During the 1840s and 1850s, students at the University of North Carolina combined censure of the Revolution's radicalism with indignation at the injustices of the Old Régime. William Hooper Haigh "read with pain" about the despotism and cruelty of feudalism, contrasting the advent of freedom in England and America with the French Revolution's Terror and war against religion. "Men," Haigh reflected, "have learned to despise riot and revolution." Jesse Harper Lindsay focused on the French Revolution's war against religion and its "madmen in the wild anarchy of freedom," but he sadly reminded his audience that the French people had been "galled to madness by the chains of oppression." John H. Bitting lamented the Revolution's descent into anarchy and a new tyranny in which even women exploded in a "storm of fanaticism." The French had proved themselves incapable of constitutionally ordered freedom.[26]

---

[24] "An Alabamian", "The One Great Cause of the Failure of the Federal Government," *SLM*, 32 (1861), 330; T. R. R. Cobb, *An Inquiry into the Law of Negro Slavery in the United States* (New York, 1968 [1858]), cxvi; John Adger, "The Revival of the Slave Trade," *SPR*, 11 (Apr. 1858), 100–35. Even after the execution of the king and the Terror, some American Protestant clergymen thought God was using barbarians to cleanse France of Catholicism: James H. Smylie, "Protestant Clergymen and American Destiny," *Harvard Theological Review*, 61 (1963), 223. In time, southern Protestants saw the revolutionaries' attacks on the Catholic Church as aimed at all religion and churches: see e.g. James A. Lyon, "Religion and Politics," *SPR*, 15 (1863), 570.

[25] W. A. Cave, *Two Sermons on the Times, Preached in St. John's Church, Tallahassee* (n.p., n.d. but War years), 10; Otey's sermon on "Christian Education," Oct. 5, 1859, quoted in William Mercer Green, *Memoir of the Rt. Rev. James Hervey Otey, D.D., LL.D., the First Bishop of Tennessee* (New York, 1885), 317–18.

[26] Haigh Diary, May 18, 1843; Jesse Harper Lindsay, Jr., in Speeches of Graduates, 1851, at UNC-NCC; John H. Bitting, "The French Revolution," in Senior Speeches, 1858, at UNC-NCC.

The War for Southern Independence spurred the preachers to new heights of anti-revolutionary rhetoric. The Presbyterian Reverend W. A. Hall of New Orleans, lecturing Confederate troops in Virginia, recalled that revolutionary France despised the Bible and closed the churches to establish a godless government. The Confederacy must stand on the Bible or meet a similar fate. French Red Republicans, the Baptist Reverend Basil Manly, Jr., wrote his father in 1861, used "Liberty, Equality & Fraternity" to conceal their "bloody and treacherous" deeds, and the Black Republicans are now using "Union" toward the same end. The Reverend Joseph Jones, of Georgia's prominent Presbyterian family, preached in Rome, Georgia: "The present reign of terror at the North reminds one of the French Revolution of 1789." For Robert L. Dabney, Virginia's outstanding theologian and social critic, "Liberty, Equality, and Fraternity" was the slogan of Marat and other mass murderers.[27]

Lay opinion paralleled clerical. In 1826 George McDuffie supposed, "All attempts which have been made in modern Europe to render government more free than the intelligence of the people would warrant have resulted in bloody and disastrous reaction." He concluded, "The people have no abstract right to any power which they cannot exercise with intelligence." *De Bow's Review,* in its first volume in 1846, struck at the French Revolution's "enthusiastic madness." Daniel R. Hundley of Alabama, who spent years as a businessman in Chicago, brought the lesson home in the 1850s: "Anti-slavery sentiments were first propagated by the ultra socialists and communists – those miserable *sans culottes,* who during the memorable French Revolution, raised the cry of *'Liberté, égalité, fraternité,'* and in the madness of their drunken folly enthroned a nude harlot in the Temple of Justice as the Goddess of Reason, the object of their admiration and worship." J. Barrett Cohen, Esq., of Charleston, in a speech to the South Carolina Historical Society, spoke for a broad spectrum of southern commentators when he branded the *philosophes* as infidels who inspired "the great social and political hydra of modern times, the French Revolution."[28]

---

[27] William A. Hall, *Historic Significance of the Southern Revolution* (Petersburg, VA, 1864); Basil Manly, Jr., to Basil Manly, Sr., Jan. 3, 1861, in Basil Manly, Jr., Papers, at UNC-SHC; J. Jones, *A Discourse Delivered ... to the Rome Light Guards and Miller Rifles* (Rome, GA, 1861), 10; *DD**, 4:56–7. The Reverend R. S. Gladney, reeling from early Reconstruction, demanded to know "What else have been all the rhapsodies of the subject of Liberty, fraternity, and equality, in France and this country, but the insane effusions of fanaticism?" Gladney, "Relation of State and Church," *SPR,* 16 (1866), 362.

[28] Edwin L. Green, ed., *Two Speeches of George McDuffie* (Columbia, SC, 1905), 23–4; *DBR,* 1 (Feb. 1846), 134; Daniel R. Hundley, *Social Relations in Our Southern States* (Baton Rouge, LA, 1979 [1860]), 16, also 148; J. Barrett Cohen, "Oration Delivered on the First Anniversary of the South Carolina Historical Society" (June 28, 1856), in *Collections of the South-Carolina Historical Society,* 2 vols. (Charleston, SC, 1857–58), 2:108–10. See the thoughtful analysis of the Virginia Convention by Dickson D. Bruce, *The Rhetoric of Conservatism: The Virginia Convention of 1829–30 and the Conservative Tradition in the South* (San Marino, CA, 1982), esp. 87, 134–6.

George Frederick Holmes held Rousseau responsible for the horrors of the French Revolution he foreshadowed and doubtless would have welcomed: [Holmes], "The Wandering Jew," *SQR,* 9 (1846), 77–8. Holmes loomed large in the formation of southern thought; for his life and work see Neal C. Gillespie, *The Collapse of Orthodoxy: The Intellectual Ordeal of George Frederick Holmes* (Charlottesville, VA, 1972). Yet assaults on the radicalism of the French Enlightenment ran into difficulty since, as self-proclaimed progressive men of the age, even the most conservative Southerners

No easy task: to hold on to the French Revolution while deploring its excesses. Instinctively, Southerners applauded the Revolution's "moderates," but not without misgivings. They backed away from the Girondists as indecisive and unprincipled. In South Carolina, Trescot, John Mathewes (a correspondent with John C. Calhoun) and David Flavel Jamison (scholar and civic leader) urged Southerners to learn from the Girondists's "blunders and follies" that only boldness avails and that concessions to mob rule prove fatal. Nathaniel Beverley Tucker of Virginia – judge, college professor, and social theorist – sneered at "the faculty of the college of the Gironde" for contributing to a radicalization the Jacobins turned against them. Howison agreed that the "philosophic Girondin" prepared the way for the "brutal Jacobin."[29]

South Carolinians deplored Jacobinism even while they organized Jacobin clubs to support nullification and later raised the tricolor as the banner of secession. Nor did Virginians express dismay at the Richmond *Whig's* call for the measures of the French Revolution to repel the Yankees. There were, it seems, Jacobins and Jacobins, and southern Jacobins were gentlemen. Anti-Jacobinism continued to provide ammunition for assorted political factions. Unionists and cooperationists labeled secessionists Jacobins. Louisa McCord, South Carolina's leading woman proslavery theorist, no less than Border State unionists, invoked the dreaded name of Robespierre in attacking radical adversaries as wild-eyed, fanatical "Red Republicans" ready to unleash the horrors of the French Revolution and Napoleonic dictatorship. When William Brownlow, east Tennessee's Methodist "fighting Parson," scored the secessionists' *"brawling Jacobin journals,"* he knew that secessionists were wearing tricolor rosettes in their hats. Andrew Johnson stood with Brownlow,

---

consciously built on certain aspects of its thought. Besides, if the evils of the Old Régime lay at the root of revolution, critics of its intellectual leaders had to temper their polemics. Thus Rives, rejecting oft-repeated propaganda, denied that radical *philosophes* caused the French Revolution, although he conceded they gave it a "false direction": Rives, *Use and Importance of History*, 40–1.

"Up to 1795," Henry May writes, "Protestantism, Republicanism, and Enlightenment seemed to most New Englanders to belong together. To separate these and range Protestantism and (American) republicanism against Enlightenment amounted to a profound and momentous upheaval. In this upheaval European revolution played a part." May notes that the attempt to Americanize the radical European combination of a new religion and a new politics – a new man and a new society – did not take deep root in America. To which we may add: certainly not in the South. See May, *Enlightenment in America*, 165, 223, quote at 196, for Virginia and the South see ch. 3.

[29] Trescot, *Washington and Adams Administrations*, 135; John R. Mathewes to Calhoun, early November, probably 1848, in *JCCP*, 26:118; [David Flavel Jamison], "Histoire des Girondins," *SQR*, 16 (1849), 53–76; [Nathaniel Beverley Tucker], "The Present State of Europe," *SQR*, 16 (1850), 290; Robert R. Howison, *A History of Virginia from Its Discovery and Settlement by Europeans to the Present Time*, 2 vols. (Philadelphia, 1846), 2:341.

Southerners chuckled at the Girondists, some of whom abhorred slavery in principle and supported the *Amis des Noirs* while their party defended the slave trade and colonial slavery as economic necessities. Southerners lost their sense of humor when business considerations compelled the Girondists to support the demands of slaveholding free coloreds of Saint Domingue for a racial equality designed to establish a biracial front of propertyholders. See Elizabeth Fox-Genovese and Eugene D. Genovese, *Fruits of Merchant Capital: Slave and Bourgeois Property in the Rise and Development of Capitalism* (New York, 1983), ch. 8.

his old foe, against secession. If forced to choose, he would prefer Black Republicans to secessionist Red Republicans.[30]

And the "Marseillaise": Defiant lowcountry gentlemen delighted in singing it during the nullification crisis. In 1856 at a concert in Staunton, Virginia, the audience roared for an encore. Staunch conservatives like the Presbyterian Reverend William Plumer Jacobs of South Carolina were "thrilled" when the young ladies of Charleston led in the singing of the "Marseillaise." The intellectually formidable Emma Holmes thought the exhibition "splendid." South Carolina's secession convention delegates arrived in Charleston to the strands of the "Marseillaise" followed by "Sweet Susan Brown, My Pretty Fair." At the reopening of the New Richmond Theater the audience sang the "Marseillaise," suitably recast in a southern version. When Beauregard assumed command in Charleston in 1861, a huge demonstration welcomed him with the "Marseillaise." The *Daily Constitutionalist* pleaded, "Oh, that when young men ask the daughters of the land for song ... they would sing the Marseillaise hymn." A. E. Blackmar of New Orleans, a music publisher, prepared a Confederate version, which young Southwesterners sang on their way to Richmond: "Sons of the South, awake to glory / A thousand voices bid you rise." When the prominent Presbyterian Reverend William Swan Plumer of Richmond rose to preach at White Sulphur Springs, the band struck up the "Marseillaise" to the delight of all and sundry. Plumer responded, "Let us begin the worship of God by singing the Marseillaise hymn of the Christian Church, 'All hail the power of Jesus' name.' "[31]

---

[30] Charles M. Wiltse, *John C. Calhoun: Nationalist, 1782–1828* (Indianapolis, IN, 1944), 88; William Watson, *Life in the Confederate Army* (Baton Rouge, LA, 1995 [1887]), 71; Donald E. Reynolds, *Editors Make War: Southern Newspapers in the Secession Crisis* (Nashville, TN, 1966), 203; "Separate Secession," in Richard C. Lounsbury, ed., *Louisa S. McCord: Political and Social Essays* (Charlottesville, VA, 1995), 206; William G. Brownlow, *Sketches of the Rise, Progress, and Decline of Secession, with a Narrative of Personal Adventures among the Rebels* (Philadelphia, 1862), 103–4; Andrew Johnson, "On the State of the Union," in Jon L. Wakelyn, ed., *Southern Pamphlets on Secession, Nov. 1860–April 1861* (Chapel Hill, NC, 1996), 305–25. See also Stuart Robinson's attack on Robert Breckenridge's "despotic and intolerant spirit" and "Jacobinical contempt" for legal procedures: "In Memoriam," *DQR*, 2 (1862), 140; and, in general, Daniel W. Crofts, *Reluctant Confederates: Upper South Unionists in the Secession Crisis* (Chapel Hill, NC, 1989), 115–16, 319. See also Supplementary References: "Jacobinism."

[31] Agnes Lee Journal, Apr. 11, 1856, in Mary Curtis DeButts, ed., *Growing Up in the 1850s: The Journal of Agnes Lee* (Chapel Hill, NC, 1984), 86; Apr. 25, 1861, in *Diary of William Plumer Jacobs*, ed. Thornwell Jacobs (Atlanta, GA, 1937), 79; Mar. 11 and May 1, 1861, Mar. 22, 1862, July 2, 1863, in John F. Marszalek, ed., *The Diary of Miss Emma Holmes* (Baton Rouge, LA, 1979), 15, 40, 138, 273; James H. Dorman, *Theater in the Ante Bellum South, 1815–1861* (Chapel Hill, NC, 1967), 166; Alicia Hopton Middleton et al., *Life in Carolina and New England during the Nineteenth Century* (Bristol, RI, 1929), 121; Nell S. Graydon, *Tales of Columbia* (Columbia, SC, 1964), 67; Richard Barksdale Harwell, *Brief Candle: The Confederate Theatre* (Worcester, MA, 1971), 55; *Daily Constitutionalist*, Dec. 30, 1860; A. E. Blackmar in Lizzie Cary Daniel, *Confederate Scrap-Book* (Nashville, TN, 1996 [1893]), 204; J. B. Grimball Diary, Sept. 8, 1832, at UNC-SHC; Sarah Lois Wadley Private Journal, Jan. 28, 1863, at UNC-SHC; for Plummer see Henry Alexander White, *Southern Presbyterian Leaders* (New York, 1911), 288. During the American Revolution, patriots organized "Councils of Public Safety"; afterwards, the appellation "Committee of Safety" usually drew on the French experience. See also Supplementary References: "Marseilles."

Those who damned abolitionism and neo-Jacobinism yet spoke as Jacobins-of-a-sort understood secession as a revolutionary act. The Richmond *Examiner* approved the French Revolution's execution of traitors. Jamison, chairing South Carolina's secession convention, proclaimed Danton's famous "To dare! to dare! and without end to dare!"[32]

Conservatives, southern as well as northern, had to reconcile their undying pride in the American Revolution with their tortured views of the French Revolution. In the South the American Revolution ignited a ferocious and protracted civil war between Whigs and Tories, neighbors and kin. The victorious Whigs welcomed the French Revolution as a worthy successor to their own, but its radical course compelled reconsideration of the American Revolution. The American Revolution did not initiate a grand social transformation, although some participants tried mightily to have it do so. From the 1830s, antislavery agitation brought a new perspective and urgency to Southerners' understanding of the underlying stakes in an American Revolution they considered their own. The more pronounced the quarrel over slavery, the more important the interpretation of the Revolution became. Both Southerners and Northerners claimed its governing principles and sought a history that legitimated their views.

The constitutional debates compelled a review of historical precedents for the establishment of a territorially extensive republic. The eighteenth-century British monarchy provided valuable instruction, positive and negative, on the workings of parliamentary institutions, convincing Americans that revolution could produce salutary political change and lasting stability. Notwithstanding the language of the Declaration of Independence, few Americans understood freedom to imply individual autonomy. Until the end of the eighteenth century, and well beyond, they defined individuals within a constraining family or community. Slavery itself did not stand as the absolute antithesis of an impracticable and undesirable individual freedom. British and American radicals embraced the full implications of the French revolutionaries' *Déclaration des droits de l'homme et du citoyen* – the first ideological formulation of systematic political individualism – but most of their countrymen did not. A good many Southerners, principally in Maryland and Virginia, frowned on slavery as incompatible with republican ideology and the freedom they were fighting for, but south of Virginia prevailing sensibilities accepted the co-existence of slavery and freedom in a republican context.[33]

Southerners credited their own revolutionary ancestors with the principle of the sovereignty of the people. They deeply resented Yankees who spoke of Massachusetts as "the mother of the Revolution." Madison's efforts at the Constitutional Convention to impose a large measure of federal authority on the states stemmed

---

[32] Richmond *Examiner*, Feb. 4, 1862; David Flavel Jamison in *Journal of the Convention of the People of South Carolina*. Danton's words: "*L'audace! l'audace! encore l'audace!*"

[33] In general see Fox-Genovese and Genovese, *Fruits of Merchant Capital*; David Brion Davis, *The Problem of Slavery in the Age of Revolution, 1770–1823* (Ithaca, NY, 1975), and for eighteenth-century proslavery thought throughout the colonies and early Republic see Larry Tise, *Proslavery: A History of the Defense of Slavery in America, 1701–1840* (Athens, GA, 1988).

in part from a widely shared belief that New England had failed to respond vigorously to the British invasion of the South. In the 1840s and 1850s Charles Carter Lee, older brother of Robert E. Lee, maintained in a series of articles for *Southern Literary Messenger* that Virginia had led the struggle against the Stamp Act. In South Carolina William Gilmore Simms, B. R. Carroll, and Dr. Joseph Johnson, mayor of Charleston, maintained that none rallied to the heroes of the Boston Tea Party as quickly as Southerners, and they chided New England for letting the South down when called upon for military assistance. The British had overrun the middle and southern states while, after 1776, New England went largely unscathed.[34]

In the 1850s, efforts to portray the American Revolution as a southern-led conservative movement increased in volume and intensity. John Peyton Little of Virginia maintained that Americans, in freeing themselves from British oppression and defending their position as slaveholders, merely exercised their rights as free Englishmen. Dew spoke volumes by mentioning the American Revolution only in passing in his *Digest of the Laws, Customs, Manners, and Institutions of the Ancient and Modern Nations,* a sweeping survey of Western Civilization that included a chapter on the seventeenth-century English revolutions and ended with a chapter on the French.[35]

The most impressive attempt at conservative interpretation came from Trescot: "To consider the American revolution as a precedent for every violent outbreak against constituted authority, is a willful and mischievous perversion of historical truth." Especially in his stunning *The Diplomacy of the Revolution* (1852), he celebrated America's readjustment of the balance of world power in accordance with the conservative principles that grounded the political order of Christendom. American independence introduced "a new power, not a new principle." George Fitzhugh of Virginia, a principal proslavery theorist, saluted the American Revolution with his customary flourish as "wise in conception" and "glorious in its execution." It "had nothing more to do with philosophy than the weaning of a calf."[36]

---

[34] Harlow W. Scheidley, *Sectional Nationalism: Massachusetts Conservatives and the Transformation of America, 1815–1836* (Boston, 1998), ch. 5, quote at 127; C. C. Lee, "The American Revolution," *SLM*, 8 (1842), 257–61; for Madison see Lance Banning, *The Sacred Fire of Liberty: James Madison and the Founding of the Federal Republic* (Ithaca, NY, 1995), 21; William Gilmore Simms, *The History of South Carolina*, 8th ed. (New York, 1860), 160; [Simms], "Critical Notices," *SQR*, n.s., 9 (1854), 234–5; B. R. Carroll, *Catechism of United States History*, 2nd ed., rev. (Charleston, copyright 1859 but this edition postwar), ch. 7. See also Supplementary References: "American Revolution in the South." For Natchez, see Samuel A. Cartwright, *Essays ... in a Series of Letters to the Rev. William Winans* (Vidalia, MS, 1843), 46.

[35] [John Peyton Little], "History of Richmond," *SLM*, 17 (1851), 605. A writer remarked that George Washington probably never read Rousseau, was no reformer, and waged no war on British institutions: "State of Parties and the Country," *SQR*, n.s., 8 (1853), 3.

[36] Trescot, *Diplomacy of the Revolution*, esp. 6, 51–6, 148; George Fitzhugh, *Cannibals All!; Or Slaves without Masters* (Cambridge, MA, 1960 [1857]), 133. For conservative interpretations of the American Revolution see also [Abel Parker Upshur], "Mr. Jefferson," *SLM*, 6 (1840), 642–50; Nelson Mitchell, *Oration Delivered before the Fourth of July Association, on the Fourth of July, 1848* (Charleston, SC, 1849), 5; [Frederick A. Porcher,] "Bancroft's History of the United States," *RM*, 2 (1857/58), 523–5; Rives, *Use and Importance of History*. College students never ceased to debate the

In 1861 Emma Holmes of Charleston saw "a singular coincidence that the first blood shed in defence of Southern Rights & Independence should have taken place April 19th, the 86th anniversary of the Battle of Lexington." She reveled in the news that Jefferson Davis would be inaugurated on George Washington's birthday. Davis, in a postwar retrospective, identified the "central idea" of the Revolution as the sovereignty of the people manifested in "distinct communities," rather than in a consolidated government. That the Revolution justified the South's own "right of revolution" against tyranny became a common theme during the 1850s. At the Alabama state legislature in 1863, William Corsan, an English businessman, heard speeches like those delivered in the legislatures of the rebellious colonies in 1776: "The same complaints of attempted tyranny, the same fervent and confident invocations of the blessings of God on the cause of right and liberty against wrong and slavery, and the same fixed resolve to conquer or perish."[37]

Civilized society and political virtue require ordered liberty. Southerners found their conception of political virtue in the American Revolution, and they considered their slave society the best chance for its realization. In the absence of the stabilizing influence of slavery, how could bourgeois societies hope to arrest anarchy like that of the French Revolution? Northern conservatives also believed that political virtue required limits to the democratization of liberty, and they, too, recoiled from Jacobinism and the radical turn in the French Revolution. In southern eyes, northern conservatives who repudiated slavery and cast their lot with an individualism based on free labor lacked an alternative vision. A rising tide of social radicalism lapped at their house built on sand.[38]

relation of the American Revolution to the French: see e.g. the debate in 1853 at Elk Fork Academy (near Nashville), as reported in Franc M. Carmack Diary, June 3, 1853, at UNC-SHC. Still, in the aftermath of the American Revolution in South Carolina, challenges to the hegemony of the planter-merchant elite in effect challenged the conservative interpretation of the Revolution: see Michael E. Stevens, "Legislative Privilege in Post-Revolutionary South Carolina," *WMQ*, 3rd ser., 46 (1989), 71–92.

[37] Apr. 30, 1861, and Feb. 20, 1862, in Marszalek, ed., *Emma Holmes Diary*, 39, 125; Jefferson Davis to J. L. Power, June 20, 1885, in Dunbar Rowland, ed., *Jefferson Davis, Constitutionalist: His Letters, Papers, and Speeches*, 10 vols. (Jackson, MS, 1923), 9:374–5; W. C. Corsan, *Two Months in the Confederate States: An Englishman's Travels through the South* (Baton Rouge, LA, 1996), 58. Henry Augustine Washington, among others, had previously expressed Davis's view: "The Virginia Constitution of 1776," *SLM*, 18 (1852), 657; for the prewar years see Michael A. Morrison, *Slavery and the American West: The Eclipse of Manifest Destiny and the Coming of the Civil War* (Chapel Hill, NC, 1997), esp. Conclusion; Sylvanus Landrum, *The Battle Is God's* (Savannah, GA, 1863), 8–9; O. S. Barton, *Sermon in St. James' Church, Warrenton, Va.* (Richmond, VA, 1861), 6–7.

[38] The North, William Gilmore Simms wrote, had nothing conservative in its morals or institutions: Simms to William Alfred Jones, June 10, 1851, in Mary C. Oliphant et al., eds., *The Letters of William Gilmore Simms*, 6 vols. (Columbia, SC, 1952–82), 5:414. For Simms's historical view, see esp. David Moltke-Hansen, "Ordered Progress: The Historical Philosophy of William Gilmore Simms," in John Caldwell Guilds, ed., *"Long Years of Neglect": The Work and Reputation of William Gilmore Simms* (Fayetteville, AR, 1988). Benjamin Morgan Palmer agreed with Simms that the North lacked the conservative institutions necessary to sustain positive freedom, but then so did Joseph Story – who argued, however, that the South did no better: B. M. Palmer, *Discourse before the General Assembly of South Carolina* (Columbia, SC, 1863), 11; James McClellan, *Joseph Story and the American Constitution: A Study in Political and Legal Thought, with Selected Writings* (Norman, OK, 1971), 52.

Simms primarily owed his reputation to his historical fiction, and one of his most important sets of interrelated novels illuminates South Carolina's experience during the Revolution. Simms regarded as imperative South Carolinians' claim to embody the spirit of the Revolution to which they had contributed disproportionately. *Woodcraft or Hawks about the Dovecote: A Story of the South at the Close of the Revolution* (1854) explores the Revolution's ultimate accomplishment and meaning. The revolutionary novels do not constitute a coherent sequence and were not written in chronological order, although characters from one frequently reappear in another. Each novel focuses upon a significant aspect of the Revolution – in *Woodcraft,* the problems of social reconstruction in the wake of a devastating upheaval.[39]

Simms saw the worst legacy of the war as the disruption of stable households, the cornerstone of a healthy society. For Captain Porgy, a member of Francis Marion's militia, reconstitution of the household depended upon disencumbering it from crippling mortgages, resuming a cycle of planting, and, above all, reassembling his slaves – his "people." Simms makes much of the mutual dependence of Porgy and his slaves. Tom, his cook and manservant, reminds his master, "You belongs to me as I belongs to you." Simms presents slavery – a hierarchical, organic social order – as a special case of the historical pattern of the mutual dependence of human beings of differing social station.[40]

Significantly, Porgy, like other Simms heroes, owes his position to his recognized standing as natural heir to leadership of a variegated rural world. Critics compare Porgy to Shakespeare's Falstaff, and Simms surely borrowed liberally from that model. Porgy's rotundity, his loudly expressed appreciation of good food and drink, his disregard for sound management, and his massive debts all contribute to his standing as a comic figure. Yet comic attributes do not detract from his effort to embody the figure of the hero. Porgy inherited his position as men in traditional societies inherit theirs. In no small part, he sustains that position against all odds because of his people's devotion. To underscore the compatibility of the mutual dependence of slavery with the freedom for which the revolutionaries fought, Simms emphasizes the crass mercenary motives of the British Colonel Moncrieff and the Scottish merchant M'Kewn, who have expropriated hundreds of slaves, including Porgy's, with the intention of reselling them in the West Indies: "South Carolina had already lost twenty-five thousand slaves, which British philanthropy had transferred from the rice-fields of Carolina to the sugar estates in the West India Islands."[41]

---

[39] All citations here will be to *Woodcraft or Hawks about the Dovecote: A Story of the South at the Close of the Revolution,* ed. Charles S. Watson (Albany, NY, 1983 [1854]). An earlier edition, entitled *The Sword and the Distaff,* appeared in 1852.

[40] Critics have frequently presented *Woodcraft* as a response to Harriet Beecher Stowe's *Uncle Tom's Cabin.* Simms said that he wrote his novel before Stowe's appeared, but he seems to have taken some satisfaction in the thought that he had helped put Stowe in her place. See letters to Hammond in Oliphant et al., eds., *Letters of Simms,* 3:5.

[41] Simms, *Woodcraft,* 35–6. Although Simms figures prominently in every general discussion of southern literature, he has yet to receive the attention he deserves. But see Mary Ann Wimsatt, *Major Fiction of William Gilmore Simms: Cultural Traditions and Literary Form* (Baton Rouge, LA, 1989)

Woodcraft assumes the compatibility of domestic slavery and ordered freedom, in contrast to the license of mercantile grasping in which anything from a bale of cotton to a man's "honor" becomes a commodity available to the highest bidder. To emphasize the importance of social continuity, Simms denies Porgy the marriage one would have expected, and Porgy bequeaths Glen-Eberley, his now-flourishing plantation, not to offspring but to a young couple who represent the union of social classes: the son of a wealthy and helpful slaveholding widow and the daughter of Porgy's own marginal ne'er-do-well overseer. The restoration of Glen-Eberley required the efforts of a variety of patriots. Simms calls for recognition of those efforts as essential to the ordered liberty the Revolution sought to preserve.

The more Southerners like Simms pondered the lessons of history, the greater their difficulty in identifying clear precedents for the predicament of their slave society. History gave with one hand and took away with the other, exposing the failings of heroes and the redeeming qualities of villains. Warnings came from various sources, including the history of ancient Rome. "The right of self-preservation," wrote Barthold Niebuhr, a historian revered in the South, "does not depend upon the innocence of those who are compelled to exercise it." For Jamison, Simms's plantation neighbor and friend, the harsh struggles between patricians and plebeians in Rome strengthened the character of both. The causes and significance of events never appeared sufficiently clear to yield neat didactic morals, and amidst the ambiguities revolutions posed special challenges. America's revolutionary origins seemed to sanctify other revolutions as crusades to free peoples from the shackles of oppression, but as successive revolutionary waves broke across Europe and, more portentously, across the Caribbean, revolution lost much of its luster. Real revolutionaries, the Baptist Reverend E. T. Winkler told South Carolina militiamen, did not confuse liberty with license and took up arms only after "every other resort had been exhausted."[42]

Shifting ideological currents called forth reassessment of Americans who sided with the British during the Revolution ("Tories") and of families with divided loyalties.[43]

and, on the figure of the hero, Renee Dye, "Sociology for the South: Representations of Caste, Class, and Social Order in the Fiction of William Gilmore Simms" (Ph.D. diss., Emory University, 1994).

[42] Barthold G. Niebuhr, *The History of Rome,* tr. Julius Charles Hare, 2 vols. (Philadelphia, 1844 [1826]), 2:85; [D. F. Jamison], "General History of Civilization in Europe," *SQR,* 3 (1843), 1–17; E. T. Winkler, *The Citizen Soldier* (Charleston, SC, 1858), 12.

[43] In the early Republic, Americans remained on guard against the return of British rule but also against mob rule at home, which Britain or other powers might turn to advantage. Among heroes of the fierce struggle against the Tories, strong voices called for a reconciliation that could block the ascent of the radicals. During the Revolution, many of those voices opposed the brutality of the suppression of the Tories, which they saw as an invitation to anarchy. See Albert H. Tillson, Jr., *Gentry and Common Folk: Political Culture on a Virginia Frontier, 1740–1789* (Louisville, KY, 1991), ch. 6; Charles Royster, *Light-Horse Harry Lee and the Legacy of the American Revolution* (New York, 1981), 31–6; Frank Lambert, " 'Father against Son, Son against Father': The Habershams of Georgia and the American Revolution," *Georgia Historical Quarterly,* 84 (2000), 1–28. Even during the Revolution but especially immediately after, pressure for the readmission of Tory exiles grew along with sympathy for their destitute wives and children, who were considered innocents. And from the end

Among the elite as well as the common folk, the Revolution became, often literally, a war between brothers. In South Carolina hardly a leading family was without Tories. Daniel Heyward, among other lowcountry planters, remained loyal to the Crown until redcoats plundered his plantation. The family of Langdon Cheves prided itself on revolutionary patriotism, but it had Tory black sheep. In Georgia in the 1820s the rival Clark and Troup factions branded each other's leaders as descendents of Tories. George Washington confessed in 1776 that Virginians shifted to the revolutionary side slowly and reluctantly. Recalcitrance and rebelliousness among slaves deepened planters' sense of dependency on British power.[44]

Violence between Patriots and Tories reached heights of ferocity and cruelty. "History," Jefferson bitterly asserted, "will never relate the horrors committed by the British army in the Southern States." He was speaking of Virginia, but South Carolina fared worse, as the British devastated the Beaufort area and, aided by Tory and Indian allies, committed atrocities elsewhere. Patriots, too, committed atrocities, but their descendants did not remember. The war provided a wonderful excuse to settle personal grudges and to rob and pillage at will. By the late 1770s, British "tyranny, oppression, and the brutal conduct of the army" – the words of Edward McCrady, Charleston's respected attorney and historian – drove Carolinians into the hands of revolutionaries who thereafter wrote a glorious chapter in American history. Yet, the Rawlins, Lowndes, Brewtons, Heywards, and Bees – the big-planter-merchant coastal elite that eventually joined the Patriots – did not believe that the enlightened government of Britain would ever kindle a revolution. British blows against Boston angered Carolinians, who themselves suffered no such direct oppression, but Charleston merchants, as well as common upcountry folk, retained strong royalist sympathies. Revolutionaries could not rely on the state militia and had considerable difficulty in recruiting troops.[45]

The fate of the family of William Bull, the pro-British if vacillating last royal Lieutenant Governor of South Carolina, suggests much about the course of regional sentiment. The British, unconvinced of Bull's loyalty, plundered his estate

---

of the War, conservative coastal planters began to regret the absence of conservative influence that the exiles might have. See Cynthis A. Kierner, *Southern Women in Revolution, 1776–1800: Personal and Political Narratives* (Columbia, SC, 1998), 97–9, 101–7.

[44] Chalmers S. Murray, *This Our Land: The Story of the South Carolina Historical Society* (Charleston, SC, 1949), 15 (Heyward); "Memoir of Langdon Cheves," in Richard C. Lounsbury, ed., *Louisa S. McCord: Poems, Drama, Biography, Letters* (Charlottesville, VA, 1996), 247 n. 4. Hugh Blair Grigsby wrote in 1860 of the attachment of the American colonies, especially Virginia, "to the parent country": Grigsby, *The Virginia Convention of 1776* (New York, 1969 [1855]), 5–8. See also Supplementary References: "Tories."

[45] Jefferson quoted in Sarah N. Randolph, *The Domestic Life of Jefferson, Compiled from Letters and Reminiscences* (New York, 1871), 35, 57; H. H. Simms, *John Taylor*, 126; Lawrence S. Rowland et al., *The History of Beaufort County, South Carolina*, 2 vols. (Columbia, SC, 1996), ch. 13; McCrady, *South Carolina, 1775–1780*, 296–8, esp. ch. 14. Historians on balance agree that the Tories outdid the Whigs in brutality: see Kierner, *Southern Women in Revolution*, 17 and literature cited. For the response to the Tory alliance with the Indians in the Georgia Piedmont, see Celestea Gentry Sharp, *Bishop, Georgia: The Ancient Roots, Rich History and Enduring Spirit of a Southern Community* (Bishop, GA, 1996), 46–7; Rogers, *Evolution of a Federalist*, Introduction, 134.

and threatened to hang slaves who refused to reveal the whereabouts of hidden valu-
ables. Bull reportedly lost the enormous sum of £6,000. An unforgiving Mrs. Bull
remained anti-British to the day she died. After the war everyone seemed to have a
personal list of Tories to be proscribed.[46]

Lingering hatred slowly gave way to reconciliation, often for practical reasons.
When the Revolution ended, social classes divided. With severe economic problems
in Charleston, leading merchants desperately needed the money and commercial
talent Tories could offer. Patriots and Tories at Goose Creek, with heavy investments in canals and other backcountry projects, needed to forget animosities and
get back to business. Shays's rebellion in Massachusetts encouraged unity, as did
antislavery stirrings in the North. But while big merchants and planters regarded
the returning Tories as a force for economic and social stability, small merchants
and artisans long took a hard line enforced with considerable violence.[47]

During the Revolution, Aedanus Burke of South Carolina, among other Patriot
leaders, supported confiscation of Tory property but counseled leniency when unscrupulous men expropriated the property of decent people whom British power
had overwhelmed. Although Pierce Butler suffered heavy economic losses for his
support of the Revolution, he recoiled from the postwar vindictiveness toward gentlemen who had tried to save their own property by proclaiming loyalty to the
Crown. General Francis ("Swamp Fox") Marion, the Pinckneys, and Patrick Henry
defied public opinion to call for leniency toward Tories. The legendary Janet Mac-
Neill of North Carolina was said to have divided her six sons between both sides
to be sure the family ended well whoever won. Across the South, prominent families divided – some cynically, some with conviction. The Habershams of Georgia
maintained cordial relations within the family despite splitting on the Revolution.
Several families in Savannah came under suspicion for trying to protect their property no matter who won, and Bishop Stephen Elliott of the Episcopal Church of
Georgia recalled Tories as mostly good if wrongheaded men.[48]

In 1851, Joseph Johnson of South Carolina portrayed the Tories as of two types:
good, misguided people and treacherous thugs. Evenhandedly and with regret,

---

[46] Kinloch Bull, Jr., *The Oligarchs in Colonial and Revolutionary Charleston: Lieutenant Governor William Bull II and His Family* (Columbia, SC, 1991), 275. In the Ball family, one son went with Tories, another with Americans: Anne Simons Deas, *Recollections of the Ball Family of South Carolina and the Comingtee Plantation* (Charleston, SC, 1978 [1909]), 84. A decade after the war, Eliza Wilkinson was still railing at the savagery of the British in the South Carolina lowcountry: Caroline Gilman, ed., *Letters of Eliza Wilkinson* (New York, 1969 [1839]), 42.

[47] Rogers, *Evolution of a Federalist,* Introduction, 101–7, 134; Walter J. Fraser, Jr. *Charleston! Charleston!: The History of a Southern City* (Columbia, SC, 1989), 166–70.

[48] Meleney, *Public Life of Aedanus Burke,* chs. 3–4; Sikes, *Pierce Butler,* 11–17; Harriott Horry Ravenel, *Eliza Pinckney* (New York, 1896), 310; William Wirt, *Sketches of the Life and Character of Patrick Henry* (Philadelphia, 1817), 419; *DNCB,* 2:56–8, 3:196, 4:181; *DGB,* 1:377–81; George Gillman Smith, *The Story of Georgia and the Georgia People,* 2 vols. (Macon, GA, 1900), 85–9; Thomas Gamble, *Savannah Duels and Duellists* (Savannah, GA, 1974 [1923]), 57, 60; Virgil Sims Davis, "Stephen Elliott: A Southern Bishop in Peace and War" (Ph.D. diss., University of Georgia, 1964), 254. In 1859 Trescot, in an address to the South Carolina Historical Society, approvingly recalled Marion's leniency: "South Carolina – A Colony and a State," *DBR,* 27 (1859), 679.

Simms, in his *Life of Marion* and *History of South Carolina,* recorded atrocities committed by both sides. Simms, in his historical works, never failed to mention that General Greene described the conflict as one in which "the parties pursued each other like wild beasts." Simms credited many Tories with honorable principles. The Patriots, he wrote, might have won them over by relying on reasoned argument instead of coercion. Simms approved of Marion's opposition to the confiscation acts. Yet in *The Partisan,* the first of his Revolutionary War novels, he has one Patriot explain to another that he finds it difficult to trust people who suddenly proclaim Patriot sympathies. "They have quite too much at stake: they have too much plate, too many Negroes, and live too comfortably to be willing to stand a chance of losing all by taking up arms against the British, who are squat close alongside of them." Lecturing in the North in 1856, Simms refused to apologize for South Carolina's large number of Tories or make them objects of reproach: "They had their arguments for Loyalty, and these were founded equally in reason and in natural sympathies. They were faithful to their old traditions – faithful to the laws and the authorities."[49]

In the 1840s and 1850s, South Carolina's unionists defended the Tories in their own way. Benjamin F. Perry, their effective upcountry editor, attributed to local "marauding bands of Tories" acts "equal in atrocity to those of their savage allies." Yet he acknowledged the sincerity of Carolinians who chose the wrong side for honorable reasons, and he approved the post-Revolution reconciliation and readiness to forgive ex-Tories and even to elect them to the state legislature. J. L. Petigru, Charleston's leading jurist, judged the Tory cause wrong and as deserving to fail, but he regarded many of the Tories as good, honorable, principled men. William J. Grayson – the celebrated poet of Beaufort, South Carolina, and a planter – considered revolutions and civil wars vicious and pointless. He knew of nothing the Dutch and Portuguese revolutions had accomplished that would not have come in time without bloodshed. In the wake of the American Revolution, was New England better governed than Canada? Southerners rebelled against British taxes, mercantilism, and political centralization only to end with worse American versions. When Porcher, Trescot, Perry, Petigru, and Grayson suggested that Tories might have been won over with persuasion, they probably had in mind important men like the Presbyterian Reverend John J. Zubly of Georgia, who championed America

[49] Joseph Johnson, *Traditions and Reminiscences of the American Revolution* (Spartanburg, SC, 1972 [1851]), 105–6, 141, 316, 543–57; Simms, *History of South Carolina,* 216 (quoting Greene), 231, 330; William Gilmore Simms, *The Life of Francis Marion,* 8th ed. (New York, 1844), 62–3, 104, 189–90, 239, 246–7, ch. 21 (confiscation); Simms, *The Partisan,* 48; [William Gilmore Simms], "South Carolina in the Revolution," *SQR,* 14 (July 1848), 470–501; Oliphant et al., eds., *Letters of Simms,* 3:525. Simms nonetheless remained generally hostile to the Tory legacy, and his more favorable remarks may be read as grudging or ambiguous. David Moltke-Hansen stresses his continuing distaste, the persistence of opprobrium attached to Tory families, and the struggle of descendants to overcome it: "Why History Mattered," *Furman Studies,* 26 (1980), 34–42. For the bitter response to Tories during the Revolution but also the beginnings of a relaxation of penalties, see Ella Pettit Everett, "Loyalism in Charleston, 1761–1784," in *Proceedings of the South Carolina Historical Association* (Charleston, SC, 1936), 3–17.

against British injustices but who feared the radicalism a revolution would unleash, ended up supporting the Crown when the Revolution came, and was branded as a traitor at the Second Continental Congress.[50]

Few men of letters ranked higher than Samuel Johnson, whose hostility to the American Revolution dimmed his star little despite his much-quoted, "Why is it that the loudest yelps we hear of liberty come from the mouths of slaveholders?" His stand encouraged a more forgiving attitude toward Americans who had supported the Crown. Among the few dissenters, Sarah Morgan thought his tirades against America characteristically narrow-minded and bigoted, and "R. C. P.", a Methodist writer of West Feliciana, Louisiana, brushed off "the pompous dogmatisms of Dr. Johnson." In contrast, Frederick Porcher of Charleston, whose family had fought on both sides, criticized George Bancroft's history of the American Revolution for failing to do justice to those who honorably supported the Crown. Porcher, defending Johnson's *Taxation No Tyranny*, called Johnson "a dogmatic moralist and a superstitious religionist" but also "a high-minded, generous and noble man" who opposed American independence honestly.[51]

The spirit of vindictiveness never disappeared completely. For a long time some southern church congregations refused to welcome former Tories. For a half-century or more, the stigma of Tory descent plagued the professional ambitions of leading citizens of the South Carolina upcountry. Parson Brownlow assailed as descendants of Tories the South Carolina nullifiers in 1832 and the secessionists in 1861, including William L. Yancey, the orator of secession. But the stigma did recede, and in time descendants of prominent Tories won public office without difficulty. Class ranks closed after the Revolution, and the effort to rehabilitate the reputation of the Tories gathered momentum during the second quarter of the nineteenth century. B. L. C. Wailes, a founder of the Mississippi Historical Society, noted that the descendants of Tories ranked among the leaders of society in Mississippi, where a number had settled after the war, and remarked, "It would answer to no good purpose therefore to annoy the over-sensitive of the present age, by rending the veil which time has spread over the 'bygones' of a past generation. Let them rest in oblivion."[52]

[50] [Benjamin F. Perry], "The Revolutionary History of South Carolina," *SQR*, 11 (1847), 775, 481–5, quote at 475; J. L. Petigru, "Oration Delivered on the Third Anniversary of the South-Carolina Historical Society" (May 27, 1858), in *South-Carolina Historical Collections*, 2:20; Richard J. Calhoun, ed., *Witness to Sorrow: The Antebellum Autobiography of William J. Grayson* (Columbia, SC, 1990), 185–8. On Zubly see also Supplementary References: "Tories."

[51] James Boswell, *The Life of Samuel Johnson, LL.D.* (New York, n.d.), 747–8. Sarah Morgan shrugged off Boswell as a "toady" and an "old Disguster," but she also thought Johnson overrated: July 13, 1862, in James I. Robertson, ed., *A Confederate Girl's Diary: Sarah Morgan Dawson* (Westport, CT, 1960), 115–16, quotes at 115. "R. C. P.", "The Relation of Christianity to Literature," *QRMECS*, 1 (1847), 183; F. A. Porcher, "Bancroft's History," *RM*, 2 (1858), 522–3.

[52] Brownlow, *Sketches of Secession*, 22–4, 70–1, and ch. 4; *DGB*, 1:252; *SQR*, 11 (1847), 481–3; Dunbar Rowland, ed., *Mississippi: Comprising Sketches of Counties, Towns, Events, Institutions, and Persons, Arranged in Cyclopedic Form*, 4 vols. (Spartanburg, SC, 1976 [1907]), 2:546. See also Janet Sharp Hermann, *Joseph E. Davis: Pioneer Patriot* (Jackson, MS, 1990), 5. In *JCCP* see: John Cunningham to J. C. Calhoun, Oct. 15, 1846 (23:492–4), Nov. 2, 1846 (521–2); Robert Cunningham to

Rehabilitation made sense. Southerners felt ever more intensely their moral and political isolation in a transatlantic world that held slavery anathema. They needed unity, not a vicarious refighting of the last war. Among other considerations, many Tories were yeomen and religious dissidents disaffected from the planter-dominated revolutionary regimes. On the eastern shore of the Chesapeake, as well as in large areas further south, the post-Revolutionary gentry needed to reattach their loyalty. Thousands of Tories in South Carolina and Georgia had fled to east Florida and, with the British cession of Florida to Spain, departed for other British colonies or – feeling betrayed by the British Crown – returned to the South. The concern for reconciliation emerged primarily among a slaveholding elite ready to welcome all who could be counted on to strengthen conservatism in a society in which democracy was getting out of hand.[53]

Momentous events in Saint Domingue clouded discussions of the American and French revolutions. A massive slave revolt erupted in Saint Domingue in 1791 – in the world's most valuable colony, which powered the French economy with more slaves than Virginia, South Carolina, and Georgia combined. It turned into a national revolution and in 1804 culminated in the Western Hemisphere's first black republic. Southern Federalists, crying that French madness was infecting their own slaves, determined to silence homegrown Jacobins. In Kentucky in 1792, the antislavery Reverend David Rice bravely spoke out against racism and, like many northern Federalists, viewed the revolution in Saint Domingue as the moral equivalent of the American Revolution. In 1793 the *United States Gazette* remarked sarcastically: "Liberty and equality, Paine and the Rights of Man are all the rage to the Eastward and in the South too, where slaveholders now address the slaves who clean their boots as 'Citizen Caesar' or 'Citizen Pompey,' and the auctioneer now cries, 'Twenty pounds for Citizen Alexander – who bids more?' "[54]

At first, the black revolution in Saint Domingue reverberated in the United States in a manner more factional than sectional. President Washington joined his fellow Virginian, Secretary of State Jefferson, in siding with beleaguered French planters, but Alexander Hamilton gained some southern support for a policy sympathetic to the black rebels. Federalist merchants along the Atlantic seaboard stood ready to do business with Toussaint L'Ouverture, whose stringent labor policy promised to sustain the transatlantic economy by keeping newly freed blacks at work on the

Calhoun, Nov. 19, 1846 (543–4), Nov. 25, 1846 (549–51). One example is Farquard Campbell, who vacillated between Patriots and Tories but was elected to the state senate of North Carolina: *DNCB*, 1:314 (Campbell), 100. In Georgia, the Philadelphia-born G. W. J. DeRenne propagated a more sympathetic revisionist view that considered many Tories as misguided fellow conservatives.

53 Keith Mason, "Localism, Evangelicalism, and Loyalism: The Sources of Oppression in the Revolutionary Chesapeake," *JSH*, 61 (1990), 23–54; Caroline Watterson Troxler, "Refuge, Resistance, and Reward: The Southern Patriots' Claims on East Florida," *JSH*, 60 (1989), 563–96.

54 William Barry Grove to John Steele, June 7, 1799, in Wagstaff, ed., *Steele Papers*, 1:169; on Rice see Jeffrey Brooke Allen, "Were Southern White Critics of Slavery Racists?: Kentucky and the Upper South, 1791–1824," *JSH*, 64 (1978), 177–8; for the *United States Gazette* (Feb. 2, 1793) see Hazen, *American Opinion of the French Revolution*, 214.

sugar plantations. Southern merchants kept a close watch but did not believe that blacks could long prevail over whites.[55]

The South welcomed French refugees from Saint Domingue but cast a wary eye on the slaves they brought with them. Citing the insurrectionary tendencies of "French Negroes," Maryland and North Carolina forbade all further black immigration, and Virginia strengthened its militia. For several decades refugees who had settled in upcountry and coastal Georgia alarmed local whites with hair-raising stories of black atrocities. Some southern newspapers published Dessalines's proclamation of "Liberty or Death" in 1804, but when Thomas Ritchie of the Richmond *Enquirer* promised to publish a full-scale account of Dessalines's massacre of whites, he had to eat his words. Protests convinced him that reportage would unsettle the slaves, and he supported measures to restrict emancipations and hem in free Negroes.[56]

In the House of Representatives John Randolph of Roanoke, opposing the impending War of 1812, said that "silent but powerful change" had infected the slaves since the American Revolution. "When the fountains of the great deep of abominations were broken up, even the poor slaves did not escape the general deluge. The French revolution polluted even them." Randolph accused New Englanders, including some who migrated to the South, of preaching radical French doctrine. As Gabriel Prosser's aborted slave revolt in Virginia showed in 1800, they had created a constant state of alarm. "I speak from facts when I say that the night-bell never tolls for fire in Richmond that the mother does not hug the infant more closely to her bosom." Meanwhile, news of black military successes in Saint Domingue astonished the ladies of the South Carolina lowcountry and raised apprehension of risings at home. Randolph spoke out against revolutionary violence while indicting slavery: "From the spreading of this infernal doctrine, the whole southern country

---

[55] Donald R. Hickey, "America's Response to the Slave Revolt in Haiti," *JER*, 2 (1982), 361–79; Alfred N. Hunt, *Haiti's Influence on Antebellum America: Slumbering Volcano in the Caribbean* (Baton Rouge, LA, 1988), 31; Duncan J. McLeod, *Slavery, Race, and the American Revolution* (London, 1974), 92. For praise of Toussaint's labor policy see e.g. [William Drayton], *The South Vindicated from the Treason and Fanaticism of the Northern Abolitionists* (Philadelphia, 1836), 265, and Cobb, *Law of Negro Slavery,* clxxxi–clxxxii. For an illustration of merchant attitude see John Smith to John Gray Blount, Jan. 28, 1793, in Alice Barnwell Keith, ed., *The John Gray Blount Papers,* 2 vols. (Raleigh, NC, 1952, 1959), 2:233. See also Supplementary References: "Haiti."

[56] T. Stephen Whitman, *The Price of Freedom: Slavery and Manumission in Baltimore and Early National Maryland* (Lexington, KY, 1997), ch. 1; Joseph I. Shulim, *The Old Dominion and Napoleon Bonaparte: A Study in American Opinion* (New York, 1952), 32; Katherine Ann McGeachy, "The North Carolina Slave Code" (M.A. thesis, University of North Carolina, 1948), 74; Hermann, *Joseph E. Davis,* 7; Charles Henry Ambler, *Thomas Ritchie: A Study in Virginia Politics* (Richmond, VA, 1913), 25.

   Southern slaveholders were not alone in suppressing evidence that challenged their preferred notions. Robert Moylan Walsh, appointed by Secretary of State Daniel Webster in 1851 to work with the British and French to respond to Haiti's conquest of the Spanish part of Santo Domingo, told of Haitian atrocities as well as the decline of the Haitian economy. Louisa McCord (among other Southerners) pounced, but abolitionists who went to Haiti – and did not find what they expected – suppressed evidence. See L. S. McCord, "British Philanthropy," in Lounsbury, ed., *Louisa S. McCord: Essays,* 313–15; Gilbert H. Barnes and Dwight L. Dumond, eds., *Letters of Theodore Dwight Weld, Angelina Grimké and Sarah Grimké, 1822–1844,* 2 vols. (Gloucester, MA, 1965), 2:663 n. 2.

had been thrown into a state of insecurity. Men, dead to the operation of moral causes, had taken away from the poor slave his habits of loyalty and obedience to his master, which lightened his servitude by a double operation; beguiling his own cares and disarming his master's suspicions and severity; and now, like true empirics in politics, you are called upon to trust to the mere physical strength of the fetter which holds him in bondage." Randolph zeroed in on the fate of the slave: "You have deprived him of all moral restraint; you have tempted him to eat of the fruit of the tree of knowledge, just enough to perfect him in wickedness; you have opened his eyes to his nakedness; armed his nature against the hand that has fed, that has clothed him, cherished him in sickness; that hand, which before he became a pupil of your school, he had been accustomed to press with respectful affection. You have done all this – and then show him the gibbet and the wheel as incentives to a sullen, repugnant, obedience." Randolph prayed, "God forbid, Sir, that the Southern States should ever see an enemy on these shores with these infernal principles of French fraternity in the van!"[57]

Calhoun brushed Randolph aside: "I cannot think our ignorant blacks have felt much of their baleful influence. I dare say more than half of them never heard of the French Revolution." Calhoun tripped: If half had not, then half had. Fugitives from Saint Domingue had brought talkative slaves to South Carolina with them. In 1822, Denmark Vesey's insurrectionary plot in Charleston offered frightening testimony to the contagion. Whites most concerned about the spread of radical democratic ideas did not trust even the white émigrés from Saint Domingue: Although victims of white Jacobins in Paris and black Jacobins at home, they had once sided with the Revolution. Saint Domingue and slave plots in the South frightened both antislavery and proslavery men and women and dampened hopes for emancipation. In the Carolinas early in the nineteenth century, Zachary Dicks and James Henderson Dickson warned fellow Quakers of a repetition of Saint Domingue if slavery were not abolished. Many listened and departed for the Midwest.[58]

---

[57] Randolph, *Annals of Congress*, 12th Cong., 1st Sess. See also Merton L. Dillon, *Slavery Attacked: Southern Slaves and Their Allies, 1619–1865* (Baton Rouge, LA, 1990), 52–3, 69–71, 86. On the reaction of lowcountry ladies see Joanna Bowen Gillespie, *The Life and Times of Martha Laurens Ramsay, 1759–1811* (Columbia, SC, 2000), 181–3. Louisa McCord also believed that, were the master–slave relation snapped, whites would shed their responsibility for blacks: "Uncle Tom's Cabin," in Lounsbury, ed., *Louisa S. McCord: Essays*, 270. Among later allusions to Randolph's speech see the Unitarian Charles A. Farley, *Slavery; A Discourse Delivered in the Unitarian Church, Richmond, Va.* (Richmond, VA, 1835), 19. In 1847 and again in 1910, Marion Harland of Virginia recalled John Randolph's words about frightened mothers: Harland, *Autobiography: The Story of a Life* (New York, 1910), 187. Abolitionists kept Randolph's words alive: see e.g. Lydia Maria Child to Mrs. M. J. C. Mason, Dec. 17, 1859, in *Letters of Lydia Maria Child* (New York, 1969 [1883]), 133.

[58] John Niven, *John C. Calhoun and the Price of Union: A Biography* (Baton Rouge, LA, 1988), 38. On the Quakers see McLeod, *Slavery, Race, and the American Revolution*, ch. 3; *A Journal of the Life and Religious Labors of Richard Jordan* (London, 1829), 13–14, 19; *DNCB*, 2:67 (Dickson); Whitman, *Price of Freedom*, ch. 4. For distrust of the émigrés see Ebenezer Pettigrew to James Iredell, Jr., July 4, 1804, in Sarah McCulloh Lemmon, ed., *The Pettigrew Papers*, 2 vols. (Raleigh, NC, 1971, 1988), 1:347–8; J. O. Bevan to Henry Jackson, Dec. 14, 1817, in Henry Jackson Papers, at UNC-SHC.

In the 1840s and 1850s southern propagandists did their best to exorcise the Haitian ghost, but to no avail. In Mississippi, memories of the black revolution drove T. C. Thornton, a college president, to the edge of hysteria when he pleaded the proslavery case in 1841. J. H. Hammond, Edward Bryan, Daniel Hundley, and James Warley Miles tirelessly repeated the refrain: French revolutionary folly brought on the Haitian Revolution; French abolitionists (the *Amis des Noirs*), and not the slaves, made the Haitian Revolution a success; blacks cannot prevail on their own; history exhibits no successful black revolt against white masters. Dr. Samuel Cartwright, a notable scientific racist, said the Haitian Revolution was a paltry affair until white fanatics meddled: "It is not physical force which keeps them in subjection, but the spiritual force of the white man's will." The Presbyterian Reverend George Howe of South Carolina remarked that French radicals unleashed revolt in the naïve belief that they could control the masses they were unleashing. Winthrop Jordan, in *White over Black,* bared a supreme irony: Until the Haitian Revolution, few Southerners doubted that slaves posed a threat to their masters; afterwards, especially after Nat Turner's revolt, they wonderfully decided that their own slaves were docile and that only abolitionist meddling rendered them discontent.[59]

The southern press returned to the horrors of Saint Domingue to justify secession in the wake of Lincoln's election. Yet, when the War went badly, General Patrick Cleburne cited the Haitian experience to urge the Confederacy to recruit black troops. He followed in the footsteps of southern editors who had long paid tribute to Toussaint's military as well as political prowess, offering their highest compliment: Toussaint thought like a white man. Tributes to "this remarkable Negro" and to this "good man and good Christian" came from such passionately proslavery men as Cobb, Simms, Dew, and Fitzhugh.[60]

The aftermath of the Haitian Revolution seemed to confirm another pet theory of the southern slaveholders – that, without the strong hand of a white master, blacks would relapse into barbarism. Saint Domingue, wrote Daniel Dennett, editor of the *Planters' Banner* of Louisiana, had been a flourishing country until blacks transformed it into "a mere waste." But what should we expect since "a more lazy, thriftless, filthy population can hardly be found in any country under the heavens?" In 1848 the Reverend William Plumer denied that slaves had the capacity to sustain a rebellion but cited Nat Turner as a negative instance of the notion that slaves who genuinely converted to Christianity never rebelled. Yankees cannot turn the South into another Santo Domingo, Basil Lanneau Gildersleeve wrote during the

[59] T. C. Thornton, *An Inquiry into the History of Slavery* (Washington, DC, 1841), pt. 5; Samuel A. Cartwright, "Slavery in the Light of Ethnology," in E. N. Elliott, ed., *King Cotton Is King and Pro-Slavery Arguments* (New York, 1969 [1860]), 724, 726; [George Howe], "The Raid of John Brown, and the Progress of Abolition," *SPR*, 12 (1860), 808–9; Winthrop D. Jordan, *White over Black: American Attitudes toward the Negro, 1550–1812* (Chapel Hill, NC, 1968), 392–402. See also Hundley, *Social Relations in Our Southern States,* 150; [J. H. Hammond], "Lecture on the North and South," *SQR,* 15 (1849), 308; Edward B. Bryan, *The Rightful Remedy, Addressed to the Slaveholders of the South* (Charleston, SC, 1850), 47; [J. Milton Clapp], "The French Republic," *SQR,* 14 (1848), 234–5; [James Warley Miles], *The Relation between the Races at the South* (Charleston, SC, 1861), 7.

[60] Cobb, *Law of Negro Slavery,* clxiv, clxxx ff., cxxxiv ("remarkable"); [Simms], *SQR,* n.s., 9 (1854), 543 ("good man"). On the response to Toussaint see also Supplementary References: "Haiti."

War, "for our negroes are better christians than their would-be liberators." Maybe so. But the Haitian Revolution created a strong sense across the South that the very subject of slavery and abolition had to be placed beyond discussion.[61]

As Southerners reassessed the French Revolution, they confronted antislavery radicalism. Southerners might defend popular sovereignty but denied that it implied emancipation. Yet the logic defied challenge: If principles of political liberty self-evidently applied to humanity as a whole, why not to slaves? The mere thought that slaves might claim freedom – and even political rights – doused southern infatuation with the revolutionary rhetoric of liberty and equality. Emancipation threatened southern material interests, but in a world infused with lofty aspirations to political virtue, unadorned self-interest did not provide an adequate defense of slavery. Prevailing political fashions frowned on unfettered self-interest as a shameful disregard of the public good. The sickening bloodshed in France provided an opportunity for Southerners to deplore violent social conflict without dwelling on their own material interests. Indeed, the horror of unfolding events reinforced the South's notion of slavery as a bulwark of civilization and as cornerstone of a responsible concept of political virtue. Even John Randolph and James Madison, who wished slavery gone, repudiated the radical implications of a French revolutionary virtue that stood exposed as façade for wanton tyranny.

Dew concluded his *Digest* with perceptible unease: The very notion of civilization depends upon slavery, which alone ensures the freedom from manual labor necessary to sustain a responsible and politically virtuous elite. Slavery did not merely permit the flowering of political virtue among the elite; it grounded the social hierarchy that provided the bulwark against the social injustices of capitalism and the political cruelty of French egalitarianism.[62]

Dew's analysis of the French Revolution set the tone for Southerners impressed by Edmund Burke's strictures but unable to swallow his evaluation as a whole. Dew criticized historians who dwelt on the French Revolution's horrors while slighting its achievements. He opened the final chapter of his *Digest*, "It has been well observed, that Revolution of France is one of the great eras of social order .... The period of its accomplishment constituted one of the grandest epochs in the history

---

[61] *Planters' Banner*, 14 (1849). Also, Cobb, *Law of Negro Slavery*, cxcvi; William S. Plumer, *Thoughts on the Religious Instruction of the Negroes of This Country* (Savannah, GA, 1848), 4, 16; B. L. Gildersleeve, "The Tontine," Richmond *Examiner*, Nov. 4, 1863, in Ward W. Briggs, Jr., ed., *Soldier and Scholar: Basil Lanneau Gildersleeve and the Civil War* (Charlottesville, VA, 1998), 132; Bruce Dain, "Haiti and Egypt in Early Black Racial Discourse in the United States," *Slavery and Abolition*, 14 (1993), 139–40; Jordan, *White over Black*, 384. Even free blacks reacted cautiously at first, rarely referring to Haiti lest they unleash a fierce white reaction. When Charleston's free people of color faced a reign of terror in 1860 and contemplated emigration, Haiti was the first choice of most: J. D. Johnson to Henry Ellison, Dec. 19, 1860, in Michael P. Johnson and James L. Roark, eds., *No Chariot Let Down: Charleston's Free People of Color on the Eve of the Civil War* (Chapel Hill, NC, 1984), 143. For the impact of Haiti in the South and evidence of blacks who invoked it down to the War despite all dangers, see Eugene D. Genovese, *From Rebellion to Revolution: Afro-American Slave Revolts in the Making of the Modern World* (Baton Rouge, LA, 1983), 96–7.

[62] Eugene D. Genovese, *Western Civilization through Slaveholding Eyes: The Social and Historical Thought of Thomas Roderick Dew* (New Orleans, 1986).

of man." For Dew, the Old Régime's oppression justified the people's violence and even excused the September Massacres. The arrogance and stupidity of aristocrats and the blundering opportunism of revolutionary moderates accounted for the ferocity of those determined to save the Revolution. Dew stressed the Old Régime's rigidities: "Changes took place in the social system, wholly at war with the political. It became necessary either to roll back the tide of civilization or else to fit the government by timely changes, to the constant revolutions which were taking place in the several organizations." France had outgrown feudal institutions: "Change or revolution became absolutely necessary." Dew chided the Bourbons for obstructing the free flow of capital. He approved the Revolution's creation of a national market and Napoleon's contributions toward creation of a European market.[63]

The middle classes had become much too powerful to be excluded from a large share in political power, and the French Revolution became a war between privileged and unprivileged property. Dew contrasted the English revolution of the 1640s with the French: "The English revolution differs from the French most strikingly in one particular. In the latter there was no appeal to precedents by the popular party; it was at once acknowledged that the past practice of the government was all against the people." Although Dew allowed that the American Revolution and Declaration of Independence influenced French thought and politics, he lamented the French Revolution's assignment of all sovereignty directly to the people, who could change the constitutional order at will. French democrats claimed inherent rights, which the acts and privileges of the monarchy had usurped. In England, both political parties claimed reverence for the Constitution and presented themselves as its rightful heirs and guarantors. The peculiarities of English society after the Norman Conquest had slowly created conditions for the emergence of a government and an opposition that could resolve differences peacefully.[64]

Innovation, Dew taught, becomes especially dangerous when the people have no experience with the exercise of rights. Moderate middle-class revolutionaries made the fatal error of courting the support of the propertyless urban masses. Dew did not hide his admiration for the Jacobins' revolutionary energy, decisiveness, and will – while recounting the savagery, horror, and folly of revolutionary excess. He maintained that the cry for equality outstripped the cry for liberty primarily as a reaction against aristocratic caste prejudices and haughtiness. Of Thermidor: "That hope of perfect liberty and perfect equality, which had fired all hearts and nerved all arms, was now gone – the sweet dreams of *democracy* were past."[65]

[63] Dew, *Digest,* quotes at 572, 579, 620; on economic policy see also Thomas Roderick Dew, *Lectures on the Restrictive System, Delivered to the Senior Class of William and Mary College* (Richmond, VA, 1829), 136. Dew's remarks on French "feudalism" prefigured those expressed by Alexis de Tocqueville in *The Old Régime and the French Revolution* (Garden City, NY, 1856), 19–20, 38–40. Dew's understanding of the relation of elites and lower classes in revolutions prefigured Vilfredo Pareto, *The Mind and Society: A Treatise on General Sociology,* tr. Andrew Bourgeois, 4 vols. (New York, 1963), 3:1431.

[64] Dew, *Digest,* 492, 562, 588. The antislavery liberal Lieber, writing *On Civil Liberty and Self-Government* under the influence of the revolutions of 1848, especially contrasted the institutions of England and France to warn against the concentration of power in the hands either of autocrats or radical democrats.

[65] Dew, *Digest,* 562, 583, 656.

2

The Age of Revolution through Slaveholding Eyes

> To my mind, the signs of war & convulsions never were stronger. I can see no immediate termination to the present state of disorder. All appear to be apt at pulling down existing political institutions, but not one able architect has risen in all Europe to reconstruct them.
>
> —John C. Calhoun (1849)[1]

During the 1820s and 1830s Americans, with politicians in the vanguard, wept over the oppressed peoples of Europe and cheered on the swelling revolutions, especially the Greek. Governor George Troup of Georgia referred to "the Greek, in his glorious struggle with the Turk." At the University of North Carolina, Representative William Shephard interpreted this "universal burst of indignant sympathy" as "a sincere tribute of deep-felt respect for her [Greece's] departed greatness." In Charleston in 1824, Catholic Bishop John England made a deep impression with an address on the suffering of the Greeks. Two years later he complained that "Greece" had become a magic word, conjuring up classical civilization and firing sympathy for the cause of freedom among Americans who were ignoring the struggle in Ireland. Joel Poinsett of South Carolina, an experienced diplomat, cautioned against sentimentalism and opposed Daniel Webster's inclination to intervene.[2]

---

[1] John C. Calhoun to Anna Maria (Calhoun) Clemson, June 15, 1849, in *JCCP*, 26:437. In contrast to Calhoun's letters to his daughter and others on the Revolution of 1848, the Panglossian letters from George Bancroft – an experienced diplomat and keen historian resident in Paris – to his wife reeked of naïveté. In M. A. DeWolfe, *The Life and Letters of George Bancroft*, 2 vols. (New York, 1908), see George Bancroft to Elizabeth Davis Bancroft, Apr. 20 and 29, Feb. 4 and 11, Aug. 6 and 13, 1849 (2:85–98).

Small town and village newspapers reprinted foreign news and comment from the periodicals of Europe and the North, as well as those of Richmond, Charleston, and New Orleans. Southern quarterlies reported in greater depth and surveyed reportage, esp. from *Edinburgh Review, London Quarterly Review, Westminster Review, North British Review,* and *Blackwood's*. Still, *De Bow's Review* regretted that American reports on revolutionary turmoil in Europe missed its significance for America's sectional struggle: *DBR*, 10 (1851), 2–3; 13 (1852), 320.

[2] Troup, "First Annual Message to the State Legislature of Georgia" (1824), in Edward J. Harden, *The Life of George M. Troup* (Savannah, GA, 1859), 222, full text 221–43; William Shephard, *An*

Southern enthusiasm for Christian Greeks against Muslim Turks slowly diminished. Francis Lieber, who fought on the side of the revolutionaries, grew disillusioned with Greek character and objectives and with the revolutionaries' incompetence. Editing *Southern Literary Messenger* in Richmond, Edgar Allan Poe shared
Lieber's disillusionment, but when he turned to Spanish tyranny in Latin America
Poe reverted to form and ignored the revolutionaries' deficiencies. In an 1856 *Southern Literary Messenger,* "L." tried to rekindle the sputtering pro-revolutionary fervor. "L." assured skeptics that the Greeks had proven heroic in war and noble in
aspirations. In social intercourse and hospitality they resembled Southerners. The
Greeks, "L." insisted, had replaced an absolutist regime with a liberal republic
and maintained the purity of a great race. Yet, to his dismay, Americans considered Greeks more "lying, treacherous and ungrateful" even than Turks. By the late
1850s those who, like Harry Hammond, still extolled the Greeks were fighting a
rear-guard action.[3]

Southern support for the European revolutions steadily became more qualified
and doubt ridden. In Virginia a troubled Thomas Ritchie, editor of the Richmond
Enquirer, deplored "the efforts of the crowned heads of Europe to crush out liberalism at home and rumors of their plans for the reconquest of Spanish America." In
Georgia, Judge Joseph Lumpkin grieved for an occupied Italy laid waste and deso-
lated. At the same time, those Southerners who publicly celebrated revolutionary
movements in Greece, South America, and Ireland often summoned them against
"aristocratic" and "monarchical" political opponents at home. W. W. Seaton of
Virginia, editor of *National Intelligencer,* sympathized with the Greek Revolution
but grew apprehensive over the lengths to which Northerners embraced that cause
and associated it with antislavery. Meanwhile, French conservatives denounced
pro-Greek Jacobins and Bonapartists as Negrophiles no less than Hellenophiles.[4]

In 1826 the Fifth Annual Meeting of the Auxilliary Society in Norfolk hailed
the South American revolutions and the progress of the British antislavery movement. A southern lady loudly proclaimed her sympathy for the Greeks. "Madam,"

*Address Delivered before the Two Literary Societies of the University of North Carolina, June 27,
1838* (Raleigh, NC, 1838), 22; Sebastian G. Messmer, ed., *The Works of the Right Rev. John England,
First Bishop of Charleston,* 7 vols. (Cleveland, OH, 1908), 5:82; for the reception of England's speech,
see William L. King, *The Newspaper Press of Charleston, S.C.: A Chronological and Biographical
History,* 2nd ed. (Charleston, SC, 1882), 166–8; J. Fred Rippy, *Joel R. Poinsett, Versatile American*
(New York, 1968), 80–1.

Shepherd hit a popular note. During the War, Bishop Elliott, for one – approving the struggle of
Christian Greeks against Muslim Turks – alluded to the modern Greeks as descendants of the ancients to whose great philosophical and political culture Christendom had fallen heir: Stephen Elliott,
"Samson's Riddle": A Sermon Preached at Christ Church, Savannah (Macon, GA, 1863), 11–12. The
flourishing of Greek names for American towns owed more to sympathy for the Greek revolution than
for ancient models: Walter R. Agard, "Classics on the Midwest Frontier," *Classical Journal,* 51 (1955),
103–4.
[3] Apr. 8, 1848, in Thomas Sergeant Perry, ed., *The Life and Letters of Francis Lieber* (Boston, 1882), 41.
[Edgar Allan Poe], *SLM,* 2 (1836), 125, 390; "L.", "Modern Greeks," *SLM,* 22 (1856), 90–6, quote at
93; [Harry Hammond], "European Correspondence," *RM,* 2 (1857/58), 496.
[4] Charles Henry Ambler, *Thomas Ritchie: A Study of Virginia Politics* (Richmond, VA, 1913), 83; Josephine Seaton, *William Winston Seaton of the "National Intelligencer"* (Boston, 1871), 155.

replied John Randolph, pointing to two ragged blacks, *"The Greeks are at your door!"* In Maryland, three white girls who proposed a society to help Greek children turned their attention to local black children instead. During the 1850s and the War years, Randolph's remarks on Greeks and blacks reverberated from Richmond to New Orleans. Southerners wondered if the European revolutionaries' appeal to arms would not tempt abolitionists to support slave insurrections. One revolution threatened to feed another.[5]

Southerners rallied to the Spanish-American revolutions, but few held out hope for the new republics. Euphoria over the revolutions in Latin America and elsewhere disguised skepticism about a world that verged on a grand new day of liberalism and constitutional democracy. While pro-expansionists in the southern press justified the filibustering of Narciso López and William Walker as contributions to the great transatlantic movement to overthrow decadent monarchies and empires, abolitionists – especially the blacks among them – grasped the connection between revolution in Europe and their own cause. A modern revolution had given birth to the United States and unleashed unprecedented political freedom and protection for individual property, including property in slaves. But these later revolutions were advancing interpretations of individual rights and freedom that undermined the legitimacy of slavery.[6]

In 1830, all along the eastern seaboard Americans cheered the fall of Charles X. In New York City James Monroe, living in obscurity and close to death, presided at a mass celebration at Tammany Hall. In Charleston, banquets shouted approval of William Gilmore Simms's poem, "The Tri-Color." Planters and their wives paraded with farmers, artisans, and workers. In time, Southern elation for the Revolution

---

[5] Randolph quoted in Powhattan Bouldin, *Home Reminiscences of John Randolph of Roanoke* (Danville, VA, 1990 [1878]), 113. Charleston's literary circles celebrated the revolutions of the 1820s: Gary Philip Zola, *Isaac Harby of Charleston, 1788–1828: Jewish Reformer and Intellectual* (Tuscaloosa, AL, 1994), 93. On southern reactions see Daniel R. Goodloe, *The Southern Platform; Or, Manual of Southern Sentiment on the Subject of Slavery* (Boston, 1858), 66–7; Jan. 12, 1863, in Kate Mason Rowland and Mrs. Morris S. Croxall, eds., *The Journal of Julia LeGrand: New Orleans, 1862–1863* (Richmond, VA, 1911), 83; William G. Shade, *Democratizing the Old Dominion: Virginia and the Second Party System, 1824–1861* (Charlottesville, VA, 1996), 63; Hugh Honour, *The Image of the Black in Western Art* (Cambridge, U.K., 1989), 4 (pt. 1), 133; Robert W. Fogel, *Without Consent or Contract: The Rise and Fall of American Slavery* (New York, 1989), 234–5.

Garrison exploded: "Ye patriotic hypocrites! ye panegyrists of Frenchmen, Greeks, and Poles!": *Liberator*, Sept. 3, 1831. In the 1840s Philip Lindsley of Tennessee, a critic of slavery, hit a raw nerve: "If the Bible be expected to achieve such miracles of passive obedience and non-resistance, why not send it to the Greeks, to teach them the grace of patience and submission, instead of furnishing them with money and arms to spread death and desolation around them?": "Negro Slavery in America," in LeRoy J. Halsey, ed., *The Works of Philip Lindsley*, 3 vols. (Philadelphia, 1866), 3:667.

[6] On the southern press see Tom Chaffin, *Fatal Glory: Narciso López and the First Clandestine U.S. War against Cuba* (Charlottesville, VA, 1996), ch. 3; on the abolitionists see Herbert Aptheker, *Abolitionism: A Revolutionary Movement* (Boston, 1989), ch. 3; for the New York *Daily Tribune*, see e.g. Apr. 28, 1851. For the reaction of northern conservatives against the European revolutions after the June Days see Michael A. Morrison, *Slavery and the American West: The Eclipse of Manifest Destiny and the Coming of the Civil War* (Chapel Hill, NC, 1997), 133–5. President George Junkin of Washington College supported the Latin American revolutions despite their being "unprepared for the enjoyment of rational liberty": *The Progress of the Age* (Philadelphia, 1851), 16–18.

of 1830 waned in its bourgeois monarchical aftermath, but even earlier concern had risen over the encouragement that revolutionary movements might offer rebellious West Indian slaves. In 1831 the Christmas Rising of some 2,000 slaves in Jamaica hung over the debate on England's Reform Bill, making even needed reforms look dicey. And in 1831, Nat Turner rocked Virginia.[7]

If Southerners had little taste for the restored Bourbon monarchy, they soon displayed as little for its bourgeois successor. They hoped the July Monarchy would prove a liberal quasi-republic, which to them meant a conservative regime. They were disappointed by Louis Philippe's refusal to rescue the Poles from czarist oppression but sighed with relief at his refusal to follow the British in West Indian emancipation. A lead article in *Southern Literary Messenger* traced the steady erosion of liberty in Europe and slighted liberal reforms as mere limitations on monarchy. It cautioned against celebration of popular violence, for continental institutions had poorly prepared the people to use liberty well. Republicans must settle for liberal monarchies in Europe. George Frederick Holmes noted that the revered Barthold Niebuhr had drawn back from the Revolution of 1830 and foreseen accelerating European decline. In a dramatic 1857 retrospect, Howard Caldwell exclaimed that Christians regretted the Revolution's course and outcome.[8]

For Simms, Louis Philippe's regime had "begun in fraud and continued in selfishness." It reeked of corruption and cynicism and disregarded popular distress. Benjamin Blake Minor fancifully accused Louis Philippe of scheming with the Catholic Church to colonize the Pacific and subvert American interests there. Trescot cheered the fall of "that miserable democratic imitation of royalty" who occupied "a throne which if a great man he might have sustained – if an honest man he would have shunned." Louisa McCord had no sympathy for "fallen dynasties, however much I may deem beggar-kings an object of pity." But she also repudiated radicals like Louis Blanc and M. Albert.[9]

---

[7] For Simms see Charles Downer Hazen, *Contemporary American Opinion of the French Revolution* (Gloucester, MA, 1964); W. P. Cresson, *James Monroe* (Chapel Hill, NC, 1946), 494; Oct. 4, 1830, in W. Emerson Wilson, ed., *Plantation Life at Rose Hill: The Diaries of Martha Ogle Forman, 1814–1845* (Wilmington, DE, 1976), 291; for the West Indies see Eugene D. Genovese, *From Rebellion to Revolution: Afro-American Slave Revolts in the Making of the Modern World* (Baton Rouge, LA, 1979), 36–7.

[8] See esp. Joseph Bassette Wilkins, "Window on Freedom: The South's Response to the Emancipation of the Slaves in the British West Indies" (Ph.D. diss., University of South Carolina, 1977); "The Liberties of People in Europe," *SLM*, 8 (1842), 613–20; [George Frederick Holmes], "Niebuhr," *MMQR*, 4th ser., 7 (1855), 556; [Howard H. Caldwell], "Victor Hugo," *RM*, 1 (1857), 270. On Niebuhr's reaction to the July Revolution see also John Edwin Sandys, *A History of Classical Scholarship*, 3 vols. (Cambridge, U.K.: vol. 1, 3rd ed., 1921; vols. 2 and 3, 2nd ed., 1908), 3:78. In 1831 Maria W. Steward, black Bostonian, urged her people to join in the vast revolutionary struggles of the day: Ruth Bogin and Jean Fagan Yellin, in Yellin and John C. Van Horne, eds., *The Abolitionist Sisterhood: Women's Political Culture in Antebellum America* (Ithaca, NY, 1994), 4.

[9] [William Gilmore Simms], "Guizot's Democracy in France," *SQR*, 15 (1849), 124; [Benjamin Blake Minor], "French and English Propagandism," *SLM*, 10 (1844), 580–1; also "British Interference," *SLM*, 10 (1844), 584–91; Trescot to William Porcher Miles, Mar. 22, 1848, in Miles Papers, at UNC-SHC; L. S. McCord to W. P. Miles, June 12, 1848, in Richard C. Lounsbury, ed., *Louisa S. McCord:*

The revolutions of 1848 delighted the abolitionists. Albert Barnes was ecstatic. James G. Birney fought in France. Southerners and Northerners fought on the revolutionary side, but Northerners had a better idea of what they were doing. Revolutionary turmoil drove French intellectuals to New Orleans, where they published newspapers and journals that were not always to southern tastes. Thus Dr. Louis Charles Roudanez, who had fought on the Parisian barricades, and Paul Trevigné, who during the War had been deeply affected by the 1848 revolution, published *L'Union* in New Orleans, which supported black rights. In 1864 Thomas Morris Chester, a free black, covered the War for the Philadelphia *Press* under the nom de plume "Rollin" – after Alexandre Auguste Ledru-Rollin, prominent 1848 radical. Refugee German and Czech "Forty-Eighters" had a worrisome impact on the Midwest. F. M. Klácel, a free-thinking poet-philosopher, edited a Czech-language newspaper in Iowa City.[10]

Still, southern newspapers responded hopefully to each uprising against decadent monarchies and aristocratic misrule and groaned over every setback to the popular cause. In the fall of 1849 Everard Green Baker, writing from his plantation in Jefferson County, Mississippi, welcomed the "mighty shocks" that convulsed the world and announced a "Glorious era for mankind," with America everywhere a beacon for the forces of "Liberty & virtue." T. M. Garret, a Whiggish student at the University of North Carolina, recorded, "The columns of the newspapers received by tonight's mail are big with sad forebodings. Hungary is almost prostrate at the feet of the Austrian monarch." From Brussels, Anna Maria Calhoun Clemson bemoaned "the fate of the poor Hungarians" and called the conduct of the Austrians "a disgrace to the 19th century." And as Southerners mourned the fate of brave peoples with dashed hopes, they wondered what revolutions bode for their own cause. Continued sympathy proceeded with hard criticism. David Mitchell, returning from his native England, was startled at the naïveté of those who hailed

Poems, Drama, Biography, Letters (Charlottesville, VA, 1996), 275, 363. Louis Blanc, a socialist, pushed the establishment of national workshops; Albert-Alexandre Martin, a revolutionary, was known as "Albert l'Ouvrier." David McCord returned from Paris to regale his friends with incidents of the great upheaval: see John Belton O'Neall, *Biographical Sketches of the Bench and Bar of South Carolina*, 2 vols. (Charleston, SC, 1859), 2:510. See also the surprising enthusiasm of Stephen F. Miller, a prominent Georgian, for British liberalization and French developments of the early 1830s: *The Bench and Bar of Georgia: Memoirs and Sketches,* 2 vols. (Philadelphia, 1858), 1:389, 2:390. The power attributed to Parisian journalists in bringing down the July monarchy captured the fancy of the Baptist Reverend J. L. Reynolds, an educational reformer who delighted to find the pen mightier than the sword. It did not take long for Reynolds and fellow Virginians to sober up: see Reynolds, *The Man of Letters* (Richmond, VA, 1849), 20.

[10] Charles C. Cole, Jr., *The Social Ideas of the Northern Evangelists, 1826–1860* (New York, 1954), 155; Louis S. Gerteis, *Morality and Utility in American Antislavery Reform* (Chapel Hill, NC, 1987), 62; C. C. Bell's articles in *EC*, 3:1348, 4:1621; R. J. M. Blackett, ed., *Thomas Morris Chester: Black Civil War Correspondent: His Dispatches from the Virginia Front* (Baton Rouge, LA, 1989), xi–xii; John Duffy, *Sword of Pestilence: The New Orleans Yellow Fever Epidemic of 1853* (Baton Rouge, LA, 1966), 5; G. Barany, "Appeal and Echo," in Béla K. Király and George Barany, eds., *East Central European Perceptions of Early America* (Lisse, Netherlands, 1977), 129.

the Revolution of 1848, displaying "total blindness to any possible dangers or misfortune happening to America or her institutions."[11]

Southern elation at the overthrow of monarchy ebbed as the revolutions of 1848 enshrined social equality along with political. In 1844 Professor Nathaniel Beverley Tucker of William and Mary suggested that class struggles in Europe demonstrated the wisdom of restricting suffrage to propertyholders. In 1850 he looked back on the Chartist demonstrations of April 1848, which plunged Britain into "anxiety and awe," and conjured up images of the Jacquerie and Wat Tyler. In truth, Tucker fairly shouted that the "contest of classes" in Europe differed essentially from previous social struggles, which had been over property rather than abstract principles. This new struggle was pitting defenders against enemies of property rights. The "absorbing question in every country in Christendom" was whether it would be governed by its collective mind or "pass under the brutal dominion of mobs." The revolutions of 1848, Tucker added, demonstrated anew that universal suffrage ends in anarchy or tyranny.[12]

Southern criticism grew progressively harsher. In an 1852 *Southern Literary Messenger*, "C. J. S." contemptuously dismissed responses to European revolutions as "expressions of hollow sympathy" that came cheap from Americans who expected them to fail. "C. J. S." believed serious study of European history would belie the notion that other peoples had the capacity to establish genuine republics. Trescot and a Professor Koeppen in *De Bow's Review* cited recent Greek revolutions to explain how the radicals' demagogy played into the hands of self-serving Russians and other imperialists. Speaking before the Virginia State Agricultural Society in 1858, J. P. Holcombe recalled the enthusiasm as nation after nation threw off "its old bondage," but bemoaned the crimes "committed in the name of liberty" and the "social and political convulsions" that attended supposed progress. What had become of France, Italy, Greece, and Spanish America? "A part has been swallowed up in the gulfs of anarchy and despotism – the rest still float above the wave, but with rudder and anchor gone."[13]

---

[11]   E. G. Baker Diary, Aug. 29, 1849, at UNC-SHC; T. M. Garrett Diary, Sept. 9, 1849, at UNC-SHC; Anna Maria Calhoun Clemson to John C. Calhoun, Oct. 26, 1849, in *JCCP*, 27:91; D. W. Mitchell, *Ten Years in the United States: Being an Englishman's Views of Men and Things in the North and South* (London, 1862), 29. For a typical early celebration of the revolutions of 1848 as the spread of American democracy, see "A Word for the Day," *Virginia Historical Register, and Literary Advertiser*, 2 (1849), 165.

[12]   Lewis Bernstein Namier, *1848: The Revolution of the Intellectuals* (Garden City, NY, 1964), 19–21; Nathaniel Beverley Tucker, "Moral and Political Effect of the Relation between the Caucasian and the African Slave," *SLM*, 10 (1844), 470–80; [Nathaniel Beverley Tucker], "The Present State of Europe," *SQR*, 16 (1850), 278–86, 292–3, quotes at 284, 285. William Hayne Simmons, writing about 1848, also warned the South about the dangers of universal suffrage: "Constitution of France," *SQR*, 16 (1850), 502–36.

[13]   "C. J. S.", "Austrian Politics," *SLM*, 18 (1852), 535. Professor Koeppen's essay on modern Greece clarified issues in the Greek Revolution: *DBR*, 13 (1852), 134–56, 217–29; W. H. Trescot, "An American View of the Eastern Question," *DBR*, 17 (1854), 285–6; James P. Holcombe, "Is Slavery Consistent with Natural Law?" *SLM*, 27 (1858), 406. Similarly, W. P. Riddell cited Dutch history to trace the

Southerners did loathe the aristocratic and reactionary European governments that threatened intervention, but some had qualms from the beginning, as many more did in time. In the lowcountry the Reverend John Hamilton Cornish reacted quickly: "Terrible news of the insurrection in Paris. What have they gained by Rebellion & expulsion of their King?" The Revolution of 1848 and the subsequent massacres appalled Whig politicians like William C. Rives of Virginia, who had had cordial personal relations with Louis Philippe and his family. In later years, as the threat of secession rose, Rives cried, "I have seen the pavements of Paris covered, and her gutters running with fraternal blood: God forbid that I should see this horrid picture repeated in my own country." Henry Hilliard of Alabama lectured the House of Representatives: "Let us not, in our impatience, forget that there is a mighty difference between reform and revolution. A reformation is brought about by the steady but gradual march of truth, while a revolution, like the earthquake, too often upheaves only to overthrow and crush." A month later, Hilliard reminded the House that France lacked institutions requisite for liberty: "The convulsion which exhibits a form so attractive to-day, may yet upturn the foundations of society, and result in the wildest anarchy." He assailed dreams of "fraternity" and attempts to solve the social question through governmental control of the economy. No recent convert, in 1839 and in 1846 Hilliard had looked "with the most unaffected anxiety" upon the strength of French infidelity and radicalism. The June Days did not surprise him.[14]

Representative David Outlaw of North Carolina, another Whig, conveyed his own apprehension to his wife, Emily, in December 1848: "The spirit of revolution is a great moral epidemic which seems to be prevailing over the whole world." He referred not only to Europe but also to Ohio, subjected to threats of a coup against a paralyzed legislature. The "ominous" events in France "tend to prove that when the country shall become very densely populated, the spirit of liberty will degenerate into licentiousness and anarchy until the people worried out of patience, will establish governments strong enough to preserve property and order." The next day he added, "The revolutionary spirit still seems to pervade the Continent of Europe and Prussia. What will ultimately be the result, I cannot say nor even consider." Attorney General Henry Bailey of South Carolina concluded as early as April that the revolution in France "has retarded, rather than advanced the cause of liberty, which is inseparable from law & order, and put back the progress of human happiness." He considered the Swiss and Germans the only Europeans with the

---

tortured course of freedom and republicanism in rebellion against tyranny: "Republic of Holland," *DBR*, 12 (1852), 282.

[14] Cornish Diary, July 21, 1848, at UNC-SHC; Rives quoted in *EC*, 3:1337; *Speeches and Addresses by Henry W. Hilliard* (New York, 1855), 125, 151–2, 10, 60, 67–8; also, Merton L. Dillon, *Slavery Attacked: Southern Slaves and Their Allies, 1619–1865* (Baton Rouge, LA, 1990), esp. 167–8, 225–7. At the time of heightened sectional tensions in the United States, turmoil in France elicited barbs at the centralization of political power in Paris as a cause of the revolution, which the revolutionaries then exacerbated. See e.g. [William Gilmore Simms], *SQR*, n.s., 2 (1850), 253; [Simmons], "Constitution of France"; [William W. Mann], "From Our Paris Correspondent," *SLM*, 16 (1850), 242–3, also 363.

experience and capacity for republican government. In late July Ellwood Fisher, a proslavery Quaker, described an antislavery North increasingly hostile to the South and wracked by a sharpening struggle between capital and labor: "I don't see how property will be able to sustain itself."[15]

The July 1848 issue of *Southern Quarterly Review* reveled in the overthrow of kings and the hard-fought enthronement of the people, but a review of Louis Blanc's *History of Ten Years* and Alphonse de Lamartine's *Three Days of February 1848* expressed misgivings. "C." considered the revolutions of 1830 more far-reaching than those of 1848 in marking a bourgeois ascendancy. A people as democratically inclined as the French and as contemptuous of inherited institutions would not return to monarchy but probably could not sustain a republic. "C." derided Louis Philippe; the confusion, decadence, and weakness of the European aristocrats; and the revolutionary burlesques that again revealed the inability of insurrectionary masses to accomplish anything except destruction. "C." credited Louis Blanc and his fellow radicals with ability, eloquence, and acute analyses of the social question but dismissed their socialistic measures as absurd defiance of economic laws. The June Days were a "tragic" assault on social order. "C." saw Blanc's socialism as a paternalistic appeal for a new serfdom, hinting at some such solution as the wave of the future. The outbreak of the Revolution of 1848 displeased Margaret Johnson Erwin of Mississippi, fluent in French and a student of French culture: "What a bloody race the French have once more turned out to be, and now they speak of a republic." In April 1848, James Mallory of Alabama, a small planter, hopefully told himself that the French had opted for "a new government on the model of the U.S.," but, even so, he feared that all Europe would suffer convulsions. By December, he was shaking his head over the turmoil that was expected to accompany the presidential election in France. The French "do not seem to understand how a great people can go through a political excitement in a peaceable manner and yield to a decision of the people." George Junkin, president of Washington College, told his students in 1851 that he held his breath over the revolutions of 1848, hoping they ended well. Junkin considered the revolutions part of a great forward movement in history, but he knew they could suffer defeat or turn radical or both. Those were not mutually exclusive alternatives. In 1864, Basil Lanneau Gildersleeve sneered, "The German 'revolution' of 1848 was one of the dreariest farces on record," replete with democratic pretenses, excesses, and blunders.[16]

---

[15] David Outlaw to Emily Outlaw, Dec. 14 and 15, 1848 at UNC-SHC; Henry Bailey to Calhoun, Apr. 20, 1848, in *JCCP*, 25:334–7; Ellwood Fisher to Calhoun, July 21, 1848, in *JCCP*, 25:608.

[16] "C.", "The French Republic," *SQR*, 14 (1848), 197–241. See also "Hurlburt's Essays," *SQR*, 14 (1848), 131–3; Margaret Johnson Erwin to Caroline Wilson, 1848, in John Seymour Erwin, *Like Some Green Laurel: Letters of Margaret Johnson Erwin, 1821–1863* (Baton Rouge, LA, 1981), 38 (Erwin admired the French while considering them "often fools," but for the Germans, "those tasteless swine," she had no good words: Erwin to Wilson, Dec. 19, 1848 [39]); Apr. 6 and Dec. 10, 1848, in Grady McWhiny, Warner O. Moore, Jr., and Race Pace, eds., *"Fear God and Walk Humbly": The Agricultural Journal of James Mallory, 1843–1877* (Tuscaloosa, AL, 1997), 85, 94; George Junkin, *The Progress of the Age* (Philadelphia, 1851), 16–18; B. L. Gildersleeve, "Schleswig-Holstein," Richmond *Examiner*, Feb. 22, 1864, in Ward W. Briggs, Jr., ed., *Soldier and Scholar: Basil Lanneau Gildersleeve and the Civil*

Beginning in May 1848, *Southern Literary Messenger* bared hopes, fears, and shifts in nuance about the February revolution. William Mann, a Virginian resident in Paris, opened his communiqués with denunciation of both the "temerity" of those who had plunged France into uncharted seas and the corruption of the fallen monarchy. He hinted of a grave danger posed by the "reckless and impetuous" Alexandre Auguste Ledru-Rollin, the radical darling of the masses. "None but republican opinions can now be safely expressed in France." In November, while silent about the June Days, Mann thought that the sooner "some military tyrant" took power, the better for France and the world. He expected another explosion and pinned his hopes for the restoration of order on General Louis Eugène Cavaignac, not Louis Bonaparte. By December he knew that prospects for a wholesome outcome were rapidly disappearing and predicted that Louis Bonaparte, a despot in waiting, would be elected president. In January 1849 he wrote, with mixed emotions, that all sensible, patriotic Frenchmen were crying, "A master! A master! Give us a master!" Cavaignac, who had presided over the slaughter of the June Days, had discredited himself. The experiment with republicanism had failed, and restoration of the Empire was a matter of time. Were Mann a Frenchman, he too would cry for a master. In the spring of 1849 he no longer believed that France would avoid another plunge into "ultra-democracy, and Terror, and Despotism." Socialists and radical republicans were preparing another bloody insurrection, and the regime was preparing to crush it.[17]

Meanwhile, Southerners were learning from *Letters of a Traveller* by William Cullen Bryant – New York's editor and poet, whom they held in high regard – that Europe was an armed camp: "France is not quite so free as she was under Louis Philippe." By February 1850 Mann started to panic as he saw the power of the radical Left waxing. He expected a coup by a radicalized army and predicted that, if the radicals instituted their Social Republic, they would drench Paris in more blood than their Jacobin predecessors had. In 1851 and again in 1852 Mann shifted to predict a Bonapartist coup, wondering that it had not already occurred. The republic had died with Napoleon's election to the presidency. The only remaining question was who would emerge as dictator.[18]

War (Charlottesville, VA, 1998), 259. Blanc had the respect of John R. Thompson, who reviewed his *History of Ten Years* (1843) and pronounced Blanc a "man of brilliant talents": [J. R. Thompson], *SLM*, 14 (1848), 333. "R. E. C.", who denounced Blanc the socialist, considered his historical writing "of high order": "The Problem of Free Society – Part Two," *SLM*, 27 (1858), 8.

[17] [William W. Mann], "The Provisional Government of France," *SLM*, 14 (1848), 301–7, 356–62, 758–60, quotes at 357, 360, 758, and "From Our Paris Correspondent," 15 (1849), 57–60, 343–4; 16 (1850), 240–1, 358–65; 17 (1851), 444–53; 18 (1852), 213–16. (Mann's reports from Paris contained much on French science and art.) An unidentified contributor judged Ledru-Rollin "a shabby imitation of Danton": "Lamartine," *SQR*, 12 (1855), 70. At first, Cavaignac looked good to Southerners who wanted a politically moderate strongman in Paris. A contributor to *De Bow's Review* described the June Days as "days of blood and slaughter" and Cavaignac as the "noblest Roman of them all" and a stern man of order. See "French Revolutionary History," *DBR*, 30 (1861), 300–1.

[18] William Cullen Bryant, *Letters of a Traveller; Or, Notes of Things Seen in Europe and America* (New York, 1850), 426–35, quote at 434.

Southern Literary Messenger published analyses of European affairs by Maximilian Schele De Vere, the University of Virginia's respected professor of modern languages. In 1849 De Vere argued that the European convulsions signaled a new era: "Never before has Europe been so universally, so deeply agitated." In contrast to the religious wars of earlier centuries and the French Revolution of 1789, February 1848 initiated a sweeping European-wide social revolution "full of bloodshed, meanness, and sadness." He saw a positive side in Eastern Europe's resurrection of the nationality of "ancient races" rooted in "the so-called low people," who had preserved ancient languages and customs in multinational empires while elites wallowed in cosmopolitanism. The revolutionary leaders had sprung from those elites. Intent on the reestablishment of national identities under their own aegis, they spoke in the name of the people they claimed to represent. They had unleashed forces they could not control, especially the ancient hatreds of Magyars and Slavs, Croats and Serbs, Poles and Russians. Power passed to revolutionaries who flew the banner of freedom but denied freedom to others. De Vere shrugged off political changes and transient republicanism as superficial, insisting that deep change came from the freeing of a nationalism destined to grow stronger.[19]

Calhoun had hopes for a particularistic German federation, much as he deplored a centralized France. De Vere implicitly disagreed, reporting that German republican ideals were crashing on particularism and that Germany's future depended on unification under authoritarian Prussia. For De Vere, the heroic revolutionary struggles in Italy again demonstrated that the people had to choose between two ideals they vainly sought to reconcile – liberty and nationalism. When the South seceded, Calhoun's love affair with Germany took an ironic turn: Prussia sided with the North, and its foreign minister explained that Prussia resolutely opposed all revolutionary movements.[20]

By the end of the 1850s nationalist calls for a "Young America" – an aggressive and influential movement for American expansionism – had passed in the South into calls for secession, with the Italian *Risorgimento* a strong model. That Italian unification had its turning point in 1861 was not lost on the southern press.

[19] Maximilian Schele De Vere, "Glimpses of Europe in 1848," *SLM*, 15 (1849), 1–10, quote at 1. The editors followed De Vere's article with one on "National Ballads" (10–15). De Vere much admired Stonewall Jackson and, in 1863, sought to arrange for a German edition of Robert L. Dabney's book on him: M. Schele De Vere to William McGuffey, July 6, 1863, in Thomas Cary Johnson, *Life and Letters of Robert Lewis Dabney* (Carlisle, PA, 1977), 280. For the rising importance of nationalism in Europe's turmoil see also [Francis Peyre Porcher], "A Plea for Italy," *RM*, 8 (1858), 214–21. Two years before the explosions of 1848 M. R. H. Garnett of Virginia cautioned that the admirable Hungarian people deserved to be free of Austrian despotism but also that they themselves oppressed Slavs: [Garnett], "Hungary and Transylvania," *SLM*, 12 (1846), 3, 80.
[20] De Vere, "Glimpses of Europe," 129–40, 193–208 (Italy), and on Schleswig-Holstein (313–315e). On the Prussians see Belle Becker Sideman and Lillian Friedman, eds., *Europe Looks at the Civil War, An Anthology* (New York, 1960), 97. In Europe in 1848, the youthful Louis Rémy Mignot, Charleston's superb landscape painter, found his sense of being a Southerner reinforced by the nationalism all around him. He spent the 1850s abroad and in New York but sided with the Confederacy. See Katherine E. Manthorne with John W. Coffey, *The Landscapes of Louis Rémy Mignot: A Southern Painter Abroad* (Washington, DC, 1996), 27.

Italian efforts at unification evoked southern applause, although in 1848 Mann, concerned about social radicalism, had jeered that no sensible Italian could be a republican. Southerners, even the unsentimental Edmund Ruffin and Louisa McCord, gave their hearts to Italian unification and especially to the romantic Giuseppe Garibaldi, whom Ruffin extolled as the giant among European leaders. When news arrived in 1861 of Garibaldi's support for the Union, Ruffin decided that he was a great soldier but not much else. By 1863 Ruffin saw in the brave soldier a destructive Red Republican.[21]

Southerners, distinguishing among Italian patriots, respected Camillo Benso di Cavour but not Giuseppe Mazzini. De Vere expressed a common judgment when he labeled Mazzini a dangerous fanatic of doubtful morals, prone to violence and ready to sacrifice honor to his abstract ideals – a zealot who told every patriotic Italian to stand ready to kill an Austrian. To James Johnston Pettigrew, who knew southern Europe firsthand, Victor Emmanuel was a "conscientiously constitutional monarch," in contrast to "Mazzini and his wretched crew of assassins." Enthusiasm for patriotic Italians did not extend to radicals, as news of revolutionary excesses and an incipient reign of terror in Vienna and Milan filtered into the southern press and raised the specter of proletarian dictatorship. Apprehensions extended to French leaders. "S. A. L." wrote in 1855, "The iron arm of military rule alone keeps down the destructive forces of socialism and materialism in France." With sarcasm and admiration, John Reuben Thompson reported from Paris on "the improving hand of Napoleon III," whose despotism was probably the best government Frenchmen could sustain. "L. C. B." maintained that Louis Napoleon used egalitarian demagogy to impose a dictatorship that France needed in order to overcome the war between labor and capital.[22]

Americans suffered a severe jolt in June 1848 when Parisian workers rose against the newly entrenched bourgeois republic. Proslavery Southerners said, "We told

---

[21] The late Armstead L. Robinson called our attention to the Italian model and Young America; W. W. Mann, "Paris Correspondent," *SLM*, 14 (1848), 340; Ruffin, Jan. 24 and June 21, 1859, June 22, 1861, Sept. 2, 1863, in *ERD*, 1:289, 2:311, 611, 3:131, quote at 1:289; Louisa McCord to Hiram Powers, Dec. 24, 1860, in Lounsbury, ed., *Louisa S. McCord: Poems*, 275, 363. See also Supplementary References: "Fuller."

[22] De Vere, "Glimpses of Europe," 196; [James Johnston Pettigrew], *Notes on Spain and the Spaniards in the Summer of 1859, with a Glance at Sardinia* (Charleston, SC, 1861), 6, 16; "C. J. S.", "Austrian Politics," *SLM*, 18 (1852), 542–3; "S. A. L.", "Theory of Life," *SLM*, 21 (1855), 400; J. R. Thompson, "Editorial Letters from Europe," *SLM*, 20 (1854), 532–4, quote at 532; "L. C. B.", "The Country in 1950 [*sic*]," *SLM*, 22 (1856), 429–30. On Cavour as a great man see *SLM*, 32 (1861), 72–3, and William Gordon McCabe, "Political Corruption," *SLM*, 34 (1862), 82. Bishop Patrick Lynch of Charleston referred to "the tragic farce of Mazzini's republic": [Lynch], "Nineveh and Its Remains," *SQR*, 16 (1849), 4; also, [A. Corcoran], "Prospects of Italy – Italian Unification," *RM*, 3 (1858), 460. For southern press reports see e.g. New Orleans *Daily Picayune*, June 29, 1849, and Milledgeville *Southern Recorder*, Sept. 18, 1860. David F. Jamison wrote, "The '15th of May' and the 'days of June' have shown the vast difference between political theories and their practical application": "Histoire des Girondins," *SQR*, 16 (1849), 76. The widely circulated and inexpensive *Daily Picayune* received firsthand reports from Paris on the overthrow of Louis Philippe, the June days, and Louis Napoleon's coup d'état from George Williams Kendall, who warned that the leaders of the radical Left were demagogues. See Fayette Copeland, *Kendall of the Picayune* (Norman, OK, 1943), 243–55.

you so," and antislavery Northerners, "Your turn comes next." Americans read about a class war that Alexis de Tocqueville called the most extensive and singular event in French history – the best armed, most furious insurrection Paris had ever known.[23]

Coinciding with American free-soil demands for exclusion of slavery from the Mexican cessions, the June Days dramatized the social chaos that accompanied a broad interpretation of individual freedom. Under intense pressure from radical workers, artisans, and petty bourgeois, the French republic established national workshops as a cure for unemployment and class warfare. The experiment ended badly. The lower classes had shed much of the blood that brought the republican wing of the bourgeoisie to power and now found themselves shortchanged economically and politically. Defiantly, they rioted, built barricades, and threatened to drive the revolution well to the left, much as the Jacobins had done. Southerners revisited the history of political revolutions and the dangers inherent in the expansion of individual political rights and democracy. Universal political freedom for individuals had never been the rule; democracy had everywhere proven unstable. Some Southerners began to think the unthinkable and reject democracy in all its forms, while the great majority sought to contain it within a constitutional framework.

The revolutions of 1848 showed how easily defense of the rights of propertied heads of households passed into defense of the rights of individuals. By the late 1840s southern social theorists and church leaders were attending closely to the "social question." Professing sympathy with "free" workers alienated and uprooted by capitalist exploitation, they found the alternative to social catastrophe not in radical democratization but in a servitude that held capitalists responsible for their laborers' welfare. The South, they boasted, had precisely the system needed.

White Southerners frowned when Yankees applauded the Revolution of 1848 for abolishing slavery in the Islands and smiled when Hawthorne, Melville, Thoreau, and Whitman gagged on the June Days. In the North, as in France, Fourierists and other radicals approved the social initiatives of the new French republic, only to be crestfallen when the bourgeois government closed down the workshops and shot rebellious workers. Many northern radicals dissociated themselves from the workers' resort to arms, and French conservatives joyously published Emerson's words of disgust at the revolution's radical turn. The women's-rights advocates who convened at Seneca Falls, New York, in July – one week after the news of June Days reached America – expressed horror at the violence unleashed by Parisian workingwomen. That was not the way it was supposed to be. Harriet Beecher Stowe, hostile to such radicalism, tried to turn the news against the South: Learn your lesson while you have time, for your slaves will prove your very own Jacobins.[24]

---

[23] J. P. Mayer, ed., *The Recollections of Alexis de Tocqueville* (London, 1948), 160.

[24] Larry J. Reynolds, *European Revolutions and the American Literary Renaissance* (New Haven, CT, 1988), xi, xii, 15–16, 19, 50–3, 154–7; Carl J. Guarneri, *The Utopian Alternative: Fourierism in Nineteenth-Century America* (Ithaca, NY, 1991), 336–41; Margaret Fuller, "The Roman Revolution: Three Letters," in Philip Rahv, ed., *Discovery of Europe: The Story of American Experience in the Old World* (Cambridge, MA, 1947), 172; Arthur A. Ekirch, *The Idea of Progress in America, 1815–1860* (New York, 1944), 54–6.

Although no less horrified, knowledgeable Southerners had long expected the insurrection of unemployed and exploited free workers and the collapse of the free-labor system into anarchy and despotism. John Randolph, Thomas Cooper, Thomas Roderick Dew, and John C. Calhoun had identified the destructive implications of the great social upheavals in Europe and predicted mounting ferocity. Years before, in 1831, the worldly and moderate Hugh Legaré had pointed to Lyons, where 15,000 workers fought pitched battles with the National Guard and suffered 600 casualties. In July 1848, James Henley Thornwell, disgusted by French "blundering," expressed sympathy for the Parisian workers whom a rapacious bourgeoisie had driven to insurrection: "A ball has been set in motion upon the relations of capital and labour, whose progress it will be extremely difficult to arrest." As late as 1859 *Southern Literary Messenger* published a long eyewitness account of the June Days that recalled the slaughter and mourned the insurgents. The slaveholders remained committed to social order at all cost. "The heart of Europe," wrote Senator Willie Mangum of North Carolina, "quakes in fear of the unknown future." The masses – unprepared for a manly liberty – were rising, and Mangum saw war as well as revolution threatening to engulf Europe. The decades-long critique of the French Revolution of 1789 reinforced the celebration of slavery as the world's great conservative republican social force.[25]

The revolutions did gratify the Protestant South by assailing the Catholic Church. In 1831 Alexander Campbell had linked religious awakening to the overthrow of "superstition, false religion, and oppressive governments," and Thornwell saw 1848 as the unfolding of prophecy. The Protestant clergy subsequently thrilled to Italian unification and the destruction of the Pope's temporal power. Everard Green Baker heard a sermon in Panola, Mississippi, "on the millennium, as one of the evidences of the coming of Christ's Kingdom was the condition of the Pope of Rome, now about to be stripped of his temporal Throne." Even so, southern opposition to social revolutions brought forth renewed respect for the Catholic Church and criticism of its detractors. For all we know, Calhoun agreed with Thornwell's opinion that Catholicism ruined pre-1789 France by opening the floodgates to unbelief and social radicalism. But that was then and 1848 was now, and Calhoun was defending the Pope as a genuine reformer and praising his "wisdom in proceeding cautiously." George Fitzhugh complimented the Pope as a "radical reformer." De Vere spoke of a brave and honest Pius IX, although "That he granted too much and too rapidly we

---

[25] Michael O'Brien, *A Character of Hugh Legaré* (Knoxville, TN, 1985), 189. For an especially interesting reaction from Louisiana see Jean Boze to Baron Henri de Ste. Gemé, Mar. 10, 1832, in Ste. Gemé Papers, at Historic New Orleans Collection. Thornwell to Matthew J. Williams, July 17, 1848, in B. M. Palmer, *The Life and Letters of James Henley Thornwell* (Richmond, VA, 1875), 310; F. Pardigon, "Episodes of the June Days, 1848," *SLM*, 29 (1859), 297–308; Henry Thomas Shanks, ed., *The Papers of Willie P. Mangum*, 5 vols. (Raleigh, NC, 1955–56), 5:680–1; see also William Harrison Shryock, *Georgia and the Union in 1850* (Philadelphia, 1926), 113–14, 202–3. J. Q. Moore supported the Party of Order but admired the courage shown by the workers during the June Days: "Louis Napoleon and the French," *DBR*, 16 (1854), 393. For another account of the dreadful conditions that led the workers of Lyons to rise up in 1831 see "R. E. C.", "The Problem of Free Society," *SLM*, 27 (1858), 413–14.

cannot doubt – his expulsion from Rome furnishes incontestable evidence." There were even kind words for the long-hated Jesuits. Holmes defended them in *Southern Quarterly* Review as supporters of social order and held their critics – followers of Rousseau, Voltaire, and the Encyclopedists – morally responsible for the Terror. In the same issue, a fifty-page essay "earnestly commended" a fair, unbiased account by an author who depicted the Jesuits as courageous Christian missionaries and pillars of social order.[26]

Those who believed that only the restoration of some form of slavery could save Europe held up the June Days as the beginning of the end of the free-labor system. According to the Presbyterian Reverend William Hutson of South Carolina, "Wealth and intelligence" must carry genuine reform, which "invariably retrogrades when subjected to the sway of the 'democratic idea.' " The American Constitution could not resist the onslaught of democracy. Slavery alone "secures us the only possible liberty which can endure the rude pressure of a fierce democracy." Holmes delivered the benediction: "The aberrations of socialism, communism, and etc., and their adaptability in Europe and the Northern States, betray the social distemper in the free societies there, and their total and unceremonious rejection at the South, proves the health, good order, and peace, which have resulted from slavery." In April 1848 William Valentine of North Carolina had rejoiced at the European revolutions; by 1851 he was horrified by the emergence of socialism and communism in England as well as France, although he, a slaveholder, agreed that – of course – no man should live off the labor of another.[27]

---

[26] Alexander Campbell in *Millennial Harbinger,* 2 (Dec. 1831), 568, and see Alexander Campbell, *Popular Lectures and Addresses* (Philadelphia, 1863), 375. Thornwell to Matthew J. Williams, July 17, 1848, in Palmer, *Thornwell,* 310; E. G. Baker Diary, Oct. 24, 1860, at UNC-SHC; James Oscar Farmer, Jr., *The Metaphysical Confederacy: James Henley Thornwell and the Synthesis of Southern Values* (Macon, GA, 1986), 110; Calhoun, "Remarks on the Mission to the Papal States," Mar. 21, 1848, in *JCCP,* 25:260; George Fitzhugh, "Southern Thought – Its New and Important Manifestations," *DBR,* 23 (1857), 343; De Vere, "Glimpses of Europe," 193; [George Frederick Holmes], "The Wandering Jew," *SQR,* 9 (1846), 90–3; "The Jesuits," *SQR,* 9 (1846), 149–203. Mann withheld support for French action in Rome, believing that the Romans lacked the ability to sustain a republic and would not long tolerate foreign intervention: "Paris Correspondence," *SLM,* 15 (1849), 501–2. In a continuing exchange of views, a contributor to *Southern Literary Messenger* criticized Joseph Bonaparte for humiliating the Pope and inciting insurrectionary mobs: "Alison's History of Europe," *SLM,* 9 (1843), 282. "W. R. H.", however, attacked papal pretensions and praised efforts to curb papal power: "Rome: Papal and Republican," *SLM,* 15 (1849), 547–51. In the 1890s John Girardeau, Thornwell's heir, still recalled those "signs of the times": George A. Blackburn, ed., *Sermons by John L. Girardeau* (Columbia, SC, 1907), 98–101. In 1831, the *Biblical Repertory and Princeton Review* welcomed the July Revolution as the sign of a new religious spirit destined to sweep away both Rome and infidelity and recharge Protestantism: "The Religious Prospects of France," *BRPR,* (1831), 383–98.

[27] [William F. Hutson], "History of the Girondists," *SPR,* 2 (1848), 396, quote at 404; G. F. Holmes, "Fitzhugh's Sociology for the South," *QRMECS,* 9 (1855), 180–201, quote at 196; Fitzhugh, "Southern Thought," 338, 350, and "Southern Thought Again," *DBR,* 23 (1857), 449–62; Valentine Diaries, Apr. 21, 1848, June 6, 1851, at UNC-SHC. James McNeill, a student at the University of North Carolina, identified despotism as Europe's continuing problem and Jacobinism, which was worse, its natural result: "Political State of Europe," in Speeches of Graduates, 1856, at UNC-NCC.

In South Carolina, George Howe of Columbia Seminary exclaimed that something like an eruption of Nature had burst upon the world. In Virginia, Nathaniel Beverley Tucker wrote to William Gilmore Simms, "Time was when I might have been less desperate, because I could have sought refuge under some emperor or king." But now, "There is no escape from the many-headed despotism of numbers, but by a strong and bold stand on the banks of the Potomac." In Georgia in 1850, Alexander Stephens made clear the shift in the popular mood in a letter to Representative Howell Cobb, recommending that unionists discredit their opponents in the gubernatorial campaign by linking them to French neo-Jacobinism: "Warn the good people of Georgia to beware of revolution – refer to France – and plant yourself against the factionalists of South Carolina." In 1852, Arthur Hopkins of Alabama wrote William Graham of North Carolina that South Carolinians were behaving like Jacobins and had to be put down. A few years later, Francis Lieber was not surprised that "the Jacobin communist [Pierre] Soulé" had joined William Walker to implant slavery in Nicaragua.[28]

J. P. Holcombe told the Virginia State Agricultural Society in 1858 that Americans had greeted the European revolutions with "generous enthusiasm" but not with wisdom. "Forgetting the ages through whose long night their fathers wrestled with this blessing [liberty], they have regarded an equal liberty as the universal birthright of humanity." Even the horrible consequences of anarchy and new despotisms did not readily dim the ardor of the North. Americus Featherman pronounced the Revolution of 1789 still in progress, with the outcome perhaps not to be settled for a century. He celebrated the uprising of the masses for liberty and republicanism, likening 1789 to the Puritan revolution of the seventeenth century as "the death blow to hereditary monarchy and the divine right of kings" but bemoaning the "insane ardor" and fierce radicalism. He reproached his own government for encouraging a pseudo-republic, "born of circumstances, but not of principles," and the wild and unsustainable schemes of radicals like Ledru-Rollin, Blanc, and Pierre Joseph Proudhon. "The French Revolution of 1848 was a beautiful illusion – a Platonic dream."[29]

The geopolitics of revolution and counterrevolution compelled excruciating debate over Russia, perceived as a rising world power. Politically informed Southerners, like Northerners and Europeans, recoiled at the westward expansion of this terrifying giant bent on conquest and the expansion of czarist despotism. The Reverend

[28] George Howe, "Secondary and Collateral Influence of the Scriptures," *SPR*, 7 (1853), 113; Tucker quoted in Farmer, *The Metaphysical Confederacy*, 155–6, and see Farmer's trenchant remarks on the impact of the revolutions of 1848 in the South. Alexander Stephens to Howell Cobb, June 23, 1851, in Ulrich Bonnell Phillips, ed., *The Correspondence of Robert Toombs, Alexander H. Stephens, and Howell Cobb* (Washington, DC, 1913): "Annual Report of the American Historical Association for the Year 1911," vol. 2), 237; Arthur F. Hopkins to William A. Graham, Apr. 6, 1852, in J. G. deRoulhac Hamilton, ed., *The Papers of William Alexander Graham*, 5 vols. (Raleigh, NC, 1957–73), 4:284; F. Lieber to G. S. Hilliard, Oct. 23, 1856, in Perry, ed., *Life and Letters of Lieber*, 291.

[29] J. P. Holcombe, *An Address Delivered before the Seventh Annual Meeting of the Virginia State Agricultural Society* (Richmond, VA, 1858), 8; Americus Featherman, "French Revolutionary History," *DBR*, 29 (1860), 673–95, and "The French Revolution of 1848," *DBR*, 30 (1861), 167–81.

E. T. Winkler described Russia and Pan-Slavism as enemies of freedom that must not be permitted to prevail; and, according to Professor W. T. Brantly of the University of Georgia, the Czar "contemplates the subjection of the world." W. C. Duncan, in *De Bow's Review,* extolled the Russian people for their heroic struggle against Napoleon but warned that the subsequent consolidation and expansion of Russian power threatened the freedom of others. A contributor to *Southern Literary Messenger* predicted that Western Europe, rotted by social conflict, would succumb to Russian despotism. Yet condemnations of Russian intervention in central Europe obscured southern relief at its antirevolutionary character.[30]

Russia's serfdom should have fit well into a projected worldwide social system based on unfree labor, but Southerners tended to view Russian lords as brutes. Robert Howison scowled that Russians treated serfs like beasts. De Bow, who regarded "despotic Russia" as "lowest in the scale of civilization" among European nations, protested the de facto enslavement of the agricultural population and the lack of a vigorous middle class. Still, with the coming of the Crimean War, Southerners — who instinctively preferred Britain's constitutional order — wrestled with their preference for a serf-based Russian social order over one based on wage labor. The Russia that loomed as a great reactionary power, hateful for its suppression of republicanism in Europe, commanded respect in the South for its firm resistance to radicalism within and without its borders. Early pro-British response to the Crimean War gave way to heightened awareness of a common bond of social relations between southern slavery and Russian serfdom.[31]

In 1853 an unsigned article on "The Destiny of Russia" in *Southern Literary Messenger* claimed that hopes for a glorious republicanism – arising from the ruins of a massive European crisis – were doomed. A new despotism was replacing a "turgid, ever-changing republicanism," and the despotic Russian Empire would be the sword of Christian expansion. In 1854 Trescot saw post-Napoleonic Europe as a new constellation of powers that featured extinction of the old German empire, an "astonishing" rise of Russia, consolidation of British rule in India, and emergence of powerful radical parties in every important European country. Lamenting the lack of a buffer between the West and Russia, especially after the sacrifice of Poland, Trescot viewed the Congress of Vienna as a mere truce among competing states. The "miserable folly" of the German revolutionaries of 1848 had brought European politics to a boil; only Russia, aiming southward at Constantinople, had a fixed policy. The British were sacrificing long-term national interests to commerce.

---

[30] E. T. Winkler, *An Address Delivered before the Philosophian and Adelphian Societies of Furman University* (Greenville, SC, 1853), 16; W. T. Brantley, *A Discourse Delivered before the Phi Kappa Society of the University of Georgia* (Athens, GA, 1852), 15; W. C. Duncan, "The Empire of Russia," *DBR,* 11 (1851), 459; "Destiny of Russia," *SLM,* 19 (1853), 41, 44. See Supplementary References: "Russia and the Crimean War."

[31] Robert R. Howison, *A History of Virginia from Its Discovery and Settlement by Europeans to the Present Time,* 2 vols. (Philadelphia, 1846), 2:121; J. D. B. De Bow, *The Industrial Resources, Statistics, &c. of the United States and More Particularly of the Southern and Western States,* 3rd ed., 3 vols. (New York, 1966 [1854]), 3:400; Horace Perry Jones, "Southern Opinion on the Crimean War," *Journal of Mississippi History,* 29 (1967), 95–117.

The European powers failed to dismember a decadent Turkey only because they could not agree on the shares. The balance of power was collapsing, and radical nationalists found new opportunities for mischief. Trescot acknowledged the long and dismal history of Russia's barbarous aristocracy and brutal serfdom but saw a new Russia in the making. A stern regime was promoting economic development and achieving "miracles" for its various peoples without obliterating their unique cultural characteristics. Trescot favored the reduction of Turkey to a Russian protectorate, thereby underscoring his predilection for concentrated state power and his impatience with Calhoun's constitutional doctrines. He alluded to the British in India as confirmation of a white, particularly Anglo-Saxon, destiny to rule Asia. England had accomplished great things, yet he feared its growing intervention in the New World and its designs on Cuba. An emergent Russia promised to stabilize international affairs and Continental social order, and Russia and England were natural allies in the maintenance of peace and commercial prosperity. Trescot counseled American neutrality in the Crimean War so long as Britain and France did not pursue expansion in the Americas. Although Russia remained a problem, even a threat, it stood as Europe's principal bastion against revolutionary madness.[32]

As an awestruck boy, Ujanirtus Allen of Virginia shook the hand of Lajos (Louis) Kossuth, revered leader of the unsuccessful Hungarian revolution of 1848. As a Confederate soldier, Allen looked back with a shudder at having "held the paw of that Hungarian 'Orangoutang.'" In between, in 1852, J. G. M. Ramsey of Tennessee, worrying about the Democratic party's prospects in the election of 1852, remarked, "Kossuthism is a weight no one can carry south of Pennsylvania and Ohio."[33]

From December 1851 to July 1852, a wildly acclaimed Kossuth toured the United States to raise money for the lifeless remains of his cause. The North gave him a hero's welcome of astonishing proportions. Some northern conservatives demurred, describing Kossuth's American supporters as infidels, radical abolitionists, socialists, and scoundrels. More often than not, Kossuth's supporters howled them down. For a while Kossuth-mania gripped abolitionists, free-soilers, Young America enthusiasts, and people in all regions – especially the Midwest. Among the celebrants were William Lloyd Garrison, Henry Ward Beecher, Cassius Clay, Abraham Lincoln, and William H. Seward. Harriet Beecher Stowe thought the Hungarian revolution should teach Americans to honor slaves who fled the South. In 1863, Ralph

---

[32] "Destiny of Russia," *SLM*, 19 (1853), 42–8; William Henry Trescot, "An American View of the Eastern Question," *DBR*, 17 (1854), 285–94, 327–50; George Frederick Holmes, "Relations of the Old World to the New," *DBR*, 20 (1856), 521. When Southerners embarked on their own war for national independence in 1861, Poland and the Poles gave them heartburn; see Supplementary References: "Poland."

[33] Ujanirtus Allen to Susan Fuller Allen, Apr. 28, 1861, in Randall Allen and Keith S. Bohannon, eds., *Campaigning with "Old Stonewall": Confederate Captain Ujanirtus Allen's Letters to His Wife* (Baton Rouge, LA, 1998), 31; Feb. 20, 1852, in William B. Hesseltine, ed., *Dr. J. G. M. Ramsey, Autobiography and Letters* (Knoxville, TN, 2002), 68. Our section on Kossuth draws freely and gratefully from Donald S. Spencer's admirable *Louis Kossuth and Young America: A Study in Sectionalism and Foreign Policy, 1848–1852* (Columbia, MO, 1977).

Waldo Emerson, who ranked Kossuth among God's elect, complained that Americans had failed in their duty to Kossuth and other European revolutionaries, and he brushed American professions of sympathy aside as mere sentimentalism.[34]

Notwithstanding early enthusiasm from secessionists, the South responded cautiously. The divines said little. The Methodist Reverend R. H. Rivers, a principal southern moral philosopher, observed that people treat a successful rebel like George Washington as a hero but scorn an unsuccessful one like Kossuth. We can only imagine how the divines would have reacted had they known of Kossuth's youthful attacks on the historical accuracy of the Bible. Kossuth figured that the biblical account of Creation must be mythical because no one was there to attest to it.[35]

Robin Okey remarks that Kossuth in exile provided a prototype for the "twentieth-century refugee leader whose agenda straddled two worlds, one relating to western radicalism, the other to a far away homeland." Kossuth moved from upper-class liberalism to a democratic radicalism that enhanced his popularity with the European and American Left but raised eyebrows in Hungary. For Northerners, Kossuth, an apostle of freedom, had to be a natural foe of slavery. Had he not congratulated the British on West Indian emancipation? Well, yes, but Kossuth now wanted to raise money from wealthy slaveholding planters, who were not charmed by the warm response he received from northern blacks. And warm it was. In 1851 a black convention in Cincinnati discussed slave insurrections and armed resistance to white violence, and delegates boldly predicted the coming of a black Kossuth. Kossuth, however, infuriated a delegation of black abolitionists in New York by suggesting that their visit would prove a political embarrassment to him, showing them the door and simultaneously asking for a financial contribution. Garrison had supported Kossuth, notwithstanding misgivings over his narrow nationalism, but recoiled when Kossuth temporized over slavery. In time, a great many early supporters repudiated Kossuth for one reason or another.[36]

Well before Kossuth became linked to a bizarre scheme to overthrow the government of Faustin I in Haiti, some important Southerners saw in him a champion of republican liberty determined to court their favor with little concern for enslaved blacks. Robert Tyler, son of the former President, tried to raise troops for a Hungarian expedition, and both Henry Foote and Pierre Soulé doggedly supported Kossuth

[34] Spencer, *Louis Kossuth and Young America*, passim.
[35] Reynolds, *European Revolutions and the American Literary*, 156–8; "Fortunes of the Republic," in Len Gougeon and Joel Myerson, eds., *Emerson's Antislavery Writings* (New Haven, CT, 1995), 143; Merton M. Sealts, Jr., *Emerson on the Scholar* (Columbia, MO, 1992), 207. In time Garrison cooled, contrasting Victor Hugo's forthright condemnation of slavery with Kossuth's temporizing: Henry Mayer, *All on Fire: William Lloyd Garrison and the Abolition of Slavery* (New York, 1998), 416–17; R. H. Rivers, *Elements of Moral Philosophy* (Nashville, TN, 1859), 272. On Kossuth's early religious writing see Robin Okey, *The Habsburg Monarchy from Enlightenment to Eclipse* (New York, 2001), 101.
[36] Okey, *Habsburg Monarchy*, 177. In addition to Spencer, *Louis Kossuth and Young America*, 76–7, see William Cheek and Aimee Lee Cheek, *John Mercer Langston and the Fight for Black Freedom, 1829–65* (Urbana, IL, 1989), 192–3.

to the end. Senator Robert Walker of Mississippi went so far as to call for American intervention in Hungary. The Blairs introduced Kossuth in St. Louis. Proslavery theorist Henry Hughes of Mississippi, in one of his many moods of self-inflation, hailed Kossuth as the John the Baptist who was preparing the world for you know whom.[37]

Southern criticism mounted as Kossuth held forth about "universal humanity" and uttered platitudes that Southerners associated with radicals, abolitionists, and sanctimonious fools. Almost every state government in the North formally invited him to speak. In the South he fared less well. When Governor Henry Foote invited him to Mississippi in defiance of widespread opposition, a small, half-hearted audience turned out in Natchez. In Louisiana a storm of protest swept the state legislature over the tendering of an invitation. Kossuth tried to recoup in Mobile by taking a strong prosouthern line, but to no avail. Although opinion remained divided in the lowcountry, the Charleston establishment froze him out and Kossuth left after two days – before the *Courier* announced his visit. John Bell, Zachary Taylor, and other southern Whigs rejected the man William G. ("Parson") Brownlow called a "humbug."[38]

Southern Quarterly Review, assessing the congressional debates on Hungary, came down forcefully for nonintervention. Subsequently, its editors scoffed that intervention had never been in the cards – Hungarians and Americans had "humbugged each other." In *Southern Literary Messenger,* Park Benjamin reported sympathetically from New York on a wild pro-Kossuth demonstration but sighed that it probably had less to do with politics or ideology than with a penchant for "pageant and spectacle." John Reuben Thompson, editor of *Southern Literary Messenger,* proved less tolerant, remarking on "the folly of the modern doctrine of intervention, as taught by Kossuth." In later years, contributors to *Southern Quarterly Review* – including William Gilmore Simms, who had been an early Kossuth supporter – linked Kossuth with Mazzini and Louis Blanc as radical visionaries and rebuked Henry Winter Davis of Maryland for defending so dangerous a charlatan.[39]

During the winter of 1851–52 Kossuth's tepid southern supporters, Democrats and Whigs alike, turned on him. In North Carolina, William Holden wrote John Ellis, "I concur with you, most heartily, in your Kossuth views. I dislike the manner in which the abolitionists cling about him, but he is not to blame for that. He has

---

37 For Kossuth's role in the plot to intervene in Haiti see John H. Komlos, *Louis Kossuth in America, 1851–1852* (Buffalo, NY, 1973), 121–6; Morrison, *Slavery and the American West,* 133–5; William E. Parrish, *Frank Blair: Lincoln's Conservative* (Columbia, MO, 1998), 46; Douglas Ambrose, *Henry Hughes and Proslavery Thought in the Old South* (Baton Rouge, LA, 1996), 66. See infra, Supplementary References: "Kossuth."

38 For Kossuth's generally cool and sometime hostile reception in the South, see also Komlos, *Louis Kossuth in America,* 121–7. For a report of divided opinion in the lowcountry see Emily Wharton Sinkler to Thomas Isaac Wharton, Dec. 22, 1851, in Anne Sinkler Whaley LeClerq, ed., *Between North and South: The Letters of Emily Wharton Sinkler, 1842–1865* (Columbia, SC, 2001), 162.

39 *SQR,* n.s., 7 (1853), 531, and "Critical Notices," *SQR,* n.s., 1 (1856), 543; "Recent Social Theories," *SQR,* n.s., 11 (1855), 254; *SQR,* n.s., 11 (1855), 543; [Park Benjamin], "Letters from New York," *SLM,* 18 (1852), 58–61, quote at 58; [John R. Thompson], *SLM,* 18 (1852), 256; [William Gilmore Simms], "Kossuth and Intervention," *SQR,* n.s., 6 (1852), 221–34.

no part nor lot with them." More important, widely circulated slanders of his cowardice in Hungary took a toll, for physical courage commanded a premium among the slaveholding "Chivalry."[40]

Kossuth's effort to raise big money in the South had poor prospects; someone ought to have told him that southern planters seldom lavished money on any cause. Kossuth apparently thought that he would win Southerners over by assuring them of his sympathy for state rights. Some unionists spurned the gambit and denounced Kossuth for pandering to secessionists. Others, wide-eyed, asked how Kossuth could, on principle, dissociate himself from northern intervention in the South while seeking American intervention in Hungary. Dr. Samuel Dickson, a luminary of Charleston's medical profession, returned to the theme in 1855, warning against intervention in Europe and prophesying that a proclamation of moral concern would provide a splendid excuse for European intervention against southern slavery.[41]

Had Kossuth stopped short of a fanciful – not to say preposterous – call for American intervention, he might have done better. Wise old heads like Henry Clay grimaced and referred him to America's historic Washingtonian policy of nonintervention in European affairs. After all, Americans heard the Farewell Address read every year in towns and villages to celebrate Washington's Birthday. Kossuth did rally proslavery expansionists of the sort who applauded the filibustering of Quitman, López, and William Walker, but they were not strong enough to prevail even in the Democratic party of the South. To the contrary, President Millard Fillmore won widespread approval for his cool response to Kossuth's bluster.[42]

William Russell Smith of Alabama, speaking in the House of Representatives in 1851, compared Kossuth's speeches to the revelations of Muhammad as exercises in deception. Simms, a strong supporter of Young America, endorsed Smith's speech, opposed intervention, and denounced Kossuth as a "humbug." Intervention did not even draw support from John Tyler, who wanted the United States to break relations with Austria over its violations of human rights in Hungary, or from Senator William Graham of North Carolina, who praised Kossuth as a patriot. In Georgia,

---

[40] W. W. Holden to John W. Ellis, Jan. 26, 1852, in Noble J. Tolbert, ed., *The Papers of John Willis Ellis,* 2 vols. (Raleigh, NC, 1964), 1:109, and for early Kossuth-mania in North Carolina see John W. Wheeler to John W. Ellis, Dec. 31, 1851 (1:105). For a defense of Kossuth against charges of cowardice in a northern journal that carried weight in the South, see "Austria in 1818–49," *BRPR,* 24 (1852), 461–2.

[41] S. H. Dickson, "Address at the Dinner of Charleston's New England Society," *SLM,* 21 (1855), 185.

[42] See e.g. J. Mills Thornton, *Power and Politics in a Slave Society: Alabama, 1800–1860* (Baton Rouge, LA, 1978), 215; David M. Potter, *The Impending Crisis, 1848–1861,* edited and completed by Don E. Fehrenbacher (New York, 1976), 197; Arthur A. Ekirch, *The Idea of Progress in America, 1815–1860* (New York, 1944), 58–62. Parson Weems reprinted Washington's Farewell Address in his celebrated biography, noting that its length was that of a typical sermon: Mason Locke Weems, *The Life of Washington. A New Edition with Primary Documents* (Amonk, NY, 1996 [1809]), 113. However, it was Jefferson, not Washington, who spoke of "no entangling alliances." For the international context of the northern reception of Kossuth as a "Hungarian Washington" and the cooler response of the South, see James A. Field, *America and the Mediterranean World, 1776–1882* (Princeton, NJ, 1969), 228–37. The generally pro-Kossuth *American Whig Review* responded angrily to Kossuth's perceived disrespect for Henry Clay in the aftermath of their meeting: "Kossuth and Mr. Clay," *American Whig Review,* 9 (1852), 374.

Senators John Berrien and William Dawson, Supreme Court Justice Eugenius Nisbet, and Methodist Bishop George Foster Pierce took every opportunity to invoke George Washington against intervention. William Valentine reported widespread revulsion in North Carolina, where Kossuth-mania had run strong. Valentine, conceding Kossuth's admirable qualities and especially his eloquence, concluded, "To say the least this man Kossuth is a presumptuous intermeddler. Though in the outset he knew the policy of this country, he presumed to enlighten the country in the true policy of Washington!" In 1855 J. A. Turner of Georgia – referring to Kossuth and Father Matthew, the Irish champion of temperance – expressed relief: "Fortunately the southern people did not join in the worship of these two foreigners with as much avidity as did the Northerners. I was proud to see it." Colonel B. F. Hunt of Charleston lashed out at the "unmitigated vanity and self-conceit" of Kossuth's attempt to embroil the United States in Central European affairs: "It is a spirit that would lead us into crusades to liberate the serfs of Russia, to restore her nationality to Poland, to heal the wounds of bleeding Hungary, to avenge the wrongs which bear down on the genius of Ireland, to succor the wretches who toil in dreary mines and waste away in the crowded factories of England, and even essay the act of gallantry in restoring the beautiful victims of Turkish grossness and open the well-guarded door of the harem; and, in the meantime, the North and the South, the East and the West, would become diverted ... and all our present greatness and internal prosperity would vanish like a fitful dream."[43]

Michael Holt, in his magisterial history of the Whig party, remarks that Kossuth became "the most disruptive and politically embarrassing foreigner to set foot in America since Citizen Genet." Euphoric receptions of Kossuth dangerously complicated American party politics, especially Whig hopes for retaining the White House in the 1852 election. Whigs and Democrats twisted and turned to court the votes of immigrants. German Protestants loved Kossuth, but German Catholics distrusted him. His anti-Catholicism and call for an Anglo-American alliance to defend liberty in Europe enraged the Irish, among others. President Fillmore and Daniel Webster maneuvered to maintain a Washingtonian foreign policy while they desperately tried to prevent interventionist Democrats, not to mention the pro-Kossuth William Seward, from profiting by Kossuth-mania. When Kossuth appealed to the American people over the heads of their politicians, he threatened to splinter the

---

43 William Russell Smith, *Kossuth and His Mission* (Washington, DC, 1851), 7, 10–11; Mary C. Oliphant et al., eds., *The Letters of William Gilmore Simms*, 6 vols. (Columbia, SC, 1952–82), 3:171 n. 83, 3:174; Lyon Gardiner Tyler, *The Letters and Times of the Tylers*, 3 vols. (Williamsburg, VA, 1884–96), 2:490–1; Hamilton, ed., *Papers of William Alexander Graham*, 4:230–1, 234; Miller, *The Bench and Bar of Georgia*, 1:80–6, 273, 316; Atticus G. Haygood, ed., *Bishop Pierce's Sermons and Addresses, with a Few Special Discourses by Dr. [Lovick] Pierce* (Nashville, TN, 1886), 40; Valentine Diaries, Feb. 28, 1852; J. A. Turner, *A Letter to Hon. N. G. Foster, Candidate for Congress* (Milledgeville, GA, 1855), 14; Hunt's text in William Way, *History of the New England Society of Charleston, South Carolina, 1819–1919* (Charleston, SC, 1920), 216–17. Smith anonymously offered a thirty-page satirical poem that ridiculed "the People," who idealized the tyrants Caesar and Napoleon: [William Russell Smith], *Kossuth Coppered, or the Banquet at the Capital of Laputa, Containing Gulliver's Great Speech* (New York, 1852), 30.

parties, the more so as southern Whigs and Democrats saw interventionism as an antislavery ploy.[44]

Kossuth probably never did understand the southern response. No doubt his gaffes and the slanders hurt him in the South, but the real problem lay elsewhere. Whatever Kossuth may have been, he had arrived as a symbol of social radicalism and of revolutionary defiance of constituted authority. The South no longer wanted any such symbols.[45]

On Independence Day 1815 in Abbeville, John C. Calhoun offered a toast: "The People – The only source of legitimate power. May France, acting on that principle, prove invincible, and may its truth and energy disperse the combination of crowned heads." Calhoun's fervor testified to his determination to claim the fundamental principles of the American Revolution for the South and reflected his hope that Europe would yet follow suit. Unlike many of his followers, Calhoun never quite lost that hope. By 1821 Calhoun still rejoiced that liberty was bursting from the womb of revolutionary Europe and frowned on the efforts of despotic regimes to crush it. "The institutions of Europe," he wrote Charles Tait of Alabama, "are deeply seated, growing out of the feudal institutions, which once spread over Christendom and pervaded all the relations of society; but the genius of the age, from causes not to be resisted, has become wholly hostile to the existing order of society .... The essence of feudalism was lords and vassals; that of the genius of the age is equality." In 1828 he wrote that liberty requires "responsible power" in the hands of men accountable to and regulated by the people. But in 1830, in the midst of the nullification struggle, he filed a caveat: The people could overthrow a tyrannical king much more easily than it could overthrow a tyrannical majority.[46]

Speaking carefully so as not to ruffle his northern political allies, Calhoun frequently returned to the question of "slavery in the abstract." When, during the 1840s, northern Whigs charged him with advocating enslavement of whites, Calhoun replied angrily. No, he never justified enslavement of whites; he merely predicted that current economic policies, if continued, would reduce white laborers to slavery. He did, however, repeatedly assert that civilized society required some form of servile labor, and he characterized free labor as disguised slavery. His "Rough

[44] Michael F. Holt, *The Rise and Fall of the American Whig Party: Jacksonian Politics and the Onset of the Civil War* (New York, 1999), 692–7, quote at 692.

[45] Clement Eaton, *The Mind of the Old South* (Baton Rouge, LA, 1964), 147. The pro-Kossuth attitude of socialists and other radicals in the North hurt him in the South. See Guarneri, *The Utopian Alternative*, 372–3. Still, the citizens of Alcorn County, Mississippi, named a town after Kossuth: Dunbar Rowland, ed. *Mississippi: Comprising Sketches of Counties, Towns, Events, Institutions, and Persons, Arranged in Cyclopedic Form*, 4 vols. (Spartanburg, SC, 1976 [1907]), 1:1005.

[46] Calhoun in Charleston *City Gazette*, July 27, 1815. In *JCCP* see Calhoun to Tait, Apr. 23, 1821 (6:9) as well as Calhoun, "Rough Draft" of the *Exposition* (10:490) and "Rough Draft of an Address to the People of South Carolina," circa Dec. 1830 (11:275). Although the *Exposition* and the *Protest* are usually treated as if a single document, they were not: see C. N. Wilson's editorial comments in *JCCP*, 10:442–3. The several drafts must be read separately for a proper appraisal of Calhoun's thought and of the extent to which he accommodated the opinions of others.

Draft" of the *Exposition* rebuked federal policy for making the rich richer and the poor poorer, and its final version predicted class war in free-labor countries. Although, for the moment, the tariff and similar usurpations preyed on the South, he noted that the laboring classes of the North faced miseries of their own. He returned to the theme often and made a special point of it in a speech in Virginia in December 1831.[47]

Calhoun did his best to keep to racial ground. Southern slavery, he told the Senate in 1836, was not merely a system of property ownership and labor organization but a system of racial control. Inadvertently, he surrendered much of his racial argument by insisting that labor alone creates wealth; that war against slavery threatened all property systems; that civilized societies live off the labor of the masses; and that racial differences give peculiar form to the essential struggle between capital and labor. He congratulated southern slaveholders for exploiting labor less than northern and European capitalists exploited their workers. Again assuring the Senate that he rejected slavery in the abstract and supported only racial slavery, he asserted the "fact" of an immutable historical law that necessitated one portion of the community's dependence upon the labor of another: "There is and always has been in an advanced stage of wealth and civilization, a conflict between labor and capital. The condition of society in the State exempts us from the disorders and dangers resulting from this conflict; and which explains why it is that political condition of the slave-holding States has been so much more stable and quiet than that of the North."[48]

A practical politician, Calhoun spoke carefully; an honest man, he refused to dissemble and assumed that his audiences grasped the nuances of his argument. With the June Days hovering over the Senate's debates on the territorial question, Calhoun warned northern capitalists that class war awaited them and that they needed a conservative alliance with the slaveholding South a great deal more than the South needed it. Important New York merchants applauded. Meanwhile, he appealed to labor to recognize that slaveholders were defending them against a national government controlled by big capital. When Arthur Brisbane and Fourierist socialists tried to enlist him in their cause, Calhoun conceded a similarity between

---

[47] "Rough Draft" of the Exposition, in *JCCP*, 10:480; on his speech in Virginia in 1831 see John Niven, *John C. Calhoun and the Price of Union: A Biography* (Baton Rouge, LA, 1988), 184; see also Crallé, "Memorandum," Dec. 4, 1831, in *JCCP*, 11:523.

[48] In *JCCP* see "Report from the Select Committee on the Circulation of Incendiary Publications," Feb. 4, 1836 (13:62–6), and "Remarks on Receiving Abolition Petitions (First Report)," Feb. 6, 1837 (13:389–91, 395, quote at 396). In 1869, the antislavery Francis Lieber recalled Calhoun's saying to him on the relation of capital to labor: "Do you not agree that slavery contains all that is good in Communism, and discards all that is bad? Slavery in this, as in so many other cases, solves problems which cannot be solved otherwise": Daniel Gilman, ed., *The Miscellaneous Writings of Francis Lieber*, 2 vols. (Philadelphia, 1881), 2:427. Calhoun was right about the relative rates of exploitation, which, as Karl Marx demonstrated, should not be confused with extent of oppression. See Robert W. Fogel and Stanley L. Engerman, *Time on the Cross: The Economics of Slavery in the Antebellum South* (Boston, 1974), esp. 107–9; Elizabeth Fox-Genovese and Eugene D. Genovese, *Fruits of Merchant Capital: Slavery and Bourgeois Property in the Rise and Expansion of Capitalism* (New York, 1983), 151–6.

his own and the socialists' analyses of capitalism, but he refused the political bait. Astonishingly, Nicholas Trist of Virginia, an experienced diplomat, swallowed it.[49]

Calhoun adhered to his professed principles and to his historical vision throughout his life, notwithstanding a hardening of constitutional interpretation and shifts on public policy. In some bad moments he yielded to tactical temptations for reasons that included his quest for the presidency. But what great leader has ever wholly overcome the temptation to identify cause with person – to believe that the cause itself might go down if his personal leadership did not prevail? Sometimes such a leader is proven right. Whatever Calhoun's personal ambitions and vanity, he believed, with reason, that if elected president he could protect the South against its northern enemies. Among southern theorists, Calhoun came closest to steering a prudent but principled course between the achievements and failures of the past and the hopes and fears of the future.[50]

Calhoun remained devoted to social order. His principles, instincts, and analytical ability told him to lean to one side or the other tactically but to commit himself to neither strategically. In the words of Clyde Wilson, editor of Calhoun's papers, "Calhoun cannot accurately be depicted as the ally of corporate wealth. In the emergent struggle of capital and labor, Calhoun was not the ally of one side. The South was not to be the ally of the capitalists, but rather the permanent balance wheel of the Union." Calhoun spoke clearly in 1836: "We are the real conservative body, equally opposed to aristocracy and agrarianism. So long as the tendency at the North was towards the former our natural union was with the democracy; but now that the democracy of the north tends to agrarianism, our natural union is the other way."[51]

In 1847 Calhoun's friends urged him to hit the social question hard and appeal to a conservative alliance between northern capitalists and southern slaveholders. Duff Green, a big capitalist concerned over the antagonism between labor and capital, advocated an appeal to northern capitalists to recognize the conservatism of southern slavery and to put down the abolitionists as part of an effort to maintain social order throughout the country. Calhoun responded in a speech in Charleston that stressed the dependence of northern prosperity on southern slave labor and denied the incompatibility of the two systems.[52]

The deeply conservative Calhoun could never accept a strategic alliance with northern labor, and by the late 1840s his hopes for such a tactical alliance with

---

[49] "Speech on the Proposal to Extend the Missouri Compromise Line to the Pacific," in *JCCP*, 25:669–70; on the socialists see Guarnieri, *The Utopian Alternative*, 376; for a useful discussion of Calhoun's use of the labor theory of value to justify slavery as a socioeconomic system, see August O. Spain, *The Political Theory of John C. Calhoun* (New York, 1951), 227, 230–3, 257, 272.

[50] The biographical and interpretive literature on Calhoun is large, but see esp. the indispensable insights and careful scholarship in Clyde N. Wilson's introductions and editorial notes to *JCCP*.

[51] Wilson, "Introduction," in *JCCP*, 13:xix, xx; Calhoun to Samuel D. Ingham, Apr. 3, 1836, in Clyde N. Wilson, ed., *The Essential Calhoun: Selection from Writings, Speeches, and Letters* (New Brunswick, NJ, 1991), 402.

[52] In *JCCP*: Duff Green to Calhoun, Mar. 4, 1847 (24:240); Calhoun's speech in Charleston, Mar. 19, 1847 (24:248–60).

the capitalists had faded. In 1847 he told the Senate, "Sir, the day that the balance between the two sections of the country – the slaveholding States and the
non-slaveholding States – is destroyed, is a day that will not be far removed from
political revolution, anarchy, civil war, and wide-spread disaster. The balance of
this system is in the slaveholding States. They are the conservative portion – always
will be the conservative portion." Privately, he observed sadly that Daniel Webster
had isolated himself by his Seventh of March Speech in favor of the Compromise of
1850 on slavery expansion: "Can anything more clearly evince the utter hopeless-
ness of looking to the North for support, when their strongest man finds himself
incapable of maintaining himself on the smallest amount possible of concession to
the South; and on points too clear to admit of Constitutional doubts?"[53]

On the verge of death, Calhoun made his last stand for southern rights in opposition to the Compromise of 1850 and left to posterity his *Disquisition on Government* and *Discourse on the Constitution*. He had just about abandoned his lifelong
struggle to save the Union. Was he primarily interested in saving slavery? Of course
he was: To him, slavery was not only a labor system but the foundation of republican social order. Northerners and Southerners shared a patriotic attachment to
the Union born of the heroic struggle to prove that "constitutional democracy"
could thrive in a geographically extensive country. The glory of the Union and its
Constitution lay in its historic compromise between peoples whose common ideals
transcended their material interests. Calhoun's last speech breathed a spirit of resignation to the catastrophe he had long foretold if the North continued its war on
slavery and southern civilization. Shortly before his death, he predicted the dissolution of the Union within ten years, probably in the wake of a presidential election.

Calhoun's most considered reflections on social as well as political relations had
emerged from his analyses of the revolutions that wracked Europe from 1789 to
1848. Southern congressmen who joined northern colleagues in 1848 in a unanimous vote of congratulations to the French people for establishing a republic secured
unanimity only because Calhoun absented himself. Although he believed monarchies finished and deservedly so, he held little hope for a republican France. In the
wake of economic depression he saw Europe succumbing to class war and hardly
ready for republican order. He foresaw anarchy and despotism, not a well-regulated
liberty, in the offing.[54]

Anna Maria Clemson, Calhoun's intellectually acute daughter and the wife of
Thomas Clemson, American minister to Belgium, wrote her father in 1846 that
Europe had strengthened her own lifelong acceptance of slavery into militant espousal. Of antislavery Europeans, she protested, "They talk of slavery. I never saw
in all my life at the South, the amount of suffering and misery that one sees here
in one month." She challenged them, "Make your working classes in Europe as
happy as our slaves, and then come back to me, and we *will talk* about the abolition

---

[53] In Wilson, ed., *Essential Calhoun*: "Speech on the Slavery Question," Feb. 19, 1847 (385), and Calhoun to Henry W. Conner, Mar. 18, 1850 (363).
[54] Calhoun quoted in Spencer, *Louis Kossuth and Young America*, 16; also, Charles M. Wiltse, *John C.
Calhoun: Sectionalist, 1840–1850* (Indianapolis, IN, 1951), 333, 338–9.

of slavery." Calhoun assured her that Europe remained sound and conservative and would continue to be unless political science fell behind the pace of material advance. Anna Maria, apparently unconvinced, bemoaned the callousness of the upper classes in the following year: "The winter has been long & severe, & the suffering among the poorer classes very great." She accepted the right to accumulate wealth but not the enormous disparity between classes and the horrible suffering. Calhoun wrote back, fretting over the deterioration of conditions in Europe and the corruption of political institutions in America.[55]

In March 1848, Calhoun confided to his son-in-law misgivings over events in Paris, "a great event, I would say a terrific one for Europe. No one will say where it will stop. France is not prepared to become a Republick." Calhoun, and Thomas Clemson, too, hoped the European powers would not intervene and thereby drive the French further to the left. He reiterated his lack of confidence in the ability of the French to sustain a republic and a week later, in a memorable speech in the Senate, he opposed the resolution to congratulate the French on their new republic. The French, he said, had declared a republic but not established one. If they proved incapable of sustaining a republic, what then? They would not return to the Bourbons or again attempt a constitutional monarchy; France was headed for a military despotism. "A revolution in itself is not a blessing." A revolution promises much and may accomplish great things, but if it goes astray, "It will do more to put down liberty under a republican form of government than any other event which could occur."[56]

Calhoun wrote Clemson again in mid-April: "Germany seems in a fair way to be completely revolutionized, and I hope permanently improved." He considered Germany a much better bet than France to establish a regime of constitutional liberty and hoped that positive developments there would have a salutary effect in France. Germany's old institutions "furnish an excellent foundation on which to erect a federal Republick like ours, a federal constitutional Government, United at least in a Zollverein league, and something more intimately united politically, than at present." Andrew Jackson Donelson of Tennessee seemed less sanguine when he wrote to Calhoun from Germany. Europe's disintegration gave him a new appreciation of the South's social system.[57]

Calhoun had written of "the present great crisis of the civilized world." The European monarchies were falling: "The intelligence and progress of the age have

[55] Anna Maria (Calhoun) Clemson to J. C. Calhoun, Sept. 27, 1846, in *JCCP*, 23:467–8; also, Ernest McPherson Lander, Jr., *The Calhoun Family and Thomas Green Clemson: The Decline of Southern Patriarchy* (Columbia, SC, 1983), 92. In *JCCP*: Calhoun to Anna Maria Clemson, Nov. 21, 1846 (23:544–5); Anna Clemson to Calhoun, Apr. 11, June 27, Sept. 13, 1847 (24:305, 551–3); Calhoun to Anna Clemson, June 10, 1847 (24:419–22). Lieber wrote Calhoun about dreadful conditions in Germany and efforts to raise money from German-Americans to alleviate suffering: Lieber to Calhoun, June 15 and 27, 1847 (24:402, 422).

[56] Calhoun to Clemson, Mar. 22, 1848, in J. Franklin Jameson, ed., *Calhoun Correspondence* (Washington, DC, 1900: "Annual Report of the American Historical Association for the Year 1899," vol. 2), 747–8.

[57] Calhoun to Clemson, Apr. 1, 13, 1848, in Jameson, ed., *Calhoun Correspondence*, 748–9. In *JCCP* see A. J. Donelson to Calhoun, Sept. 27, 1848 (26:65).

outgrown them, but it is by no means certain that they are so advanced and enlightened on political science, as to substitute more suitable ones in their place. I fear they are not." Those who proclaimed themselves the party of progress had not advanced beyond Dorrism – "that is, the right of a mere majority to overturn law and constitution at its will and pleasure." He hoped that the failure of French radicals and the success of German moderates would sober American political opinion.[58]

Calhoun's measured attitude doubtless reflected his work on his books, *Disquisition* and *Discourse,* which imposed the severe discipline of historical perspective. "I look, perhaps, with greater solicitude for the unfolding of the great events now in progress in Europe," he wrote Anna Maria, "as they afford me an opportunity to test the truth or error of the principles, which I have laid down in my elementary discourse on Government." While apprehensive about French radicalism and Continental disorder and anarchy, he remained optimistic about the outcome. To his daughter and son-in-law he expressed the hope that European civilization had progressed too far to succumb. Europe, after all, had given birth to the greatest of civilizations and surely had the resources to overcome current difficulties. He expected a long and dangerous period of disorder but was encouraged by England's stability.[59]

To other family members he sighed with relief at the failure of the English Chartists: "It was the turning point in the affairs in Europe. Had they succeeded, it would [have] been long – very long – before order and authority would be restored in Europe; but as it is, the revolutionary movements have gone, probably as far as it is destined to go, at least for the present." To Andrew Jackson Donelson he expressed gratification at the moderation of the revolution in France but no confidence in its perpetuation. In any case, any settlement would have to come to terms with the two most powerful interests in Europe: "the stock holders & the army." He worried that Russia would seize the opportunity to impose its will on Europe.[60]

---

[58] In *JCCP,* vol. 25, see: Calhoun to Clemson, Mar. 22, 1848 (263); Calhoun to James Edward Calhoun, Jr., Mar. 23, 1848 (265); "Speech on the Revolution in France," Mar. 30, 1848 (282–5); Calhoun to Clemson, Apr. 13, 1848 (313); Calhoun to John Ewing Colhoun, Apr. 15, 1848 (322–3); Calhoun to J. E. Colhoun, Apr. 23, 1848 (354); and for Calhoun's hopes for Germany see also Calhoun to Baron Friedrich von Gerolt, May 28, 1848 (441–3). For Calhoun's generally favorable opinion of the Germans and Austrians see *JCCP,* vols. 18–20. Calhoun's speech was widely reprinted in newspapers, especially in Virginia and South Carolina.

[59] J. C. Calhoun to Mrs. T. G. Clemson, Apr. 28, 1848, in Jameson, ed., *Calhoun Correspondence,* 752–3, see also Calhoun to A. J. Donelson, May 23, 1848 (428), and Calhoun to Thomas Clemson, May 26, 1848 (756–7). Wiltse, *Calhoun: Sectionalist,* 413–16.

[60] On Chartism see Calhoun to Sarah Mytton Maury, July 15, 1848, in *JCCP,* 25:591; on Russia see Calhoun to J. E. Colhoun, May 22, 1848, in *JCCP,* 25:428. Sarah Mytton Maury, a Calhoun correspondent, fed his forebodings: "Our lower and working classes are in hopeless destitution, and unless emigration and employment provide against such a result, our labourers and manufacturers will prove a more impracticable body than the 'Ouvriers' of Paris. *They will be fed*": Sarah Mytton Maury to J. C. Calhoun, Aug. 15, 1848, in *JCCP,* 25:5. Chartism's threat to mount a revolution in England agitated the expatriate southern community in Philadelphia in the late 1830s: Eliza Middleton Fisher to Mary Herring Middleton, June 11, 1839, in Eliza Cope Harrison, ed., *Best Companions: Letters of Eliza Middleton Fisher and Her Mother, Mary Herring Middleton, from Charleston, Philadelphia, and Newport, 1839–1846* (Columbia, SC, 2001), 57.

In late June, Calhoun's reservations about the French reappeared with full force. France has no prospects for popular government, he wrote his daughter, for it lacked the elements and had wrong principles. The French were opting for liberty, equality, and fraternity – but their standard of liberty was license, their kind of equality unattainable, and their fraternity incompatible with either liberty or equality. He deplored as false philosophy any claims of a state of nature in which liberty existed and scoffed at the very idea of an isolated individual. Liberty and equality precluded fraternity. Fraternity "can only exist in the social and political; and the attempt to unite it and the other two, as they would exist, in the supposed state of nature, in man, as he must exist in the former, must and ever will fail. The union is impossible, and the attempt to unite them absurd; and must lead, if persisted in, to distraction, anarchy and finally absolute power in the hands of man." If good principles did not prevail in Europe, the attempt at reform must fail. And the radical spirit in Europe now threatened America; abolitionism, its direct heir, would lead – if not speedily arrested – to the dissolution of the Union and the destruction of the American system of government. To prevent such a catastrophe Calhoun offered practical suggestions for a restructuring of the American government in accordance with the spirit and letter of the Constitution. It was now June 23. Probably, he had not received news of the June Days, but he was nonetheless filled with foreboding. Anna Maria needed no encouragement: By the first week in August she concluded that the so-called French republic was rapidly passing into a military despotism.[61]

Calhoun spoke for his own slaveholding class and for a swelling broader southern public opinion: To link political virtue to universal democracy meant to open the floodgates to anarchy and the tyranny of the mob. Many northern conservatives shared much of this viewpoint, but it was Southerners who constructed a radical critique of society and identified the free-labor system – the social relations of capitalism – as the source of the world's predicament. And they named slavery as the solution.

---

[61] Calhoun to Anna Maria Clemson, June 23, 1848, in Jameson, ed., *Calhoun Correspondence,* 758; Calhoun to A. M. Clemson, June 23, 1848, in *JCCP,* 25:497–8; Anna Maria Clemson to Calhoun, Aug. 7, 1848, in *JCCP,* 25:650.

3

"The Purest Sons of Freedom"

> There never was a Government on the face of the earth, but what permitted slavery. The purest sons of freedom in the Grecian Republics, the citizens of Athens and Lacedaemon, all held slaves.
>
> —U.S. Rep. James Jackson of Georgia (1790)[1]

Until recently, peoples of every race and continent lived in a world in which slavery was an accepted part of the social order. Europeans did not outdo others in enslaving people or in treating slaves viciously. They outdid others by creating a Christian civilization that eventually stirred moral condemnation of slavery and roused mass movements against it. Perception of slavery as morally unacceptable – as sinful – did not become widespread until the second half of the eighteenth century. Slavery, not merely serfdom, existed in Western and Central Europe as late as the Renaissance and in Russia until the mid-nineteenth century.

Neither slavery nor serfdom was racially determined. From ancient times Europeans had recruited slaves without regard to race, and whites overwhelmingly predominated among the millions of slaves held within Europe. When European overseas expansion in the fifteenth century made Africa the principal source of slaves, slavery became identified with racial stratification. Muslims and then Christians entered Africa and carried off enormous numbers, largely sold to them by other Africans. Over time Muslims, too, increasingly identified slave status with blackness, although less rigorously than Christians did. During the next four centuries it was in the vast plantation system of the Americas that both the critique and the defense of slavery came to focus on racial as well as class stratification.

Today we ask: How could Christians or any civilized people have lived with themselves as slaveholders? But the historically appropriate question is: What, after

---

[1] *Annals of Congress:* 1st Cong., 1st Sess. (Feb. 12, 1790), 1241. Hailing the great revolutionary generation of Virginia and South Carolina, David McCord of South Carolina announced, "All the greatest and freest people of antiquity, were slaveholders": "How the South Is Affected by Slave Institutions," *DBR,* 11 (1851), 349–63, quote at 357.

millennia of general acceptance, made Christians – and, subsequently, those of other faiths – judge slavery an enormity not to be endured?[2]

Southerners, defending slavery as a historically recurring and justifiable feature of well-ordered societies from ancient times to the present, recognized that they were defending racial as well as class stratification. They tirelessly reminded abolitionists that Northerners, too, had held black slaves, considered blacks racial inferiors, and treated them accordingly whether slave or free. In the protracted struggle that led to the War, most southern theorists emphasized constitutional issues, even as they maintained an extra-constitutional "right of revolution." They staunchly maintained, as southern conservatives have ever since, that the South fought for the Constitution, state rights, and self-determination. Abolitionists then, and most historians since, have no less staunchly maintained that Southerners fought to preserve slavery and that constitutional rhetoric provided a smokescreen for a massive economic and political interest.

That debate cannot be resolved because, although racial slavery provided the foundation for the southern way of life, race relations did not count for everything. The antislavery viewpoint lies closer to the truth, but millions of Southerners rallied to the Confederacy with more on their minds than slave property. Most Southerners did not own slaves, but like the slaveholders they upheld constitutional and political principles while frankly acknowledging slavery as the social foundation for their way of life. For "W. R. A." in a *Southern Literary Messenger* of 1848, slavery stood as "a great pillar of conservatism" and "the best and most enduring basis for Republican institutions." For Willoughby Newton of Virginia, a state legislator, the political and constitutional cause itself rested squarely on slavery as a "fixed fact." In 1855 Newton told cadets at Virginia Military Institute, "No event in the history of modern times, save the discovery of America itself," equaled in importance the landing of twenty African slaves in Virginia in 1620. For William Elliott, the Harvard-educated intellectual luminary of Beaufort, South Carolina, slavery in the mid-1850s was "*not wearing away* – it is merely marching southward and westward."[3]

The greater part of the South took shape as a slave society, not merely a society that permitted slavery. For southern slaveholders and nonslaveholders alike, slavery

[2] The rejection of slavery reflected a fundamental change in Western thought: see esp. David Brion Davis, *The Problem of Slavery in Western Culture* (Ithaca, NY, 1967) and *The Problem of Slavery in the Age of Revolution* (Ithaca, NY, 1975). For an abolitionist viewpoint see Albert Barnes, *The Church and Slavery* (New York, 1969 [1857]), ch. 2. Premodern societies had only scattered and ineffectual critics of slavery. Aristotle mentions some adherents of marginal sects or isolated intellectuals who followed the Sophists in treating institutions skeptically without challenging them directly. Gregory of Nyssa (late fourth century) stood alone among Church fathers in holding slavery sinful. See Peter Garnsey, *Ideas of Slavery from Aristotle to Augustine* (Cambridge, U.K., 1996), 78–9, 80–5, 238–40; also, Giuseppe Cambiano, "Aristotle and the Anonymous Opponents of Slavery," in M. I. Finley, ed., *Classical Slavery* (London, 1987), 22–41.

[3] "W. R. A.", "The Duty of Southern Authors," *SLM*, 23 (1856), 241; Newton quoted in Craig M. Simpson, *A Good Southerner: The Life of Henry A. Wise of Virginia* (Chapel Hill, NC, 1985), 155; for "fixed fact" see Newton, "Address before the State Virginia Agricultural Society," *Southern Planter*, 12 (1855), Supp., 6; William Elliott, *The Anniversary Address of the State Agricultural Society of South Carolina ... Nov. 30, 1848* (Charleston, SC, 1849), 43.

left no feature of life untouched. The American South ranks with ancient Greece and Rome among the few genuine slave societies in world history – that is, societies in which slave labor provided the basis of the social structure, the economy, and the culture. Slaves constituted about one third of the population of the South, roughly the same ratio as in fifth-century Athens and in Italy at the end of the Roman Republic.[4]

The great majority of Americans accepted slavery as an unexceptionable part of the social order until the second half of the eighteenth century, when many in the North and the South began to have moral qualms. Not until the nineteenth century did emancipationists gain confidence that a hardening public opinion presaged slavery's extinction. Christian teaching and the interests of propertyholders had long combined to sustain slavery; they now combined to undermine it. With the growing popularity of Scottish and Manchesterian political economy, notably Adam Smith's *The Wealth of Nations* (1776), an increasing segment of public opinion saw slavery as a fetter on economic and social progress. The American Revolution strikingly reinforced the new view. A gallant republic swore eternal opposition to the "slavery" imposed by the British Crown and told the world, "All men are created equal." Moral revulsion, political sensibility, and economic interest moved the northern states toward emancipation, but the southern held fast to slavery.

During the Revolutionary era, some masters freed their slaves, sometimes citing the principles of the Declaration of Independence, but southern public opinion remained proslavery. In 1777 North Carolina curbed emancipations by a law that denounced "the evil and pernicious practice of freeing slaves in this state." Ironically, in North Carolina and Tennessee free Negro males could vote until the 1830s, when pressure to curb emancipations arose in part from concern over a swelling black vote. Southerners who, like Thomas Jefferson and James Madison, favored emancipation faced shrinking prospects. In 1797 a disappointed St. George Tucker, Virginia's great legal scholar, admitted to the Congregationalist Reverend Jeremy Belknap of Boston that Virginians were much more hostile to emancipation than he had believed. Precious few Southerners thought that emancipated blacks could assimilate to Euro-American civilization and republican polity, and most emancipationists wanted the freedmen sent elsewhere. Even those who considered themselves free of racial prejudice believed that most whites would not live side by side with a race they deemed culturally if not genetically inferior. Almost all southern whites assumed that black freedmen would become the cat's paw of unscrupulous capitalists who would control their votes and destabilize republicanism. That assumption echoed one long used in Britain to justify disfranchisement of lower-class whites.[5]

---

[4] See the works of M. I. Finley, e.g., *Ancient Slavery and Modern Ideology* (New York, 1980), 80–2. Athens and a few places, not all of Greece, constituted a true slave society: Yvon Garlan, *Slavery in Ancient Greece*, tr. Janet Lloyd (Ithaca, NY, 1982), 201–3.

[5] James Morton Smith, ed., *The Republic of Letters: The Correspondence between Thomas Jefferson and James Madison, 1776–1826*, 3 vols. (New York, 1995), 1:19; John H. Russell, *The Free Negro in Virginia, 1619–1865* (Baltimore, 1913), 56–7, 81–2; on Tucker see Alison Goodyear Freehling, *Drift*

Slavery loomed over the new republic's Constitutional Convention. Southern delegates, aiming to defuse criticism of slavery, confessed it an evil while demanding measures to protect it. They declined to quarrel over abstractions like the morality of slavery when the real issue concerned state rights and the rights of propertyholders. Rufus King of Massachusetts and James Madison of Virginia agreed that the chief obstacle to a new constitution came from the divergent interests of southern slave states and northern ("eastern") states in which slavery was disappearing. George Mason, principal author of Virginia's historic Declaration of Rights, appealed to Roman history as evidence that slavery undermined republican institutions, yet he opposed ratification of the Constitution because he doubted that it would protect slave property, and he carefully worded the Declaration of Rights to reassure Virginians about the security of slave property. He dreaded outside interference more than he dreaded the evils he associated with slavery, protesting that the Constitution provided no guarantee against federal meddling in the slave states.[6]

During Virginia's close contest over ratification, each side proclaimed its determination to protect slave property, although the Constitution's potential threat to slavery drew softer Anti-Federalist protests than did the perceived northern threat to Virginia's economic and political interests. James Iredell of North Carolina, a Federalist appointed by President Washington to the United States Supreme Court, cautioned that effective federal government depended upon the courts' willingness to respect state rights. But not until the Missouri crisis of 1819 did many in the Upper South firmly and publicly link slavery to southern political interests. In North Carolina, Federalists rallied to the Constitution on a platform of state rights – or, more boldly, state sovereignty – and protection of slavery. During 1835–50 the Whig party dominated North Carolina and resolutely stood by its commitment to the Union, yet it weakened the nationalism it espoused by insisting upon constitutional protection for slavery.[7]

---

towards Dissolution: The Virginia Slavery Debate of 1831–1832 (Baton Rouge, LA, 1982), 95; for North Carolina and Tennessee see Caleb Perry Patterson, *The Negro in Tennessee, 1790–1865* (New York, 1968), 17, 27. For the negative reaction in the South to Jefferson's emancipationism see also William Frederick Poole, *Anti-Slavery Opinion before the Year 1800* (Cincinnati, 1873), 31–3. In Maryland economic, not moral, motives seem to have governed the great majority of manumissions: T. Stephen Whitman, *The Price of Freedom: Slavery and Manumission in Baltimore and Early National Maryland* (Lexington, KY, 1997), chs. 3–4. Despite brave efforts by Quakers and others, antislavery in Virginia and the Border States steadily waned after 1800 while openly proslavery sentiments waxed: Gordon E. Finnie, "The Antislavery Movement in the Upper South before 1840," *JSH*, 35 (1969), 319–42.

[6] James Madison, *Notes of the Debates in the Federal Convention of 1787* (Athens, OH, 1966), 261, 286, 295, 355; Robert A. Rutland, ed., *The Papers of George Mason*, 3 vols. (Chapel Hill, NC, 1970), 3:924, 1086, 1113. For a fresh look at the southern commitment to slavery during the ratification struggle see David L. Lightner, "The Founding Fathers and the Interstate Slave Trade," *JER*, 22 (2002), 25–51.

[7] Christopher T. Graebe, "Federalism of James Iredell in Historical Context," *North Carolina Law Review*, 69 (1990), 251–72; Henry McGilbert Wagstaff, *States Rights and Political Parties in North Carolina, 1776–1861* (Baltimore, 1906), 30–1, 155, and, generally, chs. 1 and 2; also, Lance Banning, *The Sacred Fire of Liberty: James Madison and the Founding of the Federal Republic* (Ithaca, NY, 1995), 254–5; M. E. Bradford, *A Worthy Company: Brief Lives of the Framers of the United States*

"The security the Southern States want is that their negroes may not be taken from them, which some gentlemen within or without doors, have a good mind to do." Thus spoke Pierce Butler of South Carolina, a wealthy planter, at the Federal Convention. Southern Federalists and southern Anti-Federalists quarreled over whether slavery and state rights would be safer in or out of a new Union. The Federalists pointed to at least ten provisions in the Constitution that upheld slavery, and Daniel Huger pleaded that South Carolina would need federal support to suppress insurgent blacks. Pennsylvania's Benjamin Franklin hoped for ultimate emancipation, while South Carolina's William Loughton Smith and Thomas Tudor Tucker and Georgia's James Jackson cited biblical sanction and threatened civil war.[8]

Antislavery expressions, heartfelt or as litany, reverberated in the South during and after the American Revolution. George Wythe, who taught Jefferson and John Marshall, among others, and is considered one of Virginia's greatest legal theorists, reasoned from the premise that blacks had natural rights to the conclusion that slaveholders had to sacrifice their economic interests as propertyholders, and St. George Tucker advanced a plan for emancipation. They got nowhere. George Washington, Thomas Jefferson, James Madison, and John Randolph never translated emancipationist hopes into effective political action. Virginians apologetically and abstractly called slavery immoral or a social and political evil but remained unconvinced that slaveholding endangered their immortal souls. Even Virginians embarrassed by the stigma hardly saw themselves as moral lepers, however much they regretted having been saddled with slavery and blacks in the first place. Apologists displayed southern courtesy, assuring tenderhearted Northerners that they would gladly shed the moral encumbrance if only circumstances permitted. In the 1790s emancipationism declined as the principal churches, which earlier had protested against slavery, made their peace with it. Intense hostility now greeted abolition petitions to Congress and state legislatures. In subsequent decades, Virginians expressed fewer qualms over the morality of slaveholding than over having to live with potentially rebellious black slaves or over the disquieting tendency of slaveholding to make young masters lascivious and tyrannical.[9]

Constitution (Marlborough, NH, 1982), 122, 152, 158–62, 180–1; Robert McColley, *Slavery and Jeffersonian Virginia* (Urbana, IL, 1964), 168–71; William Sumner Jenkins, *Pro-Slavery Thought in the Old South* (Gloucester, MA, 1960), 49–51, 55–6.

[8] For Butler see Thomas L. Pangle, *The Spirit of Modern Republicanism: The Moral Vision of the American Founders and the Philosophy of Locke* (Chicago, 1988), 75; William M. Wiecek, *The Sources of Antislavery Constitutionalism in America, 1760–1848* (Ithaca, NY, 1977), 16, 62–3, 82–3, 94; Paul Finkelman, *Slavery and the Founders: Race and Liberty in the Age of Jefferson* (Armonk, NY, 1996), 23 and, for constitutional sanction of slavery, ch. 1. William W. Freehling considers as certain that South Carolina would not have ratified without assurances on slavery: *The Road to Disunion* (New York, 1990), 135–6, 584 n. 30. On Georgia see A. Leon Higginbotham, *In the Matter of Color. Race and the American Legal Process: The Colonial Period* (New York, 1978), 7 and, generally, ch. 6. For an attack on the Founding Fathers for conceding this ground to the slave states, see J. E. K. Walker, "Whither Liberty, Equality, or Legality?" *New York Law School Journal of Human Rights*, 6 (1989), 299–352.

[9] John Chester Miller, *The Wolf by the Ears: Thomas Jefferson and Slavery* (New York, 1977), 17–18, 97, ch. 12; Mary Stoughton Locke, *Anti-Slavery in America: From the Introduction of African Slaves*

A few signposts: In the 1780s Virginia and North Carolina surrendered their territorial claims to Kentucky and Tennessee on the understanding that the federal
government would not intervene in their domestic relations. Tennessee entered the
Union in 1796 without controversy over slavery. The leaders of the South Carolina
backcountry embraced slavery while challenging the lowcountry gentry's domination of state politics. South Carolina's Federalists, who held considerable power for
a while, rebuked Jefferson for his hostility to slavery. Jeffersonians replied that they,
not the Federalists, were the true guarantors of slave property. In the 1790s, Rawlins
Lowndes and Charles Cotesworth Pinckney, political adversaries, agreed on slavery
as a positive good for masters and slaves alike. In Chatham County, Georgia, when
Judge Jabez Bowen (a Yale-educated New Englander) endorsed manumission in a
charge to a grand jury, the incensed jurors censured him, whereupon he threw them
all in jail and was then himself arrested for incitement to slave insurrection. In 1804
the governor, supported by the legislature, removed Judge Bowen from office. In
1806 Peter Early of Georgia, in a debate over the slave trade, vigorously defended
slavery in the U.S. House of Representatives.[10]

In 1790 the House of Representatives received a petition for federal action from
Benjamin Franklin and others in the Pennsylvania Abolition Society. Representatives from the Lower South went up in flames, pledging their states to resist, forcibly
if necessary. John Rutledge and St. George Tucker predicted armed resistance if
Congress acted. Congress eased the tension by acknowledging that it lacked power

to the Prohibition of the Slave Trade (1619–1808) (Gloucester, MA, 1965 [1901]), 160, 162; also, see
Robert McColley, *Slavery and Jeffersonian Virginia* (Urbana, IL, 1964). The Episcopalian Reverend
Henry Fry, a gradual emancipationist, recalled that the Quaker antislavery petitions of the 1780s were
dismissed "with contempt": Fry, in P. Slaughter, *Memoir of Col. Joshua Fry ... with an Autobiog-
raphy of His Son, Rev. Henry Fry* (Richmond, VA, 1880), 102. For the antislavery views as litany see
Forrest McDonald, *Novus Ordo Seclorum: The Intellectual Origins of the Constitution* (Lawrence,
KS, 1985), 50.

English travelers frequently commented on the argument from fear: Jane Louise Mesick, *The English Traveller in America, 1785–1835* (New York, 1922), 126–7. William H. Crawford of Georgia,
Roger Taney of Maryland, and Henry Clay of Kentucky condemned slavery as an evil and espoused
gradual emancipation, but they also condemned abolitionism and outside interference in southern
affairs. The press in North Carolina in the late 1820s was still insisting that slavery had few supporters and that the people of North Carolina would get rid of it if they could. Before 1840, Arkansans
showed little interest in defending slavery per se, but they generally accepted it as a fact of life: Rosser
H. Taylor, "Humanizing the Slave Code of North Carolina," *North Carolina Historical Review*, 2
(1925), 330. Orville W. Taylor, *Negro Slavery in Arkansas* (Durham, NC, 1958), ch. 3.

[10] Paul A. Rahe, *Republics, Ancient and Modern: Classical Republicanism and the American Revolution* (Chapel Hill, NC, 1992), 640; Chase C. Mooney, *Slavery in Tennessee* (Bloomington, IN, 1957),
8; William J. Cooper, Jr., *Liberty and Slavery: Southern Politics to 1860* (New York, 1983), 37, 48,
97–9; Rachel N. Klein, *Unification of a Slave State: The Rise of the Planter Class in the South Carolina Backcountry, 1760–1808* (Chapel Hill, NC, 1990); M. E. Bradford, "Rawlins Lowndes: Southern
Prophet," in *Against the Barbarians: And Other Reflections on Familiar Themes* (Columbus, MO,
1992), 136. On Bowen see Warren Grice, *The Georgia Bench and Bar*, 2 vols. (Macon, GA, 1931),
1:82–3, and Ralph Betts Flanders, *Plantation Slavery in Georgia* (Chapel Hill, NC, 1933), 289; for
Early see J. Jefferson Looney and Ruth L. Woodward, eds., *Princetonians, 1791–1794* (Princeton, NJ,
1991), 161.

to tamper with slavery. In the constitutional debates of the Mississippi Territory of the 1790s, antislavery had little support. Antislavery in the Southwest suffered further after the Louisiana Purchase, which northern Federalists criticized as a device for extending slavery westward. In 1860, William Harris, justice of the High Court of Errors and Appeals, explained Mississippi's effort in the 1830s to prohibit importation of slaves for sale as designed to strengthen slavery in the Border States by cutting off the market for excess slaves: "Mississippi intended to prevent abolition from affecting the consolidation of slavery in the extreme South." During the secession debates, J. D. B. De Bow, the powerful magazine editor, and Henry L. Benning, justice of Georgia's supreme court, warned of emancipation in the Border States once enough blacks were sold south.[11]

Southerners constantly reminded Northerners that their states would never have ratified the Constitution without guarantees for protection of slavery; that the Constitution provided a framework for the peaceful coexistence of antithetical social systems; and that attempts to keep slavery out of commonly owned territories betrayed that solemn compact. Everyone knew as much, John C. Calhoun taunted the Senate in 1848. John Archibald Campbell of Alabama, who disliked slavery and freed his few domestic slaves when he became an associate justice of the U.S. Supreme Court, never wavered in viewing the Constitution as a solemn compact between North and South to respect each other's property system. Campbell saw the expanding power of the courts as a vehicle for consolidation of political power in the hands of big commercial and financial interests, and Mississippi's Justice William Harris forcefully agreed.[12]

During the War, William Frierson Cooper of Tennessee, an old unionist, pondered Tocqueville's remark that slavery divided the sections less in material interests than in manners and morals. Northerners and Southerners, Cooper concluded, had become two distinct peoples held together only by a constitutional compact to respect each other's social system. After the War Alexander Stephens and Jefferson Davis, while treating slavery as incidental to the struggle over constitutional principles, insisted that the South entered the Union on the understanding that the North

---

[11] For a brief account see Merton L. Dillon, *Slavery Attacked: Southern Slaves and Their Allies, 1619–1865* (Baton Rouge, LA, 1990), 50–1, 101; "Mitchell v. Wells," *Mississippi*, 37 (1860), 253–4; J. D. B. De Bow, *The Industrial Resources, Statistics, &c. of the United States and More Particularly of the Southern and Western States*, 3rd ed., 3 vols. (New York, 1966 [1854]), 1:407, 2:120; Henry L. Benning, speech at Milledgeville, in William W. Freehling and Craig M. Simpson, eds., *Secession Debated: Georgia's Showdown in 1860* (New York, 1992), 123, 126–7.

[12] Calhoun, "Speech on the Oregon Bill," June 27, 1848, in *JCCP*, 25:515–16; Henry G. Connor, *John Archibald Campell: Associate Justice of the United States Supreme Court* (Boston, 1920), 70–1, 86; Justice Harris in "Mitchell v. Wells," *Mississippi*, 37 (1860), 252–3. In 1850 the Reverend A. A. Porter declared the Constitution a compact that recognized slavery, asserting that everyone at the time knew as much. "The Christian people of the South *are the South*" and ready "in the name of the Lord" to risk everything to defend their rights as slaveholders: [Porter], "North and South," *SPR*, 3 (1850), 370, 378. See also "Report of the Resolutions of the Mississippi Convention," Oct. 3, 1849, in *JCCP*, 27:69–73, esp. 70, which insisted that the Union would never have been founded without guarantees for slavery.

would respect slave property. Daniel Webster, shortly before his death, granted that Jesus and the apostles had never condemned slavery as sinful and demanded that the North enforce the Fugitive Slave Law or repudiate the constitutional compact.[13]

The antislavery crusade began in earnest in Great Britain during the last quarter of the eighteenth century. It won abolition of the British and American slave trades in 1807–08 and later accomplished its great goal with slave emancipation in Brazil in 1888. In the early days many Southerners opposed slavery, and some still did at secession. But at no time could the South be described on balance as other than proslavery. As abolitionism gained momentum, its adherents adamantly maintained the self-evident sinfulness of slavery. The more radical overrode all appeals to Scripture and the Constitution. The southern response went through phases, usually referred to as the transition from the apology for slavery as a necessary evil to the assertion of it as a positive good. The substance of both phases appeared at the beginning and lasted to the end, but critical changes occurred along the way in the preponderance of public sentiment, ideology, and political action.

The "positive good" defense of slavery had been heard from the beginning, albeit in muted tones, but it, too, went through fundamental changes. First, Southerners and many northern and British conservatives argued that it was a positive good to blacks, whom forcible transportation to and enslavement in America rescued from barbarism and paganism. Second, they stressed the positive good to whites, who, as Edmund Burke acknowledged, forged themselves into a proud, strong, freedom-loving, and eventually republican people by habituation to the power of command and the leisure made possible by the freedom from drudgery that slaves afforded. For generations afterwards, Southerners invoked Burke's tribute to the American slaveholders' "manly love of liberty." By extension, Mary Howard Schoolcraft (Mrs. Henry Schoolcraft, as she identified herself) of Beaufort, South Carolina, appealed to Burke's authority against egalitarianism and radicalism. In these two overlapping and to some extent concurrent phases, slavery as a scripturally sanctified force for social order became common coin, well illustrated by Richard Furman's *Views of the Baptists* in 1823 and Thomas Roderick Dew's *Essay on Slavery* (a review of the Virginia debates of 1831–32), both building on ample precedents.[14]

Ascriptions of positive good to blacks and whites complemented each other and merged steadily. The third and decisive phase, which proclaimed slavery the best

---

[13] William Frierson Cooper, "Notes on a Trip to Europe, 1862–1863," 142, 158, in Cooper Papers, at Tennessee State Library and Archives (Nashville); Alexander H. Stephens, *A Constitutional View of the Late War between the States*, 2 vols. (New York, 1970 [1868, 1870]), 1:10–12, 28–9; Jefferson Davis, *The Rise and Fall of the Confederate Government*, 2 vols. (New York, 1958), 1:3–14, 80. For the text of Webster's famous speech on March 7, 1850, see Samuel M. Smucker, *The Life, Speeches, and Memorials of Daniel Webster* (Philadelphia, 1881), esp. 259–60. The Reverend John Adger of South Carolina also threw Webster's words at the Yankees: "Motley's Dutch Republic," *SPR*, 15 (1862), 148.

[14] *Plantation Life: The Narratives of Mrs. Henry Schoolcraft* (New York, 1969 [1860]), 101 n.; Richard Furman, "Views of the Baptists," in James A. Rogers, *Richard Furman: Life and Legacy* (Macon, GA, 1985), and Furman, *The Pleasures of Piety and Other Poems* (Charleston, SC, 1859), 196. For invocations of Burke's compliment see also Supplementary References: "Burke."

possible foundation for civilized society in general and for a republican polity in particular, had only been whispered during the eighteenth century. It picked up momentum during the first few decades of the nineteenth and rose to a crescendo in the 1840s and 1850s. With this transformation of the proslavery argument, the southern slaveholders stood alone. The Brazilian and Cuban slaveholders who defended slavery as a positive institution for blacks and whites did not celebrate slavery as the best foundation for all social order and as the wave of the future.[15]

As secession approached, many Americans believed – on the basis of little evidence – that the South had come out of the Revolution determined to remove slavery but had become decidedly proslavery in consequence of the cotton boom. During the eighteenth century it cost Southerners, including slaveholders, nothing to be theoretically antislavery. They explained their reluctance to emancipate slaves in the commonly accepted language of the day: It was business. They needed slaves to cultivate their crops. It remained good business until Eli Whitney and the cotton boom made it even better business. John and Henry Laurens of South Carolina, planters critical of slavery, attributed their inability to press for emancipation or emancipate their own slaves in large part to overwhelming proslavery public sentiment.[16]

The Protestant evangelicals who converted – or reconverted – the South to Christianity during and after the 1790s rested their defense of slavery on biblical sanction and spurned crass economic rationales for slavery. The shaping of a higher proslavery argument began long before the political struggle over Missouri and the subsequent rise of abolitionist demands for immediate emancipation, but it proceeded hesitantly. In 1749–50 the Anglican Reverend Thomas Bacon of Maryland delivered six sermons in which he carefully reviewed biblical texts to establish slavery as part of God's order, and in the 1780s Virginians invoked Scripture as well as material interest in proslavery petitions to the state legislature. In the 1790s the Reverend William Graham expounded the scriptural defense of slavery to the senior class at Liberty Hall Academy, now Washington and Lee University. Although Graham, a Pennsylvanian, had studied with antislavery orthodox Presbyterian John Witherspoon at Princeton, he feared the consequences of emancipation: "These persons were therefore all slaves, and as Christianity found them, so it has left them with regard to their civil relations.... It does not point out any mode of their emancipation nor even suggest the propriety of it." During the Missouri controversy, southern newspapers from Virginia to Missouri published scriptural defenses of slavery, and the Richmond *Enquirer* appealed to its readers to accept the literal truth of the Bible.[17]

---

[15] For the different slave systems and their ideologies see Eugene D. Genovese, *The World the Slaveholders Made: Two Essays in Interpretation* (New York, 1969), pt. 1.

[16] See, e.g., the shared assumption of the radical antislavery Missouri *Blätter*, Apr. 21, 1861, in Steven Rowan and James Neal Primm, eds., *Germans for a Free Missouri: Translations from the St. Louis Radical Press, 1857–1862* (Columbia, MO, 1983), 182, and the northern prosouthern Samuel Seabury, *American Slavery Distinguished from the Slavery of English Theorists and Justified by the Law of Nature* (New York, 1861), 308. Gregory D. Massey, "The Limits of Antislavery in the Revolutionary Lower South: John Laurens and Henry Laurens," *JSH*, 63 (1997), 495–530.

[17] See esp. Henry F. May, *The Enlightenment in America* (New York, 1976), 329; Thomas Bacon, *Two Sermons Preached to a Congregation of Black Slaves* (London, 1749); Bacon, *Four Sermons, upon*

Proslavery apologetics began to threaten secession and war if the national government interfered with slavery. Before the Missouri controversy, defenders of slavery had tried hard to be circumspect. Circumspection intensified during the patriotic wave that swept the United States before and during the War of 1812. In general, Southerners did not reject slavery as immoral or criminal, although they did worry that slavery was economically and politically retrogressive. By 1817 state-rights advocates regrouped to fight the Bank of the United States, the federal tariff, the consolidationism of John Marshall's U.S. Supreme Court, and the attempt to block admission of Missouri to statehood. In 1828 Governor William Branch Giles of Virginia, in agreement with a truculent Governor George Troup of Georgia, transmitted to his legislature resolutions from Georgia that breathed fire – with a veiled threat of secession – over the right of a state to settle its Indian problem without federal intervention.[18]

The behavior of Thomas Jefferson provides a veritable précis of the dilemma that faced antislavery Southerners. Abolitionists claimed him, and proslavery Southerners repudiated the antislavery views he expressed in his *Notes on the State of Virginia*. At the same time, Jefferson remained a hero to advocates of state rights, who nonetheless damned his fascination with French radicalism, overcoming their embarrassment by stressing his diminishing ardor for antislavery politics and his defense of strict construction.[19]

In *Notes on the State of Virginia*, Jefferson penned a searing indictment of slavery's effects on the master class. It reverberated through decades of abolitionist criticism and caused the slaveholders no end of soul-searching, pain, and anger:

the *Great and Indispensable Duty of All Christian Masters and Mistresses* (London, 1750). For Bacon see also Wayne A. Meeks, "The 'Haustafeln' and American Slavery: A Hermeneutical Challenge," in Eugene H. Lovering and Jerry L. Sumney, eds., *Theology and Ethics in Paul and His Interpreters: Essays in Honor of Victor Paul Furnish* (Nashville, TN, 1996), 241; on the press see Larry R. Morrison, "The Religious Defense of Slavery before 1830," *Journal of Religious Thought,* 37 (1980/81), 16–17, also 26.

The 1,244 proslavery petitioners of 1784–85 appealed to Scripture as well as self-interest: Fredrika Teute Schmidt and Barbara Ripel Wilhelm, "Early Proslavery Petitions in Virginia," *WMQ,* 3rd ser., 30 (1973), 133–46; David W. Robson, " 'An Important Question Answered': William Graham's Defense of Slavery in Post-Revolutionary Virginia," *WMQ,* 37 (1980), 644–52, Graham quoted at 644. "Lectures on Human Nature Aula Libertatis, Delivered by Wm. Graham: Notes Taken by Joseph Glass, 1796," 161–9, in Graham Philosophic Society Papers, at Washington and Lee University. Also, Jewel L. Spangler, "Proslavery Presbyterians: Virginia's Conservative Dissenters in the Age of Revolution," *JPH,* 78 (2000), 111–23. Graham taught Moses Hoge, John Holt Rice, George Baxter, and Archibald Alexander, and he had considerable influence well beyond Presbyterian circles: see Morton H. Smith, *Studies in Southern Presbyterian Theology* (Phillipsburg, NJ, 1962), 65–70, 82, 93, 96; Henry Alexander White, *Southern Presbyterian Leaders* (New York, 1911), ch. 20.

18 Dice Robins Anderson, *William Branch Giles: A Study in the Politics of Virginia and the Nation from 1790 to 1830* (Gloucester, MA, 1965 [1914]), 208–9, 222–3; Ulrich B. Phillips, *Georgia and State Rights* (Antioch, OH, 1968), 159.

19 In an early version of what became a common theme by the late 1830s, Edward Brown of South Carolina concluded that Jefferson must have changed his mind since he continued to live off slaves: Brown, *Notes on the Origin and Necessity of Slavery* (Charleston, SC, 1826), 40–2.

"There must doubtless be an unhappy influence on the manners of our people produced by the existence of slavery among us. The whole commerce between master and slave is a perpetual exercise of the most boisterous passions, the most unremitting despotism on the one part, and degrading submissions on the other." In 1785 Jefferson sadly admitted that he had badly overestimated antislavery feeling in Virginia and that an acerbic reaction in firmly proslavery South Carolina strengthened the Federalists there. Twenty years later he fretted that many "virtuous men" who think slavery wrong were nonetheless following their material interests. When in 1820 the Virginia legislature ignored a plea for gradual emancipation from Governor Thomas Mann Randolph, his son-in-law, Jefferson still expressed surprise that most Virginians found slavery acceptable and that many actually considered slavery right. His surprise at Virginians is less understandable than his surprise at Southerners elsewhere, for he never set foot in North Carolina or Kentucky and knew much more about New York and Philadelphia than he did about Charleston. Neither Jefferson nor any prominent Virginian risked his political fortunes and social standing by publicly denouncing slavery.[20]

In Jefferson's memorable phrase, northern opposition to Missouri's entrance into the Union as a slave state was "a fire bell in the night." From then on Jefferson said little about slavery, although he never abandoned his lifelong wish that it would disappear. He viewed antislavery demands as a renewed Federalist effort, supported by the Clinton faction of the Republican party in New York, to lift northeastern capitalists to power. Writing to John Adams in December 1819, he expressed certainty that political quarrels over economic and foreign policy would pass, but "The Missouri question is a breaker on which we lose the Missouri country by revolt.... We never had so ominous a question." Two years later he wrote Adams, also on Missouri: "Are our slaves to be presented with freedom and a dagger?" Jefferson worried about servile insurrection but also about a congressionally dictated emancipation. He feared disunion. In 1792 he had written George Washington at length to express concern over the prospect of a North–South separation, arguing that – although both sections had discrete interests – the federal government was favoring the North. Only Washington, Jefferson believed, held the Union together.[21]

Jefferson supported extension of slavery throughout the whole of the Louisiana Purchase, convinced that dispersion of blacks would hasten emancipation. But he also believed that the Marshall Court, the demands for federal regulation of the

---

[20] Thomas Jefferson, *Notes on the State of Virginia* (Chapel Hill, NC, 1955), 155. In Edwin Morris Betts, ed., *Thomas Jefferson's Farm Book: With Commentary and Relevant Extracts from His Writings* (Charlottesville, VA, 1987), see Jefferson to Richard Price, Aug. 7, 1885 (10), and Jefferson to William A. Burwell, Jan. 28, 1805 (20). Dumas Malone, *Jefferson and His Time*, 6 vols. (Boston, 1962–81), 2:95–6, 3:480, 489–90, 5:542–3, 6:331–2, and on T. M. Randolph see 341.

[21] Jefferson to Adams, Dec. 10, 1819, and Jan. 22, 1821, in Lester J. Cappon, ed., *The Adams–Jefferson Letters: The Complete Correspondence between Thomas Jefferson and Abigail and John Adams*, 2 vols. (Chapel Hill, NC, 1959), 2:548–9, 570; Smith, ed., *Republic of Letters*, 1:24, 35. By 1817 at the latest Jefferson had abandoned hope of emancipation in his lifetime: Malone, *Jefferson*, 5:325. For Jefferson's early dread of disunion see George Tucker, *The Life of Thomas Jefferson*, 2 vols. (London, 1837), 1:551, and for the text of Jefferson's letter to Washington see 1:427–34.

economy, and the emergence of abolitionism threatened a national consolidation that would undermine republicanism and enthrone a regime dominated by high finance and big business. In resisting antislavery, the slaveholders were resisting a stalking horse for a resurgent Federalism. Jefferson's antipathy to slavery did not wane, but slavery did not rank at the top of his priorities. While Jefferson drifted, other Southerners who sincerely and even passionately opposed slavery on principle, especially those of the next generation, felt compelled nonetheless to sustain its exigencies. The paradox derived from their attempt to reconcile individual rights and male equality with the social stability that only rural households and the governance of a "natural" political elite could provide. From the Revolution to the War for Southern Independence, thoughtful Southerners viewed slavery as the last guarantee of a social order in which republicanism could flourish.

If a "turning point" is to be selected – always a risky procedure – in the prolonged crisis of the Union and the maturation of proslavery thought, it would have to be the congressional struggle of 1819–20 over the admission of Missouri to the Union. President Horace Holley, a New Englander who presided over the prestigious Transylvania University, groaned during the Missouri controversy that Kentuckians were uttering "Yankee" in "a tone of uncommon severity." Pennsylvania-reared Daniel Boone roared that he did not want to live within a hundred miles of a damned Yankee.[22]

Missouri itself did not launch the struggle over the place of slavery in the Union or over the proper interpretation of the Constitution. The former had begun during the Revolution, the latter at the federal Constitutional Convention. But both those struggles cut across sections, and Missouri created an unprecedented sectional polarization. The organization of the Arkansas Territory and the Florida question in the Adams–Onís treaty of 1819 on Spanish-American borders provoked strong antislavery outbursts at about the same time, and some Northerners ominously interpreted the Constitution's "general welfare" clause as giving Congress power to abolish slavery throughout the Union. Southern tempers rose when the northeastern Federalist Rufus King, in accents new to Congress, excoriated slavery as an absolute evil. Yet the antislavery – but hardly extremist – Joseph Story of Massachusetts, a Madison appointee to the Supreme Court, chided King for undue moderation and exploded at John Randolph's abuse of the North. According to Story, both political parties in the North stood firm for the Union, but a grave disunionist danger was rising in the South. Caught off guard by King's assault, Southerners raged. Spencer Roane, who ranked high among Virginia's luminaries, looked forward to gradual emancipation but was stunned by what he saw as a northern conspiracy. Others never forgave King for the sensation he caused with his denial that one man had a right to enslave another. For long afterwards they asked how, if King were right, any form of authority could be justified. In 1850 Senator R. M. T. Hunter of Virginia looked back on King's speech as a declaration

[22] Holley quoted in John D. Wright, Jr., *Transylvania: Tutor to the West* (Lexington, KY, 1975), 195; Boone quoted in Glover Moore, *The Missouri Controversy, 1819–1821* (Lexington, KY, 1966), 14.

of war on the South; in 1860 James P. Holcombe, a prominent Virginia lawyer and educator, recalled that the Missouri crisis provoked fears of disunion that never evaporated; and at Alabama's secession convention William Lowndes Yancey of Alabama, widely described as "the orator of secession," recalled King's words, derisively associating them with Jefferson's.[23]

Tempers rose higher as conservative Northerners, who might have been expected to respect the South's constitutional rights, spoke up against slavery. Among the more important stood Theodore Dwight: grandson of Jonathan Edwards, brother of Yale's Timothy Dwight, and editor of the New York *Daily Advertiser*. Dwight provided a preview of what the South could expect. Along with editorials against slavery in Missouri came opposition to the flogging of military personnel and to cruelty toward blacks, Indians, Eskimos, mental patients, and – we are not making it up – lobsters. Still, southern public opinion remained calm until anti-Missouri meetings swept the North, beating drums against slaveholding enemies of freedom, republican government, and economic development. Straws in the wind: Presbyterian ladies of Augusta, Georgia, withdrew their offer to endow a student scholarship at Princeton. Charles Tait of Georgia, a unionist Democrat who chaired the Senate committee on the Missouri issue, fairly choked as he shifted to a state-rights course.[24]

The depression that followed the economic crisis of 1819 led to demands for a protective tariff in the Middle States and to anger against southern obstructionism; simultaneously, it led to a strong effort to overcome economic distress by transforming Illinois into a slave state. Virginia stood at the forefront of pro-Missouri intransigence, followed by South Carolina, which suffered an abrupt end to an unparalleled period of prosperity. The rest of the Lower South showed greater willingness to compromise and concentrated on immediate economic problems. Northerners had deluded themselves that Virginians loathed slavery, underestimating Virginia's dependence on the domestic slave trade and its commitment to southern constitutional rights. More than a decade before William Lloyd Garrison and the demand 'for immediate abolition, Northerners began to doubt that gradual emancipation would occur in Virginia.[25]

---

[23] Moore, *Missouri Controversy*, 60, 119; William W. Story, *Life and Letters of Joseph Story*, 2 vols. (Boston, 1851), 1:359–63, 367; Margaret E. Horsnell, *Spencer Roane: Judicial Advocate of Jeffersonian Principles* (New York, 1986), 87–90, 174–5; James P. Holcombe, *The Election of a Black Republican President* (Richmond, VA, 1860), 3; W. L. Yancey in William R. Smith, ed., *The History of the Convention Debates of the People of Alabama* (Montgomery, AL, 1861), 248; also, Jenkins, *Pro-Slavery*, 67–9. There was a straight line from Fisher Ames (d. 1808) to William Lloyd Garrison: see Marc M. Arkin, "The Federalist Trope: Power and Passion in Abolitionist Rhetoric," *Journal of American History*, 88 (2002), 75–98; also, Ames to Thomas Dwight, Oct. 26, 1803, in *Works of Fisher Ames as Published by Seth Ames*, edited and enlarged by W. B. Allen, 2 vols. (Indianapolis, IN, 1983), 2:1467.

[24] Moore, *Missouri Controversy*, 74, 218–19; Margaret Burr DesChamps, "The Presbyterian Church in the South Atlantic States, 1801–1861" (Ph.D. diss., Emory University, 1952), 181; Charles H. Moffatt, "Charles Tait, Planter, Politician, and Scientist of the Old South," *JSH*, 14 (1948), 206–33.

[25] R. Carlyle Buley, *The Old Northwest: Pioneer Period, 1815–1840*, 2 vols. (Bloomington, IN, 1950), 2:20; Moore, *Missouri Controversy*, 18, 81–5, 242–3, 248; Alfred Glaze Smith, Jr., *The Economic*

Missouri fueled southern suspicions of national consolidation – concentration of power in Washington, not in state capitals – at a moment when John Marshall presided over a nationalist Supreme Court. In Maryland the aging Charles Carroll of Carrolton, who had introduced an emancipation bill in the legislature and manumitted thirty of his slaves, brooded over the polemics: "Something else than the exclusion of slaves from the Missouri State is at the bottom." In Virginia, John Randolph, James Madison, "Light Horse" Harry Lee, John Tyler, and Thomas Jefferson – all of whom found slavery distasteful – saw antislavery as a slogan around which moneyed interests that cared nothing for blacks were rallying northern public opinion against southern planters. To them, antislavery disguised concentration of political and economic power in the hands of a financial oligarchy determined to oppress the people.[26]

South Carolinians had a special reason for encouraging Virginia's intransigence. In December 1816, Governor David Rogerson Williams told the South Carolina legislature that a community of maroons (escaped slaves) was mounting an "alarming" threat backed by arms, ammunition, and numbers. While maroons were repelling state forces, authorities in upcountry Camden uncovered plans for a slave insurrection. In Charleston, Denmark Vesey, a slave who bought his freedom and turned revolutionary, was believed to have read Rufus King's denunciation of slavery. Vesey soured the hopes of influential Charlestonians like Isaac Harby – journalist, playwright, and a leader in the Jewish community – who had welcomed the Missouri Compromise. Robert Turnbull, who sat on the court that sentenced Vesey to death, wrote articles for the Charleston *Mercury* that were republished as a widely read book, *The Crisis* (1827), in which he fumed that congressional debate gave slaves the heady idea that they should look to the federal government for amelioration or eventual emancipation. Acknowledging the South's vulnerability to antislavery propaganda, Turnbull warned that congressional debate over slavery meant war. The danger came less from without than from within: "The enemy is amongst ourselves." When Congress openly threatened slavery in the states, "Many weak white men amongst us" would cave.[27]

Readjustment of an Old Cotton State: South Carolina, 1820–1860 (Columbia, SC, 1958), ch. 1; Pierce Butler, *The Unhurried Years: Memories of the Old Natchez Region* (Baton Rouge, LA, 1948), 47ff. On the importance of the domestic slave trade during the Missouri controversy see Duncan J. McLeod, *Slavery, Race and the American Revolution* (London, 1974), 44. On the growth of immediatism during the 1820s see David W. Blight, "Perceptions of Southern Intransigence and the Rise of Antislavery Thought, 1816–1830," *JER*, 3 (1983), 139–63.

[26] Charles Carroll to Robert Goodloe Harper, Feb. 17, 1820, in Kate Mason Rowland, *The Life of Charles Carroll of Carrollton, 1737–1832*, 2 vols. (New York, 1898), 2:320; Malone, *Jefferson*, 6:329–30; Charles Royster, *Light-Horse Harry Lee and the Legacy of the American Revolution* (New York, 1981), ch. 3; John Tyler to Dr. Henry Curtis, Feb. 5, 1820, in Lyon Gardiner Tyler, *The Letters and Times of the Tylers*, 3 vols. (Williamsburg, VA, 1884–96), 1:316 and 2:26–7; Oliver Perry Chitwood, *John Tyler: Champion of the Old South* (New York, 1939), 48. On Madison see Jennifer Nedelsky, *Private Property and the Limits of American Constitutionalism: The Madisonian Framework and Its Legacy* (Chicago, 1991), 40–1.

[27] Donald L. Robinson, *Slavery in the Structure of American Politics, 1765–1820* (New York, 1971), 406–15, 429; Herbert Aptheker, *American Negro Slave Revolts* (New York, 1943); Harvey Toliver

Madison, like Jefferson, accepted the "diffusion" theory according to which, if the slave population were spread out and thinned, slavery would decline; but he feared the worst from the agitation over Missouri. Monroe, too, saw a Federalist stalking horse but shrank from the consequences of a veto. John Taylor of Caroline, his longtime supporter, considered the Compromise a capitulation to moneyed interests and a betrayal of the South, and Thomas Ritchie threw his formidable influence against the Compromise and Monroe's "consolidationism."[28]

Ritchie, like Jefferson, wanted William H. Crawford of Georgia to succeed Monroe as president. Crawford expected northern aggression to build steadily, but like his enemy Calhoun and most Southerners he swallowed the Compromise, remarking, "If the Union is of more importance to the South than slavery [then] the South should immediately take measures for the gradual emancipation of the slaves, fixing a period for its final extinction." But if slavery took precedence over the Union, the South "should at once secede and establish a government to protect and preserve this institution. She now has the power do so without the fear of provoking a war." The Missouri agitation, Crawford added, had united the South to face any eventuality.[29]

In defense of Missouri's right to enter the Union as a slave state, William Smith of South Carolina, a Crawford ally, argued that throughout history one class had always served another, that the Bible and the experience of Greece and Rome sanctioned slavery, and that slavery uplifted the moral character of whites. Representative Robert Raymond Reed of Georgia defended the compatibility of a mild southern slavery with republican government. Representative Nathaniel Macon of North Carolina replied to the Declaration's assertion of the equality of all men: "Follow that sentiment, and does it not lead to universal emancipation? If it will justify putting an end to slavery in Missouri, will it not justify it in the old States?" "The Yankees," John Randolph exclaimed, "have almost reconciled me to negro slavery." Since they produced "revulsion" in him, he wondered about their effect on those

Cook, *The Life and Legacy of David Rogerson Williams* (New York, 1916), 130–1; Gary Philip Zola, *Isaac Harby of Charleston, 1788–1828: Jewish Reformer and Intellectual* (Tuscaloosa, AL, 1994), 95; Robert J. Turnbull, *The Crisis: Or, Essays on the Usurpation of the Federal Government by Brutus* (Charleston, SC, 1827), 15, 130–3; David Duncan Wallace, *The History of South Carolina*, 4 vols. (New York, 1934), 2:415.

[28] W. P. Cresson, *James Monroe* (Chapel Hill, NC, 1946), 346–8, 530, ch. 25; John Taylor, *Construction Construed and Constitutions Vindicated* (Richmond, VA, 1820), 291–314; Henry H. Simms, *Life of John Taylor: The Story of a Brilliant Leader in the Early Virginia State Rights School* (Richmond, VA, 1932), 164–6. R. J. Turnbull assailed the Monroe administration as worse than that of the Federalists or that of John Quincy Adams: *The South Must Purge Its Capitulators* (Charleston, SC, 1827), 8–9, 16–17. Tyler espoused the "diffusion theory": see R. Daniel Monroe, "A Republican Vision: The Politics of John Tyler" (Ph.D. diss., University of Illinois, 1999), 71–83. On the extent of secessionist threats from both sides see Moore, *Missouri Controversy*, 93–4. For anti-Missouri agitation in the North see Dillon, *Slavery Attacked*, 122–3.

[29] Crawford quoted in J. E. D. Shipp, *Giant Days; Or, the Life and Times of William H. Crawford* (Americus, GA, 1909), 168. Calhoun, who had accepted the Missouri Compromise during the crisis of 1819–20, privately if reluctantly acknowledged a willingness to renew it as a solution to the crisis of 1848–50: see Clyde N. Wilson, "Introduction," in *JCCP*, 25:xiii.

with "no scruples on the subject." In his will, Randolph freed his own 400 slaves at his death in 1833, providing for their settlement in Ohio, but he called northern antislavery a cynical ploy to deprive Southerners of their rights and freedom. He railed against federal support for internal improvements: "If Congress possesses the power to do what is proposed in this bill, they may not only exact a Sedition law – for there is precedent – but they may emancipate every slave in the United States – and with stronger color of reason than they can exercise the power now contended for."[30]

Congress expected fireworks from the irascible Randolph, but not from William Pinkney of Maryland, who had repeatedly decried slavery in no uncertain terms. In one of the most effective defenses of Missouri's right to admission as a slave state, he staked everything on the Constitution. Pinkney scorned the "prophetic fears" of those who share "the worst visions of the political philosophy of France ... I mean 'the infinite perfectibility of man and his institutions.' " (The archconservative Rufus King must have choked at that thrust.) Pinkney had sport with opponents who considered slavery incompatible with republican government and yet agreed that Missouri need not emancipate slaves already there. Do these gentlemen, he inquired, consider the quantity of slaves an issue that supersedes the antirepublican quality attributed to slavery itself? Will they tell us what the laws enacted by a republican government have to do with the republican form of government? Were not Sparta, Athens, and Rome slaveholding republics? They say that slavery arises from fraud and violence. Well, then, did our ancestors not seize this continent from Indians by fraud and violence? Did they thereby render impossible the construction of republican governments? Pinkney stuck to the Constitution, treating as irrelevant the biting criticisms of slavery he had previously uttered.[31]

In June 1820, Calhoun assured Andrew Jackson that the South and West remained firmly attached to the Union. Agitators "have, in my opinion, not only failed; but have destroyed to a great extent their capacity for future mischief." In August, Calhoun wrote in the same vein but with some uneasiness, admitting that a perceived northern threat to slave property could disrupt the Union, but later that autumn a tour of the North convinced him that northern opinion remained moderate and was isolating extremists. He repeated that theme during the next few months but tellingly remarked that he "still" hoped for a stable outcome. A year later Calhoun again was blaming politicians on both sides for agitating the slavery issue to advance

---

[30] Moore, *Missouri Controversy*, 125; for the text of Reed's speech see Stephen F. Miller, *The Bench and Bar of Georgia: Memoirs and Sketches*, 2 vols. (Philadelphia, 1858), 2:190–8; for the text of Macon's speech see W. J. Peele, ed., *Lives of Distinguished North Carolinians* (Raleigh, NC, 1907), 100–10, quote at 108. John Randolph to John Brockenbrough, Feb. 14, 1820, in Kenneth Shorey, ed., *Collected Letters of John Randolph to Dr. John Brockenbrough, 1812–1833* (New Brunswick, NJ, 1988), 27; Randolph, "Speech on Surveys for Roads and Canals," Jan. 30, 1824, in Russell Kirk, *John Randolph of Roanoke: A Study in American Politics, with Selected Speeches and Letters* (Chicago, 1964), 337–57, quote at 353.

[31] For the text of William Pinkney's speech see *SBN*, 9:226–70. John Marshall regarded Pinkney as the greatest "reasoner" he had ever met: W. W. Story, *Life and Letters of Joseph Story*, 2:494.

sectional ambitions. The next few years sobered him. In 1826 he presciently predicted that those who wished to expand federal power would reopen the Missouri question. In 1838 he confessed his regret at having supported the Compromise. In 1849, in a public address signed by 48 (out of 124) southern congressmen, Calhoun pointed to 1819 as the year the South felt itself broadsided.[32]

Governor Troup told the Georgia legislature in 1825 that Southerners were outraged by northern meddling in their affairs and that the federal government was becoming an instrument for fanaticism: "One movement of the Congress unresisted by you and all is lost. Temporize no longer. Make known your resolution; that this subject shall not be touched by them but at their peril." If slavery be a sin, he thundered, it is the sin of Southerners who alone must answer to God. Meanwhile, Ohio asked Congress and the state legislatures to consider a plan for emancipation, emphasizing the responsibility of the country as a whole for the introduction of slavery in the first place. Eight northern states endorsed the idea. Troup scorned Ohio's appeal, observing that northern meddling was only making things harder for the slaves. The South Carolina legislature, still smarting from the Vesey plot and the slavery debate in Illinois, responded with vituperation. The Mississippi legislature, too, rejected Ohio's interference but with apologies for slavery. After Andrew Jackson's election, apologetics declined and proslavery stiffened. In 1836, Acting Governor John Quitman asserted the morality and soundness of slavery as a system.[33]

By the late 1840s, southern moderates as well as radicals looked back on the Missouri struggle as fateful. Yet in 1850 when Henry Clay's Omnibus Bill – which included a fugitive slave law, abolition of the slave trade in the District of Columbia, and the admission of California as a free state – went down to defeat, they moved to extend the Compromise to the Pacific as the best way to head off or counterbalance the admission of California. Protesting renewed antislavery agitation, Augustin S. Clayton of Georgia, a leading jurist and politician, reiterated that

---

[32] In *JCCP*: Calhoun to Andrew Jackson, June 1, 1820 (5:164); Calhoun to Virgil Maxcy, Aug. 12, 1820 (5:327); Calhoun to Charles Tait, Oct. 26, 1820 (5:412–14); Calhoun to John Ewing Colhoun, Jan. 8, 1821 (5:541); Calhoun to L. W. Tazewell, June 13, 1826 (10:128–9); Calhoun to Moses Waddel, Sept. 25, 1821 (6:388); "Remarks," Jan. 11, 1838 (14:88); "Address of the Southern Delegates in Congress to Their Constituents," 1849 (26:227); also, "Discourse on the Constitution," 262. Of the 48 who signed Calhoun's "Southern Address," only two were Whigs. Whigs especially lashed out at Calhoun's bid to create a southern party: Michael F. Holt, *The Rise and Fall of the American Whig Party: Jacksonian Politics and the Onset of the Civil War* (New York, 1999), 387.

[33] Troup quoted in George White, *Statistics of the State of Georgia* (Savannah, GA, 1849), 561–2; see also Troup, "First Annual Message to the State Legislature of Georgia" (1824), in Edward J. Harden, *The Life of George M. Troup* (Savannah, GA, 1859), 242; Charles S. Sydnor, *The Development of Southern Sectionalism, 1819–1848* (Baton Rouge, LA, 1948), 151; on the impact of Illinois and Vesey see also Blight, "Perceptions of Southern Intransigence," 156, 159–60; Dunbar Rowland, ed. *Mississippi: Comprising Sketches of Counties, Towns, Events, Institutions, and Persons, Arranged in Cyclopedic Form*, 4 vols. (Spartanburg, SC, 1976 [1907]), 2:682–3, 684 (Jackson's election), 685–6 (Quitman); Mark J. Stegmaier, *Texas, New Mexico, and the Compromise of 1850* (Kent, OH, 1996), 202. The South never seriously considered the proposals for compensated emancipation, which first arose during the Revolution and resurfaced from time to time until secession: Betty L. Fladeland, "Compensated Emancipation: A Rejected Alternative," *Journal of Southern History,* 62 (1976), 169–72.

the South adopted the Constitution only after northern assurances on the safety of slave property. Jefferson Davis, who believed the Compromise had bolstered northern power, acknowledged that the South had accepted the bad business as a workable arrangement. Southerners reasonably saw the Wilmot Proviso of 1846, which would have excluded slavery from territories acquired in the Mexican War, as a failed attempt to deny the Compromise's constitutionality.[34]

Moderates who detested South Carolina's extremism – Albert Taylor Bledsoe and Robert L. Dabney of Virginia, John Belton O'Neall of South Carolina, Benjamin Hill of Georgia, Thomas Hart Benton of Missouri – viewed Missouri as a watershed for the defense of slavery and constitutional rights, which they considered as of a piece. O'Neall, a firm unionist, linked the Compromise to the Kansas–Nebraska Bill as a challenge to slave property. Hill denounced demands to repeal the Compromise as breach of faith. Benton, a Border State unionist, judged the Compromise an antislavery victory and considered antislavery agitation as northern aggression and a cloak for the national consolidation espoused by the old Federalist party. He described the Compromise as largely the work of Southerners who went a long way to preserve the Union and whose effort testified to a conciliatory spirit in the South. But he saw a great change thereafter. Until 1835, northern agitators had threatened the Union; after 1835 he "looked to the South for that danger."[35]

During the 1850s, unprecedented numbers of southern Whig and Democrat politicians came to see the Compromise as politically unwise despite Missouri's admission as a slave state, for it affronted southern honor by treating slavery as an evil. Edmund Ruffin identified the Missouri agitation as a turning point in North–South relations. W. D. Porter of Charleston lashed out at "a great and grievous error" that violated southern rights and unleashed "the spirit of fanaticism, the evil genius of this country." In 1851 the Southern Rights Association of the University of Virginia issued an "Address to the Young Men of the South" to rally against "our aggressor." The Compromise was "another legislative robbery." George Sawyer of Louisiana acknowledged that Monroe and Calhoun had swallowed hard to save the Union, but he concluded mournfully that they had thereby compromised principle. Southerners rallied to the Kansas–Nebraska Act of 1854 in part because it repealed the Compromise and thereby, from their point of view, corrected an old wrong.

---

[34] [A. M. Clayton], *Address of the Friends of Southern Rights to the People of Mississippi* (Jackson, MS, 1850), 30–40; Davis, *Rise and Fall of the Confederate Government*, 1:14–15.

[35] *DD*, 2:393, and R. L. Dabney, *Life and Campaigns of Lt. Gen. T. J. (Stonewall) Jackson* (Harrisonburg, VA, 1983 [1865]), 137; John B. Bennett, "Albert Taylor Bledsoe: Transitional Philosopher of the Old South," *Methodist History*, 11 (1972), 243–5; John Belton O'Neall, *Biographical Sketches of the Bench and Bar of South Carolina*, 2 vols. (Charleston, SC, 1859), 2:142–3; *Senator Benjamin H. Hill of Georgia: His Life, Speeches and Writings* (Atlanta, GA, 1891), 17–18; Thomas Hart Benton, *Thirty Years' View; Or, a History of the Working of the American Government for Thirty Years, from 1820 to 1850*, 2 vols. (New York, 1854), 1:5–10, 136, 623, 2:786. As David Potter observed, the compromises over slavery in the Constitution "adjourned rather than reconciled" the sectional division: David M. Potter, *The Impending Crisis, 1848–1861* (New York, 1977), 52. In 1860 a long refutation of Charles Hodges's "State of the Country" contended that the Republicans had subjected the history of the Missouri Compromise to unprecedented distortion and that only clarity could restore sectional peace: "Reply to Rev. Charles Hodge, D.D.," *VUM*, 5 (1860), 265–95.

Meanwhile, repeal drove many northern Democrats into the new Republican party. Advocates of proslavery militancy agreed that the South had been converted to their cause, but they differed on the turning point. More often than not they cited the 1830s, but in noting the years of preparation they generally accorded the Missouri controversy a special place.[36]

[36] Edmund Ruffin, "Consequences of Abolition Agitation," *DBR*, 22 (1857), 586; W. D. Porter, *Oration Delivered before the Calhoun Monument Association* (Charleston, SC, 1854), 31; Southern Rights Association of the University of Virginia, *Address to the Young Men of the South* (Charlottesville, VA, 1851), 7; George S. Sawyer, *Southern Institutes; Or, an Inquiry into the Origin and Early Prevalence of Slavery and the Slave Trade* (New York, 1967 [1858]), 349; also, "Is Southern Civilization Worth Preserving?" *SQR*, n.s., 3 (1851), 194.

Entr'acte

The Bonds of Slavery

> Aristocracies often commit very tyrannical and very inhuman actions; but they rarely entertain grovelling thoughts; and they show a kind of haughty contempt of little pleasures, even whilst they indulge in them. The effect is greatly to raise the general pitch of society. In aristocratic ages vast ideas are commonly entertained of the dignity, the power, and the greatness of man.
>
> —Alexis de Tocqueville[1]

Slavery grounded southern society and culture, differentiating the South from the North, to which it remained intimately linked. It had not always been thus. Although northern and southern settlement had been fed by slightly different currents – the one more Puritan, the other more Cavalier – both derived disproportionately from British stock and both included a large component of yeoman farm families. Slaveholding, like indentured servitude, was taken for granted by all. Only gradually did the two regions diverge, as slavery advanced in the South and receded in the North.

During the early years of the Republic, most Southerners lived comfortably with a kind of layered citizenship: citizens of the new United States but deeply rooted in their discrete states, which they were wont to call "my country," and in their local communities and households. Many Northerners of the day did the same, but fault lines appeared in the early Republic. By the Missouri crisis of 1819–20, the growing regional divergence in interests and values was clear to those who cared to notice. Today, many academics slight the significance – or deny the existence – of southern distinctiveness, arguing that Southerners were Northerners by another name even during the first half of the nineteenth century: aspiring capitalists, cultivators of conventional middle-class mores, and racists. In that perspective, the South seceded in 1861 solely to preserve ownership of human property and white supremacy.

A majority of Southerners did not agree. One did not have to be a large slaveholder to resent the mounting pressures from those they called "black Republicans." Augusta Jane Evans of Mobile – who held no special brief for slavery, which

---

[1] Alexis de Tocqueville, *Democracy in America*, tr. Henry Reeve, 2 vols. (Boston, 1873), 2:51.

she thought tended to make women indolent and spoiled – passionately defended southern independence and distinct southern political and moral values. She reflected a growing determination by Southerners to define themselves as a people apart. Surprising numbers of European and American travelers' accounts, flattering and unflattering, concurred with that image. Southerners picked and chose among those accounts, rejecting hostile comparisons and embracing the favorable. Frederick Law Olmsted, the Yankee architect and journalist, irritated Southerners with his report that slavery perpetuated the frontier conditions he associated with barbarism and that it had devastating effects on southern temperament. They dismissed his criticisms while basking in his occasional tributes to the fine qualities of southern gentlemen. Until the 1830s, British and continental travelers also published friendly accounts of the South. Thereafter, antislavery agitation intensified, and improvements in transportation permitted more liberal, middle-class travelers to join the conservative aristocrats who had previously dominated transatlantic travel. The higher the travelers' class, the more likely they would be to see planters as proper ladies and gentlemen – hospitable, warm, frank, and intellectually engaged – and to see, as did Sir Charles Lyell, the famous geologist, the relation of master and slave as akin to that of lord and retainer in old England. The aristocratic Achille Murat of France, who lived in Florida for some years, waxed lyrical over the southern planter who, accustomed to "considering himself as morally responsible for the condition of a great number of individuals," develops "a sort of austere dignity favourable to virtue." Murat found the planter "one of the most perfect models of the human race" and contrasted his "independence of views in politics and religion" with "the reserve and hypocrisy" of too many Northerners. "To his slaves he is a father rather than a master, for he is too strong to be cruel."[2]

Southerners particularly enjoyed the contrasts drawn by foreigners and sympathetic Northerners between southern gentlemen and vulgar upper-class Northerners. The Marques of Lothian called planters America's closest approximation to genuine aristocracy, as distinct from the North's more powerful and unattractive aristocracy-of-sorts in stockjobbers, low-minded capitalists, and political wire pullers. "Throughout the South, whether in city or country," wrote the Reverend W. H. Milburn, a northern Methodist, "there is an attention paid to the proprieties and courtesies of life, which I have failed to observe in some other parts of the Union – a reverence for age, deference to childhood, a polite regard for equals, a kind tone to the poor, treatment of the negro as if he were one of the family, and a truly chivalrous bearing toward women."[3]

---

[2] Frederick Law Olmsted, *A Journey in the Seaboard Slave States, with Remarks on Their Economy* (New York, 1968 [1856]), 51; Olmsted, *A Journey in the Back Country* (New York, 1970 [1860]), 412–15, 467–8; Charles Capen McLaughlin et al., eds., *The Papers of Frederick Law Olmsted*, 2 vols. (Baltimore, 1977, 1981), 2:207–8, 238–9. Jane Louise Mesick, *The English Traveller in America, 1785–1835* (New York, 1922), 67–8; Charles Lyell, *A Second Visit to the United States of North America*, 2 vols. (New York, 1849), 1:261; Achille Murat, *The United States of North America, with a Note on Negro Slavery*, 2nd ed. (London, 1833), 91–2.

[3] Marques of Lothian, "A British View of American Aristocracy," in Belle Becker Seidman and Lillian Friedman, eds., *Europe Looks at the Civil War, an Anthology* (New York, 1960), 22; E. S. Abdy, *Journal*

Not so in the North. There, the Massachusetts-born Parson Theodore Clapp of New Orleans wrote, people feared for the respectability of their position and attempted to "guard it, in a chilly isolation, by a stiff reserve." Welcomed in Kentucky on his way south, he was "treated with a more noble hospitality, a more marked and uniform kindness, than I had ever experienced in the land of the Puritans." Clapp found the "slaveholders in general possessed of a wider range of knowledge, much more refined, gentle and condescending in manners, far superior in the graces and amenities of social intercourse, to those regarded as well-bred and respectable people throughout the cities, towns, and villages of New England." Nowhere in the world "have I observed less of aristocratic pretensions, of pharisaic, cold-hearted, unsympathizing conduct toward the poor, humble, and unfortunate."[4]

Thomas Jefferson explained the difference between Southerners and Northerners to the Marquis de Chastellux: "Southerners – fiery, voluptuous, indolent, generous, candid; Northerners – cool, sober, persevering, self-interested, chicaning." In 1803–04 John C. Calhoun, then a student in New Haven, reported to cousins back home in South Carolina: Yankees "are certainly more penurious, more contracted in their sentiments, and less social than the Carolinians. But as to morality we must yield." A good look at Newport, Rhode Island, led Calhoun to doubt New Englanders' moral superiority. Governor John Tyler, Sr., of Virginia, father of the future president, spoke of Yankees as "these Northern cattle" who denigrated Virginia. Singling out the geographer Jedidiah Morse for his "silly and prejudiced opinion" of Williamsburg, Tyler feared that such views threatened the Union. The North has "nothing like that liberty of Sentiment which pervades and animates our Southern world."[5]

Not everyone agreed. During the nullification crisis in South Carolina, William Campbell Preston of South Carolina wrote to Waddy Thompson, a fellow unionist, that Southerners "lack perseverance and can only effect their object by a *coup de main*," whereas Northerners "never know when to let go what they once put their hands on." In vain Preston warned against dismissal of Yankees as vulgar, tight-fisted peddlers: "Their energy and enterprise are directed to all objects, great and small within their reach." Many Carolinians did not share his sober caution.[6]

---

of Residence and Tour in the United States of North America, 3 vols. (New York, 1969 [1835]), 1:35–6; Francis J. Grund, *Aristocracy in America: From the Sketchbook of a German Nobleman* (Gloucester, MA, 1968 [1839]), 10, 45–6, 87, 276.

[4] John Duffy, ed., *Parson Clapp of the Strangers' Church of New Orleans* (Baton Rouge, LA, 1957), 167.

[5] Jefferson to Chastellux, Sept. 2, 1785, in Julian P. Boyd, ed., *The Papers of Thomas Jefferson*, 28 vols. (Princeton, NJ, 1953), 8:468. According to Jefferson, both cherished their liberties, but Southerners trampled those of others while Northerners were solicitous. Southerners had no attachment or pretensions to religion except that of the heart, whereas he found Northerners superstitious and hypocritical. J. C. Calhoun to Andrew Pickens, Jr., May 23, 1803, and Calhoun to Alexander Noble, Oct. 15, 1804, in *JCCP*, 1:10, 13; John Tyler, Sr., to St. George Tucker, July 10, 1795, in Lyon Gardiner Tyler, *The Letters and Times of the Tylers*, 3 vols. (Williamsburg, VA, 1884–86), 3:10.

[6] W. C. Preston to Waddy Thompson, June 23, 1829, in Preston Papers, at USC; Preston quoted in C. G. Parsons, *An Inside View of Slavery: A Tour among the Planters* (Savannah, GA, 1974 [1855]), 165. Some twenty years later, a rueful "J. W. D." complained in *Southern Eclectic* that Southerners lack the

More typical was the report of a visit to New York by Louisa Quitman, daughter of John A. Quitman of Mississippi, himself a transplanted Yankee. Young Miss Quitman thought that only Southerners had "hearts that beat within the highest & noblest feelings of *honour* & *chivalry*." Yankees "cannot conceive of such exalted ideas, they have too much of Dr. Franklin spirit." The better she came to know them the greater her dislike. In the 1850s, James Johnston Pettigrew found his relatives in Philadelphia polite yet so lacking in warmth that he could not readily call them "cousin." Ella Gertrude Clanton Thomas's encounter with the "impertinence" of a Yankee "aroused all the haughty southern woman" in her. Thomas Holly Chivers of Georgia, a fine poet who lived in the Northeast, reacted to boorishness with greater wit and grace. "You are very much mistaken," he wrote an old friend in New York, "if you suppose that all men who were born in the South become offended at every fanatical turpitude perpetrated by crack-brained Northerners." During the War, the intellectually impressive Catherine Edmonston of North Carolina insisted, "The Yankee is too calculating to lose his life for mere honour. He wants 'a consideration.'" Tally Simpson of South Carolina agreed that the cool, calculating Northerners "are influenced more by self-interest than by principle."[7]

Such contrasts had become standard fare by the 1850s. To Louisa McCord of South Carolina, her beloved father, Langdon Cheves, was not "coldly calm" in grief but "(permit the anomalous expression) *passionately* calm." Dr. William H. Holcombe of Natchez, a broadly gauged man of letters, described Northerners: "Individually cautious & timid – collectively bold and courageous. Individually cool and calm – collectively excitable. Individually resorting to law or suasion – collectively to force. Individually insensible to the points of honor – collectively very much so." And Southerners: "Individually brave to rashness – collectively cautious and wise [word indistinct]. Individually excitable – collectively possessed and dignified. Individually resorting to violence – collectively to suasion. Individually sensitive to the point of honor – collectively less so, singularly calm and forbearing and forgiving."[8]

staying power of Northerners. Southern projects, often brilliant, come with a flash and die as quickly: *Southern Eclectic*, 1 (1853), 63–6.

7 Louisa Quitman to J. A. Quitman, Nov. 17, 1846, at UNC-SHC; Clyde N. Wilson, *Carolina Cavalier: The Life and Mind of James Johnston Pettigrew* (Athens, GA, 1990), 110; E. G. C. Thomas Diary, May 27, 1865, at Duke University; Chivers to Bush, Mar. 11, 1855, in Emma Lester Chase and Lois Ferry Parks, eds., *The Complete Works of Thomas Holley Chivers: Correspondence, 1838–1858* (Providence, RI, 1957), 229; Jan. 11, 1863, in Beth G. Crabtree and James Welch Patton, eds., *"Journal of a Secesh Lady": The Diary of Catherine Devereux Edmonston, 1860–1866* (Raleigh, NC, 1979), 341; Tally Simpson to Caroline Taliaferro, Nov. 12, 1860, in Guy R. Everson and Edward W. Simpson, Jr., eds., *"Far, Far from Home": The Wartime Letters of Dick and Tully Simpson, Third South Carolina Volunteers* (New York, 1994), xvii. Mary Moragné heard an eloquent speech by Mr. Custis of the board of foreign missions, "but I discovered that he was a Yankee, by a certain obsequiousness – a busy servility, so opposite to the stately indifference of the haughty Southrons – and I turned on my heel [and] mounted my horse": July 29, 1838, in Della Mullen Craven, ed., *The Neglected Thread: A Journal of the Calhoun Community* (Columbia, SC, 1951), 102.

8 "Memoir of Langdon Cheves," in Richard C. Lounsbury, ed., *Louisa S. McCord: Poems, Drama, Biography, Letters* (Charlottesville, VA, 1996), 261; W. H. Holcombe Diary, Aug. 5, 1855 (but apparently written early in the War), at UNC-SHC.

Nothing alarmed or amazed Augustus Baldwin Longstreet more than the "apathy and indifference" with which Southerners greeted "the encroachments and the pretensions of the Abolitionists." Author of the rollicking *Georgia Scenes* and a Methodist minister and college president, Longstreet doubted that another people "would have seen the fires of destruction kindled around them, as they have been kindled around us, with so little resistance, with so little emotion." William Gilmore Simms – literary light of South Carolina – wrote to his good friend, the politically powerful J. H. Hammond, that Southerners bravely followed audacious leaders but lived too far apart to move politically unless directly attacked. Hammond agreed that Southerners rushed to the field of honor on personal matters but lacked the public spirit necessary to defend their political interests. As a young man, Simms himself had written to a New Yorker, "We Southrons, you know, are creatures of impulse and prejudice"; after the War, Thomas De Leon of South Carolina laconically remarked, "The young men of the whole South are off-hand and impulsive." In short, Southerners collectively were slow to move while individually more excitable than Northerners and also prone to rashness.[9]

Much of the Southerners' self-image derived from – and was intended to reinforce – the legend that they descended from the Cavaliers. Virginians pretended to take for granted their aristocratic origins in England, and other Southerners pretended to believe them. At the beginning of the eighteenth century Robert Beverley, in *Present State of Virginia,* had Cavaliers in Virginia and Roundheads in Massachusetts. By the 1830s the vogue of Sir Walter Scott and the emergence of William Caruthers's romances sent Southerners scurrying to establish their own Cavalier family origins. In the 1850s even sophisticates like Daniel Hundley of Alabama and Thomas De Leon of South Carolina hinted at an aristocratic pedigree for the Spanish and French planters of the Carolinas and Southwest. On a visit to Bishop Stephen Elliott and his "lovely country seat" in Georgia, Sweden's antislavery Fredrika Bremer commended the "great Christian earnestness" of "one of the most beautiful examples of that old Cavalier race which gives tone and stamp to the nobler life of the Southern States." Who, then, could blame "L. M. B.", on the eve of the War, for finding the root of the difference between North and South in the descent of New Englanders from plebeian Roundheads and of aristocratic Virginians from Cavaliers.[10]

⁹ [Augustus Baldwin Longstreet], *A Voice from the South: Comprising Letters from Georgia to Massachusetts, and to the Southern States* (Baltimore, 1847), 55; Simms to Lawson, July 16, 1830, and Simms to Hammond, Jan. 28, 1858, in Mary C. Oliphant et al., eds., *The Letters of William Gilmore Simms,* 6 vols. (Columbia, SC, 1952–82), 1:3, 4:16–17; T. C. De Leon, *Four Years in Rebel Capitals* (Mobile, AL, 1892), 155; also, T. L. Clingman, "Speech in Defence of the South," Jan. 22, 1850, and "Speech on the Future Policy of the Government," Feb. 15, 1851, in *Selections from the Speeches and Writings of Hon. Thomas L. Clingman of North Carolina* (Raleigh, NC, 1877), 238, 283–4. Simms captured the positive and negative effects of rural isolation in his fiction, as shown in Mary Ann Wimsatt, *Major Fiction of William Gilmore Simms: Cultural Traditions and Literary Form* (Baton Rouge, LA, 1989).
¹⁰ Daniel R. Hundley, *Social Relations in Our Southern States* (Baton Rouge, LA, 1979 [1860]), 9–10, 27; Thomas De Leon, *Rebel Capitals* and *Belles, Beaux, and Brains of the 60s* (New York, 1974 [1907]), 10, 329; Fredrika Bremer, *The Homes of the New World: Impressions of America,* tr. Mary Howitt, 2 vols. (New York, 1853), 1:325; "L. M. B.", "The Past and the Present," *VUM,* 4 (1860),

Recurrence of the legend among people who knew it to be nonsense suggests its many polemical uses. Henry Howe, a historian, described the descendants of Cavaliers as men happily not absorbed in trade and moneygrubbing. George Fitzhugh and Ellwood Fisher, who surely knew better, conjured up Cavalier origins for Maryland and Virginia as a foundation of subsequent southern life and thought. Episcopalian ladies, Mrs. Henry Rowe Schoolcraft before the War and Mrs. Roger Pryor long after it, insisted that elite Virginians and South Carolinians had descended from Cavaliers with nary a Roundhead in their midst. For John Mitchel, the proslavery Irish radical, feudalism had bred a vanishing European nobility, and slavery was accomplishing for America what feudalism had accomplished for Europe. In the North opinion varied but, intentionally or not, lent support to southern pretensions. The abolitionist James Gillespie Birney condemned slavery's encouragement of aristocratic spirit and charged that the slaveholder acted as if "he had his patent of nobility in his pocket."[11]

Notwithstanding the abiding lure of the myth of Cavalier origins, most Southerners, including Virginians, knew that they had plebeian origins. Simms celebrated the Puritans who settled in the South, scorning their Cavalier counterparts as "restless intriguers, unstable in aim, and faithless in principle and conduct ... rapacious courtiers, seeking a selfish object." In the 1850s the Jeffersonian Hugh Blair Grigsby, a prominent contemporary historian, insisted that Roundheads, the bone and sinew of the English people, had settled Virginia: "The chivalry of Virginia is not to be traced to the miserable offshoots of the British aristocracy, but to our manners, habits, and state of affairs. We were a *slaveholding, tobacco planting, Anglo-Saxon* people."[12]

256–8. See also N. Beverley Tucker, *A Series of Lectures on the Science of Government* (Philadelphia, 1845), 218; Henry Edmund Ravenel, *Ravenel Records* (Atlanta, GA, 1898), 28–9. On the impact of Scott and Caruthers see J. B. Hubbell, "Cavalier and Indentured Servant in Virginia Fiction," *South Atlantic Quarterly,* 26 (1927), 25, 34, 35.

[11] Henry Howe, *Historical Collections of Virginia* (Charleston, SC, 1845), 156–7; George Fitzhugh, "The Revolutions of 1775 and 1861 Contrasted," *DBR,* 37 (1863), 725; Ellwood Fisher, "The North and the South," *DBR,* 7 (1849), 141; *Plantation Life: The Narratives of Mrs. Henry Schoolcraft* (New York, 1969 [1860]), 20; Mrs. Pryor, *Mother of Washington and Her Times* (New York, 1903), 216; John Mitchel, "A Tour in the South-West," *Southern Citizen,* Feb. 6, 1858; Birney to F. T. Taylor and others, July 22, 1835, in Dwight Lowell Dumond, ed., *Letters of James Gillespie Birney, 1831–1857,* 2 vols. (New York, 1938), 1:207. See also Solomon Cohen to Emma Mordecai, Jan. 8, 1866, quoted in B. W. Korn, "Jews and Negro Slavery," in Leonard Dinnerstein and Mary Dale Palsson, eds., *Jews in the South* (Baton Rouge, LA, 1973), 127. As the South seceded, a contributor to *Southern Literary Messenger* declared the coexistence of Cavalier and Puritan impossible: "Disfederation of the States," *SLM,* 32 (1861), 119.

A reaction came in the 1850s. The Cavalier legend embarrassed Virginia's college students, who associated it with "old fogeyism" – economic and social backwardness, loose morals, and lack of an honorable work ethic. Southerners condemned European aristocracies as irresponsible, corrupt, and oppressive and for fostering infidelity and secularism. They condemned the British aristocracy for plundering Ireland and India and for oppressing British laborers: John V. Thomas, "Influence of Aristocracy on Religious and Civil Liberty," *SRCR,* 4 (1856); see also Peter Carmichael, *The Last Generation: Young Virginians in Peace, War and Reunion, 1850–1900* (Chapel Hill, NC, 2005), ch. 3.

[12] William Gilmore Simms, *The History of South Carolina* (Charleston, SC, 1849), 47, 61–73; Hugh Blair Grigsby, *The Virginia Convention of 1776* (New York, 1969 [1855]), 37–8; Frank J. Klingberg

Both promoters and detractors of the Cavalier legend agreed on the superiority of slaveholders as a class and on slavery as the foundation of southern civilization. Samuel Wilson, in an account of life in the Carolinas that was originally published in 1682 and reprinted in *Historical Collections of South Carolina* in 1836, asked and answered the question of how a planter could achieve the life desired: "What commoditys shall I be able to produce, that will yield me money in other countrys, that I may be inabled to buy Negro-Slaves (without which a planter can never doe any great matter) and purchase other things for my pleasure and convenience, that Carolina doth not produce?" In Virginia, John Taylor of Caroline made the case for the superior qualities of slaveholders: "Personal slavery has constantly reflected the strongest rays of civil liberty and patriotism."[13]

Southerners then, unlike descendants who would deny the centrality of slavery, rested their claims to gentility and social superiority – if not quite to aristocracy – upon their command of slave labor. Although critical of slavery and contemptuous of racism, George Tucker of Virginia, a follower and early biographer of Jefferson, credited "that quiet ease which the habitual self-respect of the slaveholder is so likely to bestow; so that the manners of the cultivated classes in the slaveholding states differ little or nothing from those of people of rank in Europe." W. H. Sparks of Georgia brushed aside as fairy tales any notions of a descent from English Cavaliers and attributed southern virtues instead to Anglo-Saxon blood and the South's "peculiar institutions."[14] The astute Joseph Baldwin, an émigré Virginian who became a judge, political historian, and author of the much acclaimed *Flush Times of Alabama and Mississippi,* wrote of the effects of slavery: "It was seen in the pride, the individuality, the social spirit, the refined manners of the higher classes; and, with these, mingled other and worse effects on character. The proprietors of the large estates lived in luxury and elegance." The South seemed to be

---

and Frank W. Klingberg, eds., *The Correspondence between Henry Stephens Randall and Hugh Blair Grigsby, 1856–1861* (Berkeley, CA, 1952), 17, 76. The Baptist Reverend E. T. Winkler fairly screamed that those who settled the South came from the middle classes: Winkler, *The Citizen Soldier* (Charleston, SC, 1858), 5. For an author who questioned the Cavalier legend while expressing distaste for Cavaliers, see "The Early History of Virginia," *SLM,* 22 (1856), 111. George Davis of Wilmington, North Carolina, nicely balanced viewpoints by suggesting that the settlers of the Carolinas came from both exiled Puritans and the sons of defeated Cavaliers and combined the strengths of both: *Address Delivered before the Two Literary Societies of the University of North-Carolina, June 8, 1855* (Raleigh, NC, 1855), 10. For the Puritan origins of New England and the Cavalier origins of Virginia see also [Francis Lea?], "Religion in America," *SQR,* 7 (1845), 358–9.

[13] Samuel Wilson, "An Account of the Province of Carolina in America," in B. R. Carroll, ed., *Historical Collections of South Carolina,* 2 vols. (New York, 1836), 2:33; John Taylor, *Arator: Being a Series of Agricultural Essays, Practical and Political: In Sixty-Four Numbers* (Indianapolis, IN, 1977 [1818]), 124.

[14] George Tucker, *Political Economy for the People* (Philadelphia, 1859), 86; Hugh Blair Grigsby to Thomas Ritchie, Mar. 14, 1854, in "Ritchie Letters," *The John Branch Historical Papers of Randolph-Macon College* (Richmond, VA, 1916), 417. Robert R. Howison offered a well-balanced commentary on the legend, in which he assessed the actual strength of royalist immigration against its disproportionately great influence: *A History of Virginia from Its Discovery and Settlement by Europeans to the Present Time,* 2 vols. (Philadelphia, 1846), 1:282–3, 315. For the anti-Jeffersonian uses of the Cavalier legend see Merrill D. Peterson, *The Jeffersonian Image in the American Mind* (New York, 1962), 166.

re-creating "the feudal times and baronial manners of 'merrie England.'" Caste had its evils, but also its peculiar virtues: "These are the *espirit de corps,* the kindness and social courtesy, the gentleness of manners, the chivalry of bearing, the point of honor, the homage to woman, and a nice regard for reputation." Baldwin praised the intellectual cultivation: "Indeed, at the opening of the revolution, Virginia had more men of eminent character and intellect, than she or any state has had at any other period." Virginia probably could claim a higher proportion of Old World aristocratic families than other states; and its planter elite among the slaveholders actively sought identification with aristocratic tradition. The earliest settlers of Virginia, J. D. B. De Bow affirmed, were "adventurers and traders," neither Puritans nor Cavaliers, but those who built Virginia did have Cavalier blood in their veins. The planters eschewed the "traditionalism" of later lost-cause romantics as the dead faith of the living while warmly embracing "tradition" as the living faith of the dead.[15]

Pro- and antislavery Northerners described the traits of the slaveholders in ways not much different from the slaveholders' self-descriptions. Although the Reverend Moses Stuart of Andover Seminary in Massachusetts rebuked South Carolina for abuse of slaves, he testified with "deep conviction" that South Carolinians were "in general, persons of more generous feeling, more abounding hospitality, more gentlemanly comity and courtesy, more high-souled chivalry, and more ardent love and pride of country" than could be found anywhere. Pleading for peace in 1861, John Pendleton Kennedy of Maryland, prominent novelist and unionist, rejected South Carolina's political philosophy but not its people: "There is no society in the United States more worthy of esteem for its refinement, its just and honorable sentiment, and its genial virtues." Carolinians radiate "the best qualities of attractive manhood." James Kirke Paulding of New York, another successful literary man, celebrated the South as a land of learning, leisure, and gracious living.[16]

In 1836 "G. S. S.", writing in *American Monthly* of a trip to South Carolina some forty years earlier, noted that the Pinckneys, Middletons, and Horrys (among others) enjoyed "wealth, hereditary distinction, and educated talent, and service in the military fields or councils of the nation." Nathaniel Parker Willis, at the peak of his literary fame, extolled the "gracefully cavalier tone" of the Mississippi Valley's upper classes: "We shall be proud yet of our planter school of gentlemen." From the vantage point of the 1850s and 1860s, Hugh Garland, lamenting the passing of the Golden Age in his widely read biography of John Randolph, could not say enough about the glory of eighteenth-century Virginia: "Virginia's cavaliers under

---

[15] W. H. Sparks, *The Memories of Fifty Years* (Philadelphia, 1872), 21, 248–9; [Joseph G. Baldwin], *Party Leaders: Sketches of Thomas Jefferson, Alex'r Hamilton, Andrew Jackson, Henry Clay, and John Randolph of Roanoke* (New York, 1868), 153–5; [J. D. B. De Bow], "Bancroft's History of the United States," *DBR,* 15 (1853), 175–8, 185. On the critical distinction between tradition and traditionalism see Jaroslav Pelikan, *The Vindication of Tradition* (New Haven, CT, 1984).

[16] Moses Stuart, *Conscience and the Constitution* (Boston, 1850), 95; John Pendleton Kennedy, *The Border States, Their Power and Duty in the Present Disordered Condition of the Country* (n.p., 1860), 10; Paulding took a mildly antislavery stance in the 1817 edition of his *Letters from the South* but moved to proslavery in the 1835 edition.

the title of gentlemen, with their broad domain of virgin soil, and long retinue of servants, lived in a style of elegance and profusion, not inferior to the barons of England, and dispensed a hospitality which more than a half century of subdivision, exhaustion, and decay, has not entirely effaced from the memory of their impoverished descendants." The antislavery Reverend William Ellery Channing of Boston respected Southerners and, like Albert Gallatin and Benjamin Latrobe before him and William Cullen Bryant after him, praised Virginians' warmth, hospitality, and graciousness. Channing had tutored for eighteen months in Richmond: "Here I find great vices, but greater virtues than I left behind me." Virginians "*love money less* than we do." But in the end the vices outweighed their great virtues: "Could I only take from the Virginians their *sensuality* and their *slaves,* I should think them the greatest people in the world."[17]

Chief Justice John Belton O'Neall recounted eulogies to Senator Josiah James Evans of South Carolina delivered by several New England Republican Senators. Senator George Hoar of Massachusetts paid an ungrudging tribute: An "aptness for command ... makes the southern gentleman, wherever he goes, not a peer only but a prince." The majority "inherited from the great race from which they came the sense of duty and the sense of honor as no other people on the face of the earth." Their traits differed from those of men from "places where money making is the chief end of life." They had their own kind of perseverance – a "supreme and superb constancy" that set aside "personal ambition" and "temptations of wealth." Over generations they neither tired of nor were diverted from pursuit of "a great public object."[18]

A northern Presbyterian minister, a gradual emancipationist who held Southerners responsible for the crisis of 1860, nonetheless believed that the Northeast "would be greatly benefited by the importation of their impulsive generosity, the high sense of personal honor, the gentlemanly courtesy, the frank bearing and

---

[17] "G. S. S.", "Sketches of the South Santee," *American Monthly Magazine* 8 (Oct.–Nov. 1836), 313–19, 431–2; N. P. Willis in Katharine M. Jones, ed., *The Plantation South* (Indianapolis, IN, 1957), 339; Virginius Dabney, *Liberalism in the South* (Chapel Hill, NC, 1932), Channing quotes at 35 and 39; Hugh A. Garland, *The Life of John Randolph of Roanoke*, 2 vols. (New York, 1969 [1859]), 1:1; William Cabell Bruce, *John Randolph of Roanoke, 1773–1833: A Biography Based Largely on New Material*, 2 vols. (New York, 1970 [1922]), 2:116; *Memoir of William Ellery Channing, with Extracts from His Correspondence and Manuscripts*, 3 vols. (Boston, 1851), 1:83. For another antislavery defense of southern character, see "Who Is Responsible for the Current Slavery Agitation," *Presbyterian Quarterly Review*, 31 (Apr. 1860), 543.

James Redpath, a South-hating abolitionist, admitted to being surprised by the slaveholders of Savannah: "I saw so much that was noble, generous and admirable in their characters": *The Roving Editor: Or, Talks with Slaves in the Southern States* (New York, 1859), 82. Friendly travelers described Southerners as typically generous, unpretentious, and manly, whereas hostile travelers described them as rash, arrogant, and vulgar. Few reflected on the contrary descriptions as two sides of the same coin. See Kenneth R. Wesson, "Travelers' Accounts of the Southern Character: Antebellum and Early Postbellum Period," *Southern Studies*, 17 (1978), 310.

[18] John Belton O'Neall, *Biographical Sketches of the Bench and Bar of South Carolina*, 2 vols. (Charleston, SC, 1859), 1:189–90; Hoar quoted in Harvey Toliver Cook, *The Life and Legacy of David Rogerson Williams* (New York, 1916), 25–6. Robert L. Preston recalled Hoar's remarks in his *Southern Miscellanies* (Leesburg, VA, 1919), 29.

chivalrous courage of the Sunny South." A "perfect American manhood" required a blend of "the cold, angular, conscientious and economical Northerner" with "the warm-hearted, indulgent, confiding, and poetical South Carolinian." William W. Bennett, in his *Great Revival in the Southern Armies* (1876), extensively quoted the wartime speech of the Reverend Henry Bellows, who organized the Sanitary Commission, to a Unitarian assembly in New York City. Bellows declined to speculate on "how far race and climate, independent of servile institutions, may have produced a southern chivalric spirit and manner," but Southerners did have a "habit of command, a contempt of life in defence of honor or class, a talent for political life, and an easy control of inferiors .... Nor is this merely an external or flashy heroism. It is real."[19]

Upon arriving in Washington, Senator Benjamin ("Bluff Ben") Wade of Ohio, tough free-soiler and vociferous South-hater, paid his southern colleagues a back-handed tribute in saying that their arrogance forced Northerners to become abolitionists or doughface flunkies. During the War, Wendell Phillips, a towering figure in the abolitionist movement, acknowledged a generosity in the slaveholders that made them especially formidable. They scorned compensation for emancipation of the slaves, he observed, because they valued slavery as an institution. The highest of such tributes-of-sorts came from the abolitionist Reverend Nathan S. S. Beman, who spent more than a decade in Georgia and married the mother of William Yancey, the "orator of secession." In a militant Thanksgiving Day sermon in 1858, Beman warned: "Don't allow yourselves to be deceived with the idea that these men are going to allow this question to be settled by the result of a ballot .... I have lived among these men, and I know them and I tell you they mean blood." Tryphena Fox, wife of a small slaveholder in Louisiana, wrote in the same vein to her mother in Massachusetts, "The Southerners can *never* be conquered. They may all be killed, but conquered, never."[20]

Southerners themselves harped on the contrast between their chivalric values and the typically bourgeois values of Northerners, attributing differences to rival systems of social relations. As W. H. Holcombe wrote, "The pride of the North is in her dollars and cents, her factories and ships, her wooden-clocks, astute trades, and bold hardy prosperity," while that of the South is her sons – "their nobleness of soul, their true gentility, honor and manliness, in their love for native land." Frederick A. Porcher accused the North of preoccupation with moneymaking: Should life be reduced to "an increasing struggle after more?" What of "family, of kindred, and of friendly affections? Is man to become a mere money-making, cotton-spinning,

---

[19] "Who Is Responsible for the Current Slavery Agitation," 543; William W. Bennett, *A Narrative of the Great Revival Which Prevailed in the Southern Armies during the Late Civil War between the States of the Federal Union* (Harrisonburg, VA, 1989 [1876]), 29.

[20] Wade quoted in Louis Filler, *The Crusade against Slavery, 1830–1860* (New York, 1960), 224; for Phillips, as reported by Henry Yates Thompson, see Christopher Chancellor, ed., *An Englishman in the American Civil War: The Diaries of Henry Yates Thompson* (New York, 1971), 66; Beman quoted in Owen Petersen, *A Divine Discontent: The Life of Nathan S. S. Beman* (Macon, GA, 1986), 202. Tryphena Fox to Anna Rose Holder, Aug. 8, 1861, in Wilma King, ed., *A Northern Woman in the Plantation South: Letters of Tryphena Blanche Holder Fox, 1856–1876* (Columbia, SC, 1993), 130.

iron-founding machine?" The letters of Confederate soldiers to their families show a widespread belief that Yankees made a fetish of money.[21]

Southerners indulged in some ruthless self-criticism. Those born in the eighteenth century attributed the political and economic malaise of nineteenth-century Virginia to the decline of gentility, old republican virtues, and country morals. John Randolph, advising a young relative in 1807, deplored the "self-conceit" of the younger generation: "A petulant arrogance, or supine, listless indifference, marks the character of too many of our young men," who assume "airs of manhood" but "remain children for the rest of their lives." A decade later, future Governor Francis Walker Gilmer struck a somber note: "We Virginians seem to imagine ourselves an inspired and gifted people: that we are all born for lofty achievements, high exploits, & splendid renown, that we must all be lawyers, physicians, writers, speakers, &c." Gilmer thought Virginians "a smart people" but also "inclined to be lazy" and ill equipped to compete in an age that required "patient and systematic industry." J. L. Petigru, Charleston's most celebrated lawyer and an intransigent unionist, began a speech at a dinner to honor William Campbell Preston: "This dear old State of ours reminds me of a refined, rich, fat, lazy old planter who took his wine at dinner and his nap in the afternoon." Petigru's planter "employed an overseer of unsurpassed abilities and turned over the management of the large estates to him. One morning the planter woke up to find the overseer master of the plantation." Porcher contributed tender descriptions of two well-loved citizens of St. John's Berkeley. William Sinkler, a successful planter and devoted sportsman and member of Charleston's exclusive Jockey Club, was "always the master and never the slave of his passion." Thomas Gaillard, an unsuccessful planter, "was fond of literature" but may have devoted time to books that should have gone to his business.[22]

Whatever the balance, faults and virtues combined in an ideal of what it meant to be a Southerner – and especially, a southern gentleman. Slaveholders and, more generally, Southerners relied upon a cluster of privileged words to talk about themselves, blending classical and Christian concepts: duty, fame, honor, courage, frankness, pride, and dignity. As an unconverted teen-ager, James Henley Thornwell, who became the South's greatest theologian, had no wish to die "unknown, unhonored, and unsung, like the wild beasts of the field."[23]

Honor and fame have achieved their greatest sway in what the great historian Marc Bloch called "face-to-face" cultures, in which the relations among the members of a society have largely been mediated by direct interaction and formal

---

[21] "B." [W. H. Holcombe], "The New Social Propositions," *SLM*, 20 (May 1854), 295; F. A. Porcher, "Southern and Northern Civilization Contrasted," *RM*, 1 (May 1857), 104–5; Bell Irvin Wiley, *The Life of Johnny Reb: The Common Soldier of the Confederacy* (Baton Rouge, LA, 1978), 309–10.

[22] John Randolph to Theodore, Jan. 8, 1807, in *Letters of John Randolph to a Young Relative* (Philadelphia, 1834), 25–6; Gilmer quoted in Richard Beale Davis, *Intellectual Life in Jefferson's Virginia, 1790–1830* (Chapel Hill, NC, 1964), 295–6; Petigru quoted in James Petigru Carson, *Life, Letters and Speeches of James Louis Petigru: Union Man of South Carolina* (Washington, DC, 1920), 237.

[23] Thornwell quoted in James Oscar Farmer, Jr., *The Metaphysical Confederacy: James Henley Thornwell and the Synthesis of Southern Values* (Macon, GA, 1986), 60.

gestures. Devotion to honor and fame transcended the distinction between Christian and non-Christian, Western and non-Western, cultures. Cultures that attributed special importance to honor and fame were likely to contain a strong oral rather than literate component and to see the group, not the individual, as the fundamental social unit. The much-admired Spartan warriors fought to the death, looking forward to fame bestowed by a grateful community in remembrance of their names. Neither they nor other Greeks believed in an immortal soul. Medieval Christian knights also craved fame, and – to judge by college essays and correspondence – so did the southern youth who aspired to the knightly mantle. In the Virginia of George Washington and Thomas Jefferson, fame meant recognition by a cultivated elite. The democratization of society and attendant broadening of audience invited posturing and demagogy, which evangelicals feared as an appeal to the judgment of men rather than of God.[24]

Elizabeth Pringle called her beloved cousin, James Johnston Pettigrew, "My great hero and ideal of a man." Pettigrew more than most personified the state motto of North Carolina, derived from Cicero: *Esse quam Videre* – usually rendered by Southerners as "To be, not to seem." His achievements, according to William Trescot, failed to explain "the strength and breadth" of the impression he made: "The influence was in himself." Few politicians coveted fame more than the widely disliked J. H. Hammond of South Carolina, who yearned to be loved and could not understand why he was not. He told his friend Simms what he might have told himself: "You never met a man – *never* – I imagine – without asserting mastery & assaulting him furiously until – unless he turns upon you as I do with clubs & stones & mud – he is obliged to succumb." Hammond allowed that he, too, suffered from that fault, but "You are a tyrant – what can you expect from your victims." Campaigning in Tennessee for reelection to Congress in 1834, the legendary David Crockett boasted, "Most authors seek fame but I seek for justice – a holier impulse

---

[24] In the law of ancient Rome, *persona,* from which "person" is derived but which literally means "theatrical mask," referred to a man's part in society rather than to himself. Medieval individualism thereby provided the ideal through which the nobles could express the honor of their ranks. See Fred A. Cazel, Jr., ed., *Feudalism and Liberty: Articles and Addresses of Sidney Painter* (Baltimore, 1961), 255, 259; Maurice Keen, *Chivalry* (New Haven, CT, 1984), 250; Charles Phineas Sherman, *Roman Law in the Modern World,* 2nd ed., 3 vols. (New York, 1924), 2:23; Roberto Mangabeira Unger, *Law in Modern Society: Toward a Criticism of Social Theory* (New York, 1976), 168. For Greece see Eric Voegelin, *Order and History,* 5 vols. (Baton Rouge, LA, 1956), 2:192.

For medieval attitudes see Georges Duby et al., *Revelations of the Medieval World,* tr. Arthur Goldhammer, vol. 2 of Phillippe Ariès et al., eds., *A History of Private Life,* 5 vols. (Cambridge, MA, 1988). For medieval knights, honor "implied renown, good conduct, and the world's approval": Richard Barber, *The Knight and Chivalry,* rev. ed. (Woodbridge, U.K., 1970), 44; also, Johann Huizinga, *The Waning of the Middle Ages: A Study in the Forms of Life, Thought and Art in France and the Netherlands in the XIVth and XVth Centuries* (London, 1963 [1924]), 59. With the later Middle Ages and especially the Renaissance, fame and individual heroism emerged in a shift away from the collective sense: Julio Caro Baroja, "Honour and Shame: A Historical Account of Several Conflicts," in J. G. Peristiany, ed., *Honour and Shame: The Values of Mediterranean Society* (Chicago, 1966), 93–4. Eighteenth-century gentlemen considered fame a noble passion – a reward for effort, not a gift. See Douglass Adair's penetrating remarks in Trevor Colbourn, ed., *Fame and the Founding Fathers: Essays by Douglass Adair* (New York, 1974), 8–12.

than ever entered into the ambitious struggles of the votaries of that *fickle, flirting* goddess."[25]

Fame required physical as well as moral courage. Southerners, like Athenians, linked honor with freedom, dishonor with slavishness. "The love of honour," Pericles said, "never groweth old." As admirers of his celebrated "Funeral Oration," Southerners held that worthy men feared humiliation for their own failure more than death, and they responded to his remark: "Placing happiness in liberty, and liberty in valour, be forward to encounter the dangers of war." G. P. R. James observed in *History of Chivalry* (1833), a southern favorite, that the insecurity and violence of life in feudal times compelled personal courage and valor. For the slave-holding South as well: An honorable man disdained death or at least had to appear to. "We desire to live an imaginary life in the minds of others," Blaise Pascal wrote in *Pensées*. "We labour incessantly to adorn and preserve our imaginary being and we neglect the real one.... He would be infamous who would not die to preserve his honor." Euclides da Cunha, in his great book, *Rebellion in the Backlands,* recounts an incident that occurred after the fall of the Brazilian monarchy in 1889. A fierce guerrilla war broke out in the backcountry as wretchedly poor, religiously driven people of color rose against a new and oppressive regime of liberal modernizers. The uncomprehending regime demonized the rebels as adherents of a vast right-wing conspiracy and sent the army to restore order. The hardy guerrillas smashed wave after wave of troops over a painfully long time. One brigade "went to pieces along the road" and fled in panic: "Fear on this occasion had its own great heroes, men so stupendously brave that they were willing to announce to the entire country that they were cowards."[26]

How to distinguish manly courage from posturing? The Methodist Reverends Robert Newton Sledd and R. H. Rivers, with an eye on dueling, found much of what passed for courage immoral. The Presbyterian Reverend Robert Dabney separated "true bravery" from "animal hardihood." The bravest man is the best Christian because he fears God and nothing else. Dabney sternly criticized the kind of courage that emanates from the exalted pride slaveholders too easily slipped into.

[25] Elizabeth Allston Pringle, *Chronicle of Chicora Wood* (New York, 1922), 174, 218; William Henry Trescot, *Memorial on the Life of J. Johnston Pettigrew, Brig. Gen. of the Confederate States Army* (Charleston, SC, 1870), 62; Cicero, *De Officiis,* tr. Walter Miller (LCL), Bk. 1:20; Hammond to Simms, Feb. 13, 1850, in Oliphant et al., eds., *Letters of Simms,* 3:15 n. 48; *A Narrative of the Life of David Crockett of the State of Tennessee,* facsimile ed., annotated by James A. Shackelford and Stanley J. Folmsbee (Knoxville, TN, 1976 [1834]), 3. For Thomas Roderick Dew, fame and money spur most men's action in a quest that may turn ugly: *Digest of the Laws, Customs, Manners, and Institutions of the Ancient and Modern Nations* (New York, 1884 [1852]), 104.

[26] Roger Just, "Freedom, Slavery and the Female Psyche," in P. A. Cartledge and F. D. Harvey, eds., *Crux: Essays in Greek History Presented to F. F. M. de St. Croix on His 75th Birthday* (London, 1985), 175; Paul Rahe, *Republics, Ancient and Modern: Classical Republicanism and the American Revolution* (Chapel Hill, NC, 1992), 159–63; Pericles' "Funeral Oration" in Richard Schlatter, ed., *Hobbes's Thucydides* (New Brunswick, NJ, 1975), Bk. 2:secs. 43 and 44; G. P. R. James, *The History of Chivalry* (New York, 1833), 25–6; Blaise Pascal, *Pensées and the Provincial Letters,* tr. W. F. Trotten (New York, 1941), #147; Euclides da Cunha, *Rebellion in the Backlands,* tr. Samuel Putnam (Chicago, 1944), 390.

For Dabney, true courage included a healthy fear of real danger, which can be overcome by service to a worthier motive. A man could not be called brave who coolly takes a risk of which he remains unconscious. Courage has limited virtue when prompted by the spirit of personal honor, for "the sentiment of pride, the keener fear of reproach, and the desire of applause" render it inherently selfish. True courage – moral courage – overcomes fear by fear of God, a sense of duty to Him, and a desire for His approval.[27]

Edward Gibbon's *Decline and Fall of the Roman Empire,* widely read in the South, included a word of apt advice: The first qualification of a rebel is to despise life. That message came from southern women: "Better dead than a coward." Sarah Morgan wrote from Baton Rouge, "Courage is what women admire above all things." She considered her father and brothers exemplars of manhood: "I hate to see *men* uneasy! I have been so accustomed to brave, fearless ones, who would beard the devil himself." Faced with whipped and discouraged Confederate troops, she wrote, "Ladies are naturally hero worshippers. We are dying to show these unfortunates that we are as proud of their bravery as though it had led to victory instead of defeat."[28]

With expressions of envy, antislavery Northerners fretted over Southerners' display of raw courage. Joseph Story, furious over the annexation of Texas, cried that Southerners had reduced the men of Massachusetts to bondage. Southerners knew what they wanted, Yankees imitated Nero's fiddling. Jane Swisshelm – abolitionist, women's-rights activist, and newspaper editor – denounced the slaveholders as immoral, arrogant, and brutal but spoke respectfully of their "brute courage" in standing by their principles and beliefs and of their ability to bend others to their will. She scorned Northerners for a want of courage in confronting the South.[29]

In a democratic era, the quest for fame and the demand to show courage sometimes ran afoul of the southern predilection for "frankness." In the House of Representatives, John Randolph lauded Southerners' plainness of speech: "Not only as a Southern man, but emphatically, as a Planter, it belongs to him as a slaveholder." The Pennsylvania-born but thoroughly southern Josiah Gorgas had amiability in

---

27 Robert Newton Sledd, *A Sermon Delivered in the Market Street, M. E. Church, Petersburg, Va.: Before the Confederate Cadets on the Occasion of Their Departure for the Seat of War* (Petersburg, VA, 1861), 9–10; "True Courage," *DD,* 3:452–5; also, George D. Armstrong, *"The Good Hand of Our Lord upon Us": A Thanksgiving Sermon Preached on the Victory at Manassas* (Norfolk, VA, 1861), 8–9. R. H. Rivers defined virtue as "right willing" – that is, willing in accordance with the moral law dictated by God's commandment. He therefore denounced the Code Duello as resting "upon false principles of honor": *Elements of Moral Philosophy* (Nashville, TN, 1859), 137–43, 209–10, quotes at 137, 209. Rivers added, echoing LaRochefoucauld, "The very idea of hypocrisy supposes an excellence which is counterfeited" (119).

28 A. V. B. Norman, *The Medieval Soldier* (New York, 1971), 144; Edward Gibbon, *The History of the Decline and Fall of the Roman Empire,* ed. David Womersley, 3 vols. (London, 1994), 3:756; Apr. 12 and July 20, 1862, July 23, 1863, in Charles East, ed., *The Civil War Diary of Sarah Morgan* (Athens, GA, 1991), 38, 166, 523.

29 Joseph Story to Mrs. Joseph Story, in William W. Story, *Life and Letters of Joseph Story,* 2 vols. (Boston, 1851), 2:512–13; for Swisshelm see Peter Walker, *Moral Choices: Memory, Desire, and Imagination in Nineteenth-Century American Abolition* (Baton Rouge, LA, 1978), ch. 5.

mind when he wrote from Maine that he regretted not being back in Alabama: "The manners & habits of the people are so uncongenial here that one cannot help sighing after the frankness of southern manners." George McClellan – while a cadet at West Point, where he knew Thomas (Stonewall) Jackson and George Pickett – remarked, "I am sorry to say that the manners, feelings & opinions of the Southerners are far, far preferable to those of the majority of the Northerners at this place." You can speak frankly to Southerners, the Irish revolutionary John Mitchel told his countrymen: "They are very liberal and affable." Planters are "men of refined and dignified manners, with that tone of gentle voice and courtesy of demeanor which are characteristic of the South, and which I attribute in a great part to Slavery." Robert E. Lee wrote his eldest son Custis in 1852, "Frankness is the child of honesty and courage .... Above all, do not appear to others what you are not."[30]

With frankness went sincerity. William Wirt praised Judge John Tyler of Virginia for "a kind of Roman frankness and even bluntness in his manners." That attitude signaled respect even for certain abolitionists. When Gerrit Smith declared slavery a crime against the age he spoke from his heart, and therefore, Wiley Harris of Mississippi explained, "Southern representatives treated him with a respect which they refused to accord to men like Giddings or Wentworth." In Vicksburg, 15-year-old Sarah Wadley, annoyed by chit-chat, lashed out: "I had not been educated to speak words without meaning and to practice all those coquettish airs which form such an important part of conversation between ladies and gentlemen." According to Simms's *Magnolia,* "Openness of manners impresses us, as a guarantee that there is nothing in the character to be concealed .... It stands opposed to hypocrisy only." John Belton O'Neall praised Chancellor George Dargan, a political adversary, as epitome of the dignified man – without affectation or presumption and scorning to fawn on men of power and standing. O'Neall quoted an old classmate of Dargan: "He talked as frankly and as courteously with a tenant, a clerk, a servant, or a stranger, according to their respective relations with him, as with a prince of the blood." Thornwell preached abstention from flattery as a matter of morality: Men should not be led to think they are regarded more highly than they are.[31]

[30] Randolph quoted in Russell Kirk, *John Randolph of Roanoke; A Study in American Politics, with Selected Speeches and Letters* (Chicago, 1964), 358; McClellan quoted in John C. Waugh, *Class of 1846: From West Point to Appomattox: Stonewall Jackson, George McClellan, and Their Brothers* (New York, 1994), 41; Achille Murat, *America and the Americans* (Buffalo, NY, 1851), 17; John Mitchel, "A Tour in the South-West," *Southern Citizen,* Jan. 21 and 23, 1858; Lee in William J. Johnson, *Robert E. Lee the Christian* (Arlington Hts., IL, n.d.), 44. James Kirke Paulding, one of the South's strongest supporters in the Northeast, especially lauded the greater frankness that accompanied generosity and gallantry: Lorman Ratner, *James Kirke Paulding* (Westport, CT, 1992), 77. For an antislavery Northerner's tributes to the "frankness" of Cuban as well as southern planters, see John S. C. Abbott, *South and North; Or, Impressions Received during a Trip to Cuba and the South* (New York, 1969 [1860]), 23, 114. Southerners often used "candid" for "frank."

[31] William Wirt, *Sketches of the Life and Character of Patrick Henry* (Philadelphia, 1817), viii; Wiley P. Harris, "Autobiography," in Dunbar Rowland, *Courts, Judges, and Lawyers of Mississippi, 1798–1935* (Jackson, MS, 1935), 311; Sarah Lois Wadley Private Journal, Aug. 5, 1860, at UNC-SHC; [Simms?], *Magnolia,* 2 (1843), 197; O'Neall, *Bench and Bar of South Carolina,* 1:291–2; *JHTW,* 2:536. John Shelton Reed observes that, even today, manners for Southerners include the "idea of

In the eighteenth century, Josiah Quincy of New England and Andrew Burnaby of England charged Virginians with an overweening pride born of slave-ownership. The recurrent charge cut deep, and the Baptist Reverend Patrick Mell and the Methodist Reverend R. H. Rivers, notable moral philosophers, forcefully defended the slaveholders. Mell called pride "an inordinate self-esteem" and a "conceit of one's own superiority" but denied that slavery was guiltier than any other hierarchical system. A slaveholder, Mell argued, respected himself and was more likely than other men to respect others. Ownership of slaves made him *"frank, open-hearted and unsuspecting."* For Rivers, "Examples of humility as bright as can be found on earth are found among slaveholders." Basil Lanneau Gildersleeve cited Charles Francis Adams's remark that Southerners' local pride resembled that of Spanish hidalgos and Scots clansmen. Southern gentlemen, Gildersleeve commented, heard "in every conceivable tone" about their foolish pride – a pride that "played its part in making us what we were proud of being."[32]

John England, the intellectually gifted Irish-born Catholic Bishop of Charleston, said of its people: "The nature of their institutions impresses a peculiar immobility on their individual opinions and conduct. Landed wealth, descending from sire to son through a longer series than is usual with the possessions of mercantile communities, while it confers more social stability, imparts, with hereditary refinement of taste and manners, no moderate tenacity on every subject of family pride." The Randolphs, among other old Virginia families, demonstrated that Bishop England's remark applied well beyond Charleston. By the 1830s their family had declined in fortune but hardly in hauteur and sense of pedigree. Such family pride could take a toll. The Reverend A. D. Pollock complained of a respectable family in Culpeper County that had fallen on hard times. Conscious of its traditions and inherited social status, its gentlemen were too proud to work.[33]

If Jefferson Davis displayed many of the virtues of the best of his class, even his devoted wife testified that he carried his pride to a dangerous extent: He was always sure he was right. The Confederacy paid dearly for the pride of the many brave officers and soldiers who lacked the discipline and submission to military and political authority that war requires. Pride easily passed into recklessness, and Southerners, especially slaveholders, could forget the words of the Good Book: "Pride goeth before destruction, and an haughty spirit before a fall" (Proverbs, 16:18). In 1864

democratic manners": see Reed, "Flirting and Deferring: Southern Manners," in Digby Anderson, ed., *Gentility Recalled: "Mere" Manners and the Making of the Social Order* (London, 1996), 131.

[32] "Journal of Josiah Quincy, Jr., 1773," *Massachusetts Historical Society Proceedings, Oct. 1915–June 1916,* 49 (1916), 462–71; Rufus Rockwell Wilson, ed., *Burnaby's Travels through North America* (New York, 1904 [1798]), 52–7; [Patrick Mell], *Slavery. A Treatise, Showing that Slavery Is Neither a Moral, Political, nor Social Evil* (Pennfield, GA, 1844), 25, 34–6, quotes at 25, 36; R. H. Rivers, *Elements of Moral Philosophy* (Nashville, TN, 1859), 356; Basil Lanneau Gildersleeve, *The Creed of the Old South, 1865–1915* (Baltimore, 1915), 11–12, 118.

[33] Sebastian G. Messmer, ed., *The Works of the Right Rev. John England, First Bishop of Charleston,* 7 vols. (Cleveland, OH, 1908), 2:11; George Green Shackelford, *George Wythe Randolph and the Confederate Elite* (Athens, GA, 1988), 1; "Thomas Gordon Pollock, 1838–1863, biography written by his father, Abram David Pollock" (ms.), in Pollock Papers, at UNC-SHC.

Emma LeConte of South Carolina, reeling from Confederate setbacks, saw Yankees as determined to crush the southern pride and feelings of superiority they considered at the root of the rebellion, and after the War southern preachers did indeed point to the sin of pride as the root of the Confederacy's downfall.[34]

With pride went vanity. A great many succumbed. Riding a stagecoach in 1837, Susan Nye Hutchinson met Colonel Alston, who was "once a proud planter of Georgia, now of Florida – I was sorry to see that in spite of uncommon afflictions and losses he was as vain as ever." Mary Chesnut on the obnoxious behavior of the gentleman of the house: "How men can go blustering around, making everybody uncomfortable, simply to show that they are masters – and we are only women and children at their mercy! The Master [her father-in-law] is kind, and amiable when not crossed, given to hospitality on a grand scale, jovial, genial, friendly, courtly in his politeness. As absolute a tyrant as the Czar of Russia, the Khan of Tartary – or the Sultan of Turkey."[35]

So, too, was the danger of excessive loyalty to friends. Henry Augustine Washington of Virginia described Achilles as "the most perfect and illustrious representative of the Hellenic chivalry," who returned to the battlefield not in the service of his country but only when provoked by the death of a friend. Jefferson Davis, who found it hard to believe that men he trusted could behave badly, supported friends and military subordinates beyond the limits of prudence. Stonewall Jackson commanded the cream of the Virginia elite, who had to learn to dirty themselves like yeomen, but he knew the difference between manly pride and caste pretension, tolerated no nonsense, and imposed his will. The Beverleys, Carters, Harrisons, Hunters, Masons, and Randolphs grumbled but submitted – to him.[36]

Roberto Mangabeira Unger, doyen of the radical Critical Legal Studies movement, describes pride as "the bad conscience of vanity," a reading that may sell short the virtues of pride but contains a stinging insight. For pride constitutes what Unger disapprovingly calls "a holding back" – what the slaveholders considered a civilized but never cold reserve. When vanity infected pride, the slaveholders' finest qualities could degenerate into the vilest behavior. It led them to indifference to the opinion of others while it fostered violence in defense of personal and family honor. They denied concern for public approval, as if they could live in splendid

[34] William C. Davis, *Jefferson Davis: The Man and His Hour* (New York, 1991), 68–9, 71, 97, 154, 435; Feb. 18, 1864, in Earl Schenck Miers, ed., *When the World Ended: The Diary of Emma LeConte* (New York, 1959), 52.

[35] Susan Nye Hutchinson Journal, July 28, 1837, at UNC-SHC; Chesnut Diary, Dec. 8, 1861, in C. Vann Woodward, ed., *Mary Chesnut's Civil War* (New Haven, CT, 1981), 261–2.

[36] Henry Augustine Washington, "The Virginia Constitution of 1776," *SLM*, 18 (1852), 663; Stephen E. Woodworth, *Jefferson Davis and His Generals: The Failure of Confederate Command in the West* (Norman, KS, 1990), 24, 185, 314–16; Frank E. Vandiver, *Mighty Stonewall* (New York, 1957), 140. Northeasterners and Southerners who settled in the Midwest prided themselves on "manliness," but to the former it described a man who provided for his wife and children while to the latter a man with a reputation for physical courage and candor: see the arresting discussion in Nicole Etcheson, *The Emerging Midwest: Upland Southerners and the Political Culture of the Old Northwest, 1787–1861* (Bloomington, IN, 1995), 28–31.

moral isolation. Yet if the slaveholders' pride induced arrogance, it also induced the courage and independent spirit – the "dignity" – that they held dear.[37]

"Dignity," which slaveholders cherished, denoted reserve and a pride accompanied by warmth and frankness. John Belton O'Neall caught the tension well in his description of Chancellor Hugh Rutledge of South Carolina, which might readily have fit Calhoun (among many) in its portrayal of a man without fear or favor who held ostentation and parade in contempt: "His appearance was dignified in the extreme – somewhat stern, but polished beyond mistake – and his manners spoke his position and his training." Unfailingly courteous, if a bit too severe, Rutledge "was always the same model of a republican gentleman, affable and accessible, but never familiar: always gentle, but never doubtful, and on questions of principle, unyielding and immovable without reference to policy or circumstances."[38]

"Dignity" appeared frequently in tributes to eminent Southerners and in advice offered by one generation to the next. It could exist without "polish" in the rough and quasi-frontier hinterland. "Waddy Thompson *is* a man of parts," Simms wrote E. A. Duyckinck, a leading New York editor, "but scarcely of good taste. He belongs to the better class of our upper country gentry – men of worth and substance of whom the low countrymen are apt to suppose that there is a lack of real refinement and nice delicacy." On the still-rough frontier of northwest Georgia in the 1850s, Old "Squire" Willis Buell, a native Northerner who ranked as the ablest judge in Atlanta, drank much too much – as a few other hinterland southern judges were known to do on and off the bench – but local citizens showed him every respect because, drunk or sober, he always carried himself with dignity. Chivalry's grotesque juxtaposition of qualities proved endlessly fascinating: William J. Grayson said that a man could be insolent, arrogant, officious, ill-mannered, and yet honorable.[39]

The Latin *dignitas* signified the power that comes with high position, an ostentatious parade of wealth, a large retinue of servants, and, in the words of Ramsay MacMullen, historian of ancient Rome, "the holding of one's self apart, and the limitation of familiar address." Thus, for Caesar, Cicero, and Pliny, *dignitas* signified quickness to vengeance, ability to defend oneself by force, and readiness to retaliate against anyone who offended or hurt any of one's dependents. "Dignity," like "honor," offered constant temptations to excess and could reinforce tendencies to violence.[40]

No words stood higher in the self-definition of the slaveholders – of all Southerners who valued their reputations – than "honor" and "duty." Bertram Wyatt-Brown and Kenneth Greenberg agree that the southern concept of honor rested on a firm

37 Robert Mangabeira Unger, *Passion: An Essay on Personality* (New York, 1984), 200–2, quote at 200. We are indebted to Unger's bold exploration, notwithstanding reservations about his value judgments.

38 O'Neall, *Bench and Bar of South Carolina*, 1:230–1. See also Trescot's remarks on the members of the South Carolina legislature in his *Memorial to J. J. Pettigrew*, 32, and the advice of George Wythe Randolph to his nephew Lewis Randolph in 1859, in Shackelford, *G. W. Randolph*, 21.

39 Simms to Duyckinck, May 15, 1846, in Oliphant et al., eds., *Letters of Simms*, 2:165; Franklin M. Garrett, *Atlanta and Environs: A Chronicle of Its People and Events*, 3 vols. (Athens, GA, 1954), 1:292; [William J. Grayson], "The Character of the Gentleman," *SQR*, 7 (1853), 59.

40 Ramsay MacMullen, *Corruption and the Decline of Rome* (New Haven, CT, 1958), 69, 79.

commitment by yeomen as well as planters to various forms of hierarchy. In the South as in early modern Europe, reliance upon Roman models for ideas of honor, pride, shame, and reputation affirmed hierarchy in human affairs. Honor implied service to *patria*. Duty meant attention to honor and a concern for others that denoted the bestowal of a privilege. Southern educators insisted that moral philosophers inculcate a sense of duty to counteract the tendency to measure virtue by personal interest.[41]

The elusiveness of the concept of honor has bedeviled scholars and played havoc with those whose behavior scholars try to understand. The Southerners' problem was compounded, for honor as "claim-right" implies an equality of condition and respect within the community that sets the rules – that is, a right to insist that others behave in accordance with social rules that require a man to keep his word, pay his debts, and adhere to community standards of generosity and hospitality. "Gentlemen" refused challenges from those who did not qualify as gentlemen, but a denial of gentleman status intolerably affronted the poor and middling white folk whom the reigning ideology flattered as equals. From about the middle of the eighteenth century, the emphasis shifted from honor as proper behavior to reputation. Southerners made a conscious effort to adhere to the old way – "to be and not to seem" – but honor carried a contradiction difficult to hold in creative tension. It did not characterize gentlemen alone but instead implied a pattern of behavior appropriate to one's social station.[42]

Southern divines, embracing the word "honor," strove to render it consistent with the Decalogue. Thornwell, concerned with salvation, warned, "Men prate of their honour now, and swell with conceit of their dignity and beauty, but every sinner then will be deeply conscious that his honour is lost, that infamy is his lot, and that everlasting scorn and contempt must be poured upon him from the throne of God and the general assembly of the just." Nothing in these remarks nor in anything else Thornwell said or wrote challenged the essentials of the posthumous

---

[41] Bertram Wyatt-Brown, *Southern Honor: Ethics and Behavior in the Old South* (New York, 1982); Kenneth Greenberg, *Masters and Statesmen: The Political Culture of American Slavery* (Baltimore, 1985). See also Edward L. Ayers, *Vengeance and Justice: Crime and Punishment in the Nineteenth-Century South* (New York, 1984), 26, and, for the role of religion in southern honor, Stephen R. Haynes, *Noah's Curse: The Biblical Justification of American Slavery* (New York, 2002). Confederate troops filled their letters home with references to "duty" and "honor." For the yeomen during the War see James I. Robertson, Jr., in *EC*, 4:1499; for the European tradition see Andreas A. M. Kinneging, *Aristocracy, Antiquity and History: Classicism in Political Thought* (New Brunswick, NJ, 1997), ch. 1. The truly chivalric medieval knight feared nothing so much as shame: Richard W. Kaeuper and Elspeth Kennedy, *The Book of Chivalry of Geoffroi de Charny: Text, Context, and Translation* (Philadelphia, 1996), 12. A strong concept of honor may exist among people without a hierarchical class structure; specific similarities and differences must be taken into account: Frank Henderson Stewart, *Honor* (Chicago, 1994).

[42] On "claim right" see Stewart, *Honor*, esp. chs. 1 and 2; Bertram Wyatt-Brown in *EC*, 2:786–9; George Fitzhugh, "Johnson, Boswell, Goldsmith, Etc.," *DBR*, 28 (1860), 412; R. W. Kaeuper, in Kaeuper and Kennedy, eds., *Book of Chivalry*, 14, 47. Stewart instructively explores the methodological difficulties in assessing concepts of honor, demonstrating that even the most diligent scholars have not defined it satisfactorily.

tribute paid to the Bishop Stephen Elliott of Georgia by Bishop Richard Wilmer of Alabama: "He had been raised in the school of honor, whose teachings when sublimated by the grace of God, impel men to dare all consequences in the assertion and maintenance of the right." Men like Elliott did not "calculate the consequences by any standard of earthly profit," as did those who wallowed in the travesty of worldly honor; rather, they stood ready to die for their principles.[43]

With honor went "duty," the favorite word of John Randolph, John C. Calhoun, Robert E. Lee, Stonewall Jackson, and no few others. "Life," Randolph remarked, "is not so important as the duties of life." President Jasper Adams of the College of Charleston, a Calvinistic Episcopalian, declared: "There is no quality of the human character so fundamental as the possession of a high and permanent sense of duty." The Reverend William A. Smith added in Methodist accents that men have an inalienable natural right to liberty and with it rectitude and duty – a liberty to do good as the Lord has taught. Calhoun wrote his daughter Anna Maria that she must not think he expected success in his war against the corruption of the federal government. "Far higher motives impel me; a sense of duty – to do our best for our country, and leave the rest to Providence. I hold the duties of life to be greater than life itself." A day or two before Appomattox, Lee admitted to General William Pendleton that he had never thought the Confederacy could win the War without foreign intervention. It made no difference: "We had, I was satisfied, sacred principles to maintain and rights to defend, for which we were in duty bound to do our best, even if we perished in the endeavor."[44]

Alexander Stephens said after the War, "Times change, and men often change with them, but principles never! These, like truths, are eternal, unchangeable and immutable." As the pious Stephens knew, slavish devotion to duty, especially in slaveholders, risked manifestation of sinful pride and encouraged want of principle. Frances Kemble asked a planter if he were not proud of his son for remaining calm and risking his life to save the lives of people gripped by panic. He replied, "I am glad, madam, my son was not selfish." Thornwell, criticizing Immanuel Kant, wrote, "The naked sense of duty can make an obedient slave, but never make a holy man." Duty is "grand and glorious when the object of duty is first apprehended as the good." Obedience to the call of duty must flow from love. Divines hurled jeremiads against the sin of pride, and laymen kept up a barrage of self-criticism. Nothing could destroy the overweening pride that transformed the most admirable of southern virtues into the deadliest of vices. The confusion wrought by self-congratulation

---

[43] *JHTW*, 1:404–5; Richard H. Wilmer, *In Memoriam: A Sermon in Commemoration of the Life and Labors of the Rt. Rev. Stephen Elliott* (Mobile, AL, 1967), 17.

[44] Randolph quoted in Bruce, *Randolph of Roanoke,* 1:598; Jasper Adams, *Elements of Moral Philosophy* (Philadelphia, 1837), 11; William A. Smith, *Lectures on the Philosophy and Practice of Slavery* (Nashville, TN, 1856), 97; J. C. Calhoun to Mrs. T. G. Clemson, in J. Franklin Jameson, ed., *Calhoun Correspondence* (Washington, DC, 1900: "Annual Report of the American Historical Association for the Year 1899," vol. 2), 744–5; Lee quoted in Capt. Robert Edward Lee, *The Recollections and Letters of General Robert E. Lee, by His Son* (New York, 1904), 151. Anna Maria Calhoun attributed to her father the recognition that the duties of life are more important than life itself: to J. C. Calhoun, Mar. 24, 1850, in *JCCP,* 27:240.

and self-criticism played havoc with the slaveholders' character and performance. Richard Henry Wilde of Georgia, poet and politician, mischievously conjured up the arrogance easily ascribed to slaveholders, "LOVE AND PRIDE, are the only angelic sins. United, what mortal philosophy can withstand them?"[45]

In 1829 Robert Alexander Young, a free Negro spokesman in New York, published a pamphlet, *The Ethiopian Manifesto, Issued in Defence of the Blackman's Rights in the Scale of Universal Freedom,* in which he hurled a warning at the slaveholders: "Beware! know thyselves to be but mortal men, doomed to the good or evil, as your works shall merit from you. Pride ye not yourselves in the greatness of your worldly standing, since all things are but moth when contrasted with the invisible spirit, which ... within you will, to the presence of your God, be at all times your sole accuser." Thornwell said as much when he assailed vanity as the root of the sin of pride. Man refuses to admit that his knowledge can only be partial. "Pride, in the sense of self-independence and self-sufficiency is the very core of sin." With his eye on slaveholders as well as on the bourgeois modernism he was combating, Thornwell deplored man's tendency to exalt his own being, to pretend to be creator and Lord, to usurp the place of God.[46]

In 1864 the Baptist Reverend Thomas Dunaway bemoaned Southerners' rebellion against God: "How proud and rebellious," how "arrogant," how "self-reliant and self dependent." After the War, Isaac DuBose Seabrook, a descendant of prominent South Carolina families, wrote, "An unconquerable pride grew up in the hearts of this class – the pride of unchallenged domination, of irresponsible control of others, of unquestioned power, of uncriticized conduct." Each man became lord of his own domain: "He was the source of law among the slaves; and his self interest and good or ill will was the rule of his actions: the laws of the state did not readily reach him and public opinion among his own class naturally coincided with his views." In consequence, he displayed "an absolute indifference to the opinions of others: an entire independence of the objects, needs or aims of the other classes of the population." The Reverend James Lyon of Mississippi attributed the War not to slavery but to "the haughty *spirit* generated by slavery."[47]

45 Alexander H. Stephens, *A Constitutional View of the Late War between the States,* 2 vols. (New York, 1970 [1868, 1870]), 1:9; Frances Kemble, *Journal of a Resident on a Georgia Plantation in 1838–1839* (New York, 1863), 295; *JHTW,* 1:372–3; Richard Henry Wilde, *Conjectures and Researches Concerning the Love, Madness, and Imprisonment of Torquato Tasso,* 2 vols. (New York, 1842), 1:81.

46 R. A. Young, "Ethiopian Manifesto," in Herbert Aptheker, ed., *A Documentary History of the Negro People in the United States,* 4 vols. (New York, 1990), 1:91; *JHTW,* 1:405. Thornwell grounded his critique in predestinarianism, although, as Young's remarks suggest, Arminians fashioned their own counterparts. Predestination, Thornwell argued, destroys arrogance, for God saves us through no merit of our own; hence, predestination cultivates humility and tempers our sense of honor: *JHTW,* 2:186.

47 Thomas S. Dunaway, *A Sermon Delivered ... before the Coan Baptist Church, in Connection with a Day of National Fasting, Humiliation and Prayer* (Richmond, VA, 1864), 10; Isaac DuBose Seabrook, *Before and After; Or, the Relations of the Races at the South,* ed. John Hammond Moore (Baton Rouge, LA, 1967 [1895]), 46; for Lyon see Ernest Trice Thompson, *Presbyterians in the South,* 3 vols. (Richmond, VA, 1963), 2:68.

For the crowning touch in southern gentlemen's criticism of the Southern Gentleman, nothing surpassed a remark by the South Carolina born-and-bred Senator Louis Wigfall of Texas. Presumably without irony and certainly without malice, Wigfall characterized James Seddon as "a gentleman *and* a man of sense."[48]

To modern sensibilities it is a preposterous idea that a slave system could engender admirable virtues. If anything, the relation between slavery and such face-to-face "chivalric" virtues as honor, fame, and courage has discredited the virtues themselves. In our own time it seems perverse, not to say impossible, to try to separate the horror of slavery from the positive features of an ordered and interdependent social system. To Southerners and not just slaveholders, slavery was a bulwark against the corrosive effects of free labor and the loosening of the social bonds that nurtured humane social relations. A consequence was the formation of a distinct southern people.

In the 1820s Joseph Cabell, Thomas Jefferson's friend, sadly observed that slavery formed the very fabric of a southern life that emancipation would destroy. In 1826, former Governor Robert Hayne of South Carolina said of slavery, "To touch it at all is to violate our most sacred rights, to put in jeopardy our dearest interest, the peace of our country, the safety of our families, our altars, and our firesides." For Hugh Legaré of South Carolina, scholar and diplomat, those who – like John C. Calhoun – would allow states to nullify federal laws were embarking upon war and revolution; yet Legaré, too, protested against a federal government that was "interfering in the domestic concerns of society" and threatening "to control, in the most offensive and despotic manner, all the pursuits, the interests, the opinions and the conduct of men."[49]

In the 1830s Hammond lectured Congress, "We have been born and bred in a slave-country. Our habits are accommodated to them." Looking abroad, "We see nothing to invite us to exchange our own; but on the contrary, everything to induce us to prefer it above all others." Dr. Richard D. Arnold of Savannah, a unionist, spoke of slavery as a violation of abstract rights, but "So intimately is it mingled with our social conditions, so deeply has it taken root, that it would be impossible to eradicate it without upturning the foundations of that condition." When the War came, the antisecessionist Arnold warned that the Yankees would "uproot the very foundations of Southern Society." Addressing South Carolina's legislature, Governor George McDuffie deprecated West Indian emancipation, protested the horrible conditions that British capital imposed on its working class, and asserted that slavery constituted "the cornerstone of our republican edifice." McDuffie spurned appeals to mere economic interest: No southern patriot "will tolerate the idea of

[48] Wigfall quoted in Alvy L. King, *Louis T. Wigfall: Southern Fire-eater* (Baton Rouge, LA, 1970), 162.

[49] For Cabell see Phillip Alexander Bruce, *History of the University of Virginia, 1819–1919: The Lengthening Shadow of One Man,* 5 vols. (New York, 1920–22), 1:156–7; Hayne quoted in David Duncan Wallace, *The History of South Carolina,* 4 vols. (New York, 1934), 2:417; "Kent's Commentaries" (1828), *HLW,* 2:123–4.

emancipation, at any period however remote, or any condition of pecuniary advantage, however favorable."[50]

With an enormous investment in human property, even severe economic crises and questionable prospects did not render the slaveholders so pessimistic as to cause a sustained decline in the demand for slaves. From the Missouri crisis of 1819–20 to secession, Southerners denied that they defended slavery primarily from pecuniary interest, and even slaveholders who stressed economic interest refused to consider compensated emancipation and so reduce slavery to a purely economic interest. Nathaniel Beverley Tucker of Virginia, judge and college professor, had wanted to dispense with slavery, which he "excused" as an unfortunate imposition and a necessary evil; yet a decade later in 1844 he defended its morality, celebrated its mutual advantages for whites and blacks, and cited conditions in France and Britain to proclaim slavery's superiority as a labor system. That same year the renowned Langdon Cheves of South Carolinia, formerly a congressman and president of the Bank of the United States, said: "Remember! On the inviolability of the institution which is thus threatened and assailed, depends not our prosperity alone, but every blessing under heaven, which we enjoy. Every thing Southern must necessarily perish with it."[51]

As late as 1843 the editors of *Southern Literary Messenger* still described slavery as a social and political evil and called for its "gradual abolition, or amelioration," but two years later they announced, "Slavery is an element of southern civilization, and a constituent of southern society." One contributor wrote, "The great distinguishing feature of southern society is, of course, the institution of slavery." Slavery, another wrote, is "the most invaluable" of southern institutions because the "most closely and indissolubly interwoven into the texture of her social and political systems." A lead article, "American Slavery in 1857," opened defiantly: "Upon it, Southern society is based – into every fibre of which, it has inveterately cast its roots, wide and deep and is so interwoven with it, that one cannot be abolished without the destruction of the other." J. D. B. De Bow declared in his own journal: "We consider *slavery* and all questions that grow out of it, legitimate to the purposes of a magazine which claims to be essentially *Southern,* and that every effort to confound these questions with mere *politics* is a dangerous innovation."[52]

[50] [Clyde N. Wilson], ed., *Selections from the Letters and Speeches of James H. Hammond* (Spartanburg, SC, 1978), 31–2, and 126 for his applause of McDuffie's speech; Arnold to Chandler Robbins, Aug. 15, 1837, and Arnold to Jacob Waldburg, Oct. 18, 1862, in Richard H. Shryock, ed., *Letters of Richard D. Arnold, M.D., 1808–1876* (Durham, NC, 1929), 14, 108; McDuffie quoted in Wilkins, " 'Window on Freedom': The South's Response to the Emancipation of the Slaves in the British West Indies, 1833–1861" (Ph.D. diss., University of South Carolina, 1977), 87.

[51] Robert William Fogel, *Without Consent or Contract: The Rise and Fall of American Slavery* (New York, 1989), 63; "A Virginian" [N. B. Tucker], "Remarks on a Note to Blackstone's Commentaries," *SLM,* 1 (1835), 266–70; Nathaniel Beverley Tucker, "Moral and Political Effect of the Relation between the Caucasian and the African Slave," *SLM,* 10 (1844), 329–39, 470–8; Cheves, "Letter to the Charleston Mercury on Southern Wrongs, Sept. 1844," *Southern State Rights, Anti-Tariff & Anti-Abolition Tract, no. 1* (Charleston, SC, 1844), 5.

[52] "W." [of Westmoreland Co., VA], "Slavery in the Southern States," *SLM,* 9 (1843), 736; Samuel Henry Dickson, "Slavery in the French Colonies," *SLM,* 10 (1844), 268–70; [Benjamin Blake Minor], "French and English Propagandism," *SLM,* 10 (1844), 577–83; "Domestic Slavery," *SLM,* 11 (1845),

In 1848 John Archibald Campbell of Alabama, an eminent jurist and scholar who was appointed to the U.S. Supreme Court a few years later, wrote to Calhoun: "The strength of our position, is that slavery is the central point about which Southern Society is formed. It was so understood at the formation of the Constitution." In South Carolina, Frederick Porcher called slavery "an essential element in Southern civilization," and Chief Justice John Belton O'Neall, a crusader for a more humane slave code, wrote that slavery "is here so interwoven with every part of society, and so essential to life itself, that its destruction would be ours." William Elliott, another committed unionist, remarked in 1851 that slavery "has never stood so strong in the South as at this moment." Chief Justice Joseph Lumpkin saw slavery in Georgia "intimately interwoven with her present and permanent prosperity. Her interests, her feelings, her judgment and her conscience – not to say her very existence, alike conspire to sustain and perpetuate it." Other state Supreme Court justices and the many slaveholders who studied law had been trained to consider the defense of southern rights a paramount responsibility and slavery as at the heart of that defense.[53]

In 1861 the Virginia-born Lieutenant Governor Thomas Caute Reynolds of Missouri expressed confidence that no state senator would deny "We are two distinct nations, that the North and the South are different peoples." Thomas Cobb wrote to his wife Marion about Northerners: "These people hate us, annoy us, and would have us assassinated by our slaves if they dared, I know there are good people among them, but I speak of the masses. They are a *different* people from us, whether better or worse and *there is no love* between us." The Union, the Reverend H. A. Tupper of Washington, Georgia, told his flock in 1862, was "unnatural," for "that difference

515; "American Slavery in 1857," *SLM*, 25 (1857), 81; *DBR*, 10 (1851), 265. See also *DBR*, 4 (1847), 219, and "Mr. Smith" [of Virginia], "Character of the American People," *SQR*, n.s. (3rd), 2 (1857), 403. Ashbel Smith recalled that 1830s Texans understood that emancipation by Mexican law would mean "an eternal festering thorn on the side of the United States on their most exposed flank": Smith, *Reminiscences of the Texas Republic* (Galveston, TX, 1876), 53. The bishops of the Methodist Episcopal Church, replying to a fraternal address of the British Conference, rejected interference because slavery was "closely interwoven with their civil institutions": Gross Alexander et al., eds., *A History of the Methodist Church, South, The United, etc. . . .* (New York, 1894), 11. In 1851 Thornwell spoke for the Presbyterian Church of South Carolina: "Slavery is implicated in every fibre of Southern society" – a position he reiterated ten years later on behalf of the whole southern Presbyterian Church. See "Relation of the Church to Slavery" and "Address to All Churches of Christ," *JHTW*, 4:396, 454. John Fletcher assailed as not merely wrong but suicidal Mississippi's 1818 declaration of slavery as "condemned by reason and nature": *Studies on Slavery, in Easy Lessons* (Natchez, 1852), 392.

53 J. A. Campbell to Calhoun, Mar. 1, 1848, in *JCCP*, 25:215; Porcher, "Southern and Northern Civilization Contrasted," 98; J. B. O'Neall, "Address," in *Proceedings of the Agricultural Convention and of the State Agricultural Society of South Carolina* (Columbia, SC, 1846), 219; [William Elliott], *The Letters of Agricola* (Greenville, SC, 1851), 7. Lumpkin quoted in Mark Tushnet, *The American Law of Slavery: Considerations of Humanity and Interest* (Princeton, NJ, 1981), 221, and see Joseph H. Lumpkin, *An Address Delivered before the South-Carolina Institute at Its Second Annual Fair* (Charleston, SC, 1851), 13. For the judiciary, especially Judge Benning of Georgia, see J. P. Reid, "Lessons of Lumpkin: A Review of Recent Literature on Law, Comity, and the Impending Crisis," *William and Mary Law Review*, 23 (1982), 571–602. See also John Townsend, *The Doom of Slavery in the Union: Its Safety Out of It*, 2nd ed. (Charleston, SC, 1860), 3, 16–17.

in pursuits, and interests, and institutions, and education, and manners, and political and social views, has made us virtually two people – as much as any two people could be of the same language and color."[54]

Albert Taylor Bledsoe, who had spent years as a lawyer and college professor in Illinois and Ohio, said of the North: "Nowhere has [Mammon] more devout and abject worshippers, or has set up a more polluted civilization." W. R. Aylett of Virginia, a prominent planter and grandson of Patrick Henry, contrasted the "noble, generous and patriotic" sons of the South, whose character slavery shaped, with "cold, money-minded, calculating" Yankees. In a gesture unusual for a Virginian, he invoked the spirit of South Carolina to call for scorched-earth resistance to any attempt to uproot slavery from southern soil.[55]

Many Confederates doubtless fought the War primarily for their slave property – for money. In 1859 Charles De Morse, northern-born editor of the Clarksville *Northern Standard,* wrote that Texans cared nothing for slavery as an abstraction but needed more slaves: "We desire the practicality; the increase of our productions; the increase of the comforts and wealth of the population." Confederate troops sang "The Bonnie Blue Flag," oblivious to the irony: "We are a bond of brothers, native to the soil / Fighting for the property we gained by honest toil." Years after the War at a meeting of Confederate veterans, Nathan Bedford Forrest – a plain-speaking man of action – exploded upon hearing Lost Cause oratory that barely mentioned slavery. He had gone to war to keep his "niggers" and to help other white folks keep theirs. The northern-born Thomas Green Clemson, Calhoun's son-in-law, considered slavery a drag on economic development but an excellent investment all the same: "They are the most valuable property in the South, being the basis of the whole southern fabric." Confederate General Edward Porter Alexander concurred about the economic value of the slaves; after the War, recalling Lincoln's offer shortly before Appomattox of $400,000,000 to free the slaves, he said the Confederate government was crazy not to take it. He recognized that its refusal expressed the will of a people who could not be bought, but added acidly: "The trouble was that we were struggling against changes which the advance of the world in railroads & steamboats & telegraphs, in science & knowledge and commerce, & in short, civilization, had rendered inevitable."[56]

[54] *Speech of Lieut. Gov. Reynolds on the Preservation and Reconstruction of the Union* (St. Louis, MO, 1861), 3; T. R. R. Cobb to Marion Cobb, Oct. 11, 1860, in A. L. Hull, ed., "The Correspondence of Thomas Reade Rootes Cobb, 1800–1862," *Publications of the Southern History Association for 1907,* 11 (1907), 156–7; H. A. Tupper, *A Thanksgiving Discourse Delivered at Washington, Ga.* (Macon, GA, 1862), 4.

[55] Albert Bledsoe in *SR,* 5 (1869), 443–5; W. R. Aylett speech on slavery, in Aylett Family Papers, at Virginia Historical Society (Richmond). In 1854, John Forsyth of Georgia spoke confidently of two peoples at the Franklin Society of Mobile, Alabama: "The North and the South," *DBR,* 17 (1854), 361–78. Governor A. B. Moore repeatedly stressed the northern threat to slavery in his messages to the Alabama legislature and secession convention, and E. S. Dargan of South Carolina told the convention that if money were the issue, Alabama should give up its slaves: see William R. Smith, ed., *The History of the Convention Debates of the People of Alabama* (Montgomery, AL, 1861), 9, 14, 36, 93–5.

[56] Morse quoted in Randolph B. Campbell, *An Empire for Slavery: The Peculiar Institution in Texas, 1821–1865* (Baton Rouge, LA, 1989), 3; Frank Cunningham, *Knight of the Confederacy: Gen. Turner*

"The South," Leonidas W. Spratt of South Carolina began a secessionist polemic, "is now in the formation of a Slave Republic." Maria J. McIntosh, an accomplished, politically moderate, southern-born author, remarked that to write about the South without writing about slavery would be to play Hamlet without the Dane. Berkeley Grimball of South Carolina, son of a wealthy planter, hoped for a Confederacy in which Southerners "will have among themselves Slavery a bond of union stronger than any which holds the north together." In a momentous debate in Milledgeville, Georgia, in November 1860, Thomas Cobb and Robert Toombs, urging secession, extolled slavery as the heart of southern civilization. Fulton Anderson, a Whig sent by Mississippi to plead the secessionist case in Virginia, referred to slavery, "upon which rests not only the whole wealth of the Southern people, but their very social and political existence." He quoted Lincoln's "House Divided" speech as evidence of northern hostility to the South: "They are engaged in a holy crusade against slavery, [which] lies at the very foundation of our social and political fabric" – "the surest support of Christian moral order."[57]

The South's earlier apologies for slavery had come to seem an aberration. Southern leaders ostentatiously thanked the abolitionists for abusing the South. Calhoun told the Senate that abolitionist slanders had compelled reexamination of premises and produced awareness of slavery as a positive good. Without abolitionist abuse, Lumpkin averred, Southerners might have committed social and political suicide by plunging into the "folly" of emancipation, injuring both races, and causing innumerable problems for the nation and the world. Subsequently, Professor James Holcombe and John Reuben Thompson of *Southern Literary Messenger* agreed that abolitionist ferocity shook Virginians out of their lethargy and brought them to proclaim slavery intertwined with all southern life. Bishop Stephen Elliott of Georgia never abandoned his belief that the greatness of southern civilization rested upon slavery, which he called "the whole framework of our social life."[58]

Ashby (San Antonio, TX, 1960), 134. For Forrest see Russell Kirk, *The Conservative Mind in America: From Burke to Eliot*, 7th ed. (Chicago, 1986), 152; Clemson quoted in Ernest MacPherson Lander, Jr., *The Calhoun Family and Thomas Green Clemson: The Decline of a Southern Patriarchy* (Columbia, SC, 1983), 92; Gary W. Alexander, ed., *Fighting for the Confederacy: The Personal Recollections of General Edward Porter Alexander* (Chapel Hill, NC, 1989), 503. See also the reaction of L. Q. C. Lamar described in James B. Murphy, *L. Q. C. Lamar: Pragmatic Patriot* (Baton Rouge, LA, 1973), 64–5 n. 3. According to Alexander Stephens, Lincoln proposed $400,000,000 compensation for emancipation: Stephens, *Constitutional View*, 2:617.

[57] L. W. Spratt, *The Philosophy of Secession: A Southern View* (Charleston, SC, 1861), 1; Maria J. McIntosh, *Women in America: Her Work and Her Reward* (New York, 1850), 112; Berkeley Grimball to Elizabeth Grimball, Dec. 8, 1860, in J. B. Grimball Papers, at UNC-SHC. See the speeches of Cobb and Toombs in William W. Freehling and Craig Simpson, eds., *Secession Debated: Georgia's Showdown in 1860* (New York, 1992), 3–30, 32–50; for the text of Anderson's speech see James D. Lynch, *The Bench and Bar of Mississippi* (New York, 1881), 431–44, quote at 441. Important antisecessionist newspapers like the New Orleans *Picayune* agreed with the radicals that slavery was *sine qua non* for southern life: Carl R. Osthaus, *Partisans of the Southern Press: Editorial Spokesmen of the Nineteenth Century* (Lexington, KY, 1994), 66–7.

[58] Richard K. Crallé, ed., *The Works of John C. Calhoun*, 6 vols. (New York, 1851–56), 3:142; J. H. Lumpkin to Howell Cobb, Jan. 21, 1848, in Ulrich B. Phillips, ed., *The Correspondence of Robert Toombs, Alexander H. Stephens, and Howell Cobb* (Washington, DC, 1913: "Annual Report of the

The diplomat and historian William Henry Trescot of South Carolina noted that slavery had begun as an experiment but "has become the corner-stone of our social and political life." Southerners had a "duty to prove to a skeptical and hostile world that it is compatible with the great interests, the high ends, the purifying and elevating influences of Christian civilization." Slavery "informs all our modes of life; all our habits of thought." Slaveholding was largely responsible for southern republicanism, and therefore Trescot opposed resumption of the African slave trade in part because a rapid increase in the supply of slaves would encourage the emergence of an artificial aristocracy inassimilable by – and thus incompatible with – a republic. He simultaneously defended slavery as a bulwark of a constructive "aristocracy," specifying that "I am using the word philosophically, not in its popular sense."[59]

A "natural" aristocracy embodied and protected society's moral and political ideals and flourished in a genuinely democratic polity. In eighteenth-century Virginia, a classically educated gentleman dressed and carried himself in a manner befitting an upper-class station, typically rising from the English middle class into the ranks of Virginia's "aristocracy." Without an aristocratic pedigree, only money secured status. "Planter" meant farmer, not "gentleman." The gentlemen of eighteenth-century Virginia, Vernon Parrington remarked in a twentieth-century retrospect, "were bound together by caste solidarity, but they remained strikingly individual, never amenable to group coercion, expressing their convictions freely and ready to uphold their views by the code of the duel."[60]

The life of a Hungarian or Transylvanian "country gentleman," M. R. H. Garnett of Virginia (a young secessionist politician) wrote in the late 1840s, was "quite like that of a southern planter in our own country." Reverend Basil Manly told an Alabama agricultural convention, "The condition of the southern planters is an aristocracy; akin to what is termed the 'Nobility' in other countries." Belle Kearney

American Historical Association for the Year 1911," vol. 2), 94–5; James P. Holcombe, "Is Slavery Consistent with Natural Law?" *SLM*, 27 (1858), 402. [J. R. Thompson], *SLM*, 19 (1853), 583–4; Stephen Elliott, *How to Renew Our National Strength* (Richmond, VA, 1862), 5; also, *A Discourse Delivered by the Rev. J. Jones to the Rome Light Guards and Miller Rifles* (Rome, GA, 1861), 8–10; Armstrong, *A Thanksgiving Sermon*, 10; W. H. Vernor, *A Sermon Delivered before the Marshall Guards* (Lewisburg, TN, 1861), 11–13; J. J. D. Renfroe, *"The Battle Is God's": A Sermon Preached before Wilcox's Brigade* (Richmond, VA, 1863), 6. See also the shared assumption of the radical antislavery Missouri *Blätter* (Apr. 21, 1861), in Steven Rowan and James Neal Primm, eds., *Germans for a Free Missouri: Translations from the St. Louis Radical Press, 1857–1862* (Columbia, MO, 1983), 182, and the northern but prosouthern Rev. Samuel Seabury, *American Slavery Distinguished from the Slavery of English Theorists and Justified by the Law of Nature* (New York, 1861), 308. *Jefferson Monument Magazine* (1851), 194, published by the University of Virginia's student Jefferson Society, celebrated Virginia's conversion to vigorous defense of slavery. On the centrality of slavery to the divines see Mitchell Snay, *Gospel of Disunion: Religion and Separatism in the Antebellum South* (New York, 1993), ch. 1.

[59] William H. Trescot, "South Carolina – A Colony and a State," *DBR*, 27 (1859), 672–3, 676, 682; Trescot to William Porcher Miles, Feb. 8, 1859, in Miles Papers, at UNC-SHC; Trescot, "Oration," in *Collections of the South-Carolina Historical Society*, 2 vols. (Charleston, SC, 1857–58), 1:33.

[60] On "planter" see esp. Rhys Isaac, *The Transformation of Virginia, 1740–1790* (Chapel Hill, NC, 1982), 16, 131; also, Richmond Croom Beatty, *William Byrd of Westover* (New York, 1970), 20–1; Vernon Louis Parrington, *Main Currents in American Thought*, 3 vols. (New York, 1927), 2:8–9.

proudly announced that the outstanding families of Madison County, Mississippi – the Kearneys, Andrews, and Balfours – descended from the British nobility, and she traced her own family to Virginia and then back to the eleventh century. W. H. Holcombe distrusted Anglo-American snobs who knew much about their ancestors beyond the third generation, but he described his own paternal great-grandfather as "a Scotch Laird of modest estate" and claimed descent from the Habsburgs. Colonel Philemon Holcombe, who fought in the American Revolution, was "a noble specimen of the old Virginian, brave, frank, courteous, hospitable. He had the old-fashioned ideas of honor, chivalry and 'blood.' – He used to say that blood was the chief determining factor in the lives of men as it was in horses. He was charitable and generous to a fault." Slaveholders lived uneasily under the shadow of English gentlemen, displaying some sense of inferiority but refusing to cringe. Elite Southerners whom J. L. Fremantle, an Englishman, met in the Confederate army charmed him with their simultaneous display of pride in having descended from English gentlemen and in their republicanism and plebeian origins.[61]

Hammond, son of a struggling schoolteacher, claimed no pedigree when he told his son Marcellus, "The planters here are essentially what the nobility are in other countries." He sneered at England's "gawky Lords" and asserted that, individually and collectively, American slaveholders acknowledged no superiors: "They stand in the broadest light of the knowledge, civilization and improvement of the age." They exact "nothing undue, they yield nothing but justice and courtesy, even to the royal blood. They cannot be flattered, duped, nor bullied." Hammond hailed the government of South Carolina as an "aristocracy" and the wealth and education of the leaders of its colonial society: "They were real noblemen and ruled the Colony and the State – the latter entirely until about thirty years ago, and to a great extent to the present moment." "Real" meant having demonstrable merit.[62]

For Virginians in the age of Jefferson, writes Richard Beale Davis, "The English ideal of the country gentleman seemed the *summum bonum*. And he was close enough in memory to the mother country to comprehend fully the advantages and obligations of that ideal." Planters fashioned a world and worldview that "went far beyond the usual concept of the English squirearchy." If Virginia planters and English squires shared a code of manners and conduct, Virginia's planters knew how easily their sons could fall back into the yeomanry and how easily yeomen could rise to the top. The course from Jeffersonian to Jacksonian democracy took a heavy toll on a class that no longer reigned supreme. But even as elite Virginians succumbed

---

[61] [M. R. H. Garnett], "Hungary and Transylvania," *SLM*, 12 (1846), 78; Basil Manly, "An Address on Agriculture," in *Proceedings of the Agricultural Convention of the State of Alabama* (Tuscaloosa, AL, 1842), 20, republished in *Southern Agriculturalist, Horticulturalist, and Register of Rural Affairs*, 2 (1842), quote at 339. B. Kearney, "Patrician Days of Madison County" (ms.), at UNC-SHC; W. H. Holcombe, "Autobiography" (ms.), 2–3, 9–10, at UNC-SHC; June 4, 1863, in Arthur J. L. Fremantle, *Three Months in the Southern States: The 1863 Diary of an English Soldier* (Edinburgh, 1863), 174.

[62] J. H. Hammond, "Letters to Clarkson," 1845, in *Selections from the Letters and Speeches of James H. Hammond* (Spartanburg, SC, 1978), 172–3; Hammond Diary, Dec. 7, 1850, as quoted by Gaillard Hunt in Introduction to Carson, *Petigru*, v; J. H. Hammond to M. C. M. Hammond, quoted in Elizabeth Merritt, *James Henry Hammond, 1807–1864* (Baltimore, 1923), 43.

to an unprecedented democratization, they bequeathed to the rising planters of the Cotton Kingdom much in their style of living and even more in their own style of thinking.[63]

Antislavery Northerners struck no harder blows against the stereotype of the South as a land of gentlemen than southern gentlemen struck themselves, but through it all the South held high the standard. Surrounded by boorishness, Southerners made little attempt to dissemble, reacting with disgust and even shock when they ran into its manifestations. Dr. James Norcom of Edenton, North Carolina, lashed out at "our aristocrats from the Old Dominion, the hotbed of aristocracy, of bloated pride." Edmund Ruffin of Virginia, riding the cars to Raleigh in 1857, had never seen so many boorish, discourteous "gentlemen." Joseph E. Brown referred sadly to the number of public men in Georgia who drank to excess and swore profanely in public and private, and James Treadwell was elected to the South Carolina legislature despite a reputation for drunkenness and the contempt of Mary Chesnut, Louisa McCord, and Francis Lieber, among others. Samuel Walker of Louisiana, a big sugar planter, disdained the wretched *arrivistes* who thought only of money and wealth, lamenting nonetheless, "A gentleman must have money or be a philosopher and philosophers are too often paupers."[64]

Daily realities challenged the gentlemanly ideal. It is hard to keep a straight face while applying the term "aristocracy" to the hard-driving planters of Alabama and Mississippi during the flush times of the 1830s. William Tecumseh Sherman, in his early military career, frequently encountered those he called "worthless sons of broke down, proud Carolina families," boasted of "their state, their aristocracy, their age, their patriarchal chivalry and glory – all trash." A sham for has-beens or never-weres: "No people in America are so poor in reality, no people so poorly provided with the comforts of life." Sherman considered most of them men-on-the-make, *arrivistes*. Yet their pretensions and aspirations did not differ essentially from those of the earliest settlers of Virginia who came to be known as FFVs (First Families of Virginia). The upper crust of seventeenth-century Virginia had been proverbially hard, arrogant, and grasping. It took a century to transform them into a socially responsible hegemonic class. The Cotton Kingdom repeated the pattern during the nineteenth century in half as much time.[65]

---

[63] Davis, *Intellectual Life in Jefferson's Virginia*, 6–7. For a recent, statistically grounded assessment of upward mobility in the eighteenth-century South, see Robert W. Fogel in Fogel et al., eds., *Without Consent or Contract: Evidence and Methods*, 2 vols. (New York, 1992), 1:47–50. For the southern yeomanry seen as the principal bulwark against Jacobinism in a planter-led slave society in 1830, see Robert P. Sutton, "Nostalgia, Pessimism, and Malaise: The Doomed Aristocrat in Late-Jeffersonian Virginia," *Virginia Magazine of History and Biography*, 76 (1968), 41–55, esp. 49–50.

[64] James Norcom to Elizabeth Norcom, July 11, 1847, in James Norcom Papers, at North Carolina State Archives (Raleigh); Oct. 17, 1857, in *ERD*, 1:113–14; Herbert Fielder, ed., *A Sketch of the Life and Times of Joseph E. Brown* (Springfield, MA, 1883), 56; Lounsbury, ed., *Louisa S. McCord: Poems*, 323 (Treadwell); Samuel Walker Diary, Feb. 15, 1856, at Tulane University.

[65] Sherman quoted in Michael Fellman, *Citizen Sherman: A Life of William Tecumseh Sherman* (New York, 1995), 19. In addition to Thomas J. Wertenbaker's studies of colonial Virginia, which are especially good on these matters, see Edgar T. Thompson, "Natural History of Agricultural Labor in the

The slaves cast a critical eye on their masters' pretensions, although many admired the aristocratic ideal. They called white Southerners who lived up to it "de quality." Occasional responses slipped into the fawning and aping that whites chose to see and black spokesmen condemned. "It must be confessed," wrote Austin Steward, who had escaped from slavery, "that among the poor, degraded and ignorant slaves there exists a foolish pride, which loves to boast of their master's wealth and influence." Some slaves looked down on the nonslaveholders and on the slaves of poor folks: "I have heard slaves object to being sent in very small companies to labor in the field, lest that some passer-by should think that they belonged to a poor man."[66]

Much of such slave response to aristocracy reflected respect for values that echoed their African past. If white responses betrayed condescension and self-serving attempts at manipulation, they also betrayed genuine respect. Whites jumped at the chance to claim credit for instilling aristocratic virtues even in benighted slaves. When a schoolteacher from England who saw a touching love letter from a slave to his intended asked if he could have written it, she was told no, but he doubtless dictated it. The Virginian who enlightened her explained that slaves studied cultured whites carefully. Self-congratulations or no, whites not only took pleasure in the quality of their slaves, they depended upon it. John Pendleton Kennedy described Solomon, an aging slave on a Maryland plantation, "as an aristocrat of the most uncompromising stamp" who upheld the dignity of his master's family. Masters, trusting house servants to recognize "respectable," allowed them to admit guests — including passers-by who sought a night's lodgings. Lowcountry planters provided the finest tutors they could find but depended on polished black servants to train their children in the ways of ladies and gentlemen. Southwestern custom demanded that a white plantation boy have a somewhat older black playmate, often slated to become a body servant, who trained him to be a gentleman. Here and there a slave, only a boy himself, was hired out to care for and help train younger white boys.[67]

After the War, southern ladies extolled the aristocratic qualities of their favorite blacks. To Susan Dabney Smedes, dignified and trusted slaves were the strongest defenders of protocol, dignity, and aristocratic manners of the Big House. Elizabeth Pringle declared, "Negroes are by nature aristocrats" who know and appreciate what constitutes a gentleman. When, during the War, newly freed blacks arrived with pitchforks on the family plantation, she commented, "There is a certain kind

---

South," in David Kelly Jackson, ed., *American Studies in Honor of William Kenneth Boyd* (Durham, NC, 1940), 125.

[66] Austin Steward, *Twenty-Two Years a Slave and Forty Years a Freeman* (Reading, MA, 1969), 63. Whites commented widely on the attitude Steward described.

[67] Eugene D. Genovese, "'Rather Be a Nigger than a Poor White Man': Black Perceptions of Southern Yeomen and Poor Whites," in Hans L. Trefousse, ed., *Toward a New View of America: Essays in Honor of Arthur C. Cole* (New York, 1977), 79–96; Catherine Cooper Hopley, *Life in the South from the Commencement of the War*, 2 vols. (New York, 1971 [1863]), 1:237–9; John Pendleton Kennedy, "The Legend of the Chesapeake," *SLM*, 24 (1857), 225; Thomas Cary Johnson, ed., *Life and Letters of Robert Lewis Dabney* (Carlisle, PA, 1977 [1903]), 16–17; Burnette Vanstory, *Georgia's Land of the Golden Isles* (Athens, GA, 1956), 81; William Edwards Clement, *Plantation Life on the Mississippi* (New Orleans, 1952), 2.

of chivalry in the Negroes – they wanted blood, they wanted to kill some one, but they couldn't make up their minds to kill two defenseless ladies."[68]

How could southern slaveholders' defense of slavery, much less of a "natural aristocracy," provide the lineaments of southern culture broadly construed? How could large slaveholders' claims to embody aristocratic virtue bind small slaveholders and nonslaveholders, much less some slaves, to their values and worldview? In essence: The slaveholders rooted the defense of their privilege in a vision of independent rural property ownership – of rural households. Southerners need not have read Xenophon, although the better educated did, to understand what peasants in China, Africa, and Europe understood: To be happy meant to live independently, surrounded by family, on land that you (or your servants) cultivated and from which you drew the core of your sustenance. At the end of the War, Albion Tourgée – a Michigan abolitionist and Union soldier – explored, in a novel of Reconstruction entitled *A Fool's Errand,* the tense relations between blacks and whites in North Carolina, including the cruelty and violence. His protagonist, The Fool, bought a large agricultural holding on which he settled his family. The lyrical descriptions of meadows and apple trees that flowed from the pen of this doughty veteran of the war against slavery could as easily have come from the pen of a southern slaveholder or any of his many precursors who, throughout the centuries, had written of the beauties and peace of the pastoral life.

In 1726 William Byrd of Westover sang the praises of Virginia to the Earl of Orrery:

Besides the advantage of a pure air, we abound in all kinds of provisions without expense (I mean we who have plantations). I have a large family of my own, and my doors are open to everybody, yet I have no bills to pay, and half a crown will rest undisturbed in my pockets for many moons together. Like one of the patriarchs, I have my flock and herds, my bondmen and bondwomen, and every sought of trade amongst my own servants, so that I live in a kind of independence on everyone but Providence. However, though this sort of life is without expense, yet it is attended with a great deal of trouble. I must take care to keep all my people to their duty, to set all springs in motion, and to make everyone draw his equal share to carry the machine forward. Another thing, My Lord that recommends this country very much: we sit securely under our vines and our fig trees without any danger to our property.... Thus, My Lord, we are very happy in our Canaans if we could but forget the onions and fleshpots of Egypt.

Byrd went through much of his life contemptuous of business matters and the debts that crowded in on him. As he grew older, complacency turned to bitterness. He had to sell off some of his hallowed land to pay debts, and he grew increasingly depressed by the commercialization of the world he had revered.[69]

---

[68] Susan Dabney Smedes, *Memorials of a Southern Planter* (New York, 1965 [1887]), 19; Pringle, *Chronicle of Chicora Wood,* 17, 274.

[69] Byrd quoted in Lewis P. Simpson, *The Dispossessed Garden: Pastoral and History in Southern Literature* (Athens, GA, 1975), 17–18, and see ch. 1 for a superb interpretation of the origins of the southern pastoral in relation to the rise of a slave society; see also Beatty, *William Byrd,* 193, 204, 209–10.

The pastoral vision recurred decade by decade from Virginia to Texas. Durand of Dauphiné, a Huguenot traveler to Virginia, remarked in the 1680s, "There are no lords, but each is sovereign on his own plantation." Robert Beverley, in his *History and Present State of Virginia* (1705), blended the pleasures of the natural garden with those of the slave plantation to picture an emergent Arcadia. John Brickell's account of North Carolina (1737) paid tribute to the planters' lordly self-sufficiency. Jefferson, too, cherished the pastoral, bestowing special favor on Columella's *De Re Rustica* and copying lines from Horace: "Happy the man who, free from business worries, like the men of the old days, tills with his oxen his ancestral fields without being harassed by mortgages." George Washington told Lafayette in the 1780s of his life at Mount Vernon: "Under the shadow of my own Vine & my own Fig tree, free from the bustle of a camp & the busy scenes of public life." Parson Weems, accounting for George Washington's greatness, extolled rural Virginia and its "numerous herds and flocks." In 1815, Supreme Court Justice William Johnson addressed a meeting of Charleston's elite on "*Nugae Georgicae,*" portraying southern planters as the best of men because removed from urban corruption and with the leisure to pursue moral and intellectual improvement. They indulged in the pleasures of hunting, riding, and dining in moderation. Johnson's planters had little in common with farmers who worked the land solely to accumulate wealth. In the 1820s Juliana Margaret Conner of North Carolina said of insulated, self-sufficient planters like her father-in-law: "They live as it were independent."[70]

The Charlestonians who called themselves "The Chivalry" may not have swallowed this idyll, but they tried to. They surely recognized the ideal that Justice Johnson projected and, as well-read men, picked up his references: "Surrounded by his family, his dependents, his flocks and his herds, with all around him looking to him for food, for comfort, for protection or instruction, he cannot but form a high estimate of his own importance in the scale of creation." The planter's "station" compels "the faithful discharge of the great duties of life." In 1820s the St. Louis *Enquirer* drew a parallel between southern slaveholders and ancient Israelites: Southerners "move like patriarchs of old, at the head of their children and grandchildren, their

---

[70] [Durand of Dauphine], *A Huguenot Exile in Virginia; Or, Voyages of a Frenchman Exiled for His Religion,* tr. Gilbert Chinard (New York, 1934 [1687]), 110; John Brickell, *The Natural History of North Carolina* (Murfreesboro, NC, 1968 [1737]), 10, 30–1; Robert Beverley, *The History and Present State of Virginia,* ed. Louis B. Wright (Chapel Hill, NC, 1947 [1705]); Gilbert Chinard, ed., *The Literary Bible of Thomas Jefferson: The Commonplace Book of Philosophers and Poets* (New York, 1969 [1928]), 185. Washington quoted in Jean B. Lee, "Mount Vernon Plantation: A Model for the Republic," in Philip J. Schwarz, ed., *Slavery at the Home of George Washington* (Mount Vernon, VA, 2001), 20; Mason Locke Weems, *The Life of Washington. A New Edition with Primary Documents* (Amonk, NY, 1996 [1809]), 104; William Johnson, *Nugea Georgicae: An Essay Delivered to the Literary and Philosophical Society of Charleston* (Charleston, SC, 1815), 5; Juliana Margaret Conner Diary, June 21, 1827, at UNC-SHC. For similar remarks see Joseph Baldwin, *The Flush Times of Alabama and Mississippi: A Series of Sketches* (New York, 1957 [1853]), 57–8; J. L. Petigru to William Elliott, Dec. 14, 1854, in Carson, *Petigru,* 301; Alfred Moore Waddell, *Some Memories of My Life* (Raleigh, NC, 1908), 43. For persistence of the rural ideal in southern towns and cities see Avery O. Craven, *The Coming of the Civil War,* 2nd ed. (Chicago, 1957), 34–5.

flocks and their herds, their *"bondmen"* and *"bond maids"* to be *"an inheritance for their children after them,"* to be *"their bondmen forever."* A few years later, Edward Brown of South Carolina located the roots of southern slavery in biblical accounts of the flocks and herds of the Lord's people.[71]

Emily Burke described a large plantation in Georgia as "a township of itself," within its border "so many resources of convenience" that, for the most part, it seemed to exist independent of the outside world. The planter's ideal of a complete community glows in her description: "Teachers in the languages, music and the other sciences, received good salaries," and the master sought to build his own church with its own chaplain, as others around him were doing. In the 1840s, John Wistar Metcalfe managed a plantation near Natchez for his father, conscientiously distributing provisions daily and seeing to every detail, with time also to cultivate his mind, play the flute, and keep up correspondence: "Besides giving out the allowance & medicine to the sick to day I have been with the hands nearly all day. Wrote a lecture ... and read some Bancroft." Frank Steele of Mississippi told his sister in Ohio in 1859, "I am about as far out of the world now, as I could well desire – being five miles from the river and as far from my neighbors." Mary Jones of Georgia mused about the days in which "our dear children like a little flock were gathered around us – our pleasant friends and neighbors, our domestic school, our little social Bible class. Then the images of our valued servants in every nook and corner come flitting before my vision."[72]

In Texas in 1848, Rutherford B. Hayes visited the plantation of Sterling McNeal, "a shrewd, intelligent, cynical old bachelor" full of stories about himself: "Living alone he has come to think he is the 'be all' and 'end all' here." Hayes found social life in Texas generally rich and gregarious but concluded that the "haughty and imperious part of a man" grew naturally on lonely sugar plantations, "where the owner rarely meets with any except his slaves and minions." When Ashbel Smith settled in Texas, he planned a house in the country with the "the hearty comforts and appliances for field sports.... This will be my *home*, here will be my negroes, my books, horses,... my dogs and guns. Here I hope to see my friends."[73]

---

[71] St. Louis *Enquirer*, Apr. 29, 1820, quoted in Larry R. Morrison, "The Religious Defense of Slavery before 1830," *Journal of Religious Thought*, 37 (1980/81), 19; Edward Brown, *Notes on the Origin and Necessity of Slavery* (Charleston, SC, 1826), 10. Southerners commonly spoke of agriculture as the foundation of Roman republican life, but even as the Romans exalted the countryside over the cities for encouraging virtue, they valued the culture only cities could sustain. The Romans used "Rusticus" as a term of derision, implying lack of culture: see Oswald Spengler, *The Decline of the West*, tr. Charles Francis Atkinson, 2 vols. (New York, 1927–28), 2:95.

[72] Emily Burke, *Reminiscences of Georgia* (Oberlin, OH, 1850), 224–5. Metcalfe Diary, June 4, Apr. 18, 19, 1843, at UNC-SHC; Frank F. Steele to Anna Steele, Dec. 15, 1859, in Ferdinand Lawrence Steele Diaries, at UNC-SHC; Mary Jones to C. C. Jones, June 12, 1850, in Robert Manson Myers, ed., *A Georgian at Princeton* (New York, 1976), 37; also, E. Clitherall, "Autobiography" (ms.), Bk. 5, at UNC-SHC; Garnett Andrews, *Reminiscences of an Old Georgia Lawyer* (Atlanta, GA, 1970), 12–13.

[73] Charles Richard Williams, ed., *Diary and Letters of Rutherford Birchard Hayes*, 5 vols. (Columbus, OH, 1922–26), 1:254; Smith quoted in Elizabeth Silverthorne, *Plantation Life in Texas* (College Station, TX, 1986), 42; see also Silverthorne, *Ashbel Smith of Texas: Pioneer, Patriot, Statesman, 1805–1886* (College Station, TX, 1982), 64.

In the 1850s, Byrd's pastoral became a war cry. The Old Testament texts to which Byrd and his successors appealed carried a jeremiad. J. D. Lynch, historian of the Mississippi bar, began softly with Joseph Davis: "His numerous slaves, flocks and herds, beautiful grounds, extensive orchard, commodious dwelling, and large-hearted hospitality caused his home to become a bright landmark in the memory of the happy days of a prosperous country." Samuel Walker, a Louisiana sugar planter, updated Byrd with a political twist: "What can be more honorable employment for a Southern gentleman than occupation such as this? All admit that a good and wise despotism is the wisest of earthly governments." Walker could not understand the critics of slaveholding, especially the British king and his oppressed subjects: "We have an interest in governing well and wisely: We know each individual subject, nay we feed, we clothe, we tend him whilst the subjects of the old world despotisms is or may be underclothed, unfed, uncared for." Walker echoed the old refrain: "Let a Southern gentleman abide at home or let his absences be seldom and short. With his business, his library, his reviews from all parts of the earth, his crops and his garden, his fruits and his flowers and periodicals and proper idea of his responsibility to his God and he has within his grasp as near an approach to earthly contentment as is usually within the reach of mortal man."[74]

A contributor to *Southern Dial* depicted the planters as "men of extraordinary force – and freedom of thought": "Their independence is not, as at the North, the effect of a conflict with the too stern pressure of society, but the legitimate outgrowth of a sturdy love of individual liberty." John Fletcher, in his influential *Studies on Slavery,* quoted Genesis (26:14) on Isaac: "For he had possessions of flocks, and possession of herds, and great stores of servants, and the Philistines envied him." Southerners made the words of Micah, 4:4, their own: "But they shall sit every man under his vine, and under his fig tree; and none shall make them afraid: for the mouth of the Lord of Hosts hath spoken it."[75]

The worldlier planters did curse their rural isolation even while proclaiming its virtues. Simms and Trescot, complaining of its stultifying effects, considered cities necessary centers for a vigorous intellectual life. Hammond, who loudly and often proclaimed the superior virtues of southern civilization, scoffed at those who saw romance and poetry in the life of a planter, writing to Calhoun that planting was "the most laborious & harassing profession on earth. It is war without its glory." He wished for the leisure to enjoy the benefits of the rural isolation he was supposed to have. Simms wrote to Hammond's son about the wretched life of southern gentlemen who lolled around and cultivated bad habits, but, during the War, he wrote to William Porcher Miles: "Though I have no money, I have meat & bread, hog & hominy, enough to stand a siege."[76]

---

[74] Lynch, *Bench and Bar in Mississippi,* 75; Samuel Walker Diary, Feb. 17, 1856.

[75] [William M. Samford?], *Southern Dial,* 1 (Nov. 1857), 9; Fletcher, *Studies on Slavery,* 101.

[76] On Simms and Trescot see Farmer, *The Metaphysical Confederacy,* 18–19; also, Charles J. Faulkner, *Address before the Valley Agricultural Society of Virginia, at Their Fair Grounds near Winchester* (Richmond, VA, 1858), 4; Hammond to Calhoun, Sept. 10, 1842, in *JCCP,* 16:455–6; Simms to Marcus C. M. Hammond, Feb. 22, 1849, in Oliphant et al., eds., *Letters of Simms,* 2:485, and Simms to Miles, Feb. 22, 1861 (4:334).

In the 1820s James Garnett, an educator concerned with schools for girls and young women, playfully noted in a "Gossip's Manual" that the life of rural Virginians suffered from "a wearisome sameness." Hence the gossip had a duty "to provide against a calm so pernicious at once to health, spirits, and comfort" by spreading the wildest slander and innuendo. In 1840 Ebenezer Pettigrew, the son of North Carolina's bishop-designate and a successful planter and congressman, poured out his bitterness: "In the early and middle part of my life, being poor and a farmer of the swamp, I was not allowed to enter that society which I *vainly* thought I was entitled to, and solitude and seclusion was the consequence, which resulted in a great deal of my time spent in thought of men and things, looking at them through a spy glass at a great distance." John Pendelton Kennedy, a self-described "great enemy to solitude," had no one with whom to play billiards except a black man since no white man was around: "Necessity, however, knows no law, and solitude reconciles us to strange playmates."[77]

Bishop Elliott complained of a lack of gregariousness: "Living separate and apart, each upon his own estate, the planter is an independent power: he is the Lord of all he surveys, and he frames his own conduct upon the basis of individual sovereignty." Such men cannot readily be assembled in societies, "the instrumentality of the present day advancement of every science and art." Elliott spoke a half-truth. Isolation also encouraged gregariousness, for the wealthy tended to live in towns and villages near their plantations, and planters and farmers in the countryside exchanged visits with distant neighbors and joined them at church, courthouse, and village store. "While hemmed in on all sides by the blockade," Parthenia Antoinette Hague of Alabama recalled after the War, "we used to think that if no war were raging, and a wall as thick and high as the great Chinese Wall were to entirely surround our Confederacy, we should not suffer intolerable inconvenience, but live as happily as Adam and Eve in the Garden of Eden."[78]

---

[77] James M. Garnett, *Lectures on Female Education,* 4th ed. (Richmond, VA, 1825), 375; Ebenezer Pettigrew to Edmund Ruffin, Jan. 6, 1840, in Sarah McCulloh Lemmon, ed., *The Pettigrew Papers,* 2 vols. (Raleigh, NC, 1971, 1988), 2:423; Kennedy quoted in Charles W. Bohner, *John Pendleton Kennedy: Gentleman from Baltimore* (Baltimore, 1961), 170.

[78] Stephen Elliott, "Address on Horticulture," in David W. Lewes, ed., *Transactions of the Southern Central Agricultural Society* (Macon, GA, 1852), 118–19. See e.g. J. Carlyle Sitterson, "The McCollams: A Planter Family of the Old and New South," *JSH,* 6 (1940), 355–6; Weymouth T. Jordan, *Hugh Davis and His Alabama Plantation* (University, AL, 1948), 19–20; Parthenia Antoinette Hague, *A Blockaded Southern Family: Life in Southern Alabama during the Civil War* (Boston, 1889), 110–11.

PART TWO

THE INESCAPABLE PAST

The thing that hath been, it is that which shall be; and that which is done is that which shall be done: and there is no new thing under the sun.

—Ecclesiastes, 1:9

4

History as Moral and Political Instruction

The earthly city, has created for herself such false Gods as she wanted, from any source she chose – even creating them out of men – in order to worship them with sacrifices. The other city, the heavenly City on pilgrimage in this world, does not create false gods. She herself is the creation of the true God, and she herself is to be his true sacrifice. Nevertheless, both cities alike enjoy the good things, or are afflicted with the adversities of this temporal state, but with a different faith, a different expectation, a different love, until they are separated by a final judgment, and each received her own end, of which there is no end.

—Augustine[1]

Southerners needed to know from whence they came and where they were going. Hence, like other Americans, they turned to history as well as religion for moral guidance for nations and for individuals – for illumination of the rise and fall of empires and nations in consequence of incurring the wrath of God. Professor Francis Lieber, a German, who viewed his residence in South Carolina as an exile to nowhere, for once spoke for the Southerners among whom he lived so uncomfortably. In his inaugural address at South Carolina College, Lieber lauded the moral instruction of historical study, especially for "the sons of republicans, who at some future period, [may] have themselves to guide the state."[2]

John Berrien Lindsley of Tennessee, a prominent educator, reflected that Southerners' taste for the reading of history helped to account for "the high position they have always maintained among American public men" – a difference he saw between Southerners and Northerners: "The gentlemen of the South, many of them highly educated, have ample time for reading, and as a class give much attention to the study of history." Southerners, in his view, thereby learned to resist the tyranny

---

[1] St. Augustine, *The City of God*, tr. Henry Bettenson (London, 1972), 842.

[2] Daniel Gilman, ed., *The Miscellaneous Writings of Francis Lieber*, 2 vols. (Philadelphia, 1881), 1:183. On the contribution of Scottish moral philosophy to history as moral edification see Gladys Bryson, *Man and Society: The Scottish Inquiry of the Eighteenth Century* (New York, 1968), ch. 4; see also George H. Callcott, *History in the United States, 1800–1860: Its Practice and Purpose* (Baltimore, 1970), 156, 183. About half the textbooks in American history evoked God in the preface.

of the majority, while Northerners concentrated on business and welcomed centralization of political authority. Lindsley knew that Southerners drew on history to confirm the ubiquity of slavery in ancient and modern societies, including the most admirable, just as they drew on historical novels and novels of social criticism to illustrate the havoc that ensued from the spread of free labor. No doubt, frontiersmen and farmers had little time to read and many lacked the inclination. Others resembled the father of Reuben Davis in early Mississippi, a bright man of limited education and means whose "chief study was the Bible and a few volumes of history, which formed his only library."[3]

Francis Terry Leak, a planter in Mississippi, "never had sufficient confidence in human testimony to make history interesting to me." He had long thought "partisan bias, religious zeal, selfishness, & a natural love for the marvellous, render human testimony very unreliable." How could men know the truth about the past when they had so much difficulty in sorting out the truth of the everyday? Leak changed his mind: He advised his son John, a student at the University of North Carolina, to "Get acquainted with the histories of the U. States, England, Greece & Rome, as proper knowledge for every American." Leak may have foreshadowed postmodernist skepticism about the reliability of any "fact," but he did change his mind about the value of reading history – presumably because, like many others, he found that its moral and political instruction outweighed the difficulties of factual precision.[4]

Southerners did not turn to history primarily for facts about the past but for illustrative accounts of admirable and despicable human behavior, the complexities of political and moral struggles, and the tensions between long-term linear and cyclical patterns. Aware that as much art as science went into the writing of history, they were willing to draw instruction from imperfect sources, reading historical fiction as well as memoirs and biographies of great men – and great women. Columbus Morrison, a small slaveholding farmer and physician who moved from state to state, routinely made notes in his diary that countless other middling folk made in one form or another: "Reading – & hunting Squirrels" and "Engaged with Gun, Garden and History." Everyone had favorites among the ancients and moderns, with Plutarch de rigueur for those with the slightest claims to culture. Illustrative of the reading of young Southerners: Thomas Garrett of North Carolina plunged into biographies of Lorenzo di Medici, Lucrezia Borgia, and Queen Elizabeth, as well as the memoirs of Henri IV's Protestant finance minister, the duc de Sully. Virginians, according to G. C. Eggleston, expected a gentleman to read *The Federalist* and Thomas Hart Benton's *Thirty Years' View* – and, he might have added, James Madison's *Debates*. John C. Calhoun advised a young law student to read ancient history and literature and Edward Gibbon on Rome and then turn to histories of England and America, for "both ought, not only to be read, but studied." Mitchell

---

[3] J. B. Lindsley, "Table Talk," Apr. 18, 1862, in John Berrien Lindsley Papers, at Tennessee State Library and Archives (Nashville); Reuben Davis, *Recollections of Mississippi and Mississippians* (Oxford, MS, 1972 [1879]), 2.

[4] Leak Diary, Nov. 29, 1852, at UNC-SHC.

King, an ornament of Charleston's commercial and intellectual community, told aspiring young lawyers to read as much history as possible.[5]

Women may have overmatched the men. "I must enjoin you to study [history] several hours daily," Thomas Ruffin of North Carolina – later a distinguished justice of the state Supreme Court – wrote his 16-year-old daughter Catherine in 1826. "I suppose you are finishing Hume. That done, take up Miss Aiken's Memoirs of Elizabeth and James I." Mary Hamilton Campbell of Virginia read with fascination about Jefferson's view of Andrew Jackson's conduct during the Seminole War. Kate Carney of Tennessee devoured Washington Irving's multivolume biography of George Washington. Fannie Page Hume of Virginia studied an anthology of political orations. Anna Maria Green of Milledgeville, Georgia, read Julia Pardoes' history of Louis XIV and his court. Emma Holmes of Charleston found Vincent Nolte's *Fifty Years in Both Hemispheres* "one of the most interesting autobiographies I've ever read" and also explored a biography of Stephen Decatur and Matthew L. Davis's *Memoirs of Aaron Burr*. Burr's life, loves, and political intrigues excited widespread interest. The gentlemen were riveted by his alleged conspiracy to detach the Southwest from the United States, the ladies by the life of his daughter Theodosia, who married Joseph Alston of South Carolina and whose death at sea became the subject of much romantic speculation.[6]

Mason Locke "Parson" Weems's biography of Washington scored a smashing success in the South as elsewhere. William Gilmore Simms condescendingly pronounced it a wildly romantic "delightful book for the young" but acknowledged, with a touch of envy, its extraordinary popularity. Everyone in Virginia, Hugh Blair Grigsby wrote to Henry Randall in 1858, was reading William Wirt's biography of Patrick Henry, which compared Virginia's politicians negatively to their sterling predecessors of the Revolutionary era. Grigsby did not have a good opinion of it as biography but did think well of its contribution to the recapturing of Virginia's history, no small contribution since Virginians were groaning over the decline of the high aristocratic standards of their forebears and the rise of crude men-on-the-make.[7]

---

[5] Columbus Morrison Journal, Aug. 8, 1845, Jan. 28, 1846, at UNC-SHC; Thomas Garrett Diary, 1849, at UNC-SHC; George Cary Eggleston, *A Rebel's Recollections* (Baton Rouge, LA, 1996 [1871]), 3; J. C. Calhoun to Thomas J. Johnson, Mar. 20, 1836, in *JCCP*, 13:116. For King see John Belton O'Neall, *Biographical Sketches of the Bench and Bar of South Carolina*, 2 vols. (Charleston, SC, 1859), 1:372.

[6] Thomas Ruffin to Catherine Ruffin, Mar. 14, 1826, in J. G. deRoulhac Hamilton, ed., *The Papers of Thomas Ruffin*, 4 vols. (Raleigh, NC, 1918), 1:343; Mary Hamilton Campbell to David Campbell, Mar. 3, 1819, at William and Mary; Carney Diary, Jan. 2, 19, 20, Feb. 19, Apr. 16, 17, 21, 1861, at UNC-SHC; Hume Diary, Feb. 6, 1861, at UNC-SHC; Anna Maria Green Diary, Jan. 30, 1864, in James C. Bonner, ed., *The Journal of a Milledgeville Girl, 1861–1864* (Athens, GA, 1964), 46; Mar. 3 and Aug. 29, 1862, in John F. Marszalek, ed., *The Diary of Miss Emma Holmes* (Baton Rouge, LA, 1979), 28. On Burr see also Supplementary References: "Burr."

[7] Callcott, *History in the United States*, 25, 32; Lewis Leary, *The Book-Peddling Parson: An Account of the Life and Works of Mason Locke Weems* (Chapel Hill, NC, 1984), ch. 6; William Gilmore Simms, *The Life of Francis Marion*, 8th ed. (New York, 1844), Preface; also, J. O. Andrew, "Travels in the

Southern history merited special attention for those who sought to understand and honor the accomplishments of their own forebears. Simms complained loudly, if dubiously, that the youth of South Carolina knew little of their state's history and of the great political principles for which it stood. Yet southern college students studied history as they studied political economy, political theory, and much else in required courses on moral philosophy – taught usually by college presidents who, with four exceptions, were clergymen. At the College of William and Mary, President Thomas Roderick Dew, a layman, taught the most comprehensive history course in America.[8]

Separate departments of history came slowly to American colleges, with the South leading in the establishment of chairs of history. Even so, it was not until the 1820s that William and Mary and the College of Charleston introduced the first courses in American history. Throughout the United States, American history was taught at the lower levels, as fit for small boys; in later years, male academies in South Carolina and Georgia assigned *History of the United States* by the immensely popular Samuel Goodrich ("Peter Parley"), who extolled New England and largely ignored the South and slavery. Goodrich had saving graces: notably, his rough treatment of Thomas Paine. For a school text, Governor State Rights Gist – yes, that was his real name – of South Carolina recommended B. R. Carroll's *Catechism of United States History*; it went through twenty printings by 1859. J. D. B. De Bow heartily seconded Gist and also praised the American history textbooks of New York's Marcius Willson. Carroll pleaded that his book contained "*facts and not opinions,*" denied a sectional bias, and did try to be evenhanded.[9]

West," in *Miscellanies: Comprising Letters, Essays, and Addresses* (Louisville, KY, 1854), 48; Grigsby to Randall, July 25, 1858, in Frank J. Klingberg and Frank W. Klingberg, eds., *The Correspondence between Henry Stephens Randall and Hugh Blair Grigsby, 1856–1861* (Berkeley, CA, 1952), 135. For Weems's *Washington* and its impact see George B. Forgie, *Patricide in the House Divided: A Psychological Interpretation of Lincoln and His Age* (New York, 1979), ch. 1.

[8] William Gilmore Simms, *The History of South Carolina*, 8th ed. (New York, 1860), 5–6; Herbert Baxter Adams, *The College of William and Mary: A Contribution to the History of Higher Education* (Washington, DC, 1887), 55–6. Yale did not establish a department of history until 1865. Chairs of history were established at the universities of Pennsylvania (1780s), Maryland (1813), William and Mary (1821), and South Carolina (1818).

[9] See Callcott, *History in the United States*, 60, 90; *DBR*, 3 (1847), 587–8, and 5 (1848), 108. South Carolina Female Institute in *DHE*, 5:411, 416; Lawrence S. Rowland et al., *The History of Beaufort County, South Carolina*, 2 vols. (Columbia, SC, 1996), 1:383; Fletcher Institute, *Catalogue, 1854–1855* (Thomasville, GA); James Oscar Farmer, Jr., *The Metaphysical Confederacy: James Henley Thornwell and the Synthesis of Southern Values* (Macon, GA, 1986), 114–15; Daniel Walker Hollis, *University of South Carolina*, 2 vols. (Columbia, SC, 1951), 1:32; M. LaBorde, *History of South Carolina College* (Charleston, SC, 1874), 20; John Luster Brinkley, *On This Hill: A Narrative History of Hampden-Sydney College, 1774–1994* (Hampden Sydney, VA, 1994), 58, 99; Thomas G. Dyer, *The University of Georgia: A Bicentenial History, 1785–1985* (Athens, GA, 1985), 14–15. Women's schools assigned popular histories like those of Emma Willard, Goodrich, and B. R. Carroll: see Elizabeth Barber Young, *A Study of the Curricula of Seven Selected Women's Colleges of the Southern States* (New York, 1932), 4, 155–6; Dale Glenwood Robinson, *The Academies of Virginia, 1776–1861* (n.p., 1977), 14.

A glance at the range of assigned textbooks suggests an effort to impose solid standards as well as eclecticism in style, subject matter, and point of view. In 1836 the South Carolina Female Institute provided its pupils with a list of formidable books for vacation reading: Johannes von Müller's *Universal History*; Arnold Hermann Ludwig Heeren's *Modern History* and *Political System of Modern Europe*; Henry Hallam's *Middle Ages*; Charles Mill's *History of Chivalry and the Crusades*; David Ramsay's *American Revolution*; John Marshall's *Life of Washington*; and Emma Willard's *American History*. The University of North Carolina and the College of South Carolina, in their early years, assigned *Elements of History* by Abbé Claude François Millot. Hampden-Sidney taught history through Emmerich de Vattel's *Law of Nature and Nations* (1758), as did the University of Georgia. Despite a mounting campaign against Yankee textbooks during the 1850s, even South Carolinians tolerated books of quality despite northern biases and criticism of slavery. Criticism of slavery did not mean criticism of racism, and works like Jedidiah Morse's *American Geography* denounced slavery while denigrating blacks.[10]

Ancient, medieval, and modern history all enjoyed a following among both planters and middling folks. Some prominent southern intellectuals strongly preferred the ancient to the modern. George Fitzhugh, for one, while extolling ancient history for teaching great moral truths, disparaged modern history as an incoherent jumble of undigested facts, lamentably biased, and largely devoid of great men. George Frederick Holmes could not contain his glee when he noted that Barthold Niebuhr, a historian Southerners held in awe, considered modern history virtually worthless (*"ne vaut pas le diable"*). For many Southerners, however, modern history was a source of enlightenment and a moral guide. In politics and public affairs conservative Southerners appealed to historical experience, not abstract principles, to determine the course of government. Yet Dew's *Digest of the Laws, Customs, Manners, and Institutions of the Ancient and Modern Nations* – the posthumously published version of his lectures at William and Mary – exemplified how the sweep of Western Civilization established the basis for an understanding of moral philosophy, including "evidences of Christianity" and religious developments, political theory, political economy, and the arts.[11]

[10] South Carolina Female Institute in *DHE*, 5:411, 415; Farmer, *Metaphysical Confederacy*, 114–15. For the campaign against Yankee textbooks see Edgar W. Knight, ed., *Public Education in the South* (New York, 1922), 291–2; Leonora Sims to Harriet R. Palmer, May 2, 1863, in Louis P. Towles, ed., *A World Turned Upside Down: The Palmers of South Santee, 1818–1881* (Columbia, SC, 1996), 365; William C. Somerville, *Letters from Paris on the Causes and Consequences of the French Revolution* (Baltimore, 1822), 76, 91. Millot's history of England was available in eighteenth-century Charleston and in North Carolina: see James Raven, *London Booksellers and American Customers: Transatlantic Literary Community and the Charleston Library Society, 1748–1811* (Columbia, SC, 2002), 160; Stephen B. Weeks, *Libraries and Literature in North Carolina in the Eighteenth Century* (Washington, DC, 1896: "Annual Report of the American Historical Association for the Year 1895"), 200; and, for the early nineteenth century, see Charles L. Coon, *North Carolina Schools and Academies: A Documentary History, 1790–1840* (Raleigh, NC, 1915), 766.

[11] George Fitzhugh, "Ancient and Modern Art and Literature," *DBR*, 28 (1860), 80–5 (Fitzhugh mentioned – as the great men in modern history – Washington, Calhoun, the Duke of Wellington, and

If anything tempered the widespread enthusiasm for history in the South, it was the persistence of doubts about the reliability of historians who, while dependent on imperfect records, shaped their narratives to reinforce their own politics and ideology. "T. C." feared that only a few historians understood, let alone adhered to, scientific methods of proof. Robert L. Dabney, quoting Thomas DeQuincy, insisted on the historian's duty to weed out the lies and distortions that went into the making of his sources. "What is the philosophy of history," asked Simms, "but a happy conjecturing, of what might have been from the imperfect skeleton of what we know"? He separated the narrative historian from the philosophical historian, who proceeds less cautiously in his own narrative but corrects errors in interpretation of the mere narrative historian. Simms, who wrote an impressive sequence of historical romances as well as histories and biographies, bared the tension in southern thought. He acknowledged factual accuracy as absolutely essential but insisted that, to create a work of lasting value, historians must move beyond mere facts to principles and must, if necessary, speculate: "We care not so much for the intrinsic truth of history, as for the great moral truths." Simms and like-minded Southerners followed the *Poetics,* in which Aristotle declared poetry "a more philosophical and a higher thing than history: for poetry tends to express the universal, history the particular." And they followed Quintilian, who urged orators to study history for examples of their themes, including "those fictitious examples invented by the great poets," for they served as "lessons to the world."[12]

The stark history of a nation would be of scant importance or intrinsic use to mankind. Simms scornfully dismissed dates and names as of significance only to the "mere chronologist," for whom they are an end in themselves. "The chief value of history consists in its proper employment for the purposes of art!" To Simms and kindred spirits, "History itself is only valuable when it provokes this inquiry – when it excites a just curiosity – awakens noble affections – elicits generous sentiments – and stimulates into becoming activity the intelligence which it informs." For Simms, "The moral objects of the poet and the historian concern not the individual so much as the race – are not simply the truths of time, but the truths of

Lafayette); Niebuhr's correspondence quoted by [George Frederick Holmes], "Niebuhr," *MMQR,* 4th ser., 7 (1855), 548; Thomas Roderick Dew, *Digest of the Laws, Customs, Manners, and Institutions of the Ancient and Modern Nations* (New York, 1884 [1852]). In one example of resistance to system-building, James M. Walker of Charleston, a legal scholar, waved off historical theories and insisted that experience alone could guide men: *Tract on Government* (Boston, 1853), vi–vii; for a favorable review see [Robert Barnwell Rhett], "Tract on Government," *SQR,* 9 (1854), 486–520. See also Dickson D. Bruce, Jr., "The Conservative Use of History in Early National Virginia," *Southern Studies,* 19 (1980), 128–49; Callcott, *History in the United States,* 156, 183; and Supplementary References: "Dew's *Digest.*"

[12] "T. C.", "On Historical Authenticity and the Value of Human Testimony as to Facts," *SLJ,* 2 (1836), 176, 179; "Uses and Results of Church History," *DD,* 2:6–7; "The Epochs and Events of American History, as Suited to the Purposes of Art in Fiction," in William Gilmore Simms, *Views and Reviews in American Literature, History, and Fiction,* 1st ser., ed. Hugh C. Holman (Cambridge, MA, 1962 [1846]), 34, 35–6; [Simms], "Prescott's Conquest of Peru," *SQR,* 13 (1848), 136–8; [Simms], "A History of Georgia," *SQR,* 13 (1848), 470–1; J. H. Butcher, tr. and ed., *The Poetics of Aristotle* (London 1936), sec. 9:3; Quintilian, *Institutio Oratoria* (LCL), 4:Bk. XII, 4:1.

eternity, and can only cease to be so in the decay of all human sensibilities." He practiced what he preached, seeking to establish the origins of America's sectional crisis through a study of the history of South Carolina – a project he also pursued through his fiction.[13]

Reflecting on the relation of fact to fiction, Dew did not doubt the existence of the Trojan War but had "no confidence" in the details of Homer's account. Even so, Homer offered "almost the only knowledge we possess" of the war, and his portrayal of circumstances accorded "with the character of the times." Turning to the novels of Sir Walter Scott, Dew added, "Fiction possesses this trait in eminent degree." The same mixture of attitudes informed Dew's evaluation of Herodotus, "the father of history," as fundamentally sound, despite the many criticisms of his exaggerations and errors in detail. He considered Thucydides a more accurate historian and admired him as a truth seeker. Mary Howard Schoolcraft of South Carolina agreed with Dew's evaluation of Thucydides and supported her view with Tacitus' dictum that the historian, even when lacking abundant sources, must do his best to establish the record of events.[14]

The nature of historical accuracy troubled Southerners because of the importance they attributed to history as a source of moral and political instruction. Young Charles Dabney of Mississippi, an avid reader, took for granted that a man who wished to be learned "must rob history of its contents." Speaking at the University of Virginia in 1847, W. C. Rives declared history "one of the highest branches" of philosophy, specifically of the "*experimental philosophy* of the moral and social nature of man," but warned of the twin dangers of "a narrow and empirical spirit" and of "mere speculative theories." As an empirically accurate history of the rise and fall of states and empires in human progress, history – Rives insisted – reveals the "experimental results" of immutable human nature and the "great truth" that God punishes men for their transgressions. As Beverley Tucker put it, history teaches "a high moral lesson," the value of which depends on its factual accuracy.[15]

The quest for objectivity in the search for moral lessons led back to classical models and admonitions. The ancient historians most admired by Southerners preached truth in the writing of history, however much they violated their precept. The Presbyterian Reverend Joseph Atkinson read Herodotus, Thucydides, Livy, and Sallust as readily sacrificing "minute accuracy" for the "truth of nature," inventing speeches and refusing to spoil a good story "by fanatical scruples or ill-timed skepticism." Yet Polybius, who scorned fiction, maintained that the unvarnished truth

---

[13] "History for the Purposes of Art," in Simms, *Views and Reviews*, 37–8; [Simms], "Epochs and Events of American History," *SWMR*, 1 (1845), 113, 115, 117. Alexander Meek of Alabama, historian and man of letters, wrote a long poem to celebrate the moral vision of history: A. B. Meek, *Poem, Pronounced before the Ciceronian Club and Other Citizens of Alabama* (Tuscaloosa, AL, 1838).

[14] Dew, *Digest*, 42–3, 100, 125–6; *Plantation Life: The Narratives of Mrs. Henry Schoolcraft* (New York, 1969 [1860]), 166.

[15] Charles Dabney to Thomas Dabney, Feb. 15, 1853, in Susan Dabney Smedes, *Memorials of a Southern Planter*, ed. Fletcher M. Green (New York, 1965 [1887]), 141–2; W. C. Rives, *Discourse on the Use and Importance of History* (Richmond, VA, 1847), 9, 11, 13, 21; Beverley Tucker, "Macaulay's History," *SQR*, 15 (1849), 377–8.

of history alone provided "the soundest education and training for a life of active politics." Mitchell King, after praising Herodotus for distinguishing carefully between his presentation of facts and his recounting of plausible legends, singled out Polybius as an accurate historian, "indefatigable in collecting materials." In agreement, "S. A. L." cited Polybius as "the most accurate and philosophical" of the ancient historians. He commended the emphasis on moral instruction in Cicero's *De Republica* but insisted that only truth and accuracy could establish history's value.[16]

Dionysius of Halicarnassus declared historical works sanctuaries of the truth and justice that constituted the aims of all history, and one southern commentator after another invoked a notion of history as "philosophy teaching by example" without agreeing about the lessons to be derived. Only occasionally did doubts surface, as when C. C. S. Farrar warned in *De Bow's Review* of the ease with which "philosophy teaching by example" could pass into subjectivity and special pleading. Professsor Maximilian LaBorde of the College of South Carolina would not commit himself to Dionysius' characterization, asserting only that "There is a deep philosophy in history" and that the philosophy of history is the philosophy of man.[17]

History, De Bow wrote, must rise to a philosophy of history that generalizes at a high level, but since few historians have the talent, the less talented must at least display meticulousness in research. For this work De Bow preferred William Henry Prescott to Macaulay, and he linked Friedrich von Schlegel to both as contributors to a school that combined romance with accurate history. Enthusiasm for philosophical history never supplanted the obligation to aspire to factual accuracy. Robert Howison, the author of a history of Virginia, wrote of his own intentions: "*Truth* should be the first object of the historian." Philosophers of history, said Paul Hamilton Hayne, the distinguished poet, must rely upon historians' clear presentation of empirical evidence. He took the "eminently romantic" stories in Julia Pardoe's *Episodes of French History* with a grain of salt but maintained that, despite peppering her narrative with "highly coloured" details, she did not tamper with "central facts." George Frederick Holmes complimented Barthold Niebuhr for separating historical fact from "the mutilated and misunderstood legends" recorded

---

[16] [Joseph M. Atkinson], "The Puritans," *SPR*, 15 (1862), 233–4. Polybius, *The Histories*, tr. W. R. Paton, 6 vols. (LCL), 1:Bk. 1, 1; Mitchell King, *A Discourse on the Qualifications and Duties of an Historian* (Savannah, GA, 1843), 9; *DBR*, 3 (1847), 279–93; "S. A. L.", "Theory of Life," *SLM*, 21 (1855), 399–400. *Southern Quarterly Review*, describing Mitchell King as a well-known "eminent and profound jurist," reported uncritically on his *Qualifications and Duties*: *SQR*, 4 (1843), 526–7. Polybius made clear his double purpose – to train practical politicians and prepare people to bear the vicissitudes of fortune by keeping in mind the fate of predecessors. He preached moderation: Since men cannot cope with prosperity, they must behave as if it will not last. See F. W. Walbank, *A Historical Commentary on Polybius*, 3 vols. (Oxford, U.K., 1975), 1:9, 19–22.

[17] Dionysius excerpted in Arnold J. Toynbee, ed., *Greek Historical Thought* (New York, 1952), 57–8; C. C. S. Farrar, "The Science of History," *DBR*, 5 (1848), 58–64; [Maximillian LaBorde], "Rivers' History of South Carolina," *SQR*, n.s. (3rd), 2 (1857), 261. See also Supplementary References: "Dionysius."

by Livy and Dionysius of Halicarnassus and long credited by historians despite the skepticism of Giambattista Vico and others.[18]

These attitudes might appear contrary and frequently were. For how can history be celebrated for examples of moral and political excellence if the accuracy of the accounts is questionable? At times, Southerners advanced views that came disconcertingly close to the postmodernist view that history exists in the eye of the beholder. Yet, they resisted cynical attempts to shape history to fit a political agenda and did not flinch from recognition that most of the historians they admired did not support slavery.[19]

Throughout the first half of the nineteenth century, history and biography retained a hold upon the imaginations of all Americans, and more than a third of the best-sellers qualified as historical. By the 1850s the historical novel was becoming less popular, as Simms discovered to his dismay. *Southern Literary Messenger* dismissed Henry William Herbert's novel, *The Roman Traitor,* as a failure because of "the evident impossibility of interesting us in the men of antiquity by the familiar agency of fiction. We must have something in common with the dramatis personae or we will care nothing about them." Other reviewers, including some in northern periodicals, praised Herbert's novel on grounds that a well-wrought historical novel offered valuable instruction by bringing a previous epoch alive. Yet increasingly the cutting edge of literary fashion focused on contemporary individualist and subjective concerns. Southerners tended to follow these trends less rapidly than Northerners, although Augusta Jane Evans and other women writers were exploring them in the 1850s. Southerners also read modern fiction of social criticism with an eye on the emergence of dangerous radical ideologies for which history might provide an antidote.[20]

De Bow's Review, Southern Literary Messenger, and (more predictably) Charleston's *Southern Quarterly Review* touted Simms as a literary giant for his histories as well as his novels and poetry. Simms occupied a special place: "the chivalric gentleman – the accomplished scholar – the untiring defender of the South." Such literary luminaries as John Reuben Thompson and John Esten Cooke of Virginia

---

[18] DBR, 20 (1856), 520; Robert R. Howison, *A History of Virginia from Its Discovery and Settlement by Europeans to the Present Time,* 2 vols. (Philadelphia, 1846), 1:ix; [Paul Hamilton Hayne], *RM,* 4 (1858), 81, 567 (misprinted as 267); [George Frederick Holmes], "Niebuhr," *MMQR,* 4th ser., 7 (1855), 539, 546. Pardoe's *Episodes of French History* consists of charming vignettes on court life, focusing on the lives of women: Miss [Julia] Pardoe, *Episodes of French History during the Consulate and the First Empire,* 2 vols. (London, 1859); see also her *The Life of Marie de Medicis, Queen of France,* 2nd ed., 3 vols. (London, 1852). *Southern Quarterly Review,* noting Pardoe's rising reputation as a novelist, especially applauded her excellent character sketches: *SQR,* "Critical Notices," 10 (1846), 249.

[19] Dew, *Digest,* 42–3, 100, 125–6; *Plantation Life: Narratives of Schoolcraft,* 166; Charles Dabney to Thomas Dabney, Feb. 15, 1853, in Smedes, *Memorials of a Southern Planter,* 141–2.

[20] "Notices of New Works," *SLM,* 18 (1853), 647; Nina Baym, *Novels, Readers, and Reviewers: Responses to Fiction in Antebellum America* (Ithaca, NY, 1984), 240.

and Paul Hamilton Hayne of South Carolina joined the chorus. William Henry Trescot of South Carolina, himself a first-rate historian, acknowledged, in an address that damned Simms with faint praise, "the fidelity with which he has preserved its memory, the vigor and beauty with which he has painted its most stirring scenes, and kept alive in fiction the portraits of its most famous heroes." Reading Simms and others, men and women, planters, farmers, and artisans, clergymen, lawyers, and doctors all approved Sir Walter Scott's definition of the novel as "a fictitious narrative accommodated to the ordinary train of events."[21]

Those who read history through the prism of contemporary concerns read novels of contemporary social criticism the same way, transferring the more positive of Scott's depictions of medieval life to Charles Dickens's and Mrs. (Elizabeth Cleghorn) Gaskell's exposés of the social costs of industrialization. They lavished attention on Nathaniel Hawthorne primarily because they valued his literary achievements, but De Bow could not resist recommending *Blithedale Romance* as an antidote for Harriet Beecher Stowe's attacks on slavery and slaveholders. Edmund Ruffin, who also admired *Blithedale Romance* and Hawthorne's other novels, loved *The Scarlet Letter* but wished that Hawthorne had completed his unmasking of New England's vicious puritan bigotry.[22]

Among historical novelists Sir Walter Scott stood alone, and Southerners read him as much for his social history as anything else. They assumed the essential historical accuracy of his novels, as they did of Shakespeare's plays. They were less inclined to accept Scott's historical nonfiction on the French Revolution and Napoleon, which came under fire from such luminaries as Henry Lee, J. D. B. De Bow, Thomas Roderick Dew, A. B. Meek, and Joseph B. Cobb. But even critics credited his work on Scotland with the recovery and rehabilitation of Scots culture and as a welcome defense of the highland and border Scots against the hatred and scorn of the lowlanders and the English. Critics intended no slight to aesthetics when they dwelt on social history. After the War, Benjamin Perry applauded Simms for doing for colonial South Carolina what Scott had done for Scotland: He "illustrated the history, scenery, manners and customs."[23]

[21] *DBR*, 1 (Mar. 1846), 286–7, also 9 (1850), 574, and 18 (1855), 175; *SQR*, 4 (1843), 247–9; for Thompson and Cooke see *SLM*, 20 (1854), 446. Paul Hamilton Hayne, "Ante-Bellum Charleston, S.C.," *Southern Bivouac*, 1 (1885), 263; W. H. Trescot, "South Carolina – A Colony and a State," *DBR*, 27 (1859), 679; Scott quoted in Paul Johnson, *The Birth of the Modern: World Society, 1815–1830* (New York, 1991), 58. By 1820 a half million copies of Scott's books had been reprinted and sold in America: William Charvat, *The Profession of Authorship in America, 1800–1870*, ed. Matthew J. Bruccoli (New York, 1992), 35.

[22] [De Bow], "Southern Slavery and Its Assailants," *DBR*, 15 (1853), 487–8; Mar. 1, 1857, in *ERD*, 1:162–3, also Dec. 7, 1858 (1:253). Scott also annoyed De Bow by justifying Britain's contravention of international law and morality in its seizure of the Danish fleet during the Napoleonic wars.

[23] Stephen Meats and Edwin T. Arnold, eds., *The Writings of Benjamin F. Perry*, 3 vols. (Spartanburg, SC, 1980), 1:464. For a sampling of the attacks on Scott's historical writing see Henry Lee, *The Life of Napoleon Bonaparte, Down to the Peace of Tolentino and the Close of His First Campaign in Italy* (London, 1837), v, 502–3, 506, 516, 521; Dew, *Digest*, 573; *DBR*, 1 (Mar. 1846), 203; and "J. B. C." [Cobb], "Macaulay's History of England," *American Whig Review*, 11 (1850), 348. Southern fascination with Scotland's culture and painful history encouraged the reading of Margaret Oliphant

As that fabled "every schoolboy" knows, Southerners so loved Sir Walter Scott that they embraced the Middle Ages and the feudal order as their very own, equating medieval manors with their slave plantations. Southerners agreed with the French historian Augustin Thierry's judgment that Scott's *Ivanhoe* described medieval life better than any history did, and they saw in *Ivanhoe* a warning that order, even a primitive feudal order, is preferable to anarchy. Commenting on *The Talisman*, T. M. Garrett, a student at the University of North Carolina, declared, "A true lover of history can not but recognize in it a beautiful portraiture of the manners and customs of the Crusaders, their policy and the characters of the principal actors in that tragical event, while those of the Turks are fully set forth in the intercourse which they had with the Crusaders." Scott "has rendered fiction subservient to the illustration of truth" yet his fiction gives truth an interest that, by entertaining, "makes a more lasting impression upon the memory."[24]

As Mark Twain suggested, the ladies found Scott irresistible. As he did not suggest, they responded thoughtfully and with particular attention to Scott's patriotism. Mary Telfair, claiming to know *The Lady of the Lake* "almost by heart," especially admired Scott's "amor patrie." A much-impressed Mary Moragné stayed up all night to read Scott's history of Scotland. Emma Holmes had read almost all of Scott's poems and novels, but "A new interest has been excited by finding how most of the scenes, incidents & descriptions of scenery, so vividly portrayed, have been drawn from his own life & wanderings over his native land."[25]

Mark Twain, echoed by countless authorities, attributed secession to the Old South's crazy romance with Scott. Since Scott wrote for the modern world and read the Middle Ages through other than medieval eyes, and since his books sold more widely in New England than in the South, the verdict of Twain and every schoolboy appears questionable. Contemporaries who commented on Scott's popularity

(Wilson)'s series of novels, *Chronicles of Carlingford*, which absorbed John Reuben Thompson of Richmond, Mary Chesnut of Charleston, Lucy Breckenridge of Kentucky, and Anna Maria Green of Milledgeville: Chesnut Diary, Apr. 11, 1864, in C. Vann Woodward, ed., *Mary Chesnut's Civil War* (New Haven, CT, 1981), 595; Oct. 8, 1862, Aug. 28, 1863, in Mary D. Robertson, ed., *Lucy Breckenridge of Grove Hill: The Journal of a Virginia Girl, 1826–1864* (Kent, OH, 1979), 59, 136; Green Diary, June 27, 1862, in Bonner, ed., *Journal of a Milledgeville Girl*, 17. For southern reactions to Scott's novels as history and polemic, see Supplementary References: "Scott."

[24] Peter J. Bowler, *The Invention of Progress: The Victorians and the Past* (London, 1989), 22–3; T. M. Garrett Diary, Jan. 7, 1849, at UNC-SHC.

[25] Mary Telfair to Mary Few, Oct. 19, 28, 1814, in Joan E. Cashin, ed., *Our Common Affairs: Texts from Women of the Old South* (Baltimore, 1996), 86, 212; Mary E. Moragné Journal, Apr. 28, 1837, in Delle Mullen Craven, ed., *The Neglected Thread: A Journal of the Calhoun Community* (Columbia, SC, 1951), 32; Mar. 7, 1863, in Marszalek, ed., *Emma Holmes Diary*, 235; also Anna Maria Green "intensely enjoy[ed]" them: Green Diary, Jan. 10, 1863, in Bonner, ed., *Journal of a Milledgeville Girl*, 28. Twelve-year-old Elizabeth Randolph Preston of Lexington, Virginia, also claimed to know *Lady of the Lake* "almost by heart": Janet Allan Bryan, ed., *A March Past: Reminiscences of Elizabeth Randolph Preston Allan* (Richmond, VA, 1938), 96. Sally McDowell of Virginia was unusual in admitting that she disliked Scott's novels, but she, too, kept on reading them. Sally McDowell to John Miller, Mar. 29, 1856, in Thomas E. Buckley, ed. *"If You Love that Lady Don't Marry Her": The Courtship Letters of Sally McDowell and John Miller, 1854–56* (Columbia, MO, 2000), 537.

thought it especially high in the South, but the Unitarian divines at Harvard, among other political conservatives, admired him no less. As the decades rolled by, Northern enthusiasm ebbed with the decline in the popularity of all historical fiction, and conservative critics at New York's *Knickerbocker Magazine* disapproved Scott's turn from "novels" to "romances."[26]

The Calvinist divines approved Scott's social history, which they interpreted as support for conservative views. Presbyterians, who ordinarily viewed fiction with suspicion, considered his historical novels salutary for their teaching of timeless truths, but the fiery Presbyterian Reverend John Bocock of Virginia lashed out at Scott's "furious anti-puritanism," condemning him as a malignant "enemy of republican liberties." Even a warm admirer like Edmund Ruffin resented Scott's anti-slavery views and complained about his failure to understand that the worst kind of slavery was that of employer to hireling, which Scott, despite his concern for the poor, accepted. On balance, Scott got high grades. As the Reverend Jasper Adams, the Episcopalian president of the College of Charleston, explained, Scott provided an excellent antidote to French infidelity and radicalism, while he made truth-telling a moral responsibility for historians. Adams drew upon Scott's denunciation of the *philosophes*' assault on Christianity to underscore his own critique of Jefferson, Paine, and others whom he saw as undermining the Christian basis of the American nation. Indeed, the more intellectually engaged Southerners read Scott, as Russell Kirk and Richard Weaver have suggested, not so much for romance as for the social ideals of Edmund Burke.[27]

---

[26] For a critique of Twain's condemnation of Scott's alleged influence on the formation of character in the Old South (*Life on the Mississippi*), see G. Harrison Orians, "Walter Scott, Mark Twain, and the Civil War," *South Atlantic Quarterly*, 40 (1941), 342–59; Frank Luther Mott, *A History of American Magazines, 1741–1850* (Cambridge, MA, 1938), 178–9; also, Daniel Walker Howe, *The Unitarian Conscience: Harvard Moral Philosophy, 1805–1861* (Middletown, CT, 1988), 191. Rollin G. Osterweis argues for Scott's greater popularity in the South than in the North in his *Romanticism and Nationalism in the Old South* (Baton Rouge, LA, 1971), ch. 4, but see Perry Miller, *The Raven and the Whale: The War of Words and Wits in the Era of Poe and Melville* (New York, 1956), 28, 34. Southerners nonetheless did not let Scott escape without literary and political criticism. In 1813, John Randolph of Roanoke sneered that Scott's later work was "beneath criticism": Hugh A. Garland, *The Life of John Randolph of Roanoke*, 2 vols. (New York, 1969 [1859]), 2:21; "A Citizen of Alabama", "Henry W. Longfellow and His Writings," *DBR*, 26 (Apr. 1859), 363. George Fitzhugh slighted Scott in "Ancient and Modern Art and Literature," 82; see also Henry Young Webb Diary, May 2, 1843, at UNC-SHC.

[27] J. H. Bocock, "The Martyrs of Scotland and Sir Walter Scott," *SPR*, 10 (1858), 75; [Bocock], "The Reformation in England," *SPR*, 7 (1858), 175; *contra* Bocock see "Letters and Speeches of Oliver Cromwell," *SPR*, 1 (1847), 127; *ERD*, Jan. 15, 1864 (3:308), Sept. 2, 1861 (2:120–1). Jasper Adams, "Sermon Notes," in Daniel L. Dreisbach, ed., *Religion and Politics in the Early Republic: Jasper Adams and the Church–State Debate* (Lexington, KY, 1996), 100–1; Jasper Adams, *Elements of Moral Philosophy* (Philadelphia, 1837), 183–4, 345; Russell Kirk cited in George M. Curtis III and James J. Thompson, Jr., eds., *The Southern Essays of Richard M. Weaver* (Indianapolis, IN, 1987), 211. Southern reviewers displayed a critical temper while they honored Scott in the fullest measure: Grace Warren Landrum, "Sir Walter Scott and His Literary Rivals in the Old South," *American Literature*, 2 (1930), 258; Hayne, "Ante-Bellum Charleston," 266–7. See the arresting treatment of Scott's influence in Thomas E. Jenkins, *The Character of God: Recovering the Lost Literary Power of American Protestantism* (New York, 1997).

Like Scott, Oliver Goldsmith, the eighteenth-century poet, playwright, and historian, remained a great favorite into the nineteenth century in part for his moralism. Parson Weems easily sold *The Vicar of Wakefield* and other "uplifting" fiction in the South during 1795–1820. In 1839, Francis W. Pickens, a future governor of South Carolina, recommended it in an address to upcountry students. Mary Moragné immediately read it – in French translation – and found it "the only novel I know from which one can say he has received no bad impression." Fitzhugh, Simms, the Reverend John Girardeau, and Thomas Dabney were among Goldsmith's most vocal admirers, and for readers like Catherine Edmonston, Rachel Mordecai, and Mary Howard Schoolcraft, Goldsmith approached perfection: a historian and novelist who portrayed the elite and the common man in a manner that reinforced essential southern values, disdain for egalitarianism, and sympathy for the poor driven from the land in England and Ireland. Presenting hierarchy as the natural state of humanity, Scott and Goldsmith decried abuses of power and cruelty to working people while they depicted a world in which servants – like peasants, laborers, and even yeomen farmers – knew their place and respected their "betters." The deceptive social calm of that world appealed to Southerners and reinforced their distaste for bourgeois society and its burgeoning discourse of social equality. Southerners found in eighteenth-century novels a reassuring, if usually unintentional, endorsement of the superiority of slave society. But they also approved writers of a reformist bent, notably the Irish novelist and essayist Maria Edgeworth, and every bit as much as Northerners did, for purveying sound morals. On Edgeworth such habitual opponents as Thomas Jefferson, John Randolph, and John Quincy Adams agreed, and later admirers ran the gamut from the Presbyterian Reverend Moses Hoge to Lucian Minor, professor of law at the University of Virginia, to Alfred Mordecai, to the South Carolina matron who had a complete set of Edgeworth's works. But Edgeworth's novels carried a special lesson for Southerners who, like Tally Simpson, a Confederate soldier, were moved by her fictional depictions of the misery of the Irish countryside.[28]

Southerners read Edgeworth's scathing protests against the exploitation of rural workers in *Castle Rackrent* as confirmation that their own social system provided greater security to slaves than tenancy had provided to Irish peasants – a reading that must have appalled Edgeworth. Indeed, together with British parliamentary reports on labor conditions and the writings of European Tories and Socialists, a

---

[28] Sallie Bird to Saida Bird, Mar. 2, 1862, in John Rozier, ed., *The Granite Farm Letters: The Civil War Correspondence of Edgeworth and Sallie Bird* (Athens, GA, 1988), 68; Camilla Hardin to William Hardin, Nov. 3, 1862, loc. cit., 174; Elizabeth Silverthorne, *Plantation Life in Texas* (College Station, TX, 1986), 181; Leary, *Book-Peddling Parson,* 4; Moragné Journal, June 29, 1839, in Craven, ed., *Neglected Thread,* 138; George A. Blackburn, ed., *Sermons by John L. Girardeau* (Columbia, SC, 1907), 241; George Fitzhugh, "Oliver Goldsmith and Doctor Johnson," *DBR,* 28 (1860), 508; [William Gilmore Simms], "Critical Notices," *SQR,* n.s., 2 (1850), 247; on Simms's laughter see Hayne, "Ante-Bellum Charleston," 262. *Plantation Life: Narratives of Schoolcraft,* 186 n. 250; Smedes, *Memorials of a Southern Planter,* 81; Rachel Mordecai to Maria Edgeworth, June 24, 1827, in Edgar E. MacDonald, *The Education of the Heart: The Correspondence of Rachel Mordecai Lazarus and Maria Edgeworth* (Chapel Hill, NC, 1977), 129. See also Supplementary References: "Goldsmith."

galaxy of reform-minded nineteenth-century British and French novelists found a
place in southern hearts for their exposés of the oppression and misery of working
people. Edmund Ruffin of Virginia, Eliza Frances Andrews of Georgia, and George
Sawyer of Louisiana, among others, admired Mrs. Gaskell's novels, in particular
Mary Barton, for their delineations of character, vivid treatment of commonplace
incidents, and illumination of community life as well as for their exposure of British
labor conditions. Mrs. Gaskell's disgust at the plight of industrial workers and un-
wed mothers deeply impressed Southerners.[29]

The social criticism in the novels of Charles Dickens attracted wide southern interest, notwithstanding his unflattering picture of American life in *American Notes,*
for which southern ladies of the 1850s in Washington – according to Mary Gay's retrospective – were "cordially hating" Dickens. Letitia Burwell of Virginia dismissed
the distortions in *American Notes* and *Martin Chuzzlewit* as the result of Dickens's
unfamiliarity with the South. *Southern Quarterly Review* treated Dickens harshly,
for it had expected much better from a man whose social criticism it found praiseworthy. It deplored his bias against things American, noting with displeasure his
chapter on slavery, which was based on a brief trip that took him no further south
than Richmond. "Laon" excoriated Dickens in *Southern Literary Messenger* for
the "willful malignity" of *American Notes,* but such criticism provoked a reaction
from those, most notably John Esten Cooke, who regarded Dickens as a great novelist and rejected subordination of literature to politics.[30]

[29] Maria Edgeworth, *Castle Rackrent,* ed. Marilyn Butler (New York, 1993 [1800]). Aug. 20, 1861, in
      William M. Mathew, ed., *Agriculture, Geology, and Society in Antebellum South Carolina: The Pri-
      vate Diary of Edmund Ruffin* (Athens, GA, 1992), 109; Dec. 24, 1865, in Eliza Frances Andrews,
      War-Time Journal of a Georgia Girl (New York, 1907), 39; George S. Sawyer, *Southern Institutes;
      Or, an Inquiry into the Origin and Early Prevalence of Slavery and the Slave Trade* (New York, 1967
      [1858]), 264. Sawyer picked up Gaskell from a reference in Cobden's *White Slaves of England.* On
      Edgeworth see Jefferson to Cornelia Jefferson Randolph, June 3, 1811, and Martha Jefferson Ran-
      dolph to Thomas Jefferson, Nov. 24, 1808, in Edwin Morris Betts and James Adam Bear, Jr., eds.,
      The Family Letters of Thomas Jefferson (Columbia, MO, 1966), 401, 362. Dumas Malone, *Jefferson
      and His Time,* 6 vols. (Boston, 1962–81), 6:188; Russell Kirk, *John Randolph of Roanoke: A Study
      in American Politics, with Selected Speeches and Letters* (Chicago, 1964), 21, 37, 248, 442, 491; Paul
      C. Nagel, *John Quincy Adams: A Public Life, a Private Life* (New York, 1997), 230; Peyton Harri-
      son Hoge, *Moses Drury Hoge: Life and Letters* (Richmond, VA, 1899), 30; James Russell Lowell,
      ed., "A Virginian in New England Thirty-Five Years Ago," *Atlantic Monthly,* 16 (1870), 164; [Lucien
      Minor], "Alfred Mordecai Memoir," in Jacob Rader Marcus, ed., *Memoirs of American Jews,* 3 vols.
      (Philadelphia, 1955), 1:220; Caroline Couper Lovell, *The Light of Other Days* (Macon, GA, 1995),
      16; Tally Simpson to Caroline Miller, Feb. 5, 1863, in Guy R. Everson and Edward W. Simpson, Jr.,
      eds., *"Far, Far from Home": The Wartime Letters of Dick and Tully Simpson, Third South Carolina
      Volunteers* (New York, 1994), 185. Reactions against the novels of Bulwer-Lytton, Dickens, Dumas,
      and others also marked the religious press of the Northwest – without the southern emphasis on the
      evils of free labor: see Wesley Norton, *Religious Newspapers in the Old Northwest to 1861: A His-
      tory, Bibliography, and Record of Opinion* (Athens, OH, 1977), 73–5.
[30] Mary A. H. Gay, *Life in Dixie during the War,* 5th ed. (Atlanta, GA, 1979 [1897]), 83; Letitia A. Bur-
      well, *A Girl's Life in Virginia before the War,* 2nd ed. (New York, 1895), 132; "Dickens' American
      Notes," *SQR,* 3 (1843), 166–82; "Charles Dickens," *SQR,* 3 (1843), 431–48; "Laon" [of Columbia,
      SC], *SLM,* 9 (1843), 61; [John Esten Cooke], "A Letter about Dickens and Thackeray," *SLM,* 20

Although Southerners were less enthralled by Dickens than Northerners, they, too, feted him lavishly, and adoring crowds followed him through the streets. Emily Wharton Sinkler, born in Philadelphia but married into an elite South Carolina planter family, found Charlotte Brontë's *Jane Eyre* far superior to *Dombey and Son*, but she enjoyed Elizabeth Gaskell's *North and South* and its exposure of industrial conditions. Dickens's novels convinced Mary Middleton and her daughter, Eliza Middleton Fisher, that English laborers fared much worse than southern slaves, and Mary Chesnut evoked the characters in Dickens's *Old Curiosity Shop* to remind abolitionists that, in free-labor societies, masters and mistresses mistreat servants. *Nicholas Nickelby,* which bared the despair of lower-class life in England to young ladies like Letitia Burwell, had the advantage of lending itself to being read aloud in family circles. Louisa McCord and De Bow, among others, drew upon *Bleak House* for ammunition in their proslavery polemics, but not every proslavery intellectual approved their tactics. The Baptist Reverend William Richards, who edited secular journals, scathingly reviewed Dickens's assault on slavery in *American Notes,* countering that the black slaves of the South lived immeasurably better than the white wage slaves of Britain. Simms, too, poured contempt over Dickens for absorption with the life of the degraded and vicious, which made him a specialist on people of "lowly habits, low virtues and low vice," and the eminent scientist Joseph LeConte criticized Dickens's later novels as excessively didactic, complaining that *Bleak House* and *Little Dorritt* preached social reform in a manner that undercut their aesthetic power.[31]

Charles Kingsley, the Christian socialist influenced by Carlyle, had warm supporters among southern slaveholders. Elizabeth Allston said that his novels on the English poor had "done more to strengthen my faith in Slavery than anything else could have done." Every society must have its rich and poor; slavery, "a divine institution," was surely preferable to the wage-labor system. Citing Kingsley's *Yeast* and *Alton Locke,* as well as his poems, on the cruelty suffered by the laboring classes of England, Mary Chesnut concluded that all laborers, slave and free,

(1854), 469–70. "E. G." subsequently attacked Dickens's antislavery, referring to him as "the incarnation of cockney sentiment": "Slavery in the Southern States," *SQR,* 8 (1845), 322.

31 Emily Wharton Sinkler to Henry Wharton, Jan. 29, 1855, in Anne Sinkler Whaley LeClerq, ed., *Between North and South: The Letters of Emily Wharton Sinkler, 1842–1865* (Columbia, SC, 2001), 189; Burwell, *Girl's Life in Virginia,* 28; also, Harriet R. Palmer Diary, Feb. 6, 1863, in Towles, ed., *World Turned Upside Down,* 357; "Slavery and Political Economy," in Richard C. Lounsbury, ed., *Louisa S. McCord: Political and Social Essays* (Charlottesville, VA, 1995), 332–433; [De Bow], *DBR,* 13 (1852), 106; [Simms], "Critical Notices," *SQR,* n.s., 9 (1854), 224–8, quote at 225; also, Simms to the Editor of the *Magnolia Weekly,* Apr. 1863, in Mary C. Oliphant et al., eds., *The Letters of William Gilmore Simms,* 6 vols. (Columbia, SC, 1952–82), 4:428–9; Joseph LeConte, "On the Nature and Uses of Art," *SPR,* 15 (1863), 339–40. Dickens won plaudits, too, for his journal *Household Words,* primarily for its social criticism. In 1855 it serialized Elizabeth Cleghorn Gaskell's *North and South,* which focused on industrial conditions in Manchester. Emily Wharton Sinkler, for one, "enjoyed it exceedingly." Simms spoke well of its scientific material, and T. R. R. Cobb found valuable material on Polish slavery in it: *An Inquiry into the Law of Negro Slavery in the United States* (New York, 1968 [1858]), cxvii. See also Supplementary References: "Dickens."

suffered oppression. Edmund Ruffin called *Alton Locke* "a remarkable book" for its powerful indictment of the sufferings of the English poor – "their subjection to the worst evils of what I call hunger-slavery – or the slavery of labor to capital." Simms found Kingsley too much caught up in reformist fads but commendably audacious in his assaults on contemporary immoralities. He saw brilliance in *Alton Locke* but considered it greatly impaired by quasi-communist ideology and Chartist politics. *Alton Locke*'s Arminianism did not upset Simms or broad-church Episcopalians like Edmund Ruffin and Mary Chesnut, but *Princeton Review,* speaking for Calvinists, objected to "a book that exhibits almost as great a dread of Calvinism as it does of physical evil." Louisa McCord considered Kingsley "well-meaning but mischievous" and something of a "quack." When Sara Dickson discerned Kingsley's opposition to slavery, she protested in *Russell's Magazine*: "We have been taken in, we have been duped." He wallows in "silliness and mawkish sentiment." Kingsley did please race-conscious Southerners by promoting Anglo-Teutonic superiority in his best-selling *Roman and Teuton,* which contrasted vigorous northern races with the decadent Mediterraneans.[32]

After the death of Scott, Edward Bulwer (later, Bulwer-Lytton) swept the South, notwithstanding titillating newspaper reports of his marital scandals. Gentiles and Jews, unionists like William Hooper Haigh of Fayetteville, North Carolina, and state-rights radicals like Joseph Lyons of Columbia, South Carolina, were all captivated with Bulwer's novels. Edgar Allan Poe, however, blistered Bulwer as a corrupter of culture and predicted that his fame would evaporate. While Paul Hamilton

[32] Allston quoted in William Dusinberre, *Them Dark Days: Slavery in the American Rice Swamps* (New York, 1996), 357; Chesnut Diary, Nov. 25, 1861, May 13, 1862, June 14, 1862, in Woodward, ed., *Mary Chesnut's Civil War,* 243, 339, 394; [William Gilmore Simms], *SQR,* n.s., 9 (1854), 539–40; [Simms], "Critical Notices," *SQR,* n.s., 3 (1851), 289–90; *BRPR,* 23 (1851), 358. Simms, nonetheless, admired Kingsley and hoped to interest him in reviewing his poetry: Simms to Evert Augustus Duyckinck, Jan. 1, 1857, in Oliphant et al., eds., *Letters of Simms,* 3:487. In Lounsbury, ed., *Louisa S. McCord: Essays*: "Enfranchisement of Woman," 124, and "Negro and White Slavery," 187–202; [Sara I. Dickson], "Charles Kingsley's 'Two Years Ago,'" *RM,* 1 (1857), 169–74, quote at 169. *Southern Literary Messenger* acknowledged Kingsley's literary power and sincerity: *SLM,* 27 (1858), 398. Mary Jones Taylor of Maryland, from Georgia's renowned C. C. Jones family, found Kingsley's *Hypatia* "brilliant": Mary Jones Taylor to Mary Mallard, Sept. 14, 1858, in Robert Manson Myers, ed., *The Children of Pride: A True Story of the Children of the Civil War* (New Haven, CT, 1972), 443. Lucy Wood Butler and her female relatives in Charlottesville, Virginia, read Kingsley's *Sermons* together during the War and were "ready to proclaim Kingsley and his school as great reformers who throw aside the semblance of things and arrive at the very truth itself": L. W. Butler Diary, Nov. 29, 1862, at UNC-SHC. On Kingsley's racial views see Ivan Hannaford, *Race: The History of an Idea in the West* (Washington, DC, 1996), 248, 335, 345. That Kingsley's *Westward Ho!* had a strong bias against Catholic Spain did not hurt his standing among southern Protestants: Mar. 20, 1859, in *ERD,* 1:303, 2:500–1.

   Emily Wharton Sinkler complained to her brother about Charlotte Brontë's *Shirley*: "The meat is very strong and the Radicalism rather trop fort for me." Soon after the publication of the "pernicious" *Jane Eyre,* the schoolgirls of New Orleans and young ladies across the South were somehow getting copies and avidly reading a book their parents forbade them to read. Emily Wharton Sinkler to Mary Wharton, Feb. 26, 1848, and Sinkler to Henry Wharton, Jan. 31, 1850, in LeClerq, ed., *Between North and South,* 91, 107–8; Eliza Ripley, *Social Life in Old New Orleans: Being Recollections of My Girlhood* (New York, 1975 [1912]), 19–20. Some parents who barred *Jane Eyre* from home subscribed to *Harper's,* which serialized it.

Hayne proclaimed Bulwer's genius, certain that it would be sustained, E. A. Lynch of Virginia, like Poe, applauded Bulwer's genius but deplored the moral effect of his work. *Eugene Aram* did not entrance the Reverend Robert L. Dabney, who said it should have been entitled "Murder Made Amiable."[33]

Southern Literary Messenger, notwithstanding Poe's carping, published a glowing review of *Rienzi* as good history, and Francis Lieber, in his *Political Ethics,* quoted at length from *Rienzi* on the corruption of power. Many Southerners doubtless applauded Bulwer's political stance: "Democracy is like the grave – it perpetually cries, 'give,' 'give,' and, like the grave, it never returns what it has once taken." As time went on, Bulwer appeared to southern critics as a repentant sinner. John Reuben Thompson declared that in *What Will He Do with It* Bulwer emerged as "a great and constructive artist." For Mary Chesnut, *Richelieu* established "Bulwer's high place as an author!" Allowing that many of "Bulwer's earlier works are very reprehensible," Emma Holmes said, "None but a Christian could have written this tale, and I am convinced it embodies the struggles of his own soul to escape from the shackles of materialism & skepticism." Mary Moragné wrote of *Deveraux*: "What a lesson on human frailties it is!"[34]

On both sides of the Atlantic a problem gnawed at those who loved and appreciated the social value of literature, admiring artistic genius and yet worrying about the moral effects of the works that appealed to them aesthetically. For Southerners in a transatlantic world increasingly critical of slavery and slaveholders, the problem became acute in the nineteenth century. The problem: Despite good intentions, did not even the most socially critical novelists portray men, institutions, and social relations so graphically as to corrupt the morals of readers? *Southern Presbyterian Review,* chary of historical novels, complained that novels about the lower classes, even Dickens's, were generally vulgar. Hence, the writers Southerners most

---

[33] Haigh Diary, 1840s, at UNC-SHC; Haigh, after reading *Oxoniana,* waxed lyrical over tales of love and bad character: Jan. 21–22, 1844. Lyons in Marcus, ed., *Memoirs of American Jews,* 1:241; Landrum, "Scott's Literary Rivals," 270–1; Grace Warren Landrum, "Notes on Reading in the Old South," *American Literature,* 3 (1931), 67. C. Patterson praised Bulwer in "Effect of Circumstances on Character," *VUM,* 4 (1860), 194; [Paul Hamilton Hayne], "Bulwer and Dickens," *RM,* 1 (1857), 276–9; [Edgar Allan Poe], *SLM,* 1 (1834), 53–4; [Poe], "The Classics," *SLM,* 2 (1836), 222–3; E. A. Lynch, "Influence of Morals on the Happiness of Man," *SLM,* 4 (1838), 150–1; R. L. Dabney, "On Dangerous Reading," *DD,* 2:165. See also Supplementary References: "Bulwer."

[34] Eliza Middleton Fisher to Mary Herring Middleton, Oct. 4, 1839, in Eliza Cope Harrison, ed., *Best Companions: Letters of Elizabeth Middleton Fisher and Her Mother, Mary Herring Middleton, from Charleston, Philadelphia, and Newport, 1839–1846* (Columbia, SC, 2001), 74; *SLM,* 2 (1836), 197–200; Francis Lieber, *A Manual of Political Ethics* (London, 1819), 295; for the quote from Bulwer see Russell Kirk, *Redeeming the Time* (Wilmington, DE, 1998), 129. [J. R. Thompson], *SLM,* 28 (1859), 154–5; for different evaluations of *What Will He Do with It* as literary performance but agreement on its reformism see *SLM,* 29 (1859), 108–11, 212–19; also, "Schediasmata Critica," *SLM,* 16 (1850), 571–3; Chesnut Diary, Feb. 24, 1864, in Woodward, ed., *Mary Chesnut's Civil War,* 573; Mar. 4, 1863, in Marszalek, ed., *Emma Holmes Diary,* 235; Moragné Journal, Feb. 26, 1837, July 3, 1839, in Craven, ed., *Neglected Thread,* 26, 140; also, Green Diary, Nov. 29, 1864, in Bonner, ed., *Journal of a Milledgeville Girl,* 67.

admired did not escape stern rebuke. The Presbyterian Reverend A. F. Dickson captured a widespread concern, if in another context, by declaring: "The sensuous is the parent of the sensual." E. A. Lynch of Virginia criticized Alain René Lesage and Henry Fielding for inadvertently introducing youths to immorality.

Thomas Holcombe feared that even the great Johann Wolfgang von Goethe unintentionally promoted decadence by making it attractive. Augusta Jane Evans advised her friend Rachel Lyons, "Select the very highest types of character for the standard has sadly deteriorated of late in works of fiction .... In a too close imitation of Nature many of our novelists have fallen into the error of patronizing coarseness, vulgarity, and ignorance." Evans specifically reproached George Eliot, "because I think that its truth is strikingly exemplified in *Adam Bede* the most popular book of the age. The world needs elevating, and it is the peculiar province of the Novelist to present the very highest noble types of human nature." Still, a laudatory reviewer of Evans's *Beulah* worried that she, too, risked the promotion of the destructive doctrines she combated.[35]

Thomas De Quincy's *Confessions of an English Opium-Eater* met similar objections and much admiration, becoming a sought-after item in the libraries of college student societies. Mrs. Schoolcraft found *Confessions* morally uplifting, as did Benjamin Johnson Barbour in a speech to the cadets at VMI, but Edmund Ruffin and the editors of *Russell's Magazine* feared that DeQuincy was doing more to promote opium addiction than to fight it. Indeed, Lucy Breckenridge said that reading De Quincy "makes me long for a dose of laudanum." Since a good many southern ladies used laudanum, we may safely conclude that she was not merely speaking for herself. Such responses betrayed conflicted reactions to the growing interest in subjectivity that was assuming an increasingly important place in British and Northern American fiction. Southerners might have been shocked to find themselves viewed as latter-day representatives of the sensibilities of oral rather than

---

[35] *SPR*, 1 (1847), 151–2; *SPR*, n.s., 9 (1854), 224–8; [A. F. Dickson], "Life and Times of Bertrand de Guesclin," *SPR*, 16 (1866), 382; Lynch, "Influence of Morals on the Happiness of Man," 420 (Lynch included Bulwer and Byron as corruptors of morals: 276–80); Thomas B. Holcombe, "Moral Tendency of Goethe's Writing," *SLM*, 22 (1856), 187–8; Augusta Jane Evans to Rachel Lyons, Nov. 15, 1860, in Rebecca Grant Sexton, ed., *A Southern Woman of Letters: The Correspondence of Augusta Jane Evans Wilson* (Columbia, SC, 2002); "Beulah," *SLM*, 31 (1860), 247–8. William Elliott admired Fielding and Smollet, but he caviled at their vulgarity and offenses against decency: [Elliott], "Anne of Geierstein; or The Maiden of the Mist," *SR*, 4 (1829), 499. In contrast, Wade Keyes cited Fielding's politeness: *Wade Keyes' Introductory Lecture to the Montgomery Law School: Legal Education in Mid-Nineteenth Century Alabama* (Tuscaloosa, AL, 2001 [1860]), 35. *Southern Literary Messenger* recommended Fielding's *Tom Jones* as an invaluable account of social history: *SLM*, 26 (1858), 257.

On Sand see also David Outlaw to Emily Outlaw, Feb. 2 and Aug. 30, 1850, at UNC-SHC. William Alexander Percy reported that his slaveholding ancestor in Mississippi had the novels of Georges Sand but kept them away from his children: Percy, *Lanterns on the Levee: Recollections of a Planter's Son* (Baton Rouge, LA, 1973), 7. George Bancroft, who met Goethe in Germany, spoke of him more harshly than Southerners did. Bancroft thought him a genius but was repelled by the "indecency and immorality" in his work, which was "too dirty and too bestial in its conceptions." See O. W. Long, "Goethe and Bancroft," *Studies in Philology*, 28 (1931), 289; also, Lillian Handlin, *George Bancroft: The Intellectual as Democrat* (New York, 1986), 59.

literate culture, but many did sharply define heroes and villains that typically characterize oral cultures.[36]

From the 1820s onward, Benjamin Disraeli emerged as a focus of controversy. Philip Pendleton Cooke thought Disraeli had one of the world's most gifted minds, but William Hutson and the editor of *Southern Quarterly Review* thought he was writing fiction to promote his politics and nostalgia for feudalism. Rachel Mordecai, while admiring Disraeli's talent, complained to Maria Edgeworth that his novels were morally objectionable. James Walker, a prominent Charleston lawyer who reviewed Disraeli's *The Young Duke* for *Southern Review*, seized the opportunity to indict capitalist exploitation, depicting the sufferings of British laborers as much worse than anything experienced by southern slaves and denouncing the extravagance, luxury, and decadence of the British aristocracy and big bourgeoisie. Simms considered Disraeli's rosy picture of feudal times applicable to the South: "Ours is in truth not so much slavery as feudality." William Thackeray's novels enjoyed extraordinary popularity, reinforced by immensely successful lecture tours and personal connections in Charleston and elsewhere. John Reuben Thompson, the editor of *Southern Literary Messenger,* extolled Thackeray's presentation of the unpleasant side of social life in a constructive, morally wholesome manner. "No production of the day," De Bow wrote of *The Virginians* in the late 1850s, "has been more widely read in this country, and there are few writers more popular among us." But while admirers in New Orleans and Washington were reveling in it, Virginians were roiling. *Southern Literary Messenger* declared itself "out of patience" with *The Virginians* and ran a series of pieces that chastised its historical errors and misrepresentations.[37]

A sense of propriety demanded stern rejection of French novels, which when not blasphemous were likely to be sensual, coarse, outlandish: in a word, vulgar.

---

[36] *Southern Quarterly Review* praised De Quincy on several occasions, hailing his "genius" and recommending his works: *SQR*, n.s., 9 (1854), 538, and 10 (1854), 243, 521. On the popularity of *Confessions* see *DBR*, 15 (1853), 646, and 16 (1854), 334; [John R. Thompson], *SLM*, 21 (1855), 520; *Plantation Life: Narratives of Schoolcraft*, 497, and "Letters on the Condition of the African Race," Appendix, 19. Benjamin Johnson Barbour, "Address Delivered before the Literary Societies of the Virginia Military Institute," *SLM*, 20 (1854), 520–1; [Editor's Table], *RM*, 2 (1857/58), 382; Dec. 2, 1862, in *ERD*, 2:500–1; July 2, 1863, Apr. 24, Sept. 18, 1864, in Robertson, ed., *Lucy Breckenridge*, 122, 177, 197; *SQR*, n.s., 9 (1854), 538, and 10 (1854), 243, 521.

[37] Philip Pendleton Cooke, "Living Novelists," *SLM*, 13 (1847), 745; [William F. Hutson], "Fictitious Literature," *SPR*, 1 (1847), 66–78; *SQR*, 8 (1846), 513–16; Rachel Mordecai to Maria Edgeworth, Apr. 23, 1827, in MacDonald, *Education of the Heart*, 292; [James A. Walker], "The Distribution of Wealth," *SR*, 8 (1831), 171–92; [William Gilmore Simms?], *SWMR*, 2 (1845), 284–5. For *The Young Duke*'s "high favor in aristocratic circles" in Virginia, see *Marion Harland's Autobiography: The Story of a Life* (New York, 1910), 242. William Plumer Jacobs, Mary Chesnut, and Mary E. Moragné, among others, read Disraeli's work but left no clue to their attitude toward it. See Mar. 2 and July 11, 1858, in Thornwell Jacobs, ed., *Diary of William Plumer Jacobs, 1842–1917* (Atlanta, GA, 1937), 20, 24; also, George D. Martin to Susan Henry, Sept. 29, 1854, in Gustavus A. Henry Papers, at UNC-SHC. A. A. Smets, a wealthy Savannah merchant, purchased all of Disraeli's works: *DBR*, 13 (1852), 97.

For Thackeray: [J. R. Thompson], *SLM*, 15 (1849), 699–701; "Editorial Miscellany," *DBR*, 28 (1860), 122; *SLM*, 26 (1858), 75–7, 152–3, and 29 (1859), 475; "Thackeray's Miscellanies," *SLM*, 24 (1857), 151–8. See also Supplementary References: "Thackeray."

Refined gentlemen and especially ladies turned away in disgust, although the more sophisticated – like William Hooper Haigh, a young lawyer in Fayetteville, North Carolina – kept reading them. Exuding innocence, Agnes Ruffin wrote her father, Edmund Ruffin: "I have read one of the French novels, it is very different from any novel I ever read, more like history than anything else: are all the French novels written in that manner?" When Lucy Breckenridge wished to explain her displeasure with *The Confessions of a Pretty Woman* by the popular English novelist Julia Pardoe, she muttered, "I do not like it at all thus far. It is too much like French novels." John Reuben Thompson attacked Victor Hugo, Eugene Sue, and Georges Sand as decadent purveyors of immorality, while confessing admiration for their literary talents. LeConte, who wrote on aesthetics as well as science, reversed the usual complaint by finding much of French literature coldly rationalistic.[38]

Sue ranked high among French novelists who were roundly condemned and widely read. Hutson rebuked Sue and other recent writers for making evil characters attractive, even as he defended Daniel Defoe, Samuel Richardson, Tobias Smollett, and Henry Fielding. Haigh condemned *The Wandering Jew,* as well as *Matilda,* which celebrated Parisian high life and female infidelity. Catherine Edmonston denounced Sue as "a Radical, a red Republican, an admirer of the French revolution" and a man with "impossible theories." Trescot assured William Porcher Miles that he deplored Sue's "voluptuousness" and damned his book, but he still thought "It had a moral." Although *Southern Quarterly Review* welcomed Sue's *The Mysteries of Paris: Romance of Rich and Poor* for its picture of the moral decadence of free society, it repeatedly protested Sue's raw depictions of an unpleasant reality as offensive to American tastes and unlikely to teach balanced lessons. Sue's horror stories, replete with details that attracted prurient interest, should be kept away from children and the pious. One reviewer took the *Mysteries of Paris* as an opportunity to deplore the condition of the victims of the free-labor system, insisting that social and political radicalism provided no remedy; another found in the "splendid" *Wandering Jew* high moral lessons in its depiction of an unpleasant reality. In the 1850s, President William Carey Crane of Mississippi College (for women) assailed *Mysteries of Paris* for encouragement of moral degeneracy, noting that it was widely read and imitated, and Henry Watkins Miller of North Carolina's General Assembly told students at the state university to reject "Sue and his pestiferous imitators – whose productions creep through the social circle, leaving the track of their moral slime."[39]

---

[38] Haigh Diary, 1844; Agnes Ruffin to Edmund Ruffin, Oct. 17, 1833, in Edmund Ruffin Papers, at UNC-SHC; Oct. 9, 1862, in Robertson, ed., *Lucy Breckenridge,* 60; [John R. Thompson], *SLM,* 16 (1850), 638, and 20 (1854), 317–18; Joseph LeConte, "On the Nature and Uses of Art," *SPR,* 15 (1863), 321, 334. See also Sept. 20, 1862, and Jan. 1864, in Marszalek, ed., *Diary of Emma Holmes,* 200, 334.

[39] [Hutson], "Fictitious Literature," 57–78; Haigh Diary, Mar. 23 and May 16, 1844; June 12, 1863, in Beth G. Crabtree and James W. Patton, eds., *"Journal of a Secesh Lady": The Diary of Catherine Devereux Edmonston, 1860–1866* (Raleigh, NC, 1979), 406–7; Trescot to Miles, May 16, 1849, in W. P. Miles Papers, at UNC-SHC. For criticism of Sue, including *Wandering Jew,* see also [William Gilmore Simms?], *SWMR,* 2 (1845), 282–4; *SQR,* 5 (1844), 257–8, 497–516, quote at 504; also *SQR,* 8 (1845), 263, 517–18; Henry W. Miller, *Address Delivered before the Philanthropic and Dialectic*

Georges Sand's popularity came as a particularly bitter pill. In 1850, Representative David Outlaw of North Carolina found the overt sexuality in one of her novels "horrible and revolting." He could not believe that a woman could write such a book: "She is one of those monstrosities, in the shape of a woman, who sets at defiance all the rules of society, and those restraints which have been imposed upon the female sex for their own good." John Reuben Thompson would not think of giving a novel by Sand to a young lady. Yet Mary Chesnut read Sand's *Consuelo* without fuming, although her friend Louisa McCord referred to "the degraded but brilliant Georges Sand, bold in her impudence and her talent," who "often competes in obscenity with the nauseous filth spewed forth, as though with devilish scorn, by her compatriots, a Sue and a Dumas upon a community sufficiently degraded to admire them."[40]

Victor Hugo had a particularly strong if conflicted southern following despite his unwelcome religious heterodoxy. William J. Grayson, who considered *Les Misérables* the most powerful work of fiction since Scott, pronounced Hugo "a prodigious genius" and "a Titan, the more conspicuous among a generation of pigmies." Howard Caldwell, reviewing Hugo's career and works, applauded a great poet who wasted his talents on morally corrupting novels and political and ideological highjinks. "T. W. M.", in *Southern Literary Messenger,* described Hugo as a misguided heretic who plunged into abolitionism and radical projects but nonetheless deserved his fame. Whatever Lilliputian critics may say, his work is a "sublime protest" against the vices he describes.[41]

Societies of the University of North-Carolina, June 3, 1857 (Raleigh, NC, 1857), 17–18; William Carey Crane, *Literary Discourses* (New York, 1853), 94–5. For Sue's *Mysteries of Paris* and *Wandering Jew in America,* see Frank Luther Mott, *Golden Multitudes: The Story of Best Sellers in the United States* (New York, 1947), 307; for his popularity with the French in New Orleans see Feb. 4, 21, 22, 1865, in Michael Bedout Chesson and Leslie Jean Roberts, eds., *Exile in Richmond: The Confederate Journal of Henri Garidel* (Charlottesville, VA, 2001), 307, 325, 327. The Paris correspondent for *Southern Literary Messenger* cast a sigh of relief when the monarchist turned "Socialist" Sue turned out to be a timid and ineffective politician during the critical days of 1850: [William W. Mann], "From Our Paris Correspondent," *SLM,* 16 (1850), 466–97. The Methodist Bishop James O. Andrew simply reported that he had read Sue without respect: "Travels in the West," in *Miscellanies,* 48.

40 David Outlaw to Emily Outlaw, Feb. 2 and Aug. 30, 1850; [John R. Thompson], *SLM,* 17 (1851), 702; Chesnut Diary, May 6, 1862, in Woodward, ed., *Mary Chesnut's Civil War,* 333; "Enfranchisement of Woman," in Lounsbury, ed., *McCord: Essays,* 133, 187, 342. Henri Garidel of New Orleans, a Catholic, found Sand "blasphemous": Nov. 16, 1864, in Chesson and Roberts, eds., *Exile in Richmond,* 233. Mary Herring Middleton of Charleston raised no objection when her young daughter reported reading Alexandre Dumas's *Jeanne d'Arc* at school in Philadelphia: Eliza Middleton Fisher to Mary Herring Middleton, Jan. 5, 1844, in Harrison, ed., *Best Companions,* 350. Simms quoted Dumas favorably for his opposition to the corruption of Louis Philippe's regime: [Simms], "Guizot's Democracy in France," *SQR,* 15 (1849), 148.

41 Hayne, "Ante-Bellum Charleston," 335 (Grayson); [Howard H. Caldwell], "Victor Hugo," *RM,* 1 (1857), 259–71; "T. W. M.", "Les Miserables," *SLM,* 37 (1863), 434–46, 493–510, quote at 445; Elizabeth Pringle simply declared Hugo's *Les Travailleurs de la Mer* a "masterpiece": Elizabeth W. Allston Pringle, *Chronicles of Chicora Wood* (New York, 1976), 325. David Macrae, *Americans at Home* (New York, 1952 [1870]), 139. *Southern Literary Messenger* published translations of Hugo's short poems: Mary E. M. Hewitt, "Translations from the French of Victor Hugo," *SLM,* 11 (1845), 47, 118, and [Mary Bayard Devereux Clarke], tr., *SLM,* 32 (1861), 126, 146, 334–5. Hugo moved away

How were slaveholders to respond to Hugo and others who directed powerful social criticism at the misery and degradation in free-labor societies? Some applauded their exposure of the evils; some protested against their moral degeneracy or their encouragement of destructive political and religious radicalism; some tried to do both. Hugo's plays evoked a restrained but telling rebuke from a critic who, acknowledging his genius, complained that his fixation on the exciting and the unnatural was having a doleful influence on modern tastes. Hugo's work evoked pain and revulsion rather than pathos, for, despite moments of power and beauty, its "monstrous and absurd exaggeration" disfigured much of the rest. Catherine Edmonston damned *Les Misérables* as "vulgar" and as a "coarse, radical, & unprincipled" attempt to place responsibility for all human faults and frailty on "Society," and she could not "interest myself in the adventures of an ignorant convict & a Parisian grisette." Anna Maria Green of Milledgeville, Georgia, "could not enjoy this book it was too horrible," but she thought it "calculated to do much good, especially in Europe." Green, who shared Edmonston's political and social views but not her political discernment, looked forward to a revolution against oppressive conditions in Europe.[42]

George Frederick Holmes spoke up for those who rejected the appeal to social realism. He insisted that while fiction may appropriately expose the grossness in society, it must ennoble and instill virtue and morals. Holmes accused Sue of "false philosophical views," of "profligacy and libertinism," of pandering to "the vilest lusts and passions of the most degraded and contemptible of men" in the guise of social criticism, and of propagating the philosophy of Voltaire, D'Alembert, and especially Rousseau, which had engendered the horrors of the Terror. A celebration of radical Enlightenment views crossed the line, negating any acceptable moral and political instruction.[43]

Slaveholders and most southern readers approved criticisms of the new industrial order and of the plight of working people in particular; they did not approve the radical political sentiments that informed them. Here they faced a central issue: Were the villains of the new industrial order simply an old evil in new guise or were they truly something new under the sun? Did the changes of their time represent just one more cyclical turn or rather a linear change – the vaunted "progress" that from their perspective was threatening declension rather than improvement?

Great historians whom Southerners found intellectually riveting but morally and politically dubious demonstrated to them the tension between the demand that

from Christian orthodoxy, repudiating original sin along with much else and viewing Jesus as an anticlerical moral teacher.

42 "Victor Hugo's 'Les Burgraves,'" *SQR*, 6 (1844), 75–95, esp. 78, 94–9; Edmonston Diary, June 12, 1863, in Crabtree and Patton, eds., *"Journal of a Secesh Lady,"* 406–94; Green Diary, Jan. 30, 1864, in Bonner, ed., *Journal of a Milledgeville Girl*, 46. During the War, *Les Miserables* squeezed past the Yankee blockade to the delight of the Confederate troops, who could not resist translating it into "Lee's Miserables." Southerners had widely divergent views on the theater – a subject to which we shall return in a future volume – but criticism focused on its morally deleterious effects, a criticism parallel to that directed against overly explicit novels. See also Supplementary References: "Balzac."
43 [George Frederick Holmes], "The Wandering Jew," *SQR*, 9 (1846), 73–114, esp. 77.

history provide moral and political instruction and that it be empirically sound. Niccolò Machiavelli and David Hume enjoyed pride of place. Machiavelli struck many as the very embodiment of political cynicism and Hume as the progenitor of modern religious skepticism, although Southerners acknowledged the superiority of both men's historical writings. Espying amorality in the ever-problematic Machiavelli, some southern commentators gave him short shrift. Benjamin Faneuil Porter of Alabama spoke of "politicians famous for Machiavellian falsehoods and treachery," William Gordon McCabe of Virginia of the "tyrannical, treacherous and cruel" career of Philip II of Spain as illustrative of the "Machiavellian system." The Reverend John Adger of South Carolina held Machiavelli responsible not only for the sins of Philip II but of "all European statesmen of that day." The historian Robert Reid Howison of Virginia added a swipe at Macaulay for whitewashing Machiavelli – that "open and unscrupulous advocate of national knavery."[44]

Yet John Francis Mercer of Maryland protested that tyrants and their flatterers hated Machiavelli for having told the truth: "Machiavelli exposes the futility of an attempt to establish an aristocracy upon any other principles than the solid distinctions of property." Mercer's attitude of 1788 prefigured something of a Machiavelli revival in the nineteenth century. In 1822 William Somerville of Virginia cited Machiavelli's wisdom on the difficulties of effecting reforms, and in 1839 "W. R., Jr." of Lexington, Kentucky, fairly gushed over the republicanism, historical wisdom, and political genius displayed in the *Discourses on Livy,* applauding it for having replaced the obscurities of the history of the Roman Republic with a coherent analysis. Joseph B. Cobb, author of *Mississippi Scenes,* wrote of a Machiavelli "so uncharitably misinterpreted for generations past." In *Southern Literary Messenger,* Hugh Pleasants of Virginia rejected characterizations of Machiavelli as irreligious and a supporter of tyrants. To Pleasants, he was an admirable man and a staunch republican – a patriot, driven by his hatred of foreign rule and passion for Italian unification. Other prominent figures defended Machiavelli against the dangerous depiction of him as anti-Christian. At a meeting of historians in Georgia, Mitchell King explained Machiavelli's dictum that a historian should have neither religion nor country as meaning only that commitment to a creed or cause must not obscure the factual record. Historians, therefore, "will probably find it best to follow Machiavelli's rule" and proceed with "unwavering impartiality." Machiavelli himself attached no providential character to *Fortuna,* but his Christian admirers often interpreted it as the totality of externalities that men must master or succumb to, and that man had the God-given capacity to overcome it by an exercise of will – of *virtù.* Thus, the Presbyterian Reverend Thomas Smyth of Charleston, with cautious approbation, cited Machiavelli to argue that good government depended upon a religiously grounded public morality.[45]

44 Benjamin Faneuil Porter, *The Past and the Present* (Tuscaloosa, AL, 1845), 37; William Gordon McCabe, "William the Silent," *SLM,* 32 (1861), 290, and McCabe, "Political Corruption," *SLM,* 34 (1862), 81–2; [J. B. Adger], "Motley's Dutch Republic," *SPR,* 15 (1862), 106; Howison, *History of Virginia,* 1:94 n. b.
45 [John Francis Mercer?], "Essays by a [Maryland] Farmer," in Bruce Frohnen, ed., *The Anti-Federalists: Selected Writings and Speeches* (Washington, DC, 1999; originally published in the *Maryland Gazette,*

In 1857 Frederick Porcher of Charleston was impatient with critics who referred to Machiavelli more often than they read him. Porcher questioned the judgment of those who deplored Machiavelli's ethics without noting the accuracy of his historical analyses. Dew, too, cited Machiavelli as a reliable historian and interpreter of Florentine history, and, although without direct attribution, he echoed Machiavelli's critique of reliance upon mercenaries and standing armies rather than a popular militia. Dew, who thought it possible "for men to conquer their liberties too fast," assured his students that Machiavelli spoke the truth when he wrote that the cause of liberty sometimes required the shift of power to a single individual, and that Caesars and Bonapartes rode to power with the support of lower classes against the upper.[46]

The liberal Francis Lieber and the conservative George Frederick Holmes took similar positions when they joined the fray. Lieber pictured a much misunderstood and unfairly traduced Machiavelli as a historian with a "most uncommon and penetrating mind." Holmes regarded "the great Florentine" as an excellent historian and credited him with a noble heart and mind, an almost prescient instinct, and a love of liberty. For John Reuben Thompson, Machiavelli stood as "the greatest of all political authors, and the wisest of all statesmen." Most commentators concurred in praising Machiavelli as a great political philosopher as well as an authority on modern Italian history and military strategy and tactics, but they differed in assessments of his moral worth. They agreed that he compelled attention to the moral judgments that imparted meaning to an empirically accurate study of

Feb. 29 and Mar. 28, 1788), 565, 606; Somerville, *Letters from Paris*, 166, 189–90; "W. R.", Jr.", "Machiavelli's Political Discourses," *SLM*, 5 (1839), 819–26; Joseph B. Cobb, "Italian Literature," *QRMECS*, 9 (1855), 578; [Hugh R. Pleasants], "Machiavelli – The Prince," *SLM*, 12 (1846), 641–50; King, *Qualifications and Duties of an Historian*, 14; also, "W. R.", Jr.", "Machiavelli's Political Discourses," 824–5; *TSW*, 5:541–2. "W. R. H." invoked Machiavelli against the "spurious" claims of the Bishop of Rome to rule the Church: "Rome: Papal and Republican," *SLM*, 15 (1849), 547–51. For Providence and *Fortuna* see Vincenzo Cioffari, "Fortune, Fate, and Chance," *DHI*, 2:236.

In colonial times Machiavelli seems to have been more widely read in Virginia than in Charleston, where Guicciardini was in evidence. See Louis B. Wright, "The 'Gentleman's Library' in Early Virginia: The Literary Interests of the First Carters," *Huntington Library Quarterly*, 1 (1937/38), 26; Edgar Legare Pennington, "The Beginnings of the Library in Charles Town, South Carolina," *Proceedings of the American Antiquarian Society*, n.s., 44 (1934), 173. The occasional and passing references to Guicciardini did not rate him with the best historians of Greece and Rome: see e.g. [Daniel K. Whitaker], "English Views of the Literature and Literary Men, and of the Political and Domestic Character of the People of Ancient Greece and Rome," *SLJ*, 1 (1836), 427. But a writer in *Southern Presbyterian Review* referred to him as "the prince of Italian historians": *SPR*, 5 (1852), 456; also, [James Johnston Pettigrew], *Notes on Spain and the Spaniards in the Summer of 1850, with a Glance at Sardinia* (Charleston, SC, 1861), 331. The Baptist Reverend E. T. Winkler counted Guicciardini among those who "for good or evil" supported the "progress of pure democracy": Winkler, *An Address Delivered before the Philosophian and Adelphian Societies of Furman University* (Greenville, SC, 1853), 11.

46 Frederick A. Porcher, "The Nature and the Claims of Paradox," *RM*, 1 (1857), 483; Dew, *Digest*, 62, 89, 305–6, 434, quote at 477, on Florence see 405–6. Dew and others also knew Polybius' criticism of mercenaries, which doubtless influenced Machiavelli's: see e.g. Polybius, *Histories*, 1:Bk. 1, 65. Trescot may well have had Machiavelli in mind when he remarked that diplomacy requires the greatest possible concentration of power in the hands of an individual consistent with social safety: William Henry Trescot, *The Diplomacy of the Revolution: An Historical Study* (New York, 1852), 91.

history and approved of *Southern Review*'s reference to Machiavelli's "incomparable *Discourses*."[47]

In some respects, David Hume confronted Southerners with an even greater challenge. Hume's sympathy for the British monarchy and his religious and epistemological skepticism provoked consternation but not rejection of his historical writings. Dew deemed Hume's narrative of the English revolutions "exceedingly fascinating," "known to all," and extraordinarily influential. The best-educated Southerners read Hume's philosophical writings; many more read about them, especially in church periodicals; and yet many more read *History of England*. Reactions could be harsh, but for the most part they displayed a determination to distinguish between strengths and weaknesses and to acknowledge constructive contributions.[48]

So deeply did Southerners admire Hume's historical writing that they readily forgave his philosophical discourses and recommended his *History*. Samuel Henry Dickson of Charleston, an eminent physician and man of letters who admired Hume's "charming and elegant style," thought him a biased and unreliable historian, while Dr. R. D. Arnold, mayor of Savannah, extolling "the beauty of his style and the clearness of his narrative," advised his daughter Ellen to make it "your first historical book" on England. Benjamin Faneuil Porter, telling aspiring lawyers that moral quality took precedence over everything else in their profession, recommended Hume's *History of England* as second only to the Bible, to be followed by Cicero, Quintilian, and Edmund Burke. Even Mitchell King – who flayed Hume as a Tory, an "ingenious apologist" for the Stuarts, and a jaundiced commentator on the Puritans – declared unfeigned respect for Hume's great work. Joseph Atkinson added an assault on the "scurrilous merriment" in Hume's treatment of the Puritans, without noticing that Hume's main quarrel with the Puritans concerned their determination to change society according to the dictates of metaphysical speculation rather than to proceed through gradual reform. In retrospect, it is difficult to see much difference between the Southerners' view of the abolitionists and Hume's view of the Puritan regime as a republican military dictatorship designed to impose a revolutionary social and moral order.[49]

[47] *SR*, 8 (1832), 5 n.; Lieber, *Political Ethics*, 321–2 (Lieber also cited his own article on Machiavelli in the *Encyclopedia Americana*); [George Frederick Holmes], "Roman History," *SLM*, 12 (1846), 508, 510 (great Florentine); [G. F. Holmes], "Writings of Hugh Swinton Legaré," *SQR*, 9 (1846), 346–7; [G. F. Holmes], "Gibbon's Decline and Fall," *MMQR*, 4th ser., 10 (1856), 3, 28; [J. R. Thompson?], "Failure of Free Society," *SLM*, 21 (1855), 141; also, [Edward B. Bryan], "Political Philosophy of South Carolina," *SQR*, n.s., 10 (1854), 471. Bolingbroke – whom Southerners read, although more so in the early years of the nineteenth century than later – picked up from Machiavelli and had a strong influence in the South: see Joseph M. Isenberg, "Towards the Concurrent Majority: The Intellectual Development of Southern Constitutional Theory," paper presented at the Mid American History Conference (Fayetteville, AR), 1998. J. H. Merle D'Aubigné, whose history of the Reformation influenced educated southern Protestants, considered Machiavelli a "great historian" and one of "the most profound geniuses of Italy": *History of the Reformation of the Sixteenth Century*, 5 vols. (Rapidan, VA, n.d., reproduction of London edition of 1846), 69.
[48] Dew, *Digest*, 559.
[49] Samuel Henry Dickson, "Difficulties in the Way of the Historian," *SLM*, 12 (1846), 107; R. D. Arnold to Ellen Arnold, Nov. 5, 1849, in Richard H. Shryock, ed., *Letters of Richard D. Arnold, M.D., 1808–1876* (Durham, NC, 1929), 35; B. F. Porter, "The Utility, Studies, and Duties of the Profession of

The philosophically radical Thomas Jefferson and John Taylor of Caroline and the conservative Thomas Roderick Dew and William Henry Trescot all valued Hume's *History*. As a student, Jefferson, like Hamilton, had read it with enthusiasm, but he later complained to John Adams that it had done more than any other book "to sap the free principles of the English constitution than the largest standing army of which their patriot have been so jealous." Jefferson admired Hume's "fascinating style" but despised what he considered a consecration of the tyranny of kings. While extolling Thomas Paine's *Rights of Man,* Jefferson suggested circulation of an expurgated version of Hume's *History*. The histories of Hume and Gibbon, read through the eyes of Jefferson and Taylor, chronicled the cruelty and irrationalities of elites and the sufferings of the ruled. Taylor, who rejected ancient and medieval models of government as masks for tyranny and oppression, saw the British constitution as little more than a façade for class privileges that rested on deceit, fraud, and violence. He attacked the theory of checks and balances, asserting a perpetual war of classes and interests. "The moral qualities of human nature," he wrote, "are both good and evil." Aided by good government, men could exercise self-control and sound volition. Although hostile to Hume's politics, Taylor drew heavily on his analyses of the British aristocracy and the vicissitudes of political struggles in Poland, Venice, and elsewhere.[50]

Dew recognized Hume as a great historian but rejected his description of the history of religion as largely an account of "sick men's dreams"; Dew found compelling Hume's argument that polytheism arose naturally in the ancient world and that Jewish and Christian communities constantly struggled against backsliding. Dew directed his heaviest fire against Hume for misrepresentation of the reign of the Tudors, insisting that the reign of Henry VIII, although tyrannical, advanced "the great mass of the commonality." Hume was "almost culpably partial" to the Stuarts, whom Dew himself credited with spurring economic development and paving the way for substantial social advances.[51]

Hume's statism, most apparent in "The Idea of a Perfect Commonwealth," irritated Southerners. Hume preceded Jeremy Bentham in rejecting the natural-rights theory of property, for which he substituted the theory of property as a socially efficacious and proven human convention. A view of human nature that assumed everyone to be a knave out for his own interest led Hume to advocate a state strong enough to dole out a necessary measure of repression. In time Joseph Priestley and others followed Hume's lead, albeit with the radical twist that government

Law," *DBR*, 2 (1846), 150; King, *Qualifications and Duties of an Historian*, 15–16. Howison referred testily to Hume's "obtrusive love" of the Stuarts while nonetheless defending him against Macaulay's "unduly depressed" attack on Charles I: Howison, *History of Virginia*, 1:68, 257 n. a; [Joseph M. Atkinson], "The Puritans," *SPR*, 15 (1862), 253; and see Donald W. Livingston, *Hume's Philosophy of the Common Life* (Chicago, 1984), 318.

50 Jefferson to Adams, Nov. 25, 1816, in Lester J. Cappon, ed., *The Adams–Jefferson Letters: The Complete Correspondence between Thomas Jefferson and Abigail and John Adams*, 2 vols. (Chapel Hill, NC, 1959), 2:498–9; John Taylor, *An Inquiry into the Principles and Policy of the Government of the United States*, ed. Loren Baritz (Indianapolis, IN, 1919 [1814]), 58, 60, 63, 66, 70, 72 (words quoted), 85ff., 129 (on Paine), 220, 541–2.

51 Dew, *Digest*, 36, 59, pt. 2, ch. 8, quotes at 494, 509. See also Supplementary References: "English Revolutions."

should regulate property for the public welfare. William Paley, whose books were required reading in southern colleges, eschewed social radicalism but lent credence to Hume's notion that the state ought to have wide powers over property relations – a doctrine that doubtless appealed to Fitzhugh and Henry Hughes but caused shivers among the numerous southern advocates of limited government. Still, Hume's conservatism shone through his historical and political writing: He hated popular tribunals and religious fanaticism, preferred political moderation and reasonable compromise, forcefully upheld social order, and distinguished policy considerations from pretensions to scientific purity in political economy.[52]

As for the divines, they found distasteful Hume's religious skepticism and, in particular, his rejection of the intervention of Providence. Hume devoted "a great mind to the most destructive of systems," the Methodist Reverend David Seth Doggett said at Randolph-Macon College; he invested "infidelity with the garb of a profound, but false philosophy." The South's leading moral philosophers – the Episcopalian Jasper Adams, the Methodist R. H. Rivers, the Presbyterian William S. Plumer – assailed Hume as the fountainhead of Utilitarian morals. John Bocock charged Hume with celebrating "despotism" and "infidelity" and dismissed him as "an authority utterly worthless, indeed, on any religious question, except where he praises contrary to his own prejudices." Only a dullard could miss "the ever-visible leanings to despotism and to infidelity in Hume's History." But the Presbyterian Reverend Benjamin Morgan Palmer found a silver lining: While Hume, constructing "his fame as the Prince of Historians," sought to minimize religion, he – like Voltaire, Volney, and Paine – demonstrated its centrality. Thornwell savaged Hume on miracles and the argument from design but valued the powerful mind that put Christians on their mettle, "at once the indication and the cure of the disorder" of skepticism. While plunging into error, Hume exposed the weakness of prevalent philosophies. Thornwell recognized that Hume's attack on Christian doctrine flowed from his secularized version of human depravity and the prevalence of evil, his view that men could see God's goodness only through its historical manifestations, if any, and hence cannot know much about the future. But since Hume's epistemology and moral philosophy stressed the limits of reason apart from common human experience, southern conservatives could at least applaud the implicit defense of community prejudice and practical morality.[53]

52 For Hume, Priestly, and Paley on property theory and for Hume's influence on Madison see Richard Schlatter, *Private Property: The History of an Idea* (London, 1951), 242–5. See also Supplementary References: "Hume."

53 David Seth Doggett, *The Responsibility of Talent: An Address Delivered before the Franklin Literary Society of Randolph-Macon College* (Richmond, VA, 1844), 9; Adams, *Moral Philosophy*, 14–16; R. H. Rivers, *Elements of Moral Philosophy* (Nashville, TN, 1859), 123–7; William S. Plumer, *The Law of God, as Contained in the Ten Commandments, Explained and Enforced* (Harrisonburg, VA, 1996 [1864]), 408–9; [John H. Bocock], "The Martyrs of Scotland and Sir Walter Scott," *SPR*, 10 (1858), 69–70; [J. H. Bocock], "The Reformation in England," *SPR*, 7 (1858), 174; C. R. Vaughan, ed., *Selections from the Religious and Literary Writings of John H. Bocock* (Richmond, VA, 1891; originally published in *SPR* in 1853), 204, 261, 273; Benjamin M. Palmer, *Influence of Religious Belief upon National Character: An Oration Delivered before the Demosthean and Phi Beta Kappa Societies of the University of Georgia* (Athens, GA, 1845), 6–7. In *JHTW* see "Love of Truth," 2:506, and "Miracles," 3:258–62. For a strong defense of miracles see "The New Gospel of Rationalism," *DQR,*

Southerners did their best to swallow Hume's heterodoxy. Thomas Smyth charitably softened the charge of atheism to mere polytheism, while the Presbyterian Reverend C. S. Fedder allowed, "Even the infidel soul of David Hume, could find cause for thankfulness to God in the fact that he was not born a savage, and in a benighted land." Southerners applauded Hume's disgust with religious fanaticism and sectarian bigotry, and with such northern conservatives as John Adams and Joseph Story they accepted much of his political and social viewpoint; for, as M. E. Bradford has observed, "The caution of David Hume and the pessimism of St. Paul can have the same political results." Still, not many could abide Hume's expulsion of God, nor his views on slavery. While Hume thought that blacks lacked the capacity to create a civilized polity and had contributed nothing to world civilization, he considered slavery economically unsound and a fetter on social progress. Hume, like Machiavelli, won admiration in the South for brilliance of intellect and engagement with significant historical problems, but not for the moral and political lessons he propounded. Machiavelli and Hume – like all other great historians – might shape their evidence, narratives, and analyses to prove points that Southerners found uncongenial. Despite their disquiet with individual historians, Southerners turned to history as an irreplaceable source of instruction on the vicissitudes and complexities of human character and the human condition.[54]

Southerners found it difficult to balance the linear and cyclical views of history, not least because both views embodied internal conflicts and had radical as well as conservative implications. The linear could, as in St. Augustine's account, point toward the City of God or, as in numerous religious and secular variants, to the coming of the radical kingdom in the here and now. The cyclical could promise the rise and fall of all empires, including southern slaveholding society, but could also be read as justifying the persistence of fundamental features of the human condition, including slavery. For Southerners, who knew the United States as born of revolution and who valued progress (up to a point), a linear philosophy of history had to explain when progress had gone far enough. And a cyclical philosophy of history had to allow for measured progress – as in the treatment of women – and explain how human or divine intervention could save the South from going the way of countless empires from ancient to modern times.

1 (1861), 369. See also Nancey Murphy, *Theology in the Age of Scientific Reasoning* (Ithaca, NY, 1990), 35–41. For the similarity of Dew's reading of history to Thornwell's, see Farmer, *Metaphysical Confederacy*, 247–50, 257. References to the "infidel" Hume abounded: see e.g. [S. J. Cassells], "Conscience – Its Nature and Authority," *SPR*, 6 (1853), 460–1.

54 *TSW*, 9:76–7; C. S. Fedder, *"Offer unto God Thanksgiving": A Sermon* (Charleston, SC, 1861), 8; M. E. Bradford, *Remembering Who We Are: Observations of a Southern Conservative* (Athens, GA, 1985), 36. For Adams and Story on Hume see Trevor Coulborn, ed., *Fame and the Founding Fathers: Essays by Douglas Adair* (New York, 1974), 108–13; Joseph Story, *Commentaries on the Constitution of the United States*, 2nd ed., 2 vols. (Boston, 1851), 1:384–5. On Hume, slavery, and race see "Of the Populousness of Ancient Nations" and "National Character," in David Hume, *Philosophical Essays on Morals, Literature and Politics* (Georgetown, DC, 1817). George Sawyer, among other proslavery writers, accepted Hume's "Of the Populousness of Ancient Nations" (1772) as a reliable source for Roman history: Sawyer, *Southern Institutes*, 74.

Evidence from private libraries suggests that eighteenth-century Southerners read historians and philosophers – Herodotus, Polybius, Tacitus, Walter Raleigh, Beverley, Hugh Jones, William Stith, David Hume – who favored a cyclical view of history as a recurring struggle for liberty punctuated by periods of decadence and tyranny. From the Greeks they learned about cycles; from Christian eschatology they learned about a linear projection toward a denouement. Augustine taught that the City of Man is in perpetual decay, while his medieval opponents emphasized how easily a linear view could serve the purposes of a fearsome radicalism. Notably, the thought of Joachim of Floris, the Calabrian abbot, encouraged radicals, much as Augustine's encouraged conservatives. Whereas Augustine interpreted the thousand-year reign of Christ as the here and now of the Church, Joachim – as Paul Tillich has judged his teachings – offered a foretaste of the revolutionary utopianism of eighteenth-century liberalism and nineteenth-century revolutionary socialism. From the third millennium B.C. in Egypt and Sumeria through Judaic-Christian formulations to the grand systems of Enlightenment and nineteenth-century philosophers, linear interpretations have pointed toward an "end of history" in, say, the apocalypse proclaimed in Revelation or in Karl Marx's projection of a world free of oppression and exploitation. All such dreams have foundered. In the view of southern commentators, a linear view encouraged constant revolt against the structure of society while offering no alternative but unattainable and bloody fantasies. And many, with growing justification, feared that the abolition of slavery would prove the logical next step in moral and political progress.[55]

The tension between conservative and radical interpretations of history left its mark on a slaveholding class that resolutely opposed the principal tendencies of its day while congratulating itself on its commitment to well-ordered progress. In 1851 Frederick Porcher, celebrating the beauties of historical progress, declared that reason, science, and industrial development were putting an end to the stagnation of previous centuries and opening the way to an upward-and-onward march. Within a decade, he was stressing the dangers of a deceptive progressivism and the mounting perils of social disintegration, particularly rampant individualism. Defending slavery in 1857 he cried, "We have no past, to which we can fall back on; our only hope lies in invention."[56]

Southern ideas of progress drew upon various sources. Christianity taught that, for the individual, Providence means the possibility of constantly striving toward

55 Richard Beale Davis, *A Colonial Southern Bookshelf Reading in the Eighteenth Century* (Athens, GA, 1979), 125–6; R. B. Davis, *Intellectual Life in the Colonial South, 1515–1763*, 3 vols. (Knoxville, TN, 1978), 1:67–8, 378; also, Ollinger Crenshaw, *General Lee's College: The Rise and Growth of Washington and Lee University* (New York, 1969), 103; "W.", "Man's Inventions – God's Instrumentalities," *SRCR*, 1 (1852), 194–209; Paul Tillich, *A History of Christian Thought, from Its Judaic and Hellenistic Origins to Existentialism*, ed. Carl E. Braaten (New York, 1968), 334–6; Jack Lindsay, *Song of a Falling World: Culture during the Break-up of the Roman Empire (A.D. 350–600)* (London, 1948), 167–74; Eric Voegelin, *Order and History*, 5 vols. (Baton Rouge, LA, 1956–87), 4:7, 68–75. For Polybius and Vico see Supplementary References: "Historical Cycle Theorists."

56 F. A. Porcher, "Southern and Northern Civilizations Contrasted," *RM*, 1 (1857), 103. The course of Porcher's thought is skillfully analyzed in Charles J. Holden, *In the Great Maelstrom: Conservatives in Post–Civil War South Carolina* (Columbia, SC, 2002), chs. 1 and 2.

the Kingdom of God and implies divine guidance. The Enlightenment provided a secular version that posited a basic harmony in human affairs through the "invisible hand" in economics and through liberalism and democracy in politics. Southerners frequently sought to combine the two. Their college magazines and student papers generally applauded the progressive nature of the age, discerning the hand of God in the spread of commerce and technology – even the quest for gold in California – that was facilitating the spread of Christianity. They displayed considerable nervousness about the tendency of empires, ancient and modern, to sink into moral decay and disappear. Sounding a common warning in 1855, J. A. Turner of Georgia wrote, "Nations and peoples have their day, and then die out as do individuals."[57]

Porcher was wrestling with the tensions between the continuities beloved of romantic conservatives and the discontinuities that produced constructive change. He and other Southerners claimed for themselves the constructive aspects of such revolutionary upheavals as the Reformation, the English revolutions of the seventeenth century, and even the French Revolution. The conservative interpretation of the American Revolution, notable in Dew's and Trescot's historical writing and in Simms's Revolutionary War novels, balanced the similarities and contrasts of the Revolution with those of the revolutions that came before and after, emphasizing that America overcame the excesses of radicalism to assimilate measured social change to the Western legal tradition.

Following the logic of cyclical interpretation, Southerners accepted in theory the inevitability of the end of their own empire, even as they strove to extend its life as far as possible in practice. J. L. Petigru cautiously appealed to history to help people negotiate the conflicting claims of novelty and antiquity. "The adherents of antiquity, under the name of Conservatives," he told the South Carolina Historical Society, "and the partisans of progress, under the banner of Reform, wage an endless war." More imperially inclined Southerners welcomed the challenge, the potential, and the special mission, while the more pious stressed the duty of men to struggle against the evils inherent in the City of Man and to strive to enter the City of God. Together they agreed that, in preparing for the Second Coming, men had to do everything possible to perfect the world they had inherited. Like the Puritans before them, Southerners claimed the mantle of the ancient Israelites as God's Chosen People. Like the divines, Southerners of a secularist bent – and not only intellectuals – embraced cyclical theory, including a view of history as written in blood. Most hoped that America or a southern confederacy could prove an exception.[58]

[57] J. A. Turner, *A Letter to Hon. N. G. Foster, Candidate for Congress* (Milledgeville, GA, 1855), 22. And see the articles in *VUM*, 3 (1859): R. M. T. Hunter, Jr., "Advantages of Historical Study," 57–66; William Allen, "Progress of Literature," 128–33; C. M. Cauthen, "Progress," 450–3. Also, the report of a student speech at Elk Fork Academy (near Nashville) on "Destiny – A Delusion," in Franc Carmack Diary, June 3, 1853, at UNC-SHC.

[58] J. L. Petigru, "Oration Delivered on the Third Anniversary of the South-Carolina Historical Society" (May 27, 1858), in *Collections of the South-Carolina Historical Society*, 2 vols. (Charleston, SC, 1857–58), 2:9–10. Southern Christians grasped intuitively and their intellectuals consciously that, in the words of Eric Voegelin, "Jews and Christians have a disconcerting habit of outlasting the rise and

Acceptance of the fatalism implicit in cyclical theory would have discouraged an interest in history, but most theologians and secular intellectuals, hoping to shape the future of their society, rejected fatalism. The theologians held that man, by reconciling himself to God, could escape the cycle. For Robert L. Dabney, church and secular history taught that republicanism is better than despotism, that Presbyterianism is better than prelacy, that moral corruption leads to earthly ruin, and that human nature is fundamentally corrupt. In Burkean fashion, the Calvinist Dabney, like southern Arminians from their own perspective, concluded that knowledge of history would permit men to navigate safely. Calvinists like the Baptist Reverend P. H. Mell and Catholics like Bishop Patrick Lynch believed that nations and empires as well as individuals receive rewards and punishments in both this world and the next.[59]

Ministers, who figured prominently among southern historians, generally favored a providential view, but those who moved beyond moralistic essays tried to present the empirical record as honestly as possible. Even those who did not write history but preached its lessons spoke cautiously. Thornwell assumed that an account of moral government must proceed historically. For Thornwell, history records "the conception and execution of God's purposes of grace to the fallen family of man." Even as Thornwell combated the liberal theologians' attempt to deny the historicity of the Gospel, he remained faithful to Baconian induction in science. But by 1859 Thornwell, a political conservative and a unionist, feared the worst: "Our race is in ruins, but not hopelessly lost," although even in the darkest moments he believed that the hand of Providence guides history. The Methodist Reverend David Seth Doggett agreed: "The true philosophy of history is Divine Providence." Philip Schaff, the northern theologian who influenced the theologically liberal James Warley Miles as well as some theologically orthodox Southerners, said: "The idea of universal history presupposes the Christian idea of the unity of God, and the unity and common destiny of men, and was unknown to ancient Greece and Rome. A view of history which overlooks or undermines the divine factor starts from deism and consistently runs into atheism." George Frederick Holmes declared that history "becomes the noblest study which can employ the mind of the sage, when we regard it as the chart of the moral, social and intellectual advancement of mankind – showing how one nation and one era have paved the way for the superior intelligence of the next; or have fired the train which produced its ruin." At the same time history illuminated the mysteries of the cyclical rise and fall of nations. Holmes concluded, "To study history in this way is to study it philosophically."[60]

fall of political powers; and we cannot eliminate Judeo-Christian spiritual history without making nonsense of history in general." Voegelin, *Order and History*, 1:121 and 133, 418, 505.

59 "Uses and Results of Church History," *DD*, 2:12, 20–1; P. H. Mell, *Predestination and the Saints' Perseverance, Stated and Defended from the Objections of the Arminians* (Charleston, SC, 1858 [1850]), 46–7; [Patrick N. Lynch], "Nineveh and Its Remains," *SQR*, 16 (1849), 31.

60 "Revelation and Religion," *JHTW*, 3:166; "Theology as a Life in Individuals and the Church," *JHTW*, 2:35; D. S. Doggett, *A Nation's Ebenezer: A Discourse Delivered in the Broad St. Methodist Church* (Richmond, VA, 1862), 14; C. G. Memminger, *Oration on the Bible, as a Key to the Events of Sacred*

The fundamental problem steadily became more pressing: How could a slave-holding Christian South escape a cycle that begins in glory and ends in decadence and collapse? Although clerics and laymen saw a cyclical pattern in history, they distrusted grand systems of historical law, especially since they noticed the alacrity with which radicals seized upon them to justify their projects to remake the human race.

Southerners followed nineteenth-century European writing about history, including the sweeping philosophies and the rising tide of Biblical criticism. Although they did not cite Hegel's philosophy of history nearly as often as his theological and philosophical writings, they did occasionally comment on it, principally to provide one more argument in favor of the civilizing effects of slavery and of black inferiority. L. Q. C. Lamar forcefully praised Hegel to that effect, and Mrs. Henry Rowe Schoolcraft wrote in her popular *Black Gauntlet* of "Hegel's Philosophy of History, an imperishable monument to human genius."[61]

In similar spirit, William Frierson Cooper of Tennessee cited the liberal French Catholic Abbé Félicité de Lamennais and the British historian Thomas Henry Buckle on the laws of historical development: warning against a mechanical and fatalistic application, describing all such laws as tendencies with limited applications. Frierson, opposing egalitarianism and radicalism, concluded that a proper study of history leads to conservative politics. Buckle, like Comte, came in for heavy blows for a mechanical view of history that slighted human volition. "L." of Alabama acknowledged Buckle as "a resolute and fearless thinker" whose work has "some manly qualities" and ranks as "certainly one of the most philosophical works of the

---

and Profane History (Charleston, SC, 1843), esp. 533–4; G. F. Holmes, "Schlegel's Philosophy of History," in Michael O'Brien, ed., *All Clever Men, Who Make Their Way: Critical Discourse in the Old South* (Columbia, SC, 1982), 180–1. The early southern historians, notably John Smith, did not invoke "Providence" nearly as readily as the New England Puritans did. Specifically, whereas the Puritans – Bradford, Winthrop, and Cotton Mather – emphasized "desolate wilderness," linking it to Providence, their southern counterparts reveled in their own terrain as a joyous earthly invitation to settlement. Davis, *Intellectual Life in the Colonial South*, 1:67; Philip Schaff, *History of the Christian Church*, 5th ed., rev., 8 vols. (Grand Rapids, MI, 1960), 1:2. See also David B. Van Tassel, *Recording America's Past: An Interpretation of the Development of Historical Studies in America, 1607–1884* (Chicago, 1960), 10–11.

[61] L. Q. C. Lamar, Feb. 21, 1860, *Congressional Globe*, 36th Cong., 1st Sess., Appendix, 113–17; "The Black Gauntlet," in *Plantation Life: Narratives of Schoolcraft*, 405. For Hegel see also "On the True Meaning of 'Cogito, Ergo Sum,'" *North Carolina University Magazine*, 5 (1856), 67; for Hegel on race, see T. W. Hoit, *The Right of American Slavery* (St. Louis, MO, 1860), 11. Among southern theological liberals, James Warley Miles was especially influenced by Hegel: see Miles, *Philosophic Theology; Or, Ultimate Grounds of All Religious Belief Based on Reason* (Charleston, SC, 1849). Miles viewed history as "cycloidal" – as moving in cycles but without precise repetitions and, in effect, producing an upward development. On Miles see Ralph Luker, *A Southern Tradition in Theology and Social Criticism: The Religious Liberalism and Social Conservatism of James Warley Miles, William Porcher DuBose and Edgar Gardner Murphy* (New York, 1884), 145–6, 180–2. Only a few theologians read Kierkegaard, but most Southerners would have agreed with the sally he aimed especially at Hegel: "Socrates said quite ironically that he did not know whether he was a human being or something else, but an Hegelian can say with due solemnity in the confessional: 'I do not know whether I am a human being – but I have understood the System.' I for my part would rather say: 'I know that I am a human being, and I know that I have not understood the System.'" Kierkegaard quoted in Colin Brown, *Jesus in European Protestant Thought, 1778–1860* (Grand Rapids, MI, 1985), 145.

age," but he judged Buckle akin to Auguste Comte's positivism in the false premises of its one-dimensional materialism and consequent gross errors and distortions. Benjamin Johnson Barbour, speaking to the cadets at Virginia Military Institute, rejected cyclical theory as based on a false analogy from the physical world, as did Arminians like the Reverend Joseph Cummings.[62]

Those who subscribed to the cyclical pattern of history relied upon providential intervention to arrest or reverse its course, but providential intervention depended on an appeal to miracles, which the divines – Arminian and Calvinist alike – preached to their congregations. Controversy over miracles had a long history in the war between orthodoxy and liberalism. Hobbes, among other southern *bêtes noires,* did not deny miracles but considered them a thing of the distant past. In *Christianity as Old as Creation* (1730), Matthew Tindal rejected Revelation and miracles in order, he said, to defend Christianity against superstition by declaring the disappearance of miracles as "a proof for the uniqueness of [Jesus'] person and the validity of his message." Tindal provided heavy ammunition for Deists, Humean skeptics, and those who spoke as Christians while denying the Trinity and other core doctrines. With the innovations of Anthony Ashley Cooper, the third Earl of Shaftsbury, who exercised wide and deep influence in England during the first half of the eighteenth century and in Germany during the second half, an increasingly liberalized religion dispensed with miracles altogether, as Jefferson did. Hegel presented Jesus' miracles performed as encouragement to positive religion, for despite Jesus' emphasis upon charity, He had virtue rest on the authority exhibited by His power. As entirely unnatural phenomena, miracles "are the manifestation of the most *un*divine." Miracles violate the direct action of God, which "is the restoration and manifestation of oneness." Schleiermacher decried miracles as a suggestion that God's universe is ineffectual and requires divine repair.[63]

Thornwell assailed Schleiermacher, among others, for transforming Jesus into a mere prophet and moral teacher by encouraging a denial of miracles: "It is impossible to abandon the miracle and cling to any other Christianity but that which

[62] W. F. Cooper, "Notes on a Trip to Europe, 1862–1863," in Cooper Papers, at Tennessee State Library and Archives (Nashville); "L.", "Civilization in England," *QRMECS,* 13 (1859), 55–83, quotes at 54, 57, 58; Benjamin Johnson Barbour, "Address Delivered before the Literary Societies of the Virginia Military Institute," *SLM,* 20 (1854), 524; Joseph Cummings, "True Dignity of Human Nature and the Evidences of Man's Progress towards It," *SRCR,* 1 (1851), 146–53. W. L. Mead at the University of Virginia condemned Buckle's "pedantic ostentation and brazen self-complacency": Mead, "Legal Ethics," *VUM,* 4 (1860), 88. Oswald Spengler, attacking Buckle for proto-Darwinism scientism appropriate to beasts rather than men, also noted his implication that God was responsible for the miseries in history – an implication Southerners recoiled from: see *The Decline of the West,* tr. Charles Francis Atkinson, 2 vols. (New York, 1926–28), 1:371, 2:29 n.

[63] Edwin S. Gaustad, *Sworn on the Altar of God: A Religious Biography of Thomas Jefferson* (Grand Rapids, MI, 1991), 135; Henning Graf Reventlow, *The Authority of the Bible and the Rise of the Modern World* (Philadelphia, 1984), 214, 318; Tindal quoted in Jaroslav Pelikan, *Jesus through the Centuries: His Place in the History of Culture* (New Haven, CT, 1985), 182, and see, generally, 182–6; "Positivity of the Christian Religion," in G. W. F. Hegel, *Early Theological Writings,* tr. T. M. Knox and Richard Kroner (Philadelphia, 1948), 297; Schleiermacher, *Christian Faith,* excerpted in Keith Clements, ed., *Friedrich Schleiermacher: Pioneer of Modern Theology* (San Francisco, 1987), 118.

is enkindled in our own souls from the sparks of our own reason." Thornwell saw no alternative to miracles as a bulwark against rampant subjectivity, describing a religion without mysteries as "simply a religion that has no God." Southern Arminians joined in defending miracles as manifestations of God's power. Even the liberal James Warley Miles, choosing Plato over Hume, considered miracles to be divine interventions in history.[64]

The War and the impending fall of the Confederacy produced some momentary backsliding. "The day of miracles has passed," the Reverend C. Charles Minnigerode told his Episcopalian flock in 1864. God works differently now, and the South must win its own war. That message, politically useful in 1864, did not serve well after Appomattox, when the Baptist Reverend Basil Manly, Jr., returned to a more familiar theme: "Let us not be afraid of admitting the idea and the fact of a miracle. The whole system of Christianity is a stupendous series of miracles."[65]

Notwithstanding firm commitment to God's wonder-working power in history, the divines, especially the Calvinists, had noticeably less enthusiasm for a "progressive" reading of history than did many secular writers, including some conservatives, but they too struggled with the antitheses. Religious or no, Southerners took seriously Tacitus' lament, "I have to present in succession, the merciless biddings of a tyrant, incessant prosecutions, faithless friendships, the ruin of innocence, the same causes issuing from the same results, and I am everywhere confronted by a wearisome monotony in my subject matter." From Gibbon, Southerners heard that history was a path of blood and "indeed, little more than the register of the crimes, follies, and misfortunes of mankind."[66]

The religiously committed, despite strong efforts, tilted to the more pessimistic side of their long-standing quarrel with themselves over the relation of original sin and depravity to their hopes for human progress. In Charleston, Thomas Smyth delivered a eulogy on the death of President William Henry Harrison in which he reflected on the course of history and the sinful nature of man: "History is little more than a record of vain pursuits – the thwarted ambition – the disappointed expectations – the overthrow, calamity, vicissitudes and distress of individuals and of empires." Smyth, rejecting both fatalism and chance, acknowledged that the working of the Lord's will in history remains obscure.[67]

[64] *JHTW*, 3:221–76, quotes at 3:227 and 1:471; H. B. Bascom, *Sermons from the Pulpit* (Louisville, KY, 1852), 198–233; Miles, *Philosophic Theology*, 65, 189, and pt. 2, ch. 3; Robert L. Dabney, *Systematic Theology* (Carlyle, PA, 1985 [1878]), 280–3; J. L. Dagg, *Manual of Theology: A Treatise on Christian Doctrine and a Treatise on Church Order*, 2 vols. (New York, 1980 [1857–58]), 1:35; Linton Stephens to Iverson Harris, Apr. 21, 1860, in James D. Waddell, *Biographical Sketch of Linton Stephens, Containing a Selection of His Letters, Speeches, State Papers, Etc.* (Atlanta, GA, 1877), 210.

[65] Charles Minnigerode, *He that Believeth Shall Not Make Haste: A Sermon* (Richmond, VA, 1865), 9; Basil Manly, Jr., *The Bible Doctrine of Inspiration* (Nashville, TN, 1995 [1888]), 28.

[66] "Annals," Bk. 4:33, in Moses Hadas, ed., *The Complete Works of Tacitus*, tr. Alfred John Church and William Jackson Broder (New York, 1942); Edward Gibbon, *The History of the Decline and Fall of the Roman Empire*, ed. David Womersley, 3 vols. (London, 1994), 1:102, 3:526.

[67] "The Destruction of the Hopes of Man," *TSW*, 9:493–512, quotes at 502, 505–6.

Smyth's apprehensions reverberated in the sermons and secular writings of educated Southerners, who echoed Locke's denunciation of historical writing as a record of war and murder and the glorification of conquest and cruelty. C. M. Jacobs sounded a common theme: "History teaches us that governments like human systems have their regular periods of growth, maturity, decline and extinction," and he identified the general cause of their downfall as "the ignorance, avarice, wickedness and ambition of mankind." In 1858 *Southern Literary Messenger* began the New Year with a leader on "Modern Tactics": "It is indeed sad to think, that history is little else but the record of sanguinary strife." Yet, the evils of war "have not been unmixed with good." With the South staggering toward secession, the choice of topic spoke for itself, and George Armstrong, the influential Presbyterian theologian and pastor at Norfolk, developed it in *The Christian Doctrine of Slavery*: "National sin, persisted in from generation to generation – then national degradation, becoming deeper and darker as time rolls on – then national slavery, at once a punishment for sin, and a gracious provision for saving from utter extinction, and gradually restoring again to the position from which sin has dragged its victims down. Such is the order established by God." More pointedly, in *The Theology of Christian Experience*, Armstrong stressed original sin and the "sickness" of man: "History is, to a very large extent, but a record of human crime."[68]

The gloomy assessments of Smyth, Jacobs, and Armstrong cast a shadow over their defense of slavery. Thus Dew: "Trace the history of all nations, from the days of the Patriarchs down to present times, and you will find almost all governments to present one continued series of blunders and follies." Southerners brave enough to face history as a story of horrors had somehow to account for the horrors of the slaveholding regime that commanded their firm allegiance. They ended by convincing themselves that slavery, on balance, offered a measure of mitigation on the ground that it provided slaves with masters who protected them against a much worse fate. As self-deception, their dialectical gyration remains intriguing. As apologetics well short of their best efforts, it did them no honor.[69]

Protestant defenders of slavery had long viewed much of the history of Christianity as a process of decline from original standards with the triumph of "Romanism." With secession imminent, the Reverend George H. Clark, preaching in St. John's Episcopal Church in Savannah, recounted the history of empires from ancient times to modern: their expansion, enrichment, profligacy, and decline. Secession brought

[68] C. M. Jacobs, *The Re-Enslavement of Free Blacks* (Richmond, VA, 1858), 3; "Modern Tactics," *SLM*, 26 (1858), 1; George D. Armstrong, *Christian Doctrine of Slavery* (New York, 1967 [1857]), 114; G. D. Armstrong, *Theology of Christian Experience* (New York, 1858), 161, also 162–4. For a discussion of Locke's critique see Paul Rahe, *Republics Ancient and Modern: Classical Republicanism and the American Revolution* (Chapel Hill, NC, 1992), 298. "War," the Episcopalian Reverend Philip Slaughter of Virginia remarked in 1850, "is the instrument of God to punish nations": Slaughter, "John Caldwell Calhoun," *American Whig Review*, 11 (1850), 167.

[69] Thomas Roderick Dew, *Lectures on the Restrictive System, Delivered to the Senior Class of William and Mary College* (Richmond, VA, 1829), 7–8.

forth a spate of sermons warning the people of an aspiring new nation to repent
of their sins and root out the corruption and greed that brought down the Roman
Empire and indeed all the great empires, not to mention ancient Israel. Internal corruption, not the barbarians – the preachers cried – destroyed Rome. The preachers
and prominent politicians cited sacred and profane history to stress the rise and fall
of empires while they pleaded for the Confederacy to break the cycle.[70]

Secular and clerical intellectuals alike held fast to a notion that cyclical theories
of history could be proven false by a slaveholding society free of the pernicious tendencies of the past. Pointing to Roman history as a prime example of the evils of
accumulated wealth and the craving for luxury, they pondered the unwillingness or
inability of ruling strata to use wealth responsibly and to put the interests of society
above personal and class interests. Some Southerners cautiously defended the ways
in which slaveholders used and displayed wealth, hoping they would avoid a repetition of the evil tendencies of ancient slavery, but expressed deep forebodings about
replication of Babylonian and Roman patterns in Western Europe and the North,
where the evils inherent in the free-labor system were probably ineradicable. John
A. Quitman defended a proper display of wealth: "William Mercer's tastes, are perhaps aristocratic – but he may be the instrument in their gratification of much good
to the country." Following Malthus's paean to the social benefits of high consumer
spending, Thomas Cooper, Dew, Fitzhugh, and others, explicitly or implicitly, defended the planters' display of luxury. Fitzhugh, with no use for Malthus or any
other political economist, agreed that luxury promoted civilization but warned that
accumulation through the overworking and exploiting of labor became "a nuisance
and a crime."[71]

Dew condemned, at length, the nomadic barbarian conquerors of Europe and
Asia for their destructiveness, while coyly acknowledging their beneficent effects:
"They have been the scourge and renovators of the nations of the earth. Their
history uniform; true descendants of Ishmael – eternal depredators on civilized

---

[70] Reventlow, *Authority of the Bible,* 110–11. Among laymen, C. G. Memminger acknowledged that
America was subject to the historical laws of rise and fall but suggested that righteous living could
break the cycle: "An Oration on the Bible," in Henry D. Capers, *Life and Times of C. G. Memminger*
(Richmond, VA, 1893), 546. G. H. Clark, "Sermon," in Jon L Wakelyn, ed., *Southern Pamphlets on
Secession, Nov. 1860–April 1861* (Chapel Hill, NC, 1996); A. M. Randolph, *Address on the Day of
Fasting and Prayer* (Fredericksburg, VA, 1861), 9; Thomas Atkinson, *On the Causes of Our National
Troubles: A Sermon Delivered in St. James Church, Wilmington, N.C.* (Wilmington, NC, 1861), 7–8;
Edward Reed, *A People Saved by the Lord: A Sermon Delivered at Flat Rock* (Charleston, SC, 1861),
5; J. C. Stiles, *National Rectitude the Only True Basis of National Prosperity* (Petersburg, VA, 1863),
14–25. See also S. H. Higgins, *The Mountain Moved; Or, David upon the Cause of Public Calamity*
(Milledgeville, GA, 1863), 12–13; Charles Minnigerode, *Power: A Sermon* (Richmond, VA, 1964),
10; J. L. Blitch, *"Thy Kingdom Come"* (Augusta, GA, 1863), 5.

[71] Elizabeth Quitman to John A. Quitman, Dec. 5, 1835, and John A. Quitman to Elizabeth Quitman,
Dec. 9, 1835, in Quitman Papers, at UNC-SHC; Thomas Cooper, *Lectures on the Elements of Political Economy,* reproduction of 2nd ed. (New York, 1971 [1830]), 115; Dew, *Restrictive System,* 138;
Fitzhugh, "Oliver Goldsmith and Dr. Johnson," 511; also, Holt Wilson, "Cotton, Steam, and Machinery," *SLM,* 27 (1858), 171.

nations." Dew considered the moral degeneration of barbarian conquerors who establish great empires a universal law: "A rude, ignorant people, suddenly acquiring immense wealth, are sure to indulge every extravagance and vice; they can only enjoy their possessions as *sensualists* – all self-government is lost – the most shameless extravagance prevails." He criticized the tendency of nomadic conquerors to levy excessive taxes and to concentrate all power at a single spot, reducing the peoples of the hinterland to slavery. Civilized peoples, however, might escape their predecessors' fate, for wealth and luxury no longer produce the same effects: "Modern *civilized* nations are not injured by these – they are benefited; it is a semi-barbarous, rude, unenlightened people alone who are corrupted by them." Civilized nations have also gained "a decided advantage to civilized over barbarous nations" because of the growing expense of waging war. The civilized now conquer the barbarous, and no longer can barbarous peoples readily conquer even those civilized peoples who have fallen into effeminacy: "War is now a matter of science, of deliberate calculation."[72]

The ministers, with their eyes on the root of all evil, proved less sanguine, differing from secular theorists primarily in emphasis. They approved of wealth honestly gained and responsibly used, railing against a pervasive failure to apply it in the interests of society. Their logic led a number to condemn the inherently selfish tendencies evident in free-labor societies in contrast to the sober social responsibility evident in slaveholding societies. George Foster Pierce, speaking at Emory College in 1842, denounced the "convulsions of the monetary world" for threatening a moral catastrophe and stirring "the foundations of character with the upheaval, disruptive energy of an earthquake." His fellow Methodist, the Reverend J. N. Maffitt, described – in an article aptly entitled "The Almighty Dollar" – the national commercial system as a "disease": "ravenous, unsettling, and revolutionary." In 1859 the Presbyterian Reverend T. T. Castleman, speaking at Oakland College in Mississippi, launched a sustained attack on the radicalism fostered by "the greed for gain, which capital is everywhere fostering." Yet, also writing in 1859, the Reverend Dr. H. M. Denison of Charleston spoke for many in praising commerce as a great civilizer that becomes corrupt only when it propels luxury and the lure of conquest. Still hopeful for the preservation of the Union, he denied the inevitability projected by cyclical theories, maintaining that Christianity could still lead the United States to avoid the worst. It took a short step for many Southerners, clerical and lay, to embrace the argument that only slavery or an alternative form of servile labor could provide the social basis on which Christianity could flourish.[73]

---

[72] Dew, *Digest*, 18, 26, 28, 31, 94, 116, 143.

[73] George Foster Pierce, "Learning and Religion," in Atticus G. Haygood, ed., *Bishop Pierce's Sermons and Addresses, with a Few Special Discourses by Dr. [Lovick] Pierce* (Nashville, TN, 1886), 14; J. N. Maffitt, "The Almighty Dollar," *Southern Ladies' Book*, 6 (1852/53), 76; H. M. Denison, "The Commercial Spirit – Carthage," *DBR*, 28 (1860), 66–76; T. T. Castleman, "Address to the Literary Societies of Oakland College" (1859), 9, typescript at Oakland College; Harvey Tolliver Cook, *The Life Work of James Clement Furman* (Greenville, SC, 1926), 211.

The struggle to understand the course of history compelled attention to the origins, nature, and effects of war as a cycle-breaking instrument. The ancient historians to whom Southerners regularly appealed for guidance bequeathed contrary judgments. For Thucydides and Sallust, war corrupts its participants, but not for Livy – notwithstanding his condemnation of the endless atrocities he chronicled. Concern with historical cycles made even those Southerners most fascinated by "chivalry" take a sober view of war. Although the slaveholders have retained a reputation for readiness to plunge into war, they generally preferred caution. Roman history teaches men to avoid unnecessary wars, wrote the young H. Clay Pate of Virginia, for they undermine civilization and open the way to barbarism. Among many others, Judge John Archibald Campbell of Alabama, the Methodist Reverend Joseph Cummings of Virginia, and Jesse Harper Lindsay, Jr., a student at the University of North Carolina, found ample evidence in Greek and Roman history of such destructive consequences of military ambition and greed.[74]

Well before the War, the South's moral philosophers – the Calvinist Jasper Adams and the Methodist R. H. Rivers – lectured and wrote textbooks to show that, although Christianity encourages patriotism, it enjoins good will toward all nations and peoples, discourages national hatred and aggrandizement, and justifies war only as a last resort. Rivers exclaimed, "War, indeed, is a terrible calamity, even when it is resorted to in the cause of right." But in 1858, some ministers were beginning to prepare their congregations for the worst. The Reverend Adiel Sherwood preached to the Georgia Baptist Convention that the suffering of Christians signaled their devotion and worthiness. In 1861 the Episcopalian Reverend Daniel Dreher of North Carolina told his parishioners to expect war in this sinful world: "Men will trample upon the rights of one another, and human nature will resent a wrong." The Methodist Robert Newton Sledd, without glorifying, made a strong scriptural case for just war, while William S. Plumer agreed but warned that any war easily passes into aggression and robbery.[75]

Merchants took the lead in combating the cyclical theories prevalent in the Northeast since there, too, commerce figured as the principal spur to decadence. The Boston elite, in particular, preached that the spread of Christianity provided the antidote for all such cyclical tendencies and that commerce was carrying Christianity to every corner of the world. For a fine, brief discussion of the Boston elite's response to cyclical theory see the Introduction to Tamara Plakins Thornton, *Cultivating Gentlemen: The Meaning of Country Life among the Boston Elite, 1785–1860* (New Haven, CT, 1989).

74 On the ancient historians see the Editor's Introduction to Livy, *The War with Hannibal,* tr. Aubrey de Sélincourt (London, 1972), 17; H. Clay Pate, "Patriotic Discourse on Local and General History," *SRCR,* 2 (1852), 140–1; [John Archibald Campbell], "Slavery among the Romans," *SQR,* 28 (1848), 393; Cummings, "True Dignity of Human Nature," 155–7; J. H. Lindsay, Jr., "Our Free Institutions," in Speeches of Graduates, 1851, at UNC-NCC.

75 Adams, *Moral Philosophy,* 55, 99–109; Rivers, *Elements of Moral Philosophy,* 267; Adiel Sherwood, *Suffering Disciples Rejoicing in Persecution* (Atlanta, GA, 1858); George Fitzhugh, *Sociology for the South, or, The Failure of Free Society* (New York, 1965 [1852]), 170; Daniel I. Dreher, *A Sermon, June 13, 1861, Day of Humiliation and Prayer* (Salisbury, NC, 1861), 14; Robert Newton Sledd, *A Sermon Delivered in the Market Street, M. E. Church, Petersburg, Va.: Before the Confederate Cadets on the Occasion of Their Departure for the Seat of War* (Petersburg, VA, 1861), esp. 7–8; Plumer,

Pacifism offered Southerners no appealing alternative. The peace societies that arose in the North after the War of 1812, united in the American Peace Society in 1828, were led by men and women committed to the abolition of slavery and, in many cases, to women's liberation. Peace societies never took root in the South, and feeble early efforts ended with the nullification crisis. Only here and there did the South hear a pacifist voice. Daniel Lipscomb of Middle Tennessee, a Christian pacifist, opposed all wars. Thomas Grimké of South Carolina, a leader in the American Peace Society, contrasted the peaceful spirit of Christianity with the war-like ethos of the classical age. When he asked for and was refused exemption from militia duty during the nullification crisis, he became an object of opprobrium. For southern public opinion, enunciations of war usually end with the destruction of states through abdication of power to a rival ready to impose its will. When the War came, the abolitionists who had proclaimed Christian pacifism confirmed their judgment. Even abolitionists long committed to Christian pacifism decided that the Union was fighting a just war – if not a holy crusade. "In thus reconciling violent means with peaceful ends," Valerie Ziegler, historian of the peace movement, quips, "the advocates of peace conceded that sometimes the best way to love their neighbors was to coerce them."[76]

With the threat of war on the rise, Southern accents became more bellicose. Simms, an adherent of Young America's expansionism, unabashedly called for "military glory"; America must dominate other countries or they will dominate America. "War," he wrote J. H. Hammond, "is the greatest element of our modern civilization, and our destiny is conquest." As the War approached, George Fitzhugh announced, "War elevates the sentiments," and besides, frequent wars steel a nation to meet its responsibilities, while they keep the younger generation from effeminacy. Fitzhugh, doing his job as a propagandist, had assumed a new stance at a critical moment, for he had long looked askance at war as an encouragement to the maintenance of a standing army. For Northerners such arrogant and inhumane outbursts were to be expected from slaveholders. But Nathaniel Hawthorne remarked after Fort Sumter: "It was delightful to share in the heroic sentiment of the time, and to feel that I had a country – a consciousness which seemed to make me young again." And what should be said about Ralph Waldo Emerson, the philosopher of humane liberalism, who extolled the beauties of war in 1863: "The times are dark but heroic.

Law of God, 397–8. During the War, the Methodist Reverend D. S. Doggett of Richmond and the Presbyterian Reverend Drury Lacy of Fayetteville supported the Confederacy but lamented the destructive effects of all war and its enormous impetus to vice. See Doggett, *Nation's Ebenezer,* 9; Lacy, *Address Delivered at the General Military Hospital, Winston, N.C.* (Fayetteville, NC, 1863), 7–8. Much more sanguine was the Episcopalian Reverend W. T. Dalzell of San Antonio, Texas: "Thank God for the high moral virtues which this war has developed in our state and country": *Thanksgiving to God: A Sermon in St. Mark's Church, San Antonio* (San Antonio, TX, 1863), 9.

76 Valerie H. Ziegler, *The Advocates of Peace in Antebellum America* (Bloomington, IN, 1992), esp. ch. 5. In Kentucky, Robert Breckenridge's antislavery and pro-Union *Danville Quarterly Review* attributed war, as well as slavery, to man's inherent sinfulness and scoffed at the idea that war could be abolished: "Our Country – Its Peril – Its Deliverance," *DQR,* 1 (1861), 92–3.

The war uplifts us into generous sentiments. We do not often have a moment of grandeur in these hurried slipshod lives."[77]

In 1860, Robert L. Dabney – orthodox Calvinist theologian, longtime political moderate, a unionist, and soon to serve as an aide to Stonewall Jackson in the Army of Virginia – reiterated a long-standing theme of the southern clergy by declaring that, if political agitation distracts men and hinders the progress of religion, war brings calamity to the churches. Agreeing that the Bible sanctions defensive war, he denounced unprovoked war as "the most monstrous secular crime that can be committed." Since nations are normally "unjust and unscrupulous," only God can judge between them. He reflected on the Yankee invasion of Virginia: "Courage in the prosecution of a wicked attempt does not relieve, but only aggravates, the danger to the innocent party assailed, and the guilt of the assailants." Those who fight defensively and justly easily slip into a thirst for vengeance. Yet Dabney thought the near-universal applause for martial virtues instinctive and necessary "to the exercise of the noblest sentiments of the human soul." Those who cultivate peace do good, but, Dabney added, he who defends country and honor with his life "makes the contribution of supreme value."[78]

The preachers in general harbored serious reservations about war, especially the cultivation of a bellicose spirit that might undercut religious devotion; they distinguished just from unjust wars, denouncing wars of aggression as sinful and criminal. They recognized that war demoralizes a people and disrupts the holy work of the churches. Even when trying to steel Confederate troops for battle, they tried not to get carried away. At the front in Virginia in 1863, the Baptist Reverend J. J. D. Renfroe of Alabama justified the War but condemned the glorification of war itself as a satire of civilization and artifice for mass assaults on human life. Notwithstanding brave efforts, the preachers had difficulty in striking the right balance.[79]

From the great revival at Cane Ridge in 1801 to the onset of secession, the Presbyterians blamed wars for periods of religious doldrums. In January 1861, Episcopalian Bishop Thomas Atkinson stressed the destructive character of all wars, while Bishop Alexander Gregg said, "War is not *evil* in itself" since the religion of Christ sanctions patriotism as a virtue. Pronouncing the great evils of war sometimes

[77] Simms to Hammond, June 4, 1847, in Oliphant et al., eds., *Letters of Simms*, 2:322; George Fitzhugh, "Love and Danger of War," *DBR*, 27 (1860), 294–305; Simms, in *The Pro-Slavery Argument, as Maintained by the Most Distinguished Writers of the Southern States* (Philadelphia, 1853), 111; Hawthorne quoted in Andrew Delbanco, *The Death of Satan: How Americans Have Lost the Sense of Evil* (New York, 1995), 126; "Fortune of the Republic," in Len Gougeon and Joel Myerson, ed., *Emerson's Antislavery Writings* (New Haven, CT, 1995), 152.

[78] Robert L. Dabney, "The Christian's Best Motive for Patriotism," in *Fast Day Sermons* (New York, 1861), 82–3; R. L. Dabney, *Life and Campaigns of Lt. Gen. T. J. (Stonewall) Jackson* (Harrisonburg, VA, 1983 [1865]), 397–8; *DD*, quote at 1:618. The War of 1812 sapped religious interest, and in its wake the Methodists lost more than 1,200 members in South Carolina in 1817–18. Wade Crawford Barclay, *History of Methodist Missions: Early American Methodism, 1769–1844*, 2 vols. (New York, 1949), 1:127.

[79] J. J. D. Renfroe, *"The Battle Is God's": A Sermon Preached before Wilcox's Brigade* (Richmond, VA, 1863).

necessary, Gregg did not deny that war itself ranks among the greatest of evils. John Leadley Dagg, Baptist college president and theologian, noting the failure of God's covenant with Israel, located war in human nature and called for constant struggle against it through prayer. Confederate preachers, from the Episcopalian Bishop Richard Wilmer to the Baptist Reverend Sylvanus Landrum, acknowledged that war degrades and brutalizes its participants, dehumanizing them in even the most just of wars. The Methodist D. S. Doggett denounced war as a calamity that arises from human passions, adding that God used it to chastise nations for the errors of their ways and for the folly of trying to settle issues with blood. Doggett had another thought: War breeds social disorder.[80]

In November 1861 the Presbyterian Reverend T. V. Moore of Richmond acknowledged war as "an evil, and often a sore and terrible evil, and a thing at variance with the spirit of the Gospel" but preached that God uses war to discipline His people – specifically, to prevent their decline into effeminacy and the worship of Mammon. When, in 1864, the Methodist Reverend Leroy Lee reminded his congregation, "The pardon of sin, an act of God, is only practicable through sacrificial blood," he contributed, as doubtless he intended, to their resolution to continue to fight. The Reverend John Paris breathed fire in a blistering sermon on the treachery of 22 Confederate soldiers hanged for desertion in 1864, stopping to acknowledge, "War is the scourge of nations. God is no doubt chastising us for our own good." But even during the War, the soberest of preachers rejected the solution of political problems by bloodbaths and recalled the South's pleas for peaceful secession. Thus, in time-honored fashion, the Reverends T. L. De Veaux and Charles Minnigerode distinguished between just and unjust wars of aggression.[81]

With similar ambivalence, Bishop Stephen Elliott believed that great movements and nations had to pass through the tests of war as part of God's plan to use nations to perfect his purposes. Yet he cited Alexander, Caesar, and Napoleon to argue that wars of conquest invariably lead to further conquest and the inevitable corruption of the aggressive power, and a year later he branded war "a great eater, a fierce, terrible, omnivorous eater" that destroys whole peoples and societies, while also declaring that prolonged peace wreaks its own toll, corrupting peoples and

---

[80] Paul K. Conkin, *Cane Ridge: America's Pentecost* (Madison, WI, 1990), 47. Atkinson, *Causes of Our National Troubles*, 5; Alexander Gregg, *The Duties Growing Out of It, and the Benefits to Be Expected, from the Present War* (Austin, TX, 1861), 5–7; Blitch, "Thy Kingdom Come," 3; Dagg, *Manual of Theology*, 1:285; Richard H. Wilmer, *Future Good – The Explanation of Present Reverses* (Charlotte, NC, 1864), 6–7; Sylvanus Landrum, *The Battle Is God's* (Savannah, GA, 1863), 9–10; "The Apocalyptic Horses and Their Riders," in Thomas O. Summers, ed., *Sermons by the Late Rev. David Seth Doggett* (Nashville, TN, 1882), 49–50.

[81] T. V. Moore, *God Our Refuge and Strength in the War: A Discourse before the Congregations of the First and Second Presbyterian* (Richmond, VA, 1861), 6–7, 12–13; Renfroe, "The Battle Is God's," 3; Leroy M. Lee, *Redemption: Its Means – Its Effects – Its Rule. A Discourse* (Richmond, VA, 1864), 12; John Paris, *A Sermon Preached before Brig. Gen. Hoke's Brigade ... upon the Death of Twenty-Two Men* (Greensborough, NC, 1864), 12; De Veaux, *Fast-Day Sermon* (Charleston, SC, 1861), 12–13; also, Thomas S. Dunaway, *A Sermon Delivered ... before the Coan Baptist Church* (Richmond, VA, 1864), 4–5.

plunging them toward disasters. God, after all, uses war to chastise His people and set them back on a right course. Elliott quoted Heraclitus, "War is the father of all things."[82]

A good many Southerners – high and low – believed Montesquieu, who wrote, "Peace is the natural effect of trade." Dew and Calhoun were among the many who sought free trade and maximum commercial intercourse among nations, seeing war as generating social and political disasters. War, wrote President George Junkin of Washington College in Virginia, wanes in the face of economic and moral progress, and during the secession crisis, the Episcopal Reverend W. N. Pendleton cautioned his son Sandie, a student at the University of Virginia, against supporting actions that would disrupt commerce: "Commerce is not only peaceful but organizing in its nature." The Methodist Reverend John E. Edwards spoke more bluntly: Yes, world commerce brought peace, but as a function of European domination. Dew thought ancient Egypt the better for being unwarlike largely because, cut off from the world by sea and desert, it had to rely on its own resources. Less loftily did the coastal merchants and planters react negatively to threats of war, which, as W. C. S. Ventress wrote to G. Guignard in 1854, threatened to curtail exports and drive down slave prices.[83]

Calhoun, a strong critic of the Mexican War, had long argued against unnecessary wars as detrimental to free trade and economic prosperity and conducive to political centralization and corruption. No country, not even France, is so prone to war as the United States, Calhoun wrote to Thomas Clemson in 1846: "Our people are like a young man of 18, full of health & vigor & disposed for adventure of any discription [sic], but without wisdom or guidance." He feared the worst for his country: "No doubt the [Mexican] war will have its good, as well as its evil. It will afford an opportunity for the display of patriotism & valour; but it will at the same time disclose our financial weakness; involve us is a heavy debt; give a strong central tendency to our system; prevent reform, & greatly strengthen the spoils principle." Calhoun, supporting a compromise with Britain over Oregon, reiterated that war meant not only devastation and misery but also a vast concentration of federal power: "We would hear no more of State rights." In 1858 the *Southern Literary*

---

[82] Stephen Elliott, *How to Renew Our National Strength* (Richmond, VA, 1862), 7; Stephen Elliott, *Samson's Riddle: A Sermon Preached in Christ Church, Savannah* (Macon, GA, 1863), 14–15.

[83] Baron de Montesquieu, *The Spirit of the Laws*, tr. Thomas Nugent, 2 vols. (New York, 1975), 1:Bk. 20.2, quote at 316; W. C. S. Ventress to G. Guignard, 1854, in Arney R. Childs, ed., *Planters and Businessmen: The Guignard Family of South Carolina, 1795–1930* (Columbia, SC, 1957), 76; George Junkin, *The Progress of the Age* (Philadelphia, 1851), 11; W. G. Bean, *Stonewall's Man: Sandie Pendleton* (Chapel Hill, NC, 1959), 29; John E. Edwards, "Christ in History," *QRMECS*, 8 (1854), 263–4; Dew, *Digest*, 21 (Egypt), 31–5; see also William D. Thomas, "Connection of Political Economy with Natural Theology" (M.A. thesis, 1854, typescript at UVA). The Anglican Archbishop Richard Whateley, an influential figure in the South, held that the elimination of slavery and war would engender economic growth while it enhanced civilized life, but he worded his criticism of slavery cautiously, stressing economic considerations: Whateley, *Introductory Lectures on Political Economy*, 2nd ed. (New York, 1966 [1832]), 191. For Whateley's influence in the South see John Patrick Daly, "The Divine Economy: Evangelicals and the Defense of Slavery, 1830–1865" (Ph.D. diss., Rice University, 1993), 55–8.

Messenger praised the *Memoirs of the Duke de St. Simon* for demonstrating how tyrannical and warlike regimes erode a nation's resources and induce premature decay. Thomas Smyth quoted the Apocrypha: "In like manner the lightning when it breaketh forth, is easy to be seen; and after the same manner, the wind bloweth in every country. And when God commandeth the clouds to go over the whole world, they do as they are bidden."[84]

The attempt to overcome the tendencies toward corruption featured in cyclical theories of history proved no easy task for proslavery theorists. In 1861 the Reverend C. C. Pinckney of Charleston pointedly warned his congregants not to delude themselves that the superiority of their institutions, notably slavery, guaranteed escape from the pattern of imperial growth and decay: "The Chaldean monarchy, the Roman empire, the Greek republics, the South American States, were all slaveholding countries. But they have all fallen to pieces notwithstanding. Of itself, [slavery] is a mere rope of sand, with no more power, politically, than any other recognized relationship." By 1863 the preachers were reminding their flocks of another lesson from Greek and Roman history – that courageous, well-led armies can prevail over large ones, defying the most desperate odds to overcome superior numbers and materiel.[85]

The effort to make the perceived cyclical pattern end differently reappeared in an unsuccessful campaign mounted by the Presbyterian Reverend James Henley Thornwell, Bishop George Foster Pierce, and other powerful clergymen to declare the Confederacy a "Christian society." In the North, too, some clergymen warned that the Union would lose if it did not dedicate itself to Christ. In 1863 George Foster Pierce, Methodist bishop of Georgia, preaching to the state legislature of South Carolina, urged the Confederacy to amend its constitution to commit itself to Christ: "God should be acknowledged in his being, perfections, providence, and empire; not as the first great cause simply, that is philosophy; not as the universal father of a world of dependent creatures, that is poetry, sentimentalism, and may be nothing more – but as the God of the Bible, Maker, Preserver, Governor, Redeemer, Judge, Father, Son, and Holy Ghost." After the War, the Reverend T. E. Peck, speaking for many southern Presbyterians, retrospectively and respectfully took issue with Thornwell. Thornwell's doctrine, he feared, would have undermined the separation of church and state, and, he added, postwar events showed the pernicious uses to which such a doctrine could be put.[86]

---

[84] *SLM*, 26 (1858), 267. Calhoun to Clemson, May 28, 1846, in Clyde N. Wilson, ed., *The Essential Calhoun: Selection from Writings, Speeches, and Letters* (New Brunswick, NJ, 1991), 159. In *JCCP* see "Speech on the Abrogation of the Joint Occupancy of Oregon (Revised report)" (22:722), Calhoun to Sarah Mytton Maury, May 11, 1847 (24:354), and Calhoun to Clemson, July 30, 1846 (23:376–7). Thomas Smyth, *The Well in the Valley*, rev. ed. (Philadelphia, 1860), 249 n.

[85] C. C. Pinckney, *Nebuchadnezzar's Fault and Fall: A Sermon, Preached at Grace Church, Charleston, S.C.* (Charleston, SC, 1861), 11; Lacy, *Address Delivered at the General Military Hospital*; Renfroe, *"The Battle Is God's,"* 7; Minnigerode, *He that Believeth Shall Not Make Haste*, 7–8, 10–12.

[86] For Methodist ministers who supported Bishop Pierce's Christian Confederacy see Doggett, *Nation's Ebenezer*, 14; O. S. Barton, *Sermon in St. James' Church, Warrenton, Va.* (Richmond, VA, 1861),

As the Confederacy slowly succumbed, hopes that it could break the cycle evaporated. Even before the War, the Episcopalian Bishop James Otey of Tennessee preached a "lesson" (Daniel, 4:30) from the career of Nebuchadnezzar as an indication of God's plan for the rise and fall of kingdoms and states: "Their prosperity & decay in every instance are referable to nearly the same causes. God has ordained that mind & matter shall be governed by uniform laws, regular in their operation and consistent in their effects." Communities, like individuals, prosper in proportion to their "honesty, fidelity, and charity." Early in the War, in 1862, he spoke on the indestructibility of the church in a world in which nations rose and fell: "Moral Earthquakes & political convulsions shake society, overturning thrones, destroying states & kingdoms, subverting the established order of things, rending it into fragments & sending through its deep fissures the pitchy smoke of fire – flood of burning passions & maiming prejudices."[87]

Thereafter, the preachers of all denominations stepped up warnings of the transient nature of all empires, the manner in which wealth and power corrupted them, and their inevitable decline from the lofty heights to which an Alexander, Caesar, or Napoleon brought them for a historical moment. In the dark days of 1864, the Baptist Reverend Thomas S. Dunaway preached that the history of the world "has been a succession of wars and revolutions. Every age of time and every division of the earth furnishes its history of cruel war, and almost every page of the true history is written in blood." Bishop Stephen Elliott took a somewhat softer view, convinced that God uses nations to perfect His purposes and that history is the working out of those purposes even, or largely, in blood. The Baptist Reverend J. L. Burrows spoke with special urgency: "The history of nations has been the history of nations that rise, progress, decay and fall. They sin and are punished. But a nation may yet arise – pray it be our Confederacy – that rejects sin and retains God's favor." By 1865, the preachers had lost hope that the Confederacy would prove an exception.[88]

Benjamin Morgan Palmer exemplified the shift in the tone and content of the sermons. In 1863, he preached to the Georgia state legislature: "Providence is the interpretation of history. They are the two poles of the same truth: Providence aside from history is a blind enigma – history apart from Providence is a senseless fable. Both find their solution in God's purposes of grace as unfold through the church." After the War, a pessimistic Palmer concluded that the cycle of the rise, decadence, and fall would only be broken on Judgment Day. Looking back from the standpoint

---

11–12. Stonewall Jackson supported a Confederate dedication to Christ that strictly protected freedom of religion. See T. J. Jackson to W. Preston, Dec. 22, 1862, in Elizabeth Preston Allan, *The Life and Letters of Margaret Junkin Preston* (Boston, 1923), 153; George G. Smith, *The Life and Times of George Foster Pierce, Bishop of the Methodist Church, South, with a Sketch of Lovick Pierce, D.D., His Father* (Sparta, GA, 1888), 471; T. E. Peck, "Thornwell's Writings," *SPR*, 29 (1878), 421.

[87] Otey sermon of Jan. 6, 1858, at Calvary Church in Memphis, Nov. 23, 1862, in Otey Papers, at UNC-SHC.

[88] Dunaway, *Sermon in Coan Baptist Church*, 4; on Elliott see Dwyn Mounger, "History Interpreted by Stephen Elliott," *Historical Magazine of the Protestant Episcopal Church*, 44 (1975), 289; J. L. Burrows, *Nationality Insured: Notes of a Sermon Delivered at the First Baptist Church, Augusta, Ga., September 11, 1864* (Augusta, GA, 1864), 5.

of 1887, Bishop Wilmer of Alabama wrote, "The history of one age is pretty much the history of all ages." Empires and civilizations come and go: "There is, so far as human nature is concerned, 'nothing new under the Sun.' "[89]

Bishop Wilmer was not articulating a shock of recognition engendered by the fall of the Confederacy. Well before the War, the southern divines – joined by laymen like George Fitzhugh and Henry Hughes – appealed to Hesiod's invocation of "things that are, that shall be, and that went before" and joined Nathaniel Beverley Tucker in calling upon the words of Ecclesiastes: "There is no new thing under the sun." By no means did they imply, much less advocate, a static view of history. To the contrary, they predicated not merely constant change but tensions and turmoil, against which men must maintain constant vigilance and steady nerves. In their view, the world and human history proceed dynamically, ever in need of a stabilization of order that requires a sense of human fragility and an awareness of the inevitability of change, including deep change, and that can be mastered only episodically and only with God's grace.[90]

[89] B. M. Palmer, *"The Rainbow Round the Throne"; Or, Justice Tempered with Mercy* (Milledgeville, GA, 1863), 30; Doralyn J. Hickey, "Benjamin Morgan Palmer: Churchman of the Old South" (Ph.D. diss., Duke University, 1962), 242; Richard H. Wilmer, *The Recent Past from a Southern Standpoint: Reminiscences of a Grandfather* (New York, 1887), 21, 49–50.

[90] Beverley Tucker, *A Discourse on the Importance of Political Science as a Branch of Academic Education in the United States* (Richmond, VA, 1840), 7–8. In the myth that Hesiod offers in *Theogeny* and *Works and Days,* power passes from one divinity to another, but it differs from other Near Eastern myths by pointing toward an evolution that leads up to Zeus: see Albin Lesky, *A History of Greek Literature,* tr. James Willis and Cornelius de Heer, 2nd ed. (Indianapolis, IN, 1963), 92–104. Hesiod movingly chronicled the endless miseries of human history, but he refused to excuse them as the price of progress. He taught, in the words of Ivan Hannaford, "that the real choices in life are between chaos and order, the idiocy of private existence and the purpose of public life, the rule of blood and the state of being well lawed": Hannaford, *Race,* 16, also 25.

5

The Slaveholders' Quest for a History of the Common People

> History, in matter of fact, is information about human social organization, which itself is identical with world civilization. It deals with such conditions affecting the nature of civilization as, for instance, savagery and sociability, group feelings, and the different ways by which one group of human beings achieves superiority over another. It deals with royal authority and the dynasties ... and with the various ranks that exist within them. It further deals with the different kinds of gainful occupations and ways of making a living, with the sciences and crafts that human beings pursue as part of their activities and efforts, and with all the other institutions that originate in civilization through its very nature.
>
> —Ibn Khaldun[1]

In 1848, the 28-year-old Henry Augustine Washington, a lawyer in Richmond, published a remarkable essay on "The Social System of Virginia" that propelled him into a professorship of history at the College of William and Mary. For Washington – kin to George Washington, son-in-law of Nathaniel Beverley Tucker, and editor of Thomas Jefferson's papers – Virginia ranked as an anomaly in modern times or, more accurately, with parallels only in other southern slave states. Washington described Virginia's social system as "the remnant of an older civilization – a fragment of the feudal system floating about here on the bosom of the nineteenth century" and focused on the emergence of a society based upon slave and indentured-servant labor. Noting an abundance of histories of kings, rulers, and statesmen, he welcomed a marriage of history with philosophy: "We are now at last, to have a history of the PEOPLE."[2]

---

[1] Ibn Khaldun, *The Muqaddimah: An Introduction to History*, tr. Franz Rosenthal, 3 vols. (New York, 1958), 1:71. A few Southerners read Ibn Khaldun, the fourteenth-century Arab savant. To Dr. Samuel Henry Dickson, he was a great thinker and a pioneer historian of society, including its humblest. See also the work of William B. Hodgson of Savannah, a specialist on North Africa: *Notes on Northern Africa, the Sahara and Soudan* (New York, 1844), 24, 81.

[2] Henry Augustine Washington, "The Social System of Virginia," in Michael O'Brien, ed., *All Clever Men, Who Make Their Way: Critical Discourse in the Old South* (Fayetteville, AR, 1982), quotes at 238, 237. On Washington's professorship see Benjamin Blake Minor, *The Southern Literary Messenger*,

Washington stressed the isolation in country life that enabled the Virginia planter or farmer to envision himself as lord of all he surveyed. While critical of the blighting economic effects of slavery, he defended southern civilization: "Observe for a moment, if you please, the social position of the Virginia farmer. He was the head of a family, a landed proprietor, the master of indentured servants and the lord of slaves." He had no superior above him and no equal near him. Beyond the influence of general society, "with no rule of conduct but his own good will and pleasure, he lived in his forest home like a feudal baron in his lonely castle." Those "Anglo-Saxons of the woods" understood the nature of government well and did more than any other people "to solve the great social problem by which individual liberty shall be reconciled with social order."[3]

Washington returned to that theme in an address to the Virginia Historical Society in 1852, praising Virginia's early historians for useful political history but declaring, "What we now want is a history of her people – her institutions, her social and political system – her civilization – a history of Virginia in the sense in which Guizot has written the history of France, and [Thomas Babington] Macaulay the history of England." With due respect to the greatness of George Mason and others who established the principle of the sovereignty of the people in the constitution of Virginia, he insisted, nonetheless, that the experience and practical character of the people had shaped the contributions of such men.[4]

History as moral instruction required an integrated history of society, not a narrow concern with politics. Southern critics rebuked even their most revered historians for slighting social history. A reviewer in *Southern Literary Messenger* regretted that Robert Reid Howison had not devoted a single chapter of his two-volume *History of Virginia* (1846) to "*social history*" – to "the domestic manners, customs and peculiarities of the *people*," and George Frederick Holmes complained that even John Lathrop Motley's much-acclaimed *Rise of the Dutch Republic* slighted social history, in particular the character of the commercial classes.[5]

A history of the people came up against the notion that history was primarily the record of great men. Thus, James Holcombe spoke to the Virginia State Agricultural Society, much as W. M. Radford was speaking in Alabama and J. Barnett

---

1834–1864 (New York, 1905), 163. Sketching the social history of early Virginia, John Reuben Thompson followed Washington, whom he admired as a superior intellect and scholar: "Colonial Life in Virginia," *SLM*, 20 (1854), 333.

3 Washington, "The Social System of Virginia," in O'Brien, ed., *All Clever Men*, 236–8.

4 H. A. Washington, "The Virginia Constitution of 1776," *SLM*, 18 (1852), 657–8.

5 "Howison's History of Virginia," *SLM*, 14 (1848), 342; [George Frederick Holmes], "Motley's Dutch Republic," *SQR*, n.s. (3rd), 2 (1857), 430, 438. Motley's main strength, critics agreed, lay in his delineation of the character of such great figures as William the Silent and Philip II. For strong emphasis on social history in a public lecture see William Carey Crane's address to the Historical Society of Mississippi: "History of Mississippi," *SLM*, 30 (1860), 81–90. Much of the historical account of the ancient Israelites in the Bible, which Southerners accepted as authentic, recounts the action of the people, not merely their kings and leaders. "Norman-Saxon History," *VLM*, 1 (1829), 367, characterized the Old Testament and the Saxon chronicles as accounts of people's history.

Cohen and Frederick Porcher in South Carolina: "Invisible moral forces that emanate from the minds of the great thinkers of the race rule the courses of history." Paul Hamilton Hayne praised Thomas Carlyle's profound insights, grim humor, passion, and earnest opposition to the fashionable and disgraceful "pettifogging spirit" that denigrated great men. The Methodist Reverend David Seth Doggett assured his audience at Randolph-Macon College that Confucius still lives in China, much as George Washington does in the United States, and that Plato and Aristotle, Bacon and Newton, continue to influence modern thought. G. Norman Lieber credited "a few great men" and their commercial spirit with Portugal's moment of greatness. For W. C. Moragne of Edgefield, South Carolina, no nation preserves its fame for long except through "the luster reflected upon it by great men – by men of superior mental discipline and of lofty genius." The oratory in every southern hamlet on the Fourth of July celebrated America's heroes, especially George Washington, whose birthday offered a grand occasion for patriotic oratory. Mason Locke Weems's runaway bestseller, *Life of Washington,* made personal character its central theme. In 1858 a contributor to *Russell's Magazine* declared, "Take Washington from the Revolution and it becomes impracticable," for he alone had the genius to lead a Revolution and establish a nation-state.[6]

For most southern commentators, neither great men nor mass movements in themselves determine the course of history. Mass movements – peoples, classes, armies, and parties – never conquer and sustain power except under the direction of strong leaders. The ablest southern commentators intended by such reflections to undermine reliance upon abstractions, impersonal forces, and ideological constructs. A. B. Stark, in *Quarterly Review of the Methodist Episcopal Church, South,* wanted Carlyle's emphasis on the hero considered a tribute not to so-called great men but to what is "truly great and good, and noble, and godlike in man." For others, "great men" connoted not good men but men who performed great deeds.[7]

---

[6] James P. Holcombe, "Is Slavery Consistent with Natural Law?" *SLM,* 27 (1858), 401; W. M. Radford, "Success in Life," *VUM,* 4 (1859), 83; J. Barnett Cohen, "Oration Delivered on the First Anniversary of the South-Carolina Historical Society," in *Collections of the South-Carolina Historical Society,* 2 vols. (Charleston, SC, 1857–58), 2:105; F. A. Porcher, "Address Pronounced at the Inauguration of the South-Carolina Historical Society" (June 28, 1857), loc. cit., 1:11; [Paul Hamilton Hayne], *RM,* 4 (1858), 276, 279, 286; David Seth Doggett, *The Responsibility of Talent* (Richmond, VA, 1844), 9; G. Norman Lieber, "The Portuguese and Their Poet," *RM,* 4 (1858), 251; [W. C. Moragne], "The Statesman," *SPR,* 11 (1859), 531; William Gordon McCabe, "William the Silent," *SLM,* 32 (1861), 288–95; William Archer Cocke, "The Dutch Republic," *SLM,* 32 (1861), 382–3; Mason Locke Weems, *The Life of Washington. A New Edition with Primary Documents* (Amonk, NY, 1996 [1809]), see esp. Onuf's Introduction. Published in 1799, Weems's *Washington* went through twenty enlarged editions by 1825 and many thereafter. Weems, a Marylander, spent much of his life in Prince George County, Virginia. For Holmes's attack on the great-man theory see [Holmes], "August Comte and Positivism," *North British Review,* 21 (1854), 147–8.

[7] A. B. Stark, "Thomas Carlyle," *QRMECS,* 15 (1861), 416; "Hamilton and Burr," *RM,* 2 (1858), 385. Still, Julia Pardoe, whose work educated Southerners read, declared Louis XIV undoubtedly a great king who – being flawed in character and morals – fell short of being a great man: Miss [Julia] Pardoe, *Louis the Fourteenth and the Court of France in the Seventeenth Century,* 2 vols. (New York, 1847), 1:v–vi.

Yet, many of the South's most prestigious writers condemned that elitist cast of historical writing and demanded a history of the common people. Thomas Roderick Dew drew upon the "language of [François] Guizot," according to which "Only two grand figures appear on the stage of Europe, *The government* and *the people.*" Dew's youthful study of political economy cited, as foundations of Britain's wealth and power: "government; insularity; Protestantism; abundant coal, iron, and other minerals; and superior quality wool." His impressive lectures on history explored the reciprocal influence of religion and government on a people's character: "We must always in our estimate of nations, include all the various classes of society."[8]

Southerners believed that a proper understanding of social history, particularly of the common people, would strengthen a conservative slaveholding worldview. In any case, slaveholders had to face the reality expressed by a contributor from Petersburg, Virginia, to the *Quarterly Review of the Methodist Episcopal Church, South* who referred to the "humbler classes": "The time is long past when they could be disregarded in the social organization." The many who loved and often quoted Samuel Johnson welcomed his remark, "I wish to have one branch well done, and that is the history of manners of common life." As the Methodist Reverend Joseph Cummings told college students in 1851, "The comparison lies not between individuals but the masses," whose progress depends upon the spread of knowledge and spiritual awareness. Emory and Henry University's *Southern Repertory and College Review,* which published Cummings, also published H. Clay Pate, a student at the University of Virginia who called for the study of local history to unearth the lives of easily forgotten people. It would, Pate argued, deal with the world people know and want to learn more about. William Gilmore Simms ranked local histories high as source books, and John Fletcher of Louisiana commented on the prevalence of poverty or near poverty throughout history: "It is with these lower classes we have the most to do." According to Dr. Samuel Henry Dickson, a scientist and intellectual lion in Charleston, "The progress of man in civilization, his advancement in knowledge will be found as distinctly impressed upon the character of his recreations, his favorite amusements, as upon his occupations and serious pursuits," and "S. A. L." illustrated the decay of societies by reviewing the eating habits of the Greeks and Romans and the changing status of cooks.[9]

---

[8] Thomas Roderick Dew, *Lectures on the Restrictive System, Delivered to the Senior Class of William and Mary College* (Richmond, VA, 1829), 10, 12, 137; T. R. Dew, *Digest of the Laws, Customs, Manners, and Institutions of the Ancient and Modern Nations* (New York, 1884 [1852]), 427, 454. See also "Memoirs of St. Simon," *RM*, 4 (1858), 286.

[9] "Macaulay as a Historian," *QRMECS*, 5 (1851), 306; James Boswell, *The Life of Samuel Johnson, LL.D.* (New York, n.d.), 833; Joseph Cummings, "True Dignity of Human Nature and the Evidences of Man's Progress towards It," *SRCR*, 1 (1851), 146–53; H. Clay Pate, "Patriotic Discourse on Local and General History," *SRCR*, 2 (1852), 135–43; [Simms], *SQR*, n.s., 10 (1854), 249–50; John Fletcher, *Studies on Slavery, in Easy Lessons* (Natchez, MS, 1852), 29–30; Samuel Henry Dickson, "Characteristics of Civilisation," in [William Gilmore Simms], ed., *The Charleston Book: A Miscellany in Prose and Verse* (Spartanburg, SC, 1983 [1845]), 74; S. H. Dickson, "Difficulties in the Way of the Historian," *SLM*, 12 (1846), 105; "S. A. L.", "Good Eating among the Greeks and Romans," *SLM*, 21 (1855), 713–26.

Bishop William Meade's *Old Churches, Ministers, and Families of Virginia* and the Reverend William Henry Foote's volumes on Virginia and North Carolina drew especially high praise for their meticulous accounts of religious and social life. The scholarly John Archibald Campbell of Alabama, an associate justice of the U.S. Supreme Court, acclaimed Sismondi, Guizot, and Michelet as among "the great historical writers of France," applauding their insights into the social conditions and changing mores that underlaid the crises and decline of great states and empires. During the War, Basil Lanneau Gildersleeve expressed admiration for Carlyle but rejected his emphasis on great men, insisting that it is the people who make history. In 1864 the Presbyterian Reverend William A. Hall of New Orleans lectured Confederate troops in Virginia that the South needed a people's history, not another account of the few makers and shakers.[10]

The history of the common people, as Southerners read it, exuded support for their favorite cause – slavery. "The laboring classes assuredly can claim a special history," Lawrence Keitt, proslavery militant of South Carolina, told the House of Representatives in 1857, "or rather they have, in the general existence of society, a proper and distinct destiny, the evolution of which constitute a special history, and teach us under what conditions, and at what periods, those claims appeared, gathered together, and spread along the highways of civilized mankind." To Keitt, the history of the laboring classes in Europe was one of steady improvement for the masses until reversals ushered in by the emancipations of the modern era: "When the working classes stepped out of the condition of bondage, by the process of emancipation, they branched into four recurring subdivisions – the hireling, the beggar, the thief, and the prostitute – which have no general existence in slave countries, unless there have been a commencement of emancipation." Southern cities were not running red with blood, nor spending $600,000 or $1,000,000 a year to put down riots and turmoil, as Philadelphia and New York were. The convulsions that rip apart free societies did not torment ancient slave society or their medieval, Christian, serf-based successors. "The existence of slavery in all time, and in every country, is a great historical fact, the proofs of which are everywhere, in every book, in every poem, in every history, in every code to which man may have access." What exactly, Keitt asked, has philanthropy done for the slave? The offer of universal equality had produced the bloody barricades of Paris, the crushing of the English poor, huge standing armies on the Continent, and everywhere new and horrible oppression of the laboring classes. Socialism and slavery, Keitt said, now confronted each other as alternatives to barbarism, and the Bible sanctions slavery, not socialism – which, in any case, had proven unworkable.[11]

---

[10] For a response to Meade and Foote see "Old Churches and Families of Virginia," *SLM*, 25 (1857), 161–9, warmly welcoming Meade's *Old Churches, Ministers, and Families of Virginia*, 2 vols. (Berryville, VA, 1857) despite some factual errors and questionable judgments. [John Archibald Campbell], "Slavery among the Romans," *SQR*, 14 (1848), 413–14; B. L. Gildersleeve, "Congress," Richmond *Enquirer* [or *Examiner*], Feb. 20, 1863, in Ward W. Briggs, Jr., ed., *Soldier and Scholar: Basil Lanneau Gildersleeve and the Civil War* (Charlottesville, VA, 1998), 254; W. A. Hall, *Historic Significance of the Southern Revolution* (Petersburg, VA, 1864).

[11] Lawrence M. Keitt, *Slavery and the Resources of the South* (Washington, DC, 1857), 4, 5, 10.

During the 1850s, the mounting southern attack on free-labor societies carried an implicit but increasingly explicit call for a history of the oppression of the laboring classes. Charles Gayarré, Louisiana's much-admired historian, reminded readers that poor French peasants driven abroad during the seventeenth century rarely tasted meat and suffered a horrible transatlantic crossing. History as moral and political instruction recorded the travail of the lower orders of society and conveyed the strength and rationality of the slaveholders' worldview.[12]

Slaveholders, devotees of social hierarchy, had difficulty reconciling the importance of great individuals with the centrality of the common people. Some markedly limited the significance of great men. "Luther," wrote Dew, "merely gave expression to the feelings of the Age." Dew, Holmes, and George Tucker, among others, interpreted the Reformation as a long-germinating social movement, stressing the many predecessors of Martin Luther. Mitchell King, Charleston's prominent merchant-intellectual, believed that a few precious minds guided the affairs of men in part because they respectfully studied the character of ordinary men, including "the humblest citizen who drives his own wagon to a market."[13]

For George Fitzhugh, "All improvement and all discovery comes from workingmen" – a sentiment Gayarré had tacitly expressed in an erudite romp through history on the influence of the mechanical arts on the human race. Fitzhugh demanded that historians show medieval serfs as "well-souled men, who had homes, position, and place in the world," in contrast to the miserable creatures of the modern "hireling class." Fitzhugh nonetheless took respectful exception to Carlyle's view of the relation of great men to the people and to his notion that Frederick the Great embodied the characteristics of a whole people. No one man ever has much impact on the organization of society and the determination of its characteristics: "Great men are the results of the times."[14]

---

[12] Charles E. A. Gayarré, "Rise and Fall of John Law," in O'Brien, ed., *All Clever Men*, 295, 306–7; and see e.g. [G. F. Holmes], "Failure of Free Societies," *SLM*, 21 (1855), 129–41.

[13] Dew, *Digest*, 454; George Frederick Holmes, "Schlegel's Philosophy of History," originally published in *SQR* (1843), in O'Brien, ed., *All Clever Men*, 179–80, 217–18, 225; George Tucker, "A Discourse on the Progress and Influence of Philosophy," *SLM*, 1 (1835), 407; also, "Martin Luther, His Character and Times," *SLM*, 4 (1838), 596–602; Mitchell King, *A Discourse on the Qualifications and Duties of an Historian* (Savannah, GA, 1843), 10–13, quote at 13. Similarly, George McDuffie argued that if Caesar had not crossed the Rubicon then another would have: E. L. Green, ed., *Two Speeches of George McDuffie* (Columbia, SC, 1905), 21.

[14] Charles Gayarré, "Influence of the Mechanic Arts on the Human Race," *DBR*, 17 (1854), 229–44, 379–94; George Fitzhugh, "Oliver Goldsmith and Dr. Johnson," *DBR*, 28 (1860), 511; Fitzhugh, "Mr. Bancroft's History and the Inner Light," *DBR*, 29 (1860), 613. Carlyle's *Frederick the Great* was "what all histories should be, but which few are, a social history": Fitzhugh, "Frederick the Great by Thomas Carlyle," *DBR*, 29 (1860), 152–3, quote at 152; Carlyle's *Frederick the Great* was "the great work of his life": Stark, "Thomas Carlyle," 193. For praise of artisan contributions to northern cities see William D. Porter, "Value of the Arts and Sciences to the Practical Mechanic," in [Simms], ed., *Charleston Book*, 161. See also the muddled tribute to workingmen in history by the Reverend R. W. Bailey: "The Working Man," *SLM*, 14 (1848), 592–6. See also [Holmes], "Failure of Free Societies," 129–41, and [G. F. Holmes], "History of the Working Classes," *SLM*, 21 (1855), 193–203.

The assertion that men achieve greatness by moving in accord with the times and as embodiments of popular forces obscured the relation of the one to the other. John McCrady of Charleston, a respected biologist and mathematician, agreed with Guizot that the gradual establishment of social order measured the progress of civilization and that history progressed through the intellectual development of the masses, not of individuals alone. Even so, passions always threaten to distort intellectual refinement and moral judgment: "The worst vices, the most abandoned populations as well as the highest virtues, the purest society are to be found in civilized communities." In a proslavery formulation that foreshadowed the Marxist theory of "false consciousness," he said that the people exercise considerable power but not necessarily in their own best interest. William Gilmore Simms and Maximilian LaBorde of South Carolina College argued that a strong leader often imposes his will on the masses, who imagine they are thinking for themselves. He knows how to clothe his message in new garb, as if adhering to commonplaces; he makes people think they have thought it for themselves. And with a foretaste of Vilfredo Pareto's "circulation of elites," Henry Hughes of Mississippi sought a "law of succession" to explain the passage of power from one governing class to another. Republicanism based upon a politically educated and disinterested electorate alone offered a way out, and only slavery could ground it.[15]

The call for honest, empirically sound history ran into an instinctive rejection of interpretations unflattering to the South. Sectional animosity did not prevent Southerners from appreciating, if with a touch of envy, such distinguished northern historians as George Bancroft, Washington Irving, John Lathrop Motley, and William H. Prescott or even Francis Parkinson and Jared Sparks, notwithstanding their antislavery views and Unitarianism. In general, Southerners learned as much as possible from Bancroft and other northern and European antislavery historians, while they teased out everything that supported their conservatism. In 1845 Alexander B. Meek of Alabama made the questionable assertion that Southerners as well as Northerners valued Bancroft, Prescott, and Irving over Tacitus and Livy, Hume, and Gibbon. Encomia continued into the 1850s. Students at the University of Virginia, expressing pride in America's great historians, thought first of Irving, Prescott, and Bancroft; Walter Monteiro, a local luminary in Goochland County, Virginia, squirmed that the South had no historians to match them. Benjamin Perry of South Carolina, addressing the state legislature, ranked Bancroft and Prescott with the greatest of modern historians. De Bow, who settled for Bancroft's having treated slavery as fairly as any Northerner might be expected to, exulted over the emergence of a genuine American history from the culture and leisure that was replacing frontier exigencies. Bancroft, Irving, and Prescott "stand on the same pedestal of

---

[15] [John McCrady], "A Few Thoughts on Southern Civilization," *RM*, 1 (1857), 224–8; 338–49 (on Guizot), 546–56, and 2 (1857), 212–26; [Simms], "Headley's Life of Cromwell," *SQR*, 14 (1848), 507; [Maximilian LaBorde], "Characteristics of a Statesman," *SQR*, 6 (1844), 117; Henry Hughes, speech in Port Gibson, Mississippi, in 1856, "The New Governing Class," ms. in Hughes Papers, at Mississippi Department of Archives and History (Jackson).

fame with Hume, Gibbon, and Macaulay." President William Carey Crane of Mississippi College (for women) went De Bow one better, depicting Macaulay as, in some respects, even greater than Gibbon and Hume. At the beginning of the War, "R. H. C." of Eureka, Mississippi, declared, "Lord Macaulay, as a historian, stands without a rival"; and, near the end of the War, a bemused Basil Lanneau Gildersleeve recalled that criticism of Bancroft or Prescott ranked as "literary heresy."[16]

The first volume of Bancroft's *History,* appearing in the mid-1830s, emphasized the antiquity and the ubiquity of slavery. W. H. Holcombe of Natchez made extensive notes on the fifth chapter: "Slavery and the slave-trade universal except in Australia – Necessary in the passage from hunter life to agricultural life." Holcombe recorded evidence of slavery from ancient times through the Middle Ages to the present, paying special attention to the attitudes and practices of the Christian churches. Mary Howard Schoolcraft, Thomas Cobb, George Sawyer, John Monette, and J. B. De Bow relied on Bancroft's *History* to support their proslavery writings. Senator R. M. T. Hunter, in a discourse before the Virginia Historical Society, drew heavily on Bancroft's account of early colonization to establish the near omnipresence of slavery in world history. Less to southern taste, Bancroft and his friend, the prosouthern James Kirke Paulding of New York, identified an inherently unstable slavery as the cause of the decline of the Roman Empire and an impediment to America's progress. But in a factionally rent New England elite, Bancroft upheld generally conservative political views. A Democrat, he tried to limit an abolitionist influence he feared was strengthening the Whigs. For the most part he simply sidestepped southern slavery in his historical writing and in Democratic party politics.[17]

---

[16] Walter Monteiro, *Address before the Neotrophian Society of the Hampton Academy* (Richmond, VA, 1857), 7; Meek quoted in [B. F. Porter], *SQR,* 7 (1845), 258; Perry's Address in Stephen Meats and Edwin T. Arnold, eds., *The Writings of Benjamin F. Perry,* 3 vols. (Spartanburg, SC, 1980), 1:372, also, 2:277; De Bow, "Bancroft's History of the United States," *DBR,* 15 (1853), 163, 186; William Carey Crane, *Literary Discourses* (New York, 1853), 123; "R. H. C.", "Thomas Babington Macaulay," *QRMECS,* 15 (1861), 204; Briggs, ed., *Soldier and Scholar: Gildersleeve,* 174. On the Unitarianism of the New England historians see David Levin, *History as Romantic Art: Bancroft, Prescott, Motley, and Parkman* (New York, 1967), esp. 4–7, 73–7, 94–7; on their commercial success see William Charvat, *Literary Publishing in America, 1790–1850* (Amherst, MA, 1959), ch. 3. George S. Sawyer of Louisiana added Bancroft, Prescott, and Irving to his recommendation of Gibbon, Hallam, Sismondi, Montesquieu, Blackstone, Grotius, and a few others: Sawyer, *Southern Institutes; Or, an Inquiry into the Origin and Early Prevalence of Slavery and the Slave Trade* (New York, 1967 [1858]), 146–7 n. 1. J. R. Thompson published long excerpts from Bancroft's fourth volume in *SLM,* 18 (1852), 442–5. The Baptist Elder J. S. Walthall of North Carolina stressed Bancroft's celebration of Roger Williams and the struggle for religious freedom: Walthall, *Distinctive Features of the Baptists* (Raleigh, NC, 1861), 15. Jared Sparks drew accolades, especially for his collection of documents: see e.g. Fordyce Hubbard, "Life of Gen. William Richardson Davie of N.C.," *SLM,* 14 (1848), 510; William Henry Trescot, *The Diplomacy of the Revolution: An Historical Study* (New York, 1852), vii–viii, 169.

[17] W. H. Holcombe Diary, Notes in typescript, at UNC-SHC, 2:105–11; *Plantation Life: The Narratives of Mrs. Henry Schoolcraft* (New York, 1969 [1860]), 472–3; Thomas R. R. Cobb, *An Inquiry into the Law of Negro Slavery in the United States* (New York, 1968 [1858]), cxv–cxvi and esp. ch. 9; Sawyer, *Southern Institutes,* 146–7 n. 1; John W. Monette, *History of the Discovery and Settlement of the Valley of the Mississippi by the Three Great European Powers, Spain, France, and Great Britain,*

Bancroft's good relations with Simms, the Reverend James Henley Thornwell of South Carolina, and other prominent Southerners contributed to his good name in the South. Simms – like Bancroft, a celebrant of "order and progress" – launched his historical novels in 1834, advancing an ethnic interpretation strongly biased toward the Teutonic peoples. Bancroft and William Cullen Bryant promoted Simms's lecture tour in 1856, apparently unaware that Simms considered Northerners and Southerners different peoples with separate destinies. Bancroft held a dinner party in New York in honor of Thornwell at which he presented a two-volume German work on Aristotle, inscribed to Thornwell as "the most learned of the learned" from a "friend." Bancroft also corresponded with leading figures of the Georgia Historical Society.[18]

Still, with admiration went stern criticism. A contributor to *Southern Literary Messenger* bristled at Bancroft's elevation to status of America's premier historian, grumbling that he did not present both sides of a controversy fairly. While Fitzhugh acknowledged Bancroft as an honest historian of "great Industry," "great genius," and "profound learning" and as a literary artist superior even to Gibbon, Hume, William Robertson, and Oliver Goldsmith, he excoriated him for substituting the Inner Light for the Word; for extolling radical democracy and the assorted irrationalities of abstract reformers; and for ignoring the guidance of his own meticulous research, which counseled respect for tradition and experience. George William Bagby, editor of *Southern Literary Messenger,* found strengths and weakness in Bancroft, but mostly weaknesses: Bancroft lacked "the judicial mind that separates the grain from the chaff."[19]

2 vols. (New York, 1971 [1846]), 1:228–9; *DBR,* 1 (Jan. 1846), 45; 3 (1847), 421; R. M. T. Hunter, "Observations on the History of Virginia," *SQR,* n.s., 11 (1855), 477–506 (Hunter also drew on Bancroft, John Smith, Robert Beverley, and William Waller Henning to extol the Anglo-Saxon origins of Virginia); Russell B. Nye, *George Bancroft* (New York, 1964), 2, 14–17, 98–9, 101; Paulding to Bancroft, Nov. 21, 1834, in Ralph M. Aderman, ed., *The Letters of James Kirke Paulding* (Madison, WI, 1962), 151–3. See also Supplementary References: "Bancroft."

18 David Moltke Hansen, "Between Plantation and Frontier: The South of William Gilmore Simms," in John Caldwell Guilds and Caroline Collins, eds., *William Gilmore Simms and the Southern Frontier* (Athens, GA, 1997), 10, 16; W. S. Patterson to the Librarian of the University of South Carolina, Nov. 4, 1948 [*sic*]; B. M. Palmer, *The Life and Letters of James Henley Thornwell* (Richmond, VA, 1875), 537. For Bancroft and the Georgia Historical Society see William Harris Bragg, *De Renne: Three Generations of a Georgia Family* (Athens, GA, 1999), xviii, 154, on Simms see 10; David Moltke-Hansen, "Ordered Progress: The Historical Philosophy of William Gilmore Simms," in John Caldwell Guilds, ed., *"Long Years of Neglect": The Work and Reputation of William Gilmore Simms* (Fayetteville, AR, 1988), 133. Simms's *The Tricolor,* which celebrated the Revolution of 1830, stressed the ethnic component in historical destiny. De Bow also noted Bancroft's generous treatment of Charleston and South Carolina in his first volume in 1834: De Bow, "Bancroft's History," 186; *DBR,* 1 (Jan. 1846), 45, and 3 (1847), 421; [De Bow], "Carolina Political Annals," *SQR,* 7 (1845), 479. George Davis, Esq., of Wilmington invoked Bancroft's authority to complain that North Carolina's history was being written poorly: George Davis, *Address Delivered before the Two Literary Societies of the University of North-Carolina* (Raleigh, NC, 1855), 5.

19 "The Present State of Southern Literature," *SLM,* 23 (1856), 387; George Fitzhugh, "Mr. Bancroft's History and the Inner Light," *DBR,* 29 (1860), 598–613, esp. 611; [George William Bagby], *SLM,* 31 (1860), 157–8. Bagby was known as a "man about town" and a bellicose secessionist: see William

Virginians had a special grievance. In 1835, in a review of the first volume of Bancroft's *History,* Nathaniel Beverley Tucker devoted his entire space to a stinging refutation of Bancroft's account of seventeenth-century Virginia. Tucker and Edmund Randolph objected to Bancroft's depicting Virginia's royalist ancestors as opportunists who made their peace with Cromwell. For Tucker, Virginia was the product of a "chivalrous and generous race" that resisted Cromwell's usurpation. Simms wrote to John Pendleton Kennedy, "We believe that Yankee Histories of the United States are generally fraudulent from Peter Parley to George Bancroft." *Southern Literary Messenger* accused Bancroft of praising Virginia for the wrong reasons and for sneering at its genuine virtues. Contrary to Bancroft, Virginia did not support Cromwell. *Southern Literary Messenger* insisted, with Howison and other local historians, that Virginia's noble ancestors had loyally supported their king and opposed Cromwell's despotism. The irascible Edmund Ruffin saw much merit in the fifth volume of Bancroft's *History* but complained of a style "too florid and rhetorical."[20]

Even those who lived comfortably with Bancroft's treatment of slavery blanched at his enthusiasm for democracy. Frederick Porcher charged him with being "too ostentatiously partisan and the apologist of democracy," to the point of demagogy. Still, William Henry Trescot, who knew Bancroft from their days in Europe and who was no great admirer of democracy, applauded Bancroft's "very able history," and contributors to *Southern Quarterly Review* routinely referred to his "noble" history and to him as "the great American historian, Bancroft."[21]

Macaulay, too, acquired a large southern audience. Conservatives, North and South, especially valued Macaulay's social history as support for their worldview. John Reuben Thompson, reviewing his *History of England* for *Southern Literary Messenger,* commended its rich description of the life of the people. Although Thompson considered Macaulay not entirely trustworthy, he held him up as a model – "indeed a marvel" – for those who would correct the imbalance of historians and do justice to the "manners and customs" of colonial Virginians, by whom he meant primarily the men and women of the gentry. Despite exaggerations and

Pusey III, "Junius M. Fishburn (1830–1858): Professor of Latin," *Proceedings of the Rockbridge Historical Society,* 9 (1975–79), 141.

[20] [Nathaniel Beverley Tucker], "Literary Notices," *SLM,* 1 (1835), 587–91, quote at 587; Bagby agreed with Tucker's criticism in *SLM,* 31 (1860), 157–8; also, Edmund Randolph, *History of Virginia,* ed. Arthur H. Shaffer (Charlottesville, VA, 1970), 149; Simms to John Pendleton Kennedy, Aug. 5, 1852, in Mary C. Oliphant et al., eds., *The Letters of William Gilmore Simms,* 6 vols. (Columbia, SC, 1952–82), 3:174–5 (but see also Simms to Tucker, May 13, 1849 [2:526] and Simms to Evert Augustus Duyckinck, Dec. 6, 1854 [3:345]); *SLM,* 1 (1835), 587–91; Simms nonetheless appears to have rated Bancroft high as a historian: Simms to Bancroft, Jan. 15 and 26, 1858 (4:4–6, 15). Robert R. Howison, *A History of Virginia from Its Discovery and Settlement by Europeans to the Present Time,* 2 vols. (Philadelphia, 1846), 1:298–9 n. b; Edmund Ruffin, Sept. 17, 1864, in *ERD,* 3:568–9. But Bancroft's account of early Virginia pleased the Virginia-born Elwood Fisher: "The North and the South," *DBR,* 7 (1849), 141.

[21] F. A. Porcher, "Bancroft's History," *RM,* 3 (1858), 522–3; Trescot, *Diplomacy of the Revolution,* 169; "J. S. W.", "Histoire de Louisiane," *SQR,* 9 (1846), 363; *SQR,* 3 (1843), 42. See also Supplementary References: "Hildreth."

misrepresentations, Macaulay's historical and poetical imagination made him a great essayist with a passion that highlighted larger truths.[22]

To H. Clay Pate, Macaulay stood as "the best living historian," and to the Reverend Abram Burwell Brown as "profound and brilliant." Dew praised his "masterly articles" on the seventeenth-century English revolutions for their judicious account of the principal issues and correction of Hume's errors. An article in *De Bow's Review* praised Macaulay's essays for better moral instruction than Dickens's own, and Edward McCrady, Jr., found arguments to support curbs on popular democracy in Macaulay's opposition to Chartism. The politically moderate Fannie Page Hume registered Macaulay's death sadly: "Another great man gone! They seem to follow in rapid succession – & who alas! are fitted to take their places? I am sure we stand in need of wise heads & firm hearts now. Our national affairs seem to be in the hands of a parcel of fanatics – disorder reigns supreme." Accolades notwithstanding, Macaulay came in for severe criticism. The Cumberland Presbyterians' *Theological Medium*, uneasy at his enormous popularity, protested that Macaulay was unfair both to the Puritans and to Charles II. More cuttingly, a contributor to Robert Breckenridge's *Danville Quarterly Review* declared Macaulay and Hume "not morally qualified" to understand the Puritans. De Bow, however, cited Macaulay in an assault on the Puritans and, by extension, the abolitionists. Some admirers of *History of England* took umbrage at his attack on Baconian philosophy. W. S. Grayson of Mississippi, a Methodist, led the counterattack against Macaulay, for which he caught hell from a Macaulay fan.[23]

Macaulay – "the prince of modern historians," as the Presbyterian Reverend John Bocock of Virginia called him – enjoyed the respect of most of the intellectually formidable Presbyterians. Robert L. Dabney, calling for a social history of food and clothing, arts and agriculture, and amusements and the concerns of the common people, invoked Macaulay to warn nations against allowing their wealth to render them soft and pleasure loving. A contributor to *Southern Presbyterian Review* described Macaulay's pages as teeming "with the rich gatherings of a truthful mind." Benjamin Morgan Palmer hailed Macaulay's *History of England* for showing how personages of history represent the leading ideas of the age and embody "underlying principles." In an 1863 address to the South Carolina legislature,

---

[22] [J. R. Thompson], *SLM*, 15 (1849), 125–6; Thompson, "Colonial Life in Virginia," *SLM*, 20 (1854), 331–5; Thompson, *Address before the Literary Societies of Washington College* (Richmond, VA, 1850), 33; [Thompson], *SLM*, 19 (1853), 192; [Thompson], "Prescott and Macaulay," *SLM*, 22 (1856), 144–55. Thompson defended Macaulay against widespread suspicions of religious skepticism: *SLM*, 22 (1856), 318. See also Supplementary References: "Macaulay."

[23] Pate, "Patriotic Discourse," 135–43; Dr. and Mrs. William E. Hatcher, *Sketch of the Life and Writings of A. B. Brown* (Baltimore, 1886), 259; Dew, *Digest*, 559 n.; J. T. Nesbit, "Essay Writing and the Press," *DBR*, 5 (1848), 304; for McCrady see Charles J. Holden, *In the Great Maelstrom: Conservatives in Post–Civil War South Carolina* (Columbia, SC, 2002), ch. 3. Hume Diary, Jan. 18, 1860, at UNC-SHC; W. S. Grayson, "Bacon's Philosophy and Macaulay's Criticism of It," *SLM*, 29 (1859), 177–83; for a rebuttal to Grayson see [William Gordon McCabe], "Bacon's Philosophy and Macaulay's Criticism, of It: A Reply to Mr. Grayson," *SLM*, 29 (1859), 382–6; *DQR*, 3 (1863), 290; "Macaulay's History," *Theological Medium*, 4 (1849), 215–22; *DBR*, 10 (1851), 519. See also Supplementary References: "Macaulay."

Palmer brought Macaulay home with a reference to his "brilliant pages" on the struggle against oppression.[24]

What appealed to Presbyterian divines upset some others who lacked Calvinist sensibilities – notably Holmes, who snarled that Macaulay won wide and "stupid" applause for his many superficial judgments and "diseased fascinations." Fitzhugh ranked Macaulay with Milton as, at bottom, a radical Puritan and a malicious and impious misanthrope who "proposes to combine the landed and moneyed interests, and form a government of the middle classes." Besides, Macaulay hated England's Charles I, whom Fitzhugh admired. Other conservatives applauded the sentiments Macaulay expressed in a letter to Henry Stephens Randall in 1857, praising Randall's biography of Thomas Jefferson but confessing to no high opinion of Jefferson himself. Jefferson's egalitarianism, Macaulay wrote, leads to "spoilation" and class war: "Your Constitution is all sail and no anchor .... Your republic will be as fearfully plundered and laid waste by the barbarians in the twentieth century as the Roman Empire was in the fifth." When free land gives out, Macaulay warned, America will suffer a Caesar or a Napoleon. Fitzhugh never said it better.[25]

When Macaulay died in December 1859, a contributor to *Southern Literary Messenger* congratulated him for writing splendid history that workingmen read and enjoyed, while allowing a grain of truth to the charge that "he is too dazzling to be trusted, too interesting to be solid, too attractive to be true." The author then suggested that some critics praised Macaulay as an essayist primarily to denigrate his stature as a historian. He might have had in mind W. H. Holcombe of Natchez or Benjamin Perry of South Carolina or several contributors to *Quarterly Review of the Methodist Episcopal Church.* Indeed, much of Macaulay's reputation among Southerners rested on his essays. For all that, Macaulay stood high in southern

---

[24] [John H. Bocock], "The Martyrs of Scotland and Sir Walter Scott," *SPR,* 10 (1858), 69–94; "Letters and Speeches of Oliver Cromwell," *SPR,* 1 (1847), 126; "Uses and Results of Church History," *DD,* 2:10–11; "Principles of Christian Economy," *DD,* 1:15; [B. M. Palmer], "Import of Hebrew History," *SPR,* 9 (1856), 586; B. M. Palmer, *Discourse before the General Assembly of South Carolina* (Charleston, SC, 1864), 9. The Presbyterian Joseph Atkinson added a tribute to Macaulay's "grace" and "pictorial art": [Atkinson], "The Puritans," *SPR,* 15 (1862), 230–55. Judge Joseph Lumpkin of Georgia settled for a reference to "Macaulay's splendid history": *An Address Delivered before the South-Carolina Institute at Its Second Annual Fair, on the Nineteenth of November, 1850* (Charleston, SC, 1851), 7. The "historian, philosopher, and statesman Macaulay" defended religious liberty against those who would merge the functions of state and church: R. S. Gladney, "Relation of State and Church," *SPR,* 16 (1866), 354. Macaulay stressed the Germanic origins of Protestantism and the racial basis of modern freedom and progress.

[25] [George Frederick Holmes], "The Bacon of the Nineteenth Century – Second Paper," *MMQR,* 4th ser., 5 (1853), 491; [Holmes], "Recent Histories of Julius Caesar," *SR* (Baltimore), 1 (1867), 401 (Holmes added Palgrave, Prescott, Motley, Helps, Froude, and Carlyle among those with "diseased fascinations"); George Fitzhugh, "Milton and Macaulay," *DBR,* 28 (1860), 671, 673–4, 678, quote at 670; Macaulay to Randall, Jan. 23, 1857, in Appendix to Frank J. Klingberg and Frank W. Klingberg, eds., *The Correspondence between Henry Stephens Randall and Hugh Blair Grigsby, 1856–1861* (Berkeley, CA, 1952), 185. This letter had been published in *SLM,* 30 (1860), 225–8. Some questioned the authenticity of Macaulay's criticism of American institutions, but Henry S. Randall, who filed the charge, defended his attribution: "American Institutions," *SLM,* 31 (1860), 133–5.

public opinion, in no small part because of his respectful attention to the life of common people.[26]

The quest for the history of the common people encouraged an interest in the literary sources, folk cultures, and oral traditions of their own and other societies. In general, Southerners adopted Plutarch's view, "We must not treat legend as if it were history at all, but we should adopt that which is appropriate in each legend in accordance with its verisimilitude." A people's songs, satires, and comedies, William J. Rivers told the student societies of South Carolina College, reflect their moral condition and constitute "truthful sources for the delineations of history." In a discussion of chivalry and the exaltation of women, Dew remarked: "The songs of a nation are last things committed to writing, because so well remembered. Many negroes in the United States, who cannot read, know as many songs as would amount to an Iliad." The fable of *Reynard the Fox*, with a vast circulation in medieval Europe, passed down to schoolboys in America. Reynard, a trickster like Br'er Rabbit of black folklore, epitomized those who outwit stronger animals and whose cunning and dissembling exposed the folly and weakness of supposed superiors.[27]

The histories of John Gillies, William Mitford, and Jules Michelet also won applause, in part for their use of myths and oral traditions as historical sources, which, James Johnston Pettigrew said, "are seldom without some foundation in general facts." Holmes, influenced by Vico, called for the study of myth not as primitive delusion but as a sign of a stage in human development. *Southern Literary Messenger* found the earliest history of ancient and modern peoples primarily in ballads and heroic lays devoted to the great men of the age but sung by the people. One author called the early ballads of the people, rediscovered by Macaulay and others and separated from later corruptions, as evidence of historical cycles: struggles for freedom and the quest for empire, the triumph of conquest and luxury, the plunge into cultural decadence and imperial decline. Holmes in *Southern Quarterly Review*, F. Gaither in *Russell's Magazine*, and a contributor to *De Bow's Review* applauded historians like Macaulay and Barthold Niebuhr for plumbing such sources of popular culture as *El Cid* and the *Niebelungen Saga* as well as the legends and romances of Provence. G. Norman Lieber – in a brief sketch of the life, times, and work of Luiz de Camoëns – extolled *The Lusiads* for bringing to life the heroic period in

---

[26] [Lord Macaulay], *SLM*, 30 (1860), 241–50; W. H. Holcombe Diary, Jan. 22 and 30, 1855; Meats and Arnold, eds., *Writings of Perry*, 2:95; "Macaulay as a Historian," *QRMECS*, 5 (1851), 308–10; Stark, "Thomas Carlyle," 200. For Macaulay as a better essayist than historian see e.g. [Joseph B. Cobb of Longwood, MS], "Macaulay's History of England," *American Whig Review*, 11 (1850), 347–68.

[27] Plutarch, *Moralia*, tr. Frank Cole Babbitt (LCL), 5:sec. 58; William J. Rivers, "Connection of Epic Poetry with the History and Times in Which They Were Written," in *Addresses and Other Occasional Pieces* (Baltimore, 1893), 2; Dew, *Digest*, 51, 348; on Reynard see esp. Charles T. Wood, *Quest for Eternity: Manners and Morals in the Age of Chivalry* (Hanover, NH, 1970), 80–1. For an illuminating analysis of Simms's indebtedness to folk traditions see James E. Kibler, Jr., "Simms' Indebtedness to Folk Tradition in 'Sharp Snaffles,' " *SLJ*, 4 (1972), 55–68. President William Carey Crane of Mississippi College taught his female students that epics and songs provided "the earliest vehicle for all information": *Literary Discourses* (New York, 1853), 42–4, quote at 43.

Portuguese history, in which the exploits of a few great men rallied "young and old, rich and poor, noble and peasant."[28]

Admiration for the accomplishments of British, Continental, and northern historians prodded Southerners to reflect on their own performance, and their reflections hint at a regional inferiority complex. The South did, in fact, produce historians worthy of respect, although their contributions to southern thought have largely gone unappreciated. Thomas Roderick Dew, working from secondary sources, did not match Bancroft, Prescott, or Motley, but his posthumously published *Digest of the Laws, Customs, Manners, and Institutions of the Ancient and Modern Nations* offered a grand interpretation of the course of Western Civilization and the relation of culture to politics. William Henry Trescot's pioneering *Diplomacy of the American Revolution* and *Diplomatic History of the Washington and Adams Administrations* bristle with profound insights and earned him the status of "father of American diplomatic history."[29]

Most southern historians concentrated on the local, state, and regional histories their people loved to read: Captain John Smith, Robert Beverley, William Byrd, William Stith, Charles Campbell, and Robert Reid Howison on Virginia; David Ramsay and William Gilmore Simms on South Carolina; William Henry Foote of North Carolina and Virginia; William Bascom Stevens on Georgia; J. G. M. Ramsey on Tennessee; Albert Pickett on Alabama; J. F. H. Claiborne on Mississippi; François Xavier Martin and Charles Gayarré on Louisiana; A. B. Meek and John Monette on the Southwest. David Ramsay's *History of the United States* (1789) ran through six editions to 1865 and appeared in translation in French, German, and Dutch. "It is no exaggeration," writes A. H. Shaffer, "to say that David Ramsay created American history" and that his *History of the American Revolution* launched American national historiography. Ramsay himself took Jeremy Belknap and other New Englanders as models who taught the value of frugality, hard work, and rejection of aristocratic pretense. But, as Shaffer also insists, Ramsay ranked as the last of the "national" intellectuals in Charleston – and, as such, marked the end of an era. Jefferson considered Ramsay's *History of the Revolution in South*

---

[28] [George Frederick Holmes], "Lays of Ancient Rome," *SQR*, 4 (1843), 76–81; "Relations of the Ancient World," *SQR*, 5 (1844), 163–4; [F. Gaither], "Ariosto," *RM*, 6 (1859), 155; Lieber, "The Portuguese and Their Poet," 249–56, quotes at 250, 253; for Michelet see James Westfall Thompson, *A History of Historical Writing*, 2 vols. (Gloucester, MA, 1967 [1942]), 2:240–1. Daniel K. Whitaker ranked *Lusiads* with the Aeneid: "From Our Arm-Chair," *SLJ*, 2 (1836), 236. Macaulay's *Lays of Ancient Rome* was a lowcountry favorite readily quoted by Mary Chesnut: June 28, 1861, Dec. 1864, in C. Vann Woodward, ed., *Mary Chesnut's Civil War* (New Haven, CT, 1981), 84, 692; Meats and Arnold, eds., *Writings of Perry*, 3:326; R. Q. Mallard to C. C. Jones, July, 13, 1857, in Robert Manson Myers, ed., *The Children of Pride: A True Story of the Children of the Civil War* (New Haven, CT, 1972), 350. See also Supplementary References: "Ballads" and "Borrow."

[29] For the enthusiastic reception of Trescot's two volumes in the South see [William J. Grayson], "Trescot's Diplomatic History," *RM*, 2 (1857), 423–31; [John R. Thompson], *SLM*, 26 (1858), 238–9. On page vii Trescot declared *The Diplomacy of the Revolution: An Historical Study* (New York, 1852) an essay, not a history, but good history it remains.

Carolina authentic, reliable, and a candidate for translation into French. To James Knox Polk, Ramsay was the American Tacitus.[30]

Richard Beale Davis has suggested that Henning's 13-volume *Statutes at Large* (1809–23), although confined to legal development, qualifies as Virginia's most significant historical writing for the half-century before 1830, and in the 1850s John Reuben Thompson considered it a vital source for early social life in Virginia. Bancroft rated Henning's *Statutes at Large* peerless among state studies and joined Prescott, Dew, and Thomas Hart Benton in lavishing praise on Gayarré's pioneering work on Louisiana. The Duyckincks, editorial lions in New York, lauded William Byrd's *History of the Dividing Line.* Although John Hill Wheeler considered his own *Historical Sketches of North Carolina* of 1851 a chronicle, not a history, Simms rated it a superior work. It sold more copies in North Carolina than any history until well after the Second World War, and it may have been the most widely read book there after the Bible. J. G. M. Ramsey, pioneer historian of east Tennessee, who collected valuable manuscripts and wrote much of high quality, built frankly and gratefully on the work of Wheeler and Foote for his account of the early days of North Carolina. Wheeler hailed Francis Xavier Martin as one of the most learned jurists of his age and the author of the best history of North Carolina. State supreme court justice William Gaston and W. W. Holden, the politically influential newspaper editor, considered Martin a state ornament.[31]

---

[30] Richard Beale Davis, *Intellectual Life in Jefferson's Virginia, 1790–1830* (Chapel Hill, NC, 1964), 277; J. R. Thompson, "Colonial Life in Virginia," *SLM*, 20 (1854), 333; Dumas Malone, *Jefferson and His Time,* 6 vols. (Boston, 1962–81), 2:109; Arthur H. Shaffer, *To Be an American: David Ramsay and the Making of the American Consciousness* (Columbia, SC, 1991), 1 (Polk). Emma Holmes of Charleston spoke for many when she announced her delight with *History of the Revolution in South Carolina*: July 29, 1862, in John F. Marszalek, ed., *The Diary of Miss Emma Holmes* (Baton Rouge, LA, 1979), 185. Abroad, Friedrich von Gentz, in his comparison of the American and French revolutions, saluted Ramsay as judicious and reliable: *The Origin and Principles of the American Revolution, Compared with the Origin and Principles of the French Revolution,* tr. by "An American Gentleman" [John Quincy Adams], (New York, 1977 [1800]), 73; A. H. Shaffer, "David Ramsay and the Limits of Revolutionary Nationalism," in Michael O'Brien and David Moltke-Hansen, eds., *Intellectual Life in Antebellum Charleston* (Knoxville, TN, 1986), 48, 95–6. For praise of Ramsey from distinguished Charlestonians see Dickson, "Difficulties in the Way of the Historian," 108. The government of Alabama sent copies of Pickett's *History* to every state library in the country, and it quickly became a standard in Alabama's schools and private and public libraries. What Philip D. Beidler says of Pickett would serve for others: To read Pickett today "is still to sense one's self in the presence of a genuine literary and historiographic achievement": Beidler, *First Books: The Printed Word and Cultural Formation in Early Alabama* (Tuscaloosa, AL, 1999), 66, quote at 72.

[31] John Hill Wheeler, *Historical Sketches of North Carolina from 1584 to 1851,* 2 vols. (Baltimore, 1964 [1851]), 2:111 (Martin); [Simms], "Critical Notices," *SQR,* n.s., 6 (1852), 524–5; William B. Hesseltine, ed., *Dr. J. G. M. Ramsey, Autobiography and Letters* (Knoxville, TN, 2002), 5; W. W. Holden, *Address on the History of Journalism in North Carolina,* 2nd ed. (Raleigh, NC, 1881), 5–6; Evert A. Duyckinck and George L. Duyckinck, *Cyclopaedia of American Literature,* 2 vols. (New York, 1856), 1:74–7. On Wheeler's *Sketches* see W. S. Powell, *When the Past Refused to Die: A History of Caswell County, North Carolina, 1777–1977* (Durham, NC, 1977), 141, 343; on the reception of Gayarré's work see "Editorial Miscellany," *DBR,* 26 (1859), 481. William Byrd's *History of the Dividing Line betwixt Virginia and North Carolina, Run in the Year of Our Lord 1728* established itself as a literary classic, but it was not published until Edmund Ruffin's edition of 1841. *Southern Literary Messenger*

State and local historians, above all others, depend upon a meticulous sorting out of documents, but the historical societies necessary for collection emerged late and slowly in the South. Although the small size of the urban middle class there spelled meager financial resources and little state aid, dogged spirits laid a foundation for the collection of manuscripts and other historical materials. The sectional tensions of the 1840s and 1850s encouraged greater interest in their work, with substantial progress the result. Clergymen took the lead. In Mississippi, seven of the thirteen founding members of the state historical society were clergymen, and in Alabama the Reverend Dr. Basil Manly, prominent Baptist educator, wrote the constitution of the Alabama Historical Society in 1850.[32]

The Georgia Historical Society, too, owed much to the efforts of a few prominent men. William Bascom Stevens, an Episcopal priest and professor at the University of Georgia, wrote a controversial history of the state. Simms, with a few reservations, found Stevens's *History of Georgia* an "excellent work," and Cobb relied on it as a good source for colonial Georgia. Beginning in the 1820s under difficult circumstances, Joseph Vallence Bevan collected Georgia's historical documents, and in 1839 the collection went forward when Stevens and Israel Tefft launched the Georgia Historical Society. *Southern Quarterly Review* applauded the Society's publication of papers and documents and contrasted its impressive achievements with the feeble efforts of similar groups in Virginia and South Carolina. In 1843 it credited the Society with rekindling intellectual life in Savannah through its excellent lecture series, and in subsequent volumes it reviewed the publications of the state societies. By 1849 Mitchell King was warmly praising the Society's work in

published articles on the early history of Virginia by Charles Campbell and reprinted W. S. Bogart's articles from *Southern Field and Fireside*: [Bogart], "Historic Landmarks of Lower Virginia," *SLM*, 33 (1861), 115–26, 350–62.

Campbell judged William Stith an accurate and the best of Virginia's early historians but complained of his diffuse style: Charles Campbell, *History of the Colony and Ancient Dominion of Virginia* (Philadelphia, 1860), 105, 150 n. Stith earned respect for his command of primary sources and also qualified as an influential religious controversialist: Richard Beale Davis, *Intellectual Life in the Colonial South, 1515–1763*, 3 vols. (Knoxville, TN, 1978), 1:96–102, 737–41, 792. See also William Stith, *The History of the First Discovery and Settlement of Virginia* (Spartanburg, SC, 1965 [1747]).

Dr. James Gettys McCrady Ramsey studied medicine at the University of Pennsylvania and practiced in Nashville. He was a trustee of several colleges, a planter, a friend of Polk but a leader in the Whig party, an elder in the Presbyterian Church, and mayor of Knoxville; biographical information in Ramsey Family Papers, at UNC-Greensboro. Francis Xavier Martin, born in France, was appointed judge in the Mississippi Territory and then justice of the Supreme Court of Louisiana. He lived in New Bern for many years and died in 1842.

[32] [Simms], "A History of Georgia," *SQR*, 13 (1848), 470–501, quote at 470; E. Brooks Holifield, *The Gentlemen Theologians: American Theology in Southern Culture, 1795–1860* (Durham, NC, 1978), 40; Thomas McAdory Owens, *History of Alabama and Dictionary of Alabama Biography*, 4 vols. (Spartanburg, SC, 1978 [1921]), 1:28; Wayne Flynt, *Alabama Baptists: Southern Baptists in the Heart of Dixie* (Tuscaloosa, AL, 1998), 96. For the difficulties that early southern historians faced – because of the paucity of records available to them – and the heroic efforts of the early historical societies to provide a remedy, see E. Merton Coulter, "What the South Has Done about Its History," *JSH*, 2 (1936), 3–14.

collecting and preserving documents, which contemporaries feared were being lost. The historical societies won praise especially for such efforts. Ben Sanders (Mississippi's state librarian), J. F. H. Claiborne, Joseph B. Cobb, and B. L. C. Wailes inspired and led the Mississippi Historical Society and its collections, laying the basis for Claiborne's celebrated history of early Mississippi. The prestigious Academy of Sciences in New Orleans established a chapter for local history, and by 1860 the Historical Society of Louisiana at Baton Rouge was collecting manuscripts and other sources. The various "New-England Societies" that sprang up in the South, most notably in Charleston, promoted historical studies effectively and with sufficient southern partisanship to win the approval of the ever-watchful *De Bow's Review*.[33]

Complaints of inadequate progress continued nonetheless. In the 1840s, Simms complained about the paucity of documents on colonial and revolutionary South Carolina, blaming it on British domination and the ravages of the Revolutionary War. In 1851, David Hunter Strother ("Porte Crayon") writhed at the sight of the valuable historical manuscripts that were going to seed. In the early 1840s, *Southern Literary Messenger* published complaints by prominent citizens that Virginia was not doing nearly enough to preserve its colonial records. While it welcomed such publications as B. F. French's two-volume *Historical Collections of Louisiana* (1846, 1850), it pleaded for the collection of documents from Georgia and the Carolinas. In the 1850s, voices were still expressing embarrassment at the want of scholarly societies in the South, but Henry Augustine Washington struck a positive note when he congratulated the Virginia Historical and Philosophical Society for collecting the documents necessary for a proper history of Virginia.[34]

---

[33] On Stevens see Henry Thompson Malone, *The Episcopal Church in Georgia, 1733–1957* (Atlanta, GA, 1960), 74–5; Cobb, *Law of Negro Slavery*, 83. For R. D. Arnold see Richard H. Shryock, ed., *Letters of Richard D. Arnold, M.D., 1808–1876* (Durham, NC, 1929), 21 n. 1. Bishop Stephen Elliott served as president of the Georgia Historical Society: *SQR*, 2 (1842), 535; 3 (1843), 40–93; 5 (1844), 391–419; for the Savannah lectures see "Critical Notices," *SQR*, 3 (1843), 537–8. King, *Qualifications and Duties of an Historian*, 7, 23; also *SLM*, 15 (1849), 248; E. Merton Coulter, *Joseph Vallance Bevan: Georgia's First Official Historian* (Athens, GA, 1964), ch. 5; for the early days of the Georgia Historical Society see Bragg, *De Renne*, ch. 2. Zachary Taylor Leavell, "The Ante-Bellum Historical Society of Mississippi," in Franklin L. Riley, ed., *Publications of the Mississippi Historical Society* (Oxford, MS, 1905), 8:227–9; "Editorial Miscellany," *DBR*, 28 (1860), 242, 491; also, Thomas Ruffin to Catherine Ruffin, Mar. 14, 1826, in J. G. deRoulhac Hamilton, ed., *The Papers of Thomas Ruffin*, 4 vols. (Raleigh, NC, 1918), 1:343; C. C. Jones, Jr., to C. C. Jones, in Robert Manson Myers, ed., *A Georgian at Princeton* (New York, 1976), 112. George Bacon Stevens left Athens for Pennsylvania, where he became a bishop. His work drew heavy fire in Georgia as superficial and inaccurate, but a good deal of the criticism stemmed from personal animosities. Simms criticized Stevens's history, but he acknowledged its strong points: see Bragg, *De Renne*, 48–55. For reports on the Georgia Historical Society see also *Magnolia*, n.s., 1 (1842), 322, and 2 (1843), 271. See also Supplementary References: "Historical Societies in the South."

[34] William Gilmore Simms, *The Life of Francis Marion*, 8th ed. (New York, 1844), Preface; Cecil D. Eby, Jr., *"Porte Crayon": The Life of David Hunter Strother* (Chapel Hill, NC, 1960), 62; for a typical complaint see also [James Warley Miles], "Oriental Studies," *SQR*, n.s., 7 (1853), 273; H. A. Washington, "Virginia Constitution of 1776," 657–73. For a plea for the collection of Georgia's historical documents see "Judge Law's Oration before the Georgia Historical Society, Feb. 12, 1840," *Southern*

There were determined efforts in the 1840s and 1850s to increase the quantity and improve the quality of southern historical writing and to subject them to searching criticism. *De Bow's Review*'s articles by regional, state, and local historians were designed to advance a proper moral perspective and to present as accurate a factual record as possible. John Monette, a Virginia-born Mississippian, published his 1,200-page *History of the Discovery and Settlement of the Valley of the Mississippi* (1846) to provide an empirically solid account of a subject enshrouded in myth. The editor of *Southern Quarterly Review* pronounced it "magnificent" before seeing a copy, but J. F. H. Claiborne and Mann Butler, respected historians, criticized it for inaccuracies and questionable interpretations. De Bow lauded Albert Pickett's history of Alabama as a great event in southern publishing history, crediting Pickett and Gayarré with launching a genuinely southern history, although he found Gayarré and Martin lacking in critical respects. *Southern Quarterly Review* and *Southern Literary Messenger* joyfully welcomed Foote's histories of North Carolina and Virginia. Bocock effusively praised the research in a book destined to survive the tests of time. Recognizing *Sketches of Virginia* as essentially a history of religious liberty in Virginia, he declared that just about everyone was reading it and wishing it were even longer.[35]

Ladies' Book, 2 (1840), 195–6. For complaints see, in *SLM*: W. G. Minor quoted in Thomas Walker Gilmer, "Colonial History of Virginia," 7 (1841), 109–12; Charles Campbell, "Virginia Antiquities," 9 (1843), 591–2, 693–6, 728–9; "B.", "Foote's Sketches of Virginia," 16 (1850), 116–18; "The Early History of Virginia," 22 (1856), 110. For pleas for collections see Dickson, "Difficulties in the Way of the Historian," 110–11; [George Atkinson], "Civil Warfare in the Carolinas and Georgia," *SLM*, 12 (1846), 258–9; "S. T. G.", "Early History of Louisiana," *SLM*, 18 (1852), 311–12. De Bow published lengthy reports on the Parisian archives' material on the early history of Louisiana: see E. J. Forstall in *DBR*, 1 (Mar. 1846), 238–51; "French Colonial Records" (Apr. 1846), 358–9; (May 1846), 358–69. John Perkins, "Louisiana Historical Society," *DBR*, 7 (1849), 278, and 8 (1850), 97.

35 *DBR*, 11 (1851), 687–8, and 12 (1852), 57; [De Bow], "Sketch of Louisiana," *DBR*, 1 (May 1846), 383–4, and 3 (1847), 279–93; [J. H. Bocock?], "Foote's Sketches of Virginia," *SLM*, 17 (1851), 8–17; also, [J. R. Thompson], *SLM*, 22 (1856), 479. Simms, however, remarked on the "copious, warm, passionate" style that Gayarré displayed in his *Influence of Mechanic Arts*: [Simms], *SQR*, n.s., 10 (1854), 524. De Bow thought that Martin presented a storehouse of information but got lost in details and wrote dryly and inelegantly, and "J. S. W." found Martin's history of Louisiana "a work of considerable merit, but rather desultory." He gave Gayarré higher marks but also chafed under his dryness: "Histoire de Louisianne," 361–71. De Bow did not take well to Gayarré's decision to write in French, but he expressed high regard for the second volume, publishing long extracts in translation. Later notices of Gayarré's work in *De Bow's Review* were generally favorable and respectful to their author: see e.g. *DBR*, 4 (1847), 142. Monette criticized F. X. Martin's history of Louisiana for poor organization and other stylistic deficiencies and also for factual errors, but he found it a "store-house of information": Monette, *Valley of the Mississippi*, iii–iv, 1:111 n.; *SQR*, 8 (1845), 528; J. F. H. Claiborne, *Mississippi as a Province, Territory, and State, with Biographical Notices of Eminent Citizens* (Spartanburg, SC, 1978 [1860]), 1:ch. 8; Mann (incorrectly cited as Mason) Butler, "Monette's 'Early Spirit of the West,'" *DBR*, 9 (1850), 142–3. For Monette see C. G. Forshey's obituary in *DBR*, 11 (1851), 92–114. For Foote see *SQR*, n.s. (3rd), 1 (1856), 207.

De Bow's Review and *Southern Literary Messenger* expressed pleasure at George Tucker's *History of the United States*: *DBR*, 24 (1857), 112; also, "A Native of Virginia", "Mr. Jefferson," *SLM*, 7 (1841), 287–8. Samuel Henry Dickson lauded Stevens's history of Georgia: "Difficulties in the Way of the Historian," 107. Hugh Blair Grigsby reviewed Campbell's book favorably and noted

To Simms, Meek, Nelson F. Smith of Alabama, Joseph Addison Turner of Georgia, and other promoters of southern literature, a history of the common people meant more than the history of white men. They repeatedly called for attention to Indians as essential to a genuine regional literature, and Dew, among others, insisted upon the inclusion of women. A few mentioned Africans – free and slave – in passing, although mention was all they did. Southerners read a good deal about Africa and even wrote some, but they ignored African history, in contradistinction to racially biased and blatantly absurd accounts of current affairs; indeed, Southerners, like many other white Europeans and Americans, seem to have assumed that Africa had no history. They did, however, have one point to make, buttressed by much speculation and dubious statistics. George A. Baxter of Virginia, William C. Buck, editor of Kentucky's *Baptist Banner,* Thomas R. R. Cobb, a generally careful scholar, and innumerable others declared that three quarters of the people of Africa lived as slaves under especially miserable conditions. Discussions of Egypt credited whites with the marvels of its ancient civilization and assumed that blacks contributed nothing beyond servile labor.[36]

In *De Bow's Review,* Gayarré focused on early European–Indian contacts, and Franklin Smith of Mississippi explored theories of Indian origins, concluding that

improvement of his style since the earlier publication in [Grigsby], "Campbell's History of Virginia," *SLM*, 30 (1860), 209–20. Hugh Garland's *Life of Randolph* did not get off so lightly. The editors of *DBR* and *SLM* bestowed their blessings on it, but Nathaniel Beverley Tucker protested in *SQR* that Garland had cluttered it with panegyrics to Jefferson designed to make money. See [John R. Thompson], *SLM*, 16 (1850), 704; *DBR,* 10 (1851), 228; [Nathaniel Beverley Tucker], "Garland's Life of Randolph," *SQR,* n.s., 4 (1851), 41–61. *Southern Quarterly Review* returned to Garland's biography in 1857 with a softer tone effected by John Tyler, Jr., who knew Randolph in his youth and recounted his life with virtually no mention of Garland's biography: [Tyler], "John Randolph of Roanoke," *SQR,* n.s. (3rd), 2 (1857), 314–36. Virginia historians generally acknowledged the work of predecessors, albeit critically. Howison, for example, praised Stith for accuracy but criticized his inelegant style; he dismissed Beverley's history as sketchy and biased: *History of Virginia,* 1:251 n. a, 2:468.

36 Meek also sang the praises of America as a land populated by all the peoples of Europe, not only Anglo-Saxons: A. B. Meek, *Americanism in Literature* (Tuscaloosa, AL, 1844), 9. George A. Baxter, *An Essay on the Abolition of Slavery* (Richmond, VA, 1836), 22; William C. Buck, *The Slavery Question* (Louisville, KY, 1849), 16; Cobb, *Law of Negro Slavery,* passim. Also, J. Jones, *A Discourse Delivered ... to the Rome Light Guards and Miller Rifles in the Presbyterian Church of Rome, Ga.* (Rome, GA, 1861), 10; and the Northerner J. K. Paulding, in a book well received in the South: *Slavery in the United States* (New York, 1836), 40–1, 236–48. For a typical description of Africa as degraded and wallowing in heathenism see John Leighton Wilson, "The Moral Condition of Western Africa," *SPR,* 2 (1848), 79–97.

    Alexander Hewitt, who had spent several years of research in Charleston, recognized the ubiquity of slavery among civilized peoples and considered black labor indispensable for the development of South Carolina and Georgia. He nonetheless considered slavery an enormity and rejected racial justifications. He believed that Africans had as much right as Europeans to freedom and, conversely, as much right to enslave Europeans: *An Historical Account of the Rise and Progress of the Colonies of South Carolina and Georgia,* 2 vols. (London, 1779), 1:64, 20, 24–5, 2:59, 91, 94–104. Edwin C. Holland, in a well-circulated early proslavery pamphlet, cited *Rise and Progress* to establish northern responsibility for the slave trade and its horrors, and he remarked on Hewitt's admission that whites could not have survived lowcountry summers. See [Holland], *A Refutation of the Calumnies Circulated against the Southern and Western States, Respecting the Institution and Existence of Slavery among Them* (Charleston, SC, 1822), 17, 42–3.

they crossed from Asia. De Bow dubbed Henry Schoolcraft's *History, Condition, and Prospects of the Indian Tribes of America* a "great national work" and approved Pickett's *History of Alabama* in part for its extensive and generally sympathetic portrayal of Indians. But the long essays on Indian affairs in *Southern Quarterly Review* expressed a typical southern combination of admiration and disgust, and its reviews placed Indians in an unfavorable light. Maximillian LaBorde took "the greatest pleasure" in William Rivers's history of early South Carolina, with its primary research, but it reinforced LaBorde's belief in the Indians' cruel and merciless nature. In fact, although Rivers did portray the Indians of the early Carolinas as treacherous and bloody-minded, he also recorded the provocations of white rapacity and "ill-usage." The *Catechism of United States History* by B. F. Carroll, an especially popular text in South Carolina's secondary schools and recommended both by Governor State Rights Gist and De Bow, considered Indians "savages" but attributed the worst of the wars to white encroachment on Indian land and spoke of the cruelty of the whites.[37]

Southerners, like Northerners, grappled with the contradictory accounts provided by their own colonial historians. In general, the Indians emerged as jealous, vengeful, implacable, and ready to slaughter men, women, and children. Captain John Smith considered Indians savages to be turned into servants or exterminated; Robert Beverley and John Lawson discovered Spartan virtues and "noble savages"; William Stith and William Jones, acknowledging Indian virtues, focused on their ingratitude and perfidy. The well-documented Indian cruelty to prisoners of war – the penchant for prolonging tortures – induced shudders. In the 1850s, Charles Campbell's *History of the Colony and Ancient Dominion of Virginia* offered a cautious review of Indian customs and character in which the Indians suffered grave injustices but were "cunning, bloody, and revengeful." Wheeler, in his *Historical Sketches of North Carolina,* expressed some sympathy for the Indians but railed against their savagery: "Ripping infants from the wombs of their expiring mothers; roasting Christians to death by slow fire."[38]

---

[37] In *DBR* see: Charles Gayarré, "Romance of Louisiana History," 3 (1847), 449–52; for reviews of government reports on Indian history and current affairs: 5 (1848), 229–37; 6 (1848), 68–73. For J. A. Turner's praise of William Cullen Bryant's poetry for its sympathetic treatment of Indians, see "Bryant's Poems," *DBR,* 9 (1850), 583–5; also, Franklin Smith, "Origin of the American Indians," *DBR,* 3 (1847), 565–6; 19 (1855), 118; on Pickett see *DBR,* 12 (1852), 56–66, 148–69. See also Supplementary References: "Indians – Southern Attitudes."

[38] Karen Ordahl Kupperman, ed., *Captain John Smith: A Select Edition of His Writings* (Chapel Hill, NC, 1988), Introduction and pt. 3; Robert Beverley, *The History and Present State of Virginia,* ed. Louis B. Wright (Chapel Hill, NC, 1947 [1705]), 29, 38, 51–4, 192–3; Hugh Jones, *The Present State of Virginia: From Whence Is Inferred a Short View of Maryland and North Carolina,* ed. Richard L. Morton (Chapel Hill, NC, 1956), 54–62; Frances Latham Harriss, ed., *Lawson's History of North Carolina* (Richmond, VA, 1941 [1709, 1741]), 208–9; Stith, *Discovery and Settlement of Virginia;* Campbell, *History of Virginia,* ch. 6 and 168; Wheeler, *Sketches of North Carolina,* 1:37, quote at 2:366. See also Gary B. Nash, "The Image of the Indian in the Southern Colonial Mind," *WMQ,* 3rd ser., 39 (1972), 197–230. "To John Smith, Virginia was only the lengthened shadow of England": Edd Winfield Parks, *Segments of Southern Thought* (Athens, GA, 1938), 20. Beverley saw the injustice in the seizure of Indian lands and regretted that a policy of intermarriage had not been followed, for it

From Beverley on, southern historians conceded that the Indians' introduction to European methods of trade drove them to feel cheated and abused. Some eminent Southerners tried to respond fairly but did little to detract from the prevailing notion of a degraded race. Jefferson treated Indians respectfully in *Notes on the State of Virginia,* making blacks look bad in comparison. At the Literary and Philosophical Society of Charleston in 1827, Catholic Bishop John England lectured respectfully on the "Religion of American Indians" and followed with an essay in *Southern Review,* but his audience probably heard primarily that Indians were, after all, heathens.[39]

Each side accused the other of initiating the continuing Indian wars, and each side accused the other of committing the atrocities they each in fact indulged in. Westward-moving Southerners had a much harder time than Northerners because they faced a foe militarily more powerful and better organized. Whites signed – and repeatedly violated – one treaty after another that guaranteed the Indians their territory and placed westward-moving whites under Indian jurisdiction. Indian resistance often took ghastly form, and whites retaliated in kind, sometimes massacring friendly Indians along with the hostile.[40]

With a mixture of admiration and horror, Nelson F. Smith, an Alabama historian, described Indians as ingenious, witty, cunning, deceitful, and vengeful. Henry Howe said it was the English who had begun "to maltreat the harmless, unpretending, and simple natives" who grew "jealous of the power of the overbearing strangers." George Strother Gaines, an early leader in the Southwest, expressed surprise that the Indians he first encountered in Alabama were not the savages he expected. The more he saw of their practices, the more he came to think of them as

might have restrained the Indians' penchant for violence. On the continuing value of the accounts of John Smith and Beverley see Edmund S. Morgan, *American Slavery, American Freedom: The Ordeal of Colonial Virginia* (New York, 1975), 49 n. 14, 77; Davis, *Intellectual Life in the Colonial South,* 1:84, 87–91. Davis notes that colonial historians and commentators on the Indians looked for – and found to their own satisfaction – parallels with the ancient Hebrews: loc. cit., 1:148, 167–8, 173–5, 186. Southern accounts resembled Edward Gibbon's portrayal of the barbarians of ancient Germany: "They knew not how to forgive an injury, much less an insult; their resentments were bloody and implacable": *The History of the Decline and Fall of the Roman Empire,* ed. David Womersley, 3 vols. (London, 1994), 1:249.

[39] Sebastian G. Messmer, ed., *The Works of the Right Rev. John England, First Bishop of Charleston,* 7 vols. (Cleveland, OH, 1908), 5:104–59; see also the sympathetic remarks of Bishop George Foster Pierce, *Incidents of Western Travel: In a Series of Letters* (Nashville, TN, 1857), 50–1. On the deficiencies of the Indians as a race see also [Josiah C. Nott], "Aboriginal Races of America," *SQR,* n.s., 8 (1853), 59–92, also 256–7. Joseph Cobb of Georgia and Mississippi complained that American writers romanticized the Indians while denigrating blacks. Although a supporter of slavery, he considered black culture rich – much richer than Indian: see Tommy W. Rogers, "Joseph B. Cobb: Antebellum Humorist and Critic," *Mississippi Quarterly,* 22 (1969), 140–1.

[40] Seymour Dunbar, *A History of Travel in America,* 4 vols. (New York, 1968 [1915]), 1:151, 2:chs. 22 and 25; for documents on the period to 1812, see e.g. Edward J. Cashin, ed., *A Wilderness Still the Cradle of Nature* (Savannah, GA, 1994), 3–4, 73–156. Settlers in Mississippi fought a bitter war with the Creeks in 1813–14: Dunbar Rowland, ed., *Mississippi: Comprising Sketches of Counties, Towns, Events, Institutions, and Persons, Arranged in Cyclopedic Form,* 4 vols. (Spartanburg, SC, 1976 [1907]), 2:920–5.

"pretty good neighbors." Simms, in contrast, dubbed the Indians of South Carolina "half-human." Indians in his *History of South Carolina* were savage, treacherous, vengeful, and cruel, although Simms distinguished among tribes and their progress toward civilization, acknowledging that they had often been betrayed and abused by rapacious whites. In 1859, a contributor to *Southern Literary Messenger* from Wytheville, Virginia, added as evidence of the Indians' advance toward civilization their increasing participation in slaveholding – a note that Calhoun had previously sounded.[41]

Thomas Hart Benton, spokesman for the left-wing Jacksonians in the Border States, despised elite intellectuals and the press for promoting a false and sentimental account of the Indians during the Seminole War, of hiding the evidence of their atrocities, and of glorifying Osceola, the Indian leader he considered a butcher. Henry Clay, no left-wing Jacksonian, added that the disappearance of the Indians "would be no great loss to the world." For the conservatives, Holmes dismissed doctrines of racial equality and wrote that the Gypsies, North American Indians, and blacks of Saint Domingue "have shown themselves wholly incapable of civilization." Barbarian races might advance to civilization through intermixture with more advanced peoples, as Europeans had during the Middle Ages, but not all did so, not even most Asians. The Methodist Reverend William A. Smith of Virginia suggested that no savage community ever rose to a state of civilization unless lifted up by others.[42]

The leading historians of the Southwest devoted much of their books to Indians. A. B. Meek, in poetry and history, honored the Indians of Alabama in a confrontation with whites he treated as tragic. His book of poetry on the Creek War of 1813 featured William Weatherford ("The Red Eagle"), the half-Scots Indian chief he

---

[41] Nelson F. Smith, *History of Pickens County, Ala., from Its First Settlement in 1856* (Spartanburg, SC, 1980 [1856]), 40–1; Henry Howe, *Historical Collections of Virginia* (Charleston, SC, 1845), 19; Rhoda Coleman Ellison, *Early Alabama Publications: A Study in Literary Interests* (University, AL, 1947), chs. 3–4; James P. Pate, ed., *The Reminiscences of George Strother Gaines: Pioneer and Statesman of Early Alabama and Mississippi, 1805–1843* (Tuscaloosa, AL, 1998), 42, 46–7, quote at 78; W. G. Simms, *Francis Marion*, ch. 1; William Gilmore Simms, *The History of South Carolina*, 8th ed. (New York, 1860), esp. Bk. 1; "Slavery among the Indians," *SLM*, 28 (1859), 333–5. Simms congratulated J. G. M. Ramsey for his extensive depiction of Indians in early Tennessee: [Simms], "Ramsey's Annals of Tennessee," *SQR*, n.s., 8 (1853), 337–68; for Simms see also "The Colonial Era of South Carolina," *SQR*, 6 (1844), 130–63; J. C. Calhoun, "To the People of the Southern States," July 5, 1849, in *JCCP*, 26:477. For an illustration of uneasy conscience see Josiah Teeter, "Relative Interest Attached to America and Europe," *SRCR*, 3 (1854), 225–6; also, Lester W. Ferguson, *Abbeville County* (Spartanburg, SC, 1993), 5, 17. Calhoun also applauded the Iroquois "Confederacy of the Six Nations," along with the Polish Diet, as an illustration of unity in diversity that generated military strength: John C. Calhoun, "Disquisition on Government," in Ross M. Lance, ed., *Union and Liberty: The Political Philosophy of John C. Calhoun* (Indianapolis, IN, 1992), 54.

[42] Thomas Hart Benton, *Thirty Years' View; Or, a History of the Working of the American Government for Thirty Years, from 1820 to 1850*, 2 vols. (New York, 1854), 2:ch. 3; Clay quoted in Forrest McDonald, *States' Rights and the Union: Imperium in Imperio, 1776–1876* (Lawrence, KS, 2000), 100; Holmes, "Schlegel's Philosophy of History," in O'Brien, ed., *All Clever Men*, 203–4; G. F. Holmes, "Observations on a Passage from Aristotle," *SLM*, 16 (1850), 193–205; William A. Smith, *Lectures on the Philosophy and Practice of Slavery* (Nashville, TN, 1856), 123.

knew personally and praised for "dauntless gallantry." Much of Monette's massive *Valley of the Mississippi* focused on Indian wars and Indian–white relations. Monette depicted the Indians as savages who, despite many admirable qualities, tortured and took no prisoners, but he did not spare the whites for their many acts of treachery, exploitation, ingratitude, and usurpation: "History does not furnish an instance in which a civilized people, waging war with savages or barbarians, have not adopted the mode of warfare necessary to place them on an equality with their antagonists. It is impossible to adapt civilized warfare to the chastisement of savages." Monette had picked up an old theme. In the first decade of the nineteenth century the whites in much of Mississippi and Louisiana, according to Methodist preachers, knew little more about Christianity or civilized life than the Indians did. William Wirt, an advocate of peace with the Indians, wrote that frontier conditions and endless warfare had made the frontiersmen very much like the savages they confronted. Brantz Mayer – in his account of the Mexican War – suggested that the Spaniards, too, had become barbarians in their wars with barbarian Indians in Mexico.[43]

The frequent southern discussions of the much-admired James Fennimore Cooper focused on the strong impression left, especially among women, by his treatment of Indians. Although Ella Barrow found his novels "*very* interesting" and Maria Bryan praised his control of "suspense," Elizabeth Ruffin wrote to her father of *Last of the Mohicans*: "Can't say much in commendation of it; 'tis of almost ferocious nature." She duly noted the picture of Indians who were at once admirable, indeed noble, but she also noted that the novel "ends horridly and the indian trait of revenge is pictured and ruined to the very last." In 1861, Mary Chesnut caught up with Cooper's *History of the Navy* (1839) and observed, "a good book to give one a proper estimate of one's foes."[44]

Leading southern historians and critics, betraying an uneasy conscience about peoples driven from their lands and subjected to cruel oppression as the price of

---

[43] A. B. Meek, *The Red Eagle* (Montgomery, AL, 1914 [1855]) – appropriately, Meek dedicated his book to Simms; Monette, *Valley of the Mississippi,* esp. 1:249, 319–28, 339–40, 2:38–40 (quote at 40), 392–3. *Red Eagle* went through six printings in its first year and was well received in both North and South: see Beidler, *First Books,* 81 and (generally) ch. 6. On Indian decline see "The Indians of the United States – Their Past, Their Present, Their Future," *DBR,* 16 (1854), 143–9. For the Methodist preachers see the Narration of Lerner Blackman, Oct. 2, 1804, and Elisha W. Bowman to William Blake, Jan. 29, 1806, in John D. Jones, *A Complete History of Methodism as Connected with the Mississippi Conference of the Methodist Episcopal Church, South,* 2 vols. (Nashville, TN, 1908), 1:148–52, 173; William Wirt, *Sketches of the Life and Character of Patrick Henry* (Philadelphia, 1817), 240; Brantz Mayer, *History of the War between Mexico and the United States with a Preliminary View of Its Origin* (New York, 1848), 6, 133. See also Supplementary References: "Meek."

[44] Ella Barrow to Lucy Barrow Cobb, Feb. 25, 1865, in Kenneth Coleman, ed., *Athens, 1861–1865: As Seen through Letters in the University of Georgia Libraries* (Athens, GA, 1969), 114; Maria Bryan to Julia Ann Bryan Cumming, Apr. 14, 1828, in Carol Bleser, ed., *Tokens of Affection: The Letters of a Planter's Daughter in the Old South* (Athens, GA, 1996), 66; Elizabeth Ruffin Diary, Feb. 27, 1827, in Edmund Ruffin Papers, at UNC-SHC; Chesnut Diary, June 10, 1861, in Woodward, ed., *Mary Chesnut's Civil War,* 72; also, Mary Moragné Journal, Feb. 13, 1837, in Delle Mullen Craven, ed., *The Neglected Thread: A Journal of the Calhoun Community* (Columbia, SC, 1951), 23–4. For Cooper's popularity in Alabama see Ellison, *Early Alabama Publications,* 67. Much of Cooper's brand of conservatism corresponded to the main lines of southern criticism of northern society: see Steven Watts, " 'Through a Glass Eye, Darkly': James Fenimore Cooper as Social Critic," *JER,* 13 (1993), 55–74.

world progress, shed a tear for Indians doomed in a classic tragedy. They sadly acknowledged that the more the Indians assimilated white standards of civilization, settling into agriculture and commerce and building Christian churches and schools, the more whites were determined to drive them away. The Indians, wrote George Tucker, defended their land and patronage with "desperate valor and consummate address." De Bow added that – unlike blacks – proud, warlike Indians could not be enslaved for their own good; their very resistance doomed them to extinction before the power of a superior race. De Bow commented on the cruelties committed by Indians of the Southwest but, referring to the policies of the Spanish and French, offered an excuse that implicitly indicted whites: "Savages though they were, there is no doubt that the Natchez tribe felt all the sorrow of exiles in being driven from their delightful home." With "profound indignation" John Esten Cooke described white atrocities as "these massacres and murders – they were nothing less." He, too, saw a tragedy in which whites descended to the level of Indian barbarism. No cloud without a silver lining: Reverend E. T. Winkler concluded that South Carolina's colonial wars against savage Indians hardened its people to fight the American Revolution.[45]

In the 1840s Howison explored the European–Indian confrontation as tragedy. He stressed the Indians' unrivaled "skill to concert schemes of ingenious perfidy." Like Hugh Jones before him, he dwelt on their ferocity in wars waged on each other before the arrival of the Europeans, sometimes wars of extermination. Occasionally, Howison tripped over himself: He described them as "too cruel to be brave" while he noted the Rappahannock as distinguished for bravery as well as for hatred of the whites. He recounted white abuse of the Indians and, recapitulating Beverley, explained the claims of the Indians to consider the land their own. Yet he saw the inexorability of a racial conflict between a conquering people bent on economic and social development and a static people who could not transform their environment in accordance with the demands of the modern world. Howison, like William Wirt thirty years earlier, raised eyebrows by his concurrence in Patrick Henry's notion that miscegenation would solve the problem and his regret that it had not been tried.[46]

---

45 Tucker, "Discourse on the Progress and Influence of Philosophy," 420; [John Esten Cooke], "Indian Wars of Western Virginia," *SLM*, 17 (1851), 544–51; E. T. Winkler, *The Citizen Soldier* (Charleston, SC, 1858), 7. See also [George Frederick Holmes], "North American Indians," *SQR*, 5 (1844), 118–56; "The Indian Tribes of the United States," *DBR*, 17 (1854), 68–76; J. D. B. De Bow, *The Industrial Resources, Statistics, &c. of the United States and More Particularly of the Southern and Western States*, 3rd ed., 3 vols. (New York, 1966 [1854]), 2:20–9, quote at 24. The tale that Europeans taught scalping to the Indians is rent by James Axtell and William C. Sturdevant, who note that early European traders did pay bonuses for scalps of hostile Indians: "The Unkindest Cut, Or Who Invented Scalping," *WMQ*, 37 (1980), 451–72.

46 Howison, *History of Virginia*, 1:54, 231, 234–5, 287, 305 (Rappahannoc), 2:292–4 (Henry), and on white abuse and Indian claims see 1:57–60, 115–16, 237, 259–60, 445–6; Wirt, *Patrick Henry*, 240–2. For criticism of abusive policies toward the Indians by a distinguished soldier-statesman see Hugh Williamson, *The History of North Carolina*, 2 vols. (Spartanburg, SC, 1973 [1812]), 1:42–51.

In 1847 and 1848, Charles Hodge's *Biblical Repertory and Princeton Review* welcomed Howison's *History of Virginia* as the best book on the subject, and it especially welcomed his hopes for the end of slavery. See "Howison's History of Virginia," *BRPR*, 19 (1847), 224–36, and 20 (1848), 186–206, esp. 187, 204–6. This was quite a compliment since Howison did not disguise his New School bias in

Dew, Simms, W. R. Aylett, and Hugh Legaré – speaking for a swelling number of
Southerners – demanded that historians take account of women. Echoing Gibbon,
they declared denigration of women a sign of barbarism. Dew, focusing on the relative physical weakness of women, accepted the necessity for men to bear arms and
control public affairs, while he insisted that the progressive elevation of women provided the yardstick for the advance of civilization and the augmentation of virtue.[47]

"The lot of women among savages," Dew argued, "has always been found to
be painful and degrading," but the emergence of slavery eliminated many of the
horrors women had been subjected to. "The labor of the slave thus becomes a substitute for that of the woman." Woman ceases to be "a mere *'beast of burthen'*;
becomes the cheering and animating centre of the family circle." Slavery raised
woman to "the equal and idol of man." He bemoaned the "curious fact" that the
women who gained so much from slavery now were sentimentally embracing wild
schemes of emancipation. By ignoring slave women, Dew shifted the discussion
away from race and gender to class stratification and the necessity for what J. H.
Hammond later called a "mudsill." In articles for *Southern Literary Messenger* in
1835–36 and again in 1842, Dew characterized women's place in society as the great
question of the day.[48]

Those who sought to integrate women into history had a model in Elizabeth Fries
Ellet's *Women of the American Revolution,* which Simms, Wheeler, Mrs. Schoolcraft, and others praised and which John Reuben Thompson declared "an eminent
and deserved success," adding good words for her *Women of the West. Southern
Presbyterian Review* lauded *Women of the American Revolution* for doing justice
to the contributions of women while underscoring the proper place of women in

---

History of Virginia, 2:484. Even Edmund Ruffin, who thought well of Howison's *History of Virginia*
despite its antislavery bias, grumbled, "He is a federalist in party politics, & a New School Presbyterian in religion": *ERD,* Nov. 21, 1858 (1:250).

[47] "Professor Dew on Slavery," in *The Pro-Slavery Argument, as Maintained by the Most Distinguished
Writers of the Southern States* (Philadelphia, 1853), 336–41; Thomas Roderick Dew, "Dissertation
on the Characteristic Differences of the Sexes, and Women's Position in Society," *SLM,* 1 (1835),
493–512, 621–32, 672–91; see also Dew's articles in *SLM,* 2 (1836) and 8 (1842). With an eye on
America's high divorce rate, an anonymous contributor to *Southern Literary Messenger* surveyed
Roman history to conclude that a want of religion promotes abasement of women and invites social
decline: "Observations on the 'Caesars,' of DeQuincy," *SLM,* 29 (1859), 281–4. Dew wrote extensively on women in every epoch: see e.g. his remarks on Persia in *Digest,* 94–5; for similar sentiments
see *SQR,* 11 (1847), 307–8. Daniel C. Gilman, ed., *The Miscellaneous Writings of Francis Lieber,* 2
vols. (Philadelphia, 1881), 1:315. When Dew died, William Boulware, in a eulogy for the Richmond
Enquirer (Oct. 23, 1846), especially recommended his essays on women in history. "W. M. A." of
Baltimore cited Queen Semiramis of Assyria to argue for the intellectual equality of women with
men and to protest against the restrictions of their education. She did not hide her admiration for
the military qualities of that great warrior queen, who might, she acknowledged, have murdered her
husband to ascend to the throne. "W. M. A.", "The Rights of Woman," *SLM,* 8 (1842), 530–5.

[48] Benjamin Blake Minor, who edited *Southern Literary Messenger* in the 1840s, praised Dew's effort:
"This learned dissertation should be republished in handsome form, in memoriam of its author and
for the benefit of the living"; see Minor, *The Southern Literary Messenger,* 29. Hugh Legaré and
the Reverend Charles Colcock Jones, like Dew and Gibbon before them, considered the exclusion
of women a measure of Greek barbarism. See Gibbon, *Decline and Fall,* 2:811; Michael O'Brien, *A
Character of Hugh Legaré* (Knoxville, TN, 1985), 158; Charles Colcock Jones, *The Glory of Woman
Is the Fear of the Lord: A Sermon* (Philadelphia, 1847), 5–6.

politics. Simms saluted Ellet for bringing out the social and emotional dimension of politics, and "M. M." of Columbia, South Carolina, writing in *Quarterly Review of the Methodist Episcopal Church, South,* wondered that it had not been written years before, "filling up, as it does, an important hiatus in American history." In the 1850s the ladies' reading circle in Morganton, North Carolina, discussed Ellet's *Women of the Revolution,* which "completely charmed" the 20-year-old Harriett Newell Espy.[49]

To preach is one thing, to practice another. Wheeler took pains to mention the historical contributions of women, but his two-volume work contained little beyond references to a few outstanding women. David L. Swain, former governor of North Carolina and president of the University of North Carolina, complained that histories ignored women, but he limited himself to mention of Hagar, Ruth, Naomi, Queen Elizabeth, the Empress Josephine, and other elite women. Still, the focus on great women had at least one merit: For the most part it eschewed patronization. Queen Elizabeth, in particular, aroused mixed feelings. Brantz Mayer of Maryland admired her promotion of commerce and sea power, and the Methodist Reverend David Seth Doggett and James P. Holcombe ranked her as a great historical figure – "This woman of heroic spirit," as Holcombe called her. T. R. Price, Jr., of the University of Virginia saw the cycle of national glory and decline reflected in the pattern of English literature: glory with Elizabeth, decline with Victoria. But the staunchly proslavery Edwin C. Holland came down hard on Elizabeth for her support of the slave trade and general cupidity. Not surprisingly, Calvinists attacked her for religious opportunism: Bocock thought she deserved to be remembered as "the queen of Viragoes."[50]

---

49 [William Gilmore Simms], "Ellet's Women of the Revolution," *SQR,* n.s., 1 (1850), 314–54, and Drew Gilpin Faust, *A Sacred Circle: The Dilemma of the Intellectual in the Old South, 1840–1860* (Baltimore, 1977), 76; *Plantation Life: Narratives of Schoolcraft,* ch. 1; [John R. Thompson], *SLM,* 16 (1850), 320, and 18 (1852), 639–40; [William Gilmore Simms], "Critical Notices," *SQR,* 16 (1849), 270; "M. M.", "The Women of the Revolution," *QRMECS,* 4 (1850), 481; Harriett Newell Espy to Zebulon Vance, Jan. 22, 1852, in Elizabeth Roberts Cannon, ed., *My Beloved Zebulon: The Correspondence of Zebulon Vance and Harriett Newell Espy* (Chapel Hill, NC, 1971), 46. On Ellet's account of the contribution of women and the nurturing of the spirit of liberty at the fireside of the common people, see [Holmes], "Carlyle's Latter-Day Pamphlets," *SQR,* n.s., 2 (1850), 314. Southerners also appreciated Mercy Warren's history of the American Revolution: see W. H. Holcombe, "Autobiography" (ms.), 33, at UNC-SHC; [J. R. Thompson], *SLM,* 15 (1849), 370. Benjamin Blake Minor, editor of *Southern Literary Messenger,* warmly noted the historical works of Emma Willard – complimenting her for her judiciousness and for her scientific writings – but Simms considered her *Last Leaves of American History* a mere chronicle with brevity its principal virtue: [Minor], *SLM,* 12 (1846), 383, 453–4; [Simms], "Critical Notices," *SQR,* 16 (1849), 270.

50 Wheeler, *Sketches of North Carolina,* 1:xx, 2:114; *SPR,* 2 (1848), 459; David L. Swain, "Early Times in Raleigh," in W. J. Peale, ed., *Lives of Distinguished North Carolinians* (Raleigh, NC, 1898), 273–4. On Elizabeth see Brantz Mayer, *Calvert and Penn; Or the Growth of Civil and Religious Liberty in America* (Baltimore, 1852), 17; David Seth Doggett, *The Destiny of Educated Young Men* (Richmond, VA, 1848), 24; Swain, loc. cit., 273–4; [James P. Holcombe], *The Election of a Black Republican President* (Richmond, VA, 1860), 11; "The Augustan Era of English Literature" (M.A. thesis, 1858, typescript at UVA). [E. C. Holland], *Refutation of the Calumnies,* 20; for religious opportunism see "The Puritans and Their Principles," *DQR,* 3 (1863), 302–3; [J. H. Bocock], "The Reformation in England," *SPR,* 7 (1858), 174–80.

The effort to take account of women in history simultaneously supported and challenged the prevalent southern male view, which rested on the three pillars of Scripture, historical experience, and science. The Bible, as commonly understood, commanded women to submit to men and thereby sanctified social stratification, including slavery. Worried divines sought to curb the abuse of men's power over women. Here they received reinforcement from historians and scientists who provided a chivalric context that made the strong responsible for the well-being of the weak. The *Magnolia* of Savannah replied tartly to Harriet Martineau's and Captain Frederick Marryat's criticism of the special attention paid to women in America: "We are proud of it. Long may it remain a national trait of character." Thomas Smyth did not have much to say in a trite discourse on the sphere, character, and destiny of "woman," but he did remind affluent Charlestonians that Scripture accorded her a spiritual nature and forbade treating her as plaything.[51]

From tidewater to the trans-Mississippi, students pondered the "woman question" in colleges secular and religious. Respect for and protection of women as a measure of progress became a favorite theme on the campuses, with the abstraction "woman," rather than "women," the reference point. In 1841 Richard Don Wilson (a junior at the University of North Carolina) wrote that, notwithstanding regional and temporal variations, the condition of woman provides "an infallible index of the degree of civilization to which any nation has arrived." Man's greatness and his republican institutions depend upon mothers: "On woman then depends the morality of a nation – the preservation of its liberties." In the 1850s at the University of Virginia, *Jefferson Monument Magazine* declared female education the index of a nation's civilization and blamed the intellectual backwardness of women largely on a male arrogance that deprived them of opportunities. "L.", a student at the Methodist Emory and Henry College, wrote that the barbarians had used women as a drudge; the Romans refused her equity; and medieval Europeans did better with the code of chivalry but fell far short of according ordinary women the respect shown elite women. Christianity "directly fixes and declares the true position of woman as the equal and companion of man" and part of the Body of Christ. "L." defended male authority with the qualifications preached by the Church but identified abuses that cried out for correction: Law and community practice too often allowed husbands to abandon their wives; almost automatically assigned children to a divorcing husband regardless of circumstances; tolerated physical abuse; and denied women adequate property rights.[52]

---

[51] "Travels in the South," *Magnolia*, 4 (1842), 201–4; Smyth, "Sphere, Character and Destiny of Woman," *TSW*, 10:533–48; R. F. W. Allston to Adele Petigru Allston, Dec. 16, 1849, in J. H. Easterby, ed., *The South Carolina Rice Plantation, as Revealed in the Papers of Robert F. W. Allston* (Chicago, 1945), 99. In Columbia, South Carolina, ladies and gentlemen had an animated conversation in which Governor Robert Allston insisted that women exercise more influence in republics than in other kinds of governments, and also a few years later: R. F. W. Allston to Adele Petigru Allston, Dec. 16, 1849, loc. cit., 99.

[52] R. D. Wilson, "On the Influence of Women," in Junior Compositions, 1841, at UNC-NCC; "Chivalry," *JMM*, 2 (1851), 263; "L.", "Woman's Rights and Woman's Wrongs," *SRCR*, 3 (1854), 233–43, quote at 238; also, "M.", "Intellectual Equality in the Sexes," *JMM*, 2 (1851), 243–51. David Alexander

Student reaction against the oppression of women proceeded with strong caveats and assurances of conservative intent. In 1853 William Alfred Robinson devoted his graduation speech at the University of North Carolina to "Women, Her Education and Influence." For Robinson, "The great deference to woman is one of the most glorious and distinguished characteristics of modern civilization." Since American women have many more privileges and receive more respect than in most countries, "It would seem strange if here at least, she is not contented with her condition." Robinson did not wish to be misunderstood: "The esteem with which woman is regarded in this country, should not encourage them to neglect the duties which really belong to their station in life, and strive to gain a position which does not become them." Women, he asserted, "are too timid to think they have a right, much less to make a claim, which is likely to be disputed by men." Two years later, James Park of Columbia, Tennessee, devoted his senior speech to "Women's Rights" and entered the fray against those who preach "a crusade against old manners and old customs" and seek to "revolutionize society in the assertion of woman's rights and woman's independence." These reformers "would tear the maiden from the parlor, and the matron from the household, rob them of the flowing and graceful garb which has become to us the symbol of female elegance and dignity, and thrust them into the pulpit, the doctor's shop, the court-house and the senate chamber, to struggle for equality with man, and wring from him a reluctant acknowledgement of their right to unsex themselves." With something less than prescience he concluded that, after 6,000 years, it was too late to find a new mission for women.[53]

The conflicted student response had parallels. The more history Southerners read, the more the record of injustice to women rankled. But as soon as they articulated their discomfiture, they recoiled from their own boldness. "How unjust we are to women!" lamented the *Southern Botanical-Medical Journal* of Forsyth, Georgia, in 1841. Most men "*begin* to study after the age when women are married. – But women cannot study after marriage .... Fools! Give women but half [men's] opportunities, or a little of their encouragements, and they would out strip nineteen-twentieths of the men about them." In 1847 the Methodist *Southern Ladies' Companion* protested, in a long article on the feats of great women from ancient to modern times, "The deeds of great women have been too much limited to the chronicles of modern times. Recent history teems with their striking virtues, extensive sacrifices, and exalted heroism; while those illustrious in the elder times are not honored and applauded, as they should be, by the panegyric of profane historians." But by 1854 the editors were concentrating their fire on the women's-rights movement that was spurring "much excitement and discussion – particularly at the North" of alleged male oppression: "Now, that a lady could not fill the duties of wife, mother, and mistress, and at the same time those of lawyer, merchant, or clerk is too evident to require proof." The extreme woman's-rights advocates, the editors

Barnes Diary, Feb. 15, 1840, at UNC-SHC; W. R. Aylett Speech on Women, 1851–1854, in Aylett Family Papers, at Virginia Historical Society (Richmond).

53 William Alfred Robinson, "Woman, Her Education and Influence," in Speeches of Graduates, 1853, at UNC-NCC; James Park, "Woman's Rights," in Senior Speeches, 1855, at UNC-NCC.

charged, would educate young women to be "old maids." The editors chafed at the exclusion of "widows, maiden ladies, or others" from vocations for which they were qualified: "Honor, duty, gallantry, and humanity would require men to do all they can to open the door for woman's access to such profitable vocations as she may be able to fill."[54]

Henry Augustine Washington in 1847 and James Johnston Pettigrew in 1859 came as close as any to expressing the view common among the better-spirited southern conservatives that women needed the protection of men and, in consequence, must accept certain civil and political restrictions. In consequence of the evolution of the plantation and slave society, according to Washington, nowhere was woman held in higher regard than in Virginia: "Woman, at one time man's drudge, and, at another, his toy in the bosom of that isolated country life which the people of Virginia have always led, became at once his friend, companion, and guide." This improvement in her social position enabled her to improve her moral and intellectual faculties, strengthening her virtue and developing her mind. "No where has woman ever been more chaste, more lovely, more self-devoting. A Virginia mother, in the circle of her family, with her children around her, is the noblest specimen of her sex."[55]

The well-traveled Pettigrew thought Southerners had something to learn from the Spanish. He was pleased to report that Andalusian women did not perform the onerous tasks imposed in less gallant countries: "Nature never intended the weaker sex to do the work of the world. But every young lady of the better classes possesses a knowledge, more or less thorough, of the art of housekeeping." He loved the results: "The dwellings in Seville are models of neatness, and not surpassed in Holland." Pettigrew thought women enjoyed a more elevated position in Spain than anywhere else in the world: "Women being by nature not so well fitted as men to cope with adversity in the great struggle upon earth, have fortunately for them, been furnished with power of fascination and attraction which restore the balance." The Spanish have a natural disposition "to protect those who are incapable of protecting themselves, and hundreds will rush to the defence of a child where a man would probably be left to his own unaided exertions."[56]

Contradictory attitudes produced an abstract demand for the inclusion of women in history and a slighting of women by southern historians. Only a few outstanding women appeared in the histories, which passed over the women of the common people.

---

[54] "Woman," *Southern Botanical-Medical Journal,* 1 (1841), 513; *SLC,* 2 (1847), 144–7 (quote at 144), and 7 (1854), 155. The Reverend John Jones called for a history of the essential contributions made by women to sustain the Methodist itinerary: Jones, *A Complete History of Methodism as Connected with the Mississippi Conference of the Methodist Episcopal Church, South,* 2 vols. (Nashville, TN, 1908), 2:311–12. The great modern ladies identified by the Reverend David Seth Doggett included Elizabeth, Madame de Staël, Lady Jane Gray, Mary Fairfax Grieg Somerville, and Hannah Moore: Doggett, *Destiny of Educated Young Men,* 24.

[55] H. A. Washington, "Social System of Virginia," in O'Brien, ed., *All Clever Men,* 260.

[56] [James Johnston Pettigrew], *Notes on Spain and the Spaniards in the Summer of 1850, with a Glance at Sardinia* (Charleston, SC, 1861), 135–6, 255, 257–8.

From early colonial days Southerners, self-consciously and intuitively, wed belles lettres to history as they created symbols for an emerging slaveholding society. Simms dismissed Beverley's history as "puerile and contemptible," but Louis B. Wright, a twentieth-century historian, regarded *History and Present State of Virginia* (1705) as one of the earliest self-consciously American literary works: "A fierce loyalty to the new soil burned in Beverley's breast, and he did not hesitate to rebuke his fellow Virginians for depending too much, economically and socially, upon the mother country." Lewis Simpson has remarked that Beverley had a conventional project but, "In his very adherence to the Virginian tradition of the man of letters as a moral authority, [he] presents the image of the man of letters in a new guise, that of Virginia plantation master. In this semblance, an author on a remote plantation on the southern seaboard of the British colonial settlement in America assumes the role of literary authority, presiding over a symbolic extension of the cosmopolitan realm of letters. Reinforced by the careers of William Byrd II of Westover, this figure evolved into its representation by the slave masters who rebelled against the authority of king and church."[57]

Southern novelists displayed a high historical consciousness, much as southern historians wrote novels that depicted social life. George Tucker's *Valley of the Shenandoah* (1824), followed by John P. Kennedy's *Swallow Barn* and William Carruthers's *Cavalier of Virginia*, marked the emergence of a distinctly southern novel: romantic in tone, realistic in detail. For all their stereotyping of ladies and gentlemen, these novels celebrated the history of Virginia. John Esten Cooke, remembered primarily for his *Virginia Comedians*, scoffed at those who wrote history as the story of elites and called for a social history that embraced all classes. He consciously strove to contribute such a history through his novels. "Where," he asked, "are the men and manners of the revolution?" He answered that they are "only hinted at obscurely in what the world calls histories." Cooke wanted to hear about "the rude Old-Field School on the edge of the forest, and listen to the words, and watch the bright faces of these children who will make hardy patriots and devoted women."[58]

American journals, notably the sports-oriented *Spirit of the Times*, provided a wealth of social history in scores of humorous stories of the Southwest written by

---

57 [Simms], "Critical Notices," *SQR*, n.s., 1 (1856), 207; Beverley, *History and Present State of Virginia*, Introduction, xxi; Lewis P. Simpson, *Mind and the American Civil War: A Meditation on Lost Causes* (Baton Rouge, LA, 1989), 19. A southern commentator (Simms?) may have seen the very qualities Simpson discerned in Beverley's *Virginia*, but he dismissed it as "puerile and contemptible": *SQR*, n.s. (3rd), 1 (1856), 207. R. B. Davis assessed Beverley's *Virginia* as the first significant account of an American province: *Intellectual Life in the Colonial South*, 1:84, 87–91.

58 Tucker was preceded by novelists of lesser note: see Davis, *Intellectual Life in Jefferson's Virginia*, 298–301. Cooke quoted in John O. Beatty, *John Esten Cooke, Virginian* (New York, 1922), 60. *Southern Literary Messenger*, reviewing *Henry St. John*, complained that Cooke wrote too fast and published without proper revision: *SLM*, 29 (1859), 317. Edmund Ruffin could not get through *Virginia Comedians*: Feb. 2, 1859, in *ERD*, 1:278. David Hunter Strother ("Porte Crayon") of Virginia was among the first American writers to draw heavily on southern black and white mountaineer speech in his writing: Eby, *"Porte Crayon,"* 76. For the tendency of southern writers – Kennedy, Simms – to celebrate a Golden Age appropriate to the plantation tradition, see James Woodress, "The Idea of Progress: Introductory Note," *Georgia Review*, 11 (1957), 271–8, esp. 277.

the well-known Joseph Glover Baldwin, Johnson Jones Hooper, and lesser lights. Augustus Baldwin Longstreet – author of the vivid stories in *Georgia Scenes* and an influential Methodist minister, judge, and college president – had little patience with the history of emperors and elites and lamented the lack of attention to the common people. William Trotter Porter of Vermont emerged as a gifted and influential editor in New York and, beginning in 1831, built the *Spirit of the Times* into a celebrated literary and sporting journal. Porter cultivated southern writers and readers and got a warm response, especially in the Southwest. Literary contributions and subscriptions came not only from Charleston, Mobile, and New Orleans but from Selma and Huntsville, Alabama, which most Yankees were wont to think of as barbarous backwaters if they had heard of them at all. Especially after Porter discovered and promoted Hooper, other southern humorists broke into print in the increasingly prestigious *Spirit*. From 1831 to 1856, *Spirit* had an enormous circulation and commanded widespread respect for, among other things, publishing the work of men who went on to successful literary careers. Leading southern newspapers frequently republished its stories, especially humorous sketches of the Southwest. A slice of George Washington Harris's *Sut Lovingood* first appeared in *Spirit*, in which he published thereafter. Hooper's *Simon Suggs,* after serialization in the *Spirit,* ran through three editions in its first year and another three shortly thereafter. The leading southern humorists were educated Whigs who satirized, if gently, the foibles of the democratic masses whose politics they distrusted. Hooper, a Whig newspaper editor who feared frontier nihilism, exposed the dangers of market society with devastating wit while he reinforced racial stereotypes of blacks in books that sold in the thousands.[59]

[59] Eugene Current-Garcia, "Alabama Writers in the Spirit," *Alabama Review*, 10 (1957), 243–69, esp. 258–9; John Donald Wade, *Augustus Baldwin Longstreet: A Study of the Development of Culture in the South* (New York, 1924), 50; Hennig Cohen and William B. Dillingham, eds., *Humor of the Old Southwest*, 2nd ed. (Athens, GA, 1964), xiv–xv, 156, 203; John Rickards Betts, *America's Sporting Heritage, 1850–1950* (Reading, MA, 1974), ch. 1. For Hooper see Johanna Nicol Shields, "A Sadder Simon Suggs: Freedom and Slavery in the Humor of Johnson Hooper," *JSH*, 55 (1990), 641–64; and for Hooper and Baldwin see Beidler, *First Books*, ch. 7.

　　Joseph Cobb of Mississippi, author of *Mississippi Scenes* who took the work of his friend Augustus Baldwin Longstreet as a model, said that he intended his fiction as social history: see Rogers, "Cobb: Antebellum Humorist and Critic," 133–4. Longstreet in *Georgia Scenes* and Baldwin in *Flush Times* intended to fill a void in history by reporting on the customs, manners, and foibles of the common people: see James D. Hart, *The Popular Book: A History of America's Literary Taste* (New York, 1950), 142–3. In the 1850s the Baptist Reverend Hardin Taliaferro of Alabama published sketches of life in his boyhood area of western North Carolina. By no means among the best volumes of southern humor, it nonetheless contained useful material on courtship and weddings, law courts, religion, dancing, and much else: [H. E. Taliaferro], *Fisher's River (North Carolina) Scenes and Characters by "Skitt," "Who Was Thar'"* (New York, 1859). Like many a frontiersman, Henry Clay Lewis, Louisiana's celebrated humorist, was well read in classical and European literature and history: Edwin T. Arnold, "Introduction to Henry Clay Lewis," in *Odd Leaves from the Life of a Louisiana "Swamp Doctor,"* by Madison Tensas, M.D. (Baton Rouge, LA, 1997), xiii. William Russell Smith, a unionist congressman and president of the University of Alabama, became a much-touted literary satirist in Alabama: Joanna Nicol Shields, "A Social History of Antebellum Alabama Writers," *Alabama Review*, 42 (1989), 167–8.

6

World History and the Politics of Slavery

> The surest and indeed the only method of learning how to bear bravely the vicissitudes of fortune is to recall the calamities of others .... It is only indeed by the study of the interconnexion of all the particulars, their resemblances and differences, that we are enabled at least to make a general survey, and thus derive both benefit and pleasure from history.
>
> —Polybius[1]

Non-European history and cultures enchanted curious Southerners, as they did Northerners. By 1860, history for Southerners had become world history, and they took special pleasure in evidence of the ubiquity of slavery. Thomas Cobb, Georgia's legal scholar, concluded that slavery was "more universal than marriage and more permanent than liberty." He introduced his influential book, *An Inquiry into the Law of Negro Slavery*, with a discussion of its origins, development, and extent in ancient Egypt, India, Africa, and the Far East, and a review of the extent not merely of serfs but of slaves in medieval and early modern Europe. For Thomas Roderick Dew, the histories of Eastern Europe, Asia, and Africa "conclusively mark the evidence of slavery over these boundless regions." George Sawyer of Louisiana opened his proslavery tract, *Southern Institutes*, with Aristotle and other early authorities to demonstrate that the master–slave relation, in some form, provided the basis of social order.[2]

---

[1] Polybius, *The Histories*, tr. W. R. Paton, 6 vols. (LCL), 1:Bk. 1, sec. 1, 4. Polybius was also highly valued as a geographer. Southern colleges taught a good deal of geography, and courses included world as well as state and national geography: see e.g. Edwin L. Green, *A History of the University of South Carolina* (Columbia, SC, 1916), 178.

[2] Thomas R. R. Cobb, *An Inquiry into the Law of Negro Slavery in the United States* (New York, 1968 [1858]), esp. chs. 2–4, quote at 101; "Professor Dew on Slavery," in *The Pro-Slavery Argument, as Maintained by the Most Distinguished Writers of the Southern States* (Philadelphia, 1853), 246; Thomas Roderick Dew, *Digest of the Laws, Customs, Manners, and Institutions of the Ancient and Modern Nations* (New York, 1884 [1852]), 326; George S. Sawyer, *Southern Institutes; Or, an Inquiry into the Origin and Early Prevalence of Slavery and the Slave Trade* (New York, 1967 [1858]), 13–14, 19. Legal theorists cited Bodin, Grotius, Pufendorff, and Savigny to show slavery ubiquitous

Southerners believed that world history vindicated them as slaveholders and demonstrated that civilization itself rose on the backs of subjugated laborers. In 1836 a sermon entitled "Rights and Duties of Slaveholders" – delivered by the Reverend George Freeman, rector of Christ Church in Raleigh – supplemented scriptural arguments with historical ones, reviewing the omnipresence of slavery from the earliest ages as evidence against all egalitarian doctrine. Freeman's sermon stirred up a hornet's nest in northern churches, but it expressed a common southern opinion. In 1858 a planter in Alabama, rejecting the egalitarianism of the Declaration of Independence, estimated that a majority of the human race was in de jure or de facto slavery. John Fletcher of Louisiana said that forty million slaves remained in Europe and Asia and untold millions in Africa. J. L. Carey of Maryland lumped English workers and serfs with slaves to find millions in servitude in nineteenth-century Europe: "The question then is of more or less freedom." The study of history taught Southerners that slavery and personal servitude were characteristic of world history and that the free-labor system had poor prospects. Between 1800 and 1840, Baptist divines – Henry Holcombe (editor of Savannah's *Georgia Analytical Repository*), Richard Furman, and Gerald Capers of Macon – nurtured the theme, which was thereafter developed by Richard Fuller, William Richards (gifted editor of Baptist and secular journals), and E. W. Warren of Macon, who summed up: "The world never has, and never can, exist without slavery in some form." Leading Presbyterians preached the same message, among them: T. C. Thornton in *An Inquiry into the History of Slavery*, Frederick A. Ross in *Slavery Ordained of God*, S. J. Cassells in *Servitude and the Duty of Masters to Their Servants*, and Robert Lewis Dabney in *Defence of Virginia*.[3]

Fascinated by the experience of other peoples, Southerners turned to an unlikely authority: François Marie Aronet de Voltaire, a *philosophe* they often pictured as devil

and legal: [John Archibald Campbell], "Slavery among the Romans," *SQR*, 28 (1848), 425. A spate of travelogues accompanied commercial and missionary expansion, creating a thirst for knowledge and feeding romantic impulses, but during the eighteenth century they tended toward the exotic: see Kevin J. Hayes, *A Colonial Woman's Bookshelf* (Knoxville, TN, 1996), 119–21.

[3] George W. Freeman, *The Rights and Duties of Slaveholders* (Raleigh, NC, 1836), 5, 8–9, 12–13; "Influence of Slavery upon the Progress of Civilization," *American Cotton Planter and Soil of the South* (1859), 171–2; John Fletcher, *Studies on Slavery, in Easy Lessons* (Natchez, MS, 1852), 382; John L. Carey, *Slavery in Maryland, Briefly Considered* (Baltimore, 1845), 9–10; on Holcombe and Richards see Bertram Holland Flanders, *Early Georgia Magazines: Literary Periodicals to 1865* (Athens, GA, 1944), 7, 11, 77. Gabriel Capers, *Bondage a Moral Institution*, quoted in Ralph Betts Flanders, *Plantation Slavery in Georgia* (Chapel Hill, NC, 1933), 290–1; Richard Furman, "Views of the Baptists," in James A. Rogers, *Richard Furman: Life and Legacy* (Macon, GA, 1985), 283; on Furman see H. Shelton Smith, *In His Image ... But: Racism in Southern Religion* (Durham, NC, 1972), 7, 55. Richard Fuller and Francis Wayland, *Domestic Slavery, Considered as a Scriptural Institution in Correspondence,* 5th ed. (New York, 1847), 163; E. W. Warren, *Nellie Norton; Or, Southern Slavery and the Bible* (Macon, GA, 1864), 10, also 12, 33–4, 119; T. C. Thornton, *An Inquiry into the History of Slavery* (Washington, DC, 1841), ch. 1; Frederick A. Ross, *Slavery Ordained of God* (Philadelphia, 1857); [S. J. Cassells], *Servitude and the Duty of Masters to Their Servants* (Norfolk, VA, 1843); Robert L. Dabney, *Defence of Virginia (and through Her of the South) in Recent and Pending Contests against the Sectional Party* (New York, 1969 [1867]), 101.

incarnate. His *Essai sur les moeurs et l'esprit des nations* and his other works of history influenced even those who held him up to scorn. Among positive responses, William Drayton of South Carolina – in his book, *The South Vindicated from the Treason and Fanaticism of the Northern Abolitionists* – cited Voltaire's dictum that slavery was "as ancient as war; and war ancient as human nature." Among negative responses, the Reverends Hugh Dickson and William Barr of Abbeville, South Carolina, protested vehemently about white teachers at a school for Indians who suppressed the Bible and offered students the infidels Voltaire, Hume, Gibbon, and Paine. The Reverend Abram Davis Pollock of Virginia fumed at Voltaire's statue in Paris and suggested another to honor the devil. By the volatile 1850s, Southerners were describing abolitionists as Voltaire's heirs, and college students burned his books. Samuel Cartwright rebuked him for inadequate commitment to white supremacy. E. A. Lynch of Virginia placed "the detestable Voltaire" and his "concentrated malice of heart" at the head of the *philosophes,* "a band of ruffians," while George Frederick Holmes protested Voltaire's "outrageous blasphemy." A contributor to *Southern Literary Messenger,* attacking Voltaire's histories, called him an "architect of ruin" who knew how to destroy but not how to build. To John Reuben Thompson, Voltaire was "that brilliant and wicked personage."[4]

Yet even hostile Southerners who recoiled at Voltaire's religious skepticism and hostility to Christianity applauded his support for religious toleration, and they could not resist quoting him; although – like Holmes, who respected Voltaire's contributions to the philosophy of history – they might playfully excuse their "petty treason." Dew, for one, relied on his *Essai*'s account of the Persians, Hindus, Chinese, and Meso-Americans.[5]

The Scots William Robertson as well as the Northerners Washington Irving, William H. Prescott, and John Lathrop Motley were all antislavery, but their histories contributed to formation of southern ideas on slavery and race. Cobb, in *Law of Negro Slavery,* and the Reverend Alexander McCaine, in *Slavery Defended against the Attacks of the Abolitionists,* cited Robertson on the existence of slavery in the Americas

---

4 [William Drayton], *The South Vindicated from the Treason and Fanaticism of the Northern Abolitionists* (Philadelphia, 1836), 20; Hugh Dickson to John C. Calhoun, June 10, 1824, and William H. Barr to Calhoun, June 18, 1824, in *JCCP,* 9:152, 164; Pollock Diaries and Papers, 65, at UNC-SHC; Samuel Cartwright, *Essays in a Series of Letters to Rev. William Winans* (Natchez, MS, 1843); [George Frederick Holmes], "The Positive Religion," *MMQR,* 4th ser., 6 (1854), 350; E. A. Lynch, "Influence of Morals on the Happiness of Man," *SLM,* 4 (1838), 146; Lynch, "Influence of Morals on the Happiness of Man – Part Two," *SLM,* 4 (1838), 276; "History and Constitution of the Early Roman Commonwealth," *SLM,* 14 (1848), 266; John R. Thompson, "Editorial Letters from Europe," *SLM,* 20 (1854), 530. "M." of South Carolina attributed to Voltaire "malignity": "Moral Influence of Authors," *SLM,* 6 (1840), 286. *Southern Quarterly Review* acknowledged Voltaire as an early contributor to philosophical history, but it considered *Essay* "indifferent" and largely and justly forgotten: "Oevres de Vico," *SQR,* 2 (1841), 405.
5 [George Frederick Holmes], "Mrs. Gray's History of Etruria," *SQR,* 7 (1845), 212; for Holmes's respect see his "Schlegel's Philosophy of History," in Michael O'Brien, ed., *All Clever Men, Who Make Their Way: Critical Discourse in the Old South* (Fayetteville, AR, 1982), 203–4; Dew, *Digest,* esp. pt. 1, ch. 1, p. 35, also 67, 91–8. For southern reactions to Voltaire see also Supplementary References: "Voltaire."

before the arrival of the Europeans and on the widespread slavery throughout European history. Prescott and Motley especially celebrated the world-conquering spirit of the Anglo-Saxons and Teutons and their ethnic superiority. Their accounts of European expansion taught much about Latin America, something about Asia, and a bit about Africa. Robertson was a favorite among late eighteenth-century Virginians, and his reputation as a wise and reliable historian persisted during the next half-century or more. Dew began his discussion of modern history with Robertson's view that Western Civilization had undergone two great revolutions: the rise of the Roman Empire, and its decline and fall. A contributor to *Southern Literary Messenger* drew heavily on Robertson's *History of the Reign of Charles V* for an account of the republicanism of late medieval cities and the conflict between republican and monarchical forces in early modern Europe. Franklin Smith credited his notion that the Indians had originated in Asia and crossed the Baring Straits, delighting orthodox Christians and infuriating polygenesists – scientific racists who denied the unity of the human race. And like Hume, Robertson had the virtue of considering chivalry, a favorite institution in the South, a distinguishing feature of Western Civilization.[6]

Prescott played well in the Southwest, where interest in Spanish history and literature ran high. De Bow considered his *Conquest of Mexico* "indispensable" and, at Prescott's death in 1859, offered a glowing tribute that ranked him with Thucydides, Tacitus, Gibbon, and Hume. E. D. De Leon of Savannah hailed Irving for linking history with fiction in pursuit of historical truth, and "J. B. C." of Longwood, Mississippi, warmly applauded him for offering the people works that "have cheered

---

[6] Cobb, *Law of Negro Slavery*, cxl; Alexander McCaine, *Slavery Defended against the Attacks of the Abolitionists* (Baltimore, 1842), 7. On the racial/ethnic bias of Prescott and Motley – as well as of Bancroft and Parkman – see David Levin, *History as Romantic Art: Bancroft, Prescott, Motley, and Parkman* (New York, 1967), ch. 4; also, George Fredrickson, *The Black Image in the White Mind: The Debate over Afro-American Character and Destiny, 1817–1914* (New York, 1971), 98–102; Dew, *Digest*, 321, 422, 435, 446; "Rise of Despotism in Europe," *SLM*, 21 (1855), 610–18, esp. 614–15, and 22 (1856), 83–9; Franklin Smith, "Origin of the American Indians," *DBR*, 3 (1847), 566. Thornwell, at war with the Catholics, enlisted Robertson's *Charles V* against Hallam's respectful account of the clerical talent at the Council of Trent: "Romanist Arguments," *JHTW*, 3:428. De Bow paid special tribute to Robertson for illuminating the commercial revolution in advance of Henry Hallam and Arnold Heeren: J. D. B. De Bow, *The Industrial Resources, Statistics, &c. of the United States and More Particularly of the Southern and Western States*, 3rd ed., 3 vols. (New York, 1966 [1854]), 1:333, and *DBR*, 1 (Jan. 1846), 106. For the ideological context of Robertson's theory of Indian origins see Richard H. Popkin, "Pre-Adamism in 19th Century American Thought: 'Speculative Biology' and Racism," *Philosophia*, 8 (1978), 205–9. For Hume and Robertson on chivalry see Kenneth Cmiel, *Democratic Eloquence: The Fight over Popular Speech in Nineteenth-Century America* (New York, 1990), 115. For Robertson see esp. *History of the Discovery and Settlement of America*, many editions. In the late eighteenth and early nineteenth centuries Robertson's histories were standard fare in southern libraries, and the South appears to have contributed to the unusually high popularity of *History of Scotland*, which outsold Hume's *History* for awhile. See Richard Beale Davis, *Intellectual Life in Jefferson's Virginia, 1790–1830* (Chapel Hill, NC, 1964), 78, 83, 97; Frank Luther Mott, *Golden Multitudes: The Story of Best Sellers in the United States* (New York, 1947), 59–60, 305; Hennig Cohen, *The South Carolina Gazette, 1732–1775* (Columbia, SC, 1953), 152–3, 155; Henry Boley, *Lexington in Old Virginia* (Richmond, VA, 1936), 26.

the fireside of the peasant." Although John R. Thompson spoke highly of Irving, he published in *Southern Literary Messenger* an acerbic article by Severn Teackle Wallis of Baltimore, a noted authority on Spain, that handled Irving and others roughly for bias, errors, and ignorance.[7]

European claims to world domination and behavior in achieving it became subjects of intense controversy in the South. A contributor to *Southern Literary Messenger* agreed with Robertson's criticism of the Spanish oppression of the Indians and his suggestion of Indian revenge in the transmission of venereal diseases, as well as Prescott's approval of the Spanish promotion of Christianity. Hence, De Leon regretted Irving's decision not to write a history of Mexico in deference to Prescott, whom De Leon accused of pro-Spanish bias; he assumed that Irving would have treated the conquered Amerindians as sympathetically as he treated the Moors in Spain. But Irving, along with Prescott and Robertson, came under fire in *Southern Literary Messenger* for justifying the crimes of Cortez by asserting that he had accomplished much good by introducing Christianity into Mexico – implying that the end justified the means.[8]

For George Frederick Holmes, Motley's *Dutch Republic* – that "elaborate and faithful and brilliant narrative" – earned him recognition worthy of the company of Irving, Prescott, George Bancroft, and George Ticknor. For William Archer Cocke, Motley's account of the Dutch Revolution and European constitutional issues implicitly bolstered the case for southern secession. William Henry Trescot saw Motley as a genuinely philosophical historian who advanced republican principles, and George William Bagby, editor of *Southern Literary Messenger*, applauded his objectivity and fairness. The North, Bagby wrote, had finally produced a historian worthy of the encomia heretofore heaped on "that immense humbug and Yankee pet, Bancroft."[9]

---

[7] [J. D. B. De Bow], "Prescott's Conquest of Mexico," *SQR*, 6 (1844), 163–227; [De Bow], *DBR*, 1 (1846), 118; *DBR*, 26 (1859), 352. On Irving see: [E. D. De Leon], "Writings of Washington Irving," *SQR*, 8 (1845), 69–93; "J. B. C.", "The Genius and Writings of Washington Irving," *American Whig Review*, 12 (1850), 602. For Spanish history see e.g. [De Bow], "Prescott's Conquest of Mexico," 163–227; for literature see [Severn Teackle Wallis], "Spain: History, Character and Literature," *SLM*, 7 (1841), 441. Encomia greeted Prescott. John Reuben Thompson found *Philip the Second* "excellent and valuable": [Thompson], *SLM*, 28 (1859), 79. Dr. Samuel Henry Dickson of Charleston referred to Prescott's "imperishable" *Conquest of Mexico* and its "exquisite style," which a contributor to *QRMECS* from Louisville, Kentucky, found "gorgeous." See Samuel Henry Dickson, "Difficulties in the Way of the Historian," *SLM*, 12 (1846), 110; "W. H. G. B.", "Prescott's Peru," *QRMECS*, 2 (1848), 147. [John R. Thompson], *SLM*, 14 (1848), 760–1; S. T. Wallis, "Spain: Popular Errors," *SLM*, 8 (1841), 306, and Wallis, "Mr. Washington Irving," *SLM*, 8 (1842), 725–35. A favorable reviewer of the first volume of *Life of Washington* complained that a purported biography turned into a history of the Revolutionary era: "Irving's Life of Washington," *SQR*, n.s. (3rd), 1 (1856), 35–60.

[8] "Irving's Life of Columbus," *SLM*, 6 (1840), 569–70; [De Leon], "Writings of Washington Irving," 69–93; "H.", "A Few Reflections on the Conquest of Mexico by Cortez," *SLM*, 15 (1849), 635–7. "J. B. C." of Longwood, Mississippi, declared Irving's pages on Moorish culture in Spain worthy of Virgil: "Genius and Writings of Washington Irving," 605.

[9] [George Frederick Holmes], "Motley's Dutch Republic," *SQR*, n.s. (3rd), 2 (1857), 427–55; William Archer Cocke, "The Dutch Republic," *SLM*, 32 (1861), 383; Trescot to Thornwell, June 25, 1856, in Thornwell Papers, at USC; [George William Bagby], *SLM*, 32 (1861), 326; W. Archer Cocke, "Motley's

Motley's story of the heroic Dutch struggle for national independence provided Southerners a model of their own. Confederates, like the Dutch, faced superior material force but knew how to turn apparent weaknesses into real strengths, and they, too, counted on the Lord's blessing. Still, the Presbyterian Reverend John Adger and George Dabney found a flat contradiction between Motley's celebration of the Dutch war of secession and his opposition to the Confederacy. Women, most notably the ardent secessionists, warmed to Motley's studies of the Dutch revolutionary struggle for independence: Judith McGuire, Emma Holmes, Catherine Edmonston, Elizabeth Allston Pringle, and Mary Chesnut esteemed his *Dutch Republic*. When Lincoln appointed Motley minister to Austria, Emma Holmes wondered how an author who "depicted in such glowing, earnest, life-like colors the struggle of the Netherlands for liberty against the oppression of the House of Austria" could consider Southerners "rebels"? It showed, alas, "the party spirit and inconsistency too common to the age." As the Confederacy crumbled in 1865, Edmonston "derived great comfort" from Motley's demonstration in United Netherlands that a tenacious and perseverant people at bay could prevail against all odds. Southerners read what they wanted to into the work of authors unsympathetic to slavery and other of their favorite causes, but they did read them – and with full appreciation of their talents and accomplishments.[10]

Mercantile interests promoted commerce and Christianity as the great civilizing agents of world history, piquing interest in Asian cultures. Christians found support for their contention that all peoples, being descendants of Adam and Eve and

---

History of the United Netherlands," *DBR*, 32 (1862), 223–38. Thompson received *Dutch Republic* cordially, comparing Motley's talents to Prescott's: [J. R. Thompson], *SLM*, 22 (1856), 399–400. Another reviewer, who complained that *Dutch Republic* was not getting the attention it deserved, considered Motley fair-minded but sometimes incapable of refraining from interjections of fierce partisanship: "The Dutch Republic," *SLM*, 27 (1858), 241–9.

On Dutch history see also W. P. Riddell, "Republic of Holland," *DBR*, 12 (1852), 280–6. Glorification of the Dutch invited denigration of the Portuguese. According to G. Norman Lieber, the Portuguese – lacking experience in self-government – proved themselves unable to govern their colonies any better than they could govern themselves. Hence their imperial glory was brief. See Lieber, "The Portuguese and their Poet," *RM*, 4 (1858), 250.

[10] [J. B. Adger], "Motley's Dutch Republic," *SPR*, 15 (1862), 94–159; George E. Dabney, "Confederated Republicanism or Monarchism," *DBR*, 32 (1862), 119; Elizabeth Allston Pringle, *Chronicle of Chicora Wood* (New York, 1922), 138; Chesnut Diary, Aug. 14, 1861, in C. Vann Woodward, ed., *Mary Chesnut's Civil War* (New Haven, CT, 1981), 145; Judith W. McGuire, Dec. 18, 1861, in Jean W. Berlin, ed., *Diary of a Southern Refugee during the War. By a Lady of Virginia* (Lincoln, NE, 1995 [1867]), 73; Aug. 14, 1861, in John F. Marszalek, ed., *The Diary of Miss Emma Holmes* (Baton Rouge, LA, 1979), 80; Jan. 9, 1865, in Beth G. Crabtree and James Welch Patton, eds., *"Journal of a Secesh Lady": The Diary of Catherine Devereux Edmonston, 1860–1866* (Raleigh, NC, 1979), 654. Motley's account of William the Silent, regarded as the greatest of leaders in the Dutch struggle for national independence, drew renewed attention in 1861: William Gordon McCabe, "William the Silent," *SLM*, 32 (1861), 288–95; Cocke, "The Dutch Republic," 383. Without mentioning Motley, Drury Lacy invoked the Dutch struggle against Spain as lesson for Confederate soldiers: *Address Delivered at the General Military Hospital, Wilson, N.C.* (Fayetteville, NC, 1863), 11. In 1861 Motley published as a 36-page pamphlet his *The Causes of the Civil War, a Letter to the London Times*.

children of God, have a moral sense. The Jesuits and the *philosophes* both portrayed China as an ancient, rationally structured society – the very model of enlightened despotism – but the *philosophes,* most notably Voltaire, cited China to support their attacks on European institutions and practices and to discredit the Old Testament as history and the contention that morality and ethics must rest on Christian teaching. Voltaire celebrated China as the world's oldest, best-governed, and most civilized country, exemplary in rendering its subjects secure, with an Emperor responsible to public opinion and checked by institutions that prevented tyranny. Charles Flagg wrote in *Russell's Magazine* that the Chinese government, despite its cruelties, was "probably the best absolute despotism that ever existed."[11]

Brantz Mayer, in a fifty-page article in *Southern Quarterly Review,* expressed admiration for Chinese "quasi-civilization" and its thousands of years of continuity. Mayer, who had been to China in the 1820s, lamented British aggression and reported the atrocities of a war between a militarily advanced and a backward people. Widespread use of opium, he said, had undermined Chinese civilization and national power, but he hoped a commercial postwar aftermath would open the way to Christianization, not to mention material and moral progress. "This great and singular people" had been well on their way to industrial development until their political economists, fearing rapid population growth, had choked off invention and mechanization to prevent unemployment. Still, by the nineteenth century, China appeared stagnant and pitiable. In *De Bow's Review* articles and book reviews acquainted readers with the history, geography, resources, culture, and prospects of once-great world powers long in decline – India, Turkey, Holland, Greece, Spain, and, once again, especially China.[12]

---

[11] *An Essay on Universal History, The Manners, and Spirit of Nations … by M. de Voltaire,* tr. Thomas Nugent, 2nd ed. (London, 1759), pt. 4:ch. 164. Voltaire's *Essay,* available in English during the eighteenth century, included chapters on China, Japan, and other Asian countries. [Charles E. B. Flagg], "Consular Cities of China," *RM,* 2 (1857/58), quote at 510; *RM,* 3 (1858), 53; Donald E. Lach, "China in Western Thought," *DHI,* 1:353–73, and on Father Martinio Martini, the Jesuit missionary who in 1658 published an unprecedented account that introduced Chinese history to Europeans, see 358–86. Perry's expedition inspired interest in Japanese history and culture: see e.g. "Life and Literature in Japan," *SLM,* 31 (1860), 7–35.

On world commerce and Asia, better-educated Southerners learned from Baron de Montesquieu, *The Spirit of the Laws,* tr. Thomas Nugent, 2 vols. (New York, 1975), 1:Bks. 20–1. Chinese art became something of a fad in eighteenth-century France, and Brantz Mayer of Baltimore quoted Voltaire on the superiority of Chinese drama "to those monstrous farces of Shakespeare, which have been called tragedies": [Mayer], "China and the Chinese," *SQR,* 12 (1847), 26; also, Régine Pernoud, *Those Terrible Middle Ages: Debunking the Myths,* tr. Anne Englund Nash (San Francisco, 2000), 29. The Reverend J. Lewis Shuck, among other missionaries, returned from China to raise money for the Baptist missions and did well in the South, netting from $500 to $800 at several points – large sums for the time. He spoke to packed houses of people anxious to know about China and the Opium War: Thelma Wolfe Hall, *I Give Myself: The Story of J. Lewis Shuck and His Mission to China* (Richmond, VA, 1983), 74–5.

[12] Brantz Mayer, "A Nation in a Nutshell," *Baltimore Literary Monument,* 2 (1839), 274; [Mayer], "China and the Chinese," 1–51, esp. 3–7, 32, 47, quote at 47. *De Bow's Review* published informative articles, some by De Bow himself, on the history of Japan, China, and India that were marked by generally respectful accounts of their religion, languages, and cultural accomplishments: *DBR,* 1 (Apr.

A dark spot: The leaders of southern letters and education considered respect for women the measure of progress toward civilization, and historical and contemporary accounts of Muslim, Hindu, and Chinese societies stressed heathen misogyny and degradation of women. The Presbyterian Reverend J. P. Tusten, denying divine sanction for male superiority, mentioned Islam as evidence that a society that oppresses women cannot progress. An extensive article in *De Bow's Review* on "Indian Superstitions" reviewed the lamentable condition of women in India, and Flagg's article on China ended with critical pages on its abuse of women.[13]

Most commentators acknowledged the industriousness and perseverance of the Chinese people and their formidable scientific, industrial, and artistic accomplishments, but – like "H.R." in *Southern Literary Messenger* – they believed that the great Chinese and Hindu civilizations had stagnated or deteriorated during the last thousand years. In 1856 Professor John McCrady of South Carolina, a scientist and polygenesist, asserted that the high cultural achievements of China and India were a consequence of racially based superior intellects, yet a year later he argued that the inferiority of the Chinese, compared to Caucasians, made them unable to capitalize on scientific exploits like the discovery of gunpowder. Robert Dabney, sidestepping racial interpretation, observed that East Asians, Turks, Copts, and Syrians had performed well until "ages of despotism" reduced them to a "mournful degeneracy." The theme of once-great empires laid low recurred often. The Reverend W. N. Pendleton of Lexington, Virginia, referred to the once-great civilizations of Egypt and the Near East as "trampled in the dust by the lawless Arab and the sensuous Turk."[14]

1846), De Bow, "The Cotton Plant" (289–320); R. F. W. Allston, "The Rice Plant" (320–57). See also, in *DBR*: 10 (1851), 269–81, 299–313; "The Empire of Japan," 13 (1852), 541–63; Albert Wells Ely, "China in 1853," 14 (1853), 339–73; De Bow, "China and the Indies – Our 'Manifest Destiny,'" 15 (1853), 541–71; "Indian Superstitions," 16 (1854), 128–43; "Turkey – Its Commerce and Destiny," 16 (1854), 109–28. *De Bow's Review* also included a brief account of slavery in China: *DBR*, 21 (1856), 159–61. Albert Wells Ely contributed articles to promote commercial interest in the Far East, including material on the history and culture of the Dutch East Indies: "The East India Islands," *DBR*, 15 (1853), 14–36, 243–54, also De Bow, "Dutch Colonial Empire," 15 (1853), 232–7. De Bow, commenting on early Chinese civilization, also praised its royal library and silk culture: *Industrial Resources*, 3:163–5.

13 [J. P. Tusten], "Chivalry and Civilization," *SPR*, 4 (1850), 218–25; "Indian Superstitions," *DBR*, 16 (1854), 128–43; [Flagg], "Consular Cities of China," 509–21 (on women see 517–21); *RM*, 3 (1858), 49–59; "Critical Notices," *SPR*, 7 (1853), 443; "China and the Chinese," *SLM*, 7 (1841), 137–55; [W. H. Barnwell], "The Chinese," *SQR*, 2 (1842), 112–29; and for similar views expressed in articles on other subjects see e.g. John Blair Dabney, "Capt. Marryatt," *SLM*, 7 (1841), 253–76. For the barbarous treatment of women in India, see "Laws and Customs of the Hindoos," *Carolina Law Repository* (Raleigh), 2 (1815), 227–33; *Christian Repository* (Wilmington, DE), 1 (1821), 9; [William Archer Cocke], "Christianity and Greek Philosophy," *SPR*, 23 (1872), 189. The influential Montesquieu emphasized that Islamic slavery especially degraded women: *Spirit of the Laws*, 1:Bk. 15.11.

14 "H. R.", "The Slow Progress of Mankind," *SLM*, 18 (1852), 403; [John McCrady], "A Few Thoughts on Southern Civilization," *RM*, 2 (1857), 217; John McCrady, *A System of Independent Research* (Charleston, SC, 1856), 6; *DD**, 4:110; W. N. Pendleton, *Science: A Witness for the Bible* (Philadelphia, 1860), 288. For less biased remarks on the religion and culture of the ancient Asian empires, see [George Frederick Holmes], "History of Literature," *SQR*, 2 (1842), 479–84. For the "ill governed, wretched

Ancient India's philosophy, even more than its history, attracted southern inter-est. *Southern Quarterly Review*'s first volume included a long article on the British in India, with a respectful account of ancient Hindu civilization – its architecture, language, and literature. Even Thornwell, who abhorred the "monstrous mythol-ogy of the Hindoos," said that the contributions to philosophy made by "that great people" were just beginning to be discovered. There were charges and counter-charges. An anonymous reviewer chided George Henry Lewes, author of *Biograph-ical History of Philosophy,* for ignoring ancient Indian philosophy's contributions to positivism and other modern philosophies. Professor Charles Minnigerode of William and Mary derided the growing number of intellectuals who thought they had found the source of all wisdom in India.[15]

Appreciation and denigration of Asian cultures rekindled an old war. As Chris-tianity penetrated deep into the non-European world during the eighteenth and nine-teenth centuries, educated and observant Europeans and Americans found much to value in the religions Christian missionaries had gone forth to supplant. Christians interpreted the sense of right and wrong they observed in all peoples as evidence of steps toward Christ. Deists and religious skeptics, for their part, saw evidence that people could lead good, moral lives under many religions or philosophies. With the generation of 1680–1715, for the first time in the history of Christian Europe a sig-nificant number of the well educated denied that Christianity embodied a unique and superior truth. Matthew Tindall invoked Confucian ethics to question the moral uniqueness of Christianity, and G. E. Lessing pleaded for a religious conver-gence to sustain universal salvation through the emergence of a true and ultimate religion.[16]

East" – that is, the Turkish empire – see "J. B. S.", "Importance of Agriculture," *Southern Agricultur-alist and Register of Rural Affairs,* 11 (1838), 519. For the decline of the once-great Egyptian people to an "ignorant and cowardly" race, living in mud huts much inferior to southern slave cabins, see William Pinckney Starke to John C. Calhoun, Jan. 23, 1846, in *JCCP,* 22:498.

   From the earliest volumes of *Quarterly Review of the Methodist Episcopal Church, South* in the late 1840s, its editors sought to inform readers on the history, culture, and current situation of China: "China," *QRMECS,* 2 (1848), 628–36. In *QRMECS* in 1861, the Reverend W. G. E. Cunnynham of Tennessee followed an article on the history of Christian missionaries in China with a report from Shanghai on the Anglo-French invasion and the Taiping rebellion. He had confidence in the gen-uineness of the rebels' Christianity and thought their victory would enhance missionary efforts: "Christian Missions among the Chinese," *QRMECS,* 15 (1861), 532–54, and "Present Condition of China," 421–8.

[15] "The Anglo-Eastern Empire," *SQR,* 3 (1843), 199–236; also, [George Frederick Holmes], "Herder's Philosophy of History," *SQR,* 5 (1844), 295–301. For "that great people" see [James Henley Thorn-well], "Dictionary of Philosophical Sciences," *SQR,* n.s. (3rd), 2 (1857), 343, and on Hindu mythology see "Romanist Arguments for the Apocrypha Discussed," *JHTW,* 3:537; "Lewes's Philosophy," *SLM,* 25 (1857), 408–10; Charles Minnigerode, "The Greek Dramatists," *SLM,* 8 (1842), 606. Robertson wrote respectfully and in depth on India's contributions to science and art in *An Historical Disqui-sition Concerning the Knowledge Which the Ancients Had of India,* which became readily available when republished as an appendix to his *History of Scotland.* For broader attention to Asian literature see [Holmes], "History of Literature," 479–84.

[16] Carl T. Jackson, *The Oriental Religions and American Thought: Nineteenth-Century Explorations* (Westbrook, CT, 1981), chs. 1–4; Kenneth Scott Latourette, *Christianity in a Revolutionary Age,* 5

In the late eighteenth century conservative Christians, wary of anything that diminished Christianity's uniqueness, noticed the slighting of Christianity in Voltaire's adulation of Confucius and worried that the Jesuits' efforts to encourage respect for Asian peoples was inadvertently feeding this diminution. Southerners observed with concern the mounting enthusiasm in nineteenth-century New England for a synthetic world religion based upon a presumed common spirituality and biblically based ethics. Led by Ralph Waldo Emerson, the Transcendentalists, like the Harvard Unitarians before them, heralded the East Asian religions as essential elements of a new universal faith. Lydia Maria Child seemed pleased by her expectation that orthodox and liberals, as well as adherents of various non-Christian religions, would pan her three-volume *Progress of Religious Ideas* (1855) because she refused to recommend any one religion.[17]

While relativism gained little support in the South, it did make subtle inroads that worried the orthodox. Brantz Mayer considered Confucianism a moral philosophy with a virtuous social policy and Confucius all the more remarkable because he lived before Jesus with no access to Jewish teaching and tradition. Mayer concluded that Confucius "is to the Chinese what Christ is to Christians," the founder of a great religion with a "fundamental principle" akin to the Judeo-Christian Golden Rule. John Fletcher cited the teachings of Confucius as equivalent to the Golden Rule and applauded the proslavery implications.[18]

Prominent Southerners sensed the danger. The Methodist Bishop Henry Bascom scored the fashionable tendency to treat Confucius as morally equivalent to Jesus, and Francis W. Pickens, later governor of South Carolina, said that Confucianism ended in "base Superstition." For the Presbyterian Reverend Benjamin Morgan Palmer, the Chinese, although a great people, were "probably the most irreligious people on the globe, because a political idolatry has supplanted their religious feelings." Like the great Greek philosophers, Confucius created countless atheists by his distance from Christianity, the true religion. Palmer considered Hinduism pantheistic and unable to distinguish virtue from vice. In *Southern Presbyterian Review,* Enoch Pond, a Northerner, suggested that the idealist philosophies prevalent in nineteenth-century Germany and New England resembled a second edition of Buddhism. *Southern Literary Messenger* ran critiques of Buddhism

---

vols. (Grand Rapids, MI, 1958), 1:ch. 3. The Puritans, notably Cotton Mather, read the travelogues and missionary literature and commented upon Asia without undertaking a study of its religions. As commercial relations expanded in later years, so, if slowly, did knowledge of China and India. See Jackson, *Oriental Religions,* ch. 1.

[17] Owen Chadwick, *From Bossuet to Newman: The Idea of Doctrinal Development* (Cambridge, U.K., 1957), 55–6; Lydia Child to Convers Francis, July 14, 1848, in *Letters of Lydia Maria Child* (New York, 1969 [1883]), 65, and L. M. Child, *The Progress of Religious Ideas, through Successive Ages,* 3 vols. (New York, 1855), 1:vii–viii. For Western debates over Chinese religion from the seventeenth century see Lach, "China in Western Thought."

[18] [Mayer], "China and the Chinese," 37–9, quote at 39; Fletcher, *Studies on Slavery,* 411–14; also, A. B. Meek, *Americanism in Literature: An Oration before the Phi Kappa and Demosthenian Societies of the University of Georgia* (Tuscaloosa, AL, 1844), 11. Chinese religion caused endless fits. One writer, pleased with the veneration of parents, was appalled by their deification: "B.", "Chinese Worship of Parents," *VLM,* 1 (1829), 448.

by "Traveler" of Charlottesville, and the Reverend John Leadley Dagg's *Manual of Theology,* a standard Baptist text, sought to dampen enthusiasm for Eastern religions.[19]

Southern critics became even harsher as they noted a connection between a growing interest in non-Christian religions and the materialistic Yankee culture. Unitarians and infidels like Voltaire, Volney, and Gibbon waved off Christian claims to uniqueness by pointing to intimations of the Trinity in the Eastern religions. While conceding those intimations, the Presbyterian Reverend Thomas Smyth of Charleston argued that none of those triads captured the essentials of Christian doctrine. Robert Dabney brushed off Confucian and Buddhist ethics as basically pantheistic encouragements to behavior similar to modern Western materialism.[20]

---

[19] H. B. Bascom, *Methodism and Slavery* (Frankfort, KY, 1845), 65; Bascom, *Sermons from the Pulpit* (Louisville, KY, 1852), 19, 30, 56, 59–60; F. W. Pickens, *An Address on the Great Points of Difference between Ancient and Modern Civilizations* (Athens, GA, 1843), 12; [Benjamin M. Palmer], *Influence of Religious Belief upon National Character: An Oration Delivered before the Demosthean and Phi Beta Kappa Societies of the University of Georgia* (Athens, GA, 1845), 18–20; [Enoch Pond], "Philosophy in the Church," *SPR,* 4 (1850), 163–4; "Traveler", "Buddhist Superstitions," *SLM,* 25 (1857), 257–78, and "Buddhism, Its Origins, Tenets, Tendencies," 417–26; J. L. Dagg, *Manual of Theology: A Treatise on Christian Doctrine and a Treatise on Church Order,* 2 vols. (New York, 1980 [1857–58]), 1:20, 52–3. For once Palmer agreed with Lydia Maria Child, who also treated Hinduism as pantheism, but she showed more sympathy for pantheism than did southern commentators: Child, *Progress of Religious Ideas,* 1:11.

[20] [Thomas Smyth], "The Nature and Origin of the Pagan Doctrine of Triads, or a Trinity," *SPR,* 8 (1855), 560–80; [Smyth], "Further Objections to the Doctrine of the Trinity Answered," *SPR,* 9 (1855), 1–32; *DD**, 4:472, 573–4; also, [Cocke], "Christianity and Greek Philosophy," 189. Until the late nineteenth century many Americans, including the best educated, confused Buddhism with Hinduism. Buddhism proved attractive to northern liberals for whom Christianity was ethical philosophy or who sought to reduce it to the status of one religion among many. See Thomas A. Tweed, *The American Encounter with Buddhism, 1844–1912* (Bloomington, IN, 1992), xviii and ch. 1. For the southern reception of other universal histories – Raleigh, Volney, Michelet – see also Supplementary References: "Universal Histories."

Southern women, including some well outside the elite, singly and in groups read world history through Voltaire, Robertson, Prescott, and Irving. In addition to the works cited see Rachel Mordecai to Maria Edgeworth, Apr. 13, 1827, in Edgar E. MacDonald, *The Education of the Heart: The Correspondence of Rachel Mordecai Lazarus and Maria Edgeworth* (Chapel Hill, NC, 1977), 165; *Plantation Life: The Narratives of Mrs. Henry Schoolcraft* (New York, 1969 [1860]), 337, 343; Emily Wharton Sinkler to Thomas Isaac Wharton, Mar. 15, 1845, in Anne Sinkler Whaley LeClerq, ed., *Between North and South: The Letters of Emily Wharton Sinkler, 1842–1865* (Columbia, SC, 2001), 46; Jennie Speer Diary, Dec. 31, 1850, in Allen Paul Speer and Janet Barton Speer, *Sisters of Providence: The Search for God in the Frontier South (1843–1858)* (Johnson City, TN, 2000), 67; Ellen Douglas Brownlow to Mary Eliza Battle, Mar. 14, 1857, in Mary Eliza Battle Letters, at North Carolina State Archives (Raleigh); Tryphena Fox to Anna Rose Holder, Aug. 16 and Sept. 5, 1858, in Wilma King, ed., *A Northern Woman in the Plantation South: Letters of Tryphena Blanche Holder Fox, 1856–1876* (Columbia, SC, 1993), 80, 82; Harriet R. Palmer Diary, Jan. 7, 1861, in Louis P. Towles, ed., *A World Turned Upside Down: The Palmers of South Santee, 1818–1881* (Columbia, SC, 1996), 284; Sallie Bird to Saida Bird, Mar. 2, 1862, in John Rozier, ed., *The Granite Farm Letters: The Civil War Correspondence of Edgeworth and Sallie Bird* (Athens, GA, 1988), 68; Elizabeth Scott Neblett to Will Neblett, Apr. 26, 1863, in Erika L. Murr, ed., *Rebel Wife in Texas: The Diary and Letters of Elizabeth Scott Neblett, 1852–1864* (Baton Rouge, LA, 2001), 90–1; Elizabeth Muhlenfeld, *Mary Boykin Chesnut: A Biography* (Baton Rouge, LA, 1981), 51–3.

The specter of slave revolt hung over every consideration of social oppression and ensuing struggles. During the War, Mary Chesnut recalled the Sepoy Mutiny as she wondered about John Brown's failure to incite the slaves to revolt: "How long would they resist the seductive and irresistible call, 'rise, kill, and be free'?" Horrified over Sepoy atrocities, she was no less horrified by those of the British. She complimented Britain's William Howard Russell for reporting the War for Southern Independence with a measure of the objectivity he had applied to disclosure of British misrule in India. British cruelty in India drew steady fire in the southern press. While De Bow, notwithstanding his acknowledgment that India had one of the great early civilizations, hailed the British conquest as a tribute to "courage, zeal, perseverance, science and wisdom," an indignant Robert Howison of Virginia condemned it. Ujanirtus Allen of Virginia, a small slaveholder and a Confederate captain, wrote to his wife about the horrors of war in the Roman siege of Jerusalem, the Crusades, and the Sepoy Mutiny of 1857–58.[21]

Justification for missionaries' efforts to win converts to Christianity in the spreading Western empires became a central focus of reflection throughout the United States. The South boasted of its own missionaries to the Near East who, like John Adger and James Warley Miles, learned the languages and a good deal of regional history. William Brown Hodgson of Savannah – a big planter who served as U.S. representative in Algiers, Constantinople, and Cairo – achieved international recognition as a specialist on the Berbers. James Johnston Pettigrew was studying Arabic for a book on the Moors in Spain when the War abruptly ended his labors.[22]

Although a missionary movement implies belief in the superiority of one faith over others, Southerners differed among themselves on the degree of truth in non-Christian religions. In the eyes of the Baptist *Roanoke Religious Correspondent* of Danville, Virginia, Muhammad was a "great imposter" who led bandits in the imposition of tyranny over Arabia, and an essay in *Southern Literary Messenger* simply dismissed him as a demagogue. An essay on country life in *Southern Literary Journal*, probably written by Daniel Whitaker, portrayed Muslims as idle opium users. Thornwell dismissed Muhammed as a "false prophet" and Islam as "gross imposture and fraud," which – together with Rome – distorted and perverted the

---

[21] Chesnut Diary: June 6, 1861 (227), Aug. 1, 1861 (148), July 5, 1862 (409), July 18 and 21, 1862 (418), also, 440, all in Woodward, ed., *Mary Chesnut's Civil War*, quote at 409; De Bow, *Industrial Resources*, 1:107–8; Robert R. Howison, *A History of Virginia from Its Discovery and Settlement by Europeans to the Present Time*, 2 vols. (Philadelphia, 1846), 2:408; Ujanirtus Allen to Susan Fuller Allen, June 12, 1862, in Randall Allen and Keith S. Bohannon, eds., *Campaigning with "Old Stonewall": Confederate Captain Ujanirtus Allen's Letters to His Wife* (Baton Rouge, LA, 1998), 105. The Reverend Daniel Dreher compared Yankee atrocities to those committed during the Sepoy Mutiny: *A Sermon, June 13, 1861, Day of Humiliation and Prayer* (Salisbury, NC, 1861), 12.

[22] Henry Alexander White, *Southern Presbyterian Leaders* (New York, 1911), ch. 42 (Adger); *DGB*, 1:464–5 (Hodgson); Ralph Luker, *A Southern Tradition in Theology and Social Criticism: The Religious Liberalism and Social Conservatism of James Warley Miles, William Porcher DuBose and Edgar Gardner Murphy* (New York, 1884), ch. 1; Clyde N. Wilson, *Carolina Cavalier: The Life and Mind of James Johnston Pettigrew* (Athens, GA, 1990), ch. 9.

Bible and proved no rational grounds for religious conviction. Palmer, lecturing in Charleston in 1853, called Muhammed a falsifier and fanatic. The many South-erners who read medieval history encountered respectful accounts of early Muslim civilization. Gibbon and other writers on the Crusades appreciated Muslim tradi-tions of chivalric mercy and generosity. William Robertson's survey of the Muslim conquest of India treated Islam generously, and Henry Hallam pictured Muslim rulers as milder and more liberal than the Christians at Constantinople. Hallam defended Islam against charges of sexual indulgence, pointing out that Muhammad limited polygamy. Islam's power, Hallam argued, came in no small part from its austerity and self-discipline. G. P. R. James's popular *History of Chivalry* (1833) sadly recounted the Christian Crusaders' violation of truces with Muslims and sundry broken promises, and it told of priests who regarded moderation toward in-fidels as a sign of weakness. James noted that the Muslims fought with great valor and commended the moderation, tolerance, and generosity of their early rulers, coupling Caliph Haroun al Raschid with Charlemagne as a great man who led his people out of barbarism. "A barbarous epoch and a barbarous religion" had Sal-adin as a great man with a first-rate mind, moderate and merciful – the ideal of the chivalric warrior – "an exception to most of the vices of his age, his country, and his creed."[23]

In *Southern Literary Messenger* in the early 1840s, William W. Andrews, the U.S. representative at Malta, contrasted Muslim "humanity" in the Crusades with Christians' cold-blooded butchery in their conquest of Jerusalem. No one raised an eyebrow when "knights" in a lowcountry tournament turned up dressed as Saladin. Southerners' favorite Italian poets reinforced a positive view of Islam. Dante con-demned Muhammad to hell in the *Divine Comedy,* but he paid tribute to Arabic contributions to European philosophy and chivalry by placing Avicenna, Averroës, Saladin, and others in limbo. So too did Tasso, a deeply committed Christian, treat his Muslim subjects with respect. The Reverend F. W. Lewis admired the "Moorish schools of Cordova and Toledo" and their Muslim and Jewish scholars, and James Johnston Pettigrew devoted loving attention to Muslim contributions to Spanish history and culture. Severn Teackle Wallis seemed almost to regret the success of the Christian *Reconquista.* The Moorish civilization in Spain, De Bow wrote, was

---

[23] "Mahomedamism," *Roanoke Religious Correspondent,* 2 (1823), 91–3 and 143–4, quotes at 92, 143; "A Native of Goochland, Va.", "Benefits of Knowledge on Morals," *SLM,* 4 (1838); [Daniel K. Whitaker], "Country Life Incompatible with Literary Labor," *SLJ,* n.s., 1 (1837), 297; *JHTW,* 3:184, 418–19, 473; Thomas Cary Johnson, *The Life and Letters of Benjamin Morgan Palmer* (Richmond, VA, 1906), 123; Edward Gibbon, *The History of the Decline and Fall of the Roman Empire,* ed. David Womersley, 3 vols. (London, 1994), 3:chs. 50–52; William Robertson, *The History of Scotland dur-ing the Reigns of Queen Mary and King James VI* (New York, n.d., first published 1759), Appendix; Henry Hallam, *History of Europe in the Middle Ages,* rev. ed., 3 vols. (New York, 1899 [1818]), 2:49–71; G. P. R. James, *The History of Chivalry* (New York, 1833), 57, 172–3, 186, and on Saladin chs. 11 and 12, quote at 265 in ch. 13; on Saladin see also A. V. B. Norman, *The Medieval Soldier* (New York, 1971), 147–8. *Southern Quarterly Review,* invoking Carlyle, cautioned against declaring Muhammad an imposter in view of his formidable accomplishments in raising the level of civilization in the Near East: "Critical Notices," *SQR,* n.s., 1 (1850), 248. See also Supplementary References: "Islam and Muhammad" and *"Arabian Nights."*

marked by "much that was glorious." The Presbyterian Reverend W. T. Hamilton of Mobile noted that the Muslims derived their law from Moses, and the Episcopal Reverend W. N. Pendleton of Lexington, Virginia, while dismissing Muhammad as "the arch-imposter of the Koran," lauded Muslim civilization in Spain, attributing its achievements to Judeo-Christian roots. William Gilmore Simms and the Reverend James Cohen, a convert from Judaism, fulsomely praised Muslim civilization in Spain and duly credited the Arabs, notably Averroës, with introducing Aristotle to medieval Europe. Simms declared the history of Arab domination of Spain a brilliant chapter in humanity's march to civilization and national progress. Dew paid high tribute to the Muslims for creating a great civilization on the ruins of the Dark Ages and for contributions to medieval European culture. Brantz Mayer agreed with Dew, citing Washington Irving on Muslim ethics and piety: "The gallant Saracens who sustained the renown of Caliphate of Haroun el Rashid … carried conquest, chivalry, and civilization from Asia to Africa, and from Africa to Spain." William Horn Battle, Jr., in his senior speech at the University of North Carolina, credited the Crusades primarily with having brought Europe the "refinement and manners" of the Saracens.[24]

An 1850 essay (by C. A. Woodruff of Tuskegee) in *Southern Quarterly Review* on Washington Irving's two-volume *Mahomet and His Successors* concurred with Irving's assessment of Muhammad as largely responsible for the revitalization of civilized life in the Near East. Muhammad, with "genius" that bordered on "fanaticism," had brought a coherent monotheism to peoples who had sunk into idolatry and worse. Woodruff credited Islam with promotion of the Golden Rule. God sent Muhammad – "a remarkable" man, "honest in his intentions" – to a people unprepared for Christian enlightenment and yet desperately in need of a religion and ethics more advanced than their own.[25]

Pettigrew judged the Muslims in Spain more tolerant of Christians and Jews than Christians were toward Muslims and Jews during and after the *Reconquista*. Muslims fought with more "chivalric gallantry and humanity" and granted Christians "a liberty of conscience that puts contemporaneous Europe to the blush." Robert Dabney wrote that Europeans covered the Americas and Asia with blood

---

[24] William W. Andrews, "History of the Knights of Malta," *SLM* 7 (1841), 830–5; see also *SLM*, 8 (1842), 41–7, 139–45, 317–21, and 9 (1843), 163–71; Andrews, "A Historical Sketch of St. John of Jerusalem: Foundation of the Order," *SLM*, 9 (1843), 417–22, 579–87; [F. W. Lewis], "A Plea for the Study of Hebrew Literature," *SPR*, 9 (1855), 34; [James Johnston Pettigrew], *Notes on Spain and the Spaniards in the Summer of 1850, with a Glance at Sardinia* (Charleston, SC, 1861), esp. chs. 8 and 15; [Severn Teackle Wallis], "Spain in the Fifteenth Century," *SLM*, 7 (1841), 242; [De Bow], "Literature of Spain," *DBR*, 9 (1850), 66–85, quote at 69; W. T. Hamilton, "Character of Moses," *SPR*, 4 (1852), 531; Pendleton, *Science: A Witness for the Bible*, 29, 42, quote at 29; [William Gilmore Simms?], "The History of the Middle Ages," *SWMR*, 1 (1845), 381; James Cohen, "Life and Writings of Maimonides," *SPR*, 12 (1859), 410, 426; [Simms], *SQR*, n.s., 10 (1854), 513; Dew, *Digest*, 417–20; [Mayer], "China and the Chinese," 3; William Horne Battle, Jr., "Senior Speech," in Senior Speeches, 1853, at UNC-NCC; also, A. K. Merrill, "A Glimpse at the Past, and the Present," *Southern Ladies' Book,* 1 (1840), 284. For stress on Islam's embrace of Abraham see "Abraham's Position in Sacred History," *DQR*, 4 (1864), 612–14.

[25] [C. A. Woodruff], "Islamism," *SQR*, 4 (1851), 173–206, quotes at 173, 176, 182.

and rapine, and that the Castilians, "too proud for hypocrisy," committed more cruelties than the Muslims ever did. Seeking balance, J. P. Tusten maintained that Islamic civilization had been vastly superior to Christian during the Dark Ages and that Philip II's expulsion of the Moors contributed immensely to Spanish decline. Muslims had displayed "personal bravery and chivalric magnanimity" and, in Richard's siege of Acre Muslims, a much higher standard of chivalric honor than Christians, who disgraced themselves by acts of inhumanity. The Turks, Tusten added, do not lie, for they obey their oath to Allah, upholding a chivalric code of honor.[26]

The decline of Islam invited speculation on historical cycles. Woodruff saw Muslim virtues in great movements that collapsed into vice and corruption. Benjamin Morgan Palmer, echoed by Tusten, credited Islamic fatalism with Muslims' fearlessness in battle, but at the price of Islam's becoming "as fixed and unchangeable as the Pillar of Salt upon the Plains of Sodom." Islam, unlike Christianity, could not progress beyond the chivalric stage. It recognized no international law, carrying only the banner: "the Koran, tribute, or the sword." With no "principle of permanence," J. H. Hayne wrote, Muslim states crumbled when they ceased to conquer.[27]

"You are engaged in a holy war," the Reverend Joseph Jones told Confederate troops in 1861, comparing them to the Crusaders who died to "rescue the Holy Sepulchre from the infidel Moslem." Yet in 1864 the Reverend J. L. Burrows judged Arabs and Saracens "a purer race than the nominally Christian nations they subdued."[28]

Many prominent Americans, North and South, believed in the destiny of the white race to rule the colored peoples of the world. Wary Southerners suspected that northern expansionists aimed at an economic development based on free labor at home and a disguised slavery abroad, and strong southern interests opposed imperialism as a threat to America's republican institutions and an impediment to the unity necessary to defend slavery at home. Even such hardened racists as Dr. Samuel Cartwright considered British oppression of India a natural counterpart to support for American abolitionism. An American national expansion that

[26] [Pettigrew], *Spain and the Spaniards*, 124, 150, 126–7, 259–60, 269–70, quote at 124; *DD**, 4:54–5; [Tusten], "Chivalry and Civilization," esp. 211–12, 221, 223. Islamic accounts grudgingly praised the courage of the Frankish Crusaders but noted their lack of chivalric generosity toward their enemies. We found no southern notice of *Chronique arabes*, edited by Reinaud and published in Paris in 1829, but see Carole Hillenbrand, *The Crusades: Islamic Perspectives* (New York, 1999), 355–7; also, Francesco Gabrieli, ed., *Arab Historians of the Crusades*, tr. E. J. Costello (Berkeley, CA, 1984).

[27] [Francis P. Lea], "The Knights Templars," *SQR*, 9 (1846), 458–9; [Woodruff], "Islamism," *SQR*, 4 (1851), 200; Benjamin M. Palmer, *Influence of Religious Belief upon National Character*, 22; [J. H. Hayne], *RM*, 3 (1858), 352. Francis P. Lea suggested that the Muslims probably would have crushed their infidel enemies if they had not fallen on each other over booty: [Lea], "Knights Templars," 457–507. Negative judgment was compatible with admiration for such regimes as that of Mehemet Ali in Egypt: "C.", "Mehemet Ali," *SLM*, 9 (1843), 321–4.

[28] J. Jones, *A Discourse Delivered ... to the Rome Light Guards and Miller Rifles* (Rome, GA, 1861), 10; J. L. Burrows, *Nationality Insured: Notes of a Sermon Delivered at the First Baptist Church, Augusta, Ga., September 11, 1864* (Augusta, GA, 1864), 6.

allowed for exploitation of colonial peoples threatened to add more free states to the Union and hence to strengthen the economic power of northern capitalists. Southerners remained chary of siren calls from publications like *Democratic Review* that advocated sectional cooperation to subjugate the colored races through imperialism and free trade.[29]

Others found a divine imperative in white rule of colored peoples. In 1753 Jonathan Bryan, Georgia planter and businessman, spoke of "the Special Providence of Almighty God" in the conquest of heathens and in creation of a haven for the "persecuted church in some parts of Europe." A century later, the Reverend Mr. Claghorn of Alabama preached: "The law of Conquest has been recognized – from time immemorial – When a nation has been conquered – The lives & property of the vanquished are at the mercy of the Conqueror." The conqueror who acquires slaves requires obedience. Henry Young Webb, who provided the paraphrase, was reminded of man's slavery to God: "So we belong to God – we are bought with a price even the precious blood of the Son of God – and therefore we are bound to obey." Sam Milligan of Tennessee wrote to Andrew Johnson, a close political ally, that God ordained civilization through the workings of the laws of nature: "So that if the common interest require either the lands (as of the Indians) or the labor (as of the idle negro) of the vicious the idle or unproductive, the laws of civilization can take them for the good of the whole." Dew, Louisa McCord, and numerous others took for granted that two races could not coexist as equals in a given territory, that one must rule or exterminate the other, and that the white race was uniquely fit for liberty and destined to rule the colored.[30]

Nor did racial categorization end with a dichotomy between whites and non-whites. Differences among whites themselves took on a racial hue. The dismal outcomes of the revolutions in France and Latin America encouraged Southerners as well as Northerners to believe ever more strongly in the superiority of Anglo-Saxons and Teutons. Josiah Nott of Mobile, a formidable figure in the medical profession and chief southern polygenesist, rated colored races inferior to white, blacks the lowest race, and Amerindians not worth much. Nott had a much better opinion of the Chinese but still placed them below whites. Acknowledging much intermixture, he subdivided whites into many races of differing levels of ability and accomplishment – with Anglo-Saxons and Teutons highest in his ranking, well above southern Europeans. Many Southerners expressed similar views without necessarily accepting Nott's theory of separate racial origins. For Henry Timrod, South Carolina's gifted poet, the southern mind offered "that blending of the philosophic in thought

[29] Samuel Cartwright, *Essays in a Series of Letters to Rev. William Winans* (Natchez, MS, 1843), 6, 45; also, Kenneth M. Stampp, *America in 1857: A Nation on the Brink* (New York, 1990), ch. 7.

[30] [Jonathan Bryan], Aug. 13, 1753, in *Visit to the Georgia Islands* (Macon, GA, 1996 [1753]), 20; Claghorn paraphrased in Webb Diary, May 1, 1858, at UNC-SHC; Sam Milligan to Andrew Johnson, Feb. 8, 1860, in Leroy P. Graf and Ralph W. Haskins, eds., *The Papers of Andrew Johnson*, 13 vols. (Knoxville, TN, 1967–), 3:420; "Professor Dew on Slavery," in *Pro-Slavery Argument*, 410. In Richard C. Lounsbury, ed., *Louisa S. McCord: Political and Social Essays* (Charlottesville, VA, 1995), see "Diversity of the Races" (173) and "British Philanthropy" (289–90, 317–18).

with the enthusiastic in feeling, which makes a literary nation." For the Reverend William Scott, the races of Great Britain, America, and Germany were destined to rule the world, carrying freedom everywhere.[31]

The concept of a worldwide crusade for white domination did not sit well with many southern and northern conservatives, who saw it as the program of radical demagogues. The Presbyterian Reverend S. J. Cassells in the pulpit and Senator Henry Hilliard of Alabama on the stump protested that imperialist expansion turns a country inward and destroys the free institutions of the conquering country. French and British imperialism created a special difficulty for southern Christians. The Episcopalian Reverend William Norwood denied that the French had a right to invade and conquer Algeria, although he approved their introduction of Christianity. Mary Chesnut did not condemn the conquest of Algiers but flinched at the rough behavior of the French. In 1846 Thomas Clemson wrote Calhoun, his father-in-law, that the French were disgracing themselves in Algeria "for the almost acknowledged purpose of giving occupation to a redundant population & killing off the turbulent spirits that, had they been retained at home, might have disturbed the tranquility or jeopardized the consolidation of the present family upon the throne of France. France requires war to sustain itself." An appalled Episcopalian Reverend W. N. Pendleton of Lexington, Virginia, protested atrocities committed in Algeria by "a so-called Christian nation."[32]

The Reverends I. T. Tichenor and Henry M. Dennison lashed out at the British for waging war on China in the interests of an opium trade that demoralized and brutalized multitudes; but they, too, allowed that even an evil war driven by avarice advanced Christianity in China. In 1858 James Holcombe, speaking at length to the Virginia State Agricultural Society on British rule in India, conceded arbitrariness and some cruelty but praised a just and salutary regime that imposed civilized order on a people incapable of self-government. The radical secessionist Edmund Ruffin condemned the Opium War in China and William Walker as a pirate and a thug for his filibustering in Nicaragua, yet he concluded, as on the Sepoy Mutiny, that the colored races could advance to civilization only by yielding to white rule – that is, if such basically worthless people could advance at all: "the Chinese, & also the Japanese people, will be much benefited if their unimprovable despotic governments,

---

[31] Josiah Nott, *Two Lectures on the Connection between the Biblical and Physical History of Man* (New York, 1849), 36; Nott, "Acclimation," in J. C. Nott and George R. Gliddon, *Indigenous Races of the Earth* (Philadelphia, 1857), ch. 4; Reginald Horsman, *Josiah Nott of Mobile: Southerner, Physician, and Racial Theorist* (Baton Rouge, LA, 1987), 99–100; Edd Winfield Parks, ed., *The Essays of Henry Timrod* (Athens, GA, 1942), 101; W. A. Scott, "The Progress of Civil Liberty," in Robert Gross Barnwell, ed., *The New-Orleans Book* (New Orleans, 1851).

[32] S. J. Cassells, "The Relation of Justice to Benevolence in the Conduct of Society," *SPR*, 7 (1853), 89; Henry W. Hilliard, *Speeches and Addresses* (New York, 1855), 220; W. Norwood, *God and Our Country: A Sermon* (Richmond, VA, 1863), 6; for Mrs. Chesnut's not necessarily hostile reference to the French in Algiers see Mar. 14, 1862, in Woodward, ed., *Mary Chesnut's Civil War*, 308. Clemson to Calhoun, July 15, 1846, in *JCCP*, 23:320–1; Pendleton, *Science: A Witness for the Bible*, 222. For a sympathetic treatment of North African Arab resistance to French imperialism, see *Southern Cabinet of Agriculture, Horticulture, Rural and Domestic Economy*, 1 (1840), 46–8.

& customs, are broken down, even if by conquest by civilized European powers." Ruffin's views on the destiny of the white race paralleled those of proslavery conservatives well removed from his radical secessionist politics.[33]

"Christianity unquestionably binds the race together in ties unknown to nature," Thornwell wrote in 1855. "She establishes a sacred brotherhood in common origin, a common ruin, a common immortality, and a common Savior, which unites the descendants of Adam into one great family, and renders wars, discords, and jealousies as odious as they are hurtful." In 1862 Robert L. Dabney delivered a memorial sermon about "The Christian Soldier" on the duties of patriotism as consistent with Scripture: "The diversity of tongues, character, races, and interests among mankind forbids their union in one universal commonwealth." Separate nations are necessary, and governments carry a divine injunction to maintain order and resist aggression. God commands men to sustain their government "with heart and hand." Compliance is a duty: "He who extends his philanthropy so broadly as to refuse a special attachment to the interests of his own people, will probably make it so thin as to be of no account to any people."[34]

The South had to secure slaveholding whether in or out of the Union. In 1847 Simms wrote J. H. Hammond that, with disunion inevitable, the South must absorb Mexico to counterbalance the probable loss of a portion of the Border States to free soil. "The acquisition of Texas and Mexico secures the perpetuation of slavery for a thousand years." The South had confronted a political nightmare when the United States moved to annex Mexican territory. For Calhoun – along with such prominent Whigs as Alexander Stephens, John Berrien, and Parson William Brownlow – territorial annexations would blow the Union apart and impose grave racial problems as well. During the Mexican War, Calhoun asserted "a mysterious connection between the fate of this country and that of Mexico" and the need for close relations between sister republics. He described the Mexicans as little qualified for free and popular government. In 1848 Calhoun reiterated his doubts about the justice of American policy but pledged support for stern measures if whites exhausted "all manly exertions" to repel a genuine threat from racial inferiors: "I have no aversion to any race, but my sympathies are for the white race. I am not so sophisticated by misguided philosophy or false philanthropy as to lose the natural feelings which belong to me." He believed that the progress of the racially mixed Latin Americans who overthrew Spanish rule depended on the relative strength of the white element

[33] I. T. Tichenor, *Fast Day Sermon* (Montgomery, AL, 1863), 11; Henry M. Dennison, "Relation of Commerce to Christianity," *DBR*, 26 (1859), 261–2; James P. Holcombe, "Is Slavery Consistent with Natural Law?" *SLM*, 27 (1858), 405–6. In *ERD*, vol. 1: quote at Jan. 29, 1857 (29); also, Feb. 14, 1857 (33), Aug. 10, 1857 (96–7), Apr. 26, 1858 (181–2). For similar views see W. H. Holcombe, *The Alternative* (Richmond, VA, 1858), 23–4; Daniel R. Hundley, *Social Relations in Our Southern States* (Baton Rouge, LA, 1979), 316ff.; J. B. Lindsley, "Table Talk," May 16, 1862, in John Berrien Lindsley Papers, at Tennessee State Library and Archives (Nashville). Southern newspapers and periodicals viewed the Opium War as a disgrace to Britain. For a typical assault on British conduct in India and China and especially on the opium trade, see "A Few Thoughts on Slavery," *SLM*, 20 (1854), 203.

[34] In *JHTW*, 3:183–220, quote at 211, also 1:257, 349, 3:134; *DD*, 1:614–25, quotes at 614.

in their nature. The firmest of proslavery ideologues, looking askance at the movement to annex Mexico and other nonwhite countries, doubted that whites could civilize degraded races, much less bring them freedom and democracy.[35]

By 1858 Simms was describing privately sponsored invasions of Latin American countries ("filibustering") to William Porcher Miles as "the moral necessity of all Anglo Norman breed" and "the necessity of all progressive races," and in 1861 he expected the introduction of slavery to "civilize" Mexico. Waddy Thompson, contrasting Teutons and Anglo-Saxons with Mexicans, wrote: "Our race has never yet put its foot upon a soil which it has not only not kept but has advanced." W. R. Aylett of Virginia, a planter and grandson of Patrick Henry, depicted Latin Americans as unfit to rule themselves but somehow open to "Americanization" once absorbed by the United States. In 1852 even the unionist Joel Poinsett, disgusted with the incompetence and corruption of successive Mexican governments, suggested that conquest by a foreign power would prove a blessing. The next year the nationally prestigious Richmond *Enquirer* and *De Bow's Review* predicted that the progress of the next fifty years would be based on commercial concentration in the Gulf of Mexico, that control of Cuba would become a national priority, and that southern control of the Mississippi and Amazon valleys would determine the future of slavery. The ocean scientist Matthew F. Maury, writing at length over many years, dreamed of the eventual absorption of much of Latin America by the United States. From the Mexican War to secession, slaveholding spokesmen interpreted any restriction of slavery to specified geographical limits as a transparent effort to strangle slavery itself. It was a message that gathered force in the press and among politicians, and it contributed to the drift to secession. In 1861 Randolph Tucker asserted that a civilization either expands or perishes. Edward Pollard, who supported filibustering, identified the southern cause as the expansion of slavery into a world system.[36]

---

[35] Simms to Hammond, July 15, 1847, in Mary C. Oliphant et al., eds., *The Letters of William Gilmore Simms*, 6 vols. (Columbia, SC, 1952–82), 2:330–3; "Speech on the War with Mexico," in *JCCP*, 24:118, 131; "Speech on the Proposed Occupation of Yucatan" (May 15, 1848), in Clyde N. Wilson, ed., *The Essential Calhoun: Selection from Writings, Speeches, and Letters* (New Brunswick, NJ, 1991), 146–8. On racist opposition to the absorption of Mexico see Fredrickson, *Black Image in the White Mind*, 136–7. Democrats like William L. Yancey and Herchel Johnson saw opportunities to expand slave territory and linked Stephens's criticism with that of the abolitionists: Thomas E. Schott, *Alexander H. Stephens of Georgia: A Biography* (Baton Rouge, LA, 1988), 68–76; W. J. Cooper, Jr., *The South and Politics of Slavery, 1828–1856* (Baton Rouge, LA, 1978), 228–9.

[36] In Oliphant et al., eds., *Letters of Simms*, see: Simms to Hammond, July 15, 1847 (2:330–3); Simms to Miles, Jan. 25, 1858 (2:332, 4:11); Simms to Miles, Feb. 22, 1861 (4:332). Waddy Thompson, *Recollections of Mexico* (New York, 1847), 239; W. R. Aylett, speeches on "Our Pacific Possessions," "American Progress," and "Liberty, Patriotism, and Virtue," in Aylett Family Papers, 1851–1854, at Virginia Historical Society (Richmond); Joel Poinsett, "Mexico in 1852," *DBR*, 13 (1852), 353–4; article from Richmond *Enquirer* reprinted in *DBR*, 17 (1854), 281–3; John Randolph Tucker, "The Great Issue," *SLM*, 32 (1861), 166–7; Jack P. Maddex, Jr., *The Reconstruction of Edward A. Pollard: A Rebel's Conversion to Postbellum Unionism* (Chapel Hill, NC, 1974), 25–9. See also *Plantation*, 1 (1860), 1–2, 111–12; Samuel Walker, "Cuba and the South," *DBR*, 17 (1854), 524; A. W. Ely,

Conflicts within the South over an American foreign policy consistent with slave-holding interests brought to the fore difficulties inherent in constitutional doctrines of strict construction and state rights. In 1831 Calhoun maintained that social divisions threatened constitutional liberty and had to be overcome if society expected general suffrage to solve pressing problems. He agreed with John Taylor of Caroline that America lacked naturally constituted social classes, for he did not recognize as classes groups that accumulated property through fair competition. The federal government, he believed, created "artificial" classes through patronage, privilege, and monopoly. Calhoun worried about deepening sectional divisions but identified class relations as the source, accusing Northerners of unwillingness to respect slave property.[37]

Calhoun's confidence in the social and political solidity of southern slave society led him to obscure the danger inherent in the constitutional doctrines of strict construction and state rights, for while slave property dominated the South, it existed side by side with other forms of property. The Founding Fathers considered factional struggles subversive of republican virtue and social order, but the danger festered: A seemingly secure system of property may ground an effective sociopolitical consensus but at considerable risk. Although partisan rivalries look safe when factions that share a fundamental vision of society engage in intraclass warfare, messy political realities have a way of upsetting the property systems that supposedly inhibit destructive impulses. Factional struggles invite attention to specifics and tempt beleaguered minorities to seek alliances with dangerous radicals. The French Revolution provided a dramatic example of intraclass struggles that, despite the intentions of their initiators, passed into revolutionary confrontation.[38]

"Spanish and Cuban Views of Annexation," *DBR*, 18 (1855), 305–11; Louisville *Daily Courier*, Dec. 20, 1860, in Dwight Lowell Dumond, ed., *Southern Editorials on Secession* (Gloucester, MA, 1964), 360; Jeremiah Clemens of Alabama, *Congressional Globe*, 19, pt. 1, 31st Cong., 1st Sess., Feb. 20, 1850, 397; Rep. Warner of Georgia quoted in [George M. Weston], *The Progress of Slavery in the United States* (Washington, DC, 1857), 227. Also, Percy L. Rainwater, "Economic Benefits of Secession: Opinions in Mississippi in the 1850s," *Journal of Southern History* 1 (1935), 459; C. Stanley Urban, "The Abortive Quitman Filibustering Expedition, 1853–1855," *Journal of Mississippi History*, 18 (1956), 181. Important northern politicians opposed annexation on the ground that Mexico's lower races could not be assimilated: see Forrest McDonald, *States' Rights and the Union: Imperium in Imperio, 1776–1876* (Lawrence, KS, 2000), 151–3. "Every respectable reading room in the United States carried Ritchie's *Enquirer*": Carl R. Osthaus, *Partisans of the Southern Press: Editorial Spokesmen of the Nineteenth Century* (Lexington, KY, 1994), 13.

[37] Calhoun to Frederick W. Symmes, Jan. 26, 1831, for publication in the *Messenger*, in JCCP, 10:423–4; "Discourse on the Constitution," in Ross M. Lence, ed., *Union and Liberty: The Political Philosophy of John C. Calhoun* (Indianapolis, IN, 1992), 278–9, 284–5.

[38] For an insightful discussion of this problem see Roberto Mangabeira Unger, *False Necessity: Anti-Necessitarian Social Theory in the Service of Radical Democracy* (Cambridge, MA, 1987), 463–4. See also Bolingbroke, *Letters on the Study and Uses of History* and *Remarks on the History of England*. Bolingbroke was "assisted by Pope and Swift" in his attacks on Walpole and the corruption of the new bourgeoisie: Joseph M. Isenberg, "Towards the Concurrent Majority: The Intellectual Development of Southern Constitutional Theory," paper presented at the Mid American History Conference (Fayetteville, AR), 1998.

Thus, strong voices from a proslavery minority uttered grave reservations about state rights and suggested that the survival of a slave society in a modern world of contending national states required centralization of power in a national government. The issue haunted political discussions from the early days of the Republic and burst forth with a vengeance when Southerners flirted with secession. Southern Federalists, most notably lowcountry Carolinians, championed federal power as the best guarantor of slave property and only slowly reversed their judgment. In later years, southern Whigs out-shouted Democrats for state rights, but they harbored some men who supported federal consolidation.[39]

Impatient with Calhoun's doctrines, William Henry Trescot laid out with stunning brevity and intellectual acuteness a broad interpretation: History proceeds through "antagonisms," specifically nation-state rivalries. Within those nations the struggle of "opposing parties" determines policy, and fundamental social struggles lie at the heart of great party antagonisms. Hence, Trescot formulated his interpretation of the American Revolution as a conservative movement that upheld the status quo in international relations. He took the measure of the political course followed by Jefferson, Madison, and Monroe once they assumed power. Calhoun, to the end of his life, referred to Jefferson as leader of the state-rights cause but conceded that the policies of Jefferson, Madison, and Monroe dangerously strengthened the national government. He attributed the backsliding to the genius of Hamilton, whose talents and misguided patriotism he respected. Hamilton had done his work well, creating an institutional structure that protected big capital and big government against the best efforts of reformers. Madison, the ablest opponent of the First Bank of the United States, reluctantly signed the bill to charter the Second. He endorsed the tariff of 1816 and, while doubting the constitutionality of federally sponsored internal improvements, endorsed that policy, hoping for constitutional sanction through an amendment. Hard-liners who opposed Jeffersonian temporizing (Tertium Quids) expected Monroe to reverse Madison's course, but Monroe allowed sweeping internal improvements and higher tariffs. This disquieting record did not surprise Trescot, who believed that a great country had to move as a coherent unit in world politics and opposed American national consolidation on grounds of strategy and tactics, not principle. Although state rights protected southern property and institutions in a Union dominated by men hostile to the South, it would impede an independent slaveholding southern republic.[40]

---

[39] On the early Republic see Arthur H. Shaffer, *To Be an American: David Ramsay and the Making of the American Consciousness* (Columbia, SC, 1991), 80–1; John Harold Wolfe, *Jeffersonian Democracy in South Carolina* (Chapel Hill, NC, 1940), 38, 44–7. On the southern Whigs see esp. Michael F. Holt, *The Rise and Fall of the American Whig Party: Jacksonian Politics and the Onset of the Civil War* (New York, 1999). Waddy Thompson and Henry Stuart Foote, unionists, justified state rights for the United States as necessary to a sprawling republic but cautioned that Mexicans, among others, lacked the capacity and needed a central authority: Thompson, *Recollections of Mexico*, 58–9; Foote, *Texas and the Texans; Or, the Advance of the Anglo-Americans to the South-West*, 2 vols. (Austin, TX, 1935 [1841]), 2:ch. 2, and 373.

[40] William Henry Trescot, *The Diplomacy of the Revolution: An Historical Study* (New York, 1852), esp. 6, 51–6, 148; J. C. Calhoun, "Discourse on the Constitution," in Lence, ed., *Union and Liberty,*

Trescot contended with the isolationism of sober men worthy of respect. Dew, for example, had concluded from his study of the wars of the French Revolution that a nation plunged into the greatest folly when interfering in the internal affairs of others. American national greatness, according to the Methodist Reverend W. J. Sasnett, stemmed in large part from the Washingtonian doctrine of nonintervention. Benjamin Johnson Barbour warned a Fourth of July celebration at Virginia Military Institute against American meddling in other people's affairs: Foreign intervention and war propelled an ominous centralization of power at home. Mistaken pride, Trescot retorted, made Americans think they stood apart from the world, entrusted by God with a special mission, with wisdom that embodied the whole of world experience and with a future independent of the world's control. In 1849 he argued that, notwithstanding Washington's Farewell Address, the Monroe Doctrine showed that the United States no longer dared remain aloof from Europe's quarrels, which spilled into Latin America and the Pacific and threatened American commercial and political interests. Trescot tartly recalled that, at the very beginning of the Revolution, Americans sought European allies. He considered Washington's advice tactically sound but temporally bound. Washington, who wisely recognized the weakness of American power, had devised a strategy of neutrality that turned momentary weakness into long-term strength. His great accomplishment in foreign policy consisted of a maneuver to keep out of European wars from which America would gain little and become a mere cat's paw of England or France. Trescot nonetheless argued that the United States now found itself enmeshed in a system of nation-state rivalries. It could honor Washington's counsel to hold itself aloof from other nations' quarrels only when those quarrels did not threaten American national interests. Nations have a right to self-determination and a right to defend their national interests – and therefore a right to intervene if another nation threatens their socioeconomic and political system. Trescot approved the intervention of the conservative powers in French internal affairs on the grounds that the French revolutionaries threatened the social order of Europe. The war between France and Europe transcended struggles for commercial advantage and political power: It was a war for existence. Self-preservation required intervention against nations that export revolutionary ideologies.[41]

252–4. Arthur Schlesinger, Jr., fairly comments, "The last days of the Virginia dynasty turned into a confession of the impotence of Virginia doctrines": *The Age of Jackson* (Boston, 1945), 19. Alexander Hamilton's reputation in the South deserves a careful study, which would reveal some surprises. For a teaser, note that *Southern Literary Messenger* republished J. G. Baldwin's sketch of Hamilton: "The Genius and Character of Alexander Hamilton," *SLM*, 22 (1856), 371–80. Trescot drew a grim picture of the United States under the Articles of Confederation as a country without the institutions necessary to conduct a foreign policy. William J. Grayson referred to the "imbecility of the old Confederacy" and its inability to conduct a serious foreign policy. William Henry Trescot, *The Diplomatic History of the Washington and Adams Administrations, 1789–1801* (Boston, MA, 1857), 12; [William J. Grayson], "Trescot's Diplomatic History," *RM*, 2 (1857), 427.

[41] Dew, *Digest*, 659–61; W. J. Sasnett, "The United States – Her Past and Future," *DBR*, 12 (1852), 615–17; Benjamin Johnson Barbour, "Address Delivered before the Literary Societies of the Virginia Military Institute," *SLM*, 20 (1854), 513–28; William Henry Trescot, *A Few Thoughts on the Foreign Policy of the United States* (Charleston, SC, 1849); Trescot, *Washington and Adams Administrations*,

When William Porcher Miles of South Carolina castigated Louis Kossuth at the College of Charleston in 1852, De Bow demurred: Pre-1848 Hungary was medieval, feudal, and oppressive, and Kossuth was a great man entitled to the gratitude of the Hungarian people. De Bow's heart cried out for an intervention he conceded to be impractical. He had considered demands for American intervention in Europe absurd, but with the caveat that intervention must sooner or later become American policy. *Southern Literary Messenger* and *Southern Quarterly Review* rallied to Trescot's view that a United States enmeshed in a system of nation-state rivalries must intervene to protect its own interests. George Frederick Holmes and Charleston's John McCrady called for recognition that American security depended upon an active role in world affairs.[42]

These men of diverse views approached the position at which Trescot had arrived as a precocious youth. The cause of the South was inextricably bound to the struggle of the world's conservative great powers to master the social question at home and to crush radicalism abroad. For Calhoun as for Trescot, Fitzhugh, and others, the safety of peoples and nations required a world order that allowed them to work out internal antagonisms separately. Observant Southerners sensed but dared not accept that the new world order in the making would have no place for slaveholding. With the collapse of the Confederacy and the subsequent collapse of slavery in Cuba and Brazil, the South's half-subdued imperialist tendency ripened into an ideology that sought to justify European world conquest. At that, no European power reestablished slavery in other than an elaborately disguised fashion or attempted to re-create the master–slave relation as the basis for a colonial society. Consider the career of the Reverend James Lyon of Mississippi, who before and during the War led the fight in the Southwest to humanize the slave codes. A unionist who defended slavery while excoriating slaveholders for un-Christian treatment of slaves, he believed that civilization required slavery "in some form" and feared that the black race itself would perish if the South lost the War. With the War over, Lyon reconciled himself to a world order in which the white race served as a surrogate master class. Even George Fitzhugh, who defended as firmly as any the doctrine of slavery in the abstract, flirted with an imperialist solution to the social question that would make the white race of Euro-America a kind of collective master of the world's colored peoples. After the War, Fitzhugh – like many others – embraced a

---

96, 148, and ch. 2. On Trescot see David Moltke-Hansen, "William Henry Trescot," *Dictionary of American Biography*, 31 vols. (New York, 1927–77), 30:310–19, and "A Beaufort Planter's Rhetorical World: The Context and Content of William Henry Trescot's Orations," *Proceedings of the South Carolina Historical Association* (1981), 120–32; see also Eugene D. Genovese, *The Slaveholders' Dilemma: Freedom and Progress in Southern Conservative Thought, 1820–1860* (Columbia, SC, 1992), ch. 3.

42   De Bow in *DBR*, 12 (1852), 459, and 13 (1852), 101; De Bow, "Hungary in 1852," *DBR*, 13 (1852), 435, 444–5; [J. R. Thompson?], "Our Foreign Policy," *SLM*, 16 (1850), 1–6; George Frederick Holmes, "Relations of the Old World to the New," *DBR*, 20 (1856), 521–40; [McCrady], "Thoughts on Southern Civilization," 551–2. *Southern Quarterly Review* approved Trescot's *Oration Delivered before the Beaufort Volunteer Artillery* and his *Position and Course of the South* (1850): see [David F. Jamison], "The National Anniversary," *SQR*, n.s., 2 (1850), 170–91, and 3 (1851), 282–3.

version of the "people's imperialism" that offered white workers a secure place in a system of worldwide conquest.[43]

The growing defense of slavery in the abstract and the assignment of race to the status of a special case of the Social Question approached an impasse. A way out appeared before the War but achieved centrality only afterwards, when the reunited Union plunged into imperialism, proclaiming the white man's burden on a world scale. Later in the century the antebellum stirrings, previously stronger in the North than in the South, became a loud all-American shout: The white race had a historic responsibility to rule the world, civilize the heathens of Asia, Africa, and Latin America, and rightfully put them to work for the master race. When the Confederacy and slavery went down, this new racism, already popular in the North, directly served late nineteenth-century imperialist ideology. The irony: Before the War southern ideologues, led morally and to a considerable extent intellectually by impressive social theorists and theologians, had hewed to time-honored conservative principles. By minimizing the suffering of their own black slaves, they defended slavery at home all the more passionately while they struggled in the United States against an imperialist worldview that would subsequently impose unprecedented misery and mass slaughter on the world. The defeat of the slaveholders and their worldview opened the floodgates to the global catastrophe their leading spokesmen had long seen a-borning.

[43] Ernest Trice Thompson, *Presbyterians in the South*, 3 vols. (Richmond, VA, 1963), 2:56; on Fitzhugh see Eugene D. Genovese, *The World the Slaveholders Made: Two Essays in Interpretation* (New York, 1969), esp. 209–10. On the Methodist side, A. A. Lipscomb made the familiar argument that Providence smiled on the Anglo-Saxon race but also charged it with responsibility to shepherd benighted Africans: *Substance of a Discourse Delivered before the Legislature of Georgia* (Milledgeville, GA, 1860), 17–18.

7

History as the Story of Freedom

> The progress of civilization is the gradual disenthralment of the human mind from all the chains that fetter it, and is identical with the progress of human liberty.
> —George Frederick Holmes (1843)[1]

With few exceptions, Southerners pronounced themselves simultaneously progressive and conservative. They envisioned a cycle of flowering and decadence in an upward spiral of progression of human freedom, which would, in turn, propel historical progress. Slaveholders believed that men of good will should desire to extend freedom as far as possible, while recognizing that many peoples lacked the capacity to live free; that the freest societies in world history were based on slavery; and that freedom could be sustained only through subjugation of all laboring classes. Thus, they resolved to sustain a southern slave society even in a hostile world.[2]

As dedicated republicans Southerners supported freedom of speech in principle; as slaveholders they weighed freedom of speech against their sense of the exigencies of social stability. In consequence, the South came increasingly to condemn "free society." In 1825 Whitemarsh Seabrook rallied the South by calling upon Congress

---

[1] George Frederick Holmes, "Schlegel's Philosophy of History" (1843), in Michael O'Brien, ed., *All Clever Men, Who Make Their Way: Critical Discourse in the Old South* (Fayetteville, AR, 1982), 210.

[2] For the centrality of slavery to the emergence of the concept of freedom see Orlando Patterson, *Freedom*, vol. 1: *Freedom in the Making of Western Culture* (New York, 1991), esp. ch. 3. On the relation of slavery to freedom and of both to "progress" in southern proslavery theory, see Eugene D. Genovese, *The Slaveholders' Dilemma: Freedom and Progress in Southern Conservative Thought, 1820–1860* (Columbia, SC, 1991); also, Kenneth M. Greenberg, "Revolutionary Ideology and the Proslavery Argument: The Abolition of Slavery in Antebellum South Carolina," *JSH*, 42 (1976), 365–84. Eighteenth-century Southerners, reading historians and philosophers – Herodotus, Polybius, Tacitus, David Hume, and their own Walter Raleigh, Robert Beverley, Hugh Jones, and William Stith – found a recurring struggle for liberty. Their nineteenth-century descendants followed suit while they honed the defense of slavery: see Richard Beale Davis, *A Colonial Southern Bookshelf Reading in the Eighteenth Century* (Athens, GA, 1979), 125–6, and R. B. Davis, *Intellectual Life in the Colonial South, 1515–1763*, 3 vols. (Knoxville, TN, 1978), 1:67–8, 378. For a late version of history as progress toward freedom see [A. M. Venable], "Principles – Their Growth," *VUM*, 4 (1860), 213–19.

to censor the press and to refuse to discuss slavery. Almost all prominent Southerners denounced the reception of abolitionist petitions as a threat to the social and political order. They stood solidly behind the Gag Rule – "the Pearl Harbor of the slavery controversy," as William Freehling aptly calls it – which by seeming to suppress basic political freedoms split southern slaveholders from their conservative northern allies.[3]

Yet the South had long seen freedom as necessary for civilization. Thomas Cooper of South Carolina College, the old English radical and friend of Thomas Jefferson, considered himself the staunchest of champions of constitutional liberties, freedom of speech and the press in particular – a claim he emphatically reiterated during the nullification controversy of 1832. There could be no such thing as truth without it. Repressive governments acted on behalf of exploitative elites. Cooper deplored the "sedulously inculcated and perseveringly enforced" doctrine that some subjects were too dangerous to be debated publicly. He himself stood for "the RIGHT OF FREE DISCUSSION, in its fullest extent." Cooper, a nullifier and an ardent foe of the clergy, if not of Christianity itself, nevertheless said not a word against those who suppressed open discussion of slavery.[4]

So too, A. B. Meek of Alabama, a prominent historian and belles lettrist, wrote a widely cited pamphlet endorsed by William Gilmore Simms that followed John Locke and Alexis de Tocqueville in extolling free speech as indispensable to free government and in declaring democracy the parent of literature. The South's most prominent men – John C. Calhoun and Benjamin Perry of South Carolina, George Frederick Holmes of Virginia, William Stiles of Georgia – committed themselves to the defense of intellectual freedom.[5]

---

[3] William M. Wiecek, *The Sources of Antislavery Constitutionalism in America, 1760–1848* (Ithaca, NY, 1977), 131, 147 (Seabrook); William W. Freehling, *The Road to Disunion* (New York, 1990), 308. A student at the University of Virginia asserted what lurked beneath the surface of southern discussions – that until a few centuries ago, the preservation of social order required despotic governments: Gray Carroll, "Essay on the Utilitarian Spirit of the Present Day as Affecting Our Literature" (M.A. thesis, 1855, typescript at UVA).

[4] "The Right of Free Discussion," Appendix to Thomas Cooper, *Lectures on the Elements of Political Economy*, reproduction of 2nd ed. (New York, 1971 [1830]), 3–4, quote at 3. Cooper's *Lectures on the Elements of Political Science* (1829) – the second edition of *The Right of Free Discussion* – became a textbook in southern colleges: see Robert McColley, *Slavery and Jeffersonian Virginia* (Urbana, IL, 1964), 26.

[5] A. B. Meek, *Americanism in Literature: An Oration before the Phi Kappa and Demosthenian Societies of the University of Georgia at Athens, August 8, 1844* (Tuscaloosa, AL, 1844), esp. 10–11; William Gilmore Simms, *Views and Reviews in American Literature, History, and Fiction* (Cambridge, MA, 1962 [1846]), 23–4; "Onslow" [Calhoun], June 27, 1826, in *JCCP*, 10:144–5, 13:24, and see Clyde Wilson's cogent account of Calhoun's position in 13:xvii–xviii. Stephen Meats and Edwin T. Arnold, eds., *The Writings of Benjamin F. Perry*, 3 vols. (Spartanburg, SC, 1980), 1:335; William H. Stiles, *Connection between Liberty and Eloquence: An Address Delivered before the Phi Kappa and Demosthenean Societies of Franklin College* (Augusta, GA, 1852), 4, 20, 26; also, Thomas L. Pangle, *The Spirit of Modern Republicanism: The Moral Vision of the American Founders and the Philosophy of Locke* (Chicago, 1988), 142.

With the new German scholarship on Greece came an emphasis on aesthetics that took the superiority of Athenian art as evidence for the superiority of a degree of political freedom absent from Sparta.

Thomas Roderick Dew placed the struggle for freedom of thought at the center of Western Civilization, contrasting the long struggle for liberty in Europe with "grinding despotisms" of Asia and Africa, and stressing the racial characteristics of progressive peoples. He noted that nomadic conquerors tended to concentrate power at a single spot and reduce peoples of the hinterland to slavery: "All the artists, mechanics, carpenters, and workmen of skill were engaged at Babylon from the four quarters of the world. All the world was robbed by Nebuchadnezzar, to beautify and enrich Babylon. Hence results here which could not have taken place under other circumstances." He declared Greece an exception to the assertion that democratic governments starve the arts. Alexander Stephens echoed Dew in praising "the cause of the Grecian type of Civilization against the Asiatic!"[6]

Most Southerners seem to have thought that republics and limited monarchies – Frederick Porcher of Charleston added democracies – promoted art and science more readily than did monarchies and despotisms, but this presumption ran into stiff challenge. Writing from Europe in 1829, a Southerner found that even the more despotic German regimes promoted education and literature. William Hutson of South Carolina referred to "the want of that encouragement by free governments to literature, which despotisms have generally granted": History refuted Meek "at every step." Literature has never "flowered under free governments," which "take their tone from the uneducated and unrefined masses, who confine their attention to the useful and immediately practical." Despotisms, in contrast, have supported artistic freedom so long as that freedom does not subvert society's basic institutions and values. The Methodist Protestant Reverend A. A. Lipscomb seems to have spoken for many when he impatiently dismissed a false dichotomy: "Literature has flourished under monarchies and republics."[7]

Despite dissent, the centrality of intellectual freedom to well-ordered progress became something of a southern obsession. The Reverend William Scott of New Orleans wanted history written as a record of the long struggle for freedom and

---

See Jennifer Tolbert Roberts, *Athens on Trial: The Antidemocratic Tradition in Western Thought* (Princeton, NJ, 1994), 224. That the absence of political freedom leads to a decline in eloquence and great oratory as well as great historical writing has been a persistent theme from ancient times, when the spread of Asian despotism was held responsible for vulgar and demagogic rhetoric. A graduate student at the University of Virginia took for granted that free institutions made possible the flowering of Greek poetry, a treasure of world culture: Edwin Taliaferro, "The Poetry of Greece" (M.A. thesis, 1855, typescript at UVA). Dionysius among the Greeks and Tacitus among the Romans kept the theme alive: see Emilio Gabba, *Dionysius and the History of Archaic Rome* (Berkeley, CA, 1991), 8, 35–8, 42–5.

[6] Thomas Roderick Dew, *Digest of the Laws, Customs, Manners, and Institutions of the Ancient and Modern Nations* (New York, 1884 [1852]), 28, 36–7, 105, 456–8; Alexander H. Stephens, *A Constitutional View of the Late War between the States*, 2 vols. (New York, 1970 [1868, 1870]), 1:539. For the debates over the relation of freedom and despotism to the arts, see also Supplementary References: "Art and Freedom."

[7] Frederick A. Porcher, "Address Pronounced at the Inauguration of the South-Carolina Historical Society" (June 28, 1857), in *Collections of the South-Carolina Historical Society*, 2 vols. (Charleston, SC, 1857–58), 1:2; "Education in Germany," *SR*, 4 (1829), 88; [W. Hutson], "Fictitious Literature," *SPR*, 1 (1847), 57–78; A. A. Lipscomb, *The Social Spirit of Christianity, Presented in the Form of Essays* (Philadelphia, 1846), 41.

of those who fought and suffered for it. The Unitarian Reverend Theodore Clapp of New Orleans declared the nineteenth century an era of great progress and a replication of the Athens that gave birth to political freedom in the age of Pericles, only to decay in the end in a morass of corruption. J. H. Groesbeck of Cincinnati, writing in *Southern Literary Messenger,* announced that activities of the mind, not force, determine the course of history. Intellectual freedom, he wrote, sustains republics, and the legions of Caesar and Napoleon would have counted for little without a powerful idea. John McCrady, of Charleston's Museum of Natural History and with a scientist's perspective, agreed with François Guizot that the gradual establishment of social order measured the progress of civilization and that history moved forward through the intellectual development of the masses as well as of individuals: "Mind" constitutes the driving force of historical progress. McCrady feared, however, that passions threatened to distort intellectual refinement and moral judgment: "The worst vices, the most abandoned populations as well as the highest virtues, the purest society are to be found in civilized communities."[8]

In the South, concern for social order advanced in tension with enthusiasm for freedom. Episcopalian Reverend Jasper Adams, president of the College of Charleston and a respected moral philosopher, acknowledged that religion sought to control thoughts, not merely actions, and argued that Christianity – alone among the great religions – understood that control of human actions required moral restraints on thoughts. Not necessarily in disagreement, the Presbyterian Reverend James Henley Thornwell preferred an open contest between scriptural truth and heresies and errors, maintaining, "Within the limits of legitimate inquiry, we would lay no restriction upon freedom of thought." His protégé, the Reverend John Adger, nonetheless cautioned that the latitudinarian spirit was "treachery to all truth" and that – although political and religious opinion ought to suffer as little regulation and restraint as possible – during crises that threatened the vital interests of the country, those with subversive opinions must be held accountable. Thus, paeans to freedom passed into rumblings against an excess of tolerance.[9]

---

[8] W. A. Scott, "The Progress of Civil Liberty," in Robert Gibbes Barnwell, ed., *The New-Orleans Book* (New Orleans, 1851), 48; Theodore Clapp, "Discourse," New Orleans *Daily Picayune,* Sept. 30, 1849; H. J. Groesbeck, "Influence of Free Governments on the Mind," *SLM,* 1 (1835), 389–93; [John McCrady], "A Few Thoughts on Southern Civilization," *RM,* 1 (1857), 224–8, 338–49 (on Guizot), 546–56, and 2 (1857), 212–26. For George Tucker, all great revolutions sprung from and contributed to the development of thought: "A Discourse on the Progress and Influence of Philosophy," *SLM,* 1 (1835), 405–21. Catherine Macaulay, in her eight-volume *The History of England from the Accession of James I to that of the Brunswick Line,* stressed England's progression to liberty; her books were available in Charleston bookstores in the late eighteenth century: Hennig Cohen, *The South Carolina Gazette, 1732–1775* (Columbia, SC, 1953), 153.

[9] Jasper Adams, *Elements of Moral Philosophy* (Philadelphia, 1837), 50; *JHTW,* 1:483, quote at 3:11; J. B. Adger, "Responsibility for Opinions," *SPR,* 7 (1856); see also "The Phases of Society," *SPR,* 8 (1855), 201–2. Brantz Mayer saw the struggle for religious liberty as the driving force in the civilization of mass migrations promoted largely by love of wealth, lust for power, and a spirit of robbery: Mayer, *Calvert and Penn; Or the Growth of Civil and Religious Liberty in America* (Baltimore, 1852), 18–21.

On the "Impropriety" of Virginia's debate on emancipation see "Professor Dew on Slavery," in *The Pro-Slavery Argument, as Maintained by the Most Distinguished Writers of the Southern States*

The Reverend S. J. Cassells pulled no punches: "*The influence, too, of our free institutions upon the public mind* is another source of the evil we are here considering." The carelessness of these institutions imparts "false notions as to the nature and value of civil liberty" and furnishes the people "with every sort of privilege and opportunity for expressing and propagating their opinions." The exercise of maximum liberty requires a long and tedious preparation. George Frederick Holmes and George Fitzhugh, who hated the free market in commodities, also saw the need for restrictions in the marketplace of ideas. A contributor to *Southern Quarterly Review* protested in 1863, "the unbounded freedom which thought now enjoys, has opened the door for the introduction of much that is evil." The Presbyterian Reverend W. A. Hall of New Orleans told Confederate troops in 1864 that, while freedom of thought was a great step toward civilization, it was now running wild in the North. Society must establish equilibrium between the individual and the power of the masses.[10]

In the mid-1840s President Francis Wayland of Brown University, in a celebrated epistolary debate over "domestic slavery" with his proslavery fellow Baptist, William Fuller of Charleston, vigorously protested the suppression of antislavery opinion and activity in the South, as did northern antislavery moderates who professed sympathy for the South and opposition to the abolitionists. Fuller himself soon fell into bad odor in the South when he made clear that, while he did not consider slavery a sin, he did consider it an evil and supported gradual emancipation and colonization. More significant was the rising southern demand for the suppression of antislavery agitation in the North. In the aftermath of the Nat Turner revolt, Governor Floyd of Virginia demanded that Massachusetts prosecute Garrison and other abolitionists for incitement to insurrection, much as the mayor of Savannah urged Governor Otis of Massachusetts to prosecute David Walker for his call for slave insurrection. Southern state legislatures asked northern states to prohibit the printing of abolitionist literature and suppress abolitionist societies.[11]

(Philadelphia, 1853), 290. For church reactions to the Gag Rule see Mitchell Snay, *Gospel of Disunion: Religion and Separatism in the Antebellum South* (New York, 1993), ch. 1; Victor B. Howard, *Conscience and Slavery: The Evangelical Calvinist Domestic Missions, 1837–1861* (Kent, OH, 1990), 26; Robert L. Dabney, *Defence of Virginia (and through Her of the South) in Recent and Pending Contests against the Sectional Party* (New York, 1969 [1867]), 16. Dabney vigorously reasserted his commitment to freedom of thought shortly before his death: see his *The Practical Philosophy, Being the Philosophy of the Feelings, of the Will, and of the Conscience, with the Ascertainment of Particular Rights and Duties* (Harrisonburg, VA, 1984 [1897]), 394–7.

[10] [S. J. Cassells], "Relation of Justice to Benevolence in the Conduct of Society," *SPR*, 7 (1853), 97; George Frederick Holmes, "Fitzhugh's Sociology for the South," *QRMECS*, 9 (1855), 180–201; "Rationalism False and Unreasonable," *SPR*, 16 (1863), 163; William A. Hall, *Historic Significance of the Southern Revolution* (Petersburg, VA, 1864). Bishop Stephen Elliott, too, applauded the constitutional right to freedom of thought and speech but warned against excesses in class-divided society: see Virgil Sims Davis, "Stephen Elliott: A Southern Bishop in Peace and War" (Ph.D. diss., University of Georgia, 1964), 164.

[11] Wayland, in Richard Fuller and Francis Wayland, *Domestic Slavery, Considered as a Scriptural Institution in Correspondence*, 5th ed. (New York, 1847), 14–21; for the northern moderates see e.g.

Northern condemnations of abolitionist threats to dissolve the Union did not satisfy the South. In 1835 John Tyler accused abolitionists and northern clergymen of threatening southern institutions, duly noting that women were emerging in the vanguard of the antisouthern onslaught. He chose his words carefully, although it was apparent that he wanted an end to northern toleration of all such troublemakers. Nat Turner had convinced Virginians that mere discussion of slavery and emancipation could encourage slave insurrection and invite social catastrophe. John Randolph, at the end of his life, predicted that slave insurrection would follow open debate on slavery; when open debate came, he called for the arrest and prosecution of those who made incendiary pro-emancipation speeches.[12]

In the mid-1830s Calhoun told the Senate that the South had pleaded in vain with the North to suppress abolitionism before it wrecked the Union. Calhoun wrote Samuel Ingram of New Hope, Pennsylvania: "I have long made up my mind that the evil will progress till arrested by the South, which it can easily do if united, but which if not done speedily can only be done at the expense of the Union." By the late 1830s a significant portion of the southern press, backed by mass meetings, was demanding that the North suppress abolitionist newspapers as its price for southern allegiance to the Union. Condemning abolitionists for waging war on a constitutionally protected slavery, Jasper Adams, a northern-born unionist, called for suppression of abusive northern newspapers. Richard Yeadon of Charleston, a unionist who had passionately opposed nullification, wanted the North to imprison abolitionist agitators. James H. Hammond went whole hog: He wanted them hanged.[13]

Many abolitionists – and no few historians ever since – accused the southern churches of prostituting themselves to slavery in fear of hostile public opinion and of both legal and extralegal repression. The charge of cowardice did not sit well among southern Christians, who challenged their adversaries to prove the proslavery

"Who Is Responsible for the Current Slavery Agitation," *Presbyterian Quarterly Review*, 31 (1860), 536; also, David B. Chesebrough, *Clergy Dissent in the Old South, 1830–1865* (Carbondale, IL, 1996), 31. Theodore M. Whitefield, *Slavery Agitation in Virginia, 1829–1832* (New York, 1969 [1930]), 63; Alice Dana Adams, *The Neglected Period of Anti-Slavery (1808–1831)* (Gloucester, MA, 1964 [1908]), 94 (Walker); William Warren Sweet, *Virginia Methodism: A History* (Richmond, VA, 1955), 209; Lorman Ratner, *Powder Keg: Northern Opposition to the Antislavery Movement, 1831–1840* (New York, 1968), ch. 3. William J. Grayson praised Fuller's reply to Wayland but found "incautious" his suggestion that slavery might not continue: [Grayson], "Slavery in the Southern States," *SQR*, 8 (1845), 342–3.

[12] Whitefield, *Slavery Agitation in Virginia*, 73; Lyon Gardiner Tyler, *The Letters and Times of the Tylers*, 3 vols. (Williamsburg, VA, 1884–96), 1:577–8; Russell Kirk, *John Randolph of Roanoke: A Study in American Politics, with Selected Speeches and Letters* (Chicago, 1964), 149.

[13] "Remarks on the Maine Resolutions," in *JCCP*, 13:163–4, and Calhoun to Samuel Ingham, Feb. 5, 1837 (13:384); Frank Luther Mott, *A History of American Magazines, 1741–1850* (Cambridge, MA, 1938), 460–1; Adams, *Moral Philosophy*, 135–7; John C. Ellen, Jr., "Richard Yeadon," in Joseph F. Steelman et al., eds., *Essays in Southern Biography* (Greenville, NC, 1965), 17; Drew Gilpin Faust, *James Henry Hammond and the Old South* (Baton Rouge, LA, 1982), 161. Nat Turner caused such alarm among South Carolinians that men went to church and camp meetings armed: Thomas O. Summers, ed., *Autobiography of the Rev. Joseph Travis* (Nashville, TN, 1854), 149–51.

interpretation of Scripture wrong. Southerners responded indignantly to the assault on their honor and the sincerity of their religious beliefs, but indignation produced a defensiveness that obscured the measure of truth in the abolitionist charge of repression. Repression there was, and it unquestionably contributed to a growing proslavery consensus as the South reeled under the impact of slave conspiracies and abolitionist agitation. The Baptist Reverend John Caldwell of Georgia exaggerated only a little when, shortly after the War, he charged that it would have been safer to denigrate Catholicism in Rome or Islam in Constantinople than to denounce slavery in the South.[14]

Antislavery sentiment and organization in the early decades of the nineteenth century had flourished more in the South than in the largely apathetic North. Before 1830 the South had hundreds of antislavery organizations with thousands of members, although only in the Upper South and primarily in North Carolina and Tennessee. In 1827, according to the abolitionist Benjamin Lundy, there were about 106 antislavery societies in the South with 5,150 members, versus only 24 societies with 1,475 members in the North. North Carolina's fifty societies were concentrated in four Piedmont counties, most of Tennessee's in the yeoman counties of east Tennessee. Still, as early as 1803, southern antislavery societies found themselves on the defensive – in part as a consequence of the public reaction to the conspiracy in Virginia in 1800, when Gabriel Prosser unsuccessfully tried to raise a slave rebellion.[15]

Intransigent defense of slavery emerged in the South slowly out of a long history of internal struggles, beginning with fierce resistance to the earliest pressures for emancipation. As repression mounted, congregations dismissed antislavery ministers, communities expelled dissidents, and occasional murders accompanied frequent threats of violence. The Quakers emerged early as antislavery stalwarts. Stimulated by George Fox's tour of the South in the 1670s, they had established firm beachheads in Maryland, Virginia, and North Carolina and stepped up their attacks on slavery throughout the eighteenth century, purging their own meetings of slaveholders and promoting voluntary manumission of slaves. With good reason, the New School Presbyterian Reverend Albert Barnes held the Quakers up as the great antislavery model for the churches. Although many Quakers departed the South to cleanse themselves of the sin of slavery, sufficient numbers remained to torment slaveholders in North Carolina, especially after they were reinforced by the militantly antislavery Wesleyan Methodists, who had broken from the Methodist Episcopal Church and scored surprising local successes in the late 1840s. Southern Methodist preachers overwhelmingly followed the lead of John Wesley in execrating slavery, petitioning state legislatures in 1785 for emancipation. The Methodists and also the Baptists condemned slavery and urged communicants to free their slaves.

---

[14] Daniel W. Stowell, " 'We Have Sinned, and God Has Smitten Us': John H. Caldwell and the Religious Meaning of Confederate Defeat," *Georgia Historical Quarterly*, 77 (1994), 15.

[15] H. Shelton Smith, *In His Image ... But: Racism in Southern Religion* (Durham, NC, 1972), 67–70. By the end of 1831, Tennessee's 25 antislavery societies had collapsed. The cause waned even in east Tennessee, a stronghold, although emancipationist efforts continued in the mountains: Chase C. Mooney, *Slavery in Tennessee* (Bloomington, IN, 1957), 64, 69–77.

In Virginia and Maryland there was a mixed response, but further south congregations breathed defiance.[16]

When, in response to antislavery petitions, the Virginia Assembly debated emancipation in 1784, thousands countered by signing proslavery petitions with a message never before heard on a mass scale: Slavery was ordained of God. The numerous dissenting backcountry preachers who opposed slavery received little support from the laity and departed or fell silent. In colonial Georgia, a broad popular movement had successfully challenged the antislavery policy of the Establishment and secured the right to hold slaves. George Whitefield, the great evangelist, won the hearts of planters by denying the sinfulness of slavery and supporting the demand to introduce slaves into the colony. No serious challenge to slavery thereafter developed anywhere in the Lower South.[17]

"I am brought to conclude," a mournful Bishop Asbury wrote in his diary on January 9, 1798, "that slavery will exist in Virginia perhaps for ages; there is not a sufficient sense of religion nor of liberty to destroy it; Methodists, Baptists, Presbyterians, in the highest flights of rapturous piety, still maintain and defend it." Asbury reluctantly declared slavery a civil institution with which the church ought not to meddle. Virtually alone in the Carolina–Georgia lowcountry, Methodists pressed for emancipation; but, by the early 1800s, communicants were demanding

---

[16] William Warren Sweet, *Religion in Colonial America* (New York, 1865), 156; P. J. Schwarz, "Clark T. Moorman, Quaker Emancipator," *Quaker History,* 49 (1980), 28; Charles Henry Ambler, *Sectionalism in Virginia from 1776 to 1861* (Chicago, 1910), 25; McColley, *Slavery and Jeffersonian Virginia,* 154–62; D. W. Crofts, "Secession Crisis Voting Behavior in Southampton County, Virginia," in W. B. Moore, Jr., and J. F. Tripp, eds., *Looking South: Chapters in the Story of an American Region* (Westport, CT, 1989), 108–9; Albert Barnes, *The Church and Slavery* (New York, 1969 [1857]), 145–6, and Barnes, *An Inquiry into the Scriptural Views of Slavery* (Philadelphia, 1857); *Journal of that Faithful Servant of Christ, Charles Osborn* (Cincinnati, 1854), 193 (Tennessee); Francis M. Manning and W. H. Booker, *Religion and Education in Martin County, 1774–1974* (Wilmington, NC, 1974), 1; Daniel W. Crofts, *Old Southampton: Politics and Society in a Virginia County, 1834–1869* (Charlottesville, VA, 1992), 5, 90–2. For Wesley and the Methodists, see: John Nelson Norwood, *The Schism in the Methodist Episcopal Church, 1844: A Study of Slavery and Ecclesiastical Politics* (Alfred, NY, 1923), 10, 14–15, 21–2; Wade Crawford Barclay, *History of Methodist Missions: Early American Methodism, 1769–1844,* 2 vols. (New York, 1949), pt. 1; Donald G. Mathews, *Slavery and Methodism: A Chapter in American Morality, 1780–1845* (Princeton, NJ, 1965), 37–40; Cullen T. Carter, *History of the Tennessee Conference and a Brief Summary of the General Conferences of the Methodist Church from the Frontier in Middle Tennessee to the Present Time* (Nashville, TN, 1948), 94–7, 104–5; Robert M. Calhoon, *Evangelicals and Conservatives in the Early South, 1740–1861* (Columbia, SC, 1988), 125–7.

[17] In general see the pioneering work of Mary Stoughton Locke, *Anti-Slavery in America: From the Introduction of African Slaves to the Prohibition of the Slave Trade (1619–1808)* (Gloucester, MA, 1965 [1901]), and Adams, *Neglected Period of Anti-Slavery.* See also William Warren Sweet, *Religion on the Frontier, 1783–1840: The Methodists* (Chicago, 1946), 22–3; Sweet, *Virginia Methodism,* 110–11; Jon Butler, *Awash in a Sea of Faith: Christianizing the American People* (Cambridge, MA, 1990), 150–1; on Whitefield see Harry S. Stout, *The Divine Dramatist: George Whitefield and the Rise of Modern Evangelism* (Grand Rapids, MI, 1991), esp. ch. 4; Mathews, *Slavery and Methodism,* esp. 46, 53–4. The early proslavery petitions in Virginia contained at least as much scriptural argumentation as social and economic. Curiously, Cynthia Lynn Lyerly considers this "curious": *Methodism and the Southern Mind, 1770–1810* (New York, 1998), 126.

revision of the church discipline to accommodate slaveholding. As early as 1804 the Methodist Church was publishing two disciplines, one for Virginia and the northern states and another for states to the south. By 1808 proslavery forces prevailed, although they had to engage in some mopping up until 1820.[18]

The Presbyterian Church had opposed slavery but soon retreated, although as late as 1818 its General Assembly berated slavery as "utterly inconsistent" with the laws of God and the Gospel of Christ. It simultaneously characterized slaveholders as victims of circumstance, condemned "hasty emancipation," and declined to discipline dissidents. Theologically conservative ministers denied that slavery was sinful, and at least as early as the 1790s congregations, fearing slave rebellion, silenced or drove out antislavery ministers. By 1830 or so southern Presbyterians commonly referred to "our Southern Church" and "our Southern Zion."[19]

---

[18] Bishop Asbury, quoted in William Sumner Jenkins, *Pro-Slavery Thought in the Old South* (Gloucester, MA, 1960), 54; Herbert Asbury, *A Methodist Saint: The Life of Bishop Asbury* (New York, 1927), 148–52. Asbury, Coke, and James O'Kelley ran afoul of mobs that threatened to flog them.

Also, see Mathews, *Slavery and Methodism,* ch. 1, and the astute remarks in Donald G. Mathews, *Religion in the Old South* (Chicago, 1977), 72–4; Dunbar Rowland, ed., *Mississippi: Comprising Sketches of Counties, Towns, Events, Institutions, and Persons, Arranged in Cyclopedic Form,* 4 vols. (Spartanburg, SC, 1976 [1907]), 2:225 (on Griffin); Robert Nuckols Watkins, Jr., "The Forming of the Southern Presbyterian Minister: From Calvin to the Civil War" (Ph.D. diss., Vanderbilt University, 1969), 185; Butler, *Awash in a Sea of Faith,* 132–3; W. T. Smith, "Thomas Coke's Contribution to the Christmas Conference," in Russell E. Richey and Kenneth E. Rowe, eds., *Rethinking Methodist History: A Bicentennial Historical Consultation* (Nashville, TN, 1985), 44–5. David T. Bailey concludes that the antislavery church forces of the Southwest made their last stand at the Tennessee Methodist Conference in 1819: *Shadow on the Church: Southwestern Evangelical Religion and the Issue of Slavery, 1783–1860* (Ithaca, NY, 1985), 137.

In 1789 the General Committee of Virginia Baptists denounced slavery as a "violent deprivation of the rights of nature and inconsistent with a republican government"; in the 1790s, after much wavering, the Church declared slavery a civil problem. See Robert B. Semple, *A History of the Rise and Progress of the Baptists in Virginia* (Richmond, VA, 1894 [1810]), 105, 392; Mary Burnham Putnam, *The Baptists and Slavery, 1840–1845* (Ann Arbor, MI, 1913), 12–15; *ESB,* 2:811–12; Robert A. Baker, *The Southern Baptist Convention and Its People, 1607–1972* (Nashville, TN, 1974), 30; Walter Brownlow Posey, *The Baptist Church in the Lower Mississippi Valley, 1776–1845* (Lexington, KY, 1957), 94–5.

[19] Irving Stoddard Kull, "Presbyterian Attitudes toward Slavery," *Church History,* 7 (1938), 103; Calhoon, *Evangelicals and Conservatives,* 161; Andrew E. Murray, *Presbyterians and the Negro – A History* (Philadelphia, 1966), chs. 1 and 3; William Childs Robinson, *Columbia Theological Seminary and the Southern Presbyterian Church: A Study in Church History, Presbyterian Polity, Missionary Enterprise, and Religious Thought* (Decatur, GA, 1931), 27–8; Margaret Burr DesChamps, "The Presbyterian Church in the South Atlantic States, 1801–1861" (Ph.D. diss., Emory University, 1952), 135, 141–3; Sydney E. Ahlstrom, *A Religious History of the American People* (New Haven, CT, 1972), 648; George M. Marsden, *The Evangelical Mind and the New School Experience: A Case Study of Thought and Theology in Nineteenth-Century America* (New Haven, CT, 1970), 90–1. For the strength of antislavery among the southern Methodist clergy before 1810 or so see Lyerly, *Methodism and the Southern Mind,* 6, 62. In 1852 the Congregationalists, in a general convention in Albany, New York, condemned slavery: Howard, *Conscience and Slavery,* 111–12. Few ministers on the Southwestern frontier defended or attacked slavery. According to Anson West, the pioneer historian of Alabama Methodism, Mathew Parham Sturdivant and Michael Burdzem – the first ministers appointed to Alabama by the Methodist church, about 1810 – did not spend "their strength in a fruitless rage for emancipation" but instead brought the gospel to the slaves: West, *A History of*

A few illustrations of what antislavery preachers faced: James Blythe, a future Presbyterian minister, ran into a hornets' nest at Hampden-Sydney College in 1789 when he urged manumission. Three Presbyterian ministers – James Gilliland, Robert Wilson, and William Williamson – left South Carolina in 1804 because congregants took umbrage at their antislavery views. Lewis Dupré of Charleston emerged unscathed after publishing an emancipationist pamphlet in 1810, but his appeal to Scripture met stern resistance from proslavery divines. William Maxwell, a prominent lawyer in Norfolk, had to stare down threats to his life after publishing an antislavery tract in 1826. Matters got steadily worse, even in the Border States. Occasional letters in the correspondence of James Gillespie Birney indicate that he had support from several Disciples of Christ preachers in Kentucky, but in 1833 he saw little hope of rallying slaveholders south of Tennessee to emancipation even if the freedmen were sent to Africa. The antislavery Daniel R. Goodloe of North Carolina and Henry Ruffner of Virginia had to proceed with extreme caution, soft-pedaling the moral issue and concentrating on slavery's debilitating economic effects. The Reverend Dr. Eli Carruthers, for forty years a pastor of Presbyterian churches near Greensboro, North Carolina, kept his antislavery views to himself until 1861, when his announcement provoked his immediate dismissal. Only after he went north did he emerge as an antislavery spokesman.[20]

Brave antislavery ministers in the Southwest met fates that differed according to local attitudes and circumstances and their personal deportment. The Reverend Daniel DeVinne, born in Ireland about 1819 and raised in New York, helped build the Methodist Church in the Southwest, although he was uncompromisingly antislavery and taught blacks in Sabbath schools. In contrast, the Methodist Reverend Anthony Bewley, who preached against slavery in Missouri and then for ten difficult years in Arkansas as well, moved to Texas – where he survived (if barely) until the hysteria of 1860, when he was lynched. Even the most popular and powerful of preachers walked a fine line. The Reverend John Taylor described the emancipationist Baptist Reverend John Sutton as a man with great preaching talent but "a mighty scolder" who "scolded himself out of credit in the church."[21]

Methodism in Alabama (Spartanburg, SC, 1983 [1893]), 43–4, quote at 43, and 157–8; see also Bailey, *Shadow on the Church*, 31–3, 49–64, 94–6, 114–16, 140.

[20] James Gillespie Birney to Ralph R. Gurley, Dec. 3, 1833, in Dwight Lowell Dumond, ed., *Letters of James Gillespie Birney, 1831–1857*, 2 vols. (Washington, DC, 1938), 1:97; also, M. D. Moore, "Antislavery Presbyterians in the Carolina Piedmont," *Proceedings of the South Carolina Historical Association* (1954); John Spencer Bassett, *Anti-Slavery Leaders of North Carolina* (Baltimore, 1898), 56. Birney maintained wide contacts in the South with opponents as well as supporters. He and Bishop Otey of Tennessee were old friends who argued with each other respectfully: Birney to Lewis Tappan, Oct. 4, 1841, in Dumond, ed., *Birney Letters*, 2:637. When the churches rallied to the Confederacy they encountered stiff, if isolated, resistance even in the Lower South, but unconditional unionists were dismissed and went north. Resistance in the Upper South proved dangerous to the Confederate government: Daniel W. Harrison, "Protestant Clergy and Union Sentiment in the Confederacy," *Tennessee Historical Quarterly*, 23 (1965), 284–90; Haskell Monroe, "Southern Presbyterians and the Secession Crisis," *Civil War History*, 6 (1960), 351–60.

[21] West, *Methodism in Alabama*, 298–300 (DeVinne); *HT*, 1:153 (Bewley); [Rev.] John Taylor, *Baptists on the American Frontier: A History of Ten Baptist Churches of Which the Author Has Been Alternately a Member*, ed. Chester Raymond Young, 3rd ed. (Macon, GA, 1995), 210.

Migration from the South may have saved the migrants' souls and eased their consciences, but it removed potentially dangerous enemies of slavery from the region in which slavery was firmly embedded. The big losses included James Birney, who became an abolitionist leader in the Midwest. We can only wonder about the consequences of the emigration of James Hoge and his followers, for he was the son of Moses Hoge, one of Virginia's most prestigious Presbyterian ministers. Not all antislavery preachers left the South under threat. Many – like Peter Cartwright, a renowned Methodist preacher, and Barton Warren Stone, a founder of the Disciples of Christ – chose to separate themselves from a sinful community. No few migrants became abolitionist leaders in the Midwest, including James Lemen of Virginia, who campaigned to make Illinois a free state. Indignant congregations in Virginia drove the Baptist David Barrow and the Presbyterian John D. Paxton from their pulpits. Barrow and Elder George Smith of Virginia moved to Kentucky, only to find themselves embattled there, too.[22]

Repressions followed the revolution in Saint Domingue, the insurrectionary plots of Gabriel Prosser (1800) and Denmark Vesey (1822), and the Nat Turner rebellion (1831). The churches proceeded under circumstances that rendered criticism of slavery dangerous, and they promoted efforts to soften or eliminate support for emancipation. Moderates shook when the much beloved Presbyterian Reverend David Rice of Kentucky hailed the revolution in Saint Domingue as a just cause, although in time he moved from firm antislavery to support for amelioration. Methodists who faced accusations of sympathy for rebellious slaves in Virginia, South Carolina, and Mississippi assured neighbors of their support for slavery.[23]

Antislavery hopes and proslavery fears both centered on the nonslaveholders, small slaveholders, and businessmen of the Upper South. Kentucky, which only accepted slavery in the 1790s after a hard struggle, retained a large antislavery minority down to the War. Antislavery societies remained small but held the allegiance of an influential minority in the Kentucky legislature. The Presbyterian Reverend John Rankin's antislavery *Letters on Slavery* sold well in Kentucky in the mid-1820s, and an antislavery convention there in 1828 aroused little public hostility. Emancipation and colonization remained respectable throughout the 1830s, but thereafter

---

[22] Albert M. Shipp, *The History of Methodism in South Carolina* (Nashville, TN, 1983), 243–4, 302, 414–15; Ernest Trice Thompson, *Presbyterians in the South*, 3 vols. (Richmond, VA, 1963), 1:336–9, 347–8; *The Backwoods Preacher: Being the Autobiography of Peter Cartwright* (London, 1870), 244–5; Charles C. Ware, *Barton Warren Stone, Pathfinder of Christian Union: A Story of His Life and Times* (St. Louis, MO, 1932), 296–7, 304; Josiah Morrow, ed., "Tours into Kentucky and the Northwest Territory: Three Journals by the Rev. James Smith of Powhattan County, Va., 1783–1795–1797," *Ohio Archeological and Historical Quarterly*, 16 (1906), 348–401; *ESB*, 2:783–4 (Lemen); William E. Hatcher, *Life of J. B. Jeter, D.D.* (Baltimore, 1887), 204–9; Semple, *Baptists in Virginia*, 466 (Barrow) and 474 (Smith). See also Supplementary References: "Antislavery Southern Ministers."

[23] Adams, *Neglected Period of Anti-Slavery*, 110; Asa Earl Martin, *The Anti-Slavery Movement in Kentucky Prior to 1850* (New York, 1970 [1918]), 14–15, 23–4; James D. Essig, *The Bonds of Wickedness: American Evangelicals against Slavery, 1770–1808* (Philadelphia, 1982), ch. 6, esp. 120–3; William S. McFeely, *Frederick Douglass* (New York, 1991), 43. In yeomen-dominated Dickson County in middle Tennessee, emancipationist sentiment ran high until the Nat Turner insurrection: Robert E. Corlew, "Some Aspects of Slavery in Dickson County," *Tennessee Historical Quarterly*, 10 (1951), 224–48, 344–65.

repression of antislavery activities increased – especially after Amos Kendall, Jackson's postmaster general, encouraged interdiction of abolitionist literature.[24]

The abolitionists had taken the South by surprise when they introduced something new into American politics that transcended state borders: mass propaganda mailings. Even the antislavery John Quincy Adams considered the abolitionist mailings inflammatory and a potential spur to slave revolt. Abolitionist irresponsibility disgusted Adams almost as much as Postmaster General Kendall's encouragement of illegal seizures. Alfred Huger, Charleston's postmaster and a staunch unionist, told Kendall that those who seized the mail undoubtedly came not from the dregs of society but from the most respectable of families. Former Governor John Lyde Wilson may well have been among them. Southerners learned from their enemies' tactic of mass mailings. Thus, J. D. B. De Bow boasted that congressmen used their franking privilege to circulate "many thousands" of copies of the pamphlet version of Ellwood Fisher's *The North and the South,* originally published in *De Bow's Review.* J. H. Hammond warmly endorsed it; Calhoun sent copies to his friends in the North and South; prosouthern Northerners distributed it; and the southern press poured accolades over it throughout the 1850s.[25]

The emancipationists did score modest successes in the South, relying principally on economic and political arguments, but the cogency of these waned as the sectional struggle waxed. Most Southerners remained confident in the scriptural sanction of slavery. Even Robert Breckenridge, an orthodox Old School Presbyterian, W. C. Buck, editor of a Baptist journal, and Alexander Campbell, leader of the Disciples of Christ, denied the inherent sinfulness of slavery, although they questioned whether southern slavery met biblical standards. By the 1840s other influential smaller churches – Christian, Cumberland Presbyterian, and Moravian – joined the larger churches in condemning abolitionism and asserting a biblical sanction of slavery. The antislavery evangelicals had, in fact, encountered stiff resistance throughout the South from the very beginning, and the revivals seem to confirm that slaveholders could be pious Christians.[26]

[24] Adams, *Neglected Period of Anti-Slavery,* 110; Martin, *Anti-Slavery Movement in Kentucky,* ch. 2 and 46, 72–8.
[25] Richard R. John, *Spreading the News: The American Postal System from Franklin to Morse* (Cambridge, MA, 1995), ch. 7, esp. 258–60, 279. For the Fisher pamphlet see *DBR,* 7 (1849), 134 n.; [James H. Hammond], "Lecture on the North and South," *SQR,* 15 (1849), 273–311. In *JCCP* see: 26:292 n.; J. E. Calhoun, Jr. to John C. Calhoun, Mar. 19, 1849 (351); Fitzwilliam Byrdsall to John C. Calhoun, Apr. 20, 1849 (381). See also "B.", "The New Social Propositions," *SLM,* 20 (1858), 295.
[26] On Breckenridge see James C. Klotter, *The Breckenridges of Kentucky, 1760–1981* (Frankfort, KY, 1986), ch. 6; on Buck see John Lee Eighmy, *Churches in Cultural Captivity* (Knoxville, TN, 1972), 7; Durward T. Stokes and William T. Scott, *A History of the Christian Church in the South* (Burlington, NC, 1975), 69–71, 79–81; Louis C. LaMotte, *Colored Light: The Story of the Influence of Columbia Theological Seminary, 1828–1936* (Richmond, VA, 1937), 137. The Moravian Church quietly accepted the biblical sanction for slavery, and in 1850 the Moravian town fathers in Salem whipped and imprisoned a preacher who gave a girl an antislavery tract. See Kristen Martha Meyers, "Slavery among the Moravians of Salem, N.C." (unpublished ms., University of Rochester, 1975); Edward W. Phifer, "Slavery in Microcosm: Burke County, North Carolina," *JSH,* 28 (1962), 74, 77–9; Clement Eaton, *The Freedom-of-Thought Struggle in the Old South* (New York, 1964), 245–6.

After suppression of the Vesey plot in Charleston in 1822, Richard Furman, president of the South Carolina Baptist Convention, assured the governor and all and sundry that his Church was sound on slavery. His influential *Exposition of the Views of the Baptists* (1823) overcame qualms about slavery among the faithful and quieted those who feared abolitionist tendencies among the Baptists. Biblically sanctioned slavery, he explained, constituted a social system within the province of the civil authority. Then an ailing, 68-year-old hellfire preacher who knew he did not have long to live, Furman called upon masters to regard their slaves as a sacred trust to whom they owed kindness and paternal care.[27]

Repression of antislavery proceeded apace. The Gage brothers of South Carolina took to the road in 1835, Robert to New York and James to Paris. Robert wrote James that Carolinians were alarmed: "The daring and ingenious measures of the abolitionists begin to raise a storm in the South." Secession might be necessary, but he suggested lynch law as a way of avoiding it. Even the Reverend Thomas Witherspoon of Alabama openly approved of the lynching of abolitionists. The Reverend Robert Anderson of Virginia, a bit more discreetly, called upon the churches to excommunicate abolitionist ministers and leave their fate to the public. After a young Methodist preacher at LaGrange College in Alabama – which some inaccurately thought tinged with abolitionism – made passing reference to the Nat Turner revolt in a sermon, an outcry threatened him with a lynching. A throng of 2,000 turned out to hear his explanation, but he refused to apologize. Fortunately, Bishop Robert Paine, who had heard the sermon, cooled off the hotheads. He declared the hostile reaction unjust and unfounded. A fiend who would stir up an insurrection among contented slaves, he said, deserved universal execration, but his "young friend" was not such a man: "He is a Southerner. His father owned slaves, and he was born and reared among them. He would do them no harm. He would do you none."[28]

By the 1840s a number of abolitionists, encouraged by the revolutionary turmoil in Europe, were hoping for slave insurrections. Few called for violence but, as their response to Harper's Ferry demonstrated, fewer denounced it. In 1845 E. T. Winkler of Charleston alerted Basil Manly, Jr., a fellow Baptist, to "a storm brewing in the South" beneath a calm surface: "Among other causes of disquietude, the great religious movements in our country have reacted on the minds of our slaves – I could

---

[27] Richard Furman, "Views of the Baptists," in James A. Rogers, *Richard Furman: Life and Legacy* (Macon, GA, 1985); for context and effect see Edward Riley Crowther, "Southern Protestants, Slavery, and Secession: A Study in Religious Ideology, 1830–1861" (Ph.D. diss., Auburn University, 1986), 88–9, and Carolyn L. Harrell, *Kith and Kin: A Portrait of a Southern Family, 1630–1934* (Macon, GA, 1984), 28–9. In 1823 the Reverend Dr. Dalcho, pillar of the Episcopal Church, published *Practical Considerations, Founded on the Scripture, Relative to the Slave Population of South Carolina*, declaring slavery divinely sanctioned but insisting that masters provide slaves with Christian instruction. For the impact of efforts by Dalcho and others see Mason Crum, *Gullah: Negro Life in Carolina Sea Islands* (Durham, NC, 1940), 187, 201.

[28] Robert I. Gage to James Gage, in Reginald Horsman, *Josiah Nott of Mobile: Southerner, Physician, and Racial Theorist* (Baton Rouge, LA, 1987), 48–9, quote at 48; Joseph Sturge, *A Visit to the United States in 1841* (New York, 1969 [1842]), 185; R. H. Rivers, *The Life of Robert Paine, D.D., Bishop of the Methodist Church, South* (Nashville, TN, 1916), 55–7.

tell you startling facts on this subject, but I am unwilling to do so in a letter going to the North." In Alabama such prominent Methodist preachers as Elbert Sevier and William Garrett, supported by the prestigious Baptist Reverend Basil Manly, Sr., pledged to crush abolitionism and prevent dissemination of antislavery literature. In Texas Mrs. E. M. Houstoun, an English traveler, reported outrage in Galveston not only toward an abolitionist philanthropist, who was driven out, but toward a professed anti-abolitionist who just wanted to hear both sides. John Underwood of Georgia, a future congressman, wrote Howell Cobb in 1844 that abolitionists were stirring up the slaves: "We will be compelled to arm our Militia and shoot down our property in the field." And indeed James Curry, an ex-slave, reported that slaves heard and believed that if Martin Van Buren won the election of 1848, he would free the slaves.[29]

Despite a largely successful campaign at suppression, antislavery literature did penetrate the South and attracted the attention of ministers, prominent politicians, and community leaders, who responded with proslavery scriptural arguments in sermons, speeches, and diaries. The Grimké sisters had their pamphlets mailed to South Carolina under the franking privileges of Joshua Giddings, Salmon Chase, and other northern congressmen. Despite the authorities' every precaution, thousands of pamphlets flooded into South Carolina, and in at least nine incidents, citizens of Charleston and Columbia helped slaves escape to the North. The Presbyterian Reverend N. L. Rice, in a debate in Cincinnati with the abolitionist Presbyterian Reverend Jonathan Blanchard, denied the sinfulness of slavery but admitted that antislavery southern ministers could expect to be driven out of the South. William Graham of Pennsylvania, a Methodist missionary to the Choctaws of Arkansas,

---

[29] John W. H. Underwood to Howell Cobb, Feb. 2, 1844, in Ulrich Bonnell Phillips, ed., *The Correspondence of Robert Toombs, Alexander H. Stephens, and Howell Cobb* (Washington, DC, 1913: "Annual Report of the American Historical Association for the Year 1911," vol. 2), 54–5, quote at 55; Marion Elias Lazenby, *History of Methodism in Alabama and West Florida* (Nashville, TN, 1960), 210–12, 306 (Manly); Mrs. [E. M.] Houstoun, *Texas and the Gulf of Mexico; Or, Yachting in the Gulf of Mexico* (Austin, TX, 1968 [1845]), 199; E. T. Winkler to Basil Manly, Jr., Sept. 3, 1845, in Manly Papers, at UNC-SHC; Curry in John W. Blassingame, ed., *Slave Testimony: Two Centuries of Letters, Speeches, Interviews, and Autobiographies* (Baton Rouge, LA, 1977), 136. For antislavery Methodists who fled Georgia in the 1840s see Christopher H. Owen, *The Sacred Flame of Love: Methodism and Society in Ninteenth-Century Georgia* (Athens, GA, 1998), 61–2. For the changing attitude of the abolitionists toward violence see Merton L. Dillon, *Slavery Attacked: Southern Slaves and Their Allies, 1619–1865* (Baton Rouge, LA, 1990), ch. 11.

In 1849, Mary B. Carter of Virginia privately denounced slavery as a personal and national sin that required extirpation. The significance of such outbursts remains moot, especially among the women. In 1845, Mary E. Starnes of Texas recoiled from the travail of the slaves, whom she considered "an oppressed people," but her letters show her comfortable as a slaveholder and harshly anti-abolitionist. Yet, here and there even in the Deep South a slaveholder's son repudiated slavery and vowed to fight against it. Mary B. Carter to Mildred Walker Campbell, Mar. 10, 1849, and Mary E. Starnes to Sarah J. Thompson, Oct. 9, 1845, July 28, 1860, in Joan E. Cashin, ed., *Our Common Affairs: Texts from Women of the Old South* (Baltimore, 1996), 185, 257–8 (Carter), 191 (Starnes); Jaspus Rastus Nall, *Freeborn Slave: Diary of a Black Man in the South* (Birmingham, AL, 1996), 15. For elite women's response to slavery see Elizabeth Fox-Genovese, *Within the Plantation Household: Black and White Women of the Old South* (Chapel Hill, NC, 1988).

insisted in 1864 that southern merchants were generous to ministers, whose favors they courted, but "Woe to the minister who has censured popular vices, or in whose hat an abolition pamphlet has been found, or who in any way disturbs the 'patriarchal institution.' "[30]

Fear of slave unrest overlapped with other fears and sometimes rose to hysteria. In the Lower South opponents of slavery had to have nerves of steel, and many of the bravest went down. In the 1850s mobs in Alabama drove moderates out of Auburn, Watumpka, Troy, and Tuskeegee. In Georgia and Texas people long talked about how mobs whipped, hanged, or drove out even the most circumspect of critics. The New York–born Lorenzo Sherwood, who became a prominent lawyer in Galveston and was elected to the state legislature in 1855, spoke out boldly there. His antislavery views probably doomed his career, and he ensured that fate by taking cases against members of the planter elite, displaying the abrasive courtroom style Southerners associated with vulgar Yankees. His many powerful enemies saw their chance: a public meeting chaired by Pitt Ballinger, a pillar of the Texas establishment, denounced him, and a blue-ribbon committee gravely informed him that no agitation of the slavery question would be tolerated. He would not be permitted to address a public meeting to defend himself against charges of being a "nigger-lover" and a subversive. Sherwood resigned from the legislature.[31]

These repressions only hint at the fuller story historians have told at length. We cannot be certain what the outcome would have been if extensive open debate had

---

[30] George William Featherstonhaugh, *A Canoe Voyage up the Minay Sotor*, 2 vols. (St. Paul, MN, 1970 [1847]), 2:151–2; W. H. Holcombe Diary, "Notes," 2:133, at UNC-SHC; Franc M. Carmack Diary, Sept. 29–30, 1852, at UNC-SHC; Blake McNulty, "Uncertain Masters," in Moore and Tripp, eds., *Looking South*, 80–2; J. Blanchard and N. L. Rice, *A Debate on Slavery* (New York, 1969 [1846]), 200; on the flight of antislavery preachers from the South see William Graham, "Sketches from Arkansas," in Eugene L. Schwaab and Jacqueline Bull, eds., *Travels in the Old South: Selected from Periodicals of the Time*, 2 vols. (Lexington, KY, 1973), 2:425–6; Essig, *Bonds of Wickedness*, 119–20, 148–50; John C. Inscoe, *Mountain Masters: Slavery, and the Sectional Crisis in Western North Carolina* (Knoxville, TN, 1989), 243. In particular, David Walker's *Appeal* circulated widely in North Carolina.

Southern men and women did read abolitionist literature, notably *Uncle Tom's Cabin* and antislavery travelogues like those of Harriet Martineau: Chesnut Diary, Sept. 23, 1863, in C. Vann Woodward, ed., *Mary Chesnut's Civil War* (New Haven, CT, 1981), 428; William Watson, *Life in the Confederate Army: Being the Observations and Experiences of an Alien in the South during the American Civil War* (Baton Rouge, LA, 1995 [1887]), 24, 42–4. Maria Bryan Harford read Lydia Maria Child's *Biographies of Good Wives* with interest and respect and worked her way through a multivolume biography of Wilberforce. Harford felt honored that Harriet Martineau included a conversation with her in one of her books, although she found the book itself disappointing: Maria Bryan Harford to Julia Ann Bryan Cumming, Aug. 12, 1833 (Child), Feb. 10 and Mar. 11, 1839 (Wilberforce), Mar. 15 and May 1, 1838 (Martineau), all in Carol Bleser, ed., *Tokens of Affection: The Letters of a Planter's Daughter in the Old South* (Athens, GA, 1996), 164, 217, 220–1, 237.

[31] J. Mills Thornton, *Power and Politics in a Slave Society: Alabama, 1800–1860* (Baton Rouge, LA, 1978), 313; John Richard Dennett, *The South as It Is, 1865–1866* (New York, 1965 [1867]), 300–2; Maxwell Bloomfield, "The Texas Bar in the Nineteenth Century," *Vanderbilt Law Review*, 32 (1979), 266–7. See Chesebrough, *Clergy Dissent* (ch. 2) generally for the repression of clergy just before and at the beginning of the War. In the North in the late 1840s, worries over a British plot to rend the Union encouraged violence against abolitionists; in the South, some worried that Northerners were settling in Virginia to promote free labor: Ratner, *Powder Keg*, 36–41; *Southern Cultivator*, 5 (1848), 105.

been permitted. But given the prestige of the proslavery divines and the strength of their interpretation of Scripture, and given the less effective abolitionist replies, it seems unlikely that the antislavery cause could have prevailed in the South even with full freedom of speech and assembly. Even today some Christian theologians grapple with the southern claims of biblical sanction for slavery. Wayne Meeks has written that, although today all Christians know slavery to be wrong, "It is not easy to state clearly why the proslavery readers of the Bible were wrong."[32]

In the Border States as well as the plantation states, the conviction had grown that only the white race could sustain free government – at that, only a minority of the white race. Calhoun, speaking for the nineteenth-century proslavery entourage, insisted that it was "a great mistake in supposing all people are capable of self-government"; only a people who have advanced "to a high state of moral and intellectual excellence" could qualify. According to the Presbyterian Reverend Thomas Smyth of Charleston, "The government which would prove a blessing to one community might prove no blessing to another," and the Presbyterian Reverend Samuel Cassells of Savannah declared countless millions throughout the world "no more fit for freedom than children or brute animals." In Maryland, Brantz Mayer pronounced the Spanish "incompetent for self-government." T. W. Hoit of Missouri, in his largely incoherent but widely circulated *The Right of Slavery* (1860), appealed to historical experience to assert that only a tenth of the superior white race had the capacity for self-government. As time went on, the number of white peoples who passed the test shrank.[33]

Although the French ought to have qualified as members of the superior white race, Southerners took pleasure in reviling them. Polybius, one of their favorite ancient authors, warned that those who allied themselves with Gauls paid dearly for their error, for Gauls had a well-earned reputation for treachery, viciousness, and "lawless violence." Southerners, reading Caesar's *Gallic Wars* in school, learned that he had taken no chances with the Gauls "for fear of their instability." They were, Caesar wrote, "capricious in choosing a course and prone to revolution."[34]

---

[32] Wayne A. Meeks, "The 'Haustafeln' and American Slavery: A Hermeneutical Challenge," in E. Lovering and J. Summer, eds., *Theology and Ethics in Paul* (Nashville, TN, 1996), 245.

[33] J. C. Calhoun, speech to the Senate, Jan. 4, 1848, in Clyde N. Wilson, ed., *The Essential Calhoun: Selection from Writings, Speeches, and Letters* (New Brunswick, NJ, 1991), 114; *TSW*, 3:1–216, 6:22; [Cassells], "Relation of Justice to Benevolence," 98–9; Brantz Mayer, *History of the War between Mexico and the United States with a Preliminary View of Its Origin* (New York, 1848), 7; T. W. Hoit, *The Right of American Slavery* (St. Louis, MO, 1860), 23, 38. For support for the essentials of Smyth's view see: [J. B. Adger], "Motley's Dutch Republic," *SPR*, 15 (1862), 94–159; "A North Carolinian", *Slavery Considered on General Principles; Or, a Grapple with Abstractionists* (New York, 1861), 7; James Shannon, *The Philosophy of Slavery, as Identified with the Philosophy of Human Happiness* (Frankfort, KY, 1840), 28; Elisha Mitchell to J. C. Calhoun, Feb. 18, 1849, in *JCCP*, 26:293. On the complexities of the divines' view of biblical sanction for governments, see Chapter 22.

[34] Polybius, *The Histories*, tr. W. R. Paton, 6 vols. (LCL), 1:Bk. 2:7; 2:Bk. 3:3; Julius Caesar, *The Gallic War and Other Writings*, tr. Moses Hadas (New York, 1957), 76. William Lee of Virginia dissuaded Henry Lee from going to France to support the revolutionaries in 1790. William Lee explained that

Shortly before the French Revolution, William Vans Murray of Maryland claimed that the French had "little idea of the effects of a free constitution," whereas Americans understood "the freedom of democracy, without anarchy." The Belgian-born Rosalie Steir Calvert of Maryland sneered at Napoleon's coronation: "The empty heads of the French are easily turned by *Puppet Shows.*" Patrick Henry deemed the French debased by despotism and incapable of understanding rational liberty. William Somerville of Virginia, a pronounced Francophile, struggled manfully in his *Letters from Paris* (1822) to provide a positive account of French character despite the misery under the Old Régime and the excesses of the Revolution; he reluctantly concluded that the French had proven themselves "scarcely fit for anything better than the military despotism of Napoleon." When the War came, Bishop Elliott declared, "We are fighting to prevent ourselves from being transferred from American republicanism to French democracy."[35]

William Hutson ridiculed the French as shallow philosophers for whom Reason is Revelation: "The French people, with a desire for conquest and love of war, and that bigotry which has been their chief national characteristic, did pant after universal acceptance of their creed at the point of a bayonet." Twice the nations of Europe had to march to Paris to put down revolution and mass murder, and they will have to do it again; they would either finish the French off the next time or risk the slaughter of millions. From 1789 onward, J. Barnett Cohen told the South-Carolina Historical Society in 1856, "France has not been able to boast a single day of freedom."[36]

The France that had not been able to sustain a single day of freedom nonetheless produced a historian of freedom Southerners could applaud: François Guizot, whose *History of Civilization* achieved enviable popularity in the South. A contributor to *Southern Quarterly Review* and the Reverend Alexander Campbell of the Disciples of Christ ranked Guizot among the greatest, wisest, and most philosophically profound of historians. The Baptist Reverend J. L. Reynolds, speaking

the Parisians were "savage cannibals": quoted by Benjamin Perry in Meats and Arnold, eds., *Writings of B. F. Perry,* 3:20. Francis Lieber cited with approbation words by the revered Barthold Niebuhr on the weakness of French political culture: Daniel C. Gilman, ed., *The Miscellaneous Writings of Francis Lieber,* 2 vols. (Philadelphia, 1881), 1:95.

35 William Vans Murray, *Political Sketches Inscribed to His Excellency John Adams … by a Citizen of the United States* (London, 1787), 4, 10, also 22, 59; Rosalie Steir Calvert to Charles J. Stier, Jan. 25, 1805, in Margaret Law Callcott, ed., *The Mistress of Riversdale: The Plantation Letters of Rosalie Stier Calvert, 1795–1821* (Baltimore, 1991), 110; William Wirt, *Sketches of the Life and Character of Patrick Henry* (Philadelphia, 1817), 410; William C. Somerville, *Letters from Paris on the Causes and Consequences of the French Revolution* (Baltimore, 1822), 69, 133–4, 257, 373, quote at 71; Stephen Elliott, *God's Presence with the Confederate States* (Savannah, GA, 1861), 21. See also Supplementary References: "French Incapacity for Freedom."

36 [William F. Hutson], "History of the Girondists," *SPR,* 2 (1848), 394, 406; J. Barnett Cohen, "Oration Delivered on the First Anniversary of the South-Carolina Historical Society" (June 28, 1856), in *South-Carolina Historical Collections,* 2:112. Francis W. Pickens, no doubt cognizant of the flow of southern youth to study medicine in Paris, did allow that France was leading the world in "rapid progress in the exact sciences": *Science and Truth: An Address Delivered before the Literary Societies of Erskine College, S.C.* (Fraziersville, SC, 1849), 5.

at Wake Forest College, mentioned Guizot and Macaulay in the same breath with Thucydides and Tacitus, and the Episcopal Reverend W. N. Pendleton of Lexington, Virginia, quoted the Protestant Guizot on the achievement of the early medieval Church in saving Europe from barbarism. William Gilmore Simms, David Flavel Jamison, George Frederick Holmes, Francis Lieber, and John Reuben Thompson leveled serious criticism at Guizot for French chauvinism and want of caution and completeness, but they promoted him as a significant historian and social theorist. Dew followed Guizot, although critically, on the blending of Romans and barbarians in early feudalism, on the origins of chivalry, the history of the papacy, and the rise of European cities. Like Guizot, Dew viewed European history as the story of the development of representative institutions promoted primarily by the middle class, and like Guizot he played down the radical innovations and achievements of the English and French revolutions while chastising conservatives for denying the correction of past injustices.[37]

Although Holmes thought Guizot's reputation in decline in the 1850s, southern accolades continued, especially for his social history in philosophical context. In 1852 Henry Augustine Washington, a proponent of social history, called for a first-rate history of Virginia and cited as models Guizot on France and Thomas Babington Macaulay on England. James M. Walker of South Carolina and Thomas Cobb of Georgia, respected legal scholars, freely cited Guizot to bolster their accounts of medieval law and the persistence of slavery and peasant unrest during the Middle Ages. And in Adger's eyes, Guizot demonstrated the compatibility of slavery with Christianity.[38]

---

[37] "Ouevres de Vico," *SQR*, 2 (1842), 404–5; Alexander Campbell, "Amelioration of the Social State," in Campbell, *Popular Lectures and Addresses* (Philadelphia, 1863), 51; J. L. Reynolds, *The Man of Letters* (Richmond, VA, 1849), 10; W. N. Pendleton, *Science: A Witness for the Bible* (Philadelphia, 1860), 39–40; D. F. Jamison, "General History of Civilization in Europe," *SQR*, 3 (1843), 1–17, quote at 12, and 4 (1843), 157–78, quote at 159; [George Frederick Holmes], "Gibbon's Decline and Fall," *QRMECS*, 4th ser., 10 (1856), 324; Francis Lieber, *A Manual of Political Ethics* (London, 1819), 58, 130; [John R. Thompson], *SLM*, 19 (1853), 190; Dew, *Digest*, 325, 331, 341–2, 374, 399–400, 429. John R. Thompson declared Guizot's treatment of Shakespeare an especially admirable feature of his *History of Civilization*: *SLM*, 19 (1853), 190. Simms considered Guizot a superior philosophical historian who separated fact from fable and viewed his books on Corneille and Shakespeare as the work of a genuine authority. But Simms opened his review of Guizot's *Democracy in France* with disgust for its claims that France stood at the center of world culture and civilization: [William Gilmore Simms], "Prescott's Conquest of Peru," *SQR*, 13 (1848), 138; [Simms], "Critical Notices," *SQR*, n.s., 7 (1853), 533–4, and 8 (1853), 264–5; [Simms], "Guizot's Democracy in France," *SQR*, 15 (1849), 114–17. See also Stanley Mellon, "Introduction," in *François Guizot: Historical Essays and Lectures*, ed. S. Mellon (Chicago, 1972).

[38] Henry Augustine Washington, "The Virginia Constitution of 1776," *SLM*, 18 (1852), 657; James M. Walker, *The Theory of the Common Law* (Boston, 1852), 26; T. R. R. Cobb, "An Historical Sketch of Slavery," in Cobb, *An Inquiry into the Law of Negro Slavery in the United States* (New York, 1968 [1858]), ch. 7; [J. B. Adger], "Northern and Southern Views of the Church," *SPR*, 16 (1866), 393–4. J. A. Winslow praised Guizot's attack on the philosophers of the French Enlightenment for their utilitarianism and encouragement of revolutions in society and institutions: "Utilitarianism," *VUM*, 4 (1860), 297–300.

Goethe and Hegel admired Guizot, who was steeped in German philosophy and English literature. But as Stanley Mellon pithily observes, most nineteenth-century intellectuals despised him, Louis Philippe disliked him, and the middle class he served distrusted him. Heinrich Heine caught the Guizot whom Southerners admired despite his vulgar bourgeois cry of "*Enrichessez-voux*" and proclaimed Guizot "a man of resistance but not of reaction" – a man of order who undertook the practical measures necessary to bolster a bourgeois regime "as grimly threatened by the marauding stranglers of the past" as by "the plunder-seeking avant-garde of the future." No wonder that the historian William Rivers of South Carolina considered Guizot a guide to political moderation and that Louisa McCord quoted Guizot favorably as an enemy of cant. She may have had in mind the complaint filed by Elizabeth Cady Stanton that her brother drew his strongest arguments against immediate abolition from Guizot's *History of Civilization*. Southerners saw through Guizot's high-minded antislavery rhetoric when, as the July Monarchy's professedly liberal first minister, he faced demands for emancipation of the slaves in the French colonies. They saw for themselves what Tocqueville described: "He displayed the difficulties and costs of the measure, immensely exaggerated, before the Assembly. He did not hesitate, among other things, to announce officially that emancipation would cost the public treasury more than 250 million, which as it was easy to predict, gave rise to disapproving exclamations from the Chamber."[39]

A deep-seated apprehension transcended worries of slave revolt among slaveholders who celebrated freedom in human history. Suppose that free republics, instead of being the grand accomplishment toward which history pointed, had no future? As the sectional crisis deepened, this theoretical abstraction posed a frightening and urgent challenge. If the South seceded, two hostile nations would confront each other, neither able to sustain the very freedom each believed itself fighting for. In 1828 James Monroe had written Calhoun that disunion would mean wars in which "our free system of Government would be overwhelmed." Southern conservatives like Henry St. George Tucker and northern conservatives like Joseph Story repeatedly warned that disunion would compel both North and South to seek foreign alliances and impose military despotism. If the Union dissolved, Frederick Nash of North Carolina said, America would go the way of Europe and South America, with many states constantly at war and tending toward despotism. Abel Upshur of

---

[39] Heinrich Heine quoted by Guizot in *Historical Essays and Lectures*, xvii, xix; William J. Rivers, *Address Delivered before the South Carolina Historical Society on Their Twenty-first Anniversary* (Charleston, SC, 1876), 18; L. S. McCord, "Right to Labor," in Richard Lounsbury, ed., *Louisa S. McCord: Political and Social Essays* (Charlottesville, VA, 1995), 84; Elizabeth Cady Stanton to Angelina Weld and Sarah Grimké, June 25, 1840, in Gilbert H. Barnes and Dwight L. Dumond, eds., *Letters of Theodore Dwight Weld, Angelina Grimké and Sarah Grimké, 1822–1844*, 2 vols. (Gloucester, MA, 1965), 2:848–9; "The Emancipation of Slaves" (1843), in Jennifer Pitts, ed. and tr., *Alexis de Tocqueville: Writings on Empire and Slavery* (Baltimore, 2001), 225–6. Joseph Dorfman suggests that *History of Civilization* was the most popular textbook in American colleges: *The Economic Mind in American Civilization*, 5 vols. (New York, 1966), 2:700.

Virginia, a Calhoun ally, was convinced that secession would invite military despotism in the trail of vast bloodletting. "Dissolve this Union," Hugh Legaré told the House of Representatives in 1839, "and your republican institutions are gone forever." In the crises of 1850 and 1860, Southern unionists – Henry Hilliard in Alabama, W. C. Rives in Virginia, Ferdinand Jacobs and James Henley Thornwell in South Carolina – predicted that secession would lead to a reign of terror like that of the French Revolution and that a military confrontation between North and South would destroy free institutions in both. Sarah Morgan of Louisiana, a unionist who supported the Confederacy with a heavy heart, conjured up an even worse prospect: "No glory awaits the Southern Confederacy, even if it does achieve its independence; it will be a mere speck on the world, with no weight or authority."[40]

As the election of 1860 approached, unionist as well as secessionist tempers frayed. Thomas Walton of Mississippi, opposing secession and the reopening of the African slave trade, warned that international exigencies would lead an independent southern Confederacy to replicate the North's political centralization and economic protectionism. Some secession-leaning slaveholders, with substantial personal property at stake, shared those fears and pleaded for restraint; others were ready to resist Yankee aggression but deeply worried about the vast army and government apparatus it would take to defend a separate southern Confederacy. David Hunter Strother ("Porte Crayon") cringed at secession in part because he did not believe the South could win a war with the North and in part because he believed that, even if it did, it would become a third-rate power dependent upon the protection of a European country. Some unionists feared that a southern Confederacy would itself split into petty republics dependent on foreign support.[41]

Many of the staunchest proslavery Southerners, dreading the war that secession would bring, predicted reenactment of the worst episodes of ancient and modern

[40] Monroe to Calhoun, Aug. 4, 1828, in *JCCP*, 10:409; Henry St. George Tucker, *Lectures on Government* (Charlottesville, VA, 1844), 58–9, 62, 172, 181, 191, 203, 212; on Joseph Story see Peter B. Knupfer, *The Union as It Is: Constitutional Unionism and Sectional Compromise, 1787–1861* (Chapel Hill, NC, 1991), 57; Frederick Nash to Willie P. Mangum, Jan. 23, 1833, in Henry Thomas Shanks, ed., *The Papers of Willie P. Mangum*, 5 vols. (Raleigh, NC, 1955–56), 2:11–12; Claude H. Hall, *Abel Parker Upshur: Conservative Virginian, 1790–1844* (Madison, WI, 1963), 92; "Recognition of Hayti," *HLW*, 1:328; "Slavery and the Union," Dec. 12, 1849, and "Boundary of Texas and New Mexico," Aug. 28, 1850, in Henry W. Hilliard, *Speeches and Addresses* (New York, 1855), 228, 313–14; for Jemison on a new Reign of Terror see *EC*, 2:842; Ferdinand Jacobs, *The Committing of Our Cause to God* (Charleston, SC, 1850), 4, 22. In B. M. Palmer, *The Life and Letters of James Henley Thornwell* (Richmond, VA, 1875), see Thornwell to Breckenridge, Mar. 28, 1851 (477), Thornwell to Rev. Dr. Hooper, Mar. 8, 1850 (478), and Thornwell, "Our Danger and Our Duty" (Appendix 2:582); Morgan Diary, June 29, 1862, in James I. Robertson, ed., *A Confederate Girl's Diary: Sarah Morgan Dawson* (Westport, CT, 1960), 93. On the South Carolina Whigs see J. G. deRoulhac Hamilton, ed., *The Papers of William Alexander Graham*, 5 vols. (Raleigh, NC, 1957–73): James Graham to W. A. Graham, Aug. 25, 1850 (3:371), and James W. Osborne to W. A. Graham, Mar. 25, 1852 (4:267).

[41] Thomas Walton, "Further Views of the Advocates of the Slave Trade," *DBR*, 26 (1859), 51–66; Basil Lanneau Gildersleeve, *The Creed of the Old South* (Baltimore, 1915), 33; Cecil D. Eby, Jr., *"Porte Crayon": The Life of David Hunter Strother* (Chapel Hill, NC, 1960), 103; Carmack Diary, Jan. 1, 1861.

European history. Tocqueville had warned: "All those who seek to destroy the liberties of a democratic nation ought to know that war is the surest and the shortest means to accomplish it." War, he explained, may not throw up a Caesar, but it will necessarily "concentrate the direction of all men and the management of all things, in the hands of the administration." Robert Barnwell Rhett, the fiery secessionist, agreed with unionists that a southern Confederacy would have to accept national political consolidation to survive. With war on the horizon in 1861, Thomas Cobb – a pillar of the slaveholding Establishment and soon to emerge as the principal author of the Confederate Constitution – added another ominous note. A new Confederacy would have to resort to direct taxation, and "If so I am for striking at the capitalists and slave-owners."[42]

Columbia's *Daily South Carolinian* chose disunion in August 1860 despite frank recognition that "expensive Governments, standing armies and large navies" would ensue, for nothing would be worse than continued submission to Yankee tyranny. Raleigh's *North Carolina Standard* did not want to rush into the misery. It would accept, if necessary, a "military despotism" strong enough to protect the South against the Yankees and its own blacks. But in 1861 the *Standard* declared that secession meant war – and war meant turbulence among the slaves, heavy taxes, and an increasingly repressive government. The whole world would array against the South, and at home the burden would provoke the white masses to rebel. New Orleans' *True Delta* had no doubt that a southern Confederacy would require government centralization and a large military establishment. Secession, Alexander Stephens told Georgians in November 1860, will lead to demonic and bloody regimes on both sides of the new border.[43]

Unionists pressed hard the theme of secession as prelude to a war that would result in centralization of power, despotism, and destruction of civil liberties. Allison Davidson, a unionist banker in western North Carolina who joined the secessionists only when Lincoln called for troops, wrote home from Atlanta, "If ever the liberty of speech and the press was under the direct control of a despotism, it is here. God save our glorious old state from the damnation of such a lawless and desperate *Mob*." From the Union side came a sobering apologetic: The criminal secessionists, wrote Adam Gurowski, a pro-Union Pole, have forced the Union to "make use of despotism for the sake of self-defence."[44]

---

[42] Alexis de Tocqueville, *Democracy in America*, tr. Henry Reeve, 2 vols. (Boston, 1873), 2:330; Laura A. White, *Robert Barnwell Rhett: Father of Secession* (Gloucester, MA, 1965 [1931]), 88; T. R. R. Cobb to Marion Cobb, May 4, 1861, in "Correspondence of Thomas Reade Rootes Cobb, 1860–62," *Publications of the Southern Historical Association*, 11 (1907), 321. For centralization in the Confederacy and growing awareness of its necessity, see Charles W. Ramsdell, *Behind the Lines in the Southern Confederacy* (Baton Rouge, LA, 1944), 5, 61.

[43] Dwight L. Dumond, ed., *Southern Editorials on Secession* (Gloucester, MA, 1964), 157, 212, 286, 446–7; Stephens, Speech of Nov. 14, 1860, in William W. Freehling and Craig M. Simpson, eds., *Secession Debated: Georgia's Showdown in 1860* (New York, 1992), 68; Donald E. Reynolds, *Editors Make War: Southern Newspapers in the Secession Crisis* (Nashville, TN, 1966), 167, 204.

[44] Davidson quoted in Inscoe, *Mountain Masters*, 234; Oct. 1861, in Adam G. de Gurowski, *Diary*, 2 vols. (Boston, 1862–65), 108.

Love for the Union had acquired a special cast in the South: Slaveholders saw the Union as the great guarantor of their peculiar species of human property. As sectional antagonisms intensified, unionists appealed to the slaveholders to consider their interests carefully and to understand that slavery and southern political and economic interests were immeasurably safer in the Union than they would be out of it. Secessionists, in contrast, believed that the safety of slavery required a separate republic. The most clear-headed among them understood the threat to their freedom posed by hostile and militarily powerful states in America as well as Europe but considered the risk unavoidable. In the 1820s Dew, a unionist, recognized that secession might have to come but cautioned the South to consider the constitutional right to secession a last resort: "There is scarcely any event that could justify this rash step." Standing armies and all the perils of European politics would descend upon North and South and both would have to surrender constitutional liberties and sound economic policies: "So will our own country be torn to pieces, oppressed with debt, impoverished and ruined, if disunion takes place."[45]

In subsequent years Dew returned to the problem with foreboding and offered thoughts that called into question his optimistic view of humanity's upward and onward progress toward freedom. Reflecting on Greek history and on the struggle between Rome and Carthage, he attributed the warlike spirit of the Greeks to "division into so many states, and proximity to each other, always liable to attack from neighbors." Two republics, he explained, "cannot exist near each other, without one being destroyed or subjected." The protracted war between Rome and Carthage "inspired a national hatred, such is only found in republics; the conviction also that they could not remain independent of one another." He inquired, "Who does not know the arrogance of a republic after the first essay of her power has been crowned with success?" As if to answer his own rhetorical question, he referred to Rome's savage treatment of the Carthaginians, which has "given a warning to those nations who can take it, of what they may expect from the domination of a powerful republic."[46]

Lamenting the Confederate defeat in 1866, the Presbyterian Reverend R. S. Gladney of Mississippi deplored the "licentiousness and fanaticism prevalent in the United States." He cautioned that the most despotic governments had proven the most lasting, whereas free governments persisted only among a few peoples. The collapse of the federal Union and its replacement by what many Southerners saw as a nationally consolidated tyranny led to a grim conclusion, which demolished the fundamental premise of the slaveholders' view of history as a story of progress toward freedom: "*Sinful man, by his own wisdom, is not capable of establishing and maintaining free or self-government.*"[47]

---

[45]   Thomas Roderick Dew, *Lectures on the Restrictive System, Delivered to the Senior Class of William and Mary College* (Richmond, VA, 1829), 185–6.

[46]   Dew, *Digest,* 44, 241, 243, 246, 253.

[47]   R. S. Gladney, "Relation of State and Church," *SPR,* 16 (1866), 349–76, quote at 351.

PART THREE

ANCIENT LEGACIES, MEDIEVAL SENSIBILITY, MODERN MEN

No voice is wholly lost that is the voice of many men.

—Hesiod/Aristotle*

---

* As liberally translated by Harry Slochower, *No Voice Is Wholly Lost: Writers and Thinkers in War and Peace* (New York, 1945); cf. "The Works and Days," in *Hesiod,* tr. Richard Lattimore (Ann Arbor, MI, 1953, lines 763–4), and Aristotle's version, *Nicomachean Ethics,* tr. Martin Ostwald (Indianapolis, IN, 1962), 1153b-25-8.

8

In the Shadow of Antiquity

> The spirit of a people is best revealed in the words it employs with an emotional content. To a Roman, such a word was "antiquus"; and what Rome now required was men like those of old, and ancient virtue.
>
> —Ronald Syme[1]

The legacy and models of Greek and Roman antiquity have permeated Western culture, articulating, if elusively, the essence of being human. The "classics" offered archetypal representations of the human condition – its passions, its potential for heroism and baseness, its social and political nature, and its historical consciousness. The twentieth century revealed its affinity for the classical past in Freud's Oedipus complex, Jean Anouilh's resurrection of the myth of Antigone as a figure of resistance, Toni Morrison's reworking of the figure of Medea in *Beloved*, Eugene O'Neill's *Mourning Becomes Electra*, and beyond. The persisting influence of ancient culture in the contemporary world is all the more striking because of the precipitous decline in the knowledge of ancient languages even among the best-educated. Today, a passing remark that the entire world of thought is either Plato or Aristotle will predictably draw blank stares in the classrooms of elite colleges and universities; among any two hundred random college students, as few as five may have heard of Oedipus. The Ancients' philosophies of history or practice and acceptance of slavery have largely vanished from general knowledge – even if many of their representations of human nature persist in culture, often unrecognized. Such was not the case in the slaveholding South. Classical learning retained its hold on the education and culture of Southerners, who would likely have agreed with the claim of Johann Wolfgang von Goethe, whom they much admired: "When we place ourselves over against antiquity and regard it seriously with the intention of developing ourselves, only then do we gain the impression of becoming truly human."[2]

---

[1] Ronald Syme, *The Roman Revolution* (New York, 1960 [1931]), 442.

[2] Goethe as translated by Jane V. Curran, "Goethe's Helen: A Play within a Play," *International Journal of the Classical Tradition*, 7 (2002), 165.

Classical education – ancient history and literature – distinguished the southern gentleman. Jefferson, who loved Latin and touted Greek as the greatest of all languages, agreed with Thomas Cooper, president of South Carolina College, that no youth ought to be admitted to the University of Virginia who could not read Virgil, Horace, Xenophon, and Homer with facility and translate at sight a page of English into Latin. When John Rutledge of South Carolina, a future associate justice of the U.S. Supreme Court, made clear that he hated Greek and Latin, his mother fretted: Without Greek and Latin, he would lack the attributes of a gentleman. Proficiency in Greek and Latin permitted the upcountry J. L. Petigru to feel at ease among the gentlemen of Charleston. Virginians and Carolinians who moved westward garnered prestige and political influence from their command of classical languages and literature – witness, among many, William H. Crawford in Georgia, Jefferson Davis in Mississippi, and Ashbel Smith in Texas.[3]

Polish alone did not account for the southern gentleman's attachment to the classics. Basil Lanneau Gildersleeve, who became America's foremost classicist, echoed Goethe in describing the classics as "the offspring of a healthy humanity" – by which he meant that they taught historical continuity, critical perspective, and "eternal norms." Isaac Stuart delivered his inaugural address as professor of ancient languages at South Carolina College in the chamber of the State Senate, telling the governor, legislators, and local elite in attendance that the classics discipline the mind to precise thought and expression. Educators, clerical and lay, heartily agreed, drawing upon the classics to promote intellectual rigor in support of Christian values. In Kentucky, Dr. James Chambers and Judge John Rowan even squared off on the field of honor to settle rival claims to the more thorough knowledge of Greek and Latin. Rowan, who went on to the House of Representatives and the Senate, killed Chambers, thereby demonstrating superior linguistic and literary talent, to say nothing of marksmanship.[4]

---

[3] Richard Beale Davis, *A Colonial Southern Bookshelf Reading in the Eighteenth Century* (Athens, GA, 1979), esp. 22–3, 26, 100–1, 115–16; Richard M. Gummere, *The American Colonial Mind and the Classical Tradition: Essays in Comparative Culture* (Cambridge, MA, 1963), 57; Thomas Cooper to Gov. Wilson Cary Nichols, Aug. 1, 1816, in *DHE*, 5:14. Richard Barry, *Mr. Rutledge of South Carolina* (New York, 1941), 10; Lacy Ford, "James Louis Petigru," in Michael O'Brien and David Moltke-Hansen, eds., *Intellectual Life in Antebellum Charleston* (Knoxville, TN, 1986), 158; John Belton O'Neall, *Biographical Sketches of the Bench and Bar of South Carolina*, 2 vols. (Charleston, SC, 1859), 1:xv, 58, 80, 112, 288, 306, 324. See also Wayne K. Durrill, "The Power of Ancient Words: Classical Teaching and Social Change at South Carolina College," *JSH*, 65 (1999), 469–98.
[4] Basil Lanneau Gildersleeve, "The Necessity of the Classics," in Michael O'Brien, ed., *All Clever Men, Who Make Their Way: Critical Discourse in the Old South* (Columbia, SC, 1982), 404, 417–18; W. W. Briggs, Jr., and H. W. Benario, eds., *Basil Lanneau Gildersleeve: An American Classicist* (Baltimore, 1986), 291; Isaac W. Stuart, *On the Classical Tongues and the Advantages of Their Study* (Columbia, SC, 1836), 7–9, 15–17; R. Gerald Alvey, *Kentucky Bluegrass Country* (Jackson, MS, 1992), 218; J. Jefferson Looney and Ruth L. Woodward, eds., *Princetonians, 1791–1794* (Princeton, NJ, 1991), 138. On Stuart as innovator see Caroline Winterer, *The Culture of Classicism: Ancient Greece and Rome in American Intellectual Life, 1780–1910* (Baltimore, 2002), 50, 62. See also Abram Burwell Brown, "Christianity and Civilization," in Dr. and Mrs. William E. Hatcher, *Sketch of the Life and*

Throughout the eighteenth century, progressive educational views steadily gained ground – especially in France and the United States, where more and more educators denounced the classical curriculum as elitist and the residual froth of an aristocratic and decadent Europe, unsuited to modern young minds and a regrettable diversion from practical studies. In the North the classics still retained a place of honor, but a pronounced retreat was in evidence. The socially conservative (although theologically radical) Unitarians at Harvard held the line for classical studies, as did Yale, but the rumblings against classical studies grew louder as other colleges freed themselves from the influence of the leading universities of New England.[5]

By the early nineteenth century, important northern educational centers – influenced by the American Philosophical Society – were beginning to prefer "useful" learning to classical, which some, including Benjamin Rush, dismissed as "ornamental": little better than a cover for aristocratic pretension and the glorification of war. Southerners saw modernizers of this persuasion as allies of such dangerous radicals as Paine, Diderot, Brissot, and Freneau. Even in northern colleges retreat from the classics proceeded slowly, except in such hotbeds of abolitionism as Oberlin College, which dropped the "heathen classics" in 1830. By the War, however, colleges throughout the North were relinquishing the notion of education as the classically grounded formation of the Christian gentleman in favor of a more utilitarian secularization and specialization.[6]

Some southern educators like Bartholomew Carroll of Charleston worried that continued emphasis on the classics condemned southern youth to fall behind northern in "a business education." Others, like George Frederick Holmes, president of the University of Mississippi, worried that the South was falling prey to that very northern disease. "W. C.", in *Southern Quarterly Review*, pleaded for improved teaching of the classics to combat "the monstrous danger of the triumph of a frigid utilitarianism." Judges Archibald Murphey and William Gaston of North Carolina, William J. Rivers of South Carolina, and Robert G. H. Kean of Virginia

Writings of A. B. Brown (Baltimore, 1886), 145, 258–9; [Edgar Allan Poe], "The Classics," *SLM*, 2 (1836), 225; "W. H." [William H. Hall], "The Utility of Classical Studies," *Oakland College Magazine*, 2 (1858), 10–17; [George E. Dabney], "On the Study of Ancient Languages in the United States," *SLM*, 17 (1851), 329–39.

5 Lawrence Cremin, *American Education: The National Experience, 1783–1876* (New York, 1980), 406–7; Stow Persons, *The Decline of American Gentility* (New York, 1973), 179, 182, 187, 190–4; F. O. Matthiessen, *American Renaissance: Art and Expression in the Age of Emerson and Whitman* (New York, 1941), 18–19.

6 Benjamin Rush, "An Enquiry into the Utility of a Knowledge of the Latin and Greek Languages," *American Museum*, 5 (1789), 525–32; J. R. Berrigan, "Impact of the Classics upon the South," *Classical Journal*, 64 (1968), 18–20. For national trends see esp. Meyer Reinhold, *Classica Americana: The Greek and Roman Heritage in the United States* (Detroit, 1984), 30–49, ch. 2; Carl J. Richard, *Founders and the Classics: Greece, Rome, and the American Enlightenment* (Cambridge, MA, 1994), ch. 7; Frederick Rudolph, *The American College and University: A History* (Atlanta, GA, 1990), ch. 6; Larry E. Tise, *Proslavery: A History of the Defense of Slavery in America, 1701–1840* (Athens, GA, 1988), 225–6. New England colleges decreased emphasis on the classics from the 1820s: David B. Potts, *Wesleyan University, 1831–1910* (New Haven, CT, 1992), 17.

stressed classical education as a vital defense line against a utilitarian materialism subversive of southern Christian civilization.[7]

Hugh Legaré of South Carolina, one of America's most distinguished classical scholars, saw the decline of classical learning as support for irrationality and radicalism. Thomas Smith Grimké of Charleston, himself a fine classical scholar, campaigned against "the classics of heathenism" and a curriculum he regarded as largely useless for life after college, predicting that present and future intellectuals would surpass the ancients. The fruitless campaign earned him the contempt of Legaré, who consigned him to the company of those Islamic fanatics, Anabaptists, and Fifth Monarchy men among levelers who subjected literature to a "degrading, cui bono test" and who estimated "genius and taste by their value in exchange, and weigh the results of science in the scales of the money changer."[8]

Southern supporters of "practical" subjects – science, mathematics, agricultural chemistry – scored some victories, notably at Transylvania University and the University of North Carolina. Virginia Military Institute, the Citadel, and other military academies, which mushroomed in the 1840s and 1850s, slighted classical studies in emulation of West Point, which led the movement to produce engineers and to spur economic development. But at South Carolina College, presidents James Henley Thornwell and William Campbell Preston led a pro-classics backlash, and the South at large stood firm. In 1843, the University of Virginia had 33 students enrolled in classical studies; by the mid-1850s the number had grown to 259, more than in any other subject. By the advent of the War, a total of some 1,800 students had taken courses in that especially demanding program in classics, and many of their papers displayed obvious competence.[9]

Familiarity with the classics extended beyond the colleges. "American farmers," Thomas Jefferson quipped, "are the only farmers who can read Homer." In 1874

[7] Bartholomew R. Carroll to J. C. Calhoun, Aug. 8, 1845, in *JCCP*, 22:62–5; James Allen Cabaniss, *A History of the University of Mississippi* (University, MS, 1949), 18–19; [George Frederick Holmes], "Sir William Hamilton's Discussions," *SQR*, n.s., 8 (1853), 289–337; "W. C.", "Brooks' Classics," *SQR*, 14 (1848), 369–71, quote at 370; A. D. Murphy and W. Gaston, in W. J. Peele, ed., *Lives of Distinguished North Carolinians* (Raleigh, NC, 1907), 149–50, 166–7; William J. Rivers, *The Study of Greek Literature* (Columbia, SC, 1858), 7; Robert G. H. Kean, "Essay on the Advantages to Be Derived from the Classics," *SLM*, 16 (1850), 479–82; also, "Critical Notices," *SLM*, 2 (1836), 716–17. On Talmadge and Olin see Edwin A. Miles, "The Old South and the Classical World," *North Carolina Historical Review*, 68 (1971), 260.

[8] "Classical Learning," *HLW*, 2:5–51, quotes at 9, 18, 21, 22 (first published in *SR* in 1828, republished in *SLM* in 1862); *Address of Thomas S. Grimké at a Meeting in Charleston, South Carolina, Held March 29, 1831* (Philadelphia, 1831), 4, and Grimké, *Science and Literature, Past, Present, and Future* (Charleston, SC, 1827). At the University of Virginia, *VLM* provided English translations for Latin quotations: 1 (1829). Legaré's criticism of Grimké received implicit support from Stuart, *Classical Tongues*, as well as explicit support from Holmes in "Writings of Hugh Swinton Legaré," *SQR*, 9 (1846), 342–3; see "Classical Learning," *SLM*, 34 (1862), 368–75.

[9] Thomas C. Johnson, *Scientific Interests in the Old South* (New York, 1936), 27–8, 33, 35–6, 43, 91–2; Kemp P. Battle, *University of North Carolina*, 2 vols. (Spartanburg, SC, 1974 [1907]), 1:552–3; J. H. Thornwell to Gen. James Gillespie, Mar. 27, 1846, in Thornwell Papers, at USC; James McDowell Graham, "Worship of Nature," *VUM*, 3 (1859), 507–8.

George Cary Eggleston recalled Virginia planters as "Latinists" who read Virgil and Ovid for pleasure and quoted Horace and Juvenal from memory. Some, including some of the Founding Fathers, apparently relied on translations, and a thorough grounding in the ancient languages may have been lacking among others who claimed knowledge of classical writings. Certain Yankees – John Quincy Adams, for one – sneered at the superficiality of classical education in the South, singling out John Randolph of Roanoke in particular. Randolph, whose annotations in his books belie the accusation, retorted that he never met "a Yankee who knew anything about the classics." Contemptuous Northeasterners did not notice the ease with which southern boys displayed knowledge of Greek and Latin as they gained admittance to Harvard, Yale, and Princeton.[10]

The contempt was misplaced for other reasons. Knowledge of the ancient languages was declining throughout the Western world. Even in pre-Revolutionary France, the educated classes generally knew the Greeks only in French. As early as 1600 almost all the ancient classics had appeared in English, and the translations of Homer's *Iliad* by Pope and Dryden became especially popular in Europe and America. George Washington never learned Greek or Latin but read classical authors widely in translation. Sam Houston, among others, lovingly read Pope's translation, and Henry Clay, who had neither Greek nor Latin, earnestly advised his son to profit from his own misfortune.[11]

---

[10] George Cary Eggleston, *A Rebel's Recollections* (Baton Rouge, LA, 1996 [1871]), 52; Charles Fraser, *Reminiscences of Charleston* (Charleston, SC, 1969 [1854]), 86–7; *The Education of Henry Adams* (Boston, 1974), 59–60; Briggs and Benario, eds., *Gildersleeve,* 4–5. Meyer Reinhold found Samuel Miller's book "superficial and flawed": "Survey of the Scholarship on Classical Traditions in Early America," in John W. Eadie, ed., *Classical Traditions in Early America* (Ann Arbor, MI, 1976), 3. For evidence against C. F. Adams's assertion see Reinhold, *Classica Americana,* 282–3; Randolph quoted in "Early Recollections of John Randolph," *SLM,* 28 (1859), 464. See also F. V. N. Painter, "Education in the Southern Colonies," *SBN,* 10:195; Richard Beale Davis, *Intellectual Life in Jefferson's Virginia, 1790–1830* (Chapel Hill, NC, 1964), 111–12. William J. Grayson, however, saw impressive progress in classical education: Richard J. Calhoun, ed., *Witness to Sorrow: The Antebellum Autobiography of William J. Grayson* (Columbia, SC, 1990), 65–7. For Jefferson see Gummere, *American Colonial Mind and Classical Tradition,* 9, 62–3; Douglas L. Wilson, "The American Agricola: Jefferson's Agrarianism and the Classical Tradition," *South Atlantic Quarterly,* 80 (1981), 343.

   For the "deep classical training of Southern intellectuals" and their command of the original languages see Drew Harrington, "Classical Antiquity and the Proslavery Argument," *Slavery and Abolition,* 10 (1989), 70; also, Durrill, "Power of Ancient Words," 471, and Sidney J. Cohen, *Three Notable Ante-Bellum Magazines of South Carolina* (Columbia, SC, 1915), 14. For vignettes see George W. Paschal, *Ninety-Four Years: Agnes Paschal* (Spartanburg, SC, 1974 [1871]), 279–80; Henry Howe, *Historical Collections of Virginia* (Charleston, SC, 1847), 197–8. For protests against the fakery of ill-educated Southerners, see Frederick A. Porcher, "The Nature and the Claims of Paradox," *RM,* 1 (1857), 487; Robert Barnwell, Jr., to Waddy Thompson, July 17, 1860, in Waddy Thompson Papers, at USC; "Classical Study," in Ward W. Briggs, Jr., ed., *The Selected Classical Papers of Basil Lanneau Gildersleeve* (Atlanta, GA, 1992), 44–6. For the circulation of Greek and Latin works in English see also Supplementary References: "Translations."

[11] Reinhold, *Classica Americana,* 118–19, 216 (Houston), 224–5; Richard, *Founders and the Classics,* 36–7 (Washington). J. Drew Harrington has found Clay's frequent references to ancient history and literature accurate: "Henry Clay and the Classics," *Filson Club Quarterly,* 61 (1987), 239, 246.

At the end of the eighteenth century, classical knowledge had been widespread among southern middling folk as well as gentlemen, and down to secession they continued to receive a solid classical education. In Virginia, William Byrd, a big planter, and George Wythe Randolph, a leading educator, read some Greek and Latin every day. Byrd added Hebrew and also had French, Italian, and Dutch. A number of planters and merchants read throughout their lives, among them Landon Carter, Charles Cotesworth Pinckney, David and Louisa McCord, Jefferson Davis, John C. Breckenridge, and Henry Winter Davis, as well as Mirabeau B. Lamar, president of the Republic of Texas, and Dr. J. G. M. Ramsey, Tennessee's leading historian. After the War, Robert E. Lee examined students at Washington College in Greek. Henry Timrod and his friends spoke, read, and played word games in Latin. John G. ("Ghost") Eliot, who taught at fine academies, conversed in Greek with his former classmate, James Knox Polk. Edwin Holland of Charleston put his classical knowledge to work in his *Refutation of the Calumnies Circulated against the Southern and Western States, Respecting the Institution of Slavery* (1822), and a good many classically informed proslavery pamphlets followed suit.[12]

A small but noticeable number of Southerners enhanced command of Latin and Greek with knowledge of Hebrew. During the eighteenth century, Nicholas Trott, first chief justice of South Carolina, drew on Hebrew as well as Greek and Latin to transform his charges to grand juries into lectures on natural law. In later years the Reverends Basil Manly, Jr., James Boyce, George Buist, and Francis Sampson acquired reputations as Hebrew scholars, and such laymen as John Fletcher, Samuel Cartwright, and L. L. Gibbes drew on their reading knowledge of Hebrew for proslavery arguments. Despite early resistance, Presbyterian, Episcopalian, and other theological seminaries required Hebrew and Greek. Baptist and Methodist seminaries also taught both, and some secular colleges offered Hebrew. The Presbyterian Reverends Robert Dabney and James Henley Thornwell and the Unitarian

---

[12] Byrd may well have been the unnamed collaborator with William Burnaby on a translation of his lifelong favorite Petronius: Louis B. Wright, ed., *The Prose Works of William Byrd of Westover: Narrative of a Colonial Virginian* (Cambridge, MA, 1966), 4, 11. George C. Rogers, Jr., *Charleston in the Age of the Pinckneys* (Columbia, SC, 1980), 122–3; George Green Shackelford, *George Wythe Randolph and the Confederate Elite* (Athens, GA, 1988), 34; David McCord to William Porcher Miles, Oct. 15, 1846, in W. P. Miles Papers, at UNC-SHC; William C. Preston to Waddy Thompson, July 17, 18??, in Preston Papers, at USC; William C. Davis, *Jefferson Davis: The Man and His Hour* (New York, 1991), 7, 14, 16, 20–1, 82; Capt. R. E. Lee, *The Recollections and Letters of General Robert E. Lee, by His Son* (New York, 1904), 213–14, 314; William J. Cooper, Jr., *Jefferson Davis, American* (New York, 2000), 18, 25; J. William Jones, *Personal Reminiscences of General Robert E. Lee* (Baton Rouge, LA, 1989 [1875]), 248; William C. Davis, *Breckenridge: Statesman, Soldier, Symbol* (Baton Rouge, LA, 1974), 14; Bernard C. Steiner, *Life of Henry Winter Davis* (Baltimore, 1916), 17 n. 5, 42; Philip Graham, *The Life and Poems of Mirabeau B. Lamar* (Chapel Hill, NC, 1938), 6–7; William B. Hesseltine, ed., *Dr. J. G. M. Ramsey, Autobiography and Letters* (Knoxville, TN, 2002), 48, 52–3; Henry T. Thompson, *Henry Timrod: Laureate of the Confederacy* (Columbia, SC, 1928), 28–9; *DNCB*, 2:145 (Eliot). See also Dec. 30, 1842, and Jan. 1, 1844, in Ferdinand Lawrence Steele Diaries, at UNC-SHC; Samuel Agnew Diary, Aug. 31, 1863, at UNC-SHC. Since not every Latin teacher knew Greek, a local minister might tutor pupils: see e.g. Philip Slaughter, *A Brief Sketch of the Life of William Green, LL.D., Jurist and Scholar, with Personal Reminiscences of Him* (Richmond, VA, 1883), 14 n.

Reverend Theodore Clapp agreed that a minister without Hebrew and Greek placed himself at the mercy of a linguistically competent church establishment.[13]

The private academies that flourished across the South taught the classics to a substantial number of children from "middling" as well as affluent families, and every state had a few outstanding and long-lived classical academies: Mount Zion and Willington in South Carolina; Concord and Hanover in Virginia; Caldwell's Academy and Bingham's Hillsborough Academy in North Carolina; Richmond and Sunbury in Georgia; Greene Springs in Alabama; Elizabeth Academy in Mississippi; and others in Louisiana, Florida, and Texas. In South Carolina, the Reverend William Best's Academy counted among students who went on to distinguished careers Isaac Harby, a strong advocate of having ancient authors read in the original languages. Governor State Rights Gist of South Carolina credited Mount Zion's training in Greek and Latin for his easy entrance into Harvard. David L. Swain of North Carolina and Benjamin F. Perry of South Carolina, both upcountry rustics and future governors, had a first-rate academy teacher in Asheville, who delighted them by reading Homer aloud in class. Cassius Clay, who became an abolitionist, learned Latin in the Kentucky Bluegrass. In the most improbable places, dedicated and unheralded teachers educated the youth in their charge. William Lowry, Esq., an Irish Protestant graduate of Dublin University and a "thorough Scholar," tutored Thomas Bayne, who later graduated from Yale College and became a planter in Monroe County, Georgia. James Petigru Boyce, teaching theology at Furman College in South Carolina, recruited poor boys who lacked the requisite linguistic

---

[13] L. L. Hogue, "The Sources of Trott's Grand Jury Charges," in Herbert A. Johnson, ed., *South Carolina Legal History: Proceedings of the Reynolds Conference, University of South Carolina, December 2–3, 1977* (Spartanburg, SC, 1980), 25; for Trott (ca. 1662–1740) as a Hebrew scholar see also Richard Beale Davis, *Intellectual Life in the Colonial South, 1515–1763,* 3 vols. (Knoxville, TN, 1978), 2:575–6; Basil Manly, Jr., to Rev. and Mrs. B. Manly, Feb. 12, 1861, in Manly Papers, at UNC-SHC; William A. Mueller, *A History of Southern Baptist Seminary* (Nashville, TN, 1959), 89–90 (Boyce); William Buell Sprague, *Annals of the American Pulpit,* 9 vols. (New York, 1859–69), 4:74, 7:395, 768 (Buist); "Memoirs of Francis S. Sampson, D.D.," *DD,* 3:411, 428–30 (Sampson); John Fletcher, *Studies on Slavery, in Easy Lessons* (Natchez, MS, 1852); James Denny Gillory, "The Pro-Slavery Arguments of Dr. Samuel A. Cartwright," *Louisiana History,* 9 (1968), 210; for Gibbes see Lester D. Stephens, *Science, Race, and Religion in the American South: John Bachman and the Charleston Naturalists, 1845–1895* (Chapel Hill, NC, 2000), 101. Among those with good Hebrew see Louis B. Wright, "Richard Lee II, a Belated Elizabethan in Virginia," *Huntington Library Quarterly,* 2 (1938), 19; Francis Lieber, "On the Study of Foreign Languages" (1837), in Daniel C. Gilman, ed., *The Miscellaneous Writings of Francis Lieber,* 2 vols. (Philadelphia, 1881), 1:499–535; Charles Edward Leverett, Jr., to Milton Leverett, Apr. 13, 1858, in Frances Wallace Taylor et al., eds., *The Leverett Letters: Correspondence of a South Carolina Family, 1851–1868* (Columbia, SC, 2000), 63; "A Thoroughly Educated Ministry" (1883), *DD,* 2:656–77, 3:52; Theodore Clapp, "Discourse," New Orleans *Daily Picayune,* Feb. 10, 1850; *JHTW,* 3:429; [F. W. Lewis], "A Plea for the Study of Hebrew Literature," *SPR,* 9 (1855), 32–55; [B. M. Palmer], "Import of Hebrew History," *SPR,* 9 (1856), 582–610. *Southern Review* published an introduction to the study of Hebrew through a lengthy review of Moses Stuart's *Grammar of the Hebrew Language*: *SR,* 5 (1830), 5–32. The skeptics: Gildersleeve to Emil Hübner, Feb. 7, 1858, and Gildersleeve to W. D. Whitney, Mar. 6, 1858, in Ward W. Briggs, ed., *The Letters of Basil Lanneau Gildersleeve* (Baltimore, 1987), 33, 36; Henry Bascom, "Classical Learning Not an Essential Prerequisite to the Christian Ministry," *QRMECS,* 1 (1847), 357–8; "Craft's Fugitive Writings," *HLW,* 2:143. For Hebrew in southern schools see Supplementary References: "Hebrew."

skills, worked them hard, and demanded the excellence appropriate for Baptist preachers.[14]

From the long-settled Southeast to the rough Southwest, academy students read, in the original, Homer's *Iliad*, Plutarch's *Lives*, Caesar's *Commentaries*, Virgil's *Aeneid*, and selections from Xenophon, Cicero, Horace, Livy, Sallust, and possibly Plato, Aristotle, and Pliny. George McDuffie established the record at Willington Academy by memorizing 1,212 lines of Horace in ten days. In a single term at an academy in Richmond in 1860, Edmund Ruffin, Jr., had to recite 150 lines a day from Lucretius, six from Thucydides, an unspecified number from Livy – and a hundred lines from *Don Quixote*. South Carolina College required entering freshman to be able to read the Gospel of St. John in Greek, and the University of Georgia required substantial portions of Cicero, Virgil, Horace, Juvenal in Latin, and John's Testament and Acts in Greek. At Washington College in Virginia, students were required to read about a thousand pages in Greek. Even the University of Alabama, which shifted toward a military-school curriculum in the 1850s, required Caesar's *Commentaries*, Virgil's *Bucolics*, six books of the *Aeneid*, and six of Cicero's *Orations*. Southerners who attended the frequent public oral examinations took pride in the performance of the students.[15]

Throughout America, the education of girls and young women usually ignored Greek and Latin. Only an occasional Martha Jefferson Randolph learned Greek and Latin either at home or in one of the Catholic schools to which a surprising number of southern Protestants sent their children, especially their daughters. Varina Howell Davis, well educated in Greek and Latin, had been tutored for twelve years in Natchez. Sarah Clayton, from a planter family in Georgia, had insisted on being

---

[14] *SBN*, 10:276; John Hill Wheeler, *Historical Sketches of North Carolina from 1584 to 1851*, 2 vols. (Baltimore, 1964 [1851]), 1:ch. 7, 132; on Richmond see Lollie Belle Wylie, ed., *Memoirs of Judge Richard H. Clark* (Atlanta, GA, 1898), 217. Gary Philip Zola, *Isaac Harby of Charleston, 1788–1828: Jewish Reformer and Intellectual* (Tuscaloosa, AL, 1994), 10, 16; Walter Bryan Cisco, *States Rights Gist: A South Carolina General of the Civil War* (Shippensburg, PA, 1991), 20–3; on Swain and Perry see Clement Eaton, *The Mind of the Old South* (Baton Rouge, LA, 1964), 116–17; Benjamin Franklin Riley, *History of Conecuh County, Alabama* (Blue Hill, ME, 1964 [1881]), 30; T. Bayne, "Autobiographical Sketch" (ms.), 5–6, at UNC-SHC; T. George, "James Petigru Boyce," in Timothy George and Davis S. Dockery, eds., *Baptist Theologians* (Nashville, TN, 1990), 252–3; Hugh Wamble, "James Petigru Boyce," *ESB*, 1:184. On Wilson see Columbus Morrison, "Family Autobiography," opening page, at UNC-SHC; [George Frederick Holmes], "Munford's Homer," *SQR*, 10 (1846), 2. Southern classical academies advertised their ability to prepare students to enter college above the freshmen level, and the best did so: see e.g. E. Merton Coulter, "Meson Academy, Lexington, Georgia," *Georgia Historical Quarterly*, 42 (1958), 139–40; Elbert W. G. Boogher, *Secondary Education in Georgia, 1732–1858* (Philadelphia, 1933), 57. See the tributes in J. S. Buckingham, *The Slave States of America*, 2 vols. (New York, 1968 [1842]), 1:253–4, and Frederick Law Olmsted, *A Journey in the Back Country* (New York, 1970 [1860]), 130. Both *DBR* and *SQR* announced and evaluated Greek and Roman dictionaries, grammars, and anthologies.

[15] Our discussions of curricula are based on a review of academy and college catalogues, contemporary diaries and commentaries, and college histories. See also John M. McBryde, Jr., "The South Carolina College in the Late Fifties," *Sewanee Review*, 18 (1910), 334, as well as Supplementary References: "Classical Education."

tutored in Latin. A great many women read ancient history and literature in translation. After 1820 or so some female academies did offer Latin and a few Greek, and the best of them – Raleigh Academy (North Carolina), Judson College (Alabama), Wesleyan Female College (Georgia), Mary Sharpe College (Tennessee) – taught ancient history and literature and increasingly offered Latin or Greek as an elective alternative to French. Judson added Hebrew, and Mary Sharp required Greek. During the 1850s, the teaching of Latin in women's schools increased in the older states and the Southwest.[16]

Still, efforts to provide classical education for women met heavy opposition. Speaking for many, Charles Fraser, Charleston's eminent artist, condemned such teaching and deplored the curricula of the female institutes and colleges in general as unsuitable to woman's condition. Those who considered young ladies incapable of mastering the mysteries of the classical languages got some rude shocks. In far-off Texas in 1839, young ladies celebrated the news from Pendleton, South Carolina, where 13- and 14-year-old girls outshone the boys in an examination in Greek and Latin. The diaries and letters of the better-educated women of the elite – Mary Howard Schoolcraft; Phoebe Yates Pember and Emma Holmes of South Carolina; Catherine Edmonston and Mary E. Moragné; Cornelia Phillips Spencer of North Carolina; Margaret Junkin Preston of Virginia; Sarah Morgan of Louisiana – contain knowledgeable references to Greek and Roman myths and literature and some quotations from the original languages. Elisha Mitchell, geologist and Presbyterian minister, prescribed a course of classical study for his daughters. Seventeen-year-old Emma LeConte, Joseph's daughter, read Latin and taught it to her younger siblings. Latin was the favorite subject of Susan Dimock, who became North Carolina's first woman physician after the War. Jewish women seem to have been especially well read in the classics: Phoebe Yates Pember of South Carolina referred knowledgably to the military prowess of Hannibal and Caesar; Rachel Mordecai of North Carolina doted on the Greek myths; and Clara Solomon of Louisiana enthusiastically quoted Quintilian. Yet a classical education remained a luxury for ladies and never became part of the ideal of southern womanhood.[17]

[16] Davis, *Intellectual Life in Jefferson's Virginia*, 43–5; Frances Leigh Williams, *Plantation Patriot: A Biography of Eliza Lucas Pinckney* (New York, 1967), 109; Elizabeth Barber Young, *A Study of the Curricula of Seven Selected Women's Colleges of the Southern States* (New York, 1932), 4, 25, 54–7, 125–6; Mrs. I. M. Blandin, *History of Higher Education in the South Prior to 1860* (Washington, DC, n.d.), 82, 233, 238, 257; Clement Eaton, *Jefferson Davis* (New York, 1977), 23; Sarah "Sallie" Conley Clayton, *Requiem for a Lost City: A Memoir of Civil War Atlanta and the Old South*, ed. Robert Scott Davis, Jr. (Macon, GA, 1999), 57; Elizabeth W. Allston Pringle, *Chronicles of Chicora Wood* (New York, 1976), 50–1. Also, Archibald Thomas Robertson, *Life and Letters of John Albert Broadus* (Philadelphia, 1909), 331; Francis Terry Leak Diary, May 3, 1853, at UNC-SHC; Harold W. Mann, *Atticus Haygood: Methodist Bishop, Editor, and Educator* (Athens, GA, 1965), 7; Sarah Lois Wadley Private Journal, 1860, at UNC-SHC; Edgeworth Bird to Sallie Bird, Aug. 21 and 23, 1863, Apr. 19, 1864, in John Rozier, ed., *The Granite Farm Letters: The Civil War Correspondence of Edgeworth and Sallie Bird* (Athens, GA, 1988), 138, 141, 163; Richmond Female Institute circular for 1854, part of the Manly Letterbook, in Manly Papers. See also Supplementary References: "Women and the Classics."

[17] Fraser, *Reminiscences*, 110–13; Lester W. Ferguson, *Abbeville County: Southern Lifestyles Lost in Time* (Spartanburg, SC, 1993), 27; Newman Seminary Catalog, 1851; Fletcher Institute Catalogue,

Some young men and women, not all of them affluent, learned Greek and Latin at home – especially those from devout families, who wanted their sons to know the Greek version of the New Testament. The many rural and town folks who submitted their own poems to newspapers had to be careful not to plagiarize ancient authors, for even in frontier Alabama editors and printers would recognize (say) Horace in any disguise. Among accomplished Latinists, Edmund Pendleton, George Wythe, and Lewis Minor Coleman learned Greek and Latin from their mothers. The Baptist Reverend Richard Furman, who spent only the briefest time in school, acquired at home the basis for proficiency in Greek, Latin, and Hebrew. A few prominent men, notably Petigru and Representative E. S. Dargan of North Carolina, taught themselves Greek and Latin while working as laborers in their early years.[18]

Across the South, a broad agreement prevailed about the uses and, especially, the intrinsic value of classical culture, which many honored as an important guide to human affairs. Representative William B. Shepherd of North Carolina thought no European or American "who values his reputation for sanity" could doubt the importance of the classical languages and literature. Professor George E. Dabney of Richmond College, Virginia, defended the classics against the "wild innovator," who "would bid us fling away at once this rubbish of the past." William J. Rivers, respected for his teaching and writing on both ancient and modern history, linked the defense of the classics to demands for an American, and distinctly southern, literature. Judge J. L. Lumpkin of Georgia strongly endorsed the classical curriculum, but like many others he also pleaded for the addition of modern languages, civil engineering, and the sciences necessary to nineteenth-century life. Such divided loyalties were common as Southerners tried to balance the wisdom of the ancients with the needs and promises of modernity. In 1845, Benjamin Faneuil Porter counseled students at the University of Alabama against denigration of the present and

1854/55; Mrs. D. G. [Louise Wigfall] Wright, *A Southern Girl in '61: The War-Time Memories of a Confederate Senator's Daughter* (New York, 1905), 19; *DNCB*, 4:282 (Mitchell); Emma LeConte Diary, Feb. 28, 1864, in Earl Schenck Miers, ed., *When the World Ended: The Diary of Emma LeConte* (Lincoln, NE, 1987), 68; *DNCB*, 2:70 (Dimock); Phoebe Yates Pember, *A Southern Woman's Story: Life in Confederate Richmond*, ed. Bell Irwin Wiley (Macon, GA, 1959 [1879]), 111, 112; Maria Edgeworth in Edgar E. MacDonald, *The Education of the Heart: The Correspondence of Rachel Mordecai Lazarus and Maria Edgeworth* (Chapel Hill, NC, 1977); Solomon Diary, Mar. 13, 1862, in Elliott Ashkenazi, ed., *The War Diary of Clara Solomon: Growing Up in New Orleans, 1861–1862* (Baton Rouge, LA, 1995), 282; see also Caroline Gilman, ed., *Letters of Eliza Wilkinson* (New York, 1969 [1839]), 42.

18 William Wirt, *Sketches of the Life and Character of Patrick Henry* (Philadelphia, 1817), 47; on Wythe see also Herbert W. Benario, "The Classics in Southern Higher Education," *Southern Humanities Review*, 7 (1977), 17; J. L. Burrows, *The Christian Scholar and Soldier: Memoirs of Lewis Minor Coleman* (Richmond, VA, 1864), 19–20; William H. Pease and Jane H. Pease, *James Louis Petigru: Southern Conservative, Southern Dissenter* (Athens, GA, 1995), 7, 15; Sarah Woolfolk Wiggins, "E. S. Dargan," *EC*, 2:444. For the Greek New Testament as the one book students had to read in all four years see W. M. Wightman, *Inaugural Address Delivered at the Opening of the Southern University, Greensboro, Ala.* (Marion, GA, 1859). Dabney's proficiency in Latin owed much to the encouragement of his sister: Thomas Cary Johnson, *Life and Letters of Robert Lewis Dabney* (Carlisle, PA, 1977), 26–7.

romanticization of the past. The Reverend Joseph Cummings carried a similar message to students at Emory and Henry College: "Misplaced is reverence for the past age of wisdom. This is the true olden time."[19]

Frederick Adolphus Porcher, professor of belles lettres at the College of Charleston, opened fire on the spurious classicism he saw in Hiram Powers's statue of Calhoun in a toga. "We asked for our statesman, and have received a Roman senator. We asked for the citizen of the nineteenth century, and have received a specimen of the antique. We asked for our Calhoun, the Carolina planter, and have received an elaborately carved stone." Porcher declared the pre-Reformation ages "dark" because they "shut themselves behind the veil of antiquity." Ignoring the voice of the people, "They lived for antiquity, wrote for antiquity," and posterity has rewarded them with derision. In 1858 Petigru's presidential address to the South-Carolina Historical Society touched directly upon such southern concerns: "The students of antiquity, under the name of conservatives, and the partisans of progress, under the banner of reform, wage an endless war."[20]

Defending the claims of antiquity, J. H. Lumpkin, Jefferson, Grayson, Legaré, Francis Lieber, and Thomas Roderick Dew viewed Greek language and culture as peerless for, in Lieber's words, "simplicity, purity, conciseness, vigor, beauty and elegance." Legaré found Greek literature and art "by far the most extraordinary and brilliant phenomenon in the history of the human mind." No translation could convey the "bitter and contemptuous emphasis, and the powerful effect" of Demosthenes' oratory or the "eloquent horror and astonishment with which Cicero exclaims against the crucifixion of a Roman citizen."[21]

[19] William B. Shepherd, *An Address Delivered before the Two Literary Societies of the University of North Carolina, June 27, 1838* (Raleigh, NC, 1838), 8; [Dabney], "Study of Ancient Languages," 329–39, quote at 331; Rivers, *Study of Greek Literature*, 3, 5, 14; Joseph H. Lumpkin, *An Address Delivered before the South-Carolina Institute at Its Second Annual Fair* (Charleston, SC, 1851), 36–8. Benjamin Faneuil Porter, *The Past and the Present* (Tuscaloosa, AL, 1845), 5–6; Joseph Cummings, "True Dignity of Human Nature," *SRCR*, 1 (1851), 155–7. "A Dialogue on Oratory," in Moses Hadas, ed., *The Complete Works of Tacitus*, tr. Alfred John Church and William Jackson Broder (New York, 1942), Sec. 12.22:752–3; Quintilian, *Institutio Oratoria* (LCL), 1:Bk. 2:21–2. Tacitus recommended ancient authors but combated fear of innovation. For rejection of the Renaissance's establishment of static ancient models of perfection, see "Intellectual and Moral Relations of the Fine Arts," *SLJ*, n.s., 1 (1837), 485, and William Allen, "Progress of Literature," *VUM*, 3 (1859), 128–33; cf. Régine Pernoud, *Those Terrible Middle Ages: Debunking the Myths*, tr. Anne Englund Nash (San Francisco, 2000), 25, and ch. 2.

[20] Frederick Adolphus Porcher, "Modern Art," in O'Brien, ed., *All Clever Men*, 321–2, 336; J. L. Petigru, "Oration Delivered on the Third Anniversary of the South-Carolina Historical Society," *Collections of the South-Carolina Historical Society*, 2 vols. (Charleston, SC, 1857–58), 2:9–10.

[21] Lumpkin, *Address Delivered before the South-Carolina Institute*, quote at 36; Calhoun, ed., *Witness to Sorrow*, 164; Hugh S. Legaré, "The Greek Language," in [William Gilmore Simms], ed., *The Charleston Book: A Miscellany in Prose and Verse* (Spartanburg, SC, 1983 [1845]), 290; *HLW*, 2:15–16; "On the Study of Foreign Languages," in Gilman, ed., *Miscellaneous Writings of Lieber*, 1:499–535; Thomas Roderick Dew, *Digest of the Laws, Customs, Manners, and Institutions of the Ancient and Modern Nations* (New York, 1884 [1852]), 150. Stuart considered Latin the greatest of languages and the embodiment of taste, elegance, and economy of style: *Classical Tongues*, 7–9. James Warley Miles and George William Bagby commended the annotated student editions prepared

The many southern defenses of the inimitable beauty of the ancient languages represented a direct – if not always explicit – attack on the proliferation of translations and flew in the face of a transatlantic tide. On both sides of the Atlantic, translations were everywhere. At Austin College in Texas, Professor Rufus William Bailey warned of the perils of even the best translation of Homer's *Iliad*. Translations simply would not do. N. C. Brooks of Baltimore wondered how people who read classical authors in translation hoped to profit much, and the private correspondence of slaveholders, including the politically prominent, indicates that many shared his wonder. Holmes, in his inaugural address as president of the University of Mississippi, dismissed translations from the Greek and Latin as caricatures that failed to impart "a thousandth part of the riches imbedded in those languages."[22]

During the eighteenth century, Southerners had begun to make their own contributions to translation. In 1846 Nathaniel Beverley Tucker, himself an able translator, lauded William Munford's translation of the *Iliad* as comparable to Pope's. Robert Howison, the historian, rated it superior to Cowper's, while George Frederick Holmes and Professor C. C. Felton of Harvard praised it as a credit to Virginia and the South. Governor John L. Wilson of South Carolina, author of *The Code of Honor*, translated in verse "Cupid and Psyche" from Apuleius' *Golden Ass*, winning plaudits from *Southern Quarterly Review* and *Magnolia* for his excellent annotated adaptation.[23]

by Augustus Sachtleben (principal of a classical school in Charleston) and President Brooks of Baltimore Female College: see [Miles], "Septem contra Thebas," *SQR*, n.s., 8 (1853), 514–20, and Bagby, *SLM*, 31 (1860), 160, 320.

[22] Rufus William Bailey, "Homer," *SLM*, 23 (1856), 109–12; R. D. Arnold to E. F. Finney, July 9, 1854, in Richard H. Shryock, ed., *Letters of Richard D. Arnold, M.D., 1808–1876* (Durham, NC, 1929), 68; T. J. Jackson to Thomas Jackson Arnold, Apr. 1856, and Jackson to Laura A. Jackson Arnold, Feb. 19, 1859, Apr. 23 and May 1, 1860, in Thomas Jackson Arnold, *Early Life and Letters of General Thomas J. ("Stonewall") Jackson* (Richmond, VA, 1957 [1916]), 301, 268, 279–80, 300–1; N. C. Brooks, "Greek and Latin Versification," *SQR*, 2 (1842), 72; George Fredrick Holmes, *Inaugural Address, Delivered at the Occasion of the Opening of the University of the State of Mississippi* (Memphis, TN, 1849), 16. "A." of Williamsburg, Virginia, accepted translations in principle but insisted that no satisfactory English translation of Plato existed: "Plato against the Atheists," *QRMECS*, 4 (1850), 387–8, 392; see also his own translation of Crito in *QRMECS*, 4 (1850), 544–53.

[23] Simms to G. F. Holmes, Feb. 3, 1846, in Mary C. Oliphant et al., eds., *The Letters of William Gilmore Simms*, 6 vols. (Columbia, SC, 1952–82), 2:139; [Nathaniel Beverley Tucker], *SLM*, 12 (1846), 445–6, 448–52; also, *SQR*, 9 (1846), 528; Robert R. Howison, *A History of Virginia from Its Discovery and Settlement by Europeans to the Present Time*, 2 vols. (Philadelphia, 1846), 2:465–6; on Felton see F. V. N. Painter, *Poets of Virginia* (Richmond, VA, 1907), 45. *Southern Quarterly Review* warmly praised Wilson's work from *Golden Ass* in 10 (1854), 236, as did *Magnolia*, n.s., 2 (1843), 112–13. Holmes felt compelled to defend *Golden Ass* against filthy interpretations and illustrations: [Holmes], "The Wandering Jew," *SQR*, 9 (1846), 84–5. Simms feared that it might, indeed, be too racy for the ladies but welcomed a new edition (1853) as marked by beautifully poetic moments and an aid "equally to history and philosophy": [Simms], *SQR*, 10 (1854), 235–6.

For Hugh Blair Grigsby as translator from the Greek, see Grigsby to Randall, Mar. 18, 1861, in Frank J. Klingberg and Frank W. Klingberg, eds., *The Correspondence of Henry Stephens Randall and Hugh Blair Grigsby, 1856–1861* (Berkeley, CA, 1952), 183–4. For leading classical scholars see E. L. Shepard, "Nathaniel Pope Howard," in W. Hamilton Bryson, *Legal Education in Virginia, 1779–1979: A Biographical Approach* (Charlottesville, VA, 1982), 305. O. H. Cooper, "Reminiscences

In defending the classics, southern conservatives spoke for a deeply entrenched slaveholding class, just as northern conservatives spoke for a declining commercial bourgeoisie no longer able to exercise cultural hegemony even over the industrial bourgeoisie of the heartland. By the 1830s the challenge to classical education was rising even in the South, and it grew stronger in the 1840s. Southerners who focused on economic development – W. F. Maury, Philip Lindsley, Thomas Grimké – pressed for reforms in southern education but made little headway. The University of Nashville's President Lindsley tried to rein in the classics in favor of courses on government, manufacturing, and commerce, as well as gymnastics and fencing. The German experience demonstrated to Stephen Elliott, a leading Charleston intellectual, the compatibility of teaching the classics while vigorously pursuing the sciences – but only with teachers of high quality. In 1838 *Southern Literary Messenger* published "The Learned Languages" by the influential literary impresario Mathew Carey of Philadelphia, who called for reform in teaching methods, reduction of time allotted, and (implicitly) restriction of classical languages to young men of the privileged classes. A university professor tartly replied that the South continued to value and study the classics in the original languages.[24]

Even in the South, some professors of theology and some laymen as well had long recognized a tension between Christianity and the classics, and the tendency to find the Greek and Roman classics alarming if admirable steadily spread. Resistance to the inclusion of pagan Greek and Roman authors in the curriculum had begun at Harvard in the seventeenth century; in the nineteenth century, Charles Sumner protested that the classics' military and nationalistic ardor was contrary to

---

of Colonel Ashbel Smith," *Alcalde*, 9 (1922), 1007; Elizabeth Silverthorne, *Ashbel Smith of Texas: Pioneer, Patriot, Statesman, 1805–1886* (College Station, TX, 1982), 231, 1007; O'Neall, *Bench and Bar of South Carolina*, 1:368–70 (King); 2:402–6 (Holland), 2:575, 577 (Walker); Thomas Smyth, *Autobiographical Notes, Letters, and Reflections* (Charleston, SC, 1914), 181 n. 5 (Howe). William Burke translated the *Aeneid* for *SLM*: 16 (1850), 145–63, 641–9; 19 (1853), 449–56. The drawings of John Izard Middleton, "the first classical American archeologist," reflected impressive classical scholarship: see Charles Eliot Norton's appraisal in Charles R. Mack, ed., *The Roman Remains: John Izard Middleton's Visual Souvenirs of 1820–1823* (Columbia, SC, 1997), 18–25. For Munford see [Holmes], "Munford's Homer," 1–45; *SQR*, 2 (1842), 273–4. *Southern Quarterly Review* published an excerpt, and *Southern Literary Messenger* recommended it as an ornament to Virginia: *SLM*, 1 (1835), 768–70, and 12 (1846), 61; for its reception see Davis, *Intellectual Life in Jefferson's Virginia*, 113. The Duyckincks of New York acknowledged the translation's grace and accuracy but regretted the want of "poetic gusto": Evert A. Duyckinck and George L. Duyckinck, *Cyclopaedia of American Literature*, 2 vols. (New York, 1856), 1:74–7. Reinhold has described it as "the most distinguished translation of a classical work by an American of the early national period": *Classica Americana*, 224–5.

24 Allan Nevins, *Ordeal of the Union*, 2 vols. (New York, 1947), 1:546–7; Clement Eaton, *The Freedom-of-Thought Struggle in the Old South* (New York, 1964), 217–18; Anne M. Boylan, *Sunday School: The Formation of an American Institution* (New Haven, CT, 1988), 54. [Stephen Elliott], "Education in Germany," *SR*, 4 (1829), 98, 101; Mathew Carey, "The Learned Languages," *SLM*, 2 (1836), 557–61, 693–6; also, Carey, "Learned Languages," *SLM*, 3 (1837), 11–13. "Plea for Classical Learning: Moore's Latin Prosody," *SLM*, 12 (1846), 30–3; [William J. Grayson], "Slavery in the Southern States," *SQR*, 8 (1845), 317; [Henry Charles Lea], "The Greek Symposium and Its Materials," *SLM*, 11 (1845), 625–30; Lucian Minor, "Study of the Latin and Greek Classics," *SLM*, 1 (1835), 213; [Poe], "The Classics," 231–3.

the spirit of the Sermon on the Mount. During the eighteenth century in Charleston, as elsewhere, some who acknowledged the *Iliad* and the *Aeneid* as great poetry rejected them as morally unsuitable tales of slaughter and oppression. Thomas Peck of Union Theological Seminary in Richmond said God had selected the Hebrews as His Chosen People, not the more civilized Greeks. Peck saw in Greek philosophy false belief and a tendency toward atheism, despite its contributions to intellectual development and rational thought as preparatory for the reception of Trinitarian Christianity. Opposition to classical curricula as pagan especially resonated through the South and Midwest. Thomas Smith Grimké denounced the classics as "un-American and anti-Christian," and Benjamin Johnson Barbour, speaking at Virginia Military Institute, declared the Bible – not the classics – the guide of human progress.[25]

Defense of the classics made strange bedfellows. In 1832, in a carefully worded address to the Literary and Philosophical Society of Charleston, the Catholic Bishop John England lauded classical education, denied that Greek and Roman authors could be properly understood in translation, stressed ancient history and literature as powerful antidotes to the dangerous cult of progress, derided the demand for a more "practical" education, and recommended Homer, Demosthenes, Virgil, Caesar, Horace, and Cicero as stylistic models. As for charges of ancient pagans' morally corrupting influence on southern youth, England wryly observed that all sensible educators and well-regulated schools expurgated works assigned to students. The Presbyterian Calvinist John Bocock of Virginia said Greek poetry breathed "a beautiful, refined and delicate taste" with a sinless passion that pointed toward redemption and that the great Greek writers – Socrates, Plato, Aristotle, Sophocles, Euripides, Pericles, and Demosthenes – prepared the world for the coming of Christ.[26]

---

[25] "The Place of Ancient Greece in the Providential Order of the World," in Thomas E. Peck, *Miscellanies,* ed. T. C. Johnson, 3 vols. (Richmond, VA, 1895–97), 2:202–16; George M. Marsden, *The Soul of the American University: From Protestant Establishment to Established Nonbelief* (New York, 1994), 42–4; Edwin A. Miles, "The Young American Nation and the Classical World," *Journal of the History of Ideas,* 35 (1974), 272; Reinhold, *Classica Americana,* 157–8, 194 ("un-American"), 237, 338; Benjamin Johnson Barbour, "Address Delivered before the Literary Societies of the Virginia Military Institute," *SLM,* 20 (1854), 526–8. On Latin as requisite for English see Francis Cummins, *The Spiritual Watchman's Character and Duty* (Charleston, SC, 1795), 17; Richmond Croom Beatty, ed., *Journal of a Southern Student, 1846, with Letters of a Later Period* (Nashville, TN, 1944), 67–8; Francis H. Smith, *Introductory Address to the Corps of Cadets of the Virginia Military Institute,* 2nd ed. (Richmond, VA, 1856), 11; Circular for Horner's Oxford Classical and Mathematical School, Nov. 23, 1860, in Henry Thomas Shanks, ed., *The Papers of Willie P. Mangum,* 5 vols. (Raleigh, NC, 1955–56), 5:378–9. Basil Gildersleeve, of all people, expressed doubts: *Hellas and Hesperia: Or, the Vitality of Greek Studies in America* (New York, 1909), 56–7. For Poe's affinity for "classical values" and romantic stance as an effort to recapture a classical worldview, see Darlene Harbour Unrue, "Edgar Allan Poe: The Romantic as Classicist," *International Journal of the Classical Tradition,* 1 (1995), 112–19. On the gradual shift away from the classics in the Midwest see Walter R. Agard, "Classics on the Midwest Frontier," *Classical Journal,* 51 (1955), 108–9.

[26] Sebastian G. Messmer, ed., *The Works of the Right Rev. John England, First Bishop of Charleston,* 7 vols. (Cleveland, OH, 1908), 7:337–70; C. R. Vaughan, ed., *Selections from the Religious and Literary Writings of John H. Bocock* (Richmond, VA, 1891), 539–40, 198–281, quote at 198. England

Yet even with expurgation to curb pagan influence, a problem remained. In 1842 a contributor to *Southern Literary Messenger* warned that even ancient writers like Juvenal, who launched "bold, impetuous, uncompromising" attacks on vice, inadvertently advertised them. The author admired Aristophanes but feared that his ribald style, brutal assaults on individuals, and exposure of the dark side of human nature would feed the popular penchant for vulgarity and make vice attractive to impressionable minds. The Episcopalian Reverends Philip Slaughter and Charles Minnigerode combated the tendency of educated Virginians to take Cicero, Horace, and other Roman authors as moral guides more or less equal to Jesus. Religious skepticism, even more than paganism, troubled Southerners, who admired the learning of Pliny the Elder but chafed at his scorn for Greek adulation of the gods and his failure even to mention Jesus or Christianity, while his *Natural History* exalted the natural world as god, "sacred, eternal, boundless, self-contained."[27]

Southerners delighted in histories of the ancient world as well as in the original sources. The popularity of Charles Rollin's *Ancient History* rivaled that of Gibbon's *The History of the Decline and Fall of the Roman Empire*. A best-seller in the early Republic, *Ancient History* had greater sales in Richmond than in Philadelphia. Rollin's picture of republican Rome as a model of virtue pleased those who sought a disciplined political order in America. Jefferson and Randolph, as well as John Adams, warmly recommended Rollin, and Poe studied his voluminous work in college. Rollin's popularity nonetheless slowly faded, although women's schools continued to assign him. Holmes found Rollin's history "amiable but weak … more suitable for the nursery than the library." Holmes also found John Gillies's *History of Ancient Greece, Its Colonies and Conquests* (1786) "weak and worthless," and

---

returned to the theme at Franklin College in 1840: Peter Guilday, *The Life and Times of John England: First Bishop of Charleston (1786–1842)*, 2 vols. (New York, 1927), 2:20–2, 37. For selection and expurgation see e.g. Alva Woods, *Valedictory Address … at the Close of the Seventh Collegiate Year of the University of the State of Alabama* (Tuscaloosa, AL, 1837), 36; Charles L. Coon, ed., *The Beginnings of Public Education in North Carolina*, 2 vols. (Raleigh, NC, 1908), 1:74–5. Hampden-Sidney assigned Horace in its grammar school, "the indelicate parts excepted": John Luster Brinkley, *On This Hill: A Narrative History of Hampden-Sydney College, 1774–1994* (Hampden-Sydney, VA, 1994), 55; also, James Edward Scanlon, *Randolph-Macon College, 1825–1967* (Charlottesville, VA, 1983), 61; for expurgated editions in the North see Winterer, *Culture of Classicism*, 91–2. Isaac Stuart, uncomfortable with censorship, asked students to interpret texts for themselves: Durrill, "Power of Ancient Words," 482–5.

27 H. B. Grigsby, "Oration," *SLM*, 29 (1859), 85; "L. M. B.", "Importance of Classical Education," *VUM*, 3 (1858), 111; "B.", "Greek and Roman Poets," *SLM*, 8 (1842), 372–3, quote at 372; Charles Minnigerode, "The Greek Dramatists," *SLM*, 9 (1843), 99–100; "Bulwer," *SLM*, 14 (1848), 234; Slaughter, *William Green*, 50, 57–8; Pliny the Elder, *Natural History: A Selection*, ed. John F. Healy (London, 1991), Bk. 2:2, 14, 20, 54; Dew, *Digest*, 359, 363. For Pliny's influence on Byrd's *Dividing Line* see Wright, ed., *Prose Works of William Byrd*, 24. King and Couper built on Pliny in their work on agriculture in South Carolina: Mitchell King, *The History and Culture of the Olive* (Charleston, SC, 1846), 15 and 28 (Couper). A few Southerners read Pliny the Younger, but many more knew of his account of Nero's brutal treatment of Christians from Foxe's *Book of Martyrs*. Philip Howard judged him second-rate and untrustworthy in social and political commentary: "Pliny the Younger," *SLM*, 10 (1844), 361. Even so, *Southern Literary Messenger* published Howard's translations of "Letters of Pliny the Younger": *SLM*, 10 (1844), 444–5, 505–6, 608–14.

a reviewer for *Southern Quarterly Review* fumed, "The transition from Gillies to Grote is like exchanging the drivelling loquacity of imbecile old age for the quick intelligence and vigorous reflection of inquiring manhood." Despite sneers, Gillies graced the shelves of the better private libraries in Virginia and became popular among southern college students and conservatives who appreciated its condemnation of republicanism as well as democracy. Gillies, a Scot, flaunted the virtues of monarchy, and his account of the difficulties in maintaining republican institutions in a democratic atmosphere influenced the Virginia constitutional debates. In the 1820s Nicholas Tazewell, among other conservative Virginians, recommended Gillies as a corrective to radical democratic illusions, and in the 1850s George Sawyer respectfully cited him as an authority for his own account of slave society in Greece.[28]

Southerners from Thomas Jefferson to George Fitzhugh and the intellectually sophisticated Mary Moragné (of upcountry South Carolina) were very much taken with Oliver Goldsmith's *History of Greece* and *Roman History,* which described gradual descent into opulence and enervation and attributed the ruin of Athens and Rome to their imperialism. Holmes, in contrast, regarded Goldsmith's history of Rome as "ludicrous" and "child's babble." The reaction to Rollin, Gillies, and Goldsmith showed that the more learned Southerners thirsted for heavier fare. Such readers embraced the scholarly Arnold Heeren, although he held Greek slavery responsible for squeezing out and degrading free labor. Dew accurately noted, "Heeren admits that without slaves in Greece the upper classes would never have obtained great mental pre-eminence." But Heeren had also written, "We may at least be permitted to doubt, whether they were too dearly purchased by the introduction of slavery." Southerners who cherished state rights and localism had to like Heeren's insistence that no single Greek city eclipsed all others.[29]

---

[28] For dismissal of Rollin and Gillies see [George Frederick Holmes], "Cimon and Pericles," *SQR*, n.s., 3 (1851), 341; [Holmes], "Athens and the Athenians," *SQR*, 11 (1847), 278–9; [Holmes], "Revival of the Black Arts," *MMQR*, 4th ser., 6 (1854), 205; [Simms] "Critical Notices," *SQR*, n.s., 1 (1856), 533, and [Simms], *SWMR*, 1 (1845), 149; [Holmes], "Grote's History of Greece," *SQR*, n.s. (3rd), 2 (1856), 89. For Gillies's *Greece* in Virginia see Davis, *Intellectual Life in Jefferson's Virginia,* 83; Hugh Blair Grigsby, *Discourse on the Life and Character of the Hon. Littleton Waller Tazewell* (Norfolk, VA, 1860), 74. Davis erred in asserting that Gillies exhibited "a strong Whig bias especially welcome to Jeffersonian Republicans." See also Supplementary References: "Modern Historians of the Ancient World."

[29] Harrington, "Antiquity and the Proslavery Argument," 63 (Jefferson); George Fitzhugh, "Oliver Goldsmith and Dr. Johnson," *DBR*, 28 (1860), 508–9; Mary E. Moragné Journal, Mar. 22, 1839, in Delle Mullen Craven, ed., *The Neglected Thread: A Journal of the Calhoun Community* (Columbia, SC, 1951), 114; [George Frederick Holmes], "Roman History," *SLM*, 12 (1846), 507–12, quote at 509. For imperialism and luxury see e.g. [Oliver Goldsmith], *Pinnack's Improved Edition of Dr. Goldsmith's History of Greece, Abridged for the Use of Schools* (Philadelphia, 1845), 164. Goldsmith cribbed extensively from Rollin and Temple Stanyan: see Jennifer Tolbert Roberts, *Athens on Trial: The Antidemocratic Tradition in Western Thought* (Princeton, NJ, 1994), 157. Schools across the South assigned Oliver Goldsmith's histories: Calhoun Winton, "The Southern Book Trade in the Eighteenth Century," in Hugh Amory and David D. Hall, *A History of the Book in America:* vol. 1, *The Colonial Book in the Atlantic World* (Cambridge, MA, 2000), 240; Young, *Curricula of Women's Colleges,* 4; Dale Glenwood Robinson, *The Academies of Virginia, 1776–1861* (n.p., 1977), 14; Coon, *North Carolina Schools,* 765–6, 786.

George Grote's *History of Greece* influenced southern thinking in part through the writings of Cobb, Sawyer, and others on Greek slavery, although Augusta Evans, a voracious reader, surprised herself by wading through the ten volumes. Grote's insistence on race and ethnicity as central to a scientific history reinforced leading southern notions; *Southern Quarterly Review* proclaimed his *History* essential to every library. With studies of ancient slavery attracting special attention, many leading commentators were generous in evaluations of the work of learned and talented antislavery authors like Henri Wallon (*Histoire d'esclavage dans l'antique*) and Edouard Biot (*D'abolition de l'esclavage ancién en occident*). Cobb and Campbell approved Wallon's emphasis on Christianity's humanization of ancient slavery, much as they approved the similar emphasis in Biot and in Traplong's *D'influence du Christianisme sur le droit des Romains.*[30]

Poe, among many, regarded Barthold Niebuhr as the greatest modern historian of Rome, a first-rate intellect, simultaneously artist and scientist, and "a truly great man." LaBorde commended Niebuhr's superior mind and original research. For Holmes, the erudite, penetrating, "incomparable" Niebuhr introduced "a new

Arnold H. L. Heeren, *Ancient Greece,* tr. George Bancroft, new ed. (London, 1847), 122–5; King and De Bow in *DBR,* 1 (Jan. 1846), 85; J. D. B. De Bow, *The Industrial Resources, Statistics, &c. of the United States and More Particularly of the Southern and Western States,* 3rd ed., 3 vols. (New York, 1966 [1854]), 1:332; Francis Lieber, *A Manual of Political Ethics* (London, 1819), 32, 181, 331; "Relations of the Ancient World," *SQR,* 5 (1844), 161–2, 179–80; "Condition of Women in Ancient Greece," *SQR,* 16 (1850), 325–6; "Oeuvres de Vico," *SQR,* 2 (1841), 409; Porter, *Past and Present,* 23. For Heeren's "profound" studies of North African peoples see William Brown Hodgson, "Grammatical Sketch and Specimens of the Berber Language," *Transactions of the American Philosophical Society,* n.s., 4 (1834), 36. *Southern Quarterly Review* discussed extensively the translation of Heeren's *Historical Researches into the Principal Nations of Antiquity* and other works. The editors praised Heeren's style and scholarship but did not think him suitable for the classroom: *SQR,* n.s. (3rd), 2 (1857), 458. Heeren laid responsibility for "the fall of Greece" to no small degree on the decay of popular religion. He agreed with scholars who blamed the subversive teachings of the philosophers but maintained that Greek religion was implausible and untenable to begin with: A. H. L. Heeren, *Ancient Greece,* tr. George Bancroft, 2nd ed. (New York, 1842 [1823]), ch. 16.

30 Augusta Evans to Rachel Lyons, Jan. 21, 1860, in Rebecca Grant Sexton, ed., *A Southern Woman of Letters: The Correspondence of Augusta Jane Evans Wilson* (Columbia, SC, 2002), 10. In *SQR* see: 11 (1847), 492; 12 (1847), 521–2, 523–31; [Simms], "Critical Notices," 9 (1854), 266, 536; [Holmes], 3 (1843), 109–42. See also [Holmes], "Grote's History of Greece," 89–124; *SQR,* n.s., 8 (1853), 264–5, and 9 (1854), 536; [Holmes], "The Bacon of the Nineteenth Century," *MMQR,* 4th ser., 5 (1853), 337; [Holmes], "Blakey's History of Logic," *MMQR,* 4th ser., 4 (1856), 527; "Critical Notices," *SQR,* 11 (1847), 492. *Southern Literary Messenger* also frequently praised Grote's history. For Wallon and Biot: Thomas R. R. Cobb, "Historical Sketch of Slavery," in Cobb, *An Inquiry into the Law of Negro Slavery in the United States* (New York, 1968 [1858]), ch. 2 (Egypt), ch. 5 (Greece), ch. 6 (Rome), ch. 7 (Christianity); [John Archibald Campbell], "Slavery among the Romans," *SQR,* 14 (1848), 431–2. Cobb trusted Wallon's authority on Egypt and the relation of Christianity to ancient and medieval slavery. Campbell invoked Wallon on the historical ubiquity of slavery: "Slavery throughout the World," *SQR,* n.s., 3 (1851), 305–39; see also A. B. Meek, *Romantic Passages in Southwestern History, Including Sketches and Essays* (Mobile, AL, 1857), 68; Agnew Diary, Apr. 1, 1864. Campbell also acknowledged his obligation to the "great erudition" of Wallon, Biot, and Traplong. On slavery as the basis of all ancient republics see, among many, "J.", "The National Anniversary," *SQR,* n.s., 2 (1850), 179–80. See also Supplementary References: "Modern Historians of the Ancient World."

and more scientific history," separating Roman history from a cobweb of myth. Niebuhr was a great historian and a great man who stood out in "an age of insincerity and pretension." Niebuhr downgraded politics, advancing the primacy of popular history and culture. By highlighting racial antipathies and struggles in patrician–plebean conflicts, he contributed to the emergence of racialist ideology, which required a scientifically accurate history of the ordinary peoples who constituted a "race."[31]

Henry Augustine Washington, addressing the Virginia Historical Society, credited "the immortal Niebuhr" with establishing the centrality of race and religion in Roman society. Greece, Washington added, showed that democracy worked only within a dominant race. The emphasis on race also emerged in the work of the French historian Augustin Thierry, who focused on the peasantry and the purported racial characteristics of the contending social classes. With Niebuhr, Thierry contributed to the shift in historical writing toward a social history that slid into racialist ideology. De Bow, Mitchell King, and contributors to *De Bow's Review* and *Southern Quarterly Review* treated Niebuhr as the foremost historian of Rome of their day, and Dew drew upon "the immortal labors of Niebuhr" to shore up his own doctrine of white superiority. Among the few who struck a discordant note, Simms dismissed the "coldly inquisitive" Niebuhr as a narrow empiricist: "We prefer one Livy to a cloud of such witnesses as M. Niebuhr."[32]

Southerners relied, above all, on Edward Gibbon's *The History of the Decline and Fall of the Roman Empire,* although it provoked howls of rage for its caustic treatment of Christianity: "While that great body [the Empire] was invaded by open violence, or undermined by slow decay, a pure and humble religion gently insinuated itself into the minds of men, grew up in silence and obscurity, derived new vigor from opposition, and finally erected the triumphant banner of the cross on

---

[31] [E. A. Poe], "Critical Notices," *SLM,* 2 (1836), 125, 127; [Poe], "The Classics," 228; [Maximilian LaBorde], "Rivers' History of South Carolina," *SQR,* n.s. (3rd), 2 (1857), 263–4. [Holmes], "Roman History," 508; [Holmes], "Niebuhr," *MMQR,* 4th ser., 7 (1855), 530, 535, Holmes noted (at 537) Niebuhr's debt to Aristotle and Cicero. See also "History and Constitution of the Early Roman Commonwealth," *SLM,* 14 (1848), 266. Holmes sadly acknowledged that Niebuhr's *The History of Rome* (tr. Julius Charles Hare, 2 vols., Philadelphia, 1844 [1826]) attracted only scholars: "Niebuhr," 548. For "the great Niebuhr" see Thomas B. Holcombe, "Moral Tendency of Goethe's Writing," *SLM,* 22 (1856), 186, and "L. M. B.", "The Past and the Present," *VUM,* 4 (1860), 259. James M. Walker of Charleston cited Niebuhr as authority on the significance of Twelve Tables for Rome's diverse races: *Theory of the Common Law* (Boston, 1852), 8. See also Supplementary References: "Modern Historians of the Ancient World."

[32] Henry Augustine Washington, "The Virginia Constitution of 1776," *SLM,* 18 (1852), 663–5, quote at 664. A review of Augustin Thierry's *Histoire de la Conquête de l'Angleterre par les Normandes* declared, "Of the work of M. Thierry we can hardly speak in terms of adequate praise. It is history as it should be – careful scholarship, a lively style and freedom from all prejudices": "Norman-Saxon History," *VLM,* 1 (1829), 367–8. Dew, *Digest,* 208, 216; [Simms], "Epochs and Events of American History," *SWMR,* 1 (1845), 111 n.; *DBR,* 13 (1852), 210; Mitchell King, *A Discourse on the Qualifications and Duties of an Historian* (Savannah, GA, 1843), 5–6; "Relations of the Ancient World," *SQR,* 5 (1844), 161, 178–9. Holmes praised Michelet's *Histoire Romain* in "Ante-Roman Races of Italy," *SQR,* 7 (1845), 265–84, but the editors would not recommend Michelet's "speculative dissertation" because it was not up to Niebuhr's standards: *SQR,* 11 (1847), 504–8.

the ruins of the Capitol." His biting irony was lost on no one, least of all southern Christians. Nor were they much assuaged by the evenhandedness of his judgment on Christianity's effects on Roman valor: "If the decline of the Roman Empire was hastened by the conversion of Constantine, his victorious religion broke the violence of the fall, and mollified the ferocious temper of the conquerors." But Albert Taylor Bledsoe suggested that Gibbon's "sophisms and sneers" at Christianity marred "the otherwise splendid pages of his *Decline and Fall*."[33]

In the 1840s few Southerners disagreed with Legaré that, among the historical productions of the eighteenth century, only *Decline and Fall* had withstood the criticism of the nineteenth. Holmes saluted *Decline and Fall* as "imperishable," "noble," and "classic," while he chastised Christians for failing to reply satisfactorily to Gibbon's skepticism, omissions, ambiguities, misrepresentations, and distortions. Criticism mounted in the 1850s, as J. Athearn Jones, J. H. Bocock, William Gilmore Simms, and Mitchell King charged that anti-Christian bias made Gibbon unreliable. Both the Catholic Bishop John England and the anti-Catholic Presbyterian Reverend Robert Breckenridge lashed out at Gibbon's derisive view of Christianity's triumph over the Empire. Gibbon's assault on Christianity carried much that Protestants applauded as directed against priesthood, monasticism, popery, bigotry, and the assorted evils associated with Catholicism. For the Baptist Reverend J. L Reynolds it was enough that Gibbon had ridiculed such papist errors as the doctrine of transubstantiation. Thornwell found good use for *Decline and Fall* in polemics against Catholics over the Apocrypha and the Immaculate Conception, and he noted its suggestion that a lack of idolatry made Islam in some respects preferable to Catholicism.[34]

---

[33] Edward Gibbon, *The History of the Decline and Fall of the Roman Empire*, ed. David Womersley, 3 vols. (London, 1994), 1:446; 2:511; chs. 15 and 16 esp. focus on Christianity. For a searching critique see Jaroslav Pelikan, *The Excellent Empire: The Fall of Rome and the Triumph of the Church* (New York, 1987); Albert T. Bledsoe, "Introduction," in Philip Slaughter, *Man and Woman; Or, the Law of Honor Applied to the Solution of the Problem, Why Are So Many More Women than Men Christians* (Philadelphia, 1860), xvii.

[34] Dew, *Digest*, 362; [Holmes], "Roman History," 507 (quoting Legaré and pronouncing it "noble"); [Holmes], "Gibbon's Decline and Fall," *MMQR*, 4th ser., 10 (1856), 323, 328–32; J. Athearn Jones, "Ballads of History – The Vision of Julian the Apostate," *SLM*, 17 (1851), 645; [Simms], *SQR*, n.s., 8 (1853), 255; King, *Qualifications and Duties*, 16–17; J. H. Bocock, "Divine Purpose in the Classics," *SPR*, 15 (1862), 36–7; also, [Thomas V. Moore], *SLM*, 20 (1854), 1; "H. C. M.", "The Doom of Paganism and the Fall of Rome," *SLM*, 14 (1848), 325–7; J. L. Reynolds, *Church Polity: Or, the Kingdom of Christ in Its Internal and External Development*, 2nd ed. (Richmond, VA, 1849), 208; "Romanist Arguments for the Apocrypha Discussed," *JHTW*, 3:419, 420 n. 1 (Thornwell did not cite Gibbon on the Immaculate Conception but see *Decline and Fall*, 3:180); Messmer, ed., *Works of John England*, 5:290; Robert Breckenridge in James C. Klotter, *The Breckenridges of Kentucky, 1760–1981* (Frankfort, KY, 1986), 89; "Not Ashamed of the Gospel," in *Sermons by the Right Reverend Stephen Elliott, D.D., Late Bishop of Georgia* (New York, 1867), 44; [Joseph M. Atkinson], "The Puritans," *SPR*, 15 (1862), 230. Hostility to Gibbon led to some absurd criticisms of his style by Breckenridge and J. B. Harrison, "English Civilization," in O'Brien, ed., *All Clever Men*, 78; [Park Benjamin], "Letters from New York," *SLM*, 15 (1849), 186; "Progress of Liberal Principles," *MMQR*, 33 (July 1851), 447. Tazewell did not like Gibbon's "diction," although he admired his scholarship; he despised Hume's politics but admired his style: Grigsby, *Littleton Waller Tazewell*, 81. A. A. Lipscomb

Although Gibbon did not disguise his hostility to slavery as immoral, inhumane, economically retrogressive, socially debilitating, and politically dangerous, Southerners found enough in his text to support their own views. Blanton Duncan of Kentucky, a conditional unionist, nicely summed up Gibbon's attraction for those who had the sectional struggle uppermost in their minds. Kentuckians know that slavery "is right and of divine origin – that it is no drawback on our prosperity and happiness. The greatest of empires, notably those of Rome, Greece, and Egypt, were slaveholding, and their highest civilization was during the strongest era of slavery." Duncan risked some liberties in associating Gibbon with his own assertion that "The decline and fall of the Roman Empire began with the abolition of slavery, and so does our decline begin through the attempts of the Abolitionists." The Reverend Thornton Stringfellow of Virginia even enlisted Gibbon to support his argument for the humane character of slavery in the Christian South. So too, Gibbon reinforced the conservative view, according to which democratic governments tend to become debased and collapse when too much power accrues to "an unwieldy multitude." Although few Southerners appreciated Gibbon's defense of hereditary monarchy as the best if not only bulwark against democratic excess, many lauded his contempt for the excess: "The multitude is always prone to envy and censure." And Gibbon supplied a running critique of the deadly effects of the high taxation required by imperial centralization.[35]

On slavery in Roman history, Southerners drew upon Gibbon cautiously. Christian Southerners found themselves in an awkward corner when antislavery men attributed the waning of ancient slavery to what Horace Greeley called "the advancing light of Christianity." Proslavery men had no problem crediting Christianity as a great civilizing force in overcoming, say, the corruption and moral decadence of the Romans, but they denied its responsibility for reforms for which they had little taste. They drew upon Gibbon and others who suggested that slavery's softening and decline had resulted primarily from economic pressures. Gibbon influenced southern racial thinking primarily by his impatience with the Tacitus-inspired fashionable romance with the barbarism of ancient Germans and by his description of the harshness of slavery among the Goths, Burgundians, and Franks. Gibbon admired the civilization of the Ethiopians, distinguished them from African Negroes,

---

mischievously took Gibbon's explanation for the success of Christianity as confirmation of its moral power: *The Social Spirit of Christianity, Presented in the Form of Essays* (Philadelphia, 1846), 14. John Randolph, upon his conversion, thought to burn the work of the infidel Gibbon but reconsidered: [N. B. Tucker], ed., "Mss. of John Randolph," *SLM*, 2 (1836), 462. Southerners had cheap and abridged editions of Gibbon: [Holmes], "Gibbon's Decline and Fall," 321.

[35] Duncan in Louisville (KY) *Daily Courier*, Jan. 14, 1861; Thornton Stringfellow, "The Bible Argument," in E. N. Elliott, ed., *Cotton Is King and Pro-Slavery Arguments* (New York, 1969 [1860]), 481–4, also 462 n. Stuart Robinson relied on Gibbon as historian of biblical slavery: *Slavery, as Recognized in the Mosaic Civil Law* (Toronto, 1865), 31; also Fletcher, *Studies on Slavery,* 289–90. James M. Walker cited Gibbon for the impact of Aristotle and the Stoics on medieval legal theory: *An Inquiry into the Use and Authority of Roman Jurisprudence in the Law Concerning Real Estate* (Charleston, SC, 1850), 11, 19. On slavery see Gibbon, *Decline and Fall,* 1:67–70, 152, 1007–8; on monarchy, taxation, and bureaucracy see 1:61, 181–8; quote on demagogy at 3:1024. Scholars now debate Gibbon's claim of excessive taxation.

and declared them olive-skinned Arabs. He agreed with his friend David Hume, whose generalizations reinforced scattered remarks in the *Decline and Fall* on black inferiority.[36]

Calhoun and Sawyer, among others, urged the *Decline and Fall* on those who asked for advice on historical reading. Gibbon's accounts of the Roman Empire in the East, the Vandals in North Africa, and the Muslims and other great conquerors reinforced his lesson on the Roman Empire in the West: Conquest breeds luxury, which breeds the relaxation of martial and civic virtues, which breeds decadence and decline. As secession and war approached, Southerners pondered another of Gibbon's favorite themes, elaborated with particular clarity in his extended treatment of the reign of Justinian: Nostalgic attempts to restore past glories fail.[37]

In reading Greek and Roman literature, educated Southerners sought aesthetic pleasure as well as moral guidance, and they especially admired the craft of the Ancients' literary style. Herotodus, whom many referred to as "the father of history," was no less the father of Greek prose, according to George Frederick Holmes. "No style of writing," Thomas Jefferson wrote his grandson, "is so delightful as that which is all pith, which never omits a necessary word, nor uses an unnecessary one." The finest models? Tacitus, "the first writer in the world," and Sallust. An Alabaman ordinarily critical of John C. Calhoun recommended his speech on banking to readers of the *United States Telegraph*: Calhoun had perhaps surpassed Tacitus "in brevity and perspicuity" and equaled Euclid "in certainty of demonstration." Quintilian won Southerners' respect for style but disdain for his separation of form from moral instruction and practical concerns.[38]

---

[36] Horace Greeley, *History of the Struggle for Slavery Extension* (New York, 1856), 1; Gibbon, *Decline and Fall*, 1:67–70. For especially influential expressions of the proslavery view see Dew, *Digest*, 306–7; [Campbell], "Slavery among the Romans," 391–432, and 400–3 on economic imperatives. For appreciation of Gibbon on the economics of Roman emancipation see also [Grayson], "Slavery in the Southern States," 345. Baron de Montesquieu's authority lent credence to the notion that Christianity had abolished slavery in Europe: *The Spirit of the Laws*, tr. Thomas Nugent, 2 vols. (New York, 1975), 1:Bk. 15.8. Gibbon, *Decline and Fall*, 1:ch. 9, 2:727–8; "Of National Characteristics," in David Hume, *Philosophical Essays on Morals, Literature, and Politics* (Georgetown, DC, 1817), 217–32. Thomas Cobb cited Gibbon on Germanic slavery: *Law of Negro Slavery*, cxi. A contributor to *Southern Literary Messenger* decried Roman aggression in Germany but said that it spread civilization to a barbarous people: "The Romans in Germany," *SLM*, 17 (1851), 37–44.

[37] Calhoun to Thomas J. Johnson, Mar. 20, 1836, in *JCCP*, 13:116–17; George S. Sawyer, *Southern Institutes; Or, an Inquiry into the Origin and Early Prevalence of Slavery and the Slave Trade* (New York, 1967 [1858]), 146–7 n. 1.

[38] Thomas Jefferson to Jefferson Randolph, Dec. 7, 1808, in Edwin Morris Betts and James Adam Bear, Jr., *The Family Letters of Thomas Jefferson* (Columbia, MO, 1966), 369; Alabaman quoted by Clyde N. Wilson in *JCCP*, 12:xxxvi; Quintilian, *Institutio Oratoria*, 4, Bk. 10, 1:32, 73, 101; "Classical Study," in Briggs, ed., *Classical Papers of Gildersleeve*, 44–5; George Fitzhugh, "Frederick the Great by Thomas Carlyle," *DBR*, 29 (1860), 152; [George Frederick Holmes], "History of Literature," *SQR*, 2 (1842), 495. For Holmes, Tacitus was the most "original" Roman historian, without whom Machiavelli could not have written: "Napoleon III and Augustus Caesar," *SQR*, n.s., 10 (1854), 4. According to Meek, Sallust was the most elegant Roman historian: *Romantic Passages*, 73. Poe lauded Thucydides, Tacitus, and Plutarch as stylists superior to modern historians: [E. A. Poe], "The Classics," *SLM*, 2 (1836), 227; see also [Holmes], "Gibbon's Decline and Fall," 341. Tacitus' style

The best-educated Southerners read Herodotus, Thucydides, Livy, Tacitus, Sallust, and Polybius, but many more learned ancient history from Plutarch's *Parallel Lives of the Noble Grecians and Romans,* reinforced by Shakespeare's plays – which drew heavily on it, as did such other favorites as Montesquieu, the French historian Charles Rollin, and especially Oliver Goldsmith. William Henry Holcombe of Natchez suspected that Plutarch's *Lives* had a greater influence on the development of human character and sentiment than any book except the Bible. In humble farmhouses *Lives* became a virtual bible, although usually in translation. In Virginia an edition of Plutarch was considered a handsome prize for a boy who led his class at school. Southerners valued Plutarch as a moralist who glimpsed the truths of Christianity, and his heroes struck a chord among southern gentlemen as models of heroic virtue who stood on principle and selflessly served the very people who scorned and persecuted them.[39]

From the Ancients, Southerners drew seemingly universal moral and political lessons of greatness and decadence, which they unflinchingly applied to their own society. John Francis Mercer, a prominent politician in early republican Virginia and then Maryland, read Suetonius' *Lives of the Twelve Caesars* as an indictment of Rome's extraordinary descent into "surpassing wickedness." Others found in Petronius' *Satyricon* a protest against the corruption of Nero's day, the passion for luxury, and an arrogant world conquest that generated social instability at home. Legal scholars – notably, Thomas Cobb and George Sawyer – mined *Satyricon* and Apuleis' *Golden Ass* for information on slave statuses and treatment. And since knowledge of Roman slave life comes almost entirely through the eyes of masters and other freemen, Petronius and Apuleis stand out for providing invaluable insight

has occasioned centuries of debate: see e.g. Ronald Syme, *Tacitus,* 2 vols. (Oxford, U.K., 1958), 1:v; T. A. Dorey, ed., *Tacitus* (London, 1969), Introduction, chs. 5 and 7. For Herodotus as "father" see Sawyer, *Southern Institutes,* 131; Howison, *History of Virginia,* 2:311.

    Poe admired Sallust and his *Jurgurthine War:* [Poe], *SLM,* 2 (1836), 391–3, and a contributor to *Southern Quarterly Review* hailed Sallust as the "greatest of Roman historians," whose *Catiline Conspiracy* and *Jugurthine War* sparkled with profound insights into human character: "History of Literature," *SQR,* 2 (1842), 512–13; "Mutual Influence of National Literatures," *SQR,* 12 (1847), 314. In criticizing Macaulay's essay on Catiline, "R. H. C." reexamined and supported Sallust's version: "Catiline's Conspiracy," *QRMECS,* 15 (1861), 521. The editors of *SQR* thought Sallust too philosophical to be understood by schoolboys and recommended that he be read before Tacitus, thereby suggesting that Tacitus, too, should be studied later: *SQR,* n.s., 12 (1855), 504. We cannot here discuss some writers who would deserve full treatment in a comprehensive study, but see Supplementary References: "Roman Writers" (*Appian* and *Nepos*).

39 W. H. Holcombe Diary, Jan. 31, 1855, at UNC-SHC; for Plutarch as prize see Susan Dabney Smedes, *Memorials of a Southern Planter,* ed. Fletcher M. Green (New York, 1965 [1887]), 9; Mary Hübner Walker, *Charles W. Hübner: Poet Laureate of the South* (Atlanta, GA, 1976), 30; [Holmes], "Cimon and Pericles," 341. Wirt admired Livy's depiction of "the grandeur of the Roman character": *Patrick Henry,* 13; for Plutarch's popularity see Reinhold, *Classica Americana,* 39, 152, 257. For the South see Walter B. Edgar, "Some Popular Books in Colonial South Carolina," *South Carolina Historical Magazine,* 72 (1971), 177; Roberts, *Athens on Trial,* 158; Paul A. Cantor, *Shakespeare's Rome: Republic and Empire* (Ithaca, NY, 1976), esp. 41–2, 67. For Plutarch's impact on European writers influential in the South, see Martha Walling Howard, *The Influence of Plutarch in the Major European Literature of the Eighteenth Century* (Chapel Hill, NC, 1970), 10–11, 46–52, 58–60, 60–3, 195.

into the perspective of the enslaved. In criticizing Rome's moral decadence while displaying pride in its accomplishments, Livy also foreshadowed Southerners' own ambivalence toward America. Livy had his eye on Rome's early greatness but feared that "of late years wealth has made us greedy, and self-indulgence has brought us, through every form of sensual excess, to be, if I may so put it, in love with death, both individual and collective."[40]

Southerners recognized the strong fictional element in the work of the ancient historians but admired them nonetheless. "T. C." found Livy's tales "silly" and "void of all authority," while Samuel Henry Dickson wanted to weep over the German critics' demolition of his "pleasant and spirit-stirring fictions." While crediting Livy with republican sympathies, Hugh Pleasants referred to his history as a "splendid romance" that "heightens hatred of tyrants." Patrick Henry must have agreed, for he read Livy through once a year, at least early in his life. Holmes turned on Plutarch as garrulous and full of devices and fictions. Yet Southerners defended the authenticity of the ancient sources upon which their own work depended, as did William Browne Hodgson of Savannah in his acclaimed history of the Berbers. The Baptist Reverend W. T. Brantley used Suetonius, a "Roman historian of undoubted veracity," as a reliable witness to the early history of Christianity. Thomas Caute Reynolds found "the gossiping Suetonius" valuable for the study of early Spanish ballads, and Frederick Porcher valued "the anecdotal, gossiping, scandal-loving Suetonius" as "the best illustrator of Tacitus." Charles Minnigerode lauded Herodotus for a "truly republican spirit."[41]

---

40 [John Francis Mercer?], "Essays by a [Maryland] Farmer" (1788), in Bruce Frohen, ed., *The Anti-Federalists: Selected Writings and Speeches* (Washington, DC, 1999), 621; for Suetonius on social life under Tiberius see *QRMECS*, 9 (1855), 8–9, 21; Cobb, *Law of Negro Slavery*, 101; Sawyer, *Southern Institutes*, xcii, 85, 101. Apuleis exposed cruelties excessive even for the times: see Yvon Thebert, "The Slave," in Andrea Giardina, ed., *The Romans*, tr. Lydia G. Cochrane (Chicago, 1993), 144. On imperial arrogance see Petronius, *The Satyricon*, tr. P. G. Walsh (Oxford, U.K., 1996), 113, and [G. F. Holmes], "Recent Histories of Julius Caesar," *SR* (Baltimore), 1 (1867), 395. On *Satyricon* and *Golden Ass* for approximations of slave voices see William Fitzgerald, *Slavery and the Roman Literary Imagination* (Cambridge, U.K., 2000), 3, 55–6. Samuel Davies found a forecast of Jesus in Suetonius' *Lives*: "The Mediatorial Kingdom and the Glories of Jesus Christ" (1756), in Ellis Sandoz, ed., *Political Sermons of the American Founding Era, 1730–1805* (Indianapolis, IN, 1991), 189; for Suetonius on the Christian clergy see "Have the Clergy Conferred Important Temporal as Well as Spiritual Blessings on Mankind," *SLJ*, n.s., 1 (1837), 163; Livy, *The War with Hannibal*, tr. Aubrey de Sélincourt (London, 1972), 15 (Editor's Introduction). For Livy's pessimism see Emilio Gabba, *Dionysius and the History of Archaic Rome* (Berkeley, CA, 1991), 20–3. For the reading of Suetonius in the eighteenth-century South see Davis, *Intellectual Life in the Colonial South*, 2:507, 576; Arthur Floyd Upshur and Ralph T. Whitelaw, eds., "Library of the Rev. Thomas Teackle," *WMQ*, 2nd ser., 23 (1943), 300.

41 "T. C.", "On Historical Authenticity," *SLJ*, 2 (1836), 189; Samuel Henry Dickson, "Difficulties in the Way of the Historian," *SLM*, 12 (1846), 107; Holmes, "Writings of Legaré," 341; [Holmes], "History of Literature," 514; [Holmes], "Napoleon III and Augustus Caesar," 12–27; Holmes, "History of the Working Classes," *SLM*, 21 (1855), 193; [Holmes], "Roman History," 510; Hodgson, "Berber Language," 25, and W. B. Hodgson, *Notes on Northern Africa, the Sahara and Soudan* (New York, 1844), 32; W. T. Brantly, "The Bible and the Word of God," in *Sermons* (Charleston, SC, 1858), 26; [Thomas Caute Reynolds], "Ticknor's History of Spanish Literature," *SQR*, n.s., 2 (1850), 101; Frederick Porcher, "Address," in *South-Carolina Historical Collections*, 1:113–14 n.; Minnigerode,

Tacitus offered generations of Southerners insights into the problems of their own times by delineating the latent resentments of the Roman masses and the menace their crowd psychology posed to the social order. From him, Southerners learned of Tiberius' shrewd remark that it is better to leave great vices alone than to manifest inability to suppress them. Tacitus had another asset: In *Germania*, intending to instruct Romans rather than to glorify barbarians, he celebrated the virtues of a primitive and vigorous people not yet corrupted by the negative side of civilization. Southerners who spoke as defenders of the family against Yankee barbarians reveled in Tacitus' linking of Germanic manliness, valor, and nobility to love for women and children, even as they disapproved of his hostility toward Christians.[42]

Sallust's *Jugurthine War* taught Southerners to condemn the corruption that had led Rome, Assyria, Persia, and Greece to ruin. Sallust called for resistance to demagogues like Catiline, who sought to rally the dispossessed masses. In 1848 a contributor to *Southern Quarterly Review,* warning of dire consequences from an American victory over Mexico, recalled Sallust's bon mot that it is easier to start wars than to finish them. And *Jugurthine War* gave secessionists a boost, for Sallust, a self-proclaimed moderate, admired men of action and despised temporizers. Robert Dabney singled out Sallust, as well as Horace, to denounce prodigality, covetousness, and the spirit of unbridled acquisitiveness as harbingers of social deterioration. Sallust preached a natural aristocracy of merit and, despite a reputation for personal corruption and greed, unsparingly exposed Roman crimes, vice, corruption, and bloodletting. Sallust, like Tacitus, harked back to Thucydides, whose bleak view of human nature foreshadowed the Christian doctrine of original sin. Tacitus, in particular, combined his gloomy view of human nature with a capacity to celebrate human achievement, courage, and strength. Tacitus and Sallust effected a fundamental shift in focus from public affairs to the judicious weighing of the strength and weaknesses of noble and base individuals. Senator Benjamin W. Leigh of Virginia pretended to leave open the question of whether Andrew Jackson

"Greek Dramatists," 98; [Hugh R. Pleasants], "Machiavelli – The Prince," *SLM,* 12 (1846), 641; Wirt, *Patrick Henry,* 4, 13; also, "History and Constitution of the Early Roman Commonwealth," *SLM,* 14 (1848), 267, 273. Hugh Blair Grigsby had Henry reading Livy "many times": *The Virginia Convention of 1776* (New York, 1969 [1855]), 145. On Americans' view of Livy as pro-republic see M. N. S. Sellers, *American Republicanism: Roman Ideology in the United States Constitution* (New York, 1994), ch. 13. Andrew G. Magrath quoted Suetonius, Sallust, and Pliny on the proper wife and mother: "The Condition of Woman," *SQR,* 10 (1846), 160–1.

42 Gian Biaggio Conte, *Latin Literature: A History,* tr. Joseph B. Solodow, rev. by Don Fowler and Glenn W. Most (Baltimore, 1994), 533–44, esp. 537–8; on the family see Stelio Cro, "Classical Antiquity, America, and the Myth of the Noble Savage," in Wolfgang Haase and Meyer Reinhold, eds., *The Classical Tradition in the Americas,* 1st vol. (New York, 1994), pt. 1:384–5. For Tacitus as a critic of corruption see Francis Walker Gilmer, *Sketches, Essays and Translations* (Baltimore, 1828), 68. Dew accepted Tacitus' account of the early Germans: *Digest,* 323–4. *Germania* provided a model for Charles Gayarré and Franklin Smith in their studies of American Indians: Gayarré, "Romance of Louisiana History," *DBR,* 3 (1847), 449–51; Smith, "Origin of the American Indians," 566–7. Porcher considered Tacitus invaluable for southern youth: "Address" (1857), in *South-Carolina Historical Collections,* 1:12–13.

would be remembered for good or ill: He suggested that, if for good, Jackson would find a Plutarch; if for ill – for abuse of power – a Tacitus or Sallust.[43]

Through the centuries Christians have applauded Flavius Josephus' *Antiquities* and *The Jewish War* for the use of Jewish tradition and for their rich data on early Christian history, but Jews themselves have distrusted the accounts of a Jew whose career many found distasteful. Southerners, from Samuel Davies to James Henley Thornwell, accepted Flavius Josephus as a reliable authority on Jewish doctrine, history, geography, agriculture, and politics. Some cited Josephus to demonstrate the existence and forms of slavery in Israel and even the presence of some black African slaves. As secession loomed, Josephus offered an inspiring account of the heroism of a small nation against the world's greatest power, although he duly stressed that it lost, in no small part, because of its internal divisions. Edmund Ruffin provided a poignant end point: Preparing to commit suicide after Appomattox, he pondered at length Josephus' account in *Antiquities* of the mass suicide of the Jewish rebels.[44]

Plato presented a unique challenge. From William Byrd II in the early eighteenth century, Southerners ranked the "divine Plato" among the greatest of philosophers, and an increasingly conservative South saw in his criticism of the Sophists welcome confirmation of his poor opinion of democracy. But Southerners distrusted much in Plato's philosophy and political thought. In 1856 a contributor to *Southern Quarterly Review* dismissed him, oddly enough, as a mere empiricist. Jefferson – for whom Epicureanism, properly understood, most approximated his own views – despised the *Republic*, probably more so because the orthodox Augustine considered Plato the greatest of the pagan philosophers and the father of theology. Jefferson believed that the neo-Platonists, Athanasius, and Calvin had corrupted the pure teachings of Jesus. He lumped Aristotle's *Politics* with Plato's *Republic* as examples of the system-building he considered methodologically unscientific, politically dangerous, and ignorant of the institutions necessary to sustain individual liberty. The Presbyterian Reverend Thomas Peck denounced the *Republic* as a mischievous appeal to abstract theories that project Utopias and undermine social order. The Plato who advocated a community of women and children disgusted Southerners; Francis Lieber called him a "communist."[45]

---

43 William Stith, *A Sermon Preached before the General Assembly at Williamsburg, March 2, 1745–6* (Williamsburg, VA, 1745–6), 33; "War and Its Incidents," *SQR*, 13 (1848), 1–54, quote at 6. *De Bow's Review* reviewed favorably a new translation of Sallust's *Jugurthine War*: *DBR*, 10 (1851), 595. Wirt was fond of quoting Sallust: *Patrick Henry*, 105 n., 177. "Christian Economy," *DD*, 1:12–15, 26; Sallust, *The Jugurthine War / The Conspiracy of Catiline*, tr. S. A. Handford (London, 1963), 35, 41. Saint Augustine cited Sallust and Cicero to insist that a republic had to be founded on justice: *The City of God*, tr. Marcus Dods (New York, 1950), quotes at Bk. 1:5, 10, and Bk. 7:3, also Bk. 2:17–21, Bk. 3:17, Bk. 5:12; [Benjamin W. Leigh], *Speech of the Hon. Mr. Leigh of Virginia on the Expunging Resolution* (Washington, DC, 1836), 3; Syme, *Tacitus*, 2:526, and regarding Sallust and Tacitus on human motivation see 269. On Sallust's shady political career see [Maximilian LaBorde], "Characteristics of the Statesman," *SQR*, 6 (1844), 115.

44 Davies, "Mediatorial Kingdom," in Sandoz, ed., *Political Sermons*, 185; *JHTW*, 3:560; Edmund Ruffin, June 16, 1865, in *ERD*, 3:936–40. See also Supplementary References: "Josephus" and "Eusebius."

45 Kevin Berland et al., eds., *The Commonplace Book of William Byrd II of Westover* (Chapel Hill, NC, 1996), 140 (#178); James Mercer Garnett, "Odds and Ends," *SLM*, 2 (1836), 357; "Oeuvres

Some well-educated Southerners apparently read the *Republic* as unfriendly to slavery, but others, who read *Laws,* saw that Plato accepted slavery as a feature of society. Cobb and Sawyer attributed to Plato as well as Aristotle the notion that slavery was essential to a sustainable republicanism based on freedom and equality of citizens. Dew, notwithstanding strong reservations, acknowledged Plato's intellectual greatness. Plato, like Aristotle and Xenophon, warned of the consequences of democratic excesses and mob rule and reinforced the common view that a free and sovereign rabble was capable of destroying society and incapable of creating a viable new order – and hence that the lawlessness of the people assured the emergence of a tyrant. Southern educators and theorists rested much of their social thought and their defense of slavery on that very idea.[46]

Southerners found much more in Aristotle than a defense of slavery, but proslavery polemists did find much in his *Politics* and *Nichomachean Ethics* to support their views. Hugh Legaré maintained that, for Aristotle, "The relation of master and slave is just as indispensable in every well ordered state, as that of husband and wife, or the other domestic relations." Holmes, explicitly following Dew, heralded the passage in *Politics* on some people as fit for slavery and taunted the abolitionists that no one had yet satisfactorily replied. Aristotle's definition of man as a political

de Vico," *SQR,* 2 (1842), 405; Porter, *Past and Present,* 21; *SQR,* 8 (1845), 259–60; Jasper Adams, *Elements of Moral Philosophy* (Philadelphia, 1837), 1–6. For the empiricist see "History of Philosophy," *SQR,* n.s. (3rd), 2 (1856), 223; Jefferson to Adams, Feb. 5, 1814, in Lester J. Cappon, ed., *The Adams–Jefferson Letters: The Complete Correspondence between Thomas Jefferson and Abigail and John Adams,* 2 vols. (Chapel Hill, NC, 1959), 2:432–3; Peck, *Miscellanies,* 2:162–3; Francis Lieber, *On Civil Liberty and Self-Government,* 3rd ed., rev., ed. Theodore D. Woolsey (Philadelphia, 1874 [1853]), 43–4. For Augustine on Plato see Werner Jaeger, *Humanism and Theology* (Milwaukee, WI, 1943), 46, 52–3. Henry Stuart Foote echoed Jefferson's sneers in *Texas and the Texans,* 2 vols. (Austin, TX, 1935 [1841]), 2:34. Benjamin Perry admired Plato but railed at his community of women: Stephen Meats and Edwin T. Arnold, eds., *The Writings of Benjamin F. Perry,* 3 vols. (Spartanburg SC, 1980), 1:468. For Jefferson on Plato see Dumas Malone, *Jefferson and His Time,* 6 vols. (Boston, 1962–81), 6:190–7; for Jefferson on Athanasius and Calvin see Edwin S. Gaustad, *Sworn on the Altar of God: A Religious Biography of Thomas Jefferson* (Grand Rapids, MI, 1991), 132. Most students knew Plato through *Gorgias,* admired as an attack on radicalism: see "Schediasmata Critica: Platonis Gorgias," *SLM,* 16 (1850), 350–1. For Jefferson on Epicureanism see Lee Quinby, "Thomas Jefferson: The Virtue of Aesthetics and the Aesthetics of Virtue," *American Historical Review,* 87 (1982), 352–6; Peter S. Onuf, "The Scholars' Jefferson," *WMQ,* 50 (1993), 684. Dew protested that the Epicurean characterization of the gods as indifferent to human events "virtually robbed man of the divinity": *Digest,* 58. R. H. Rivers expressed the common southern view of Epicureans as exponents of inordinate gratification of the appetites: *Elements of Moral Philosophy* (Nashville, TN, 1859), 41. For a broad critique of Epicureanism as a flawed response to the "absurdities" of Stoicism, see "Influence of the Fine Arts on the National Character," *SLM,* 30 (1860), 202–3, quote at 203. For praise of Aristotle over time see [J. F. Mercer?], "Essays by a [Maryland] Farmer," in Frohen, ed., *Anti-Federalists,* 563; "A Southron", "Thoughts on Slavery," *SLM,* 4 (1838), 737–47, esp. 738; "Ancient Greece: Her History and Literature," *SLM,* 14 (1848), 136–9; "History of Philosophy," *SQR,* n.s. (3rd), 2 (1856), 223; *JHTW,* 2:462–3, 3:663; Pendleton, *Science: Witness for the Bible,* 26; "Slavery in the Church Courts," *DQR,* 4 (1864), 522.

46 Cobb, *Law of Negro Slavery,* lvix, see also lx–x, 4–5; Sawyer, *Southern Institutes,* 14; [Campbell], "Slavery among the Romans," 417; Dew, *Digest,* 123, 209–10. Plato's *Republic* is not antislavery: see Glenn R. Morrow, *Plato's Law of Slavery in Its Relation to Greek Law* (Urbana, IL, 1939), 129–31. For Xenophon see also Supplementary References: "Greek Writers" (*Xenophon*).

animal provided a foundation for Southerners' political and social theory. Calhoun, who ranked Aristotle as a giant, advised young men to study his treatises on government, and in 1860 Senator James Chesnut invoked *Politics* to ground South Carolina's right of resistance in the formula that government is "natural and prescriptive – God-made, not man-made." Dew believed that Aristotle perceived "the great truth, that all governments perish by pushing to excess their peculiar principles," and that "The best government is a well-tempered popular constitution, in which the popular element is strong and active." So too, George Fitzhugh and others pointed out that Aristotle rejected Plato's notion of a community of women as contrary to the experience of mankind.[47]

Fitzhugh spoke for most southern commentators when he placed the "absurdities of Plato" at the root of the harebrained socialistic schemes of Louis Blanc, Pierre-Joseph Proudhon, and assorted Yankee radicals to remake the world. Aristotle, reinforced by a dose of Thomas Carlyle, provided the antidote. H. R. M. Garnett, in a straight-faced comment in *Southern Quarterly Review,* suggested that Plato's recommendation of a philosopher-king had had a fair test in the ill-fated ascendancy of the noble and generous Marcus Aurelius. Holmes weighed in against Plato as a dogmatic forerunner of Utopian dreamers, and a decade later he offered a qualification with which Fitzhugh probably agreed: Plato's wild, socialistic dreams, like those of modern socialists, should be understood as an earnest protest against the social and moral disorder of his times.[48]

And yet Southern Christians could not turn their backs on Plato, much less on Aristotle. A much weightier matter than slavery and politics hung over them. In answer to Tertullian's famous question, most southern commentators embraced

---

[47] "Constitutional History of Greece," *HLW,* 1:428–30; [George Frederick Holmes], "Some Observations on a Passage from Aristotle," *SLM,* 16 (1850), 193–4; [Holmes], "Slavery and Freedom," *SQR,* n.s. (3rd), 1 (1856), 74–5; [Holmes], "Philosophy and Faith," *MMQR,* 4th ser., 3 (1851), 191. Aristotle's theory of the natural slave has faced long-standing criticism: see Peter Garnsey, *Ideas of Slavery from Aristotle to Augustine* (Cambridge, U.K., 1996), 107–27. Some scholars interpret Aristotle as implicitly criticizing existing slavery: see Wayne Ambler, "Aristotle on Nature and Politics: The Case of Slavery," *Political Theory,* 15 (1987), 390–410; and Mary Nichols, "The Good Life, Slavery, and Acquisition: Aristotle's Introduction to Politics," *Interpretation: A Journal of Political Philosophy,* 11 (1983), 171–83. Antebellum disputants did not read him that way. Paul A. Rahe, *Republics, Ancient and Modern: Classical Republicanism and the American Revolution* (Chapel Hill, NC, 1992), 35; Calhoun to A. D. Wallace, Dec. 17, 1840, in *JCCP,* 15:389; Chesnut cited in "Horace Greeley's Lost Book," *SLM,* 31 (1860), 212; Dew, *Digest,* 210; George Fitzhugh, "Southern Thought – Its New and Important Manifestations," *DBR,* 23 (1857), 339; Fitzhugh, "The Revolutions of 1776 and 1861 Contrasted," *SLM,* 35 (1863), 719–20. For France see George Huppert, *The Style of Paris: Renaissance Origins of the French Enlightenment* (Bloomington, IN, 1999), 74.

[48] George Fitzhugh, "Black Republicanism in Athens," *DBR,* 23 (1857), 21–3, quote at 21; Fitzhugh, "The Politics and Economies of Aristotle and Mr. Calhoun," *DBR,* 23 (1857), 163–70; "Marcus Aurelius," *SQR,* n.s., 6 (1852), 360–413; [George Frederick Holmes], "Herder's Philosophy of History," *SQR,* 5 (1844), 276–8; [Holmes], "Bacon of the Nineteenth Century," 342–3. For attacks on Plato see also [Magrath?], "Condition of Woman," 152; [M. R. H. Garnett], "Life and Speeches of John C. Calhoun," *SQR,* 9 (1846), 215; "A South Carolinian", "Slavery and Political Economy," *DBR,* 21 (1856), 334; "Python", "The Relative Moral and Social Status of the North and South," *DBR,* 22 (1857), 228.

Athens in the service of Jerusalem. Thornwell, following Augustine, greeted Plato and Aristotle as harbingers of Christianity, crediting Aristotle's philosophy as the nearest approximation of the truth of Scripture and praising Plato's philosophy as a glimpse of the immortality of the soul. But there were rumblings. The Methodist John E. Edwards objected to considering Socrates, Plato, Plutarch, and other good men "sort of Christians by anticipation," and Thomas Smyth, Henry Bascom, Samuel Benedict, and J. S. Lamar – Calvinists and Arminians – held Plato and the neo-Platonists responsible for spawning Arianism and corrupting Christianity. Dew wavered over the Greeks' "indistinct" notion of the hereafter. Daniel Whitaker bypassed as fruitless the thesis that Plato prefigured Trinitarianism. William Archer Cocke denounced both Platonism and Aristotelianism as incompatible with Christianity.[49]

During the democratic upsurge from Jefferson to Jackson, John Taylor of Caroline, Edmund Ruffin, and A. B. Meek concluded that Greek political philosophers were humbugs. Greek models of government – aristocracy, monarchy, democracy – could serve only as negative examples for the United States, which had a splendid opportunity to create a genuine republic resistant to tyrant and mob alike. Still, Southerners of all stripes were not about to abandon the Greek legacy. In 1832, Jesse Burton Harrison of Virginia wrote in *Southern Review*, "The model of a republic for America is given by Pericles in his funeral oration in Thucyidides: it must be a republic that can incorporate refinement, taste, and luxury into a system of equality as available agents, or there must be provision for them as for friction in a machine." For Dew, the history of both ancient Greece and Rome taught the creative force of democracy and the evils of democracy unchecked: "Democracies never have strong police, in the modern sense of the term; every man is considered

---

[49] In *JHTW* see "Lectures in Theology" (1:27, 175–6) and "Discourses on Truth: The Ethical System of the Bible" (2:462); see also [Thornwell], "Plato's Phaedon," *SQR*, n.s. (3rd), 1 (1856), 415–29. John E. Edwards, "Christ in History," *QRMECS*, 8 (1854), 255; "Further Objections to the Doctrine of the Trinity Answered," *TSW*, 9:177–85; Bascom, "Classical Learning Not Prerequisite," 347–58; Samuel Benedict, *The Blessed Dead Waiting for Us: A Sermon* (Macon, GA, 1863), esp. 6; J. S. Lamar, *The Organon of Scripture; Or, the Inductive Method of Biblical Interpretation* (Philadelphia, 1860), 35–58. For appreciations of Plato's views on the soul see W. Carey Crane, "Speculative Philosophy, Cui Bono?" *SLM*, 10 (1844), 358; A. J. X. Hart, *The Mind and Its Creations: An Essay on Mental Philosophy* (New York, 1853), 47; "R. E. C.", "The Problem of Free Society," *SLM*, 27 (1858), 3; John V. Thomas, "Influence of Aristocracy on Religious and Civil Liberty," *SRCR*, 4 (1856), 239; James Warley Miles, *Philosophic Theology; Or, Ultimate Grounds of All Religious Belief* (Charleston, SC, 1849), pt. 2, ch. 5; for the Reverend John S. Grasty see William S. Powell, *When the Past Refused to Die: A History of Caswell County, North Carolina, 1777–1977* (Durham, NC, 1977), 409; Meats and Arnold, eds., *Writings of B. F. Perry*, 1:336; *RM*, 3 (1858), 89–90. For Augustine's influential evaluation see *City of God*, Bk. 8. Dew, *Digest*, 57; "W." [prob. D. K. Whitaker], "Pond's Plato," *SQR*, 11 (1847), 436–9, 441; Francis W. Pickens, *Science and Truth* (Frazierville, SC, 1849), 3, 6–7; [William Gilmore Simms], "Critical Notices," *SQR*, n.s., 2 (1850), 245–6; [William Archer Cocke], "Christianity and Greek Philosophy," *SPR*, 23 (1872), 208–10, but see also Cocke, "Moral Philosophy and Christianity," *SPR*, 22 (1871), 4, 25. F. W. Pickens insisted that the ancients lacked the doctrines of original sin and immortality of the soul but arrogantly pursued human perfectibility: Pickens, *An Address on the Great Points of Difference between Ancient and Modern Civilizations* (Athens, GA, 1843), 11–12.

a sort of police officer, and is bound to guard the public safety." Dew brooded that Athenian hegemony and wealth had encouraged citizens to loll at home and leave defense and war to mercenaries. Rome followed suit, ruined by the lack of a strong middle class and by dissension and threats against property. In the 1850s Campbell, Cobb, Sawyer, and John Fletcher combed both *Iliad* and *Odyssey* for evidence of the widespread existence of slavery. Fletcher added a learned but painfully dull linguistic tour de force on slavery throughout ancient Greece.[50]

Not surprisingly, different Southerners had different favorites among ancient authors. Former Governor James Hamilton of South Carolina declared Homer's poetry the "unapproachable great model," and at Austin College, Texas, Rufus Bailey declared Homer the sun and Virgil his reflective moon. William Byrd II, Samuel D. Davies, and Jefferson Davis, among others, doted on Virgil. Dew admired Virgil's understanding of the hereafter, and Calvinists, following Augustine, read Virgil as recognizing the coming of Christ. Virgil's *Georgics* appealed to Americans for its conviction that farming was the backbone of the republic and its exhortation to regenerate communities after long periods of warfare. Judge Joseph Lumpkin extolled Virgil as "the Sir Walter Scott of Italy" for his celebration of agriculture and rural life, and Fitzhugh quoted him at length on the responsibility of rich to poor. Especially to southern tastes, Virgil's *Bucolics* (*Eclogues*) offered the wisdom of the peasant-warrior as the source of his moral and material self-sufficiency.[51]

Horace enjoyed an especially wide following. "There has been no philosopher since Horace," roared the hyperbolic Fitzhugh, "and his philosophy is expressed in four words: 'Est modus in rebus.' " Horace criticized luxury, extravagance, and selfishness – as well as the foibles and weaknesses of slave masters – but he also

---

[50] John Taylor, *An Inquiry into the Principles and Policy of the Government of the United States*, ed. Loren Baritz (Indianapolis, IN, 1919 [1814]), esp. 71–146; E. Ruffin, Jan. 22, 1864, in *ERD*, 3:315–16; Meek, *Americanism in Literature*, 16; J. B. Harrison, "English Civilization," in O'Brien, *All Clever Men*, 82; Dew, *Digest*, 187, 189, on Rome and Carthage see 241, 268. [Campbell], "Slavery throughout the World," 314–15; Cobb, *Law of Negro Slavery*, lvix–lxii; Sawyer, *Southern Institutes*, 75, 86–7, 94, 97, and Essay III; Fletcher, *Studies on Slavery*, 281, 383–4, 526, 537–54; also, "B.", "Greek and Roman Poets," *SLM*, 8 (1842), 367–8; Homer, *The Iliad*, tr. Robert Fagles (London, 1990), Bk. 13: lines 281–2 (p. 272), and Bk. 15: lines 170–1 (p. 315); Dew, *Digest*, 51. See also J. Joubert, "Writers of Antiquity," *SLM*, 9 (1843), 31. Joshua N. Danforth proclaimed Homer "the prince of poets": "Influence of the Fine Arts on Moral Sensibilities," *SLM*, 10 (1844), 109. For the "Homeric Question" see, e.g.: *SQR*, 11 (1847), 486–93; "The Homeric Question," *SLM*, 13 (1847), 698–701; "Ancient Greece," *SLM*, 14 (1848), 132–3. Women knew Homer primarily through Pope's translations: Margaret Hayne Harrison, *A Charleston Album* (Ringe, NH, 1953), 67; Gilman, ed., *Letters of Eliza Wilkinson*, 42. Octavia Le Vert, however, quoted Homer and Virgil easily in Greek and Latin: Frances Gibson Satterfield, *Madame Le Vert: A Biography of Octavia Walton Le Vert* (Edisto Island, SC, 1987), 142–3.

[51] James Hamilton, "An Address on the Agriculture and Husbandry of the South," *Southern Agriculturalist, Horticulturalist, and Register of Rural Affairs*, 4 (1844), 303; Rufus William Bailey, "Homer," *SLM*, 23 (1856), 109–12, esp. 111–12; Berland et al., eds., *Commonplace Book of William Byrd*, 166–7 (#394); Dew, *Digest*, 57; *DBR*, 2 (846), 115; Samuel D. Davies, "A Classical Recreation," *SLM*, 37 (1863), 44; Augustine, *City of God*, Bk. 10:27. Lumpkin, *Address Delivered before the South-Carolina Institute*, 37; George Fitzhugh, "Southern Thought – Again," *DBR*, 23 (1857), 456–7. For the Fourth Eclogue as a foretelling of Christ see John Edwin Sandys, *A History of Classical Scholarship*, 3 vols. (Cambridge, U.K.: vol. 1, 3rd ed., 1921; vols. 2 and 3, 2nd ed., 1908), 3:5–6.

celebrated the individual's joy in communal activities. In *De Bow's Review*, Dr. W. Albert called upon Horace when insisting on the health of citizens as a public responsibility and proposing restoration of the ancient Roman public baths to prevent disease; he wanted new people's palaces, graced by masterpieces of art and including gymnasia, libraries, and lecture rooms. James Madison and Charles Carroll of Carrolton drew on Horace to justify the American Revolution and to warn against the susceptibility of the masses to demagogic rhetoric. Southerners enlisted Horace in the defense of slavery, the more easily since southern colleges had long made his work required reading. Slaveholders had to love Horace for his "I hate the common mob" and his famous reference, derived from Plato's *Republic,* to the multitude as "the many-headed beast." In 1854 Benjamin Johnson Barbour invoked him on patriotism and on the indelibility of one's country of origin on those who leave it. George Parsons Elliott of Beaufort, South Carolina, addressing the South Carolina militia in 1852, and, at the front a decade later, Captain Ujanirtus Allen, who would die at Chancellorsville, and Tally Simpson, who also died in battle in 1863, all quoted Horace: "*Dulce et decorum est pro patria mori*" [It is sweet and fitting to die for one's country]. And in 1864 Catherine Edmonston quoted Horace to express her bitterness toward the Yankees. In 1865, with the War lost, a disconsolate Mary Chesnut quoted from Horace's odes, "I have had my hour."[52]

Southerners could pay a man no greater tribute than to characterize him as "Roman." Thus, Thomas Jefferson called Nathaniel Macon of North Carolina, Speaker of the House of Representatives, "*the last of the Romans,*" and John Randolph of Roanoke called him "the wisest and best man" he knew. George Frederick Holmes, Hugh Legaré, and Macon himself exalted Cicero as a model republican citizen. David Street of Tennessee pronounced Calhoun comparable to Cicero, a statesman whose devotion to republican principles cost him his life but left for posterity a name that conjured up virtue and love of freedom. Alexander Stephens took Cicero's dialogues as the model for his *Constitutional View of the War Between the States.*[53]

The Episcopalian Reverend Jasper Adams, president of the College of Charleston, and the Reverend Theodore Clapp, leader of New Orleans' Unitarians, turned to Cicero to support their discussions of truth, duty, hypocrisy, friendship, honor, and piety. James Henley Thornwell, doyen of orthodox southern Calvinists, found "more affinity with the Gospel in Cicero, than in the whole tribe of utilitarians." *Southern Quarterly Review* and *Southern Literary Messenger* recommended Cicero

---

[52] *SLM*, 1 (1835), 712–14, and 2 (1836), 93–4; "B.", "Grecian and Roman Literature," *SLM*, 8 (1842), 371; for selections from Horace see e.g. *SLM*, 14 (1848), 506, and 16 (1860), 354; George Fitzhugh, "Mr. Bancroft's History and the Inner Light," *DBR*, 29 (1860), 608; W. Albert, *DBR*, 2 (1846), 228–39. For Horace on slave masters see Fitzgerald, *Slavery and Roman Literary Imagination*, 18. On Roman baths see Christopher Dawson, *Medieval Essays* (Garden City, NY, 1959), 35. Among the many invocations of Horace's bon mot on the impossibility of expelling nature (Odes, 3:1), see Dew, *Digest*, 78–9; [J. H. Bocock], "Bledsoe's Theology," *SPR*, 8 (1855), 526. See also Supplementary References: "Roman Writers" (*Horace*).

[53] For quotes on Macon see Wheeler, *Historical Sketches of North Carolina*, 1:xx, 2:39, 435–6; Holmes, "Writings of Legaré," 333–7; David A. Street to Calhoun, May 25, 1844, in *JCCP*, 18:619.

as the culmination of Roman moral ideas and font of the notion that duties must be the starting point for all philosophies worthy of the name.[54]

Occasionally, Cicero drew stinging criticism. Rome's legacy, wrote "R. H. C." of Eureka, Mississippi, "will be valuable only so far as it illustrates the works of Marcus Tullus Cicero," but, alas, Cicero ruined himself by being "vain" and "excessively proud of his services." A contributor to *Southern Literary Messenger* spoke of Cicero as a man "whose brilliant intellect understood everything while his faint heart believed nothing." James Walker of Charleston, a legal scholar of parts, lumped him unflatteringly with Plato, Locke, and Calhoun as men who dreamed of an ideal government and then demanded that existing governments conform. But more Southerners found Cicero congenial to their emerging version of a Burkean conservatism that relied on experience and probability. Cicero steadfastly sided with the aristocracy, warning that preservation of traditional values and a stable society depended upon the political flexibility only a morally sound aristocracy could provide. Cicero's political and social thought, however vague, enabled Fitzhugh, Sawyer, and Cobb to link his view of slavery to that of the revered Aristotle. And in *Magnolia*, "Aristeus" wrote of the Greeks and Romans who bore witness to "the principle of aristocracy, so deeply rooted in human nature, so inseparably linked with property and distinction."[55]

Thornwell cited Seneca – as well as Plato, Pythagoras, Cicero, and Claudius – in defining true slavery as voluntary surrender to sin. Seneca, in his celebrated Forty-Seventh Letter ("Slaves"), foreshadowed the southern version of the Golden Rule: "Treat your slave as you would wish your superior to treat you." His view of private property stressed the duties and responsibilities of propertyholders to the public at large. He condemned the mistreatment of slaves, insisting that well-treated slaves would fight for their masters: "We do not acquire them as enemies. We make them such." Seneca, well aware of growing slave violence, pleaded for humane treatment that would secure slavery by encouraging slaves to accept their lot. Jefferson Davis opened his *Rise and Fall of the Confederate Government* with Seneca's dictum: "*Felix et prosperum scelus virtus vocatur*" [A pleasing and rewarding crime is called a virtue].[56]

---

54 Adams, *Moral Philosophy*, title page, 11, 45, 56, 179, 253–62, 303; Theodore Clapp, "Sermon," New Orleans *Daily Picayune*, Mar. 19, 1848, and Oct. 27, 1850; *JHTW*, 2:492, 542, 586, 607–8, quote at 462.

55 "R. H. C.", "Catiline's Conspiracy," 523–4; "A Few Thoughts on Cicero," *SLM*, 16 (1850), 499; [James M. Walker], *Tract on Government* (Boston, 1853), 49. For Charles Pelham, Cicero lacked originality: "Cicero's De Officiis," *SQR*, n.s. (3rd), 2 (1856), 204–7, 213; Cicero, *De Officiis*, tr. Walter Miller (LCL), Bk. 1.8. Holmes, "Bledsoe on Liberty and Slavery," *DBR*, 21 (1856), 143; Fitzhugh, "Politics and Economies of Aristotle and Calhoun," 165–6; Cobb, *Law of Negro Slavery*, xcii; Sawyer, *Southern Institutes*, 69; Aristeus, "On Agriculture – As an Occupation," *Magnolia*, 3 (1841), 307. On Cicero's conservatism see esp. Syme, *Roman Revolution*, 319–20, 351; see also Supplementary References: "Roman Writers" (*Cicero*).

56 "Christian Doctrine of Slavery," *JHTW*, 4:417–19; "Letter 47," in *The Stoic Philosophy of Seneca: Essays and Letters of Seneca*, tr. Moses Hades (New York, 1958), 191–207, quote at 193. For admiration of Seneca the moralist see Christopher Gadsden, *The Times, Morally Considered* (Charleston, SC, 1843), 27; C. C. Jones to C. C. Jones, Jr., Oct. 15, 1860, in Robert Manson Myers, ed., *The Children*

The "universally admired compositions of Ovid," as *Southern Literary Journal* called them, also earned Southerners' admiration for their contributions to the philosophy of history and hostility to tyranny and absolute power. Southerners from Baltimore to Charleston read Ovid. Colleges and women's schools required students to read *Art of Love* and *Metamorphoses,* as teachers appealed to some of Ovid's love poetry for instruction in manners and language. He alone in Roman times followed the Greeks in asserting that women had as much capacity for and right to sexual satisfaction as men. Ovid acutely explored masters' fears of becoming dependent on their slaves, and Thomas Cobb and George Sawyer turned to him – and also to Horace, Martial, Livy, Nepos, and Pliny the Elder – for extended discussions of slavery in Roman social life and, specifically, for accounts of affectionate relations between Roman slaveholders and their house slaves.[57]

Ovid's depiction of sexual license, homosexuality, bisexuality, and other offenses against southern taste produced qualms, partially allayed by the praise of Ovid found in ancient and modern writers whom Southerners most admired: Tacitus, Dante, Tasso, Goethe, Corneille, Racine, Cervantes, and Pope. "B." praised Ovid's work but deplored its tendency to "effeminate and deprave the youthful mind." Joseph B. Cobb of Mississippi, a Methodist and an Ovid enthusiast, lamely censured *Art of Love* "for its pernicious counsels and sensual inclinations" and for the "splendid, vivacious diction and the glowing fervor of versification," which pervert youthful sensibilities. The Presbyterian Reverend William S. Plumer of Richmond agreeably recalled: "Ovid, in a grave work addressed to Augustus, advises the suppression of theatrical amusements as a grand source of corruption."[58]

Roman writing on agriculture attracted considerable attention, more for its moral aspects than its technical. Cato, in *De Agri Cultura,* depicted agriculture as a barrier to mean-spirited acquisitiveness and applauded landowners who lived on their estates as *patrofamilias* to all in their charge. Simultaneously, he wrote of slaves as virtual beasts of burden: to be driven, bought, and sold for economic convenience. His famous calculation that it paid to work slaves to death in seven years angered those Southerners who preached paternalism. The Reverend H. N. McTyeire condemned Cato's recommendation to dispatch old slaves, adding, "But that was two centuries before the Christian era, and among the heathens." More appealing to Southerners was Cato's insistence on corporate identity and solidarity

---

of Pride: A True Story of the Children of the Civil War (New Haven, CT, 1972), 615. On Seneca and slavery see Garnsey, *Ideas of Slavery,* 57–8, 68–9, 150–1, 239–40; Thebert, "The Slave," in Giardina, ed., *Romans,* 160–1; P. A. Brunt, *Studies in Greek History and Thought* (Oxford, U.K., 1993), 372. On property see Richard Schlatter, *Private Property: History of an Idea* (New York, 1951), 26. On Roman decadence see "S. A. L.", "Good Eating among the Greeks and Romans," *SLM,* 21 (1855), 714. Jefferson Davis, *The Rise and Fall of the Confederate Government,* 2 vols. (New York, 1958).

57 "J. P. W.", "Literary Coincidences," *SLJ,* 2 (1836), 452; Cobb, *Law of Negro Slavery,* ch. 6, esp. lxxxv–lxxxviii; Sawyer, *Southern Institutes,* 65–6 n. 2, 73, 87, 97. See also Supplementary References: "Roman Writers" (*Ovid*).

58 "B.", "Grecian and Roman Literature," 370; Joseph B. Cobb, "Roman Literature," *QRMECS,* 12 (1853), 90–2, quote at 91; William S. Plumer, *The Law of God, as Contained in the Ten Commandments, Explained and Enforced* (Harrisonburg, VA, 1996 [1864]), 493.

over individual presumption and on the slow growth of institutions over generations and centuries. Although Southerners got a smattering of Varro's philosophy through Augustine's *City of God*, they were more interested in his agricultural writing. Varro's scattered remarks on slave treatment reinforced the picture of slave life as grim. The "learned Varro" (as the Reverend James L. Reynolds called him), directly and through his influence on Virgil's *Georgics*, reinforced the notions that farmers made better citizens than townsmen and that free workers rather than valuable slaves should be given the most dangerous tasks.[59]

Cato's demand for the destruction of Carthage ("*delenda est Carthago*") shocked southern sensibilities. From John Francis Mercer in 1788 to the Reverend William A. Hall during the War, leading Southerners denounced the brutal policy of "that stupid old fool" and "that majestic and useless character." J. D. B. De Bow, who preferred commerce to war and plunder, ruefully mused that every schoolboy knew the genius and spirit of Rome to be military. De Bow expressed displeasure over the destruction of a Carthage he admired as a brave and resourceful commercial state. Other contributors to *De Bow's Review* commended Carthage's commercial spirit over Rome's aristocratic militarism, and J. H. Hammond, without mentioning Cato or Carthage, flayed the Greeks and Romans for their anticommercial attitudes. But it was Henry Watkins Miller of North Carolina's General Assembly who, in 1857, put his finger on the sorest point: Northern fanaticism was threatening to do to the South what "Roman cupidity and ambition" had done to Carthage. More critically, Mary Chesnut called the Carthaginians a "luxurious people" who "could not endure the hardship of war." The Reverend Henry Dennison noted that commercially great Carthage succumbed to a wild thirst for luxury: "The military genius of Rome triumphed over the base hirelings and undisciplined masses and factions of Carthage." The South, Dennison warned, would escape the vicious cycle Carthage epitomized only if it lived up to its professions of being a Christian society.[60]

---

[59] Cato, "On Agriculture," in *Cato and Varro*, tr. William Davis Hooper (LCL), sec. 5 (13–15); H. N. McTyeire, *Duties of Christian Masters*, ed. Thomas O. Summers (Nashville, TN, 1859), 120. For Jefferson's revulsion at Cato on slave labor see Harrington, "Antiquity and the Proslavery Argument," 62. For criticism of Cato's callousness see also [William Drayton], *The South Vindicated from the Treason and Fanaticism of the Northern Abolitionists* (Philadelphia, 1836), 30, and [Campbell], "Slavery among the Romans," 401–2. Thomas Clay of Georgia probably had Cato in mind in his protest against slaveholders who drove slaves mercilessly: see *Narrative of James Williams, an American Slave, Who Was for Several Years a Driver on a Cotton Plantation in Alabama* (New York, 1838), viii. Yet Cato called for proper feeding and other measures as necessary for profit maximization, and his slaves had more to eat than the average Egyptian peasant: see Dorothy J. Crawford, *Kerkeosiris: An Egyptian Village in the Ptolemaic Period* (Cambridge, U.K., 1971), 130. For Cato as reactionary see Arnold Toynbee, *Hannibal's Legacy: The Hannibalic War's Effects on Roman Life*, 2 vols. (London, 1965), 2:515–17. For Cato the Elder, Varro, and Pliny as guides for southern agricultural reformers, see Lumpkin, *Address Delivered before the South-Carolina Institute*, 37. Varro, "On Agriculture," in *Cato and Varro*, Bk. 1:sec. 17 (307). For Varro and Columella see Supplementary References: "Roman Writers" (*Varro*).

[60] [J. F. Mercer?], "Essays by a [Maryland] Farmer," in Frohen, ed., *Anti-Federalists*, 626–7; "A Few Thoughts on Cicero," *SLM*, 16 (1850), 496 ("useless"); William A. Hall, *Historic Significance of the Southern Revolution* (Petersburg, VA, 1864), 7; *DBR*, 1 (1846), 101, 200–1; De Bow, *Industrial Resources*, 1:302 (De Bow) and 3:27 (Hammond); Dew, *Digest*, 253; Chesnut Diary, Mar. 19, 1862, in

With countless other readers before and since, Southerners immersed themselves in Greek and Roman literature for insight into the human condition, and by no means principally to find support for slavery. Like the German historian Arnold Heeren, whom they much admired, they valued Greek comedy as political farce and for its record of social decay. In *Southern Literary Messenger,* Thomas Moore approved the satires of Juvenal and Horace, and he praised Tacitus for exposing the domestic corruption of Roman households. Joseph B. Cobb applauded Horace for directing his odes "against the growing effeminacy and degeneracy of the times" – a judgment implicitly sustained by the Presbyterian Reverend William S. Plumer of Virginia, who cited *Ode to the Romans* as saying, "Brave men are made by brave men." Holmes and Fitzhugh enlisted Aristophanes and Juvenal in polemics against woman's rights and free love.[61]

Southerners delighted in Greek and Roman exposés and satires of the demos, the seamier side of democracy, and the pandering of demagogic orators. Holmes, Fitzhugh, and Dew paraded the virtues of slave society and excoriated the vices of free society and the excesses of the Athenian demos. They reveled in Aristophanes' satires on ancient evils that were being replicated in the modern world. Dew loved Aristophanes' *Wasps* and *Clouds* for revealing the Sophists' destructive effect on morals. The comedies aimed "to make men better in the state, to admonish and instruct" and to "lampoon and ridicule the foibles and vices of individuals." From William Stith in the mid-eighteenth century to Jasper Adams and J. D. B. De Bow, Southerners summoned Juvenal's condemnation of Roman corruption, class rigidity, and passion for conquest and his warnings not to expect government to cure society's every ill.[62]

The sketches of slave life and master–slave relations in the Greek and Roman comedies pleased Southerners by upholding slavery while rebuking ill treatment of

C. Vann Woodward, ed., *Mary Chesnut's Civil War* (New Haven, CT, 1981), 31; Henry M. Dennison, "Commerce – The Harbinger of Civilization," *DBR,* 26 (1859), 156–8, and "The Commercial Spirit – Carthage," 28 (1860), 69–73. For pro-Carthaginian writers in *De Bow's Review* see J. Gadsden, "Commercial Spirit at the South," *DBR,* 2 (1846), 127, and W. P. Riddell, "Republic of Holland," *DBR,* 12 (1852), 284. For the Carthaginian peace see also Thomas Roderick Dew, *Lectures on the Restrictive System, Delivered to the Senior Class of William and Mary College* (Richmond, VA, 1829), 185–6; Henry W. Miller, *Address Delivered before the Philanthropic and Dialectic Societies of the University of North-Carolina* (Raleigh, NC, 1857), 27. Southerners admired Hannibal: see e.g. "Hannibal and Bonaparte," *SLM,* 14 (1848), 421–35.

61 Heeren, *Ancient Greece* (2nd ed.), 321–5; [Thomas V. Moore], "Christianity and the Fall of the Roman Empire," *SLM,* 20 (1854), 2–3; Cobb, "Roman Literature," 86; Plumer, *Law of God,* 359; [Holmes], "Philosophy and Faith," 200; [Holmes], "Grote's History of Greece," 116–17; on luxury and corruption in the satires, see also [Holmes], "History of Literature," 511–12; [Holmes], "The Sibylline Oracles," *MMQR,* 4th ser., 6 (1854), 498–9; Fitzhugh, "Black Republicanism in Athens," 21, 23–6. Edwin Taliaferro considered Aristophanes the best of those Greek writers who used their talent destructively: "The Poetry of Greece" (M.A. thesis, 1855, typescript at UVA).

62 [Holmes], "History of Literature," 493–4; [Holmes], "Cimon and Pericles," 344; Dew, *Digest,* 121–2, 124, 129–31, quote at 129; Stith, *Sermon Preached before the General Assembly,* 33; Adams, *Moral Philosophy,* 85, 172, 278–9; De Bow, "Some Thoughts on Political Economy and Government," *DBR,* 9 (1850), 262 n.; Porter, *Past and Present,* 33. See also Supplementary References: "Greek Writers" (*Aristophanes*).

slaves. Aristophanes displayed contempt for people who chose slavery over death. Plautus ridiculed caste class barriers but did not encourage social leveling; he projected, in the words of Erich Segal, an aristocracy based on "wit, not birth." Plautus' slaves never seek emancipation; indeed, clever slaves who betray rather than serve their masters end badly.[63]

George Sawyer of Louisiana derided the ostentation of wealthy Roman slaveholders, against whom "Juvenal, above all, aimed the poisoned shafts of satire." Sawyer praised Plautus' comedies for making readers "thoroughly acquainted with slave life on every side." John Archibald Campbell of Alabama, a respected associate justice of the U.S. Supreme Court, enlisted Plautus, as well as Juvenal and Martial, to inveigh against "debauched Romans" and the "explosions of their rage and violence" against brutalized slaves who "unquestionably endured great suffering" and "appalling experiences." Plautus and Horace, who found the slave trade abhorrent, lent credence to Campbell's claim that in all epochs slave traders called forth opprobrium from respectable slaveholders. Not even Cato's approbation overcame Roman antagonism toward slave traders, said Campbell, citing the "generally approved" advice of Plautus "to place no trust in those fellows."[64]

Slaves appear in Plautus' extant twenty plays of second-century B.C. and at the center of the plots in nine. Usually clever, some slaves look a lot brighter than their masters. *Captivi (Captives)* encouraged audiences to consider slaves human beings worthy of decent treatment. Slaves and lower-class freedmen who provided most of the actors in Rome built rapport with their audiences with frequent reminders that actors – slaves or no – would be beaten for poor acting.[65]

---

[63] Erich Segal, *Roman Laughter: The Comedy of Plautus* (Cambridge, MA, 1968), 13–18, 29, 104–5, 142, 166–7. Plautus was the most successful comic poet in the ancient world, and Shakespeare and Molière "found him indispensable"; the comedies of Menander, the Athenian "comic dramatist" who influenced Plautus and whose plays were produced all across the Greek-speaking world, followed Aristotle on slavery: David Wiles, "Greek Theatre and the Legitimation of Slavery," in Léonie Archer, ed., *Slavery and Other Forms of Unfree Labour* (London, 1988), 53–67; also, Konstan, *Greek Comedy and Ideology* (New York, 1995), 166.

[64] Sawyer, *Southern Institutes*, 79–80, 82, 90 n. 4, 93–5, 97, quotes at 65–6 n. 2, 95; [Campbell], "Slavery among the Romans," 395–6, 404–5, quotes at 404, 395; [Campbell], "Slavery throughout the World," 318. Cobb cited Juvenal frequently: *Law of Negro Slavery*, ch. 6. Leonard Bacon, antislavery Congregationalist pastor in New Haven, also noted the proslavery context of Juvenal's criticism of Roman slavery: Bacon, *Slavery Discussed in Occasional Essays from 1833 to 1846* (New York, 1846), 45 n. For the assignment of Plautus see e.g. McBryde, "The South Carolina College in the Late Fifties," 334.

Juvenal, like Seneca, upheld the humanity of slaves against those who sought to dehumanize them: Fitzgerald, *Slavery and the Roman Literary Imagination*, 7, and for Plautus and other satirists on the symbiotic relation of master and slave, see ch. 1. Kathleen McCarthy stresses "the investment socially dominant Romans had in Plautine comedy" and its view of slaves as "simple, playful, joyous": *Slaves, Masters, and the Art of Authority in Plautine Comedy* (Princeton, NJ, 2000), ix, 23. For slave traders as despised figures in Roman literature see Fitzgerald, *Slavery and Roman Literary Imagination*, 74–5.

[65] See esp. Timothy J. Moore, *The Theater of Plautus: Playing to the Audience* (Austin, TX, 1998), 3–4, 10–11, 40, 181–96. *Captivi* exposes the tension between notions of the innate slave inferiority of slaves and the slaves' flattering of the master's self-image by acceptance of enslavement: see William

David Konstan calls Plautus' *Asinaria* a superior example in Roman comedy "of sheer Saturnalian perversity, the elevation of the slave and humiliation of the master" in consequence of his sheer greed. In *Captives* a master and his slave, captured and enslaved together, exchange identities to allow the master to be released to carry home a ransom demand. The slave who assumes the role of the captured master suffers terribly but nobly when his captors discover the deception. In the end he is discovered to have been a freeman all along, illegally sold off by another slave, who is then sternly punished. "In this and in practically all Roman comedy," writes Bernard Knox, "the finale is a restoration of the characters to their proper station."[66]

Plautus' *Captives* reminded southern slaveholders of ancient slave revolts, which southern scholars thought frequent. Cobb, citing Herodotus and the antislavery Henri Wallon, mentioned a revolt at Tyre in which armed slaves "massacred the freemen, and took possession of the city." He added Tacitus and Cicero to suggest: "In every slaveholding state the intimate terms of companionship of the master and slave necessarily give the slave frequent opportunity for committing violence upon the master unknown to any other person." Cobb quoted Cato's "Our slaves are our enemies." Sawyer, pointing to "frequent insurrections among the slaves," concluded that Roman masters reasonably feared violent retaliation. He scored Roman slavery as uniquely brutal, recalling Tacitus' account of 400 slaves put to death for the murder of a master as well as the vicious treatment meted out by Roman ladies to female attendants.[67]

G. Thalmann, "Versions of Slavery in the *Captivi* of Plautus," *Ramus: Critical Studies in Greek and Roman Literature,* 25 (1996), 114, 116–17. For the clever slave who effects role reversal with his master, promotes dissipation, and undermines social norms, see esp. William S. Anderson, *Barbarian Play: Plautus' Roman Comedy* (Toronto, 1993), 76–7, 101, 113, 116, 134.

   Vulnerability to corporal punishment distinguished slaves from free men, and the comedies portrayed slaves as preoccupied with it. For harsh physical punishment of slaves (including torture) in Plautus, Juvenal, and other satirists see esp. Segal, *Roman Laughter,* ch. 5; Robert Saller, "Corporal Punishment, Authority, and Obedience in the Roman Household," in Beryl Rawson, ed., *Marriage, Divorce, and Children in Ancient Rome* (Oxford, U.K., 1991), 153. Cobb referred to Plautus frequently in his chapter on Roman slavery, and he cited *Captivi* in *Law of Negro Slavery,* lxxxvii n. and ch. 6; see also Sawyer, *Southern Institutes,* Essay 18 and pp. 70–1, 85–6, 95–7. For Plautus' popularity in eighteenth-century Virginia see George K. Smart, "Private Libraries in Colonial Virginia," *American Literature,* 10 (1938), 38. See also Supplementary References: "Roman Writers" (*Terence*).

[66] David Konstan, *Roman Comedy* (Ithaca, NY, 1983), quote at 55 (Asinaria), and 57–72; Bernard Knox, *Word and Action: Essays on the Ancient Theater* (Baltimore, 1979), 362. Greek comedy reinforced the notion that the slave may be beaten with impunity and so remains a "boy": see esp. Konstan, *Greek Comedy and Ideology,* 27. Plautus "ultimately validates existing social arrangements": Alalisa Rei, "Villains, Wives, and Slaves in the Comedies of Plautus," ch. 7 (99–108) in Sandra R. Joshel and Sheila Murnaghan, eds., *Women and Slaves in Greco-Roman Culture: Differential Equations* (London, 1998), 104. In Roman theater, Segal points out, quest for gold always has a specific end beyond accumulation for its own sake: *Roman Laughter,* 60, 100. This, too, would correspond with professed southern attitudes.

[67] Cobb, *Law of Negro Slavery,* lvii, xcii, xcvii–xcviii, also lxxvii; Sawyer, *Southern Institutes,* Essay 4, esp. 58, 97, quote at 111. J. W. Cummins, a northern Catholic, supported Sawyer: Cummins, "On Slavery, the Union and the Catholic Church," New Orleans *Daily Picayune,* June 2, 1850. Southerners frequently alluded to the murder of Pedanius Secundus, an Urban Prefect, in 61 A.D. and the execution of his 400 slaves.

Commentators said little about something they knew well: Most of Greece, including Athens, did not suffer from slave revolts, but Sparta faced constant danger from its helots. Prevention and suppression of helot risings obsessed the Spartans, who more than once appealed to Athens and other city-states for aid. Indeed, Thucydides maintained that Sparta's institutions arose in no small part to assure control of helots – a judgment some eminent scholars support. Its helots provided the material basis for a rentier state that perpetually assigned free men to military service. The Spartans impressed their helots into supplementary military service, rewarding them with emancipation. By the fifth century these numerous *neodamodeis* posed a danger to a state for which they had little affection.[68]

Southerners confronted the charge that slavery undermined Roman military spirit and contributed to imperial decline. The Reverends A. A. Porter and J. W. Tucker taunted Northerners that agricultural states prevailed militarily over commercial states: Sparta over Athens, Macedonia over Greece, Rome over Carthage. Thomas Cooper, John C. Calhoun, William Harper, J. H. Hammond, Samuel Cartwright, and Robert L. Dabney all asserted that slavery strengthened nations militarily. "The armies of the commonwealth of Sparta and Rome, the feudal barons of the middle ages," Campbell wrote, "exhibit the best specimens of soldierly bearing and personal prowess that history affords." According to Henry Hughes of Mississippi, the martial virtues of the Roman army declined after the pacification of the Mediterranean world and the deterioration of the "governing class" into little more than "a gang of robbers." If, as some said, slavery engendered "habits of indolence and effeminacy," the cause lay in the evil influence of excessive affluence on marriage and the family. Campbell and "H. C. M." of Virginia attributed the fall of Rome to the decline of religious spirit and credited Christianity with saving civilization from the ensuing ruins. The Baptist Reverend Dr. Basil Manly, however, refused to concede any relation between slavery and "indolence, voluptuousness, and profligacy."[69]

---

[68] Paul Cartledge, *Spartan Reflections* (Berkeley, CA, 2001), esp. ch. 10; Rahe, *Republics,* chs. 5–6; Donald Kagan, *The Outbreak of the Peloponnesian War* (Ithaca, NY, 1991), 10, 24–7, 30–3, 71, 79, 85–6, 121, and Kagan, *The Peace of Nicias and the Sicilian Expedition* (Ithaca, NY, 1991), 10, 46–7, 258, 294. Alfred S. Bradford denies that helotry and fear of helots were at the core of the Spartan system: "The Duplicitous Spartans," in Anton Powell and Stephen Hodkinson, eds., *The Shadow of Sparta* (London, 1994), 59–85. Southerners often conflated slaves and helots when discussing slave revolts.

[69] [A. A. Porter], "North and South," *SPR,* 3 (1850), 354; J. W. Tucker, *God's Providence in War: A Sermon* (Fayetteville, NC, 1862), 8–9; [Thomas Cooper], "Slavery," *SLJ,* 1 (1835), 193; Calhoun, "Speech on the Proposal to Extend the Missouri Compromise Line," in *JCCP,* 25:670; W. Harper, *SLM,* 4 (1838), 628; [Clyde N. Wilson], ed., *Selections from the Letters and Speeches of James H. Hammond* (Spartanburg, SC, 1978), 128; Samuel Cartwright, *Essays in a Series of Letters to Rev. William Winans* (Natchez, MS, 1843), 54; [Campbell], "Slavery among the Romans," 409–11, 415, quotes at 411, 415; Henry Hughes, ms. of speech on "The New Governing Class" delivered in Port Gibson, Mississippi (1856), in Hughes Papers, at Mississippi Department of Archives and History (Jackson); "H. C. M.", "The Doom of Paganism," 325–7; Dr. [Basil] Manly, "An Address Delivered before the Alabama State Agricultural Society on 7th December 1841," *Southern Agriculturalist, Horticulturalist, and Register of Rural Affairs,* 2 (1842), 339. Also, *DBR,* 10 (1851), 108; "The United States as a Military Nation," *DD*,* 4:124–5; E. A. Miles, "Old South and the Classical World," 266–7.

Caius Cassius, "a senator of great distinction," in Campbell's words, warned of the rebellious temper of Roman slaves and advocated extreme measures against "the scum of mankind collected from all quarters of the globe." Dr. Samuel Cartwright of Louisiana and E. A. Pollard of Virginia argued that Greco-Roman enslavement of whites violated God's racial arrangements and provoked rebellion from racially equal slaves. They congratulated the South for avoiding that error and for its efforts to lift up an inferior race.[70]

The influence of ancient texts on southern racial attitudes and rationalizations remains difficult to evaluate. Roman comedies did lend support to the southern stereotype of slaves as lazy and insolent, mendacious and untrustworthy, thieving and amoral. Medieval lords in Western Europe and Russia characterized their slaves and serfs in similar terms; masters of serfs and slaves agreed that they had a duty to rein in their dependents' immorality and vice. It was Herodotus who introduced the West to the idea of distinct ethnicities. In time the principal division perceived by Europeans separated the Anglo-Saxons, Celts, and Teutons from Mediterranean peoples. Pliny the Elder referred to Europe as "nurse of a people who have conquered all nations" and added that Italy became "the sole parent of all the races of the world"; neither he nor Cicero invoked "race" in its current meaning or as biologically grounded. Although Cicero sometimes suggested that some peoples seemed naturally fit for slavery, he wrote, "In fact, there is no human being of any race who, if he finds a guide, cannot attain to virtue." In later centuries racial ideologues pounced on such casual stereotypical judgments by ancients as Quintilian's reference to Asians as "naturally given to bombast and ostentation."[71]

Tacitus emerged as the spiritual father of Germanic and even of French racism. Jacques Barzun writes ironically, "Tacitus, if anyone, deserves burning in effigy for starting the powerful race-dogma of Nordic superiority." Although Barzun stresses that Tacitus had no such intention and, as Alan Davies puts it, "did not think in racial categories," promoters of the myth of Nordic moral simplicity and love of liberty built on Tacitus' claim that an unmixed racial stock explained the strength of the German tribes' social order. Ancient history reinforced the case for the historical ubiquity of slavery but not for white or Anglo-Teutonic superiority. When Greeks and Romans called other peoples "barbarians," they ranged far from the racialists of

---

[70] [Campbell], "Slavery among the Romans," 406; Cartwright, *Essays in Letters to Winans,* 9; Edward A. Pollard, *Black Diamonds Gathered in the Darkey Homes of the South* (New York, 1968 [1859]), 82; also, "A North Carolinian", *Slavery Considered on General Principles; Or, a Grapple with Abstractionists* (New York, 1861), 16–18, 24.

[71] Jacques Barzun, *The French Race: Theories of Its Origins and Their Social and Political Implications Prior to the Revolution* (New York, 1932), 11–12; Peter Mason, "Classical Ethnography and Its Influence on the European Perceptions of the Peoples of the New World," in Haase and Reinhold, eds., *Classical Tradition in the Americas,* pt. 1:145–8; Pliny the Elder, *Natural History,* Bk. 3:1.5, 39.42; Cicero, *De Re Republica; De Legibus* (LCL), 1:10.30; Quintilian, *Institutio Oratoria,* 4:Bk. XII, 10:17. On slave stereotypes see Victoria Cuffel, "The Classic Greek Concept of Slavery," *Journal of the History of Ideas,* 27 (1966), 333; Keith Hopkins, *Conquerors and Slaves* (Cambridge, U.K., 1978), 121; David Brion Davis, *Slavery and Human Progress* (New York, 1984), 32–3; Peter Kolchin, *Unfree Labor: American Slavery and Russian Serfdom* (Cambridge, MA, 1987), 94, 98, 100–1, 241–2.

later times. They enslaved and emancipated peoples of all races, usually explaining their inferiority as a consequence of environmental and historical circumstances.[72]

Accounts of the progress of civilization, southern commentators agreed, must begin with Egypt – "that acknowledged parent of the arts and sciences of Greece," as *Southern Quarterly Review* called it. Although Egyptian art generally portrayed both free and enslaved blacks as dignified figures, southern scholars claimed support for some of their pet contentions. Dew, Cobb, and Sawyer studied ancient monuments for evidence of Egyptian slavery and race relations. Dew, an admirer of ancient Egyptian civilization, accepted Herodotus' account of Egypt as peopled by "a black race with wooly hair" but insisted that the Egyptians themselves were "Shemites" who ruled over the black Africans in their midst. He concluded that several races inhabited Egypt and that "the one approaching to white was the ruling race, while the negroes were always subjects and slaves." Cobb claimed that Africans enslaved in Egypt 1,600 years before Christ "were the same happy negroes of this day," although he added, " 'Prejudice of color' does not seem to have been so great as at this day."[73]

Muddled racial debate wracked the Old South, as it wracks our own time. For Dew, Greece contained two "great races," the Dorians and the Ionians, with an insurmountable "gulf of separation" between them. He began his discussion of Roman history with the original racial elements in Italy, but neither there nor elsewhere did he clarify "race." With similar vagueness, John McCrady of the College of Charleston assured students that Greco-Roman achievements stemmed from racial superiority. Perspicacious Southerners saw a trap – a threat to white unity – in interpretations that placed some white peoples over others. R. M. T. Hunter, Jr., a student at the University of Virginia, worried about the "antipathies" of the Greeks toward "the so-called barbarian" peoples of Persia and other countries. General Felix Huston, speaking at the Nashville Convention in 1850, ridiculed Daniel Webster for saying that the ancient Greeks included racial arguments in defense of slavery. Nonsense, Huston retorted: Greeks enslaved mostly other Greeks. In the North, antislavery blacks and whites enlisted ancient history against racism by stressing the nonracial basis of Greek and Roman slavery. If Southerners advanced mutually exclusive interpretations, they closed ranks on the political essentials. From ancient

---

[72] "Germany and Its Tribes," in *The Complete Works of Tacitus,* tr. Alfred John Church and William Jackson Broder, ed. Moses Hadas (New York, 1942), 709–10; Barzun, *French Race,* 21–5; Jacques Barzun, *Race: A Study in Modern Superstition* (New York, 1937), 11, 27–8, quote at 11; also, Alan Davies, *Infected Christianity: A Study of Modern Racism* (Kingston, Ontario, 1988), esp. ch. 2, quote at 37. For a refutation of the interpretation of Tacitus as a racial thinker see Ivan Hannaford, *Race: The History of an Idea in the West* (Washington, DC, 1996), 81–2, and for Roman racial attitudes see chs. 1 and 2. On Greco-Roman racial attitudes see Frank Snowden, *Blacks in Antiquity: Ethiopians in the Greco-Roman Experience* (Cambridge, MA, 1970); A. N. Sherwin-White, *Racial Prejudice in Imperial Rome* (Cambridge, U.K., 1967), esp. 12–13, 32, 60–1, 101.

[73] [A. H. Everett], "Ancient Egyptians," *SQR,* 2 (1842), 5–55; "Relations of the Ancient World," 5 (1844), 158–9; "Mutual Influence of National Literatures," 12 (1847), 311; [Campbell], "Slavery among the Romans," 393–4; "General History of Civilization in Europe," *SQR,* 3 (1843), 3–7, quote at 4; Dew, *Digest,* 91–3; Cobb, *Law of Negro Slavery,* xlvi; Sawyer, *Southern Institutes,* 24. See also Supplementary References: "Ancient Egypt."

sources and the most prestigious historians of their own day, they found – to their own satisfaction – much of what they considered necessary to uphold their doctrine of the efficacy of slavery and their claims of white supremacy.[74]

Professor Maximilian LaBorde of South Carolina College told an apocryphal story of an old man left standing in a crowded Greek Assembly. A Spartan rose and yielded his seat, whereupon the Athenians erupted in cheers. "The Lacedaemonians," LaBorde remarked, "practice virtue, Athenians know how to admire it." Yet Athens held the hearts of many Southerners. Jennifer Tolbert Roberts, in *Athens on Trial,* finds "ironically, indeed," that the most positive reaction to classical Athens in pre–twentieth-century America came from southern proslavery theorists. She mentions Dew, Calhoun, Holmes, and Fitzhugh and could have added others. "The soil of Athens is consecrated ground" – so said Holmes in 1847, as he pronounced Athens' brief ascendancy the most fascinating of historical epochs. Meanwhile, *De Bow's Review* depicted Sparta as a precursor of the radicalism of the French Revolution of 1848.[75]

Dew attributed the decline of Greece to Athens' imposition of hegemony, with high taxation and levying of tribute. The demos used its power to soak the rich at home. A corrupt, volatile, rabble-controlled judicial system rendered private property insecure: "It was as dangerous to be rich under the Athenian democracy as under a Turkish despotism." Athenian supremacy "made the Athenian democracy the most extraordinary multitude – the most *singularly constituted mob,* recorded on the page of history." All the same, he preferred democratic Athens to aristocratic Sparta. Athens exhibited "change and activity," lived for the future, and embodied Greek glory; Sparta, "fixed and stationary," lived for the past. Greece taught Americans "the true value of the democratic principle" and "the great blessings of

---

[74] Dew, *Digest,* 196, 191, 211–15; John McCrady, *A System of Independent Research* (Charleston, SC, 1856), 6; R. M. T. Hunter, Jr., "Advantages of Historical Study," *VUM,* 3 (1859), 64; Felix Huston, *Military Strength of the Southern States and the Effects of Slavery Therein, Addressed to the Southern Convention* (Nashville, TN, 1850), 12–13; William Hamilton, "An Address to the New-York African Society for Mutual Relief" (1809), in Herbert Aptheker, ed., *A Documentary History of the Negro People in the United States,* 4 vols. (New York, 1990), 1:53. (Huston erred but made his point: Most slaves in Greece were not Greek but white foreigners.) Dew, like Huston, bristled at dismissals of the ancient Persians as barbarians. In the *Digest* he lauded ancient Persia and its influence on Greek culture. Persian religion bore "an analogy to the Jewish" and foreshadowed some Christian doctrine: see *Digest,* 91–8, esp. 91.

[75] LaBorde quoted by Mary Chesnut, Aug. 1, 1862, in Woodward, ed., *Mary Chesnut's Civil War,* 422. LaBorde probably took the incident from the version in Cicero, *De Senectute,* tr. William Armistead Falconer (LCL), secs. 18.63–64. Roberts, *Athens on Trial,* 192–3; [Holmes], "Athens and the Athenians," 273–321; also, [William Hayne Simmons], "Constitutions of France," *SQR,* 16 (1850), 520, 529; M. R. H. Garnett, *An Address Delivered before the Society of Alumni of the University of Virginia* (Richmond, VA, 1852); "French Revolutionary History," *DBR,* 30 (1861), 296. On Sparta see Rahe, *Republics,* chs. 5 and 6. See generally E. A. Miles, "Old South and the Classical World," 271–2. Plato and Xenophon, pictured as Spartaphiles, were much more critical of Sparta than was the radical democrat Rousseau: see Paul Cartledge, "The Socratics' Sparta and Rousseau's," in Stephen Hodkinson and Anton Powell, eds., *Sparta: New Perspectives* (London, 1999), ch. 11.

our federative system." Dew described Sparta as "a little band of soldiers, supporting themselves over a people that detested them," facing warlike neighbors while contending with their own brutally treated helots. Apparently influenced by Montesquieu's judgment that Spartan helotry combined the worst features of slavery and serfdom, Dew credited the Athenians with treating their slaves gently. He recoiled at Plutarch's account of the Spartans' treacherous murder of 2,000 helots to whom they had promised emancipation in return for military service. Spartan helotry, which Dew considered slavery, constituted "the main pillar on which the whole fabric rested." Slaves and an equitable division of property sustained a warrior ruling class. The Spartans were a people born to command – stern, selfish, and haughty and with little benevolence, amiability, or mercy. Although Athens gave undue weight to the collective will against the individual, Dew believed that it shone over Sparta because of the much wider scope it gave to individual talent and initiative.[76]

Today it might seem strange to hear Sparta trotted out as an example of republicanism rather than tyranny. Since the French Revolution commentators have found in Athens, not in Sparta, a glimmer of the respect for individual freedom that later ages came to prize. The image of Sparta as a totalitarian and militaristic embodiment of pure evil reached new heights in the twentieth century when the Nazis embraced Sparta and invested it with a Nordic racial character. Yet during the long time in which Athens held sway over the Aegean, Sparta enjoyed a reputation for the rule of law and for championing the rights and interests of the city-states. Indeed, the generation of American Founding Fathers preferred stable Sparta to tumultuous and mob-ridden Athens, and so had such southern favorites as Machiavelli, Guicciardini, and Montesquieu. Thomas Paine, a southern pet hate, loved Athens. The *Federalist* encouraged an interpretation of Sparta as a mixed government; Samuel Adams of Massachusetts called upon Boston to become a Christian Sparta; and John Taylor of Caroline contrasted the Spartan aristocracy favorably with the British bourgeoisie. Although Jefferson deplored Sparta's "military monks" – a term he borrowed from Montesquieu – he viewed Athens as a corrupt commercial city. When in 1814 Francis Scott Key wrote of "the land of the free, and the home of the brave," he was adapting the common American description of Sparta. Calhoun called Sparta and Rome "the two most distinguished governments of antiquity, both in respect to permanence and power." Both Sparta and Rome had the dual executives Calhoun was recommending for the United States. Pondering Sparta's victory in the Peloponnesian War, Southerners noted Thucydides' descriptions of a chaotic and violent Athenian democracy and Aristotle's and Xenophon's

---

[76] Dew, *Digest*, 18, 44, 61, 74, 76–9, 174–5, 180–4, 84, 101, 202–3, 206–10, 219, 241, 243, 246, quotes at 76, 79; Montesquieu, *Spirit of the Laws*, 1:Bk. 15.15–16, 9. Dew appealed to his students to resist the "demon of fanaticism" and "stand firm and resolute as the Spartan band at Thermopylae." Since the Spartans had been smashed at Thermopylae, Ludwell Johnson suggests that Dew was saying more than he intended in "an apocalyptic vision of the future": "Between the Wars," Part 2 of Susan H. Godson et al., *The College of William & Mary: A History*, 2 vols. (Williamsburg, VA, 1993), 1:247. Thucydides' story (retold by Plutarch) of the slaughter of the 2,000 liberated helots is probably true: see Cartledge, *Spartan Reflections*, 128–30.

criticism of democratic excesses and mob rule. J. D. B. De Bow, for his part, hailed Sparta over Athens as illustrative of a regime of law.[77]

Southerners especially appreciated Spartan community discipline and Plutarch's paean to Lycurgus: "He bred up his citizens in such a way that they neither would nor could live by themselves; they were to make themselves one with the public good." Robert Dabney contrasted Spartan simplicity to the conspicuous consumption and the excesses of the rich, although after the War he opposed the very idea of public schools as radicalism "derived from heathen Sparta," replacing the parent with the state. In Virginia, James Holcombe, George Junkin, Judith McGuire, and George Frederick Holmes lauded the Spartan spirit, and the Reverend Henry Ruffner declared: "It takes Spartan mothers to rear Spartan men."[78]

Southerners who trumpeted themselves as humane masters and who, like "Preston Souther" of Virginia, hoped to find Sparta a model for a well-ordered slave society were appalled by its treatment of helots. Cobb admitted Spartan cruelty and sheer viciousness while cautioning against hyperbole. No less disturbing, enthusiasm for Spartan austerity and egalitarianism rose to a crescendo among such eighteenth-century French radicals as Rousseau, Helvetius, Mably, and Babeuf; indeed, the bloodthirsty Saint-Just drew upon Plutarch's account of Sparta to limn his own profile of a new society. Nor did Sparta's militarized education of its youth go down well in the South. It took male children away from their families and put them in the hands of the state. Modern society, Nathaniel Beverley Tucker enjoined, must avoid the "absurdity" of the Spartans, who protected themselves against social upheaval by submitting to a state discipline that made them virtual slaves. Holmes, Groesbeck, Henry Augustine Washington, and Frederick Porcher especially scorched the Spartan educational system for producing, in Porcher's words, "an absolute negation of self, and a surrender of the whole person, body and soul." In contrast, Parson Weems gushed over Spartan military prowess in his best-selling *Life of Washington,* and Judge J. H. Lumpkin of Georgia commended Sparta's "austere laws," which "made war a trade" and gave children a military education that "rendered them not only undaunted on the field of battle, but illustrious for their courage and love of liberty."[79]

77 John C. Calhoun, "Discourse on the Constitution and Government of the United States," in Ross M. Lance, ed., *Union and Liberty: The Political Philosophy of John C. Calhoun* (Indianapolis, IN, 1992), 373–4; J. D. B. De Bow, "Law and Lawyers – No. 1," *DBR,* 19 (1855), 306.

78 Plutarch, *The Lives of the Noble Grecians and Romans,* tr. John Dryden, ed. and rev. by Arthur Hugh Clough, 2 vols. (New York, 1992), 1:75; "Christian Economy," *DD,* 1:9–10, 14–15, 26, and "Free School System," *DD*,* 4:194; James P. Holcombe, "Is Slavery Consistent with Natural Law?" *SLM,* 27 (1858), 413; George Junkin, *The Progress of the Age* (Philadelphia, 1851), 16; Judith W. McGuire, Feb. 22, 1862, in Jean V. Berlin, ed., *Diary of a Southern Refugee during the War, by a Lady of Virginia* (Lincoln, NE, 1995 [1867]), 94; [Holmes], "Athens and the Athenians," 273–321; Henry Ruffner, *Early History of Washington College* (Richmond, VA, 1890), 10. On Sparta and southern reactions to its culture, see Supplementary References: "Sparta."

79 "Preston Souther", "Miss Murray's Travels," *SLM,* 22 (1856), 459–60; Cobb, *Law of Negro Slavery,* lxiiii–lxv; Nathaniel Beverley Tucker, "Moral and Political Effect of the Relation between Caucasian Master and African Slave," *SLM,* 10 (1844), 477; [Holmes], "William Hamilton's Discussions," 309; H. J. Groesbeck, "American Social Elevation," *SLM,* 2 (1836), 35; H. A. Washington, "Virginia

Proslavery southern theorists and educators considered the condition of women the measure of a civilized society, and they judged Athens and Sparta accordingly. Athenians considered men brave, magnanimous, reserved, rational, and self-controlled but considered women fearful, vindictive, loquacious, irrational, and self-indulgent. Although Aristotle exaggerated the status and power of Spartan women, they did have more rights – including property rights and access to public education – than Athenian women. Athenians, President A. A. Lipscomb of the University of Georgia said, treated women miserably, whereas Spartans gave them too much liberty, encouraging their widely reputed licentiousness. Neither Athens nor Sparta equated women with slaves, but in neither did women enjoy anything remotely like equity with men. Controversy continued to rage: Athens or Sparta as model for the South? A. B. Meek of Alabama spoke for Athens' "social, political and intellectual superiority"; Basil Gildersleeve for the identification of the South with Sparta and the North with Athens. On balance southern opinion favored Sparta. But every proslavery Southerner could agree with Holmes in attributing both the intellect of Athens and the heroism of Sparta to the moral and material effects of their respective systems of servitude.[80]

Greek culture culminated in Rome, the Reverend William Hall told Confederate troops, and the consolidation of the Roman Empire brought the "highest development of law and government and social civilization." Still, for Henry Augustine Washington, Francis Lieber, and Robert Howison, among many Southerners, the ancient republics established what Hugh Legaré called the "despotism of the society over the individual." In Greece and Rome, Howison wrote, "freedom was rather nominal than real."[81]

William Hooper of North Carolina depicted Romans as driven, by luxury and corruption, from being a nursery of heroes to a "residence of musicians, pimps,

Constitution of 1776," 659–60; [F. A. Porcher], "Political Institutions of Sparta and Athens," *SQR*, n.s. (3rd), 2 (1856), 457, and *DBR*, 1 (Mar. 1846), 270–3; Roberts, *Athens on Trial*, 192–3, 197; for Saint-Just and the French revolutionaries see Harold T. Parker, *The Cult of Antiquity and the French Revolutionaries: A Study of the Development of the Revolutionary Spirit* (Chicago, 1937), ch. 14, esp. 160. On southern reactions to Spartan education see also Supplementary References: "Sparta."

[80] Lipscomb, *Social Spirit of Christianity*, 48; Meek, *Romantic Passages*, 54–5, 168; Gildersleeve, *Hellas and Hesperia*, 95; Briggs and Benario, *Gildersleeve*, 52; [Holmes], "Athens and the Athenians," 273–321. In southern denunciations of the Greeks for mistreatment of women the Spartans came off better than the Athenians, but not always by much: see e.g. E. A. Lynch, "Influence of Morals on the Happiness of Man," *SLM*, 4 (1838), 277–9; [J. L. Martin], "The Women of France," *SLM*, 5 (1839), 297–303; Edward C. Bullock, *True and False Civilization: An Oration Delivered before the Erosophic and Philomathic Societies of the University of Alabama* (Tuscaloosa, AL, 1858), 10.

[81] William A. Hall, *Historic Significance of the Southern Revolution* (Petersburg, VA, 1864), 6; "Constitutional History of Greece," *HLW*, 1:435, 437–40, quote at 435, and "Demosthenes" (1:475–6); H. A. Washington, "Virginia Constitution of 1776," 659–60; Lieber, *Manual of Political Ethics*, ch. 13; Lieber, *On Civil Liberty and Self-Government*, ch. 4; Gilman, ed., *Miscellaneous Writings of Francis Lieber*, 1:227, 232–4, 240, 271–2; Howison, *History of Virginia*, 2:120; "L. M. B.", "The Past and the Present," *VUM*, 4 (1860), 260; also, Richard, *Founders and the Classics*, 9. On Greek suppression of individuality see also "Mr. Smith" [of Virginia], "Character of the American People," *SQR*, n.s. (3rd), 2 (1857), 401–2.

panderers, and catamites." Thomas Cooper considered the Romans bandits and ruffians. President Thomas Newton Wood of the University of Alabama referred to "the stern Roman" and "his natural ferocity." Basil Gildersleeve, a great classicist, described the Romans of the Empire as a "canting, lying, thievish race." Joseph LeConte asserted that the joyous Greeks had produced a wonderful art, but the Romans, oppressed by a sense of sin and religious obligation, produced no native art. William Campbell Preston joshed to Waddy Thompson, "There have been two great dispensations in Civilization, the Greek & the Christian." The Reverend E. T. Winkler, citing Augustine, deemed the greatest of Roman virtues merely splendid sins.[82]

Southern opinion generally favored Greek culture over Roman. For A. J. Roane, Charles Scott Venable, and a contributor to *Southern Quarterly Review,* the Romans reproduced pale copies of Greek philosophy and literature. Southerners, nonetheless, read the Romans for their ethics and moral philosophy and accepted their claims to being practical men who shied away from Greek speculations. Yet, nineteenth-century Southerners echoed the view of the Roman Empire prevalent in seventeenth-century England and France that Roman civilization was superior to any in modern times, notwithstanding their acceptance of the judgment of Tacitus and Sallust that the end of the Carthaginian threat had introduced into the Roman Republic widespread corruption and lust for power. A few Southerners rejected both Greek and Roman culture, muttering with W. G. Minor about "fickle Greece" and "unprincipled Rome" – to the disgust of Holmes, who considered Roman history the most important of all histories.[83]

[82] William Hooper to James Iredell, Apr. 26, 1774, in Don Higginbotham, ed., *The Papers of James Iredell,* 2 vols. (Raleigh, NC, 1976), 1:231–2; for Cooper see E. A. Miles, "Old South and the Classical World," 260–1; Thomas Newton Wood, *An Address Delivered before the Two Literary Societies of the University of Alabama* (Tuscaloosa, AL, 1840), 5; B. L. Gildersleeve "Historical Parallels," Richmond *Enquirer,* Oct. 28, 1863, in Ward W. Briggs, Jr., ed., *Soldier and Scholar: Basil Lanneau Gildersleeve and the Civil War* (Charlottesville, VA, 1998), 121; W. C. Preston to Waddy Thompson, Sept. 7, 1857 (typescript), in Preston Papers, at USC; Joseph LeConte, "On the Nature and Uses of Art," *SPR,* 15 (1863), 337–8, 338, cf. Barthold G. Niebuhr, *The History of Rome,* tr. Julius Charles, 2 vols. (Philadelphia, 1844), 1:lxvii; E. T. Winkler, *Commencement Address at Baptist Theological Seminary in Greenville, S.C.* (Charleston, SC, 1861), 12. For harsh criticism of the Romans see "History and Constitution of the Early Roman Commonwealth," *SLM,* 14 (1848), 270–1; "S.A.L.", "Theory of Life," *SLM,* 21 (1855), 399–400; "Some Thoughts on Social Philosophy," *SLM,* 22 (1856), 314. According to a Methodist critic, Athens created tragic drama and the "magnificent productions of the human intellect": "The Greek Tragic Drama," *QRMECS,* 14 (1860), 571.

[83] "History of Philosophy," *SQR,* n.s. (3rd), 2 (1856), 228; C. S. Venable, *An Address Delivered before the Alumni of the University of Virginia* (Richmond, VA, 1859), 17; A. J. Roane, "American Literature – Northern and Southern," *DBR,* 24 (1858), 176–7; on the reputation of the Roman Empire in early modern England and France see Louis Auchincloss, *La Gloire: The Roman Empire of Corneille and Racine* (Columbia, SC, 1996). W. G. Minor quoted in Thomas Walker Gilmer, "Colonial History of Virginia," *SLM,* 7 (1841), 112; [Holmes], "Roman History," 505–8, and [Holmes], "History of Literature," 506. H. J. Groesbeck considered Greek and Roman culture of a piece: "Influence of Free Governments on the Mind," *SLM,* 1 (1835), 392.

For dismissals of Roman literature as derivative and weak see "Literature in Ancient Rome," *SWMR,* 1 (1845), 17–25, 312–17, and J. Quitman Moore, "American Letters," *DBR,* 28 (1860), 657.

As Southerners struggled to balance freedom and order in republican Athens and Rome, their professed commitment to the political rights of the individual sometimes clashed with the corporatist tendencies and exigencies of slave property. Dew wrote with special clarity: "Governments of antiquity, no matter of what kind, were considered as possessing every power. There were *no constitutions*, limiting their authority, no reserved rights to individuals. The state was every thing – the individual only became important through the state." Private property remained insecure, and the bourgeois concept of "absolute" property remained unknown: "Ancient governments aspired to the regulation of every thing." Liberty in the ancient world, he continued, "consisted principally in the share a man had *in* the government, not freedom *from its action. Perfect equality was perfect liberty.* The government might be the most complete despotism on earth, but if each one had his equal share in that despotism, then he had liberty." The ancients "had not arrived at that cardinal principle, growing out of feudalism and Christianity, that neither *one,* the *few,* nor the *many* have a right to do what they please; that unanimous millions have no right to do what is unjust; that absolute power is not for frail, mortal man."[84]

Three lessons: (1) Colonial Americans, northern and southern, had learned from Thucydides that a colony could survive independent of its mother country. (2) "The republics of Greece and Rome," Representative William Shepherd of North Carolina announced in 1838, "were based upon the principle of the rights of men" and left a legacy for opponents of the despotic monarchies of modern Europe. (3) During the political debates of the 1850s, Southerners recalled that neither the ordinances of Sparta's Lycurgus and Athens' Solon nor Rome's Twelve Tables frowned on slavery. Conservative Southerners nevertheless had to be wary of modern appeals to ancient republicanism. The French revolutionaries who had been taught by Cicero, Livy, and Plutarch to admire republican virtue and its heroes willfully smashed everything old, even replacing the calendar, while they offered themselves as the legitimate heirs of the classical world.[85]

Arthur Middleton of Charleston embraced the view of Johann Joachim Winckelmann that ancient Greece represented the childhood of Europe and the source of its culture: Maurie D. McInnis in collaboration with Angela D. Mack, *In Pursuit of Refinement: Charlestonians Abroad, 1740–1860* (Columbia, SC, 1999), 69. For an echo of Cato's remark that if Romans embraced Greek literature they would lose their empire, see [Daniel K. Whitaker?], "English Views of the Literature and Literary Men," *SLJ,* 1 (1836), 416–17. Southerners found much to admire in the Greeks as northern enthusiasm waned: E. A. Miles, "Young American Nation and the Classical World," 263, 273. For different appraisals of Greek and Roman studies in Europe see Eliza Butler, *The Tyranny of Greece over Germany* (New York, 1935), and Frank M. Turner, *The Greek Heritage in Victorian Britain* (New Haven, CT, 1981), 2–3, 8, 447–51. On shifting American attitudes toward the Greeks see Susan Ford Witshire, "Jefferson, Calhoun, and the Slavery Debate: The Classics and the Two Minds of the South," *Southern Humanities Review,* 11 (1977), 33–40.

84 Dew, *Digest,* 202–4. Although Greek literature included egalitarian visions, Aristophanes (among other great Greek writers) could imagine the destruction of private property and male prerogatives but not the destruction of slavery: see Yvon Garlan, *Slavery in Ancient Greece,* tr. Janet Lloyd, rev. ed. (Ithaca, NY, 1982), 130–6.

85 Gummere, *Colonial Mind and Classical Tradition,* 97; Shepherd, *Address before Two Literary Societies,* 19; on the 1850s debates see *Powers of the Government of the United States – Federal, State,*

Enthusiasm for Germany arose in the South in part from Germany's love affair with the ancient Greeks. In 1829 Stephen Elliott, Charleston's intellectual luminary, held up Germany as a model for political decentralization and the confederation of small states. The U.S. Constitution, according to Alexander Stephens, provided a federalism that combined the advantages of republics with those of monarchy, thereby securing the people's rights and liberties. In upholding strict construction, the South was upholding the federal principle of government against the imperial: "The cause of the Grecian type of Civilization against the Asiatic!" George Fitzhugh, who admired the Greeks for sending out colonists to establish independent states, chided the English for ignoring that lesson in the settlement of America. In several respects the familiar classical models had little to offer the Jeffersonian vision of republicanism, which rested upon the hegemony of a yeomanry. Plato and Aristotle thought good government safest in or near urban centers in which citizens and nearby farmers participated actively in political life. The considerable distances that separated the South's rural population undermined the model, and Jefferson's southern successors cast a wary eye on the direct democracy of New England townships. Ancient history and political thought reinforced Southerners' trust in republican representation rather than dictatorship, oligarchy, or radical democracy.[86]

For Dew, the Roman conquest of Macedonia had "consequences equally disastrous to the conquerors and the conquered," for it turned the Romans from aspiring to be the arbiters of the world to aspiring to be its masters. Roman centralization bred oppression, corruption, and decline. Dew wrote respectfully of the achievements of the ancient despotisms of the Near East and Asia but expressed reservations

---

and Territorial: Speech of Hon. James A. Stewart of Maryland on African Slavery (Washington, DC, 1856), 10. Parker, *Cult of Antiquity and French Revolutionaries*, 3; R. A. Leigh, "Jean-Jacques Rousseau and the Myth of Antiquity in the Eighteenth Century," in R. R. Bolgar, ed., *Classical Influences on Western Thought A.D. 1650–1870* (Cambridge, U.K., 1979), 155.

[86] Elliott in Briggs, ed., *Soldier and Scholar: Gildersleeve*, 4, and [Elliott], "Education in Germany"; also, *HLW*, 2:299; Alexander H. Stephens, *A Constitutional View of the Late War between the States*, 2 vols. (New York, 1970 [1868, 1870]), 1:169–70, 539, quote at 539. See also Madison to Jefferson, Oct. 24 and Nov. 1, 1787, in James Morton Smith, ed., *The Republic of Letters: The Correspondence between Thomas Jefferson and James Madison, 1776–1826*, 3 vols. (New York, 1995), 1:496; James Madison, "Commonplace Book," in William T. Hutchinson et al., eds., *The Papers of James Madison* (Chicago, 1962–), 1:20–1; Fitzhugh, "Revolutions of 1776 and 1861 Contrasted," 718. For the influence of Greek political thought see esp. Thomas L. Pangle, *The Spirit of Modern Republicanism: The Moral Vision of the American Founders and the Philosophy of Locke* (Chicago, 1988), 101–3. E. C. Kopff, "Gildersleeve in American Literature: The 'Kaleidoscopic Style,'" in Briggs and Benario, eds., *Gildersleeve*, 50–61. Richard, *Founders and the Classics*, 159; Reinhold, *Classica Americana*, 228–9; also, Ellen Meiksins Wood and Neal Wood, *Class Ideology and Ancient Political Theory: Socrates, Plato, and Aristotle in Political Context* (New York, 1978), 259, 265. George Frederick Holmes and James M. Walker hailed Solon for giving Athenians the best constitution they would receive: [Holmes], *SQR*, 11 (1847), 290–1; [Walker], *Tract on Government*, 11. Shepherd dubbed Lycurgus "the wisest of lawgivers": *Address Delivered before the Two Literary Societies*, 15. Polybius, who influenced southern judgments, credited Lycurgus with giving Sparta the "best form of government" and "laws that secured Sparta's strength through an equal distribution of landed property": Polybius, *The Histories*, tr. W. R. Paton, 6 vols. (LCL), 2:Bk. 4:81, 3:Bk. 6:10, 45–9, quote at Bk. 4:81.12.

about overly consolidated government, speculating that ancient Egypt owed some of its greatness to decentralization: "Great consolidated empires unfavorable to individual energy and greatness; they are without a history." Even so, Dew dreaded secession, for the Greek experience showed small states more vulnerable than large to internal disorder and coups. In 1861, James S. Clark provided a variation at Alabama's secession convention when he opposed separate state secession, recalling the Greek experience to argue that small states invariably become dependent on strong ones.[87]

The peculiar combination of individuality and community coercion in the trial of Socrates proved endlessly disturbing. Cicero recommended governments in which aristocracy balanced authoritarian kingship against mass democracy, but he knew them to be fragile. Polybius and Tacitus taught the virtues of mixed governments but warned of the near impossibility of their being sustained. Tacitus remarked in the *Annals* that a mixed constitution "is easy to commend but not to produce; or, if it is produced, it cannot be lasting." The mixed governments among the ancients that Southerners most admired had a decided aristocratic bias.[88]

Still, both radical democrats and conservative republicans appealed to ancient history to support their modern views. Typical outbursts: In Mobile, Arthur Hopkins, a prominent Whig lawyer and businessman, invoked Roman history to blast secessionists and abolitionists alike while venting his spleen on the immigrants and emancipated slaves who, he claimed, had created a new and barbarous race that destroyed Roman civilization. In Virginia, Julia Tyler, bemoaning what she considered abolitionists' attempts to wreck the Union, wrote that southern women had learned from the Greek city-states and subsequent history how factional intriguers break up happy confederations. Thomas Hart Benton of Missouri spoke for Border State unionists and radical democrats in citing Greek and Roman history on the beauties of popular participation in government and the evils of oligarchies.[89]

Benton's clash with Calhoun exposed the chasm between radical and conservative appeals to ancient history. Benton traced the origins of the doctrine of nullification

---

[87] Dew, *Digest*, 18, 44, 174–5, 180–4; 241–3, 246, 61–2, quotes at 18, 181, 253; for Clark see William R. Smith, ed., *The History of the Convention Debates of the People of Alabama* (Montgomery, AL, 1861), 82. For a view similar to Dew's see H. A. Washington, "Virginia Constitution of 1776," 665–6.

[88] "Annals," Bk. 4:33, in Hadas, ed., *Works of Tacitus*. Referring to Athens as "extremely democratic," Dew thought that the labor of 400,000 slaves made it simultaneously "aristocratical": *Digest*, 81, 100–1. On the aristocratic bias of the ancient writers who applauded mixed governments, see Andreas A. M. Kinneging, *Aristocracy, Antiquity and History: Classicism in Political Thought* (New Brunswick, NJ, 1997), 215–28; Gabba, *Dionysius and the History of Archaic Rome*, 205. Americans understood the Roman constitution mainly through Polybius: see Sellers, *American Republicanism*, 46; also, Benario, "The Classics in Southern Higher Education," 16; Dickson D. Bruce, Jr., "The Conservative Use of History in Early National Virginia," *Southern Studies*, 19 (1980), 137–8.

[89] A. F. Hopkins to W. A. Graham, Apr. 6, 1852, in J. G. deRoulhac Hamilton, ed., *The Papers of William Alexander Graham*, 5 vols. (Raleigh, NC, 1957–73), 4:286; Julia Gardiner Tyler, *A Letter to the Duchess of Sutherland and Ladies of England, in Reply to Their "Christian Address" on the Subject of Slavery in the Southern States* (Richmond, VA, 1853), 4; Thomas Hart Benton, *Thirty Years' View; Or, a History of the Working of the American Government for Thirty Years, from 1820 to 1850*, 2 vols. (New York, 1854), see e.g. 1:290–2, 335–7 (on Calhoun), 411.

to Calhoun's obsession with the division of power exemplified by the Roman Tribunate. Calhoun drew on Barthold Niebuhr but ignored Livy and Edward Gibbon, who characterized the Tribunate as dominated by corrupt demagogues and oppressors of the people in whose name they spoke – a characterization echoed by Southerners whom Calhoun respected. Livy acknowledged that some tribunes tried to relieve the distress of the poor but concluded that they succeeded only in stirring up class envy and sacrificing community interests to their constituents' selfish demands. Calhoun's silence is the more surprising since Livy preached, as did Calhoun himself, the need for unity against outsiders and disruptions caused by internal social and party strife. Representative Lemuel Dale Evans of Texas echoed Livy, protesting that the Roman government Calhoun admired promoted dangerous social conflicts. Daniel Whitaker snarled that the Tribunate "prostituted individual judgment to the nod of the common people." Edward B. Bryan agreed with Calhoun on the Tribunate as a fine balance of patricians and plebs, but Dew and the Reverend William Stiles, both of whom recognized the Tribunate as counterweight to an arrogant and oppressive aristocracy, stressed its susceptibility to demagogy and corruption by patricians. Augustus Baldwin Longstreet observed that the people had raised the tribunes against the patricians only to see them vie for power, so that the interests of the people were "entirely overlooked."[90]

Athens versus Sparta, democracy versus oligarchy, freedom versus tyranny, aristocrats versus plebs – the special significance that these ideological quarrels over Greek history had for southern slaveholders became, if anything, more strikingly apparent in their consideration of Roman history, specifically of the radical agrarian reforms of the Gracchi. Conservative Southerners, including ardent proslavery theorists, cautiously approved of the Gracchi. Benjamin Faneuil Porter of Alabama included the Gracchi along with Homer and Virgil among the lasting treasures from the collapse of ancient civilization. Southerners nevertheless commonly used

---

[90] Benton, *Thirty Years' View*, 1:290–2, 411; in *JCCP*: 11:494, 12:90–1, also 11:416, 13:7. John C. Calhoun, *A Disquisition on Government and Selections from the Discourse* (Indianapolis, IN, 1953), 70ff.; Livy, *The Early History of Rome*, tr. Aubrey de Sélincourt (London, 1971), Bk. 3:66–8, 4:54–6, 5:10–11; Livy, *Rome and Italy*, tr. Betty Radice (London, 1982), Bk. 7:27; Gibbon, *Decline and Fall*, 1:90–1, 3:991–2 and 1023–1104; for Evans see E. A. Miles, "Old South and the Classical World," 269; [Daniel K. Whitaker?], "Democracy in America," *SLJ*, 4 (1838), 278; Dew, *Digest*, 236–7; William H. Stiles, *Connection between Liberty and Eloquence: An Address Delivered before the Phi Kappa and Demosthenean Societies of Franklin College* (Augusta, GA, 1852), 14–15, 29; [Edward B. Bryan?], "Political Philosophy of South-Carolina," *SQR*, n.s., 7 (1853), 129–30; Augustus Baldwin Longstreet, *Fast-Day Sermon: Delivered in the Washington Street Methodist Episcopal Church, Columbia, S.C.* (Columbia, SC, 1861), 5. F. W. Pickens remarked ambiguously that the tribunes preserved "the political power of classes and interests": *Difference between Ancient and Modern Civilizations*, 7. In 1787 William Vans Murray of Maryland sympathized with the oppressed Roman plebs: *Political Sketches Inscribed to His Exellency John Adams* (London, 1787), 39–41, 15–16. Contra Calhoun, see the negative assessments of the Tribunate in Syme, *Roman Revolution*, esp., 16, 65, 145, and D. C. Earl, *Tiberius Gracchus: A Study in Politics* (Bruxelles-Bercheim, 1963), 46–7. Southerners knew Shakespeare's *Coriolanus*, which picked up Plutarch's portrayal of the Tribunes as unsavory: Cantor, *Shakespeare's Rome*, 43, 61–2, 97.

"agrarianism" as an epithet for assorted radicalisms and cried out with the Richmond *Whig* against the "unjust, loose, revolutionary principle of Agrarianism."[91]

Tiberius and Caius Gracchus, sons of a consul and censor, were alarmed by the concentration of wealth and land in a few hands and the decline of the middle class, and they sought to redistribute public lands. In the version of history familiar to John Taylor of Caroline and generations of Southerners, wealthy Romans had established their large estates primarily by evicting peasants, importing slaves, and throwing hundreds of thousands of the dispossessed on the dole. Pliny, condemning the Empire's luxury-loving decadence, rendered the famous judgment, echoed through the ages, that large landed estates had ruined Rome [*Latifundia perdidere Italiam, jam, vero et provincias*]. A Sicilian slave revolt and a lesser revolt on the mainland spurred Tiberius to radical agrarian reforms. The last 20,000 of the 60,000 or so slaves surrendered in 132 B.C. and were butchered. Tiberius Gracchus' agrarian laws redistributed but did not equalize property, but like Caesar and Augustus afterwards he spoke in the name of dispossessed and socially threatened free men. Rebuked as a traitor to his class, he had, in fact, proceeded with the support of and in consultation with a powerful faction of the ruling class. He was nonetheless assassinated – as was his brother and successor Caius Gracchus. The defeat of the Gracchi ushered in an aristocratic reaction and a decisive commitment to slave labor.[92]

Pondering the history of social struggles in Greece and Rome, leading Southerners of various political stripes drew conservative conclusions. For George McDuffie, Roman liberty collapsed in the struggle between patricians and plebeians and the resultant anarchy, violence, and despotism. For Hugh Legaré, usually at political loggerheads with McDuffie, democracy needed to be reined in by constitutional republicanism. For William Frierson Cooper of Tennessee, the Romans taught a valuable lesson by advancing people from lower offices to higher only after they had acquired the requisite experience. Politically ambitious southern planters had to tread carefully. After all, Plutarch and Shakespeare on Coriolanus related the troubling experience of haughty nobles who neglected to show respect for the people. Plutarch had sport with aristocrats who pretended to scorn popularity while secretly craving it. In 1861 Elliott Fletcher, a wealthy planter in Arkansas's Mississippi River Valley, advised his fellow planters: "We must stoop to conquer sometimes, or else an arrow sped by a vulgar hand may find a crevice in our armor of pride, and wound us to the quick." Southern commentators accepted Plutarch's judgment that the Roman aristocrats had become extraordinarily avaricious and unjust and that the

[91] Porter, *Past and the Present*, 6; Richmond *Whig*, Mar. 19, 1860, reprinted in Dwight Lowell Dumond, ed., *Southern Editorials on Secession* (Gloucester, MA, 1964), 60. Abel Parker Upshur defined agrarianism as that which "seeks to give to idleness and vice the hard earnings of industry and virtue": "The True Theory of Government," *SLM*, 22 (1856), 410. Also on agrarianism see e.g. *DBR*, 20 (1854), 299–300; "The Great Issue," *SLM*, 32 (1861), 164; E. Merton Coulter, *Daniel Lee, Agriculturalist: His Life North and South* (Athens, GA, 1972), 6; Frank H. Alfriend, "A Southern Republic and a Northern Democracy," *SLM*, 35 (1863), 284–5.

[92] Taylor, *Inquiry*, 66; Max Weber, *The Agrarian Sociology of Ancient Civilizations*, tr. R. I. Frank (London, 1976), 395; Hopkins, *Conquerors and Slaves*, ch. 1; Conte, *Latin Literature*, 118. See also Supplementary References: "Roman Writers" (*Pliny*) and "Gracchi."

Gracchi had been upholding the honor of their class. Sallust grudgingly acknowl-edged that the Gracchi were attempting to defend the people against the rapacity of reactionary aristocrats, much as his hero, Caesar, would do later.[93]

Barthold Niebuhr's appealing combination of conservatism and liberalism deeply influenced southern responses. Niebuhr considered the patricians exploiters and, siding with the plebs, he showed that the agrarian law's distribution of public lands did not threaten private property; southern commentators agreed that the Gracchi sought to balance property in society, not destroy it. Recent scholarship confirms that Tiberius and his party designed the agrarian law to distribute to the poor re-claimed arable pasturelands appropriated by the rich and did not strike at efficient latifundia. Thus, George Fitzhugh and J. D. B. De Bow interpreted the work of the Gracchi as an essentially conservative attempt at a massive land redistribution designed to restore a healthy peasantry that could defend the state. While they rec-ognized the conservative virtues of the old regimes in Spain, Russia, and Eastern Europe, they condemned their reactionary social policies. Fitzhugh, the most rad-ical of the proslavery theorists, blamed land monopoly in modern Europe for the slavery of white labor to capital. The progress of civilization did arise from sys-tems in which a few held most of the land, but he insisted that wealth and luxury had ruined ancient Rome. Influenced by Goldsmith's popular *History of Rome*, Fitzhugh drew a parallel between Roman and American efforts to counteract the accumulation of landed property and concluded that great estates undermined the paternalism necessary to maintain a slave society.[94]

---

[93] "On the Election of the President and Vice-President of the United States," in Edwin L. Green, ed., *Two Speeches of George McDuffie* (Columbia, SC, 1905), 21; *HLW*, 2:367–442, 277–8; William Frierson Cooper, "Notes on a Trip to Europe," 31, in Cooper Papers, at Tennessee State Library and Archives (Nashville); Fletcher quoted in Carl H. Moneyhon, *The Impact of the Civil War and Re-construction on Arkansas: Persistence in the Midst of Ruin* (Baton Rouge, LA, 1994), 57; Livy, *Early History of Rome*, Bk. 4:12–13; Sallust, *Jugurthine War*, 41–2, and *Conspiracy of Catiline*, 153, 157; on Sallust's treatment of the Gracchi see the incisive remarks of Ronald Syme, *Sallust* (Berkeley, CA, 1964), 170–1. See also Livy's criticism of the selfish behavior of the great landowners who thwarted needed reforms: *Rome and Italy*, Bk. 6 and Bk. 7:17. If anything, Livy read the agrarian struggles back into the earliest phases of Roman history on the strength of little evidence. Niebuhr approved of Livy's discussion of the early agrarian laws – "He forgets his prejudices": Niebuhr, *History of Rome*, 2:80 n. 59. Southerners held the latifundia responsible for the destruction of the yeomanry and the increased dependence on slaves, which ruined the Roman Empire. See e.g. [Thomas V. Moore], *SLM*, 20 (1854), 1–5. Dionysius of Halicarnassus, whom many Southerners cited and some actually read, dated the "perpetually slaying and banishing" to the time of Caius Gracchus, who "destroyed the harmony of the government": Earnest Cary, ed. and tr., *The Roman Antiquities of Dionysius of Halicarnassus*, 7 vols. (LCL), 1:Bk. 2:11.

The influence of Montesquieu among the leaders of southern thought cannot be doubted. He val-ued the early Romans' rough equality in rural property and thought the subsequent concentration of property a principal factor in the decline. He favorably quoted Tiberius Gracchus' call to the nobility to meet its responsibilities. See Baron de Montesquieu, *Considerations on the Causes of the Great-ness of the Romans and Their Decline*, tr. David Lowenthal (New York, 1965, first English translation 1734), 41.

[94] Arnoldo Momigliano, "Niebuhr and the Agrarian Problems of Rome," *History and Theory*, 21 (1982), 1–15; "History and Constitution of the Early Roman Commonwealth," *SLM*, 14 (1848), 266; Alvin H. Bernstein, *Tiberius Sempronius Gracchus: Tradition and Apostasy* (Ithaca, NY, 1978), 122,

The slaveholders' affection for the Gracchi stemmed in large part from their sense that a slave society required a strong and loyal yeomanry to bolster it. Livy and Sallust tempered that romance with the yeomanry. Livy maintained that the commons, once in power, were just as corrupt as aristocrats. Sallust carefully distinguished smallholders from proletarians and excoriated both the tyranny of the mob and the tyranny of the oligarchy, suggesting that those ambitious for power should look for support to the poor, who – with nothing to lose – will rally to those who have something to offer. Southerners could hardly miss the irony. Yet the proslavery Reverend Benjamin Morgan Palmer, as conservative politically as he was theologically, exulted in "the agrarian law of Moses," which created smallholdings. Nathaniel Beverley Tucker saw the revolutionary era that began in 1789 as an effort to remedy deep social ills by the redistribution of property. In Jeffersonian fashion, he assumed that a stable republicanism required a strong and politically experienced peasantry, which France lacked. The militantly proslavery Louisa Mc-Cord, author of a book-length poem entitled *Caius Gracchus,* called the Gracchi "my *bona fide* heroes," who acted "nobly" and "in a good cause": "I confess to being a thorough upholder of the people's rights." Few elite Southerners sympathized with those Roman aristocrats who became enraged because Caius Gracchus, rising to speak, faced the populace rather than the senators. Edward A. Pollard expressed admiration for the Gracchi and disgust with the Roman aristocracy: "With the Gracchi perished the liberties of the Eternal City."[95]

Southern slaveholders had mixed feelings about the Roman aristocrats' reaction to Tiberius Gracchi's self-righteousness and skirting of legality. As ardent admirers

137–8, 158. George Fitzhugh, "The Conservative Principle," *DBR,* 22 (1857), 458; Fitzhugh, "Reaction and the Administration," *DBR,* 25 (1858), 546–7; Fitzhugh, "Private and Public Luxury," *DBR,* 24 (1858), 49–52; Fitzhugh, "Public Lands of Rome and America," *DBR,* 24 (1858), 428–31; Fitzhugh, *Cannibals All!; Or Slaves without Masters* (Cambridge, Mass, 1960 [1857]), 29; "The States of Europe – Spain, Part 1," *DBR,* 13 (1852), 377; "Hungary in 1852," *DBR,* 13 (1852), 435–9, 443–4; De Bow, "The Character and Causes of the Crisis," *DBR,* 24 (1858), 53; W. C. Duncan, "The Empire of Russia," *DBR,* 11 (1851), 557. Goldsmith, in his popular Roman history, attributed to the Gracchi hostility to corruption and oppression and placed justice on their side against the selfish aristocrats of the Senate. See *Oliver Goldsmith's Roman History, for the Use of Schools,* revised and corrected by William Grimshaw (Philadelphia, 1835), ch. 18.

At a time when Rome's Italian allies did not qualify for citizenship, only citizens benefited from the redistribution of land under the law of 133 B.C. Caius Gracchus later revived a proposal to extend citizenship to Latins: see C. Nicolet, *The World of the Citizen in Republican Rome,* tr. P. S. Falla (Berkeley, CA, 1980), 38, 40. For Niebuhr's attitude toward the agrarian laws and southern responses, see Supplementary References: "Modern Historians of the Ancient World."

95 Livy, *The War with Hannibal,* tr. Aubrey de Sélincourt (London, 1972), Bk. 23:4; Sallust, *Jugurthine War,* ch. 5, and on the poor see 87–90, 123–5; [Palmer], "Import of Hebrew History," 600; [Nathaniel Beverley Tucker], "The Present State of Europe," *SQR,* 16 (1850), 277–323, esp. 289; L. S. McCord to W. P. Miles, June 12, 1848, in Richard C. Lounsbury, ed., *Louisa S. McCord: Poems, Drama, Biography, Letters* (Charlottesville, VA, 1996), 274–5, and for McCord's text see 161–232. E. A. Pollard, "Modern Analogies of the Roman History," *SLM,* 24 (1857), 354–5. For muted expressions of sympathy for the Gracchi that highlighted the evils against which they struggled, see [Campbell], "Slavery among the Romans," 409, 412–13; *The American Text-Book: Being a Series of Letters, Addressed by 'An American', to the Citizens of Tennessee, an Exposition and Vindication of the Principles and Policy of the American Party* (Nashville, TN, 1855), 33.

of Cicero, they knew of his defense of the murder of the Gracchi as "justifiable." Reviewing the history of Sparta and Rome, Cicero concluded that tyrannical regimes rose in the wake of the demagogic agitation of "the agrarian issue." He lashed out at the abolition of debts. What does it mean, "except that you buy a farm with my money; that you have the farm, and I have not the money"? "Even the man who denies that they were good," Seneca wrote, "will admit they were great men." Caesar, accused of continuing the Gracchi's sedition, portrayed himself as a pillar of law and order who promoted wise reforms to head off more radical measures. Augustine treated the Gracchi as seditious but as responding to Roman greed and corruption by dividing "among the people the lands which were wrongfully possessed by the nobility." John Taylor of Caroline, no fan of Augustine, remarked in words that recalled Augustine's, "The murder of the Gracchi is a proof that usurpation can only be corrected in infancy."[96]

While deploring the demagogy of the Gracchi, Dew acknowledged that Tiberius Gracchus sought to relieve the burdens placed on the lower orders by a "hateful" aristocracy; but like all demagogues, Tiberius did not know when to stop: "If any order in society have property and talents, they immediately become restless until they can get a share in the government, for the principal action of all government is on property, and the owner of property does not like to see it touched, except by his consent." Dew, who credited Augustus with restoring order by reestablishing the security of property, pilloried the aristocrats of ancien régime France for failing to institute necessary reforms while it still had time. Dew approved of the "agrarian division" of property, on which Spartan power had rested. Had such a rough equality of landholding prevailed under conditions of free labor, it would have constituted an injustice and produced a population of worthless idlers. But since the larger part of the population were "slaves," their labor made possible the transformation of freemen into a caste of warriors.[97]

---

[96] Syme, *Roman Revolution*, 60; "To Marcia on Consolation," in Seneca, *Moral Essays*, tr. John W. Basore, 3 vols. (LCL), 2:Bk. 6, 16:4; Cicero, *De Officiis*, Bk. 2:12, 2:23; Julius Caesar, *The Gallic War and Other Writings*, tr. Moses Hadas (New York, 1957), 139, 284. Augustine, *City of God*, Bk. 3:24; Taylor, *Inquiry*, 66. Caesar protected debtors against gouging but reassured creditors by eschewing debt moratoria and promoting cautious land distribution: Zvi Yavetz, *Plebs and Princeps* (Oxford, U.K., 1969), 44–8; also Yavetz, *Julius Caesar and His Public Image* (Ithaca, NY, 1983), chs. 1 and 4. The Gracchi stood high as models for southern oratory – a subject we shall treat in a separate volume.

[97] Dew, *Digest*, 78–9 (Lycurgus), 255, 257, 259, 287, 582, 604–5, quotes at 78–9. Dew, harshly criticizing the Jurgurthine War, denounced Marius as an even greater and more dangerous demagogue than the Gracchi (260). Dew recognized the plebs of early Rome as part of a dominant class that replenished itself from below, much as the dominant classes of England were to do in later centuries: "Both the people of Rome and the people of England have been able to make but slow progress against an aristocratic order thus consolidated and recruited": *Digest*, 218–19, 222, 224–5, quote at 225. Once the rich plebeians satisfied their political ambitions, the poor had difficulty finding spokesmen and champions: P. A. Brunt, *Social Conflicts in the Roman Republic* (London, 1971), 58–9, 72–3. For criticism of Dionysius and Plutarch for obscuring the inclusion of the plebs in Rome's subsequent power and conquests, see "History and Constitution of the Early Roman Commonwealth," *SLM*, 14 (1848), 275–8. Henry Augustine Washington, among others, lauded the plebs as "the great Roman commons": "Virginia Constitution of 1776," 664.

In 1855 Holmes replied to abolitionists who claimed that slavery and the dispossession of the peasantry had ruined the Roman republic. To Holmes, the Gracchi did not intend to undermine slavery. He saw the greedy expropriations of the rich and the sops to the poor as two sides of a corrupting process. Southern slaveholders had learned their lessons well and now presided over a social system and republican political order that protected the interests of a vigorous yeomanry. The "legitimate agrarianism of the Gracchi" and their wise policy of land redistribution had nothing in common with the wild and destructive radicalism of modern socialism.[98]

For southern slaveholders, the aftermath of the fall of the Gracchi carried a special omen. The efforts of the tribunes to protect the people against aggrandizement and oppression had driven Roman conservatives to support dictatorships. Caesar's military conquests had permitted the mass migration of proletarianized former peasants, simultaneously strengthening slavery at home. Caesar, no revolutionary, had led a revolution that sorely disappointed the more rapacious of his supporters and those who hoped for expropriation of the rich. Ever-wary Southerners took the measure of Caesar's course, ready for strong measures to protect their slave society but not ready to pay the price of Caesarism.[99]

The Gracchi offered Southerners a great bonus: Cornelia, mother of the Gracchi and the most frequently invoked model of southern motherhood. Cornelia took "upon herself all the care of the household and the education of her children," Plutarch wrote, and proved herself "so discreet a matron, so affectionate a mother, and so constant a noble-spirited widow [that] Tiberius seemed to all men to have done nothing unreasonable in choosing to die for such a woman." Cornelia stood, above all, for a mother's duty to train her sons to a high sense of honor and service. Plutarch remarked that many Romans held her responsible for goading her ill-fated sons into promulgating the radical agrarian laws "because she frequently upbraided her sons, that the Romans as yet rather called her the daughter of Scipio, than the mother of the Gracchi." For Plutarch, "It was most admirable to hear her make mention of her sons, without any tears or signs of grief, and give the full account of all their deeds and misfortunes, as if she had been relating the history of

---

[98] George Frederick Holmes, "Ancient Slavery," *DBR*, 20 (1855), 617–37; [Holmes], "Greeley on Reforms," *SLM*, 17 (1851), 260–1, 270–2. Gildersleeve allowed that the rise of the latifundia and weakening of the yeomanry contributed to the decline of Rome, but he, too, implicitly divorced the concentration of landholding from ownership of slaves: Gildersleeve, "Taxation of the Middle Class," Richmond *Enquirer*, Dec. 7, 1863, in Briggs, ed., *Soldier and Scholar: Gildersleeve*, 191–2; also, [Campbell], "Slavery among the Romans," 419–26. During the 1820s, "Caius Gracchus" wrote a series of proslavery articles for the Richmond *Examiner*: Tise, *Proslavery*, 53. Francis Lieber, after returning North, praised the Gracchi's efforts to arrest the latifundia, which choked the yeomanry and corrupted the regime: Lieber, *Slavery, Plantations, and the Yeomanry* (New York, 1863), 4–5.

[99] "The Social Causes of the Decline of Ancient Civilization," in Weber, *Agrarian Sociology of Ancient Civilizations*; Hopkins, *Conquerors and Slaves*, 59–67, 105–6; Pierre Dockès, *Medieval Slavery and Liberation*, tr. Arthur Goldhammer (Chicago, 1982), 51–7, 205–6; Syme, *Roman Revolution*, 52–3. Colonization was important to the Gracchan reforms: "In colonizing abroad, Caesar was the authentic successor of Caius Gracchus": E. T. Salmon, *Roman Colonization under the Republic* (Ithaca, NY, 1970), 113–23.

some ancient heroes." Plutarch defended her against the charge that she was devoid of natural feelings: "They who thought so were themselves more truly insensible not to see how much a noble nature and education avail to conquer any affliction." He seems to have admired Cornelia's response as essentially manly.[100]

Cornelia, when asked about her jewels, replied that her jewels were her sons (*Haec ornamenta mea sunt*). Southerners, male and female, made her declaration their own great symbol of southern womanhood. Savannah's *Ladies' Magazine* opened its first issue, in 1819, by declaring that only Cornelias who raised their sons to valor could ensure the safety of the Republic. N. Buchanan of Virginia praised the mother of John Randolph as "that lady worthy to have been the mother of the Gracchi." Parson Weems invoked Cornelia and her jewels in his *Virginia Almanack*. Nathaniel Beverley Tucker wrote, in his college text on political science, "Are not the names of Washington and Henry, and Jefferson and Madison, and Marshall and Randolph, all her [Virginia's] *property? Are not these her jewels?*" Robert Y. Hayne, Henry A. Washington, C. C. Memminger, Louisa McCord, George Sawyer, and Daniel R. Hundley – prominent proslavery theorists all – invoked Cornelia no less effusively. Cornelia and her jewels rang through congressional speeches and in prominent southern journals. *Southern Literary Messenger* offered Cornelia as the model for young ladies. George Frederick Holmes opened a long essay on Hugh Legaré in *Southern Quarterly Review* with Cornelia and her jewels; in a textbook designed for the education of young men and women, William Gilmore Simms hailed South Carolina's sons as her jewels. Reverend T. O. Summers, praising the Charleston Orphan Asylum in 1854, remarked that Charlestonians have a right to say, "These are my jewels." When Thomas Dabney decided to leave Virginia for Mississippi, his neighbors gave him a dinner party, toasting him as an exemplar of Cornelia's boast of her sons.[101]

---

[100] Plutarch, *Lives*, 2:355–6, 360. Tacitus expressed a view that became common in the South when he railed at child-raising by irresponsible nurses and insisted that mothers raise their own sons in the manner of Cornelia: Tacitus, "Dialogus de Oratoribus," in *Tacitus*, tr. W. Peterson, rev. M. Winterbottom (LCL), secs. 28–29 (307–8). The alternate ideal woman was the farmwife, whose qualities in some ways accorded to the ideal of the lady and in some ways did not: see D. Harland Hagler, "The Ideal Woman in the Antebellum South: Lady or Farm Wife," *JSH*, 66 (1980), 405–18; Hagler does not mention Cornelia, whose qualities accorded with the essentials of both models. A contributor to *Southern Literary Messenger* seems to have something of the sort in mind when he wrote that, to the dignity of the Roman matron, the southern woman adds the nobler qualities of the Christian mother: "A Few Thoughts on Slavery," *SLM*, 20 (1854), 198.

[101] For Buchanan's reminiscence see William Cabell Bruce, *John Randolph of Roanoke, 1773–1833: A Biography Based Largely on New Material*, 2 vols. (New York, 1970), 1:32; on Weems see Lewis Leary, *The Book-Peddling Parson: An Account of the Life and Works of Mason Locke Weems* (Chapel Hill, NC, 1984), 55, 62; N. Beverley Tucker, *A Series of Lectures on the Science of Government* (Philadelphia, 1845), 371. For Hayne and H. A. Washington see O'Brien, ed., *All Clever Men*, 253; Memminger, "Address at the Opening of the Female High & Normal School in Charleston, SC, 1859," *DHE*, 5:271, also 272; Sawyer, *Southern Institutes*, 376; Daniel R. Hundley, *Social Relations in Our Southern States* (Baton Rouge, LA, 1979 [1860]), 122–3; "Female Education," *SLM*, 1 (1835), 521; Holmes, "Writings of Legaré," 321; William Gilmore Simms, *The History of South Carolina*, 8th ed. (New York, 1860), 390; Thomas O. Summers, *Talks, Pleasant and Profitable* (Nashville, TN, 1854), 74; Smedes, *Memorials of a Southern Planter*, 31. D. Macaulay gushed over Cornelia in *The*

The ideological uses to which attention to women in history could be put before and after the War emerged with special clarity in the frequent appeals to Cornelia's memory. Southern men, drawing on Plutarch, lectured each other on their duty to be worthy of such a noble mother. A reviewer slapped Michelet's history of Rome hard for an unflattering portrait of Cornelia that compared her to Lady Macbeth. Cornelia's virtues shone forth all the more strongly in light of the reputation of the aristocratic women of Rome, about whom Ronald Syme comments, "There names were more often heard in public than was expedient for honest women; they became politicians and patrons of the arts." We might add: too often, little more than trollops. Southern gentlemen did not cite the ancient authors who attributed to women dangerous sexual appetites and passions that, at the least, rendered them prone to be seduced. The staunch and faithful Cornelia, who as a widow refused an offer of marriage from King Ptolemy and chose to raise her children by herself, provided a silent counterpoint.[102]

A woman's highest attainment was considered by southern women to be as the mother of great men.[103] Writing in the *Southern Ladies' Companion* in 1853, a southern lady cheerfully accepted a subordinate place for women in society: "Man must strive. He was made for action. It is his life. He must enter into the arena where truth and error are in deadly conflict, and must struggle and conquer or fall …. She enters not the arena of political debate, it is true; but she forms minds and habits from which emanate the laws of government." Contemporaries compared Louisa McCord to Cornelia, commenting on McCord's "masculine" qualities – by which they meant her formidable intellect and rough polemical style as well as her tall, strong, physical bearing. The southern love affair with Cornelia did not abate after the War. Bledsoe, in *Was Davis a Traitor?* (a strong defense of southern constitutional principles), boasted that the defeated South retained her wealth: "her moral wealth – the glory of her Jacksons, her Sidney Johnstons, her Lees, her Davises, and of all who have nobly died or suffered in her cause. These are her imperishable jewels." W. H. Sparks and William Porcher DuBose exulted similarly, and Mrs. Roger [Sara Agnes] Pryor of Virginia began her book on George Washington's mother by observing, "The mothers of famous men survive only in their sons."[104]

Patriot's Catechism, or The Duties of Rulers and Ruled (Washington, DC, 1843), x–xiii, 67–8 – a pamphlet endorsed by such prominent Southerners of different politics as Rives, Calhoun, and Benton. Simms credited Chevalier Bayard's mother for instilling his combination of modesty and fearlessness: *The Life of Chevalier Bayard: "The Good Knight"* (New York, 1847), 10.

[102] Plutarch, *Lives,* 2:384. For Cornelia see also Supplementary References: "Gracchi."

[103] See e.g. Shackelford, *George Wythe Randolph and the Confederate Elite,* 10; Meats and Arnold, eds., *Writings of B. F. Perry,* 2:59.

[104] "C. Virginia S.", "Woman. Her Position and Office," *SLC,* 6 (1852/53), 267; "Afterword," in Lounsbury, ed., *Louisa S. McCord: Poems,* 424–65; A. T. Bledsoe, *Is Davis a Traitor; Or, Was Secession a Constitutional Right Previous to the War of 1861?* (Baltimore, 1866), 4–5; W. H. Sparks, *The Memories of Fifty Years* (Philadelphia, 1872), 101; for DuBose see Ralph Luker, *A Southern Tradition in Theology and Social Criticism: The Religious Liberalism and Social Conservatism of James Warley Miles, William Porcher DuBose and Edgar Gardner Murphy* (New York, 1884), 16 n. 4; Mrs. Pryor, *Mother of Washington and Her Times* (New York, 1903), 1. Among the Founders only James Wilson of Pennsylvania praised the women of antiquity: Richard, *Founders and Classics,* 72–3.

The gentlemen who extolled Cornelia, being steeped in Roman history, knew they were celebrating women who raised their sons to be statesmen and warriors – women with minds of their own who held strong political views and ideals. Still, the gentlemen were admiring themselves as "jewels." And southern ladies and gentlemen alike believed that Cornelia had spurred her jewels to revolutionary efforts in an essentially conservative cause.[105]

---

[105] Some recent historians have challenged the long-held version and suggested that Cornelia, having lost her husband and then her older son, did not want her remaining son sacrificed. See Pierre Grimal, *Love in Ancient Rome,* tr. Arthur Treen, Jr. (Norman, OK, 1980), 186–91; Susan Dixon, *The Roman Mother* (Norman, OK, 1987), 179.

9

Coming to Terms with the Middle Ages

> The Middle Ages are not a kind of waiting-room between two different worlds, but the age which made a new world, the world from which we come and to which in a sense we still belong .... Medieval Christendom is the outstanding example in history of the application of Faith to Life: the embodiment of religion in social institutions and external forms.
>
> —Christopher Dawson[1]

The forging of a modern slave society without adequate models and precedents challenged the imagination of the South's leaders of public opinion. The novelty of their project seemed to foreclose appeals to historical precedent, and yet the full implications of their own concepts of freedom and equality made useful historical precedents at the same time both necessary and unrealizable. Antiquity had had slave societies, and throughout history most societies, including those of Europe, had included slavery. But in the modern world of expanding capitalism, industrialization, bourgeois individualism, and Enlightenment liberalism, southern slave society appeared increasingly anomalous, the more so since embedded in the world's most democratic republic. For the South to build a modern slave society, no ritualistic defense of the past would serve. An enfranchised nonslaveholding majority found aristocratic pretensions distasteful. The South was rent by competing visions of the good society – the good slave society. Slaveholders who most clearly understood the novelty of the world they were building understood also that it rested on the master–slave relation. Most nonslaveholders – arguably, even in Border States – accepted slavery in principle but often resisted many of its implications, especially the challenge to their Jeffersonian democratic values.

In the United States and Europe conservatives and liberals, reactionaries and revolutionaries all declared themselves the true heirs of the ages and defenders of Western Civilization, its institutions and values. All claimed historical and spiritual continuity with the European past. The eighteenth century's devotion to the

---

[1] Christopher Dawson, *Medieval Essays* (Garden City, NY, 1959), 7, 15.

Enlightenment and to "progress" encouraged disdain for the "backwardness" of the Middle Ages, but by the beginning of the nineteenth century European Romantics were promoting a renewed appreciation for medieval culture. The most thoughtful intellectuals in Great Britain and in the American South understood that the momentous changes of their own era dwarfed any that had occurred between the Middle Ages and the onset of the industrial revolution.[2]

By no means were all southern intellectuals fond of the Middle Ages. Daniel Whitaker, editor of *Southern Literary Journal,* saw a "semi-barbarous and feudal age" dominated by a "supercilious order of nobles" and a "corrupt and debasing aristocracy" with "profligate manners" and an "overbearing and tyrannical temper." Whitaker would not have swallowed Wendell Phillips's contemptuous portrayal of the southern elite as an "aristocracy" fit for the thirteenth and fourteenth centuries. Yet while most southern intellectuals criticized medieval backwardness, they were drawn to what they saw as the divinely inspired, the permanent, and the admirable in the medieval legacy. Ambivalence produced strange contortions. The planters of Carolina contemptuously ignored Locke's grand program to create a hereditary nobility of "Landgraves" and "Caciques," but later Carolinians manifestly longed for the trappings of the medieval aristocracy that had simultaneously repelled and attracted their forebears.[3]

Southerners did not delude themselves that they had or wanted a refurbished medieval society: They did not confuse plantations with manors, slaveholders with feudal lords, or slaves with serfs. Yet they reveled in reading Malory's *Morte d'Arthur,* in the histories of Jean Froissart and Henry Hallam, in Abelard and Héloise, and sometimes even, as with Plowden Weston of South Carolina, in collecting medieval manuscripts.[4]

Thomas Roderick Dew's *Digest of the Laws, Customs, Manners, and Institutions of the Ancient and Modern Nations* divided European history into two parts, ancient and modern, and linked the Middle Ages, together with the Renaissance

---

[2] On the proximity of the Middle Ages to the Victorians, see Walter E. Houghton, *The Victorian Frame of Mind* (New Haven, CT, 1957), esp. 1–6.

[3] On Phillips see Howard R. Floan, *The South in Northern Eyes, 1831 to 1861* (New York, 1958), 13; [Daniel K. Whitaker], "Rienzi," *SLJ,* 2 (1836), 213–14; for the reflections of a descendant of early planters on their attitudes see Samuel Gaillard Stoney, *Plantations of the Carolina Low Country* (Charleston, SC, 1938), 14. For a wartime description by a hostile Northerner of southern life and sensibility as reminiscent of "feudal times," see George H. Hepworth, *The Whip, Hoe, and Sword: Or, The Gulf Department in '63* (Baton Rouge, LA, 1979 [1864]), 78.

[4] During the eighteenth century, medieval forms and motifs steadily declined in southern architecture. For a brief and sober introduction to the southern fascination with the Middle Ages, see Francis Pendleton Gaines, *The Southern Plantation: A Study in the Development and the Accuracy of a Tradition* (Gloucester, MA, 1992 [1924]); Rollin G. Osterweis, *Romanticism and Nationalism in the Old South* (Baton Rouge, LA, 1971), 52–3; on Weston see John B. Irving, *A Day on Cooper River,* ed. Louisa Cheves Stoney, 2nd ed. (Columbia, SC, 1932 [1842]), ix; Richard Beale Davis, *Intellectual Life in the Colonial South, 1515–1763,* 3 vols. (Knoxville, TN, 1978), 3:1145; also, Herbert A. Johnson, *Imported Eighteenth-Century Law Treatises in American Libraries, 1700–1790* (Knoxville, TN, 1978), xiii, xxiii, xxv; W. Hamilton Bryson, *Legal Education in Virginia: A Biographical Approach* (Charlottesville, VA, 1982), 7–8. See also Supplementary References: "Froissart."

and Reformation, to civilized modern nations "that sprang from the ruins of the Roman Empire." He reviled the "barbarism" of the Dark Ages, which reached its nadir about the tenth century, focusing on their low level of agricultural production, commerce, and manufacturing and the wretched conditions of the servile masses. Dew described the aristocracy – its roots in violence, plunder, and injustice – as "An assemblage of individuals, isolated landed possessors – each one setting himself up for himself, a complete spirit of individuality prevailed." Surrounded by "trembling slaves," the feudal lord saw himself as master of all he surveyed, and he "must have been the proudest being on earth." The typical early lord had "that sentiment of personality, of individual liberty, which the barbarian had in the forest." Only two things guaranteed the lord's honor: the "nature of the contract and the sword." A man's word, his loyalty, had to stand like a rock. Rural isolation made the lord psychologically and morally dependent upon his family and prepared to do something Dew considered vital to the progress of civilization – elevate, if gradually, the status of women. While Dew was laying out the essentials of an emerging slaveholders' interpretation, most – although by no means all – northern intellectuals were echoing Voltaire's denunciation of the Middle Ages as contemptible.[5]

Slaveholders, proclaiming themselves modern men who scorned restoration of any past age, insisted on a historical and divinely sanctioned continuity between medieval culture and their own. During the 1840s and 1850s they saw the Middle Ages as simultaneously deformed – by backwardness, superstition, and rigidity – while ennobled by great achievements. William Gilmore Simms, deploring the "supposed degradation of society and the ignorance fancied to have been then present," applauded Thomas Carlyle's and Orestes Brownson's efforts to promote a more positive view of the Middle Ages. The editors of *Southern Presbyterian Review* protested the widespread failure to appreciate the medieval roots of modern political institutions. The Baptist Reverend E. T. Winkler, cautioning against too easy a denigration of the Dark Ages, pointed to the survival and strengthening of Christianity despite barbarous times. Southerners, above all, saw a disastrous rupture between the Middle Ages and the bourgeois world of the North.[6]

---

[5] For this and the following paragraphs see Thomas Roderick Dew, *Digest of the Laws, Customs, Manners, and Institutions of the Ancient and Modern Nations* (New York, 1884 [1852]), 212, 321–40, quotes at 325–6, 331–2. On Voltaire see Toby Burrows, "Unmaking 'The Middle Ages,' " *Journal of Medieval History*, 7 (1981), 129–30. George Frederick Holmes divided European history much as Dew did, but he acknowledged the usefulness of separating the Middle Ages from the ancient world for some purposes: George Frederick Holmes, "Schlegel's Philosophy of History," originally published in *SQR* (1843), in Michael O'Brien, ed., *All Clever Men, Who Make Their Way: Critical Discourse in the Old South* (Fayetteville, AR, 1982), 219–20. In England, "modern" history had long meant post-ancient. Dew was hearkening back to a model that was being discarded elsewhere.

[6] [William Gilmore Simms?], "The History of the Middle Ages," *SWMR*, 1 (1845), 379–80; "Critical Notices," *SPR*, 8 (1855), 601; E. T. Winkler, *The Pulpit and the Age* (Charleston, SC, 1856), 8. Among the many interpretations of the Middle Ages as "a creative epoch" see "Sir J. Stephens' Lectures on the History of France," *SQR*, n.s., 6 (1852), 447; E. A. Lynch, "Influence of Morals on the Happiness of Man," *SLM*, 4 (1838), 145, and Lynch, "Feudalism in the Nineteenth Century," *SLM*, 15 (1849), 465–72; Edward C. Bullock, *True and False Civilization: An Oration Delivered before the Erosophic and Philomathic Societies of the University of Alabama* (Tuscaloosa, AL, 1858), 11–12.

Proslavery intellectuals made a daunting attempt to reconcile slavery to the modern world, cultivating an appreciation of the medieval foundation of the best features of the modern age. Thus, they welcomed the refusal of romantics like François-René de Chateaubriand and Sir Walter Scott to glorify the Enlightenment as a new beginning in world history and appreciated the Romantics' belief that the infinite manifests itself in all ages. In particular, they valued the rediscovery of Christian-based medieval organicism by Saint-Simon and even the socialists, who looked forward to a new type of organic society. They fought to restore respect for authority against democratic leveling.[7]

In reconciling history as high moral lesson with respect for the empirical record, Southerners found a kindred spirit in "glorious old Froissart," author of *Chroniques de France, d'Angleterre, d'Ecosse, de Bretagne, de Gascogne, de Flandre et lieux circonvoisins,* an account of the Hundred Years' War from 1328 until 1400 and beyond. They especially esteemed Froissart, their favorite medieval historian, for his craftsmanship. Simms declared him "a great artist" who did as much with his contemporary documents as they did for him and provided a model for historical reconstruction. Southerners admired Froissart's chivalric reading of history, with great men performing noble deeds and bringing a sense of order to the chaos around them. In 1865 *The Life and Times of Bertrand du Guesclin,* by David Flavel Jamison of Charleston, led Catherine Edmonston back to Froissart, "the fountain head" and a "wonderful book, which should be almost a 'vade mecum' in a boy's education."[8]

Southerners relied, too, on Henry Hallam's *A View of the State of Europe during the Middle Ages* (1818), his *Constitutional History of England* (1827), and his later *Introduction to the Literature of Europe during the Fifteenth, Sixteenth and Seventeenth Centuries.* Hallam's mistrust of lower-class unrest and opposition to the Reform Bill of 1832 may well have seemed congenial to many southern readers. Dew drew on Hallam for his depiction of social conditions in the Middle Ages and medieval chivalry and, with evident relish, cited Hallam's judgment that English laborers fared less well materially before than after their emancipation. With northern conservatives like Chancellor James Kent of New York, Southerners accepted Hallam's view of the early lords as men who began by protecting their peasants after the collapse of ancient Roman authority but who afterwards became their oppressors. Men as ideologically diverse as Mitchell King, Henry Hughes, George

---

[7] See Supplementary References: "Medieval Studies."

[8] For "the glorious old Froissart" see J. Athearn Jones, "Ballads of History – The Vision of Julian the Apostate," *SLM,* 17 (1851), 646; [Simms], "Ramsey's Annals of Tennessee," *SQR,* n.s., 8 (1853), 341; William Gilmore Simms, *The Life of Francis Marion,* 8th ed. (New York, 1844), 103; Mar. 19, 1865, in Beth G. Crabtree and James W. Patton, eds., *"Journal of a Secesh Lady": The Diary of Catherine Devereux Edmonston, 1860–1866* (Raleigh, NC, 1979), 680–1; *SLM,* 26 (1858), 267; Samuel Agnew Diary, July 9, 1862, at UNC-SHC. Dew drew upon Froissart for his own account of peasant insurrections and other matters: *Digest,* 342, 496. See also Supplementary References: "Froissart."

Sawyer, and Francis Lieber recommended Hallam, and W. C. Rives and Margaret Junkin ranked him with Macaulay as a great historical critic.[9]

Hallam had a host of admirers among the South's most influential intellectuals. They applauded the clarity of his style; his knowledge of literature as well as history; his exposure of medieval backwardness and superstition; and his attacks on Scholasticism. *De Bow's Review* called Hallam's *Constitutional History of Britain* "indispensable," and *Southern Quarterly Review* found it a useful weapon against British repression in Ireland. And they, like other Southerners, applauded his insistence on the omnipresence of slavery in world history and its persistence alongside serfdom in medieval Europe.[10]

James Henley Thornwell, however, took a negative view of Hallam, deriding his tribute to the Council of Trent and – with Simms, A. B. Meek, and Hugh Legaré – questioning the accuracy and depth of his scholarship. Thornwell feared the influence of Hallam's generous treatment of the medieval Catholic Church on the southern youth who were reading him in school. George Frederick Holmes, who took a friendly view of the Catholic Church, nonetheless found Hallam silly, although a decade later he cited him as an authority on the omnipresence of servile labor in history and gave him high marks for his work on Rabelais.[11]

Jean Charles Léonard Simonde de Sismondi's 16-volume *Histoire des républiques italiennes au moyen age* – or the 1832 one-volume abridgement in English – received considerable attention from Southerners who liked his version of human freedom and individual rights and his protest against the social costs of industrial capitalism. G. C. Grammer, in *Southern Quarterly Review*, cited Sismondi's foreshadowing of George Fitzhugh's indictment of free labor. Sismondi also foreshadowed – and doubtless influenced – Dew in presenting medieval commercial

---

[9] Dew, *Digest,* 330, 338–40, 350, and pt. 2:ch. 8 on English liberties; Joseph Kent, *Commentaries on American Law,* 2nd ed., 4 vols. (New York, 1832), 3:494–501; John Belton O'Neall, *Biographical Sketches of the Bench and Bar of South Carolina,* 2 vols. (Charleston, SC, 1859), 1:372 (King); Douglas Ambrose, *Henry Hughes and Proslavery Thought in the Old South* (Baton Rouge, LA, 1996), 191–2; George Sawyer, *Southern Institutes; Or, an Inquiry into the Origin and Early Prevalence of Slavery and the Slave Trade* (New York, 1967 [1858]), 146–7 n. 1; Francis Lieber, *A Manual of Political Ethics* (London, 1819), Dedication, 193, 238, 331; Francis Lieber, *On Civil Liberty and Self-Government,* 3rd ed., rev., ed. Theodore D. Woolsey (Philadelphia, 1874 [1853]), 237. Dew's *Digest* sparkles with references to Hallam's authority. "The circumstances we now condemn," Dew wrote, "including the power of the Papacy and the work of the monasteries, constituted, according to Hallam, the bridge which brought the Latin language over the *chasm* of the dark ages." He also favorably cited Hallam's criticism of Luther's Antinomian tendencies: Dew, *Digest,* 330, 338–40, 350, 444 (Luther).

[10] For the reception of Hallam in the South see Supplementary References: "Hallam."

[11] A. B. Meek, *Americanism in Literature: An Oration before the Phi Kappa and Demosthenian Societies of the University of Georgia* (Tuscaloosa, AL, 1844), 17; [Simms?], "History of the Middle Ages," 382–3; J. H. Thornwell, "Romanist Arguments for the Apocrypha Discussed," *JHTW,* 3:428 (Lynch's remarks reprinted as an Appendix, 3:759). Thornwell may also have been infuriated by Hallam's slighting remark – if he knew it – about the "general obscurity" of the style of Bacon's *Novum Organum*: Hallam quoted by John Edwin Sandys, *A History of Classical Scholarship,* 3 vols. (Cambridge, U.K.: vol. 1, 3rd ed., 1921; vols. 2 and 3, 2nd ed., 1908), 2:340.

city-states as the seedbed of representative political institutions. The republican Sismondi scorned egalitarianism and radical democracy and favored a distribution of power that Southerners could find congenial: "General ideas exercise a durable influence only on minds capable of comprehending them. Let liberty exist for all; but let power remain with those who can distinguish the means by which to attain [them]."[12]

Sismondi became increasingly congenial to Southerners as he moved from an early devotion to laissez-faire toward criticism of the cruelties of early industrialization and support for an economic *étatisme* that indicted big capitalists as a threat to individual liberty. Sismondi favored government regulation of production and profits and protection of workers, including their right to join unions. His political economy clearly influenced Dew, who saw the progress of industrialization as irreversible but worried that bourgeois social relations could not sustain social peace as serfdom and slavery could. Class war had accompanied the severing of the organic ties of serfs to lords and the onset of liberty for the masses. Liberation had led to the peasant rebellions of the fourteenth century, to Wat Tyler's revolt in England, and to the great peasant war in Germany in Luther's time. "The hope of freedom produces sullenness and insubordination on the one side, and revenge and cruelty on the other." As long as the dependence of black slaves on their masters remained complete, kindness would continue to mark social relations, but "when the law interposes and inspires [the] negro with notions of freedom, then there is insolence on the one side and revenge and cruelty on the other." Incidentally, the aristocratic Tylers of Virginia prided themselves on their descent from Wat Tyler, which permits us to wonder at their response to *Russell's Magazine*'s depiction of that rebellion as essentially a slave revolt.[13]

---

[12] J. C. L. Sismondi, *A History of the Italian Republics,* ed. Wallace K. Ferguson (Gloucester, MA, 1970), 217; G. C. Grammer, "The Failure of Free Society," *DBR,* 19 (1855); Dew, *Digest,* pt. 2:chs. 4, 5, and 8. "A Lady of Georgia" chided Harriet Beecher Stowe that much could be said for the old feudal principle of placing the weak under the protection of the strong: "Southern Slavery and Its Assailants," *DBR,* 16 (1854), 59. *Southern Quarterly Review* lavished praise on Sismondi's *Historical View of the Literature of the South of Europe* and his "great work" on the history of France: [Thomas Caute Reynolds], "Ticknor's History of Spanish Literature," *SQR,* n.s., 2 (1850), 133; "Stephens' Lectures on France," 443. Reynolds judged him "careful and accurate" as well as "thoughtful and philosophical" (133). For Sismondi as a reliable historian of medieval Spain and the Crusades see *SR,* 5 (1830), 66.
 Notably, Southerners frequently cited or paraphrased his work with or without attribution, but Simms did acknowledge his debt to Sismondi for his own account of the life of the Chevalier Bayard: W. G. Simms, *The Life of Chevalier Bayard: "The Good Knight"* (New York, 1847), vii. For study and appreciation of Sismondi see William Frierson Cooper, "Notes on a Trip to Europe," 31, in W. F. Cooper Papers, at Tennessee State Library and Archives (Nashville). Although Sismondi became a religious skeptic, he was well grounded in the Calvinism of the Huguenots, which made him especially attractive to Presbyterians and Baptists. References to Sismondi's *Italian Republics* turn up in plantation records, regrettably without critical comment: see e.g. William Harris Bragg, *De Renne: Three Generations of a Georgia Family* (Athens, GA, 1999), 18; Harry Clemons, *The Home Library of the Garnetts of "Elmwood"* (Charlottesville, VA, 1957), 7.

[13] Dew, *Digest,* 203–4, 333, 398–401, 406, 495–9 (quotes at 398, 495). Dew considered mercantilist restrictions on free trade a relic of feudalism and an obstacle to economic and social progress: *Essay*

During the 1840s and 1850s, when Dew's analyses became standard fare in academies and colleges, influencing the emerging worldview of the master class, Sismondi's following (in turn) continued to grow. A good many southern Protestants doubtless approved of Sismondi's attacks on the papacy, his belief that Christianity softened the relation of masters to slaves and serfs, and his critique of bourgeois society. Sismondi's work justified admiration for medieval society and the sense that individual freedom was as secure then as now. And Southerners preoccupied with the claims of state rights approvingly noted Sismondi's respect for the advantages of diversity and localism among the Italian republics.[14]

The first issue of *Southern Quarterly Review* (1841), reviewing *Italian Republics* favorably and at length, emphasized its support for unity, the duty to watch leaders carefully, the subversive force of party spirit, the dangers of unbounded prosperity and excessive accumulation of wealth in the hands of a few, and the fragile balance between the honor due heroic popular leaders and the common unfitness for freedom of those who rally to them. T. M. Garrett, a student at the University of North Carolina, drew a hard political conclusion: "Few are fit to rule."[15]

Still, no sensible Southerner confused the slave plantation with the medieval manor, although some colonial Virginians with more than one plantation called their home place "the manor plantation." A chasm separated medieval manors from the modern slave plantations that produced staples for a world market. Seigniorial estates, never entirely self-sufficient, did enter into international commodity production as propitious economic conditions emerged. Eastern Europe accelerated market production during and after the sixteenth century, but it had long existed without strong ties to external markets. Modern slave plantations, in contrast, had no social or economic rationale outside the expanding world market from which they arose. Every modern slaveholder necessarily had to be a kind of businessman whose ability to survive, not to mention prosper, depended upon the supply of and demand

---

on the Interest on Money, and the Policy of the Laws against Usury (Shellbanks, VA, 1834), 8. Lyon Gardiner Tyler, *The Letters and Times of the Tylers*, 3 vols. (Williamsburg, VA, 1884–96), 1:38–41; "Slavery in England," *RM*, 5 (1859), 23. For an illustration of the continuing excoriation of the feudal lords as oppressors see "A Citizen of Alabama", "Henry W. Longfellow and His Writings," *DBR*, 26 (1859), 370. But, criticizing Sismondi's quasi-socialism, a commentator wrote, "Neither morals nor politics are legitimately portions of the science of political economy": *SR*, 4 (1829), 3.

[14] For a critical view of Sismondi see *SLM*, 2 (1836), 197–8; "W. R. H.", "Rome: Papal and Republican," *SLM*, 15 (1849), 547–51; "Rise of Despotism in Europe," *SLM*, 21 (1855), 610–18; T. R. R. Cobb, *An Inquiry into the Law of Negro Slavery in the United States* (New York, 1968 [1858]), xcvii; Sawyer, *Southern Institutes*, 146–7 n. 1; John Fletcher, *Studies on Slavery, in Easy Lessons* (Natchez, MS, 1852), 31–2; *SLM*, 28 (1850), 311–13. Probably, Sismondi also influenced Augustus Baldwin Longstreet, who would have liked to restructure state legislatures to allow for the veto of legislation by representatives of such corporate groups as agriculture, commerce, and manufacturing. "Notes on a Trip to Europe, 1862–1863," in W. F. Cooper Papers; Donald Wade, *Augustus Baldwin: A Study in the Development of Culture in the South* (New York, 1924), 138; A. B. Meek, *Romantic Passages in Southwestern History* (New York, 1857), 133–4.

[15] "History of the Italian Republics," *SQR*, 1 (1842), 157–73; T. M. Garrett Diary, June 14 and 15, 1849, at UNC-SCH; Garrett also praised Cardinal Ximenes for his "firmness."

for slaves and the commodities they produced. The great cultural and political struggles for the soul of the Old South raged between the ideals of a slaveholding southern society and those of the capitalist world in which it was necessarily enmeshed. The same irreconcilable tendencies raged within the plantation world itself, testifying to the Southerners' continuing effort to define and defend their distinct social vision.[16]

Southerners equated slavery and serfdom only for limited purposes, but they saw both as the social bases for rejection of the market as an adequate standard for human relations. However greedy, selfish, and acquisitive, southern slaveholders did not justify their economic activity by a straightforward appeal to the profit motive. Rather, they held that gentlemen needed money to provide for those they called "my family, white and black." Their often intense yearning for wealth and power exemplified little of the historically specific spirit of capital accumulation – of making money to make more money.[17]

Slaveholders celebrated their link to medieval lordship, but as good republicans they pilloried "aristocracy." Proslavery theorists, clerical and lay, saw the Middle Ages as a continuum of class stratification and recognized the extent to which, as twentieth-century scholarship has amply confirmed, white chattel slavery coexisted with serfdom in Western as well as Eastern Europe on a large scale. Proslavery theorists thus emphasized the compatibility of slavery with serfdom and the reduction of the many to the direct control of the few. And, more explicitly than medieval lords had, southern slaveholders proclaimed themselves protectors of the lower classes and guardians of public order. When – borrowing a term from Sir Walter Scott – they referred to themselves as "The Chivalry" and as functional equivalents of the European nobility, they were speaking not only of the graces, accomplishments, and aristocratic virtues they aspired to but also of their commitment to organic social relations as the basis for civilized life.[18]

Proslavery theorists never found it easy to balance their conflicting views of medieval social order. In one view, the emancipation of the serfs and the onset of market relations devastated the lives of the peasants and the poor, now transformed into wage slaves who had to shift for themselves or starve. In the other, emancipation and economic progress introduced individual freedom and republican government.

---

[16] W. C. Duncan implicitly distinguished Russian serfdom from southern slavery and explicitly distinguished it from the residual Russian slavery: "The Empire of Russia – Part 2," *DBR*, 11 (1851), 525–53, 561–2; see also De Bow, "Hungary in 1852," *DBR*, 13 (1852), 433–54.

[17] Notwithstanding extensive criticism, much of it valid, the great work of Karl Marx and Max Weber remains the indispensable introduction to these problems. For our own interpretation see Elizabeth Fox-Genovese and Eugene D. Genovese, *Fruits of Merchant Capital: Slavery and Bourgeois Property in the Rise and Expansion of Capitalism* (New York, 1983); also, Eugene D. Genovese, *The World the Slaveholders Made: Two Essays in Interpretation* (New York, 1969).

[18] On white slavery, not merely serfdom, in medieval and early modern Europe see the voluminous researches of Charles Verlinden as summarized in his *Beginnings of Modern European Colonization* (Ithaca, NY, 1970). In a swelling literature see Pierre Dockès, *Medieval Slavery and Liberation*, tr. Arthus Goldhammer (Chicago, 1982), and Ruth Mazo Karras, *Slavery and Society in Medieval Scandinavia* (New Haven, CT, 1988).

The proslavery theorists who praised the virtues of stable peasant communities and paternalistic benevolence harbored few illusions about the rigors of medieval life or the tendency of medieval lords to treat their peasants horribly, even as they protected them from competing lords. Oppression of the peasantry implicitly threatened the proslavery argument, which insisted that the wage-labor system had severed the historical link between rulers and ruled, replacing humane organic social relations with the callous and brutal relations of the cash nexus. Proslavery theorists, unable to reconcile these mutually contradictory positions, simply discussed them separately without cross-references.

The South's foremost social theorists drew upon the Scottish Historical School's theories of historical stages of economic development. The reasoning that viewed the age of democratic revolution as human progress could view the emergence of feudalism through the same lens. Thus, Henry Hughes, speaking in Port Gibson, Mississippi, explained the rise of feudalism out of the ashes of the Roman Empire as natural, necessary, and positive. He depicted the ruling warrior lords as guarantors of the peasants' sustenance and applauded the priesthood for tempering the warrior spirit. George Fitzhugh wrote in one of his wilder moments: "In the palmy days of royalty, of feudal nobility, and of Catholic rule, there were no poor in Europe." An article in *De Bow's Review,* possibly also by Fitzhugh, reported no paupers, financial crises, or unemployment in the Middle Ages, only responsible nobles and a Church that looked after the less fortunate. George Frederick Holmes was sure that medieval serfs fared better than modern free laborers. Nathaniel Beverley Tucker and James Holcombe, two of Virginia's most respected political theorists, regretted that many descendants of emancipated British and Irish serfs had sunk into degradation far worse than their ancestors had suffered.[19]

William Hutson of South Carolina, whose polemically charged historical commentary enlivened *Southern Presbyterian Review,* acknowledged – while scorning Benjamin Disraeli's "hankering after the barbarous massiveness of feudalism" – that the barons had defended the poor and established an "old bulwark" in "a community of interest." Lord and peasant "prospered or decayed together; there was loyalty and love – and the affections were not entirely the product of money." Modern Europe had no such bulwark: "The capitalist is too sordid to desire it – the social slave too ignorant and too puffed up with fancied rights to consent." The socialistic workshops of revolutionary Paris in 1848 offered new proof that the end of serfdom had shattered the organic unity of society. Hutson thanked God that

---

[19] Henry Hughes, ms. of speech on "The New Governing Class" delivered in Port Gibson, Mississippi (1856), in Hughes Papers, at Mississippi Department of Archives and History (Jackson); George Fitzhugh, "Southern Thought," *DBR,* 23 (1857), 345; George Fitzhugh, *Sociology for the South: Or the Failure of Free Society* (New York, reproduction of 1854 edition), 35; "The Character and Causes of the Crisis," *DBR,* 24 (1858), 27–32; [George Frederick Holmes], "Some Observations on a Passage from Aristotle," *SLM,* 16 (1850), 197; [Holmes], "Slavery and Freedom," *SQR,* n.s. (3rd), 1 (1856), 81–3; Nathaniel Beverley Tucker, "Moral and Political Effect of the Relation between the Caucasian and the African Slave," *SLM,* 10 (1844), 333; James P. Holcombe, "Is Slavery Consistent with Natural Law?" *SLM,* 27 (1858), 408, 412; also, [John Archibald Campbell], "Slavery among the Romans," *SQR,* 28 (1848).

South Carolina had a black "peasantry without political rights" and that "our social slaves are not our equals."[20]

A chapter on "Slavery in the Middle Ages" in George Sawyer's *Southern Institutes* distilled long-evolving themes, notably disgust for the post-emancipation
lords: They were little better than nineteenth-century capitalist landlords who expelled peasants from the land by enclosures of common lands or emancipation,
both of which severed the peasants' ties to the land. But Sawyer also singled out
two great forces for humanity and protection of the lower classes: the influence of
Christianity and the power of the crown. He applauded the Catholic Church for
its defense of slaveholders' property rights. His logic cast the southern slaveholders as rightful heirs to the best in the Middle Ages – as reformed and enlightened
Christians who represented the finest traditions of the old aristocracy and a Christianity cleansed of medieval corruption. As keepers of republican virtue, modern
slaveholders could collectively replace the crown as protector of the poor.[21]

Even Daniel Hundley of Alabama, living as a businessman in Chicago during
the 1850s, deplored the decline of seigniorialism, which had left the peasants of the
British Isles no better off than the serfs: "It may be that the old order of things,
the old relationship between landlord and villein, protected the latter from many
hardships to which the nominal freemen of the nineteenth century are subjected by
the blessed influences of free competition and the practical workings of the good
old charitable and praiseworthy English maxim: 'Every man for himself, and the
devil take the hindmost.'" Hundley acknowledged the benefits of a periodic infu-
sion of fresh, vigorous, middle-class blood into the master class; but, like others, he
stressed the negative effects of leveling and had no sympathy for the revolutionary
overthrow of the Old Régime in France or for the new assaults on the remnants of
the feudal regimes in Europe.[22]

---

[20] [William F. Hutson], "Fictitious Literature," *SPR*, 1 (1847), 67 (on Disraeli); [Hutson], "History of
the Girondists," *SPR*, 2 (1848), 377–413, quotes at 405–6, 410.

[21] Sawyer, *Southern Institutes*, ch. 6, supplemented by 28, 123, 134ff., 252–5, 381; also, Fletcher, *Studies
on Slavery*, 380–1. Frederick A. Porcher, among others, assailed the antislavery Duchess of Sutherland for the removal of peasants from her land: Porcher, "Southern and Northern Civilization Contrasted," *RM*, 1 (1857), 105, and Porcher, "Conflict of Labour and Capital," *RM*, 3 (1858), 293–4; also,
"R. E. C.", "The Problem of Free Society – Part One," *SLM*, 27 (1858), 406. For a Catholic counterpart see Augustine Verot, *A Tract for the Times: Slavery and Abolitionism* (Charleston, SC, 1861), 4.

   Sawyer and other Southerners who attacked the modern enclosures drew upon eighteenth-century
works like that of "Scotus Americanus," who published a pamphlet in 1773 to encourage immigration to North Carolina. He condemned the enclosures and the passage of estates to a new class of
dissipated and conscienceless commercial landowners. Their tenants, he protested, no longer have
"access to their masters." "Scotus Americanus" contrasted the peasants' wretchedness with the ostensibly good treatment afforded the blacks of the Carolinas: "Information Concerning the Province
of North Carolina," in William K. Boyd, ed., *Some Eighteenth Century Tracts Concerning North
Carolina* (Raleigh, NC, 1927), 430, 445.

[22] Daniel R. Hundley, *Social Relations in Our Southern States* (Baton Rouge, 1979 [1860]), 16, 134
(quoted), 148; also, Sawyer, *Southern Institutes*, 381. For parallel thoughts see Haigh Diary, May 18,
1843, and Columbus Morrison Journal, June 30, 1845, both at UNC-SHC.

With increasing boldness proslavery theorists, including the divines, extended their critique of wage labor into a critique of emancipation of the serfs. The Presbyterian Reverend George Armstrong of Norfolk – disgusted by the Roman practice of granting patriarchs power of life and death over wives, children, and slaves – credited Christianity with humanizing the social relations of ancient slave society. William ("Parson") Brownlow, spokesman for the east Tennessee nonslaveholders, criticized the French Revolution for dumping the peasants onto the marketplace. The proslavery Samuel Nott of Massachusetts, much cited in the South, considered France a mess from the Revolution on and saw the emancipation of serfs there and elsewhere as a withdrawal of protection and security.[23]

But what were slaveholders and their theorists to do about the extensive historical evidence of the oppression and degradation of peasants and urban poor? It appalled the leading lights of southern thought – Thomas Cobb, Thomas Cooper, Thomas Roderick Dew, George Tucker, J. D. B. De Bow, Louisa Susanna Mc-Cord. Dew summed up their judgment of the condition of the masses in one word: "wretched." Over time, more and more Southerners acknowledged that much of the lords' vaunted protection of peasants and burghers resembled a protection racket. In 1850 Edward Bryan suggested, "The hardships of the feudal system were perhaps greater than those which have prevailed since the world began." The warlike barons in their castles who sought glory and power had little sympathy for their dependents, virtual slaves who were expected to be grateful to a lord who shielded them from the ravages of other lords. W. M. Burwell of Virginia deplored the burdensome restrictions on commerce and denounced the robber-nobles who preyed on those they claimed to be shielding: "In the feudal ages every castle was a fortress, and every baron exacted pay for protection, or permission to traverse his narrow domain."[24]

"These palaces," James Johnston Pettigrew remarked, "are painful evidence of the preponderance of a few, commanding the services of thousands to minister to their luxury." Pettigrew was protesting the enormous gap between rich and poor that persisted throughout nineteenth-century Europe. Hugh Legaré expressed disgust at the unpaved and incredibly filthy streets he saw in the Rhineland in 1835 and reflected, "Who that sees what their condition is now ... can wonder that they found it intolerable then?" Dew interpreted the medieval peasant wars as

[23] George D. Armstrong, *Christian Doctrine of Slavery* (New York, 1967 [1857]), 59–60; W. G. Brownlow and A. Pryne, *Ought American Slavery to Be Perpetuated: A Debate* (Miami, 1969 [1858]), 21; Samuel Nott, *Slavery, and the Remedy; Or, Principles and Suggestions for a Remedial Code* (Boston, 1856), 36, 87–8. Among the abolitionists, George B. Cheever in particular gave the slaveholders an unintended boost when he wrote of medieval serfdom, "The reality was still that of slavery": *The Guilt of Slavery and the Crime of Slaveholding, Demonstrated from the Hebrew and Greek Scriptures* (New York, 1969 [1860]), xviii. Even medieval jurists sometimes confused the categories "slave" and "serf."

[24] Dew, *Digest*, 322, 326; Edward Brown, *Notes on the Origin and Necessity of Slavery* (Charleston, SC, 1826), 37; Edward B. Bryan, *The Rightful Remedy, Addressed to the Slaveholders of the South* (Charleston, SC, 1850), 20; W. M. Burwell, "Overland and Ocean Routes between the Southwest and Europe," *DBR*, 26 (Jan. 1859), 5. The insistence that feudalism provided security to serfs in a barbarous age continued despite criticism of the condition of the laborers: see e.g. R. S. Breck, "Duties of Masters," *SPR*, 8 (1855), 271.

"partaking mostly of the character of servile insurrections," replete with butchery on both sides, treachery of kings and lords who made promises of amnesty they had no intention of keeping, and the savage violence of insurgents who killed, burned, and raped on a grand scale. Cobb thought no one should be surprised to learn that the brutal treatment of the medieval peasants provoked frequent revolts. Conservatives devoted to social order that they were, these modern slaveholders viewed the European peasant risings with no little sympathy.[25]

College students, following their professors' lead, joined the negative chorus on medieval society. The Reverend Jasper Adams, president of the College of Charleston, termed the Middle Ages a period in which "violence and bad faith were equally the chief characteristics." At the University of North Carolina during the 1850s, John Henderson McDade had nothing good to say: "The moral condition of Europe was sunk in barbarism, superstition and licentiousness." Jesse Harper Lindsay, Jr., spoke of "the feudal system of the Middle Ages and its chivalry" as "possessing still the despotic character of the [imperial Roman] parent." William Horn Battle, Jr., deplored the prevalence of papal power in the eleventh century and feudalism's oppression of the common people. Thomas Berriman Wade agreed that feudalism had retarded the nobler sentiments: "Superstition, ignorance, idolatry and all the direful train of evils incident to this were fully developed." In the face of this onslaught, only the ideal of chivalry, which Southerners prized highly, survived. Wade saw a turning point with eleventh-century warrior knights' efforts to cultivate chivalry. Rufus Brooks Mann praised Americans as "a go-ahead people" but considered chivalric ideals necessary to modern life.[26]

Wayne Gridley's *Slavery in the South* (1845) struck a common note, citing Gibbon on the decline of European slavery and arguing that economic conditions led to the freedom of the medieval serfs and benefited the bourgeoisie more than the serfs or lords. A year later George Calvert, in *Scenes and Thoughts in Europe,* paid generous tribute to the feudal nobility in its rise to power, but he emphasized its subsequent degeneration into a closed and effete caste that oppressed the people and kindled the hostility of a dangerous bourgeoisie poised to finish it off. The conflict aggravated the aristocrats' worst quality, the "feeling of superiority over one's fellows, mere personal pride." He drew the lesson for southern slaveholders: Cultivate republican manners, stay close to your lower classes, and maintain the manly virtues.[27]

---

[25] [James Johnston Pettigrew], *Notes on Spain and the Spaniards in the Summer of 1850, with a Glance at Sardinia* (Charleston, SC, 1861), 24–5, 330; *HLW*, 1:123 (Legaré refers to "Munster" but he surely meant "Münzer" – at the time he was living in the house in which Thomas Münzer, the Anabaptist leader of a great sixteenth-century peasant rising, had been born); Cobb, *Law of Negro Slavery*, cxiv–cxv; Dew, *Digest*, 495–8. G. P. R. James, whom Southerners considered a solid source, maintained without elaboration that lower-class resistance to nobles' oppression had important if indirect effects on the Crusades: *The History of Chivalry* (New York, 1833), 200–3.

[26] Jasper Adams, *Elements of Moral Philosophy* (Philadelphia, 1837), 191. The speeches of Lindsay (1851), Battle (1853), and McDade (1852) are at UNC-NCC: Speeches of Graduates; that of Wade (1858) is at UNC-NCC: Senior Speeches.

[27] [George Henry Calvert], *Scenes and Thoughts in Europe, by an American* (New York, 1846), 32–3; Wayne Gridley, *Slavery in the South: A Review of Hammond's and Fuller's Letters and Chancellor*

Proslavery theorists argued that emancipation of the serfs had served the interests of a new and especially brutal capitalist class and of landlords who yielded to the temptations of a burgeoning marketplace. George Tucker of Virginia maintained that a decline in the value of labor had led to the emancipation of European slaves and serfs and soon would lead to the emancipation of serfs in Russia and, eventually, to the emancipation of American slaves. Tucker, America's ablest theorist of economic development, reasoned – from Ricardian and Malthusian premises and from his painstaking statistical studies of the effects of industrialization, population growth, and the workings of the world market – that slavery had no future because the price of free labor was falling to the bare minimum necessary to reproduce the labor force. In time sane people would choose to exploit free workers at rock-bottom wages rather than assume the burden of raising and caring for slaves.[28]

The South's leading political economists – Jacob Cardozo, De Bow, and Dew – did not dispute Tucker's reasoning, but since (unlike Tucker) they were strongly proslavery, they faced a conundrum. For if it armed them to bash the bourgeoisie for a wage slavery that outdid all previous forms of labor organization in brutality and callousness, so too did it cast doubt on the historical viability of slavery as an alternative. Tucker always insisted that the viability of slavery was ultimately a market question and that emancipation of the slaves would come about through the operation of the market rather than through bloody political interventions. Almost every southern writer agreed that "economic forces" compelled the abolition of serfdom, although most offered a racial qualification Tucker ridiculed: White Europeans possessed superior racial qualities that suited even the masses for responsible freedom, provided they received adequate Christian instruction. The qualification presented problems for the slaveholders' argument that emancipation had been a catastrophe for those same masses who needed protection against bourgeois exploitation and blind market forces. Only social stratification and the subordination of labor seemed to offer resolution of this baffling contradiction, although it was widely assumed that the servitude of presumed racially superior Europeans would be mild and hedged about with a large panoply of rights.[29]

Harper's Memoir on the Subject (Charleston, SC, 1845), 15. Some version of the argument remained in vogue. Villeinage and slavery, a contributor to *Russell's Magazine* wrote, disappeared from England with the emergence of the middle class and in response to economic and political pressures, not in response to Christian influence: "Slavery in England," *RM*, 5 (1859), 19–29.

[28] This was a running theme in Tucker's many books: see e.g. *Progress of the United States in Population and Wealth in Fifty Years* (New York, 1964 [1855]), 110, and *Political Economy for the People* (Philadelphia, 1859). Tucker defended his view of economic development and the fate of slavery within it in an address to the Virginia Historical and Philosophical Society: "A Discourse on the Progress and Influence of Philosophy," *SLM*, 1 (1835), 414–16.

[29] George Frederick Holmes expressed cogently the principal points of agreement among Southerners on the end of serfdom: "Observations on a Passage in the Politics of Aristotle Relative to Slavery," *SLM*, 26 (Apr. 1850), 193–205. For a few supporting texts, see: Cobb, *Law of Negro Slavery*, xlvii, xcix–c, cxii–cxiii, cxxvii–cxxviii; *HLW*, 2:289–90; George Fitzhugh, "The Valleys of Virginia – The Rappahannock," *DBR*, 27 (June 1959), 618; Edmund Ruffin, "The Different Advantages of Large and Small Farms," *Farmers' Register*, 4 (1837), 567; T. W. MacMahon, *Cause and Contrast: An Essay on the American Crisis* (Richmond, VA, 1862), 29–31.

"The present condition of the laboring classes in Great Britain," wrote Cobb, "differs from personal bondage chiefly in the name. Necessity and hunger are more relentless masters than the old Saxon lords .... When time and labor of one person are by any means not purely voluntary, the property of another, [then] the former is a slave and the latter is a master." Pointing to outright slavery in Russia and Turkey, Cobb added that in Hungary and Transylvania "The serfs rise but little above the state of slavery." Slavery, in fact if not in name, would survive until Christian enlightenment purified the heart of man and rendered everyone content "to occupy that sphere for which his nature fit him." The proslavery theorists asserted that direct ownership of human beings in a competitive modern economy compelled masters to take care of their investments and to accept instruction on their Christian duties. This assertion, too, supported an interpretation of free labor as the worst of all possible social arrangements. William Henry Trescot wrote that, with an unraveling social structure, England faced a new class struggle – as the United States would soon have to do. The fate of constitutional freedom, he wrote, depended on the outcome of the struggle to ground it in social relations appropriate to a new stage in human history. Like other proslavery writers, Trescot effectively repudiated everything medieval that might appear morally obnoxious and a fetter on material progress, at the same time holding on to everything that appeared morally superior in social relations.[30]

The critique of the emancipation of the serfs and their subsequent expulsion from the land ought to have raised the question of the proper relation of southern yeoman to planter, for it explicitly argued that the country folk needed the protection of paternalistic lords. But the question drowned in paeans to republican virtue and racial unity. The yeomen did not want to hear about the pastoral beauties of tenancy, although even before the War more southern whites were driven into tenancy, sharecropping, and part-time labor for planters than was recognized at the time. The yeomen despised planters who put on aristocratic airs, but they constantly heard dismaying descriptions of the fate of plain folk in capitalist countries.

Whether from conviction or strategy or both, proslavery ideologues idealized the yeomen in a manner that fit, if awkwardly, into the projection of historical continuity. These sturdy freemen, tried and true, contributed to a solid, stable, religiously grounded community that in one popular version recalled the world of the Celtic clans. It was a romance that obscured much. For just as the slaves were not serfs, so southern yeomen were neither tenants of lordly estates nor formally free but dependent peasants nor the equivalent of farmers in northern market society. The South was developing as a historically unique slave society with historically unique class relations. Its plantation slavery left room for a substantial yeomanry of a distinct social type – or, better, types – that occupied freeholds but remained only weakly integrated into the market. In this respect, too, the world of the plantation ranged

---

[30] Cobb, *Law of Negro Slavery*, cxxxi, also, cxix–cxx; William H. Trescot, *The Position and Course of the South* (Charleston, SC, 1850), 5–6. M. R. H. Garnett agreed that Hungarian peasants were oppressed but described their conditions as mild, making no reference to slavery: [Garnett], "Hungary and Transylvania," *SLM*, 12 (1846), 75–7.

far from that of the medieval manor while it sought an analogous social stability and tried to preserve a sense of being a "traditional" order.

The feudal political system offered southern republicans another opportunity to play *sic et non,* mostly *sic.* On the *non,* John Taylor of Caroline – who hated the medieval aristocracies and feudal political institutions – considered the doctrine of a balance of power between king and lords a swindle to ensure their joint domination of the lower orders, and George McDuffie of South Carolina, who sprang from the yeomanry, simply dismissed feudalism and all its works as reactionary. Henry Augustine Washington, however, protested the "deep-rooted prejudice against the feudal system." Like John C. Calhoun, he traced the modern concept of individual rights to feudalism and its aristocracy and federalism to the ancient and medieval European tradition of sovereign communities. The Magna Carta was the "great prototype" of the 1776 Constitution of Virginia, and the spread of German feudalism saved Europe from plunging into decadence: "The Feudal System has become the keystone of the arch that supports modern liberty and civilization." A contributor to *Southern Literary Messenger* explained that the ancient barbarians who looted and enslaved other peoples maintained among themselves a standard of freedom and a basically republican spirit. He regretted that that spirit made every lord the master of all he surveyed but was pleased it discouraged absolute monarchy and centralized power.[31]

The learned Hugh Legaré expressed cautious approval both of the French kings and the revolutionaries who overcame feudal anarchy and the vestiges of serfdom. The feudal constitution established under the successors of Charlemagne, he said, spread over almost all of Christendom: "With this singular external structure were complicated the consequences of a conquest, the relation of a superior and inferior race, of lord and villein.... There was no social union, no country to serve, no government to obey." Legaré nonetheless lauded English feudalism for providing the basis for the emergence of modern institutions: "England is the nation of Europe whose laws, whose manners, whose whole constitution of society, have been most thoroughly penetrated with the spirit of the feudal system." To Legaré, all the feudal establishments were "a nursery for this spirit of refractory independence." He concluded: "In these, as well as in other respects, modern society has

---

[31] John Taylor, *An Inquiry into the Principles and Policy of the Government of the United States,* ed. Loren Baritz (Indianapolis, IN, 1919 [1814]), 23–5, 114; E. L. Green, ed., *Two Speeches of George McDuffie* (Columbia, SC, 1905), 24–6; Henry Augustine Washington, "The Virginia Constitution of 1776," *SLM,* 18 (1852), 660–1, 666, quotes at 660, 666; J. C. Calhoun, "Speech on the Force Bill," Feb. 16, 1833, in *JCCP,* 12:76. The editor of *Southern Literary Messenger* praised Washington's speech as excellent: "Rise of Despotism in Europe," *SLM,* 21 (1855), 610–18. Edward B. Bryan reinforced the point by noting that the disreputable Rousseau understood and damned the medieval origins of representative government: "Political Philosophy of South Carolina," *SQR,* n.s., 10 (1854), 471–4; also, [David J. McCord], "Political Elements," *SQR,* n.s., 10 (1854), 394–5. J. Quitman Moore of Mississippi relegated feudalism to the grave, but he too noted its lasting contribution to a modern republicanism that stood against radical democracy: "Feudalism in America," *DBR,* 28 (1860), 615–24.

been thoroughly imbued with the spirit of the feudal aristocracy, or, rather, of the military democracy formed by the Teutonic conquerors of Europe."[32]

The lectures of southern educators – the best published as college textbooks, notably Dew on history and Nathaniel Beverley Tucker on political science – inculcated a sense of continuity from medieval constitutionalism to the southern version of modern republicanism. So, too, Thomas Burke Burton's student address to the graduating class of 1852 at the University of North Carolina expressed a southern respect for the legacy of feudal institutions in rejecting radical proposals to abolish property qualifications for voting: "The advocates of the proposed change, in order to arouse our indignation, tell us that the present principle of representation is a remnant of the Feudal system – that it is a scion of that parent by which Europe was enslaved. As well may they condemn the Christian Religion because it has been marked by popish superstition and made the means of temporal power."[33]

Here, southern thought took an ironical turn. "There is something exceedingly melancholy," Dew wrote, "in contemplating the overthrow of the old feudal and municipal liberties of Europe." The aristocracy had fought long and hard for its independence, and the revolution had, after all, "caused torrents of blood to be spilt." Consolidation prevailed: "Europe wanted more repose and security than baronial and city governments could afford, and the rapid increase of regal power, consolidating all the elements of society into a sort of homogenous whole, alone could satisfy the want." Dew knew that the Americans who had risen against the British Crown heralded the "myth of the ancient constitution," as Forrest McDonald calls it, which Americans understood as rooted in the medieval notion that a just government rests on the consent of the governed.[34]

Among more modern commentators, Lord Acton commended Calhoun's interpretation of the American Constitution as "the very perfection of political truth," combining with "the realities of modern democracy the theory and the securities of medieval freedom." Joseph Schumpeter wrote that the medieval Catholic thought did not countenance political authoritarianism: "The divine right of monarchs, in particular, and the concept of the omnipotent state are creatures of the Protestant sponsors of the absolutist tendencies that were to assert themselves in the national states." Ellis Sandoz has added that the very notion of the American Constitution's establishment of a government of laws, not men, represented "an anti-modernist embodiment of medieval principles of order."[35]

No contemporary spoke for the slaveholders to their complete satisfaction on feudalism or any other subject, but Dew approximated a consensus on the essentials. Contrasting Europe as the birthplace of liberty and the fountainhead of human progress with a despotic and static Asia, he identified Caucasian racial superiority

[32] "Constitutional History of Greece," *HLW*, 1:375, 419–20.
[33] T. B. Burton, in *Speeches of Graduates*, 1852, at UNC-NCC.
[34] Dew, *Digest*, 433; Forrest McDonald, *The American Presidency: An Intellectual History* (Lawrence, KS, 1994), 17–20; Richard Schlatter, *Private Property: History of an Idea* (New York, 1951), 91–3.
[35] Acton quoted by C. N. Wilson, ed., in *JCCP*, 12:xxx; Joseph A. Schumpeter, *History of Economic Analysis*, ed. Elizabeth Boody Schumpeter (New York, 1954), 92; Ellis Sandoz, *A Government of Laws: Political Theory, Religion, and the American Founding* (Baton Rouge, LA, 1990), 235.

as the underlying cause while allowing great climatic advantages of the temperate zone. The British constitution, he averred, qualified as "perhaps the most beautiful phenomenon of modern times," and British juridical history echoed "the old Jewish plan"; the Magna Carta, paradoxically, was the child of Norman despotism, yet the foundation of British liberties. Dew traced modern republicanism back to European feudal institutions. Feudalism encouraged private wars, anarchy, confusion, and "individual oppression" but spawned chivalry, national languages, and the beginnings of modern culture. Even its despotisms, being decentralized, left more room for moral and political progress than centralized regimes did. Feudalism's feeling of honorable obligation and manly loyalty "was the conservative principle of society; and was to feudal monarchies as valuable as patriotism in republics." The steady expansion of individual freedom had propelled the material and moral progress of Christian civilization but now threatened to destroy its own great work. Modern slavery was the rightful heir of medieval social relations and the necessary solution to "the social question." Dew understood the contradiction in the process he was describing as well as the dilemma it posed for the slaveholding class.[36]

Harry Hammond of South Carolina lovingly described medieval lords and knights off to battle or the hunt as villagers gazed in "amazement at the display of beauty and magnificence." He regretted their passing but took comfort that villagers still had the Catholic Church for counsel and charity. Participants in debates over medieval social, economic, and political developments saw the Church as social mediator. Many devout Protestants who could not stomach much of the Church's ecclesiology and theology praised it as a civilizing force that had softened the harshest features of medieval society. The sympathy of Holmes, who flirted with conversion to Catholicism, is not surprising, nor is that of the Episcopalians Thomas Roderick Dew, Frederick Porcher, or George Fitzhugh. Even Thomas Cooper grudgingly acknowledged the Church's beneficial role. He especially hated the Presbyterians but had no fondness for any clergy and certainly not for the Roman, yet his lectures on political economy at the College of South Carolina generously credited the Church with having used its accumulated riches in a way morally superior to anything seen since. Dew credited the Church and its monasteries with advancing European civilization, humanizing and stabilizing social relations, and defending the poor and oppressed against the feudal lords' rapacity. Dew gave his students an evenhanded account of the doctrinal and political struggles between Catholics and Protestants and expressed admiration for the medieval popes' defense of the people against their lords, for promoting civilized life through Truce of God and Peace of God, for permitting social mobility in a rigidly structured society, and for defending

---

[36] Dew, *Digest*, 36–7, 340, 461, 465, 469. For an elaboration see Eugene D. Genovese, *The Slaveholders' Dilemma: Freedom and Progress in Southern Conservative Thought, 1820–1860* (Columbia, SC, 1991). The significance of the feudal legacy, including the Magna Carta, for the development of modern constitutionalism – especially in the version that southern conservatives have always appreciated – is well defended in Fred A. Cazel, Jr., ed., *Feudalism and Liberty: Articles and Addresses of Sidney Painter* (Baltimore, 1961), esp. 13, 256, 263–4, and in Sandoz, *Government of Laws*, 33–5, 87–8, 201–2.

institutional autonomy against the demands of a centralizing state: "With all its faults and vices, the church was the most democratic institution in Europe before the rise of the cities."[37]

Porcher deplored the vast prejudices that interfered with a proper evaluation of the Middle Ages, and he criticized Protestants, including the leaders of the Reformation, for undervaluing the social stability and discipline the Catholic Church had imposed on an anarchic society. He defended the Church's insistence on a celibate clergy, wrote glowingly of Pope Gregory VII, commended the concern for the poor, and even had a few good words for the Jesuits. Porcher and James Johnston Pettigrew, while conceding that the Spanish Inquisition eventually turned into a horror, defended it as a proper effort to put down conspiracies against the Crown fomented by hypocrites who secretly maintained loyalty to Muslim and Jewish forebears and by Protestants all too prone to revolution.[38]

Most Southerners, like Gibbon, saw the Crusades as driven by savage fanaticism. As early as 1818, in an Address to the Clarisophic Society at the College of South Carolina, a precocious 15-year-old C. G. Memminger called the Crusades "stupendous monuments of human credulity" even as he credited them with opening the East to commerce and enlightenment. Dew judged the Crusades "the most stupendous monument of human folly, which has ever been produced by a fanatical superstition operating on an ignorant world" but paid tribute to their contributions to civilization and commercial development. In 1833, G. P. R. James's popular *History of Chivalry* offered another view – a grim account of the disgraceful behavior of the Christians Crusaders at Constantinople, including their indulgence in cannibalism, contrasting it with the behavior of Near Eastern Christians who lived peacefully for long periods in Muslim Palestine and who were appalled by the horrors perpetrated by the Crusaders. Still, James granted that the Crusades were a flawed effort to repel a mounting danger from Muslim imperialism, and he denied that Christian atrocities outstripped those of others in those barbarous times.[39]

---

[37] [Harry Hammond], "European Correspondence," *RM*, 2 (1857/58), 37–8, quote at 37; Thomas Cooper, *Lectures on the Elements of Political Economy*, reproduction of 2nd ed. (New York, 1971 [1830]), 8; Thomas Roderick Dew, *Lectures on the Restrictive System, Delivered to the Senior Class of William and Mary College* (Richmond, VA, 1829), 137–40; Dew, *Digest*, 333–4, 371, 378, 379, 387, 391–6, 402, 449, and, generally, pt. 2:ch. 3, quotes at 378, 391. For the Church as the guardian of social order and defender of the poor and oppressed, see "The Study of History," *SQR*, 10 (1846), 133. E. A. Lynch, striving for a balanced view of Dark and Middle Ages, deplored the "debasement of our species" but acknowledged great advances in learning and the arts. He saw feudalism and the Church as abusive but credited the clerics with having restored civilized life: Lynch, "Influence of Morals on the Happiness of Man," 145.

[38] F. A. Porcher, "False Views of History," *SQR*, n.s., 6 (1852), 31–8; [Pettigrew], *Spain and the Spaniards*, 322. The essential and often heroic contributions of the Church to the relief of the poor is amply demonstrated by Michel Mollat, as are the efforts of Louis IX of France and other kings whom Southerners were wont to see as opponents of increasing bourgeois exploitation: *The Poor in the Middle Ages: An Essay in Social History*, tr. Arthur Goldhammer (New Haven, CT, 1986). But for a more typical southern assessment of the Jesuits as purveyors of "a well planned scheme of universal domination," see "Ignatius Loyola," *QRMECS*, 3 (1849), 603–18, quote at 603.

[39] Edward Gibbon, *The History of the Decline and Fall of the Roman Empire*, ed. David Womersley, 3 vols. (London, 1994), 3:727; Memminger, "The Art of Printing," in Henry D. Capers, *Life and Times*

In 1846 a disgusted contributor to *Southern Quarterly Review* (probably Francis P. Lea) described as "folly" a Christian crusade against infidels that ended with the spectacle of some Christians protecting other Christians against still other Christians. He sadly described the Knights Templars' promising beginnings and brave fighting in Europe – followed by their succumbing to vice and corruption in the Near East, lured by wealth and opportunities for plunder. An article in the University of Virginia's *Jefferson Monument Magazine* referred to the "constant depredation, and perpetual war, anarchy and despotism" that marked the medieval state. The fanatical spirit of the Crusades, like that of the witch craze in seventeenth-century New England, prefigured the fanaticism that Southerners saw in abolitionism and its root in what William Rivers, a South Carolina historian, referred to as "the spreading fanaticism of a universal brotherhood."[40]

In 1851 Claudius Saunders, a student at the University of North Carolina, said of the medieval Church: "Its salutary efforts in restraining the violence of feudal anarchy in a measure atoned for the many evils practised within its own pale." For Saunders, the monks had preserved learning and the Crusaders spread Christianity, although it took the Reformation to free men's minds. He said no more than leading southern intellectuals were already saying with increasing boldness – some, like John Berrien Lindsley, increasingly suspicious of radical attacks on established religion, including those by Protestant reformers. J. M. Boyd, a student at the University of Virginia, expressed the sentiments of many when he wrote that the Catholic Church alone saved Europe during the long night of the soul that followed the collapse of the Roman Empire: "At a time when the world was one scene of violence and depravity, the Church was the centre and embodiment of all the good that survived."[41]

---

of *C. G. Memminger* (Richmond, VA, 1893), 495; Dew, *Digest,* 394–7, quote at 391 (Dew pointedly condemned the murder of Jews in the Rhineland); James, *History of Chivalry,* 72, 76–7, 284–5, for Christian atrocities see 148–9 and on cannibalism under Boemond see 139, 163; for chivalry see chs. 1 and 15. For attempts at a balanced view see also [George Frederick Holmes], "Gibbon's Decline and Fall," *MMQR,* 4th ser., 10 (1856), 331; [Holmes], "The Bacon of the Nineteenth Century," *MMQR,* 4th ser., 5 (1853), 350. Michaud's *History of the Crusades* was commended as rich in new data and balanced interpretation: *SQR,* n.s., 8 (1853), 255–6; [J. R. Thompson], *SLM,* 19 (1853), 318. For a portrayal of the Crusades as disasters that watered the flowering chivalry necessary to defend Christian Europe against a barbarian Muslim onslaught, see [J. P. Tusten], "Chivalry and Civilisation," *SPR,* 6 (1851), 218.

40 [Francis P. Lea?], "The Knights Templars," *SQR,* 9 (1846), 457–507; *Jefferson Monument Magazine* (Charlottesville), 2 (1851), 262; "The Crusades," *SQR,* n.s. (3rd), 1 (1856), 343–83; William J. Rivers, *Address Delivered before the South Carolina Historical Society on Their Twenty-first Anniversary* (Charleston, SC, 1876), 11, 20. For the Crusades as "a superstitious zeal" and a "fanatical spirit" that nonetheless saved Europe from "the corrosive influences and intellectual darkness of Islam," see "J. B. C." [Cobb], "Macaulay's History of England," *American Whig Review,* 11 (1850), 349. E. Boyden agreed that the Crusades transformed religious inspiration into a morally diseased fanaticism: "The Epidemic of the Nineteenth Century," *SLM,* 31 (1860), 365–74.

41 Claudius B. Saunders, "Progress of Civilization," in Speeches of Graduates, 1851, at UNC-NCC; J. B. Lindsley, "Memoranda," June 4, 1863 , in John Berrien Lindsley papers, at Tennessee State Library and Archives (Nashville); J. M. Boyd, "Roman Catholicism and Free Institutions," *VUM,* 4 (1860), 341–53, quote at 343–4. Even some Presbyterian divines credited the Catholic Church and the

John Fletcher, in his influential *Studies on Slavery,* commended the Catholic Church and the popes for having pacified and civilized Europe during the Dark Ages. Noting the Church's refusal to declare slavery sinful, he recommended Bishop John England's essays on its historical relation to slavery and emancipation. Thomas Cobb, Robert Dabney, and George Fitzhugh – as well as the author of an article for *Russell's Magazine* entitled "Slavery in England" – made much of the Church's continued recognition of slavery in medieval Europe, reminding Southerners that it had never assailed the rights of masters nor encouraged the insubordination of slaves. In the Southwest, A. B. Meek of Alabama celebrated "the fierce and fiery chivalry of Spain" in the De Soto expedition, "accompanied by a pious priesthood ever bearing aloft the symbol of Christianity"; after the War, J. F. H. Claiborne of Mississippi described the Spanish conquerors of Louisiana as "a troop of cavaliers": "a race of heroes, bold, arrogant, and generous, who believed it their mission to carry the religion of Christ, by conquest, into the territories of the infidel." The "Castilian chivalry" did not stoop to the commission of atrocities like Sherman's march to the sea and the devastation of the Valley of Virginia.[42]

Like many British Victorian intellectuals, Southerners passed over the Renaissance and Early Modern eras and – like John Stuart Mill, Thomas Arnold, and other British intellectuals – saw themselves as living in an age of transition from "feudal" to some "modern" times yet to be determined. Walter Houghton writes, "From their perspective it was the medieval tradition from which they had irrevocably broken." As late as 1869–70 Baldwin Brown could claim, "Until quite recently,... our modes of thought and speech, our habits of action, our forms of procedure in things social and political, were still feudal." Thomas Carlyle, John Ruskin, and Thomas Arnold viewed their era as one of "decaying feudalism." Edward Bulwer-Lytton captured the tension: "We of a certain age belong to the new time and the old one. We are of the time of chivalry as well as the black Prince of St. Walter Manny. We are of the age of steam."[43]

Southerners very much resembled the British in treating the centuries between the Middle Ages and the present as an extension of the Middle Ages. Both the

---

monasteries with accomplishments – notably education of the leading classes, preservation of learning, and promotion of the early universities: L. Stanton, "Inaugural Address," in Oakland College Board of Trustees, *Addresses on the Inauguration of Rev. Robert L. Stanton* (Oakland, MS, 1851), 11–14. For a harsh student attack on the medieval church for corruption and political tyranny see J. B. Thompson, "Religion and Learning in the Middle Ages" (M.A. thesis, 1854, typescript at UVA).

[42] Fletcher, *Studies on Slavery,* 256–9, 266–7; T. R. R. Cobb, "An Historical Sketch of Slavery," in Cobb, *Law of Negro Slavery,* ch. 7; "Slavery in England," *RM,* 5 (1859), 26–7; Robert L. Dabney, *Defence of Virginia (and through Her of the South) in Recent and Pending Contests against the Sectional Party* (New York, 1969 [1867]), 186, 203–4; George Fitzhugh, *Sociology for the South,* and *Cannibals All!; Or Slaves without Masters* (Cambridge, MA, 1960 [1857]); Meek, *Romantic Passages,* 48, 80–1; J. F. H. Claiborne, *Mississippi as a Province, Territory, and State, with Biographical Notices of Eminent Citizens* (Spartanburg, SC, 1880 [1978]), 2.

[43] This argument is elegantly developed by Houghton, *Victorian Frame of Mind,* esp. 1–3, where all these citations may be found. For specifics see John Stuart Mill, *The Spirit of the Age,* ed. F. A. von Hayek (Chicago, 1942), 6; James Baldwin Brown, "The Revolution of the Last Quarter Century," in *First Principles of Ecclesiastical Truth: Essays on Church and Society* (London, 1871).

British and Southerners felt themselves heirs of a series of intellectual revolutions, most notably the Reformation but also the Renaissance, the scientific revolution, and the Enlightenment. Southerners' conviction that slavery was a humane and just social order gave them special reason to defend features of medieval social relations, although their relations to medieval religious thought, which encompassed the majority of medieval intellectual traditions, were more complex.

Some southern intellectuals, clerical and lay, contemptuously dismissed Scholasticism as worthless abstractions that retarded science; others credited it with formidable contributions to Christian thought, modern philosophy, and science. Thornwell applauded Albertus Magnus for introducing Aristotle into thirteenth-century Europe and demonstrating that a science of the infinite is impossible, and he admired much in Thomas Aquinas' *Summa,* but had no doubt that the Scholastics' speculations had prepared the way for the infidelity and incoherence of modern philosophy. Regrettably, neither he nor any other southern divine offered sustained criticism, but certain medieval writers touched a wide southern audience well beyond the ranks of the intellectual elite.[44]

Boethius' *The Consolation of Philosophy* and Thomas à Kempis's *Imitation of Christ* ranked close to John Bunyan's *Pilgrim's Progress* as favorites. Boethius turned up in southern homes and on college reading lists with surprising frequency. Boethius had been a principal figure in the transmission of patristic doctrine to the Latin Middle Ages, and his codification of Trinitarianism influenced Thomas Aquinas as well as Dante. His translation, preservation, and synthesis of Greek sources may have contributed to Southerners' understanding of medieval philosophy, but he owed his greater renown to *The Consolation of Philosophy* (525 A.D.), written in prison while awaiting execution by the Ostrogoth King Theodoric. As a Trinitarian in a regime presided over by the Arian Theodoric, Boethius called for the reconciliation of faith and reason, offering strong support to the Trinitarians of later centuries in their struggle against the inroads of Unitarianism. Southerners were led to Boethius not only by their ministers but, ironically, by Edward Gibbon, who described *The Consolation* as "a golden volume" worthy of the leisure of Plato or Cicero but who saw him, as Philip Schaff tended to, as basically an ethical philosopher in the tradition of Plato and Seneca and not a Christian at all.[45]

---

[44] In *JHTW*, see 1:34–5, 49, 193, 334–40, 470, 519–25, 579, 604–5; 3:18–25, 131, 140, 153, 173, 180–9, 230, 235, 271–2, 498. For attacks on Scholasticism as worthless see: *SR*, 1 (1828), 89; Edwin Hubbell Chapin, "Anniversary Address Delivered before the Richmond Lyceum," *SLM*, 5 (1839), 726; and J. S. Lamar, *The Organon of Scripture; Or, the Inductive Method of Biblical Interpretation* (Philadelphia, 1860), 118. For positive assessments see "History of Philosophy," *SQR*, n.s. (3rd), 2 (1856), 230. Professor Charles Scott Venable of South Carolina College defended the Scholastics' philosophical contributions: *An Address Delivered before the Alumni of the University of Virginia* (Richmond, VA, 1859), 18. George Frederick Holmes considered the Schoolmen as "unjustly neglected": [Holmes], "Blakey's History of Logic," *MMQR*, 4th ser., 8 (1856), 516. See also Charles Henry Foster, who attributed to Abelard the rise of religious skepticism and its attendant political views: "Blaise Pascal," *SLM*, 27 (1858), 64. For a Methodist defense of contributions of the Middle Ages to philosophy see L. I. Gogerty, "Scholasticism – Abelard," *QRMECS*, 12 (1858), 41–59. See also Supplementary References: "Nominalism and Realism."

[45] Gibbon, *Decline and Fall*, 2:550–3, quote at 553, and 2:chs. 21 and 39. See also Supplementary References: "Boethius and Thomas à Kempis."

Boethius' *Consolation* taught a hard lesson that strengthened Southerners during the War: Since worldly success does not always crown good and virtuous deeds, good people must brace themselves for the worldly success of the ungodly. The answers to the most difficult and trying questions must belong to the individual – must be transformed "into ourselves in the innermost chambers of our being." He whose riches and honors have been arbitrarily stripped away, who is "blinded by grief" and "sunk in lamentation over his losses," in the end glimpses the greater riches "of his inclusion in that greater and more real reality." Southerners who considered themselves good people, besieged in a transatlantic world increasingly dominated by enemies of religion and social order, could read: "To oppose evil men is the chief aim we set before ourselves. Though the band of such men is great in numbers, yet it is to be contemned: for it is guided by no leader, but is hurried along at random only by error running riot everywhere." To South Carolinians or Mississippians Boethius could be talking about the rising tide of abolitionism.[46]

Thomas à Kempis, like Boethius, called upon reason to support religious faith and promoted the principles of the "common life" as a guide to a holy and devout life. His *Imitation of Christ* (1418) counseled the peace that could come from a turning away from the ways of the world and toward "believing, confessing, preaching." It attracted the attention of educated women of the coastal Carolina–Georgia elite, including Mary Chesnut and Mrs. Henry Rowe Schoolcraft. But the Presbyterian Dabney questioned its view of salvation and spoke of the darker ages of Christianity and of Thomas à Kempis's "perverted piety." Thornwell expressed similar concerns about Boethius.[47]

Many Southerners paid little mind to Protestant theologians' occasional reservations about the Catholicism of Boethius, à Kempis, or Dante and his "immortal" *Divine Comedy.* Indeed, if the abolitionist George Cheever wished to infuriate Southerners, he could not have done it more effectively than by opening and closing his *Wanderings of a Pilgrim* (1865) with quotations from Dante, whom well-educated Southerners loved and regarded as their own.[48]

---

[46] Thomas à Kempis, "Imitation of Christ," in Irwin Edman, ed., *Consolation of Philosophy* (New York, 1943), 8. John Edwin Sandys minimized the Christian quality of *Consolation:* see *History of Classical Scholarship,* 1:151–258, 646.

[47] Chesnut Diary, Feb. 19, 1865, in C. Vann Woodward, ed., *Mary Chesnut's Civil War* (New Haven, CT, 1981), 72; *Plantation Life: The Narratives of Mrs. Henry Schoolcraft* (New York, 1969 [1860]), 321; Robert L. Dabney, *Systematic Theology* (Carlisle, PA, 1985 [1878]), 702; *DD,* 1:645–6; *JHTW,* 1:192–3, 470, 472.

[48] George Cheever, *Wanderings of a Pilgrim in the Shadow of Mont Blanc and the Jungfrau Alp* (Glasgow, 1865), x, 367. For the "immortal" Dante see A. J. X. Hart, *The Mind and Its Creations: An Essay on Mental Philosophy* (New York, 1853), iii, and "T. W. M.", "Les Miserables," *SLM,* 35 (1863), 438; for the "divine" Dante see [A. Corcoran], "Prospects of Italy – Italian Unification," *RM,* 3 (1858), 460. Those who had no Italian learned something of Italian literature from Leigh Hunt's *Stories from the Italian Poets* (1846) and from Sismondi's *De la litterature du midi de l'Europe,* which J. R. Thompson recommended as learned, accurate, and the product of a man of cultivated philosophical taste: *SLM,* 14 (1848), 263. For Catherine Edmonston, *De la litterature* qualified as "rather a dull work, but useful, especially for tracing the downward course of the Italian muse just now. From Tasso to Goldoni and Gozzoli. What a fall!": Aug. 29, 1862, in Crabtree and Patton, eds., *"Journal of a Secesh Lady,"* 247.

The Reverend E. T. Winkler described *Divine Comedy* as "the grandest, sweetest, and most tender epic that ever poured its passion into human speech." For Dew, the Italians had produced the greatest of early modern literature, with Dante and Petrarch the "morning stars." Augusta Jane Evans of Mobile considered *Divine Comedy* "far superior" to *Paradise Lost*. An array of leading southern intellectuals offered homage to Dante, among them Hugh Legaré, Joseph B. Cobb (author of *Mississippi Scenes*), Margaret Junkin Preston of Virginia, the Baptist Reverend Richard Furman, the Presbyterian Reverends George Howe and R. L. Dabney, and William Holcombe of Natchez. Dante's opposition to papal intervention in secular affairs drew praise, and De Bow, in a stretch, put him in a proslavery polemic by suggesting that the oppression of the British poor exceeded even Dante's imagination of hell. But perhaps most important, his southern admirers could see Dante, as Cheever did, as a premature Protestant.[49]

There were other favorites, most notably *Pilgrim's Progress* and *Grace Abounding* by "the immortal" John Bunyan, as the Baptist Reverend Hosea Holcombe of Alabama dubbed him. Clement Eaton has written that between 1800 and 1860 "thousands of planter families" read Bunyan, fascinated by the allegory of Beulah Land and the Celestial City. The Reverend John Landrum was probably not the only Southerner who knew *Pilgrim's Progress* almost by heart. De Bow and Simms were captivated by it in their youth, and countless women in the South took it as the model for their own spiritual progress – or backsliding. Richard Furman's long poem "The Pleasures of Piety" compared the effects of twelve years of imprisonment on Bunyan's writing of *Pilgrim's Progress* to those of John's banishment to the Isle of Patmos, where he held direct conversation with God and wrote the Book of Revelation.[50]

[49] E. T. Winkler, *An Address Delivered before the Philosophian and Adelphian Societies of Furman University* (Greenville, SC, 1853), 12, also 19; Dew, *Digest*, 521; Evans to Rachel Lyons, Jan. 4, 1860, in Rebecca Grant Sexton, ed., *A Southern Woman of Letters: The Correspondence of Augusta Jane Evans Wilson* (Columbia, SC, 2002), 2; Linda Rhea, *Hugh Swinton Legaré: A Charleston Intellectual* (Chapel Hill, NC, 1934), 53; Joseph B. Cobb, "Italian Literature," *QRMECS*, 9 (1855), 238, 245; "Notebook," 1850s, in Margaret Junkin Preston Papers, at Washington and Lee University; Richard Furman, *The Pleasures of Piety and Other Poems* (Charleston, SC, 1859), 162, 178–84; George Howe, "Secondary and Collateral Influences of the Sacred Scriptures," *SPR*, 7 (1853), 119; Thomas Cary Johnson, ed., *Life and Letters of Robert Lewis Dabney* (Carlisle, PA, 1977), 334, 457; W. H. Holcombe Diary, Jan. 17 and Feb. 4, 1855, at UNC-SHC; J. D. B. De Bow, *The Industrial Resources, Statistics, &c. of the United States and More Particularly of the Southern and Western States*, 3rd ed., 3 vols. (New York, 1966 [1854]), 1:24. Hart, in Mobile, quoted Ariosto's *Orlando Furioso* on the frontispiece of his *Mind and Its Creations*. See Supplementary References: "Dante."
[50] Hosea Holcombe, *A History of the Rise and Progress of the Baptists in Alabama* (Philadelphia, 1840), 32; Clement Eaton, *The Mind of the Old South* (Baton Rouge, LA, 1964), 177–8; H. P. Griffith, *The Life and Times of Rev. John G. Landrum* (Charleston, SC, 1992 [1885]), 240; Paul Hamilton Hayne, "Ante-Bellum Charleston," *Southern Bivouac*, 1 (1885), 262 (Simms); Furman, *Pleasures of Piety*, 45, 61–4; also, William Harris Hardy and Toney A. Hardy, *No Compromise with Principle: Autobiography and Biography of William Harris Hardy* (New York, 1946), 28 (Alabama in the 1840s); Agnew Diary, May 23, 1864; William S. Powell, *When the Past Refused to Die: A History of Carswell County, North Carolina, 1777–1977* (Durham, NC, 1977), 409; Henry L. Poe, "John Bunyan," in Timothy George and David S. Dockery, eds., *Baptist Theologians* (Nashville, TN, 1990), 26–48; Jan. 24 and Feb. 14, 1858, in Paul D. Escott, ed., *North Carolina Yeoman: The Diary of Basil Armstrong*

Thomas Smyth recommended Richard Baxter, one of the most eminent of seventeenth-century English divines and theologians. Baxter's *Saints' Everlasting Rest* smoothed the way for Susan Catherine Botts of Richmond, among others, to enter the Presbyterian Church. Thornwell snorted a bit about Baxter's Arminianism, but the southern churches, including the Presbyterian, admired Baxter, whose *Christian Directory* offered a bonus in a chapter of advice to masters on their duties to servants. American slaveholders read it during the seventeenth century, and the Reverend C. C. Jones, Georgia's foremost missionary to the slaves, drew on it directly in the middle of the nineteenth. George Whitfield, whose sermons were still read in the South during the nineteenth century, strongly recommended Baxter, and Methodist preachers brought *Imitation of Christ* and *Everlasting Life* to camp meetings. Arminians and Calvinists both read *Saints' Everlasting Rest,* if usually in abridgement; it became one of the most popular books in the South and with the Confederate troops. Devotional and spiritual reading provided an important bridge between Southerners and the Middle Ages.[51]

The Middle Ages offered an indispensable foundation – and justification – for many cherished southern beliefs despite practices they believed they themselves had overcome and left behind. Whether in religion or social relations, the Middle Ages illuminated for Southerners the tension between continuity and change. Medieval history comforted them, too, with reassurances about the ubiquity of slavery, dependency, and hierarchy, while simultaneously reminding them of their own allegiance to modernity. How much of the old could they carry and still embrace the best of their own time? How much could they relinquish and still sustain their distinct values and social system? They knew that the medieval world was not – never could be – theirs. But they determined to preserve its most admirable features as they fought to build a bulwark against the morally corrosive features of the modernity that was breaking upon them.

Thomasson, 1853–1862 (Athens, GA, 1996), 189, 190. Basil Lanneau Gildersleeve assumed that educated Southerners also knew Bunyan's *The Holy War*: see Gildersleeve, *The Creed of the Old South* (Baltimore, 1915), 61. Bunyan was also immensely popular in the colonial North, especially with *Grace Abounding* (his spiritual autobiography) and *Pilgrim's Progress*: see Kevin J. Hayes, *A Colonial Woman's Bookshelf* (Knoxville, TN, 1996), 44.
51 *TSW,* 5:153–6 (Smyth's list of books that Christians should have at home included Foxe's *Book of Martyrs*, Bunyan's *Pilgrim's Progress*, Law's *Serious Call*, and everything by Baxter, Edwards, and Whitfield); A. B. Van Zandt, *"The Elect Lady": A Memoir of Mrs. Susan Catherine Bott, of Petersburg, Va.* (Philadelphia, 1857), 118; *JHTW,* 3:387. See also Supplementary References: "Baxter."
   William Law trailed Bunyan in popularity but not by much; more nineteenth-century Southerners may have read the former's *Serious Call to a Devout and Holy Life* (1728) than read à Kempis's *Imitation of Christ*. Law tried to mediate between pietism and rationalism without reducing Christianity to mere moralism: see Jaroslav Pelikan, *The Christian Tradition: A History of the Development of Doctrine,* 5 vols. (Chicago, 1989), 5:49–59, 149, 152–3. Nathaniel Russell Middleton, who grew up in coastal South Carolina early in the nineteenth century, tried to mold his life according to the aphorism in *Serious Call*: "If religion is worth anything, it is worth everything": "Reminiscences," in Alicia Hopton Middleton et al., *Life in Carolina and New England during the Nineteenth Century* (Bristol, RI, 1929), 202. Paeans to Law and *Devout Life* were scattered through such publications as *Charleston Gospel Messenger and Protestant Episcopal Christian Register* – see e.g. 1 (1824).

10

The Chivalry

> Now the man Moses was very meek, above all the men which were upon the face of
> the earth.
>
> —Numbers, 12:3

Gone With the Wind and the many novels about the grace and charm of life in the
Old South have taught a popular view of Southerners' attachment to the concept
of chivalry, but even the more historically sophisticated remain vague about the actual place of chivalry in southern culture, missing its medieval source. The chivalry
of the Middle Ages, as Richard Kaeuper demonstrates, rested upon – and uneasily
bridged – contradictory allegiances to Christianity and to violence, producing tensions that persisted in Southerners' attempts to defend their ideal of chivalry in their
unique modern slave society.[1]

The medieval ideal of meekness in the ferocious warrior and of ferocity in the
meekest of men lay at the heart of the southern ideal of the gentleman, which
chivalry inspired and informed across differences of region and social class. The
Presbyterian Reverend Frederick Ross and his doctrinal and political arch-foe, the
Methodist Reverend William G. Brownlow, for once saw eye to eye. Ross, scion of
a planter family in Virginia, taunted the abolitionists: "Oh sir, if slavery tends in
any way to give the honor of chivalry to Southern young gentlemen towards ladies,
and the exquisite delicacy of heavenly integrity and love to Southern maid and matron, it has then a glorious blessing with its curse." Brownlow, a spokesman for
the plain folk of east Tennessee and a plebeian to his core, defiantly exclaimed during a debate with an abolitionist in Philadelphia, "Yes, gentlemen, ours is the land
of chivalry, the land of the muse, the abode of statesmen, the home of oratory; the
dwelling place of the historian and the hero."[2]

---

[1] Richard W. Kaeuper, *Chivalry and Violence in Medieval Europe* (New York, 1999). The southern
version of the ideal combined the original medieval model with its late medieval and Renaissance
transformations.
[2] Frederick A. Ross, *Slavery Ordained of God* (Philadelphia, 1857), 20; W. G. Brownlow and A. Pryne,
Ought American Slavery to Be Perpetuated: A Debate (Miami, 1969 [1858]), 271.

In language that became steadily more popular during the nineteenth century, worthy southern youth were "knights." Jefferson Davis invoked the term frequently in his account of the War, as when he praised General John B. Macgruder as "knightly." To the Presbyterian Reverend Benjamin Morgan Palmer, Wade Hampton was "the Chevalier Bayard of the South – the chivalrous knight 'without fear and without reproach.'" Even after the War, Carolinians spoke of Micah Jenkins, John Ashe, and Abner Nash as knights, and Mary Gay of Georgia wrote, "Our Bayard sans peur et sans reproche, General Lee." Frank Ticknor in 1893: "The knightliest of the knightly race / Who since the days of old / Have kept the lamp of chivalry." As late as 1905, Rabbi Bennett Elzas declared that South Carolina stands "for culture, for chivalry, and for exalted citizenship, for higher ideals than which no people ever possessed."[3]

In 1927 William Faulkner chose Bayard for the name of the restless, self-destructive protagonist of his first novel, *Flags in the Dust*. This fictional flying ace of the early 1920s evokes an earlier Bayard Sartoris, subject of the reminiscences of Aunt Jenny, "who told them of the manner of Bayard Sartoris' death prior to the second battle of Manassas." Linking the Confederate Bayard explicitly to the southern chivalric tradition and its medieval origins, Faulkner depicts this aide-de-camp of Jeb Stuart as possessing "merry blue eyes" and a "high colored face" that "wore that frank and high-hearted dullness which you visualize Richard the First as wearing before he went crusading." In Faulkner's tale, Bayard and Jeb Stuart together embody the glory and pointless daring of the southern chivalric tradition at its close. At one point Stuart, having captured a Yankee captain, proposes to go by a Yankee cavalry picket to provide his prisoner with a mount. "'Will General Stuart, cavalry leader and General Lee's eyes'" the officer queries, "'jeopardize his safety and that of his men and his cause in order to provide for the temporary comfort of a minor prisoner of his sword?'" Such action, the captured officer continues, "'is not bravery: it is the rashness of a heedless and headstrong boy.'" And he reminds Stuart that fifteen thousand men lie between him and the horse. "'Not for the prisoner, Sir,' Stuart replied haughtily, 'but for the officer suffering the fortune of war. No

---

[3] Jefferson Davis, *The Rise and Fall of the Confederate Government*, 2 vols. (New York, 1958), 2:233; Thomas Cary Johnson, *The Life and Letters of Benjamin Morgan Palmer* (Richmond, VA, 1906), 273–4; John Peyre Thomas, *The History of the South Carolina Military Academy* (Columbia, SC, 1991 [1893]), 159 (Jenkins); George Davis, *Address Delivered before the Two Literary Societies of the University of North-Carolina* (Raleigh, NC, 1855), 21 (Ashe); Henry W. Miller, *Address Delivered before the Philanthropic and Dialectic Societies of the University of North-Carolina* (Raleigh, NC, 1857), 20 (Nash); Mary A. H. Gay, *Life in Dixie during the War*, 5th ed. (Atlanta, GA, 1979 [1897]), 205; also, T. C. De Leon, *Belles, Beaux and Brains of the 60's* (New York, 1974 [1907]), 202; Frank Ticknor, "The Virginians of the Valley," in Lizzie Carrie Daniel, *Confederate Scrap-Book* (Nashville, TN, 1996 [1893]), 232; B. A. Elzas, "Address of Greeting," *Proceedings of the Centennial Celebration of South Carolina College, 1805–1905* (Columbia, SC, 1905), 127. Myrta Lockett Avery quoted *Harper's Weekly* for 1861 as referring to Jefferson Davis as "the Bayard of the Senate, *sans peur et sans reproche*": *Dixie after the War* (New York, 1918 [1906]), 49. Chivalry glorified the power of the knight but no less his duties and responsibilities: Richard Barber, "Chivalry and the Morte Darthur," in Elizabeth Archibald and A. S. G. Edwards, eds., *A Companion to Malory* (Woodbridge, U.K., 1996), 22–3.

gentleman would do less.'" Nor would any gentleman refrain from violence when circumstances required it.[4]

Chivalry encompassed conflicting conceptions of the knight and the gentleman: the former accentuated the special claims of the aristocracy; the latter the kind of equality that joined all members of the nobility into a single class, from hidalgos to grandees, despite wide differences in wealth and worldly standing. Both models contributed to the great popularity of Miguel Cervantes' *Don Quixote* and to the South Carolina elite's image of itself as "The Chivalry."

At Miami University in Ohio in 1846, the contentious Francis Lieber held forth on "The Character of the Gentleman": "The character of the gentleman produces an equality of social claims, and supersedes rank, office or title. It establishes a republic of intercourse, as we speak of the republic of letters." He cited Plato on the gentleman as one who acts kindly toward slaves, family, and all others in his power. Lieber had no patience with South Carolinians who styled themselves "The Chivalry" – which to his disgust they pronounced "chiv-AL-ry" – but they applauded his published address enthusiastically, seeing themselves reflected in his portrait. Lieber respected true gentlemen of any rank and scorned a society that "loses its capacity of acknowledging greatness."[5]

The South, the Baptist Reverend Iveson Brookes of South Carolina proclaimed, embraced the title "chivalric" with pride, "not in abolition sarcasm, but in the true import of the term." The South, not the slaveholders alone. Brookes and William Gilmore Simms appreciated the appeal of chivalry to the plain folk, much as Johann Huizinga, in the twentieth century, wrote that fifteenth-century chivalry was second only to religion as the strongest of ethical conceptions to crown a hierarchical social system in which learning and military prowess were fused "in the chivalric ideal: hero and sage." For several centuries, chivalry's preeminence as an ideal rested on its very exaggeration of generosity, ferocity, and passion, as rich burghers imitated the values of the nobility.[6]

The literature of the Middle Ages and the early Renaissance shaped Southerners' understanding of the chivalry they celebrated as their own. *Chansons de Geste*, most notably *Chanson de Roland*, as well as Malory's *Morte d'Arthur*, told of wandering minstrels' praise of knights as the image of knightly generosity and Christian

---

4   William Faulkner, *Flags in the Dust*, ed. Douglas Day (New York, 1973), 13–14, 21. Initially, *Flags in the Dust* was not published in its entirety but only (in 1928) in an abbreviated version entitled *Sartoris*.

5   Elsewhere, Lieber quoted Hegel as replying to the adage that no man is a hero to his valet, "This is true, most true, not however because no hero is a hero, but because a valet-de-chambre is a valet-de-chambre." Daniel C. Gilman, ed., *The Miscellaneous Writings of Francis Lieber*, 2 vols. (Philadelphia, 1881), 1:227, 232–4, 240, 271–2; also, John S. Wise, *The End of an Era* (Boston, 1900), 22. *Southern Quarterly Review* warmly commended Lieber's lecture: 11 (1847), 262–3. Franklin Minor of Virginia added that obedience to a master did not degrade the southern slave, who was "more of a gentleman" than the law-flouting whites of Boston: "Address Delivered before the Virginia State Agricultural Society," *Southern Planter*, 15, (1855), 373.

6   Iveson L. Brookes, *A Defence of the South against the Reproaches of the North* (Hamburg, SC, 1850), 32. On the emergence of knights as a hereditary caste in the early twelfth century see A. V. P. Norman, *The Medieval Soldier* (New York, 1971), ch. 7, including a discussion of the Church's teaching knights charity to the poor, protection of the weak, and the liberality of alms.

virtue that passed into the modern age, nowhere more strongly than in the South. To idealistic Southerners, aristocratic virtues included gallantry, contempt for money-grubbing (but not for money), classical education, polished manners, and a high sense of personal and family honor – virtues frequently evoked in publications, on the stump, and in speeches at public celebrations and college commencements. The Middle Ages was a favorite theme, and no one noticed that many of the purported chivalric virtues had arisen with commercial *grands bourgeois* and courtiers of the Renaissance and of early modern national states.

Even though Renaissance writers often described chivalry with greater self-consciousness than the medieval predecessors who lived it, Southerners slighted their contributions. For at the beginning of the sixteenth century the Italian diplomat Baldassare Castiglione developed, in his *Book of the Courtier,* what would become the classic picture of the chivalrous gentleman – the courtier. Castiglione and his contemporaries presented courtly virtues as products of feudal and manorial life. Their writings helped to transform the medieval knight into the gracious and courtly gentleman, thereby minimizing both the Christianity and the violence that distinguished medieval chivalry itself.[7]

Living in what long remained a frontier society and amid a potentially dangerous slave population, Southerners infused the more urbane and courtly version of chivalry with the Christianity and violence of the medieval prototype. In remote areas west of the Mississippi and as far off as California, Southerners – following the haughty planters of the lowcountry – styled themselves "The Chivalry." In biographies of exemplars of the chivalric tradition, William Gilmore Simms and David Flavel Jamison wrote with their eyes on their beloved South. Simms's biography of the Chevalier Bayard portrayed its hero as the paragon of knightly chivalry and Christian piety and virtue; in the dedication to John Izard Middleton, Simms wrote: "You will not be displeased, at least, that in pursuing the career of so perfect a character as that of the Chevalier, distinguished par excellence as without reproach, I should, at the same time, have naturally thought of yours."[8]

David Flavel Jamison, a prominent Charlestonian who served in the state legislature and then presided over South Carolina's secession convention, wrote a two-volume biography of Bertrand du Guesclin, a heroic military leader of fourteenth-century France. Mary E. Lee of Charleston published a poem about Guesclin in

---

[7] Castiglione was much better received in the South than in the North: Louis B. Wright, *The Cultural Life of the American Colonies, 1607–1763* (New York, 1957), 137; on Castiglione's popularity see e.g. [William Wirt et al.], *The Old Bachelor* (Richmond, VA, 1810), 36. "Xy" identified the spirit of chivalry with roaming adventurers rather than the settlers and builders of stable communities. In his view, feudalism obliterated the chivalric public spirit by encouraging vassals to focus entirely on their own local affairs: "Blondel and Richard Lion-Heart," *VLM*, 1 (1829), 171–2. Régine Pernoud insists that courtliness emerged from the life of the castles, not from the Renaissance cities: *Those Terrible Middle Ages: Debunking the Myths,* tr. Anne Englund Nash (San Francisco, 2000), 72.

[8] W. G. Simms, *The Life of Chevalier Bayard: "The Good Knight"* (New York, 1847), Dedication, 1, 71. Chivalry declined with feudalism, but the sixteenth century brought renewed interest in France: Richard Cooper, "Notre histoire renouvelée: The Reception of the Romances of Chivalry in Renaissance France," in Sydney Anglo, ed., *Chivalry in the Renaissance* (Woodbridge, U.K., 1990), 175–91.

Southern Literary Messenger, and Mary Chesnut, a Guesclin devotée, read Jamison's manuscript before publication. They and others accorded Guesclin hero status for bold exploits on behalf of French chivalry, although James Johnston Pettigrew reported from Europe that the Spanish still recalled him as "a vile assassin." When Jamison published his biography the Reverend D. F. Dickson pronounced it "the only solid literary production of the South during the memorable four years of the late war."[9]

For all Guesclin's glamour, he embodied more than a little chivalric violence and was more of a Jeb Stuart with a dash of Nathan Bedford Forrest than a Robert E. Lee. In contrast, southern youth, reading *Morte d'Arthur* in school, found a different world in Sir Eitor's pronouncement over Launcelot, the fallen epitome of knightly virtues: "Thou wast the meekest man and the gentlest that ever ate in hall among ladies, and thou wert the sternest knight to thy mortal foe that ever put spear to the rest." This medieval ideal, C. S. Lewis observed, makes a double demand on human nature: "It taught humility and forbearance to the great warrior because everyone knew how much he needed that lesson. It demanded valour of the urbane and modest man because everyone knew that he was likely as not to be a milksop." Gentleness implies sympathy without condescension: "There but for the grace of God, go I."[10]

John Wise, appealing to such a view of chivalry, said of his father, Henry A. Wise, that he impressed a stranger as "the gentlest, the tenderest, the most loving, the most eloquent, the most earnest, the most fearless, the most impassioned, or the

---

[9] David Flavel Jamison, *The Life and Times of Bertrand du Guesclin: A History of the Fourteenth Century* (Charleston, SC, 1864; French translation, Paris, 1866); Mary E. Lee, "Bertrand du Guesclin: A Historical Ballad," *SLM*, 13 (1847), 636–7; Chesnut Diary, May 13, 1861, in C. Vann Woodward, ed., *Mary Chesnut's Civil War* (New Haven, CT, 1981), 72; [James Johnston Pettigrew], *Notes on Spain and the Spaniards in the Summer of 1850, with a Glance at Sardinia* (Charleston, SC, 1861), 192; [A. F. Dickson], "Life and Times of Bertrand de Guesclin," *SPR*, 16 (1866), 376–84, quote at 378; also, Alton Taylor Loftus, "A Study of Russell's Magazine: Ante-Bellum Charleston's Last Literary Periodical" (Ph.D. diss., Duke University, 1973), 217.

[10] C. S. Lewis, "The Necessity of Chivalry," in *Present Concerns* (New York, 1986), 13–14, and quoting Malory. The following discussion draws upon this fine essay; see also the perceptive remarks of Roberto Mangabeira Unger, *Passion: An Essay on Personality* (New York, 1984), 269.

G. P. R. James's *The History of Chivalry* (New York, 1833) depended heavily on French sources, but Southerners added English, understanding that chivalry rose on a social structure no less hierarchical than the French but with considerably more class and caste fluidity. See Richard W. Kaeuper and Elspeth Kennedy, *The Book of Chivalry of Geoffroi de Charny: Text, Context, and Translation* (Philadelphia, 1996), 9, and Kaeuper, *Chivalry and Violence*, 112–13. William Robertson, popular in the South, discussed at length Mahabarata and chivalry in the caste system of India: "An Historical Disquisition Concerning Ancient India," in *The History of Scotland during the Reigns of Queen Mary and King James VI* (New York, n.d., first published 1759), Appendix, 85–90. On the need of warlike aristocracies for "an ideal form of manly perfection" with an ascetic aspect, see Johann Huizinga, *The Waning of the Middle Ages: A Study in the Forms of Life, Thought and Art in France and the Netherlands in the XIVth and XVth Centuries* (London, 1963 [1924]), 47, 55, 58–9, 66–7, 93–4, 115, and (generally) ch. 3. Huizinga depicted compassion, sacrifice, and fidelity as erotic as well as religious contributions to chivalry, recalling from Hippolyte Taine that chivalric pride and honor grounded a later patriotism. See also Joseph Schumpeter, *Imperialism and Social Classes: Two Essays* (New York, 1955), 143.

fiercest man he had ever met." John Wise described his brother Jennings – by reputation a hotspur – as gentle, tender, loving, deferential to his mother, considerate
toward the humblest of his servants and, withal, as fearless and as uncompromising "as the fiercest knight who ever entered the lists." And he added, reflecting on
his own experience in the Confederate army, "An officer to be really efficient must
add to the qualities of courage and firmness those of nurse, monitor, and purveyor
for grown-up children, in whom the humps of improvidence and destructiveness are
abnormally developed."[11]

An unidentified eighteenth-century Charlestonian proclaimed, "A man's word
must be better than his bond, because unguaranteed. A woman's name must never
pass his lips except in respect; a promise, however foolish, must be kept .... If he
wrongs any man he must offer his life in expiation. He must always be ready to fight
for the State or his lady." A half century later, John Manning, soon to be governor
of South Carolina, toasted the Richland Light Dragons: "At once the ornament and
protection of our city. As citizens, they are peaceful and patriotic – as soldiers generous and brave." The Presbyterian Reverend Robert Dabney wrote to his brother
of a Dr. Wilson, "an old Virginian in the true sense of the word, mild, polite, and
courteous, and still natural and dignified." The Virginia gentleman, Nathaniel Beverley Tucker told an audience at the College of William and Mary, is "courteous
and manly – gentle and not fearful." The gravestone of Henry St. George Tucker,
Beverley's brother, read: "meek but unbending; rigid in morals, yet indulgent to all
faults but his own."[12]

The disdain of some prominent Romans for men's display of womanly weakness,
especially tears, influenced medieval and southern views of chivalry. Livy decried
the "womanish and useless tears" shed by the peoples of Spain who faced Hannibal's onslaught. In that spirit Mary Hawes said her Presbyterian father in Rockland
County, Virginia, "had the true masculine dislike for womanly tears" and "drilled
us from babyhood to restrain the impulse to cry." Yet, while sharing Livy's disdain for cowardice, few Southerners objected to tears. James Roberts Gilmore, a
northern abolitionist who wrote as "Edmund Kirke," remarked that no chivalric
Southerner was ashamed to weep "like a woman." The cadets at Virginia Military
Institute, who longed to go to the front in 1861, wept openly when assigned to stay
behind to guard the arsenal. R. T. Coles of Alabama reported that General Hood
"was as sympathetic as a woman" when one of his officers was badly wounded. Of

[11] Plutarch, *The Lives of the Noble Grecians and Romans*, tr. John Dryden, ed. and rev. by Arthur Hugh
Clough, 2 vols. (New York, 1992), 1:234; Wise, *End of an Era*, 5, 94, 347. Joseph Story's eulogy to
John Marshall referred to his tenderness and the "romantic chivalry in his feelings": W. W. Story, ed.,
The Miscellaneous Writings of Joseph Story (Boston, 1852), 680.
[12] Richard Barry, *Mr. Rutledge of South Carolina* (New York, 1942), 24; Manning's toast in Jean Martin
Flynn, *The Militia in Antebellum South Carolina Society* (Spartanburg, SC, 1991 [1917]), 4; Dab-
ney to C. W. Wilson, Nov. 22, 1844, in Thomas Cary Johnson, ed., *Life and Letters of Robert Lewis
Dabney* (Carlisle, PA, 1977 [1903]), 83; N. B. Tucker, "Valedictory Address," *SLM*, 13 (1847), 570;
gravestone quoted in David M. Cobin, *Henry St. George Tucker: Jurist, Teacher, Citizen, 1780–1848*
(Stephens City, VA, 1992), 1.

James Southall, Martha Montgomery of North Carolina wrote, "I hear he cried like a child."[13]

Simms's biography of Bayard reminded readers of the other side of this womanly softness: The chivalrous knight mourns a fallen comrade by buckling on his armor for a renewed attack. Dabney wrote of Confederate troops on their way to the front: "A stalwart set of fellows, sun-burnt, raw-boned, and bearded; but they all wept like children. They will fight none the less for that." Troops wept at Dabney's sermon, not with "unmanly tears." The tough Irish troops in the Confederate army reputedly wept as readily as babies. John T. Morgan of the Alabama state legislature spoke to the secession convention of "that sort of patriotism which glows in the burning cheek and glisters in the falling tear." When James Johnston Pettigrew fell in battle, a friend described him in a manner at once stereotyped yet personally accurate: "gentle and soft as a woman in all offices of friendship, yet true as steel to all his obligations and duties." Southerners did not limit their appreciation of warriors' capacity for womanly gentleness nor restrict the attribution of chivalry to the officer corps. The Presbyterian Reverend Joseph Atkinson of Raleigh wrote: "The true history of this war will show that nobler instances of knightly courtesy, of generous valour and of chivalric enterprise, have not been found [more readily] among the best and bravest of our officers, than among the men subject to their authority."[14]

Southerners expected their countrymen to understand softness as a proper complement to strength. In memoirs and eulogies they spoke of men of feminine softness who embodied the gentler Christian virtues of charity and compassion. In the 1820s Francis Walker Gilmer of Virginia noted that John Randolph's eloquence made "hearty warriors," not only women and old men, weep. The South, wrote John Perkins, Jr., of Mississippi in 1853, will yet demonstrate "that cultivated refinement, that educated and gentle chivalry, that proud and almost haughty jealousy of right, that Burke says, always attaches to the Slaveholder – making liberty not only an enjoyment, but a privilege and giving its possessor something more noble and liberal than is elsewhere found." Benjamin Morgan Palmer's wartime funeral oration on General Maxcy Gregg captured the general sentiment, "He belonged to

---

[13] Livy, *The War with Hannibal*, tr. Aubrey de Sélincourt (London, 1972), Bk. 25:37; [Mary Virginia Hawes Terhune], *Marion Harland's Autobiography: The Story of a Life* (New York, 1910), 75; Edmund Kirke [James Roberts Gilmore], *My Southern Friends* (New York, 1963), 180; James Lee Conrad, *The Young Lions: Confederate Cadets at War* (Mechanicsburg, PA, 1997), 42 (VMI). Jeffrey D. Stocker, ed., *From Huntsville to Appomattox: R. T. Cole's History of the 4th Regiment, Alabama Infantry, C.S.A., Army of Northern Virginia* (Knoxville, TN, 1996), 70; Martha (Pipkin) Montgomery to Mary A. Wynns, circa 1839, in L. C. and E. S. Lawrence Letters, at North Carolina State Department of Archives (Raleigh).

[14] Joseph M. Atkinson, *God, the Giver of Victory and Peace* (Raleigh, NC, 1862), 12; James P. Gannon, *Irish Rebels: Confederate Tigers: The 16th Louisiana Volunteers, 1861–1865* (Campbell, CA, 1998), 24; Simms, *Chevalier Bayard*, 241; Dabney quoted in Johnson, ed., *R. L. Dabney*, 232, 237; Morgan in William R. Smith, ed., *The History of the Convention Debates of the People of Alabama* (Montgomery, AL, 1861), 46; Clyde N. Wilson, *Carolina Cavalier: The Life and Mind of James Johnston Pettigrew* (Athens, GA, 1990), 204. On the romantic sensibility of southern military men see Lesley J. Gordon, *General George J. Pickett in Life and Legend* (Chapel Hill, NC, 1998), 100–1.

that elect class of the brave and true, whose hands are strong in the great battle of life, but who love with a woman's heart at home."[15]

In a wartime biography designed principally for Britons, Catherine Cooper Hopley, an English teacher in Virginia who knew Stonewall Jackson well, portrayed him as the epitome of "The Christian Hero" and chivalric knight, always ready to devote himself to others with "a zeal so womanly, as to evoke the gibes of coarser natures." Hopley described Jefferson Davis after First Manassas: "Mildness and gentleness are the prominent expressions; kindness, benevolence, then a touch of sadness strikes you." On Davis's reputation as a devout Christian: "Meek devotion marks his bearing in the presence of the Almighty." General Richard Taylor called Davis a man who "could soothe the feelings of these officers with a tenderness and delicacy of touch worthy of a woman's hand"; he added that General William H. T. Walker of Georgia, who fell in the battle of Atlanta, "might have come from the pages of old Froissart." The Baptist Reverend J. B. Jeter's pamphlet *A Mother's Parting Words to Her Soldier Boy,* which made a deep impression on the troops, considered Christian meekness intrinsic to chivalry in defense of faith and home. "The southern gentleman," wrote George Fitzhugh, "is the outgrowth of Chivalry and Christianity – the knight-errant, civilized and softened down. Chivalric piety, virtuous and devoted gallantry to women, truth, honor and romance, were the distinguishing traits of the gentlemen whom Richard Coeur de Leon led to the walls of Jerusalem, and who tilted at Ashmont and Montalban."[16]

Medieval culture often depicted Jesus "as mother." In The Song of Roland, Charlemagne not only breaks down in tears upon hearing of the death of Roland, he faints. His doughty warriors emulated him. Southerners frequently applied "womanly" to strong men, much in the manner of the chivalric warriors of earlier times, who invoked Mary as well as Jesus ("*Christus Victor*") to capture the ideal combination of gentleness, humility, and fierceness in battle. Thus, James West Pegram of Virginia, who had two big plantations in Mississippi, nursed his ill children with

---

[15] Francis Walker Gilmer, *Sketches, Essays and Translations* (Baltimore, 1828), 21 n.; John Perkins, Jr., *An Address Delivered before the Adelphic and Belle-lettres Societies, of Oakland College ... On the Duty of Drawing from the History and the Theory of Our Government Just Views of Individual and National Life* (Port Gibson, MS, 1853), 17–18. Among the many who praised men they admired for their vigorous action – and gentleness and softness – see James Holmes, *"Dr. Bullie's" Notes: Reminiscences of Early Georgia and of Philadelphia and New Haven in the 1800s,* ed. Delma Eugene Presley (Atlanta, GA, 1976), 40, 66; B. M. Palmer, "Address Delivered at the Funeral of Gen. Maxcy Gregg," ms. in the Palmer Papers, at USC; F. W. Brandon in Anson West, *A History of Methodism in Alabama* (Spartanburg, SC, 1983 [1893]), xii.

[16] Catherine Cooper Hopley, *"Stonewall" Jackson, Late General of the Confederate States Army: A Biographical Sketch, and an Outline of His Virginian Campaigns* (London, 1863), v, 43; Catherine Cooper Hopley, *Life in the South from the Commencement of the War,* 2 vols. (New York, 1971 [1863]), 2:18; Richard Taylor, *Destruction and Reconstruction* (New York, 1992 [1889]), 19; George Fitzhugh, "Johnson, Boswell, Goldsmith, etc.," *DBR,* 27 (Apr. 1860), 412. In the *Iliad* and *Odyssey,* Achilles, Odysseus, Agamemnon, Phoenix, Patroclus, Antichus, and Telemachus (among others) broke down in tears, as did Aeneas and Anchises in Bk. 4 of "Aeneid," in *Virgil's Works,* tr. J. W. Mackail (New York, 1950).

what the Richmond *Whig* in 1844 described as "womanly tenderness." Stephen Miller's biographical sketches of eminent members of the Georgia bar resorted to similar expressions: George D. Anderson, "mild and courteous"; Robert Augustus Beall, "kindness of heart"; Paul Coalson, "modest and unassuming"; William C. Dawson, "of manner gentle and affections mild." Of the formidable Augustus S. Clayton, Miller noted that – despite his quick temper and periodic fits of passion – his was a spotless character devoted to truth and justice, and gentle in its manners. William H. Macfarland, eulogizing Benjamin Leigh Watkins at a memorial meeting at the Virginia Historical Society, described a man with delicate, "well-nigh effeminate" features whose sincerity marked him a man both "bland and resolved." Margaret Junkin Preston wrote of the "womanish" character of the heroic Turner Ashby, and of William Campbell Preston, "Never was there anything more beautiful than [his] woman-like tenderness." Of the fallen young Willy Preston: "His love and care for his father had a womanly tenderness to it." Sarah Morgan of Louisiana described the qualities of the gentleman she sought in a husband: "principle as firm and immovable – as the rock of Gibalta [Gibraltar] and a sense of honor as nice and delicate as a woman's, and a noble, generous, pure heart."[17]

If much pretense reinforced the slaveholders' self-image as the chivalric gentleman, it was not so much as to invalidate the ideal as a standard of conduct. Slaveholders credited Christianity with mandating respect for women and paternalism in master–slave relations. As a standard of properly Christian and chivalric conduct, paternalism bade masters accept duties, responsibilities, and a code that made the ultimate test of the gentleman the humane treatment of his slaves. Yet all knew that slaveholding paternalism, when faithfully observed, also followed the chivalric mode: It included violence.

Historically, chivalry – medieval, southern, or other – has rested on violence or, what comes to the same thing, the threat of violence. Medieval chivalry, according to Richard Kaeuper, had a bloody-minded side manifested in a "prickly sense of honor," an "insistence on autonomy," and a "quick recourse to violence." Like paternalism, chivalry provoked men, not least by the magnitude of its demands, to

---

[17] Jaroslav Pelikan, *Mary through the Centuries: Her Place in the History of Culture* (New Haven, CT, 1996), 27; *Song of Roland*, tr. Dorothy L. Sayers (Harmondsworth, U.K., 1971), secs. 68 and 177–178 – for Charlemagne's reaction see Sayers's splendid introduction. Richmond *Whig*, Nov. 1, 1844; Stephen F. Miller, *The Bench and Bar of Georgia: Memoirs and Sketches*, 2 vols. (Philadelphia, 1858), 1:20, 23, 201, 302, and 186 (Clayton); William H. Macfarland, "Eulogy on Benjamin Leigh Watkins," *SLM*, 17 (1851), 123; "Dirge for Ashby" and "William C. Preston," in Margaret Junkin Preston Papers, at Washington and Lee University; M. J. Preston Journal, Sept. 3, 1862, in Elizabeth Preston Allan, *The Life and Letters of Margaret Junkin Preston* (Boston, 1903), 148; May 21, 1862, in Charles East, ed., *The Civil War Diary of Sarah Morgan* (Athens, GA, 1991), 61–2. For the depiction of Jesus as mother, see Carolyn Bynum, *Jesus as Mother: Studies in the Spirituality of the Middle Ages* (Berkeley, CA, 1984). For the impact of the chivalric ideal in softening the warrior code of the European aristocracy, see Andreas A. M. Kinneging, *Aristocracy, Antiquity and History: Classicism in Political Thought* (New Brunswick, NJ, 1997), 72–3.

compensate through violence informed by a particular ferocity born of religious passion. The terrible hardships and suffering of war metamorphosed into a crusade for Christ and provided the aura of quasi-martyrdom. In medieval chivalric literature, violence exhilarated knights and grounded their very identity. In Louisiana the historian Charles Gayarré applauded the early European explorers for their chivalric spirit; J. D. B. De Bow, while conceding their "valor, endurance, intrepidity," damned their "criminal and groveling desires." The beauties of chivalric poetry could not "veil the deformities of a picture in which avarice, blood and slaughter, command so prominent a place." De Bow recoiled from a culture that refined cruelty in the service of systematic and heartless tyranny. Cheering *Don Quixote* for deflating chivalric myths, he sneered at the "mock heroic, Quixotic chivalry" that preferred war to peace.[18]

For Thomas Roderick Dew, the chivalric "spirit of honor" guided the love of arms and the romantic urge for adventure toward the protection of women and the weak. Dedicated to "progress," he responded with mixed feelings to the prevalent interpretation that had gunpowder end the era of medieval chivalry by making the common man equal to any knight in battle. Dew took pleasure in the symbiosis of gentle knight and ferocious warrior. He saw the spirit of liberty only among the propertied and educated classes and thus by itself incapable of causing the Revolution. That spirit had to permeate the masses, with religion providing the necessary instrument. He found the Puritans somewhat ridiculous but saluted their "great character" – their zeal, perseverance, courage, and cool judgment. On balance: "It was precisely this spirit of the puritan, meek before his God but violent towards men, which made them so formidable in battle, slaying their enemies, as they said, hip and thigh."[19]

The two students at the University of Virginia who drew pistols might have avoided the prescribed expulsion but did not: They drew their pistols in the presence of a young lady. College students could get away with almost anything except such disrespect. A romantic youth, writing his junior-year composition at the University of North Carolina in 1841, presented the prevalent view with a melodramatic flourish. Richard Don Wilson's essay "On the Influence of Woman" declared the days of chivalry over: "Those high toned sentiments which imagined the Knights of bygone centuries are no more." No longer does the Knight seek adventures to impress his lady or challenge a brother Knight to a battle for her hand. No longer does he "guard her rest beneath night's holy vault." Yet woman's influence remains, and "the spirit of gallantry lives on among us." He ended: "Daughters of Carolina, 'Land of the beautiful and the brave, the fair and the chivalric.' It is yours to

---

[18] The foundations of chivalry in violence are explicated in Kaeuper, *Violence and Chivalry*, 7–8, 143, 205–6, quotes at 7–8. On martyrdom see also Kaeuper and Kennedy, *Geoffroi de Charny*, 37. Charles Gayarré, "Romance of Louisiana History," *DBR*, 3 (1847), 453–4; see also *DBR*, 5 (1848), 4; 1 (May 1846), 411; 9 (1850), 80–2.

[19] Thomas Roderick Dew, *Digest of the Laws, Customs, Manners, and Institutions of the Ancient and Modern Nations* (New York, 1884 [1852]), 341–3, 351, 353, 545 n., 433–4.

elevate – to give tone – and character to the age.... The chivalry of Carolina is here and look to you to reward their toils."[20]

The feudal aristocracy, especially through its religion, had sought an ethos that would bind other classes to itself – to bring the Christian life down to earth and carry its own life up to heaven. The ideal also bound the aristocracy and even the monarch to those they sought to rule – bound them in what Mikhail Bakhtin has called a dialogic or symbiotic relation in which each side, however unequally, becomes hostage to the values that unite them in a society. The chivalrous Christian knight, above all others, embodied this ethos. G. P. R. James referred to chivalry as "a military institution, prompted by enthusiastic benevolence, sanctioned by religion." James quoted *Ordène de chevalerie fabliaux* on the expectations of aspirants to chivalry: "To speak the truth, to succor the helpless and oppressed, and never to turn back from an enemy." No squire, in James's view, achieved knighthood without a convincing display of religious faith. Charles Mills, whose history of chivalry was assigned in southern schools, described religion as "the arch" of chivalry and the Church as the mortar that bound society's disparate elements.[21]

Chivalry, from its origins, had insisted upon the sanctity of the chivalric knight's devotion to his lady. Although as much observed in neglect as in practice, its ideals of fealty and of deference to women left a lasting mark upon Western Civilization and inaugurated a steady – if painfully slow – rise in women's status and improvement in their treatment. In South Carolina A. G. Magrath traced the manners of modern gentlemen to the feudal system, and Charles Carroll referred to "the punctilious laws of knight-errantry, the substitute for merciless assault and private assassinations." Carroll celebrated chivalry for rescuing women from their miserable status as objects of exploitation and for insisting they be protected and cherished as precious human beings. Alabama's prominent Methodist Reverend A. A. Lipscomb agreed but argued that Christianity corrected the "romantic extravagancies of chivalry" that hemmed women in.[22]

British and Northern travelers and sojourners extravagantly reinforced southern self-esteem about manners, testifying that southern men showed an exalted respect for their ladies. During a ten-year stay in Virginia, D. W. Mitchell observed that respectable people of all ranks, including workingmen, were judged by the civility

[20] Charles Coleman Wall, Jr., "Students and Student Life at the University of Virginia, 1825–1861" (Ph.D. diss., University of Virginia, 1978), 272; R. D. Wilson, "On the Influence of Woman," in Junior Compositions, 1841, at UNC-NCC; see also Charles Woodward Hutson [a student at the South Carolina College] to Dear Father, Feb. 2, 1857, in *DHE*, 3:433.

[21] Mikhail Bakhtin, *Rabelais and His World*, tr. Hélène Iswolsky (Cambridge, MA, 1965); James, *Chivalry*, 18, 28, quote at 28; Charles Mills, *The History of Chivalry; Or Knighthood and Its Times* (Philadelphia, 1844), 16.

[22] "A. G. M." [Andrew G. Magrath?], "The Condition of Woman," *SQR*, 10 (1846), 163; C. C. Carroll, "Woman," in [William Gilmore Simms], ed., *The Charleston Book: A Miscellany in Prose and Verse* (Spartanburg, SC, 1983 [1845]), 135; A. A. Lipscomb, *The Social Spirit of Christianity, Presented in the Form of Essays* (Philadelphia, 1846), 52; *DD**, 4:503.

of their behavior, especially toward women. The Reverend William Henry Milburn, a northern Methodist who spent six years in Alabama, thought that men treated women more reverently and courteously in the South than elsewhere, addressing them with simple respect rather than affectation or condescension. Southerners like "C." in *Southern Literary Messenger* credited slavery for providing the basis for southern respect and deference toward women.[23]

The Northeast, too, displayed something of a cult of the gentleman – hearkening back to medieval knights and Renaissance courtiers and embracing the same compound of gentleness and valor as the South – but it was a cult in rapid decline, largely restricted to dwindling enclaves of commercial *grands bourgeois* in a few cities.[24] Northern tributes reinforced the widespread southern fascination with The Chivalry, but the tributes were not only to gentle manners. In 1843 an antislavery Northerner who believed, inaccurately, that the planters of the South Carolina lowcountry descended from English Cavaliers described them in *Knickerbocker's Magazine*: "Finer horsemen, more skilled marksmen, hardier frames for pugilistic feats, or a quicker eye and prompter hand for a game at fence, the world cannot produce." He judged them generally "of liberal learning and generous dispositions; frank and courteous" and a "hot-blooded chivalry upon which they are too apt to pride themselves, noble and humane in all their impulses." Julia LeGrand of New Orleans esteemed the gentlemen of her native Maryland, "so kind, so generous, so brave, so gallant to women" and exemplifying "the graces of chivalry as well as its sturdy manhood." In contrast, the Philadelphia-born Emily Wharton Sinkler of coastal South Carolina wrote teasingly to her sister Mary that "chivalrous and bullying" were "pretty much synonymous."[25]

The evolution of medieval chivalry complicated Southerners' efforts to claim it as a model for their slave society. The shift in the function of the knight between

---

[23] D. W. Mitchell, *Ten Years in the United States: Being an Englishman's Views of Men and Things in the North and South* (London, 1862), 68, 91; William Henry Milburn, *Ten Years of Preacher-Life: Chapters from an Autobiography* (New York, 1859), 321–2; Kenneth R. Wesson, "Travelers' Accounts of the Southern Character: Antebellum and Early Postbellum Period," *Southern Studies*, 17 (1978), 311–13; "C.", *SLM*, 1 (1834), 84. In the Southwest in 1835 and again in 1859, Richard Cobden, the English liberal, found a "real deferential respect paid to women": Mar. 19, 1859, in *The American Diaries of Richard Cobden*, ed. Elizabeth Hoon Cawley (Princeton, NJ, 1952), 154.

[24] Stow Persons, *Decline of American Gentility* (New York, 1973), esp. 29. For the rural ideal in New England see Tamara Plakins Thornton, *Cultivating Gentlemen: The Meaning of Country Life among the Boston Elite, 1785–1860* (New Haven, CT, 1989).

[25] "Sketches of South Carolina," in Eugene L. Schwaab and Jacqueline Bull, eds., *Travels in the Old South: Selections from the Periodicals of the Times*, 2 vols. (Lexington, KY, 1973), 2:329; June 10, 1863, in Kate Mason Rowland and Mrs. Morris S. Croxall, eds., *The Journal of Julia LeGrand: New Orleans, 1862–1863* (Richmond, VA, 1911), 77; Emily Wharton Sinkler to Mary Wharton, Feb. 21, 1850, in Anne Sinkler Whaley LeClerq, ed., *Between North and South: The Letters of Emily Wharton Sinkler, 1842–1865* (Columbia, SC, 2001), 109. Many of the Union troops who poured contempt on the Southerners' claims to chivalry grudgingly acknowledged Southerners' hospitality, courtesy, elegance, refinement, and cultivation: Randall C. Jimerson, *The Private Civil War: Popular Thought during the Sectional Conflict* (Baton Rouge, LA, 1988), 132.

the eleventh and fourteenth centuries had brought a shift in the ideal. So long as quasi-anarchy lasted, a knight had to fight to the death and could not afford to be chivalrous. He had to prevail through "prowess." As the knights were drawn into the armies of kings and lords, prudence cautioned mercy toward defeated foes lest their own side lose the next round – and forfeit substantial ransoms. The penchant for fearlessness, not to say recklessness, provided the main spur to the fame they coveted. But increasingly they came to cherish a reputation for loyalty, generosity, courtesy, justice, and Christian bearing – upon the qualities celebrated by such southern favorites as Froissart, who glorified medieval knights and rarely noticed their lapses from the chivalric ideal. These knightly rules were rarely applied to treatment of the lower classes. Knights hardly scrupled when they saw a chance to rape peasant girls and, on occasion, women of the privileged classes as well.[26]

As the wounded John Brown awaited execution in 1859, Lydia Maria Child appealed directly to the chivalry of Governor Henry Wise of Virginia. Acknowledging her abolitionism, she requested permission to nurse Brown and gave her word to say or do nothing to offend Virginia sensibilities. With a formally courteous letter that oozed ironic condescension, Wise persuaded her to stay home: "A few unenlightened and inconsiderate persons, fanatical in their modes of thought and action, might molest you, or be disposed to do so; and this might suggest the imprudence of risking any experiment upon the peace of a society very much excited by the crimes with whose chief author you seem to sympathize so much." The circumstances vexed a southern gentleman: "I could not permit an insult ever to woman in her walk of charity among us, though it be one who whetted knives of butchery for our mothers, sisters, daughters, and babes."[27]

Yes, the claims were inflated. Albert Gallatin Brown of Mississippi told the House of Representatives in 1854 that, since Southerners had black slaves to do menial work, "The wives and daughters of our mechanics and the laboring men stand not an inch lower in the social scale than the wives and daughters of our governors, secretaries, and judges." Presumably, some gullible Southerners and Northerners believed him. But no similar claim about the equal standing of women of different classes appeared in the sober reflection of J. G. M. Ramsey, Tennessee's leading historian and a radical democrat who in 1858 explained to L. W. Spratt, South Carolina's militant advocate for reopening the African slave trade, that slavery

---

[26] Chivalry softened the rules of war among knights but the common people continued to suffer atrocities. "As a code," Richard Kaeuper writes, "chivalry had next to nothing to do with ordinary people at all": *Violence and Chivalry*, 185. Here and elsewhere we have also drawn upon Maurice Keen, *Chivalry* (New Haven, CT, 1984); Sidney Painter, *French Chivalry: Chivalric Ideas and Practices in Medieval France* (Ithaca, NY, 1940); Charles T. Wood, *The Quest for Eternity: Manners and Morals in the Age of Chivalry* (Hanover, NH, 1970); and Huizinga, *Waning of the Middle Ages*. Keen's criticisms of Painter and Huizinga do not touch points at issue here. In the 1840s *Southern Literary Messenger* published a good deal on the history and characteristics of chivalry and the medieval knights – for example, an extended history of Malta and its famous knights by William Winthrop and William W. Andrews.

[27] For the Child–Wise correspondence see *Letters of Lydia Maria Child* (New York, 1969 [1883]), 103–7, esp. Child to Wise, Oct. 26, 1859 (104), and Wise to Child, Oct. 29, 1859 (106).

undergirded southern chivalry as the foundation for the separation of Northerners and Southerners into distinct peoples and nations.[28]

Hostile contemporaries as well as modern historians – not all of them damn-yankees – have ridiculed southern identification with the old nobilities. When Fannie Kemble found nothing aristocratic about Philadelphia, her lowcountry husband responded that she would have to go to Charleston to find an American aristocracy. When she did go south, she fumed that southern ladies' accounts showed lowcountry planters to be as "idle, arrogant, ignorant, dissolute, and ferocious as that medieval chivalry to which they are fond of comparing themselves." J. L. Fremantle, an Englishman with the Confederate army, whimsically noted the showering of tobacco juice on stagecoach passengers by "the Southern Chivalry on the roof." Stephen Douglas's wife remarked that in some men what passed for southern chivalry was but "ill-bred impertinence." Especially during the War, the more disgruntled yeomen derided the "chivalry" of political adversaries among the gentry. Marcus Woodcock of middle Tennessee, surveying the "squalid, miserable, and thievish-looking persons" he met in a campaign in Mississippi, spoke contemptuously of the "brilliant, wonderful, and chivalric Southern Conthieveracy." Woodcock fought for the Union and so his blast might have been expected. But what of F. Stanley Russell, Confederate patriot and soldier from a yeoman family, who – writing his father from the front – grimly recalled the blather from "our Southern chivalry" about how the Yankees could not or would not fight? Russell learned differently. The many southern women who refused to flee in the face of the advancing Yankee troops defied southern propaganda that had long depicted the Yankees as devoid of all chivalrous impulse and likely to commit "outrages" (rapes).[29]

To the abundant evidence of lapses from prescribed chivalric norms and even of flagrant hypocrisy, William Henry Holcombe of Natchez added criticisms of both medieval and southern chivalric behavior: indisposition to industry and "the dead consumption of capital in pursuit of pleasure," dueling, and impatience with legal restraint. Holcombe considered Southerners chevaliers by blood and instinct and recognized that slavery provided the social basis for "the tone, bearing, and superiority of a gentleman of elevated position." He appreciated the South's attachment to chivalry and its success in preserving more of it than other societies. Living up

---

[28] Brown quoted in James Byrne Ranck, *Albert Gallatin Brown: Radical Southern Nationalist* (New York, 1937), 127; Ramsey to L. W. Spratt, Apr. 23, 1858, and "Autobiography," in William B. Hesseltine, ed., *Dr. J. G. M. Ramsey, Autobiography and Letters* (Knoxville, TN, 2002), 168–70.

[29] Frances Kemble, *Journal of a Residence on a Georgia Plantation in 1838–1839* (New York, 1863), 286; Margaret Armstrong, *Fannie Kemble, A Passionate Victorian* (New York, 1938), 169, 339; Apr. 28, 1863, in Arthur J. L. Fremantle, *Three Months in the Southern States: The 1863 Diary of an English Soldier* (Edinburgh, 1863), 56; Mrs. Douglas quoted in Gay, *Life in Dixie during the War*, 99; J. Mills Thornton, *Power and Politics in a Slave Society: Alabama, 1800–1860* (Baton Rouge, LA, 1978), 170; Kenneth W. Noe, ed., *A Southern Boy in Blue: The Memoirs of Marcus Woodcock, 9th Kentucky Infantry (U.S.A.)* (Knoxville, TN, 1996), 75; F. Stanley Russell to Papa, Jan. 1, 1864, in Douglas Carroll, ed., *The Letters of F. Stanley Russell: The Movement of Company H Thirteenth Virginia Regiment* (Baltimore, 1963), 51. For the response of the women see Stephen V. Ash, *When the Yankees Came: Conflict and Chaos in the Occupied South, 1861–1865* (Chapel Hill, NC, 1995), ch. 1.

to chivalric standards of civility and graciousness – and to the cultivation of a rich intellectual life and a distinguished tradition of political leadership – required the leisure provided by freedom from manual labor. Holcombe attributed the cause of southern attachment to chivalry to "the comparative absence of the principles of its destruction": first, to "the prevalence of a mechanical & commercial or trading and industrial spirit – which destroys the ideal and reduces everything to a utilitarian standard," second, to "the power of religious fanaticism endeavoring to abolish all human institutions" and ultimately "establish a peculiar spiritual kingdom upon earth," and third, to "the power of skepticism and infidelity – that mocking spirit which derides alike religion and honor – and is thoroughly mercenary, sensual, and devilish." Finally, "Great cities, dense population, diversity of pursuits, rapidity of communication, and the democratic principle in the sense of levelling down," he wrote, "all prevail more extensively at the North than at the South, and all are more or less inimical to the perpetuity of the spirit of chivalry."[30]

"The age of chivalry is gone: that of sophisters, economists and calculators has succeeded: and the glory of Europe is extinguished forever." Thus wrote Edmund Burke in 1793, outraged by the execution of Marie Antoinette. More than a half-century later, *Southern Literary Messenger,* mourning the passing of John C. Calhoun and James Hamilton, lamented that chivalric figures were giving way to the sort described by Madame Germaine De Staël as "merely eating, drinking, bargain-making men." Yet Charles Kingsley – the Anglican priest, Christian socialist, and defender of the poor – thought differently: "The age of chivalry is never past so long as there is a wrong left unredressed on earth," and most Southerners probably concurred or at least wanted to. If, as James Johnston Pettigrew feared in 1859, chivalry had become a term of reproach in much of the transatlantic world, he hoped the next age would rediscover its virtues.[31]

Southerners' chivalric ideals owed much to literary sources, but their favorite literary models were never exclusively – or even predominantly – medieval. They drew freely upon an eclectic array of authors who admired the same characteristics as they. Thus, their portrait of Christian gentlemen borrowed from pre-Christian authors who blended romance with tough-mindedness. College professors who assigned Ovid had predecessors in the medieval exponents of chivalry who turned to Ovid and Virgil for notions of courtly love. Southerners learned from Xenophon,

---

[30] "Notes," W. H. Holcombe Diary, n.d. (probably 1860s), 2:173–5, at UNC-SHC.

[31] *The Works of the Right Honourable Edmund Burke,* 3rd ed., 12 vols. (Boston, 1869), 3:331; "The Great Monarchs of France," *SLM,* 25 (1857), 407; *SLM,* 26 (1858), 56; J. D. Douglas, "Charles Kingsley," *EDT,* 612; [Pettigrew], *Spain and the Spaniards,* 142–3. J. P. Tusten expressed another ambiguous view that resonated. Chivalry, which he considered primarily English, did its work in time and place but ceased to serve well as Christian civilization grew: [Tusten], "Chivalry and Civilisation," *SPR,* 6 (1851), 209–10, 224. For the laments of Northerners about the passing of chivalry from their own society see Perry Miller, *The Raven and the Whale: The War of Words and Wits in the Era of Poe and Melville* (New York, 1956), 34; also Frances Trollope, *Domestic Manners of the Americans* (Gloucester, MA, 1974 [1832]), 257. For an example of occasional southern impatience with the sentimentality attached to medieval chivalry and ridicule of Burke and the novel-reading men and women who celebrate it, see "M.", "Fields of Heroism," *SLM,* 9 (1843), 190–1.

among other ancients, to value men who combined generosity toward friends with ferocity toward enemies, and they learned from Ovid and his medieval admirers to take a sympathetic view of women's sensibilities and just claims to recognition. Every schoolboy had to read Caesar, who proclaimed that no Roman would abandon loyal allies, just as (ideally) no medieval knight ever betrayed a trust, deserted a good man, or ignored a starving widow or child. Plutarch, too, taught virtues that easily merged with the chivalric ideal: He wrote of Pericles' "equitable and mild temper" and of his "high spirit and feeling" – characteristics that combined to control his passions and encourage generosity toward adversaries.[32]

The ancient legacy had a dark side that resonated with the slaveholders' sense of the world, and their favorite ancient texts readily reinforced their more dangerous attitudes. Even the devout Christians among them often forgot the terse warning of the Epistle of James (1:20): "The wrath of man worketh not the righteousness of God." Thomas Roderick Dew warned his students that Homer's Achilles displayed some of the less admirable qualities of the chivalrous knight: "He loved his own honor and fame more than the cause of Greece." Passion, not reason, moves the principal characters in Homer's epics. In the *Iliad*, which Eric Voegelin calls a study in the pathology of heroes, such lordly wrath becomes "a legal institution" that resembles a medieval feud, and the violation of a man's honor induces "an upheaval of emotion, tending to inflict damage on the transgressor, with the ultimate purpose of compelling formal compensation and recognition of the rightful relation between them." This rationale helps to justify wrath as vital to the maintenance of social order. Achilles provided a model of a man ready to die for the glory that established a man's right to be free – and to defend the personal reputation by which he would be remembered. The elegy of the Spartan Tyrtaeus rendered the much-heralded manly virtues secondary to that of a "savage valor," exemplified in the slaughter of enemies. Those of savage valor fight for country, right or wrong, and find dying for it "honorable and sweet." The Romans, who doubted personal immortality, strove to be remembered in this world.[33]

---

[32] Here, as in so many other instances, their use of sources depended heavily upon the availability of the relevant works, many of which had not been retranslated or reprinted for centuries. That neither Virgil nor Ovid intended their work to be read in a chivalric spirit is beside the point. Some such questionable reading influenced Southerners, especially those who read expurgated editions. Keen, *Chivalry,* 112; Elizabeth Rawson, *The Spartan Tradition in European Thought* (Oxford, U.K., 1969), 48; Julius Caesar, *The Gallic War and Other Writings,* tr. Moses Hadas (New York, 1957), 34; on Ovid see Michael Grant, *Roman Literature* (Baltimore, 1964), 208–9; Norman, *Medieval Soldier,* 145; Richard Barber, *The Knight and Chivalry,* rev. ed. (Woodbridge, U.K., 1970), 72. During the Renaissance, chivalry was considered an inheritance from Antiquity: Cecil H. Clough, "Chivalry and Magnificence in the Golden Age of the Italian Renaissance," in Anglo, ed., *Chivalry in the Renaissance,* 38–9. On Ovid's *Ars Amatoria* in eleventh-century thought see Pernoud, *Those Terrible Middle Ages,* 24.

[33] Dew, *Digest,* 351; Eric Voegelin, *Order and History,* 5 vols. (Baton Rouge, LA, 1956–87), 2:83, 89–90. For the importance of "undying glory" see Paul A. Rahe, *Republics, Ancient and Modern: Classical Republicanism and the American Revolution* (Chapel Hill, NC, 1992), 44; Pierre Grimal, *Love in Ancient Rome,* tr. Arthur Tain, Jr. (Norman, OK, 1980), 173; and Dean A. Miller, *The Epic Hero* (Baltimore, 2000), 334. "B. M. S." of Augusta, Georgia, protested against the promotion of religion

Most Southerners acquired much of their familiarity with the chivalric tradition from the sixteenth-century flowering of the literature of chivalry, notably by the Italian and Iberian writers Ludovico Ariosto, Torquato Tasso, their beloved Miguel de Cervantes, and Luis Vaz de Camões, the great Portuguese poet whom they knew (following the usual English spelling) as Camöens. Hugh Legaré noted that leading critics esteemed the heroic ballads of medieval Spain more than any other body of literature for their spirit of Christianity and chivalry. Spanish history and literature caught the fancy of educated Southerners especially among cultivated circles in the Southwest, where Nashville's elite lavished accolades on George Ticknor's three-volume *History of Spanish Literature*. In 1850 De Bow, reviewing Ticknor and S. T. Wallis's *Glimpses of Spain,* lauded Spanish literature but also Cervantes's satirical dissection of the "preposterous" chivalric Spanish romances. College professors made an effort to introduce southern youth to the classics of Iberian literature, including Camöens's *Os Lusiadas* [The Lusiads]. Tasso – Camöens's slightly younger Italian contemporary, fellow epic poet, and rival for the utmost esteem – enjoyed a modest but enthusiastic southern audience that included Robert Bolling, "the dominant poet and writer of pre-Revolutionary Virginia." The University of Virginia's *Virginia University Magazine* ranked Tasso among the great figures of world literature, and *Southern Literary Messenger* put him in the company of Michelangelo, Rafael, and Shakespeare.[34]

While Mary Chesnut's social circle discussed Tasso's *Jerusalem Delivered,* a certain William Joshua Grant, branding it risqué, ordered his daughter to cease reading. The ladies wondered what he was fussing about. *Jerusalem Delivered* posed the moral problem of the limits of Christian charity in the duel: Do you kill an opponent whose sword has been broken? Christian charity would seem to say no, and Tancredi, Tasso's hero, tries to spare his pagan adversary. Professors of moral philosophy taught southern youth that men who claimed title to "The Chivalry" must show generosity and respect to a defeated enemy, since subversion of another's reputation was a criminal attack on his person. Tasso has Argante, a brave and cruel warrior, scorn the offer of mercy and renew his charge. Tancredi must kill him, much as Virgil had Aeneas kill Turnus. For when an adversary is – like a Yankee abolitionist – a fanatic who lives outside the code, even the most devout Christian gentleman has no honorable alternative.[35]

---

through fear of death. Duty should be at issue, not fear: "Death, Doubts and Immortality," *SLM*, 7 (1841), 379–82. For Tyrtaeus see Supplementary References: : "Greek Writers" (*Tyrtaeus*).

34 "Early Spanish Ballads," *HLW*, 2:303; J. H. Ingraham, *The Sunny South; Or, the Southerner at Home* (New York, 1968 [1860]), 122. Dew traced the literature that arose from troubadours as Provençal in origin, recounting songs and poems with little special interpretation; see *Digest*, 417–18. See also Supplementary References: "Iberian Literature" and "Tasso."

35 Mary E. Moragné Journal, July 4, 1837, in Delle Mullen Craven, ed., *The Neglected Thread: A Journal of the Calhoun Community* (Columbia, SC, 1951), 43; Aug. 29, 1862, in Beth G. Crabtree and James W. Patton, eds., *"Journal of a Secesh Lady": The Diary of Catherine Devereux Edmonston, 1860–1866* (Raleigh, NC, 1979), 247; Chesnut Diary, Sept. 24, 1861, in Woodward, ed., *Mary Chesnut's Civil War*, 202; also, Tally Simpson to Anne Tallulah Simpson, Apr. 5 and 28, 1863, in Guy R. Everson and Edward W. Simpson, Jr., eds., *"Far, Far from Home": The Wartime Letters of Dick*

Clyde Wilson, in his biography of James Johnston Pettigrew, holds that the South's revival of chivalry had an ascetic tendency; indeed, Pettigrew lauded the austere side of Spanish dignity, with its martial ideal of self-sacrifice. For him, its knightly ideal corresponded to a republican as well as a feudal temper and provided Southerners with a splendid model of qualities at once military and Christian – with the asceticism typical of all warlike aristocracies. "Warlike aristocracies," Johann Huizinga has remarked, "need an ideal form of manly perfection" requiring sacrifice, fidelity, and compassion. "G. W. M." declared Spain the land of "chivalry and romance," with a chivalric spirit "highly honorable to the nation."[36]

No continental writer enjoyed as much esteem as Cervantes, and most Southerners read *Don Quixote* in English translation or even in French, some in Spanish. An entranced Jefferson read it in Spanish and berated his daughter, who was doing the same under her aunt's tutelage, for not applying herself more diligently. *Don Quixote* together with Sterne's *Tristram Shandy* figured among the few notable exceptions in the young William Wirt's library, which consisted largely of law books. *Don Quixote*'s many readers mined it for a variety of different political lessons. John Taylor of Caroline invoked it to satirize the big capital's Paper Aristocracy

---

and Tully Simpson, Third South Carolina Volunteers (New York, 1994), 207–8, 221. The correspondence of a lowcountry woman and her daughter, who was living in Philadelphia, suggests that they and their friends admired and discussed *Jerusalem Delivered*: see Eliza Middleton Fisher to Mary Herring Middleton, Dec. 27, 1844, in Eliza Cope Harrison, ed., *Best Companions: Letters of Eliza Middleton Fisher and Her Mother, Mary Herring Middleton, from Charleston, Philadelphia, and Newport, 1839–1846* (Columbia, SC, 2001), 418. Also, Rosalie Stier Calvert to Isabelle van Havre, Oct. 25, 1816, in Margaret Law Callcott, ed., *The Mistress of Riversdale: The Plantation Letters of Rosalie Stier Calvert, 1795–1821* (Baltimore, 1991), 304. For Tasso and the debate see Loren Scanarelli Seem, "The Limits of Chivalry: Tasso and the End of the Aeneid," *Comparative Literature*, 42 (1990), 116–25; G. W. F. Hegel, *Early Theological Writings*, tr. T. M. Knox and Richard Kroner (Philadelphia, 1948), 190; E. Brooks Holifield, *The Gentlemen Theologians: American Theology in Southern Culture, 1795–1860* (Durham, NC, 1978), 37–8. See also Frederick Robertson Bryson, *The Point of Honor in Sixteenth-Century Italy: An Aspect of the Life of a Gentleman* (New York, 1935), esp. ch. 1 and 107–8. Bryson stresses the continuing influence of Aristotle and the specifically Aristotelian emphasis on virtue as valor and justice.

[36] Wilson, *Carolina Cavalier*, 54–5, 228; Huizinga, *Waning of the Middle Ages*, 66; "G. W. M.", "The Spaniards, Their Character and Customs," *SLM*, 5 (1839), 519–20; [Severn Teackle Wallis], "Spain in the Fifteenth Century," *SLM*, 7 (1841), 242; Julio Caro Baroja, "Honour and Shame: A Historical Account of Several Conflicts," in J. G. Peristiany, ed., *Honour and Shame: The Values of Mediterranean Society* (Chicago, 1966), 92; [De Bow], "Literature of Spain," *DBR*, 9 (1850), 70; Dew, *Digest*, 417–20; Julian Pitt-Rivers, "Honour and Social Status," in Peristiany, ed., *Honour and Shame*, 23. On chivalry Dew also drew upon the *Edda* and other Norse literature.

Sarah Morgan, Eliza Frances Andrews, and Margaret Junkin Preston were among the ladies who read Spanish, and *El Cid* and *Don Quixote* ranked high among their favorites. Catherine Edmonston and others got *El Cid* through Corneille's *Le Cid*, upon which much of the French-reading elites of Europe relied: see Marek Jan Chodakiewicz, "Affinity and Revulsion: Poland Reacts to the Spanish Right, 1936–1939 (and Beyond)," in M. J. Chodakiewicz and John Radzilowski, eds., *Catholic and Right: Essays on Spain and Poland in the Nineteenth and Twentieth Centuries* (forthcoming). Stonewall Jackson taught Spanish to Margaret Junkin: Mary Price Coulling, *Margaret Junkin Preston: A Biography* (Winston-Salem, NC, 1993), 79.

while the unionist James Legaré, intending no flattery, called South Carolina "a modern La Mancha."[37]

George Fitzhugh loved *Don Quixote*. Cervantes exposed the absurdities of knight-errantry but "unfortunately expelled, at the same time, the new elements of thought which chivalry and Christianity had introduced into modern literature." Fitzhugh's heart went out to Don Quixote – "Don Quixote mad, is the noblest, because the most chivalrous and disinterested of all the heroes of Epic poetry; he is but a drivelling, penitent dotard when he recovers" – but his brain went out to Sancho Panza, in his view the wisest man in literature except for Solomon, for Sancho Panza measured everything against experience and common sense. When "Don Quixote" jousted with "Ivanhoe" at the tournament at Fauquier Springs in Virginia in 1845, the Richmond *Enquirer* saw no need to explain its reference to "the renowned Knight of La Mancha." Even clergymen found *Don Quixote* edifying. He who wages war on southern slavery, the Presbyterian Reverend Ferdinand Jacobs preached in Charleston in 1850, "should with the Knight of La Mancha, become the universal redresser of grievances, and set about righting all the affairs of earth." In 1853 the Methodist Reverend George Richard Browder of Kentucky "sat up very late" reading *Don Quixote*: "Think many people might be benefited by reading the exploits of the crazy old knight. The book is a splendid Burlesque."[38]

Lewis Simpson, the leading modern interpreter of southern letters, has suggested that Hamlet, Prince of Denmark, and Don Quixote, Knight of the Sad Countenance, may be seen as "symbolic prototypes of the poet and the man of letters" and as

---

[37] Thomas Jefferson to Mary Jefferson, May 23, 1790, Jan. 22, 1791, in Edwin Morris Betts and James Adam Bear, Jr., eds., *The Family Letters of Thomas Jefferson* (Columbia, MO, 1966), 56–7, 70–1; Dumas Malone, *Jefferson and His Time*, 6 vols. (Boston, 1962–81), 2:4, 3:170; John P. Kennedy, *Memoirs of the Life of William Wirt, Attorney-General of the United States*, 2 vols. (Philadelphia, 1850), 1:57, 247; [Wirt et al.], *Old Bachelor*, 90; Russell Kirk, *John Randolph of Roanoke: A Study in American Politics, with Selected Speeches and Letters* (Chicago, 1964), 21; John Taylor, *An Inquiry into the Principles and Policy of the Government of the United States*, ed. Loren Baritz (Indianapolis, IN, 1919 [1814]), 41; James Legaré, quoted in Robert Nicholas Olsberg, "A Government of Class and Race: William H. Trescot and the South Carolina Chivalry, 1860–1865" (Ph.D. diss., University of South Carolina, 1972), 125. For *Don Quixote* in French see Mrs. Burton [Constance Cary] Harrison, *Recollections Grave and Gay* (London, 1912), 3. John R. Thompson, editor of *Southern Literary Messenger*, said there could never be too many translations of *Don Quixote*: *SLM*, 19 (1853), 520. Arnold Hauser has remarked that in Spain chivalry had its strongest late-medieval resurgence, and in Spain the disillusionment that accompanied its dissolution was greatest: *The Social History of Art*, 2 vols. (London, 1951), 1:399.

[38] George Fitzhugh, "What Shall Be Done with the Free Negroes," Appendix to *Sociology for the South: Or the Failure of Free Society* (New York, reproduction of 1854 edition), 288; Fitzhugh, *Cannibals All!; Or Slaves without Masters* (Cambridge, MA, 1960 [1857]), 252; Rollin G. Osterweis, *Romanticism and Nationalism in the Old South* (Baton Rouge, LA, 1971), 4–5 (on the tournament); Rosena H. Lassiter to Susan E. Southall, May 26–29 and Oct. 1, 1865, in L. C. and E. S. Lawrence Letters; Moragné Journal, Aug. 16, Oct. 13 (quote), 1838, in Craven, ed., *Neglected Thread*, 103; Elizabeth Ruffin Diary, Feb. 5, 1827, in Edmund Ruffin Papers, at UNC-SHC; also, William Harris Bragg, *De Renne: Three Generations of a Georgia Family* (Athens, GA, 1999), 22. Pettigrew, an acute student of Spanish culture, especially applauded Cervantes's character delineations: *Spain and the Spaniards*, 141–3.

"the first poets to know not only an isolation of the self in history but an isolation of history in the self." Although Simpson is not here discussing the Old South, he captures its mood or, better, its fear: "Shakespeare and Cervantes are motivated by a tension toward the dread knowledge that the displacement of society is irreversible."[39]

Alain-René Lesage's *Gil Blas* provided the early eighteenth-century bridge between the heroic and often deeply Christian chivalric literature of the sixteenth century and the transformation of that tradition in later eighteenth- and early nineteenth-century novels. Much influenced by *Don Quixote,* Lesage gave his wonderful picaresque romp a Spanish setting, although it is unmistakably French in spirit and written in French. Eighteenth-century Charleston bookstores carried Lesage in both French and English, and *Gil Blas* turned up in planters' libraries in North Carolina. *Gil Blas* seems to have been the most popular foreign book in eighteenth-century Maryland, except for Voltaire's histories. In the early nineteenth century it was assigned in French courses at the universities of North Carolina and Virginia. Tryphena Fox improved her French by reading it and having her husband read it to her.[40]

Southerners' vision of chivalry drew also on classic seventeenth-century French drama, openly engaged with the implications of chivalry for the emerging world of courtly and urban civility. Of the great trio – Pierre Corneille, Jean-Baptiste Poquelin Molière, and Jean Racine – Corneille, probably best known for *Le Cid,* hewed closest to the Spanish and Italian traditions, drawing upon ancient and chivalric sources for his tragedies. Many of Molière's "comedies" have a dark edge, and he provided a link between the waning chivalric tradition and the domestic fiction of the following century. Racine drew heavily upon classical literature, history, and mythology, although his preoccupation with love and honor testified to a considerable – albeit indirect – influence of the chivalric themes.[41]

Pupils from age 10 on read Racine and Molière. Jefferson discovered Racine early and inserted four extracts in his Commonplace Book, the only such he left in French. Racine and Corneille pleased the staunchly Calvinist Reverends George Howe and Jasper Adams as well as the successful Charleston merchant Mitchell King. Southerners who faulted Corneille for his devotion to absolute monarchy respected him as the poet of patriotism par excellence, the more so since his Horace

[39] Lewis P. Simpson, "The Southern Republic of Letters and *I'll Take My Stand,*" in William C. Havard and Walter Sullivan, eds., *A Band of Prophets: The Vanderbilt Agrarians after Fifty Years* (Baton Rouge, LA, 1982), 73.

[40] Hennig Cohen, *The South Carolina Gazette, 1732–1775* (Columbia, SC, 1953), 124, 136, 137; Stephen B. Weeks, *Libraries and Literature in North Carolina in the Eighteenth Century* (Washington, DC, 1896: "Annual Report of the American Historical Association for the Year 1895"), 201, 206. We use "Lesage," rather than "Le Sage," as recommended in Joyce M. H. Reid, ed., *The Oxford Dictionary of French Literature* (Oxford, U.K., 1976), 348. Most Southerners preferred "Le Sage" and even bestowed upon him a noble status he did not possess. See Supplementary References: "Lesage and Rabelais."

[41] For a classic formulation of the transition to courtly and urban social standards, see Norbert Elias, *The Civilizing Process: The History of Manners,* vol. 1, tr. Edmund Jephcott (Oxford, U.K., 1978).

taught that patriotism could generate madness – as when carried to the excess of Horace's killing his wife's brother in the name of loyalty to Rome, his *patria*. No doubt Corneille's appeal was enhanced by his celebration of chivalry's combination of a generosity laced with barbarous violence and of the joys of killing and loving.[42]

By the mid-eighteenth century, medieval chivalry was being transformed into an increasingly bourgeois domestic courtesy. Henry Fielding and Samuel Richardson were immensely popular in Virginia and the Carolinas in the late eighteenth century and were still read across the South in the nineteenth despite Fielding's raciness. The young Elizabeth Ruffin "took a small peep" at *Tom Jones* and wrote teasingly in her diary: "Don't be alarmed my delicate readers, am sorry to shock any one of your senses by such an UNLADY-LIKE and ungenteel confession." But Fielding's Squire Weston presented a paternalistic country gentleman of a kind Southerners liked to relate to. Mary Chesnut struck a common note when she took Sir Charles Grandison as an exemplar of the chivalrous gentleman. The novels of George P. R. James, who represented the British government in Virginia for a while, had enormous sales throughout the United States. James's *History of Chivalry* (1831) and his novels of knights and chivalry caught southern fancy, and Edward Bulwer-Lytton's *Pelham* also became something of a rage with its chivalric themes. Catherine Edmonston and Mary E. Moragné, among others, read a great deal of Bulwer-Lytton during the War, entranced by *Deveraux* and its fondness for the medieval chivalry.[43]

---

[42] "Fontenelle", "Life of Corneille," *SLM*, 8 (1842), 647–52; Jane Tayloe Lomax Worthington, "French Dramatists," *SLM*, 9 (1843), 76–9. William Howard Adams, *The Paris Years of Thomas Jefferson* (New Haven, CT, 1997), 30; Malone, *Jefferson and His Time*, 6:188; George Howe, "Secondary and Collateral Influences of the Sacred Scriptures," *SPR*, 7 (1853), 119; Daniel L. Dreisbach, ed., *Religion and Politics in the Early Republic: Jasper Adams and the Church–State Debate* (Lexington, KY, 1996), 105; Mitchell King, *A Discourse on the Qualifications and Duties of an Historian* (Savannah, GA, 1843), 20. Also, Elizabeth Ruffin to Edmund Ruffin, Jan. 6, 1840, in Edmund Ruffin Papers; Eliza Ripley, *Social Life in Old New Orleans: Being Recollections of My Girlhood* (New York, 1975 [1912]), 17. For the social views of Corneille and Racine, especially as evidenced in their treatment of Roman subjects, see Louis Auchincloss, *La Gloire: The Roman Empire of Corneille and Racine* (Columbia, SC, 1996). Racine's *Brittanicus* depicted Nero as a youth who displayed generosity as well as sadism and traced the course of the domination of the latter trait. Molière, among other French intellectuals, established the principle of tolerance, asserting that nonbelievers could behave in a more Christian manner than many Christians: George Huppert, *The Style of Paris: Renaissance Origins of the French Enlightenment* (Bloomington, IN, 1999), 99.

[43] Among many works on the relation between the novel and society in the eighteenth century, see esp. Ian Watt, *The Rise of the Novel: Studies in Defoe, Richardson and Fielding* (Berkeley, CA, 1957). Elizabeth Ruffin Diary, Feb. 5, 1827, in Edmund Ruffin Papers; Chesnut Diary, Apr. 15, 1861, in Woodward, ed., *Mary Chesnut's Civil War*, 52. For Fielding and Richardson in the South see Sarah McCulloh Lemmon, *Parson Pettigrew of the "Old Church": 1744–1807* (Chapel Hill, NC, 1970), 12; Columbus Morrison Journal, June 4, 1846, at UNC-SHC; Alfred C. Mordecai of Richmond, in Jacob Rader Marcus, ed., *Memoirs of American Jews*, 3 vols. (Philadelphia, 1955), 1:228; George Cary Eggleston, *A Rebel's Recollections* (Baton Rouge, LA, 1996 [1871]), 52–3; *SLM*, 26 (1858), 257; Aug. 10, 1865, in Sarah Woolfolk Wiggins, ed., *The Journals of Josiah Gorgas, 1857–1878* (Tuscaloosa, AL, 1995), 185. For Fielding's readers see also Maria Bryan Harford to Julia Ann Bryan Cumming, Mar. 11, 1839, in Carol Bleser, ed., *Tokens of Affection: The Letters of a Planter's Daughter in the Old South* (Athens, GA, 1996), 239; Rhoda Coleman Ellison, *Early Alabama Publications: A Study*

The palm for chivalric knight *par excellence* went to Turner Ashby of Virginia. Ashby's wartime heroics struck terror into the Yankees and reached such heights of daring – some said recklessness – that Stonewall Jackson, his famously bold commanding officer, had to rein him in or at least try to. Ashby's chafing under authority became notorious, as did his cavalry's lack of discipline, which more than once took a heavy toll on the Confederate war effort. Jackson, himself known for unorthodox and fierce tactics and for being the strictest of disciplinarians, swallowed hard, and when Ashby died he described his loss as irreparable. Robert Barton, who served under Ashby and admired his horsemanship and performance at tournaments, declared him "a gallant fellow" but "a man of few accomplishments and not much capacity as an officer." But Captain Ujanirtus Allen of Virginia, a small slaveholder, sadly reported to his wife that the Confederacy had lost "one of the most gallant cavalry officers the world has ever produced," and Colonel Alexander Fleet lamented "the terrible loss of Gen. Ashby – a second Marion." In the balanced judgment of General Richard Taylor, who opposed Ashby's promotion to brigadier general, he and his troops were valiant but undisciplined and hopeless romantics. Taylor invoked the language of Bossuet, " 'Tis beautiful, but 'tis not war." Taylor thought the Confederacy had lost the best cavalry officer he had ever known. Charles William Trueheart reported from the front to his mother in Galveston that the "partisan leader" Ashby deserved to be "celebrated" and "famous" because, brave to a fault, he never failed to rally his troops in the face of adversity.[44]

---

in Literary Interests (University, AL, 1947), 65, 117; Clement Eaton, *The Freedom-of-Thought Struggle in the Old South* (New York, 1964), 59.

On James see G. Harrison Orians, "Walter Scott, Mark Twain, and the Civil War," *South Atlantic Quarterly*, 40 (1941), 346–9; *SQR*, 5 (1844), 530–4. On James's readership see Chesnut Diary, May 6, 1862, in Woodward, ed., *Mary Chesnut's Civil War*, 334; Edmonston Diary, Aug. 21, 1860, Aug. 26, 1862, Feb. 24 and June 12, 1863, in Crabtree and Patton, eds., *"Journal of a Secesh Lady,"* 9, 243, 366, 406. See also Maria Bryan to Julia Ann Bryan Cumming, Apr. 15, 1833, in Bleser, ed., *Tokens of Affection*, 152. Mary Moragné wrote of Deveraux: "What a lesson on human frailties it is!": Journal, Feb. 26, 1837, July 3, 1839, in Craven, ed., *Neglected Thread*, 26, 140. The prolific G. P. R. James, who died in 1860, was enormously popular throughout America: James D. Hart, *The Popular Book: A History of America's Literary Taste* (New York, 1950), 79. Mary Gay, who knew and liked James, referred to "the English novelist whose star rose and set before 1860: Gay, *Life in Dixie during the War*, 12. Simms was among those who found James wonderfully warm in correspondence and conversation: Simms to John Esten Cooke, Jan. 29, 1859, in Mary C. Oliphant et al., eds., *The Letters of William Gilmore Simms*, 6 vols. (Columbia, SC, 1952–82), 4:114.

44 The principal source for this sketch of Ashby is Frank Cunningham, *Knight of the Confederacy: Gen. Turner Ashby* (San Antonio, TX, 1960), from which all material and quotations not otherwise cited are drawn. See also Thomas A. Ashby, *Life of Turner Ashby* (New York, 1914); Perceval Reniers, *The Springs of Virginia: Life, Love, and Death at the Waters, 1775–1900* (Chapel Hill, NC, 1941), 159–60. For a critical account of Ashby's war record see John Bowers, *Stonewall Jackson: Portrait of a Soldier* (New York, 1989), 114 and, generally, ch. 7. Our account of Ashby is an expanded version of Eugene D. Genovese, "The Chivalric Tradition in the Old South," *Sewanee Review*, 108 (2000), 180–98. For a recent appraisal of Ashby as symbol, see Paul Christopher Anderson, *Blood Image: Turner Ashby in the Civil War and the Southern Mind* (Baton Rouge, LA, 2002).

Frank E. Vandiver, *Mighty Stonewall* (College Station, TX, 1957), 216, 248, 254, 273, 279; Robert T. Barton, in Margaret Barton Colt, *Defend the Valley: A Shenandoah Family in the Civil War* (New York, 1994), 156; Ujanirtus Allen to Susan Fuller Allen, June 12, 1862, in Randall Allen and Keith

A good many Yankees agreed. No Confederate officer, with the possible exception of Stonewall Jackson, struck such fear into the Union army or so clearly won its respect. Brigadier General David Hunter Strother ("Porte Crayon"), a Virginian who fought for the Union, reported: "Ashby has played his part handsomely in disputing our advance, displaying a great deal of personal boldness and military tact in checking so large a column as ours with his small force." Upon learning of Ashby's death, Strother remarked, "What better end for a gallant and chivalrous gentleman? He was a man limited in mental prowess but of grave and generous nature .... He died gallantly."[45]

Since Ashby descended from English cavaliers, royalist refugees from Cromwell's regime, he would seem the perfect representative of Virginia's Chivalry. Alas, his forebears were not planters at all, and his family had fallen on hard times. With their lineage and a proud record of service during the Revolution and the War of 1812 they did, however, achieve sufficient respectability to be well connected socially despite straitened economic circumstances. Turner Ashby proved a good and morally upright student and a respectable slaveholding farmer, but he spent years working principally as a merchant.

When Ashby fell, no one thought excessive the tributes to his chivalric virtues that a host of soldiers, poets, and ladies rushed to pay him. Poems and eulogies poured out of the South's better-known writers, including R. C. Ambler, John Esten Cooke, Margaret Junkin Preston, John R. Thompson, and Frank Ticknor, in addition to passionate scribblers. Preston, "the poetess of the Confederacy":

> Bold as the Lion-Heart –
> 　Dauntless and Brave;
> Knightly as knightliest
> 　Bayard could crave;
> Sweet – with all Sidney's grace –
> 　Tender as Hampden's face –
> Who shall fill the space,
> 　Void by his grave?

S. Bohannon, eds., *Campaigning with "Old Stonewall": Confederate Captain Ujanirtus Allen's Letters to His Wife* (Baton Rouge, LA, 1998), 102; Alexander Fleet to Marie Fleet, June 13, 1862, in Betsey Fleet and John D. P. Fuller, *Green Mount: A Virginia Plantation Family during the War* (Charlottesville, VA, 1962), 137; Taylor, *Destruction and Reconstruction*, 77; Charles William Trueheart to Mary Trueheart, Dec. 12 and 26, 1861, in Edward B. Williams, ed., *Rebel Brothers: The Civil War Letters of the Truehearts* (College Station, TX, 1995), 35–7; also R. L. Dabney, *Life and Campaigns of Lt. Gen. T. J. (Stonewall) Jackson* (Harrisonburg, VA, 1983 [1865]), 327–8.

　Grady McWhiney and Perry D. Jamieson, in *Attack and Die: Civil War Military Tactics and the Southern Heritage* (University, AL, 1982), argue that the culture of "attack and die" stemmed from the Celtic clans, but it probably derived no less and even more directly from Anglo-French chivalry: cf. Kaeuper, *Chivalry and Violence*, 146. For descriptions of the troops from Alabama and Texas as undisciplined – but courageous and effective even without officers to command them – see Stocker, ed., *From Huntsville to Appomattox*, 31; Clyde Lottridge Cummer, ed., *Yankee in Gray: The Civil War Memoirs of Henry Ebenezer Handerson with a Selection of His Wartime Letters* (Cleveland, OH, 1962), 46.

45　Strother, Mar. 19, June 18 and 28, 1862, in Cecil D. Eby, Jr., ed., *A Virginia Yankee in the Civil War: The Diaries of David Hunter Strother* (Chapel Hill, NC, 1961), 17, 60.

Sallie B. Putnam of Richmond: "The brave, gallant, daring young cavalier of Virginia had fallen." Mary Boykin Chesnut: "Drop a tear for Turner Ashby, the hero of the Valley. They say he is killed! All things are against us." Jefferson Davis: "the stainless, fearless cavalier." T. C. De Leon: "True knight – doughty leader – high-hearted gentleman .... Chivalric – lion-hearted – strong armed." Cornelia Peake McDonald of Winchester: "the gallant soldier, the enemy so dreaded."[46]

As a knight at southern-style tournaments in North Carolina and Virginia, Ashby had ridden without peer. It may be doubted that any young Virginian ever crowned as many Queens of Love and Beauty. Usually riding without bridle or saddle and dressed as an Indian warrior, he took the name Knight of the Black Prince or Knight of Hiawatha. A joyful foxhunter and sportsman, he put his extraordinary horsemanship, unflinching courage, and careful study of military tactics to various uses. In 1852 he organized the Mountain Rangers to defend the local folk who complained of being abused and assaulted by rowdies employed in building a railroad through the area. (The workers' side of the story has gone unrecorded.) The Mountain Rangers maintained order for years and then constituted the nucleus of Company A, Seventh Virginia Cavalry, C.S.A., which Ashby led into battle, often against heavy odds.

Ashby also tried his hand at politics, but despite immense personal popularity he failed to win an election, perhaps because of his Whiggery and his strong unionism. Although a slaveholder, he hoped that Virginians would, in time, find a way to phase out slavery. A supporter of the Constitutional Union party's John Bell for the presidency in 1860, he did not hesitate to stand with his state during the secession crisis, offering to support Henry Wise's threatened coup d'état against the supposedly wavering Governor John Letcher. For Ashby, as for Robert E. Lee, "duty" came before all else in life.

The endless tales of Ashby's chivalric demeanor contain the usual quotient of romance, but most ring true. Shortly before the War he hosted a party to which he invited a visiting Yankee gentleman, a known Republican. Another guest, a young hotspur uninstructed in the rules of respect, abused the Yankee verbally and then challenged him to the field of honor. Ashby intervened: A Virginia gentleman did not countenance discourtesy toward his guests and took any such insult as directed at himself. Ashby, whose skill with weapons approximated his skill with horses, accepted the challenge hurled at his guest, and the hotspur, apparently in his cups but not suicidal, backed off. During the War some unionist women in West Virginia asked permission to leave for the North. Assuring Ashby that they carried no contraband, they offered to submit to a search. He granted permission to leave but added, "The gentlemen of Virginia do not search ladies' trunks or their persons."

---

[46] De Leon, *Belles*, 202; [Sallie B. Putnam], *Richmond during the War; Four Years of Personal Observation. By a Richmond Lady* (New York, 1867), 139; Chesnut Diary, June 13, 1862, in Woodward, ed., *Mary Chesnut's Civil War*, 385; Cornelia Peake McDonald, June 20, 1862, in Minrose C. Gwin, ed., *A Woman's Civil War: A Diary, with Reminiscences of the War from March 1862* (Madison, WI, 1992 [1875]), 63, also 254–7, 265–8. For an Englishwoman's tribute to Ashby see Catherine Cooper Hopley, *"Stonewall" Jackson*, 94–5. The other quotations are from Cunningham.

Thus did Ashby emerge as the ideal southern chivalric warrior: the fierce but gentle knight who would lead men into battle but protect wronged men as readily as he would protect women. In the words of a lady of his neighborhood, "He was a person of very deep feelings, which would not have been apparent to strangers, from his natural reserve of manner; but there was no act of friendship or kindness he would have shrunk to perform, if called upon." In Charlottesville, Lucy Woods Butler heard that Ashby's body had been taken up by "the men whom he had led so bravely on to the battle with the foe, to whom he had been 'gentle as a parent': Strong, hardened men wept, and sayd they loved him better than any one, even their fathers." The commanding officer of the Union forces that entered Winchester asked a black waiter about Ashby. The waiter described Ashby as a favorite of the community – a "true gentleman, sober and considerate." He remarked that not all Confederate officers behaved as well as Ashby did, but added, "You know, we can tell who are gentlemen."[47]

According to countless testimonials, Ashby's life embodied the highest ideals of southern chivalry. Southerners thought of Ashby as G. P. R. James, a favorite British author, thought of Guesclin and Bayard: as a man who rises in "the midst of corrupted times to shame the vices of the day by still showing one more true knight." In southern eyes Turner Ashby qualified as pious, moral, temperate, gallant, honorable. A veritable modern knight. A legend in his own time. But *Chevalier sans reproche*? Could Christian believers in original sin and human depravity believe that any human could pass that test? G. K. Chesterton commented on a character in a novel: "If he is not always the Good Knight, he is always the man who would judge men in the last resort by whether they approximated to being Good Knights." Southerners understood *chevalier sans reproche* in the original meaning: a man who, although by no means spotless, could not be charged with cowardice, meanness, or the dishonoring of a lady. Ashby and those who tried to approach his high standards may not have qualified as saints, but they represented the hopes of a proud people determined to forge a great southern future.[48]

Centuries after the medieval warfare evoked by chivalry proper had given way to new forms of warfare, tournaments – with an increasingly ritualistic cast – enjoyed great popularity in the South. On the eve of secession, when tournaments were almost disappearing in the North, Daniel Hundley of Alabama called the South the center of neo-medieval tournaments. Hundley derided the pretentious parvenu planters he called "Cotton Snobs" for their ostentatious playing as knights-errant, parading like peacocks before their ladies at pseudo-medieval tournaments. Hundley's genuine southern gentlemen dressed rather carelessly, lived unostentatiously, and carried themselves with a quiet sense of being a New World version of European

47 E. A. Pollard, *Southern History of the War*, 2 vols. (Fairfax, VA, 1977 [1866]), 1:398; Lucy Woods Diary, June 9, 1862, at UNC-SHC; for the black waiter see David Hunter Strother, Mar. 19, June 18 and 28, 1862, in Eby, ed., *Virginia Yankee*, 63–4.

48 James, *History of Chivalry*, 52; G. K. Chesterton, "The Messenger of the Snow: A Preface," *Chesterton Review*, 25 (1999), 7. On the meaning of *chevalier sans reproche* see Keen, *Chivalry*, 174.

nobility. The southern gentleman delighted in the quiet and peace of country life. "No matter what may be the Southern Gentleman's avocation, his dearest affections usually centre in the country." Hundley doubtless romanticized, but many of the young men who flocked to the summer vacation resorts to play at knight-errantry qualified as the finest products of their class, even if others did not. The ladies enjoyed the tournaments immensely. At the beginning of the 1850s Emily Wharton Sinkler, wife of a lowcountry planter, sent her family in Philadelphia a rich account of a tournament in Pineville, South Carolina, attended by about 200 ladies from Charleston to Columbia, some looking on from their carriages but most occupying stands expressly provided for them. At the end of the decade, Esther Simons Palmer sent her daughter Harriet a report of a well-attended tournament that "went off handsomely" with 13 knights, "mostly handsomely dressed." Rosena Lassiter of North Carolina failed to attend the tournament in Murfeesboro only because her elaborate dress was not ready.[49]

Educated Southerners knew something of the checkered relations between tournaments and Christianity. When tournaments appeared at the beginning of the twelfth century, perhaps a bit earlier, the Church roundly condemned them – but not effectively, to judge by evidence of their growing popularity and the repetitions of the condemnations. By 1130 A.D. Pope Innocent II was denouncing tournaments for wantonness, human slaughter, and un-Christian rashness and arrogance, and Pope Gregory IX incorporated the ban on tournaments into canon law. In the eyes of the Church, tournaments embodied a cult of violence and a near occasion for the seven deadly sins. Medieval tournaments often were murderous. Twelfth-century Church Councils refused burial in consecrated ground to those killed in them. While the ideals of feudal and religious chivalry were at odds, tournaments continued until changes in the art of war brought about their decline. "Earning honor by prowess," writes Richard Kaeuper, "appears throughout most chivalric literature as complementary to the worship of God."[50]

---

[49] Daniel R. Hundley, *Social Relations in Our Southern States* (Baton Rouge, LA, 1979 [1860]), 55, 174–5; Emily Wharton Sinkler to Thomas Isaac Wharton, Apr. 1851, in LeClerq, ed., *Between North and South*, 149–51; Esther Simons Palmer to Harriet R. Palmer, Apr. 28, 1859, in Louis P. Towles, ed., *A World Turned Upside Down: The Palmers of South Santee, 1818–1881* (Columbia, SC, 1996), 241; Rosena H. Lassiter to Susan E. Southall, Oct. 20, 1865, in L. C. and E. S. Lawrence Letters. On the South as tournament center see Esther J. Crooks and Ruth W. Crooks, *The Ring Tournament in the United States* (Richmond, VA, 1936). Many of those whom Hundley considered southern gentlemen did not dress or act as he claimed. But then, his book combines much of value with many indefensible assertions.

[50] Kaeuper, *Violence and Chivalry*, 48, 135; Kaeuper and Kennedy, *Geoffroi de Charny*, 33; also, Willis B. Glover, *Biblical Origins of Secular Culture: An Essay in the Interpretation of Western History* (Macon, GA, 1984), 24–5. On the medieval tournaments see esp. Keen, *Chivalry*, 84, 90–3, and chs. 5 and 11; Painter, *French Chivalry*, 47, 89; Huizinga, *Waning of the Middle Ages*, 71.
    In the tenth and eleventh centuries the Church, no longer able to direct military aggressiveness toward non-Christian targets, concentrated on establishing civilized rules for warfare among Christians. Robert C. Stacey observes, "The First Crusade was in this respect a counsel of despair": "Age of Chivalry," in Michael Howard et al., eds., *The Laws of War: Constraints on Warfare in the Modern*

Promotion of the Truce and Peace of God, which curbed feudal warfare, also curbed the income and sport of the knights, who – romance aside – lived largely off violence and plunder. With warfare reduced, tournaments served as schools for military training and for the display of prowess. Descriptions of early tournament battles read much like those of actual knightly warfare: bloody, raucous, and marked with corpses and maimed bodies. They permitted the legal settlement of personal scores in accordance with reigning mores.

With the mellowing of late medieval society, tournaments mellowed, too; in the end, they did contribute to the spread of chivalry. Even more than the Crusades, they promoted the evolving knightly virtues of largesse and courtesy as well as physical prowess. The element of play eventually crowded out the murderously martial, but something of the old spirit of feudal warfare lingered. Henry Dickson, a prominent Charleston physician, wrote: "Let the [medieval] tournament be remembered – the product and passion of Christian chivalry – where the bright eyes of gentle and Christian woman watched the progress of the headlong duel, or gazed on the mingled throng of the fiery melee and adjudged the prize to the panting and bloody conqueror. These have gone by." More acidly, Bishop John England of South Carolina, echoing the original hostility of the Catholic Church to the chivalric code, blamed southern tournaments for fostering the barbarism of dueling.[51]

In the United States tournaments persisted primarily as southern events, but the North had its own. One ostensibly small difference in the sporting events at agricultural fairs reflects the cultural separation of North and South. During the 1850s, northern agricultural fairs drew fire at home for promoting horse races in which women rode astride, jockey style – a practice disdained in the South, where women commonly rode sidesaddle. For Southerners, the tournaments did recapture the original meaning of chevalier as mounted warrior, although their formalized ring tournaments never approximated the bloody medieval jousts described in *Ivanhoe* with which Mark Twain mistakenly confused them.[52]

World (New Haven, CT, 1994), 27. In time, state and Church saw the tournaments as a threat to social order, if only because of the danger posed by the massing of armed men and possibilities for hatching conspiracies. On state intervention as well as the Church's opposition to tournaments from the beginning, the difficulties of enforcement, and the accommodation see Richard Barber and Juliet Barber, *Tournaments: Jousts, Chivalry and Pageants in the Middle Ages* (Woodbridge, U.K., 1989), ch. 6.

51 Henry Dickson, "Characteristics of Civilisation," in Simms, ed., *Charleston Book,* 74–5; Sebastian G. Messmer, ed., *The Works of the Right Rev. John England, First Bishop of Charleston,* 7 vols. (Cleveland, OH, 1908), 7:423–49; "The tournament may fairly be described as the central ritual of chivalry": Richard Barber, *The Knight and Chivalry,* rev. ed. (Woodbridge, U.K., 1970), 155. By the end of the Middle Ages, the state claimed a monopoly of licit violence and few defended dueling as a proper manifestation of manly prowess, although the practice continued: Kaeuper, *Violence and Chivalry,* 307. For the German experience with tournaments promoted by the state see William H. Jackson, "Tournaments and the German Chivalric Renovatio: Tournament Discipline and the Myth of Origins," in Anglo, ed., *Chivalry in the Renaissance,* 77–91.

52 Albert Lowther Demaree, *The American Agricultural Press, 1819–1860* (New York, 1941), 220–1; Orians, "Walter Scott, Mark Twain, and the Civil War," 344–5. G. P. R. James, however, recommended the descriptions in *Ivanhoe* as valuable: *Chivalry,* 40.

Virginia led in tournaments, and South Carolina had the most lavish south of Virginia, supplemented in the lowcountry with cavalry tilts by military horse companies. In Virginia the most prestigious occurred at Fauquier White Springs, about fifty miles west of Washington, where – during vacation season, amid hounds and hunters – one tournament followed another. "The knights rode at a ring instead of each other and wore bright silks instead of shining armor," writes Percival Reniers, "but otherwise they were as close as possible to their medieval models." The more fashionable ladies dressed in appropriate medieval-style sleeves, bodices, and skirts. In 1858 G. P. R. James described Fauquier's uniquely grand setting: "A broad, flat area, of several acres, surrounded by high banks, shaded with embowering trees, under which the judges sit, would inspire something like the ancient feats of arms, and we might expect to see the lances shivered, and the helmets dashed away, were not the age of chivalry really past."[53]

Thomas Roderick Dew and Nathaniel Beverley Tucker, among other prominent figures, delivered ceremonial orations at Fauquier, although Dew cast a cold eye on the original medieval tournaments as "very little better than barbarous shows." He did approve of the martial sports of ancient Greece, open to all rather than restricted to a warrior caste, and thus a knighthood of the whole people. He also approved of southern tournaments, which dispensed with medieval barbarism and recaptured that ancient republican flavor. Dew urged southern "knights" to remember that knighthood had grown out of the Dark Ages, which failed to recognize the rights of womanhood, and that it was devised "to arrest the downward progress of civilization; that all true knights must be honorable, courteous, liberal, clement, loyal, devoted to woman, to arms, to religion." Tournaments served as military training schools and reinforced the regional martial spirit. "Knights" rode at the ring rather than at each other – but the ring was no easy conquest. A young man had to practice at it all year round. To prevail and pay tribute to his lady, he had to ride at full speed and lift the ring without jarring the hook on which it rested.[54]

---

[53] George A. Rogers and R. Frank Saunders, Jr., *Swamp Water and Wire Grass: Historical Sketches of Coastal Georgia* (Macon, GA, 1984), 181; for the participation of the South Carolina militia in Independence Day festivities that included tournaments, see Flynn, *Militia in South Carolina*, 144; Reniers, *Springs of Virginia*, 125, 156–7; G. P. R. James, "Virginia's Country Life," in Schwaab and Bull, eds., *Travels in the Old South*, 2:526–7 (originally published in *Knickerbocker Magazine*).

[54] Dew, *Digest*, 68–71. For Dew's speech at Fauquier see Reniers, *Springs of Virginia*, 159. The words are Renier's paraphrase, with a few words from Dew included as subquotation. Dew did not mention Oliver Goldsmith's *History of Greece*, which Southern students read, but their views were similar. Goldsmith criticized the medieval tournaments at class-bound, in contrast to the games of ancient Greece, which he described as national events open to all classes. [Oliver Goldsmith], *Pinnack's Improved Edition of Dr. Goldsmith's History of Greece, Abridged for the Use of Schools* (Philadelphia, 1845), 45–6. Dew also knew of the similar analysis in Arnold H. L. Heeren, *Ancient Greece*, tr. George Bancroft, 2nd ed. (New York, 1842 [1823]), 129. As Dew suggested, by the end of the Middle Ages tournaments had become expensive to stage and became aristocratic events staged for great events of state: see Barber and Barber, *Tournaments*, 1–2. Without reference to the medieval tournaments, E. F. Rockwell also praised the Greek games as a reflection of religion in which the whole community participated: "Superiority of the Greeks in Literature and the Fine Arts," *SPR*, 15 (1862),

In North Carolina and in the parts of Maryland dominated by the rural gentry, jousting and tournaments also persisted. During the 1850s Davidson, North Carolina, prided itself as much on its tournaments as on its barbecues. Representative David Outlaw found the tournaments in Warrenton Springs tame enough for his Whiggish soul, for "the knights are in but little danger of life and limb." He was not enthusiastic about the fancy ball, a "thing equally foolish and ridiculous in this country." To Governor J. W. Ellis the Warren County tournaments had the trappings of *Ivanhoe*, and at Fayetteville in 1860 schoolgirl Malinda Ray reported with relish: "This morning I went to the Donaldson Academy to the Tournament which the boys had. Charlie Watts won & crowned – Kate Shepherd, Jennie, Lilly, Agnetta, & Kittie were the maids of honor." And so across the South, as the gentry moved westward. Citizens admired gentlemen like General Charles R. Floyd of Camden County, Georgia, for their hospitality and fondness for tournaments and boat races. Tallahassee, Florida, celebrated Washington's birthday with a ring tournament that had a frontier touch: The participants dressed as Indians, and the winner was dubbed Knight of the Miccosukie. Tournaments thrived at Alabama's state fairs in the 1850s. Greensboro, a small town, attracted folks from miles around to tournaments and balls. Jackson, Mississippi, held fairs with separate tournaments for boys under 13 and for those between 13 and 19.[55]

The tournament burst forth anew almost immediately after Appomattox. Southerners – coping with the trauma of defeat, frustration, impoverishment, and military occupation – attended agricultural fairs and other events that advertised tournaments. Confederate troops, especially cavalrymen, returned to have a good time in a manner connected to the past and their community's self-image. White Southerners of all ranks flocked to the postwar tournaments, perhaps in unprecedented numbers. John Houston Bills, a planter in western Tennessee who whiled away his spare hours early in 1866 reading tales of the Crusades, reported on October 12: "To day the great and long expected 'Tournament' Comes – off 1200 to 1500

199–200. Simms saw the medieval tournaments as a training ground for war: *Chevalier Bayard*, 71. See Osterweis, *Romanticism and Nationalism*, ch. 1, for descriptions of tournaments in Virginia and South Carolina. For a superb literary rendering see Allen Tate's novel, *The Fathers* (New York, 1938), 61–6.

55 Jean H. Baker, *The Politics of Continuity* (Baltimore, 1973), 11; Chalmers Gaston Davidson, *The Plantation World around Davidson* (Davidson, NC, 1969), 77; David Outlaw to Emily Outlaw, Sept. 4, 1850, at UNC-SHC; Noble J. Tolbert, ed., *The Papers of John Willis Ellis*, 2 vols. (Raleigh, NC, 1964), 1:137–8; Malinda B. Ray Diary, Dec. 23, 1860, in David A. Ray Papers, at UNC-SHC. On the role of westward-migrating slaveholders in spreading the culture of those of the eastern states, see James David Miller, *South by Southwest: Planter Emigration and Identity in the Slave South* (Charlottesville, VA, 2002). On Georgia: J. Holmes, *"Dr. Bullie's" Notes*, 105 n. On Florida: Herbert J. Dougherty, *Richard Keith Call, Southern Unionist* (Gainesville, FL, 1961), 139; Betram H. Groene, *Ante-Bellum Tallahassee* (Tallahassee, FL, 1971), 146–7. On Alabama: William Edward Wadsworth Yerby, *History of Greensboro, Alabama from Its Earliest Settlement*, ed. Mabel Yerby Lawson (Northport, AL, 1963 [1908]), 17–18; Weymouth T. Jordan, *Ante-Bellum Alabama: Town and Country* (Tallahassee, FL, 1957), 133. On Mississippi: James H. Stuart to Adelaide L. Stuart, Nov. 18, 1859, and Edward Stuart to Annie E. Stuart, Dec. 2, 1859, in Mayes-Dimitry-Stuart Papers, at Mississippi Department of Archives and History (Jackson).

persons attend it – the Tilting is Verry spirited, a dozen or more Knights enter the Contest – Brewer of Holly Springs, Missi[ssippi] – Wins the prize, a fine horse for which was paid $350 – Betty Neely was crowned queen of Love & Beauty – Genl Billy Jackson Capt Hurt & several Ladies stay with us and attend the Con[t]est." The tournament continued into the following day with "a verry spirited Contest": "After a Crowning & Ludicrous show of green horns riding – the thing closed – all went off well – no riotous Conduct on the part of Actors or audience." In 1906 Myrta Lockett Avery explained that postwar tournaments provided a respite for a weary people and sport for cavalry: "The tournament was to the South what base-ball is [now] to the nation." Tournaments eventually waned in North Carolina and probably elsewhere when blacks started to hold tournaments of their own, satiriz-ing whites and appropriating the chivalric mantle for themselves.[56]

"The press of the North," the Reverend John Adger had protested during the War, "has long been accustomed to sneer at those chivalrous notions upon which the Southron prides himself." In New York after the War, editors of *The Nation*, appalled by the continued enthusiasm for southern tournaments, raged:

Any country in which it is the custom, in our day, to assemble in great crowds to watch men doing these things in broad daylight, in the midst of great public distress, dressed up in fantastic costumes, and calling themselves "disinherited knights," "knights of the sword," "knights of the lone star," and pretending to worship a young woman from a modest wooden house in the neighborhood as the "queen of love and beauty," and to regard the bestowal of a shabby theatrical coronet by her as the summit of earthly felicity, we need not have the least hesitation in pronouncing semi-civilized.[57]

What, indeed, could be more absurd than the spectacle of a defeated and oc-cupied people pretending that their ideals, aspirations, and mores lived on despite political and military collapse? Was not the defiant prancing of brave young men who had lost a ghastly four-year war a demonstration of bad taste? What was a civilized person to think of treating young ladies from modest wooden houses as if they were queens of love and beauty? How else but "semi-civilized" ought one to describe those who called themselves disinherited knights and now reveled in tour-naments "in broad daylight?"[58]

[56] See e.g. the Diary and Journal of Flavellus G. Nicholson of Mississippi, Aug. 17, 1865, Jan. 22, 1866, at Mississippi Department of Archives and History (Jackson); William McKee Evans, *Ballots and Fence Rails: Reconstruction on the Lower Cape Fear* (Athens, GA, 1967), 211–16. On the tradi-tion of satirizing white dances and manners, see esp. Roger D. Abrahams, *Singing the Master: The Emergence of African American Culture in the Plantation South* (New York, 1992), xvii, 27, and (generally) Bills Diary, Feb. 24, Oct. 12 and 13, 1866, at UNC-SHC; Avery, *Dixie after the War* (New York, 1918 [1906]), 172. For the postwar boom in tournaments see Ted Ownby, *Subduing Satan: Re-ligion, Recreation, and Manhood in the Rural South, 1865–1920* (Chapel Hill, NC, 1990), 70–6.

[57] [J. B. Adger], "Motley's Dutch Republic," *SPR*, 15 (1862), 150; "The Southern Transformation," *The Nation*, 8 (Nov. 8, 1866), 371.

[58] See Ernest McPherson Lander, Jr., *The Calhoun Family and Thomas Green Clemson: The Decline of Southern Patriarchy* (Columbia, SC, 1983), 235; for the image of General Lee at the tournaments see Thomas L. Connely, *The Marble Man: Robert E. Lee and His Image in American Society* (New York, 1977), 101.

Twentieth-century conservatives have debated the relative merits of Robert E. Lee, Stonewall Jackson, and Nathan Bedford Forrest as exemplars of the chivalric ideal. Allen Tate – who later wrote insightful, if wildly inaccurate, biographies of Jefferson Davis and Stonewall Jackson – abandoned his plan to write on Lee, for the more he studied Lee's career the more disgusted he became that Lee had sacrificed the South's chance for victory by fighting a gentlemen's war in the great chivalric tradition. Tate accused Lee of egotism in putting his cherished Virginia ideals above the duty he himself constantly advocated. The War, Tate and Andrew Lytle argued, was not a gentlemen's war but a new type of war: a people's war that required revolutionary ruthlessness toward civilians and soldiers alike. In their view, Jackson and Forrest, like Grant and Sherman, understood as much and did whatever was necessary to win. Since the fate of the southern nation hung in the balance, they were right, Lee wrong.[59]

Richard Weaver has excoriated the Union army for its own modern war, describing it as largely free of previous restraints and designed to break the will of a whole people at any cost. The Confederate army fought in an older manner, although considering Forrest's tactics it might not have continued to do so if the War had lasted much longer. In *Ideas Have Consequences,* Weaver celebrated "the splendid tradition of chivalry" for its "formal cognizance of the right to existence not only of inferiors but also of enemies." He assailed the demand for unconditional surrender, which "impiously puts man in the place of God by usurping unlimited right to dispose of the lives of others." In contrast, "chivalry was a most practical expression of the basic brotherhood of man." In the pursuit of brutality, the modern age has exceeded the cruelest of previous ages: "Cruelty is refined and, at least, discriminates its objects and intentions. The terrible brutalities of democratic war have demonstrated how little the mass mind is capable of seeing the virtue of selection and restraint," it ignores the chivalric distinctions between babe and adult, between the sexes, between combatant and noncombatant. "This is the destruction of society through brutality." In the wake of the horrors of two world wars, Weaver developed his theme further in *Visions of Order*: "The modern war against war has not succeeded." War itself, Weaver urged, may be an ineradicable consequence of human nature, and chivalry's rules of warfare may well be the only alternative to modern barbarism.[60]

Weaver's predecessors credited chivalry with the transformation of warfare from indiscriminate slaughter to civilized behavior toward a fallen enemy. For the Reverend Robert Newton Sledd during the War, the Yankees inflicted a barbarism that would have disgraced the Middle Ages. Dew summarized the characteristics of

---

[59] "R. E. Lee," "A Hero and Doctrinaire of Defeat," and "A Retrospect on Bedford Forrest and His Critter Company," in M. E. Bradford, ed., *From Eden to Babylon: The Social and Political Essays of Andrew Lytle* (Washington, DC, 1990), esp. 98, 136, 146–53.

[60] Richard M. Weaver, *Ideas Have Consequences* (Chicago, 1948), 175, 33; Weaver, *Visions of Order: The Cultural Crisis of Our Times* (Baton Rouge, LA, 1964), 108–9; Mary Gay included George Mc-Clellan with Washington and Lee as men who respected "ideas of civilized and Christian warfare": *Life in Dixie during the War*, 244. For a critique of the charge of Union atrocities see Mark E. Neely, Jr., *Retaliation: The Problem of Atrocity in the American Civil War* (Gettysburg, PA, 2002).

chivalry at its best: "Love of arms, romantic spirit of adventure, courtesy of manners, the point of honor, and devoted and respectful attention to the female sex." To such Southerners, feudalism's code of a moral obligation to maintain fidelity to lord or vassal had provided the foundation for social order – which, when broken, left the sword as the only recourse. Yet Dew also cited Jean de Joinville's *Vie de St Louis* to show how little knights thought of persons of low birth, and he did not underestimate the murderous impulses of medieval chivalry, especially when combined with religious fanaticism. He pointed with wrath to the Crusaders who, with "Deus vult!" on their lips, "massacred, without distinction, thousands of the inhabitants of the Holy Land." Remarking on the terrible slaughters of the peasant insurrections, Dew castigated the lords whose oppression provoked them and the peasants who reacted with comparable brutality: "The spirit of chivalry, then at its height, was totally at war with both the order of society which furnished the insurgents, and their brute and ruffian-like mode of carrying on wars." Nor did the chivalric code benefit common soldiers. When Henry II captured Stephen's Castle in 1153, he spared the knights but executed sixty archers. For long afterwards brutal treatment of civilians persisted. The Hundred Years' War, which raged off and on from 1337 to 1453, slaughtered civilians on an unprecedented scale and, contrary to the romantic notions of Weaver and others, introduced "peoples' war" against whole communities. The wars of the Middle Ages, A. F. Dickson exclaimed in 1866, far outdid the War for Southern Independence in sheer savagery.[61]

Weaver maintained silence on the atrocities committed against black troops, whose very humanity the Confederate army frequently disdained. The slaughter of black troops at Fort Pillow in Tennessee in 1864 sickened even some of the perpetrators. A Confederate soldier wrote his mother, "I hope I may never see a Negro soldier," fearing that if he did he would not act like "a Christian soldier." Milton Barrett, an upcountry South Carolina yeoman, noted casually that his unit took 1,000 white but only two black prisoners, having killed some 500 blacks. And in "refugeeing" blacks, some planters shot recalcitrant slaves rather than let them flee,

---

[61] Robert Newton Sledd, *A Sermon Delivered in the Market Street, M. E. Church, Petersburg, Va.: Before the Confederate Cadets on the Occasion of Their Departure for the Seat of War* (Petersburg, VA, 1861), 19; Dew, *Digest*, 45, 333 (fidelity), 351–2 (Joinville), 354–5, 342–3 (chivalry at its best), 393 (Crusaders), 499 (peasant insurgents); [Dickson], "Life of de Guesclin," 376–8. See also Dabney, *Lt. Gen. T. J. (Stonewall) Jackson*, 36, as well as "Southern Chivalry and Total War" (168) and "Lee the Philosopher" (171–80) in George M. Curtis III and James J. Thompson, Jr., eds., *The Southern Essays of Richard M. Weaver* (Indianapolis, IN, 1987), for Dabney on Jackson's doctrine of total war see 192–3. For other southern defenses of Jackson and criticisms of Lee on "total war" see Osterweis, *Romanticism and Nationalism*, 91–2.

Fewer Southerners read Joinville than Froissart, but a good many read G. P. R. James, who relied heavily on Joinville's account of the Crusade of St. Louis. James wrote that, with the possible exception of Froissart, "Joinville offers the most original, simple, and delightful painting of times and manners long gone by": James, *Chivalry*, xi–xii, also 30 n. 2. On the unchivalric nature of medieval warfare see: John Gillingham, "An Age of Expansion, c. 1021–1204," Norman Housely, "European Warfare, c. 1200–1320," and esp. Christopher Allmand, "War and the Non-Combatant in the Middle Ages," all in Maurice Keen, ed., *Medieval Warfare: A History* (Oxford, U.K., 1999), 83, 133, 252–72.

convinced that such recalcitrance displayed impudence, disobedience, ingratitude, and insufferable presumption.[62]

Walter Herron Taylor, Lee's adjutant, wrote his sister in the summer of 1863 to express dismay and outrage over the prospect of black troops in an army of occupation. Taylor could not understand how the black troops, who – he had no doubt – had lived with good masters "in happy Virginia homes," could now serve the occupier. David Holt, a Confederate soldier, deemed the sight of black troops "more than 'Johnnie Reb' could stand," and he could only assume that the Yankees were forcing them to fight against their old masters. A Confederate soldier yelled at black troops on the Union side: "Damn you, you are fighting against your master." Confederate soldiers showed black Union troops a disquieting lack of quarter in battle. Emma Holmes had a special worry that the execution of captured black troops would provoke Yankee retaliation against Confederate troops yet failure to execute would provoke slave insubordination. Even the deeply pious William P. J. Pegram of Virginia considered it "perfectly" correct to slaughter captured black troops, since they posed a direct threat to a properly constituted Christian social order. Pegram nevertheless accepted the late decision to recruit black troops into the Confederate army. Racism accounted for part of the hardening of the heart that flowed from the brutality of war. But not all. John Sibley, seeing his comrades shot down during the battle of Vicksburg in 1863 and preparing to meet another Yankee assault, was "astonished at my own indifference." "My God," he wondered, "what kind of people will we be."[63]

---

[62] Confederate soldier quoted in Brian Steel Wills, *A Battle from the Start: The Life of Nathan Bedford Forrest* (New York, 1992), 190–1; Milton Barrett to Jesse and Caroline McMahan, Aug. 1, 1864, in J. Roderick Heller III and Carolyn Ayres Heller, eds., *The Confederacy Is on Her Way Up the Spout: Letters to South Carolinians, 1861–1864* (Athens, GA, 1992), 123; Julie Saville, *The Work of Reconstruction: From Slave to Wage Labor in South Carolina, 1860–1870* (New York, 1994), 35. For horror at and acceptance of the massacres of black troops see Garidel Diary, Apr. 20 and Aug. 16, 1864, in Michael Bedout Chesson and Leslie Jean Roberts, eds., *Exile in Richmond: The Confederate Journal of Henri Garidel* (Charlottesville, VA, 2001), 119, 199. On the atrocities committed against black Union troops see esp. James McPherson, *The Negro's Civil War: How American Negroes Felt and Acted during the War for the Union* (New York, 1965), 216–22.

[63] Walter Herron Taylor to Mary Lou Taylor, Aug. 1, 1863, and Walter Herron Taylor to Bettie Taylor, Aug. 1, 1864, in R. Lockwood Tower with John S. Belmont, eds., *Lee's Adjutant: The Wartime Letters of Colonel Walter Herron Taylor, 1862–1865* (Columbia, SC, 1995), 65, 179; Thomas D. Cockrell and Michael B. Ballard, eds., *A Mississippi Rebel in the Army of Northern Virginia: The Civil War Memoirs of Private David Holt* (Baton Rouge, LA, 1995), 287; July 17, 1863, in John F. Marszalek, ed., *The Diary of Miss Emma Holmes* (Baton Rouge, LA, 1979), 282; Peter S. Carmichael, *Lee's Young Artillerist: William R. J. Pegram* (Charlottesville, VA, 1995), 131, 158–9; Jimerson, *Private Civil War*, ch. 4, quote at 113; also, Rufas H. Barrier to Mathias Barrier, Aug. 6, 1864, in Beverley Barrier Troxler and Billy Dawn Barrier Auciello, eds., *"Dear Father": Confederate Letters Never Before Published* (n.p., 1989), 60. See also William Dunsinberre, *Them Dark Days: Slavery in the American Rice Swamps* (New Haven, CT, 2000), 167; Leon Litwack, *Been in the Storm So Long: The Aftermath of Slavery* (New York, 1979), 87–93; Anne J. Bailey, "A Texas Cavalry Raid," in Ralph A. Wooster, ed., *Lone Star Blue and Gray: Essays on Texas in the Civil War* (Austin, TX, 1995), 257–72; also Wooster and Wooster, "Rarin' for a Fight," loc. cit., 67; John T. Sibley to E. P. Ellis, Mar. 10, 1863, in Bell Irvin Wiley, *The Life of Johnny Reb: The Common Soldier of the Confederacy* (Baton Rouge, LA, 1978), 35.

Reflecting back on the War, Phoebe Yates Pember, who had nursed Confederate troops at Chimborazo hospital in Richmond, found "one of the remarkable features of the war" in a lack of hatred for the Yankees and a readiness to understand that two opposing armies were fighting for what they thought right. That attitude changed as the Yankees committed what Southerners viewed as atrocities, and bitterness deepened when the Yankees recruited black troops. Southern hostility to black troops undoubtedly was rooted in the prevailing assumption of racial superiority as well as in class attitudes that recalled medieval warfare. Chivalric knights seldom showed Christian compassion toward rebellious peasants, to say nothing of heretics and nonbelievers. The Peace of God and Truce of God marked the beginnings of a common – if much ignored – agreement to refrain from attacking women and children, common laborers and the poor, who were not supposed to serve as combatants. When, as often happened, such men did enter the fray, no mercy need be shown. "In the ordinary circumstances of battle," writes Robert C. Stacey, "a knight ought not kill another knight if it was possible instead to capture him for ransom. Armed peasants and townsmen could be massacred at will." The Church's impassioned protests availed little.[64]

George Washington, with long experience in war and concluding that the world had had enough of "Knight-errantry and mad-heroism," called upon Scripture to counsel that nations study war no more. After the War, Basil Gildersleeve recalled the words of Pindar, "A sweet thing is war to those who have not tried it." A staunch Confederate, Gildersleeve identified "selfish hatred" as the spur to war: "It is the hell-fire to which we owe the heat that is necessary to some of the noblest as to some of the vilest manifestations of human nature. Righteous indignation, sense of injustice, sympathy with the oppressed, consecration to country, fine words all, fine things, but so many of the men who represent these fine things perish."[65]

The problem that tormented antebellum Southerners only deepened over time: Can a society committed to equality create a synthesis of the best in all its people or will it propel a downward leveling to a common mediocrity? Southerners were simultaneously striving to live as a modern people and to recapture the virtues of a bygone era, on the understanding that, as C. S. Lewis warned his twentieth-century contemporaries, "The knightly character is art not nature – something that needs to be achieved, not something that can be relied upon to happen."[66]

---

[64] Phoebe Yates Pember, *A Southern Woman's Story: Life in Confederate Richmond,* ed. Bell Irwin Wiley (Macon, GA, 1959 [1879]), 86; Stacey, "Age of Chivalry," in Howard et al., eds., *Laws of War,* 30. With consolidation of papal and monarchical power, the state increasingly punished errant knights for murder, assault, theft, pillage, and sexual violence. The state implemented its claim to a monopoly of licit violence, which the knights had long taken for granted as their own. See Kaeuper, *Violence and Chivalry,* 20–1, 36–8, 102, 106, 225–9; Keen, ed., *Medieval Warfare,* Introduction, 7.

[65] Washington to Chastellux, Apr. 25 and May 1, 1788, in W. B. Allen, ed., *George Washington: A Collection* (Indianapolis, IN, 1988), 394; Lee quoted in Curtis and Thompson, eds., *Southern Essays of Richard Weaver,* 172; Basil Lanneau Gildersleeve, *The Creed of the Old South, 1865–1915* (Baltimore, 1915), 61, 64–5, Pindar quote at 61.

[66] Lewis, *Present Concerns,* 16.

Like Alaric, the barbarian conqueror of Rome, southern men who presented themselves as The Chivalry declared their readiness in battle to find either a kingdom or a grave. More often than not, they failed to live up to their own standards. To acknowledge those lapses is to say what Edward Gibbon said of the "fearless and fanatic" knights of the Crusades: "They neglected to live, but they were prepared to die, in the service of Christ." That the practice of an ideal usually falls short of its preaching goes without saying, but the effect of the ideal itself on the lives of the men, high and low, who aspire to fame or simply to think of themselves as decent and "useful" cannot be negated.[67]

Well before the War, orators and writers often told the ladies that the age of chivalry had passed but then added that they could nonetheless count on their young gentlemen to behave according to its canons. The War brought a renewed emphasis on the religious dimension of medieval chivalry, and those divines who, like Bishop Leonidas Polk, buckled on the sword could cite the example of the medieval warrior-priest: fierce in battle and tender in ministering to his flock. The Presbyterian Reverend C. S. Fedder of South Carolina, preaching in 1861, referred to "that chivalric courtesy and lofty self-sacrificing patriotism which has made the Southern name a synonym for honor, hospitality and valor." And the Reverend Henry Niles Pierce of Mobile reminded his congregants that knights prayed before trials of personal combat. William Gilmore Simms accorded to the Chevalier Bayard, that epitome of the chivalric knight, "a wonderful modesty." Although Josef Stalin probably never performed a chivalrous act in his breathtaking career as socialist state-builder and mass murderer, he instilled a spirit that made millions sacrifice their lives for a cause. G. I. Kotovski, a Bolshevik cavalry officer and military hero, knew how to "pulverize the enemy." Stalin's kind of man: "The bravest among our most modest commanders and the most modest among the brave."[68]

Augusta Jane Evans's vastly popular novel, *St. Elmo*, appeared shortly after the War in 1867. *St. Elmo* opens with a duel, witnessed but not understood by the very young Edna Earle, Evans's heroine. Shortly thereafter Edna, now orphaned, finds herself in the home of the wealthy mother of St. Elmo, the victor of the duel – and thereby murderer of the opponent, who had provoked him. The novel bears directly upon the South's relation to the amalgam of Christianity and violence that characterized chivalry. St. Elmo, an emotionally wounded and essentially good man, manifests in his despair a restless violence, while Edna, who is good as gold but vulnerable to sanctimony and moral arrogance, manifests a romanticized Christianity. In Evans's view, their eventual marriage reunites qualities that are essential to any society but destructive when divorced from each other. Evans was not writing a

---

[67] Edward Gibbon, *The History of the Decline and Fall of the Roman Empire*, ed. David Womersley, 3 vols. (London, 1994), 2:134.

[68] *Song of Roland*, sec. 127; C. S. Fedder, *"Offer unto God Thanksgiving": A Sermon* (Charleston, SC, 1861), 7; Henry Niles Pierce, *Sermons Preached in St. John's Church, Mobile* (Mobile, AL, 1861); "A. G. M.", "The Condition of Woman," *SQR*, 10 (1846), 164; Simms, *Chevalier Bayard*, 3; *DD**, 4:429; Stalin quoted in Lars T. Lih et al., eds., *Stalin's Letters to Molotov, 1925–1936* (New Haven, CT, 1995), 94 n. 4. In the medieval code, a knight must avoid boasting, act modestly, and shun the sin of pride: Kaeuper and Kennedy, *Geoffroi de Charny*, 23.

latter-day defense of chivalry so much as an indictment of the capitalist society of the North, which she saw as divorcing morality from power, confining morality to a sanitized and impotent domestic sphere, and allowing amoral power free rein to run the public world.

Evans's bitter criticism of capitalism's tendency to sever morality from power betrays scant trace of her compatriots' pre-War turn to history for guidance and justification. Her St. Elmo has a strong resemblance to dark Romantic and Gothic heroes. But, in a new guise, St. Elmo bears traces of the chivalric ideal of morality and power that at least some Southerners aspired to follow. And some, at their best, had succeeded. Among them was the upright, honored, and beloved Nathaniel Macon of North Carolina, who counseled a young follower: "Remember, you belong to a meek state and just people."[69]

---

[69] Macon quoted in *DNCB*, 4:186; Jefferson quoted in William S. Price, Jr., "Nathaniel Macon, Planter," *North Carolina Historical Review*, 78 (2001), 199; Calhoun, "Remarks at a Dinner at Shocco Springs," Sept. 2, 1842, in *JCCP*, 16:441. "The purest and best of men are the humblest, and have the least confidence in themselves, because they compare themselves, not with an imperfect standard, but with the purity of God": [S. J. Barnett], "Buckle's History of Civilization," *SPR*, 17 (1866), 198. On Macon see John Hill Wheeler, *Historical Sketches of North Carolina from 1584 to 1851*, 2 vols. (Baltimore, 1964 [1851]), 1:xx, 2:39, 435–6.

Chivalric Slave Masters

If I could reconcile it to myself I should be very much disposed to act upon your suggestion and sell all my negroes except enough for servants. But I cannot bring myself to [consider] them merely as property. They are human beings – placed under my control, and for whose welfare I am to some extent responsible.

—Rep. David Outlaw of North Carolina[1]

"It is wise, too, in relation to the civilized world around us," wrote Chancellor William Harper of South Carolina, "to avoid giving occasion to the odium which is so industriously excited against ourselves and our institutions. For this reason, public opinion should, if possible, bear down even more strongly on masters who practise any wanton cruelty on their slave." Harper issued a warning heard across the South: "The miscreant who is guilty of this not only violates the law of God and of humanity, but as far as in him lies, by bringing odium upon, endangers the institutions of his country, and the safety of his countrymen."[2]

The slaveholders did not see themselves as many contemporaries or most historians have seen them. As their diaries and letters attest, they could hardly believe it when, during the War, thousands of presumably loyal and contented slaves deserted to the Yankees and told horror stories. To be a gentleman, James Holcombe told the State Agricultural Society of Virginia in 1858, meant to be a kind master. The Christian South refused to view slaves as mere chattel, and Holcombe believed public opinion would provide a guarantor against cruelties. Mary Howard Schoolcraft took umbrage at northern ridicule of southern chivalry, insisting that Southerners taught the young to defend the weak, notably the slaves in their charge. Henry Garrett, a law student in Mississippi, wrote in 1861: "We all know the Southern heart and how it rebels against anything like oppression." J. L. Fremantle, an Englishman

---

[1] David Outlaw to Emily Outlaw, Jan. 19, 1849, at UNC-SHC. Outlaw complained bitterly to his wife that their slaves were not paying their way and were stealing everything in sight.

[2] "Chancellor Harper on Slavery," in *The Pro-Slavery Argument, as Maintained by the Most Distinguished Writers of the Southern States* (Philadelphia, 1853), 64–5.

with the Confederate army, said that even the "wildest Texans" showed kindness and compassion to those in distress.[3]

When Miss Gibbs, a college teacher, asked Jefferson Davis for a few words to guide the women of the South, he replied, *"For My Fellow-countrywomen:* Be ye slow to anger, swift to forgive, and hold fast to the charity that raises the lowly, with the self-respect that stoops not to the haughty." Davis considered the nick-naming of slaves by owners as disrespectful. Varina Davis attributed to her husband a truly generous temper, "best illustrated toward his inferiors" – the women, children, and slaves he considered in need of patrons to control them. Davis expected deference but would not let slaves outdo him in courtesy. Davis's classmate and lifelong friend, Albert Sidney Johnston, was – in the words of his son – a man who brooked no insults but was "gentle to women and children, tender to the weak and suffering, gracious to subordinates and dependents." An "indulgent husband, father, and master," he taught his son, William Preston Johnston, "A man has no right to inflict upon any creature of God unnecessary pain." Southerners maintained that no gentleman would dream of oppressing slaves or anyone else deemed in his charge, but requiring obedience and subordination was not oppression. A master who abused his slaves, Rose Harlow Warren wrote long after the War, would strike his wife or beat his horse: "The abolition of slavery has unfortunately not obliterated this brute from the annals of our country."[4]

There is no point in laughing. A curious web of notions and emotions remains to be untangled.

The ancients had taught that a gentleman must be a good master, simultaneously stern and kind, but precisely because masters should despise their slaves they should not speak harshly to them. In *Memorabilia*, Xenophon's Socrates stressed a master's duty to make "subordinates willing and obedient." In *Oeconomicus* he explained, "Husbandry helps train men for corporate effort," adding "Nobody can be a good farmer unless he makes his labourers both eager and obedient." Slaves "need the stimulus of good hopes no less, nay, even more than free men, to make them steadfast." A southern gentleman had the ideal knight's sense of justice. Those who aspire to be just, Cicero wrote, must be so toward the humblest

---

[3] J. P. Holcombe, "Is Slavery Consistent with Natural Law?" *SLM*, 27 (1858), 403, 407; H. A. Garrett Diary, Mar. 25, 1861, in John K. Bettersworth, ed., *Mississippi in the Confederacy: As They Saw It* (Baton Rouge, LA, 1961), 47; Apr. 20, 1863, in Arthur J. L. Fremantle, *Three Months in the Southern States: The 1863 Diary of an English Soldier* (Edinburgh, 1863), 41; *Plantation Life: The Narratives of Mrs. Henry Schoolcraft* (New York, 1969 [1860]), 206. For the masters' shock at the desertion of their slaves see Eugene D. Genovese, *Roll, Jordan, Roll: The World the Slaves Made* (New York, 1974), 97–112; Willie Lee Rose, *Rehearsal for Reconstruction: The Port Royal Experiment* (New York, 1964).

[4] Jefferson Davis to Miss Gibbs, in Lizzie Carrie Daniel, *Confederate Scrap-Book* (Nashville, TN, 1996 [1893]), 129; William C. Davis, *Jefferson Davis: The Man and His Hour* (New York, 1991), 80, 188–9, 219; William Preston Johnston, *The Life of General Albert Sidney Johnston* (New York, 1997 [1879]), quotes at 735, 149, 9; Rose Harlow Warren, *A Southern Home in War Times* (New York, 1914), 11. Warren expressed a common lost-cause theme: see e.g. *Confederate Veteran*, 1 (1893), 171. In 1832 Johnston emancipated Randolph, his body servant, who chose to remain with him and, after Johnston's death, with his family (248). Postwar tributes to Davis featured his idyllic relations with his slaves: *Confederate Veteran*, 1 (1893), 5.

slaves: "They must be required to work; they must be given their due .... No occasion arises that can excuse a man for being guilty of injustice." With Ciceronian spirit, Philip St. George Cocke's *Plantation and Farm Book* (1852), which planters bought to keep accounts, advised masters to remember "Like master, like man" and to set an example. " 'Tis but just and humane, when they have done their duty, to treat them with kindness, and even sometimes with indulgence."[5]

Masters thought they knew what God and their consciences expected – and what their neighbors expected or should have expected. Many tombstones in old southern graveyards identify "kind" and "affectionate" masters. How often did anyone bother to ask the slaves if they agreed and were in a position to answer frankly? Tombstones speak especially to families, to grandchildren and generations to come. We find engraved on them what the closest survivors wanted to convey.

In 1817, Attorney General William Wirt's *Life and Character of Patrick Henry* extolled Patrick Henry as a model master, husband, and father. Fifty years later Caroline Pinckney Seabrook, when asked for her impressions of Calhoun, began with an encomium to him as master as well as husband and father. "Many of the Negroes enquired kindly for you," R. F. W. Allston wrote his young son in 1860. "You must try to be a good boy, in order to treat them judiciously and well, when Papa is gone. Strive to think justly, to act wisely and diligently." Judge Daniel Coleman of the Alabama Supreme Court, commending his soul to Christ, left a last letter to his wife and children: "The children must be obedient to their Mother, and loving and kind to their brothers and sisters, kind to the servants and just to everybody." John Berkeley Grimball, wealthy lowcountry planter, commented on the death of a friend: "Mr. Tillman was a kind man to the Negroes, and an excellent planter." J. H. Adams wrote, "Mr. Vinson was always a strictly moral man discharging with fidelity all the duties of life – an affectionate husband, a kind parent, a humane master & an honest man." John Belton O'Neall, the much-admired jurist who crusaded for humane slave laws, offered biographical sketches of the eminent men of the South Carolina bench and bar that coupled "kind master" with affectionate husband or father as a supreme tribute to his subject's character. Stephen Miller, in *Bench and Bar of Georgia,* wrote of Augustus S. Clayton: "As a husband, father, and master, none could have been more kind, affectionate, and gentle." Kate Stone of northern Louisiana wrote, "We admire Dr. Carson greatly. He is such a humane master and good Christian." George White, explaining the many reasons citizens of Georgia named a county after Nathaniel Macon of North Carolina, said that his slaves had good reason to mourn his death, for "Never had slaves a kinder master."[6]

5 Glenn R. Morrow, *Plato's Law of Slavery in Its Relation to Greek Law* (Urbana, IL, 1939), 45–6; Xenophon, "Memorabilia," Bk. 3:4, 8, and "Oeconomicus," Bk. 5:1, 15–16, in *Memorabilia, Oeconomicus, Symposium; Apology,* tr. E. C. Merchant and O. J. Todd (LCL); Cicero, *De Officiis,* tr. Walter Miller (LCL), Bk. 1.13, 1:19; [Philip St. George Cocke], "Plantation and Farm Instruction, Regulation, Inventory and Account Book," 4, copy in Barbour Papers, at UVA.
6 William Wirt, *Sketches of the Life and Character of Patrick Henry* (Philadelphia, 1817), 402; Caroline Pinckney Seabrook to Charles Edward Leverett, Mar./Apr. 1867, in Frances Wallace Taylor et al., eds., *The Leverett Letters: Correspondence of a South Carolina Family, 1851–1868* (Columbia, SC, 2000), 421; R. F. W. Allston to Charles Pettigrew Allston, Nov. 8, 1860, in J. H. Easterby, ed., *The South*

In 1849 William Elliott told the members of the State Agricultural Society of South Carolina what they wanted to hear, that they were kind masters whose greatest fault was indulgence: "Against *insubordination alone,* we are severe." According to Daniel Hundley of Alabama, gentlemen scorned masters who behaved like brutes. The parvenu planters he called "Cotton Snobs" were not brutal; to the contrary, they indulged their slaves at the cost of community discipline and safety. He attributed to Cotton Snobs the worst of motives: a craving for the respectability that only a reputation as a humane master could provide. Everard Green Baker, a 23-year-old planter near Natchez and no Cotton Snob, illustrated the attitudes Hundley cited. After whipping a slave for "misbehaving," Baker expressed regret for a loss of self-control: "I allowed myself to get too much into a passion – I have resolved to be more guarded in the future & not to allow passion such absolute sway thereby exposing me to the ill will of the world, & making me a much unhappier man."[7]

Slaveholders, including the most pious, stoutly defended slavery as a system of organic social relations that, unlike the market relations of the free-labor system, created a bond of interest that encouraged Christian behavior. When interest and humanity clashed, piety and honor demanded a decision for humanity, but slaveholders considered a social system good if it kept clashes to a minimum. Schoolcraft had put her finger on a prime concern: Sensible slaveholders understood that brutality, neglect, and inconstancy provoked covert or overt slave resistance that, in turn, threatened social order. Slaves learned that slaveholders' theory and practice held gentleness and sternness as complementary. Slaves did not perceive the balance as their masters did, nor did they accept their masters' notion of justice. The Reverend Charles Pettigrew of North Carolina, who hoped for the day "there was not a slave in the world," instructed his sons, "There is no such thing as having an obedient & useful Slave, without the painful exercise of undue and tyrannical authority .... To manage *negroes* without the exercise of too much passion, is next to an impossibility, after our strongest endeavors to the contrary; I have found it so. I would therefore put you on your guard, lest their provocations should on some occasions transport you beyond the limits of decency and christian morality." Still, good treatment required firmness. In response to an insurrectionary scare in 1802, Pettigrew called for stern repression: "I wish it may be properly quelled – lenity will not do it – it will only make the worse."[8]

Carolina Rice Plantation, as Revealed in the Papers of Robert F. W. Allston (Chicago, 1945), 169; Coleman quoted in Anson West, *A History of Methodism in Alabama* (Spartanburg, SC, 1983 [1893]), 527; J. B. Grimball Diary, Jan. 17, 1851, at UNC-SHC; J. H. Adams to J. H. Thornwell, Oct. 27, 1852, in Thornwell Papers, at USC; John Belton O'Neall, *Biographical Sketches of the Bench and Bar of South Carolina,* 2 vols. (Charleston, SC, 1859), 1:166, 287, 289, 2:235, 400, 483, 547, 565; Stephen F. Miller, *The Bench and Bar of Georgia: Memoirs and Sketches,* 2 vols. (Philadelphia, 1858), 1:175 and passim; John Q. Anderson, ed., *Brokenburn: The Journal of Kate Stone, 1861–1868* (Baton Rouge, LA, 1955), 41; George White, *Statistics of the State of Georgia* (Savannah, GA, 1849), 404.

[7] William Elliott, *The Anniversary Address of the State Agricultural Society of South Carolina* (Charleston, SC, 1849), 37; Daniel R. Hundley, *Social Relations in Our Southern States* (Baton Rouge, LA, 1979 [1860]), 64, 184–7; Everard Green Baker Diary, June 1, 1849, at UNC-SHC.

[8] *Plantation Life: Narratives of Schoolcraft,* 79–80; Sarah McCulloh Lemmon, *Parson Pettigrew of the "Old Church": 1744–1807* (Chapel Hill, NC, 1970), 89–90. For a clergyman's particularly blunt

Men who doubled as planters and military officers – George Washington and Andrew Jackson among them – cautioned masters to issue orders in good temper and never abusively, yet to condone no disobedience. Washington enjoyed a reputation as a humane master, since he enforced the same rule with his soldiers, slaves, and all others subject to his authority. His instructions, published in the widely circulated *Affleck's Cotton Plantation Record and Account Book,* told his overseer to "see that the sick be cheered and encouraged, and some extra comforts be allowed them." Treat them gently but firmly: "Be constantly with your people … for when an over-looker's back is turned, the most of them will slight their work or be idle altogether." Yet, punishment accomplished little and often produced greater evils. Washington restricted his affection to a few personal servants and spoke gruffly to the others. He kept his distance, much in the manner of the military officer he was. He disliked slavery, the more so as he grew older, and provided for wholesale emancipation of his own slaves in his will.[9]

Joseph G. Baldwin, an acute commentator on southern mores and personalities, left a telling portrait of Andrew Jackson that may have exaggerated his virtues but delineated the southern ideal of a plantation gentleman: "As a neighbor, Jackson was the soul of kindness and generosity. To the poor he was a father." Jackson "neither wasted nor hoarded, was neither exacting nor indulgent; was a discreet manager, without undue anxiety or driving energy." Jackson provided a model: "A kind master, he tried to govern his slaves the way a Scottish chieftain governed his clan, or a Hebrew patriarch his tribe, not like a slave-driving planter who held lands and negroes, mules and ploughs as so much stock in trade, of value only as they were profitable." Jackson himself wrote, "I could not bear the idea of inhumanity to my poor negroes." And yet he did not shrink from use of the whip or even of chains.[10]

Every southern slaveholder, according to the model, was supposed to treat his slaves as part of his "family, white and black" and yet keep his head above water in a competitive market. While managing the work of his slaves, supervising their lives, paying bills, and getting the crop out, he was simultaneously to be gentle, forbearing, and kind – but stern, even severe, when duty, dignity, and preservation of authority required. His character and reputation depended upon his ability to resolve the attendant contradictions. Mr. Moultrie of Alabama met the challenge, at

defense of slaveholders who treated slaves well largely out of self-interest, see T. C. Thornton, *An Inquiry into the History of Slavery* (Washington, DC, 1841), 89–91.

9 Frances Leigh Williams, *Plantation Patriot: A Biography of Eliza Lucas Pinckney* (New York, 1967), 116; *Affleck's Cotton Plantation Record and Account Book* contained bits of advice for planters, although (as the title suggests) it was designed to allow planters and farmers to keep their own farm diaries and a record of income and expenditure. Washington's instructions were often excerpted by agricultural journals for the benefit of those who did not use Affleck's volume: see e.g. *American Cotton Planter,* 2 (Dec. 1854), 353–6. For a sensitive evaluation of Washington's dual role of planter and military commander see Ulrich Bonnell Phillips, *Life and Labor in the Old South* (Boston, 1948), 250.

10 Joseph Glover Baldwin, *Party Leaders* (New York, 1868), 297–8; Jackson quoted in Ardra Walker, "Andrew Jackson: Planter," *East Tennessee Historical Society's Publications,* 15 (1943), 30–2. For a tribute to Andrew Jackson as slave master from a "plain farmer": G. W. Featherstonhaugh, *Excursion through the Slave States* (New York, 1968 [1844]), 50.

least in the eyes of fellow planters. According to the editor of *Soil of the South,* who inspected his plantation, Moultrie enforced "strict discipline among his negroes, and better fed or clothed negroes we have never seen."[11]

A master determines the performance of subordinates, so a featured speaker told the Virginia Central Agricultural Society in 1859: "An attentive master makes a good overseer and good Negroes." The well-read John Hartwell Cocke, a notable slave-holding critic of slavery, instructed his overseer in a manner that reads like a gloss on the defense of capital punishment in Hegel's *Philosophy of Right*: "If you punish only according to justice and reason, with uniformity, you can never be too severe, & will be the more respected for it, even by those who suffer." For Cocke, justice and humanity required that dutiful slaves be treated with "kindness, and even sometimes with indulgence," and he branded as "absolutely mean and unmanly" the whipping of a slave from passion or malice. Stephen Henderson of Louisiana, who emancipated his slaves in his will, inveighed against abolitionists and fanatics who sought to incite slaves to disobedience. Henderson demanded that his people be well treated while they remained slaves, but at the same time, "There must be strict discipline." Plowden Weston of South Carolina, whose plantation rules circulated widely in southern periodicals, could forgive an overseer's errors of judgment but "never can or will excuse any cruelty, severity, or want of care towards the negroes." Not to be misunderstood, he added, "For the well being, however, of the negroes, it is absolutely necessary to maintain obedience, order, and discipline."[12]

In North Carolina the pious James Greenlee whipped a slave for bad conduct. Disconcerted, he prayed, "Enable me to discharge all my duties in a proper manner." William Valentine, a lawyer who lived on his father's plantation in Hertford County, reported that the family performed the "most disagreeable but necessary duty" of whipping slaves for stealing: "Slaves we have raised and have ever been well treated, as well as we know how, and according to the nature of master and slave as this relation exists among us." Such an event "disharmonizes, distresses, and mortifies owners of slaves," but "It was our duty to meet it with firmness and enforce family right, that is, redress wrong."[13]

Slaveholders lived on a high wire. They had to balance a public stake in the decent treatment of slaves; a compelling need to support their authority at almost any cost; and a psychological as well as ideological need for reassurance that they were kind as well as stern. Passion, Fannie Kemble wrote, could outweigh interest: "The

---

[11] "The Batchelor Farmer," an account by the editor of *Soul of the South,* as reprinted in *American Cotton Planter,* 2 (Aug. 1854), 253.

[12] Hill Carter, "Address Delivered before the Virginia Central Agricultural Society," *Southern Planter,* 20 (1859), 274–5; [Cocke], "Plantation and Farm Instruction," 4–5; William Kauffman Scarborough, *The Overseer: Plantation Management in the Old South* (Athens, GA, 1966), 74; "Heirs of Stephen Henderson v. P. A. Rost, et al." (1850), in *Exec's 5 La. Ann. 458n.;* "Rules on the Rice Estate of P. C. Weston of South Carolina" (1856), in Ulrich B. Phillips, ed., *Plantation and Frontier, 1649–1863,* 2 vols. (New York, 1969 [1910]), 1:11.

[13] Greenlee Diary, Nov. 15, 1848, at UNC-SHC; Valentine Diary, Jan. 1, 1851, at UNC-SHC; "Hargrove v. Redd," in Helen Tunnicliff Catterall, ed., *Judicial Cases Concerning Slavery and the Negro,* 4 vols. (Washington, DC, 1919–37), 3, pt. 1:103.

instances in which men, to gratify the immediate impulses of passion sacrifice not only their eternal but their evident, palpable, positive worldly interest, are infinite. Nothing is commoner than for a man under the transient influence of anger to disregard his worldly advantage." Charles Dickens, having visited America, found what he considered unimpeachable evidence of atrocities and impatiently dismissed the argument from pecuniary interest as psychologically naïve.[14]

John Taylor of Caroline offered what became a southern motif in which the master's concern for his own reputation, as well as his material interest, weakened any inclination to overdriving. In the free-labor system, to the contrary, the market disguised the relation of master and man and imposed a "slavery, in which the sufferer is ignorant of his tyrant, and the tyrant is remorseless, because he is unconscious of his crime." A half-century later, David Hubbard of Alabama replied to Republicans that no man who let a slave die for want of provisions could live in a southern state. Isaac Holmes of South Carolina, reputedly kind and indulgent to servants, set out to punish a slave woman. She drowned herself. Sick with grief and blaming himself, he considered himself shamed in the eyes of the white community. When James Petigru pleaded with Benjamin Allston to save a slave family from separation, he appealed to his chivalry.[15]

Notwithstanding good intentions, pious hopes, and modest accomplishments, the lapse of practice from the Christian–chivalric ideal of slave management challenged public reputations while constituting an irrefutable indictment of slavery itself. Educators, clerical and lay, sent up flares. The Methodist Reverend D. S. Doggett warned that an inherently corrupt public opinion countenances "in civilized life a multitude of vices, some of which would be esteemed a disgrace to uncultivated man." Southerners weighed the power of public opinion but knew better than to trust it. They had in front of them history's most famous and instructive case: Faced with hostile public opinion, Pontius Pilate – notwithstanding his proconsular powers – caved in to pressure to crucify Jesus. It was public opinion, David McCord wrote, that favored Philip over Demosthenes; that crushed the great men of Athens and corrupted Rome; that put down Cicero and Cato while raising up Marius and Scylla, and Caesar; that led to the persecution of Jews during and after the Middle Ages, the wars of religion, the witch trials, the St. Bartholomew

---

[14] Frances Kemble, *Journal of a Residence on a Georgia Plantation in 1838–1839* (New York, 1863), 43; Charles Dickens, *American Notes for General Circulation* (Harmondsworth, U.K., 1972 [1842]), 271, 275–7.

[15] John Taylor, *An Inquiry into the Principles and Policy of the Government of the United States,* ed. Loren Baritz (Indianapolis, IN, 1919 [1814]), 305–6; David Hubbard, Speech on "The Terriorial Question," *Congressional Globe,* 31st Cong., 1st Sess., App. 946; Mar. 12, 1863, in John F. Marszalek, ed., *The Diary of Miss Emma Holmes* (Baton Rouge, LA, 1979), 238; Elizabeth Allston Pringle, *Chronicle of Chicora Wood* (New York, 1922), 10. Dolly Sumner Hunt of Georgia described the Reverend Thomas Burge, her husband, as "a gentleman of the Old South, devoted to his family, his church, and caring for his slaves as for his children": James I. Robertson, Jr., ed., *The Diary of Dolly Lunt Burge* (Athens, GA, 1962), ix. For a tribute to a Presbyterian minister as an exemplary "husband, father, and master" see A. L. Phillips, "Historical Sketch of the Presbyterian Church of Fayetteville," in Harriott Sutton Rankin, *History of the First Presbyterian Church, Fayetteville, North Carolina* (n.p., 1928), 27.

Day massacre, and the bloody assizes. And now a northern public opinion, aroused by abolitionists, threatened to isolate, expropriate, and destroy the South.[16]

Responding in the mid-1830s to the charge of cruelty to slaves, the Reverend James Smylie of Mississippi urged fellow Mississippians not to be provoked by the abolitionists but to strive for Christian benevolence: "Let us, as masters, not be hindered from rendering to our slaves that which is just and equal. They are 'our households.'" Justice Joseph Lumpkin of Georgia's Supreme Court wanted slave laws tightened but also relaxed, in accordance with Christian duty – that is, when relaxation did not threaten the slaveholders' security. Counseling both resistance to abolitionist provocations and avoidance of undue harshness, Lumpkin gave "un-qualified approval" to a combination of self-interest, humanity to the slave, and respect for the ties that bound master and slaves. Slaveholding constitutes a "family or social compact," and "The very strength and security of the South consists in the loyalty of our Negro population to their owners."[17]

Southerners admitted cases of extreme cruelty to slaves but asserted their infrequency, assuring themselves that public opinion ostracized, if it did not punish, guilty parties. Yet critics had forced the slaveholders onto the defensive long before the rise of militant abolitionism. In the 1770s, thirty years after the slave uprising at Stono, South Carolina, and the promulgation of a harsh slave code, Governor William Bull declared, "The state of slavery in this province is as comfortable as such a state can be." Lauding "our Negro Law and the humanity of the masters," Bull added: "Not but that there are monsters of cruelty [who] sometimes appear, who are punished and abhorred." Presumably, monsters of cruelty did not include the government of South Carolina itself, which as late as 1791 sentenced two blacks to be burned alive for murdering their overseer. Sixty years later the usually hardheaded Louisa McCord challenged her cousin, Mary Cheves Dulles of Philadelphia, on *Uncle Tom's Cabin*: "Why! have you not been at the South enough to know, that our gentlemen dont keep mulatto wives, not whip negroes to death nor commit all the various other enormities that she describes?" As late as 1913 Mrs. R. M. Grune, a descendant of middling slaveholders in Alabama, still maintained that "many" slaveholders never whipped their slaves. She acknowledged the existence of vicious masters but insisted that "upright just citizens" scorned them.[18]

---

[16] "The Baptism of Fire," in Thomas O. Summers, ed., *Sermons by the Late Rev. David Seth Doggett* (Nashville, TN, 1882), 63; [David J. McCord], "Slavery and the Abolitionists," *SQR*, 15 (1849), 168–70. Wade Keyes of Alabama cited Plutarch's *Phocius* to make law students wary of public applause and the pressure of public opinion: *Wade Keyes' Introductory Lecture to the Montgomery Law School: Legal Education in Mid-Nineteenth Century Alabama* (Tuscaloosa, AL, 2001 [1860]), 33. See also Supplementary References: "Thomas à Kempis."

[17] James Smylie, *Review of a Letter from the Presbytery of Chillicothe to the Presbytery of Mississippi on the Subject of Slavery* (Woodville, MS, 1836), 53; J. H. Lumpkin, "Dudley vs. Mallery – Mallery vs. Dudley," in *Reports of Cases in Law and Equity Argued and Determined in the Supreme Court of the State of Georgia*, 4 (1848), 65–6; also, Paul DeForest Hicks, *Joseph Henry Lumpkin: Georgia's First Chief Justice* (Athens, GA, 2002), 127.

[18] L. S. McCord to Mary Cheves Dulles, Oct. 9, 1852, in Richard Lounsbury, ed., *Louisa S. McCord: Poems, Drama, Biography, Letters* (Charlottesville, VA, 1996), 294; Mrs. R. M. Grune to H. C. Nixon, Mar. 21, 1913, in Nixon Collection, at Alabama Department of Archives and History (Montgomery);

Slaveholders weighed their responsibilities to keep order in the community against pressures of practical circumstance at home. In 1834 a planter in Virginia began simply: "Harmony among neighbors is very important in the successful management of negroes." Even a good manager should expect trouble when his policies varied significantly from those of his neighbors. In any locality, one or two bad managers could ruin the efforts of all. "It does no good," agreed a clergyman, "to enforce discipline on your own plantation, if the next planter does not. Looseness in one engenders discontent and insubordination on another."[19]

Leaders of public opinion did their best to uphold the honor and reputation of the slaveholders and simultaneously defend a social system that taxed patience and ingenuity to the limit. Agricultural societies, awarding premiums for the best-managed plantations, included humane treatment of slaves in good management. In 1846 in Alabama, a committee of the Barbour County Agricultural Society acknowledged abuses and recommended fearless exposure and correction, despite the danger that northern abolitionists would exploit such frank admission: "Your Committee feels well warranted in adding that the master who could disregard all those motives for good treatment of slaves, must be brutal indeed, and must be so obtuse in his intellect as to act against the plainest principles of reason. For such cases your Committee invokes the rigid enforcement of the laws, and the expression of a strong condemnation by public sentiment." The Committee claimed "a gradual improvement" in treatment of slaves but nonetheless called for efforts "to convince all, that interest, humanity and religion, alike, demand kindness to slaves, and that the law frown on those who treat their slaves inhumanely." The clergy reinforced the theme frequently, even stridently. A master must provide his slave with food and raiment, James Henley Thornwell preached, not only because it is good policy but in fear of the damnation of his own soul.[20]

Paradoxes abounded. Bennet Barrow of Louisiana, a hard taskmaster, whipped his slaves often. He tracked runaways and shot them in the legs. Disgusted with one slave who shirked and then ran off to steal a neighbor's hogs, he whipped him "severely" and swore to shoot him if he tried it again. Yet nothing so outraged Barrow as mistreatment of slaves – as he defined mistreatment. Sternness and severity were one thing, neglect and cruelty another. The one sustained good order; the other subverted it. Barrow could not contain himself when a wealthy planter of high social standing whipped a slave to death and escaped conviction. When an uncle abandoned an elderly runaway slave to his fate, Barrow muttered, "Dunbar treats him verry badly. Old & cripple, a verry Bad Example, he shall not stay in this

Kinloch Bull, Jr., *The Oligarchs in Colonial and Revolutionary Charleston: Lieutenant Governor William Bull II and His Family* (Columbia, SC, 1991), 17.
[19] "H. C.", "On the Management of Negroes," *Southern Agriculturalist*, 8 (July 1834), 369–70; "A Minister of the Gospel", "'Tatler' on the Management of Negroes," *Southern Cultivator*, 9 (June 1851), 84; also, W. H. Sparks, *The Memories of Fifty Years* (Philadelphia, 1972), 120–1; *TCWVQ*, 2:493.
[20] Chalmers S. Murray, *This Our Land: The Story of the Agricultural Society of South Carolina* (Charleston, SC, 1949), 92; "Management of Slaves – Report of a Committee of the Barbour County Agricultural Society," *Southern Cultivator*, 4 (Aug. 1846), 113; *JHTW*, 4:379–97.

neighborhood." Barrow, the hard taskmaster, made himself obnoxious to some of his slaveholding neighbors by his complaints about their severity to slaves.[21]

Those who sang the praises of community sentiment and its wonderful advantages for slaves appealed to evidence. From Virginia to Texas, notorious slaveholders – most notably those who killed slaves – found it advisable to relocate in some far-off place. Although juries might be loath to acquit even when faced with damning evidence, the wretch could face the wrath of irate citizens. Anna Matilda King of Georgia, horrified at the news that a planter had whipped a boy of 12 or 14 years to death and then promptly departed for Savannah, wrote her brother: "Now if this Dr. Moffet gets clear – I think the abolishionists may well talk of cruelty to slaves." Even masters with a genuine complaint about their slaves responded strangely. In Kentucky a master vigorously but vainly opposed the execution of a slave who had shot and wounded him. And what are we to make of the recollection of Litt Young, who had been a slave in Mississippi? – His master spent $500 to buy a slave condemned to hang for the murder of his previous master. If true, the community had to believe, notwithstanding the slave's conviction, that he had killed a monster in self-defense.[22]

Although juries seldom convicted a malicious and negligent master, they did so on occasion and sometimes on circumstantial evidence – which suggests that the master's neighbors considered him a savage. Public opinion expressed circumspect approval for a slave who killed a barbaric overseer or even a barbaric master. Slaveholders knew the risk of condoning the act while they whispered, "He got what he deserved." Throughout centuries of slavery some whites, confronted by gross inhumanity to slaves, protested and testified at trials. Usually, newspapers ignored the evidence of outrages committed against slaves but sometimes waxed indignant and fueled campaigns to punish vicious masters. In South Carolina, 83 prosecutions for cruelty led to 31 convictions. Occasionally, sadistic murderers got their just deserts. Judge John Belton O'Neall sentenced two white men to death for the "cruel and

[21] Edwin Adams Davis, ed., *Plantation Life in the Florida Parishes of Louisiana, 1836–1846, as Reflected in the Diary of Bennet H. Barrow* (New York, 1943), 148, 202, 227, 239, 262 (entries for 1839–42). Notable if less frequent was the characterization of a southern lady according to the degree of her kindness to her slaves: see e.g. A. B. Van Zandt, *"The Elect Lady": A Memoir of Mrs. Susan Catherine Botts of Petersburg, Va.* (Philadelphia, 1857).

[22] Anna Matilda King to Thomas Butler King, Aug. 8, 1858, in Thomas Butler King Papers, at UNC-SHC; Marion B. Lucas, *A History of Blacks in Kentucky,* 2 vols. (Lexington, KY, 1992), 1:50; Litt Young in Norman R. Yetman, ed., *Life under the "Peculiar Institution"* (New York, 1970), 337. See also Catherine Cooper Hopley, *Life in the South from the Commencement of the War,* 2 vols. (New York, 1971 [1863]), 1:216–17; Frederick Law Olmsted, *A Journey in the Seaboard Slave States, with Remarks on Their Economy* (New York, 1968 [1856]), 622; Francis Terry Leak Diary, Aug. 24, 1852, at UNC-SHC; Joe Gray Taylor, *Negro Slavery in Louisiana* (Baton Rouge, LA, 1963), 226. Murderers of slaves also ran off to escape prosecution as well as the anger of their neighbors. See e.g. Scarborough, *Overseer,* 95. For enforcement of laws in South Carolina against cruel masters see A. E. Keir Nash, "Negro Rights, Unionism, and the Greatness of the South Carolina Court of Appeals: The Extraordinary Chief Justice John Belton O'Neall," *South Carolina Law Review,* 21 (1969), 167–73. James B. Battle, the slaveholder in North Carolina's famous *State v. Will,* believed Will innocent and is believed to have spent $1,000 in his defense: *DNCB,* 1:112.

inhuman murder" of a fugitive slave on whom they had turned dogs loose. Although one of them, Thomas Motley, hailed from a wealthy Charleston family, Governor John L. Manning refused a pardon and called out the militia to prevent a rescue. It was 1854, at the height of sectional tensions, but hanged they were.[23]

More typical were events in Georgia, where masters who were found guilty got off with modest fines more appropriate to misdemeanors. An example: A woman who killed a slave by "undue correction" was fined $214.28. Most whites indicted for manslaughter of slaves – where, by definition, intent to kill was unclear – were acquitted. Here and there, a brave soul like Joseph Vallance Bevan, Georgia's prominent historian and editor, risked his career to see that whites were prosecuted even when the community thought it impolitic. Captain J. G. Richardson of Louisiana made dangerous personal enemies by enforcing laws against cruelty to slaves. Richardson made no bones about his attitude: Duty first, consequences afterwards. Less dramatically, whites reported and former slaves attested that irate citizens, often women, strenuously demanded intervention by community leaders against brutal masters.[24]

Public opinion usually proves most powerful in small communities, and the prevalence of small towns and villages in the South offered considerable scope for social, political, and religious leaders to encourage humane treatment of slaves by all those, high and low, who valued respectability. But there were strong countertendencies. First, the typical pretensions to lordship, with its attendant demand for obedience and deference, made slaveholders overcome their craving for respectability and defy anyone who questioned their behavior, judgments, and probity. Second, the rural isolation of plantations shielded many offenders from the eyes of the community. And third, the spirit of neighborliness, which induced reluctance to intrude into another's affairs, led to toleration of a master who violated norms, especially if he seemed a decent fellow in other respects. Citizens intervened against bad masters

---

[23] Fredrika Bremer, *Homes of the New World: Impressions of America*, 2 vols. (New York, 1853), 2:512; R. Q. Mallard, *Plantation Life before Emancipation* (Richmond, VA, 1892), 42–4; Gavin Diary, Nov. 9, 1855, at UNC-SHC; Lyle Saxon et al., *Gumbo Ya-Ya: A Collection of Louisiana Folk Tales* (New York, 1945), 236–8; Ivan E. McDougle, *Slavery in Kentucky, 1792–1865* (Westport, CT, 1968 [1918]), 91–2; A. E. K. Nash, "Reason of Slavery: Understanding the Judicial Role in the Peculiar Institution," *Vanderbilt Law Review*, 32 (1979), 39–40; Jean Martin Flynn, *The Militia in Antebellum South Carolina Society* (Spartanburg, SC, 1991 [1917]), 17 (Motley). For black testimony on white efforts to punish cruel masters see Ophelia Settle Egypt et al., eds., *Unwritten History: Autobiographical Accounts of Ex-Slaves* (Washington, DC, 1968 [1945]), 2, 5, 103, 107; Jeff Hamilton, *My Master: The Inside Story of Sam Houston and His Times, as Told to Lenoir Hunt* (Austin, TX, 1992), 23–4. For other black attestations see: George Teahmoh Journal, Parts 1 & 2 (ms. p. 32), in Library of Congress, "Slave Papers"; Lou Smith in George Rawick, ed., *The American Slave: A Composite Autobiography,* 19 vols. (Westport, CT, 1972), South Carolina, 7 (pt. 1), 302; Delicia Patterson in Julius Lester, ed., *To Be a Slave* (New York, 1968), 52.

[24] E. Merton Coulter, *Joseph Vallance Bevan: Georgia's First Official Historian* (Athens, GA, 1964), 56–7; Francis DuBose Richardson, ms., p. 43, in Richardson Memoirs, at UNC-SHC; "Letter of Mary Woodrow to the Mayor of Alexandria, Va.," June 21, 1813, in Library of Congress, "Slave Papers"; Mary A. Thrift to George N. Thrift, May 17, 1859, at Duke University; "A Young Planter", "Communication," *Carolina Planter*, 1 (July 15, 1840), 209–10. Also, Ralph Betts Flanders, *Plantation Slavery in Georgia* (Chapel Hill, NC, 1933), 241–3.

only with the utmost discretion, lest slaves get the idea that their masters' power over them had narrow limits. Such a prospect tempted juries to acquit masters who were guilty of palpable cruelty and murder.[25]

Since immorality in the home spilled into society, Southerners, like the Greeks and Romans before them, accepted a measure of community concern with private morals but demurred from the Greco-Roman assumption that the state should regulate private morals. Slaveholders, writing to and for each other, repeatedly rebuked outsiders, including close friends and neighbors, who interfered in the master–slave relation. Yet some intervention could not be avoided. Informal and quasi-spontaneous community action against gross individual behavior became the *via media*. Fear of encouraging slave insubordination hovered over all. John Mills of Bayou Sarah, Louisiana, wrote his cousin, "You must know that unless there is order and subordination kept up, amongst the negroes, they would be masters instead of slaves." That theme reverberated throughout the press, which expressed frequent apprehension that insurrections follow relaxation in enforcement of masters' authority. President T. C. Thornton of Centenary College in Mississippi was sure that public opinion reined in bad masters and rendered cases of cruelty rare. In an inadvertent tribute to slave resistance, he added that hostility of slaves toward cruel masters spurred good masters to greater vigilance toward malefactors.[26]

How far did Thornton's assurances extend? In 1760 John Rutledge – the eminent Attorney General of South Carolina, a wealthy planter who enjoyed the society of the most prominent families in aristocratic Charleston – prosecuted Jared Mangin, a dissolute assistant overseer. Mangin, after twice losing jobs for drunkenness and sexual relations with slave women, killed one who resisted his advances. A public outraged at the crime reacted even more harshly when Mangin sneered that she was worth no more than his employer owed him anyway. Gentlemen only

---

[25] Countryside and small towns grounded southern slave society, as James Johnston Pettigrew kept in mind when he wrote his sparkling book, *Notes on Spain and the Spaniards in the Summer of 1859, with a Glance at Sardinia* (Charleston, SC, 1861). In societies like those of Spain and the Old South, direct personal contact – rather than anonymous relations – becomes paramount and persona becomes as significant as office. Since hierarchy establishes positions in families and small communities, a man's authority is taken for granted. Within, he need not compete; without, he must constantly uphold his honor against challenge. Competition without requires readiness to yield to public opinion rather than to a hierarchical superior. The individual courts public opinion so that presumed equals pronounce him worthy. See J. G. Peristiany, "Introduction," in Peristiany, ed., *Honour and Shame: The Values of Mediterranean Society* (Chicago, 1966), 11. Reputation and public acknowledgment, Julian Pitt-Rivers remarks, must support a person's self-estimation or else his honor reduces to vanity and pretense, inviting ridicule and contempt; Pitt-Rivers, "Honour and Social Status," in Peristiany, *Honor and Shame*, 22.

[26] For slaveholders' warnings to each other, see e.g. "Alpha", "War of the Fanatics," *Southern Eclectic*, 2 (1853), 67, and James C. Coggesbal's "Report of the State Comptroller," quoted in Caleb P. Patterson, *The Negro in Tennessee, 1790–1864* (Austin, TX, 1922), 79; Mills quoted in Leslie Howard Owens, *This Species of Property: Slave Life and Culture in the Old South* (New York, 1976), 77; Thornton, *Inquiry into History of Slavery*, 85–7, 110; also, Philip J. Schwarz, "Forging the Shackles," in David J. Bodenhamer and James W. Ely, eds., *Ambivalent Legacy: A Legal History of the South* (Jackson, MS, 1984), 129.

twenty years removed from the Stono slave revolt consulted their interests and their consciences. Fearing a violent slave response if lower-class whites had open season on slave women, they urged Rutledge, who needed no urging, to do his duty. Getting a conviction and a death sentence required all of Rutledge's formidable legal and political skills, but he prevailed. Outraged public opinion, instead of cheering, recoiled, and Rutledge found himself under fire. Did Rutledge and the judge have to go that far? Gentlemen wanted a conviction but not a hanging. The hanging of a white man could give slaves dangerous ideas. Austin Steward and other ex-slaves acidly recorded the extent to which public opinion protected brutal masters by approving stern discipline and condemning indulgence.[27]

Reeling from the Denmark Vesey slave conspiracy of 1822 in Charleston, R. J. Turnbull and Edwin C. Holland reassured the world – and themselves – that the leading planters of the lowcountry shunned hard masters as monsters. But John Randolph of Roanoke exploded in a letter to his friend Dr. John Brockenbrough: "What man is worse received in society for being a hard master? Who denies the hand of a sister or daughter to such monsters?" Some Southerners first read those words in *Southern Literary Messenger* in 1836, and many more read them on the eve of the War when quoted in Hugh Garland's biography of Randolph and in Frederick Law Olmsted's *Seaboard Slave States*. The ostracism demanded by Randolph ran afoul of delicate personal circumstances. The cream of the planter class intermarried on a large scale and crystallized into a social elite. To ostracize kinsmen was no easy matter. And how could you ostracize a whole family, especially one tied by marriage to your own, for the transgressions of one or two scoundrels?[28]

The same public opinion that detested cruel masters also feared disruption of the white community. Thomas Jefferson did not speak of slaves when he warned Martha Randolph, his newly married daughter, "The ill-will of a single neighbor is an immense drawback on the happiness of life, and therefore their good will cannot be bought too dear." A cruel master could be a splendid chap in other respects, much as a kind master could be a nuisance or a scamp. In South Carolina in 1860 the neighbors of John Magill, owner of 189 slaves, ranked him among the most hated planters on Waccamaw Peninsula. His savagery included quasi-starvation. Yet Magill – vestryman in the Episcopal Church, member of the elite Winyah Indigo Society, trustee of All Saints Academy – moved easily in the highest social echelons. He also contributed generously toward the building of a Methodist church. Who

---

[27] Richard Barry, *Mr. Rutledge of South Carolina* (New York, 1942), 78–82; Austin Steward, *Twenty-Two Years a Slave and Forty Years a Freeman* (Reading, MA, 1969 [1857]), 19–20.

[28] [Edwin Holland], *A Refutation of the Calumnies Circulated against the Southern and Western States, Respecting the Institution and Existence of Slavery among Them* (Charleston, SC, 1822), 50–3; [N. B. Tucker], ed., "Mss. of John Randolph," *SLM*, 2 (1836), 462 (avarice alone, Randolph also wrote, drove and sustained the slave trade); Randolph to Brockenbrough, Sept. 25, 1818, in Kenneth Shorey, ed., *Collected Letters of John Randolph of Roanoke to Dr. John Brockenbrough, 1812–1833* (New Brunswick, NJ, 1988), 19; Hugh A. Garland, *The Life of John Randolph of Roanoke*, 2 vols. (New York, 1969 [1859]), 2:101; Olmsted, *Seaboard Slave States*, 620 n.; William Dusinberre, *Them Dark Days: Slavery in the Rice Swamps* (Athens, GA, 2000), 423.

knows what his pastor – the Reverend James M. Belin, himself a slaveholder known as a kind master – thought. So far as we know, he kept quiet.[29]

The chivalric spirit directed toward slaves could get you killed, as evidenced by Joseph Bond, one of the biggest planters in Georgia. When an overseer on a neighboring plantation beat one of Bond's slaves, Bond rode to his home to chastise him. The overseer killed Bond, pleaded self-defense, and got off. Judge Richard H. Clark, who recounted the incident, commented that Bond "regarded his slaves as part of his household" and considered "a wrong done the meanest of them was a wrong done to him." Those who swore that bad masters called forth scorn and rejection were not lying: They were simply being selective. Transplanted Yankees like S. S. Prentiss and visitors like Eleanor Baker, writing privately, supported that contention. Prentiss, in a letter to his brother in Maine in 1831, described the slaves of Mississippi as "kindly treated"and probably as "fully as happy as their masters." Public opinion, he had no doubt, did not tolerate cruelty. Mrs. Baker, visiting Charleston in 1848, privately noted that cruel planters were rare and invariably discussed by the gentry with the utmost distaste. Even Bishop John England, neither mendacious nor naïve, declared, "The owner who would treat his slave unkindly or cruelly would not be sustained by public opinion, and nothing would more sink a man in public estimation than the character of a cruel master." Elite families, he thought, led more modest slaveholders in ostracizing brutal masters – especially parvenus not yet tightly connected to the elite or not so wealthy that the hands of their daughters could prove irresistible to gentlemen who had fallen on hard times. Catherine Cooper Hopley reported that respectable Virginians scorned and even ran off brutal masters, although usually masters who had previously fallen into disfavor for immorality. A Methodist clergyman in Alabama got a taste of the community ostracism Southerners liked to talk about. A church court acquitted the Reverend James Boatwright of Greensborough of charges of brutality to his slave. It is doubtful that he was guilty, but he had to retire from the ministry anyway. His congregants thought him guilty and refused to attend his church.[30]

"There were tales circulated of cruelty on neighboring plantations," shuddered Kate Stone, "tales that would make one's blood run cold. And yet we were powerless to help." She credited those tales after the War, but did she at the time? Ladies and gentlemen must be given the benefit of the doubt. The most telling support for Kate Stone's "powerless to help" came from diaries and letters of planters who

---

[29] Thomas Jefferson to Martha Randolph, May 8, 1791, in Edwin Morris Betts and James Adams Bear, Jr., *The Family Letters of Thomas Jefferson* (Columbia, MO, 1966), 80; James L. Michie, *Richmond Hill Plantation, 1810–1868: The Discovery of Antebellum Life on a Waccamaw Rice Plantation* (Spartanburg, SC, 1990), 34–5, 40–2, 46, 113, 118.

[30] Lollie Belle Wiley, ed., *Memoirs of Judge Richard H. Clark* (Atlanta, GA, 1898), 30, 33, 156–7; Dunbar Rowland, ed. *Mississippi: Comprising Sketches of Counties, Towns, Events, Institutions, and Persons, Arranged in Cyclopedic Form*, 4 vols. (Spartanburg, SC, 1976 [1907]), 2:688 (Prentiss); Mrs. E. J. W. Baker Journal (1848), 16, at UNC-SHC; Sebastian G. Messmer, ed., *The Works of the Right Rev. John England, First Bishop of Charleston*, 7 vols. (Cleveland, OH, 1908), 4:425–49; Hopley, *Life in the South*, 1:216–17; West, *Methodism in Alabama*, 557.

dutifully noted the willful murder of slaves without comment. In a violent world, prudence reinforced southern reserve and simple neighborliness encouraged people to mind their own business. A scenario: Can one believe the stories that Mr. Johnson Smith-Jones, a devoted churchgoer, treats servants atrociously? After all, there are two sides to every story. It would be reassuring to hear his side, but no gentleman – and certainly no lady – would dream of questioning another about such matters.[31]

Not everyone chose prudence. In 1828 Rufus Anderson of Alabama, a prominent state senator with a notoriously violent temper, went off to Tennessee to kill his sister's husband for abusing her and shot him to death in broad daylight. Defended by the politically powerful Felix Grundy, Anderson was acquitted. Five years later Anderson beat a slave woman to death. He was arrested, tried, and acquitted. Gideon Frierson, a local lawyer, denounced the man and the verdict, excusing a man for shooting a sister's abusive husband but not for beating a slave woman to death. Anderson then went to Frierson's office with the explicit intention to kill him. This time justice was rendered. Frierson struck first, crushing his skull. No indictment: self-defense.[32]

Commentary on these matters more often than not came from women, native and foreign. Fredrika Bremer believed that Joel Poinsett of South Carolina – the diplomat, planter, and unionist – deplored slavery and viewed the degradation of blacks as due to their enslavement, not to their race. Poinsett told her that public opinion was steadily reducing the incidence of brutality, but she wondered. In Richmond, her hosts spoke with distaste of a wealthy acquaintance who treated his slaves savagely. Why then, she asked, did they accept invitations to his party? Well, he had a lovely wife and daughters whose feelings they could not bear to hurt. Yes, thought Bremer as she declined to accompany them to the party, and besides he is rich.[33]

Respectable Southerners scorned neighbors who failed to provide for their old slaves, and Mary Howard Schoolcraft, among many, denied abolitionist accusations of neglect. Nasty behavior toward the elderly stirred dissatisfaction among the slaves of the area. A Virginian wrote home from France in 1860 to inquire about the condition of his old slaves. "They must be very helpless; and will soon, if not now, require the personal attention of a young negro. Suggest some mode of making them comfortable the balance of their lives, and at the present or a less expense." All well and good, but in most cases the elderly slaves who did fare decently benefited from minimal support from their masters while younger slaves provided much

[31] Anderson, ed., *Brokenburn*, 8. See e.g. Bills Diary, Mar. 21, 1861, at UNC-SHC; Paul C. Cameron to W. P. Mangum[?], 1835, in Henry Thomas Shanks, ed., *The Papers of Willie P. Mangum,* 5 vols. (Raleigh, NC, 1955–56), 2:291.

[32] N. F. Smith, "History of Pickens Co., Ala.," in Carl Elliott, ed., *Annals of Northwest Alabama,* 2 vols. (Tuscaloosa, AL, 1958–59), 1:107–8.

[33] Bremer, *Homes of the New World,* 2:511. For the continuation of such patterns with respect to unsavory landowners after the war, see Hortense Powdermaker, *After Freedom: A Cultural Study in the Deep South* (New York, 1939), 271; John Richard Dennett, *The South as It Is: 1865–1866* (New York, 1965 [1867]), 84.

more. At that, few slaves lived to age 60. Even those who lived past 65 contributed income to their masters, since many remained sufficiently productive to pay for those who did not.[34]

In 1871 a Georgia planter "denounced, with bitter curses, his negroes, saying that they had abandoned him, when set free and left him to starve in his old age, knowing as they did, what he had intended to do for them if he could have had his own way." Where interest and humanity coincided, public opinion offered slaves a modicum of protection. A different story came from areas in which they did not coincide. From the middle of the eighteenth century to the final decades of the old regime, scandalized public opinion in Maryland proved helpless to stem the influx of newly emancipated elderly blacks into Baltimore.[35]

Masters of Christian conscience or any conscience at all recognized that the dos and don'ts of the *Decalogue* qualified their demand for obedience from their slaves. Ownership of human beings nevertheless invited morally weak or practically ineffective masters to commit atrocities they would not have dared commit under other circumstances. A few unscrupulous masters ordered slaves to steal from neighbors. Others, who never gave such orders, winked at thefts, which softened the burden of their providing food and supplies. Ingenious slaves took advantages of white greed. In Natchez in the 1850s, blacks stole copies of the *Courier* and sold them to "respectable" whites, who cheerfully took the discount. On a grander scale, a man was caught using a slave to run an illegal ferry line in Virginia, but – since the law debarred slaves from testifying against whites – it was the slave, not his master, who suffered punishment. A few masters or mistresses ordered a slave to murder a spouse, relative, or neighbor. "We sent Kirkland to the penitentiary for seven years," Alexander Stephens wrote his brother, in 1840. "Kirkland had arranged with Mr. Farmer's slave woman to poison her mistress." In South Carolina in 1849, Martin Posey tried to get rid of his wife by enrolling the services of a black conjuror to whom the slaves ascribed great magical powers. In 1833 a shocking case in Mississippi became the focus of Mrs. Trollope's novel *Jonathan Jefferson Whitelaw*. Alexander McNutt, the reform-minded governor of Mississippi and a literary figure of some note, lived under the shadow of suspicions, pressed hard by Henry S. Foote, that he had ordered his slaves to kill his business partner. The account was widely believed.[36]

---

[34] Virginian quoted in Phillips, *Life and Labor in the Old South,* 175; Catterall, ed. *Judicial Cases,* 3:154, 491–2, 597.

[35] Jeffrey R. Brackett, *The Negro in Maryland: A Study in the Institution of Slavery* (Baltimore, 1899), 149; August Meier and Elliott Rudwick, eds., *From Plantation to Ghetto: An Interpretive History of American Negroes* (New York, 1966), 67. On the attention given old slaves by young see Genovese, *Roll, Jordan, Roll,* 519–23; on life expectancy and the productivity of old slaves see Robert William Fogel, *Without Consent or Contract: The Rise and Fall of American Slavery* (New York, 1989), 53 (Figure 7).

[36] For black testimony see *Slave Life in Georgia: A Narrative of the Life, Sufferings, and Escape of John Brown, a Fugitive Slave* (Savannah, GA, 1972 [1855]), 22; Ronald Killion and Charles Waller, eds., *Slavery Time When I Was Chillun Down on Marster's Plantation* (Savannah, GA, 1973), 118; Egypt et al., eds., *Unwritten History,* 46; Rawick, ed., *American Slave,* pt. 3:9, 13, 94 (Arkansas), 94, 208

What to do about bad masters who doubled as good chaps in the white community – who did not blaspheme, drink heavily, indulge in miscreant sexual behavior, or behave uncivilly toward neighbors? What to do when those acknowledged by peers as ladies and gentlemen committed atrocities and even murdered slaves in moments of high dudgeon? After all, gentlemen who murdered gentlemen in a rage usually got off on grounds of self-defense and were forgiven. And what to do about rich and powerful men who, utterly indifferent to the opinion of others, defied the community with impunity? Need anyone be surprised to encounter some masters without conscience?

Slaveholders protested that every social system suffered unspeakable atrocities because men are frail creatures bound to abuse power. Exactly so. The slaveholders lost the argument at the very moment they thought they had won it. For if all social systems require concentration of some men's power over others, and if the sinful nature of all men tempts them to abuse it, then slavery, which especially concentrates power, stands convicted as the least defensible of human relations. A contributor to *Southern Literary Messenger* argued that slavery did not of itself undermine morals but might do so in the hands of evil men. He counseled that Southerners avoid absurd and extreme proslavery claims.[37]

The abolitionist William Goodell ridiculed "the *'Chivalry'* to which our American nobility of woman-whippers lay claim." Cassius Clay's road to abolitionism began with a drunken overseer who tried to rape a slave. In 1858 Charles Whipple of New York's Reform Tract and Book Society had no doubt that many slaveholders were much more humane than the law allowed, but he suggested that just as many were not. Pointedly, Whipple observed that even the better sort were liable to

---

(Missouri), pt. 4:13, 185 (Georgia), 17, 291 (Florida); Yetman, ed., *Life under the "Peculiar Institution,"* 182. For the newspapers see John Hebron Moore, *The Emergence of the Cotton Kingdom in Old Southwest: Mississippi, 1770–1860* (Baton Rouge, LA, 1988), 276, and for the ferryman see A. Leon Higginbotham, Jr., and Barbara K. Kopytoff, "Property First, Humanity Second: The Recognition of the Slave's Human Nature in Virginia's Civil Law," *Ohio State Law Journal,* 50 (1989), 518. For other evidence see Kenneth S. Greenberg, *Honor and Slavery* (Princeton, NJ, 1997), ch. 2; Bell's Adm'r v. Troy, *35 Ala. 184.* Alexander Stephens to Linton Stephens, Apr. 5, 1840, in James D. Waddell, ed., *Biographical Sketch of Linton Stephens, Containing a Selection of His Letters, Speeches, State Papers, Etc.* (Atlanta, GA, 1877), 24. Also, Sept. 8 and 17, 1774, in Hunter Dickinson Farish, ed., *Journal and Letters of Philip Fithian: A Plantation Tutor of the Old Dominion, 1773–1774* (Charlottesville, VA, 1957), 245, 252. Mark A. Keller, " 'The Guv'ner Waz a Writer': Alexander G. McNutt of Mississippi," *Southern Studies,* 20 (1981), 396–400; Rowland, ed., *Mississippi,* 1:348–9; *DNCB,* 1:29; Mason W. Stephenson and D. Grier Stephenson, Jr., " 'To Protect and Defend': The Supreme Court of Georgia and Slavery," *Emory Law Journal,* 25 (1976), 592–3. J. S. Buckingham reported a master who had his slave kill a white man and who beat the rap because the slave could not testify against him: *The Slave States of America,* 2 vols. (New York, 1968 [1842]), 2:168–9. For a woman who offered a reward to her slaves to kill another woman, see Nathaniel Cheairs Hughes, Jr., *Liddell's Record* (Baton Rouge, LA, 1985), 23, and for further evidence of slaves ordered to kill for whites see Thomas D. Morris, *Southern Slavery and the Law, 1619–1860* (Chapel Hill, NC, 1996), 284–6. Masters who ordered slaves to kill can be found through history in every part of the world: see e.g. Ruth Mazo Karras, *Slavery and Society in Medieval Scandinavia* (New Haven, CT, 1988), 111–12.

37 "J. A. W.", "De Servitude," *SLM,* 20 (1854), 425.

behave badly in a fit of sudden anger. Lydia Maria Child twisted the knife, much as Harriet Beecher Stowe did in *Uncle Tom's Cabin*. "Lucky accidents" was how Child replied to a proslavery Virginian's testimony to the kindness of masters and mistresses: "If any one *chooses* to be a brutal despot, your laws and customs give him complete power to do so."[38]

From the perspective of the slaves and to our own cold eye, the protection offered by the slaveholders' internalization of Christian and chivalric values did not add up to much. We can, however, shudder at what life would have been like without even that much. Self-serving slaveholders learned from Edward Gibbon, "A nation of slaves is always prepared to applaud the clemency of their master, who, in the abuse of absolute power, does not proceed to the last extremes of injustice and oppression." However much the slaveholders did violence to their own rules of conduct – not to mention their rationally calculated social and economic interests – the struggle of the many to justify themselves to themselves made them less dangerous human beings.[39]

---

[38] William Goodell, *Views of Constitutional Law, in Its Bearing upon American Slavery,* 2nd ed. (Utica, NY, 1845), 73; H. Edward Richardson, *Cassius Marcellus Clay: Firebrand of Freedom* (Lexington, KY, 1976), 12; Charles K. Whipple, *Family Relations as Affected by Slavery* (Cincinnati, 1858), 6–7; Lydia Maria Child to Mrs. M. J. C. Mason, Dec. 17, 1859, in *Letters of Lydia Maria Child* (New York, 1969 [1883]), 135.

[39] Edward Gibbon, *The History of the Decline and Fall of the Roman Empire,* ed. David Womersley, 3 vols. (London, 1994), 2:88.

12

Chivalric Politics

Southern Ladies Take Their Stand

> Whilst our fathers, brothers, and friends contend on the gory fields for the rights of freemen, we would gladly assist in every way within the sphere of women's influence.... We claim a share in the lives of our brave countrymen; they are fighting for our common rights – we with willing hearts if feeble hands, are engaged in a soul-inspiring cause. We expect not, nor do we wish a voice in the councils of our nation.
>
> —"A Rebel Daughter of Alabama" (1862)[1]

Southern women, more so than northern, accepted exclusion from voting and political office as natural and proper and scored those who tested the boundaries of good taste. A lady expressed political opinions, but of course she deferred to the opinions of father, brother, or husband. Despite extraordinary pretense and interminable blather, sensible men, northern and southern, acknowledged women's interest in politics within the bounds of accepted etiquette, which required a southern lady to deride "petticoat politicians," eschew public controversy, and indignantly deny that she would dream of "meddling" in civic affairs. A gentleman did not refuse to hear her opinions, much less presume to question her Christian principles and loyalty to the South.[2]

The Romans' literary image of aristocratic mothers, Susan Dixon comments, gave them standing as "disciplinarians, custodians of Roman culture and traditional morality" – a role akin to that of fathers. Roman mothers of the elite had a duty to train their sons for service to the state and their daughters to train sons of their own. Southern women learned of Roman mothers who compelled action

---

[1] "A Rebel Daughter" quoted in William Edward Wadsworth Yerby, *History of Greensboro, Alabama from Its Earliest Settlement,* ed. Mabel Yerby Lawson (Northport, AL, 1963 [1908]), 48.

[2] In 1808, Rosalie Eugenia Calvert, the Belgian-born member of a planter family in Maryland, condemned women who were "making themselves ridiculous discussing politics at random without understanding the subject." An ardent Federalist, she herself voiced a strong interest in politics: Ida Gertrude Everson, *George Henry Calvert: American Literary Pioneer* (New York, 1944), 31. Similarly, Mrs. Gabriel Manigault of South Carolina rejected women's direct participation in politics, but her letters bristled with partisan bitterness as Federalists faced Jeffersonians: George C. Rogers, *Charleston in the Age of the Pinckneys* (Columbia, SC, 1980), 135.

from sons who might have preferred to avoid it: Volumnia, mother of Coriolanus; Cornelia, mother of the Gracchi; Julia, mother of Marc Anthony; Aggrippina, wife of Germania, who stood ready to die with her husband in war. Tacitus told entrancing stories of the heroism of German women and of the manner in which they steeled their men for battle, but Edward Gibbon, in his *Decline and Fall of the Roman Empire,* added a cautionary lesson: "Whilst they affected to emulate the stern virtues of man, they must have resigned that attractive softness in which principally consist the charm and weakness of woman." Gibbon's *Decline and Fall,* nonetheless, sparkles with tributes to the political power, talent, sagacity, humanity, and sheer ability of Roman and Byzantine women and of women raised to power in later monarchies. Thus Victoria of Gaul ruled "with a manly vigour." Theodora rallied her cringing husband and his Byzantine court to face acute danger: "If flight were the only means of safety, yet should I disdain to fly. Death is the condition of our birth; but they who have reigned should never survive the loss of dignity and dominion." But Gibbon, like Livy, limned the record of the blind ambition and wanton cruelty of others.[3]

Southern women found a lesson that served them well during the War. In 539 A.D., when the great Byzantine General Belissarius entered Ravenna in triumph over the Goths, the women spit in the faces of sons and husbands who had failed to preserve their freedom without outside help. Oliver Goldsmith, whose writings Southerners warmed to, added grudging admiration for the "masculine" education of Spartan women – "bold, frugal, and patriotic, filled with a sense of honor, and a love of military glory." Spartan mothers sent their sons to war with a shield and an admonition, "Return with it or upon it." "Shield-dropper" became a severe reproach to level at cowards. And from the *Iliad*: Helen of Troy taunts a shirking Paris, "So, home from the wars! / Oh would to god you'd died there."[4]

In Virginia in 1853, Julia Gardner Tyler – northern wife of John Tyler, the former president – ridiculed the Duchess of Sutherland and her abolitionist sisters who accused southern women of political ignorance and indifference: "Politics is almost universally the theme of conversation among the men in all their coteries and social gatherings, and the women would be stupid indeed, if they did not gather much

---

[3] Susan Dixon, *The Roman Mother* (Norman, OK, 1987), opening sentence of the second paragraph of the unpaginated Preface, ch. 1, and 109–10. In Moses Hadas, ed., *The Complete Works of Tacitus,* tr. Alfred John Church and William Jackson Broder (New York, 1942), see "Annals," Bk. 1:40–1, 69, and "Germany and Its Tribes," 712–13; Edward Gibbon, *The History of the Decline and Fall of the Roman Empire,* ed. David Womersley, 3 vols. (London, 1994), 1:149–50, 170–1, 193, 244, 311, 313–19; 2:252–4, 321, 563, 576, quotes at 2:576, 1:244; Livy, *The Early History of Rome,* tr. Aubrey de Sélincourt (London, 1971), Bk. 1:47. For the important role of women in the politics of the Roman Empire see Pierre Grimal, *Love in Ancient Rome,* tr. Arthur Train, Jr. (Norman, OK, 1980), chs. 7 and 8.

[4] Gibbon, *Decline and Fall,* 2:677; Oliver Goldsmith, *History of Greece from the Earliest State to the Death of Alexander the Great,* 2 vols. (New York, 1845), 1:73; Homer, *The Iliad,* tr. Robert Fagles (London, 1990), Bk. 3: lines 499–500 (p. 60). On the Spartan mothers, "shield-droppers," and contemporary opposition to the code of chivalry see Albin Lesky, *A History of Greek Literature,* tr. James Willis and Cornelius de Heer, 2nd ed. (Indianapolis, IN, 1963), 111. William Byrd II noted the Spartan mother who told her cowardly son to get himself character or die and hide his shame: Kevin Berland et al., eds., *The Commonplace Book of William Byrd II of Westover* (Chapel Hill, NC, 1996), 152 (#292).

information from this abundant source." Southern women, she said, stood guard against the intrigues of foreigners who sought to undermine southern interests and thereby subvert the Union. The Reverend W. H. Milburn, a northern Methodist assigned to the South, underscored Tyler's observations: "Their constant and intimate association with husband, father, brothers, incites them to the study of graver topics, with an interest in higher themes than is customary in our crowded and hard-driven society."[5]

Southern women argued with each other and with their husbands, sometimes heatedly, over elections and court decisions. They filled the galleries of the state legislatures and Congress, rated the oratorical performances, complimented their favorites, and berated their hates. In plantations and town families, men read aloud pamphlets, newspapers, and political speeches and women read to each other, as when Fannie Page Hume read "Mr. Barbour's fine speech at the inauguration of the Clay statue – it was a noble tribute." Women's diaries recorded political commentary, invitations to politically sponsored social events, attendance at rallies, and responses to electoral victories and defeats.[6]

Still, opposition to female participation in politics ran deep. During the congressional debate over statehood for Missouri, John Randolph of Roanoke vigorously objected to the crowd of women in the galleries who spilled onto the floor: "Mr. Speaker, what pray are all these women doing here, so out of place in this arena? Sir, they had much better be at home attending to their knitting." Frances Trollope, visiting Congress some years later, defended the women in her own caustic way. The House of Commons had to exclude ladies, for Englishwomen, being lovely, distracted the Members of Parliament – but no such problem could arise in America.[7]

---

5 Julia Gardiner Tyler, *A Letter to the Duchess of Sutherland and Ladies of England* (Richmond, VA, 1853), 4; William Henry Milburn, *Ten Years of Preacher Life: Chapters from an Autobiography* (New York, 1859), 326. John R. Thompson, editor of *Southern Literary Messenger,* stopped the presses to make room for Tyler's reply to the Duchess of Sutherland, explaining that it deserved the widest circulation: Editor's Introduction, *SLM,* 19 (1853), 120. See also "The Affectionate and Christian Address of Many Thousands of the Women of England to Their Sisters, the Women of the United States of America" – signed by the Duchess of Sutherland, other prominent aristocrats, and eventually 560,000 women – in Richard C. Lounsbury, ed., *Louisa S. McCord: Political and Social Essays* (Charlottesville, VA, 1995), Appendix 1, and McCord from the Charleston *Mercury* (Aug. 10, 1853), reprinted as "A Letter to the Duchess of Sutherland by a Lady of South Carolina," in *Essays,* ch. 12, where McCord declares that women by instinct side with the oppressed (351) and rips the British ladies for their callousness toward the misery suffered by the Irish and by British laborers. See another reply to the "Ladies of England" and to Stowe: "E." [of Charleston], "Woman's True Mission," *SLM,* 19 (1853), 303–6. For an early warning about the strength of women in the abolitionist movement see [William Drayton], *The South Vindicated from the Treason and Fanaticism of the Northern Abolitionists* (Philadelphia, 1836), 180–2. On the relation of domestic concerns to foreign policy, the correspondence between a mother in Charleston and her daughter in Philadelphia contains numerous informed comments on Texas, Oregon, and the danger of war with England: Eliza Cope Harrison, ed., *Best Companions: Letters of Eliza Middleton Fisher and Her Mother, Mary Herring Middleton, from Charleston, Philadelphia, and Newport, 1839–1846* (Columbia, SC, 2001).

6 Fannie Page Hume Diary, Mar. 27 and June 22, 1860, at UNC-SHC; also, Kate Carney Diary, Aug. 1–5, 1859, at UNC-SHC.

7 William Cabell Bruce, *John Randolph of Roanoke, 1773–1833,* 2 vols. (New York, 1970 [1922]), 2:628; Frances Trollope, *Domestic Manners of the Americans* (Gloucester, MA, 1974 [1832]), 225–6.

A half-century after Randolph's outburst, Josephine Seaton described the curious contradictions that beset southern men. Randolph's defense of slavery in Missouri, she said, had less to do with his professed constitutional principles than with his aversion to being led by a majority and to his "Ishmaelite" nature. He considered satire a cruel female device and "shuddered" when a woman resorted to it. He opposed the participation of women – and ministers, too – in politics because their vital callings required deference accorded to no politician. But Randolph had another reason: "I am well aware that ladies are as delicate as they are charming creatures, and that, in our intercourse with them, we must strain the truth as far as possible. Brought up from their earliest infancy to disguise their real sentiments (for a woman would be a monster who did not practice this disguise) it is their privilege to be insincere, and we would despise [them], and justly too, if they had that manly frankness, which constitutes the ornament of our character, as the very reverse does of theirs."[8]

Randolph did enjoy the company of well-educated women: "Female society, in my eye, is an indispensable requisite in forming the manly character." To his nephew Theodore he wrote that without female society men would degenerate into brutes. He recognized the intellectual power of certain women, not merely by the standards of their sex but in comparison with men. Shortly after Randolph's death, *Southern Literary Messenger* saluted the many intellectually remarkable women of the French elite, including Charlotte Corday, who assassinated Paul Marat, radical cheerleader for the Reign of Terror. Mary Moragné of South Carolina, among other Southerners, approved Corday's tyrannicide, and Justice Henry K. Nash of North Carolina's Supreme Court, on learning that Union General Benjamin Butler had insulted the ladies of New Orleans, wrote Thomas Ruffin: "Butler may yet find a Charlotte Corday in the land of the Creole."[9]

In sophisticated Charleston, gentlemen earnestly discussed the place and rights of women in a well-ordered republic. In the debate over female education, a substantial number of southern men rejected notions of women's intellectual inferiority. On rare occasions a prominent Southerner like Thomas Ritchie, the powerful editor of the Richmond *Enquirer* and leader of the Richmond Junto, even suggested

---

[8] Josephine Seaton, *William Winston Seaton of the National Intelligencer* (New York, 1970 [1871]), 150–1; Randolph quoted in Bruce, *Randolph of Roanoke,* 2:417.

[9] For Randolph's views see Bruce, *Randolph of Roanoke,* 1:630; Kenneth Shorey, ed., *Collected Letters of John Randolph of Roanoke to Dr. John Brockenbrough, 1812–1833* (New Brunswick, NJ, 1988); Randolph to William Thompson, Dec. 31, 1800, in Hugh A. Garland, *The Life of John Randolph of Roanoke,* 2 vols. (New York, 1969 [1859]), 2:101, 1:167, also 165; *Letters of John Randolph to a Young Relative* (Philadelphia, 1834), 236, 249–50. Randolph would probably not have contradicted the story that George Bancroft refused to accept a wager from a southern lady over a literary reference, explaining that he had been warned about the wide and deep reading of plantation ladies: *Confederate Veteran,* 1 (1893), 74.

[J. L. Martin], "The Women of France," *SLM,* 5 (1839), 297–303; Mary E. Moragné Journal, Jan. 20, 1837, in Delle Mullen Craven, ed., *The Neglected Thread: A Journal of the Calhoun Community* (Columbia, SC, 1951), 19; Henry K. Nash to Thomas Ruffin, May 23, 1863, in J. G. deRoulhac Hamilton, ed., *The Papers of Thomas Ruffin,* 4 vols. (Raleigh, NC, 1918), 3:243. When the ladies of New Orleans insulted occupying Yankee troops, General Benjamin Butler ordered them treated like common whores.

(albeit timidly) consideration of women's suffrage. Still James H. Hammond, as might be expected, while paying misty-eyed tribute to the exemplary character of his wife, mother, or mother-in-law, characterized women as "mostly fools and savages and not to be called either civilized or thinking or reasonable beings."[10]

The slave, James Holcombe told the Virginia State Agricultural Society in 1858, "scarcely labors under any personal disability to which we may not find a counterpart in those which attach to other incompetent classes – the minor, the lunatic, and the married woman." Henry Hughes of Mississippi, a bright social theorist, mingled contempt with the usual paeans to women's moral superiority. The South, in proud recognition of women's superior virtues, treated them like queens, not cooks and chambermaids, but Harriet Beecher Stowe's *Uncle Tom's Cabin* confirmed Hughes's conviction that women were intellectually inferior and hence must remain dependents: "That book is womanish & I am afraid absurdly unprincipled; written by a woman clearly." In 1856, Hughes assured a mercifully small audience in New Orleans: "Fat makes beauty and orders repose; women are fatter than men, and their fat settles their status. It is not natural for women to be politicians and strong-minded; political women are social excrescences. Nature has settled woman's social status. They have not physical power to be anything other than home folk."[11]

The Reverend John Girardeau appealed to Scripture to justify exclusion of women from sacred office and politics. Girardeau denied that women were inferior in intellect and piety and argued that, since women carry the special burdens of procreation and nurturing, justice and equity require that they be relieved of public burdens. Most clerics and laymen supported exclusion of women from politics, not on grounds of intellectual inferiority or the burdens of procreation but on grounds of intellectual difference. Men and women have different sorts of minds and different spheres of action.[12]

Anna Maria Calhoun, a teen-ager with her father's brain and determination, adamantly insisted on joining him in Washington to help with his work. John C. Calhoun, whose correspondence reveals that he discussed domestic and foreign politics with a number of southern and European women, replied to his beloved daughter: "I am not one of those who think your sex ought to have nothing to do

[10] R. F. W. Allston to Adele Petigru Allston, Dec. 16, 1849 (from Columbia), in J. H. Easterby, ed., *The South Carolina Rice Plantation, as Revealed in the Papers of Robert F. W. Allston* (Chicago, 1945), 99; Mitchell King Diary, Dec. 1, 1852, at USC; Charles Henry Ambler, *Thomas Ritchie: A Study in Virginia Politics* (Richmond, VA, 1913), 120; Dec. 15, 1850, in Carol Bleser, ed., *Secret and Sacred: The Diaries of James Henry Hammond, a Southern Slaveholder* (New York, 1988), 213, also, 82, 261, 194.

[11] James P. Holcombe, "Is Slavery Consistent with Natural Law?" *SLM*, 27 (1858), 403; Sanford M. Lyman, Jr., ed., *Selected Writings of Henry Hughes: Antebellum Southerner, Slavocrat, Sociologist* (Jackson, MS, 1985), 40, 185–6.

[12] George A. Blackburn, ed., *The Life and Work of John L. Girardeau* (Columbia, SC, 1916), 217–18; also, D. G. M. Wharton, "Women's Rights," *South-Western Monthly* (Nashville), 1 (1852), 146; Jean E. Friedman, *The Enclosed Garden: Women and Community in the Evangelical South, 1830–1900* (Chapel Hill, NC, 1985), 13. For arguments from sexual difference see B. M. Palmer, *The Family in Its Civil and Churchly Aspects: An Essay in Two Parts* (Richmond, VA, 1876), 59; Henry W. Hilliard, "Women – Her True Sphere," in *Speeches and Addresses by Henry W. Hilliard* (New York, 1855), 479–80.

with politicks. They have as much interest in the good condition of the country as the other sex, and tho' it would be unbecoming of them to take an active part in political struggles, their opinion, when enlightened, cannot fail to have a great and salutary effect." Anna Maria became her father's confidante. Her political influence cannot be gauged precisely, but – in the words of Clyde Wilson, editor of *The Papers of John C. Calhoun* – she was "perhaps closer to him in mind and temperament than anyone on earth." In 1848 Gustavus Henry of Tennessee, a leading politician, confided in his 14-year-old daughter, Susan: "I hope you will never think of getting married, till you are at least Twenty years old. I cant spare you sooner than that, and you know you and I are confidants." He reminded Susan of her promise to consult him when she did consider marriage: "I hope with your advantages and my knowledge of men we can make a very good selection." He urged her not to think of marrying until she had finished school and then focus on a "first rate gentleman," never a "second rate man."[13]

In Alabama the talented novelist Augusta Jane Evans corresponded about politics with Confederate congressman J. L. M. Curry. In Texas, John H. Regan, senator and later Confederate Postmaster General, valued the political opinions of Edwina, his Virginia-born wife. Mrs. Regan played the game well, and when gentlemen at her dinner parties turned to politics, she discreetly withdrew but placed herself just outside the door so as not to miss a word. George Wythe Randolph of Virginia, Confederate Secretary of War, had five political "intimates": three men; Mary, his wife; and Mollie, his niece and special confidante. And while the widespread rumors about Varina Davis's political influence over her husband Jefferson Davis were maliciously inspired and wildly exaggerated, she did have his ear. Some men argued, much as Louisa McCord did, that women's physical weakness offset any plausible claims to intellectual parity; some denied the intellectual parity; almost all agreed on women's moral superiority or special qualities.[14]

---

[13] J. C. Calhoun to A. M. Calhoun, Mar. 10, 1832, in J. Franklin Jameson, ed., *Calhoun Correspondence* (Washington, DC, 1900: "Annual Report of the American Historical Association for the Year 1899," 2 vols.), 2:316; also, Charles M. Wiltse, *John C. Calhoun: Nullifier, 1829–1839* (Indianapolis, IN, 1949), 167; C. N. Wilson, "Introduction," in *JCCP,* 11:xxxi; G. A. Henry to Susan Henry, Mar. 14, 1848, in Henry Papers, at UNC-SHC. For Calhoun's correspondence with other women see *JCCP,* vol. 25: xix; Mary D. Campbell to Calhoun, Dec. 10, 1847 (7–8); Sarah Mytton (Hughes) Maury to Calhoun, Jan. 29, 1848 (155). Sarah Maury, author of *Statesmen of America* (London, 1846) and *An Englishwoman in America* (London, 1848) and who married into a Virginia family, corresponded with Henry Clay and other American luminaries and dedicated *Statesmen* to her friend James Buchanan. See also Anne Fontaine Maury, *Intimate Virginiana: A Century of Maury Travels by Land and Sea* (Richmond, VA, 1941), 127–8, 314. When Patrick Henry defended himself against charges that he abandoned his principles, he did so in a long letter to his daughter, Betsy Aylett: Patrick Henry to Betsy Aylett, Aug. 20, 1796, in William Wirt, *Sketches of the Life and Character of Patrick Henry* (Philadelphia, 1817), 385–7. Octavia Walton Le Vert translated government documents for her father and recorded the senatorial debates over Jackson's removal of federal deposits: *DGB,* 2:617–19. Peter V. Daniel of Virginia, associate justice of the U.S. Supreme Court, had as political confidante his unmarried daughter Elizabeth, a broadly cultured woman: John P. Frank, *Justice Daniel Dissenting: A Biography of Peter V. Daniel, 1784–1860* (Cambridge, MA, 1964), 53, 230.

[14] "Jabez Lamar Monroe Curry" and "Augusta Jane Evans," *BDC,* 156, 180; Ben H. Proctor, *Not without Honor: The Life of John H. Reagan* (Austin, TX, 1962), 145–6; George Green Shackelford, *George*

The emergence of important women editors mocked demands that women refrain from public controversy. A few prominent cases: the Massachusetts-born Sarah Porter Hillhouse reputedly became the first woman editor in Georgia. In 1803 her husband published the *Monitor,* a newspaper in Washington, Georgia; when he died two years later, she maintained it with about 800 subscribers until replaced by her son eight years later. Mary Edwards Bryan of Georgia, who had begun to publish stories at age 14, became literary editor of *Georgia Literary and Temperance Crusader* in 1859, left after a year to become a correspondent for the more prestigious *Southern Field and Fireside,* and, after the War, edited a political newspaper in Natchitoches, Louisiana. In North Carolina the Reverend Sidney Bumpass and his wife Frances Webb Bumpass founded *Weekly Messenger,* a Methodist newspaper. Shortly after he died, she assumed editorship, defying convention. She bowed to public pressure and had a man run it as managing editor, but when he proved incompetent she dropped the façade. *Weekly Messenger* flourished under her editorship for the next twenty years.[15]

Women bore, largely in silence, their assignment to an inferior place in society and even within the household, but few tolerated the contempt that sometimes accompanied it from men who were not gentlemen. Their own male kin and friends harbored no such attitudes. If ladies did not take personally expressions of contempt for women who did not know their place, they did tease their gentlemen about the stereotypes. Juliet Upshur made her 20-year-old brother Abel a pair of breeches when he started a career at law that ended with his becoming Secretary of State in the Tyler administration. She wanted to give him "a badge of royalty" to mark his "only superiority over that tribe of insignificant beings – women."[16]

In 1850 Representative David Outlaw of North Carolina sent his wife Emily, whose intelligence he much admired, his reflections on Randolph's outburst in Congress thirty years earlier. Outlaw distanced himself from "the length and breadth" of Randolph's words, but he, too, deplored the crowds of women who choked the Capitol each day, many outrageously flirtatious and dressed at the height of fashion: "Ladies had no business to be present where men contended for victory & empire any more than they had to be in military camp because things frequently occur there which are unfit for them to hear." He disparaged "he-women, if I may be permitted to coin such a word, [who] have the good traits of neither sex, and what is revolting in both." During the 1840s and 1850s, Outlaw frequently wrote to keep

Wythe Randolph and the Confederate Elite (Athens, GA, 1988), 98; also Eli N. Evans, *Judah P. Benjamin: The Jewish Confederate* (New York, 1988), xviii, 139–40 on Varina Howell. For Augusta Jane Evans's friendship with Beauregard, who said that he read *Beulah* with tears in his eyes, see T. Harry Williams, *P. G. T. Beauregard: Napolean in Gray* (Baton Rouge, LA, 1955), 160.

15 *DGB,* 1:456 (Hillhouse) and 130–1 (Bryan); Frances A. Bumpass, *Autobiography and Journal,* ed. Eugenia H. Bumpass and Mrs. F. A. Butler (Nashville, TN, 1899), 38; *DNCB,* 1:268. Mrs. Bumpass also taught school, drawing upon her knowledge of Greek, among other subjects.

16 Claude H. Hall, *Abel Parker Upshur: Conservative Virginian, 1790–1844* (Madison, WI, 1963), 15. Mary E. Moragné read aloud Lieber's chapter on women in *Stranger in America,* calling it "a very fair and flattering, but not too flattering criticism": Sept. 24, 1839, in Craven, ed., *Neglected Thread,* 161.

his wife up to date on political news, although he could not resist an occasional for-mulaic self-rebuke: "I have written more politics this morning than usual – It is not I know a very interesting subject to you." David Outlaw knew no such thing.[17]

John Quitman of Mississippi, from his earliest days as a Democratic politician, sprinkled letters to his wife with political news despite concession to the ritual: "I scarcely know what to say to you in my letters. Matters of legislation will not I know interest you, and nothing else is worthy of notice." His reports on legisla-tion and politics became more detailed as time went on. He paraded accounts of his steadfast devotion to principle and of the painful contrast between his sterling behavior and the shabby behavior of others. In later years he wrote his daughters, Louisa and Antonia, in much the same vein. They responded by encouraging his political radicalism, especially when he came under fire from unionists and other adversaries. Louisa, who approved Calhoun's opposition to Mexican annexations, warned her father of the potential threat of absorption of an "ignorant" and "dis-orderly" Catholic rabble, and she boiled at male indifference in Natchez toward the Cuban filibusterers she admired.[18]

Rosalie Eugenia Calvert hosted a barbecue to promote her brother-in-law's cam-paign for the state legislature. Varina Davis helped frank 2,780 letters for her hus-band in 1859: "It gave me great pleasure to be doing something which seems to bring us nearer to each other." And Varina Davis, like many other women, regularly ex-changed detailed political news, primarily with her mother. When their men ran for office, mothers, wives, and daughters battered kin, friends, and acquaintances who did not rally around.[19]

The ladies did not always agree with, much less rubber-stamp, their men's polit-ical opinions and actions. While John Marshall fumed about the menace of rev-olutionary France, Polly, his anti-British wife, demurred. Sarah Childress Polk, a self-effacing helpmeet, dutifully read newspapers for President James Knox Polk but let her husband know when she thought his preferred policies silly. In eastern North Carolina, the popularity of the young, politically promising Abner Vail de-clined after he published an article that bruised female sensibilities.[20]

[17] David Outlaw to Emily Outlaw, Feb. 14, 1850, Dec. 10, 1849, and, generally, letters from the 1840s and 1850s, in Outlaw Papers, at UNC-SHC.

[18] J. A. Quitman to Emily Quitman, Jan. 19 and Feb. 2, 1828, Jan. 10, 1836, Oct. 1, 1850, Eliza Quit-man to John A. Quitman, Jan. 30, 1847, and Louisa Quitman to J. A. Quitman, June 31, 1847, in Quitman Papers, at UNC-SHC; also, Robert E. May, *John A. Quitman: Old South Crusader* (Baton Rouge, LA, 1985), 204, 240. Henry A. Wise wrote his wife regularly on political matters, in which she evinced a keen interest: John S. Wise, *The End of an Era* (Boston, 1900), 38.

[19] Everson, *Calvert*, 32; Hudson Strode, *Jefferson Davis*, 3 vols. (New York, 1955–64), 1:328; also, Susan Nye Hutchinson Journal, Mar. 10 and July 17, 1832, at UNC-SHC; Moragné Journal, Jan. 14, 1837, in Craven, ed., *Neglected Thread*, 16–17; Hume Diary, Jan. 31 and Feb. 7, 1860; Mary Blount Petti-grew to William Sheppard Pettigrew, Dec. 22, 1842, in Sarah McCulloh Lemmon, ed., *The Pettigrew Papers*, 2 vols. (Raleigh, NC, 1971, 1988), 2:547; Stephen Meats and Edwin T. Arnold, eds., *The Writ-ings of Benjamin F. Perry*, 3 vols. (Spartanburg, SC, 1980), 2:59.

[20] Frances Norton Mason, *My Dearest Polly: Letters of Chief Justice Marshall to His Wife, with Their Background, Political and Domestic, 1779–1831* (Richmond, VA, 1961), 59–60; Anson Nelson and

Floride Calhoun took little interest in politics, but during the 1820s, while her husband served as Secretary of War, she lobbied informally for his military appropriations measures and presidential aspirations. Calhoun's opponents considered Floride Calhoun the ringleader of a petticoat lobby. A waggish John Quincy Adams complained that she – a charming and successful hostess – was pushing her husband's presidential candidacy at her dinner parties. Some years later she endangered her husband's fortunes by insisting that they snub the controversial Margaret Eaton, discourteously referred to as "Peggy," whose professions of chastity were accepted by the gallant Andrew Jackson. Calhoun probably could not have avoided a break with Jackson anyway but surely did not need his wife's contribution to it. As for Margaret Eaton, Calhoun and his supporters believed she exercised a malicious political influence over her husband John Eaton and Jackson.[21]

By the 1830s abolitionists were taking seriously southern women's proslavery feelings and political radicalism. In Danville, Kentucky, James Birney "had a real bout on Saturday with a company of Ladies" over slavery, whereas Texas revolutionaries rejoiced at the support they were getting from proslavery Kentucky women. Gerrit Smith of New York related "an incident, to show what a fiend even woman, gentle and lovely woman, may become after she has fallen under the sway of the demon of slavery." A professed Christian lady in New York hoped the antislavery Reverend Dr. Samuel H. Cox would visit Georgia: "I should love to see him tarred and feathered, and his head cut off and carried on a pole around Savannah." David Ruggles of New York, a free black abolitionist, began his tract on *The Abrogation of the Seventh Commandment by the American Churches*: "Nothing is more easily demonstrable than the fact that slavery owes its continuance in the United States chiefly to the women." Ruggles scorned the "slaveholding ladies of the South" who occupied the highest ranks of southern society and "notoriously" drove their slaves ferociously, proving themselves "inexcusably criminal." And he chided northern women for not standing up against slavery.[22]

Nullification provided new opportunities for politically inclined ladies. Shortly before the crisis broke, antislavery Mrs. Basil Hall, to her chagrin, found South

---

Fanny Nelson, *Memorials of Sarah Childress Polk* (Spartanburg, SC, 1980 [1892]), 94; Ebenezer Pettigrew to James Iredell, Jr., Aug. 6, 1806, in Lemmon, ed., *Pettigrew Papers,* 1:393–4 (Vail).

[21] John Niven, *John C. Calhoun and the Price of Union: A Biography* (Baton Rouge, LA, 1988), 103, 167. See Hemphill's Introduction to *JCCP,* 7:xxvii; Virgil Maxcy to Calhoun, Apr. 6, 1829, Calhoun to Samuel D. Ingraham, May 4, 1831, Duff Green to John B. Helm, May 20, 1831, in *JCCP,* 11:17, 378–9, 386–8. For a sympathetic yet balanced account of Margaret Eaton see John Marszalek, *Petticoat Affair: Manners, Mutiny and Sex in Andrew Jackson's White House* (Baton Rouge, LA, 2000). Marszalek maintains that much of the gossip about her stemmed not from evidence of sexual improprieties but from her bold behavior, which defied social customs and seemed unladylike.

[22] James Birney to Theodore Weld, July 21, 1834, in Gilbert H. Barnes and Dwight L. Dumond, eds., *Letters of Theodore Dwight Weld, Angelina Grimké and Sarah Grimké, 1822–1844,* 2 vols. (Gloucester, MA, 1965), 1:161; *HT,* 2:5; *Letter of Gerrit Smith to Rev. James Smylie of the State of Mississippi* (New York, 1837), 28; Ruggles in Dorothy Porter, ed., *Early Negro Writing, 1760–1837* (Boston, 1971), 481–3, Ruggles quote at 478. During congressional debates over abolitionist petitions and the Gag Rule, Southerners knew that signatures came primarily from churchwomen. See William Lee Miller, *Arguing about Slavery: The Great Battle in the United States Congress* (New York, 1996), chs. 6 and 19.

Carolina's proslavery ladies ever ready to debate. At a party in Columbia at the De-Saussures: "I had as tough an argument regarding slavery with some ladies as ever Basil had on any subject with gentlemen." Maria Henrietta Pinckney earned fame for her little book, *The Quintessence of Long Speeches, Arranged as a Political Catechism,* which offered an effective summary of state-rights political creed, and she joined Governor James Hamilton in importing a cargo of sugar to challenge the hated tariff. Harriet Martineau, that well-traveled and famous British intellectual, found that South Carolinians regarded Pinckney as a pillar of the nullification party. Upcountry women at huge antitariff and pro-nullification rallies provided homespun as symbols of resistance, and some of the "nullification quilts" woven from their dresses were prized well into the twentieth century. William Lowndes drew a sharp reprimand from Mrs. Daniel Horry for supporting the tariff of 1816 – "the worse thing done since universal suffrage." Governor John Floyd of Virginia privately denounced Andrew Jackson for threatening South Carolina, while his wife more fiercely described Jackson as "a bloody, bawdy, treacherous lecherous villain." In Abbeville, South Carolina, Uncle Jack read to the family circle a speech by Henry Wise of Virginia, which Mary Moragné found a "Brilliant & dazzling flow of thought – making up a string of biting invective against poor old crumbling Jackson."[23]

The presidential campaign of 1840 engaged southern and northern women, with the Whigs the stronger sponsors and beneficiaries. Evangelical churches discouraged women's participation in politics, but even they could not restrain large numbers during and after 1840. Women made flags for the Whigs and slipped political statements into presentations at rallies. If no women made speeches, strictly defined, some carried party banners and, from all accounts, contributed markedly to the wild excitement at rallies and barbecues. During that campaign, some politicians in Georgia, most notably Governor George Towns, turned to their wives as principal consultants. In Virginia, Robert Tyler – son and political adviser to President Tyler – consulted his northern-born wife carefully, regarding her as an intellectual equal. Self-deprecatingly, she teased that she wrote "all the pathetic and romantic parts" of his speeches, and he "the law and reason."[24]

---

[23] Una Pope-Hennessey, ed., *The Aristocratic Journey: Letters of Mrs. Basil Hall Written during a Fourteen Months' Sojourn in the United States* (New York, 1931), 209; Rogers, *Charleston in the Age of the Pinckneys,* 153; Harriet Martineau, *Retrospect of Western Travel,* 2 vols. (London, 1838), 1:229; William W. Freehling, *The Road to Disunion* (New York, 1990), 279; Douglas Summers Brown, *A City without Cobwebs: A History of Rock Hill, South Carolina* (Columbia, SC, 1953), 72–3; Mrs. Horry quoted in David Duncan Wallace, *The History of South Carolina,* 4 vols. (New York, 1934), 2:420; Mrs. Floyd quoted in Arthur C. Cole, *The Whig Party in the South* (Gloucester, MA, 1962), 20 n. 59; Moragné Journal, Jan. 15, 1837, in Craven, ed., *Neglected Thread,* 17.

[24] Lollie Belle Wiley, ed., *Memoirs of Judge Richard H. Clark* (Atlanta, GA, 1898), 345; Elizabeth Tyler Coleman, *Priscilla Cooper Tyler and the American Scene, 1816–1889* (University, AL, 1955), 79; Richard J. Carwardine, *Evangelicals and Politics in Antebellum America* (New Haven, CT, 1993), 31–5; R. G. Gunderson, "The Southern Whigs," in Waldo W. Braden, ed., *Oratory in the Old South, 1828–1860* (Baton Rouge, LA, 1970), ch. 3; Robert Gray Gunderson, *The Log-Cabin Campaign* (Frankfort, KY, 1957), 4, 135–9; Richard Zuber, *Jonathan Worth: A Biography of a Southern Unionist* (Chapel Hill, NC, 1965), 40; Wiley, ed., *Clark Memoirs,* 29, also 344. For the effort of the Whigs to

Men pictured the little lady as dutiful helpmeet to a father or a husband whose politics she made her own, but the growth of women's political independence became more obvious with each passing decade. Forty or fifty women crowded into Mississippi's constitutional convention in 1832 to hear the debate on election of judges – hardly the most exciting of issues. It took pro-temperance petitions by ladies of Jackson to move the state legislature to tighten Mississippi's liquor laws in 1854. Sallie Eola Reneau of Grenada, Mississippi, campaigned in the 1850s for state aid to education, receiving respectful attention of the state legislature, which, in response, chartered a state female college but then could not fund it.[25]

Ladies of South Carolina spoke forcefully at home, as well. It is hard to believe that Louisa Susanna McCord and Mary Boykin Chesnut did not influence their husbands, although James Chesnut must have found Mary's carping a heavy cross to bear. In 1847 when Francis Lieber wanted William Campbell Preston to read a speech by Senator Charles Sumner of Massachusetts on white slavery, he told Sumner to send a copy to Preston's wife, explaining that Preston would ignore an abolitionist tract unless she pressed it upon him. In 1859 Alexander Sands, advocate of women's higher education, reminded the students at Richmond's Hollins Female Institute that women profoundly influenced the nation's social development and had a duty to uphold slavery, "intertwined with the dearest and best interests of your homes and firesides." Sands appealed for intervention within women's proper sphere. As custodians of their communities' religious life, they must also be crystal clear on slavery's biblical sanction.[26]

Rosalie Roos – Bremer's antislavery sister-Swede, teaching in Charleston – knew only one woman who was unconvinced of slavery's divine sanction. The Philadelphia-born Emily Wharton Sinkler got an unpleasant surprise when she learned that Mrs. Russell Middleton, a woman noted for her broadly liberal religious views, was strongly proslavery and pro-secession. Lotte Yancey, who sat in the gallery during South Carolina's debate over the Compromise of 1850, rejoiced when hostile citizens yawned down Benjamin Perry's "submissionist" speech. Elizabeth Rhett assured her husband, Robert Barnwell Rhett, that South Carolina was bravely rallying to his secessionist cause. On a visit to Charleston in 1850, Fredrika Bremer

mobilize women during the campaign of 1840 see Elizabeth R. Varon, "Tippecanoe and the Ladies, Too: White Women and Party Politics in Antebellum Virginia," *Journal of American History*, 82 (1995), 494–521. See also Hutchinson Journal, Nov. 12, 17, 20, 1840; Mary Jane Chester to Elizabeth Chester, May, 15, 1841, in Mary Jane Chester Papers, at UNC-SHC. The presidential campaign of 1848 agitated the girls at the Columbia Female Institute in Tennessee. "They voted the other day," a jubilant Susan Henry informed her father, a prominent Whig politician, in a letter full of political commentary, "and Taylor was elected by a majority of 25." Susan Henry to Gustavus A. Henry, Nov. 11, 1848, in Henry Papers.

[25] May, *Quitman*, 54; Dunbar Rowland, ed., *Mississippi: Comprising Sketches of Counties, Towns, Events, Institutions, and Persons, Arranged in Cyclopedic Form*, 4 vols. (Spartanburg, SC, 1976 [1907]), 2:203, 537.

[26] Francis Lieber to Charles Sumner, May 28, 1847, in Thomas Sergeant Perry, ed., *The Life and Letters of Francis Lieber* (Boston, 1882), 211; A. H. Sands, "Intellectual Culture of Woman," *SLM*, 28 (1859), 330–2.

found elite women "more irritable and violent" than their men in defense of slavery and radicalism. The political testiness Roos and Bremer found in Charleston extended across the South. Daniel Webster's effort to conciliate the South with his Seventh of March Address earned him the opprobrium of abolitionists as well as supporters of slavery. Mary Jones of Georgia, wife of the Presbyterian Reverend Charles Colcock Jones, protested: "He does not mean to open our veins and bleed us to death by abolishing the Fugitive Slave Bill; but by confining us and our property to the original limits, he will put his hand around our necks and strangle us to death. This seems to my mind to be his present position with regard to the right of the South." Although Virginia Tunstall Clay, wife of the senator from Alabama, arrived in Washington with apparently little interest in politics, she refused to associate with Northerners unsympathetic to southern rights. A few years later southern women were congratulating Representative Preston Brooks of South Carolina for his caning of Charles Sumner in the Senate.[27]

By the time of secession, southern women had established a reputation as more ultra than their men. In 1861 William Howard Russell, the British correspondent, found the women of the Brown family of Tennessee not only fierce secessionists but capable of doing "the whole slave doctrine first rate." The celebrated pianist Louis Moreau Gottschalk of New Orleans, a unionist who went north during the War, expressed dismay at the extremism of both northern and southern women. An English traveler in South Carolina recorded women's demands for radical action. A lady in Georgia exclaimed that she loved Thomas Cobb's four- and five-hour secessionist speeches and would listen without fatigue were he to go on for seventy-five hours. In Charleston, at the fateful convention that split the Democratic party, women opened their homes to radical delegates and those who might be won over; they left moderates to swelter at night in the heat of packed hotels. If female gossip be credited, after Stephen Douglas emerged as the nominee the wives of radical senators prevailed on Mrs. Benjamin Fitzpatrick of Alabama to persuade her husband to decline the proffered vice-presidential nomination. What Sallie Putnam of Richmond said of Virginia's secession convention could have been said about every

[27] Rosalie Roos to Olof Gustaf Roos, Apr. 4, 1853, in R. Roos, *Travels in America, 1851–1855,* tr. Carl L. Anderson (Carbondale, IL, 1982), 80, 276; Emily Wharton Sinkler to Mary Wharton, Apr. 11, 1851, in Anne Sinkler Whaley LeClerq, ed., *Between North and South: The Letters of Emily Wharton Sinkler, 1842–1865* (Columbia, SC, 2001), 148; on Lotte Yancey and Elizabeth Rhett see John Barnwell, *Love of Order: South Carolina's First Secession Crisis* (Chapel Hill, NC, 1982), 138–9, 146; Fredrika Bremer, *Homes of the New World: Impressions of America,* 2 vols. (New York, 1853), 1; Mary Jones to C. C. Jones, June 20, 1851, in Robert Manson Myers, ed., *A Georgian at Princeton* (New York, 1976), 193; C. Bleser and F. M. Heath, "The Clays of Alabama," in Carol Bleser, ed., *In Joy and in Sorrow: Women, Family, and Marriage in the Victorian South, 1830–1900* (New York, 1991), 143. For an excellent and well-documented discussion of the secessionist radicalism of elite ladies before and during the War, see Armstead L. Robinson, *Bitter Fruits of Bondage: The Demise of Slavery and the Collapse of the Confederacy, 1861–1865* (Charlottesville, VA, 2005), esp. 164–5. In North Carolina Willie P. Mangum, Jr., playfully wrote his cousin Martha about a chap who was having a devil of a time with his favorite, who, taking high ground on southern rights, chafed at his support for the Compromise: Willie P. Mangum, Jr., to Martha Mangum, July 16, 1850, in Henry Thomas Shanks, ed., *The Papers of Willie P. Mangum,* 5 vols. (Raleigh, NC, 1955–56), 5:182–4.

other southern state's convention: "Every prominent delegate had his own partisans among the fair sex. Every Woman was to some extent a politician."[28]

Secessionists capitalized on the powerful legacy of women's contributions to
the Revolutionary War. William Gilmore Simms's *Magnolia* published accounts
of women's efforts for the revolutionary cause and the new nation while it supported female education and assailed those who disparaged female intellect. In the
mid-1840s the Reverend William Henry Foote of North Carolina recalled that the
patriotic young ladies of Mecklenburg County demanded that their men fight with
the nobility, courage, and manliness it took to qualify as guardians of the weaker
sex. In North Carolina some fifty ladies signed the pro-revolutionary Edenton Tea
Party Declaration and showed a patriotic zeal that John Wheeler, the historian,
said was even greater than their men's. Wheeler lauded the nurses and women who
farmed to provide for their families and, like Foote, honored women who exhorted
their men to die rather than live as slaves.[29]

Mrs. Henry Rowe Schoolcraft, recalling the heroism of southern women in the
Revolution, confidently predicted that if war followed secession, "The daughters of
the South will develop the same chivalrous love of justice and nobility of purpose."
The Augusta *Daily Constitutionalist,* which had supported Steven A. Douglas in
1860, announced: "We appeal to the women of the land. If they would keep our
fair South free from the curse of negro equality; would keep forever the slave in the
kitchen and the cabin, and out of the parlor." This blatant appeal to women's Negrophobia culminated in a challenge to rouse husbands, sons, and brothers by a gift
of "a blue rosette, a smile, and a ticket to – VOTE FOR SECESSION."[30]

Consider the responses of Keziah Brevard of Tennessee, Lucy Wood of Virginia,
Malinda Ray of North Carolina, and Sarah Lois Wadley of Mississippi. In 1860 a
tremulous Keziah Brevard prayed for peace and reconciliation, although two weeks
earlier she had written, "It is time for us to show the rabble of the North we are

[28] W. H. Russell, Mar. 12, 1861, in Martin Crawford, ed., *William Howard Russell's Civil War: Private Diary and Letters, 1861–1862* (Athens, GA, 1992), 11; Louis Moreau Gottschalk, *Notes of a Pianist,* ed. James Behrend (New York, 1964 [1881]), 205–6; "An Englishman in South Carolina," in Eugene L. Schwaab and Jacqueline Bull, eds., *Travels in the Old South: Selections from the Periodicals of the Times,* 2 vols. (Lexington, KY, 1973), 2:563–4; Roy Franklin Nichols, *The Disruption of American Democracy* (New York, 1948), 291, 305, 334–5; [Sallie B. Putnam], *Richmond during the War; Four Years of Personal Observation. By a Richmond Lady* (New York, 1867), 17.

[29] *Magnolia,* 4 (Apr. 1842), 249; William Henry Foote, *Sketches of North Carolina, Historical and Bio-graphical, Illlustrative of the Principles of a Portion of Her Early Settlers* (New York, 1846), 510–11; DNCB, 2:44; John Hill Wheeler, *Historical Sketches of North Carolina from 1584 to 1851,* 2 vols. (Baltimore, 1964 [1851]), 2:90, 152, 408.

[30] *Plantation Life: The Narratives of Mrs. Henry Schoolcraft* (New York, 1969 [1860]), 145, also, 458–9 and ch. 7; Augusta *Daily Constitutionalist,* Jan. 1, 1861. Secessionists also called upon woman's "superior intuition" to advance their cause. In the aftermath of John Brown's raid, the *Gazette* of Lexington, Virginia, declared southern women's support for secession a "historical fact." From the beginning of the sectional struggle women had intuitively grasped "the propriety of the measure long before the dull and slated brain of man could perceive and respond to the necessity": quoted in Henry Boley, *Lexington in Old Virginia* (Richmond, VA, 1936), 88. On southern women's support for slav-ery and their Negrophobia see Elizabeth Fox-Genovese, *Within the Plantation Household: Black and White Women of the Old South* (Chapel Hill, NC, 1988).

not to be murdered in cold blood because we own slaves." Before Southerners freed "such a multitude of half barbarians, they would give up their lives." In October 1860 Lucy Wood wrote Waddy Butler of Florida, her fiancé, that she "was very much interested" in John Bell, presidential candidate of the Constitutional Union party. "As the ladies have been exhorted to exert their influence with the Gentlemen, for him, you must excuse me for attempting it in an indirect manner." Butler, alas, was a Democrat, and as Florida prepared to secede, he needled his unionist fiancée: "I heard of an old lady, living on this island, who said she would first send her sons to fight the Yankees and when they were killed she would go herself." By January 1861, Lucy's unionism was crumbling, notwithstanding her anger at "the extremely revolting" proposal to reopen the African slave trade. "I have no political opinion, and have a peculiar dislike to all females who discuss such matters." Yet by April, Lucy had become a militant secessionist. "We are expecting a dispatch every moment, stating that Virginia has left at last this inglorious, disagreeable Union." She lowered the Union flag "with my own hands." In August she met Mr. Strong, "a handsome young Gentleman," but, since he had not yet joined the army, "I, of course, cannot like him very much." In December reports of the surrender of 7,000 troops in Tennessee caused "blushes." Such cowardice! Such disgrace! And women, prevented from fighting, must bear it.[31]

So, too, in Fayetteville in 1860, Malinda Ray cheered Bell's unionist campaign. In January 1861 Ray and her fellow teen-age academy students begged for and got time off to watch the boys' military drill at the arsenal. In March she attended a southern-rights meeting and cheered the fall of Fort Sumter. A month later she was pleased to see a unionist speaker howled down at another meeting. When Lincoln called for troops, she said, "As N. C. can never fight against her Sister states she will leave the Union as soon as the Legislature is called," and on the eve of secession she thrilled to the lowering of the Union flag: "No one can imagine how glad I was when I saw it descending the staff." Later, she commented, "I think now that the Congress has done nothing. They had better go to fighting & then it will be over all the sooner. And that I am so anxious for a fight & perhaps my only brother killed for I know one cannot always have Bethel Church battles. Yet I think that will be the only thing that would make the North yield." A battle at Manassas "might do some good."[32]

Sarah Lois Wadley, in her teens, shared the unionism of Lucy Wood and Malinda Ray, as she noted the "great excitement" in 1860 over the coming election: "God grant that it may not be the cause of the breaking up our glorious Union." Yet she considered the Union already rent by an abolitionist fanaticism that fanned dissension and insurrection: "Better far for us would be civil war than this dreadful incubus which hangs over us now, this continued wrangling and bitter malediction

---

[31] Brevard Diary, Oct. 12, 23, Dec. 1, 1860, at UNC-SHC. In the L. W. Butler Papers, at UNC-SHC, see Lucy Wood to Waddy Butler, Oct. 12, 1860, Jan. 21, 1861, Apr. 16, 1861, Aug. 6, 1861; Waddy Butler to Lucy Wood, Dec. 14, 1860; and Lucy Wood (Butler) Diary, Feb. 27, 1862.

[32] Malinda B. Ray Diary, Nov. 5, 1860, Jan. 27, Mar. 15, Apr. 17, 22, May 22, July 13, 1861, in David A. Ray Papers, at UNC-SHC.

with which we are persecuted." A would-be suitor, who irritated her by writing with undue familiarity, enraged her by finding war preparations in Columbia,
South Carolina, amusing. How could he be so utterly devoid of patriotism to treat
grave matters with levity? How dare he insult her by such behavior? In April the
news arrived from Fort Sumter: "Oh! rather every man, woman, and child perish upon the soil that gave them birth and from which they draw their sustenance
rather than call down the curses of our free Forefathers upon the degenerate race
who could stoop to ask admittance again into a Union of name when there is hatred and treachery in the hearts of those with whom we have been united." While
in Amite, Louisiana, Sarah Wadley pondered "a woman's lot to wait and pray" and
wished she were a man. "But I am not; my spirit often makes me chafe at the reg-
ulations which it is right a woman should submit to, and I will not encourage it
by giving way to vain wishes and vauntings 'if I were a man.'" In March 1862, depressed over the fall of Fort Donelson, she wished only that Confederate troops
fight bravely, for "submission," the great horror, meant disgrace and bitter death.[33]

When the South seceded, northern threats of war met scorn and defiance from
southern women who worried that their men would temporize. "I have fears,"
wrote a lady from South Carolina. "Some of the men sent to the [secession] convention have twice backed out .... They have twice put the State in a ridiculous
position." From Montgomery, Thomas Cobb kept his wife Marion abreast of the
political infighting at the launching of the Confederacy and the militancy of the
ladies, who were excluded from the galleries during the convention's closed sessions
and responded with outrage. Bishop Stephen Elliott's wife expected her sons to
defend their state, although, as a mother, she feared for them. Hester, her impetuous daughter, worried that Georgia would not secede – in which case she planned
to move to South Carolina. "Do they think," wrote an indignant Susan Cornwall
of Georgia, "that we are as degraded as our slaves, to be whipped into obedience
at the command of our self-styled masters?" Kate Carney uttered a "Hurrah for
Tennessee" when it refused to acquiesce in Lincoln's call for troops: "If she will
now secede, I will no longer be ashamed of her." A few weeks later "the men of
Tennessee" won her heart "for turning out so bravely in defense of their home."[34]

The South had fiercely stalwart unionist women, as well. During the War, unladylike outbursts that called for violent retribution came from pro-Union and pro-
Confederate women alike. In Virginia, Mary Payne of Culpeper County, a hotel
owner, blamed fire-eating politicians for a secession she "violently opposed." Susan
Hall, Sarah Shaw, and their tenant-farmer husbands dreaded "a Negro war" and
saw no reason to leave the Union over slavery. In Tennessee unionist women read,

[33] Sarad Lois Wadley Private Journal, Oct. 26, Dec. 19, 1860, Apr. 21, 1861, Mar. 2, 1862, at UNC-SHC.

[34] Unidentified lady to Caroline Elliott, quoted in Robert Nicholas Olsberg, "A Government of Class
and Race: William H. Trescot and the South Carolina Chivalry, 1860–1865" (Ph.D. diss., University of South Carolina, 1972), 245; A. L. Hull, ed., "The Correspondence of Thomas Reade Roots
Cobb, 1860–1862," *Publications of the Southern Historical Association,* 11 (1907), 147–56, 161–3,
164, 171–2; Virgil Sims Davis, "Stephen Elliott: A Southern Bishop in Peace and War" (Ph.D. diss.,
University of Georgia, 1964), 182–3; Susan Cornwall Diary, Jan. 31, 1861, at UNC-SHC; Carney
Diary, Apr. 18 and May 3, 1861, also Mar. 21 and 25, 1861.

discussed, and cheered the speeches of such Yankee favorites as Edward Everett. Marcus Woodcock, a Southerner who fought for the Union, loved the unionist ladies of Tennessee for "making numerous little speeches of encouragement to us to follow the ruthless enemy and subjugate or exterminate him." And having studied the correspondence of Union troops with their families, Bell I. Wiley concluded, "The women were the most spirited of patriots." Women's militancy sometimes drew gentle rebukes from their men. N. J. Brooks of Georgia reported to his family on the carnage in Virginia in 1862, commenting that war was no way to settle political disputes: "Men love to fight too well ever to need the example and persuasion of women to excite them to war." Not that southern women outdid northern in warlike stridency.[35]

Confederate troops protected the rights as well as the persons of their women. "It is to perpetuate the liberties and honors you proudly enjoy," Ira Woodruff wrote his cousin Mattie, "that I leave the bosom of my friends and especially those who lie near to my heart." Edwin Bass of Georgia rebuked his mother and sister, who had urged him not to rush to service: "Your interests and rights, my Mother and Sister must [be] defended and fought for too .... Your liberties and rights are dear and sweet to you. Who shall fight to defend them if not your own sons and brothers?" Southern gentlemen had to quail before an outburst like Georgia King's to her brother Tip. Writing from Milledgeville, Georgia, where the state legislature was meeting, she exploded, "All the women are RIGHT – but it is strange to say, there are MANY MEN quite willing to be ruled by the Yankee and the nigger! – I suppose you see that New York has passed the law for UNIVERSAL SUFFRAGE – ALL the niggers!" And then there was the young man under pressure to join the Confederate army on the eve of his marriage to a Charleston belle. She replied delicately to a gentleman who teasingly asked if she would not like to keep him home for awhile: "If he had not promptly volunteered for the defense of our State, he never could have entered this house; and, indeed, he could not have had access to

---

[35] Daniel E. Sutherland, *Seasons of War: The Ordeal of a Confederate Community, 1861–1865* (New York, 1995), 35–6; Elizabeth Maney Bowman to Susan Maney Boddie, Dec. 19, 1859, in Joan E. Cashin, ed., *Our Common Affairs: Texts from Women of the Old South* (Baltimore, 1996), 161, and for the diverse political views of women (especially the unionists) and their reactions to secession see 209–301; Kenneth W. Noe, ed., *A Southern Boy in Blue: The Memoir of Marcus Woodcock, 9th Kentucky Infantry (U.S.A.)* (Knoxville, TN, 1996), 98; Ira Woodruff to Cousin Mattie, Nov. 6, 1861, and Edwin Bass to His Sister, Apr. 22, 1861, in Mills Lane, ed., *"Dear Mother: Don't Grieve about Me. If I Get Killed, I'll Only Be Dead"* (Savannah, GA, 1990), 4–6, 82; N. J. Brooks to His Family, July 14, 1862, loc. cit., 161.

The women of the upper South split over the War, but those who supported the Confederacy developed a reputation for intransigence: see Cynthia DeHaven Pitcock and Bill J. Hurley, eds., *I Acted from Principle: The Civil War Diary of Dr. William M. McPheeters, Confederate Surgeon in the Trans-Mississippi* (Fayetteville, AR, 2002), 46–8; William G. Brownlow, *Sketches of the Rise, Progress, and Decline of Secession, with a Narrative of Personal Adventures among the Rebels* (Philadelphia, 1862), 384; Bart Rhett Talbert, *Maryland: The South's First Casualty* (Berryville, VA, 1995), 63. For the secessionist militancy of women in divided families see L. Minor Blackford, ed., "The Great John B. Minor and His Cousin Mary Face the War: Correspondence," *Virginia Magazine of History and Biography*, 61 (1953), 439–49; Bell I. Wiley, *The Life of Billy Yank: The Common Soldier of the Union* (Baton Rouge, LA, 1978), 18–19.

any parlor in the city again. No woman of Carolina would for a moment tolerate
a coward." John B. Lamar of Georgia, brother-in-law of the old unionist Howell
Cobb, received a letter from his niece, 10-year-old Mary Ann Lamar Cobb. She
expected war and announced that she would fight if she could: "I think if Southern men have any bravery in them, they will fight, and I think if they do fight they
will gain the victory, for the right is on their side." Sallie Law of North Carolina,
who devoted her life to charitable causes, regretted having "only one son to lend to
the Confederate Armies." Ladies who spoke up for the Union did not have an easy
time, even in their own families. Adele Petigru got rough with Mrs. Joseph Hunter,
suggesting it was time for people like the Hunters to move north.[36]

The fall of Fort Sumter overwhelmed Mary Gaillard of Charleston: "Then came the
flooding tide in gushing streams from my pent-up heart and I felt how good God
was. At sunrise I got up and took my Bible [and read] in the 12 and 13 verses of
one chapter of Nahum, 'I have afflicted thee, but thou shall be afflicted no more.
For now I will break the yoke off thee, and burst thy bonds asunder.'" From Virginia, Catherine Cooper Hopley of England reported that secessionist women were
egging their men on. Schoolgirls at the Baptist seminary in Warrenton, where Hopley taught, longed to play Confederate marching music as they waved their brothers
off to war. At the fall of Fort Sumter, Annie Maney hoped that the Yankees could
now be "exterminated."[37]

Brigadier General David Hunter Strother, a Virginian who chose the Union army,
bitterly recounted the intransigent "Rebel dames and maides" and "She-braggarts"
in Winchester. General Peter Joseph Osterhaus could not promise to refrain from
making war on women since they were the fiercest of rebels. Eliza Goodwyn, wife of
the mayor of Columbia, watched her house burn during Sherman's march, thought
of her six sons – two already dead – and lamented that she did have not six more
to offer. The ferocity with which the women upheld secession appalled Yankee soldiers. "Damn you women," shouted a soldier, "You are the ones keeping up the
war." In 1865, William C. P. Breckenridge, Confederate army officer, wrote, "The
people in parts of Georgia, Alabama & the Carolinas are ready to submit; but the
real country is the army – it and the vast majority of the women are unconquered &
unconquerable." J. L. Fremantle, an Englishman with the Confederate army, was

[36] Georgia King to Tip King, Nov. 13, 1860, in Thomas Butler King Papers, at UNC-SHC; Wallace,
History of South Carolina, 3:152; Mary Cobb quoted in Nichols, *Disruption of American Democ-
racy*, 367; DNCB, 4:29–30 (Law); Adele Petigru Allston to Mrs. Joseph Hunter, May 15, 1861, in
J. H. Easterby, ed., *The South Carolina Rice Plantation, as Revealed in the Papers of F. W. Allston*
(Chicago, 1945), 176.

[37] Gaillard quoted in James Oscar Farmer, Jr., *The Metaphysical Confederacy: James Henley Thornwell and the Synthesis of Southern Values* (Macon, GA, 1986), 285; Catherine Cooper Hopley, *Life in
the South from the Commencement of the War*, 2 vols. (New York, 1971 [1863]), 1:258, 268–9, 281–5,
326, 2:104; Charles Royster, *The Destructive War: William Tecumsah Sherman, Stonewall Jackson,
and the Americans* (New York, 1991), 22, 35, 37, 86–7, 187. On the bloody-minded hatred of Yankees among the women of Louisiana see Charles P. Roland, *Louisiana Sugar Plantations during the
Civil War* (Baton Rouge, LA, 1997 [1957]), 123–4.

convinced that women reacted to the Yankees more violently than their men – more violently "than it is possible for a European to conceive."[38]

General Albert Sydney Johnston addressed his troops in 1862: "The eyes and hopes of eight millions of people rest upon you; and you are expected to show yourselves worthy of your lineage, worthy of the women of the South, whose noble devotion in this war has never been exceeded." The religious press, condemning desertion, called on women to keep their men in the army. In the pulpit the Presbyterian Reverend J. W. Tucker of Fayetteville, North Carolina, asked women to stiffen their men's willingness to fight, and Confederate troops relied on wives behind Yankee lines to maintain morale. Years later, John Sharp Williams asked an old veteran to explain the dogged resistance of Mississippi's troops: "Oh, God, John, everybody knew we were whipped." Why did you continue? "We were afraid to stop." Afraid of what? "Afraid of the women at home, John. They would have been ashamed of us."[39]

Although Julia Le Grand had little use for Jefferson Davis, she proudly noted that he complimented the women of Vicksburg for preferring ceaseless Yankee shelling to submission. There and everywhere, women uttered the Spartan cry: Come back victorious or dead. The ladies had a long history of hardening the backbone of their men during sectional crises, with grim consequences for those southern men who fought for the Union and found themselves at sword's point with their mothers and sisters. After the War, Northerners who went south pronounced the women intransigent and less reconciled than the men.[40]

Even Natchez, a city suspected of bourgeois capitulationism, had its fierce militants. Mrs. Andrew Wilson proved so staunch that the Federals exiled her to Atlanta.

---

[38] Strother, Mar. 25, 1862, in Cecil D. Eby, Jr., ed., *A Virginia Yankee in the Civil War: The Diaries of David Hunter Strother* (Chapel Hill, NC, 1961), 21; for Osterhaus see Emilie Riley McKinley, Sept. 9, 1863, in Gordon A. Cotton, ed., *From the Pen of a She-Rebel: The Civil War Diary of Emilie Riley McKinley* (Columbia, SC, 2001), 48 (Riley, a transplanted Yankee, became an intransigent rebel). In Arthur J. L. Fremantle, *Three Months in the Southern States: The 1863 Diary of an English Soldier* (Edinburgh, 1863), see Diary, May 28, 1863 (140), and Postscript (308).

[39] Address of Gen. A. S. Johnston to his troops (Apr. 1862) and Williams quote in James W. Silver, ed., *Mississippi in the Confederacy: As Seen in Retrospect* (Baton Rouge, LA, 1961), 115, 182; on the religious press see Willard E. Wight, "The Churches and Confederate Cause," *Civil War History*, 6 (1960), 370; J. W. Tucker, "God's Providence in War," in David B. Chesebrough, ed., *"God Ordained This War": Sermons on the Sectional Crisis, 1830–1865* (Columbia, SC, 1991), 237; on the pleas from Confederate troops see LeGrand James Wilson, *The Confederate Soldier* (Memphis, TN, 1973 [1902]), 49–50, 66–7, 71. For a celebration of the rebel ladies of east Tennessee by a contemporary historian see William B. Hesseltine, ed., *Dr. J. G. M. Ramsey, Autobiography and Letters* (Knoxville, TN, 2002), ch. 13.

[40] Julia Le Grand Journal, excerpted in John K. Bettersworth, ed., *Mississippi in the Confederacy: As They Saw It* (Baton Rouge, LA, 1961), 2:103; Walter L. Fleming, *Civil War and Reconstruction in Alabama* (Cleveland, OH, 1905), 231; John Richard Dennett, *The South as It Is: 1865–1866* (New York, 1965 [1867]), 347. For those who joined the Union army see e.g. Carney Diary, Apr. 28, 1861; John Rozier, ed., *The Granite Farm Letters: The Civil War Correspondence of Edgeworth and Sallie Bird* (Athens, GA, 1988), 132, 143; Parke Rouse, Jr., *Cows on the Campus: Williamsburg in Bygone Days* (Richmond, VA, 1973), 59–60. For the defection of Southerners to the Union army see Richard Nelson Current, *Lincoln's Loyalists: Union Soldiers in the Confederacy* (Boston, 1992), 4, 47, 48, 66–7, 84–5.

A woman with the pseudonym "Gamma" published a poem in the Natchez *Courier* in 1862:

> My Love a slave? A coward's thought and creed!
> Far better, Love, to weep above thy grave.
> Go! arm thyself, and join the strong fight!
> There is no wrong a freeman may not right.
> Swear! swear! that on thy native hills, God-given,
> Thou'lt tread them as a master, and wilt never
> Surrender them to slaves! 'Tis writ in heaven:
> "The South IS free and SHALL BE FREE forever."[41]

Julia Fisher, who did outstanding work in creating a Ladies Aid Society to relieve southern hospitals, wrote in 1862, "I should feel that my life and labors were well paid for, if only I live long enough to know that our liberty was won.... I am willing to suffer and die if it can only aid a cause of far more importance ... your country is next to your God: in my heart they seem connected." A year later she rebuked her unionist brother, declaring her "hatred" and "contempt" for the Yankees: "I would choose poverty and suffering with the South: It has become part of my religion." The wartime diaries of Mary Chesnut, Emma Holmes, and Catherine Edmonston – to mention only the most famous – demonstrate considerable knowledge, acute judgments, and passionate concern with military as well as political affairs.[42]

Grady McWhiney, biographer of General Braxton Bragg, writes, "He made the mistake of following the advice of his wife. Her views were often based on whim or rumor, but she constantly instructed him." Eliza ("Elise") Bragg, a spirited plantation mistress and kin to several great planter families of Louisiana and South Carolina, offered her husband solicitous counsel: "Dear husband, please do not trust the Tennessee troops. Put the Tennesseans where your batteries can fire upon them if they attempt to run. Lead them into action yourself and shame them into fighting." (Elise Bragg preferred the troops from Mississippi and Louisiana.) When General Bragg scored a tactical victory, she grumbled, "You have, it is true, made a very rapid march but without defeating your wary foe .... I have a high opinion of Gen. Buell's abilities, & feel that he has drawn you into a very precarious position." She proposed countermeasures. Much less presumptuous women confused their husbands by demanding military as well as political news. "I have written you a great deal about your *esposo*, and how much he loves you," Stonewall Jackson wrote his wife. "What do you want with military news?"[43]

[41] Theodora Britton Marshall and Gladys Crail Evans, *They Found It in Natchez* (New Orleans, 1939), 184; Bettersworth, ed., *Mississippi in the Confederacy*, 76.

[42] Julia Fisher to Rebecca Bryant, May, 25, 1862, and Julia Fisher to James W. Bryant, Mar. 1, 1863, in Arch Frederic Blakely et al., eds., *Rose Cottage Chronicles: Civil War Letters of the Bryant–Stephens Families of North Florida* (Gainseville, FL, 1998), 118, 209.

[43] Grady McWhiney, *Braxton Bragg and Confederate Defeat* (New York, 1969), 217, 324–5; John Bowers, *Stonewall: Portrait of a Soldier* (New York, 1989), 118.

When Jefferson Davis proposed in 1864 to recruit blacks into the Confederate army, Catherine Edmonston of North Carolina raged at "that silly Congress" for considering recruitment of black troops and for promising freedom to those who enlisted. "Can one credit it?" She went to the heart of the ideological impasse: "We give up a principle when we offer emancipation as a reward or a boon, for we have hitherto contended that slavery was Cuffee's normal condition, the very best position he could occupy."[44]

As the War dragged on, women, like men, displayed war-weariness. Some wondered if it was all worthwhile. More impressive – astounding – was their dogged determination to continue. In Virginia 28 women petitioned Confederate Secretary of War James Seddon to let them raise a female regiment to repel the Yankees who were bloodying their countryside. If women were permitted to fight, Sarah Morgan complained, they would set an example for the men. Sally Bradford kept her husband out of the army to take care of their plantation and two dozen slaves, but twitted him: "The place for a man is on the field. Just give me a chance to fight! Just give me a chance to fight and see where I'll be!" In 1863 William Corsan, an English businessman, reported the outburst of "a pretty Creole lady" who wanted to trample and spit upon the dead bodies of the hated Yankees: "If the men had half the spunk which the women have, New Orleans would be ours again." Elsewhere Corsan heard complaints that the young women gave no peace to men not in the army.[45]

Like Ellen House, who dearly loved her brothers, other women announced they would rather have their husbands, sons, and brothers die in battle than fail in their duty. Sarah Morgan had brothers she considered the soul of bravery: "I would despise them if they shrunk back." Mary Chesnut announced that, were she a man, she would emulate Lord Nelson's "Victory or Westminster Abbey." Judith McGuire quoted a woman who feared for the life of her wounded husband but nonetheless wanted him to continue to fight for his country and not "to stand back, like some women's husbands." The women of the South, wrote Phoebe Yates Pember, who performed heroically at Chimborazo hospital in Richmond, were "openly

---

[44] Nov. 20 and Dec. 30, 1864, in Beth G. Crabtree and James W. Patton, eds., *"Journal of a Secesh Lady": The Diary of Catherine Devereux Edmonston, 1860–1866* (Raleigh, NC, 1979).

[45] For the argument that southern women displayed increasing hostility to the Confederate war effort see Drew Gilpin Faust, *Mothers of Invention: Women of the Slaveholding South in the American Civil War* (Chapel Hill, NC, 1996); for the petition from the ladies of Virginia see Gary W. Gallagher, *The Confederate War: Popular Will, Nationalism, and Strategy* (Cambridge, MA, 1996), 77. Sally Bradford in Myrta Lockett Avary, ed., *A Virginia Girl in the Civil War, 1861–1865. Being a Record of the Actual Experiences of a Wife of a Confederate Officer* (New York, 1903), 235–6; Charles East, ed., *The Civil War Diary of Sarah Morgan* (Athens, GA, 1991), xxiv; W. C. Corsan, *Two Months in the Confederate States: An Englishman's Travels through the South*, ed. Benjamin H. Trask (Baton Rouge, LA, 1996 [1863]), 16, 91. For the militancy of the women early in the War and expressions of wanting to fight like the men – but also for signs of eventual war weariness in many – see Stephen V. Ash, *When the Yankees Came: Conflict and Chaos in the Occupied South, 1861–1865* (Chapel Hill, NC, 1995), ch. 2. Carol Bleser, in her Series Editor's Prefaces to southern women's diaries, implicitly sides (as do we) with Gallagher against Faust on the staunchness of southern women during the War: see e.g. Bleser, in Cotton, ed., *From the Pen of a She-Rebel*, xi–xii.

and violently rebellious" before the War and, "incited their men to struggle in support of their views."[46]

Christian women were not supposed to be bloody-minded, but the Yankee invasion threw them off balance. Harriet Palmer was "very glad" to hear that Abner Doubleday had died at Fort Sumter after firing the first Union gun, "because if he had not died there he would have been hung anyhow by us." A young Virginian with a husband in the army cried, "I am sure I do not hate our enemies. I earnestly hope their souls may go to heaven, but I would like to blow all their mortal bodies away, as fast as they come upon our soil." Ellen House in Federal-occupied Tennessee, who felt "perfectly fiendish," confessed: "I would kill a Yankee and not a muscle quiver." She "hated" Yankees. The sight of a Yankee with one arm or leg made her "glad," and she only wished it upon "the whole Yankee nation." Sarah Morgan and Eliza Frances Andrews struggled not to hate the enemies Jesus had commanded them to love, but Andrews could not believe that "when Christ said, 'Love your enemies,' he meant Yankees."[47]

In 1863 Phoebe Yates Pember spent an evening with a "particularly pious" group of men and women in Richmond: "The feeling here against the Yankees exceeds anything I could imagine, particularly among good Christians." The pious ladies demanded Yankee blood. One wanted a skull to keep her toilette trinkets in. Pember, a Jew, congratulated herself for having been born into a "nation and a religion that did not enjoin forgiveness on its enemies, that enjoyed the blessed privilege of praying for an eye for an eye, and a life for a life, and was not one of those for whom Christ died in vain." The gentlemen seconded her in good-sport repartee. She did not let go: "I proposed that till the war was over they should all join the Jewish Church, let forgiveness and peace and good will alone and put their trust in the sword of the Lord and Gideon."[48]

---

[46] Mar. 13, 1863, in Daniel E. Sutherland, ed., *A Very Violent Rebel: The Civil War Diary of Ellen Renshaw House* (Knoxville, TN, 1996), 115; Randall C. Jimerson, *The Private Civil War: Popular Thought during the Sectional Conflict* (Baton Rouge, LA, 1988), 160–1; July 31, 1862, in East, ed., *Diary of Sarah Morgan*, 182; Chesnut Diary, Oct. 15, 1861, in C. Vann Woodward, ed., *Mary Chesnut's Civil War* (New Haven, CT, 1981), 217; Judith W. McGuire, Feb. 28, 1864, in Jean V. Berlin, ed., *Diary of a Southern Refugee during the War. By a Lady of Virginia* (Lincoln, NE, 1995 [1867]), 255; Phoebe Yates Pember, *A Southern Woman's Story: Life in Confederate Richmond*, ed. Bell Irwin Wiley (Macon, GA, 1959 [1879]), 24. During the War, foreign travelers credited the ladies with an especially bitter hatred of the Yankees and especially their women. Even in Union-occupied Baltimore, the pro-Union Ernest Duvergier de Hauranne – friend of the late Alexis de Tocqueville – was astonished at the firmly proslavery views of the well-to-do women he met there late in the War: R. H. Bowen, ed., *A Frenchman in Lincoln's America*, 2 vols. (Chicago, 1974), 2:481–5. Some southern women armed themselves for self-defense, and a few fought in Confederate ranks: see June 5, 1863, in Fremantle, *Three Months*, 173.

[47] Harriet Palmer Diary, Apr. 13, 1861, in Louis P. Towles, ed., *A World Turned Upside Down: The Palmers of South Santee, 1818–1881* (Columbia, SC, 1996), 294; George Cary Eggleston, *A Rebel's Recollections* (Baton Rouge, La, 1996), 84–6 and ch. 4; Feb. 26, 1864, Oct. 1865, in Sutherland, ed., *Diary of Ellen Renshaw House*, quotes at 108, for "hated" see 188; June 10, 1862, in East, ed., *Diary of Sarah Morgan*, 112; Apr. 16, 1865, in Eliza Frances Andrews, *War-Time Journal of a Georgia Girl* (New York, 1907), 149.

[48] Pember, *Southern Woman's Story*, 168. Some women admitted to being joyful at the sight of the suffering Yankees in Confederate hospitals: Ash, *When the Yankees Came*, 69–70.

Emma Holmes of the Charleston elite welcomed secession as a "revolution won-derful in the rapidity with which it has swept the country." At the end of the War she cheerfully reported that Yankee troops held rebel women responsible for their men's determination to continue a hopeless conflict. When a Yankee officer railed that the South already would have surrendered if not for its intransigent women, Cor-nelia Peake McDonald of Winchester mused that Yankees badly underestimated the tenacity of southern men. Long after the War, southern women were boast-ing of their successful efforts to spur on the troops and also plunging into literary controversies in defense of the Lost Cause and the constitutional justification for secession.[49]

No doubt many southern women held moderate political views, and for all we know – the evidence defies measurement – most may have opposed disunion even in dissent from the views of fathers and husbands. "We are alarmed from time to time about the national bonds," Rosalie Eugenia Calvert cried out in 1808 against talk of disunion. "If Madison continues the same system as Jefferson we shall be on the brink of civil war." During the nullification crisis, Sophia Hunt in Woodville, Mis-sissippi, received alarming news from her father in Columbia, South Carolina; ap-palled by the prospect of disunion, she lashed out, "May heaven avert such an awful event – as must ensue; unless the minds of the rulers be changed." In 1851, Mar-ion Henry of Tennessee wrote her husband Gustavus that she had been reading the speeches of Daniel Webster, "a great man." She contemplated great danger for the Union when Webster and Henry Clay died: "There are thousands of hot-headed men hearing such things from men of influence who will rush madly on to destruction and involve us all in one common ruin." She prayed that God would thwart them.[50]

In *Ghosts of the Confederacy*, Gaines Foster warns against exaggeration of the militancy of Confederate women, for both northern and southern men enjoyed and may have heightened the image of the southern woman as the most intransigent of Confederates. Strong-minded women like Julia Gilmer's mother-in-law read widely on political matters, refused to be stampeded by extremists, and prided themselves on making up their own minds. Some rallied to the unionists. "I won't put up a sou for the success of this [independence] movement," Carolina Pettigrew Carlson of South Carolina wrote in 1860, viewing secessionism as an attempted coup by ex-tremists like Representative Lawrence Keitt. She found the prospect of being deliv-ered into their hands "horrible and grotesque." Several years earlier she had warmly approved a pamphlet by her brother James Johnston Pettigrew against reopening of the African slave trade and read it aloud to a neighboring small planter. In Virginia, Fannie Page Hume deplored "a real disunionist speech" in late December 1860 and

[49] Feb. 13, 1861, and Mar. 4, 1865, in John F. Marszalek, ed., *The Diary of Miss Emma Holmes* (Baton Rouge, LA, 1979), 1, 402; Cornelia Peake McDonald, Apr. 27, 1863, in Minrose C. Gwin, ed., *A Woman's Civil War: A Diary, with Reminiscences of the War from March 1862* (Madison, WI, 1992 [1875]), 126; Rose Harlow Warren, *A Southern Home in War Times* (New York, 1914), 75. On the literary efforts see Sarah E. Gardner, *Blood and Irony: Southern White Women's Narratives of the Civil War, 1861–1937* (Chapel Hill, NC, 2004).

[50] Rosalie Eugenia Calvert, quoted in Everson, *Calvert,* 31; Sophia Hunt to Dr. John Hughes, Nov. 4, 1832, in Hughes Papers, at Mississippi Department of Archives and History (Jackson); Marion Henry to Gustavus Henry, Jan. 4, 1851, in Henry Papers.

spent several days poring over the newspaper accounts of "conservative" speeches by politicians more to her taste. Rejecting radicals of both sides, she walked out of the Senate gallery in the middle of a speech by William Seward that she deemed "not worth listening to," but she also expressed disgust at a "violent and abusive" public letter by southern radicals. She prayed for the Union. In Richmond in 1861, when the crisis descended, unionist women crowned John Baldwin, a politician from western Virginia, with a wreath of roses for his speech against secession.[51]

Examples of the political moderation of southern women could be multiplied; indeed, for all we know, unionist women outnumbered secessionist. But the secessionists spoke more loudly and resolutely, and although the ladies could strengthen the resolve of unionist male kin, they could less easily moderate the views of radical kin. As presumed nurturing, pacific, timid creatures, they acted as expected in taking moderate stands. Acting true to form they could be patted on the head and reminded that big, strong men had to make the hard decisions for militant action and for war. Still, radical women sometimes only seemed more militant than husbands, whose political alliances compelled prudence. John Pendleton Kennedy, a unionist, recoiled from the secessionism of the South Carolinians he encountered at White Sulphur Springs in 1851. He found David McCord more moderate than most but heard that his wife, Louisa, was anything but. Yet the McCords shared the same political outlook. In any case, southern women and men shifted from unionism to secessionism in a flash as the crisis deepened and some new northern assault on southern rights came to light.[52]

Radical women found themselves in a more favorable position than their moderate sisters – ironically, because of the same persistent stereotype. For if nurturing creatures could take no more Yankee insolence and demanded – or conveyed their feelings through withering silence – a counterattack against assaults on southern honor and manhood, what man could fail to act? In Richmond a Jewish shopkeeper told his usually "nervous" and timid wife that Virginia had seceded, only to hear, "Goodness knows it is time." Did the radicals outnumber the moderates among the southern ladies? How could we possibly know? How do we place innumerable women like the middle-class Mary Jeffreys Bethell of North Carolina or the aristocratic Meta Morris Grimball of South Carolina, who preferred peace and moderation but who slowly abandoned faith in northern intentions? The number of moderates and radicals matters much less than meets the eye, for the intensity lay with the extremists, as it usually does.[53]

---

[51] Gaines M. Foster, *Ghosts of the Confederacy: Defeat, the Lost Cause, and the Emergence of the New South* (New York, 1987), 29–30; J. A. Gilmer Diary, Sept. 1861; Clyde N. Wilson, *Carolina Cavalier: The Life and Mind of James Johnston Pettigrew* (Athens, GA, 1900), 130; Hume Diary, Feb. 29, Aug. 22, Nov. 6, 29, Dec. 4, 5, 1860; Alexander F. Robertson, *Alexander Hugh Holmes Stuart, 1807–1891* (Richmond, VA, 1925), xvii (Baldwin later signed Virginia's Ordinance of Secession).

[52] Richard Lounsbury, ed., *Louisa S. McCord: Poems, Drama, Biography, Letters* (Charlottesville, VA, 1996), 8 n. 16.

[53] Herbert T. Ezekiel and Gaston Lichtenstein, *The History of the Jews of Richmond from 1769 to 1917* (Richmond, VA, 1917), 148; also, Virginius Dabney, *Richmond: The Story of a City* (Garden City, NY, 1976), 161; Bethell Diary, Apr. 29, 1861, at UNC-SHC; M. M. Grimball Diary, Apr. 14, 15, 22, 1861, at UNC-SHC.

Prevalent male notions of honor and aggressive masculinity positioned politically radical women to pressure their men in a way and to an extent moderates never could. They held their men's feet to the fire, demanding actions in accordance with professed standards of honor and manhood. Self-critical southern men had long complained about their inability to act together as a people – to do as a people what men readily did as individuals when under threat or insult. By 1860 the women of the South had gone a long way toward compelling their men to overcome that self-proclaimed disability.

PART FOUR

A CHRISTIAN PEOPLE DEFEND THE FAITH

If our principles are true, the world must come to them .... It is not the narrow question of Abolitionism or Slavery – not simply whether we shall emancipate our Negroes or not; the real question is the relations of man to society, of States to the individual, and of the individual to States – a question as broad as the interests of the human race .... The parties in this conflict are not merely Abolitionists and Slaveholders; they are Atheists, Socialists, Communists, Red Republicans, Jacobins on the one side, and the friends of order and regulated freedom on the other.

—James Henley Thornwell

13

A Christian People

[Southerners] have progressed as far in civilization, and in many respects, much farther than any people in the whole country. A very large portion of them are confessedly pious, as well as intelligent. Taken as a whole, they are eminently entitled to be regarded a religious people as any other people on the face of the globe.

—William A. Smith (1856)[1]

Charlestonians had a "fashionable but shameful vice," so the intellectual Eliza Lucas Pinckney, probably America's first agriculturalist with claims to greatness, mused in 1741: They ridiculed religion, "pretending" to disbelief. In the late 1760s, James Iredell of North Carolina, a future U.S. Supreme Court justice, penned a scathing indictment of the supercilious wealthy coastal planters who considered religious people "morose," "unreflecting," and "unsocial" or "unsound." In the 1820s Margaret Hunter Hall, British aristocrat, found wealthy residents of Charleston, Columbia, and Savannah still indifferent to religion, and as late as 1839 the Reverend Moses Drury Hoge protested French infidelity among the Virginia gentry.[2]

But by 1836, President Thomas Roderick Dew of the College of William and Mary announced that "the enlightened portion of the world" considered infidelity a sign of weak mind or heart: "The argument is now closed forever, and he who now obtrudes on the social circle his infidel notions, manifests the arrogance of a literary coxcomb, or that want of refinement which distinguishes the polished gentleman." In the 1850s and 1860s, Bishops William Meade of Virginia and Stephen

---

[1] William A. Smith, *Lectures on the Philosophy and Practice of Slavery* (New York, 1969 [1856]), 189.

[2] Pinckney quoted in James Turner, *Without God, Without Creed: The Origin of Unbelief in America* (Baltimore, 1985), 53; "Essay on Religion," in Don Higginbotham, ed., *The Papers of James Iredell*, 2 vols. (Raleigh, NC, 1976), 1:8–11, quote at 9; see also Iredell's subsequent "Essay on Religion" (1769), 1:36–9; Una Pope-Hennessey, ed., *The Aristocratic Journey: Being the Outspoken Letters of Mrs. Basil Hall Written during a Fourteen Months' Sojourn in America, 1827–1828* (New York, 1931), 230; Peyton Harrison Hoge, *Moses Drury Hoge: Life and Letters* (Richmond, VA, 1899), 80; also George Chalmers, "Political Annals of the Province of Carolina," in B. R. Carroll, ed., *Historical Collections of South Carolina*, 2 vols. (New York, 1836), 2:291–2; Eugene M. Sirmans, *Colonial South Carolina: A Political History* (Chapel Hill, NC, 1966), 71, 99–100, 231–2, 254–5.

Elliott of Georgia exulted in the decline of infidelity and the advance of evangelicalism. Dew, Meade, and Elliott claimed victory in a long, hard-fought struggle that
had begun with the great religious revival at Cane Ridge in 1801.[3]

A resurgent Christianity was doing battle against the Deism that had arisen in
the seventeenth century, rejecting Revelation and seeking God in nature. Thomas
Paine's deistic *Age of Reason* had pervaded southern and northern colleges alike.
Young rebels found in it an ideal way to taunt parents, although after graduation
from college most settled into churches. Southern Deists did not match northern
in founding organizations, producing journals like *Temple of Reason,* or writing books like Ethan Allen's anticlerical *The Only Oracle of Man* (1784). The
churches, North and South, may have exaggerated the danger in order to promote
their revivals. New Jersey's Philip Freneau, the widely acclaimed poet of the Revolution, charged that *Age of Reason* would have remained largely unread if not
for the hysterical opposition, and in Virginia it was said that more people were
reading *Age of Reason* than the Bible. Deism and skepticism, although waning,
remained influential until about 1830. Deism attracted some prominent Virginians – notably, Thomas Jefferson and St. George Tucker – but its prevalence among
planters, if ever it existed, did not last long. David Ramsay doubted Deism's hold
in South Carolina over more than a few prominent planters and merchants. Toussaint L'Ouverture in Saint Domingue and Gabriel Prosser in Virginia did wonders
for religious orthodoxy.[4]

During the boyhood of Charles Fraser, Charleston's eminent artist, the men of
the Revolution had still held sway in Charleston. A rough lot – jovial, warm, hospitable – they had little regard for religion, told smutty stories, drank to excess,
and frequented races and cockfights. They spent the Sabbath at home, riding and
hunting in "noisy relaxation." Church was for women. Not until the great revivals of the 1830s did most men keep the Sabbath and condemn immorality, even
if they continued to fall into it. By 1850 the celebrated poet William J. Grayson reported that, although gaiety remained, religion and sobriety now shaped everyday
life. Charlestonians kept Lent. Churches more than doubled, and Bible societies
and Sabbath schools flourished. Georgia and the states to the west went through a

---

[3] Thomas Roderick Dew, "Address to the Students of William and Mary," *SLM*, 2 (1836), 768; William
Meade, *Old Churches, Ministries, and Families of Virginia*, 2 vols. (Berryssville, VA, 1978 [1857]),
1:25–6, 399; "Sixteenth Sermon" (1866), in *Sermons by the Right Reverend Stephen Elliott, D.D.,
Late Bishop of Georgia, with a Memoir by Thomas Hanckel, Esq.* (New York, 1867), 165.

[4] A. C. McGiffert, *Protestant Thought before Kant* (Gloucester, MA, 1971), 212–16; Kenneth Scott
Latourette, *Christianity in a Revolutionary Age*, 5 vols. (Grand Rapids, MI, 1958), 1:31–3; for the
campuses see Daniel Walker Howe, *The Unitarian Conscience: Harvard Moral Philosophy, 1805–
1861* (Middletown, CT, 1988), 84; Clement Eaton, *The Freedom-of-Thought Struggle in the Old
South* (New York, 1964), 14–17; Sydney E. Ahlstrom, *A Religious History of the American People*
(New Haven, CT, 1972), 366–8; [Rev.] John Taylor, *Baptists on the Frontier. A History of the Bap-
tist Churches of Which the Author Has Been Alternately a Member,* ed. Christopher Raymond Young
(Macon, GA, 1995), 113–14; on Freneau and the reaction see E. Brooks Holifield, *The Gentlemen
Theologians: American Theology in Southern Culture, 1795–1860* (Durham, NC, 1978), 51–3, and
Henry F. May, *The Enlightenment in America* (New York, 1976), 38, 71–2, 135–7, 327. For the course
of Deism in the South, see Supplementary References: "Deism."

similar metamorphosis. In the late eighteenth century Jesse Lee, the great Methodist evangelist, declared the people of Georgia "ungovernable." St. Mary's, while good for cattle, was "a poor place for piety and morality." By 1807 Lee found Hancock County much improved, thanks in part to the Baptists and a great camp meeting of 3,000 to 4,500 sober and orderly people, rich and poor, white and black. In the 1820s wives converted husbands; churches sprang up; and frontier violence, gambling, and drinking diminished markedly. By the 1850s, with new revivals, churches flourished in frontier counties.[5]

William Wells Brown, a Kentucky-born slave who had escaped from his master (his white father), considered the slaveholders' version of Christianity a massive self-deception. Even so, "A more praying, preaching, psalm-singing people, cannot be found than the slaveholders at the South." Europeans, marveling at Americans' everyday religious conversation and zealous disputation over church doctrine and polity, wondered that professed Christians could own slaves. Northern abolitionists called slaveholders heathens and hypocrites, citing the small number of southern church members and buildings as proof that slavery dulled religious and moral sensibilities. In influential travelogues of the 1850s, Frederick Law Olmsted – antislavery journalist and architect, most notably of New York's Central Park – announced that he had found fewer church buildings and estimated that Northerners spent three times as much on their church buildings. The Reverend Thornton Stringfellow replied that in 1850 the Southeast had proportionately more church buildings per worshipers than the Northeast.[6]

Numbers games resolved little, and the argument shifted to the quality of the buildings. Emily Burke, a Northerner, scoffed at the rural South's rough log buildings that "the people in the country are obliged to call a church." Burke saw only barns: "a frame covered slightly with boards," with "neither bell, cupola, or glass windows." Virginia's leading clergymen sadly told similar stories. As the churches

[5] Charles Fraser, *Reminiscences of Charleston* (Charleston, SC, 1969 [1854]), 64–6; Richard J. Calhoun, ed., *Witness to Sorrow: The Antebellum Autobiography of William J. Grayson* (Columbia, SC, 1990), ch. 3; Eola Willis, *The Charleston Stage in the XVIIIth Century: With Social Settings of the Times* (Columbia, SC, 1924), 168. See also Robert E. Brunhouse, ed., "David Ramsay, 1749–1815: Selections from His Writings," *American Philosophical Society*, n.s., 55, pt. 4 (1965), 173; Anne Sinkler Whaley LeClerq, ed., *Between North and South: The Letters of Emily Wharton Sinkler, 1842–1865* (Columbia, SC, 2001), 17 (James Hervey Greenlee, a devout small slaveholder from North Carolina, visited Charleston in the 1850s and reported in the same vein as Grayson: Diary, May 22–23, 1852, Apr. 11, 1858, at UNC-SHC); Jesse Lee to the editor of *Farmer's Gazette* of Athens, Georgia, Aug. 8, 1807, in Ulrich B. Phillips, ed., *Plantation and Frontier, 1649–1863*, 2 vols. (New York, 1969 [1910]), 2:284–6; Minton Thrift, *Memoir of the Rev. Jesse Lee, with Extracts from His Journals* (New York, 1969 [1823]), 232–3, 257–8, 300–6. For the trajectory of the revivals see also Supplementary References: "Revivals."

[6] *The Narrative of William Wells Brown, A Fugitive Slave* (Reading, MA, 1967 [1848]), 56; Frederick Law Olmsted, *A Journey in the Back Country* (New York, 1970 [1860]), 102; Thornton Stringfellow, "Statistical View of Slavery," in E. N. Elliott, ed., *Cotton Is King and Pro-Slavery Arguments* (New York, 1969 [1860]), 525–6. For the wretchedness of country church buildings in western Georgia and eastern Alabama see John S. C. Abbott, *South and North; Or, Impressions Received during a Trip to Cuba and the South* (New York, 1969 [1860]), 128–9. Abbott noted that what the South calls "fanaticism" the North calls "religion" (58). See Supplementary References: "Church Membership."

accommodated growing congregations by tacking sheds onto the sides of their buildings, the more barnlike the buildings seemed. Early log churches had no floors and wooden shutters and no glass for the windows. Split logs provided uncomfortable seats. Not many pulpits offered a touch of elegance.[7]

Wealthy southern towns were not famous for piety in their early days, and often the only preaching was at the courthouse or statehouse. Thomas Jefferson described Charlottesville to Thomas Cooper in 1822: "We have four sects, but without either church or meeting-house. The court-house is the common temple, one Sunday in the month to each. Here, Episcopalian and Presbyterian, Methodist and Baptist, meet together, join in hymning their Maker, listen with attention and devotion to each others' preachers, and all mix in society with perfect harmony." Throughout the South, then and long afterwards, denominations took turns at courthouse preaching. Since Richmond had no regular church buildings at the end of the eighteenth century, as late as 1815 Episcopalians and Presbyterians used the Capitol regularly, Baptist and Catholic itinerants occasionally. In the 1820s Anne Royall, the Virginia-born editor whose slashing journalism terrified Washington politicians, reported throngs at courthouse preaching in Huntsville and other towns in Alabama that still lacked church buildings. Long afterwards, Bishop Otey drew large crowds to his courthouse preaching on swings through Tennessee, and well into the nineteenth century Episcopalians, struggling against heavy competition and too weak in number to build a church, preached at the courthouse.[8]

---

[7] C. G. Parsons, *An Inside View of Slavery: A Tour among the Planters* (Savannah, GA, 1974 [1855]), 112; Abbott, *South and North*, 128; Emily P. Burke, *Reminiscences of Georgia* (Oberlin, OH, 1850), 147. Catherine Cooper Hopley, an Englishwoman, testified much as did Burke: Hopley, *Life in the South from the Commencement of the War*, 2 vols. (New York, 1971 [1863]), 1:56. So did clergymen and church groups: see Robert B. Semple, *A History of the Rise and Progress of the Baptists in Virginia* (Richmond, VA, 1894 [1810]), 198; P. H. Hoge, *Moses Drury Hoge*, 74; "Minutes of Board of Trustees, 1809–1867," Lexington First Church, M. E. C., S., Kentucky Conference, Lexington District, Papers at Duke University; Walter Brownlow Posey, *The Presbyterian Church of Old Southwest, 1778–1838* (Richmond, VA, 1952), 102; *ESB*, 1:17–20; Julia Murfree Lovelace, *A History of Siloam Baptist Church, Marion, Alabama* (Birmingham, AL, 1943), 8–9.

[8] Jefferson to Cooper, Nov. 2, 1822, *DHE*, 3:212; *DGB*, 886; Alexander G. Brown, "Methodism in Richmond, Va.," in Edward Leigh Pell, ed., *A Hundred Years of Richmond Methodism* (Richmond, VA, n.d.), 27; Samuel Mordecai, *Richmond in By-Gone Days* (Richmond, VA, 1860), 154, 157–64; also, William Hatcher, *Life of J. B. Jeter, D.D.* (Baltimore, 1887), 114; Anne Newport Royall, *Letters from Alabama, 1817–1822* (University, AL, 1969), 119, 204; Otey Diary, Sept. 21–25, 1848, and passim, at UNC-SHC; Albert M. Shipp, *The History of Methodism in South Carolina* (Nashville, TN, 1983), 406; Francis Taylor Diary, June 17, 1792, June 22, 1794, May 3 and Dec. 13, 1795, Sept. 11 and 28, 1796, at UNC-SHC; Henry Thompson Malone, *The Episcopal Church in Georgia, 1733–1957* (Atlanta, GA, 1960), 62, 70, 79; Sarah McCulloh Lemmon, *Parson Pettigrew of the "Old Church," 1744–1807* (Chapel Hill, NC, 1970), 23; for Louisiana see Hodding Carter and Betty W. Carter, *So Great a God: A History of the Episcopal Church and of Christ Church Cathedral, 1805–1955* (Sewanee, TN, 1955), 56. The churches made a feeble impression in Richmond in the 1790s, but Methodist circuit riders brought a new era. Jews had a Synagogue as early as 1789, but Baptists did not build their first church until 1800, Presbyterians and Catholics not until the second decade. See Virginius Dabney, *Richmond: The Story of a City* (Garden City, NY, 1976), 68. By 1860, Richmond had nearly forty houses of worship for eleven denominations as well as Jews and Catholics.

Schoolhouses could also provide a room for Sunday services, and sometimes a congregation preferred it to another denomination's church building. College chapels served as places of worship for the community, not the campus alone, and ordained college professors proved popular as preachers. Then too, churches made heavy use of the Masonic and Oddfellows lodges, which sprang up early in towns and even small villages. Catholics without a building of their own in Tuscaloosa and St. Augustine ignored the hierarchy and celebrated Mass in Masonic halls. As late as 1859 and 1860 in Nashville, the Oddfellows provided facilities for the Church of the Advent (Catholic) and the Episcopal Church.[9]

Scarcity and roughness did not characterize churches and courthouses everywhere. In South Carolina churches as well as courthouses were the most impressive of the public buildings, as Baptists vied with Episcopalians and Presbyterians for architectural distinction. Paul Hamilton Hayne, the celebrated poet, noted "the number and elegance of these sacred buildings" in Charleston and designated St. Michael's, the oldest, as "one of the noblest examples of ecclesiastical architecture in America, perhaps in the world!" J. S. Buckingham, among antislavery British travelers, found the Independent Presbyterian Church of Savannah, which cost $120,000 and served the planter-merchant elite, "as substantial as it is elegant." As time went on, most denominations across the South built impressive churches. In the slave-rich but cash-poor world of plantations, villages, and thinly spread

---

[9] Franklin M. Garrett, *Atlanta and Environs: A Chronicle of Its People and Events*, 3 vols. (Atlanta, GA, 1954), 1:240, 247–9, 291; James Holmes, *"Dr. Bullie's" Notes: Reminiscences of Early Georgia and of Philadelphia and New Haven in the 1800s*, ed. Delma Eugene Presley (Atlanta, GA, 1976), 201; Laura Jervey Hopkins, *History of St. John's Episcopal Church, 1858–1950: Congaree, South Carolina* (n.p., n.d.), 12; Otey Diary, Aug. 29, 1854; Francis M. Manning and W. H. Booker, *Religion and Education in Martin County, 1774–1974* (Wilmington, NC, 1974), 59–60; Massenburg Journal, Dec. 25, 1842, at UNC-SHC; E. G. Baker Diaries, May 3 and Nov. 12, 1857, Feb. 20, 1859, at UNC-SHC; Ray Holder, *William Winans: Methodist Leader in Antebellum Mississippi* (Jackson, MS, 1977), 53; Dorothy Orr, *A History of Education in Georgia* (Chapel Hill, NC, 1950), 24. For the centrality of college chapels in community religious life, see Ernest C. Hynds, *Antebellum Athens and Clarke County, Georgia* (Athens, GA, 1974), 107; R. H. Rivers, *The Life of Robert Paine, D.D., Bishop of the Methodist Church, South* (Nashville, TN, 1916), 45–6; Charles S. Sydnor, *A Gentleman of the Old Natchez Region: Benjamin L. C. Wailes* (Durham, NC, 1938), 215; Emily Caroline Douglas, "Autobiography" (ms.), 114–15, at LSU. J. Packard, "Recollections of the Old Chapel," in William A. R. Goodwin, *History of the Theological Seminary in Virginia and Its Historical Background*, 2 vols. (Rochester, NY, 1923), 1:344. Frank M. Braly to Amanda Braly, Oct. 3, 1853, in Braly Family Papers, at University of Arkansas (Fayetteville). On the lodges see Herschel Gower et al., eds., *Pen and Sword: The Life and Journals of Randal W. McGavock, Colonel, C.S.A.* (Nashville, TN, 1959), 378, 492; Hudson Diary, Apr. 1, 1852, at UNC-SHC; Steven C. Bullock, *Revolutionary Brotherhood: Freemasonry and the Transformation of the American Social Order, 1730–1840* (Chapel Hill, NC, 1996), ch. 5; James C. Bonner, *Georgia's Last Frontier: The Development of Carroll County* (Athens, GA, 1971), 56; Minnie Clare Boyd, *Alabama in the Fifties: A Social Study* (New York, 1931), 13; William M. Baker, *The Life and Labors of the Rev. Daniel Baker, D.D., Pastor and Evangelist*, 3rd ed. (Philadelphia, n.d.), 259; Cornish Diary, Oct. 14, 1860, at UNC-SHC; Gail Williams O'Brien, *The Legal Fraternity and the Making of a New South Community, 1848–1882* (Athens, GA, 1986), 30; Cornish Diary, Jan. 1, 1847, Feb. 22, 1848, Mar. 19, 1854, at UNC-SHC; Peter Guilday, *The Life and Times of John England: First Bishop of Charleston (1786–1842)*, 2 vols. (New York, 1927), 1:203, 317, 2:241; J. J. O'Connell, *Catholicity in the Carolinas and Georgia: Leaves of Its History* (Westminster, MD, 1964 [1879]), 108, 213.

population, denominations had a difficult time raising money to build churches. Southerners, nonetheless, flocked to services with or without church buildings, assembling in the open air or at a schoolhouse or courthouse, or in private homes. Some ministers resorted to preaching in stores and taverns, Episcopalian Bishop J. H. Otey of Tennessee in an "oyster house" next to a dancing academy.[10]

Every community had some pious people – referred to by the Reverend Samuel Agnew of Mississippi as "supporters" and "encouragers" – who attended and contributed generously to churches they did not join but raised their children in. Among many, Thomas Dabney of Virginia and Mississippi, a strong church supporter, had his sons christened but, feeling unworthy, long deferred his own christening. Pastors struggled with the pious who considered themselves unworthy. The young Andrew Jackson did not join a church, but Peter Cartwright, the great frontier evangelist, knew him as a man who deeply respected and supported religion. Some conscientious Christians did not join because they could not submit to the authority of their preferred church, while others did their best to live as Christians but recognized their sinfulness – they drank, gambled, and worse. In Midway, Georgia, a reputedly irreligious man contributed a handsome fifty dollars to the Reverend Daniel Baker, but how could a man who earned his living by keeping a billiards room join the Church? In Virginia Dr. Fleet left the Baptist church rather than face excommunication for drinking and dancing.[11]

Politicians, who left better biographical records than most other people, could not bring themselves to own up in front of fellow parishioners or submit to stiff church discipline. Among those who never joined a church or joined only late in life, U.S. Secretary of the Treasury William H. Crawford of Georgia promoted the American Bible Society, contributed to several churches, and regularly read the Bible to his family. Senator Nathaniel Macon of North Carolina faithfully attended the Baptist church with his slaves. The dashing Jennings Wise of Virginia was, in the words of his brother John, "as punctilious in church attendance as an elder," known for the "unaffected piety" with which he prayed every night before retiring. William Gregg, the South Carolina industrialist, prayed and professed Christianity but was not baptized until shortly before his death. Although James Chesnut rarely

[10] Chalmers Gaston Davidson, *The Last Foray: The South Carolina Planters of 1860. A Sociological Study* (Columbia, SC, 1971), 89; Paul Hamilton Hayne, "Ante-Bellum Charleston, S.C.," *Southern Bivouac*, 1 (1885), 194; J. S. Buckingham, *The Slave States of America*, 2 vols. (New York, 1968 [1842]), 1:121; also, Lawrence S. Rowland et al., *The History of Beaufort County, South Carolina*, 2 vols. (Columbia, SC, 1996), 119; Malone, *Episcopal Church in Georgia*, 56–7; Carolyn L. Harrell, *Kith and Kin: A Portrait of a Southern Family, 1630–1934* (Macon, GA, 1984), 27; Posey, *Presbyterian Church of Old Southwest*, 102–3. See also Supplementary References: "Preaching."

[11] Samuel Agnew Diary, Jan. 13, 1857, at UNC-SHC; *The Backwoods Preacher: Being the Autobiography of Peter Cartwright* (London, 1870), 117; W. M. Baker, *Daniel Baker*, 96–7; Clement Eaton, *The Mind of the Old South* (Baton Rouge, LA, 1964), 179; also, Susan Dabney Smedes, *Memorials of a Southern Planter*, ed. Fletcher M. Green (New York, 1965 [1887]), 152; L. A. (G.) McCorkle Diary, Aug. 23, 1847, at UNC-SHC; also, Taylor, *Baptists on the Frontier*, 292.

attended church, his wife Mary, famous for judging him harshly, certified him a better Christian than most.[12]

John Randolph confessed to his friend Dr. Brockenbrough that for years his sense of unworthiness had kept him from communion. "If I can not be a member of the Church," the future Presbyterian Reverend Thomas Gordon Pollock wrote as a college student, "I will at any rate be a member of the Congregation." General Robert E. Lee, describing himself as "a poor sinner" and "unworthy," could not bring himself to join until 1853, at age 46. As General James Johnston Pettigrew lay near death during the War, he refused the sacrament, explaining to the Episcopalian Reverend P. N. Wilmer that he had faith but lacked worthiness. Wilmer said he had never seen a better example of Christian resignation in death.[13]

Lucilla Agnes McCorkle wondered whether a camp meeting had "enlarged and warmed up" Christian hearts. Were sinners "convicted & converted"? Or were they merely gratifying their senses, seeking novelty, and pursuing the excitement some confuse with religious ardor? Church-going young ladies felt unable to submit to a discipline that, among other inconveniences, prohibited dancing. The genuinely pious among them felt horribly sinful. The daughters of Robert E. Lee tormented themselves: "I do wish I was a Christian!" Agnes cried. Fearing that she did not feel her Savior's presence, she prayed, "Oh, that I could believe there was a place in Heaven for me." Sarah Lois Wadley waited until her twenties to join the Episcopal church, and a sense of inadequacy dogged her still. A stirring sermon from Romans made Barbara Ann Love long to join Christ's church, but she hesitated: "Oh that I were not a forgetful hearer and could do as I am bid." She feared she "would act like some of the members, not conform to his law & then I would be worse than all the rest which I feel that I am. I know that I am a poor unworthy Sinner." Lucy Breckenridge read the Bible and religious literature regularly, attended the Episcopal church faithfully, yet could not join: "I may not be able to prove myself a consistent member of the church. So few people do, and I am not as good naturally as other people."[14]

---

[12] Chase C. Mooney, *William H. Crawford, 1772–1834* (Lexington, KY, 1974), 16; William S. Price, Jr., "Nathaniel Macon, Planter," *North Carolina Historical Review*, 78 (2001), 205–7, and *DNCB*, 4:186; John S. Wise, *The End of an Era* (Boston, 1900), 91; Rembert W. Patrick, *Aristocrat in Uniform: General Duncan L. Clinch* (Gainesville, FL, 1963), 10–11 (Clinch); Cornish Diary, Jan. 18, 1862 (Gregg); Elisabeth Muhlenfeld, *Mary Boykin Chesnut: A Biography* (Baton Rouge, LA, 1981), 52. See also Supplementary References: "Church Membership."

[13] John Randolph to John Brockenbrough, Sept. 15, 1818, in K. Shorey, ed., *Collected Letters of John Randolph of Roanoke to Dr. John Brockenbrough, 1812–1833* (New Brunswick, NJ, 1988), 18; A. D. Pollack, "Thomas Gordon Pollack" (ms.), 190, at UNC-SHC; Thomas L. Connely, *The Marble Man: Robert E. Lee and His Image in American Society* (New York, 1977), 190; Clyde N. Wilson, *Carolina Cavalier: The Life and Mind of James Johnston Pettigrew* (Athens, GA, 1990), 204; George Lee Simpson, Jr., *The Cokers of Carolina: A Social Biography of a Family* (Chapel Hill, NC, 1956), 40. See also J. Marion Sims, in Sims, *The Story of My Life* (New York, 1884), 118; Hanson Diary, Nov. 23, 1859 (slave), at UNC-SHC.

[14] McCorkle Diary, Aug. 23, 1847; Agnes Lee quoted in Connely, *Marble Man*, 180; Sarah Lois Wadley Private Journal, May 1, 1865, at UNC-SHC; Love Diary, Feb. 14, 1858, in Curry Hill Plantation

Parents, children, and other relatives of leading ministers devoted time and money to a church they never joined or joined only after years of soul-searching. One or both parents of such eminent ministers as the Baptists John Jeter and Patrick Hues Mell did not join although they attended services, participated in church activities, and had reputations for piety. The Baptist Reverend John Landrum baptized his pious mother when she was 70 years old. Richard Furman's first wife died without professing faith, and his second wife, daughter, and a son who struggled with doubts all his life joined only at a late date. James Jones, nephew of the renowned Reverend Charles Colcock Jones, did not become a member of the Presbyterian church until he was 25, and John Newton Waddel – son of the Reverend Moses Waddel, the South's greatest teacher – not until he was 30.[15]

Young men had an especially hard time submitting to church discipline, and a sense of sinfulness often extended into middle age, even afflicting those who had not indulged in youthful escapades. Yet the prevailing stern view of original sin and corrupt human nature did not lead to morbidity; the divines' relentless preaching against "concupiscence" did not imply contempt for bodily pleasures, and a good many Southerners clearly enjoyed life to the fullest. Most would have agreed with Philip Schaff, the Mercersburg theologian, that concupiscence should be located not in the body but in the soul and should be understood not as sensuousness in itself but as "the preponderance of the sensuous, the lusting of the flesh against the spirit."[16]

"Some persons confound faith with assurance," the Reverend (later Bishop) Nicholas Cobbs protested in 1841, "and think they cannot have a saving faith unless they are certain of being converted and accepted." John Ellis, embarking on a successful gubernatorial race in North Carolina, resisted a call to enter the Episcopal church: "I do not feel sufficiently the weight and burden of my sins. There is not with me, a sufficiently repentant sorrow for my transgressions. I wish to have this feeling." The Reverend John Parker assured Ellis that God would strengthen him. Elizabeth Scott Neblett, wife of a small slaveholder in east Texas, as well as the young Sarah Lois Wadley from a plantation family in Mississippi, invoked "Help thou my unbelief" (Mark, 9:24), which the Reverend Stuart Robinson explained as "Lord, I believe, help thou my unbelief." Neblett added, from the Book of Daniel, that she felt weighed in the balance and found wanting. Ministers cautioned against allowing moments of doubt to lead to despair. South Carolina's

---

Records, at Georgia State Department of Archives and History (Atlanta); also, J. Jackson to Henry Jackson, 1825, in Jackson–Prince Papers, at UNC-SHC; Sept. 14, 1862, in Mary D. Robertson, ed., *Lucy Breckenridge of Grove Hill: The Journal of a Virginia Girl, 1826–1864* (Kent, OH, 1979); James S. Guignard to John G. Guignard, Aug. 25, 1839, in Arney R. Childs, ed., *Planters and Businessmen: The Guignard Family of South Carolina, 1795–1930* (Columbia, SC, 1957), 27.

[15] Hatcher, *Jeter*, 9; P. H. Mell, Jr., *Life of Patrick Hues Mell* (Louisville, KY, 1895), 11 n.; H. P. Griffith, *The Life and Times of Rev. John G. Landrum* (Charleston, SC, 1992 [1885]), 11; James A. Rogers, *Richard Furman: Life and Legacy* (Macon, GA, 1985), 96–7; Henry Alexander White, *Southern Presbyterian Leaders* (New York, 1911), 421 (Waddel); James O. Breeden, *Joseph Jones, M.D.: Scientist of the Old South* (Lexington, KY, 1975), 52.

[16] Philip Schaff, *History of the Christian Church*, 5th ed., rev., 8 vols. (Grand Rapids, MI, 1960), 3:826–7.

illustrious Reverend Dr. James Henley Thornwell wrote, "At some seasons in their history, all earnest minds have been tortured with the agony of doubt .... Intense conviction is rooted in the storms of spiritual conflict. He alone believes deeply who has doubted deeply; and he alone can estimate the preciousness of assured faith, who has experienced the anguish of its birth." Indeed, the prominent Baptist Reverends H. E. Taliaferro and I. T. Tichenor of Alabama faced protracted struggles to overcome their doubts.[17]

Expressions of piety – and doubt – poured out during the War. Bishop Cobbs of Alabama, seeking to combat widespread doubts and backsliding among Episcopalians, wrote, in *The Doubting Christian Encouraged,* of those with the deepest religious feelings: "Where there is much grace, there is commonly the most humility." Thomas Ruffin, Jr., C.S.A., wrote his distinguished father from the front in 1862, "There is no place where God's power appears so great. We all feel, then, that without him there is no hope for us, no door of escape." Jefferson Davis, Robert E. Lee, and "Stonewall" Jackson credited God with each of their victories, and Margaret Junkin Preston reported that Virginians were convinced that Jackson's military successes were a consequence of his constant prayer.[18]

Dolly Burge of Middle Georgia, a devout Methodist absorbed in church work, constantly resisted a slide into unbelief or un-Christian behavior: "I have but few evidences that I am a Christian. O shall I thus pass through the world a doubting unbelieving child? Is it never for me to say, 'Abba Father'?" Anna Maria Green of Milledgeville found her heart cold. "I do not know what is my trouble exactly," she wrote in January 1861, "I fear I have no religion that my heart is not right." Two weeks later, deeply moved by a powerful sermon in a Methodist church, she "forcibly felt the truth." In another two weeks she felt terribly fallen from her sense of commitment. She wondered what would become of her: "My doubts are truly fearful." She questioned the very existence of God: Was Christianity "a cunningly devised fable?" At six months: "I still strive to be a Christian, may God help my efforts and grant me his peace." By 1864 she did not deserve God's love: "Yet still

---

[17] Cobbs quoted in Greenough White, *A Saint of the Southern Church: Memoir of the Right Reverend Nicholas Hammer Cobbs* (New York, 1897), 67; John H. Parker to John W. Ellis, Mar. 8, 1858, in Noble J. Tolbert, ed., *The Papers of John Willis Ellis,* 2 vols. (Raleigh, NC, 1964), 1:184–6; also, Cornish Diary, Feb. 3, 1852; Diary, Apr. 12, 1852, in Erika L. Murr, ed., *A Rebel Wife in Texas: The Diary and Letters of Elizabeth Scott Neblett, 1852–1864* (Baton Rouge, LA, 2001), 34–5; Stuart Robinson, *Discourses of Redemption* (New York, 1866), 41; Wadley Private Journal, July 26, 1863; J. H. Thornwell, "Memoir of Dr. Henry," in Michael O'Brien, ed., *All Clever Men, Who Make Their Way: Critical Discourse in the Old South* (Fayetteville, AR, 1982), 428; H. E. Taliaferro, *The Grace of God Magnified: An Experiment Tract* (Charleston, SC, 1859); on Tichenor see Wayne Flynt, *Alabama Baptists: Southern Baptists in the Heart of Dixie* (Tuscaloosa, AL, 1998), 69.

[18] Nicholas H. Cobbs, *The Doubting Christian Encouraged,* 4th ed. (Uniontown, AL, 1864), 11; Thomas Ruffin, Jr., to Thomas Ruffin, Oct. 14, 1862, in J. G. deRoulhac Hamilton, ed., *The Papers of Thomas Ruffin,* 4 vols. (Raleigh, NC, 1918), 3:261; M. J. Preston Journal, July 1, 1862, in Elizabeth Preston Allan, *The Life and Letters of Margaret Junkin Preston* (Boston, 1923), 145; R. L. Dabney, *Life and Campaigns of Lieut.-Gen. Thomas J. Jackson (Stonewall Jackson)* (Harrisonburg, VA, 1983 [1865]), 100, 107–8, 229–30, 531, 585–6, 640, 710.

I trust him for I feel his love and the power of Jesus intercessions and I can never doubt my Savior's love."[19]

Competing theologies and church doctrines induced confusion, with predestinarianism a stumbling block for many. Chief Justice John Marshall regularly attended and contributed generously to the Episcopal Church but held off joining, apparently because of Unitarian inclinations. Ashbel Smith, who became a leading politician and educator in Texas, attended Episcopalian, Methodist, Presbyterian, and Lutheran churches in North Carolina and read deeply in the Bible and religious literature – but with serious theological reservations that long delayed his entrance into the Episcopal Church. L. Q. C. Lamar, a rising politician, and Joseph LeConte, a distinguished scientist, and William Gilmore Simms, the South's most prestigious novelist, were believers and church supporters, but theological qualms kept all three from membership. Counterpoints: David Johnson, pleased that his brother joined a church, did not care which. He considered it "immaterial as the leading doctrines of all the protestant Churches are substantially the same and the ceremonials I regard as mere conventional forms." The Reverend J. O. Andrew was taken by the piety and excellent character of a Methodist woman in Texas who did not know or care whether her church was Methodist Episcopal or Republican Methodist.[20]

Religious revivals appeared across Western Europe about 1830, in part as a reaction by both aristocrats and peasants against the liberalization of Christian doctrine, and before long campus revivals led to a noticeable decline in student drinking, dueling, and hell-raising. The fervor of American revivals nonetheless stunned Europeans. Alexis de Tocqueville commented on "men, full of fanatical and almost wild enthusiasm, which hardly exists in Europe." He suspected a dose of insanity in people who traveled great distances through rough terrain to listen to discourses at camp meetings. Revivals and camp meetings receded in the North while they long remained vigorous in the South. Methodists led a revival in 1826–27 that extended from Virginia to Georgia and then westward. Stores and schools shut down.

---

[19] See e.g. Mar. 29, Apr. 21, May 18, 1848, and Jan. 13, 1849, in James I. Robertson, Jr., ed., *The Diary of Dolly Lunt Burge* (Athens, GA, 1962), 13, 15, 19, 33, quote at 19; Green Diary, Jan. 20, Feb. 3 and 24, May 5, 1861, Nov. 14, 1862, Jan. 1, 1863, Nov. 8, 1864, in James C. Bonner, ed., *The Journal of a Milledgeville Girl, 1861–1867* (Athens, GA, 1864), 11–15, 23, 57.

[20] Meade, *Old Churches*, 2:223–4 (Marshall); Elizabeth Silverthorne, *Ashbel Smith of Texas: Pioneer, Patriot, Statesman, 1805–1886* (College Station, TX, 1982), 29; Wirt Armistead Cate, *Lucius Q. C. Lamar: Secession and Reunion* (Chapel Hill, NC, 1935), 26–7; William Dallas Armes, ed., *The Autobiography of Joseph LeConte* (New York, 1903), 17; Lester D. Stephens, *Joseph LeConte: Gentle Prophet of Evolution* (Baton Rouge, LA, 1982), 5; W. G. Simms to Justus Starr Redfield, May 4, 1856, in Mary C. Oliphant et al., eds., *The Letters of William Gilmore Simms*, 6 vols. (Columbia, SC, 1952–82), 3:431; David Johnson to E. C. Johnson, Oct. 3, 1852, in Francis Johnson Scott, ed., "Letters and Papers of Governor David Johnson and Family, 1810–1855," Appendix to *Proceedings of the South Carolina Historical Association* (1941), 16; "Travels in the West," in J. O. Andrew, *Miscellanies* (Louisville, KY, 1854), 95. Sallie Bird's Aunt Carrie died at peace. She placed all trust in her Savior but regretted not showing her love for Him by joining the church: Sallie Bird to Saida Bird, July 1861, in John Rozier, ed., *The Granite Farm Letters: The Civil War Correspondence of Edgeworth and Sallie Bird* (Athens, GA, 1988), 5.

Turner Saunders had seen many camp meetings in his time but nothing quite like those of Alabama in 1828, when the smaller averaged 1,500. Around Nashville, William McKendree and his brethren drew 6,000 and more. In 1829 Methodists held four-day town-based "protracted meetings" with an eye toward stimulating a national revival. Even Memphis, a river town regarded as a hotbed of infidelity, responded to the Methodist circuit riders, and the towns of the interior displayed growing sobriety. By the 1840s camp meetings were annual affairs, lasting a few days to two weeks or more. Old-timers who preferred spontaneity to scheduled events thought the careful organization and emphasis on good order threatened to turn revivals into social affairs accompanied by routine expressions of piety.[21]

Religious revival swept the Southeast in the midst of the nullification crisis, the Nat Turner revolt, and the Virginia debate over emancipation. The Reverend James Furman remembered 1831–32 as "memorable years" for South Carolina Baptists. The revival of the early 1830s was indeed a boon to the churches, converting leaders of society and opening the way for the rise of younger, better-educated, and more aggressive preachers. The new evangelicals, like their predecessors, helped stabilized the social order. An astonished William J. Grayson singled out Daniel Baker, the great Presbyterian evangelist, for overcoming sectarianism and promoting Christian unity in men who were politically at sword's point. The unionist J. L. Petigru, hearing that the people of Beaufort, South Carolina, were becoming more religious yet more committed to state rights, remarked sardonically, "For as it is the business of religion to wean us from the world, the object may be well promoted by making the world less fit to live in." Petigru mocked, "Many excellent men have thought the making a hell upon earth is a good way of being sure of a place in heaven." Religious fanaticism would follow the political fanaticism of the nullifiers without undoing it: "Our little fellow Pinckney has been vastly devout for six months, without any visible change in the filthiness of the outer man."[22]

[21] Paul Tillich, *A History of Christian Thought: From Its Judaic and Hellenistic Origins to Existentialism*, ed. Carl E. Braaten (New York, 1972), 449–50; on European revival see also Claude Welch, *Protestant Thought in the Nineteenth Century*, 2 vols. (New Haven, CT, 1972), 1:192 n. 5; Alexis de Tocqueville, *Democracy in America*, tr. Henry Reeve, 2 vols. (Boston, 1873), 2:161; John Walker Diary, May 16, 1826, at UNC-SHC; Susan Nye Hutchinson Journal, Nov. 10, Dec. 6 and 7, 1826, Apr. 9, 1827, at UNC-SHC; *The Life and Times of Judge Junius Hillyer: From His Memoirs* (Tignall, GA, 1989), 100; Marion Elias Lazenby, *History of Methodism in Alabama and West Florida* (Nashville, TN, 1960), 118 (Saunders); E. E. Hoss, *William McKendree: A Biographical Study* (Nashville, TN, 1916), 197; James Porter, *Compendium of Methodism* (Boston, 1851), 157–8; George G. Smith, *The History of Georgia Methodism from 1786 to 1866* (Atlanta, GA, 1913), 269–70; Gerald M. Capers, Jr., *The Biography of a River Town. Memphis: Its Heroic Age* (Chapel Hill, NC, 1939), 64–6. For the revivals of the 1840s, see Supplementary References: "Revivals."

[22] Harvey Tolliver Cook, *The Life and Work of James Clement Furman* (Greenville, SC, 1926), 16, 18, 28; Grayson, *Witness to Sorrow*, ch. 3; Petigru, letter to an unspecified person, in W. J. Grayson, *James Louis Petigru: A Biographical Sketch* (New York, 1866), 120–1; Petigru to William Elliott, Nov. 14, 1831, in James Petigru Carson, *Life, Letters and Speeches of James Louis Petigru: Union Man of South Carolina* (Washington, DC, 1920), 86; see also Supplementary References: "Revivals." For the relation of religious revival to the political crisis in South Carolina, see esp. Stephanie McCurry,

From Virginia to Texas, revivals prepared the South to meet the abolitionist offensive. Anne Tuberville Davis returned from an 1838 camp meeting in Johnston
County, North Carolina, convinced that she would never forget "the revolution of
the glorious events which occurred on that consecrated ground .... It was indeed
a time of the outpouring of the Holy Spirit of our merciful God, in the awakening and conversion of sinners, and the sanctification of believers." The Reverend
John Girardeau exulted, "Who of us can forget the wonderful scenes of the great
revival of 1846? The hardest hearts were melted." In 1833 at Dandridge, Tennessee, according to George Gillespie, "Almost every person there has joined with the
Presbyterian or Methodist Church."[23]

In Virginia in the summer of 1831 a memorable religious revival among blacks
and whites transfixed Nat Turner as well as those against whom he raised his hand.
Louisiana Hubbard, recounting her lifelong effort to live as a good Christian, pronounced the Turner rebellion a warning and perhaps a blessing for a people who
now had to turn their faces to God. The Presbyterian Reverend Abram David
Pollock described a "considerable awakening" in the early 1830s that brought together Methodists and Baptists. The Baptist Reverend John Jeter, in the Northern
Neck of Virginia, recalled the summer of 1831 as "memorable" for the religious
revivals of all evangelical Christian denominations. Baptists and Methodists long
remembered 1844–45 and the years immediately thereafter as a great time in which
southern withdrawals from the national churches stimulated enormous revivals.[24]

In the early days, several denominations cosponsored extensive camp and protracted meetings, but in time each denomination – Methodist, Baptist, Presbyterian,
and even Episcopalian – tended to sponsor its own. Camp meetings brought the
gentry and no few sophisticated professionals together with middling and poor
folks, providing a powerful counterweight to social antagonisms. Some of the richest planters attended, and some sent hands to perform services in preparation for
the camp meetings. From Virginia to Georgia, especially in the upcountry, wealthy
planters and professionals mingled freely with yeomen and poorer folks. Moses
Hoge was struck by how many of the better-educated and more affluent citizens
of North Carolina appeared at camp meetings with the poorest of the poor. A
successful camp meeting, said the Methodist Reverend Anson West, simply had to

*Masters of Small Worlds: Yeoman Households, Gender Relations, and Political Culture of the Ante-
bellum South Carolina Low Country* (New York, 1995).

23 A. T. (Beale) Davis Diary, Oct. 28, 1838, at UNC-SHC; George A. Blackburn, ed., *Sermons by John L.
Girardeau* (Columbia, SC, 1907), 238, also 247; Thomas H. Pope, *The History of Newberry County,
South Carolina*, 2 vols. (Columbia, SC, 1973), 1:233; Griffith, *Landrum*, 66–9, 80, 116–17; Hynds,
Antebellum Athens, 108; Martha R. Jackson Journal, July 22, 1835, in Jackson–Prince Papers; George
Gillespie to Elizabeth Gillespie, Feb. 16, 1833, in Caswell Papers, at UNC-SHC (on Tennessee). On
religion, politics, and temperance in Alabama see J. Mills Thornton III, *Power and Politics in a Slave
Society: Alabama, 1800–1860* (Baton Rouge, LA, 1978), 318.

24 Hubbard Diary, dated Sept. 29, 1832 but probably 1831, at UNC-SHC; Pollock Diaries, 1832–1833
(pp. 15–16, 19, 30, 34–5), at UNC-SHC; J. B. Jeter, *Memoir of Mrs. Henrietta Schuck, the First American Female Missionary to China* (Boston, 1846), 17–18; also, *ESB*, 2:794.

include both. Great meetings in Tennessee often drew 5,000 to 10,000 people with a record turnout of 20,000, and in Jackson, Tennessee, Herndon Haralson reported on "great Electioneering" by preachers and politicians alike. Stephen Mallory of Florida, a Catholic, was not about to pass up a large meeting of his Methodist constituents. Politicians had to be seen in church.[25]

"It is not the Custom," Philip Fithian, a northern tutor, wrote from the Northern Neck in the 1770s, "for Gentlemen to go into Church til Service is beginning, when they enter in a Body, in the same manner as they come out." The fashionably late gentlemen talked business before and after service and then dined together. Charles Bruce, Presbyterian planter in Southside, Virginia, sadly observed that many people went to church primarily for recreation, social intercourse, business news, and gossip. At the University of Georgia in the early 1840s, J. L. M. Curry went to church because attendance was required and because it was the best place to meet girls. Especially in the 1850s, the devout complained about parishioners who attended church mainly to see or be seen and to socialize inside and outside church. James Mallory, a small planter in Alabama, grumbled about inattention to good sermons. Mrs. E. M. Houstoun, on tour from New Orleans to Texas, found churches filled but doubted the depth of conviction. Bishop Otey rebuked congregants who arrived without prayer books and assumed "the appearance of spectators at a show." The Presbyterian Reverend James Henley Thornwell wondered whether those who jammed churches on Sullivan's Island had much genuine religion. The Methodist Bishop George Foster Pierce, on a tour of the Southwest, confessed to "impatience and disgust with those drowsy, yawning men ... who never feel the quickening impulse of a generous Christian emulation."[26]

[25] For planters sending hands see John D. Jones, *A Complete History of Methodism as Connected with the Mississippi Conference of the Methodist Episcopal Church, South*, 2 vols. (Nashville, TN, 1908), 2:269; J. G. Clinkscales, *On the Old Plantation: Reminiscences of His Childhood* (Spartanburg, SC, 1916); S. A. Jones to Sarah P. Hamilton, Oct. 28, 1842, in B. C. Yancey Papers, at UNC-SHC; Ernest Trice Thompson, *Presbyterians in the South*, 3 vols. (Richmond, VA, 1963), 1:141 (Hoge); Anson West, *A History of Methodism in Alabama* (Spartanburg, SC, 1983 [1893]), 56; also, [James Holt Ingraham], *The South-West. By a Yankee*, 2 vols. (n.p., 1966 [1835]), 2:166; Walter Brownlow Posey, *Frontier Mission: A History of Religion East of the Southern Appalachians to 1861* (Lexington, KY, 1966), 25; Haralson Diary, July 21, 1839, at UNC-SHC; Joseph T. Durkin, *Stephen R. Mallory: Confederate Navy Chief* (Chapel Hill, NC, 1954), 91. See also Supplementary References: "Revivals."

[26] P. V. Fithian, Dec. 13, 1773 (quoted), July 10, 1774, in Hunter Dickinson Farish, ed., *Journal and Letters of Philip Vickers Fithian: A Plantation Tutor of the Old Dominion, 1733–1744* (Charlottesville, VA, 1957), 29, 137; on Charles Bruce see W. C. Bruce, *John Randolph of Roanoke, 1773–1833*, 2 vols. (New York, 1970), 2:140; also, *SBN*, 10:658–9. Allan Kulikoff, *Tobacco and Slaves: The Development of Southern Cultures in the Chesapeake, 1680–1800* (Chapel Hill, NC, 1986), 236–7; Jesse Pearl Rice, *J. M. L. Curry: Southerner, Statesman and Educator* (New York, 1948), 21; "Nella", "Sights, Sounds and Thoughts at Church," *SLM*, 24 (1857), 43–5; "Inefficiency of the Pews," *SLM*, 24 (1857), 324–5; Mallory Journal, June 14 and 21, 1846, Mar. 12, June 18 and 25, 1854, in Grady McWhiny, Warner O. Moore, Jr., and Robert Pace, eds., *"Fear God and Walk Humbly": The Agricultural Journal of James Mallory, 1843–1877* (Tuscaloosa, AL, 1997), 51, 189, 194; Mrs. [E. M.] Houstoun, *Texas and*

On pins and needles awaiting the arrival of a beloved kinswoman from far away, Mary Dean confessed to lack of attention to Mr. Granberry's sermon. Basil Armstrong Thomasson, a North Carolina yeoman, fumed at inattentive, flirtatious young men in church. From St. Andrew's Episcopal Church near the Ashley River, Alicia Hopton Middleton reported: "Here, of a Sunday morning, would gather from miles around, the planters and their families, some in carriages with liveried coachmen and footmen, many on horseback, always in time for a neighborly chat and exchange of gossip before as well as after, service." When a man married, he confirmed his respectability by attending church regularly. Anyone who found himself in court wanted to be known as a steady churchgoer, since courtroom oratory made much of religion and since judges and juries noted the religious standing of plaintiffs, defendants, and witnesses.[27]

Rural as well as town folk often attended church several times a week: services on Sunday and perhaps prayer meeting and songfests on Wednesday; sometimes the church trials of backsliders on Saturday. Dr. Thomas Edward Cox, a churchgoing Virginia Baptist, recorded the occasions he did not attend church: his illness or his daughter's, severe rainstorms, a broken buggy. Ministers groused about people who seized upon some excuse to skip services. The Reverend John Hamilton Cornish of Aiken, South Carolina, had no patience with the excuse of bad weather: "The shops & stores have been thronged. There has been a good deal of whooping & yelling about the streets." Often, the ministers were too hard on their people. The pelting rains typical of the South, supplemented by occasional snowstorms, created serious obstacles. Even in the larger cities streets became impassable. Mary Jane Chester, a student at the Columbia Female Institute in Tennessee, complained that the disagreeable weather had kept the whole school away from church. When one heavy rain kept the Hutchinsons at home, they read one of Dr. Kollock's sermons, and Susan "offered in my poor way – a prayer." It rained so hard one night

the *Gulf of Mexico; Or, Yachting in the New World* (Austin, TX, 1968 [1845]), 192; Otey Diary, Aug. 6, 1854; Thornwell to A. J. Witherspoon, June 17, 1851, and Thornwell to Thomas E. Peck, July 1, 1851, in Benjamin Morgan Palmer, *The Life and Letters of James Henley Thornwell* (Richmond, VA, 1875), 350, 352; George F. Pierce, *Incidents of Western Travel: In a Series of Letters* (Nashville, TN, 1857), 246.

27 Mary Dean to James Norman, in Susan Lott Clark, ed., *Southern Letters and Life in the Mid 1800s* (Waycross, GA, 1993), 67; Oct. 5, 1856, in Paul D. Escott, ed., *North Carolina Yeoman: The Diary of Basil Armstrong Thomasson, 1853–1862* (Athens, GA, 1996), 151–2. Also, Jack Kenny Williams, *Vogues in Villainy: Crime and Retribution in Ante-Bellum South Carolina* (Columbia, SC, 1959), 95; A. H. Middleton, "Family Record," in Alicia Hopton Middleton et al., *Life in Carolina and New England during the Nineteenth Century* (Bristol, RI, 1929), 9; Henry T. Garnett to Thomas Ruffin, July 28, 1829, in Hamilton, ed., *Papers of Thomas Ruffin*, 1:506–7; A. B. Van Zandt, *"The Elect Lady": A Memoir of Mrs. Susan Catherine Botts of Petersburg, Va.* (Philadelphia, 1857), 38, 91. On newly married men see Buckingham, *Slave States*, 1:546. In compensation for a dull sermon, Flavellus Nicholson had a few pleasurable moments with his "little Dulcinea": Nicholson Diary-Journal, July 8, 1860, at Mississippi Department of Archives and History (Jackson). The Cumberland Presbyterian Reverend Jacob Clark of Missouri said that the presence of community leaders at church drew people to church, but he feared that the effects were superficial: "Sermon," *Theological Medium*, 2 (1847), 389.

that Mary Eliza Eve Carmichael could not get out in the morning but heard an excellent sermon later in the day. A disconsolate Frances Webb Bumpass thought the rain too heavy for travel and felt "little profited" by reading until the evening, when she "read some in Wesley's Journal," conversed with her husband, and found "my hard, cold heart was somewhat touched." In bitter cold weather on one Sunday, Elizabeth Curtis Wallace of Norfolk County, Virginia, stayed home and sang hymns; Sarah Alexander, chafing because of the distance to church and the long two-sermon days, stayed home and read the Bible to her slaves.[28]

Some denominations agreed to offer the Lord's Supper jointly – a practice that brought people together in a special fellowship. Usually, people attended three services, with dinner between the second and third. In the countryside and villages, folks went home for dinner between services, taking with them those who lived too far to make a return journey. More affluent Virginia planters opened their homes to feed neighbors and friends. Between morning and afternoon services, people met strangers at lunch tables servants set up in the nearby woods, discussed the week's events and scandals, exchanged political views, and sometimes got mail from the postmaster.[29]

[28] Thomas Edward Cox Diary, Jan. 8, Apr. 14, May 27 and 29, June 4, June 11, 1854, at UNC-SHC; Cornish Diary, Dec. 24 and 25, 1853. At UNC-SHC see: Chester Diary, Dec. 20, 1840; Hutchinson Journal, Apr. 9, 1827; Carmichael Diary, Feb. 11, 1841; Bumpass Diary, Mar. 12, 1842; Carney Diary, 1859–1860. See also Diary, Apr. 3, 1864, in Eleanor P. Cross and Charles B. Cross, Jr., eds., *Glencoe Diary: The War-Time Journal of Elizabeth Curtis Wallace* (Chesapeake, VA, 1968), 102; Sarah Alexander to Clifford Alexander, Feb. 20, 1853, in Marion Alexander Boggs, ed., *The Alexander Letters, 1787–1900* (Athens, GA, 1980 [1911]), 176. For heavy attendance at various functions see R. L. Dabney, *Life and Campaigns of T. J. Jackson*, 90; John Hebron Moore, *The Emergence of the Cotton Kingdom in Old Southwest: Mississippi, 1770–1860* (Baton Rouge, LA, 1988), 144–5. For weather and roads see V. Dabney, *Richmond*, 99; M. E. E. Carmichael Diary, Feb. 11, 1841 (Augusta, GA); Anna Matilda King to Thomas Butler King, Aug. Jan. 27, 1955, in Thomas Butler King Papers, at UNC-SHC.

  Some had a more attractive kind of social motive for church attendance: to hear the music, especially in the Catholic churches. The Catholic Pauline DeCaradeuc Heyward of Aiken, South Carolina, went to church three times one Sunday. She was in fact religious but was especially drawn by the "delightful music." See "Journal of P. DeC. Heyward," Apr. 18, Aug. 24 (quoted), 1864, in Mary D. Robertson, ed., *A Confederate Lady Comes of Age: The Journal of Pauline DeCaradeux Heyward, 1863–1888* (Columbia, SC, 1992), 44, 56. Eliza Middleton Fisher, a low-church Episcopalian who loathed the Oxford Movement, attended a Catholic Mass to hear Haydn: Eliza Middleton Fisher to Mary Herring Middleton, Jan. 14, 1841, in Eliza Cope Harrison, ed., *Best Companions: Letters of Eliza Middleton Fisher and Her Mother, Mary Herring Middleton, from Charleston, Philadelphia, and Newport, 1839–1846* (Columbia, SC, 2001), 173. For additional Protestant tributes to the music at Catholic Masses see George Mason to George Mason, Jr., May 20, 1787, in Robert A. Rutland, ed., *The Papers of George Mason,* 3 vols. (Chapel Hill, NC, 1970), 2:881; J. H. Bills Diary, Mar. 8, 1846, at UNC-SHC; W. P. Mangum to Charity Mangum, Sept. 2, 1843, in Henry Thomas Shanks, ed., *The Papers of Willie P. Mangum,* 5 vols. (Raleigh, NC, 1955–56), 1:195; Apr. 18, 1857, in *ERD,* 1:175; Carney Diary, May 20, 1860.

[29] Margaret Burr DesChamps, "The Presbyterian Church in the South Atlantic States, 1801–1861" (Ph.D. diss., Emory University, 1952), 57, 89; Mary A. H. Gay, *Life in Dixie during the War,* 5th ed. (Atlanta, GA, 1979 [1897]), 150–1; Burke, *Reminiscences of Georgia,* 148; Reginald May, *Eldon*

Many churchgoers displayed the latest fashions. Anne Tuberville Davis saw "the love of many waxing cold, and some few withdrawing from our church for the purpose of mingling more freely in the fashionable pleasures, and sinful amusements of the age." Religious profession itself became something of a fad among young ladies. The Reverend Christopher Gadsden, rector of St. Luke's Episcopal Church in Charleston, chided parishioners about "so many false and sinful motives" among professed Christians: "Can you be surprised that he does not sit in the gay church of fashion?" Juliana Margaret Connor disdained evangelical preachers and religious enthusiasm. Curiosity drove her to a camp meeting of "great assemblage." She and her friends wanted "to see the show." To her surprise, she found ladies "dressed in their finest and best style," as if at a party or the theater. It was like "an exchange or public resort, where the gentlemen transacted business, the candidates electioneered and the belles and beaux displayed their beauty and gallantry – but one would never have supposed it a place of worship." Ministers saw civilizing influences. Especially in quasi-frontier areas, church attendance signaled civility and separation from the riffraff that David Holt recalled from a rough boyhood among fellow slaveholders in Woodville, Mississippi: "The counteracting influences were home and church." Writing after the War, he added that "religious, sober, pure, and righteous" women saved Mississippi.[30]

So too, church arrangements reduced distractions and frivolity. Men and women generally sat separately, although city folks sometimes violated the code, and families sat together in some churches. A boy's move from the women's section (where he sat with his mother) to the men's denoted a rite of passage. Sexual separation required some adjustments – even the most fashionable churches provided spittoons for gentlemen. J. S. Wise recalled with some frustration that to court one of the Presbyterian young ladies in upcountry Virginia, you had to escort her to church. Young gentlemen sent written requests for the privilege.[31]

Drayton; Or, Crises, Intellectual and Moral. A Story for the Young (Nashville, TN, 1886), 12; Randolph Whitfield and John Chapman, *The Florida Randolphs, 1829–1978*, 2nd ed. (Atlanta, GA, 1987), 82. The rural southern style of churchgoing irritated New Englanders: see e.g. Owen Petersen, *A Divine Discontent: The Life of Nathan S. S. Beman* (Macon, GA, 1986), 28–9.

[30] Davis Diary, Dec. 1838; Thomas D. Cockrell and Michael Ballard, eds., *A Mississippi Rebel in the Army of Virginia: The Civil War Memoirs of Private David Holt* (Baton Rouge, LA, 1995), 11; also, Camila Davis Trammel, *Seven Pines: Its Occupants and Their Letters* (Houston, TX, 1986), 62; James H. Elliott, ed., *Tributes to the Memory of the Rev. C. P. Gadsden, with Thirteen of His Sermons* (Charleston, SC, 1872), 241; Juliana Margaret Conner Diary, Aug. 4, 1827, at UNC-SHC. Nancy McDougall of Port Gibson, Mississippi, versified: "Some go there to laugh and talk / Some go there for speculation / Some go there for observation / Some go there for things to view / Some go there their dress to show / Some go there to meet a friend / Some go there to doze and nod / But few go there to worship GOD": McDougall Papers, 1832, in N. McD. Robinson Collection, at LSU.

[31] John Richard Dennett, *The South as It Is, 1865–1866* (New York, 1965 [1867]), 48; *SBN*, 10:659; Ted Ownby, *Subduing Satan: Religion, Recreation, and Manhood in the Rural South, 1865–1960* (Chapel Hill, NC, 1990), 130–1; Wise, *End of an Era*, 241–2. The pious Kate Carney of Tennessee acknowledged her pleasure at the attention paid by gentlemen at church: Carney Diary, Feb. 20, Apr. 10, May 8 and 15, 1859, at UNC-SHC.

Nonbelievers and antirevivalists broadcast – and exaggerated – the sexual indulgences on the margins of the camp meetings. To hear the critics, people who collapsed into an ecstasy of awe, love, and fear of God thereupon copulated in the bushes. Slanderers picked up every reference to "camp meeting babies" and expressed horror at the behavior of the young folks. The Baptist Reverend John Jeter admitted that the camp meetings could become occasions for frivolity, dissipation, and vice: "Satan usually attends camp meetings and trains his servants for mischief." (Curiously, no historian has correlated the time of conception of Yankee babies with presence of youth at psalm-singing social-reform meetings.) Bishop William Meade's *Old Churches* (1857) recounted a steady shift over the years of Virginia's churches from places for social gathering to places of genuine worship. His fellow divines across the South, while never ceasing their jeremiads, said as much themselves.[32]

With such notable exceptions as the early New England Puritans, vast numbers of people seldom struggle with theology and church doctrine. Yet the many churchgoing Southerners, like Northerners, noted the texts of the sermons and left accounts of their doctrinal content. Secular journals and newspapers often published notices of sermons and discourses and sometimes published the texts. Diaries of men and women reflect religious concerns and familiarity with the Bible. Among secular luminaries, Mitchell King of Charleston, with a command of theology worthy of the ablest divines, scrutinized the doctrine of every sermon, pronouncing one "absurd," "heretical," and "hateful," another full of "vague undefined generalities." Prominent politicians – among them Confederate Secretary of the Treasury Christopher Memminger of South Carolina, Governor Zebulon Vance of North Carolina, and Ashbel Smith, an architect of Texas independence and statehood – won reputations as serious biblical scholars. While on duty with the Confederate army, Dr. S. G. Welch wrote his wife about the hard-drinking, gambling son of former President John Tyler, a former divinity student. "Tyler is one of the most wicked and profane men I ever knew, but he is a very intelligent man and is generous and high-minded." Tyler had frequent exchanges with the chaplain: "It is highly amusing, for he is hard to handle in an argument over Scripture."[33]

[32] Camp meetings served as places for chaste wooing among the respectable: see e.g. Maria Bryan to Julia Ann Bryan Cumming, Dec. 21, 1826, and Jan. 22, 1827, in Carol Bleser, ed., *Tokens of Affection: The Letters of a Planter's Daughter in the Old South* (Athens, GA, 1996), 17–18, 30.

[33] Hatcher, *Jeter*, 158; Durward T. Stokes and William T. Scott, *A History of the Christian Church in the South* (n.p., 1973), 25–6; Mitchell King Diary, Oct. 3, 1853, and Oct. 21, 1855, at USC; Layton W. Jordan, "Schemes of Usefulness," in Michael O'Brien and David Moltke-Hansen, eds., *Intellectual Life in Antebellum Charleston* (Knoxville, TN, 1986), 216; Frances Gray Patton, "Introduction," in Elizabeth Roberts Cannon, ed., *My Beloved Zebulon: The Correspondence of Zebulon Vance and Harriett Newell Espy* (Chapel Hill, NC, 1971), xvii; Silverthorne, *Ashbel Smith*, 135; for North and South see Lewis O. Saum, *The Popular Mood in Pre–Civil War America* (Westport, CT, 1980), xix, 8. On Tyler see Spencer Glasgow Welch to his wife, Apr. 5, 1863, in *A Confederate Surgeon's Letters to His Wife* (New York, 1911), 53–4, also Jan. 3, 1864 (85–6). Joseph LeConte's scientific writings

John Randolph of Roanoke was "never so free from uneasiness as when reading the Bible or hearing an able preacher." Henry Foote, who attracted public attention as a particularly erratic and nasty politician in Mississippi and Tennessee, demanded sermons that had something to say. In Georgia, the Stephens brothers, Alexander and Linton, corresponded with each other and with friends on the character and significance of miracles, their belief in an afterlife, and their impatience with Universalism. When Linton joined the Presbyterian Church, Alexander advised, "Read your Bible – make it your text-book of faith." Linton chuckled over his learned brother's error in a scriptural citation.[34]

The few Universalist preachers in the South, facing considerable hostility, saw in the widespread interest in church doctrine an opportunity to attract the curious to their own sermons. So did the yeoman-based Disciples of Christ, criticized for being cold and overly intellectual. "Oh Heavenly father," James Hervey Greenlee of North Carolina prayed, "Instruct us in the great doctrines of salvation by grace." He criticized doctrine even in sermons he admired, grumbling about Mr. Kerr's on the Resurrection: "Have heard the same arguments & sermon often before." William Valentine sputtered that a Baptist minister was entitled to his opinions but ought not teach heretical doctrine on baptism as if it were the Word of God. Nicholas Massenburg, a Methodist, judged Brother Norwood's sermon "able and forceful, but not sound."[35]

Reputedly unintellectual Baptist laymen showed themselves vigorous disputants. The Reverend Samuel Agnew of Mississippi, an Associate Presbyterian, had to deal

demonstrate command of the Bible. He remembered the text of a sermon a half-century after he heard it: William Dallas Ames, ed., *The Autobiography of Joseph LeConte* (New York, 1903), 117.

[34] John Randolph to John Brockenbrough, May 29, 1815, in Shorey, ed., *Letters of Randolph to Brockenbrough*, 12; Dunbar Rowland, ed., *Mississippi: Comprising Sketches of Counties, Towns, Events, Institutions, and Persons, Arranged in Cyclopedic Form*, 4 vols. (Spartanburg, SC, 1976 [1907]), 2:162, 171 (Foote). On the Stephens brothers see e.g. A. H. Stephens to Linton Stephens, Feb. 28 and May 5, 1840, and Linton to Alexander, Apr. 21 and Sept. 8, 1860, May 31, 1870, in James D. Waddell, ed., *Biographical Sketch of Linton Stephens, Containing a Selection of His Letters, Speeches, State Papers, Etc.* (Atlanta, GA, 1877), 20–1, 25, 210, 312–13; also, Henry Cleveland, *Alexander H. Stephens in Public and Private: With Letters and Speeches Before, During, and Since the War* (Philadelphia, 1866), 233, 333, 558–60.

In Tuscaloosa, Alabama, Columbus Morrison – a small slaveholder left with three children – mourned the death of his wife of only four years: "I have been impressed with the importance of religion and indulge the hope that Christ is my God & Savior." The first "exercises" he taught his children admonished, "Love God & your fellow creatures." Morrison wondered, "What is man? Where is he? and what is he doing?" He replied, "A soul is a spirit, a living principle emanated from God, clothed with a body adapted to his wants, and endowed with a capacity to expand without limit in knowledge and enjoyment. His abode is on earth an atom in the creation of Him who is author and ruler of thousands of worlds." Morrison stressed man's duty to God to repent and seek salvation: Columbus Morrison Journal, May and Dec. 1845, at UNC-SHC.

[35] See the correspondence of a Universalist preacher in the Bain Papers for the 1850s: Carter E. Boren, *Religion on the Texas Frontier* (San Antonio, TX, 1968), 268–73. At UNC-SHC see: Greenlee Diary, Sept. 17, 1848, and Mar. 10, 1850 (for Greenlee's more measured criticism of Wightman on doctrinal matters see Oct. 4, 1854); Valentine Diaries, Sept. 9, 1850; Massenburg Farm Journal, Mar. 22, 1835; Thomas M. Garrett Diary, July 1, 21, 1849. See also Supplementary References: "Universalism."

with a Mr. Wilks, "who would argue ad infinitum in favor of the peculiar doctrines of the Baptist Church." After church services, congregants invited preachers to dinners that featured hot debates over predestination or some other point of theology. In Georgia, Eliza Frances Andrews recalled a staunch Baptist planter with a Methodist slave. "They used to have some high old religious discussions together." As a seminary student, William Porcher DuBose, a future Episcopal theologian, carried on fervent discussions with his slave coachmen about interpretation of biblical texts.[36]

Folks may not have expected breathtaking originality in every sermon, but they did expect fresh thought, and everyone felt free to criticize substance and artistry. In the South Carolina upcountry, the early Scots-Irish settlers brought their own stools to sit on during services at Ebenezer Church in York County so that – the story goes – they would have something to throw if the preacher offended them. In later years, Henry Young Webb of Alabama grew irritable when the Reverend Mr. Smith had "nothing very striking" to say and tried to get away with mere quotations from the Psalms. Stonewall Jackson, who reputedly slept during sermons, stirred when he heard a new topic or idea. Juliana Margaret Connor of Chesterville, South Carolina, suffered through one dull sermon: "Had the discourse interested me I should have been much annoyed by the crying of the infants." Catherine Thom almost walked out on "a very metaphysical and stupid sermon." Preachers learned that poorly educated "Crackers" followed serious talks and grasped matters supposedly beyond them. The Episcopalian Josiah Gorgas muttered that he would attend church more often if he could find an edifying preacher. Basil Armstrong Thomasson, a teacher and small farmer in western North Carolina who remarked frequently on the quality of Methodist and Baptist sermons, judged the local preaching good but fumed at lapses. Arriving late to hear a poor sermon from the Reverend James Minish, Thomasson "did not lose much." His favorite put-down for uninspiring preachers: "Tried to preach."[37]

The learned Thomas Ruffin of North Carolina "never heard our religion preached in greater Gospel Purity" than by Bishop Ravenscroft: "There was no new-fangled notion, no metaphysical subtlety, no effort to draw off the attention of the hearers from devotion to the Deity & make the Preacher the object to be considered."

---

[36] Agnew Diary, Mar. 16, 1857; W. P. DuBose, "Reminiscences" (ms.), 60, at UNC-SHC; Eliza Frances Andrews, *War-Time Journal of a Georgia Girl* (New York, 1908), 321.

[37] *Life and Times of Junius Hillyer*, 46; Henry Young Webb Diary, Oct. 2, 1853, and Mar. 1, 1858, at UNC-SHC; Thomas Jackson Arnold, *Early Life and Letters of General Thomas J. ("Stonewall") Jackson* (Richmond, VA, 1957 [1916]), 252; Conner Diary, June 14, 18??; C. G. R. Thom to Pembroke Thom, Jan. 16 and 30, 1864, in Catherine Thom Bartlett, ed., *"My Dear Brother": A Confederate Chronicle* (Richmond, VA, 1952), 125, 140; Thomas Cary Johnson, ed., *Robert Lewis Dabney* (Carlisle, PA, 1977 [1903]), 88; Nicholson Diary, Sept. 23, 1860; June 27, 1858, in Sarah Woolfolk Wiggins, ed., *The Journals Josiah Gorgas, 1857–1878* (Tuscaloosa, AL, 1995), 21. On not losing much see e.g. Thomasson Diary, Mar. 9, 1856, in Escott, ed., *North Carolina Yeoman*, 129, and for "tried to preach" see the references to the Reverend John Webster, Apr. 15, 1855 (77), the Reverend Franklin Moss, Aug. 17, 1855 (84), and the Reverend James Minish, Sept. 18, 1856 (139). Virginia Hawes recalled both the intellectual content and oratorical style of preaching in Virginia in the 1840s: [Mary Virginia Hawes Terhune], *Marion Harland's Autobiography: The Story of a Life* (New York, 1910), 95.

David Outlaw made Ruffin's point negatively: He found the Reverend Mr. Butler's sermons "eloquent" but much too "rhetorical."[38]

Thomas W. Henry, a slave raised as a Catholic, eventually became a minister in the African Methodist Episcopal Church; he converted to Methodism after he heard doctrinal challenges at a camp meeting. The Reverend John Cornish reported several vigorous debates over theology with laymen. Cornish, Bishop Otey, and other Episcopalians became embroiled in doctrinal discussions with young ladies who had converted to Catholicism but wavered when confronted by scriptural readings and doctrinal arguments. The Confederate army was famous for vigorous debates among various Protestants, Catholics, Jews, and nonbelievers. But rural churchgoers demanded "practical sermons." Frontier Baptist and Methodist preachers who knew little theology and relied wholly on the presence of the Holy Spirit might offer a version of Bunyan's *Pilgrim's Progress* on the soul's conflicts, trials, and conversions. With time, the intellectual level of the preachers rose, but the challenge remained to bring the truth of the Gospel to bear on everyday life. "Mr. Paxton preached on the doctrine of Election from Ephesians 1st 4–6," reported James Hervey Greenlee. "Preached a good sermon and as I thought made the doctrine plain from Scripture proof." Greenlee, having heard the Reverend Mr. Gibbs give "a plain & instructive sermon," prayed, "Oh Lord carry home the important doctrine of repentance." Calls to repentance were standard fare, but the more powerful moved troubled sinners. In Columbus, Georgia, James Norman, hearing a sermon on the parable of the prodigal son, went home to read the text. Willie Mangum, a not especially pious politician, was brought up short by "one of the most powerful sermons" he had ever heard. He thought he could now put his daily concerns in a perspective that had been eluding him.[39]

The rustic John Houston Bills applauded "practical sermons" and excoriated pedantic ones. In the University of Virginia chapel in Charlottesville, Bills heard a sermon in which the Reverend Mr. Ruffner "preached nonsense, making God the Author of sin in all its forms, from the eating of the Apple in the Garden down to throwing *High Dye* and Back Gammon, he degrades the deity by perversion of his text, 'The Lord Reigneth.'" The Reverend Robert L. Dabney of Virginia, convinced that Presbyterians paid attention to the theology of sermons, worried that they connected intellectually and remained unmoved spiritually.[40]

[38] Thomas Ruffin to Anne M. Ruffin, Sept. 3, 1823, quoted by H. S. Lewis, "Formation of the Diocese," in Lawrence Fushee London and Sarah McCulloh Lemmon, eds., *The Episcopal Church in North Carolina, 1701–1959* (Raleigh, NC, 1987), 125; David Outlaw to Emily Outlaw, Apr. 21, 1850, in Outlaw Papers, at UNC-SHC; see also Greenlee Diary, July 10, 1853.

[39] Jean Libby, ed., *From Slavery to Salvation: The Autobiography of Rev. Thomas W. Henry of the A. M. E. Church* (Jackson, MS, 1994), 8; Cornish Diary, Aug. 10, 1843, Oct. 1855; Cockrell and Ballard, eds., *Mississippi Rebel: Memoirs of David Holt*, ch. 25; Greenlee Diary, Aug 1, 1852, Aug. 17, 1849, also May 9 and 23, July 4, 1847, Oct. 6, 1854; E. Clitherall, "Autobiography" (ms.), Dec. 6, 1858, at UNC-SHC; James Norman to Mary Dean, June 22, 1851, in Clark, ed., *Southern Letters*, 75–6; Willie P. Mangum to Charity A. Mangum, Dec. 5, 1825, in Shanks, ed., *Papers of W. P. Mangum*, 1:209.

[40] Bills Diary, May 18, 1851; Johnson, ed., *Dabney*, 110.

Painful ups and downs dogged the struggle to live a Christian life. In 1831 the high-church Episcopalian Dr. James Norcom, whom the escaped slave Harriet Jacobs portrayed as a lecherous ogre, urged his son to proceed slowly and carefully rather than play the "revival convert," since genuine conversion – a lasting conversion in depth – must proceed slowly and thoughtfully. Recovering from a severe illness, Norcom felt compelled to face his grievous sins and throw himself on God's mercy. In 1837 he urged his son to remember that "practical piety" ought to be "easy and convenient" and "does not require that a man should fail to make provision for his household, or that he should neglect his worldly interest." Norcom comforted Mary Harvey, who had qualms about her new pastor's views of apostolic succession: "So long as he gives you pious discourses containing precepts to guide you in the practice of life, I do not think it wise to be so exclusive."[41]

Unlike Norcom, most southern Episcopalians remained low church. The high-church party attracted mainly a minority of affluent planters of Virginia and the Carolinas, although in the 1830s the diocese of North Carolina ranked among the most high-church in America. Bishop Levi Silliman Ives, attracted by the Oxford movement, endorsed auricular confession and ended by converting to Catholicism. Some of North Carolina's most prominent public men, notably Chef Justice Thomas Ruffin and George Badger, reacted against Ives's course and promoted extensive discussion among the faithful on intricate matters of church doctrine. Women – who loomed large in the recovery of the Episcopalian Church from its post-Revolution malaise – responded first to evangelical doctrine and then to the high-church doctrines ascendant under Bishops Ravenscroft and Ives. But they did not follow Ives to Rome. Charles Todd Quintard, who succeeded Otey as bishop of Tennessee, also sympathized with the Oxford Movement, and Bishop Nicholas Cobbs of Alabama advocated a *via media* between high-church and low-church doctrine and practice.[42]

---

[41] James Norcom to Benjamin Rush Norcom, Aug. 13, 1831, Nov. 20, 1833, James Norcom to John Norcom, Apr. 4, 1837, and James Norcom to Mary Harvey, Mar. 4, 1848, in James Norcom Papers, at North Carolina State Archives (Raleigh). The 63-year-old Norcom finally joined the Episcopal Church in 1839. The last eleven years of his life suggest an honest conversion. "If his conversion was insincere," writes Richard Rankin, "he was a gifted actor": *Ambivalent Churchmen and Evangelical Churchwomen: The Religion of the Episcopal Elite in North Carolina, 1800–1860* (Columbia, SC, 1993), 115. Shortly after the War, J. H. Bills heard Mr. Thompson preach against the Apostolic succession and commented, "very unprofitable preaching, though he is perhaps right in his theory": June 17, 1866, also July 11 and Dec. 28, 1868.

[42] Rankin, *Ambivalent Churchmen and Evangelical Churchwomen*, ch. 2; Arthur H. Noll, ed., *Doctor Quintard, Chaplain, C.S.A. and Second Bishop of Tennessee, Being His Story of the War (1861–1865)* (Sewanee, TN, 1905), 7, 156; Walter C. Whitaker, *History of the Protestant Episcopal Church in Alabama* (Birmingham, AL, 1898), chs. 4 and 16. Ellen Douglas Brownlow, who had long admired Ives, wrote Mary Eliza Battle that good Episcopalians were "horrified at the course of Dr. Ives": Brownlow to Battle, Mar. 10, 1853, in Mary Eliza Battle Letters, at North Carolina State Archives (Raleigh); also, Wadley Private Journal, Jan. 12, 1863. Judith McGuire extolled the preaching as well as the gentlemanly character of the Reverend Joseph Wilmer, who was passing through Virginia on his way to Europe on a Confederate errand. But, "The Doctor is too High Church for my views": Feb. 20 and Sept. 24, 1863, in Jean W. Berlin, ed., *Diary of a Southern Refugee During the War, by a Lady of Virginia* (Lincoln, NE, 1995 [1867]), 192, 239. For anti-Tractarianism in Virginia and the Carolinas see also Elizabeth Wright Weddell, *St. Paul's Church, Richmond Virginia: Its Historic Years*

When the landlady of William H. Crawford of Georgia, a leading contender for the presidency, referred to "a mighty good sermon," Crawford sneered: "Mrs. A., I presume you are like my mother, who would go to church and hear the verriest jackass preach and say, 'a mighty good sermon, a mighty good sermon.'" Crawford to the contrary, southern women did not much trail southern men in thoughtful doctrinal commentary, although they often settled for "one of the most delightful sermons" or "the best sermon" or "an excellent sermon from the first of Kings" or "one of the best Preachers I have ever heard." Thus Mahalia Roach heard a "delightful sermon from Brother James" in the afternoon and a "fine sermon" from him in the evening. Harriett Newbell Espy wrote Zebulon Vance about "a most excellent sermon," and Elizabeth Catherine Palmer paid tribute to the preaching of James Warley Miles. Amanda McIntosh wrote her husband in only general terms about sermons in Taylorville, North Carolina; his letters to her contained detailed accounts of the sermons he heard in Raleigh. From the Atlantic seaboard to Texas, matrons, young ladies, and girls exchanged and discussed religious tracts, printed sermons, and biblical commentaries, reading alone and with relatives and friends.[43]

The ladies responded tartly if the content of a sermon did not live up to form. An elderly Presbyterian who attended a Methodist church said her piece to the

and *Memorials*, 2 vols. (Richmond, VA, 1931), 1:15–16, and Stephen B. Barnwell, *The Story of an American Family* (Marquette, MI, 1969), 65. For Ives see *DNCB*, 3:256–7. On the impact of Badger's anti-Ives pamphlet see John Norcom to James Norcom, Dec. 5, 1849, in James Norcom Papers.

43 Crawford quoted in Garnett Andrews, *Reminiscences of an Old Georgia Lawyer* (Atlanta, GA, 1970), 59; for Crawford's local reputation as committed Christian and a serious student of religion, see George W. Paschal, *Ninety-Four Years: Agnes Paschal* (Spartanburg, SC, 1974 [1871]), 135–6. Mahalia Roach Diary, Nov. 13, 1853 ("delightful"), in Roach–Eggleston Papers, at UNC-SHC; Espy to Vance, Jan. 31, 1853, in Cannon, ed., *My Beloved Zebulon*, 175; correspondence of Amanda and A. C. C. McIntosh for 1848, at UNC-SHC. Also, Ann C. Furman to J. C. Furman, Apr. 2, 1837, in Cook, *Furman*, 76 ("delightful"); M. J. Chester to Elizabeth Chester, May 15, 1841 ("best"), in Mary Jane Chester Papers, at UNC-SHC; Carmichael Diary, Feb. 7, 1841 ("excellent"), also Oct. 22, 1837; Elizabeth Catherine Palmer to Esther Simons Palmer, June 29, 1847, in Louis P. Towles, ed., *A World Turned Upside Down: The Palmers of South Santee, 1818–1881* (Columbia, SC, 1996), 115 ("ever heard"); E. M. Ross to Lucy Taylor, Sept. 16, 1858, in Catherine Thom Bartlett, ed., *"My Dear Brother": A Confederate Chronicle* (Richmond, VA, 1952), 28.

For women's reading see also Fannie Page Hume Diary for 1860, at UNC-SHC; L. W. Butler Diary, Sept. 16, 1861, at UNC-SHC; McCorkle Diary, Oct. 28, 1847; Jeter, *Henrietta Shuck*, 45–51; Clitherall, "Autobiography," Dec. 1, 1859, June 8 and Oct. 22, 1860. Also, Hutchinson Journal, Feb. 11, Aug. 12 and 13, Sept. 7, 1827, May 20, July 15, 1838, May 12, 1839; C. Beatty Diary, Sept. 5 and 8, 1843, 13, at UNC-SHC; A. F. Simpson to Leah and Rebecca Simpson, Oct. 19, 1844, at UNC-SHC; Carney Diary, Jan. 2, 9, 23, Mar. 16, 17, Apr. 23, Nov. 6, 14, 1859; Hume Diary, Nov. 11, 1860. Mary E. Moragné Journal, Jan. 23, 1842, in Delle Mullen Craven, ed., *The Neglected Thread: A Journal of the Calhoun Community* (Columbia, SC, 1951), 225; Ellen Douglas Brownlow to Mary Eliza Battle, Feb. 7, 1857, in M. E. Battle Letters. For women who studied published biblical commentaries see Jane Wofford Wait, ed., *History of the Wofford Family: Direct Descendants of Captain Joseph Wofford* (Spartanburg, SC, 1928), 55; Cornelia Peake McDonald, Jan. 8, 1863, in Minrose C. Gwin, ed., *A Woman's Civil War: A Diary, with Reminiscences of the War from March 1862* (Madison, WI, 1992 [1875]), 98. For women's comments on the substance of sermons see Elizabeth Fox-Genovese, *Within the Plantation Household: Black and White Women of the Old South* (Chapel Hill, NC, 1988), 44 n. 13. See also Rankin, *Ambivalent Churchmen and Evangelical Churchwomen*, ch. 2.

Reverend Joseph Travis: "Poor preach, Joe." Lucille McCorkle said of Mr. Scales's sermon on sanctification: "I do not rightly get the drift of his discourse – I was going to say argument – but he presented none except his own experience." Kate Carney found a visiting minister "not very intellectual," but Elizabeth Randolph of Virginia proudly wrote her daughter, Mary Braxton Randolph Carter, "I know of no place where there is more orthodox preaching than Warrenton." Mary Watters of North Carolina chose one church because she believed it freer of error than the others. Martha Foster of Alabama dismissed the preaching of the Disciples' Reverend Mr. Casky, who knew nothing of deeper truths.[44]

Ladies rarely provided specifics, but they said freely what gentlemen probably felt as strongly: They expected their preachers to move them. When Brother Hamil preached on "What is truth," Lucille McCorkle did not "for a moment doubt his sincerity," for "he seemed so earnest so truthful, his mind seemed to GLOW." Anne Beale Davis heard a touching missionary discourse that drew her to the message of love. Mr. Slaughter's few "stirring remarks" struck Fannie Page Hume "like the muttering of distant thunder," but she expected more than emotion. Mr. George "was not as interesting as usual," although he gave "a good sermon from 1st Peter, 1st chap. & 3rd, 4th, & 5th verses." Susan Nye Hutchinson was "particularly pleased" with Mrs. Smelt for opening a discussion of the difference between regeneration and conversion, which she had thought synonymous. Still enthralled by theological disquisition a decade later, Hutchinson participated in a "spirited and delightful conversation" with the Reverend Mr. Pharr and others on subjects "more metaphysical than religious." She beamed when the Reverend Mr. Davis made "some very appropriate remarks upon original sin" at the funeral of a friend. In Alabama, Mr. Hillhouse's sermon on the 113th Psalm surprised Martha Gaston, a Presbyterian who thought there was not much more to say on its theme but now discovered there was. Maria Bryan Harford of Georgia, who commented knowledgably on theology, remarked of her 14-year-old sister Sophia, "Her mind is remarkably well informed in Scripture, but as to its special bearing upon herself or her own responsibility, it appears to me that she never thinks of it, or at least never realizes it." Sarah Gayle of Alabama, who always found the Atonement "a dark subject," confessed to "uneasiness in thinking of it." She appreciated the unusually clear and "most excellent" exposition preached by Judge Taylor in the Methodist Church.[45]

---

44 Thomas O. Summers, ed., *Autobiography of the Rev. Joseph Travis* (Nashville, TN, 1854), 34; McCorkle Diary, Sept. 4, 1847, and Dec. 4, 1848; Elizabeth Randolph to Mary Braxton Randolph Carter, Apr. 12–13, 1825, in Randolph Papers, at LSU; Mary Watters to Richard Quince, Feb. 16, 1836, in Quince–Waters Papers, at UNC-SHC. Kate Carney, a Presbyterian, went to hear Dr. Boardman preach only to find someone else in the pulpit, "of whom we got very tired." She did not like Dr. Vinson, whom she heard regularly, "half as much" as Dr. Boardman, but even Vinson sometimes preached an "excellent" sermon: Oct. 23, 1859, Feb. 14 and Apr. 3, 1860.

45 Davis Diary, Apr. 12, 1840; Hume Diary, Jan. 8 and 29, 1860, also May 15 and June 16, 1980 (Slaughter); Carney Diary, Mar. 6, 1860; Hutchinson Journal, May 27 and July 12, 1827, Sept. 14, 1837; Martha Gaston to Jane Gaston, Nov. 22, 1824, in Joan E. Cashin, ed., *Our Common Affairs: Texts from Women in the Old South* (Baltimore, 1996), 169, 173; Sarah Gayle Diary, May 1833, at UNC-SHC; Maria Bryan to Julia Ann Bryan Cumming, May 14, 1829, May 25 and Sept. 3, 1840, in Bleser, ed., *Tokens of Affection*, 97, 288, 301.

Elizabeth Ruffin of Virginia, who demanded "solid arguments," commented acerbically on preachers who resorted to "the superficial appearance of oratory and eloquence [that] tickles our ear." Still, she was glad she took the long and lonely ride to church: "The Bishop pretended to nothing like elegance or oratory but the discourse was excellent, plain, intelligible and suited to the comprehension of the lowest capacity, brought forth many clear illustrations to exemplify the subject so perfectly as to exclude all possibility of a misunderstanding." She responded differently to a sermon at the Methodist Church, "There is so little edification to be received from Methodism, so mistaken is their notion of disapprobation in Theological researches and attainments." She did not agree that "personal feeling, conviction, and conversion" provided "as powerful an instrument of convincing the reason and enlightening the understanding as a greater degree of Biblical knowledge."[46]

Dolly Sumner Hunt Burge of Middle Georgia, a devout Methodist who commented thoughtfully on the theology of sermons, was annoyed by a poor discussion of the denial of the Holy Ghost: "This was not satisfactorily explained." She thought that the Reverend Mr. Thomas delivered an "interesting sermon" but less good than another she had heard from the same text. When Mary Hamilton Campbell accompanied her parents to Colonel Campbell's for dinner, the entire party discussed new Methodist Church doctrines until close to midnight. Certain questions provoked interdenominational squabbles, most notably over infant baptism but also over the Lord's Supper and the nature of heaven and hell. Eliza Frances Andrews found "funny" the attempts of the Episcopalian Mrs. Sims and the Baptist Mrs. Meals to convert each other in friendly conversations. Lucy Breckenridge was not at all pleased with the preaching of the Reverend Mr. McGuire, for he was, in her estimation, folksy to the point of silliness and not Episcopalian at all. She spent Sunday nights with her brother Gilmer and others in theological discussions: "I always drink in anything doctrinal very eagerly." She heard some bad theology preached in Tennessee, and it distressed her.[47]

If ladies got rough with preachers who insulted their intelligence, the strains of the war years made them rougher. Sarah Morgan of Baton Rouge heard "a long stupid sermon from that insufferable bore, Mr. Garie." It gave her "a dreadful headache." It was bad enough that he had little to say; it was worse that he said his little three times over: "Does it not seem the ministry is overstocked with fools?" The

---

[46] Elizabeth Ruffin Diary, Feb. 23 and 25, Mar. 4, 1827, in Edmund Ruffin Papers, at UNC-SHC. Elizabeth Ruffin did not share the religious skepticism of her famous father, Edmund Ruffin.

[47] Dolly Burge, Mar. 19, 1848, and May 19, 1861, in Robertson, ed., *Diary of Dolly Lunt Burge*, 11, 73; M. H. Campbell to David Campbell, June 11, 1820, at William and Mary. For theological quarrels see, for example: Davis Diary, Nov. 11, 1838; Beatty Diary, June 27–28, 1843; Hume Diary, Feb. 3, 1861; Jan. 1, 1865, in Andrews, *War-Time Diary*, 71; Aug. 11, 1862, in Robertson, ed., *Lucy Breckenridge*, 18–20, also Sept. 22, 1862 (49). Mary Chesnut read and discussed theology and religious literature, but – true to her conviction that religion should be a private matter – she removed all prayers and biblical passages when she prepared her diary for publication: Muhlenfeld, *Mary Boykin Chesnut*, 52. Southern women who were living in Washington, Philadelphia, and other northern cities vigorously debated the apostolic succession, the Oxford Movement, and other religious subjects: see Eliza Middleton Fisher to Mary Herring Middleton, Mar. 19, 1840 (118–19), and Apr. 30, 1845 (446), in Harrison, ed., *Best Companions*; Margaret Bayard Smith, *The First Forty Years of Washington Society* (New York, 1965 [1906]), 341.

Reverend Mr. Garie made the most beautiful passages from the Bible ("those I cry over alone") seem absurd. She tried to read hymns while he was droning on, but his chatter kept intruding. "I do not feel like a Christian. I shall never go to hear him again. Better to remain at home, than to feel so wickedly disgusted in church." Contravening accepted practice at the end of the service, she dropped to her knees "to render thanks for having heard the last of it." That was on September 16, 1862. On October 19, she solved her problem. An Episcopalian, she passed up the Reverend Mr. Garie to hear a "great sermon" by a Methodist. Mary Chesnut joined Mary Preston and her mother at church: "The preacher was so dull, and we sat far off, very near the door indeed. So we bad old women fell to whispering, and even to noiseless laughter, as the conversation grew interesting. We enjoyed our scolding, too, as we walked home."[48]

During the War, the Methodist Reverend Luther Smith, professor of Greek at Emory, offended Anne Maria Green with chit-chat when she tried to engage him in serious conversation. Mary Gay remarked without surprise that Methodist women were reading "theological books." Even the less intellectual contended with the doctrinal implications of daily events. In a cave during the siege of Vicksburg, Mrs. James H. Loughborough described a "silvery glow of moonlight, within the darkened earth – beautifying my heart with lighter and more hopeful thoughts." She thought, "Whatever the sins of the world may have brought to us – however dark and fearful the life to which man may subject us, our Heavenly Father ever blessed us alike with the sun's warmth and the moon's beauty – ever blessed us with the hope that, when our toil and travail here are ended, the peace and the beautiful life of heaven will be ours."[49]

In the late 1850s on camp ground, Mississippi planter Everard Green Baker implored, "Oh God strengthen me in good resolve, enable me to grow better as I grow older, & teach me to live in accordance with thy holy laws, for Jesus Christs sake." And again: "May the fear and love of God, direct me in all my doings." Baker captured a determination to make home the focal point of religious commitment in everyday life, and to raise children accordingly. Shephard Pryor of Georgia wrote Penelope, his wife, from the army in 1861, "You must try to raise our children to the best of your ability, and I am satisfied that if you do that they will be raised right. Learn them to love and fear God." You may soon be a widow and they orphans, "But you have a promise in the Holy Book that will hold you up in your trials; that He will be a father to the fatherless and a husband to the widow. Then go on, keep the faith, which you have in Him, pray to Him daily."[50]

---

[48] Sept. 21 and Oct. 19, 1862, in Charles East, ed., *The Civil War Diary of Sarah Morgan* (Athens, GA, 1991), 269, 313; Chesnut Diary, Dec. 21, 1863, in C. Vann Woodward, ed., *Mary Chesnut's Civil War* (New Haven, CT, 1981), 511–12.

[49] Anne Maria Green, Aug. 19, 1863, in Bonner, ed., *Journal of a Milledgeville Girl,* 38; Gay, *Life in Dixie during the War,* 223; Mrs. James M. Loughborough, *My Cave Life in Vicksburg, with Letters of Trial and Travel* (Spartanburg, SC, 1988 [1864, 1882]), 71, also, 13, 114–15, 165.

[50] E. G. Baker Diary, Oct. 17, 1858, and Feb. 8, 1849; S. Pryor to Penelope Pryor, Aug. 17, 1861, in Mills Lane, ed., *"Dear Mother, Don't Grieve about Me. If I Get Killed, I'll Only Be Dead"* (Savannah, GA, 1990), 50.

New Year's Eve was a day for reflection. At the end of 1840, M. W. Philips of Mississippi looked back on a year of "sorrows and anxieties," praying, "Thou Ruler of the world, judge with mercy and punish with moderation, guard and protect us, guide our footsteps, that we may not stumble in thy paths, and keep us ever the same." For Samuel Hairston of North Carolina, a rich and prominent planter, "This last day of the year brings with it melancholy reflections. How many of its days have been misspent, and how often have we strayed from the path of duty." Ferdinand Lawrence Steel of Mississippi, a farmer, reiterated his faith in the wisdom and goodness of the Lord. God could raise him "from adversity to prosperity, but I wish to be any thing He would have me to be. I believe in the dispensation of His Providence towards me." James Hervey Greenlee of North Carolina responded to an outstanding sermon from Dr. Morison by contemplating Judgment Day and men's infidelity: "The affairs of time engross their attention to pile up trash but eternity will reveal their worthlessness. Oh that men would learn true wisdom to Love & fear *God.*" In eastern Virginia, Catherine Cooper Hopley, an Episcopalian visiting a Baptist Church, reported on "the simple unostentatious piety in these rural worshippers, assembled in a modest little building beneath the forest trees." John Walker of Virginia, a planter at a Methodist quarterly meeting after an illness, reported, "I hope to feel always thankfull to my blessed Master for his wise doings with me." He hoped for a good year "if it is used with prudence and fear unto the Lord," and he sought "the lowest seat in Glory thinking myself worthy of no higher one." H. G. Evans of Mississippi went to live with his older brother and a planter, praying, "Lord help him to do right and prosper him in doing." John Houston Bills of Tennessee, in good health and circumstances as he turned 70 after the War: "I thank almighty God, the giver of Good Gifts."[51]

With the Episcopal Church in ruins after the American Revolution, mothers and grandmothers had kept the faith alive by religious instruction of the children. For diverse reasons in early nineteenth-century Europe and America, mothers taught their children rather than expose them to wrong influences. The education of some of the South's most prominent clergymen, including Cornelius Walker and John Girardeau, began with their mothers' instruction. Girardeau learned to read at age 5, taught by a mother who used the Bible as her textbook, no doubt invoking it when she "corrected me soundly" for swearing. With striking frequency women prayed for God's guidance as they went about their daily chores. "To the language of the Fathers, of men, of angels," wrote Charlotte Beatty of Louisiana, "I oppose neither antiquity nor numbers, but the single word of Eternal majesty. I little heed the words of men whatever may have been their sanctity, nor am I anxious."[52]

---

[51] Franklin L. Riley, ed., "Diary of a Mississippi Planter," *Publications of the Mississippi Historical Society,* 10 (Oxford, MS, 1909), 339; Hairston Diary, Dec. 31, 1845, at UNC-SHC; Ferdinand Lawrence Steele Diaries, Jan. 1, 1844, at UNC-SHC; Greenlee Diary, Sept. 24, 1848; Hopley, *Life in the South,* 1:356; Walker Diary, Dec. 19, 1826; H. G. Evans Diary, Jan. 25, 1856, at Mississippi Department of Archives and History (Jackson); Bills Diary, July 29, 1870.

[52] W. A. R. Goodwin, "Northern Influences," in Goodwin, ed., *Theological Seminary in Virginia,* 1:439; C. E. Grammer, "The Rev. Dr. Cornelius Walker," loc. cit., 1:620; George A. Blackburn, ed., *The Life and Work of John L. Girardeau* (Columbia, SC, 1916), 10, 13. P. Johnson, *The Birth of the Modern* (London, 1987), 728–9; Van Zandt, "Elect Lady," 26–7, 84; M. R. Jackson Journal, May 12,

Reading aloud in groups – especially the family circle – became standard practice in North and South, lowcountry and backcountry, and publishers learned that it encouraged the young to learn to read for themselves. The Bible and published sermons dominated family reading circles, followed by political speeches circulated as pamphlets or published in newspapers, and by poetry and novels. As a rule, discussion followed. Each husband and wife had a favorite passage to serve as a text for informal sermons. The family of the busy A. J. Broadus, Virginia's celebrated Baptist preacher, usually proceeded without him in the evenings. When he attended, he sometimes included sight translations of Plato and, on Sundays, read religious poetry to his wife and children. As with eminent ministers, so with eminent politicians. W. H. Crawford drilled his children in the Bible, reading it aloud, favoring the Psalms.[53]

On Sundays in town and country, those who missed church for one reason or another read the Bible or sermons or selections from favorites like Bunyan or Baxter, and Sundays also featured religious readings to servants. The head of household offered exegesis and led discussion, or called on a visitor to do so. James Hervey Greenlee and his wife often read religious tracts and political speeches together, she usually reading to him because his eyes were bad. He did read aloud two sermons on "the great supper": "Oh Lord impress more forcibly divine truth on our hearts and minds & enable us to give a reason for the hope that is in us." They read "Flavell on Keeping the Heart, which is one of the most practical works I have ever read." When fathers were away, mothers or the oldest child led the reading, and daughters read to mothers and vice versa. Husbands and wives sometimes studied the same book separately and then exchanged views. Reading together the Bible, Milton, novels, or some other favorite marked many a courtship.[54]

A religious press barely existed in America in 1800. In the eighteenth and early nineteenth centuries, denominational journals reached the South Carolina backcountry when a solitary subscriber like Mrs. David Rogerson Williams passed issues on to neighbors and friends. By 1830, however, the religious press had become a power in both North and South. More than 600 publications had a combined circulation of 400,000. Methodist itinerants supplemented meager incomes by selling printed sermons, periodicals, and gospel music, largely of southern origin, to the common people. The abolitionist Albert Barnes, fuming at the proslavery ministry in the

1834, in Jackson–Prince Papers; Beatty Diary, Apr. 18, 1843. For expressions of daily piety among South Carolina women see Mark M. Smith, *Mastered by the Clock: Time, Slavery, and Freedom in the American South* (Chapel Hill, NC, 1997), ch. 2.

53 David D. Hall, *Cultures of Print: Essays in the History of the Book* (Amherst, MA, 1996), 31, 56–61; Mooney, *Crawford*; Archibald Thomas Robertson, *Life and Letters of John Albert Broadus* (Philadelphia, 1909), 331.

54 Greenlee Diary, Jan. 11, May 29, July 19, 1847, Apr. 3, 1849, Jan. 27, Mar. 17, 1850, Jan. 19, 1851, quote at Feb. 27, 1853; also, Sarah Eve Adams Diary, Dec. 3, 1813, at UNC-SHC; Hutchinson Journal, Oct. 1, 1826; Louisa Quitman to John A. Quitman, Feb. 1847, at UNC-SHC; Roach Diary, Feb. 3, 1853; Magruder Diary, Nov. 19, 1854, at UNC-SHC; Hume Diary, June 22, 1860; Wadley Private Journal, Mar. 4, 1863. On courtship reading see e.g. the correspondence for 1851–53 in Cannon, ed., *My Beloved Zebulon*, as well as V. Dabney, *Richmond*, 135–6, and Steven M. Stowe, *Intimacy and Power in the Old South: Ritual in the Lives of the Planters* (Baltimore, 1987), 117.

South, ruefully noted that throughout America the religious press exerted enormous influence over the mind of churchgoers. Methodist Bishop O. P. Fitzgerald, looking back after the War, asserted confidently that the boys and girls in church-going families grew up with denominational journals that often provided their principal reports on the outside world. David Moltke-Hansen estimates that in the 1850s Southerners subscribed to religious journals at a rate of one for fifty to sixty whites, or one in ten families. Those journals were often passed along to neighbors and sometimes read aloud to groups. Moncure Conway recalled that on Sunday his Methodist family in Virginia was allowed to read only the Bible and the *Christian Advocate*. Presbyterian journals, noted for their focus on educated clergy, displayed an especially high intellectual level. So it is difficult not to stand in awe at the news that Cornelia Jones Pond's mother in Liberty County, Georgia, taught her to read from them.[55]

Churches published newspapers, usually weeklies, and journals as well. While agricultural journals had a hard struggle in Alabama and Georgia, and literary journals came and went, religious journals proved well based and long-lived. Religious journals ranged from those heavy on theology and doctrine to those that focused on church affairs and moral uplift. Across the South, their subscribers included people of various socioeconomic standing. By the 1830s denominations were publishing journals as part of their campaign to raise the intellectual standards of southern ministries, to contribute to the development of a distinctive southern literature, and to guide the increasing number of better-educated congregations. Apparently, in 1850 the Presbyterians circulated their journals and newspapers more widely in proportion to membership than other denominations: 6,500 subscribers among 35,476 members in the South Atlantic States. Presbyterian newspapers had an average circulation of 1,300, which compared favorably with an average of 872 for the political newspapers in the same area. Thornwell and his entourage held forth at *Southern Presbyterian Review*, but *Central Presbyterian* had its own stars in Robert Dabney and Moses Drury Hoge. Methodists, Baptists, and others published a similar range of journals, and in 1859 J. R. Graves's contentious *Tennessee Baptist* had the largest circulation of any denominational journal in the South: 13,000 subscribers in Tennessee, Arkansas, Mississippi, and Louisiana.[56]

---

[55] Harvey Toliver Cook, *The Life and Legacy of David Rogerson Williams* (New York, 1916), 188; Albert Barnes, *The Church and Slavery* (New York, 1969 [1857]), 26–7, 31–3; O. P. Fitzgerald, *Fifty Years: Observations – Opinions – Experience* (Nashville, TN, 1903), 26; David Moltke-Hansen, "The Expansion of Intellectual Life: A Prospectus," in O'Brien and Moltke-Hansen, eds., *Intellectual Life in Antebellum Charleston*, 382–3 n. 28; Elizabeth Ruffin Diary, Feb. 18, 1827; Peter Walker, *Moral Choices: Memory, Desire, and Imagination in Nineteenth-Century American Abolition* (Baton Rouge, LA, 1978), 32 (Conway); Josephine Bacon Martin, ed., *Life on a Liberty County Plantation: The Journal of Cornelia Jones Pond* (Darien, GA, 1974), 3. *Alabama Baptist*, launched in 1835, continued under various titles until 1866: Rhoda Coleman Ellison, *Early Alabama Publications: A Study in Literary Interests* (University, AL, 1947), 89. The Reverend E. T. Winkler of Charleston described *Alabama Baptist* as "indeed, the only truly Southern paper that the Bapts. have": E. T. Winkler to Basil Manly, Jr., Sept. 3, 1845, in Basil Manly, Jr., Papers, at UNC-SHC.

[56] Bertram Holland Flanders, *Early Georgia Magazines: Literary Periodicals to 1865* (Athens, GA, 1944), vii; *DCA*, 493 (Tennessee Baptist); Thompson, *Presbyterians in the South*, 1:43. *Southern Presbyterian Review* (Columbia) stood out as the most intellectually formidable religious journal in the

The planters of eighteenth-century South Carolina had good private libraries and generously supported dissemination of books. Thereafter, religious literature circulated widely throughout the South. In the early nineteenth century Jesse Lee vigorously promoted the sale of his book in Virginia, reportedly selling some 4,000 copies. In later years the Baptists of Virginia waxed ecstatic over the sales of Jeremiah Jeter's critique of the doctrines of the Disciples of Christ ("Campbellism"). "It is well known," William Hatcher wrote, "that it was extensively read by representative men, and was also popular with the masses." The Baptists of the Lower South thought highly of John Leadley Dagg's *Manual of Theology,* and many knew it through frequent excerpts in denominational journals. Methodist circuit riders distributed vast numbers of books and pamphlets, many of them works of history, biography, travel, philosophy, and ethics, and the Presbyterians distributed 3,000 copies of their post-secession statement of purpose. Albert Taylor Bledsoe's dense and closely argued *Theodicy* had six printings in six years.[57]

In South Carolina, John Belton O'Neall noted with admiration that the educated lowcountry gentry had long had a penchant for reading sermons and theology. The Reverend Dr. Thomas Smyth drew up a long list of Christian books for the home that included Foxe's *Book of Martyrs,* Bunyan's *Pilgrim's Progress,* Law's *Serious Call,* and the works of Baxter, Jonathan Edwards, and George Whitfield, plus eleven works specifically for women. In Mississippi, Everard Green Baker's list of a dozen or so religious books included Locke, Newton, and Watson as well as Grotius, Paley, and Alexander on "evidences of Christianity." He resolved to read and reread Scripture, "satisfied, that the truest happiness we can have upon this earth results, from religious feelings & upon that alone depends our happiness hereafter."[58]

South, but see also *Central Presbyterian* (Richmond), *True Witness* (New Orleans), *North Carolina Presbyterian* (Fayetteville), and *Presbyterian Herald* (Louisville). In addition the New School did well with *Presbyterian Witness* (Knoxville) and circulated the *Christian Observer* of Philadelphia.

57 Edgar W. Knight, *Public Education in the South* (New York, 1922), 38–9; on Jesse Lee see Alexander M'Caine to Sterling Ruffin, July 19, 1805, in Hamilton, ed., *Papers of Thomas Ruffin,* 1:83; Hatcher, *Jeter,* 364; Robert G. Gardner, "The Alabama Female Athenaeum and John Leadley in Alabama," *Alabama Baptist Historian,* 5 (1969), 3–32; Wade Crawford Barclay, *History of Methodist Missions: Early American Methodism, 1769–1844,* 2 vols. (New York, 1949), 2:431–3; Thompson, *Presbyterians in the South,* 2:34; J. B. Bennett, "Albert Taylor Bledsoe: Transitional Philosopher of the Old South," *Methodist History,* 11 (1972), 60. During the eighteenth century an estimated 60 percent of free white Marylanders of all classes owned books, primarily the Bible and religious tracts: Joseph Tower Wheeler, "Books Owned by Marylanders, 1700–1776," *Maryland Historical Magazine,* 35 (1940), 337–53. Also, "Library of Edmund Berkeley, Esq.," *WMQ,* 2 (1894), 250; Louis B. Wright, "Richard Lee II, a Belated Elizabethan in Virginia," *Huntington Library Quarterly,* 2 (1938), 7.

58 John Belton O'Neall, *Biographical Sketches of the Bench and Bar of South Carolina,* 2 vols. (Charleston, SC, 1859), 2:8; *TSW,* 5:153–6; "List of Books on Christianity" in Baker Diaries, July 29, 1855, Aug. 22, 1861 (quoted). Also, H. S. Lewis, "Formation of the Diocese," in London and Lemmon, eds., *Episcopal Church in North Carolina,* 162–3; Walker Diary, Jan.–Feb. 1831. For Baxter see also "Libraries in Colonial Virginia," *WMQ,* 2 (1894), 174. Smyth may have known that the few books found in the homes of farmers on the Georgia frontier included *Pilgrim's Progress* and Baxter's *Call* and *Saints' Rest:* see Paschal, *Ninety-Four Years,* 25, 131–2. Professor Rufus Bailey of Austin College in Texas ranked Bunyan with Homer and Shakespeare among the greatest figures in literature: "Homer," *SLM,* 22 (1856), 109. Baptists found a hero in Bunyan: William A. Mueller, *A History of Southern Baptist Seminary* (Nashville, TN, 1959), 25.

Reports of itinerant booksellers (colporteurs) suggest an enormous circulation of religious tracts. Cash-strapped yeomen wanted tracts, and ministers and ladies' church groups took pains to provide them. Since colporteurs had long done a flourishing business in the South, their outstanding success in the Confederate army came as no surprise. The Reverend Moses Drury Hoge, for one, won fame by running the Union blockade to bring thousands of Bibles into the Confederacy from Europe. The salaries of colporteurs rarely exceeded a pittance, and *Southern Literary Messenger* saluted them as humble men who visited and comforted the poor. In Texas, Sumner Bacon distributed thousands of Bibles in English and Spanish, largely at his own expense, despite much trouble from ruffians who almost killed him. The American Tract Society sponsored colporteurs in 1841, and within five years some five hundred were in the field, mostly in the South and West, supplemented by those recruited by separate churches. Because they were itinerants, colporteurs had to reassure every community that they were coming to do God's work, not William Lloyd Garrison's; an occasional abolitionist colporteur caused grief to the rest. Word of an untoward incident spread, as in the case of Amos Dresser, a northern abolitionist convicted in Nashville for selling abolitionist tracts along with Bibles. He denied only that he passed the tracts on to slaves. During the fierce sectional debate within the northern-based American Tract Society in the late 1850s, Thomas Smyth went to some lengths to reassure the South that the colporteurs were sound on slavery and under effective supervision.[59]

Few if any writers on religious matters had a greater impact on southern sensibility than England's Hannah More. Her "fervor, simplicity, and considerable power" and the "directness and brevity" of her inexpensive books, in the words of Paul Johnson, caused a sensation, and Calvinists and Arminians alike cheered her message of good works, duty, and obedience to constitutional authority. Her books reached more Britons of all classes than those of Maria Edgeworth, Sir Walter Scott, Mrs. Radcliffe, and Lord Byron combined and made her the first author to sell a million copies. In *Thoughts on the Importance of the Manners of the Great to General Society* (1788), More laid out her principal theme: The privileged classes must set an example for society, especially for the poor. In America during 1790–1825,

---

[59] *DCA*, 300; Cornish Diary, Feb. 22, 1842; *HT*, 1:93–4; "The Inefficiency of the Pulpit," *SLM*, 24 (1857), 107; Chase C. Mooney, *Slavery in Tennessee* (Bloomington, IN, 1957), 16–17 (Dresser). For assessments of the colporteurs see DesChamps, "Presbyterian Church in the South Atlantic States," 83; Thompson, *Presbyterians in the South*, 1:318–419; Beth Barton Schweiger, *The Gospel Working Up: Progress and the Pulpit in Nineteenth-Century Virginia* (New York, 2000), 67–8; Anne C. Loveland, *Southern Evangelicals and the Social Order, 1800–1860* (Baton Rouge, LA, 1980), 35; Richard J. Carwardine, *Evangelicals and Politics in Antebellum America* (New Haven, CT, 1993), 39; William W. Bennett, *A Narrative of the Great Revival Which Prevailed in the Southern Armies during the Late Civil War between the States of the Federal Union* (Harrisonburg, VA, 1989 [1876]), ch. 5.

Other proselytizers had a vastly different experience in Texas. James Burke traveled through Texas for the Cumberland Presbyterian Church for forty years without hostile incident and without having to carry a weapon: *HT*, 1:249–50. During the 1820s the American Tract Society became the chief force in the mass circulation of religious books, distributing five million tracts in addition to books and magazines. The ATS published some 300 books and 600 tracts after 1826 – some proslavery, none antislavery – and came under increasingly heavy fire in the North during the 1850s. See *TSW*, 9:460, 472–3, 489; *DCA*, 53; Louis Filler, *The Crusade against Slavery, 1830–1860* (New York, 1960), 268.

Parson Weems sold sermons only slowly but did well with Hannah More's works. Several large printings sold out in five months. Fears in England of a domestic replay of the French revolution ran high, and More added immensely to her reputation by entering the lists against Rousseau and Thomas Paine's *Rights of Man*. Yet Parson Weems and Margaret Bayard Smith, who chronicled life in Washington, thought More overwrote sentimentally; stylistic criticism aside, Southerners chafed at the enthusiasm shown by Northerners like Lyman Beecher, who gushed, "I love her better than ever." Southerners knew that More was a friend of British emancipationists, yet they swallowed and even put her to proslavery use. In 1836 the Louisville *Baptist Banner* excerpted More's story of a slave who drowned after giving his place in a lifeboat to two children. William H. Holcombe suffered some discomfiture when he recalled that More's moral principles guided his mother, who became antislavery and left Virginia for the North. Firmly proslavery, he moved to Natchez. Still, More helped shape his mother's distrust of modern literature and fashions. The ever-vigilant George Fitzhugh lumped More with Wilberforce and Thomas Clarkson as purveyors of "rosewater philosophy," but most Southerners, mesmerized by her piety and moral teaching, forgave her antislavery peccadilloes.[60]

The divines themselves sensed that many congregants learned more Christian moral philosophy from More than from college professors and theologians. Bishop Meade – scoring the dry, philosophical, "moral" preaching of the Episcopalians of the eighteenth and early nineteenth centuries – credited her with helping "to elevate and evangelize the style of preaching in the Church." The Methodist Reverend Mr. Means hoped for a new Hannah More to bring a "vigorous style" as well as virtue and morals "to warn the wealthy and gladden the poor." Zebulon Vance sent books by More to his fiancée, Harriett Newell Espy, and they became her constant companions. The Presbyterian Reverend John Girardeau named a daughter "Hannah More." The South's most intellectually accomplished women throve on More: Augusta Jane Evans, Mary Howard Schoolcraft, Rachel Mordecai Lazarus, Catherine Edmondston, and Eliza Frances Andrews. Susan Catherine

---

[60] Johnson, *Birth of the Modern*, 382–3; Mona Scheuermann, *In Praise of Poverty: Hannah More Counters Thomas Paine and the Radical Threat* (Lexington, KY, 2002), 3, 9, 12, 70, 210; also, Latourette, *Christianity in a Revolutionary Age*, 1:177, 2:257; Lewis Leary, *The Book-Peddling Parson: An Account of the Life and Works of Mason Locke Weems* (Chapel Hill, NC, 1984), 15; Smith, *Washington Society*, 370–1; Charles Beecher, ed., *Autobiography, Correspondence, Etc. of Lyman Beecher*, 2 vols. (New York, 1871), 1:174; on *Baptist Banner* see David T. Bailey, *Shadow on the Church: Southwestern Evangelical Religion and the Issue of Slavery, 1783–1860* (Ithaca, NY, 1985), 225 or 235; W. H. Holcombe, "Autobiography" (ms.), 32–3, at UNC-SHC; George Fitzhugh, "Slavery Aggressions," *DBR*, 28 (1860), 138. For More's antislavery see Scheuermann, *In Praise of Poverty*, 84. On Fitzhugh's contempt for More's sentimentality: She saw nothing wrong with child labor since it built character, and she deplored the "sentiment" that encouraged coddling of disreputable poor: Scheuermann, *In Praise of Poverty*, 157–8, 222.

Lowcountry families read in concert Hannah More's *Book of Private Devotion* (1845) and other works: see e.g. Emily Wharton Sinkler to Henry Wharton, Mar. 1, 1850, and Emily Wharton Sinkler to Mary Wharton, May 30, 1850, in LeClerq, ed., *Between North and South*, 112, 128. For examples of the lavish praise of Hannah More and her salutary moral influence, see: Webb Diary, May 2, 1843; A. A. Lipscomb, *The Social Spirit of Christianity, Presented in the Form of Essays* (Philadelphia, 1846), 52, 81–2, and Lipscomb, *The Relation of the Anglo-Saxon Race to Christian Womanhood* (Macon, GA, 1860), 21; Franc M. Carmack Diary, June 19, 1853, at UNC-SHC.

Botts, a veritable Presbyterian saint in Petersburg, Virginia, joined the Church under the influence of More's *Practical Piety*.[61]

In *Journey through the Seaboard Slave States* (1856), Frederick Law Olmsted left a vivid picture of a "Cracker" church in Georgia. A good many blacks were sitting in back, dressed more neatly than most of the fifty or so whites in attendance. The leisurely coming and going of whites and blacks displeased Olmsted, and the shrieking offended his sense of propriety. Dogs came and went, and open windows let in the neighing and braying of horses and mules. Olmsted recounted the "meaningless" harangues of the preacher, who raked atheism, socialism, and other isms over the coals and especially had it in for Fourier, Tom Paine, Voltaire, "Roosu," the Pope of Rome, and Joe Smith. The preacher eschewed violent language but constantly cried aloud in a curiously conversational tone that held his audience:

A-ah! why don't you come to Christ? ah! What's the reason? Is it because he was of *low birth*? ah! Is that it! *Is it* because he was born in a manger? ah! Is it because he was of humble origin?... Or is it – is it because .... It can't be – it can't be .... Perhaps you don't like the messenger – is that the reason? I'm the Ambassador of the great and glorious king; it's his invitation, 'taint mine. You mustn't mind me. I ain't no account. Suppose a ragged, insignificant little boy should come running in here and tell you, "Mister, your house's afire! would you mind the ragged, insignificant little boy, and refuse to listen to him, because he didn't look respectable?

The Georgia preacher appealed to wives to convert husbands and turned to the sorrows of parents of dead children, pleading for prayers to spare the departed the torments of hell. A few in the pews declared for Christ then and there. An astonished Olmsted recorded the sympathetic response of a congregation that included wealthy slaveholders and others more prosperous than their rude dress made them appear. He concluded that the preacher and his flock thought alike on essential matters. Olmsted himself found the service in bad taste and rather absurd but impressive nonetheless.[62]

The rural South harbored many congregations as insulated and ignorant as Olmsted assumed that one in Georgia to be. Baptist and Methodist country preachers

---

[61] Meade, *Old Churches,* 1:26; A. Means, "God in Jesus Christ," in William T. Smithson, ed., *The Methodist Pulpit South* (Washington, DC, 1858), 118; Harriett Newell Espy to Zebulon Vance, Oct. 9, 1852, in Cannon, ed., *My Beloved Zebulon,* 132; Blackburn, ed., *Life and Work of Girardeau,* 27; Augusta Jane Evans to J. L. M. Curry, Nov. 10, 1862, in Curry Hill Plantation Records; *Plantation Life: The Narratives of Mrs. Henry Schoolcraft* (New York, 1969 [1860]), 66; Rachel Lazarus to Maria Edgeworth, Jan. 1, 1835, in Edgar E. MacDonald, *The Education of the Heart: The Correspondence of Rachel Mordecai Lazarus and Maria Edgeworth* (Chapel Hill, NC, 1977), 265; June 17, 1863, in Beth G. Crabtree and James W. Patton, eds., *"Journal of a Secesh Lady": The Diary of Catherine Devereux Edmonston, 1860–1866* (Raleigh, NC, 1979), 406; Feb. 12, 1865, in Andrews, *War-Time Diary,* 93; Van Zandt, *"Elect Lady,"* 48. Also, Judith W. McGuire, June 1, 1861, in Berlin, ed., *Diary of a Southern Refugee,* 25; Jan. 21, 1824, in W. Emerson Wilson, ed., *Plantation Life at Rose Hill: The Diaries of Martha Ogle Forman, 1814–1845* (Wilmington, DE, 1976), 173; Hume Diary, Sept. 30, 1860; Gaillard Hunt, *As We Were: Life in America, 1814* (Stockbridge, MA, 1993 [1914]), 78.

[62] Frederick Law Olmsted, *A Journey in the Seaboard Slave States, with Remarks on Their Economy* (New York, 1968 [1856]), 454–61. Olmsted discerned smugness among the blacks: "I have no doubt they felt they could do it with a good deal more energy and abandon, if they were called upon."

proved fair game for northern correspondents who saw only disreputable ("jack-leg") ignoramuses. Yet, in 1849 "Southern Traveller" reported in *Knickerbocker Magazine* that Georgia's Crackers included substantial yet illiterate slaveholders, and that the licentiousness of nearby mining villages gave way to sobriety among these country folks. In 1855 "A Pedagogue" writing for *Putnam's Monthly* gave an account of Hard-Shell Baptists in the interior of Georgia: "They are generally very plain people, indulging in no ostentation or luxury, mostly of moderate means, and for their proverbial honesty and promptness in paying debts may be called the Quakers of the South." Quiet, cordial, and gracious to strangers, they "hate all popular innovations upon manners and beliefs." Even the most ignorant preacher had to know his Bible well because congregants would catch him out if he did not.[63]

An elderly lady said of the hellfire Methodist Reverend James Dannelly, "If he did not edify, he would be sure to scarify." Yet George McDuffie found Dannelly edifying as well as scarifying and judged his sermon among the ablest he had ever heard: "It told the truth, the whole truth, and nothing but the truth, though in the roughest possible manner." Everywhere there were great exhorters like the Reverend Joshua K. Speer of the Disciples of Christ in Tennessee, who had little learning and did not always reason logically but whose fiery eloquence and manifest piety made even the learned weep. Sarah Lois Wadley, accustomed to worldly Vicksburg, observed whites and blacks at a communion table near Amite, Louisiana. Spider nests infected the church's roof; the windows had no panes, only rude shutters. Still the ladies, rich and poor alike in the "heterogeneous" congregation, dressed color-fully, and the circuit rider in the pulpit spoke gracefully and movingly. "I enjoyed it very much more than I expected." Bishop George Foster Pierce described the world of his youth in the Barnwell District of South Carolina, in which crude Methodist preachers wrought better than they knew: "a log house, a congregation of poor, obscure people; an unlettered preacher, but full of zeal and faith, expecting the presence and unction of the Holy Ghost upon the word, the power of God revealed in awakening and conversion."[64]

Had Olmsted paid attention to the South's theologians and sophisticated ministers, he would have known that the Cracker preacher was telling his congregation what the former were telling theirs. If that preacher railed against the great infidels of the radical Enlightenment and the French Revolution, so did well-educated elite pastors. Even if he did not read a denominational journal – he may well have – newspapers reported the names and doings of the Antichrist. Ignorant preachers knew that "at the North," during the Millerite craze of the 1840s, husbands murdered

---

[63] In Eugene L. Schwaab and Jacqueline Bull, eds., *Travels in the Old South: Selections from the Periodicals of the Times,* 2 vols. (Lexington, KY, 1973), see: "Georgia Life and Scenery," 2:411–14, and "Pedagogue in Georgia," 2:543–50. For reports similar to that of Olmsted see Hopley, *Life in the South,* 1:57–8; Parsons, *Inside View of Slavery,* 27–8, 92; Oct. 7, 1854, in Suzanne L. Bunkers, *The Diary of Caroline Seabury, 1854–1863* (Madison, WI, 1991), 37; Feb. 9, 1844, in Lester B. Shippee, ed., *Bishop Whipple's Southern Diary, 1843–1844* (New York, 1968), 77.

[64] On Speer see *Reminiscences of B. F. Manire of Preachers and Churches in Mississippi* (n.p., n.d.), 3; Wadley Private Journal, July 14, 1861; George G. Smith, *The Life and Times of George Foster Pierce, Bishop of the Methodist Church, South, with a Sketch of Lovick Pierce, D.D., His Father* (Sparta, GA, 1888), 11–12.

wives and parents poisoned children in one of those waves of Yankee fanaticism that provided an impetus to abolitionism. They knew that soaring divorce and suicide rates were shaking the North. They knew of the frightful bloodletting in the class war of the Paris June Days of 1848. And they knew of the Seneca Falls women's-rights convention in 1848, which they viewed as bringing the anarchic spirit of Paris to their doorsteps. Except for crude expression, the sermon Olmsted heard did not differ from any number of those delivered in the best-educated circles in Charleston, Columbia, Richmond, Nashville, Natchez, and New Orleans.[65]

So, too, the most polished town and college ministers often preached to the common folk of the countryside. The sedate style of the lowcountry Episcopalians and the shouting Baptist and Methodist congregations of the frontier displayed a common theological orthodoxy and social conservatism. Thomas Peck fairly remarked that Thornwell, the greatest of southern theologians, held no views peculiar to himself but spoke for "the great mass of the Church." When Girardeau, a Thornwell protégé, preached to blacks and poor whites in South Carolina, he adjusted the intellectual level of his sermons but struck the same themes. He took the understanding of the common people as a guide for theologians, referring to "the same thing we confess in our prayers, which often represents a scriptural theology more accurately than do our speculations." The Methodist Reverend William Sasnett, a professor at Emory College, could have written that Cracker preacher's sermon: Christians, having routed the infidelity of Hobbes, Hume, Voltaire, Paine, and Rousseau, were threatened by a more insidious infidelity – that of the liberal theologians who undermined faith in the Bible. Among many culprits, Sasnett singled out the Germans Immanuel Kant, F. W. J. Schelling, and G. W. F. Hegel, the British Thomas Carlyle and Harriet Martineau, and the Americans Ralph Waldo Emerson and Theodore Parker. The overwhelming majority of notable southern divines said as much.[66]

Preachers, high and low, knew what they stood for and against, and for good or ill they taught their people well. Primarily, they taught them how to express the thoughts, feelings, hopes, and fears that welled up from their own everyday lives. Abram Burwell Brown, a well-educated Baptist preacher and college professor, commented – in his inaugural sermon as pastor to a well-to-do congregation in Hampton, Virginia – on the style of country preachers. He reminded his congregation of Paul's performance in Athens: "To be willing in the midst of a highly polished people, to be accounted rude and ignorant from *failure* in disposition to exhibit his knowledge, displayed a moral heroism of a high order. Paul had

---

[65] The Presbyterian Reverend John Girardeau and the Methodist Bishop Henry Bascom, preaching to the elite, stressed the poverty and suffering of Jesus in pretty much the same way as that Cracker preacher did: Blackburn, ed., *Sermons by Girardeau*, 176; H. B. Bascom, *Sermons from the Pulpit* (Louisville, KY, 1852), 172, 182, also 188, 255–6.

[66] Peck quoted in Morton H. Smith, *Studies in Southern Presbyterian Theology* (Philipsburg, NJ, 1987), 173; Joseph B. Mack, "Work among the Negroes – Part Two," in Blackburn, ed., *Sermons by Girardeau*, 71; John L. Girardeau, *The Will in Its Theological Relations* (Columbia, SC, 1891), 306; William J. Sasnett, *Progress: Considered with Particular Reference to the Methodist Episcopal Church, South*, ed. T. O. Summers (Nashville, TN, 1855), 121–2; also, William Mercer Green, *Memoir of Rt. Rev. James Hervey Otey* (New York, 1885), 317–18.

considerable learning which might have secured him respect among the Greeks, if in singleness of heart he had determined to know nothing among them save Jesus Christ, and Him crucified." Brown stressed Jesus' poverty and hoped Virginians had not grown too jaded to respond to the simple message of the Cross.[67]

After the War, Junius Hillyer – a college-educated judge, congressman, and planter – thought back on his boyhood in upcountry Georgia. A Baptist, he recalled preachers with little learning and imperfect command of language but with "sound practical good sense and extensive knowledge of human nature, and of the human heart." They lived among the people and knew them. They "had a knowledge of the Scriptures both thorough and minute; and added to all this, and above all, they had a daily walk with God, and a religious life that Paul would with joy have commended."[68]

[67] See Brown's sermons in Dr. and Mrs. William E. Hatcher, *Sketch of the Life and Writings of A. B. Brown* (Baltimore, 1886): "First Sermon," 97–98, 105; "Sermon in Charlottesville, Va.," 122, 130–1; "Christianity and Civilization," 150–1.

[68] *Life and Times of Junius Hillyer*, 103.

14

Unity and Diversity among the Faithful

> In my Father's house are many mansions .... I am the way, the truth, and the life: no man cometh unto the Father, but by me.
>
> —John, 14:2, 6

The slaveholding South took pride in its religious toleration, and Jews and Catholics freely attested that they found the South more hospitable than the North. Even religious skeptics could advance in politics and social life as long as they committed no gross indiscretions. Especially in South Carolina and Georgia, any number of prominent men admitted to agnosticism or were strongly suspected of being free thinkers without suffering ostracism.[1]

A good many colonial southern planters, much like their contemporaries among European aristocrats, eschewed religion but at the risk of encouraging social disorder. Voltaire himself wanted his lawyer, tailor, valet, and even his wife to believe in God: "If they do I shall be robbed less and cheated less." He asked dinner companions who flaunted unbelief in front of servants if they wanted their throats cut. Touring the mid–nineteenth-century South, both the slavery apologist Solon Robinson and the antislavery Frederick Law Olmsted found religiously skeptical planters who, convinced that religion was necessary for the maintenance of social order, publicly expressed little of their private views.[2]

In 1851 John Hill Wheeler, a historian, portrayed seventeenth-century North Carolina as a bastion of religious toleration. On Governor William Tryon, "He was free from all religious intolerance, as he was destitute of any religious principles."

---

[1] Agnostics and other nonbelievers included Howell Cobb, Augustin Clayton, George McDuffie, Benjamin Peppoon, James Cochran, Robert Augustus Beal, Armistead Burt, and Harry Toulmin of Preston, Alabama. Some of these gentlemen converted late in life.

[2] Voltaire quoted by Owen Chadwick, *The Secularization of the European Mind in the Nineteenth Century* (Cambridge, U.K., 1993), 10, and ch. 9; Herbert Anthony Kellar, ed., *Solon Robinson: Pioneer and Agriculturalist: Selected Writings,* 2 vols. (Indianapolis, IN, 1936), 2:279–80; Olmsted to Charles Brace Loring, Dec. 1, 1853, in Charles Capen McLaughlin, ed., *The Papers of Frederick Law Olmsted, 1822–1857,* 2 vols. (Baltimore, 1977, 1981), 2:234. See also William Sumner Jenkins, *Pro-Slavery Thought in the Old South* (Gloucester, MA, 1960), 206.

Wheeler might have been writing about James H. Hammond, of South Carolina's political elite, who wanted to believe but could not satisfy himself that he did. Hammond considered religion a requisite for social order and especially for keeping the lower classes content with their lot. Hammond could sound like Voltaire: "Let Priests reign a while yet over those who require hell & devils to restrain them." In his open letters on slavery to Thomas Clarkson, the British Christian emancipationist, Hammond described the religious character of the slaveholding South as he saw it: "The piety of the South is unobtrusive. Our sects are few, harmonious, pretty much united among themselves, and pursue their avocations in humble peace."[3]

Although religious tolerance flourished in the slaveholding South, honest critics had enough evidence to make a plausible case for the opposite. The religious rhetorical fratricide in the war between Calvinists and Arminians in east Tennessee provided wonderful sport for heathens and anticlericals, with its all-time lows for vulgarity, meanness, demagogy, mendacity, slander, and libel. The Reverend J. R. Graves, foremost leader of an ultra-Calvinistic Baptist sect, employed a talent for invective rivaled only by that of Parson William Brownlow, Tennessee's fiery Methodist preacher and Whig politician, who damned Calvinists and Democrats as Satan's disciples. In 1848 the Presbyterian Reverend Frederick A. Ross, a familiar figure at revivals on both sides of the Ohio, stunned an audience of 2,000 with a tirade against Methodist doctrine. President Charles Collins of Emory and Henry College rebutted tartly, and the ensuing ruckus got uglier as Brownlow and Graves entered the fray. The Reverend Stephen Morgan, a contentious Presbyterian, became locally famous for his aphorism: "Brethren there are three things God-Almighty never made, and never intended should be: a mule, a mulatto and a Methodist."[4]

[3] John Hill Wheeler, *Historical Sketches of North Carolina from 1584–1851*, 2 vols. (Baltimore, 1964 [1851]), 1:30, 49; Hammond quoted in Drew Gilpin Faust, *James Henry Hammond and the Old South* (Baton Rouge, LA, 1982), 262; [Clyde N. Wilson], ed., *Selections from the Letters and Speeches of James H. Hammond* (Spartanburg, SC, 1978), 133–4. Wheeler picked up an old theme. John Brickell, writing on North Carolina in the 1730s, paid tribute to the widespread religious tolerance: *The Natural History of North Carolina* (Murfreesboro, TN, 1968 [1737]), 36.

[4] Morgan quoted in Wilma Dykeman, *The French Broad* (New York, 1955), 325; Tommie W. Rogers, "F. A. Ross: Huntsville's Belligerent Clergyman," *Alabama Review*, 22 (1969), 54–6; E. Merton Coulter, *William G. Brownlow: Fighting Parson of the Southern Highlands* (Knoxville, TN, 1971), 87. For James R. Graves as the most powerful Baptist in the Southwest in the 1850s and for Landmarkism as the product of a long history of doctrinal intransigence, see Richard T. Hughes and C. Leonard Allen, *Illusions of Innocence: Protestant Primitivism in America, 1630–1875* (Chicago, 1988), ch. 4. For Brownlow's viciousness in the local political context see Noel C. Fisher, *War at Every Door: Partisan Politics and Guerrilla Violence in East Tennessee, 1860–1869* (Chapel Hill, NC, 1997), 11–15, and Michael F. Holt, *The Rise and Fall of the American Whig Party: Jacksonian Politics and the Onset of the Civil War* (New York, 1999), 847, 926. Graves provoked a ruckus with incessant attacks on Alabama's leading Baptists. See B. F. Riley, *History of the Baptists of Alabama from the Time of Their First Occupation of Alabama in 1808, until 1894* (Birmingham, AL, 1895), 98, 263–4, 277. Riley records that, in early nineteenth-century Alabama, Baptists sometimes resorted to physical violence against intradenominational rivals (18, 68–9). For trouble caused by the Hard-Shells in Alabama's Baptist churches see Wayne Flynt, *Alabama Baptists: Southern Baptists in the Heart of Dixie* (Tuscaloosa,

A spate of widely circulated books paralleled these lecture-circuit doings, and intemperate articles burned up the pages of denominational journals. Graves's 570-page *The Great Iron Wheel* went through 17 editions by 1856, sweeping the Border States and the upcountry of the cotton states. Acknowledging its impact, Brownlow went off across Tennessee and North Carolina to deliver lengthy counterattacks that culminated in 1856 in *The Great Iron Wheel Examined* (1856). Graves's *Great Iron Wheel* sold more than 100,000 copies and was passed around and read aloud in Baptist circles. Brownlow claimed a like number for his *Great Iron Wheel Examined*. He may have exaggerated, but its sales doubtless reached tens of thousands. The Methodist Reverend Anson West, a contemporary church historian, admitted that Graves had driven people to the Baptists until Brownlow saved the day. The controversy created a bonfire of responses and inspired a spate of polemical novels, as well.[5]

Graves opened with chapters designed to destroy the reputation of John Wesley, the founder of Methodism, indicting him for heresy, blasphemy, apostasy, egomania, corruption, deceit, and sexual impropriety. Graves never let anyone forget that Wesley had supported the British during the American Revolution, thereby exposing himself as pro-monarchy and pro-tyranny. Meanwhile, Graves repeatedly insisted that the Methodist Church had betrayed what was said to be Wesley's opposition to episcopacy. In sections of *The Great Iron Wheel*, Wesley appears as a decent quasi-republican, vainly struggling against the usurpations of American bishops.[6]

The irrepressible Graves was just warming up. The Methodist Church was no more Christian than the hated Church of Rome. All Protestant churches, except his own Baptist sect, emanated from the Catholic Church, that infamous Whore of Babylon. How could the offspring of a whore qualify as a Christian church? Only Baptists could trace their lineage back through Christ to John the Baptist; only they were unencumbered by connection with ancient and medieval Catholicism. The Methodists arose within the Catholic-spawned Anglican Church, which, in Graves's reckoning, Jesus had denounced along with the Catholic Church as "a *harlot* and an *abomination*." Graves's onslaught made the Episcopalians and Methodists cross, and they did not respond kindly. Neither did the Presbyterians and others, who "must adopt the primitive form of Church government before they can be recognized as Christian Churches." Embrace of episcopacy proved Methodists advocates of social hierarchy and monarchism – "anti-American, and a threat to our national liberties." As for Presbyterian polity, it was a thinly disguised episcopacy and hence Presbyterians were no better. Never mind that Graves took every opportunity to enlist Presbyterians against Methodists; at those moments,

AL, 1998), 32–4; also, J. R. Graves, *Trilemma: Or, Death by Three Horns*, 2nd ed. (Texarkana, TX, 1881 [1860]), 120–4, 198–9, 206–7.

[5] Anson West, *A History of Methodism in Alabama* (Spartanburg, SC, 1983 [1893]), 721–5.

[6] In a later work, *The Little Iron Wheel* (Nashville, TN, 1857), 144, Graves reiterated: "Episcopal Methodism is plainly and incorrigibly anti-Wesleyan." For a brief and sober appraisal of Wesley and the British Methodists' disdain for republicanism see Mark A. Noll, *America's God: From Jonathan Edwards to Abraham Lincoln* (New York, 2002), 69, 219.

Presbyterians like Ross became respectable and faithful Christians despite doctrinal errors.[7]

Graves found in Methodism the two-horned beast depicted in the Book of Revelation. Methodism imposed a church discipline that transformed communicants into *"tax-gatherers and spies, or informers."* Money-grubbing Methodist ministers lived off duped communicants; their camp meetings promoted fornication and hypocrisy; and their class meetings imposed tyranny. The crusher: Methodism crossed the Atlantic in the form of an unidentified old woman who arrived in New York in 1766: "Thus we see the precious seed deposited already in America through the direct influence of *woman*."[8]

The Baptist Graves met his match in the Methodist Brownlow, who took second place to none as a master of invective, innuendo, and an instinct for the jugular. Witness the response of John Mitchel – influential newspaper editor, proslavery Irish nationalist, and a Protestant who hated the Know-Nothings: Mitchel described Brownlow, who had joined the Know-Nothings, as "a Methodist preacher, who once preached with pistol and a bowie-knife on the Bible before him; who is systematically, chronically, frantic in his personal abuse of all and sundry, and is generally understood to be perfectly ready to gouge any fellow-creature at a moment's notice."[9]

Brownlow opened *Great Iron Wheel Examined* with chapters that lumped Graves with the Presbyterian Ross. He had special reason to hate Ross, who (unlike Graves or himself) hailed from a planter family. Brownlow choked when Andrew Johnson referred to Ross's impeccable reputation as a gentleman. For while Brownlow pursued one manifestation of the Antichrist in Calvinism, he pursued another in the Democratic party, which Johnson led in east Tennessee. Long after the War, the Methodist Bishop O. P. Fitzgerald of North Carolina described both Brownlow and Johnson as men "whose vocabulary abounded in expletives and superlatives, with a genius for invective and a passion for combat" that suited stormy times "they helped to make more stormy." Political animosities reinforced the religious. Ross demanded suppression of the Methodist Church as a threat to the Republic, and widespread Methodist support for the Know-Nothings fueled the vituperation of their detractors.[10]

---

[7] J. R. Graves, *The Great Iron Wheel; Or, Republicanism Backwards and Christianity Reversed* (Nashville, TN, 1856), 33, 291 ("anti-American"), 499 n.; Richard P. Heitzenrater, *Wesley and the People Called Methodists* (Nashville, TN, 1995), 247. In contrast, Basil Manly, Sr., maintained friendly relations with Methodists and other doctrinal opponents: see Thomas J. Nettles, ed., *Southern Baptist Sermons on Sovereignty and Responsibility,* 2nd ed. (Harrisonburg, VA, 1995), 71, 24.

[8] Graves, *Great Iron Wheel,* 128.

[9] Mitchel quoted in William Dillon, *Life of John Mitchel,* 2 vols. (London, 1888), 2:71–2. Brownlow had a shootout with Landon Carter Haynes, a rival editor. He also unsuccessfully challenged William G. Swan, another editor, to a duel and called Swan a coward for refusing: Fisher, *War at Every Door,* 12.

[10] O. P. Fitzgerald, *Fifty Years: Observations – Opinions – Experience* (Nashville, TN, 1903), 151. Ross inherited a small fortune but lost it in bad investments. He entered the ministry without wealth or slaves: T. W. Rogers, "Dr. Frederick A. Ross and the Presbyterian Defense of Slavery," *JPH,* 45 (1967), 113–15. For the political imbroglio see Richard J. Carwardine, *Evangelicals and Politics in*

With no evidence Brownlow pronounced Ross "a man of *color*," whose anti-Methodist viciousness had been endorsed by his synod in Tennessee. Why, then, did some people object that he, William Brownlow, spoke harshly? "Let them consider WHAT it is we are replying to – not merely this *degraded and slanderous blackguard – this illegitimate son of an old negro wench – this adulterous descendant of an old Scotch Tory* – but all the RULING ELDERS AND MINISTERS OF THE LATE SYNOD OF TENNESSEE." So, it was not the person of Ross that counted, although "he is the embodied personification of all my conceptions of a villain." No. It was the incredible performance of his church in following its "sable leader" in his "falsehood and detraction." True, Ross had Caucasian features but please note "the *copper color,* the *wooly head,* and other similar appendages of the *negro.*" Further on, "that PRINCE of calumniators" went from being a "man of *color*" to a "nigger." Brownlow, while attributing to Ross much greater talent than Graves, called him a broken-down minister who had fled to Alabama because he could not answer Brownlow's masterly arguments.[11]

Brownlow further expressed disgust that Graves would drag personal matters into religious disputes. No honest Christian would do such a thing, although everyone knew that a former congressman had caned Graves on the streets of Nashville for casting aspersions upon the character of a lady, and that a jury had acquitted the perpetrator on grounds of justifiable outrage. Brownlow himself never stooped so low, for – as was well known – he had a spotless character. He neither smoked, nor drank, nor attended horse races or theaters. And in truth, he did cut an exemplary figure, at least for Eliza, his widow, who considered him "the kindest man I ever knew." Brownlow had Graves out to line his own pocket and puff up his ego. Why, Graves could not even claim originality, for he had baldly "*filched*" his slanders and abuse from the work of the "Reverend Slander" (Ross). Few men had "gained so much notoriety, or prostituted a larger stock of *ordinary talents* to baser purposes than this man Graves!" Graves was "a man who cannot elevate himself above the level of a common blackguard – a man who habitually indulges in language toward other Christian denominations which would hardly be tolerated within the precincts of Billingsgate, or the lowest fish-market in London!" A "vagabond politician," Graves made "ruffian-like attacks upon private character" – a "*gasometer*," whose brain was "a mass of living, creeping, crawling, writhing, twisting, turning, loathsome vermin."[12]

Antebellum America (New Haven, CT, 1993), 115–16, 228–9. Brownlow also made vicious attacks on Dr. J. G. M. Ramsey and others who disagreed with him over railroad policy. See William B. Hesseltine, ed., *Dr. J. G. M. Ramsey, Autobiography and Letters* (Knoxville, TN, 2002), 42–3.

[11] William G. Brownlow, *The Great Iron Wheel Examined; Or, Its False Spokes Extracted* (Nashville, TN, 1856), xiii, 103, 144–5, 162.

[12] William G. Brownlow, *Sketches of the Rise, Progress, and Decline of Secession, with a Narrative of Personal Adventures among the Rebels* (Philadelphia, 1862), 19; Eliza Brownlow quoted in Nancy Wooten Walker, *Out of a Clear Blue Sky: Tennessee's First Ladies and Their Husbands* (Cleveland, TN, 1971), 168; Brownlow, *Great Iron Wheel Examined,* Preface, 20 ("gasometer"), 23, 46, 262–4 (with a full-page illustration of the caning). Graves denied that he indulged in personal attacks: *Little Iron Wheel,* 203–4.

Brownlow depicted Graves, editor of the most widely read Baptist journal in the South, as an emotionally twisted extremist whom most good Baptists held in contempt. Brownlow, cleverly attempting to isolate him, carefully restricted his allegation of "TREASON AGAINST GOD" to Baptists who refused communion with other Baptists, and included lengthy protests by "respectable" Baptists against Graves's assorted polemics. But he went too far in a denigration of Graves that implicitly applied to all Baptists when he referred to Roger Williams of Rhode Island, a Baptist idol since colonial days, as a bigot undeserving of his reputation as an apostle of religious toleration. And although Brownlow pretended to respect Presbyterians, he could not resist invoking Thomas Jefferson's broadsides against them as bigots and reactionaries and against Calvinism in general as blasphemy and absurdity.[13]

The leading figures in this spectacular display of Christian disputation self-consciously spoke for the yeomanry and middling folks of the upcountry. Even the plantation-born Ross, himself a slaveholder, represented that largely nonslave-holding constituency until he repaired to Huntsville, where he was more careful to watch his mouth or, rather, to turn his gift for mordant wit against abolitionists. Graves's grim view of the "direct influence of *woman*" and his gratuitous assertion of a divinely decreed perpetuity of black enslavement both appeared in the middle of a book that read like a hymn to social and political democracy and a blistering of all forms of hierarchy, elitism, and social stratification. Repeatedly and worshipfully, he invoked Jefferson and the Declaration of Independence in support of the inalienable Rights of (white) Man.

Graves had a considerable following among the upcountry yeomen, but plantation ladies and gentlemen despised his vulgarity. Although Graves was firmly proslavery and later supported the Confederacy, Brownlow reminded one and all of Graves's Yankee origins and smeared him as a closet abolitionist. The penultimate chapter of *Examined* dwelt on Graves's supposed disloyalty to the South and on the need to purge traitors at a time when Yankee aggression was driving honest Southerners to calculate the value of the Union. This from Brownlow, who emerged – with Andrew Johnson, his political *bête noire* – as a hero of resistance to the Confederacy and became the first Republican governor of Tennessee. But then, Brownlow, only a few years after his violent denunciations of the unspeakable "nigger" Ross, sounded like Ross, Johnson, and George Fitzhugh of Virginia in describing slavery as the natural condition of the laboring classes regardless of race. In a debate with the Reverend Mr. Pryne of New York, Brownlow came down hard on the side of "slavery in the abstract." For good measure, he borrowed heavily (without attribution) from Ross's *Slavery Ordained of God* for his own *Sketch of Secession,* which sold 75,000 copies within a year of publication in 1862. Brownlow, like Ross, reaffirmed that slavery had been historically ubiquitous and that Jesus never preached against it. During and after the War, Brownlow and Andrew Johnson managed not to blush when they announced that – of

---

[13] Brownlow, *Great Iron Wheel Examined,* esp. 149–51, 174, 186 ("Treason against God"), and 270–7 for Baptist attacks on Graves.

course – they had never really supported the slavery they had long so extravagantly defended.[14]

Much to the disgust of the planters of the slaveholding heartland, the Christianity professed by all parties to the polemical war in east Tennessee took a beating. But if Christian planters and their ladies suffered embarrassment, they received compensation: Every such outrage reassured them of their own superiority to those democratic yeomen for whom Graves, Brownlow, and Johnson proudly spoke.

Arminians and Calvinists went after each other hammer and tong in theological and ecclesiastical debates. Mutual recriminations sometimes turned into mudslinging diatribes against the character of ministers and sometimes of whole congregations. Even those who avoided personal remarks slipped into grossly unfair characterizations of each other's positions. Accuse an opponent of Antinomianism and you might just as well accuse him of abolitionism. The two isms became firmly linked, and Arminians, defending free will, and Calvinists, insisting upon predestination, plunged into tortured dialectics to tarnish each other. Each accused the other of making God responsible for sin. They had splendid precedents. The staunchly orthodox Charles Hodge of Princeton Seminary lamented that during the early Reformation Catholics, Lutherans, and Arminians abused Calvin, of all people, for Universalism, Arianism, Nestorianism – even for Islamic tendencies – and that Calvinists abused everyone else for just about everything.[15]

During the revivals of the early nineteenth century, Methodists complained bitterly of the callous treatment they received at the hands of the Calvinists, and the Methodists returned – or initiated – the blows. Peter Cartwright and other frontier preachers spared Calvinists little since they could hardly show courtesy to people who tried to kill men's souls. Yet the viciousness most denominational spokesmen recalled with shudders by 1840 rose to greater heights north of the Ohio River, and even greater among southern yeomen than planters. The Reverend Lovick Pierce

---

[14] See W. G. Brownlow and A. Pryne, *Ought American Slavery to Be Perpetuated: A Debate* (Miami, 1969 [1858]); Brownlow, *Sketch of Secession*, 25, 108–9, 289–90. On the sales of *Sketch* see James D. Hart, *The Popular Book: A History of America's Literary Taste* (New York, 1950), 114–16. For Johnson's views on slavery and "slavery in the abstract" see, in Leroy P. Graf and Ralph W. Haskins, eds., *The Papers of Andrew Johnson*, 13 vols. (Knoxville, TN, 1967–): "First Inaugural Address as Governor of Tennessee" (2:172–83); "To the Freemen of the First Congressional District of Tennessee," Oct. 15, 1845 (1:252); "Speech at Evans Crossroads," May 26, 1849 (1:498–507); "Speech on the Gag Resolution," U. S. House of Representatives, Jan. 31, 1844 (2:133–46); "Address to State Democratic Convention," Nashville, TN, Jan. 8, 1856 (2:352–6); "Speech at Raleigh, N.C.," July 24, 1857 (2:477); "Speech on Popular Sovereignty and the Right of Instruction," Feb. 23, 1858 (3:61–2); "Speech on the Homestead Bill," U. S. Senate, May 20, 1858 (3:159–202); "Speech on Harper's Ferry Incident," Dec. 12, 1859 (3:334, 335); "Acceptance of Vice-Presidential Nomination," Nashville, TN, July 2, 1864 (7:7–10); "Speech at Logansport, Indiana," Oct. 4, 1864 (7:218–30).

[15] Charles Hodge, *Systematic Theology*, 3 vols. (Grand Rapids, MI, 1993 [1871]), 1:467; for a brief account of the mudslinging during the sixteenth century see Jaroslav Pelikan, *The Christian Tradition: A History of the Development of Doctrine*, 5 vols. (Chicago, 1989), 4:336. For a Calvinist response to the charge that Calvinist predestation veers to Universalism, see P. H. Mell, *Predestination and the Saints' Perseverance Stated and Defended, from the Objections of Arminians in a Review of Two Sermons by Rev. Reneau* (Harrisonburg, VA, 1995 [1850]), 66–7.

told his son George, a future bishop, about the terrible days in the late eighteenth century when Methodists arrived in the frontier Barnwell District of South Carolina, about twenty miles from Augusta: "In this better day we have no conception of the hate, the denunciation, the vengeance." Hard-Shell Baptists dominated the country, he added, and many of their preachers were drunks who vilified Methodists. In Virginia, when Baptist preachers forbade their flock to attend Methodist preaching, Peter Cartwright chuckled that natural curiosity sent Baptists flocking to hear the Methodists they were told to shun. In return, the Baptist Reverend J. B. Jeter of Virginia recalled the bad old days of 1800 when a Methodist class leader subjected him to severe heckling, although many local Methodists condemned his intolerance.[16]

Most denominations accepted outsiders at communion, but the Baptists generally did not. Since to refuse communion meant – or was taken to mean – unwillingness to recognize another as a Christian at all, Methodists pilloried Baptists for refusing to commune with them and with other Baptists. Presbyterians, recognizing Methodists as fellow Christians, welcomed them and others to communion, but not without controversy. In 1808, when the Synod of North Carolina noted that the Methodists were slandering Presbyterian clergymen and discouraging shared communion, the Synod advised its flock to shun contact and rebuked those ministers who invited Methodists to share pulpits. Methodists in North Carolina did, however, take communion in Episcopal churches, while in later years the Presbyterian Thomas Smyth of Charleston protested loudly about Episcopalian refusal to admit other Christians to communion. The issue remained thorny and engendered much zigzagging. The anti-Calvinist Bishop John Starke Ravenscroft of North Carolina did not exclude others but did discourage Episcopalians from communion in other churches. Low-church Episcopalians viewed communion as a privilege only for the converted, rather than as a means of grace.[17]

John Leadley Dagg, a premier Baptist theologian, allowed that a large part of the Christian community, including many Baptists, considered close (or closed)

---

[16] T. Scott Miyakawa, *Protestants and Pioneers: Individualism and Conformity on the American Frontier* (Chicago, 1964), 127–8; George G. Smith, *The Life and Times of George Foster Pierce, Bishop of the Methodist Church, South, with a Sketch of Lovick Pierce, D.D., His Father* (Sparta, GA, 1888), 10–11, 15; *The Backwoods Preacher: Being the Autobiography of Peter Cartwright* (London, 1870), 53; William Hatcher, *Life of J. B. Jeter, D.D.* (Baltimore, 1887), 114. See also Supplementary References: "Unitarians."

[17] On the refusal of Baptists to commune with other Baptists see Herman A. Norton, *Religion in Tennessee, 1777–1945* (Knoxville, TN, 1981), 31. William Henry Foote, *Sketches of North Carolina, Historical and Biographical* (New York, 1846), 462–3; Massenburg Farm Journal, Apr. 7, 1835, Mar. 1843, at UNC-SHC; *TSW*, 1:5; H. S. Lewis, "Formation of the Diocese," in Lawrence Foushee London and Sarah McCulloh Lemmon, eds., *The Episcopal Church in North Carolina, 1701–1959* (Raleigh, NC, 1987), 142–4 (Ravenscroft). The question of close communion threatened to rend the Disciples in 1829: R. L. Harrison, "Early Sacramental Theology," in Kenneth Lawrence, ed., *Classic Themes of Disciples Theology: Rethinking the Traditional Affirmations of the Christian Church (Disciples of Christ)* (Fort Worth, TX, 1986), 82–3; Franc M. Carmack Diary, Jan. 31, 1861, at UNC-SHC. On Episcopalian communion see Richard Rankin, *Ambivalent Churchmen and Evangelical Churchwomen: The Religion of the Episcopal Elite in North Carolina, 1800–1860* (Columbia, SC, 1993), ch. 2.

communion offensive, and in his customarily gentle tone he urged Baptists to recognize as Christians ministers who did not baptize according to Scripture. But, he
added, they could not preach in Baptist churches. The not-so-gentle Graves held
that those who practiced open communion thereby confessed to not taking seriously
their own interpretation of Scripture. The fiercely independent Baptist congregations went their own way, and many accepted parishioners who communed with
other churches. Similarly, the Associated Presbyterian Church stood against open
communion, but parishioners in Mississippi stood by the Reverend Samuel Agnew,
who offered communion to Methodists and others.[18]

No issue in religion or politics aroused more animosity than adult baptism and
total immersion, pitting Baptists against the field. In the Middle Ages, the great debates over the sacraments had centered on the Eucharist, on which the Council of
Trent of 1545–63 spent more time than all the other sacraments combined. During
the Reformation, appealing to Scripture, Anabaptists rejected and Luther upheld
infant baptism. In the South baptismal processions to the river intrigued the unconverted, who turned out in droves for the show, and no few found themselves
converted. Clergymen went for each other's throats. Resident William Hooper of
Wake Forest College resigned as pastor of an Episcopalian church and defected to
the Baptists because of their support for adult baptism. (He had been provoked during the baptismal rite by a 2- or 3-year-old child who cursed him in words worthy of
a sailor.) The Episcopalians, trying to defuse the issue, caught hell from both sides.
Bishop Ravenscroft denied that the Bible ordained only one form of baptism and
acknowledged that many Episcopalians preferred total immersion to sprinkling.
The scholarly Presbyterian Reverend Robert Lewis Dabney devoted twice as much
space in his *Systematic Theology* to baptism as to the Lord's Supper.[19]

18 J. L. Dagg, *Manual of Theology: A Treatise on Christian Doctrine and a Treatise on Church Order,*
2 vols. (New York, 1980 [1857–58]), 2:224–5, 288–9; Graves, *Great Iron Wheel,* ch. 38; Samuel Agnew Diary, Oct. 14, 1860, and May 8, 1864, at UNC-SHC. For some sociopolitical implications of
the debate see Ernst Troeltsch, *The Social Teachings of the Christian Churches,* tr. Olive Wyon, 2
vols. (London, 1950), 2:483. The Reverend Hosea Holcombe deplored the factional warfare among
Alabama Baptists, but he insisted on the need to maintain doctrinal purity: Holcombe, *A History of
the Rise and Progress of the Baptists in Alabama* (Philadelphia, 1840), ch 4.

19 Jaroslav Pelikan, *The Melody of Theology: A Philosophical Dictionary* (Cambridge, MA, 1988)), 22,
24, 81. On Luther see also A. C. McGiffert, *Protestant Thought before Kant* (Gloucester, MA, 1971),
53–4. On the processions see [Rev.] John Taylor, *Baptists on the Frontier. A History of the Baptist
Churches of Which the Author Has Been Alternately a Member,* ed. Christopher Raymond Young
(Macon, GA, 1995), 188, Editor's Note; Pelikan, *Christian Tradition,* 4:52–9, 203ff., 297–9. George
Washington Paschal, *History of Wake Forest College,* 2 vols. (Wake Forest, NC, 1935), 1:411; also,
Sermons for 1835, in Otey Papers, at UNC-SHC; Marshall DeLancey Haywood, *Lives of the Bishops of North Carolina from the Establishment of the Episcopate in that State Down to the Division
of the Diocese* (Raleigh, NC, 1910), 63; Robert L. Dabney, *Systematic Theology* (Carlyle, PA, 1985
[1878]), 439, 773–4, 758–88, 800–16; also, Haigh Diary, Apr. 25, 1844, at UNC-SHC. For Thomas
Smyth's intervention see *TSW,* 9:515–29. In Charleston in 1838 the Lutheran Reverend John Bachman and Catholic Bishop John England debated transubstantiation, but the polemics passed into an
extended quarrel over baptism: see Sebastian G. Messmer, ed., *The Works of the Right Rev. John
England, First Bishop of Charleston,* 7 vols. (Cleveland, OH, 1908), 1:57–288. Joseph B. Cobb, Mississippi's celebrated humorist, had a grand time ridiculing the bitter quarrels between Baptists and

Lovick Pierce of Georgia censured Baptists for using the trivial issue of baptismal immersion to exclude Christians from communion. Trivial for whom? A surprised Olmsted found two rich but rough-hewn planters in northern Mississippi heatedly discussing an unsatisfactory Episcopalian sermon on immersion. The Reverend Samuel Agnew did not understand why some people walked out on his sermon on baptism when he had tried so hard not to give offense. The wonder is that Agnew thought it possible to discuss baptism inoffensively. He was lucky, for congregations in various denominations dismissed pastors without even a "by-your-leave" for preaching the wrong side of infant salvation.[20]

In North and South both – from the early days of interdenominational frontier rivalry – Methodists raked Calvinists over the coals on the issue of infant baptism. Arminians attributed to Presbyterians and Calvinists damnation of the unbaptized. They cleverly intertwined two separate issues: adult baptism, which might be read as implying damnation of the unbaptized; and predestination, which had no real bearing since Calvinists did not claim that God always condemned those who did not live long enough to receive the sacrament. With countless others, Moncure Conway's mother defected to the Methodists because she believed that Calvinists preached infant damnation.[21]

The most formidable Baptists and Presbyterian theologians entered the fray. The Baptist Richard Furman of South Carolina and the Presbyterian Moses Hoge of Virginia upheld adult baptism, referred to the inscrutability of God's grace, and denounced the "obnoxious sentiment" that attributed to Calvinists the automatic damnation of unbaptized infants. Thomas Smyth, ministering to Charleston sophisticates, published *Infants Die to Live: Solace for Bereaved Parents* and congratulated Calvinists for being the first to overthrow the dogma of infant damnation. Calvinist doctrine went down hard anyway since it conceded condemnation of unelected infants to hell. Yet, Dabney and most southern Calvinist theologians included infants in a process of election extolled as the happy fate of the great mass of mankind. He and Charles Hodge, summing up orthodox Presbyterian doctrine, suggested that God probably saved most unbaptized infants and intended the salvation of the great majority of all people.[22]

Methodists over immersions and other minor matters while they ignored the broad area of agreement between them on Christian essentials: Cobb, *Mississippi Scenes; Or, Sketches of Southern and Western Life and Adventure, Humorous, Satirical, and Descriptive, Including the Legend of Black Creek* (Philadelphia, 1851), 17–19.

[20] Lovick Pierce, "Paul's Commission to Preach," in William T. Smithson, ed., *The Methodist Pulpit South* (Washington, DC, 1858), 192; Frederick Law Olmsted, *A Journey in the Back Country* (New York, 1970 [1860]), 133; Agnew Diary, Jan. 26, 1862; Julia Gilmer Diary, Feb. 1859, at UNC-SHC; also, C. Beatty Diary, June 27–28 and Nov. 9, 1843, at UNC-SHC.

[21] B. W. McDonnold, *History of the Cumberland Presbyterian Church* (Nashville, TN, 1899), 70–1; Peter Walker, *Moral Choices: Memory, Desire, and Imagination in Nineteenth-Century American Abolition* (Baton Rouge, LA, 1978), 27 (Conway). The issue of infant damnation, vigorously debated in the twelfth century, had a long history: see Pelikan, *Christian Tradition,* 3:111. For the Baptist struggle with the Disciples see Supplementary References: "Disciples of Christ."

[22] T. J. Nettles, "Richard Furman," in Timothy George and Davis S. Dockery, eds., *Baptist Theologians* (Nashville, TN, 1990), 159; Morton H. Smith, *Studies in Southern Presbyterian Theology*

Notwithstanding such endless and even virulent quarreling among and within denominations, Southerners continued to proclaim their religious tolerance proudly, while they arraigned the intolerance manifest wherever abolitionism was making headway. Irritated by widespread praise of the Puritans, F. A. Porcher told the South Carolina Historical Society in 1857 that it was the Cavalier settlers in the South who had blazed the way for Christianity and religious toleration. George Sawyer of New Orleans condemned "New England Conscience" for the witchcraft craze and for the persecution of Baptists and Quakers. The South, according to Dr. E. H. Barton, president of the New Orleans Academy of Science, had minimal sectarian warfare: "No bigotry, no ridiculous humbugs about women's rights, false philanthropy or pseudo religion, each attends to his own business." A. Clarkson of Mississippi wrote in *De Bow's Review,* "The Northern are by courtesy called the 'free states'; but, in reality, the only true, civil, or religious freedom that now lives in the world, is to be found in the Southern slaveholding States."[23]

Despite impressive testimony of southern toleration, leading divines had to plead for restraint and perspective in doctrinal disputation. General Charles Lee of Berkeley County, Virginia, left a will that forbade his being buried within a mile of a Presbyterian or Baptist meeting house, for "I have kept so much bad company while living, that I do not choose to continue when dead." The Baptist Reverend John Taylor lamented, "I once thought, if all the people on the earth could be Christians we should have a paradise here," but in the wake of extended revivals, he found that "brother" had become commonplace and "lost its sacred quality." To his disgust, great difficulties arose from personal bickering: "The most frivolous thing will

---

(Phillipsburg, NJ, 1962), 91, 307 (on Hoge); Benjamin Griffin, *History of the Primitive Baptists of Mississippi from the First Settlement by the Americans, Up to the Middle of the XIXth Century* (Jackson, MS, 1853), 20; "Infants Die to Live," *TSW,* 10:140–286; Smyth added a number of articles on infant baptism and immersion: 10:331–447. Dabney, *Systematic Theology,* 779; *DD,* 1:251–3; also, Hodge, *Systematic Theology,* 1:27, 2:298–9. For other Presbyterians see T. E. Peck, *Miscellanies,* ed. T. C. Johnson, 3 vols. (Richmond, VA, 1895–97), 3:221; George D. Armstrong, *The Theology of Christian Experience* (New York, 1858), 212; Armstrong, *The Doctrine of Baptism: Scriptural Examinations* (New York, 1857), pt. 3; John L. Girardeau, *The Will in Its Theological Relations* (Columbia, SC, 1891), 481. Orthodox Calvinists squirmed over charges that their doctrine consigned at least some infants to damnation: see e.g. Stuart Robinson, *Discourses of Redemption* (New York, 1866), 89–99.

[23] F. A. Porcher, "Address Pronounced at the Inauguration of the South Carolina Historical Society" (June 28, 1857), in *Collections of the South-Carolina Historical Society,* 2 vols. (Charleston, SC, 1857–58), 1–17; George S. Sawyer, *Southern Institutes; Or, an Inquiry into the Origin and Early Prevalence of Slavery and the Slave Trade* (New York, 1967 [1858]), 288–93; *Anniversary Discourse of E. H. Barton, A.M., M.D., President, before the New Orleans Academy of Sciences* (New Orleans, 1856), 26; A. Clarkson, "Basis of Northern Hostility," *DBR,* 28 (1860), 11. On the absence of witch-hunting in Virginia see Philip Alexander Bruce, *Institutional History of Virginia in the Seventeenth Century,* 2 vols. (Gloucester, MA, 1964 [1910]), 1:288. The colonial proprietors of South Carolina insisted on belief in God but initially resisted narrow demands that would have discouraged immigration. The Constitution of 1778 granted religious freedom to all who professed belief in God and in a future state of rewards and punishments. The Constitution of 1790 permitted the incorporation of Jewish synagogues and Catholic churches. See James Lowell Underwood, *The Constitution of South Carolina,* 4 vols. (Columbia, SC, 1992–94), 3:chs. 1–4.

stir up factions." Internal intrigues weakened churches in confrontation with other churches. Surrounded by Roman Catholics, the Methodist Reverend Mr. Cottrell of Pensacola complained that "misrepresentation, calumny and slander" by some in his own church were undermining him. Calls for Protestant cooperation proliferated in the politically dangerous 1850s. Disinclined to exaggerate differences between Calvinists and Arminians, the Presbyterian Reverend George Armstrong of Norfolk stressed agreement on core doctrine, reminding audiences that the real faith of many a man was better than his creed. George Foster Pierce, Methodist Bishop of Georgia, exhorted, "Life is too short to be wasted in frivolous disputes even about matters of conscience. Christianity is too precious and noble and vast to be scandalized by contentions in the Church."[24]

To Thomas Smyth of Charleston, religious bigotry was "a mental aberration, a form of religious insanity," and he reminded his readers and congregants of St. Cyprian's dictum, "Outside the Church there is no salvation." Insisting that God demands allegiance to Christ through one of the branches of His church, Smyth invoked the words of Jesus: "He that is not with me is against me, and he that gathereth not with me, scattereth" (Luke, 11:23). He added, forcefully, "But mark what the church is. It is not the Episcopalian, Baptist, or Presbyterian. The Church is a company of men who have received the Spirit." John Leadley Dagg, who held a hard Calvinistic theological line for the Baptists, deplored the bitterness among professed Christians. "Different creeds, and different ecclesiastical organizations, have divided those who bear his name into hostile parties, and Christianity has been disgraced, and its progress retarded. The world has seen hatred and persecution where brotherly love ought to have been exhibited; and Christ has been crucified afresh, and put to open shame, by those who claim to be his disciples." The Methodist Reverend Dr. Charles Parsons compared the several Christian denominations to railroad cars drawn by the same engine and bound for the same station. The Methodist Bishop Robert Paine doubtless approved: He had been raised a Calvinistic Baptist.[25]

When interdenominational polemics got as hot as hellfire, voices rose to demand courtesy and kindness, some with personal reasons for wanting restraint. The Baptist Reverend Hardin Taliaferro of Alabama had some sport with Methodist idiosyncrasies but denied intention "to slur that most excellent denomination of Christians." Taliaferro's pious late mother had been born, raised, and died a Methodist. Editors who "neither asked nor gave any quarter to heresy" courted reputations as tolerant men in their everyday doings. "Yet – bless their bigoted souls!" cried Methodist Bishop Fitzgerald, "they were the kindest of neighbors" who hated heresy but loved the heretic as a brother. Then there was LeGrand James

---

[24] Henry Howe, *Historical Collections of Virginia* (Charleston, SC, 1845), 191 (Lee); Taylor, *Baptists on the Frontier,* 205; Cottrell Diary, Nov. 9, 1855, at UNC-SHC; Armstrong, *Theology of Christian Experience,* 16–23; G. F. Pierce, "Devotedness to Christ," in Smithson, ed., *Methodist Pulpit South,* 58.

[25] *TSW,* 3:136; Thomas Smyth, *The Well in the Valley,* rev. ed. (Philadelphia, 1860), 15–17, 42, 44; Dagg, *Manual of Theology,* 2:11; R. H. Rivers, *The Life of Robert Paine, D.D., Bishop of the Methodist Church, South* (Nashville, TN, 1916), 102, 152 (Parsons).

Wilson, a staunch Presbyterian who had no problem with Methodist believers in "that horrible doctrine" just so long as they did not practice it. Wilson admired the Methodist chaplain with whom he served during the War but did not comment on what he thought the chaplain was practicing.[26]

Sincere Christians recoiled from bigotry – as they understood it. A good many ministers practiced admirable self-criticism, which often led them to exaggerate the discord. Understandably so: Every act of bigotry among Christians is one too many. All honor to those who recoiled. But self-criticism notwithstanding, every clergy-man, being human, might find bigotry in the doctrine of another and devotion to principle in his own. Dabney remarked after the War, "Now, everybody condemns other people's *bigotry;* yet every carnal man is naturally a bigot as soon as he ceases to be a mere indifferentist." Doctrinal steadfastness by no means denoted intol-erance, much less bigotry. In South Carolina the Episcopal Reverend Dr. Christo-pher Gadsden told the Presbyterian Reverend John Girardeau that the older he got the less denominational he became. Girardeau confessed the opposite for himself. Gadsden expressed surprise, "I thought you were growing in grace," whereupon Girardeau replied, "My denominational creed teaches me that there are other sheep not of the Presbyterian fold; and the older I get the more heartily do I believe it; hence as I grow in grace, I am growing in denominationalism."[27]

If the intransigent ministers had had their way, the South would have suffered the extensive religious intolerance that many outsiders attributed to it. But the in-transigents did not have their way; their congregants balked. The more heavily slaveholding the area, the more readily churchgoers, led by the planter elite, reacted against religious prejudice and told their preachers to tone down the rhetoric. In the 1820s the few Presbyterians in Sunbury, Georgia, attended the Baptist Church, and, sure enough, a terrible row broke out between Baptist and Presbyterian min-isters. "The disputants were both learned men," James Holmes recalled. "Greek met Greek, and as linguists they had few equals." A dispute over the definition of two Hebrew words ended in angry words about close communion and personal al-lusions. The congregation was appalled. The Presbyterian Reverend Joseph Stiles, a man often flattered, got a shock when in private gatherings he spoke rudely of the Methodists. His congregants did not take it well. Maria Bryan's father "seemed very uneasy, aggrieved and disturbed" by Stile's invective. Mr. Bryan replied, "I am really sorry to see that you feel so, and to hear you talk in such a manner. You are injuring yourself and carving out work for future repentance. Leave them alone, the weapons of *your* warfare are not carnal." Church leaders had to be careful not to seem mean-spirited. Bishop Thomas Atkinson of North Carolina was not about to prevent the burial of a pious woman next to her husband's grave in church ground because she did not belong to the Episcopal Church: "It would I think be considered

---

[26] [Hardin E. Taliaferro], *Fisher's River (North Carolina) Scenes and Characters by "Skitt," "Who Was Thar'"* (New York, 1859), 42; Fitzgerald, *Fifty Years,* 27; LeGrand James Wilson, *The Confederate Soldier* (Memphis, TN, 1973 [1902]), 15, 26.

[27] DD, 2:653; Gadsden and Girardeau quoted in R. A. Webb, "The Presbyter," in George A. Blackburn, ed., *The Life and Work of John L. Girardeau* (Columbia, SC, 1916), 213.

something like persecution after death." John Walker of North Carolina, a devout Methodist, noted, "Miss Betsy Prince died this day in full triumph of faith in the Baptist Church." In 1832 he witnessed a Methodist minister's administering of the Lord's Supper to Baptists and Disciples: "All uniting in receiving it that I never saw before. May the Lord speedily bring all denominations of christians to unite together." He asked God to forgive the Disciples' Reverend Dr. Duval for berating his communicants who communed with the Methodists.[28]

In Clarksville, Tennessee, the Episcopalian Marion Henry opened her home to Baptists for a meeting. She sighed with relief when Mrs. Reynolds behaved: "The old lady was very friendly and did not abuse the Episcopalians at all scarcely." A few years later she again had a house full of visiting Baptists. Mrs. Lewis wrote her about the impending meeting of the Methodists, asking that she take care of Mrs. Ervin: "as we are aware the hospitality of all denominations are called upon at such times." Whenever the Baptists met in Savannah the Presbyterian Reverend Willard Preston entertained them.[29]

In 1851 John Houston Bills, a prosperous western Tennessee planter returning from Europe, heard a shipboard sermon by the Reverend Dr. Chouls. "But [Chouls,] being a Baptist, refuses to read the Episcopal service which is so appropriate for Voyagers – Bigots will be bigots forever." In 1858 Bills welcomed "a great day for our Presbyterian friends" and saluted the Reverend Dr. Grundy as "a preacher of great power." For some reason he "greatly regretted, the total want of Charity amongst pretended followers of Christ" who refuse to commune with fellow Christians. Bills inclined to the Reformed theology, but in March 1845 he entertained delegates to the Methodist quarterly meeting and listened attentively to the sermons. In April he went to the Baptist Church to hear Dr. Gayle; six months later, he attended an Episcopal church in the morning, an African church later in the day, and a Baptist church in the evening. In December he participated in a St. John's Day Masonic parade and dinner. In Washington in 1846, he attended a Presbyterian service with President and Mrs. James K. Polk, and in Quebec, a Catholic mass. Shortly after the War, Bills heard a sermon against the apostolic succession: "very unprofitable preaching, though he is perhaps right in his theory."[30]

---

[28] James Holmes, *"Dr. Bullie's" Notes: Reminiscences of Early Georgia and of Philadelphia and New Haven in the 1800s*, ed. Delma Eugene Presley (Atlanta, GA, 1976), 164–5; Atkinson to Ruffin, Feb. 22, 1857, in J. G. deRoulhac Hamilton, ed., *The Papers of Thomas Ruffin*, 4 vols. (Raleigh, NC, 1918), 2:549; Maria Bryan to Julia Ann Bryan Cumming, Jan. 1, 1827, in Carol Bleser, ed., *Tokens of Affection: The Letters of a Planter's Daughter in the Old South* (Athens, GA, 1996), 21–2, also Maria Bryan to Julia Ann Bryan Cumming, Apr. 3, 14, 1828, Apr. 13, 1829, and pp. 61, 64, 94 for Maria Bryan's acid remarks on ministerial feuds between Presbyterians and Baptists. John Walker Diary, Apr. 19 and July 30, 1832, at UNC-SHC; also, Susan Nye Hutchinson Journal, May 26, 1838, at UNC-SHC. Stiles's son, the Reverend Robert Stiles, emerged as a principal figure in the Episcopal Church: Elizabeth Wright Weddell, *St. Paul's Church, Richmond Virginia: Its Historic Years and Memorials,* 2 vols. (Richmond, VA, 1931), 2:555–6.

[29] Marion Henry to Gustavus A. Henry, July 23, 1843, and Marion Henry to Susan Henry, Sept. 26 and Oct. 18, 1848, at UNC-SHC; *Sermons by Willard Preston, D.D., Late Pastor of the Independent Presbyterian Church, Savannah, Georgia,* 2 vols. (Philadelphia, 1857), 1:30.

[30] J. H. Bills Diary, July 27, 1851 (Chouls), June 20, 1858 (Grundy), 1845–1846, at UNC-SHC.

However tolerant of the opinions of others, Bills held fast to his own. On an Episcopalian convocation in 1859: "They preach the succession by the imposition of hands and sadduce my daughter Clara from her church & Bishop Otey lays his human sinful hands upon her by way of Confirmation; as though it would do good. Away with such trifling with the King of Kings – God alone can do good." Bills did not quarrel with daughter Clara or other Episcopalians in his family and recorded without a sign of rancor the baptism of Laura Prudence Polk, his 4-year-old grand-daughter, in the Episcopal Church. On another occasion, he complimented the Episcopalian Reverend Mr. Gray on a fine sermon.[31]

Adherents of one denomination contributed freely to the support of other denominations. Thus the Episcopalian convention that elected Stephen Elliott bishop met in a Methodist church in Clarksville, Georgia, on land donated by James Brannon, who stipulated that the building be made available to all denominations. In the 1820s the Episcopalians of North Carolina proved so generous in donating money to other churches that Bishop Ravenscroft rebuked them for forgetting their own church's dire straits and for holding the misdirected notion of "equal regard for all denominations." John Marshall of Virginia, Alexander Templeton Black of South Carolina, John Blackford of Maryland, John A. Quitman of Mississippi, and Robert Toombs of Georgia were merely a few of the many wealthy slaveholders who contributed generously to churches other than their own. Toombs contributed to the Methodist Church and its colleges partly because of old schoolboy ties to Bishop Pierce, but he also contributed to the Catholic Church and its orphanage: "I always try to honor God Almighty." These politicians knew that their constituents approved of contributions to churches other than their own. No surprise, then, that the 250 or so proslavery volunteers in Montgomery, Alabama, went off to Kansas after being blessed by a Methodist minister in a Baptist church.[32]

Those who have believed the South a land of religious bigots have confused realms. A Southerner, priding himself on frankness, would not pretend to accept another's religion as good, pure, and reasonable – as true – as his own. If a neighbor wanted to play the fool and damn his soul to perdition, that was his business. So long as he "walked orderly" and did not disturb the peace, judgment could safely be left to the Lord. Up to a point, Southerners shared Gibbon's approbation of the religious tolerance of Roman conquerors, but they winced at his cynicism: "The various modes of worship, which prevailed in the Roman world, were all considered by the people,

---

[31] Bills Diary, May 8, 1859 (quoted), May 28, 1865, May 20, 1866; also, June 17, 1866, July 11 and Dec. 28, 1868.

[32] Olin Jackson, ed., *A North Georgia Journal of History*, 2 vols. (Alpharetta, GA, 1992), 1:81; Ravenscroft quoted in H. S. Lewis, "Formation of the Diocese," in London and Lemmon, eds., *Episcopal Church in North Carolina*, 126; Frances Norton Mason, *My Dearest Polly: Letters of Chief Justice John Marshall to His Wife, with Their Background, Political and Domestic, 1779–1831* (Richmond, VA, 1961), 42; Douglas Summers, *A City without Cobwebs: A History of Rock Hill, South Carolina* (Columbia, SC, 1953), 75–6; Fletcher M. Green, ed., *Ferry Hill Plantation Journal* (Chapel Hill, NC, 1961), xiv; Robert E. May, *John A. Quitman: Old South Crusader* (Baton Rouge, LA, 1985), 108; Pleasant A. Stovall, *Robert Toombs: Statesman, Speaker, Soldier, Sage* (New York, 1892), 10–11, 373.

as equally true; by the philosophers, as equally false; and by the magistrate, as equally useful. And thus toleration produced not only mutual indulgence, but even religious concord." The editors of *Cumberland Presbyterian Theological Medium* in effect replied to all such arguments on behalf of the whole southern clergy: "It is true that intolerant prejudice and bigotry are no part of religion [and] it is equally true that disregard to the distinction between truth and error constitutes no part of that religion." An old southern joke contrasts northern and southern tolerance: Yankees say, "You worship God in your way, and we'll worship Him in ours." That does fine for those to whom religion does not much matter. Those who think it does matter prefer the southern version: "You worship God in your way, and we'll worship Him in His." Tolerance of error requires belief in truth. Those who consider all questions open cannot readily tolerate those who think they have found truth and who act on it.[33]

Fierce debates between Calvinists and Arminians and between rival types of each drew enormous crowds to the churches. The wildest of political debates did not exceed their partisanship and rough language. When Disciples and Methodists debated in Carrollton, Mississippi, in 1851, Sarah Watkins reported "as much stamping of feet and applauding as if they had been at a theater or some such place." Especially in the Border States, preachers railed against infidels, heathens, and atheists when they referred, say, to "Campbellites" (Disciples). The "Campbellites" and everyone else gave as good as they got.[34]

Most denominations invited rival ministers to their pulpits. Exchanges became common between, as well as within, Calvinistic and Arminian churches. In Georgia in 1840 Methodists, Baptists, and Presbyterians often opened their pulpits to the Episcopalians, who rarely reciprocated, although over time Episcopalians, too, veered toward closer relations. Polemical rough stuff shocked the tender sensibilities of genteel travelers, but the debates frequently took place in a church presided over by a pastor who invited his rival to share the pulpit. Often the rival had the pulpit to himself, to be answered at a subsequent church service. Presbyterians and Methodists ripped each other up and wounded each other's feelings, but the Reverend Anson West of Alabama, himself a tough debater, testified that a healthy sense of humor contained the damage. More likely than not, after a brutal exchange, the ministers continued their debate over dinner. The Methodist Reverend A. H. Mitchell, who had derided those "fed on the husks of Calvinism," dined afterwards with the Presbyterian Reverend Mr. McCorkle and commented on the many

---

[33] Edward Gibbon, *The History of the Decline and Fall of the Roman Empire,* ed. David Womersley, 3 vols. (London, 1994), 1:56; "A True but Startling Thought," *Theological Medium,* 4 (1848), 22. John L. Girardeau insisted that Christianity justly claimed "the right to be the only religion of the race," since other religions are false: *Discussions of Theological Questions,* ed. George A. Blackburn (Harrisonburg, VA, 1986 [1905, written in 1890s]), 5. John Shelton Reed comments that, even today, "Theoretical hostility toward other groups, other communities, and other regions is often combined with a sort of workaday pluralism that lets folks get along pretty well most of the time": "The Same Old Stand," in "Fifteen Southerners", *Why the South Will Survive* (Athens, GA, 1981), 26.

[34] Sarah E. Watkins to Letitia A. Watkins, Nov. 7, 1851, in E. Grey Dimond and Herman Hattaway, eds., *Letters from Forest Place: A Plantation Family's Correspondence* (Jackson, MS, 1993), 47.

newspapers about. "Yes," McCorkle replied, "I use them to be fed on the husks of Calvinism."[35]

In 1807 John Early, later a Methodist bishop, found the sparring with Baptists on the Cumberland circuit unpleasant, and fearing that the Baptists "have done much harm" he congratulated himself on the "gracious time" the Lord bestowed on his effort "to kill Calvinism." Still, when the Baptist Reverend Mr. Dawson's wife died, he asked Early to preach the funeral service since she had been a devout Methodist. The Baptist Reverend Jesse Mercer and the Methodist Reverend Daniel Duffie, who had reputations for polemical ferocity and as good haters of denominational rivals, worked closely together in support of the Troup faction in Georgia politics.[36]

South Carolinians of every denomination expressed unfeigned respect for the learned and irenic Unitarian Reverend Dr. Samuel Gilman of Charleston. Yet Presbyterian polemics against Catholicism did not much exceed in harshness their polemics against Unitarianism. The Presbyterian Reverend Thomas Smyth and the Catholic Bishop John England had tense public exchanges with Gilman and each other, although they maintained civility, respect, and even personal warmth. The Lutheran C. F. Bansem found the population of the Beaufort District of South Carolina divided among Presbyterian, Methodist, Episcopalian, and Baptist churches: "By the ministers of the first two denominations, a fraternal regard was always manifested to your licentiate, and they willingly availed themselves of his assistance. No such attention was shown by the ministers connected with the Anglican Church." The Baptists, he added, also remained aloof. But personalities were often more responsible for reactions than denominational affiliation. In another place, Baptists and Episcopalians might have exuded warmth and the Presbyterians and Methodists ice.[37]

When exchanging pulpits and hearing each other preach, ministers of one denomination looked at others with a discriminating eye, focusing on their piety and effectiveness. As professionals, they appreciated each other's talents. The Methodist Reverend George Richard Browder's diary sparkles with tributes to Baptist ministers. The Reverend W. H. Milburn, who noted "little or no intercourse" between his Methodist Episcopal Church and the Methodist Protestant Church, attended an MPC funeral service in 1850, confessing, "I felt I had never listened to so wonderful a preacher, and I think so still after having heard most of the renowned pulpit orators in England and America."[38]

---

[35] Robert Nuckols Watkin, Jr., "The Forming of the Southern Presbyterian Minister: From Calvin to the Civil War" (Ph.D. diss., Vanderbilt University, 1969), 370 (on Georgia); Massenburg Farm Journal, 1839–1842; Dr. and Mrs. William E. Hatcher, *Sketch of the Life and Writings of A. B. Brown* (Baltimore, 1886), 197; West, *Methodism in Alabama*, 690, and on the consequences of refusing pulpit access see 222. See also Supplementary References: "Interdenominational Cooperation."

[36] John Early Diary, July 31, Aug. 2, Sept. 13, 1807, at UNC-SHC; W. H. Sparks, *The Memories of Fifty Years* (Philadelphia, 1872), 128.

[37] *TSW*, 9:323–5; Bansemer Journal, 1841–1842, opening page, at UNC-SHC.

[38] Richard L. Troutman, ed., *The Heavens Are Weeping: The Diaries of Richard Browder, 1852–1856* (Grand Rapids, MI, 1987), Sept. 27, 1852 (57), July 20, 1854 (82), July 30, 1863 (162), Aug. 8, 1863

Ministers constituted part of a social and intellectual slaveholding elite in circumstances that encouraged personal friendships. In the 1790s, John Marshall regularly had dinner with the select Barbecue Club, which consisted of thirty or so of the most powerful men in Richmond. The Episcopalian Reverend Mr. Buchanan and the Presbyterian Reverend Mr. Blair – witty, fun-loving chaps – kept their own congregations merry and immensely enjoyed each other's company. In later years a less structured conviviality marked the cities and towns of the South. Ministers attended and often preached at the funeral of a minister from another denomination and attended weddings and funerals of members of each other's families. It seemed to George Freeman that just about all of Raleigh, led by ministers of every denomination, turned out for the Bishop Ravenscroft's funeral in 1830. The Reverend J. P. Justin, a Baptist, delivered the "solemn discourse" at the funeral of the Presbyterian Willard Preston, and ministers from other denominations added a few words. A sick minister would be visited and prayed for by the ministers of every local church.[39]

Bishop James Otey of Tennessee graciously cooperated with other churches but drew hard lines when necessary. While unfailingly courteous, he gave no quarter in ecclesiastical disputes. Yet in an emergency he did not hesitate to turn over his pulpit to a Presbyterian rather than to a fellow Episcopalian. His friendships extended widely, and he judged men by their Christian sincerity and character. Typically, he appreciated the Cumberland Presbyterian Reverend Dr. Porter as "an intelligent man and of liberal mind." In Brandon, Mississippi, he performed the marriage of a Methodist preacher to the daughter of another Methodist preacher. Otey's friend, the Presbyterian Reverend Dr. Elisha Mitchell – after whom the highest mountain peak in North Carolina was named – died on an expedition. Mitchell's friends asked Otey to preach. Otey also preached the funeral service of one of his communicants in the Presbyterian Church to which the young man's family belonged.[40]

The Reverend John Hamilton Cornish of South Carolina, an Episcopal priest, arrived in the lowcountry from the North. The high-church Cornish went in and out of hot water among low-church congregants but got along fine with adherents of other denominations. Cornish preached at a Baptist church, which received him well, and at Baptist and Methodist funeral services, and he and his wife enjoyed the "panoramas" at the local Baptist church, particularly the rendition of "Pilgrim's Progress." In 1844 the Unitarian Reverend Samuel Gilman and the Presbyterian Reverend Benjamin Palmer invited Cornish to join an interdenominational temperance movement and give the opening prayer at its meeting. Meanwhile Cornish dined with Methodist, Baptist, and Presbyterian ministers. In the 1840s and 1850s

(163); William Henry Milburn, *Ten Years of Preacher Life: Chapters from an Autobiography* (New York, 1859), 295.

39 Albert J. Beveridge, *The Life of John Marshall*, 4 vols. (Boston, 1916), 3:182–3; Samuel Mordecai, *Richmond in By-Gone Days* (Richmond, VA, 1860), 159; George W. Furman to Thomas Ruffin, Mar. 15, 1830, in Hamilton, ed., *Papers of Thomas Ruffin*, 2:8; S. K. Talmadge, "Biographical Sketch," in *Sermons by Willard Preston*, 1:31–2; Cornish Diary, July 20 and Oct. 30, 1858, at UNC-SHC.

40 William Mercer Green, *Memoir of the Rt. Rev. James Hervey Otey, D.D., LL.D., the First Bishop of Tennessee* (New York, 1885), 60, 115, 117, 120, 123–4, and "Unity of the Church" (1843), 214–82; Otey Diary, Apr. 14, 1854 (Cumberland minister), Oct. 6, 1852.

he reported full congregations with Jews and Catholics as well as "the most radical Presbyterians." Cornish cultivated the friendship of his Jewish neighbors, and Rabbi Pasnowsky enrolled his own three sons in Cornish's school. In the late 1850s Cornish recounted the funeral of William Pitser Miller, at which the Presbyterian Reverend Mr. Thompson read the Episcopal burial service. Cornish attended the funeral of W. A. Schmidt at the Methodist Church, at which a Presbyterian Reverend J. Halstead Carroll preached the sermon. Cornish then received Schmidt's body in the Episcopal cemetery, where he was laid to rest alongside his wife. Cornish's relations with Carroll sometimes got touchy, but he recorded Carroll's sermon at the funeral of James D. Legaré as "a brilliant effort."[41]

Interdenominational cooperation zigzagged. Formal ruptures in church agreements in the early 1840s did not end local cooperation, which, if anything, became stronger in the towns and villages. Formalities did not much matter. When disputes arose between pastors of two denominations, they appealed to a leading man in a third to mediate. The denominations fought each other to establish a foothold in early Texas, but the visiting Methodist Reverend J. O. Andrew, invited to preach in Presbyterian churches, found them getting along surprisingly well. Still, cooperation did not always run smoothly. In Lexington, Virginia, Episcopalians in 1840 held their first service in the Presbyterian church, and the Presbyterians then contributed generously to the building of an Episcopal church. Washington College, a Presbyterian stronghold, nonetheless opposed the establishment of Virginia Military Institute primarily from fear of an Episcopalian influx into Lexington. Several denominations did fine in building a church to be shared by all in Mobile, but in a Mississippi village the Reverend William Winans called upon Methodists to build a church open to "Orthodox Christians of all denominations" since the Episcopalians kept their building "exclusively for themselves." Alas, Winans then got into a brawl with the Presbyterian pastor and accused him of trying to appropriate an interdenominational ("union") church in Woodville. As the sectional crisis reached white heat and the War came, interdenominational cooperation soared and sniping declined markedly. Confederate soldiers reacted against sermons that spouted denominational special pleading.[42]

---

[41] Cornish Diary: July 22, 1844, Aug. 23, 1844 (temperance); on non-Episcopalians at his church see July 26, 1846 (quoted) and May 23, 1856; Nov. 28 and June 30, 1848, June 11–12, 1849; on Carroll see Aug. 3, 1859, and Mar. 10, 1860; July 24, 1860; Feb. 9, 1861; Dec. 14, 1864. On Jews see Jan. 16, May 22, Aug. 17, Sept. 14, 1854, July 16, Oct. 30, 1855, Feb. 11, 1856; also, Jacob Rader Marcus, ed., *Memoirs of American Jews*, 3 vols. (Philadelphia, 1955), 1:150–1, 2:294, 3:135.

[42] On the formal ruptures see Paul K. Conkin, *The Uneasy Center: Reformed Christianity in Antebellum America* (Chapel Hill, NC, 1995), ch. 8; for an illustration of peacemaking see Otey Diary, Aug. 6, 1856; William R. Hogan, *The Texas Republic: A Social and Economic History* (Austin, TX, 1969), 203–4; J. O. Andrew, "Travels in the West," in *Miscellanies: Comprising Letters, Essays, and Addresses* (Louisville, KY, 1854), 109; Henry Boley, *Lexington in Old Virginia* (Richmond, VA, 1936), 30–1; Ollinger Crenshaw, *General Lee's College: The Rise and Growth of Washington and Lee University* (New York, 1969), 59–60, 87; Charles D. Bates, *The Archives Tell a Story of the Government Street Presbyterian Church, Mobile, Alabama* (Mobile, AL, 1959), 13 (Mobile); Ray Holder, *William Winans: Methodist Leader in Antebellum Mississippi* (Jackson, MS, 1977), 145, Winans quoted at 211; Willard Eugene Wight, "Churches in the Confederacy" (Ph.D. diss., Emory University, 1957),

Presbyterian, Methodist, and Baptist churches had cooperated closely to win souls to Christ in the early nineteenth century. As the Awakening advanced, interdenominational rivalry and tempers flared. The negative responses of congregants, particularly in the plantation belt, called the churches back to Christian charity. Ministers cooperated in Bible societies, in the building of schools, in missions to slaves, and in patriotic festivities, although they continued doctrinal debates and snarls while going to extraordinary efforts to help each other out. Ministers attended the laying of cornerstones for each other's churches and supported concerts and other fund-raising activities. When a denomination had too few communicants to build a church, another shared its own. Small denominations had to turn to others; thus, the Lutherans of South Carolina often held services in Methodist churches. When the Richmond Methodist church burned down in 1835, Dr. William Plumer, Presbyterian pastor, made his own church available. Churches — or, rather, their leaders — cooperated in temperance societies. The passing observation of Columbus Morrison, a much traveled jack-of-all-trades, had parallels in every community: "Grand Military Parade — Great procession including the scholars and teachers of the Baptist, Methodist & Presbyterian Sunday schools."[43]

There was nothing surprising when P. H. Pitt of Alabama, the Presbyterian son of a lifelong Episcopalian, went to hear the Presbyterian Reverend Dr. Armstrong preach in a Baptist church in Selma — or when Mitchell King of the Charleston elite reported that the visiting Baptist Reverend Mr. McLeod preached in his Presbyterian church and received lavish hospitality. When Kate Carney attended church in the morning but skipped afternoon service to read *Lady of the Manor,* she violated an unstated rule, which, according to the not especially pious Frederick Porcher, required a good Christian to hear two sermons every Sunday. When Methodists gathered in Nashville for a conference, Mayor Randal McGavock reported, "All the pulpits of the City are occupied by Methodist preachers." Cumberland Presbyterian Reverend Frank M. Braley of Arkansas preached in the Cane Hill Methodist Church and invited its pastor to preach in his. Braley extolled religion as the bond of family, society, and political union — of all worthy social compacts that unite people across denominations by kindness, affection and love.[44]

ch. 3; Bell Irvin Wiley, *The Life of Johnny Reb: The Common Soldier of the Confederacy* (Baton Rouge, LA, 1978), 187. For the tangled course of the Border State churches see E. Merton Coulter, *The Civil War and Readjustment in Kentucky* (Gloucester, MA, 1966), 394–400.

43 Columbus Morrison Journal, July 4, 1846, at UNC-SHC; Herbert J. Doherty, *Richard Keith Call, Southern Unionist* (Gainesville, FL, 1961), 137; Cornish Diary, Nov. 5, 1840, Dec. 28, July 7, Oct. 19, 1858; James C. Bonner, *Georgia's Last Frontier: The Development of Carroll County* (Athens, GA, 1971), 59–60; Edward Leigh Pell, ed., *A Hundred Years of Richmond Methodism* (Richmond, VA, n.d.), 36–7. For Moravian contributions to the building of Episcopal churches see Haywood, *Bishops of North Carolina,* 153; for Episcopal–Methodist church-sharing see Albert Sidney Thomas, *A Historical Account of the Protestant Episcopal Church in South Carolina, 1820–1857: Being a Continuation of Dalcho's Account, 1670–1820* (Columbia, SC, 1957), 256; for the Lutherans and Methodists see Lutheran Church in America (South Carolina Synod, History of Synod Committee), *A History of the Lutheran Church in South Carolina* (Columbia, SC, 1971), 218.

44 Pitt Diary, Apr. 4, 1850, also Oct. 23, 1851, at UNC-SHC; Mitchell King Diary, May 11, 1852, at USC; Kate Carney Diary, Apr. 22, 1860, at UNC-SHC; F. A. Porcher, "The Nature and the Claims

Denominational loyalties did not prevent Calvinists, Arminians, or those not tied to denomination or creed from seeking the best preacher available. Hearing a good preacher from another denomination went a long way toward overcoming prejudices and encouraging fellowship, and, more often than not, folks would hear the best of another denomination's preachers. Let Lovick Pierce arrive, and not even Calvinists would pass him up. The most dedicated Arminians turned out to hear the touring Presbyterian Reverend Daniel Baker; when he hit Beaufort, South Carolina, in 1830, the Methodist, Baptist, and Episcopal pastors invited him to take their pulpits. The zealous Disciples usually behaved unpleasantly toward ministers of other denominations, but in 1850 their congregation in Texas responded warmly to a sermon delivered in one of their churches by the eloquent Methodist Bishop Pierce of Georgia.[45]

Class prejudices as well as religious led wealthy Episcopalians to turn up their noses at Baptist and Methodist preachers, but Julia Marsh Patterson left the Baptist Reverend Mr. Binney's sermon on the goodness of God full of admiration. William Haigh, another Episcopalian, reported all of Raleigh on tiptoe in expectation of the arrival of the celebrated Methodist Reverend Mr. J. N. Maffitt. Haigh missed Maffitt's last sermon but got an earful from friends: "The crowd that heard him this evening are perfectly enraptured, carried away with the sublimity of his thoughts and his masterly eloquence. He is said to have surpassed their highest expectations, and to have shown himself to be a great Orator." Haigh's impression of Methodists improved when they converted and reformed an old, debt-ridden, whoring alcoholic who had abandoned his family. Representative David Outlaw of North Carolina found the Methodists ludicrous but approved of the Reverend Mr. Morgan's sermons in Washington. Well-to-do Presbyterians shared with Episcopalians a snooty attitude toward Baptists and Methodists. Zebulon Vance observed confusion when the Methodists had their annual conference in Asheville but acknowledged some fine preaching, most notably from Dr. William Wightman of Charleston. James Hervey Greenlee, a devout Presbyterian planter, went to hear Baptist, Methodist, and Episcopalian preachers and generally ranked them high. He pronounced a Methodist sermon one of the best he had heard.[46]

The staunchly Presbyterian Currys of northwest Georgia traveled thirty miles to attend their own church, but most people saw no such need or had little choice. A

---

of Paradox," *RM*, 1 (1857), 486; May 2, 1858, in Herschel Gower et al., eds., *Pen and Sword: The Life and Journals of Randal W. McGavock, Colonel, C.S.A.* (Nashville, TN, 1959), 468; F. M. Braly Diary, Aug. 4, Sept. 1, Dec. 3 (quoted), 1854, in Amanda Braly Papers, at University of Arkansas (Fayetteville).

45 William M. Baker, *The Life and Labours of the Rev. Daniel Baker, D.D., Pastor and Evangelist (1791–1857)*, 3rd ed. (Philadelphia, n.d.), 146; Frederick Law Olmsted, *A Journey through Texas; Or, a Saddle-Trip on the Southwestern Frontier* (Austin, TX, 1978 [1857]), 84–5; George F. Pierce, *Incidents of Western Travel: In a Series of Letters* (Nashville, TN, 1857), 114–15.

46 J. M. Patterson Journal, Aug. 1850, in B. C. Yancey Papers, at UNC-SHC; Haigh Diary, Aug. 12, 14 (quoted), 28, 1844; Zebulon Vance to Harriett Newell Espy, Oct. 7, 1852, in Elizabeth Roberts Cannon, ed., *My Beloved Zebulon: The Correspondence of Zebulon Vance and Harriett Newell Espy* (Chapel Hill, NC, 1971), 129, 135; Greenlee Diary, Sept. 22, 1850, Feb. 20, 1852, Nov. 17, 1861, at UNC-SHC. For illustrations of cross-attendance in the South see Supplementary References: "Interdenominational Cooperation."

few Baptists without a church in a Methodist stronghold might hold services in a private home, but even so, some wanted to attend a more formal service – as did Stonewall Jackson's mother, a Presbyterian who joined the Methodist Church for want of one of her own. Mary Moragné heard the Reverend Charles Colcock Jones preach in the Presbyterian church one Sunday morning and later the same day attended the Baptist church, followed by the Methodist.[47]

The diaries of slaveholders suggest that a great many attended more than one service, often at churches of different denominations. Most settled for two. Presbyterians and Episcopalians readily attended each other's churches, especially when the Episcopal minister had Calvinist leanings. Martha Ogle Forman, an Episcopalian and a planter's daughter in Maryland, frequently attended the local Methodist church, where she found excellent preaching, and occasionally Presbyterian and Catholic churches as well. Dolly Burge of Middle Georgia, a devout Methodist, attended Presbyterian services and commented thoughtfully on the sermons – occasionally with annoyance, more often with approbation. She also did much of her charitable work in the Presbyterian "Ladies Sewing Society." The Presbyterian Malinda Ray, at school in Fayetteville, simply found the Methodist church more convenient.[48]

Frontier "union churches" were shared by several denominations, none of which had enough communicants or resources to build a church of their own. Folks attended service no matter who was presiding and did not welcome sectarian discourtesy from the pulpit. Associate Presbyterian Reverend Samuel Agnew responded patiently when hassled by a Methodist parishioner. The Episcopalians of Botecourt County, Virginia, got upset with the Reverend William McGuire when he offered communion but omitted the morning service. He explained that it ran on too long and that, well, Methodists and Presbyterians do get tired. John Houston Bills grumbled that the Episcopal services during Lent lasted too long: "Too much of a good thing, this keeping of *Lent*." William Holcombe of Natchez did not think much of blacks, but he insisted that he much preferred a pious black man to a doctrinally rigid white man.[49]

---

[47] Curry Hill Plantation Records, 1820s, at Georgia State Department of Archives and History (Atanta); R. L. Dabney, *Life and Campaigns of Lieut.-Gen. Thomas J. Jackson (Stonewall Jackson)* (Harrisonburg, VA, 1983 [1865]), 10; Mary E. Moragné Journal, Feb. 25, 1838, in Della Mullen Craven, ed., *The Neglected Thread: A Journal of the Calhoun Community* (Columbia, SC, 1951).

[48] Merriman Diary, May 14, 1850, at UNC-SHC; Forman Diary, in W. Emerson Wilson, ed., *Plantation Life at Rose Hill: The Diaries of Martha Ogle Forman, 1814–1845* (Wilmington, DE, 1976); Mar. 5 and 7, 1848, in James I. Robertson, Jr., ed., *The Diary of Dolly Lunt Burge* (Athens, GA, 1962), 9; M. B. Malinda Ray Diary, Sept. 9, 1860, Oct.–Nov. 1860, in David Ray Papers, at UNC-SHC. Presbyterians dominated the area around Davidson College in North Carolina, and planters attended whether Presbyterians or no: Chalmers Gaston Davidson, *The Plantation World around Davidson* (Davidson, NC, 1969), 20.

[49] Agnew Diary, Feb. 26, 1857; Aug. 11, 1862, in Mary D. Robertson, ed., *Lucy Breckenridge of Grove Hill: The Journal of a Virginia Girl, 1826–1864* (Kent, OH, 1979), 18–19; Bills Diary, Mar. 28, 1858; W. H. Holcombe Diary, Sept. 16, 1855, at UNC-SHC. On mixed ("union") churches see Frederick Law Olmsted, *A Journey in the Seaboard Slave States, with Remarks on Their Economy* (New York, 1968 [1856]), 251–2; Henry Thompson Malone, *The Episcopal Church in Georgia, 1733–1957*

Members of a close family sometimes chose different denominations. The Episcopalian Reverend Mr. Cornish called on Mrs. Perry and her two daughters: "She is
a Baptist – her elder daughter a Methodist – the other in suspense." Basil Manly,
Sr., had a Baptist mother, a Catholic father, and Quaker kin. Basil became a Baptist minister; his brother Matthias, a supreme court justice of North Carolina, was
a Catholic; another brother, Charles, governor of North Carolina, became an Episcopalian. Abram Burwell Brown of Virginia joined his parents' Methodist church
but became a Baptist minister. John Blackford, an Episcopalian who married a
Presbyterian, had children in both churches and a daughter who became a Catholic.
The Holcombes of Virginia took their children to their Methodist church on Sunday morning but allowed them to accompany their uncle to his Presbyterian church
later in the day.[50]

Any and every pattern might appear in the same family. John Cox Winder of
North Carolina, christened as a Presbyterian, became an Episcopalian, married
a Baptist, attended her church, agreed to have his son raised in her church, and
eventually returned to the Episcopal. John Walker, a devout Methodist planter,
prayed fervently that he might meet his beloved and recently deceased "Campbel-
lite" Aunt Hannah in heaven. When the Reverend Samuel Agnew's Methodist aunt
died, he wondered about her views of salvation and wished he had known her better.
Benjamin Morgan Palmer's sister Mary married an Episcopalian minister. Ellison
Capers, son of Methodist Bishop William Capers, also became a bishop – in the
Episcopal Church.[51]

In the social circles of the elite, Episcopalian and Presbyterian planters were
hard to distinguish, the more so as Presbyterian ministers showed up in the pulpit
dressed like Episcopalian priests. In part, the standard of dress separated lowcountry and upcountry sensibilities. James Norman allowed that a Presbyterian
had preached a fine sermon, but "He was dressed in a gown after the fashion of
the Episcopalians which somewhat shocked my Presbyterian notions of propriety."
Still James Holmes wrote that Bishop Elliott manifested his "pure catholic spirit" in
his respect and affection for the Presbyterian Reverend Mr. Preston. Holmes added
that Elliott maintained cordial relations with Richard Fuller, a kinsman who left the
Episcopal Church for the Baptist. In North Carolina, relations between the Episcopalians and Moravians could hardly have been warmer. Bishops Ravenscroft, Ives,

(Atlanta, GA, 1960), 93; Edward L. Ayers, *Vengeance and Justice: Crime and Punishment in the Nineteenth-Century South* (New York, 1984), 120.

50 Cornish Diary, Aug. 21, 1854; Hatcher and Hatcher, *A. B. Brown*, 27; *DNCB*, 4:209 (Burwell); Green,
ed., *Ferry Hill Plantation Journal*, xxii–xxiii, 97; also, Ray Diary, Oct. 8, 1860; James A. Rogers,
Richard Furman: Life and Legacy (Macon, GA, 1985), 209; Walker Diary, Apr. 20, 1833; W. H. Holcombe, "Autobiography" (ms.), 51–2, at UNC-SHC; Timothy George, " 'Faithful Shepherd, Beloved
Minister': The Life and Legacy of Basil Manly, Sr.," *Alabama Baptist History*, 27 (1991), 15.

51 Arch Frederic Blakey, *General John H. Winder, C.S.A.* (Greenville, FL, 1990), 41; Walker Diary, Aug.
13, 1849; Agnew Diary, Feb. 5, 1861; Mary C. Oliphant et al., eds., *The Letters of William Gilmore
Simms*, 6 vols. (Columbia, 1952–82), 3:323 n. 177 (Palmer); J. G. deRoulhac Hamilton, ed., *The Papers of William Alexander Graham*, 5 vols. (Raleigh, NC, 1957–73), 5:172 n. 52 (Capers).

and Atkinson – who did not always have kind words for other denominations – loved the Moravians, who returned the compliments.[52]

Intermarriage did not necessarily produce conversions. Calvinistic Episcopalians attracted to the Presbyterian Church resisted because of its strictures on dancing. An Episcopalian like Henry Wise of Virginia attended the church of a Presbyterian wife but did not join it. John Berkeley Grimball, lowcountry South Carolina Presbyterian, finally joined a church after years of faithful attendance. He wound up a communicant of his wife's Episcopal church, doubtless in part to please her but perhaps also because it took an easier view of social gaiety. Lowcountry residents credited intermarriage with the close relations of Episcopalians and Presbyterians. Fredrika Bremer's eyebrows lifted when the "highly-esteemed and beloved" Unitarian Mr. Gilman of Charleston presided over the wedding of an Episcopalian and a Catholic. In intermarriages the husband and wife usually attended church together, alternating between their preferences rather than going off to church separately. James Knox Polk deferred to the Presbyterian sensibilities of his wife, Sarah, only to follow his own inclinations and join the Methodist Church after her death. The poet Charles W. Hübner was raised in a Lutheran family but joined his bride's Methodist church and, after her death, his second wife's Presbyterian church. Representative James Pugh of Alabama, a Presbyterian, switched to the Episcopalians when he married. The elite churches took a liberal view of such personal sensibility. Prominent families and lesser folk split religiously for reasons other than marriage. Arminians found themselves convinced by Calvinist ministers or vice versa. Personal rebellions against parental authority appeared here and there, especially since parents usually accommodated.[53]

Every community contained pious, churchgoing people who cared little for doctrinal differences or could not decide who had the better case. Those who cared enough to want to stay within either the Arminian or Calvinist orbit had ample choices. The Episcopal Church prided itself on its latitudinarianism. Arminians

[52] James Norman to Mary Dean Norman, Nov. 3, 1861, in Susan Lott Clark, ed., *Southern Letters and Life in the Mid 1800s* (Waycross, GA, 1993), 114; Holmes, *"Dr. Bullie's" Notes,* 143 (quoted), 232; Haywood, *Bishops of North Carolina,* 23, 153; also, J. B. Grimball Papers, at UNC-SHC.

[53] Craig Simpson, *A Good Southerner: The Life of Henry A. Wise of Virginia* (Chapel Hill, NC, 1985), ch. 1; Meta Morris Grimball Diary, Sept. 9, 1863, at UNC-SHC; James Oscar Farmer, Jr., *The Metaphysical Confederacy: James Henley Thornwell and the Synthesis of Southern Values* (Macon, GA, 1986), 172; Ethel Trenholm Seabrook Nepveux, *Sarah Henry Bryce, 1825–1901: A Glimpse at a Remarkable Woman in the Turbulent Civil War Era* (Charleston, SC, 1994), 17; for Edisto see I. Jenkins Mikell, *Rumbling of the Chariot Wheels* (Charleston, SC, 1923), 230; Fredrika Bremer, *Homes of the New World: Impressions of America,* 2 vols. (New York, 1853), 1:274; *DNCB,* 1:368–9, 2:76; Mary Hübner Walker, *Charles W. Hübner: Poet Laureate of the South* (Atlanta, GA, 1976), 20, 67; *BDC,* 357 (Pugh); Carwardine, *Evangelicals and Politics,* 75. For reasons other than marriage see Bethell Diary, Apr., Aug. 10, Sept. 25, 1864, at UNC-SHC; [P. Cartwright], *Backwoods Preacher,* 36–7; *BDC,* 86–8, 195, 228. Prominent religious leaders like the Methodist Bishop Daniel Asbury of South Carolina and the Reverend Sidney D. Bumpass were born into religiously mixed marriages and found their way to one or the other side or ended by joining a third church: William Buell Sprague, *Annals of the American Pulpit,* 9 vols. (New York, 1859–69), 7:127, 814.

chose among the Methodists, the Cumberland Presbyterians, the Disciples of Christ, or even some Baptist churches. Calvinists had the Presbyterian and Baptist churches. For those who felt as comfortable in one denomination as another, respect for family tradition often guided the choice. Thomas Ruffin did not regard denominational differences as being of much importance but "for that very reason" urged his son to choose the Episcopal Church: "I have long considered it very proper for each person to attach himself to that persuasion which he can not only call *a* Church of *God*, but also *the* Church of his *Fore Fathers*." Charles Lockhart Pettigrew, who wanted to join a church "and fight under the banner of my lord and redeemer," could not decide between the Episcopal and the Presbyterian. Charles Biddle Shepard, his uncle, counseled that he ought to join the church of his worthy parents, and so he did. When James M. Legaré presented himself as a candidate for entrance into the Episcopal Church in Aiken, South Carolina, he escaped an examination on the validity of baptism. Cornish explained that Legaré "does not wish to think it not valid, lest he should cast a painful imputation upon the faith of his parents, & dishonor or offend them." Susan Nye Hutchinson reacted testily when Mrs. B. expressed distress over her predilection for the Methodists, for surely the effort of a stranger to draw her away from the church of her parents was simply cruel. Harriett Newell Espy, who married Governor Zebulon Vance of North Carolina, found herself an orphan at age 9 sent to live with pious Methodist kin. Her parents had been Presbyterians, and she held firm to their faith with no difficulty from her stepparents.[54]

Kinfolk seldom made a fuss over intermarriages. To the great joy of both sets of parents, Joseph Jones – son of the celebrated Presbyterian Reverend C. C. Jones – married Caroline Smelt Davis, daughter of a Baptist minister. The bride's father officiated, and the groom's offered the benediction. With varying consequences, even ministers married out of their denomination. Sometimes a wife switched to her husband's church, as the devoutly Presbyterian wife of the Baptist Reverend John Landrum did after a few years of marriage. Richard Furman, the eminent Baptist minister, had an Episcopalian father and a Baptist mother. His wife, Elizabeth Haynsworth, remained an Episcopalian. The Methodist Bishop Robert Paine's second wife was the daughter of a Presbyterian minister.[55]

---

[54] Thomas Ruffin to William K. Ruffin, Dec. 31, 1826, in Hamilton, ed., *Papers of Thomas Ruffin*, 1:369 (Thomas Ruffin's parents had in fact been Methodists, but we may suppose he chafed at their having left the church of their own parents); Charles Lockhart Pettigrew to Ebenezer Pettigrew, Sept. 19, 1831, and Charles Biddle Shepard to Charles Lockhart Pettigrew, Oct. 1, 1831, in Sarah McCulloh Lemmon, ed., *The Pettigrew Papers*, 2 vols. (Raleigh, NC, 1971, 1988), 2:164, 167; Cornish Diary, Apr. 29, 1848; Hutchinson Journal, Dec. 28, 1837; F. G. Patton, "Introduction," in Cannon, *My Beloved Zebulon*. A kind of reverse case: Eliza S. Schley of Texas did not take it lightly when her mother seemed on the verge of defecting to the Campbellites: Eliza S. Schley to Sarah Rootes Jackson, Apr. 29, 1840, in Jackson–Prince Papers, at UNC-SHC.

[55] James O. Breeden, *Joseph Jones, M.D.: Scientist of the Old South* (Lexington, KY, 1975), 66; H. P. Griffith, *The Life and Times of Rev. John G. Landrum* (Charleston, SC, 1992 [1885]), 142–3; Carolyn L. Harrell, *Kith and Kin: A Portrait of a Southern Family, 1630–1934* (Macon, GA, 1984), 15, 18; R. H. Rivers, *Robert Paine*, 59. The Lumpkins of Georgia began as Methodists but became Baptists. One son, Governor Wilson Lumpkin, remained a Baptist, but another, Chief Justice Joseph Henry

The first two Jews elected to the U.S. Senate, both from the slave states, married Christians. P. G. T. Beauregard's sister and other prominent Louisianans married Jews. Several of the nine children of Joseph Marx, a Jew and one of Richmond's most prominent citizens, married Gentiles. Gustavus A. Meyers, a prominent lawyer in Richmond and president of the prestigious Richmond Club, married the daughter of William Branch Giles; Meyers and some other prominent Jews of Richmond who married Christians remained practicing Jews. Margaret Bain Cameron, daughter of Duncan Cameron (one of the biggest planters in North Carolina), married George W. Mordecai in 1853. The attempts to brand John Slidell of Louisiana a Jew after his sister married August Belmont did not damage his political career. Jesse Mercer, the eminent Baptist minister and educator, married Nancy Simons of Wilkes County, Georgia, a Christian widow of a prominent Jew. The Sephardim, who predominated in the early Jewish immigration, married more easily into Christian families than the Ashkenazi, who predominated after 1830. Jewish law, rigorously enforced in Charleston, prohibited marriage out of the faith, but the synagogue in New Orleans made it easy – perhaps under pressure from French-speaking Jews who had long-standing cordial relations with French-speaking Christians. Salomon de Rothschild of Paris, visiting New Orleans in 1861, expressed astonishment at the extent of intermarriage.[56]

David Wyatt Aiken courted a young lady whose father gave consent despite denominational difference, but her mother remained unreconciled "because she believed unhappiness would be the result of an Episcopalian marrying into a Presbyterian family." John Brownrigg heard that his brother had joined the Methodists and worried about the effect on his mother, who was in mourning and badly shaken by the death of her husband. Edgeworth Bird, a planter in Hancock County, Georgia, was reared a Catholic by his mother but married a Presbyterian, who raised their children in her church. His wife Sallie, Presbyterian or no, had attended Catholic

---

Lumpkin, became a Presbyterian. See Paul DeForest Hicks, *Joseph Henry Lumpkin: Georgia's First Chief Justice* (Athens, GA, 2002), 10–11.

[56] On Jewish–Christian intermarriage see Robert Douthat Meade, *Judah P. Benjamin: Confederate Statesman* (New York, 1943), 6–7, 48–50; Leon Hühner, "David Yulee, Florida's First Senator," *Publications of the American Jewish Historical Society*, 17 (1917), 5–6, 19, 31; on Mrs. Yulee's strong religious convictions see Virginia Clay-Clopton, *A Belle of the Fifties: Memoirs of Mrs. Clay of Alabama* (New York, 1905), 54; Marcus, ed., *Memoirs of American Jews*, 1:17, 154–60; Virginius Dabney, *Richmond: Story of a City* (Garden City, NY, 1976), 83; George Green Shackelford, *George Wythe Randolph and the Confederate Elite* (Athens, GA, 1988), 127; Herbert T. Ezekiel and Gaston Lichtenstein, *The History of the Jews of Richmond from 1769 to 1917* (Richmond, VA, 1917), 62; Jean Bradley Anderson, *Piedmont Plantation: The Bennehan–Cameron Family and Lands in North Carolina* (Durham, NC, 1985), 46; Louis Martin Sears, *John Slidell* (Durham, NC, 1925), 14; Spright Dowell, "Jesse Mercer," *ESB*, 2:849. For Sephardim and Ashkenazi see James William Hagy, *This Happy Land: The Jews of Colonial and Antebellum Charleston* (Tuscaloosa, AL, 1993), 85, 163–4; Elliott Ashkenazi, *The Business of Jews in Louisiana, 1840–1875* (Tuscaloosa, AL, 1988), 35, 166–7; for Rothschild see Marcus, ed., *Memoirs of American Jews*, 3:104; also, Harriet Elizabeth Amos, "Social Life in an Antebellum Cotton Port: Mobile, Alabama, 1820–1860" (Ph.D. diss., University of Alabama, 1976), 136.

schools and sent her children there. Edgeworth Bird, who suffered from his religious "isolation," was delighted to find Sallie reading and enjoying the work of Catholic Bishop John England of Charleston. During the War, Bird wrote his "Dear, dear Darling" Sallie of his love for and trust in her and of his discomfiture with the widening "chasm between us." He groaned about his children's baptisms and rearing as Presbyterians, but, "Between our hearts, darling, there is a *bond* nothing can ever disunite, for God and a pure love have cemented them."[57]

John Wesley, the founder of Methodism, had forbidden marriage to the unconverted, but southern Methodists did not understand "unconverted" to include members of other Christian denominations. Quakers, however, expelled those who, like Jonathan Worth of North Carolina, married out of the faith. J. R. Graves projected a nightmare: A Baptist wants to marry a Methodist woman; her father objects and then relents – provided that the suitor agree to convert or attend her church or let her raise the children as Methodists. That is how the Catholics work, Graves fumed, and Methodists are no better.[58]

Particularly in the Southwest, ministers were often in short supply, and bride and groom could not be picky. When an Old School Presbyterian couple found a Methodist the only preacher available, they gratefully turned to him. Ministers of one denomination performed wedding and funeral services in churches other than their own when members of the family split in their allegiances. Not everyone adjusted: Mary Ellen Norman, for one, did not "fancy having been married by a Methodist – perhaps it is wrong, but you know I am every whit a Presbyterian."

---

[57] David Wyatt Aiken Autobiography (ms.), 16, at UNC-SHC; John Brownrigg to Capt. John Hunter, Oct. 29, 1791, at UNC-SHC; Edgeworth Bird to Sallie Bird, Apr. 21, 1862, and July 17, 1864, in John Rozier, ed., *The Granite Farm Letters: The Civil War Correspondence of Edgeworth and Sallie Bird* (Athens, GA, 1988), 136, 175.

Intermarriage between Catholics and Protestants was by no means rare and in fact occurred in a number of prominent families. See e.g. Robert A. Rutland, ed., *The Papers of George Mason*, 3 vols. (Chapel Hill, N. C. 1970), 2:882 n.; Joseph W. Cox, *Champion of Southern Federalism: Robert Goodloe Harper of South Carolina* (Port Washington, NY, 1972), 212; Charles Hartridge, ed., *The Letters of Robert Mackay to His Wife: Written from Ports in America and England, 1795–1816* (Athens, GA, 1949), 186, Editor's Note 113; R. D. W. Connor, "William Gaston: A Southern Federalist of the Old School and His Yankee Friends, 1778–1844," *Proceedings of the American Antiquarian Society*, n.s., 43 (1933), 383; Jon Wakelyn, "Catholic Elites," in Randall M. Miller and Jon L. Wakelyn, *Catholics in the Old South: Essays on Church and Culture* (Macon, GA, 1983), 229; Judith Ann Benner, *Sul Ross: Soldier, Statesman, Educator* (College Station, TX, 1983), 15; Edward L. Tucker, *Richard Henry Wilde: His Life and Selected Poems* (Athens, GA, 1966), 15, 261 n. 39; Edgeworth Bird to Sallie Bird, Aug. 15, 1863, and July 17, 1864, in Rozier, ed., *Granite Farm Letters*, 136, 174, quote at 136.

[58] Herbert Asbury, *A Methodist Saint: The Life of Bishop Asbury* (New York, 1927), 45; West, *Methodism in Alabama*, 174; Richard Zuber, *Jonathan Worth: A Biography of a Southern Unionist* (Chapel Hill, NC, 1965), 12; Graves, *Great Iron Wheel*, 488–90. A. C. Dayton's Baptist novel, *Theodosia Ernest: Heroine of the Faith*, sold well in the South; it concerned a woman married to a tyrannical Presbyterian who tried to suppress her faith. Robert L. Dabney likened its slander of Presbyterians to the abolitionist slanders peddled in *Uncle Tom's Cabin*. See Dabney, "Review of Theodosia Ernest," *Central Presbyterian*, 25 (1859), 1.

Complaints arose primarily when, say, a local Methodist family preferred to have a wedding performed by a Baptist minister despite the availability of one of their own.[59]

Ministers looked back on the polemically bloody days of the early nineteenth century and shuddered, although their own days remained bloody enough. Down to the 1840s and 1850s, when relations among denominations became more genteel, disputants who preached civility did not always practice it. Even when personally civil, they spoke out against heretical and seductive doctrines that threatened the unwary with damnation. Ministers had always berated each other – often fairly – for unchristian personal attacks, but increasingly they reassured themselves and their congregations that, no matter how sharply they criticized error, they intended no personal aspersions. Typically, in 1858 the Universalist Reverend Hope Bain complained that most southern ministers did not know their Bible well enough to appreciate the proper view of salvation as universal. Still, "They are good men & entitled to the respect & confidence of their several congregations."[60]

Robert L. Dabney, assailing Alexander Campbell and the Disciples for Pelagianism, Socinianism, and nasty rhetoric, insisted that Presbyterians distinguished sin from sinner and hurled anathema at no man, not even Unitarians and Pelagians. The Lutheran John Bachman, who doubtless felt as Dabney did, reacted angrily to suggestions that his doctrinal criticisms of the Episcopalians contained personal assaults. But the Reverend Mr. Cornish, among others, took his criticisms personally. Relations remained strained, although they shook hands and behaved politely in the home of William Gregg, the prominent industrialist who set out to cool the feud and whom neither wished to alienate. Thornwell never wanted to give personal offense, but being a rough polemicist he could hardly avoid it. In 1836 Thornwell heard that he had offended local Methodists "by some rough and unchristian expressions about shouting." He was abashed: "I was wrong in saying what I did. I sinned and sinned grievously; and shall, by permission of God, make an acknowledgement tomorrow." Years later Bishop Lynch, after a pummeling by Thornwell, inquired if he thought Catholics had no feelings. Thornwell's antipathy for Catholics notwithstanding, he winced at Lynch's protest.[61]

Solon Robinson, traveling in Georgia in 1851, remarked that the Baptist–Methodist disputations had a salutary effect: "Both are constantly exercising a rivalry which results in great benefit to the whole country." Pressures mounted on ministers

---

[59] Mary Ellen Norman to James Norman, Jan. 3, 1862, in Clark, ed., *Southern Letters and Life,* 141; Ferdinand Lawrence Steele Diary, Dec. 10, 1850 (complaint), at UNC-SHC; Peyton Harrison Hoge, *Moses Drury Hoge: Life and Letters* (Richmond, VA, 1899), 93.

[60] "Discourse on Hell," 1858, in Bain Papers, at UNC-SHC. For a Baptist plea for restraint in debates see J. S. Walthall, *Distinctive Features of the Baptists* (Raleigh, NC, 1861), 4.

[61] *DD,* 1:324; Cornish Diary, Aug. 21, 23, 1848, July 1, Aug. 18, 1849; Thornwell, Sept. 5, 1836, Private Journal, 141, at Historical Foundation of the Presbyterian and Reformed Churches (Montreat, NC). Efforts to criminalize expressions of nonbelief made little headway. In 1796, for example, the Tennessee legislature considered but rejected the idea: Robert H. White, ed., *Messages of the Governors of Tennessee:* vol. 1, *1796–1821* (Nashville, TN, 1952), 8.

to create an atmosphere of mutual toleration and cooperation without sacrifice of doctrine. The accounts of denominational cooperation, rivalries, and bitter quarrels reveal, above all, passionate commitment to the Word of God as offered in the Holy Bible. Southern Christians, in most churches, stood for one or another orthodoxy and rejected the doctrinal liberalism that was making steady headway in the North – a distinction fraught with enormous consequences for civil as well as church polity.[62]

[62] Kellar, ed., *Solon Robinson*, 2:471; also, Sarmiento's *Travels in the United States in 1847*, tr. Michael Aaron Rockland (Princeton, NJ, 1970), 196–7.

15

War over the Good Book

> If the scriptures do not justify slavery, I know not what they do justify. If we err in maintaining this relation, I know not when we are right – truth then has parted her usual moorings and floated off into an ocean of uncertainty.
>
> —Ferdinand Jacobs[1]

"A large portion of the Northern States believe slavery to be a sin," a worried John C. Calhoun told the Senate in 1837, "and would believe it to be an obligation of conscience to abolish it, if they should feel themselves in any degree responsible for its continuance." The North was falling prey to those who "have been taught to hate the people and institutions of nearly one half of this Union." Calhoun subsequently denounced proposals to abolish slavery in the District of Columbia as first steps toward abolition in the states: "There is no code of morals which justifies the doing of that indirectly which is forbidden to be done directly."[2]

Religion became the *sine qua non* for the South's defense of slavery. In 1790 Representative James Jackson of Georgia appealed to Scripture to persuade Congress to refuse to consider Quaker antislavery petitions. Thereafter, the appeal to the divine sanction – and condemnation – of slavery grew steadily. Robert Y. Hayne of South Carolina, in his famous debate with Daniel Webster of Massachusetts in 1830, conceded that northern ministers were scoring successes in branding slavery a sin. In 1836 J. K. Paulding, a prosouthern New Yorker, began his book *Slavery in the United States* with a chapter on the testimony of the Bible and closed with a chapter that charged abolitionists with "prostituting the Old and New Testaments." In 1839 Duff Green, a politically influential businessman close to Calhoun, argued, "We believe we have most to fear from organized action upon the consciences and fears of slaveholders themselves; from the insinuations of their dangerous heresies into our schools, our pulpits, and our domestic circles." Ten years later Professor

---

[1] Ferdinand Jacobs, *The Committing of Our Cause to God* (Charleston, SC, 1850), 20.
[2] In *JCCP* see "Remarks on Receiving Abolition Petitions (Revised Report)," Senate, Feb. 6, 1837 (13:393–4), and "Address to the Republican Members of Congress" (14:382).

Elisha Mitchell of the University of North Carolina warned Calhoun that many people in the Border States doubted slavery's divine sanction.[3]

Both sides in the great congressional debate of 1850 over slavery in the territories invoked Scripture. In the Senate it was a Whig unionist, George Badger of North Carolina, who most effectively expounded the scriptural foundations of slavery. Robert Allston, one of South Carolina's most powerful planter-politicians, wrote his wife that the churches were becoming more important than political organizations in the struggle over slavery. As Alabama seceded, J. L. M. Curry, Mobile's rising political star, pleaded with the Border States: "An infidel theory has corrupted the Northern heart." In Natchez, W. H. Holcombe, a prominent physician and man of letters, held northern religious journals responsible for the adherence of Maryland, Kentucky, and Missouri to the Union. "The pulpit," Mary Gay of Georgia recalled years later, "became a rostrum from which bitter invective of the South flowed in Niagara torrents."[4]

In 1844 the churches erupted over the slavery issue. The General Conference of the Methodist Church, America's largest denomination, met amidst political storms: congressional suppression of antislavery petitions (the "Gag Rule"), the annexation of Texas, James Birney's abolitionist presidential campaign, anti-Catholic riots in Philadelphia, and tensions over slavery in the nominating conventions of the Democratic and Whig parties. The principal question at the conference concerned acceptance of James Andrew, a slaveholder, as a bishop. William Capers and H. N. McTyeire observed that, as a simple matter of logic, a church that excluded slaveholders from the episcopate ought to exclude them from the ministry and, indeed, from the laity. Capers, like John Early, had previously been passed over for bishop because he owned slaves; he now cited John Wesley to the antislavery men.

---

[3] William Sumner Jenkins, *Pro-Slavery Thought in the Old South* (Gloucester, MA, 1960), 51–2; Robert Y. Hayne, Jan. 25, 1830, in Herman Belz, ed., *The Webster–Hayne Debate on the Nature of the Union: Selected Documents* (Indianapolis, IN, 2000), 45. Lieber, however, admonished Webster for acknowledging that the Bible did not explicitly condemn slavery: Lieber to George S. Hilliard, 1850, in Thomas Sergeant Perry, ed., *The Life and Letters of Francis Lieber* (Boston, 1882), 243. J. K. Paulding, *Slavery in the United States* (New York, 1836), chs. 1 and 10, quote at 282; Duff Green in *Southern Review,* as excerpted in Julius R. Ames, comp., *"Liberty"* (n.p., 1839), 2; Elisha Mitchell to Calhoun, Feb. 1, 1849, in *JCCP,* 26:263. Other northern and Border State correspondents sent Calhoun reports on the effects of antislavery preaching and religious publications: in *JCCP* see Ezra D. Pruden [of New Jersey] to Calhoun, Oct. 4, 1848 (26:77), and Henry B. Goodwyn [of Maryland] to Calhoun, Feb. 6, 1849 (26:280).

[4] For Badger see W. J. Peele, ed., *Lives of Distinguished North Carolinians, with Illustrations and Speeches* (Raleigh, NC, 1898), 195; Robert F. W. Allston to Adele Pettigrew Allston, Nov. 25, 1850, in J. H. Easterby, ed., *The South Carolina Rice Plantation, as Revealed in the Papers of Robert F. W. Allston* (Chicago, 1945), 105; Curry quoted in Charles B. Dew, *Apostles of Disunion: Southern Secession Commissioners and the Causes of the Civil War* (Charlottesville, VA, 2001), 57; W. H. Holcombe Diary, "Notes," 2:133, at UNC-SHC; Mary A. H. Gay, *Life in Dixie during the War,* 5th ed. (Atlanta, GA, 1979 [1897]), 14. In 1808, Congress debated severe penalties, including death, for international slave traders. Southern congressmen objected that, since the Northerners who wanted draconian measures appealed to Mosaic Law, they would have to acknowledge that the Bible sanctioned slavery. See Matthew E. Mason, "Slavery Overshadowed: Congress Debates Prohibition of the Atlantic Slave Trade to the United States, 1806–1807," *JER,* 20 (2000), 69.

Yes, Wesley opposed slavery, but, no, he did not try to force his opinion down the Church's throat.⁵

Southern delegates to the Conference appealed to conservative northern and Border State brethren by taking the high ground of acknowledging slavery to be an evil, a gambit that cost nothing since "an evil" meant different things to different people. They wanted civil rather than ecclesiastical adjudication because Scripture neither characterized slavery as sin nor warranted exclusion of slaveholders from the Church. Led by William A. Smith of Virginia, who had been calling for the secession of the southern churches since 1836, they demanded strict construction of church constitutions, much as they demanded strict construction of the Constitution of the United States. Stephen Olin of Vermont explained to James Andrew, "You know I love you, and you know I do not blame you for the course you have taken, and yet I shall vote for the [antislavery] resolution tomorrow. It is the only way to save the Church in the North; the South will go off, but it will do so en masse and united. If we do not pass this resolution, the North will go off in fragments, and there will be only strife and bitterness." The bitterness came anyway and on all sides. George Foster Pierce of Georgia predicted that if the Church drove the Southerners out it would slide into apostasy and abandon the distinctive features of Methodism, notably the itinerant ministry that served small rural churches.⁶

The antislavery Reverend Peter Cartwright, who had departed the South, recalled in 1856 how early Methodist efforts to stamp out slavery were undermined

⁵ For the text of Capers's speech see Albert M. Shipp, *The History of Methodism in South Carolina* (Nashville, TN, 1883), 479–92; Holland N. McTyeire, *A History of Methodism* (Nashville, TN, 1886), 38. For the southern reaction to the rejection of Capers and Early see William Warren Sweet, *Virginia Methodism: A History* (Richmond, VA, 1955), 207–8, 213. Quarrels over slavery continued in churches of the plantation South and of the Border States into the 1830s. The Methodists in Mississippi, for example, felt compelled to clarify their position in 1835, dissociating themselves from abolitionism. Conversion of blacks increased thereafter. See John D. Jones, *A Complete History of Methodism as Connected with the Mississippi Conference of the Methodist Episcopal Church, South*, 2 vols. (Nashville, TN, 1908), 2:347, 411. James Smylie, an acknowledged power in the Presbyterian Church in Mississippi and Louisiana, delivered a controversial proslavery sermon in Port Gibson in 1836. Although some ministers and congregants urged him to desist, he won considerable support within all denominations. Much of the criticism of his sermon may have come from proslavery men annoyed at his stress on the responsibilities and duties of masters toward slaves. See Randy J. Sparks, "Mississippi's Apostle of Slavery: James Smylie and the Biblical Defense of Slavery," *Journal of Mississippi History*, 51 (1989), 98–103.

⁶ John Nelson Norwood, *The Schism in the Methodist Episcopal Church 1844: A Study of Slavery and Ecclesiastical Politics* (Alfred, NY, 1923), 33, 59–60; Gross Alexander et al., *A History of the Methodist Church, South* (New York, 1894), 15–37; A. H. Redford, *History of the Organization of the Methodist Episcopal Church, South* (Nashville, TN, 1871), esp. 331–61; Marion Elias Lazenby, *History of Methodism in Alabama and West Florida* (Nashville, TN, 1960), 118 (on Saunders); E. E. Hoss, *William McKendree: A Biographical Study* (Nashville, TN, 1916), 276; on Olin see George G. Smith, *The History of Georgia Methodism from 1786 to 1866* (Atlanta, GA, 1913), 178–9, 252–3, quote at 179; G. F. Pierce, "Bishop Andrew," in William T. Smithson, ed., *In Memoriam* (New York, 1871), 6–7; *Journal of the General Conference of the Methodist Episcopal Church* (New York, 1844), 157. In 1844 the Methodist bishops ruefully admitted that little remained of the itinerancy in a number of Conferences. In 1871 Pierce grimly protested the retreat from biblical orthodoxy that he had foreseen.

by "ruffle-shirted" preachers who bought slaves or who married planters' daughters and courted the slaveholders. "Then they began to apologize for the evil; then to justify it, on legal principles; then on Bible principles till lo and behold! it is not an evil, but a good! it is not a curse but a blessing." Yet Cartwright denied that slavery was per se a sin. He blamed fanatical abolitionists for provoking the split of 1844 and for driving Southerners out of the Church. The great majority of southern Methodists, he believed, would have remained loyal to the national church and in time would have effected emancipation. He recoiled also from the hard line taken by Northerners in response to abolitionist pressure when they scuttled their previous agreement to divide church property amicably. James Porter, a Northerner who wrote *Compendium of Methodism* in 1851, did not recoil: He welcomed the split of 1844, noting that by the late 1820s southern Methodists were embracing the righteousness of slavery.[7]

The categorization of slavery as sin alienated a good many wavering ministers, especially in the South. John Witherspoon, William Plumer, Moses Drury Hoge, and Benjamin M. Smith, disgusted by the abolitionists, fell silent. In the 1830s an illuminating public quarrel embroiled the Methodist Reverend William Winans of Mississippi and his nephew, the Disciples' Matthias Winans of Ohio. The Disciples, still being shunned by other churches, felt persecuted. When Matthias Winans, an abolitionist, made slavery a prime issue, his uncle William replied: "Depend upon it, the South will see universal ruin overwhelm all, before they will submit to interference in this matter, by any power on earth." Southerners would "bring themselves in the last ditch, defending what they believe to be their own rights, against the intrusion of their neighbor."[8]

Henry Bidleman Bascom's version of the southern Methodist position in *Methodism and Slavery* attracted much interest and even pleased the Methodist-baiting J. R. Graves of the Landmark Baptists. Bascom explained that the Church had always considered slavery an "evil" but had not denied slaveholders communion.

---

[7] *The Backwoods Preacher: Being the Autobiography of Peter Cartwright* (London, 1870), 130–2, 157, 375–6, and chs. 27–28, quotes at 131, 157; J. James Porter, *Compendium of Methodism* (Boston, 1851), 175–6, 182–6. In the 1830s antislavery feeling seemed to be rising in Kentucky until the abolitionists got nasty. The courageously antislavery colonizationist Robert J. Breckenridge grew increasingly bitter toward abolitionists as he fought for gradual emancipation. See *BRPR*, 21 (1849), 582–607; also, Jeffrey Brooke Allen, "The South's 'Northern Refutation' of Slavery: Pre-1830 Kentucky as a Test Case," *Southern Studies*, 20 (1981), 351–61. In 1861, Breckenridge's resolutely pro-Union *Danville Quarterly Review* reiterated, "The abolition movement has been *free-thinking* in religion": "Our Country – Its Peril – Its Deliverance," *DQR*, 1 (1861), 85.

[8] James D. Essig, *The Bonds of Wickedness: American Evangelicals against Slavery, 1770–1808* (Philadelphia, 1982), ch. 6; William S. McFeely, *Frederick Douglass* (New York, 1991), 43; Margaret Burr DesChamps, "The Presbyterian Church in the South Atlantic States, 1801–1861" (Ph.D. diss., Emory University, 1952), 146–7, 150–1; Winans quoted in Ray Holder, *William Winans: Methodist Leader in Antebellum Mississippi* (Jackson, MS, 1977), 118. See also "On Slavery: Selected Letters of Parson Winans, 1820–1844," ed. Ray Holder, *Journal of Mississippi History*, 46 (1984), 323–54. David Rice, William McKendree, David Barrow, and other prominent men continued to preach against slavery, but their influence waned, especially as antislavery ministers departed the South. For the contribution of southern émigrés to northern abolitionism see Philip J. Schwarz, *Migrants against Slavery* (Charlottesville, VA, 2001).

The Bible itself, he insisted, sanctions slavery and does not advocate the replacement of one social evil by potentially worse evils. Bascom confidently expected the South, if left alone, to move responsibly toward emancipation: "We do not mean to say that the Bible favors slavery, or that slavery is not an evil; what we insist upon is, that the Bible treats it as a jural arrangement in human governments, which the Church has no right to assail or disturb, beyond proper efforts to bring master and slave into the fold of Christ." The antislavery Bishop Francis Asbury had convinced Bascom a number of years before, in 1812, that the Church must treat slavery as a civil institution. The organization of the Methodist Episcopal Church, South in 1845 ended Bascomesque concessions to northern sensibilities, after which proslavery ministers spoke out more often and more vigorously, reducing the qualms of the faithful.[9]

On July 7, 1845, in an uncharacteristic flash of enthusiasm, Calhoun certified Bascom's book as "the ablest production which has yet appeared against the fanatical agitation of the subject of Abolition." When he urged James H. Hammond to review this "very able production," Hammond shot back that he found the book "rude, undigested, disconnected & confused." Especially infuriating was the treatment of slavery as an evil "only *permitted* & *regulated*, not *ordained* by God." Southrons, Hammond cried, must stand on the Word, and the Word ordained slavery. Calhoun pleaded that *Methodism and Slavery* provided a powerful antidote to the "poison" that the abolitionist Cassius Clay was disseminating in Kentucky. Hammond begged to differ and pointed to the Methodists of South Carolina, who were rebuking it. A flustered Calhoun finally allowed that he had read Bascom only "cursorily." Hammond, relieved that Calhoun was seeing the light, reiterated that slaveholders must abandon apologetics. Calhoun agreed on the need to take high ground.[10]

The Baptist split between northern and southern churches, like the Methodist, had roots in long-standing southern resentments, most notably against the Home Missionary Society's exclusion of slaveholders. Southern reaction reached white heat by 1840, although northern Baptist newspapers did not swing decisively to antislavery until a few years later. At the 1844 session of the Triennial Convention, Bostonians assailed their brethren from Alabama for supporting the appointment

[9] H. B. Bascom, *Methodism and Slavery* (Frankfort, KY, 1845), 66; M. M. Henkle, *The Life of Henry Bidleman Bascom* (Nashville, TN, 1857), 38, 385; J. R. Graves, *The Little Iron Wheel* (Nashville, TN, 1857), 8–13.

[10] In June 1845, Calhoun, writing to his son-in-law, described Bascom's *Slavery and Methodism* as "one of the fullest & most powerful vindication[s] of the South & its institutions, which has yet appeared. It will do great good." See the correspondence for 1845 in *JCCP*: Calhoun to Thomas G. Clemson, June 23 (21:598); as well as Calhoun to Thomas B. Stevenson, July 7; Hammond to Calhoun, July 20; Calhoun to Hammond, Aug. 2; Hammond to Calhoun, Aug. 18; Calhoun to Hammond, Aug. 30; Hammond to Calhoun, Sept. 26; Calhoun to Hammond, Sept. 20 – in *JCCP*, 22: 12–13, 13–14, 31–3, 50–1, 79–83, 100–2, 171–4, 176–8. On the drop in moral qualms see Ralph Flanders, *Plantation Slavery in Georgia* (Chapel Hill, NC, 1933), 179. The editors of *Southern Literary Messenger* cited Calhoun to praise Bascom's work on slavery: "Domestic Slavery," *SLM*, 11 (1845), 528; [J. R. Thompson], *SLM*, 15 (1849), 63–4. See also Supplementary References: "Antiabolitionist Bible Arguments in the North."

of slaveholders as missionaries. Southerners protested that they were being purged at the behest of fanatics. The antislavery Francis Wayland wrote Jeremiah Jeter of Richmond, "You will separate of course. I could not ask otherwise. Your rights have been infringed." The organizers of the Southern Baptist Convention cautioned, "Let not the extent of this disunion be exaggerated. At the present time it involves only the Foreign and Domestic Missions of the denomination. Northern and Southern Baptists are still brethren. They differ in no article of faith. They are guided by the same principles of gospel order." Then the salvo: "We will never interfere with what is Caesar's. We will not compromise what is God's."[11]

Separation of the churches wrenched thoughtful Americans as little else could have. Abolitionists, proslavery militants, and moderates agreed that the separation of the churches rendered the survival of the Federal Union itself moot. Among the Presbyterians, Charles Hodge of Princeton had prefigured the response to the schisms of 1844–45 during the earlier Presbyterian schism of 1837, which touched on slavery only indirectly. For Hodge, America was becoming two nations in feeling and must soon become two nations in fact. Calhoun, Abel Upshur, and the Reverends William Plumer and Richard Fuller predicted that church splits would wreck the Union and lead to sectional bloodshed. The prospect of separation delighted William Lloyd Garrison. The secession of the antislavery "come-outers" in the early 1840s and the subsequent secession of the Southerners in 1844–45 intensified criticism of slavery within the northern churches and the interdenominational mission societies, which never went as far as the abolitionists desired although far enough to infuriate Southerners. Southern secessionists shared Garrison's enthusiasm. The separation of the churches, John T. Morgan approvingly told Alabama's secession convention, "opened the way to our present condition."[12]

Southern Christians of every denomination, joined by religious skeptics, now rallied to their Methodist brethren. South Carolina's distinguished Langdon Cheves exulted, "The Methodist Episcopal Church of the South have set us a noble example,

[11] William Wright Barnes, *The Southern Baptist Convention, 1845–1953* (Nashville, TN, 1954), 12–13; *Proceedings of the Southern Baptist Convention, Held in Augusta, Georgia, May 8–12, 1845*, 17, 19; E. C. Routh, "Foreign Mission Board," *ESB*, 1:457–74 (Wayland quoted at 457–60); Mary Burham Putnam, *The Baptists and Slavery, 1840–1845* (Ann Arbor, MI, 1913), chs. 3–5. Of the 293 individual delegates who established the Southern Baptist Convention in Augusta in 1845, 241 hailed from Georgia and South Carolina: see Jesse C. Fletcher, *The Southern Baptist Convention: A Sesquicentennial History* (Nashville, TN, 1994), 10.

[12] John R. McKivigan, *The War against Proslavery Religion: Abolitionism and the Northern Churches, 1830–1865* (Ithaca, NY, 1984), 66–9, 92, 126–7, and ch. 5 on the "Come-Outer" sects; C. C. Goen, *Broken Churches, Broken Nation: Denominational Schisms and the Coming of the American Civil War* (Macon, GA, 1985), 55, 74–5, and 94 on Fuller; for Garrison's speech of July 4, 1844, see Truman Nelson, ed., *Documents of Upheaval: Selections from William Lloyd Garrison's Liberator, 1831–1865* (New York, 1966), 123; Morgan in William R. Smith, ed., *The History of the Convention Debates of the People of Alabama* (Montgomery, AL, 1861), 367. William A. Smith of Virginia looked back on the Presbyterian split of 1837 as largely driven by the slavery question: *Lectures on the Philosophy and Practice of Slavery* (Nashville, TN, 1856), 20 n. By 1861, Benjamin Morgan Palmer was proclaiming that South and North had been two nations from the beginning: "A Vindication of Secession and the South," *SPR*, 14 (1861), 175.

which, if our opponents persist, we shall be obliged to imitate." The Charleston *Mercury* called the schism the beginning of the dissolution of the Union. Governor Hammond asked: "If Christians are compelled to divide on account of Slavery how can unbelievers hold together?" Unfazed, in an address to the state legislature, he commended southern Methodists for their "becoming spirit." News of the Methodist schism stunned Thomas Ritchie, a usually upbeat Virginia unionist, for at that very moment moderates were celebrating the advent of the Polk administration, which they hoped would cool off sectional antagonisms. Henry Clay blanched at the sundering of religious ties, for ministers, he pleaded, ought always be governed by love, however much politicians might not be. Even the most powerful of commercial ties, Clay predicted, would not overcome the destructive effects of church separations. Calhoun, reading the news with foreboding, sent word to William Capers in New York, where the Methodists had been meeting, that he would much appreciate a visit from him and Augustus Baldwin Longstreet on their way home. The consequence "both as it relates to Church and State, demand the gravest attention on the part of the whole Union, and the South especially." Southerners would recall Calhoun's warning down through the War years.[13]

Southern divines, most of them with little taste for political extremism, encouraged the unionists. While staunchly defending "southern rights," most divines had resisted secession until Lincoln's election or a year or two earlier. By no means of one mind, the divines divided within rather than between churches. Among the most influential Methodists, H. N. McTyeire firmly supported secession, while Bishop Pierce opposed it until the last minute. Episcopalian bishops split, but all eventually fell in line. While Bishops William Meade, J. H. Otey, and Nicholas Cobbs were standing by the Union, Bishops Leonidas Polk, Stephen Elliott, and Francis Rutledge were joining the secessionists. John Brown's raid at Harper's Ferry hardened secessionist inclinations, and Bishop Rutledge of Florida delighted the fiery secessionist Edmund Ruffin, saying that he seceded from the Union when South Carolina did. Lincoln's call for troops proved the last straw for some of the most committed unionists – Meade, Otey, and C. T. Quintard, who would succeed Otey as bishop in Tennessee. Judith McGuire said of Bishop Meade that "The old gentleman" held out until Lincoln's call, when he "could stand it no longer." On Thanksgiving Day

[13] Langdon Cheves, "Letter to the Charleston Mercury on Southern Wrongs," Sept. 1844, in *Southern State Rights, Anti-Tariff and Anti-Abolition Tract #1* (Charleston, SC, 1844), 5; Charleston *Mercury*, June 14 and 20, 1844; Hammond quoted in Drew Gilpin Faust, *James Henry Hammond and the Old South* (Baton Rouge, LA, 1982), 247; see also Hammond to the Legislature, Nov. 26, 1844, in [Clyde N. Wilson], ed., *Selections from the Letters and Speeches of James H. Hammond* (Spartanburg, SC, 1978), 101. Charles Henry Ambler, *Thomas Ritchie: A Study in Virginia Politics* (Richmond, VA, 1913), 259; Chester Forrester Dunham, *The Attitude of the Northern Clergy toward the South, 1860–1865* (Toledo, OH, 1942), 2 (Clay); Calhoun to Capers, June 4, 1844, in *JCCP*, 18:708, and see Calhoun's reiteration in 1850: *JCCP*, 27:199–200; for echoes of Calhoun's warning see e.g. "Christianity versus Philanthropy," *SLM*, 34 (1862), 575. In 1843 and early 1844, evangelicals complained of religious backsliding; afterwards they found large and earnest audiences for their revivals. Hunter Dickinson Farish, *The Circuit Rider Dismounts: A Social History of Southern Methodism, 1865–1900* (Richmond, VA, 1938), 18.

1860 in Tennessee, Otey and Quintard reviled the secessionists as demagogues, but they too defected when Lincoln called for troops.[14]

The radical tide had been rising, but not until the end of the 1850s did it prevail with the most revered southern Baptist ministers. Richard Fuller, a southern hero for his scriptural defense of slavery in a much-discussed debate with Francis Wayland, moved from Charleston to Baltimore. There, in an address to the American Colonization Society in 1851, he counseled moderation, open debate, and mutual concessions. Rejecting "positive good" arguments, he called for gradual emancipation. Fuller nonetheless became president of the Southern Baptist Convention and chaired the committee that welcomed the Confederacy. In the view of *Southern Quarterly Review* – and growing numbers of Southerners, including unionists – the Wayland–Fuller debate effectively exhausted the argument. The Reverend J. B. Jeter of Virginia, longtime unionist, wrote to the Reverend J. A. Broadus in 1860: "The time has come when we must have an adjustment of our difficulties with the North, or go out of the Union. The incessant agitation of the slavery question, and the sectional policy of the North can no longer be endured." He confessed that he clung "with great tenacity" to the Union, but his tenacity had limits. When Virginia seceded, he became an ardent Confederate.[15]

Not until 1860 did the Baptists of South Carolina, Alabama, and Mississippi officially describe the Union as a failure and call for secession. In the end, secessionism rang in the Baptist pulpits of the South Carolina upcountry and carried a majority of that long-unionist area. When the Reverend James Furman, who supported the radicals, debated the unionist Benjamin Perry in Greenville in 1860, he considered the scriptural argument won and concentrated his fire on the northern abuse of the Constitution and southern property rights. A dismayed Perry stopped going to church.[16]

---

[14] Richard J. Carwardine, *Evangelicals and Politics in Antebellum America* (New Haven, CT, 1993), 188–9; George G. Smith, *The Life and Times of George Foster Pierce, Bishop of the Methodist Church, South, with a Sketch of Lovick Pierce, D.D., His Father* (Sparta, GA, 1888), 436; William Mercer Green, *Memoir of the Rt. Rev. James Hervey Otey, D.D., LL.D., the First Bishop of Tennessee* (New York, 1885), 91, 93; Ruffin, Jan. 4, 1861, in *ERD*, 1:524. On the pro-secession bishops see Greenough White, *A Saint of the Church: Memoir of the Right Reverend Nicholas Hammer Cobbs* (New York, 1897), 171–2; H. Shelton Smith, *In His Image ... But: Racism in Southern Religion* (Durham, NC, 1972), 175; J. H. Otey to James W. Patton, Feb. 2, 1861, in Otey Papers, at UNC-SHC; James Welch Patton, *Unionism and Reconstruction in Tennessee, 1860–1869* (Chapel Hill, NC, 1934), 5, 16; Judith W. McGuire, June 18, 1861, in Jean W. Berlin, ed., *Diary of a Southern Refugee during the War, by a Lady of Virginia* (Lincoln, NE, 1995 [1867]), 32. See also Supplementary References: "Secession – Clerical Support and Opposition."

[15] On Furman see David B. Chesebrough, ed., *"God Ordained This War": Sermons on the Sectional Crisis, 1830–1865* (Columbia, SC, 1991), 144–5, and Barnes, *Southern Baptist Convention*, 44; "Critical Notices," *SQR*, 8 (1845), 253; J. B. Jeter to J. A. Broadus, Dec. 11, 1860, in William Hatcher, *Life of J. B. Jeter, D.D.* (Baltimore, 1887), 261–2. Broadus saw deep political divisions among Baptist ministers but said they got along fine: Broadus to Cornelia Taliaferro, Jan. 22, 1861, in Archibald Thomas Robertson, *Life and Letters of John Albert Broadus* (Philadelphia, 1909), 179, 182.

[16] *EC*, 1:13; Harvey Tolliver Cook, *The Life and Work of James Clement Furman* (Greenville, SC, 1926), 195–201; Lillian Kibler, *Benjamin F. Perry: South Carolina Unionist* (Durham, NC, 1946), 317, 337, 362. Many Baptist ministers had come from the North and tended toward unionism: see *EC*, vols.

Long-standing collaboration with Old School stalwarts at Princeton had strengthened the unionism of the southern Presbyterians; and, despite Lincoln's election,
John Adger and others turned back attempts to force a sectional split in the Old
School. When the South seceded and the southern Presbyterians did establish their
own national church, James Henley Thornwell, on behalf of the Synod of South
Carolina, issued "Reasons for Separate Organization": The slavery agitation "has
transferred to the Church all the bitterness of the political feud. An Assembly composed of members, one half of whom believe the other half ought to be hanged,
denouncing each other, on the one hand as rebels and traitors, and on the other
hand, as *tyrants* and *oppressors,* would be anything but an edifying spectacle."
As a coda, William Capers, Sr., an especially prestigious overseer, summed up the
thoughts of countless laymen and ministers in a letter to Louis Manigault at the
end of October 1861: "Am afraid before quietude is restored, there will be blood
shed. The Southern States have remained in the Union too long."[17]

Presbyterian preachers entered the lists as passionate Confederates, all the more
passionate because so many had resisted secession. Thornwell defected with the
first wave when Lincoln won the election, and Robert Dabney with the second wave
when Lincoln called for troops. The Reverend John Girardeau, Thornwell's protégé, argued in verse:

> Sons of the South, Arise! Arise!:
> Shoulder to shoulder, hand to hand,
> For freedom's rights together stand;
> Or, wrapped in one unfolding pall,
> In the last pass of freedom fall.[18]

The separation of the churches accelerated a decades-long slide into bitter sectional invective in both North and South. The early abolitionists came either from
the South or from a then still slaveholding North. Having experienced slavery firsthand and been outraged by its horrors, they were little inclined to see slaveholders
as demons. Succeeding generations of abolitionists were prone to regard all slaveholders as infamous. To consider slavery a sin might not mean considering every

---

1 and 2. Most Baptist preachers seem to have stood by the Union into the 1850s but then defected
in two waves: W. H. Daniel, "Southern Baptists in the Confederacy," *Civil War History*, 6 (1960),
389–401.

[17] William Childs Robinson, *Columbia Theological Seminary and the Southern Presbyterian Church:
A Study in Church History, Presbyterian Polity, Missionary Enterprise, and Religious Thought* (Decatur, GA, 1931), 36–8, 44–6; James Stacy, *A History of the Presbyterian Church in Georgia* (Atlanta,
GA, 1912), 15–25; T. E. Peck, *Miscellanies*, ed. T. C. Johnson, 3 vols. (Richmond, VA, 1895–97), 2:292
(Clay); Claude H. Hall, *Abel Parker Upshur: Conservative Virginian, 1790–1844* (Madison, WI, 1963),
85–6; "Reasons for Separate Organization," *JHTW*, 4:439–45; William Capers, Sr., to Louis Manigault, Oct. 31, 1860, in James M. Clifton, ed., *Life and Labor on Argyle Island: Letters and Documents
of a Savannah River Rice Plantation, 1833–1867* (Savannah, GA, 1978), 309.

[18] Haskell Monroe, "Southern Presbyterians and the Secession Crisis," *Civil War History*, 6 (1960),
351–60; George A. Blackburn, ed., *The Life and Work of John L. Girardeau* (Columbia, SC, 1916),
348. On *Southern Presbyterian* see Jonathan Worth to James McNeill, Mar. 16, 1861, in J. G. de-
Roulhac Hamilton, ed., *The Correspondence of Jonathan Worth*, 2 vols. (Raleigh, NC, 1909), 1:135.

slaveholder a wanton sinner, but it did encourage impatience with amelioration and a preference for confrontation. After the schisms of 1844–45, northern Baptists and Methodists did hold slavery sinful but refused to indict slaveholders as sinners or deny communion to thousands of Border State slaveholders. With rising vehemence, however, the abolitionists tended to label all northern as well as southern churches as diabolical. In 1834 Professor Edward Dromgoole Sims of the Methodist Randolph-Macon College, visiting New England, found people "unduly agitated" over "this delicate subject" of slavery. Abolitionists and even free-soilers demanded militancy. The platform of the sagging Free Soil party in 1852 indicted slavery as "a sin against God and a crime against man, which no human enactment nor usage can make right." The abolitionist George Cheever counterpoised "freedom and Slavery, truth and falsehood, justice and oppression, God and the Devil." The country, he said, had become "a battle-ground of religious principle against a wretched political expediency, and of God's authority in national affairs against the spirit of conquest, covetousness, oppression, and diplomatic fraud and selfishness." Horace Greeley's New York *Tribune* saluted Lincoln for turning his debate with Stephen Douglas into "a contest for the Kingdom of Heaven or the Kingdom of Satan," and a northern farmer wrote Lincoln: "It is no less than a contest for the advancement of the kingdom of Heaven or the kingdom of Satan."[19]

Southern voices, too, grew harsher. The Baptist Reverend Thornton Stringfellow of Virginia labeled as "baptized infidels" Yankees who called themselves Christians while they preached heresy and social and political radicalism. For Wayne Gridley, Francis Wayland practiced "Protestant Jesuitry." For Representative James Stewart of Maryland, the antislavery men "go after strange gods of their own creation." For Senator Louis Wigfall of Texas, they were "pretended followers of Christ." The Reverend Joseph Jones of Georgia, addressing Confederate troops, described abolitionism as "pure infidelity," "the child of the Devil," and "a vast insurrection against God and man." The Reverend Joel Tucker, taking the pulpit in Fayetteville, North Carolina, proclaimed "a conflict of truth with error – of the Bible with Northern infidelity – of a pure Christianity with Northern fanaticism – of liberty with despotism – of right with might."[20]

[19] For the different waves of southern abolitionists in the North see James L. Huston, "The Experiential Basis of the Northern Antislavery Impulse," *JSH*, 56 (1990), 609–40; Sims, July 20, 1834, in W. Alexander Mabry, ed., *The Diary of Edward Dromgoole Sims, June 17–August 3, 1834* (Richmond, VA, 1954), 18; McKivigan, *War against Proslavery Religion*, 150; George B. Cheever, *God against Slavery; And the Freedom and Duty of the Pulpit to Rebuke It as a Sin against God* (Cincinnati, 1857), 69; New York *Tribune* quoted in Harold Holzer, ed., *The Lincoln–Douglas Debates: The First Complete, Unexpurgated Text* (New York, 1994), 43; a northern farmer quoted in Robert W. Johannsen, ed., *The Lincoln–Douglas Debates of 1858* (New York, 1965), 9; Carwardine, *Evangelicals and Politics*, 269 (Cheever), 297. Also, [D. K. Whitaker], "Channing's Duty of the Free States," *SQR*, 2 (1842), 152; [D. J. McCord], "Slavery and the Abolitionists," *SQR*, 15 (1849), 192–3. The Reverend Alexander McCaine of South Carolina seemed surprised by the debate in the Methodist Protestant Church in 1842 in which the abolitionists denounced conservatives in what he felt was unspeakable language: Alexander McCaine, *Slavery Defended against the Attacks of the Abolitionists* (Baltimore, 1842).

[20] Wayne Gridley, *Slavery in the South* (Charleston, SC, 1845), 12; James A. Stewart, *Powers of the Government of the United States – Federal, State, and Territorial* (Washington, DC, 1860), 8; *Speech*

Even northern moderates raised southern hackles. Charles Hodge of Princeton – the most powerful voice among Northerners who denied the sinfulness of slavery and scorched abolitionism – disapproved of slavery, voted Republican, and supported the Union. In 1861 *Southern Presbyterian Review,* the Augusta *Constitutionalist,* and other southern religious and secular publications blistered Hodge for his unionist "State of the Country," in effect calling him a traitor to a cause he had never embraced. Hodge believed the South would face catastrophe if it failed to transform its slave system in accordance with the Christian model and institute reforms that would speed emancipation.[21]

Political moderates of various stripes tried desperately to shift the sectional debate from Scripture to economic and political exigencies. Thomas Roderick Dew pointed to biblical history to show the mutual support of an agricultural Palestine and a manufacturing and commercial Phoenicia. In 1848 Representative David Outlaw of North Carolina and his wife shared worries over an agitation stirred up "by men who know nothing of our actual conditions, or of the practical bearings of the question which they attempt [to] discuss. It tries a man's patience, not a little." Outlaw lashed secessionists as irresponsible men full of "braggadocio and abuse." Slavery was "an existing fact" to be treated by "practical men." In 1860

of the Hon. Louis T. Wigfall, of Texas: In Reply to Mr. Douglas, and on Mr. Powell's Resolutions (Washington, DC, 1860), 8; J. Jones, *A Discourse Delivered … to the Rome Light Guards and Miller Rifles* (Rome, GA, 1861), 10; J. W. Tucker of North Carolina, *God's Providence in War: A Sermon Delivered in Fayetteville, N.C.* (Fayetteville, NC, 1862), 11; also, "American Slavery in 1857," *SLM,* 25 (1857), 87–8; J. A. Turner, *A Letter to Hon. N. G. Foster, Candidate for Congress* (Milledgeville, GA, 1855), 31. R. L. Dabney, among others, used "Baptized infidelity" in his assaults on liberalism: see Sean Michael Lucas, " 'Hold Fast that Which Is Good': The Public Theology of Robert Lewis Dabney" (Ph.D. diss., Westminster Theological Seminary, 2002), 60. Southern Baptists who went north to raise money for their colleges appreciated the warm response but caviled at the preaching. J. S. Purifoy, traveling in Connecticut, heard "nice, pretty sermons, but lacking the spirit of Jesus and Him crucified." Purifoy quoted in George Washington Paschal, *History of Wake Forest College,* 3 vols. (Wake Forest, NC, 1935–43), 2:122; see also W. E. Hill, "Address," in Harriott Sutton Rankin, *History of First Presbyterian Church, Fayetteville* (n.p., n.d.), 72.

[21] E. N. Elliott of Mississippi included two of Hodge's essays in his important book, *Cotton Is King and Pro-Slavery Arguments* (New York, 1969 [1860]). For the southern reaction to Hodge's "State of the Union" see e.g. J. H. Rice, *SPR,* 14 (1861), 1–44; also, Caroline L. Shanks, "The Biblical Anti-Slavery Argument of the Decades 1830–1860," *Journal of Negro History,* 16 (1931), 134–5. *Princeton Review* had long made clear its distaste for slavery: in *BRPR,* see: [Hodge], "Slavery. By William E. Channing," 8 (1836), 268–306; review of C. C. Jones's *Religious Instruction of the Negroes,* 15 (1843), 22–41; review of the works of George Junkin, William Graham, and William Wisner, 16 (1844), 545–81; "Howison's History of Virginia," 20 (1848), 186–206; and Robert J. Breckenridge, "The Question of Negro Slavery and the New Constitution of Kentucky," 21 (1849), 582–607. On the complexity of Hodge's position see Mark A. Noll, "The Bible and Slavery," in Randall M. Miller et al., eds., *Religion and the American Civil War* (New York, 1998), 59–60, and Richard J. Carwardine, "The Politics of Charles Hodge," in John W. Stewart and James H. Moorhead, eds., *Charles Hodge Revisited: A Critical Appraisal of His Life and Work* (Grand Rapids, MI, 2002), 247–97. For the evolution of Hodges's views on slavery, see Stewart, "Introducing Charles Hodge to Postmoderns," in *Hodge Revisited,* 31–5; also, Allen C. Guelzo's more questionable "Charles Hodge's Antislavery Moment," loc. cit., 299–325. See also Supplementary References: "Anti-abolitionist Bible Arguments in the North."

John Berrien Lindsley of Tennessee tried to dampen the scriptural fireworks. Slavery a sin? A divine institution? Nonsense. It was a political and economic fact of life with no end in sight. With secession imminent, Lindsley dismissed the Republican party's theory of the incompatibility of free and slave labor, convinced that northeastern businessmen preferred peaceful separation to economic disruption, but he saw the Northwest as the lynchpin of the Union. If the United States had remained confined to the eastern seaboard, he believed, it would have already dissolved.[22]

The efforts to shift away from the Bible proved vain not because Southerners slighted political and economic arguments. Far from it. But they could no more readily divorce politics and economics from religion than many Northerners. Few Southerners would have disagreed with George Frederick Holmes: "In all countries and among all nations, the religion of the people is the chief influence in determining their character." General John W. A. Sanford, Alabama's commissioner to the Texas secession convention in 1861, recalled the efforts of southern moderates to try to save the union from "the sacrilegious hands of the ruthless despoiler." The Reverend A. H. H. Boyd of Winchester, Virginia, a New School Presbyterian pastor with good credentials as a unionist, thought that – despite much pretense to religion – America was suffering from widespread infidelity thinly disguised as philanthropy. In consequence, such wild schemes as socialism and abolitionism were fomenting bitter sectional hatreds and undermining social order. Boyd detected disunionism in an abolitionist fanaticism that was exhausting the patience of southern unionists. He did not expect the South to bear further encroachment upon its constitutional liberties.[23]

Northern abolitionists damned the churches as bulwarks of slavery – in Parker Pillsbury's words, as *spiritual and ecclesiastical plantations.*" Harriet Beecher Stowe scored orthodox Christianity and especially Calvinism in such novels as *The*

---

[22] Thomas Roderick Dew, *Digest of the Laws, Customs, Manners, and Institutions of the Ancient and Modern Nations* (New York, 1884 [1852]), 24; David Outlaw to Emily Outlaw, July 28, 1848, at UNC-SHC; J. B. Lindsley, "Table Talk," Nov. 9, 1860, June 18, 1861, May 8, 1862, in John Berrien Lindsley Papers, at Tennessee State Library and Archives (Nashville); also, John C. Inscoe, *Mountain Masters: Slavery, and the Sectional Crisis in Western North Carolina* (Knoxville, TN, 1989), 114. In the Northwest the Protestant churches and religious press became steadily more antislavery but nonetheless long took a critical view of the abolitionists. By the 1850s – especially during the political explosion over Kansas–Nebraska – moderation gave way and the religious press openly supported the Republican party. See Wesley Norton, *Religious Newspapers in the Old Northwest to 1861: A History, Bibliography, and Record of Opinion* (Athens, OH, 1977), 43 and ch. 5.
  Sally McDowell of the Shenandoah Valley viewed slavery in a manner similar to that of Lindsley. The daughter of Virginia's Governor James McDowell, she shared his disquiet over slavery but conceded, "I think slavery will exist as long as the world. My heart bleeds for the poor creatures very often, but I don't think their condition will ever be remedied." Sally McDowell to John Miller, Sept. 15, 1855, in Thomas E. Buckley, ed., *"If You Love That Lady Don't Marry Her": The Courtship Letters of Sally McDowell and John Miller, 1854–56* (Columbia, MO, 2000), 388.

[23] George Frederick Holmes, "Greece and Its History," *QRMECS*, 9 (1855), 54; *Journal of the Secession Convention of Texas* (Austin, TX, 1861), 73; A. H. H. Boyd, *Thanksgiving Sermon, Delivered in Winchester, Va.* (Winchester, VA, 1860), 10–12, 15.

Minister's Wooing. She devoted a chapter of *A Key to Uncle Tom's Cabin*, which sold 90,000 copies in the first month of publication, to quotations from proslavery southern divines. "The influence of the clergy," Stowe wrote, "is looked upon by our statesmen as a most serious element in making up their political combinations." George Cheever referred to slaveholders as "Christians, so-called" and ridiculed their expressions of piety. Daniel Alexander Payne, a future bishop of the African Methodist Church who had been forced to close his school for black children in Charleston, joined the philanthropist Lewis Tappan of Massachusetts in denying that a slaveholder could be a Christian. Stephen Foster enlivened abolitionist meetings by denouncing churches that did not censure slavery unequivocally as "combinations of thieves, robbers, adulterers, pirates, and murderers." The Methodist Church was "more corrupt than any house of ill fame in New York." Foster and Thomas Parnell Beech made a specialty of disrupting church services. Beech did three months in jail when the Quakers of Newburyport had had enough of his antics.[24]

Angelina Grimké and Theodore Weld aimed at individuals as well as churches, condemning preachers for "connivance at cherished sins ... truckling subserviency to power,... clinging with mendant sycophancy to the skirts of wealth and influence,... humoring of pampered lusts,... cowering before bold transgression when it stalks among the high places of power with fashion in its train." For Gerrit Smith, prominent New York abolitionist, a "bastard Christianity" supported slavery with a clergy "the most guilty and corrupting body of men in the land." The southern-born Quaker Charles Osborne described slaveholders as "the vilest of sinners." Yet as late as 1885, R. Abbey of North Carolina, who had courageously supported the Union during the War, was still fuming at abolitionist characterizations of slavery as the "sum of all villanies" and of the southern church as "a slave-trader and slave-breeder."[25]

---

[24] Stacey M. Robertson, *Parker Pillsbury: Radical Abolitionist, Male Feminist* (Ithaca, NY, 2000), 5–6; Harriet Beecher Stowe, *A Key to Uncle Tom's Cabin* (Port Washington, NY, 1968 [1853]), 193; on the sales of *Key* see James D. Hart, *The Popular Book: A History of America's Literary Taste* (New York, 1950), 112; Daniel Alexander Payne, *Recollections of Seventy Years* (New York, 1968 [1888]), 51; Stephen Foster, *The Brotherhood of Thieves* (Boston, 1844), 9–11; George B. Cheever, *The Guilt of Slavery and the Crime of Slaveholding, Demonstrated from the Hebrew and Greek Scriptures* (New York, 1969 [1860]), xix, 376 n.; also, H. Mattison, *The Impending Crisis of 1860; Or, the Present Connection of the Methodist Episcopal Church with Slavery and Our Duty in Regard to It* (New York, 1858), 110. In general see McKivigan, *War against Proslavery Religion*, chs. 1 and 2; Louis Filler, *The Crusade against Slavery, 1830–1860* (New York, 1960), 77; Ronald G. Walters, *The Antislavery Appeal: American Abolitionism after 1830* (Baltimore, 1976), 41; Lewis Perry, *Radical Abolitionism: Antislavery and the Government of God in Antislavery Thought* (Ithaca, NY, 1973), 100–1, 107–9. Frederick Douglass avoided Foster's vulgarity, but he, too, charged the churches with timidity and worse: see William S. McFeely, *Frederick Douglass* (New York, 1991), 102, 124. James Birney published the anticlerical *American Churches, the Bulwarks of Slavery* (Newburyport, MA, 1834).

[25] Grimké and Weld quoted in Walters, *Antislavery Appeal*, 43; Gerrit Smith quoted in Avery O. Craven, *The Growth of Southern Nationalism, 1848–1861* (Baton Rouge, LA, 1953), 207, and Perry, *Radical Abolitionism*, 179, but see also *Letter of Gerrit Smith to Rev. James Smylie of the State of Mississippi* (New York, 1837); *Journal of that Faithful Servant of Christ, Charles Osborn* (Cincinnati, 1854),

Radical abolitionist rhetoric drowned temperate antislavery voices. Fewer and fewer in North and South alike heeded antislavery sermons by men like James Freeman Clarke of Kentucky, who spoke of "many very kind masters – very many." The slaves had rather too little than too much to do: "There is often a strong attachment between master and servant, very different from the mercenary relation which exists so much among ourselves between employer and domestic." Clarke, a Unitarian, regarded the spirit of the Bible as antislavery, but he acknowledged that Jesus did not reject slaveholders or characterize slavery as intrinsically sinful.[26]

Albert Barnes, a principal abolitionist theologian, defended his colleagues in the New School Presbyterian Church against the radicals' vituperation. He claimed that most Christian ministers abhorred slavery; that his church had a creditable antislavery record; and that even in the South proslavery ministers spoke only for a small minority of clergy and laity. The churches simply lacked the power to serve as the bulwark of slavery. Barnes then contradicted himself: "There is not power enough out of the Church to sustain [slavery] if the Church were wholly detached from it and arrayed against it." Slavery lacked the "vital energy" to maintain itself without church support. Slavery alone divided the Union, which consisted of one people united "in customs, in law, and religion." Barnes again contradicted himself: "Slavery touches on society at a thousand different points; and it is impossible that there should be *any* institution in a region where slavery prevails which will not be more or less affected by it."[27]

During the War, Edward Everett Hale surprised few Southerners when he translated antislavery doctrine into the language of Wall Street. Hale identified manufacture, commerce, and religion as special Yankee gifts and called upon the federal government to introduce Christian civilization into a benighted South. Nor did George Julian, who had long pronounced the struggle over slavery as between God and the devil, surprise them when he carried abolitionist logic to the end and demanded the execution of Jefferson Davis and Robert E. Lee.[28]

When advances in geology (among other things) led James Birney to doubt the divine inspiration of the Bible in addition to such specifics as eternal rewards

461; R. Abbey, *Peter: Not an Apostle but a Chattel. With a Strange History* (Nashville, TN, 1885), 5, 18, 42. Douglass's attitude toward Christianity was ambiguous at best: Donald B. Gibson, "Faith, Doubt, and Apostasy," in Eric J. Sundquist, ed., *Frederick Douglass: New Literary and Historical Essays* (New York, 1990), 84–98. Among abolitionist tracts, Theodore D. Weld's *The Bible against Slavery* (Pittsburgh, PA, 1864 [1837]) scored the greatest public success.

26 James Freeman Clarke, *Slavery in the United States* (Boston, 1843), 6, 14–15.

27 Albert Barnes, *The Church and Slavery* (New York, 1969 [1857]), 7, 14–15, 20, 23–4, 28–30, 46–8, 68–9, 169, quote at 23–4. In 1860 Cheever praised the early Presbyterian Church for its efforts to exclude slaveholders and extirpate slavery but lamented its subsequent backsliding: Cheever, *Guilt of Slavery*, 98–100, 426. When the emancipationist campaign of 1849–50 in Kentucky failed, its leaders blamed northern abolitionist excesses but also the temporizing of the churches: see *BRPR*, 21 (1849), 582–607.

28 For Hale see Gardiner H. Shattuck, Jr., *A Shield and a Hiding Place: The Religious Life of the Civil War Armies* (Macon, GA, 1987), 20; "Dangers and Duties of the Hour" (1865), in *Speeches on Political Questions by George W. Julian* (New York, 1872), 264–8; G. W. Julian, "The Trial of Jefferson Davis," Apr. 30, 1866, *Congressional Globe,* 39th Cong., 1st Sess., 2282–5.

and punishment and the miraculous birth of Jesus, Birney gave up on the letter of the Bible and demanded that abolitionists stand instead on the inspiration of the Holy Spirit. Angelina Grimké, J. V. Himes, Charles Fitch, and George Storrs turned to Millerism. Lydia Maria Child testified that she was "passing through strange spiritual experiences." LaRoy Sunderland, who helped found the abolitionist Wesleyan Methodist Church in 1843, turned to pantheism and then to spiritualism. Theodore Weld, who had "a direct communion with God," lost faith in all creeds. Cassius Clay professed Christianity but doubted the immortality of the soul. Frances Wright's Nashtoba settlement in Tennessee declared against religion and marriage as well as against slavery. The religious skeptic William Herndon – Lincoln's abolitionist friend and law partner and a fan of Theodore Parker, liberal theologian of Boston – predicted that enlightened man would become his own Providence and Redeemer. Lydia Maria Child tended to agree: "More and more, I feel that every sort of salvation we do attain to in this life must be worked out by ourselves." John Pierpont and Richard Hildreth abandoned Christianity for secular rationalism. Jane Swisshelm, anti-Christian abolitionist, gloated that slavery was indeed Christian. Nathaniel Rogers, a "come-outer," considered the established churches as "Popery, only Protestantized" and considered the Bible "useful" only to the extent that it registered "human understanding" and as without authority over individual conscience.[29]

Most abolitionists, however, maintained with Henry Clark Wright that the churches had to be revitalized. Thus James Redpath repudiated not Christianity but "Churchianity." Paul Tillich, the formidable twentieth-century Protestant theologian, properly chastised the person who has no use for "organized religion" but claims to be deeply religious: "It is nonsense because in his personal religiousness – excuse this terrible word – he is dependent on the tradition of the church for every word, every symbol that he might use in prayer, in contemplation or in mystical experience. Without the community of speaking, there is no speaking whatsoever, and without an inner speaking, there is no spiritual life whatsoever." The theologically liberal Reverend Theodore Clapp of New Orleans and the orthodox Reverend Thomas Smyth of Charleston preached that very message.[30]

---

[29] Walters, *Antislavery Appeal*, 2, 18, 47–51; Clement Eaton, *The Mind of the Old South* (Baton Rouge, LA, 1964), 99; David Herbert Donald, *Lincoln's Herndon: A Biography* (New York, 1948), 59–60, 289–92; Lydia Maria Child to Convers Francis, July 14, 1848, in *Letters of Lydia Maria Child* (New York, 1969 [1883]), 65; Perry, *Radical Abolitionism*, 110–13, 120–2, 127, 157; also, David Brion Davis, *Slavery and Human Progress* (New York, 1984), 14, 149, and on Swissholm see Peter Walker, *Moral Choices: Memory, Desire, and Imagination in Nineteenth-Century American Abolition* (Baton Rouge, LA, 1978), 97. Lydia Maria Child, who found little essential Christianity in the doctrines of the various churches, adhered to "the moral precepts of the New Testament": Child, *The Progress of Religious Ideas, through Successive Ages*, 3 vols. (New York, 1855), 1:137.

[30] For "Churchianity" among abolitionist women opposed to organized religion, see Anna M. Speicher, *The Religious World of Antislavery Women: Spirituality in the Lives of Five Abolitionist Lecturers* (Syracuse, NY, 2000), 61–2; Paul Tillich, *A History of Christian Thought: From Its Judaic and Hellenistic Origins to Existentialism*, ed. Carl E. Braaten (New York, 1972), 477–8; Clapp's sermon in New Orleans *Daily Picayune*, Mar. 19, 1848; Thomas Smyth, *The Well in the Valley*, rev. ed. (Philadelphia, 1860), chs. 3 and 17.

The leading proslavery polemicists tried to present the thought of their opponents accurately, quoting *in extenso* and in context from books, sermons, and discourses they identified. In a contrast historians have failed to notice, antislavery polemicists offered caricatures of proslavery authors and unidentified texts they did not name. Antislavery Northerners who privately acknowledged James Henley Thornwell as an intellectual giant did not quote or cite his proslavery writings. Only rarely did abolitionist literature suggest that a proslavery writer might be honest, broadly cultured, theologically learned, or competent in exegesis. Yet, although many Southerners shrilly denounced John Quincy Adams, William Ellery Channing, Ralph Waldo Emerson, and Francis Wayland, many others engaged them respectfully. "The cunning malice of John Quincy Adams, father of the antislavery party" was matched by kindly expressions. E. F. Rockwell, speaking at Davidson College in North Carolina in 1851, quoted Adams's "elegant language" on religious faith. The fiery proslavery Catherine Edmonston remarked compassionately if with condescension that the "poor old man" allowed himself to be seduced by unprincipled abolitionist fanatics. When Adams died, *Southern Literary Messenger* published generous tributes to a great and pious man.[31]

Southerners took the measure of Channing as a formidable intellectual opponent. He did suffer nasty ad hominem attacks but also enjoyed respect and admiration. In the 1840s Channing drew fire for his religious heterodoxy but compliments for the restraint with which he criticized the South and slavery. His cultural criticism won applause from W. J. Tuck of Memphis and William Gilmore Simms

---

[31] "Disfederation of the States," *SLM*, 32 (1861), 128; E. F. Rockwell, *Inaugural Address before the Board of Trustees of Davidson College* (Salisbury, NC, 1851), 18. For tributes to Adams in *SLM*, 14 (1848): A. J. Crane, 293–301; E. L. Magoon, 334–5; and H. M. Brackenridge, 519–20. President William Carey Crane of Mississippi (women's) College referred to "the gifted but eccentric" John Quincy Adams: Crane, *Literary Discourses* (New York, 1853), 14.

Occasionally, an abolitionist quoted a slaveholder in the manner of Sarah Grimké, who quoted C. C. Jones's admission that slaves were prevented from reading the Bible: Sarah M. Grimké, *An Epistle to the Clergy of the Southern States* (New York, 1836), 12. However, the antislavery Leonard Bacon, a moderate critical of radical abolitionists, discussed Dew's *Review of Debates* at length, critically but "with no little admiration": *Slavery Discussed in Occasional Essays from 1833 to 1846* (New York, 1846), 91–6, quote at 91. The silence on Thornwell was appalling in view of his unquestioned stature. A comical exception is LaRoy Sunderland's description of the orthodox Calvinist Thornwell in the 1830s as a Methodist: see Sunderland, *The Anti-Slavery Manual: Containing a Collection of Facts and Arguments on American Slavery*, 3rd. ed. (New York, 1839), 51. Daniel Webster, Edward Everett, and J. W. Alexander of Princeton praised Thornwell's intellect and oratory: B. M. Palmer, *The Life and Letters of James Henley Thornwell* (Richmond, VA, 1875), 62. Henry Ward Beecher graciously acknowledged, "By common fame Dr. Thornwell was the most brilliant debater in its [Presbyterian] General Assembly": quoted in Louis C. LaMotte, *Colored Light: The Story of the Influence of Columbia Theological Seminary, 1828–1936* (Richmond, VA, 1937), 70; see also John Miller Wells, *Southern Presbyterian Worthies* (Richmond, VA, 1936), 46. Even northern newspapers sympathetic to the South, which often published proslavery articles on Scripture, demonstrated little acquaintance with the intellectually strongest southern efforts. See Howard C. Perkins, "The Defense of Slavery in the Northern Press on the Eve of the Civil War," *JSH*, 9 (1943), 528. Wayland's *Elements of Moral Science* (1835), which laid down the antislavery case as well as anything available, was widely read in the South: see also Supplementary References: "Wayland."

("beautiful little essay"). In a fifty-page critique of Channing's antislavery writing, Daniel Whitaker acknowledged him a foremost man of letters. Channing had superiors in erudition and scholarship, but Whitaker lauded "the masculine vigor of his mind, the pure and elevated tone of his thoughts, the free, fearless and liberal spirit by which his writings are distinguished, and, above all, by his evident sincerity and great earnestness of purpose."[32]

When Channing died, Simms's *Magnolia* lamented, "The nation has lost a strong man." Never mind his antislavery views; he exhibited "the purest and holiest purposes of humanity." *Southern Literary Messenger*'s handsome tribute by Henry Theodore Tuckerman, a Northerner, hailed Channing as a teacher of ethics and a pursuer of truth, if marred by "egotism." Gently critical of his philosophy and theology, Tuckerman left the impression of a basically good if flawed man. Julia LeGrand of New Orleans, who had no use for Channing's philosophy, said his sermons breathed a Christian spirit even if not in ways orthodox churches would approve.[33]

Leading southern journals commended the contributions of antislavery Northerners – but usually on other subjects. *De Bow's Review* published an article by Horace Greeley on rivers and harbors. Simms rebuked Greeley for antisouthern bigotry but praised his valuable commentary on the Crystal Palace industrial exhibition in New York. *Southern Quarterly Review* thought George Cheever's defense of capital punishment first-rate. *Southern Literary Messenger* admired Thoreau's depiction of rural life in *Walden* and, as late as 1860, applauded Julia Ward Howe for the moderation of her book *A Trip to Cuba*. Lydia Maria Child's *Biographies of Good Wives* charmed the editor of *Southern Quarterly Review,* who described Child as a woman of superior intellect and literary style. He even complimented the "eccentric" Theodore Parker as one of the "bright erratic stars" of Massachusetts, whose thoughtful and graceful words Southerners should appreciate, notwithstanding his antisouthern diatribes. So, too, M. R. H. Garnett, Virginia's proslavery polemicist, complimented Parker as "one of the best writers of New England." *Southern Quarterly Review* scolded Albert Barnes for his antislavery reading of *Philemon*, at the same time noting his theological learning and talent. De Bow recommended Asa Mahan's *The True Believer* as "abounding in precious consolations for the

---

[32] W. J. Tuck, "The Mind, Its Powers and Results," *SLM*, 10 (1844), 665; [Willliam Gilmore Simms], *SWMR*, 1 (1845), 439; [Daniel K. Whitaker], "Channing's Duty of the Free States," *SQR*, 2 (1842), 130–77, quote at 130; *SQR*, 2 (1846), 539. As early as 1836, Senator Benjamin Watkins Leigh of Virginia painfully noted the shift in Channing's antislavery stance from moderation to increasing harshness: *Speech of Mr. Leigh on the Question of the Reception of Certain Memorials from Citizens of Ohio, Praying Congress to Abolish Slavery within the District of Columbia* (Washington, DC, 1836), 5–8. Channing had good friends and dinner partners among proslavery Southerners who lived or "summered" in the Northeast: see e.g. Eliza Middleton Fisher to Mary Herring Middleton, Dec. 31, 1840 (166), Apr. 22, 1841 (211), in Eliza Cope Harrison, ed., *Best Companions: Letters of Eliza Middleton Fisher and Her Mother, Mary Herring Middleton, from Charleston, Philadelphia, and Newport, 1839–1846* (Columbia, SC, 2001).

[33] *Magnolia*, n.s., 1 (1842), 327; Henry Theodore Tuckerman, "Channing," *SLM*, 15 (1849), 25–31; Kate Mason Rowland and Mrs. Morris S. Croxall, eds., *The Journal of Julia LeGrand: New Orleans, 1862–1863* (Richmond, VA, 1911), Feb. 28, 1863 (162).

thoughtful, the afflicted, or pious mind." Bishop William Meade, seeking to guide the Episcopal Church toward evangelicalism, expressed his indebtedness to *Practical View of the Prevailing Religious System of Professed Christians* by the English abolitionist William Wilberforce.[34]

If some weak southern ministers supported slavery in fear of the wrath of their communities and if self-interest motivated ministers who themselves owned slaves, an impressive number – probably the great majority – supported slavery because they firmly believed that the Bible sanctioned it. Biographies of ministers show courageous men who defended slavery on principle and believed every word they said. Decades of impressive scholarship, close textual analysis, and skillful argumentation enhanced the beliefs of pastors, denominational leaders, and scripturally informed secular theorists. We cannot know what the outcome of the struggle would have been if the divines had failed to make a solid scriptural case for slavery: The South might then itself have been rent over slavery. If many slaveholders would have turned away from churches rather than surrender their human property, many others were primarily concerned with their own spiritual salvation. But southern evangelicals, having cited chapter and verse, successfully enlisted the Bible to unify the overwhelming majority of slaveholders and nonslaveholders in defense of slavery as ordained of God. The antislavery spokesman failed to demonstrate that the Bible repudiated slavery; primarily, they appealed to the ideals of the Enlightenment and Declaration of Independence.

Some ministers' diaries do show struggles with conscience. A few set out to refute the abolitionist argument only to end up accepting it. In the 1830s Reverend William Henry Brisbane of Charleston, editor of a Baptist journal, freed his twenty slaves and settled them in Ohio. When forced from his pulpit, he went north to join the antislavery forces. The extent of the quarrels within slaveholding families will never be known, but consider one example (reported by a family slave) in which a Tennessean sharply rebuked his sister with the warning that she could not be simultaneously a Christian and a slaveholder. But conversion worked in both directions, and the number of Southerners drawn to an antislavery reading of the Bible appears to have been small. John McCullough, a Presbyterian Pennsylvanian, had been a

---

[34] Horace Greeley, "River and Harbor Improvement," *DBR,* 4 (1847), 291–6; [William Gilmore Simms], "Critical Notices," *SQR,* n.s., 9 (1854), 535–6; *SQR,* 1 (1847), 3 (Cheever); *SLM,* 20 (1854), 575 (Thoreau); [John R. Thompson], *SLM,* 30 (1860), 235 (Howe); "Critical Notices," *SQR,* 8 (1845), 252–3; *SQR,* n.s., 1 (1850), 264; "Critical Notices," *SQR,* 9 (1846), 539 (Child); [M. R. H. Garnett], *The Union, Past and Future: How It Works, and How to Save It,* 4th ed. (Charleston, SC, 1850), 35. On Meade see Allen C. Guelzo, "Ritual, Romanism, and Rebellion: The Disappearance of the Evangelical Episcopalians," *Anglican and Episcopal History,* 62 (1993), 554. A brother of Governor Wilson Lumpkin and Judge J. H. Lumpkin of Georgia was named William Wilberforce Lumpkin (b. 1829): Paul DeForest Hicks, *Joseph Henry Lumpkin: Georgia's First Chief Justice* (Athens, GA, 2002), 51. The proslavery William B. Hodgson of Savannah admired Thomas Foxwell Buxton and Wilberforce, citing them against the African slave trade: William B. Hodgson, *Notes on Northern Africa, the Sahara and Soudan* (New York, 1844), 54–5.

confirmed abolitionist, but after he settled in Texas he accepted slavery as "ordained of God" and supported the proslavery wing of the Presbyterian Church.[35]

John Early, riding circuit in Virginia and North Carolina before he became a distinguished Methodist bishop, preached to both races and avoided the subject of slavery but drove slave traders – "among the blackest characters" – from his services. In 1813 a "much distressed" Early inherited his father's property and "dreaded" having "to engage in disagreeable things." He had become a slaveholder: "Oh degrading appellation and unhappy situation." Soon, he agreed to buy the slaves left to his mother. In 1814, seeking a new overseer, he reiterated that he found the business "disagreeable" but learned to live with it. How could he live with it? Slavery, however disagreeable, was not sinful.[36]

The proslavery reaction grew fierce, with accusations that abolitionists assaulted property rights and the racial order and, worse, assaulted southern honor: "The abolitionist," Joseph Stiles cried, "robs me of my *right of character*." Worst of all, abolitionists mocked Christianity. Many southern commentators acknowledged that early antislavery agitation had avoided denunciations of slaveholders and appealed to sensibility and interest; they acknowledged, too, that most clergymen in New England, even after 1830, supported Channing's soft tone against Garrison's vituperation. Still, they saw such efforts as of no avail. The increasingly powerful abolitionists placed Southerners under moral opprobrium.[37]

---

[35] Weld, *Bible against Slavery*, 14; also, Carolyn L. Harrell, *Kith and Kin: A Portrait of a Southern Family, 1630–1934* (Macon, GA, 1984), 125; Ophelia Settle Egypt et al., eds., *Unwritten History of Slavery: Autobiographical Accounts of Ex-Slaves* (Washington, DC, 1968), 110; Richard B. Hughes, "Old School Presbyterians: Eastern Invaders of Texas, 1830–1865," *Southwestern Historical Quarterly*, 74 (1971), 328.

[36] In 1785, when the Methodist Reverend Thomas Coke preached against slavery in Virginia, a woman offered a mob £50 to give him a hundred lashes but found no takers: W. T. Smith, "Thomas Coke's Contribution to the Christmas Conference: A Study in Ecclesiology," in Russell E. Richey and Kenneth E. Rowe, *Rethinking Methodist History: A Bicentennial Historical Consultation* (Nashville, TN, 1985), 44. John Early Diary, June 9 and Nov. 24, 1812, Jan. 4 and Nov. 15, 1813, Jan. 23, 1814, at UNC-SHC. Antislavery agitation in Virginia in the 1830s stressed economic and political arguments while downplaying the biblical and moral. Charles Henry Ambler, *Sectionalism in Virginia from 1776 to 1861* (Chicago, 1910), 192–3. In Kentucky, however, antislavery agitation, centered in the churches, stressed biblical and moral arguments: see Asa Earl Martin, *The Anti-Slavery Movement in Kentucky Prior to 1850* (New York, 1970 [1918]), 84–7. For the weakness of antislavery organization in the Border States see Gordon E. Finnie, "The Antislavery Movement in the Upper South before 1840," *JSH*, 35 (1969), 319–42. For a brief review of the historiography see Harrold Stanley, *The Abolitionists and the South, 1831–1861* (Lexington, KY, 1995), ch. 1.

[37] McKivigan, *War against Proslavery Religion*, 58–9; John Robinson, *The Testimony and Practice of the Presbyterian Church in Reference to American Slavery* (Cincinnati, 1852), 35–8, 67; Walter Brownlow Posey, *Presbyterian Church in the Southwest, 1778–1838* (Richmond, VA, 1952), 76–82, 89–90; Robert Nuckols Watkins, Jr., "The Forming of the Southern Presbyterian Minister: From Calvin to the Civil War" (Ph.D. diss., Vanderbilt University, 1969), 446; Victor B. Howard, *Conscience and Slavery: The Evangelistic Calvinist Domestic Missions, 1837–1861* (Kent, OH, 1990), 26–7; Joseph C. Stiles, *Modern Reform Examined* (Philadelphia, 1857), 47. The anarchism of Garrison and Henry C. Wright gave most abolitionists heartburn. John Greenleaf Whittier, for example, complained that they were doing the cause enormous harm: Whittier to Sarah and Angelina Grimké,

In any case, with the call for immediate emancipation, the abolitionists moved from "hate the sin but love the sinner" to hatred of slaveholders themselves as evil personified, spurring antislavery in the North but ending its slim hopes in the South. The political and economic crises of the late 1840s and 1850s produced a sense of a decline in everyday morality – for which someone or something had to be held responsible. God was punishing America for its sins, slavery the most dreadful of them all. The Reverend Leonard Bacon, one of New England's leading antislavery voices, pleaded – in words made famous by Lincoln without attribution – that if slavery is not wrong, nothing is wrong. The Reverend Ferdinand Jacobs returned the fire: "If the scriptures do not justify slavery, I know not what they do justify." William Garrison, Lucy Stone, Theodore Parker, and Lucretia Mott ruled slavery beyond debate, along with adultery, burglary, and piracy. The militantly proslavery Albert Taylor Bledsoe of Virginia and a good many other Southerners recognized a declaration of war when they were handed one.[38]

During Virginia's debate over emancipation in 1831, John Thompson Brown of Petersburg demanded to know, "In what code of ethics is it written that slavery is so odious?" Jesus "came into the world to reprove sin. Yet he rebuked not slavery." Hugh Lawson White of Tennessee, Whig presidential candidate in 1836, declared that the South held slavery "sacred." Alexander Stephens said the morality of slavery rested "upon a basis as firm as the Bible" and would be sustained "until Christianity be overthrown." The South, in the words of Charles Clark, Mississippi's wartime governor, would not "abandon its cherished and Christian institution of domestic slavery."[39]

"Let us open these Holy Scriptures," where we shall find that the Apostles considered "slavery as an *established* as well as *inevitable condition of human society.*" So James H. Hammond, hardly the most pious of men, began his public letter to Thomas Clarkson, the British emancipationist. Those who did rise to defend slavery seldom failed to cite chapter and verse. Chancellor William Harper's essay, "Slavery in the Light of Social Ethics," first published in the 1830s, exercised an influence down to secession comparable to the writings of Dew and Calhoun. Harper, like Dew and Calhoun, preferred secular argument but appealed to Scripture to undercut abolitionism. Louisa McCord and George McDuffie in South Carolina, Willie Mangum in North Carolina, Jefferson Davis and L. Q. C. Lamar in Mississippi,

---

Aug. 14, 1837, in Gilbert H. Barnes and Dwight L. Dumond, eds., *Letters of Theodore Dwight Weld, Angelina Grimké and Sarah Grimké, 1822–1844,* 2 vols. (Gloucester, MA, 1965), 1:423.

[38] Bacon, *Slavery Discussed in Occasional Essays,* x; Albert Taylor Bledsoe, "Mr. Bledsoe's Review of His Reviewer," *SLM,* 23 (1856), 20.

[39] Brown quoted in Alison Goodyear Freehling, *Drift towards Dissolution: The Virginia Slavery Debate of 1831–1832* (Baton Rouge, LA, 1982), 153; White quoted in William J. Cooper, Jr., *The South and the Politics of Slavery, 1828–1856* (Baton Rouge, LA, 1978), 59; Stephens in the House of Representatives quoted in E. Ramsay Richardson, *Little Aleck: A Life of Alexander H. Stephens* (Indianapolis, IN, 1932), 110; Clark to the Mississippi Legislature in John K. Bettersworth, ed. *Mississippi in the Confederacy: As They Saw It* (Baton Rouge, LA, 1961), 151.

Sampson Harris in Alabama, Ashbel Smith in Texas – the list could be extended – all invoked Scripture in defense of slavery. When a politician cited Scripture, he had to get it straight, for many of his constituents could embarrass him by recognizing a serious error. At a Breckenridge rally in 1860 at Port Gibson, Mississippi, J. B. Thrasher delivered much of a long speech extemporaneously but read aloud the portion published as *Slavery a Divine Institution,* not daring to risk an error in biblical references.[40]

Southern preachers had to be careful with biblical citations. A mere grumble from a few congregants would send others scurrying to check their Bibles. The Baptists of Richmond and the Northern Neck may have merely smiled when – as often happened – their beloved Reverend Jeremiah Jeter misidentified biblical citations, but the Reverend Mr. Tuft, congressional chaplain, was less fortunate, messing up a biblical text in his prayer in Congress and thereby appalling William Hooper Haigh of North Carolina. Barbara Ann Love, a student in Georgia who read sermons carefully, picked up a minister's misquotation from Timothy. Nor could preachers depart with impunity from denominational doctrine. Even theologically well-grounded ministers sometimes tripped, as did one poor chap who delivered a staunchly Calvinistic sermon on the perseverance of the saints and then led his congregation in a hymn that included, "With shame of soul I do confess / A real saint may fall from grace." As in the pulpit, so before the bar of justice. John Fletcher of Louisiana, in his *Studies on Slavery,* offered an extended review of scriptural arguments from the original Hebrew and Greek that won accolades from both clerical and lay scholars. George Sawyer, also of Louisiana, observed in his *Southern Institutes* that since Mosaic Law grounded society's constitutions and mores, "It is as much the province of the jurist as the priest, to discuss all theological and moral questions, so far as they affect the interpretation and force of the laws of the land."[41]

[40] *Letters and Speeches of Hammond,* 121, 123; Chancellor Harper, "Slavery in the Light of Social Ethics," in Elliott, ed., *Cotton Is King,* esp. 552, 556, 562; "Enfranchisement of Woman," in Richard Lounsbury, ed., *Louisa S. McCord: Political and Social Essays* (Charlottesville, VA, 1995), 122; Henry Thomas Shanks, ed., *The Papers of Willie P. Mangum,* 5 vols. (Raleigh, NC, 1955–56), 2:374; William C. Davis, *Jefferson Davis: The Man and His Hour* (New York, 1991), 195; James B. Murphy, *L. Q. C. Lamar: Pragmatic Patriot* (Baton Rouge, LA, 1973), 45; Sampson W. Harris, *Speech on the Bill to Organize a Territorial Government for the Territory of Oregon* (Washington, DC, 1848), 13; Elizabeth Silverthorne, *Ashbel Smith of Texas: Pioneer, Patriot, Statesman, 1805–1886* (College Station, TX, 1982), 135, 147; J. B. Thrasher, *Slavery: A Divine Institution* (Port Gibson, MS, 1861). Calhoun, according to his daughter, read the Bible "constantly, & earnestly, & conversed often & beautifully about it." His life was governed by "simple faith" and he avoided creedal discussions: Anna Calhoun Clemson to Charles Edward Leverett, May 20, 1867, in Frances Wallace Taylor et al., eds., *The Leverett Letters: Correspondence of a South Carolina Family, 1851–1868* (Columbia, SC, 2000), 426–7.

[41] Hatcher, *Jeter,* 333; Haigh Diary, Mar. 9, 1844, at UNC-SHC; Love Diary, Feb. 14, 1858, in Curry Hill Plantation Records, at Georgia State Department of Archives and History (Atlanta); B. W. McDonnold, *History of the Cumberland Presbyterian Church* (Nashville, TN, 1899), 315–16; see also Holder, *William Winans,* 162 (for the blunders of the Reverend D. S. Doggett); George S. Sawyer, *Southern Institutes; Or, an Inquiry into the Origin and Early Prevalence of Slavery and the Slave Trade* (New York, 1967 [1858]), 17–18, 29, 147–8, quote at 18 (for Fletcher's influence on Sawyer see

In 1858 Thornwell boasted: "Our Theological Professors are preachers upon a large scale – Preachers not only to preachers, but to all the congregations of the land. In their studies they are putting forth an influence which, like the atmosphere, penetrates to every part of the country." Thornwell was delighted by the reception accorded his sermon on slavery: "It has taken remarkably well, much beyond my expectation." His sermon electrified Charleston in 1850, evoking demands for its publication and distribution across the South. Its popularity rivaled publications of the Episcopalian George W. Freeman, the Presbyterian John Adger, the Methodist H. N. McTyeire, and the especially influential pamphlets of the Baptist Thornton Stringfellow. A number of Southerners, some of them prominent, confessed to qualms about slavery before they studied the scriptural arguments of Stringfellow and others. Stringfellow turned around William Campbell Preston and Jeremiah Jeter and elated Edmund Ruffin, who needed no turning. John Leadley Dagg's *Manual of Theology,* with its scriptural defense of slavery, became the first textbook in systematic theology used in southern Baptist theological seminaries. Charles Campbell's *History of the Colony and Ancient Dominion of Virginia* based a scriptural justification of slavery on Stringfellow, Thornwell, and George Armstrong of Norfolk.[42]

Many Southerners thought that preachers should stay out of politics altogether, and many more – probably a substantial majority – objected to the use of pulpits to advance political causes. When a minister entered politics directly he risked his personal reputation within the church and, as Bishop Otey complained, he risked the reputation of the church with the general public. By 1850 nine slave states formally disqualified ministers from holding office. Easier said than done: A flock of ministers sat in Congress and state legislatures. Churches that eschewed political pronouncements hosted political meetings and constitutional conventions without a murmur of protest. Where and how to draw the line between religion and politics? The Richmond *Examiner,* among other newspapers, criticized ministers both for meddling in politics and for being insufficiently partisan in defense of the South.[43]

132). For tributes to Fletcher see George D. Armstrong, *The Christian Doctrine of Slavery* (New York, 1967 [1857]), 119 n.; Thrasher, *Divine Institution*; Memphis *Daily Appeal*, Feb. 22, 1853; Thomas R. R. Cobb, *An Inquiry into the Law of Negro Slavery in the United States* (New York, 1968 [1858]), 7; Mar. 10, 1857, in *ERD*, 1:165; R. H. Rivers, *Elements of Moral Philosophy* (Nashville, TN, 1859).

[42] "Theology, Its Proper Method and Its Central Principle," *JHTW*, 1:445 n. 1. Thornwell to Gen. James Gillespie, June 17, 1850; Waddy Thompson was among the politicians who sought Thornwell's guidance on biblical matters: Thompson to Thornwell, Apr. 13, 1848 – both in Thornwell Papers, at Historical Foundation of the Presbyterian and Reformed Churches (Montreat, NC). W. C. Preston to Waddy Thompson, July 22 and Aug. 10, 1857, in Preston Papers, at USC; Charles Campbell, *History of the Colony and Ancient Dominion of Virginia* (Spartanburg, SC, 1965 [1860]), ch. 48; Anne C. Loveland, *Southern Evangelicals and the Social Order, 1800–1860* (Baton Rouge, LA, 1980), 187–8. In the late 1830s the Reverend Leander Ker of Pennsylvania, who had spent a few years in Florida, claimed to have been antislavery until he studied the question closely: Leander Ker, *Slavery Consistent with Christianity*, 3rd ed. (Weston, MO, 1853), 22; *ERD*, 1:327. See also Supplementary References: "Proslavery Religious Tracts."

[43] Green, *Otey*, 204; Adger to Thornwell, Sept. 30, 1850, quoted in John Barnwell, *Love of Order: South Carolina's First Secession Crisis* (Chapel Hill, NC, 1982), 135–6.

The Presbyterians, most notably in South Carolina, were proud heirs of the Scots Church, which had a tradition of political preaching that extended at least as far back as its seventeenth-century resistance to the divine right of kings. During the crisis of 1850, the Reverend John Adger wrote Thornwell that, as a minister of Christ and no politician, he saw the issue between secession and abolition: "I find myself unable to pray except as a *partisan*. I can not help feeling that we are in a contest, and praying that God give *us* the victory." The Reverend Thomas Smyth wrote that "true religion and sound politics" were intimately connected: "The well being of the one is the well being of the other." He opposed the use of the pulpit as a political forum, but he insisted that sound preaching had to impart the Christian principles necessary to the political life of a moral community. Smyth, a unionist, reluctantly endorsed secession on (he said) moral not partisan political grounds.[44]

Ministers inculcated in their flock moral imperatives in political choice, which usually translated into a defense of the scriptural justification for slavery. Rural folk considered their pastors' opinions carefully. So, too, the most influential ministers exercised political power indirectly through close friendships with politicians who respected their judgment or did not want them for enemies. Bishop Pierce of Georgia, who usually avoided politics in the pulpit, did not always agree with Robert Toombs, Alexander Stephens, or Richard M. Johnson, but he had their ear, and vice versa. Henry Clay courted and received the support of Pierce and of the Methodist Reverends Henry Bascom of Kentucky and William Winans of Mississippi. The Reverends Augustus Longstreet and James Henley Thornwell did not always agree politically – Longstreet hated the Know-Nothings, Thornwell voted for them – but each maintained good relations with Calhoun. The Episcopalian Bishop Christopher Gadsden attended Yale with Calhoun, and they remained fast friends. When Gadsden was terminally ill, he carefully read and approved Calhoun's last publication. In Georgia the openly political Baptist Reverend Jesse Mercer carried his county for Troup and Crawford, earning the hostility of Governor Lumpkin, who accused the Church itself of political intervention.[45]

[44] Smyth quoted in Edward Riley Crowther, "Southern Protestants, Slavery, and Secession: A Study in Religious Ideology, 1830–1861" (Ph.D. diss., Auburn University, 1986), 4; Thomas Smyth to David Magie, Dec. 24, 1860, in Smyth, *Autobiographical Notes, Letters, and Reflections* (Charleston, SC, 1914), 564. On the Scottish tradition see Watkins, "Southern Presbyterian Minister," 114–15.

[45] Carwardine, *Evangelicals and Politics*, ch. 1, esp. 41; on Winans see Cooper, *South and Politics of Slavery*, Prologue, and James Byrne Ranck, *Albert Gallatin Brown: Radical Southern Nationalist* (New York, 1937), 62; on the indirect political influence of the Methodist ministers see Carwardine, "Methodist Ministers and the Second Party System," in Richey and Rowe, eds., *Rethinking Methodist History*, 144. For the response of the rural folk to their preachers see John Hebron Moore, *The Emergence of the Cotton Kingdom in Old Southwest: Mississippi, 1770–1860* (Baton Rouge, LA, 1988), 145. Even in late antebellum times, as Loveland observes, in some parts of the South voting was still oral, and the people knew how their ministers voted: *Southern Evangelicals*, 118. On Pierce and Mercer see the reflections of W. H. Sparks, *The Memories of Fifty Years* (Philadelphia, 1872), 79–80, 83; on Gadsden see William Buell Sprague, *Annals of the American Pulpit*, 9 vols. (New York, 1859–69), 5:510–14; on Clay see E. Brooks Holifield, *The Gentlemen Theologians: American Theology in Southern Culture, 1795–1860* (Durham, NC, 1978), 78, and E. Merton Coulter, *George Walton Williams: The Life of a Southern Merchant and Banker, 1820–1903* (Athens, GA, 1976),

That the Bible sanctioned slavery: Such became the conviction of pious and not-so-pious Southerners. Thomas Cooper, who took the Bible lightly, protested, "I do not know a more bold, a more impudent, a more unprincipled, unblushing false-hood, than to say that *slavery is inconsistent with the laws of God,* if the Bible is assumed as the repository of those laws." Cooper, like William Gregg the in-dustrialist and De Bow, spokesman for the commercial interest, was delighted that all social classes united on the scriptural defense of slavery. John Witherspoon of Virginia wrote his wife, "Nothing has so prostrated our Southern country in point of domestic improvement, as Slavery. And yet I believe African Slavery, lawful and not unchristian." The Reverend Dr. Henry Ruffner recalled that – during the row stirred up in 1847 in Virginia by his pro-emancipation *Address to the People of West Virginia* – "No one, so far as I remember, took the abolitionist ground that slaveholding was a sin." Indeed, a year earlier, Robert R. Howison's *History of Virginia* called slavery a moral and social evil, said most Virginians wanted it gone, and predicted emancipation at a pace consistent with social safety; but Howison, too, acknowledged slavery's biblical sanction. In his diary, Mitchell King asked "What are those who deny the divine origin of servitude of slavery" and answered: "Fanatics – Atheists." A new publication or organization usually issued an anti-abolition statement like that which launched *The Pioneer* in Augusta: "We believe that the institutions of the South are founded in the *immutable laws* of the God of Nature."[46]

"The whole Southern mind with an unparalleled unanimity," wrote the Sweden-borgian W. H. Holcombe of Natchez in 1861, "regards the institution of slavery as righteous and just, ordained of God, and to be perpetuated by man." Travelers had found Holcombe's declaration close to the truth in the 1840s and 1850s. William Chambers reported that Southerners everywhere accepted slavery as historically ubiquitous and divinely sanctioned. A Virginia planter reminded Marianne Finch that Jesus never condemned slavery and that Paul "rather encouraged it." Dur-ing the War the emphatically pro-Union Ernest Duvergier de Hauranne described the typical resident of St. Louis as strongly influenced by proslavery pastors and priests: "Whoever speaks against [slavery] is a blasphemous infidel and a hateful demagogue. The Southerner is the most interesting example of what a combina-tion of education and self-interest can produce in the way of infatuation, blindness and injustice." Mark Twain's mother in Kentucky accepted slavery as righteous: "She had never heard it assailed in any pulpit, but she had heard it defended and

23. On Mercer see also Ulrich Bonnell Phillips, *Georgia and State Rights* (Yellow Springs, OH, 1968), 102–3.

[46] [Thomas Cooper], "Slavery," *SLJ*, 1 (1835), 188; Gregg, *DBR*, 30 (1861), 103; J. D. B. De Bow, *The Interest in Slavery of the Southern Non-Slaveholder* (Charleston, SC, 1860), 5; John Witherspoon to Susan Witherspoon, May 23, 1837, in Witherspoon–McDowall Papers, at UNC-SHC; Mitchell King Diary, May 9, 1862, at USC; Henry Ruffner quoted in Ambler, *Sectionalism in Virginia,* 24–5; Robert R. Howison, *A History of Virginia from Its Discovery and Settlement by Europeans to the Present Time,* 2 vols. (Philadelphia, 1846), 1:219–22, 2:228–9, 389–96, 444–5, 517–20. For Howison's later views on slavery see esp. his long series of articles on the "History of the War," *SLM,* 1862–1864. Pi-oneer quoted in J. S. Buckingham, *The Slave States of America,* 2 vols. (New York, 1968 [1842]), 2:83.

sanctified in a thousand; her ears were familiar with the Bible texts that approved it." In her experience, "The wise and the good and the holy were unanimous in the conviction that slavery was right, righteous, sacred, the peculiar pet of the Deity, and a condition which the slave himself ought to be daily and nightly thankful for." Presumably, Twain knew that countless Southerners were checking their pastors' sermons against their Bible.[47]

"South Carolinians, you know, are 'old fogies,'" Mrs. Henry Schoolcraft wrote, "and consequently *they* do not believe with the Abolitionists, that *God* is a progressive being; but that throughout eternity *He* has been the same; perfect in wisdom, perfect in justice, and perfect in love to all his creatures." That perfect God had spoken: "Neither the Bible, nor the Apostles, nor Jesus Christ, ever condemned the institution of slavery as a sin." Eliza Frances Andrews of Georgia, thinking back in 1908 as a socialist, mused, "I myself honestly and conscientiously believed the institution of slavery to be as just and sacred as I now hold it to be the reverse." Hiram B. Tibbetts of Louisiana, a New England–born planter, wrote his brother in Massachusetts in 1848, "If it is sinful to own Negroes treated as I treat mine, I am willing to live and die under the sin. I feel no misgivings about it at all." Solomon Northup recalled his former master, a Baptist preacher and farmer in Avoyelles Parish, Louisiana: "It is but simple justice to him when I say, in my opinion, there never was a more kind, noble, candid Christian man than William Ford …. Were all men such as he, Slavery would be deprived of more than half its bitterness." Ford, Northup noted, never questioned the righteousness of slavery.[48]

In 1838, Bennet Barrow, a sugar planter in Louisiana, felt that Northerners "openly speaking of the sin of Slavery in the southern states – on the floor of Congress – must eventually cause a separation of the Union." William Valentine of North Carolina, a politically moderate Clay Whig, dated sectional strife from the Missouri crisis of 1819 but thought matters much more perilous in 1850. The trouble had

---

[47] William H. Holcombe, "The Alternative: A Separate Nationality, or the Africanization of the South," *SLM*, 32 (1861), 81; William Chambers, *Things as They Are in America* (London, 1854), 355; Marianne Finch, *An Englishwoman's Experience in America* (New York, 1969 [1853]), 313; Ernest Duvergier de Hauranne, *A Frenchman in Lincoln's America: Huit Mois en Amerique: Lettres et Notes de Voyage, 1864–1865*, 2 vols. (Chicago, 1974), 1:311; Twain quoted in Louis D. Rubin, Jr., *William Elliott Shoots a Bear: Essays on the Southern Literary Imagination* (Baton Rouge, LA, 1975), 31–2. On religion in encouraging southern unity on slavery and a hardening of the political line against the North, see also James Oscar Farmer, Jr., *The Metaphysical Confederacy: James Henley Thornwell and the Synthesis of Southern Values* (Macon, GA, 1986), 9, 14, and Mitchell Snay, *Gospel of Disunion: Religion and Separatism in the Antebellum South* (New York, 1993).

[48] *Plantation Life: The Narratives of Mrs. Henry Schoolcraft* (New York, 1969 [1860]), iii–iv, 54; Eliza Frances Andrews, *War-Time Journal of a Georgia Girl* (New York, 1907), 13; Hiram B. Tibbetts to John C. Tibbetts, Dec. 28, 1848, in John C. Tibbets Correspondence, at LSU; Solomon Northup, *Twelve Years a Slave* (New York, 1970 [1854]), 90. Mrs. Schoolcraft knew whereof she spoke. In eighteenth-century theology, God the Creator who remained the same generated a creation that changed over time. But gradually theologians began to project God Himself as changing with His creation – as Himself in a process of perfection: see Arthur J. Lovejoy, *The Great Chain of Being: A Study in the History of an Idea* (New York, 1960), 316–17.

started when a few early abolitionists, disreputable religious fanatics, claimed the Bible and converted "the ablest divines of the Northern States." But Valentine took solace, for "they have long since been driven from the field," routed by Southern divines armed with the Bible and reason.[49]

In 1856 the Methodist Reverend William A. Smith of Virginia felt humiliated to confess that "not a few" Southerners remained confused about slavery and suffered "great embarrassment." But the great religious revival of 1857–58 emboldened John Adger to claim that a "calm and quiet" review of Scripture had overcome southern doubts, eased consciences, and effected a "complete revolution of sentiment." He celebrated the unity of the southern churches: "It prepares the whole people to stand as one man. It is a conviction that will make patriots, and if need were, martyrs. There is no earthly power that can overcome a whole people when animated by such convictions!" Thomas Smyth, too, found growing unity against northern "atheists, infidels, communists, free-lovers, rationalists, Bible-haters, anti-Christian levelers and Anarchists." To the South "is given the high and holy keeping above all conservators, of the whole Bible, and nothing but the Bible; and of that liberty of conscience, free from the doctrines and commandments of men." Recalling the words of Jesus, Smyth felt certain that – so long as the South stood upon that rock – "the gates of hell shall not prevail against it." The New School Reverend Frederick Ross heartily agreed with his Old School Presbyterian brethren that southern slaveholders were convinced as never before of biblical sanction. On the eve of the War, William Gregg declared slavery "rooted in nature, and sanctified by the Bible," and he saw no reason to change his mind afterward. During the War, Parson Brownlow, soon to be Republican governor of Tennessee, continued to deny that the Bible rejected slavery. Even Southerners who later accepted the end of slavery gracefully continued to believe that, although slavery may have been a social evil, it was no sin.[50]

[49] Jan. 14, 1838, in Edwin Adams Davis, ed., *Plantation Life in the Florida Parishes of Louisiana, 1836–1846, as Reflected in the Diary of Bennet H. Barrow* (New York, 1943), 105–6; Valentine Diaries, Jan. 26, 1850, at UNC-SHC. Southerners had long been hearing the scriptural defense of slavery from the pulpit and, increasingly, in addresses to their agricultural societies and in secular publications: see e.g. A. M. Clayton's paper for the Mississippi State Bureau of Agriculture, "Advancement of the Agricultural Interests of the South," *DBR*, 26 (1859), 229, as well as Robert Collins's prize-winning essay for Georgia's Southern Central Agricultural Society, "Essay on the Treatment and Management of Slaves," published in *Southern Cultivator* in 1852 and republished in James O. Breeden, ed., *Advice among Masters: The Ideal in Slave Management in the Old South* (Westport, CT, 1980), 17.

[50] Smith, *Philosophy and Practice of Slavery,* 15; John B. Adger, "The Revival of the Slave Trade," *SPR*, 9 (Apr. 1858), 102–3; Smyth quoted in Perry Miller, *The Life of the Mind in America from the Revolution to the Civil War* (New York, 1965), 94; Frederick A. Ross, *Slavery Ordained of God* (Philadelphia, 1857), 101–2; [William Gregg], "Southern Patronage to Southern Imports and Domestic Industry," *DBR*, 30 (1861), 102; William G. Brownlow, *Sketches of the Rise, Progress, and Decline of Secession, with a Narrative of Personal Adventures among the Rebels* (Philadelphia, 1862), 108–9. Brownlow's views were influential across the North and Border States. His *Secession*, better known as *Parson Brownlow's Book*, sold 100,000 copies in the first three months: Frank Luther Mott, *Golden Multitudes: The Story of Best Sellers in the United States* (New York, 1947), 166. Lutheran ministers

Abolitionists, more often than not, preached less from the Bible on slavery than from the Declaration of Independence and the secular ideology of the Enlightenment. Angelina Grimké, who announced, "The Bible is my ultimate appeal in all matters of faith and practice," summed up by citing the Declaration of Independence first and only then the Bible. Henry Ward Beecher's pulpit exhortation, "Peace Be Still," scoffed at proslavery biblical arguments, but as Mark Noll has observed, "Although he said it would be an easy thing to refute the proslavery biblical arguments, he did not adduce even a single text to that end."[51]

In 1836 a group of emancipationist Presbyterians in Kentucky made some extraordinary assumptions in a passionate assessment of the evils of slavery. After eighteen pages on the Declaration of Independence and natural rights, they finally got to the Bible: "If any man can fairly show that the Bible countenances such slavery as existed in the days of the apostles, he would construct a more powerful argument against the divine origin of our own religion than infidelity has ever yet invented. A religion that sanctions a system of atrocious cruelty can never have come down from heaven." Eighteenth-century Deists had found nothing in the Bible attributable to God that men judged immoral and unreasonable, and now, antislavery divines – professed Calvinists at that – said that if the Bible sanctioned slavery then it should be rejected as the work of the devil. Presumably, they believed that the Bible offered no such sanction. Still, traveling in the Northeast in the 1840s, the Presbyterian Reverend W. T. Hamilton of Mobile got a shock: An abolitionist bluntly told him that, if the Bible were proven to sanction slavery, he would abandon the Bible. Hamilton warned that while fanatical, reckless, indeed "crazy" abolitionists constituted only a small minority in the North, they were winning great numbers to their view of slavery as sinful. Beriah Green asked his fellow abolitionists, Elizur Wright, Jr., and Theodore Weld, what would become of cherished "self-evident truths" if they acknowledged that the Bible sanctioned slavery? What would come of the authority of the Bible's claims to divine authority? Ross chided Albert Barnes: "You find it difficult to persuade men that Moses and Paul were moved by the Holy Ghost to sanction the philosophy of Thomas Jefferson!" Every one of the "self-evident truths" of the second paragraph of the Declaration of Independence, Ross scoffed, is simply false.[52]

---

continued to argue about the biblical standards for slavery as late as 1868: *EC*, 3:961 (Lutherans). Like countless others, William Frierson Cooper, a well-read moderate, considered the Mosaic Code and the entire Bible as sanction for slavery: "Notes on a Trip to Europe, 1862–1863," 147, in Cooper Papers, at Tennessee State Library and Archives (Nashville).

[51] Angelina Emily Grimké, *Appeal to the Christian Women of the South* (New York, 1969), 3, 16, quote at 3; Henry Ward Beecher, "Peace Be Still," in *Fast Day Sermons* (New York, 1861), 286–9; Mark A. Noll, "The Bible and Slavery," in Randall M. Miller et al., eds., *Religion and the American Civil War* (New York, 1998), 45.

[52] Committee of the Synod of Kentucky, *An Address to the Presbyterians of Kentucky, Proposing a Plan for the Instruction and Emancipation of the Slaves* (Newburyport, KY, 1836), 21–2; W. T. Hamilton, *Duties of Masters and Slaves Respectively; Or, Domestic Servitude as Sanctioned by the Bible* (Mobile, AL, 1845), 3–4, 7–8, quote at 3; Green to Wright and Weld, Oct. 22, 1838, in Barnes and

Abolitionist assertions outraged Christian sensibilities. Reverend John Pierpont of Connecticut considered Jesus an abolitionist, but if Jesus did not preach against slavery, "Then I say, he didn't do his duty." Since Pierpont was a Unitarian he did not have to explain how the Son of God could fail to do His duty. Henry Wright, when asked if he would yield to evidence that the Bible sanctioned slavery, demurred: "I would fasten the chain upon the heel of God and let the man go free." The Bible would then be "a lie and a curse." Lucretia Mott, preaching in Philadelphia, denied the divine inspiration of the Bible itself and recognized as truths only concepts that appealed to individual conscience. The orthodox William Goodell was convinced that the Bible held slavery sinful but, shaken by aggressive proslavery responses, wrote *American Slave Code* to sidestep the biblical critique of slavery and offer a legal one.[53]

In Cincinnati in 1846, N. L. Rice challenged the abolitionist Jonathan Blanchard, a skillful debater, to show exactly where the Bible condemns slavery as sinful. Blanchard talked about anything and everything and, when pressed to the wall, restricted himself to definitional quibbles. George Armstrong and others pounced on Barnes, Channing, Wayland, and Wright for arguing or implying that the Bible's divinity would be disproved if it were found to sanction slavery. Wayland drew fire from Fuller for writing that if the Bible sanctioned slavery then "The New Testament would be the greatest curse that was ever inflicted on our race." *Southern Presbyterian Review* mockingly paraphrased Theodore Parker: "If the Bible teaches this or that doctrine, it ought to be burnt or thrown away." The Reverend James Petigru

---

Dumond, eds., *Letters of Weld and Grimké*, 2:710; Ross, *Slavery Ordained of God*, 103–4, 123–5, quote at 97.

By the 1850s antislavery New Englanders insisted that the churches could not acknowledge New Testament toleration of slavery without sacrificing a large section of public opinion to infidelity: see Robert Bruce Mullin, "Bible Critics and the Battle over Slavery," *JPH*, 61 (1983), 219. For a representative blast at abolitionists who quoted Jefferson, not the Bible, during the debates in the Protestant Methodist Church in 1842, see McCaine, *Slavery Defended*, 18–19. The Methodist Reverend John Caldwell of Newman, Georgia, a unionist, criticized southern slavery for falling short of the Abramic model, but he sadly chided abolitionists for readiness to abandon the Bible because it sanctioned slavery: Caldwell, *Slavery and Methodism: Two Sermons Preached in the Methodist Church in Newman, Georgia* (Newman, GA, 1865), 19–20.

53 Perry, *Radical Abolitionism*, 122 (Pierpont), 49 (Wright); Lucretia Mott, "Abuses and Uses of the Bible," in Dana Green, ed., *American Sermons: The Pilgrims to Martin Luther King, Jr.* (New York, n.d.: "Library of America"), 123–8; Walters, *Antislavery Appeal*, 42 (Goodell). For an example of southern reaction see Samuel J. Cassells's condemnation of the remarks by William C. Wisner, a leading abolitionist in New York, that if the Bible recognized slavery then it should be rejected: [S. J. Cassells], *Servitude and the Duty of Masters to Their Servants* (Norfolk, VA, 1843), 4. J. W. Cummins, speaking for the Catholics in a lecture in New York in 1850 – which the *Daily Picayune* published in New Orleans – protested vehemently against those who said that if the Bible supported slavery, it should be amended: Cummins, "On Slavery, the Union and the Catholic Church," New Orleans *Daily Picayune*, June 2, 1850. In 1861 Robert Breckenridge's antislavery and pro-Union *Danville Quarterly Review* still bristled at the abolitionists' willingness to set aside the Bible if shown to sanction slavery: "L." [Robert W. Landis?], "The Relation which Reason and Philosophy Sustains in the Theology of Revelation," *DQR*, 1 (1861), 47.

Boyce of Charleston, a staunch unionist who was emerging as a leading Baptist theologian, dismissed the Unitarian Parker as devoid of genuine Christian spirit. The
Baptist Reverend P. H. Mell railed at "madmen" who would abandon the Bible if it
were shown to be proslavery; the Reverend Stuart Robinson of Kentucky shook his
head over a "whole class of thinkers" who discuss ethics as if "the Bible must come
to them rather than they come to the Bible."[54]

"If the word of God does sanction slavery," the Reverend James Pennington of
Hartford, Connecticut, thundered, "I want another book, another repentance,
another faith, and another hope!" Bypassing the Word, Pennington (a free black)
declared: "Slavery is condemned by the general tenor and scope of the New Testament." Long after the War a black preacher in Doswell, Virginia, said that the
slaves in his neighborhood thought white folks had no religion because they got it
from the Bible, not from direct revelation. In a pamphlet devoted to a recitation of
slave insurrections, Joshua Coffin characterized slavery as "the sum of all villainies"
and echoed the warnings of Gerrit Smith and Barnes that a proslavery Bible would
create infidels.[55]

Southern ministers respected the Reverend Dr. Asa Mahan, president of Oberlin
College, as a learned man. Professor R. H. Rivers of Wesleyan College in Alabama
called him "a profound and accurate thinker," but the Reverend Joseph Stiles could
not contain himself when he quoted Mahan as saying, "We are constrained to admit either that slavery is right or the Bible not of God. If I felt myself forced to take
one or the other of these positions, I freely confess that for one I should take the latter." Stiles appended to his *Modern Reform Examined* a series of quotations from
Garrison, Wright, and other leading abolitionists who repudiated the Bible. The
master, Stiles wrote, was preparing a backward people for eventual freedom: "The
very law of human rights, therefore, which gives ultimate freedom to the slave, gives
present authority to the master." The Reverend George Howe of South Carolina,
a man not given to rages, came close when abolitionists suggested that if God con-
dones slavery, men should become atheists. William J. Grayson of Charleston, a
firm unionist, complained that antislavery Protestants were far exceeding Catholics
in setting the Bible aside. Bishop Thomas Atkinson of North Carolina, another

---

54 J. Blanchard and N. L. Rice, *A Debate on Slavery* (New York, 1969 [1846]); Armstrong, *Christian Doctrine of Slavery*, 82–5, 100–1; Richard Fuller and Francis Wayland, *Domestic Slavery, Considered as a Scriptural Institution in Correspondence*, 5th ed. (New York, 1847), 174–5; "Sufficiency of Scrip-tures," *SPR*, 7 (1853), 255; Boyce cited in William A. Mueller, *A History of Southern Baptist Semi-nary* (Nashville, TN, 1959), 25, 33–4; P. H. Mell, *Predestination and the Saints' Perseverance Stated and Defended, from the Objections of Arminians in a Review of Two Sermons by Rev. Reneau* (Harrisonburg, VA, 1995 [1850]), 24; Stuart Robinson, *Slavery, as Recognized in the Mosaic Civil Law* (Toronto, 1865), 28. For scathing attacks on Barnes on this point see John Fletcher, *Studies on Slavery, in Easy Lessons* (Natchez, MS, 1852), 16–17, 97–9.

55 Pennington quoted in David E. Swift, *Black Prophets of Justice: Activist Clergy before the Civil War* (Baton Rouge, LA, 1989), 236; Joseph B. Earnest, *The Religious Development of the Negro in Vir-ginia* (Charlottesville, VA, 1914), 97 n. 96; Joshua Coffin, *An Account of Some of the Principal Slave Insurrections, Which Have Occurred, or, Have Been Attempted, in the United States and Elsewhere, during the Last Two Centuries* (New York, 1860), 7, 35; *Letter of Gerrit Smith*, 69.

unionist, almost lost his temper when abolitionists admitted they would scorn the Bible if it were proven to be proslavery. Alexander Campbell, who found slavery distasteful, could not swallow the abolitionist doctrine of inherent sinfulness. His Disciples of Christ had their greatest strength in the Border States, and he tried to speak softly: "I know some men, and have heard of others, who candidly aver the resolution to abandon the Bible *so soon as it is made evident that it sanctions the relation of master and slave.* Such is their faith in their own reason, and such their preference for natural law, that, if any sacrifice is to be made, they will sacrifice the Bible to their theory rather than their theory to the Bible. I have nothing to say at this time to such *Christians* as these!"[56]

John Fletcher traced the abolitionists' heresy to his pet hates among the thinkers of the Enlightenment, and R. H. Rivers expressed disgust for those who would discard the Bible because it was at odds with their social and political notions. Solon Robinson accused the abolitionists of ignoring or distorting the Bible and of turning more people into infidels than all the publications of Voltaire, Paine, and Owen put together. Dabney tried turn-it-around sarcasm: "If slavery is in itself a sinful thing, then the Bible is a sinful book."[57]

[56] Rivers, *Moral Philosophy,* 68, 99–100; Stiles, *Modern Reform Examined,* 73, 77, 111, 140–2; [George Howe], "The Raid of John Brown, and the Progress of Abolition," *SPR,* 12 (1860), 797; "E. G." [William J. Grayson], "Slavery in the Southern States," *SQR,* 8 (1845), 336–7; Thomas Atkinson, *On the Cause of Our National Troubles: A Sermon Delivered in St. James Church, Wilmington, N.C.* (Wilmington, NC, 1861), 10; [Alexander Campbell], "Our Position on American Slavery," *Millennial Harbinger,* 16 (1845), 234. Campbell pursued a course that led to public acceptance of his church in the South as no threat to slavery: David Edwin Harrell, Jr., *A Social History of the Disciples of Christ,* vol. 1, *Quest for a Christian America: The Disciples of Christ and American Society to 1866* (Nashville, TN, 1966), 59, 67–8, 97–101, 104–9, 121–7; also, Carter E. Boren, *Religion on the Texas Frontier* (San Antonio, TX, 1968), 32–3.
    During the War, Alexander Gregg (Episcopalian bishop of Texas), among others, returned to the theme: Gregg's remarks in Charles Gillette, *A Few Historic Records of the Church in the Diocese of Texas, during the Rebellion* (New York, 1865), 35; also, Ferdinand Jacobs, *A Sermon for the Times; Preached in Fairview Presbyterian Church, Perry County, Ala.* (n.p., 1861), 3–4; on Mahan see also Robert Newton Sledd, *A Sermon Delivered in the Market Street, M. E. Church, Petersburg, Va.: Before the Confederate Cadets on the Occasion of Their Departure for the Seat of War, Sunday, Sept. 22d, 1861* (Petersburg, VA, 1861), 21. De Bow noted Stile's "admirable" *Modern Reform Examined* more than once: *DBR,* 23 (1857), 559, 561–70. In the early 1840s George Junkin, president of Miami University in Ohio, blistered those abolitionists who would scrap the Bible: Junkin, *The Integrity of Our National Union vs. Abolitionism* (Cincinnati, 1843), 14–15.

[57] Fletcher, *Studies on Slavery,* 18–19, 97–9, 138, 174–6, 180–2; Rivers, *Moral Philosophy,* ch. 6, pt. 2; Herbert Anthony Kellar, ed., *Solon Robinson: Pioneer and Agriculturalist: Selected Writings,* 2 vols. (Indianapolis, IN, 1936), 2:265. See also the attack on Wayland and Barnes by a northern missionary long in residence in the South: David Brown, *The Planter: Or, Thirteen Years in the South, by a Northern Man* (Upper Saddle River, NJ, 1970 [1853]), 192–3, 243–4; R. L. Dabney, *Life and Campaigns of Lieut.-Gen. Thomas J. Jackson (Stonewall Jackson)* (Harrisonburg, VA, 1983 [1865]), 169. Tongue-in-cheek J. O. Andrew defended missions to the heathens: If the Bible could not save such souls, "I confess I shall be in great danger of turning skeptic": Andrew, "Essays on Missions," in *Miscellanies: Comprising Letters, Essays, and Addresses* (Louisville, KY, 1854), 296. Other Georgians were not so light-hearted. The Reverend P. H. Mell ripped the Reverend Russell Reneau for suggesting that if the Bible could be shown to advocate Calvinism he would preach from it no more: Mell, *Predestination and the Saints' Perseverance,* 15–16. Whereas Solon Robinson reviled northern

The Baptist Thornton Stringfellow of Virginia summed up an outcry that could be heard from the pulpits of every denomination in the South, urban or rural, polished or down-home: "There is something else in the world to corrupt religion and morals besides slaveholders and slavery. There are *isms* at the North whose name is Legion. According to the universal standard of *orthodoxy,* we are compelled to exclude the *subjects* of these isms from the pale of Christianity." Stringfellow focused on social trends. In the North these isms "have been nurtured into *organized* existence"; in the South, "a man might wear himself out in travel, and never find one of these isms with an *organized* existence." During the War, the Reverend Thomas Dunaway, another Virginia Baptist, reiterated, "The word we are called upon to preach to you is not a refined, philosophical system. In the soil of our simple faith, *isms* can take no root."[58]

In North Carolina the Reverend William Greely was said to be raising moral consciousness by his exposure of "the monster evil" of the socialism of Owen, Fourier, and the Millerites and, especially, by his defense of marriage. In Tennessee, Harrod Clopton Anderson, a unionist planter who fervently prayed against secession, added: "May the south be never tinged with infidel notions of the north and their many isms." James D. B. De Bow, editor of the prestigious *De Bow's Review,* appealing to – and trying to speak for – the nonslaveholders, wrote of their adherence to "the simple truths of the Gospel and the faith of their fathers" and resistance to "isms." The common people "have not run hither and thither in search of all the absurd and degrading isms which have sprung up in the rank soil of infidelity." They "are not Mormons or Spiritualists, they are not Owenites, Fourierists, Agrarians, Socialists, Free-lovers or Millerites." They "prefer law, order, and existing institutions to the chaos which radicalism involves."[59]

Bishop Pierce, in a scathing criticism of the South's deficiencies and failure to reform its slave system, nevertheless told the state legislature of Georgia in 1863 that "the Southern people, with all their faults – vices if you please – have never corrupted the gospel of Christ." The South, Reverend J. Henry Smith of North Carolina preached, had been "exempt from the radicalism, infidelity, fanaticism, ultraism and the countless forms of error, lawlessness and riot that blind and madden so many communities." He thanked God for "Christian institutions" that made it possible, and he coupled its religious orthodoxy to the prevalence of the master–slave relation. Emma Holmes in Charleston and Tally Simpson at the front expected a

clergymen as hypocrites, the Massachusetts-born Reverend Theodore Clapp of New Orleans purred that sincerity and good intentions lay behind the ministers' infidelity: [Solon Robinson], "Negro Slavery at the South," *DBR,* 7 (1849), 213; Theodore Clapp, "Thanksgiving Sermon," New Orleans *Daily Picayune,* Dec. 22, 1850.

58 Thornton Stringfellow, "Statistical View of Slavery," in Elliott, ed., *Cotton Is King,* 527–8; Thomas S. Dunaway, *A Sermon Delivered ... before the Coan Baptist Church, in Connection with a Day of National Fasting, Humiliation and Prayer* (Richmond, VA, 1864), 9.

59 William Hooper Haigh Diary and Letters, July 16, 1844; Anderson quoted in Chase C. Mooney, *Slavery in Tennessee* (Bloomington, IN, 1957), 157; De Bow, *The Southern Non-Slaveholder,* 8. J. H. Hammond said that Southerners simply laughed at Mormonism and Millerism: *Letters and Speeches of Hammond,* 133–4.

Confederate victory because of the superior piety of the southern people. Bishop Alexander Gregg of Texas had the same expectation, but he added that it was slavery that allowed the South to resist the heresies of "Unitarianism, Universalism, transcendentalism, Mormonism, spiritualism, and higher-lawism."[60]

---

[60] G. F. Pierce, "The Word of God a Nation's Life," in *Sermons of Bishop Pierce and Rev. B. M. Palmer* (Milledgeville, GA, 1863), 5; James Henry Smith, *Sermon at Greensboro* (Charleston, SC, 1863), 5; Apr. 12 and Sept. 15, 1861, in John F. Marszalek, ed., *The Diary of Miss Emma Holmes* (Baton Rouge, LA, 1979), 25–6, 90; Tally Simpson to Caroline Miller, July 14, 1862, in Guy R. Everson and Edward W. Simpson, Jr., eds., *"Far, Far from Home": The Wartime Letters of Dick and Tully Simpson, Third South Carolina Volunteers* (New York, 1994), 136; Gregg in Gillette, *A Few Historic Records*, 35.

The War brought renewed celebration of southern Christian orthodoxy and denunciation of Yankee apostasy: see e.g. Bishop William Meade's sermon in Elizabeth Wright Weddell, *St. Paul's Church, Richmond, Virginia: Its Historic Years and Memorials,* 2 vols. (Richmond, VA, 1931), 1:141–7. Lieutenant James Norman of Columbus, Georgia, wrote to his wife from the front in January 1862: "Freedom and independence is the Southron's birthright." Southerners have a right to "worship our own God, & to perpetuate & enjoy our own institutions": James Norman to Mary Norman, Jan. 5, 1862, in Susan Lott Clark, ed., *Southern Letters and Life in the Mid 1800s* (Waycross, GA, 1993), 142.

16

Slavery

Proceeding from the Lord

> The thing proceedeth from the Lord. We cannot speak unto you bad and good.
>
> —Genesis, 23:50

"If slavery be thus sinful," the Baptist Reverend Thornton Stringfellow wrote in a widely read essay, "it behooves all Christians who are involved in the sin, to repent in dust and ashes, and wash their hands of it, without consulting with flesh and blood." So said the theologically liberal Unitarian Theodore Clapp of New Orleans. So said the ultra-orthodox Baptist J. R. Graves, who "would lift my voice in thunder tones" against slavery were it proven unscriptural. The Reverend Alfred Watson of the Episcopal Diocese of North Carolina as well as college presidents George Addison Baxter and T. C. Thornton concurred. The Methodist Reverend Thomas Burge of Middle Georgia and the Presbyterian Thomas ("Stonewall") Jackson of Virginia told their wives they would free their slaves if convinced of the sinfulness of slavery. Our whole struggle, so Linton Stephens wrote to his brother Alexander, turns upon the single issue of slavery as right or wrong. "If it is wrong, everybody ought to do all that can be done, consistently with a prudent regard to circumstances, to abolish it." An incredulous Episcopalian Reverend Richard Adgate Lipscomb of Alabama asked Frederick Law Olmsted if he really thought Southerners would tolerate slavery if they believed it sinful. The antislavery President Francis Wayland of Brown University, for one, did not doubt the sincerity of Southerners who made such assertions.[1]

---

[1] Thornton Stringfellow, "Bible Argument," in E. N. Elliott, ed., *Cotton Is King, and Pro-Slavery Arguments* (New York, 1969 [1860]), 461; Theodore Clapp, *Slavery: A Sermon* (New Orleans, 1838), 5, 7; J. R. Graves, *The Little Iron Wheel* (Nashville, TN, 1857), 17; Alfred A. Watson, *Sermon before the Annual Council of the Diocese of North Carolina* (Raleigh, NC, 1863), 13; George A. Baxter, *An Essay on the Abolition of Slavery* (Richmond, VA, 1836), 5, 16; T. C. Thornton, *An Inquiry into the History of Slavery* (Washington, DC, 1841), 173; Nov. 8, 1864, in James I. Robertson, Jr., ed., *The Diary of Dolly Lunt Burge* (Athens, GA, 1962), 98; John Bowers, *Stonewall Jackson: Portrait of a Soldier* (New York, 1989), 24; Linton Stephens to Alexander H. Stephens, June 29, 1860, in James D. Waddell, *Biographical Sketch of Linton Stephens, Containing a Selection of His Letters, Speeches, State Papers, Etc.* (Atlanta, GA, 1877), 224; Charles Capen McLaughlin, ed., *Papers of Frederick Law*

James Henley Thornwell established the essentials without direct reference to slavery. Man's knowledge differs in kind from God's: "How arrogant to arraign His wisdom at our bar!" Men must submit to God's will, accepting the arrangements of His providence and the unequal distribution of His favors: "Let us not be tempted to censure or repine. It is enough that God does it. That word God is a guarantee that all is right." In 1860 Thornwell replied to those who denounced slavery as contrary to morality: "If I know the character of our people, I think I can safely say, that if they were persuaded of the essential immorality of Slavery, they would not be backward in adopting measures for the ultimate abatement of the evil." In 1861, a fatally ill Thornwell wrote his son Gillespie, who was off to war, "There is nothing worth living for but the glory of God, and I do most devoutly wish that your eyes may be opened to see the transcendental importance of eternal things. You have but one soul, and if you lose that, all is lost forever.[2]

From the great eighteenth-century evangelist George Whitefield onward, defenders of slavery pointed to Genesis, 15:14, in which the great patriarch Abraham prepared for war with his "armed and trained servants, born in his own house, three hundred and eighteen." In the 1850s John Fletcher of New Orleans cited leading scholars to show that Abraham's "household" included slaves over whom he ruled and that God's covenant with him required their maintenance, governance, and protection. If war comes, "The South, like Abraham in olden time, 'will arm their trained servants,' and go to war, SHOUTING UNDER THE BANNER OF THE ALMIGHTY." George Sawyer of New Orleans, lawyer and proslavery theorist, added that Abraham trafficked in slaves before and after the covenant in accordance with "universal custom" and "international and common law." Henry Hughes of Mississippi held up Abraham's household as a model for a new world order in which all labor, regardless of race, would thrive under a benign servitude.[3]

Olmsted, 1822–1857 (New York, 1977, 1981), 2:171–2 n. 11; Richard Fuller and Francis Wayland, *Domestic Slavery, Considered as a Scriptural Institution in Correspondence*, 5th ed. (New York, 1847), 21–2, for Fuller's declarations see 3, 135; also, John Patrick Daly, "The Divine Economy: Evangelicals and the Defense of Slavery, 1830–1865" (Ph.D. diss., Rice University, 1993), 209. For similar secular expressions see [William J. Grayson], "Slavery in the Southern States," *SQR*, 8 (1845), 334; W. T. Hamilton, *Duties of Masters and Slaves Respectively; Or, Domestic Servitude as Sanctioned by the Bible* (Mobile, AL, 1845), 5; John Fletcher, *Studies on Slavery, in Easy Lessons* (Natchez, MS, 1852), 46–7; [E. J. Pringle], *Slavery in the Southern States, by a Carolinian* (Cambridge, MA, 1852), 44.

[2] In *JHTW*: 1:205, 3:205, 4:539; J. H. Thornwell to Gillespie Thornwell, June 19, 1861, in Thornwell Papers, at USC (Gillespie was killed in battle in 1863). Also J. L. Dagg, *Manual of Theology: A Treatise on Christian Doctrine and a Treatise on Church Order*, 2 vols. (New York, 1980 [1857–58]), 1:85–6.

[3] Fletcher, *Studies on Slavery*, 9, 23, 221; George S. Sawyer, *Southern Institutes; Or, an Inquiry into the Origin and Early Prevalence of Slavery and the Slave Trade* (New York, 1967 [1858]), 25, 30, quote at 30; N. B. Tucker, "A Lecture on Government," *SLM*, 3 (1837), 211–12; Henry Hughes, *Treatise on Sociology, Theoretical and Practical* (New York, 1968 [1854]), 82–3. The chorus included Protestants and Catholics, divines and laymen: George W. Freeman, *The Rights and Duties of Slaveholders* (Raleigh, NC, 1836), 7; J. B. Thrasher, *Slavery: A Divine Institution* (Port Gibson, MS, 1861), 8–9; Augustin Verot, *A Tract for the Times: Slavery and Abolitionism* (Baltimore, 1861), 5, 13. Abraham's 318 slave soldiers suggest a total slave population in his household of a thousand or so: Gordon J.

Some abolitionists suggested that Abraham's relations with his servants, whatever their legal status, set high standards of humanity. Others described Abraham as ruler of a household of free men in a nonslaveholding society. Most abolitionists saw no relation at all between Abraham and southern slaveholders, thereupon plunging into circular argument. Sarah Grimké dismissed the suggestion that Abraham held slaves "a mere slander"; Angelina Grimké reasoned that, since Abraham and Sarah worked alongside their laborers, those laborers could not have been slaves. In criticizing the antislavery historian Henri Wallon for conceding Abraham's slaveownership, George Cheever devoted page after page to an attempt to establish that the Israelites held property in labor services, not in men. Since Abraham had no fixed residence and more than a thousand "servants" to control, John Rankin called it absurd to think he held them as slaves rather than as retainers. Samuel Crothers argued that since Abraham was a good man he could not have behaved like a southern slaveholder, and George Bourne – who defined slavery as the deprivation of human rights – therefore concluded that Abraham's people could not have been slaves. Proslavery theorists rejected the major premise, maintaining that their slaves (like Abraham's) had human rights sustained by law and custom, and they noted that the Bible listed Abraham's slaves along with his beasts, his wife Sarah, and other property. "Do you tell me," asked the New School Reverend Frederick Ross of Huntsville, Alabama, sardonically, "that Abraham, by divine authority, made these servants part of his family, social and religious? Very good. But he still regarded them as his slaves .... Every Southern planter is not more truly a slaveholder than Abraham." Zephaniah Kingsley of Florida, a proslavery merchant-planter who rejected as nonsense theories of white superiority and black inferiority, maintained that masters who treated slaves properly could rely on their loyalty and willingness to serve as soldiers.[4]

The virtues of Abraham, the patriarch and "father of all them that believe" (Romans, 4:11), set the standard for the individual and society. God entrusted to Abraham the seed of David and Jesus, enabling him to accumulate wealth to support his people in a household that served as a model for church and state. For

---

Wenham in Wenham, ed., *World Biblical Commentary,* 2 vols. (Waco, TX, 1987), 1:314. On the biblical household model and the slavery debate see Wayne A. Meeks, "The 'Haustafeln' and American Slavery: A Hermeneutical Challenge," in E. Lovering and J. Summer, eds., *Theology and Ethics in Paul* (Nashville, TN, 1996), 232–53.

4 Sarah M. Grimké, *An Epistle to the Clergy of the Southern States* (New York, 1836), 7; Angelina Emily Grimké, *Appeal to the Christian Women of the South* (New York, 1969), 6; George B. Cheever, *The Guilt of Slavery and the Crime of Slaveholding, Demonstrated from the Hebrew and Greek Scriptures* (New York, 1969 [1860)]), 47 n., 138–9, chs. 3, 4, 11, 15, and 28; John Rankin in William H. Pease and Jane H. Pease, eds., *The Antislavery Argument* (Indianapolis, IN, 1965), 122; Samuel Crothers, *Strictures on African Slavery* (Rossville, OH, 1833); also, Theodore D. Weld, *The Bible against Slavery* (Pittsburgh, PA, 1864), 53–4; Albert Barnes, *An Inquiry into the Scriptural Views of Slavery* (Philadelphia, 1857), ch. 3, esp. 76–7; [George Bourne], *A Condensed Anti-Slavery Bible Argument; By a Citizen of Virginia* (New York, 1845), 34–5; Frederick A. Ross, *Slavery Ordained of God* (Philadelphia, 1857), 151–2; Zephaniah Kingsley, *The Patriarchal or Co-Operative System of Society,* 2nd ed. (n.p., 1829); Ronald G. Walters, *The Antislavery Appeal: American Abolitionism after 1830* (Baltimore, 1976), 50–1. And see Richard Schlatter, *Private Property: History of an Idea* (New York, 1951), 87–8.

the Methodist Reverend L. D. Huston, "In all the relations of life as husband, father, master, and patriarch, he was a model of manly virtues." For the Presbyterian Reverend George Armstrong and the Baptist Thornton Stringfellow, the Abramic family provided the foundation for the Church, for slavery, for all Christian social organization.[5]

Most abolitionists argued that the Israelites practiced a mild form of indentured servitude or that the Year of Jubilee in effect prevented indenture from passing into slavery or that Israelite workers were actually wage laborers. William Wisner gently rebuked Theodore Weld, his fellow abolitionist, for the bold assertion that Israelites bought slaves in order to assimilate them to their families as freedmen. The Unitarian James Freeman Clarke protested that, in denying the facts of Israelite slavery, the abolitionists "wish to prove too much"; Clarke preferred to appeal to the spirit of the Bible. Important antislavery northern moderates, notably Leonard Bacon of New Haven, had no patience with abolitionists who denied the existence of biblically sanctioned slavery in Israel. Discernibly annoyed, George Bancroft, America's premier historian, chided Angelina Grimké for denying the existence of Israelite slavery. Moses Stuart, John Hersey, and Francis Wayland agreed with the Southerners that ancient Israel had had two discrete types of servitude – enslavement of foreigners and indentured labor for Israelites – although they characterized Mosaic Law as specific to time and place and without relevance to the current disputes about slavery. The quarrel passed to linguistic ground. William Henry Brisbane, Albert Barnes, and other abolitionists denied – erroneously – that the Hebrew *ebed* and Greek *doulos* could signify "slave." Southern critics replied correctly that *ebed* and *doulos* included slaves.[6]

---

[5] L. D. Huston, "Characteristics of Abraham's Faith," in William T. Smithson, ed., *The Methodist Pulpit South* (Washington, DC, 1858), 229; George D. Armstrong, *The Doctrine of Baptism: Scriptural Examinations* (New York, 1857), 4–8, 252–5, 306–7, 312; Thornton Stringfellow, *Slavery: Its Origin, Nature, and History, Considered in the Light of Bible Teachings, Moral Justice, and Political Wisdom* (New York, 1861), 36; also, George Junkin, *The Integrity of Our National Union vs. Abolitionism* (Cincinnati, 1843), 19–21; Ferdinand Jacobs, *The Committing of Our Cause to God* (Charleston, SC, 1850), 12–13; [R. S. Breck], "Duties of Masters," *SPR*, 8 (1855), 266–83. For a typical secular invocation of Abraham see "Barbour County Agricultural Society, Committee Report, 1846," in James O. Breeden, ed., *Advice among Masters: The Ideal in Slave Management in the Old South* (Westport, CT, 1980), 8.

[6] Weld, *Bible against Slavery*, 40–1; for Weld and Wisner see Robert H. Abzug, *Passionate Liberator: Theodore Dwight Weld and the Dilemmas of Reform* (New York, 1980), 162–3; James Freeman Clarke, *Slavery in the United States* (Boston, 1843), 14–15, quote at 14; Leonard Bacon, *Slavery Discussed in Occasional Essays from 1833 to 1846* (New York, 1846), iii–iv, 25, 33–4. George Bancroft to Angelina Grimké, Jan. 25, 1838, in Gilbert H. Barnes and Dwight L. Dumond, eds., *Letters of Theodore Dwight Weld, Angelina Grimké and Sarah Grimké, 1822–1844*, 2 vols. (Gloucester, MA, 1965), 2:848–9, 525; Moses Stuart, *Conscience and the Constitution* (Boston, 1850), 26–7, 45–6; John Hersey, *An Appeal to Christians on the Subject of Slavery*, 2nd ed. (Baltimore, 1833), 68–70; William Henry Brisbane, *Slaveholding Examined in the Light of the Holy Bible* (New York, 1847 [1817]), iv–viii, ch. 1. On Wayland see Caroline L. Shanks, "The Biblical Anti-Slavery Argument of the Decades 1830–1860," *Journal of Negro History*, 16 (1931), 143. Angelina Grimké's position on Israelite slavery was ambiguous but open to Bancroft's strictures: see her *Appeal to Christian Women*, 3–4. Sarah M.

LaRoy Sunderland, the fiery Methodist abolitionist who grudgingly acknowledged Israelite servitude, asserted that, apart from use as punishment for crime, servitude was voluntary and temporary. He embraced Exodus, 21:21 ("And if a man smite his servant, or his maid, with a rod, and he die under his hand; he shall be surely punished. Notwithstanding, if he continue a day or two, he shall not be punished: for he is his money.") Servants could not have been property: "The meaning is, the servant's labor was to the master for the time being, the same as money." Cheever admitted, in *The Guilt of Slavery* (1860), that *ebed* and *doulos* stood for a wide swath of dependencies, but he denied that slavery could have existed in Judea, for if it had then it would have spread widely and taken deep root, as it always does. For good measure, he interpreted even seven-year indenture as a form of free-labor contract. His earlier *God against Slavery* (1857) had acknowledged Israelite slavery but as one of many Jewish rebellions against God's laws.[7]

Abolitionists focused on the Year of Jubilee, according to which slaves should be freed every fifty years. In 1822, Richard Furman of South Carolina replied that the Year of Jubilee had applied only to fellow Israelites in limited servitude and that masters held foreign-born slaves in perpetuity. Wayland interpreted God's commandment to enslave the Canaanites in perpetuity as historically specific, not a general license. Jesus, he argued, taught meekness and submission to slaves, but their very enslavement encouraged the vices He everywhere combated. As the Reverend Richard Fuller quickly saw, Wayland had surrendered the argument from Jubilee, even if God's command to the Israelites to slaughter and enslave the Canaanites was historically specific. Since He surely could not have commanded them to sin, slavery could not be sinful. Thomas Cobb and the Reverend George Howe, among others, warned that the Bible sustains slavery as a duty, not merely as a right. To the abolitionist argument that "forever" in the Bible meant "to the year of Jubilee," Cobb replied that Israelite law forbade strangers to possess land and thus the enslaved had no land to which they could return to claim emancipation lawfully. Cheever retorted that two kinds of servants, Hebrew and foreign, could not imply two sets of contradictory laws. Thus he averred what he had to prove – that whenever the word "forever" came up with reference to enslavement, it could only mean the longest period acceptable to contractual relations.[8]

Grimké wrote of Israelite "servitude" but insisted that it bore no relation to southern slavery: *Epistle to the Clergy,* 6–7. Stuart Robinson of Kentucky observed that all leading linguists agreed that *ebed* and *doulos* included slaves: *Slavery, as Recognized in the Mosaic Civil Law* (Toronto, 1865), 4–5; also, Fletcher, *Studies on Slavery,* 506–37; Thrasher, *Divine Institution,* 6–7; George D. Armstrong, *The Christian Doctrine of Slavery* (New York, 1967 [1857]), 19–21. See also Supplementary References: "Israelite Servitude."

7 LaRoy Sunderland, *The Anti-Slavery Manual: Containing a Collection of Facts and Arguments on American Slavery,* 3rd ed. (New York, 1839), 33, 40, quote at 33; Cheever, *Guilt of Slavery,* chs. 2, 10, 11, and 12; George B. Cheever, *God against Slavery; And the Freedom and Duty of the Pulpit to Rebuke It as a Sin against God* (Cincinnati, 1857), 72–3, 99–100, and ch. 25; also, Barnes, *Scriptural Views,* ch. 3. The moderately antislavery Alexander Campbell scoffed at the characterization of Israelite labor as free labor: [Campbell], "Our Position on American Slavery," *Millennial Harbinger,* 16 (1845), 196.

8 Furman, "Views of the Baptists," in James A. Rogers, *Richard Furman: Life and Legacy* (Macon, GA, 1985), 277–8; Fuller and Wayland, *Domestic Slavery,* 49–52, 59–60, 77–84, 178, 181–2; [George

That God commanded, not merely allowed, the Israelites to hold slaves (Deuter-
onomy, 20:10–16) became a proslavery staple. In 1840 the Reverend Mr. Crowder
of Virginia said, "In its moral aspect, slavery was not countenanced, permitted, and
regulated by the Bible, but it was positively instituted by God Himself – he had, in so
many words, enjoined it." Running for a seat in the Texas legislature in 1855, Ashbel Smith said, "That which is once right in the eyes of God is always right." T. C.
Thornton of Mississippi recalled that God commanded the Israelites to destroy the
men, women, and children of Canaan. Man cannot reject or call sinful that which
God has commanded. The coming of the War brought a spate of sermons from
such clergymen as Thomas Smyth that emphasized God's specific command.[9]

Abolitionists said Israelites treated "servants" without rigor, while the Reverend
E. W. Warren of Georgia said the reverse. The more cautious Armstrong and J. D. B.
De Bow said Israelite slaves fared neither better nor worse than did southern slaves,
but others claimed that the Israelites exercised legal powers over their slaves far beyond those permitted by southern law. Stringfellow concluded: "It is certain that
God interposed to give Joseph the power in Egypt, which he used, to create a state,
or condition, among the Egyptians, which substantially agrees with patriarchal and
modern slavery."[10]

Biblical references to a servant's right to ask to be held in perpetual servitude at
the end of his seven-year term provoked another row. A servant whose indenture
was up could decide to remain permanently with his master by having his ear bored
in the household doorway and reciting, "I love my master, my wife, and my children; I will not go out free" – thus the idea of permanent servitude accompanied a
declaration of love, which had to be reciprocated by the master. As a sign, the door-
post transcended household nourishment and protection designated by hearth or

---

Howe], "The Raid of John Brown, and the Progress of Abolition," *SPR*, 12 (1860), 792; Thomas
R. R. Cobb, *An Inquiry into the Law of Negro Slavery in the United States* (New York, 1968 [1858]),
xliii, xxxviii n. 2, xlii; Theodore Clapp, "Thanksgiving Sermon," New Orleans *Daily Picayune*, Dec.
22, 1850; Cheever, *God against Slavery*, 151–2. John Henry Hopkins, the Episcopalian Bishop of
Vermont, cited Leviticus, 25:10, to demonstrate that the Year of Jubilee applied only to Israelites: *A
Scriptural, Ecclesiastical, and Historical View of Slavery from the Days of the Patriarch Abraham
to the Nineteenth Century* (New York, 1864), 10–11; also, James Shannon, *The Philosophy of Slavery, as Identified with the Philosophy of Human Happiness* (Frankfort, KY, 1840), 15–17; Freeman,
Rights and Duties of Slaveholders, 7; "Slavery," *SPR*, 9 (1856), 350–1. William B. Hayden, a northern
moderate, caustically remarked that the Israelites, left to themselves, would have enslaved each other
and that the Year of Jubilee "operated only in favor of Hebrew servants": Hayden, *The Institution of
Slavery Viewed in the Light of Divine Truth* (Portland, ME, 1861), 11, quote at 13.

9 Crowder quoted in Joseph Sturge, *A Visit to the United States in 1841* (New York, 1969 [1842]), 184;
   Ashbel Smith quoted in Elizabeth Silverthorne, *Ashbel Smith of Texas: Pioneer, Patriot, Statesman,
   1805–1886* (College Station, TX, 1982), 135; Thornton, *Inquiry into Slavery*, 61–5, 81–2. See also
   Supplementary References: "Slavery Commanded."

10 Cobb, *Law of Negro Slavery*, xli; Daniel R. Hundley, *Social Relations in Our Southern States* (Baton
   Rouge, LA, 1979 [1860]), 366–7; E. W. Warren, *Nellie Norton; Or, Southern Slavery and the Bible*
   (Macon, GA, 1864), 42; J. D. B. De Bow, "Origin, Progress, and Prospects of Slavery," *DBR*, 9 (July
   1850), 16; Armstrong, *Christian Doctrine of Slavery*, 11; "Slavery and the Bible," *DBR*, 9 (1850), 283;
   Stringfellow, "Bible Argument," in Elliott, ed., *Cotton Is King*, 473.

granary because, in the recent interpretation of Dean Miller, it signified "protective, separable identity" within the household. R. H. Rivers, president of Wesleyan College in Alabama, reveled in the provisions to allow the Israelite servants to enslave themselves permanently. Well might he have reveled. The invocation of "love," which imposed a requirement upon master as well as slave, represented something new and infused the idea of "property" with a human content. Cheever again said too much (for his own position) when he referred to the boring of the ear as a way of protecting an old or infirm servant from being thrown on his own resources. To southern slaveholders Cheever was describing their own practice.[11]

Proslavery men had much the better of the historical argument. Israelites did hold slaves as well as indentured servants. Modern scholarship vindicates those who drew on a wide variety of sources, including Flavius Josephus' *Antiquities* and *The Jewish War,* to document the existence of slavery in Israel and the two systems of servitude. "No competent judge," wrote the Reverend W. T. Hamilton of Mobile, a principal opponent of scientific racism, "no one with the least pretension to scholarship" could deny the prevalence of slavery among the Jews. The Old Testament, writes Isaac Mendelsohn, "justifies perpetual slavery of Canaanites, but demands the release of the Hebrew defaulting debtor in the seventh year and of those who sold themselves, or were sold, in the year of jubilee." Jubilee, writes Christopher Wright, proclaimed liberty to Israelites enslaved for debt and restoration of land to those compelled to sell it because of economic need. Jubilee primarily aimed to protect the poorer and weaker Israelite families. The historical scholarship of the early nineteenth century had said as much, and by the 1850s A. A. Porter, De Bow, and T. W. MacMahon confidently declared the scriptural argument settled in favor of the South.[12]

---

[11] Dean A. Miller, "Biblical and Rabbinic Contributions to an Understanding of the Slave," in William Scott Green, ed., *Approaches to Ancient Judaism: Theory and Practice* (Missoula, MT, 1978), 191; R. H. Rivers, *Elements of Moral Philosophy* (Nashville, TN, 1859), 331–2; Cheever, *Guilt of Slavery,* ch. 1, and Cheever, *God against Slavery,* 155–6. Also, Hans Walter Wolff, *Anthropology of the Old Testament* (London, 1974), 199; E. E. Urbach, "The Laws Regarding Slavery as Sources for Social History of the Period of the Second Temple, the Mishnah and Talmud," in J. G. Weiss, ed., *Papers of the Institute of Jewish Studies, London* (Jerusalem, 1966), 23, 26–7. For ear-boring: Exodus, 21:6–7.

[12] Hamilton, *Duties of Masters and Slaves,* 6, and 10–11 on Jubilee; Christopher J. H. Wright, "Jubilee, Year of," in David Noel Freedman, ed., *The Anchor Bible Dictionary* (New York, 1992), 3:1025–30; [A. A. Porter], "North and South," *SPR,* 3 (1850), 338–9; "Slavery and the Bible," *DBR,* 9 (1850), 281; T. W. MacMahon, *Cause and Contrast: An Essay on the American Crisis* (Richmond, VA, 1862), 7. McMahon appealed to the work of Reverend Dr. Henry Van Dyke of Brooklyn and Rabbi Morris Raphall of New York City. In *Fast Day Sermons* (New York, 1861) see Raphall, "Bible View of Slavery," 227–46, and Van Dyke, "The Character and Influence of Abolitionism," 127–76. In the early debate among New England Puritans, the proslavery John Saffin identified the two types of Israelite servitude: see Louis Ruchames, ed., *Racial Thought: America,* vol. 1: *From the Puritans to Abraham Lincoln: A Documentary History* (Amherst, MA, 1969), 1:53–8. See Isaac Mendelsohn, *Slavery in the Ancient Near East* (New York, 1949), 123, also 90. See also Urbach, "Laws Regarding Slavery," 3–4, 12, 32, 84; Harry M. Orlinsky, *Ancient Israel,* 2nd ed. (Ithaca, NY, 1960), 11, 81–2, 119; Roland de Vaux, *Ancient Israel,* 2 vols. (New York, 1965), 1:175–7; Bernard S. Jackson, "Biblical Laws of Slavery: A Comparative Approach," in Léonie Archer, ed. *Slavery and Other Forms of Unfree*

The abolitionists did draw blood on the question of the African slave trade. Proslavery ministers themselves saw the trade as an egregious violation of the biblical prohibition of "man-stealing" (Exodus, 21:16; 1 Tim., 1:10), but in the 1850s – when southern radicals tried unsuccessfully to reopen the slave trade – political, economic, and ideological arguments threatened to overwhelm scriptural and moral arguments. Slaveholders' doubts about the loyalty of white workers played an important part. In 1856 Governor Adams of South Carolina, who called for reopening the trade, cited fear of white laborers: Better to have "savage" Africans than "a species of labor we do not want, and which is, from the very nature of things antagonistic to our institutions." The radical L. W. Spratt reacted with chagrin when the Confederacy refused to countenance a reopening of the African slave trade: "*Our whole movement is defeated.* Slavery cannot share a government with democracy," and the South will require yet another revolution, no matter how painful. Lower South militants found some support from Virginians concerned about a growing labor shortage.[13]

George Fitzhugh of Virginia and William Goulden of Georgia, among the South's prominent unionists, thought that renewed importation of Africans would strengthen slavery and the southern position in national politics. Some Southerners who opposed reopening nevertheless supported repeal of the federal prohibition of the trade since it stamped slavery as immoral. At Alabama's secession convention in 1861, John T. Morgan argued that if the African slave trade were morally objectionable, so would the interstate trade in slaves have to be. At that, he claimed that the African trade had the virtue of bringing heathens to be Christianized, whereas domestic trade dealt in Christian slaves. In 1864 a special committee of the Presbyterian church in the Confederacy considered providential the transportation of African pagans to Christian America, but added that "God's inscrutable plan" provided no excuse to reconstitute the trade on a plea that good can come from evil. It pleaded for humanization of the slave codes while reiterating support for slavery as scriptural. By the laws of political economy the slave trade injured society, but even if not, no economic advantage should tempt Christians to defy God's commandment against man-stealing. The biblical model calls for a "patriarchal," "domestic" slavery, but the renewed trade would bring in "savages" who would have to

---

Labour (London, 1988), ch. 6. For the distinction between temporary and permanent Israelite slaves in proslavery polemics see also Supplementary References: "Israelite Servitude."

[13] In general see Ronald T. Takaki, *A Pro-Slavery Crusade: The Agitation to Reopen the African Slave Trade* (New York, 1971), esp. 27–8, 72–4, Adams quoted at 49; L. W. Spratt, "The Philosophy of Secession," appended to John E. Cairnes, *The Slave Power: Its Character, Career, and Probable Designs,* 2nd ed. (Newton Abbot, U.K., 1863), 393, 398; Spratt quoted in Emory Thomas, *The Confederate Nation, 1861–1865* (New York, 1979), 44; for concern about a labor shortage in Virginia see A. L. Scott in *Proceedings of the Southern Convention Held in Savanna, Georgia, Dec. 1856,* Supplement to *DBR* (1857), 211, 216–17. In the 1830s the press censored news of strikes in southern cities, some spurred by opposition to the use of slaves in industry: Julia A. Flisch, "The Common People of the Old South," *Annual Report of the American Historical Association,* 1 (1908), 139–40. See also Supplementary References: "Christianization – Slave Trade and Slavery."

be disciplined severely. Hence, southern resumption of the slave trade would defy the Bible.[14]

Abolitionists, notably R. P. Stanton, Brisbane, and Cheever, struck back. If slave trading was sinful then so was the slavery that profited from the initial sin. Slaveholders, in turn, denied that adherence to slavery implicated them in a sin implicit in its origins and maintained that some good had come from the sinful trade. Cheever answered that since the Bible commands return of stolen property, slaveholders must surrender their slave property without compensation. Representative Robert H. Smith of Mobile and the conservative Reverend N. L. Rice of Cincinnati replied that, if that were so, Americans should return all their stolen land to the Indians. William Hayden of Maine added that the biblical injunction against man-stealing had not prohibited Israelites from buying people who had been enslaved in heathen countries. They missed the chance to cite Exodus, 22:3, which commands that thieves must make restitution or be sold into slavery.[15]

When the Mormons compelled national attention to polygamy, they caught hell from abolitionists and slaveholders alike. Abolitionists and slaveholders each saw polygamy as the natural outcome of the other's moral degeneracy. In 1856 the Republican party branded slavery and polygamy "twin relics of barbarism," while the southern press called Mormonism a fraud and "the lying legends of stupid and wicked imposters." Louisa McCord linked polygamy to socialist and communist challenges to the family, and Henry Watkins Miller of the North Carolina General Assembly linked "*Mormonism,* that hyena of modern debasement," to Fourierism, free love, and abolitionism. Although the Mormons appealed to God's higher law and to the Constitution of the United States – which they interpreted, in the Calhoun manner, as guarantor of local rights – Southerners were not impressed, although Stephen Douglas refused to support federal legislation to curb Mormon polygamy as unwarranted federal intervention in local affairs.[16]

---

[14] Morgan in William R. Smith, ed., *The History of the Convention Debates of the People of Alabama* (Montgomery, AL, 1861), 195–200.

[15] R. P. Stanton, *Slavery Viewed in the Light of the Golden Rule* (Norwich, CT, 1860), 5–7, 10–11; Brisbane, *Slaveholding Examined,* 168–70 for the American and Foreign Antislavery Society; Cheever, *Guilt of Slavery,* chs. 2 and 30; Robert H. Smith, *An Address to the Citizens of Alabama, on the Constitution and Laws of the Confederate States of America* (Mobile, AL, 1861), 18; J. Blanchard and N. L. Rice, *A Debate on Slavery* (New York, 1969 [1846]), 369; Hayden, *Institution of Slavery,* 10. Bishop Francis Patrick Kenrick, a prestigious Catholic theologian, offered an ingenious defense of the difference between slavery and slave trade: Although the original title to the slaves taken in the wars and slave trade was defective, defective titles are "healed" by the lapse of a long time: Hugh J. Nolan, *The Most Reverend Francis Patrick Kenrick: Third Bishop of Philadelphia, 1830–1851* (Philadelphia, 1984), 241–2.

[16] R. S. Gladney, "Relation of State and Church," *SPR,* 16 (1863), 356; "Rationalism False and Unreasonable," *SPR,* 16 (1863), 180; Richard Lounsbury, ed., *Louisa S. McCord: Political and Social Essays* (Charlottesville, VA, 1995), 139, 141; Henry W. Miller, *Address Delivered before the Philanthropic and Dialectic Societies of the University of North-Carolina* (Raleigh, NC, 1857), 20–1, quote at 21; Arthur Charles Cole, *The Era of the Civil War, 1848–1870* (Urbana, IL, 1987 [1919]), 184. Among

Abolitionists reacted with public outrage and private satisfaction to the Mormons' defense of polygamy, which plunged Southerners into a quandary. The youthful John S. Wise of Virginia shocked family and friends by asserting that Benjamin Morgan Palmer's defense of slavery applied to polygamy as well. The antislavery divines countered: If Southerners were right that the Word sanctioned slavery, then it also sanctioned polygamy. Replying to the charge that polygamy denigrated the family, the Mormons pictured it as an antidote for the disintegration of family life that evangelicals were railing against. In reply to William Ellery Channing and others who pressed the analogy of slavery to polygamy, Southerners – including Robert Dabney, Albert Taylor Bledsoe, and the Catholic Bishop Augustin Verot – held that the Old Testament tolerated but did not sanctify polygamy and that Jesus condemned it. In contrast, Moses introduced slavery to the Israelites under God's command; and Jesus condemned polygamy but not slavery. Channing and Wayland described polygamy as widespread and lawful in Jesus' time without drawing His condemnation. Fuller replied: To the contrary, neither Greek nor Roman law permitted polygamy, and "The gospel does forbid, and did at once abolish polygamy." The early Church never excluded slaveholders but did resolutely exclude polygamists.[17]

R. H. Rivers pointed to polygamy's degradation of women: "It makes her a slave; her power and influence are gone, and her light is quenched." Marriage should "promote individual and domestic happiness, and especially the happiness of women." Other theologians added that the Church testified against evils but had no right to try to extirpate evils through politics. Some abolitionists, notably the Reverend Rufus Clark of New Hampshire, had Moses regulate but not abolish slavery, polygamy, and other evils because of the underdeveloped moral sensibilities of a people who

attacks on polygamy see [Grayson], "Slavery in the Southern States," 342; John Leighton Wilson, "The Moral Condition of Western Africa," *SPR*, 2 (1848), 88. For southern responses to the Mormons, see Supplementary References: "Mormons."

[17] John S. Wise, *The End of an Era* (Boston, 1900), 145–6; Robert L. Dabney, *Systematic Theology* (Carlisle, PA, 1985 [1878]), 410–13; Albert Taylor Bledsoe, *An Essay on Liberty and Slavery* (Philadelphia, 1856), 151–2; Verot, *Tract for the Times*, 6; Joseph C. Stiles, *Modern Reform Examined* (Philadelphia, 1857), 10–11; Fuller in Fuller and Wayland, *Domestic Slavery*, 10–12, 183–4, quote at 11; also, "The Judicial Law of Moses," in T. E. Peck, *Miscellanies*, ed. T. C. Johnson, 3 vols. (Richmond, VA, 1895–97), 1:163–5; A. J. Roane, "Reply to Abolitionist Objections to Slavery," *DBR*, 20 (1856), 648–9; Robinson, *Slavery, as Recognized in the Mosaic Civil Law*, 40–2. Henry J. Van Dyke of Brooklyn supported the southern position: "The Character and Influence of Abolitionism," in *Fast Day Sermons*, 140–3. For the argument that God permitted polygamy in the Old Testament and thus it became a sin only when Jesus declared it so in His new dispensation, see Ross, *Slavery Ordained of God*, 44–5; Hopkins, *View of Slavery*, 36–40, ch. 29. For secular formulations see esp. "Domestic Slavery," *SLM*, 11 (1845), 520–1; Cobb, *Law of Negro Slavery*, 57–8; Sawyer, *Southern Institutes*, 45–6; E. Boyden, "The Epidemic of the Nineteenth Century," *SLM*, 31 (1860), 369. For the southern argument on polygamy addressed to yeomen see [Gabriel Capers], *Bondage a Moral Institution, Sanctioned by the Scriptures of the Old and New Testaments, and the Preaching and Practice of the Saviour. By a Southern Farmer* (Macon, GA, 1837), 63. For an early statement of the southern position see "Lectures on Human Nature Aula Libertatis, Delivered by Wm. Graham: Notes Taken by Joseph Glass, 1796," 131–2, in Graham Philosophic Society Papers, at Washington and Lee University.

had to be brought to higher standards. In the enlightened nineteenth century, people had no such excuse. Clapp angrily rejected the notion that Moses opportunistically accommodated to the Jews' hardness of hearts: "Was there ever a more wretched subterfuge than this? Is it not the vilest of sophisms?" Did it not make Moses "a cunning, sagacious, unprincipled temporizer?" Clapp expanded his blast to include Jesus and Paul. An indignant Stuart Robinson of Kentucky opened fire on those determined to discredit the Bible itself by arguing that, since Moses tolerated such evils as slavery, he could not have spoken with divine inspiration.[18]

In fighting scriptural battles, both sides considered decisive the designation "sin" or the ambiguous "moral evil." By the 1820s southern Baptists and Methodists were denying that slavery constituted a "a question of morals at all." In 1835 in Clinton, Mississippi, a large public meeting resolved that slavery was "not felt as an evil, moral or political, but ... a blessing both to master and slave." In 1845, Fuller equated "sin" with "moral evil" and then bluntly denied that slavery was either. Thomas Ritchie, editor of the Richmond *Enquirer* and boss of the politically powerful Richmond Junto, clung with many other defenders of slavery to the idea that slavery was not sinful but was in some sense a moral evil. In the 1850s Sawyer excoriated the "thousands" of Southerners who still considered slavery a moral evil: "The day is coming when every man must record his vote and man his post. 'He that is not for us is against us: He that gathereth not with us, scattereth abroad.' " On the eve of secession Thrasher and an anonymous Mississippian asked how, since the Old Testament and the New both recognized slavery, a Christian could consider it immoral and sinful. Why, even the pope dared not go that far.[19]

Nothing infuriated Southerners more than the common abolitionist assertion that Jesus had remained silent on slavery in order to ward off great violence and disorder in a society in which slavery was deeply embedded. Gabriel Capers of

---

[18] Rivers pressed this attack in *Moral Philosophy*, 288–91; see also Fletcher, *Studies on Slavery*, 219–30, and, generally, William Sumner Jenkins, *Pro-Slavery Thought in the Old South* (Gloucester, MA, 1960), 220–1. Rufus W. Clark, *A Review of the Rev. Moses Stuart's Pamphlet on Slavery, Entitled Conscience and the Constitution* (Boston, 1850), 25–6; Clapp, *Slavery*, 10–11; Robinson, *Slavery, as Recognized in the Mosaic Civil Law*, 3, 13–14. Jesus said that Moses suffered the Israelites to put away their wives "because of the hardness of your hearts" (Matt., 19:8). The abolitionists' suggestion that Paul's teaching on slavery is comparable with Moses' attribution of "hardness of heart" in his instructions on divorce, writes Guenther Haas, "does not bear scrutiny. It has no explicit scriptural support parallel to Jesus' comments on divorce in Matt. 19:7–8": "The Kingdom and Slavery: A Test Case for Social Ethics," *Calvin Theological Journal*, 28 (1993), 76.

[19] Furman, "Views of the Baptists," in Rogers, *Furman*; Wayland in Fuller and Wayland, *Domestic Slavery*, 35–8; Charles S. Sydnor, *Development of Southern Sectionalism, 1819–1848* (Baton Rouge, LA, 1948), 122 (Ritchie); Sawyer, *Southern Institutes*, 386; Thrasher, *Divine Institution*, 5–6; "A Mississippian", "Slavery – The Bible and the 'Three Thousand Parsons,' " *DBR*, 26 (1859), 45, 50. For attempts to come to terms with "moral evil" see *TSW*, 5:166, 9:479–80; W. S. Grayson, "The Constitution of Man and Slavery," *DBR*, 22 (1857), 76; [Patrick Mell], *Slavery. A Treatise Showing that Slavery Is Neither a Moral, Political, nor Social Evil* (Pennfield, GA, 1844), 9. For a review of the "word game" see Christopher H. Owen, *The Sacred Flame of Love: Methodism and Society in Nineteenth-Century Georgia* (Athens, GA, 1998), 52–3.

Georgia, in a pamphlet aimed at the yeomanry, fairly shouted that nothing would have justified Paul's call to slaves to obey masters who "held them in bondage contrary to the precepts of the Bible." Here and there an abolitionist also objected. Barnes's argument that Jesus withheld criticism of slavery for prudential reasons angered Cheever, for whom Jesus had no more need to denounce slavery than idolatry. He had come to fulfill the law of the Old Testament, and the Golden Rule had already said everything necessary. When an antislavery professor at the University of Virginia wrote that Jesus did not bother with slavery because of its mildness under the Romans, incensed Southerners replied – and many Northerners agreed – that the historical record showed ancient slavery as more brutal than southern. In the mid-1830s William Drayton of South Carolina said that ancient slaves were treated more harshly than modern and yet Jesus had not condemned slavery. Charles Taggart, to the applause of William Gilmore Simms, told the Unitarians of Nashville that Jesus witnessed a Roman slave system "more absolute and objectionable" and more "abject and degrading" than anything seen in America.[20]

For the proslavery divines, the argument from prudence could apply just as well to the southern states, and – more damning – made Jesus out to be an opportunist or a coward. Samuel Sewall of Massachusetts, in his early antislavery essay of 1700, had referred to Tacitus' account of the murder of Pedanius Secundus that led to the execution of his four hundred slaves. Despite such atrocities neither Jesus nor His apostles had condemned Roman slavery per se. And in 1773 Robert Nisbet reasoned in *Slavery Not Forbidden by Scripture* that, had Jesus considered slavery sinful, He would certainly have preached against it as he did against other socially entrenched sins. In the 1830s and 1840s George Addison Baxter of Virginia, Patrick Mell of Georgia, and Richard Fuller of South Carolina criticized Francis Wayland for arguing for Jesus' "expediency." Wayland pleaded that he would be ashamed to depict Jesus as an opportunist; by "expediency" he meant only prudence. Jesus commanded only that which people were prepared to hear. To have gone further would have provoked slave rebellion and brutal repression. His teachings created the moral atmosphere in which people could change their hearts and minds. By teaching personal accountability, Jesus undermined slavery, for masters could not simultaneously follow His teachings and employ measures necessary to sustain their power. Fuller retorted that in plain English expediency means "truckling and trimming,"

---

[20] [Capers], *Bondage*, 12; Cheever, *Guilt of Slavery*, chs. 28 and 29; for the antislavery professor see J. B. Bennett, "Albert Taylor Bledsoe," 207 n. 38; [William Drayton], *The South Vindicated from the Treason and Fanaticism of the Northern Abolitionists* (Philadelphia, 1836), 28–9, 93; Charles M. Taggart, *Slavery and Law, in the Light of Christianity* (Nashville, TN, 1851), 5; [William Gilmore Simms], "Critical Notices," *SQR*, n.s., 5 (1852), 254. For a similar argument by an earlier Unitarian see Charles A. Farley, *Slavery; A Discourse Delivered in the Unitarian Church, Richmond, Va.* (Richmond, VA, 1835), 17. The Apostles upheld slavery in seven passages: 1 Cor., 7:20–1; Eph., 6:5–9; Col., 3:22; 1 Tim., 6:1; Titus, 2:9–10; Phil., 10–18; 1 Peter 2:18–19; and see the discussion in Kevin Giles, "The Biblical Argument for Slavery: Can the Bible Mislead? A Case Study in Hermeneutics," *Evangelical Quarterly*, 66 (1994), 3–17. Southerners also invoked Jesus and the centurion in defense of slavery: see e.g. "Tract #10 Reviewed," *SWMR*, 2 (1845), 291. For proslavery and antislavery comparisons of ancient and modern slavery, see Supplementary References: "Slavery, Ancient and Modern Compared."

whereas Jesus called men to a new life, and the Apostles risked everything to preach against sin. Appealing to history, Fuller refuted Wayland's contention that Christianity had led to slave emancipation in Europe, adding that slavery, not merely serfdom, still existed in Christian Europe. In any case Southerners, who much admired Cicero, knew of his contempt for the "pernicious doctrine" that made expediency the measure of the morally right. Sawyer and other secular writers expressed outrage at the implication that Jesus and early Christians behaved like opportunists.[21]

Thornwell fumed. Since the abolitionists could not claim the Word against slavery, they turned to the Holy Spirit and a complacent Jesus unwilling to provoke disastrous social revolutions, leaving a great moral evil to the slow evolution of the human spirit. Well then, why did abolitionists not practice what they say Jesus preached and leave the slave states to evolve toward freedom slowly? Just after the War, Elias Dodson of North Carolina wrote to Thomas Ruffin that God had placed the curse of slavery on men in the wake of the Fall: "Christ and his apostles found this curse but did not aim to remove it but to mitigate it." Dodson groaned, "If the Yankees had preached and written as Christ and his apostles, this civil war had never been." The abolitionist Harriet Beecher Stowe replied sardonically to such arguments: "Neither Christ nor his apostles bore any explicit testimony against the gladiatorial shows and the sports of the [Roman] arena, and, therefore, it would be right to get them up in America." Jesus condemned wanton killing, Southerners replied, rejecting the analogy.[22]

[21] Samuel Sewall, "The Selling of Joseph," in Ruchames, ed., *Racial Thought*, 1:51–2; Baxter, *Essay on the Abolition of Slavery*, 18; see Wayland's Fifth and Seventh Letters in Fuller and Wayland, *Domestic Slavery*, and Fuller's reply, 205, 221; Cicero, *De Officiis*, tr. Walter Miller (LCL), Bk. 2:3; Sawyer, *Southern Institutes*, 106–7. [Mell], *Slavery*, is largely a critique of Wayland. In contrast to Protestant commentators, A. J. X. Hart of Mobile, a Catholic, credited medieval Catholicism with the abolition of slavery in Europe: *The Mind and Its Creations: An Essay on Mental Philosophy* (New York, 1853), 17–18, 78, 83.

[22] "Christian Doctrine of Slavery," in *JHTW*, 4:407; Elias Dodson to Thomas Ruffin, Feb. 16, 1866, in J. G. deRoulhac Hamilton, ed., *The Papers of Thomas Ruffin*, 4 vols. (Raleigh, NC, 1918), 4:50; Harriet Beecher Stowe, *A Key to Uncle Tom's Cabin* (Port Washington, NY, 1968 [1853]), 194–5, 201, quote at 200; for an attack on Stowe for treating the Bible with contempt see "Stowe's Key to Uncle Tom's Cabin," *SQR*, 8 (1853), 216. See also A. J. Roane, "Reply to Abolitionist Objections to Slavery," *DBR*, 20 (1856), 649–50; "E. G." [William J. Grayson], "Slavery in the Southern States," *SQR*, 8 (1845), 335, 338–40; Clapp, "Thanksgiving Sermon"; [John Archibald Campbell], "Slavery among the Romans," *SQR*, 28 (1848), 391–432; Daniel K. Whitaker, "Channing's Duty of the Free States," *SQR*, 2 (1842), 148–9; also, Fuller and Wayland, *Domestic Slavery*, 196–8. Antislavery southern divines also fell back on the Spirit: in William A. R. Goodwin, *History of the Theological Seminary in Virginia and Its Historical Background*, 2 vols. (Rochester, NY, 1923), see C. E. Grammer, "Rev. Dr. William Sparrow," and Grammer, "Social Life of the Hill," 1:384, 388, 578–601, as well as R. H. McKim, "Seminary during the War," 2:185. Lydia Maria Child admitted that the Apostles and the early Church accepted slavery as a social given, but she dubbed them egalitarians who prepared the way for emancipation in a community with a latent antislavery consciousness: Child, *The Progress of Religious Ideas, through Successive Ages*, 3 vols. (New York, 1855), 2:197, 3:182, 184, 189, 280–4, 428–9.

Northern antislavery moderates like Noah Webster opposed immediate emancipation because they understood that slavery constituted the heart of the southern social order, which would be shaken to its foundations by abrupt action: Stow Persons, "The Cyclical Theory of History in Eighteenth

Prudential considerations aside, the proslavery ministers asked why Jesus did not exclude slaveholders from the church, much as He had driven money changers from the temple and excluded polygamists? Fuller recalled that Jesus baptized slaveholders, and George Howe noted that all churches mentioned in the New Testament embraced both slaveholders and slaves. Leonard Bacon did not hide his irritation with antislavery brethren who denied that the Apostles' churches welcomed slaveholders. The evidence "cannot be got rid of without resorting to methods of interpretation which will get rid of anything." The radicals "torture the Scriptures into that which the anti-slavery theory requires them to say." Granted, condemnation of slavery would have provoked violence on a scale judged impermissible; granted (with P. R. Coleman-Norton, a recent contributor to a continuing debate) that Paul, like Jesus, "must have had enough sense to see that, since almost the entire economic system of his era was established on slavery, any convulsive changes inaugurated by him, if carried to completion, would have resulted in the ruination of contemporary civilization." Even so, the Roman state had not objected to personal emancipations, and no legal or political obstacle prevented Jesus and the Apostles from commanding Christians to desist from slaveholding. They gave no such command, as Charles Taggart pointed out.[23]

Paul's Epistle to Philemon invited fits of temper. Paul addressed Philemon as "our dearly beloved and fellow laborer" – that is, as a fellow Christian – and urged him to forgive his slave for unspecified transgressions. Neither in Philemon nor Colossians nor anywhere else did Paul suggest emancipation; he asked Philemon to treat Onesimus as a valued servant of Christ. Abolitionists argued that Paul's request proved slavery sinful, their adversaries, that it demonstrated acceptance of slavery and concern for humane treatment. The Baptist Reverend E. W. Warren of Georgia and the Catholic Bishop Augustin Verot of Florida agreed that God only forbade the Israelites to return fugitives to heathen slaveholders. Not a word in Philemon condemns slavery as *malum in se* or criticizes slavery at all.[24]

Century America," *American Quarterly*, 6 (1954), 158; Victor B. Howard, *Conscience and Slavery: The Evangelic Calvinist Domestic Missions, 1837–1861* (Kent, OH, 1990), 22. The argument from the extent of slavery and the potential horrors of slave revolt recurs in recent discussions, as reviewed by Joseph E. Capizzi, "A Development of Doctrine: The Challenge of Slavery to Moral Theology" (Ph.D. diss., University of Notre Dame, 1998), 22–3. J. W. Cummins of Maryland assailed the Jesus-as-opportunist argument from the Catholic viewpoint: Cummins, "On Slavery, the Union and the Catholic Church," New Orleans *Daily Picayune*, June 2, 1850. *Southern Literary Messenger* wrote of Father Cummins's "elaborate and brilliant discourse," reporting that it was received well by an awestruck audience in New York: Park Benjamin, "Letters from New York," *SLM*, 16 (1850), 371–2, quote at 372.

23 [Howe], "The Raid of John Brown," 793–4; Bacon, *Slavery Discussed*, 180; P. R. Coleman-Norton, "The Apostle Paul and the Roman Law of Slavery," ch. 13 of Coleman-Norton, ed., *Studies in Roman Economic and Social History in Honor of Allan Chester Johnson* (Princeton, NJ, 1951), 171; Taggart, *Slavery and Law*, 5. For an excellent analysis of he implications of Jesus' refusal to command Christians to refrain from slaveholding see Haas, "The Kingdom and Slavery," 81.

24 William J. Richardson, "Principle and Context in the Ethics of the Epistle to Philemon," *Interpretation: A Journal of Bible and Theology*, 22 (1968), 310–11. For recent discussions that find no evidence

Growing up in Tarsus, Paul had probably encountered few slaves, but he must have encountered many when he passed through the great slave market of Tyre on his way to Jerusalem and its teeming small slaveholdings. As Southerners knew, when Paul wrote 1 Corinthians at least a fifth and perhaps a third of the population of Corinth was enslaved; another third were freedmen, some descended from former slaves whom Julius Caesar sent out as colonists. Paul observed that many slaves fared much better than did free laborers. His Epistle manifested his "theology of the calling," which demanded fidelity to Christ in every earthly occupation and status. It contained no criticism of slavery.[25]

The assertion that Paul advocated emancipation rests on ethical inferences drawn especially from 1 Corinthians, 7:21. But, as J. Albert Harrill delicately warns, "Nothing in the passage implies that Paul was considering the question of whether the social institution of slavery ought to be abolished or not. Paul's explicit topic is the manumission of baptized slaves. Ethical inferences about slavery as a general phenomenon of the Greco-Roman world should be drawn from Paul's statement only with great caution."[26]

Guenther Haas, John G. Nordling, P. R. Coleman-Norton, and others have held that Paul's call to masters to meet the conditions taught by Jesus would, if heeded, have undermined the system. Their reasoning recapitulates and develops a line of thought projected by early and politically moderate opponents of American slavery. In a 1773 pamphlet that provoked fierce debate, Benjamin Rush remarked that while the Bible did not condemn slavery, it did condemn a multitude of sins that inexorably arose out of it. During the first decade of the nineteenth century the antislavery Baptist Friends of Humanity in Kentucky assailed proslavery arguments based on the Abramic household and the Noahic curse and identified slavery's inherent inducement of "pride, covetness and cruelty" among slaveholders. In later

---

for antislavery in Paul and that specifically refute the abolitionist interpretation of Philemon, see Joseph A. Fitzmyer, *The Letter to Philemon: A New Translation with Introduction and Commentary* (New York, 2000), esp. 19–20, 31–5; Coleman-Norton, "The Apostle Paul," in Coleman-Norton, ed., *Studies in Roman Economic and Social History*, 167–72. On the rival interpretations of Philemon see also Supplementary References: "Philemon."

[25] On Paul's theology of the calling, see esp. S. Scott Bartchy, *ΜΑΛΛΟΝ ΧΡΗΣΑΙ: First-Century Slavery and the Interpretation of 1 Corinthians 7:12* (Missoula, MT, 1973), 50, 173–4. Albert Barnes made the astonishing assertion that Jesus never came in contact with slavery at all: *Scriptural Views*, ch. 7. For Jesus' acquaintance with slaves and slavery see also Jennifer A. Glancy, *Slavery in Early Christianity* (New York, 2002), 129. On Corinthian slavery see Donald Engels, *Roman Corinth: An Alternative Model for the Classical City* (Chicago, 1990), 15–16, 30–1, 83; Paul Cartledge, *Spartan Reflections* (Berkeley, CA, 2001), 136. On Corinth as a large slave market in Greco-Roman times see Sawyer, *Southern Institutes*, 114 and n. 2. George A. Baxter stressed that Paul preached to slaveholding churches everywhere: *Essay on the Abolition of Slavery*, 20.

[26] J. Albert Harrill, "Paul and Slavery: The Problem of 1 Cor. 7:21," *Biblical Research*, 39 (1994), 5; also, John G. Nordling, "Christ Leavens the Culture: St. Paul on Slavery," *Concordia Journal*, 24 (1998), 43–52; William J. Richardson, "Principle and Context in the Ethics of the Epistle to Philemon," *Interpretation: A Journal of Bible and Theology*, 22 (1968), 306–7. S. Scott Bartchy renders a straightforward and sound judgment: "As Christians moved into the second century, they continued to share with their pagan contemporaries the view that slavery was an integral part of civilization." Bartchy, "Slave, Slavery," *Dictionary of the Later New Testament and Its Developments* (Downers Grove, IL, 1997).

years John S. C. Abbott, the northern historian and political moderate, observed
that many Christian masters treated their slaves badly; he wondered what, then,
should be expected from the many nonbelieving masters? George Bourne and Albert Barnes argued that if the Bible does not specifically condemn slavery, it nonetheless lays down general moral principles that slaveholders proved incapable of
upholding – that, in other words, the Bible implicitly condemned slavery through
its injunctions against a long list of sins intrinsic to the reduction of men to property. Proslavery theorists, jurists, and divines emphatically denied that southern
slavery reduced men to property and crafted an elaborate refutation to demonstrate
that southern law and custom recognized the human rights of slaves. While the
slaveholders rejected the notion that slavery was evil and oppressive beyond what
must be expected of any social system, they acknowledged the difficulties of bringing their own system up to Abramic standards.[27]

Southern theologians did not simply proclaim that they were marching behind
the Lord of Hosts against the Antichrist. They seized upon the War to underscore
their long-building campaign of reform to protect slave families, repeal the laws
against slave literacy, and punish cruel masters. Before and during the War, southern divines professed confidence in the South's ability to institute necessary reforms,
but some had doubts. When the Disciples' Alexander Campbell rejected the abolitionist argument on sinfulness, he wondered whether the South could in fact bring
its slavery up to an Abramic standard. With deepening sectional crisis, secession,
and the War, most divines agreed that if God had indeed sanctified slavery, He had
put the Christian South on its mettle. Either it met Abramic standards or God
would send the heathens of the North to punish them, much as he had sent heathens of old to punish recalcitrant Israelites.[28]

Proslavery theologians believed that slavery encouraged moral evil to a lesser extent than did the North's free-labor system. But the more perceptive antislavery

---

[27] Benjamin Rush, *An Address to the Inhabitants of the British Colonies upon Slavekeeping* (Philadelphia, 1773), and Lester B. Scherer, "A New Look at Personal Slavery Established," *WMQ*, 3rd ser.,
30 (1973), 645–52; William Warren Sweet, *Religion on the Frontier: The Baptists, 1783–1830: A Collection of Source Material* (New York, 1931), 82–5, 564–96, quote at 568; John S. C. Abbott, *South
and North; Or, Impressions Received during a Trip to Cuba and the South* (New York, 1969 [1860]),
74–5; [Bourne], *Anti-Slavery Bible Argument*, 7–9; Albert Barnes, *The Church and Slavery* (New
York, 1969 [1857]), 42–3. Among recent studies see Haas, "The Kingdom and Slavery," 86; Nordling,
"Christ Leavens the Culture," 43–52; Coleman-Norton, "The Apostle Paul," in Coleman-Norton,
ed., *Studies in Roman Economic and Social History*, 165, 173. During the War, *Danville Quarterly
Review* – as voice of the pro-Union orthodox Presbyterians in Kentucky – reiterated its condemnation of slavery as un-Christian without, however, calling it *malum in se*: "Slavery never did and never
can exist per se." Imperfect masters have unlimited power, which no man can sustain without falling
into sin: "Slavery in the Church Courts," *DQR*, 4 (1864), 516, quote at 520. William B. Hayden of
Maine, pleading for sectional peace in 1861, acknowledged that the Bible sanctioned slavery but argued that slavery, biblically regulated, would end in emancipation. Hence, he opposed holy war and
urged patience with the South: Hayden, *Institution of Slavery*, 15, 24–8.

[28] [Campbell], "Our Position on American Slavery," 234. For this paragraph and the following see Eugene D. Genovese, *A Consuming Fire: The Fall of the Confederacy in the Mind of the White Christian
South* (Athens, GA, 1998); also, Daniel W. Stowell, "'We Have Sinned, and God Has Smitten Us':
John H. Caldwell and the Religious Meaning of Confederate Defeat," *Georgia Historical Quarterly*,
77 (1994), 1–38.

and proslavery proponents saw that the reforms necessary to meet Abramic standards would, in effect, end slavery and transform the social system into a version of serfdom. Immense structural difficulties impeded any such transition, and thus the reformers found themselves constantly at bay. The test of slavery's compatibility with the Gospels lay in reform sufficient to limit the moral evils – necessitated by mankind's fall – to the minimum associated with the Abramic standard. The War, then, was God's judgment on his sinful Chosen People, who were weighed in the balance and found wanting.

Fatefully, Southerners used their scripturally weakest suit – Noah's curse on his son Ham – to maximum political effect. Properly, the abolitionists condemned it as a fraud. "Cursed be Canaan. A servant of servants shall he be unto his brethren" (Genesis, 9:25 and generally 9:18–27). Japheth, Shem, and Ham found Noah, their father, asleep, drunk, and naked – or so the passage has usually been understood – and Ham disrespectfully had sport at his father's expense. In consequence, Noah cursed Canaan, Ham's son. His offspring would be servants of Shem, and Shem would dwell in the tent of Japheth. How white supremacists could turn Japheth into an imperial lord remains a mystery. Max Weber has suggested that, in fact, the tent-dwelling Japhethites were probably merchants. Nothing at all in the Bible says that Africans descended from Ham, although apologists for racial slavery said they did and gained the support of some eminent scientists who claimed to trace racial descent. And there it was: a grand religio-scientific justification for white enslavement of blacks.[29]

Noah's curse as justification for enslavement predated the European conquest of America and had little to do with race. Jerome and Augustine cited it to account for slavery per se, not for racial slavery. Augustine rejected the notion that Japheth, Shem, and Ham represented different races: Shem, circumcised Jews; Japheth, uncircumcised Greeks; Ham, heretics. Augustine referred to Noah's nakedness and subsequent curse as "pregnant with prophetic meanings, and veiled in mysteries." He said that nothing in Scripture links the Egyptians, Ethiopians, or others to Ham, and he noted that Jesus descended from Shem ("named"). Augustine interpreted the "enlargement" of Japtheth to refer to the Church of Christ, not to a race or empire. Medieval theorists, attributing purity of blood to nobles, traced it to Japheth. They had free commoners descend from Shem and their slaves from Ham, but those slaves were white. Not until the Middle Ages did many Christians, Jews, or Muslims identify blacks as descendants of Ham, although some such identification had appeared in ancient Israel. By the sixteenth century some Christian theologians were taking racial ground, and toward the end of the century racial interpretation swept England. In later centuries application of the Noahic curse to blacks had

---

[29] Southern politicians readily invoked the curse, some to support the notion of perpetual slavery. See e.g. [Thomas Caute Reynolds], *Speech of Lieut. Gov. Reynolds on the Preservation and Reconstruction of the Union* (St. Louis, MO, 1861), 2. On the Japhethites as merchants see Max Weber, *Ancient Judaism*, tr. and ed. Hans H. Gerth and Don Martingale (Glencoe, IL, 1952), 35. As to the notion that God punished the progeny of sinners in perpetuity, Exodus (20:5) says in refutation: "The Lord thy God am a jealous God, visiting the iniquity of the fathers upon the children unto the third and fourth Generation of them that hate me."

special import in Germany, which emerged as the center of theological and philosophical speculation.[30]

From tidewater to Texas – from before the time of William Byrd to the War and
beyond – ministers and laymen, the well educated and the ignorant, routinely referred to blacks as "sons of Ham." Southern congressmen appealed to the Noahic
curse to justify enslavement of blacks, as Senator William Smith of South Carolina
did in 1818 in a debate over the Fugitive Slave Law and James Hammond in the debate over the Gag Rule. In the 1820s the eminent Reverend Frederick Dalcho and the
Richmond *Enquirer* injected the curse into the Missouri controversy. The Presbyterian Reverend William Plumer presented a more benign version when he opened
his *Religious Instruction of the Negroes* (1848) with Ethiopia's stretching its hand
to God after the Africans had been dispersed among other races to uplift them. In
1859 the Arkansas Baptist convention reasserted the curse as racially specific.[31]

John Fletcher gave the curse a particularly nasty twist, attributing it to miscegenation – to Ham's marrying a descendant of Cain. Fletcher, Thrasher, Joseph
H. Lumpkin, and the Reverends Iveson Brookes and J. R. Graves interpreted the
curse to mean that God ordained the white race to rule the world and that slavery would continue until the end of time. Among the Baptist divines, Basil Manly
invoked Noah's curse to contend that blacks had made little progress, and E. W.
Warren simply insisted that the Canaanite slaves of Israelites descended from Ham.

[30] Augustine, "On the Trinity," in Philip and Henry Wace, eds., *Nicene and Post-Nicene Fathers,* 2nd
ser., 14 vols. (Peabody, MA, 1995), 1:15–25, 16:2; Saint Augustine, *The City of God,* tr. Marcus Dods
(New York, 1950), Bk. 16; Maurice Keen, *Chivalry* (New Haven, CT, 1984), 157; on Augustine see
also Ivan Hannaford, *Race: The History of an Idea in the West* (Washington, DC, 1996), 94–5. Benjamin Braude has traced the vicissitudes of the Noahic curse through the Middle Ages: "The Sons of
Noah and the Construction of Ethnic and Geographical Identities in the Medieval and Early Modern
Periods," *WMQ,* 3rd ser., 54 (1997), 103–42. On racialist interpretation from the sixteenth century
onward see Hannaford, *Race,* 183; on Germany see Marian E. Musgrave, "Literary Justifications of
Slavery," in Reinhold Grimm and Jost Hermand, eds., *Blacks and German Culture* (Madison, WI,
1986), 8–9. For the American debate see Thomas Virgil Peterson, *Ham and Japheth: The Mythic
World of Whites in the Antebellum South* (Metuchen, NJ, 1978).

[31] In eighteenth-century Virginia, Hugh Jones supported the Japheth–Shem–Ham derivation of races:
*The Present State of Virginia: From Whence Is Inferred a Short View of Maryland and North Car-
olina,* ed. Richard L. Morton (Chapel Hill, NC, 1956), 50–3. Peterson, *Ham and Japheth,* 45 (Smith),
96–7 (Schaff and Ross); for Dalcho and the Missouri crisis see Larry R. Morrison, "The Religious
Defense of Slavery before 1830," *Journal of Religious Thought,* 37 (1980/81), 18; for Hammond and
the congressmen see William Lee Miller, *Arguing about Slavery: The Great Battle in the United States
Congress* (New York, 1996), 32–42; Robert McColley, *Slavery and Jeffersonian Virginia* (Urbana,
IL, 1964), 123; Sept. 25, 1863, in Christopher Chancellor, ed., *An Englishman in the Civil War: The
Diaries of Henry Yates Thompson* (New York, 1971), 89; Randolph B. Campbell, *An Empire for Slav-
ery: The Peculiar Institution in Texas, 1821–1865* (Baton Rouge, LA, 1989), 212; William S. Plumer,
Thoughts on the Religious Instruction of the Negroes of This Country (Savannah, GA, 1848), 3; Carl
H. Moneyhon, *The Impact of the Civil War and Reconstruction on Arkansas: Persistence in the Midst
of Ruin* (Baton Rouge, LA, 1994), 60–1. Prominent clergymen who invoked the curse and referred
to "Sons of Ham" included John Girardeau, Benjamin M. Palmer, Stephen Elliott, G. W. Freeman,
Samuel Dunwoody, Alexander McCaine, G. W. Freeman, Howell Cobb, J. T. Wightman, W. Rees, and
Joseph Jones. The Vatican did not officially denounce the Hamitic myth until 1864: Maria Genoino
Caravaglios, "A Roman Critique of the Pro-Slavery Views of Bishop Martin of Natchitoches, Louisiana," *Records of the American Catholic Historical Society of Philadelphia, Pa.,* 83 (1972), 76–7.

Dr. Samuel Cartwright, stressing physical characteristics, provided spurious science; other proslavery writers, most notably Northerners like Josiah Priest, associated a black presence with evil.[32]

Some leading proslavery divines rejected the racial interpretation as unscriptural and unscientific. Dabney did not doubt black inferiority but did doubt the curse, considering it "not essential to our argument." The Reverend Samuel Seabury, a proslavery northern Episcopalian, accepted black descent from Ham but denied that the curse gave whites the right to enslave blacks. He criticized racism as such and read the Bible as sanctioning slavery per se. The theologically liberal Reverend James Warley Miles of Charleston carefully demonstrated that the Noahic curse had no relation to the black race, and instead he turned to science to establish black inferiority and a special fitness for slavery. John Adger, S. J. Cassells, William Hamilton, Ferdinand Jacobs, Joseph Stiles, James Henley Thornwell, and J. L. Wilson shied away from the association of the curse with blacks, and George Howe and John Bachman emphatically rejected it. Thornton Stringfellow and Benjamin Morgan Palmer made much of the curse to justify the enslavement of blacks but agreed that the Bible sanctioned slavery regardless of race. The Reverends Frederick Ross in Alabama, William White and Stuart Robinson in Kentucky, and Philip Schaff in the North denied that slavery would last forever since Christianization was preparing the blacks for better things.[33]

---

[32] Thrasher, *Divine Institution*, 8–9; Iveson L. Brookes, *A Defence of the South against the Reproaches of the North* (Hamburg, SC, 1850), 3; also, Brookes, *A Defence of Slavery against the Attacks of Henry Clay and Alex'r Campbell* (Hamburg, SC, 1851), 8–9, 20–1, 30; on Graves see Timothy George and David S. Dockery, eds., *Baptist Theologians* (Nashville, TN, 1990), 234–6; Fletcher, *Studies on Slavery*, 443–7, 471–3, 482; Ron Bartour, "American Views on Biblical Slavery, 1835–1865," *Slavery and Abolition*, 4 (1983), 42–4; Harold Wilson, "Basil Manly, Apologist for Slaveocracy," *Alabama Review*, 15 (1962), 42–3; Warren, *Nellie Norton*, 104; Samuel Cartwright, *Essays in a Series of Letters to Rev. William Winans* (Natchez, MS, 1843). Moses Stuart invoked Noah's curse to show that slavery preceded the Flood: *Conscience and the Constitution*, 23.

Josiah Priest also insisted that the Canaanites were black: *Bible Defense of Slavery and Origins, Fortunes, and History of the Negro Race,* 5th ed. (Glasgow, KY, 1852). Chief Justice Joseph Lumpkin of Georgia's Supreme Court, an Old School Presbyterian, repeatedly cited the Noahic curse to support proslavery decisions: Mason W. Stephenson and D. Grier Stephenson, " 'To Protect and Defend': Joseph Henry Lumpkin, the Supreme Court of Georgia, and Slavery," *Emory Law Journal*, 25 (1976), 579–608. Lumpkin was favorably impressed with Priest's book: Paul DeForest Hicks, *Joseph Henry Lumpkin: Georgia's First Chief Justice* (Athens, GA, 2002), 131–2. But his decisions assumed that Africans under southern tutelage were making steady progress toward civilization: see "Seaborn C. Bryan vs. Hugh Walton," in *Reports of Cases in Law and Equity Argued and Determined in the Supreme Court of the State of Georgia*, 14 (1854), 186–7. The origins of the Canaanites remain obscure: see Keith N. Schoville, "Canaanites and Amorites," in Alfred J. Hoerth et al., eds., *Peoples of the Old Testament World* (Grand Rapids, MI, 1994), 157–9.

[33] Robert L. Dabney, *Defence of Virginia (and Through Her of the South) in Recent and Pending Contests against the Sectional Party* (New York, 1969 [1867]), 104; Samuel Seabury, *American Slavery Distinguished from the Slavery of English Theorists and Justified by the Law of Nature* (New York, 1861), 223–5, 272–3; [James Warley Miles], *The Relation between the Races at the South* (Charleston, SC, 1861), 18–19; [George Howe], "The Mark of Cain and the Curse of Ham," *SPR*, 3 (1850), 417–18; John Bachman, *The Doctrine of the Unity of the Human Race Examined on the Principles of Science* (Charleston, SC, 1850), 241–3; B. M. Palmer, *"The Rainbow Round the Throne"; Or, Justice Tempered with Mercy* (Milledgeville, GA, 1863), 31–2; Stringfellow, "Bible Argument," in Elliott,

For Thomas Roderick Dew, the Noahic curse permitted but did not mandate enslavement of blacks. Dew identified Ham as the founder of an ancient Egyptian civilization he himself regarded with great respect, and he identified Abraham as the Shemite founder of the "Jewish nation." Dew recognized the Phoenicians as Shemites and as great merchants who established stable government, founded cities, and promoted peace, emerging as one of the most civilized people of their day. The racial myth nonetheless swept the South, making the educated and the uneducated alike comfortable with racial slavery. Other important lay proslavery theorists, notably Edmund Ruffin and Thomas Cobb found nothing in Scripture or science to convince them that blacks descended from Ham.[34]

As Abraham Lincoln saw, a painful problem inhered in the South's scriptural defense of slavery: The Bible sanctioned slavery per se but not racial slavery. Abolitionists taunted proslavery adversaries to defend the logical implication of their argument – that God sanctioned the enslavement of whites and any others as well as blacks. The antislavery northern Reverend Taylor Lewis eloquently stressed the damning point that modern slavery differed from biblical precisely in being racial. Cheever and Barnes pointed out that the Bible nowhere singled out blacks for opprobrium. "Where is the sentence," Cheever demanded to know, "in which God ever appointed you, the Anglo-Saxon race, you the mixture of all races under heaven, you, who cannot tell whether the blood of Shem, Ham, or Japheth mingles in your veins." In 1864, Cheever excoriated the oppression of blacks in and out of slavery and denied that race is an exception to the "Law of Love." Racial prejudice, he said, is "our national sin." The abolitionist war on racism, not merely slavery, was all the more courageous since racial interpretation of the Noahic curse was at least as popular in the North as in the South.[35]

---

ed., *Cotton Is King*, 463, 506; Robinson, *Slavery, as Recognized in the Mosaic Civil Law*, 8–9; also, Preston Graham, Jr., *A Kingdom Not of This World: Stuart Robinson's Struggle to Distinguish the Sacred from the Secular during the Civil War* (Macon, GA, 2002), 114–15; H. M. White, ed., *Rev. William S. White, D.D., and His Times (1800–1873): An Autobiography* (Richmond, VA, 1891), 117.

[34] Thomas Roderick Dew, *Digest of the Laws, Customs, Manners, and Institutions of the Ancient and Modern Nations* (New York, 1884 [1852]), 10, 17, 20, 32–5; William K. Scarborough on Ruffin in *ERD*, 1:xxxii, xxvi, xxxi; Cobb, *Law of Negro Slavery*, xxxv–xxxvi. Since Abraham, Isaac, and David were Shemites (Chron., 1:17–42), so was Jesus, as noted by Samuel Cartwright, *Essays in a Series of Letters to Rev. William Winans*. Ross lost sight of Jesus, commenting, "Shem will ever be lower than Japheth": *Slavery Ordained of God*, 30.

[35] Taylor Lewis, in *Fast Day Sermons*, 177–226; Cheever, *Guilt of Slavery*, v, 179–83, 192–3, chs. 11 and 41; Cheever, *God against Slavery*, 94, quote at 101–2; George B. Cheever, *Rights of the Coloured Race to Citizenship and Representation; And the Guilt and Consequences of Legislation against Them* (New York, 1864), 5, also 25–7; Barnes, *Scriptural Views*, 88–9, 207–9. Also, Stanton, *Slavery Viewed in the Light of the Golden Rule*, 11–12. The antislavery movement in Kentucky and across the Border States contained a good many adherents who bravely condemned racism as well as slavery: Jeffrey Brooke Allen, "Were Southern White Critics of Slavery Racists? Kentucky and the Upper South, 1791–1824," *JSH*, 64 (1978), 169–90. For abolitionist efforts nationally to combat racism, including the racism in its own ranks, see Paul Goodman, *Of One Blood: Abolitionism and the Origins of Racial Equality* (Berkeley, CA, 1998). For an expression of firm antiracism see Lydia Maria Child to Lemuel Shaw, July 1, 1861, in John G. Whittier, ed., *Letters of Lydia Maria Child* (New York, 1969 [1883]), 146. On the popularity of the curse in the North see Adelaide Avery Lyons, "Religious Defense of Slavery in the North," *Trinity College Historical Society Historical Papers*, ser. 13 (Durham,

Since abolitionists doubted that many Southerners would countenance justifi-cation of white enslavement, they focused on the nonracial nature of the very Is-raelite slavery most of them denied even existed. In particular, they shredded the assertion that had blacks descending from Cain as well as from Ham and Canaan. Theodore Weld derided the Noahic curse as "the Vade mecum of slaveholders, and they never venture abroad without it." George Bourne reminded Southerners dryly that blacks believed whites themselves to be the descendants of Cain: "a controversy with which I feel no disposition to interfere." Bourne was not making it up. The Reverend Charles Gentry, a black preacher in northwestern North Carolina, ex-plained the origin of the white race: Adam and his progeny were "black as jet," but when God confronted Cain with his crime against Abel, Cain turned white. The marginality of the racial Noahic curse to the defense of slavery per se had emerged in the early debates in Puritan New England. Samuel Sewall, denouncing slavery, had blacks descend from Cush, not Ham. John Saffin replied that the origin did not matter since the Bible sanctioned slavery in general.[36]

As the scriptural argument for slavery passed into a defense of slavery in the abstract, the leading southern divines did what abolitionists felt sure they would not do: They agreed that the enslavement of blacks provided only a special case of the argument for slavery. At a debate in Cincinnati 1846 the abolitionist Reverend James Blanchard quoted the reply of the *Alabama Baptist* to a newspaper editor in Vermont who had accused southern clergy of defending slavery as rabidly as fire-eating politicians. *Alabama Baptist* refused to dissemble: "He says we endorse the sentiment of George McDuffie – '*slavery is the best possible relation between the employer and the laborer*' and '*we repudiate that old-fashioned doctrine, that all* MEN *are born equal.*' THIS IS EXACTLY OUR POSITION." The Noahic curse loomed large in T. C. Thornton's *Inquiry into Slavery* (1841), which dwelt on the long history of indigenous black slavery in Africa and on the white slavery in Eu-rope that still continued, overtly in Russia and covertly in Britain. R. H. Rivers appealed to the Noahic curse to deny that he advocated the enslavement of whites but then presented slavery as unifying the interests of labor and capital and pro-ducing happier workers than the free-labor system. In contrast, the most vigorous northern scriptural defenses of slavery concentrated on the curse and ignored slav-ery in the abstract. Now, it was one thing to say that slavery would continue as one social relation among many, but it was quite another to advocate slavery as

---

NC, 1919), 17, 25. The myth appeared among black leaders, although none read it to support white supremacy: see Mia Bay, *The White Image in the Black Mind: African-American Ideas about White People, 1830–1925* (New York, 2000), 46–7, 51, 105–6.

[36] Weld, *Bible against Slavery*, 46; Barnes, *Church and Slavery*, 16; [Bourne], *Anti-Slavery Bible Argu-ment*, 23–4, quote at 24; Gentry quoted in [Hardin E. Taliaferro], *Fisher's River (North Carolina) Scenes and Characters by "Skitt," "Who Was Thar'"* (New York, 1859), 188–9; also, James O. Buswell, Jr., *Slavery, Segregation, and Scripture* (Grand Rapids, MI, 1964), 32–3; William Cheek and Aimee Lee Cheek, *John Mercer Langston and the Fight for Black Freedom, 1829–65* (Urbana, IL, 1989), 91; Samuel Sewall, "The Selling of Joseph" (1700), and Saffin's reply in Ruchames, ed., *Racial Thought*, 1:46–56. Saffin attracted a bigger audience in defense of slavery than Sewell did: Jon Pahl, *Paradox Lost: Free Will and Political Liberty in American Culture, 1630–1760* (Baltimore, 1992), 59. Unlike most Puritans, Saffin denigrated blacks as cowardly, cruel, and vicious: Winthrop D. Jordan, *White over Black: American Attitudes toward the Negro, 1550–1812* (Chapel Hill, NC, 1968), 199–201.

the necessary and proper condition of labor. The former statement renders the latter theologically permissible but does not constitute an endorsement of it as social policy. Thus, the divines had to move from theology to history, political economy, and moral and social philosophy, much as the moral and social philosophers had to move to theology to justify their proposed solution of the Social Question through the enslavement of the laboring classes.[37]

Proslavery ministers of all denominations – as well as secular writers – fell back on the curse, but some genuinely learned and honest men among them did read both Scripture and history as confirming God's sanction for the enslavement of peoples of all races. Those who tried to prove that blacks but not whites were fit for slavery ran afoul of two difficulties: Some of the most prestigious southern divines rejected a racial interpretation of biblical slavery; and many of those who accepted it could not justify identifying the enslaved peoples of biblical times with Africans. For them, the Bible sanctioned enslavement regardless of race. The curse merely placed the blacks in a special category, with all blacks fit for slavery along with many whites.[38]

This scripturally and intellectually weakest point in the biblical defense of slavery emerged as the politically strongest. It gripped public opinion more firmly than any other. We live with the consequences of the ensuing tragedy.

How strong intrinsically were the abolitionist and proslavery appeals to Scripture? Americans of today might not think this a significant question, but millions of nineteenth-century Americans cared passionately. To speak bluntly: The abolitionists did not make their case for slavery as sin – that is, as condemned in Scripture. The proslavery protagonists proved so strong in their appeal to Scripture as to make comprehensible the readiness with which southern whites satisfied themselves that God sanctioned slavery.

Christian churches and other churches and temples today proclaim, persistently and forcefully, the sinfulness of racism and of slavery. With no difficulty, their theologians enlist Scripture to demonstrate the sinfulness of racism, but not the sinfulness of slavery. To this day, the southern theologians' scriptural defense of slavery as a system of social relations – not black slavery but slavery per se – has gone unanswered, although some recent efforts deserve respectful consideration. If the abolitionists did not come close, neither, more recently, has the Catholic church or the Southern Baptist Convention. The Anglican Reverend Kevin Giles of Australia

---

[37] Blanchard and Rice, *Debate on Slavery*, 358; Thornton, *Inquiry into Slavery*, 9–10 and passim; Rivers, *Moral Philosophy*, pt. 2:ch. 6 (1860 edition). The Reverend Irem W. Smith, in Connecticut, cited Jesus' concern for the poor and the oppressed and then assumed that he had replied to the specifics of the proslavery argument: *American Slavery; A Prayer for Its Removal* (Middletown, CT, 1860), 4.

[38] Despite Cartwright and a few others, proslavery polemicists frankly admitted that Jewish slave law, in the words of one, "knew no distinctions of color": [Maurice Mayer], "Slave Laws of the Jews," *RM*, 5 (1859), 102. For recent critiques of racial interpretations of the Noahic curse, see: Gene Rice, "The Curse that Never Was (Genesis, 9:18–27)," *Journal of Religious Thought*, 29 (1972), 5–27; Gunther Wittenberg, " 'Let Canaan Be His Slave,' " *Journal of Theology for Southern Africa*, 74 (1991), 46–56.

speaks uneasily of fellow theologians who continue to grapple with this problem: "We are so sure that the Bible does not support slavery, we fail to see just how compelling their arguments were in their day – and for that matter still are."[39]

Could the abolitionists have done better? Could a stronger hermeneutic (method of scriptural interpretation) have provided the resources to establish the abolitionist case on traditional Christian grounds? Mark Noll, a great and theologically sophisticated historian, has suggested as much. Noll offers the arresting argument that a faulty hermeneutic imposed severe rigidity on both proslavery and antislavery theologians and that peculiarly American conditions prevented a turn to the alternative hermeneutics offered by African Americans, Catholics, and certain Reformed Protestants. Noll's illuminating discussion clarifies much but does not demonstrate how any of the alternatives could ground antislavery Christian doctrine in Scripture. Guenther Haas's challenge remains unanswered: "Where an ethic of redemption is given primacy over an ethic of creation, the structure of a created moral order is lost, and one drifts about on a sea of historicism (and its implicit relativism)." Personal redemption in Christ does have implications for the necessary reformation of the social structure, but "No existing social structure is absolutely corrupt and therefore needs to be totally condemned. In some way every social structure participates in some way in God's created order." Thus, Haas continues, "Slavery is never directly condemned because it embodies, albeit it in a perverted form, God's creational order for the relationship between subordinate and superior in a work situation. To condemn slavery outright would be to reject aspects of the creational structure for work that remains intact even in the institution of slavery."[40]

Northerners and Southerners "read the same Bible." Or so Abraham Lincoln declared in his Second Inaugural Address. But Lincoln knew they did not read it the same way or grant it the same authority. The war over the Good Book revealed a larger, more extensive war over the very meaning of Christianity – specifically, over the relation of the revealed Word of God to the Holy Spirit and the demands of individual conscience.

---

[39] Giles, "Can the Bible Mislead?" 12. Antislavery cannot be deduced from natural-rights philosophy, as Alasdair MacIntyre demonstrates: *Are There Any Natural Rights* (Brunswick, ME, 1983: "The Charles F. Adams Lecture at Bowdoin College"). Proslavery men also appealed to the doctrine of natural rights, but with no greater success than scored by their adversaries. See Eugene D. Genovese, *The Slaveholders' Dilemma: Freedom and Progress in Southern Conservative Thought, 1820–1860* (Columbia, SC, 1992), ch. 2.

[40] Mark A. Noll, "The Bible and Slavery," in Randall M. Miller et al., eds, *Religion and the American Civil War*, ch. 2; Haas, "The Kingdom and Slavery," 74–89, esp. 83–6.

17

The Holy Spirit in the Word of God

> The Apostle's words, "The Letter killeth, but the spirit giveth life," do not refer to
> figurative phrases ... but rather plainly to the law, which forbids whatever is evil.
> —Augustine[1]

Beneath the common Protestant Christianity professed by North and South, a chasm
widened not only in constitutional interpretation and vision of social order but in
theology. During the seventeenth and eighteenth centuries, acrimonious debate
shook the long-standing pillars of Christian belief: authority of Scripture; Revelation; the divinity of Jesus; the afterlife; the very existence of God. By the nineteenth
century the doctrines of original sin, human depravity, the Trinity, and much else
were receding in Western Europe and in the northern states of the American Union,
where the social relations of transatlantic capitalism shook the ground on which
Christian orthodoxy and a conservative worldview could be sustained. In the South,
however, slavery permitted them to flourish. Before the War and beyond, the South
resisted the principal theological and philosophical tendencies of the age, and the
southern churches, Arminian and Calvinist, stood firm for orthodoxy. Flannery
O'Connor, explaining the difference between twentieth-century Northerners and
Southerners, suggested that a great many more Southerners than Northerners still
believe in original sin.[2]

---

[1] Augustine, "A Treatise on the Spirit and the Letter," in Philip Schaff, ed., *Nicene and Post-Nicene Fathers,* 1st ser., 14 vols. (Peabody, MA, 1995), 5:7.5 (85). Augustine interpreted Paul as warning that the
formal Word could encourage sin among those not touched by the Holy Spirit.
  It seemed to many Southerners that the northern churches had abandoned orthodoxy, but the most
careful critics focused on direction rather than extent. Even the more liberal northern churches resisted
materialism and secularism, but Southerners saw them as losing the battle. For resistance in northern churches see Mark Y. Hanley, *Beyond a Christian Commonwealth: The Protestant Quarrel with
the American Republic, 1830–1860* (Chapel Hill, NC, 1994), 90–2; also, Steven E. Woodworth, *While
God Is Marching On: The Religious World of Civil War Soldiers* (Lawrence, KS, 2001), esp. ch. 3.

[2] See Jaroslav Pelikan's magisterial *The Christian Tradition: A History of the Development of Doctrine,* 5 vols. (Chicago, 1989), esp. vol. 5; Sally Fitzgerald, ed., *The Habit of Being: Letters of Flannery
O'Connor* (New York, 1979), 302–3. Samuel Clarke defended the concept of God and the afterlife

Demotion of Jesus from Second Person of the Trinity to a moral philosopher became fashionable in the late eighteenth century, enlisting the talents of Thomas Jefferson, Benjamin Franklin, and Joseph Priestley among those who sought to disentangle the "mythical" from the "real" Jesus. Bishop Meade recalled that Episcopalian preaching in Virginia at the beginning of the nineteenth century had been substituting morality for religion, as English clergymen took their texts less from Scripture than from Plato, Cicero, and Epictetus. Meade described their American counterparts as preaching from Hugh Blair, Lawrence Sterne, and the *Spectator*: "It is no wonder that the churches were deserted and the meeting-houses filled." For Priestley, the eminent scientist credited with discovery of oxygen and a celebrated Unitarian pastor, Jesus ranked slightly above Socrates as a moral philosopher. Jefferson reshaped the Gospels to produce a quadrilingual "Life and Morals of Jesus," which left out everything the orthodox thought essential but he found unreasonable. Rejecting divine inspiration as well as miracles, Jefferson purged the Gospels of falsehood and irrationality with a scissors-and-paste job that featured Jesus as a splendid moralist in a true Bible based on reason. Along the way Jefferson turned Paul into "the first corruptor" of Jesus' doctrines, Athanasius into an "impious dogmatist," and Calvin into "an atheist" and a worshiper of "Daemonism." In 1866 the Reverend Stuart Robinson of Kentucky recapitulated the orthodox answer: Christian morality has no greater claims than the morality of Socrates or Plato unless grounded in acceptance of Jesus as Savior. Robinson had no patience with those who, confronted by the difficulties of exegesis, sought to rewrite the Gospels in accordance with "the 'advanced thought' above" or "the Jacobinical philanthropism of popular opinion below."[3]

Jefferson did not publish his modest effort – the so-called "Jefferson Bible" appeared long after his death – but his contempt for Christianity as traditional Christians understand the term did not remain a secret. The Reverend Iveson Brookes of Georgia spoke of Jefferson's "mistaken and strange notions of universal liberty and equality" and his "expurgated Bible" as promoting the worst sort of infidelity.

vigorously enough to impress even Voltaire, but he suffered Anthony Collins's bon mot that no one had doubted the existence of God until Clarke tried to prove it: Claude Welch, *Protestant Thought in the Nineteenth Century*, 2 vols. (New Haven, CT, 1972, 1985), 1:36 and, on original sin, 1:263–5. A caveat: Across the United States from the mid-1820s, "The voices contending for the mantle of orthodoxy became a cacophony": Mark A. Noll, *America's God: From Jonathan Edwards to Abraham Lincoln* (New York, 2002), 293.

3 William Meade, *Old Churches, Ministries, and Families of Virginia*, 2 vols. (Berryville, VA, 1978 [1857]), 1:25–6, 399; Francis I. Fesperman, "Jefferson's Bible," *Ohio Journal of Religious Studies*, 4 (1976), 78–82; Charles Mabee, "Thomas Jefferson's Anti-Clerical Bible," *Historical Magazine of the Protestant Episcopal Church*, 48 (1979), 474–6; Thomas Jefferson to Benjamin Waterhouse, June 26, 1822 (Athanasius), and Jefferson to William Short, Apr. 13, 1820 (Paul), in Dickinson W. Adams, ed., *Jefferson's Extracts from the Gospels* (Princeton, NJ, 1983), 405, 392; Thomas Jefferson to John Adams, Apr. 11, 1823, in Lester J. Cappon, ed., *The Adams–Jefferson Letters: The Complete Correspondence between Thomas Jefferson and Abigail and John Adams*, 2 vols. (Chapel Hill, NC, 1959), 2:591 (Calvin); Stuart Robinson, *Discourses of Redemption* (New York, 1866), 54, 152, 391, 402, quote at 391. For a sympathetic treatment of Jefferson's religious views see Edwin S. Gaustad, *Sworn on the Altar of God: A Religious Biography of Thomas Jefferson* (Grand Rapids, MI, 1991).

Robert Howison's *History of Virginia* (1847) castigated Jefferson for denigrating Jesus. A contributor to *Southern Literary Messenger* charged that Jefferson's moral philosophy reeked of the irreligion of French radicalism. George Sawyer of Louisiana, a notable proslavery theorist, indignantly branded Jefferson's version of the New Testament and his rejection of Mary's virginity as "blasphemous." Unitarians, skeptics, and nonbelievers all appealed to Enlightenment philosophy more readily than to the Bible, forcing a shift in religious discourse even for the orthodox – among whom especially the Presbyterians embraced science, citing its compatibility with religion – and exposing deep tension between the Scottish Enlightenment and Calvinist orthodoxy.[4]

To southern theorists the defense of civilization itself required a defense of slavery against the onslaught of apostasy and nihilism, which they traced to an ascendant transatlantic bourgeois worldview and erosion of essential Christian doctrine. Waging war against both German philosophical idealists and French materialists, they culled support for a Christian conservativism appropriate to their slaveholding society from other philosophers, most of whom choked at being used in the proslavery cause. In the 1850s the southern religious and college press concentrated fire on atheism, agnosticism, and pantheism, linking them to abolitionism and political radicalism. The principal target shifted. Charles Hodge of Princeton Theological Seminary and leading southern intellectuals, clerical and lay, considered the materialism implicit in pantheism more dangerous than atheism, arguing that if God is everything, He is nothing. James Henley Thornwell dreaded agnosticism: Atheists, being anti-God, might be won to belief; agnostics, believing in nothing, could be converted to nothing. "Practical atheists abound" the Reverend William Plumer fumed in 1864; pantheism, a "monstrous system" was akin to antitheism – by its own logic a "very stupid and very wicked" de facto atheism. Sidney Bumpass, editor of the Methodist *Weekly Messenger,* criticized preachers and religious writers for concentrating on Voltaire, Paine, and others he grouped as infidels instead of on David Friedrich Strauss, who represented a more formidable challenge to Christian doctrine than passé atheism.[5]

---

[4] Iveson L. Brookes, *A Defence of the South against the Reproaches of the North* (Hamburg, SC, 1850), 8, 22; Robert R. Howison, *A History of Virginia from Its Discovery and Settlement by Europeans to the Present Time,* 2 vols. (Philadelphia, 1846), 2:299; "J. T. C." [John T. Clarke], "Mr. Rives' Address," *SLM,* 13 (1847), 574–5; George S. Sawyer, *Southern Institutes; Or, an Inquiry into the Origin and Early Prevalence of Slavery and the Slave Trade* (New York, 1967 [1858]), 207–8. As Sawyer saw, the litmus test of orthodoxy was becoming the virgin birth: *DCA,* 264. Between Catholics and Protestants the bone of contention soon became the Immaculate Conception.

   Mark A. Noll aptly observes that the move of Jonathan Blanchard, Albert Barnes, Henry Ward Beecher, and Gerrit Smith from the Word to the Spirit "led directly or indirectly to the theological liberalism of the last third of the twentieth century": "The Bible and Slavery," in Randall M. Miller et al., eds., *Religion and the American Civil War* (New York, 1998), 51, also, Noll, *America's God,* 49; on the tension in Presbyterianism see Noll, "The Irony of the Enlightenment for Presbyterians in the Early Republic," *JER,* 5 (1985), 149–75.

[5] For Harry Hammond of South Carolina, the French Revolution and the Terror taught what happens with worship of the Goddess of Reason: [Hammond], "European Correspondence," *RM,* 2 (1857/58),

By the nineteenth century a substantial portion of the educated classes in Europe seemed no longer to believe in revealed religion. Christians as different as William Wilberforce, Friedrich Schleiermacher, and Pope Pius IX considered new historical studies a threat to religion more dangerous than science. A counterattack against extreme rationalism and skepticism ranged from an inflexible defense of orthodoxy, at one end, to romantic flights of fancy, at the other. Philosophically, romantics tried to classify subject with object to reconcile man with nature. Like the rationalists, they could not accept the Bible as literally true, and they, too, understood Jesus as what Jaroslav Pelikan has referred to as "the poet of the Spirit." Schleiermacher placed "feeling" at the center of his theology, and Samuel Taylor Coleridge, who powerfully influenced New England, followed suit. G. W. F. Hegel, whose own philosophical project undermined Christian orthodoxy as much as any, quipped that if the emphasis on feeling were justified then dogs would be the most religious of beings.[6]

James Henley Thornwell, like Hegel, took Schleiermacher's "feeling" to mean "subjective emotion" and a plunge into airy psychology. Schleiermacher had intended a sense of immediate awareness of and total dependence upon God, the ground of being beyond subject and object, but he was open to the criticism. As the Baptist theologian Timothy George has put it, his "turn to the subject" transformed

---

40. For the connection between abolitionism, infidelity, and German heresies that undermined faith in the Bible, see [Patrick Hues Mell], *Slavery. A Treatise, Showing that Slavery Is Neither a Moral, Political, nor Social Evil* (Pennfield, GA, 1844); "Domestic Slavery," *SLM*, 11 (1845), 524–5.

[Charles Hodge], "Theology in Germany," *BRPR*, 25 (1853), 430; Charles Hodge, *Systematic Theology*, 3 vols. (Grand Rapids, MI, 1993 [1871]), 1:23, 242, ch. 3, 309, 329–30; Thornwell to Holmes, June 17, 1856, in B. M. Palmer, *The Life and Letters of James Henley Thornwell* (Richmond, VA, 1875), 398–9; *JHTW*, 1:53–4, 206–7, 491–512; 3:264–71; *Weekly Messenger,* May 15, 1851; William S. Plumer, *The Law of God as Contained in the Ten Commandments, Explained and Enforced* (Harrisonburg, VA, 1996 [1864]), ch. 14, quotes at 114–15, 117; see also "W.", "Man's Inventions – God's Instrumentalities," *SRCR*, 1 (1852), 194–209, as well as *SRCR*, 1 (1851), 4; Charles S. Stringfellow, *VUM*, 3 (1858), 71; *TSW*, 46; Robert L. Dabney, *Systematic Theology* (Carlisle, PA, 1985 [1878]), 14, 22–6, 249–50, 289–91, 617. In the 1890s John L. Girardeau, attacking Schleiermacher, again made pantheism the prime enemy: *Discussions of Theological Questions,* ed. George A. Blackburn (Harrisonburg, VA, 1986 [1905, written in 1890s]), 75–86, 134, 277, quote at 86. In the 1850s and during the War, Albert Taylor Bledsoe and an array of preachers still feared widespread atheism, primarily in the North: Bledsoe, *A Theodicy; Or, Vindication of the Divine Glory, as Manifested in the Constitution and Government of the Moral World* (New York, 1853), 24; A. H. H. Boyd, *Thanksgiving Sermon Delivered in Winchester, Va.* (Winchester, VA, 1860), 12–13; William Norwood, *God and Our Country: A Sermon* (Richmond, VA, 1863), 3–4, 10–11; I. T. Tichenor, *Fast-Day Sermon* (Montgomery, AL, 1863), 1; "Rationalism False and Unreasonable," *SPR*, 16 (1863), 246–8; Plumer, *Law of God*, 115–28.

6 In general see Pelikan, *Christian Tradition,* 5:174, 199–201, and ch. 4; also, Jaroslav Pelikan, *Jesus through the Centuries: His Place in the History of Culture* (New Haven, CT, 1985), 189 and ch. 16; B. M. G. Reardon, *Religion in the Age of Romanticism: Studies in Early Nineteenth Century Thought* (Cambridge, U.K., 1985), esp. 2–5, 8, 14, 29, 110. For Hegel's quip see Welch, *Protestant Thought,* 1:94. For the generations between 1680 and 1815 see Willis B. Glover, *Biblical Origins of Secular Culture: An Essay in the Interpretation of Western History* (Macon, GA, 1984), 9–10. For Coleridge's *Aid to Reflection* (1825) in America see James Turner, *Without God, Without Creed: The Origins of Unbelief in America* (Baltimore, 1985), 106–7.

"Thus saith the Lord" into "It seems to me." Schleiermacher's intentions notwithstanding, the churches' preaching of "feeling" encouraged men to stay home and leave church to women. Although Schleiermacher's view of religion deeply penetrated the North, only slowly did Southerners like Thomas Peck and Basil Manly, Jr., single him out for criticism in their reaction to the mounting denial of basic doctrine and the divine inspiration of Scripture. Thornwell considered Schleiermacher, like Strauss, a disguised Deist and recoiled from something Schleiermacher did not intend but left himself open to: diminution of Jesus to moral philosopher. For Thornwell, Schleiermacher and his liberal admirers had created a man-centered religion. (Karl Barth would later criticize Schleiermacher for leading to a theology that ended in "the death of God.") Thornwell thought Schleiermacher right to make feeling the essence of religion but wrong to make feeling, "subjectively considered," a sense of absolute dependence on God. Thornwell found nothing moral in dependence per se since people could know themselves to be in the hands of God and yet hate his power. The virtue lay not in the sense of dependence but in love of that dependence. Besides, "The accomplished Schleiermacher could make no more of sin than Fichte or Hegel."[7]

In 1847 an anonymous contributor to *Southern Quarterly Review* casually referred to Hegel as "a man of decided genius," and soon a few of the most accomplished intellectuals, mostly divines, were studying his work. Mary Howard Schoolcraft referred to his *Philosophy of History* as "an imperishable monument to human genius," and L. Q. C. Lamar took comfort in its historical treatment of slavery and race. T. W. Hoit of Missouri, in a widely circulated racist diatribe entitled *The Right of American Slavery*, cited the English translations of Hegel's *Philosophy of History* and Schlegel's *Philosophy of the History of Man* to denigrate Africans.[8]

Although Hegel influenced the theologically liberal James Warley Miles and his *Philosophic Theology*, almost all Southerners who knew Hegel rejected his objective idealism. Southerners also had an intense distaste for system-building and should have loved Søren Kierkegaard's sally: "Socrates said quite ironically that he did not

---

7 Paul Tillich, *A History of Christian Thought, From Its Judaic and Hellenistic Origins to Existentialism*, ed. Carl E. Braaten (New York, 1972), 392–4; Welch, *Protestant Thought*, 2:ch. 1. See also Colin Brown, *Jesus in European Protestant Thought, 1778–1860* (Grand Rapids, MI, 1985), ch. 3; Timothy George, "Revival of Baptist Theology," in Timothy George and David S. Dockery, eds., *Baptist Theologians* (Nashville, TN, 1990), 16; T. E. Peck, *Miscellanies*, ed. T. C. Johnson, 3 vols. (Richmond, VA, 1895–97), 2:49; Basil Manly, Jr., *The Bible Doctrine of Inspiration* (Nashville, TN, 1995 [1888]), 50–1. In *JHTW* see quote at 2:470, 3:222–6, quote at 1:505; Karl Barth, "Concluding Unscientific Postscript on Schleiermacher," in Clifford Green, ed., *Karl Barth: Theologian of Freedom* (Minneapolis, MN, 1991), 66–90, quote at 80. See also Supplementary References: "Schleiermacher."

8 "American Literature – 1," *SQR*, 11 (1847), 157–60, quote at 154, which included rare good words about objective idealism; "Black Gauntlet," in *Plantation Life: The Narratives of Mrs. Henry Schoolcraft* (New York, 1969 [1860]), 405; L. Q. C. Lamar, Feb. 21, 1860, in *Congressional Globe*, 36th Cong., 1st Sess., App. 113–17; T. W. Hoit, *The Right of American Slavery* (St. Louis, MO, 1860), 11–12 (Hoit's publisher claimed a sale of 500,000 for its two editions); also, *DBR*, 20 (1856), 520. Hegel's *Philosophy of History* was translated into English in 1857.

know whether he was a human being or something else, but an Hegelian can say with due solemnity in the confessional: 'I do not know whether I am a human being – but I have understood the System.' I for my part would rather say: 'I know that I am a human being, and I know that I have not understood the System.'" *Southern Presbyterian Review* led the barrage against Hegel's objective idealism. D. H. Hill, with an eye on the "Left-Hegelians" from whose ranks Ludwig Feuerbach and Karl Marx sprang, derided the "ignorant or rash scholars" who embraced Hegel's philosophy. Hegel, he wrote, reduced theology to a branch of philosophy and the Trinity to discoverable philosophical truth. George Howe fell back on a saw: God gave the English the seas, the French the land, and the Germans the clouds. New England's Enoch Pond said Hegel, Immanuel Kant, Friedrich von Schelling, and other German philosophers had no fixed principles. He and another writer in *Southern Presbyterian Review* complained that they denied God's authority and made men aspire to be gods.[9]

Thornwell damned Leibniz, Hegel, Johann Gottlieb Fichte, and Friedrich von Schelling for endless speculation, for "aspiration to omniscience," and for reluctance "to accept any constitutional beliefs." He judged pantheism and positivism alike in their rejection of a personal God and a divine Creation. Ever since Locke, Thornwell grumbled, English philosophy, too, has been largely "a confession of human ignorance."[10]

Hegel, portraying Jesus as a divinely inspired human being who preached virtue as an emanation of man's being, subordinated Revelation to Reason. God's will and morality lie within us. Hegel thereby gave a mighty impetus to the transformation of Christianity into a code of ethics. He viewed the doctrine of original sin as a projection by people who regarded themselves chosen yet had to confront the corruption of everyday life. The doctrine of original sin offered solace in degradation and excused their direct responsibility. Hegel implicitly rejected the Pauline doctrine of the Atonement and the orthodox understanding of the Trinity. His anthropology led to Feuerbach and on to Marxism. Dethroning theology as Queen of

---

[9] Kierkegaard quoted in Brown, *Jesus in Protestant Thought*, 145; D. H. Hill, "The Bible, and Not Reason, the Only Certain and Authoritative Source of Our Knowledge," *SPR*, 7 (1853), 335–7, quote at 335; [George Howe], "The Genuineness of the Pentateuch," *SPR*, 4 (1850), 258; [Enoch Pond], "Objections to the German Transcendental Philosophy," *SPR*, 4 (1851), 333–4; "Sufficiency of the Scriptures," *SPR*, 7 (1853), 243. Plumer quoted Kant approvingly on morals in his *Law of God*, 9. Thornwell, although usually respectful, sometimes treated Kant harshly: *JHTW*, 3:118–20, 128, 144–5. Feuerbach was especially popular among the German intellectuals who emigrated to America in the wake of the Revolution of 1848. George Eliot celebrated Feuerbach and promoted the English translation of his *Essence of Christianity*. See Hanley, *Beyond a Christian Commonwealth*, 112–16. See also Supplementary References: "Hegel."

[10] In *JHTW* see 1:494, 3:84–6, 98, 148–9, 265, quotes at 86; James Oscar Farmer, Jr., *The Metaphysical Confederacy: James Henley Thornwell and the Synthesis of Southern Values* (Macon, GA, 1986), 193. For Schelling as a pantheist see also [Enoch Pond], "Coleridge," *SPR*, 2 (1861), 51. Daniel K. Whitaker found much to praise as well as criticize in Fichte. He thought Fichte had refuted the charge of atheism and that his idealism was at war with Transcendentalism: [Whitaker], "Critical Notices," *SQR*, 10 (1846), 253–4.

the Sciences, he subsumed it in an all-encompassing philosophy of transcendence. S. J. Barnett, Esq., pithily expressed the southern response when he extolled the-ology as the "sanction and sanctifier of knowledge." William Porcher Miles, who acknowledged Hegel's metaphysics as profound, deplored the influence of objective idealism and the materialism it paradoxically encouraged. The Methodist Reverend W. Rees of Austin, Texas, called for vigilance against Hegel and "the barren and icy rocks of atheism, that would resolve God into a dead idealism." A deistic and skep-tical age was trying "to philosophize God out of His own creation." A contributor to *Southern Presbyterian Review* noted that, for Hegel, human self-consciousness was the only route to an understanding of God. And in truth, Hegel had trans-formed God into an objectified self-consciousness, conflating the nature of God and man, but to the day he died he maintained that his philosophy, far from being atheistic, explicated Christianity.[11]

With mounting fervor, southern journals in the 1850s placed rival understandings of Christian doctrine at the heart of the broader sectional struggle. *Southern Liter-ary Messenger* tirelessly reiterated that the North's "isms" assaulted the principle of authority, biblical or other. George Frederick Holmes saw the centuries-long strug-gle between science and religion as being in an especially hazardous phase. Faith and "evidence of things not seen" lay at the foundation of all reasoning, whatever the philosophical method: "If there be an impassable chasm between religious faith and scientific knowledge, religion must ultimately be the sacrifice." Holmes denied that science could solve the ultimate mysteries of the universe. The North, John Randolph Tucker went to far as to protest in 1861, hated the South's "religion – its Bible – its God."[12]

Protestant churches that loudly affirmed orthodoxy were abandoning doctrines long considered *sine qua non*. The churches' inadequate responses to the scien-tific revolution encouraged the equation of Christianity with obscurantism, and, increasingly, nineteenth-century cultural leaders slighted theology as an effete pas-time. The heterodox measured the intellectual respectability of theology by the extent to which it met the tests of philosophy cloaked as science.[13]

[11] G. W. F. Hegel, *Early Theological Writings*, tr. T. M. Knox and Richard Kroner (Philadelphia, 1948), esp. 159–60, 224–5, 226 n. 51; for an appraisal of Hegel on Jesus see Brown, *Jesus in Protestant Thought*, ch. 2; [S. J. Barnett], "Buckle's History of Civilization," *SPR*, 17 (1866), 214; [William Porcher Miles], "Philosophy of Spinoza," *SQR*, 16 (1849), 79; W. Rees, *A Sermon on Divine Provi-dence* (Austin, TX, 1863), 3, 5; "Rationalism False and Unreasonable," 176. Barnett was following St. Anselm's *"credo ut intelligam"* [I believe in order to understand].

[12] "Northern Mind and Character," *SLM*, 31 (1860), 343; "B.", "The New Social Propositions," *SLM*, 20 (1858), 294–306, esp. 297; see also "J. A. W.", "De Servitude," *SLM*, 20 (1854), 425–7; [George Frederick Holmes], "Philosophy and Faith," *MMQR*, 4th ser., 3 (1851), 186, 206, 209–10, quotes at 206, 209; [Holmes], "Alchemy and the Alchemists," *MMQR*, 4th ser., 8 (1856), 468–86; [Holmes], "The Positive Religion," *MMQR*, 4th ser., 6 (1854), 332–3; [John Randolph Tucker], "The Great Issue," *SLM*, 32 (1861), 170. On Strauss, H. H. Milman, and the controversies, see Supplementary References: "Bible Criticism."

[13] For the movement to subsume religion – not merely theology – under philosophy, see Brown, *Jesus in Protestant Thought*, ch. 2.

David Friedrich Strauss's widely read *Life of Jesus,* translated by George Eliot, had made Jesus all too human. Americans were also hearing from such German theologians as Ferdinand Christian Bauer that historical theology must replace dogmatics. The radical Unitarian Theodore Parker of Boston provided an influential translation of W. M. L. deWette's *Critical and Historical Introduction to the Canonical Scripture of the Old Testament,* and George Freeman Clarke translated Karl von Hase's Straussian *Life of Jesus.* If before the War few Americans questioned the existence of Jesus, the groundwork had long been laid. Adoring Bostonians packed Parker's church and turned out by the thousands for his lectures, which argued that the great truths of Christianity stood apart from the Word and were available through human intuition. Although many "respectable" New Englanders loathed Parker and the more traditional Unitarians thought him extreme, Southerners primarily noticed his popularity. They also noticed that Parker, William Ellery Channing, John Gorham Palfrey, and other antislavery Northerners accepted German higher criticism and denied the Trinity, the virgin birth, and other dogmas. For Thomas Thornton of Mississippi, abolitionism was the logical consequence of religious subjectivism; for Frederick Porcher, Parker and Lyman Beecher "put to shame the irreverent infidelity of Voltaire"; for a contributor to *Southern Quarterly Review,* the northern clergy "prostitutes itself to the level of the blackguard."[14]

German theologians who turned to history to demonstrate the truths of Christianity undermined faith thereby, however unintentionally. Thus, H. S. Reimarus and Gottfried Lessing pioneered in a historical criticism of the Bible that eroded faith in miracles, and Strauss demanded that faith in Jesus be bolstered through historians' judgment of His life. When higher criticism aimed at establishing the authorship and historical authenticity of the Bible, literalists took the bait and made defense of the historicity of Jesus the acid test of faith. Karl Barth, surveying the ruins, sardonically referred to "the none too dignified flight of the cleverest brains into the study of history."[15]

---

[14] T. C. Thornton, *An Inquiry into the History of Slavery* (Washington, DC, 1841), 184–6; F. A. Porcher, "The Nature and the Claims of Paradox," *RM,* 1 (1857), 488; "The North and the South," *SQR,* n.s., 1 (1855), 2–4. Parker was Garrison's pastor and strongly influenced him. Prominent women abolitionists questioned the authority of Scripture: Anna M. Speicher, *The Religious World of Antislavery Women: Spirituality in the Lives of Five Abolitionist Lecturers* (Syracuse, NY, 2000), ch. 3; Lydia Maria Child, *The Progress of Religious Ideas, through Successive Ages,* 3 vols. (New York, 1855), 2:154–84. Planters Samuel Perkins Allison of Kentucky and George Jones of Georgia read Strauss's *Life of Jesus:* Olmsted to Charles Brace Loring, Dec. 1, 1853, in Charles Capen McLaughlin, ed., *Papers of Frederick Law Olmsted, 1822–1857,* 6 vols. (Baltimore, 1977–), 2:234 (Allison); William Harris Bragg, *De Renne: Three Generations of a Georgia Family* (Athens, GA, 1999), 22 (Jones).

[15] On the corrosive effect of historical studies on confidence in the infallibility of the Word see Pelikan, *Christian Tradition,* 5:243–4, Barth quoted at 75; Hans W. Frei, *The Eclipse of Biblical Narrative: A Study in Eighteenth and Nineteenth Century Hermeneutics* (New Haven, CT, 1974), 10–11, 82–4. Adolph von Harnack, from the liberal side, saw a natural tendency in Christianity to verify its articles of faith but also wanted its universal and supernatural character upheld against "our wavering knowledge of nature and history": Harnack, *Outline of the History of Dogma,* tr. Edwin Knox Mitchell (Boston, 1957), 1–2, quote at 2. In the 1850s the higher criticism made little impact on the southern churches, but it began to shake the northern.

A good minister – or so the Presbyterian Reverend Francis Cummins of Abbeville, South Carolina, remarked – knows the Bible to be coherent and, when properly understood, never self-contradictory. Everyone agrees, William Hobby of Georgia was sure, that "The Bible alone contains the revealed will of God" and His moral law. The New School Reverend Joseph Stiles: "If we let go the word of God, where shall we fix our hold?" The Old School Reverend Thomas Smyth: "Reason has, in all ages, rendered man shamefully unreasonable." Smyth rebuked the ignorance, arrogance, and illusions of self-sufficiency of philosophers as a great source of error. Reason must be understood as the interpreter of the Bible, but not its legislator or judge. Southern as well as northern Calvinists denied that science contradicted the Bible and followed Thomas Reid and the Scottish Enlightenment in separating subject from object to account for a real world outside human consciousness.[16]

Smyth spoke for most clergymen when, referring to Francis Bacon as "the father of philosophy," he simultaneously extolled science as the handmaiden of religion and set limits to science's access to knowledge. Even in Eden, Thornwell said, man depended not merely on nature and reason but also on divine Revelation. Thornwell resisted the contention that God must remain unknowable, and in later years the Reverend John Girardeau, invoking Charles Hodge, remarked, "The Bible republishes natural theology."[17]

The Presbyterian Reverend Robert Lewis Dabney of Virginia, a formidable theologian, told his students that faith did not demand acceptance of Scripture as God's word without rational evidence. Faith supports "right reason" by recognizing, "on reasonable grounds," the infallibility of the Word, but the Word, independent of reason, does not settle everything: "The whole process of salvation, however spiritual, must also be rational." Dabney criticized rationalists who denied the infallibility

---

[16] Francis Cummins, *The Spiritual Watchman's Character, Call, and Duty* (Charleston, SC, 1795), 4 (quoted), 7–8; [William Hobby], *Remarks upon Slavery, Occasioned by Attempts Made to Circulate Improper Publications in the Southern States. By a Citizen of Georgia*, 2nd ed. (Augusta, GA, 1835), 3; J. C. Stiles, *National Rectitude the Only True Basis of National Prosperity* (Petersburg, VA, 1863), 10; *TSW*, 9:27–8, 35, 54.

[17] *TSW*, 5:538; "Theological Lectures," in *JHTW*: 1:31, 53–73, 87, 107, 113, 121–2, 127, 142, 342; Girardeau, *Theological Questions*, 4, 44. When Thornwell declared moral philosophy a branch of theology, he spoke for an interdenominational southern consensus: E. Brooks Holifield, *The Gentlemen Theologians: American Theology in Southern Culture, 1795–1860* (Durham, NC, 1978), 127. Southern theologians embraced Baconian induction, convinced that a scientific theology must appeal to the data of Nature but also that scientists who claim to "prove" their theories never actually do so. Divines contributed articles on science to secular journals, and secular writers contributed articles on religion to denominational journals. For John Bachman, if nature's data seemed at variance with the Bible, then the Bible had to be reexamined to find the error in interpretation. See John Bachman, *The Doctrine of the Unity of the Human Races* (Charleston, SC, 1850), and Jay Schuler, *Had I the Wings: The Friendship of Bachman and Audubon* (Athens, GA, 1995), 214. For the compatibility of geology with revealed Christianity by a professor of natural science, see E. F. Rockwell, *Inaugural Address before the Board of Trustees of Davidson College* (Salisbury, NC, 1851), 15. The indispensable introduction to the centrality of Baconian induction to American religious thought is Theodore Dwight Bozeman's *Protestants in an Age of Science: The Baconian Ideal and Antebellum American Religious Thought* (Chapel Hill, NC, 1977).

of the Word and who wound up doubting everything and knowing nothing. In a wartime tribute to "The Christian Soldier," Dabney echoed a famous passage in Pascal's *Pensées,* "For the heart is nobler, wiser, greater than the head. The speculations of the head are cold and devoid of moral trait. It is the impulses of the heart which characterize man as a moral being."[18]

Although the South, like the North, pursued scientific interests, it effectively resisted the spread of skepticism. The orthodox countered Hume, whose professed defense of religion denied that the existence of an all-powerful, all-wise, all-good God could be inferred from the design of nature. Augustine, too, had appealed both to nature and the Bible, but for him observation helps determine belief only by providing testimony and remaining subject to authoritative interpretation. With the fragmentation unleashed by the Reformation, Jansenism, and Jesuitical "probablism," probability increasingly became the standard of authority.[19]

The first natural science that threatened Christianity was geology, with its mid–eighteenth-century historical accounts at variance with Genesis on the creation of the world. Of all the sciences, J. J. Ampère wrote in 1855, geology is especially popular with Americans for it touches "aux deux chers plus interêts de la société americaine – la religion et la richesse." Still, theologians well into the nineteenth century were interpreting geological findings as supportive of Scripture. Perhaps Harvard, Yale, and other colleges might have invested less heavily in scientific education had they taken the measure of the impending challenge. By 1850, when they began to appreciate the stakes, most divines were continuing to deny any contradiction between religion and science.[20]

The orthodox answered that the Bible was infallible but its interpreters were not. Hodge, Thornwell, and John Leadley Dagg saw no problems with astronomy and geology: They viewed the dating of the earth, like the Copernican system, as within the sphere of an empirical investigation that helped Christians better understand the words of the Bible. Albert Taylor Bledsoe, mathematician and unchurched theologian, saw no reason for apprehension that the forward movement of science would encourage man's presumption, which "is, indeed, the natural offspring of ignorance, and not of knowledge." The Methodist Reverend A. Means of Georgia announced that science, purged of infidelity and materialism, was now safely at the service of Scripture. Among laymen, Thomas Clingman lectured on the compatibility of science and religion, and Edmund Ruffin, John Reuben Thompson, and William Gilmore Simms welcomed Hugh Miller's *Testimony of the Rocks* as undermining biblical literalism while demonstrating the compatibility of geology and

[18] *DD,* 1:116, 181, also 3:152–72; Robert L. Dabney, *Sacred Rhetoric: A Course of Lectures on Preaching* (Richmond, VA, 1870), 191–2, quote at 189; Holifield, *Gentlemen Theologians,* 80–1. Augustine wrote, "Academic philosophy has so prevailed as to be still more wretchedly insane by doubting all things": "On the Trinity," in Philip and Henry Wace, eds., *Nicene and Post-Nicene Fathers,* 2nd ser., 14 vols. (Peabody, MA, 1995), 3:211.
[19] Nancey Murphy, *Theology in the Age of Scientific Reasoning* (Ithaca, NY, 1990), ch. 1.
[20] Herbert Hovenkamp, *Science and Religion in America, 1800–1860* (Philadelphia, 1978), 119, 122; J. J. Ampère, *Promenade en Amérique,* 2 vols. (Paris, 1855), 1:323.

religion. The Reverend J. C. Mitchell, pastor of the Second Presbyterian Church of Mobile, credited Hugh Miller with "forcefully" asserting that inferior races cannot survive competition with superior races.[21]

Dabney had qualms. Before and more strongly after the War, when southern orthodoxy started to unravel, he denied science's competence to evaluate the six-day Creation and protested concessions by theologians as invitations to skepticism. Dabney complained that Miller's *Testimony of the Rocks,* which purported to defend theology in the light of geology, actually undermined it by making the Bible depend on science and philosophy. Like the abolitionist Albert Barnes, Miller made philosophy the standard of truth. Augustus Baldwin Longstreet depicted the War as struggle between a "Christ-taught band" and a "science-taught band." Thornwell welcomed articles in *Southern Presbyterian Review* by the eminent scientist Joseph LeConte that considered the object of the sciences to be establishment of "the universality of law" and "unity in the midst of diversity." LeConte struggled to defend Calvinist orthodoxy, but after the War he slid toward theological liberalism and appealed less to the Bible than to natural theology. Natural science to him became the ultimate arbiter of biblical truth. Indeed, Dabney did not think theologians should teach science at all since – apart from an occasional John Bachman – they did it superficially and, awed by scientific complexities, easily made disastrous concessions to materialism. In 1869, Dabney arraigned even orthodox theologians for inadvertently yielding to materialism and for blindness to the extent and force of "the ulterior tendency" in modern thought. He predicted that within two or three generations skepticism and infidelity would overwhelm Christianity in elite circles and in the educational system: "After a time the church will have more trouble with her defenders than with her assailants; for the spirit of these sciences is essentially infidel and rationalistic."[22]

Religious leaders generally dismissed theories of evolution as anti-Christian, but as Darwinism spread they had increasing difficulty upholding the compatibility of

[21] Jon H. Roberts, *Darwin and the Divine in America: Protestant Intellectuals and Organic Evolution, 1859–1900* (Madison, WI, 1988), 22–3; Hodge, *Systematic Theology,* 1:165; *JHTW,* 3:218–20, 275–6; J. L. Dagg, *Manual of Theology: A Treatise on Christian Doctrine and a Treatise on Church Order,* 2 vols. (New York, 1980 [1857–58]), 1:ch. 2; Bledsoe, *Theodicy,* 19. A. Means, "God in Jesus Christ," in William T. Smithson, ed., *The Methodist Pulpit South* (Washington, DC, 1858), 115; *Selections from the Speeches and Writings of Hon. Thomas L. Clingman of North Carolina* (Raleigh, NC, 1877); July 8, 1859, in *ERD,* 1:315–16; [J. R. Thompson], *SLM,* 17 (1851), 192; [William Gilmore Simms], "Critical Notices," *SQR,* 3 (1851), 274–5; J. C. Mitchell, *A Bible Defence of Slavery and the Unity of Mankind* (Mobile, AL, 1861), 30–1. For Testimony of the Rocks see Bozeman, *Protestants in an Age of Science,* 95, 106–7.

[22] *DD,* 2:73–4; Dabney, *Systematic Theology,* 139–41, 253–63 (it is unclear how Dabney reconciled his position with his insistence that faith did not demand acceptance of the divinity of Scriptures in advance of rational evidence); Ernest Trice Thompson, *Presbyterians in the South,* 3 vols. (Richmond, VA, 1963), 2:454–5; John Donald Wade, *Augustus Baldwin Longstreet: A Study of the Development of Culture in the South* (New York, 1924), 267–8; J. LeConte, "Morphology and Its Connection with Fine Art," *SPR,* 12 (1859), 104–5; Lester D. Stephens, *Joseph LeConte: Gentle Prophet of Evolution* (Baton Rouge, LA, 1982), 130–1 and ch. 12.

science and religion. The orthodox looked to "evidences of Christianity" to support their theology but with diminishing success. Before the War the divines held their own, and with few exceptions southern clergymen agreed that natural science, properly interpreted, confirmed Scripture. The more theology became "liberal" in its concessions to the new science, the weaker the hold of religion on the thinking of intellectuals and ordinary men. In the popular mind, as well as in the highest intellectual circles, scientists emerged as the arbiters of truth.

In politics as in science, southern theologians found themselves at bay. Although in Europe the confessional Protestant churches and the Catholic Church offered stiff resistance to theological liberalism, their brand of conservatism – deeply compromised with monarchical political reaction – did not play well in republican America. The course of both European and American theological conservatism proved excruciatingly complex and contradictory, but it is clear that conservatives who supported the Prussian state bet on an unreliable horse. In the second half of the century, marked by German imperial unification and the consolidation of the Union in America, the new regimes accommodated to the culture as well as to the economics of industrialism and threw their weight on the side of the secularists and the liberal divines who tailed them.[23]

By the eighteenth century, the most influential shapers of European and American religious opinion had already gone a long way toward transforming faith into rational assent. While vigorously combating Deism, they capitulated to the Deist concept of a God whose claims rested upon an ability to compel intellectual assent to natural law. It did not take long to decide that God's demand to be worshiped – even God's existence – depended upon divine adherence to man-made morality. Southern divines, challenging this view at every turn, prefigured James Turner's conclusion in *Without God, Without Creed*: "Religion caused unbelief. In trying to adapt their religious beliefs to socioeconomic change, to new moral challenges, to novel problems of knowledge, to tightening standards of science, the defenders of God slowly strangled him. If anyone is to be arraigned for deicide, it is not Charles Darwin but his adversary Bishop Samuel Wilberforce, not the godless Ingersoll but the godly Beecher family."[24]

Struggles over the Bible and the U.S. Constitution centered on the relation of Word to Spirit and understanding of the Holy Spirit. Southerners indicted the northern

[23] For the confessional churches' response in Britain, Germany, and America to theological liberalism and their political position, see Walter H. Conser, *Church and Confession: Conservative Theologians in Germany, England, and America, 1815–1866* (Macon, GA, 1984).

[24] Turner, *Without God, Without Creed*, 63, 73, quote at 86–7. Modern secularization, M. H. Abrams comments, did not delete and replace religious ideas; rather, it assimilated and reinterpreted them as "constitutive elements in a world view founded on secular premises": Abrams, *Natural Supernaturalism: Tradition and Revolution in Romantic Literature* (New York, 1971), 13. Professions of infidelity receded steadily in America in large part because of religious liberalism's concessions to secularism, which left "progressively less to be infidel about," and in the twentieth century the concept of infidelity virtually disappeared in the churches: Martin E. Marty, *The Infidel: Freethought and American Religion* (Cleveland, OH, 1961), 14.

churches for substituting the subjectivism of individual conscience for the Word of the Bible – and the Constitution. The orthodox upheld the Holy Spirit, objectively understood, charging that liberals reduced it to the spirit of everyman. The liberals' retreat into a subjectively conceived spirit threatened Protestantism's effort to replace the hierarchical, sacramental Catholic Church with unmediated direct access to the Word. The radical revivalists of New York's Burned-Over District preached both Word and Spirit, but the Spirit seemed to be almost everything. Southerners knew Antinomianism when they saw it and drew a straight line from this "deepest depravity of the human heart," as Plumer called it in Richmond, to abolitionism. Defending the Word against skeptics and backsliders, the Episcopalian Reverend C. P. Gardner of St. Luke's Church in Charleston allowed that Scripture did not contain the whole of God's Word but quickly added that the Spirit did not contradict the testimony of Scripture. Lest he be misunderstood, he expressed admiration for Thornwell and Calhoun.[25]

For Thornwell, although God had committed Himself to written documents as the abiding standard of faith, the Bible and Spirit were equally essential to Protestantism. In a passionate outburst he cautioned, "The Word alone cannot save us; it is the means but not the source of life. The Bible without the Spirit is a dead letter, as the spirit without the Bible is a lying delusion. The Spirit *and* the Bible, this is the great principle of Protestant Christianity." He implicitly followed Justin, the early Christian martyr, in acknowledging truths other than those in the Bible and in Christianity's absorption of all truth. But he flayed liberals for introducing "havoc and desolation" by replacing the Bible as an authoritative standard of faith with "dim intimations of sentiment and feeling, chastened and regulated by the natural sympathy of earnest and awakened minds." Thornwell continued, "Let the authority of the Bible be destroyed, and Christianity must soon perish from the earth. Put its doctrines upon any other ground than a 'thus saith the Lord,' and every one of them will soon be denied." Paul "knew nothing of an inspiration of the Spirit as contradistinguished from an inspiration of the letter." Faith signals "recognition of God in the Word" and "knows God's voice." Without the Bible, reference to

---

[25] Plumer, *Law of God*, ch. 11, quote at 79; Ernst Troeltsch, *The Social Teachings of the Christian Churches,* tr. Olive Wyon, 2 vols. (London, 1950), 2:478–81; Whitney R. Cross, *The Burned-Over District: The Social and Intellectual History of Enthusiastic Religion in Western New York, 1800– 1860* (New York, 1965), 198; Sydney Ahlstrom, *A Religious History of the American People* (New Haven, CT, 1972), 4, 476, 603; C. P. Gardner, in James H. Elliott, ed., *Tributes to the Memory of the Rev. C. P. Gadsden, with Thirteen of His Sermons* (Charleston, SC, 1872), 111–14, 120, 122. "Holy Ghost" and "Holy Spirit" were used interchangeably, Southerners usually preferring "Ghost." People in all religious camps labeled as "Antinomian" opponents they wished to discredit. Methodists and New School Presbyterians did this to orthodox Calvinists: see e.g. Zebulon Crocker, *The Catastrophe of the Presbyterian Church in 1837* (New Haven, CT, 1838), 77–8. On the relation of these theological currents to political radicalism see Carl T. Guarnieri, *The Utopian Alternative: Fourierism in Nineteenth-Century America* (Ithaca, NY, 1991), 68, 115–20, 154, 278–83. For Old School Presbyterian fears of Antinomian tendencies in the New School, see Morton H. Smith, *Studies in Southern Presbyterian Theology* (Phillipsburg, NJ, 1962), 96–100, 140. The Baptist Hosea Holcombe also saw Antinomianism as a problem in his church: *A History of the Rise and Progress of the Baptists in Alabama* (Philadelphia, 1840), 50, 292.

the Holy Spirit becomes a mere expression of the spirit of man and leads to fanaticism. Since "the most enormous crimes" may be committed in the name of religion, "Those who reject the Word under the pretence of being led by the Spirit are guilty of madness as well as error."[26]

Similarly, John Girardeau, a Thornwell protégé, granted that the "inward witness of the spirit" attests to the Holy Ghost but emphasized that the spirit is delivered to the soul, not derived from it. Although faith comes from within, "The Scriptures are an external, ultimately authoritative standard or rule." God's witness comes from without: "If the Bible is one standard, and our experience is another, or if our experience determines the Bible and not the Bible our experience, there is an end to the discussion." The acerbic Reverend Frederick Ross of Alabama, addressing a New School Assembly in New York in 1856, professed himself terrified that when Yankees finally recognized the divine sanction of slavery, as he was sure they would, their penchant for fanaticism and excess would make them so ultra-proslavery that Southerners would have to restrain them. More seriously: "The question is in a nutshell, it is this: *Shall man submit to the revealed word of God or to his own will?*"[27]

Southern Arminians and Calvinists forcefully contrasted northern backsliding with their own orthodoxy and drew sociopolitical conclusions. In the wake of the Denmark Vesey insurrectionary plot of 1822, Richard Furman called abolitionism an assault on the principle of authority, subversive of family and all government. Even the more temperate Richard Fuller considered the war against slave property nothing short of a war against the principle of private property and berated northern divines for abandoning the Word upon which the proslavery case rested. Thomas (later, "Stonewall") Jackson, a Presbyterian layman, saw abolitionism as "the prelude to anarchy, infidelity, and the ultimate loss of free responsible government." Slavery was biblically sanctioned, preached the Baptist Reverend Patrick Hues Mell of Georgia, a professor of ancient languages who recognized no code of morals other than that contained in the sacred Scriptures. Dagg spoke for all wings of the southern Baptist church when he described the Bible as "the perfect source of religious knowledge, and the infallible standard of religious truth." Biblical manuscripts passed through various hands and translators and hence they differ, but not in essentials: "Revelation never contradicts or sets aside the teachings of natural religion."[28]

---

[26] In *JHTW*: 1:34–5, 49; 3:468; 3:18–19, 25, 153, 173, 180–9, 605, quotes at 180–1, 18, 25, 173. On Justin Martyr see Paul Tillich, *Christian Thought,* 27–8. For "The Letter killeth, but the spirit giveth life" (2 Cor., 3:6) see J. S. Lamar, *The Organon of Scripture; Or, the Inductive Method of Biblical Interpretation* (Philadelphia, 1859), 94–5. See also Supplementary References: "Spirit of Christianity."

[27] "The Signs of the Times – In the Church," in *Sermons by John L. Girardeau,* ed. George A. Blackburn (Columbia, SC, 1907), 116–17; Frederick A. Ross, *Slavery Ordained of God* (Philadelphia, 1857), 39, quote at 81.

[28] Furman, "Views of the Baptists," in James A. Rogers, *Richard Furman: Life and Legacy* (Macon, GA, 1985), 281–2; Richard Fuller and Francis Wayland, *Domestic Slavery, Considered as a Scriptural Institution in Correspondence,* 5th ed. (New York, 1847), 2–3, 170–3; Jackson quoted in James I. Robertson, Jr., *Stonewall Jackson, the Man, the Soldier, the Legend* (New York, 1997), 234; [Mell],

Among the Methodists, Bishop Henry Bascom considered the Bible "without doubt or question, as the unerring, unimprovable standard of truth and goodness." Methodists "renounce and abjure all tests and standards, except the Word of God, and the evidence of facts and experience." Bascom sounded the common theme: Natural theology and the sciences demonstrate God's existence and relation to man, but God's nature is known only through Revelation. The Bible settled the slavery question in favor of the slaveholders, and "Slavery as a question of *morality,* can only be settled *by an appeal to the revealed will of God.*" In 1835 the Irish Methodist Adam Clarke opened fire on the reduction of the Holy Spirit to the spirit of man. The Reverend Thomas Boswell of the Memphis Methodist Conference: Since the Spirit operates through the Word, men must fly to Christ or suffer eternal damnation. The power of the largely unlettered Methodist preachers, wrote Bishop George Foster Pierce, stemmed from their zeal and faith, "expecting the presence and unction of the Holy Ghost upon the word, the power of God revealed in awakening and conversion."[29]

The Christianity of Northerners, one contributor to *Southern Quarterly Review* tartly observed, was not necessarily the Christianity of others. Another contrasted the purity of southern religion to "*the northern fungi,* which disfigure the Tree of Life." For Thornwell and Holmes, too, liberals espoused not a different view of Christianity but an essentially different religion. Abraham Lincoln disagreed, John Brown agreed. When local ministers sought to pray with Brown as he awaited execution, he refused: "We do not worship the same God."[30]

More than once Thornwell cited Jesus' warning that those who sin against the Holy Ghost will not be forgiven – in Thornwell's paraphrase, "are damned forever." Southern divines – Thornwell, Robert Breckinridge, Willard Preston – returned again and again to that terrifying warning as they indicted northern churches for substituting egotistical subjectivism for the Holy Ghost. Louisa McCord assailed abolitionism and all social radicalism: "This is indeed the sin not to be forgiven, the sin against the Holy Ghost and against the spirit of God." Add the sermons on

Slavery: A Treatise, 9; Dagg, *Manual of Theology,* 1:21, 54, also 22–5; on Williams see Timothy George, "Revival of Baptist Theology," in George and Dockery, eds., *Baptist Theologians,* 20.

[29] H. B. Bascom, *Sermons from the Pulpit* (Louisville, KY, 1852), 19, 30, 56, 59–60, quotes at 19, 56; H. B. Bascom, *Methodism and Slavery* (Frankfort, KY, 1845), 65; on Clarke see Thomas A. Langford, ed., *Wesleyan Theology: A Sourcebook* (Durham, NC, 1984), 40; Thomas L. Boswell, "Salvation in Its Individual Relations," in Smithson, ed., *Methodist Pulpit South,* 208–9, 218; George G. Smith, *The Life and Times of George Foster Pierce, Bishop of the Methodist Church, South, with a Sketch of Lovick Pierce, D.D., His Father* (Sparta, GA, 1888), 11–12, quote at 12.

[30] "Milman's History of Christianity," *SQR,* 4 (1843), 261–2; "F. P. L." [Francis P. Lea?], "Religion in America," *SQR,* 7 (1845), 371–2, quote at 372; "Standard and Nature of Religion in Three Sections," *JHTW,* 3:9–182; [George Frederick Holmes], "Morell's Philosophy of the Nineteenth Century," *SLM,* 16 (1850), 385–96; Merrill D. Peterson, *John Brown: The Legend Revisited* (Charlottesville, VA, 2002), quote at 18. On two religions, Thornwell foreshadowed J. Gresham Machen's *Liberalism and Christianity* (Chicago, 1923); see also D. G. Hart, *Defending the Faith: J. Gresham Machen and the Crisis of Conservative Protestantism in Modern America* (Baltimore, 1994).

"baptized infidelity" and the message becomes clear: The Yankees were committing the one sin God would not forgive.[31]

Theological quarrels over Word and Spirit brought to the surface the social and political implications of radically different understandings of "benevolence." Martin Luther spoke of "the wrath of His severity," and long afterwards Protestants looked to God as Supreme Judge. But as liberalism became more influential, God emerged primarily as Pure Love – a forgiving father who eschewed eternal punishment. If wrath and love coexisted as two characteristics of one divine personality, the deepening emphasis on the latter characteristic resulted in a subtle, hesitant, and partially disguised metamorphosis of doctrine. Professedly orthodox northern churches slowly absorbed many of the assumptions and much of the rhetoric of their liberal adversaries. God became much less wrathful and much more forgiving – except for His wrath against slaveholders.[32]

A quarrel had arisen over the relation of the Old Testament to the New. An admittedly impressionistic survey of scattered texts from which the southern divines preached does not sustain the commonly held view that Northerners appealed primarily to the teachings of the New Testament and Southerners to the Old. Most Southerners – notwithstanding the Disciples of Christ ("Campbellites"), who stood squarely on the New Testament – upheld the unity of the Bible and resisted efforts to have the New Testament repeal the Old.[33]

Luther himself did not, as often charged, equate the Old Testament with Law and the New with Gospel. He saw Jesus as reaffirming the Law and the Holy Spirit as guiding Moses. But since, according to Scripture, Jesus bore the penalty for man's sin, Baptists – as well as Lutherans who felt themselves in a state of grace – could slip into Antinomianism and decide they need not obey the moral law of the Old Testament. The call to reject the Old Testament picked up momentum and culminated at the end of the nineteenth century with Adolf Harnack: "To have rejected

---

[31] *JHTW*, 1:113–14, 2:365; R. S. Breckenridge, *The Knowledge of God, Objectively Considered* (New York, 1858), 255–7; *Sermons by Willard Preston, D.D., Late Pastor of the Independent Presbyterian Church, Savannah, Georgia*, 2 vols. (Philadelphia, 1857); "Negro-mania," in Richard Lounsbury, ed., *Louisa S. McCord: Political and Social Essays* (Charlottesville, VA, 1995), 226; also, "Doctrine of the Trinity," in William T. Brantly, *Sermons* (Charleston, SC, 1858), 115. ["All manner of sin and blasphemy shall be forgiven unto men: but the blasphemy against the Holy Ghost shall not be forgiven unto men.... And whosoever speaketh a word against the Son of man, it shall be forgiven him: but whosoever speaketh against the Holy Ghost, it shall not be forgiven him, neither in this world, neither in the world to come": Matt., 12:31–2; see also Mark, 16:16, and Luke, 12:12.]

[32] Luther quoted in Pelikan, *Christian Tradition*, 4:132.

[33] For the view that Northerners preferred the New Testament and Southerners the Old, see Charles S. Sydnor, "The Southerner and the Laws," *JSH*, 6 (1940), 6; also, Edward L. Ayers, *Vengeance and Justice: Crime and Punishment in the Nineteenth-Century South* (New York, 1984), 28. In the 1840s the Methodist Protestant Reverend A. A. Lipscomb felt it necessary to defend the unity of the two Testaments: *Our Country: Its Danger and Duty* (New York, 1844), 29, and *The Social Spirit of Christianity, Presented in the Form of Essays* (Philadelphia, 1846), 19–20. Augustine defended the Old Testament and its continuity with the New against the Manicheans, who derided the former as paganism. See Jaroslav Pelikan, *The Mystery of Continuity: Time and History, Memory and Eternity in the Thought of Saint Augustine* (Charlottesville, VA, 1986), 6–7, 73.

the Old Testament in the second century was a mistake that the main body of the church was correct in avoiding; to retain it in the sixteenth century was a historical fate that the Reformation was not yet in a position to escape; but to go on considering it within Protestantism as a canonical authority after the nineteenth century is the consequence of a paralysis of religion and church."[34]

By 1861 the tendency to downgrade the Old Testament had proceeded so far in Europe and in the North that southern theologians began to worry about its possible inroads in the South. Simms and a few others remained cool toward the Old Testament without appreciating their approximation to the view of the left wing of the Reformation, which set the Gospels, not the Decalogue, as the standard for ethical action and which, in effect, politicized the Word. William Lloyd Garrison and others in the abolitionist and peace movements, concluding that the teachings of Jesus flatly contradicted the works of the Old Testament's God of Wrath, embraced the one and repudiated the other. But then Thomas Paine, a southern *bête noire,* had long before (in his *Age of Reason*) described the Old Testament as abhorrent and contemptible.[35]

Yet for the orthodox and prestigious Presbyterian Reverends George Howe and Thomas Smyth of South Carolina, the Old Testament and the New alike were the Word of God and confirmed the Trinity. The New Testament, Thornwell wrote, "professes no new revelations in morality; it is only a commentary on the Law and the prophets." Girardeau found absurd the notion that the New Testament negated the unchangeable divine law of the Old Testament, and he cited Jesus' assurance, "Think not that I am come to destroy the law, or the prophets: I am not come to destroy, but to fulfill" (Matt., 5:17). Girardeau reiterated that the New Testament dispensation is the "culmination, the crowning development of the old economy." Dabney added, "There is no mercifulness in the Son that was not equally in the Father."[36]

In New England, Samuel Hopkins's benevolent God was not benevolent enough to satisfy Nathaniel Taylor and the rising generation of theologians. In Taylor's

<hr/>

[34] On Luther see Pelikan, *Christian Tradition,* 4:168–70; Timothy George, "John Gill," in George and Dockery, eds., *Baptist Theologians,* 92; Harnack quoted in Jaroslav Pelikan, *The Melody of Theology: A Philosophical Dictionary* (Cambridge, MA, 1988), 113.

[35] William Gilmore Simms to William Porcher Miles, Feb. 26, 1860, in Mary C. Oliphant et al., eds., *The Letters of William Gilmore Simms,* 6 vols. (Columbia, SC, 1952–82), 4:199; for Garrison see Valerie H. Ziegler, *The Advocates of Peace in Antebellum America* (Bloomington, IN, 1992), 106–7; on the radical Reformation see Henning Graf Reventlow, *The Authority of the Bible and the Rise of the Modern World* (Philadelphia, 1984), ch. 3. For the setting and effects of Paine's remarks see Noll, *America's God,* 83–4. William Green of Virginia, a leading jurist and Episcopalian, considered the Old Testament historically unreliable: Philip Slaughter, *A Brief Sketch of the Life of William Green, LL.D., Jurist and Scholar* (Richmond, VA, 1883), 17, 51.

[36] Smith, *Southern Presbyterian Theologians,* 113 (Howe); *TSW,* 9:188; Thornwell, "Morell's Philosophy of Religion," *JHTW,* 3:69; John L. Girardeau, *The Will in Its Theological Relations* (Columbia, SC, 1891), 423–4; Girardeau, *Theological Questions,* 320; Dabney, *Systematic Theology,* 513. For the Holy Spirit of the Gospels as fulfillment of Old Testament law see "Milman's History of Christianity," *SQR,* 4 (1843), 282–3, and for a Southerner's harsh attack on those who divorced the Testaments see Stuart Robinson, *Discourses of Redemption* (New York, 1866), 47–8; also, Hodge, *Systematic Theology,* 3:331.

view, Hopkins's God seemed to be sending just about everyone to hell, while Dabney accused Taylor, Barnes, N. S. S. Beeman, and all antislavery proponents of having abandoned Calvinism for Socinianism. He spoke highly of the "great and good Jonathan Edwards" but criticized deviations from Calvinist orthodoxy that Edwards's successors had turned into apostasy. The New England theologians, in Dabney's view, made benevolence God's central quality at the expense of His self-proclamation as a "consuming fire," transforming benevolence into a doctrine of utilitarian selfishness and marketplace ethics.[37]

Hopkins's ideas of "benevolence" and "love" stressed a common identity, and Nathaniel Taylor, taking utilitarian ground, identified sin as moral evil. Southerners, for their part, wanted no part of a universe that lacked a God of Wrath and no part of the notion that, since man had never fallen, God had nothing to be wrathful about. "Depravity," Dagg replied, "is natural to man; it is born with him, and not acquired in the progress of life." Every child is born of depraved parents. Yet southern preachers had to proceed cautiously in this matter, for they could turn congregations cold by overdoing the torments of hell while seeming to slight God's benevolence and their congregants' own feelings of mutual love. When the Methodist William Winans spoke of benevolence, he referred to a minister for whom "no form of human suffering or want ever failed to arouse his sympathy, or put in requisition his efforts for its removal." Southerners and conservative Northerners alike grasped the political implications of the New England version of benevolence. In a proslavery pamphlet, Gabriel Capers of Georgia asserted that abolitionists appealed to the spirit of the New Testament in an effort to make it contradict the incontrovertible evidence of the Old. For the southern divines, Christian ethics divorced from a Christian love inherent in the Atonement descended into a self-righteousness that identifies sin with sinner and finds the locus of sin in social relations and institutions – a trap pious abolitionists tried to avoid.[38]

---

[37] Allen C. Guelzo, *Edwards on the Will: A Century of American Debate* (Middletown, CT, 1989), chs. 3 and 8; Dabney, *Sacred Rhetoric*, 28–9; Dabney, *Systematic Theology*, 169, 100–1, 296–7, 508–10, quote at 100.

[38] Dagg, *Manual of Theology*, 1:153–4, quote at 153; on Winans see William Buell Sprague, *Annals of the American Pulpit*, 9 vols. (New York, 1859–69), 7:401–7, quote at 407, and see the perceptive remarks of Paul K. Conkin, *The Uneasy Center: Reformed Christianity in Antebellum America* (Chapel Hill, NC, 1995), 106–7, 217–18; [Gabriel Capers], *Bondage a Moral Institution, Sanctioned by the Scriptures of the Old and New Testaments, and the Preaching and Practice of the Saviour. By a Southern Farmer* (Macon, GA, 1837), 4. Since abolitionists say that the New Testament repeals the Old, wrote J. B. Ferguson of Tennessee, let us by all means consult the New on slavery: *Address on the History, Authority, and Influence of Slavery* (Nashville, TN, 1850), 14.

For the southern version of benevolence especially through women's church work, see Anne C. Loveland, *Southern Evangelicals and the Social Order, 1800–1860* (Baton Rouge, LA, 1980), ch. 6. For a preacher who could not walk that tightrope see Mary E. Moragné Journal, Oct. 25, 1839, in Della Mullen Craven, ed., *The Neglected Thread: A Journal of the Calhoun Community* (Columbia, SC, 1951), 165–6. The Baptist Patrick H. Mell reacted testily to any suggestion that Hopkins ought to be considered a Calvinist: *Predestination and the Saints' Perseverance, Stated and Defended from the Objections of the Arminians* (Charleston, SC, 1858 [1850]), 20. In *America's God*, 131–3, Noll defends the claims of Hopkins, Bellamy, and New Divinity to a large measure of agreement with Edwards. For a critique of the New Divinity's claims to orthodoxy see Joseph Haroutunian, *Piety versus Moralism: The Passing of the New England Theology* (New York, 1932), 34–5, 38, 152. Haroutunian

Southerners understood that, for better or worse, Romanticism had brought the self to center stage. Yankee benevolence, Wayne Gridley of South Carolina wrote in the 1840s, had "nothing in common with the pure and noble sentiment of Christian benevolence" and was "the offspring of inordinate vanity, the love of excitement, or the bastard ambition, which seeks power by other than ordinary and legitimate modes." In an explicit defense of social hierarchy, S. J. Cassells identified God's benevolence and justice as essentially the same: Justice is "the principle which regulates our conduct towards others, according to the relations existing between us"; benevolence is the same, "associating itself with hearty good-will to others." To slight justice means to slight benevolence, and vice versa. Only God can adjust these virtues perfectly. Cassells chuckled that abolition societies existed only in states without slavery. In the name of benevolence, he argued, free societies promoted hatred against the South and cynically undermined blacks themselves, who received better treatment in the South than laborers, black or white, in the North. Thornwell weighed in against the attempt to make benevolence God's greatest if not sole perfection. "Wisdom, justice, truth" and other attributes of God condition God's benevolence. Nature, too, "speaks as loudly of justice as of love." For Southerners, the liberal doctrine of benevolence played stalking horse to abolitionism and political radicalism. Theologically orthodox Northerners agreed.[39]

The bitter quarrel centered on the nature of man as well as God. William Ellery Channing, in his famous Baltimore sermon of 1819 on "Unitarian Christianity," asked opponents for a God worthy of humanity's love and trust. Channing's call to believers to look beyond the Word to the Spirit did not in itself offend the orthodox, but he displayed little interest in the Word at all. In contrast, the overwhelming majority of southern Christians demanded that man prove himself worthy of God,

---

sardonically concludes (254) that Nathaniel Taylor abandoned "the sovereignty of God, the dependence of man on God, the doctrines of election, total depravity, and regeneration. On these subjects he waxed profound and unintelligible."

[39] Wayne Gridley, *Slavery in the South: A Review of Hammond's and Fuller's Letters, and Chancellor Harper's Memoir* (Charleston, SC, 1845), 2; Samuel J. Cassells, "Relation of Justice to Benevolence in the Conduct of Society," *SPR,* 7 (1853), 85–6, 90–1; J. Thornwell, "Principles of Moral and Political Economy," *SPR,* 7 (1853), 14–15; see also Dagg, *Manual of Theology,* 1:76–7. Among orthodox Northerners, Samuel J. Baird scorned the prevalent New England notion of benevolence: Baird, *A History of the New School and of the Questions in the Disruption of the Presbyterian Church in 1836* (Philadelphia, 1868), 176. Leander Ker of Missouri denounced New England benevolence as self-serving: *Slavery Consistent with Christianity,* 3rd ed. (Weston, MO, 1853), vi, 34–6. For the view under attack see e.g. Lydia Maria Child, *An Appeal in Favor of that Class of People Called Africans* (Boston, 1833), 29; Lydia Maria Child to Gov. Wise, Oct. 26 and 29, 1859, in *Correspondence between Lydia Maria Child and Gov. Wise and Mrs. Mason of Virginia* (Boston, 1860), 3, 7.

Southerners rejected what they perceived as a waxing northern view of "moral government," which derived from the abandonment of original sin and the embrace of abolitionism. New Divinity men made God a governor who tended toward universal salvation rather than an angry and offended God. Hopkins recommended adherence to antislavery and other social causes as a way for Christians to find humility by seeking good for the downtrodden. His benevolence encouraged condemnation of all slaveholders as unfit for a republican polity. See esp. James D. Essig, *The Bonds of Wickedness: American Evangelicals against Slavery, 1770–1808* (Philadelphia, 1982), 40, 89–91; Charles C. Cole, Jr., *The Social Ideas of the Northern Evangelists, 1826–1860* (New York, 1954), 38, 44–5, 105–9, 119.

whose omnipotence, omniscience, and goodness they did not question. Thornwell maintained that, unlike Aristotle and the ancients, the typical modern philosopher began "with consciousness, and confounding thought with existence, reality with knowledge, has made the laws of thought the regulative and constitutive principles of being." God then became "a complement of primitive cognitions." Arguing against subjective individualism, Thornwell held that the Word presupposed faith and constituted its only ground: hence the need for "an instituted ministry."[40]

"God restrains us," Thomas Smyth preached, "by the principle of fear and allures us by the principle of love." In 1850 James Henry Greenlee, a Presbyterian planter in McDowell County, North Carolina, paraphrased in his diary the Reverend Dr. R. H. Morrison's sermon on how God looks with favor upon those who fear Him: "Our fear should be filial & not servile, fear him as an obedient and affectionate child fears a parent for he is the parent of all Love him give him our Supreme love fear to offend him desire his ways Love his services delight in his commandments walking in his ordinances blameless and the life death and sufferings of our Lord and saviour Jesus Christ & his full atonement is the hope of the true child of *God.*" The Reverend C. P. Gadsden preached in Charleston that God, pronouncing Himself a "consuming fire" and a "jealous God" (Deut., 4:24), announced His "consuming justice." Arminians stood with Calvinists. Bishop Bascom related "the self-love of infidelity" to "the sickly charity of Utopian reformers" who separate punishment from sin. The Gospel of universal brotherhood and peace, he said, also makes clear the necessity for stern punishments. Jesus used His power not only to save the virtuous but also "to subdue and destroy his enemies."[41]

In *Southern Presbyterian Review,* E. P. Rogers protested creeping liberalism at the ostensibly orthodox Andover Seminary in Massachusetts, deploring its instruction as incompatible with sound doctrine and the Westminster catechism. Fearing that New England doctrines were spreading across the North, especially in Congregationalist churches, Rogers summoned orthodox New Englanders like Samuel Baird to denounce Andover's abandonment of the Calvinist "Federal Theology" and the concept of original sin. Thornwell, whose own experience as a student at Andover had left a bad taste, charged the New Divinity with "laying the foundations broad and deep of a new phase of philosophical infidelity – an infidelity more dangerous, because more subtle, than that of Bolingbroke and Hume, which pretends reverence while it really insults, which, like Judas, betrays the Son of man with a kiss." Two years later Thornwell spoke of the attempt to construct theology from consciousness: "We must try our hearts by [the divine life], and not it by our hearts." New England theologians "have made the Bible an appendix to their shallow and sophistical psychology, and their still shallower and more sophistical ethics."[42]

---

[40] Pelikan, *Christian Tradition,* 4:325–7; "Unitarian Christianity," in *A Selection From the Works of William E. Channing, D.D.* (Boston, 1855), 179–233; "Personality of God," *JHTW,* 1:494. On "an instituted ministry" see "Election and Reprobation," *JHTW,* 2:189.

[41] *TSW,* 9:417 and 5:244; Greenlee Diary, June 9, 1850, at UNC-SHC; Elliott, ed., *Tributes to C. P. Gadsden, with His Sermons,* 224–6; Bascom, *Sermons from the Pulpit,* 90–1, 177.

[42] E. P. Rogers, "Orthodoxy in New England," *SPR,* 7 (1853), 52–60, quote at 53; "The Office of Reason in Regard to Revelation" and "Discourse upon Being Inaugurated as Professor of Theology," *JHTW,* 3:216, 1:582; also, Baird, *New School,* 213.

Samuel Johnson emerged in theological quarrels over the origins and nature of sin. Johnson had a large and appreciative southern audience, notwithstanding his opposition to the American Revolution, his detestation of slavery, his impatience with racism, and his doubts about the Noahic curse. Thomas Smyth, among others, welcomed Johnson's eloquence on faith in an afterlife and on the reasonableness of Trinitarianism as well as his ridicule of the rosy view that basically good human beings rely upon reason, study the universe, and abide by its laws: "Whatever is the cause of human corruption, men are evidently and confessedly so corrupt, that all the laws of heaven and earth are insufficient to restrain them from crimes." Isaac Domingos of Georgia, at the front in Virginia with the Confederate army, provided a typical southern version as he reminded his son and daughter that everyone has an immortal soul: "So now my last words of advice to you is to seek God and our blessed Savior in the pardon of your sins. For you are all sinners, for through Adam's disobedience sin came into this world and came upon every man and the children of man." Not surprisingly, then, Thomas Roderick Dew opened his history of Western Civilization with an account of the Fall, and John Fletcher of New Orleans, in his *Studies on Slavery,* came down hard in defense of an orthodox version of original sin. For liberals, since the doctrine of original sin stood in opposition to Enlightenment ideas of a progressive improvement in the human condition, it had to go – and with it, hell and eternal damnation. The very idea of grace had to go, too, for it undermined faith in man's ability to make himself.[43]

Rejection of original sin had a long history. In its modern phase, Jonathan Edwards had combated the views of John Taylor, the prestigious English divine who thought that Adam simply missed the mark by failing to distinguish between good

Robert Breckenridge's *DQR*, 1 (1861), 352–4, referred to "the Andover riddle – the conjugation of the verb to sin, in the passive voice." George M. Marsden cites Andover as a classic case of seminaries that began by defending orthodoxy against modernist error and heresy and eventually succumbed: Marsden, *Reforming Fundamentalism: Fuller Seminary and the New Evangelicalism* (Grand Rapids, MI, 1987), 214. For orthodox Southerners who studied at Andover in its early years see Preston Graham, Jr., *A Kingdom Not of This World: Stuart Robinson's Struggle to Distinguish the Sacred from the Secular during the Civil War* (Macon, GA, 2002), 15.

43   James Boswell, *The Life of Samuel Johnson, LL.D.* (New York, n.d.), 1160; *TSW*, 9:95; Isaac Domingos to Joseph and Tallulah Domingos, Apr. 19, 1864, in Mills Lane, ed., *"Dear Mother: Don't Grieve about Me: If I Get Killed, I'll Only Be Dead"* (Savannah, GA, 1990), 289–91; Thomas Roderick Dew, *Digest of the Laws, Customs, Manners, and Institutions of the Ancient and Modern Nations* (New York, 1884 [1852]), pt. 1:ch. 1; John Fletcher, *Studies on Slavery, in Easy Lessons* (Natchez, MS, 1852), 433–4.

For Johnson's popularity in the South see Rhoda Coleman Ellison, *History of Huntingdon College, 1854–1954* (University, AL, 1954), 124–5; [William Wirt], *The Old Bachelor* (Richmond, VA, 1810), 34; Paul Hamilton Hayne, "Ante-Bellum Charleston," *Southern Bivouac,* 1 (1885), 335; *SLM*, 27 (1858), 196; E. G. Baker Diary, Feb. 21, Mar. 2, July 14, 1849, at UNC-SHC; Mrs. David Hillhouse to Col. Elisha Porter, Jan. 26, 1787, in Marion Alexander Boggs, ed., *The Alexander Letters, 1787–1900* (Athens, GA, 1980 [1911]), 19; Franc M. Carmack Diary, Jan. 6, 18??, at UNC-SHC; George Fitzhugh, "Johnson, Boswell, Goldsmith, Etc.," *DBR*, 28 (1860), 414, 417; Thomas Cary Johnson, ed., *Life and Letters of Robert Lewis Dabney* (Carlisle, PA, 1977), 22; *Plantation Life: Narratives of Schoolcraft*, 33, 163, 565; also, Peyton Harrison Hoge, *Moses Drury Hoge: Life and Letters* (Richmond, VA, 1899), 37; Dr. and Mrs. William E. Hatcher, *Sketch of the Life and Writings of A. B. Brown* (Baltimore, 1886), 246.

and evil and that, coming into the world neither righteous nor sinful, individuals make sinful choices out of their passions. Samuel Hopkins protested, "If I give up this doctrine [original sin], I must give up Christianity," and angry orthodox Calvinists soon accused him of doing just that. Hopkins appealed to those who hoped to save orthodoxy by a doctrinal development designed to draw the teeth of Unitarian and other heterodox challenges. He acknowledged human depravity but denied the imputation of Adam's guilt to his progeny, arguing that without sin there would be no redemption and joy in salvation. Hopkins strove to follow Jonathan Edwards, but, in the sound assessment of Joseph Haroutunian, "In reality he deserted his master." Step by step he adopted his opponents' premises and "moralized" his theology. Jonathan Mayhew and the liberals championed a gospel centered on a good, moral, Christian life rather than on the glory of God. The New Divinity struck its Calvinist colors: "It was Calvinism soiled and bruised in its struggle against the humanitarianism of the age, exaggerated here, distorted there, sheepish and worried, and weakening." New England Calvinists who identified with Nathaniel Taylor abandoned original sin early. Taylor threw down the gauntlet in 1828 and, to the horror of most Southerners, his views influenced the debates that led to the Presbyterian split of 1837. During the post-War debate over the proposed reunion of Old and New Schools, Dabney, among others with long memories, would remain unforgiving.[44]

In the North, too, the orthodox fought Taylor tenaciously and with considerable success but could not stem the retreat from the doctrine of original sin. Ostensibly Calvinist churches in New England saw human beings as prey to their passions rather than as inherently sinful. Commenting on the testy debates in Boston and Cambridge, Unitarians mocked nominally Calvinist New Divinity men for shedding "the five points of Calvinism." H. Shelton Smith and Rosemary Radford Reuther have wryly remarked that affluent Bostonians repeated the Calvinist Federal Theology on Sunday but on Monday decided that Adam's sin had nothing to do with them or pertained only to the lower classes – an attitude that slowly penetrated the principal denominations of the North. Yale College, long a bastion of orthodox Calvinism, no longer taught the doctrine of imputation, and the orthodox howled at what Ashbel Green branded a shamefaced surrender to the Unitarians. It took little perspicacity to recognize that the modernizers were embracing radical individualism and sloughing off the corporatist tendencies of the Christian tradition. And southern critics had more than a little perspicacity.[45]

Yet the great Methodist revival, which began in Britain and swept across the Atlantic, placed heavy emphasis on original sin and human depravity. John Wesley considered the Fall *sine qua non* for Christian belief, and in 1851 James Porter spoke

---

[44] H. Shelton Smith, *Changing Conceptions of Original Sin: A Study in American Theology since 1750* (New York, 1955), 11–19; Ahlstrom, *Religious History of the American People*, 406–9; Haroutunian, *Piety versus Moralism*, esp. ch. 2 (15–42), quotes at 40, also 120–1, for Mayhew see 11, 48–9, 53, summary quote on the New Divinity at 60.

[45] Smith, *Original Sin*, 19, 26–7, 99–104, 125; Rosemary Radford Reuther, *The Radical Kingdom: The Western Experience of Messianic Hope* (New York, 1970), 40; W. B. Posey, *The Presbyterian Church in Old Southwest, 1778–1838* (Richmond, VA, 1952); George M. Marsden, *The Evangelical Mind and the New School Experience: A Case Study of Thought and Theology in Nineteenth-Century America* (New Haven, CT, 1970), 34–9.

for the Methodist Episcopal Church (North) in upholding those doctrines while he stressed God's grace. Southerners questioned how well northern Methodists were upholding Christian orthodoxy on these matters; increasingly, they thought they espied creeping Pelagianism in their northern brethren and rededicated themselves to a hard line.[46]

New Divinity tried to develop the work of Jonathan Edwards by locating human depravity solely in the will and recognizing the ability of repentant sinners to earn salvation. Perhaps their most striking departure from Calvinism came in their rejection of the imputation of Adam's sin and Christ's righteousness. They thereby fed, if inadvertently, the notion of universal salvation. For New Divinity men, as Allen Guelzo writes, "Christ did not die on behalf of any individuals. His atonement was intended to justify God for forgiving sinners – not to justify men." Christ, that is, made possible repentance by making it possible for God to justify Himself in His forgiveness of sinners. That God needed to justify Himself went down hard in Dixie, where Calvinists debated respectfully the difficulties presented by original sin and imputation. Thornwell and Dabney acknowledged that original sin remains enveloped in a mystery man cannot unravel but emphatically denied that the doctrine was inherently unjust.[47]

Since Southerners preferred to leave heresy mania to the descendants of New England witch-hunters, southern Presbyterians reacted slowly to charges of heresy against Albert Barnes and Lyman Beecher in the 1830s, although – despite acquittals by the Presbyterian National Assembly – the debates revealed that Barnes and Beecher had abandoned basic Calvinist doctrine. Even southern Methodists, who welcomed every sign of defection from Calvinism, looked askance at defections from the doctrine of original sin, especially when coupled with abolitionism. Barnes and Beecher, like Samuel Hopkins and Joseph Bellamy, staunchly opposed slavery.[48]

New Divinity and New Haven theologians faced formidable challenges from Transcendentalists and others who thought they had not gone far enough. In 1858, Horace Bushnell traduced Calvinists for preaching that sinful mankind retained

---

[46] Troeltsch, *Social Teachings of the Christian Churches*, 2:721–2; James Porter, *Compendium of Methodism* (Boston, 1851), 204–7, 231–5, 243–4.

[47] Allan C. Guelzo, "Jonathan Edwards and the New Divinity," in Charles G. Dennison and Richard C. Gamble, eds., *Pressing toward the Mark: Essays Commemorating Fifty Years of the Orthodox Presbyterian Church* (Philadelphia, 1986), 160–3, quote at 161; *DD*, 1:229–81. For Thornwell on original sin and his rejection of "numerical identity," see his review of Baird in *JHTW*, 1:515–68.

[48] Smith, *Original Sin*, ch. 6, esp. 125–33. Smith, who treats the abolitionists and theological liberals sympathetically, concludes that Barnes, Beecher, and their New School supporters retreated from orthodoxy while claiming to sustain it. For Barnes on original sin see also George P. Hutchinson, *The Problem of Original Sin in American Presbyterian Theology* (Nutley, NJ, 1972), 16. John R. McKivigan observes that conservative New Englanders hardened their religious orthodoxy in response to the abolitionists' reliance on liberal theology but then retreated from the doctrine of original sin: *The War against Proslavery Religion: Abolitionism and the Northern Churches, 1830–1865* (Ithaca, NY, 1984), 179, 180. For the biblical grounding of the Federal Theology see esp. Romans, 5:12. Southerners remarked that no ecclesiastically sanctioned execution of witches occurred in colonial Virginia: see e.g. *SLM*, 2 (1836), 283; Howison, *History of Virginia*, 1:284–5, 2:151.

no affinity for God: "Total depravity was made total, in such a sense as to leave the soul no receptivity for God whatever." For Bushnell, human nature – however much corrupted – retains "the original divine impress." He was caricaturing Yankee Calvinists, who did, however, leave themselves open in a manner their southern brethren did not. "Total depravity," Thornwell preached in 1850, "was never used to express the degrees of positive wickedness attaching to human nature," nor was it ever "employed to convey the idea that men were as wicked as they could be, or that there were no differences of moral character among them." He distinguished between "the man of unblemished honour and integrity" and "the low and unprincipled knave or cut-throat." Baptists and Methodists agreed.[49]

The southern war against liberalism extended to the cult of free love, which the ladies in Mary Chesnut's circle saw as peculiarly New England. In the 1830s James Smylie of Mississippi, in a famous proslavery discourse, stressed the patriarchal family and warned, "The licentiousness of the female character in France ... is a true test of the effects of the Rights of Women" espoused by Godwin, "one of the High Priests of the abolition of marriage." When North Carolina seceded, F. H. Smith and Henry Burgwyn, preparing for military service, agreed that New Englanders "ruled partly by strong minded women, have become so corrupted by infidelity & free love associations, etc. as to be completely rotten & unworthy of any connection." Yet, contrary to a good many overly zealous Southerners, few Northerners who abandoned original sin embraced free love. But northern free lovers espoused theological liberalism or repudiated Christianity altogether. Southerners could not resist having some fun on the subject. The Baptist Reverend Patrick Mell of Georgia drolly noted that Miss Grimké asserted from personal experience that slavery deadens the moral sense and that even females looked upon "lewdness" – apparently, black nudity – with indifference or worse. "Far be it from me," Mell mocked, "to complain of Miss Grimké or to accuse her of falsehood. She is a very honest lady, and doubtless spoke the truth – *as far as her* CONFESSION *goes.*"[50]

Western culture has come a long way since Jean-Jacques Rousseau transformed sin into a social phenomenon in which corrupt society drives a basically good humanity into sin. Christian theology had long maintained creative tension between

[49] "Religious Nature and Religious Character," in Horace Bushnell, *Sermons,* ed. Conrad Cherry (New York, 1985), 26, also 29–33; "Theological Lectures: Original Sin," *JHTW,* 1:309; Dagg, *Manual of Theology,* 1:152; Nathan Bangs in Langford, ed., *Wesleyan Theology,* 51. For the acceptance of gradations of sin and punishment see *JHTW,* 1:425, and Girardeau, *The Will,* 463, 480–1; Sebastian G. Messmer, ed., *The Works of the Right Rev. John England, First Bishop of Charleston,* 7 vols. (Cleveland, OH, 1908), 6:330; and for Bushnell's complex attitude, see Daniel Walker Howe, "The Social Science of Horace Bushnell," *Journal of American History,* 70 (1983), 305–22.

[50] Smylie quoted in Randy J. Sparks, "Mississippi's Apostle of Slavery: James Smylie and the Biblical Defense of Slavery," *Journal of Mississippi History,* 51 (1989), 103; Chesnut Diary, June 16, 1861, in C. Vann Woodward, ed., *Mary Chesnut's Civil War* (New Haven, CT, 1981), 101; for Smith and Burgwyn see Archie K. Davis, *Boy Colonel of the Confederacy* (Chapel Hill, NC, 1998), 50; [Mell], *Slavery,* 26 n. For a typical attack on northern free love that singles out the Universalist Hosea Ballou, see Sawyer, *Southern Institutes,* 243–4. On the extent of free love and cultural extremism in the North see John C. Spurlock, *Free Love: Marriage and Middle-Class Radicalism in America, 1825–1860* (New York, 1988).

sin as lapse from God and sin as a direct offense against God. The swing toward inwardness reinforced a concentration on individual experience and rendered the sin personal in a new way. In the words of the historian Claude Welch, "It is I who am a lost soul, sinful and defiled, in search of cleansing and renewal." Creation, Fall, and Redemption were losing their collective significance and becoming reenactments in each person's life. Northern evangelicals continued to plead for self-reformation, but an increasing number moved toward a social action that conceded much to Rousseau and to such Christian Socialists as Charles Kingsley and J. M. Ludlow. For the religious radical and utopian socialist George Ripley, "The purpose of Christianity is to redeem society as well as the individual from all sin."[51]

The theological shift to the left carried westward from New England the notion that people sin primarily because they are besieged by temptations of their upbringing in family and society. When Timothy Dwight – who taught Lyman Beecher, Moses Stuart, and Nathaniel Taylor – argued for human depravity on the basis of all human experience, he looked old-fogeyish to the swelling number of theological liberals and radicals, but his pupils' rejection of the wellsprings of original sin made him look like an apostate to the orthodox. Led by Charles Finney, northern revivalists preached that conversion must be followed by a life dedicated to Christian virtue as manifested in a war against social sins. Together with romantic secular reformers, they breathed an egalitarian spirit and sought social reconstruction through the purging of personal sin; they thus transformed the doctrine of sin as a personal rebellion against God into a political issue. (These revivalists rarely noticed that they risked committing the sin of pride – the ultimate act of rebellion against God – by granting godlike status to man.) Theodore Weld carried the logic forward, describing anyone who held slaves, even by inheritance, as "a joint partner in the original sin." For John Humphrey Noyes, who appalled most northern churchmen, the overthrow of all government meant a "universal emancipation from sin"; for the eminently more respectable Lyman Beecher, the creation of an earthly utopia meant the institution of God's law.[52]

Dabney, too, considered sin as mere negation ("lack of conformity to God's will") but sought its root in the original corruption of the soul, not in unjust social relations. For the orthodox, reduction of sin to privation or lapse made God the cause of evil by implying a deficient creation of man. Crying that we know the sin is in ourselves, Hodge rebuked Schleiermacher for reducing it from an objective offense against God to individual subjectivity; Thornwell described sin as

---

[51] Welch, *Protestant Thought,* 1:28, 40, 48–9; for Augustine's view see Harnack, *Dogma,* 338; Ripley quoted in Guarnieri, *Utopian Alternative,* 3. On Rousseau's discovery of the root of his doctrine of social sin in apocalyptic theories in Judaism and early Christianity, see Reuther, *Radical Kingdom;* also, for Rousseau and Voltaire on original sin see Ernst Cassirer, *The Philosophy of the Enlightenment,* tr. Fritz C. A. Koelin and James P. Pettegrove (Boston, 1951), 138–9, 141, 155–6.

[52] Lewis Perry, *Radical Abolitionism: Antislavery and the Government of God in Antislavery Thought* (Ithaca, NY, 1973), 43–6, 51, 68, quotes at 51, 68. On the impact of the Enlightenment see Tillich, *Christian Thought,* 288–91. With only peripheral exceptions, southern Baptists held to original sin despite bitter internal quarrels over other matters: Benjamin Griffin, *History of the Primitive Baptists of Mississippi* (Jackson, MS, 1853), 58–67.

a real power of evil, not a mere privation of goodness. Alexander Stephens, who criticized the Universalists for rejecting eternal punishments, described the devil as a person who tempted frail mortals. Willard Preston, lowcountry Presbyterian, ridiculed the appeals of Hume, Bolingbroke, and Voltaire to a merciful God whom they stripped of all sense of justice. Girardeau, reaffirming Augustine, saw sin as flagrant disobedience and direct offense and "the infliction of misery." Liberal theologians, he protested, trivialized sin as a deprivation of happiness. Southerners surely would have enjoyed Kierkegaard's reply to those for whom sin was mere ignorance or "missing of the mark." He pointed out that, if so, then sin does not exist at all since it is a manifestation of consciousness.[53]

Joseph Story recalled that, in late eighteenth-century Massachusetts, hellfire preachers offended their congregations by dwelling on the sinfulness of man. The New England divines, from the early Puritans to the leaders of the Great Awakening, had preached the doctrine of original sin. The change described by Story was occurring in Virginia by the turn of the century. William Wirt, in *The Old Bachelor* (1810), referred tongue-in-cheek to preachers who apologized for mentioning sin and hell. Hell and the devil, Robert Howison wrote in his *History of Virginia* (1846), receded until the Second Great Awakening restored them in the public mind. Liberalization of doctrine proceeded apace in New England and, if more slowly, in the West. It shrank to a whisper in the South.[54]

The retreat from orthodoxy permitted abolitionists to rework the very definition of Christian. "Slaveholding," writes Bertram Wyatt-Brown, a sympathetic historian of abolitionism, "became the cardinal sin in the antinomian theology, for men were judged solely according to their relationship to slavery, a radical departure in scriptural interpretation." He concludes: "Something of the dignity and awesomeness of divinity, as it had been perceived for centuries, was displaced by an identification of sin with certain cultural arrangements and virtue with others." The early Emerson, who saw sin as privation and nonentity, made an exception for slavery as absolute evil. Holy War could be the only outcome.[55]

---

[53] Dabney, *Systematic Theology*, 136; Hodge, *Systematic Theology*, 2:134–40; *JHTW*, 1:380, 382–3, 393, 402–3; "Salvation through Christ Alone," in *Sermons by Willard D. Preston*, 1:41; Girardeau, *The Will*, 237, 246–9, quote at 253; Girardeau, "Sanctification by Grace," in *Sermons*, 48; Søren Kierkegaard, *The Sickness unto Death*, tr. Walter Lowrie (Princeton, NJ, 1941), 109. Jerry H. Walls remarks that if Christ offers a way of salvation, it is difficult to see how Christians can abandon the idea of eternal punishment: *Hell: The Logic of Damnation* (Notre Dame, IN, 1992), 3, 7.

    The notion of sin as deprivation of goodness arose with Platonism. A persistent tendency of southern Calvinists and Arminians to accuse the each other of backsliding obscured the measure of their agreement. Wesley stood with Calvin in holding that Adam's sin led to total depravity, and Methodist theologians like John Fletcher, Adam Clarke, Nathan Bangs, and Richard Watson followed suit. But in their version, Paul Conkin remarks, "Depravity lost its sting." See the selections from the leading Methodist theologians in Langford, ed., *Wesleyan Theology*; Conkin, *Uneasy Center*, 68.

[54] "Autobiography," in W. W. Story, ed., *The Miscellaneous Writings of Joseph Story*, 2 vols. (Boston, 1852), 1:10; [Wirt], *Old Bachelor*, 213; Howison, *A History of Virginia*, 2:184–5.

[55] Bertram Wyatt-Brown, *Yankee Saints and Southern Sinners* (Baton Rouge, LA, 1985), 22, 23; Merton M. Sealts, Jr., *Emerson on the Scholar* (Columbia, MO, 1992), 130. Unlike the radicals, Emerson continued to plead for compensated emancipation but as sound social policy, not property right.

Without a deep-seated belief in human corruption, the divinity of Jesus would be unthinkable. Hence, the retreat from the doctrine of original sin accompanied a watering down of Trinitarianism. In New England during the 1730s, Jonathan Edwards confronted both a deepening Arminianism and anti-Trinitarianism. During the nineteenth century, even theologically liberal southern divines shared the "hearty dislike" expressed by the secular *Russell's Magazine* of "that German radicalism and infidelity that strips the Bible of its inspiration and Christ of his divinity."[56]

Christians have killed and been killed over the concept of the triune God. Edward Gibbon, a southern favorite despite his religious views, deemed Trinitarianism a thinly disguised tritheism and a cynical ploy by the Church fathers to manipulate the residual polytheism of the common people. Yet he conceded that Arianism "might satisfy the cold and speculative mind," while the Nicene Creed's "merits of faith and devotion, was much better adapted to become popular and successful in a believing age." Southerners winced. Some took to heart his "melancholy truth" that Christians suffered immeasurably greater severities from other Christians than from infidels. Dew approved Julian the Apostate's attempt to curb religious fanaticism and intolerance and criticized Theodosius the Great for having "persecuted Arianism."[57]

A Christian in-joke: He who denies the Trinity will lose his soul; he who strives to understand it may lose his mind. For nonbelievers and many theological liberals, the concept of the Trinity is a worthless abstraction if not sheer nonsense. But to others, a non-Trinitarian Christianity ranks as an oxymoron and an invitation to rip up Christianity by its root. For Trinitarians the mysterious existence of Jesus as simultaneously God and man – "the Word made flesh" – separates Christianity from all other religions and embodies its claims for the redemption of humanity. The eminent Baptist Reverend Basil Manly told a story: "A young man once said to Dr. Parr, conversing on the subject of the Trinity, 'I will not believe anything I cannot understand.' 'Then, young man,' said he, 'your creed will be the shortest I know of.' "[58]

Trinitarianism means one God in three persons, but the very idea of "person" has changed over the centuries as theologians have pondered the limits of the analogy to human personhood. Secular thought since the eighteenth century has visualized "person" as a unique, self-initiating, and self-determining individual and has viewed modern notions of freedom, equality, and democracy as resting on a core idea of

[56] Smith, *Original Sin*, 10–11; A. C. McGiffert, *Protestant Thought before Kant* (Gloucester, MA, 1971 [1911]), 110–12; [Augustus Sachtleben], "Schaff's Germany," *RM*, 1 (1857), 155–6. For liberal southern theologians who remained Trinitarians see James Warley Miles, *Philosophic Theology: Or, Ultimate Grounds of All Religious Belief Based on Reason* (Charleston, SC, 1849), pt. 2:ch. 4, and William Porcher DuBose, *Turning Points in My Life* (New York, 1912), 104–7. See also Supplementary References: "Trinitarianism."

[57] Edward Gibbon, *The History of the Decline and Fall of the Roman Empire*, ed. David Womersley, 3 vols. (London, 1994), 1:580, quote at 2:33, 3:ch. 54. Gibbon demonstrated the extensive political strength of Arianism down to the early Middle Ages: 1:chs. 21 and 22, and the running account in vols. 2 and 3. Dew, *Digest*, 315–16; also, *TSW*, 9:82.

[58] Basil Manly, *Divine Efficiency Consistent with Human Activity* (Tuscaloosa, AL, 1849), 12. Philip Schaff spoke for all Trinitarians when he complained of the inadequacy of language to express the unique, mysterious, and indispensable notion of a triune God: *History of the Christian Church*, 5th ed., rev., 8 vols. (Grand Rapids, MI, 1960), 3:676–7.

personal autonomy. Liberal Protestants have followed suit, although with some discomfiture. Schleiermacher relegated the Trinity to an appendix in his *Christian Faith* and denied its indispensability to Christianity.[59]

The self-proclaimed orthodox Lyman Beecher, who defended the doctrine of the Trinity vigorously in his early years, mentioned it less over time and with little discernible conviction. Horace Bushnell developed a spirited defense-of-sorts of the Trinity that made the orthodox choke. Declaring God directly related to His creatures, he described the Trinity as "symbol"; in an effort to translate the concept into ordinary language, he appealed to the imagination as alone able to grasp it. If Bushnell had intended to do no more than emphasize the ultimate mystery, he might not have aroused the ire of the orthodox. But as he made clear, his defense of the Trinity formed part of his largely aesthetic vision of the content of Christianity. The South had its own version. The Reverend Theodore Clapp of New Orleans, protesting against the distortion of Unitarian views, complained that the American public judged ministers, first and foremost, by their stand on the Trinity. Quoting "I am the resurrection and the life," he acknowledged Jesus' "divinity" but treated Jesus basically as a prophet. Clapp came close to describing Trinitarians as tritheists. In contrast, D. H. Hill wrote in *Southern Presbyterian Review* that "This unity in Trinity is, undoubtedly, mysterious and incomprehensible. But it is not unreasonable and beyond the capacity and limits of reason to discover or comprehend. But so is all that relates to God and things supernatural and divine."[60]

These knotty theological debates, which try the patience of the practical or the non-philosophically inclined, have critical social and political implications. No simple dichotomy between Trinitarianism and social corporatism versus anti-Trinitarianism and individualism would bear examination, but a tendency toward correlation does exist and did exist in the minds of orthodox Southerners. Anti-Trinitarianism correlates nicely with the bourgeois individualism of modernism, whereas revolts of both the antibourgeois Left and Right have repeatedly fallen back on Trinitarian theology.

According to Jürgen Moltmann, a prominent "liberation theologian," "The problem with monotheism is a political one, namely the notion of a divine monarchy in heaven justifies earthly domination." Moltmann notwithstanding, southern theologians had the wit to put a social or interpersonal understanding of the Trinity

---

[59] Ted Peters, *God as Trinity: Relationality and Temporality in Divine Life* (Louisville, KY, 1993), 34–7; Pelikan, *Christian Tradition*, 1:223–4. In criticizing non-Trinitarian monotheism, specifically Islamic, Girardeau stressed interpersonality as a model of human social relations: *Theological Questions*, 8–12, 403–4. See also Supplementary References: "Trinitarianism."

[60] Vincent Harding, *A Certain Magnificence: Lyman Beecher and the Transfiguration of American Protestantism, 1775–1863* (Brooklyn, NY, 1991), 112–13, 181–2, and 487 n. 36; Bushnell, *Sermons*, esp. 39–41; Theodore Clapp, New Orleans *Daily Picayune*, Feb. 20, 1848, Mar. 4, Apr. 30, 1849, Jan. 6, 1850; D. H. Hill, "The Bible," *SPR*, 7 (1853), 478. For Bushnell's controversial formulation on the Trinity see Robert Bruce Mullin, *The Puritan as Yankee: A Life of Horace Bushnell* (Grand Rapids, MI, 2002), 134–8, 172–5. Prominent women abolitionists rejected the divinity of Christ: Speicher, *Religious World of Antislavery Women*, ch. 3. Lydia Maria Child concluded that, strictly speaking, no monotheistic religion had ever existed: Child, *Progress of Religious Ideas*, 2:181, 3:423–4.

to conservative uses. They understood the Trinity as relation and grasped its significance for social life. Breckenridge, Dabney, and Thornwell complained about the
awkwardness of "person" as applied to God. Breckinridge taught that each "person" of the Trinity "is really God," although none exclusively so: "Moreover, the
essence of God must be considered absolutely, the person, relatively." The Trinity includes "the idea of relation, as paternity, filiation, procession." For Dabney,
the three persons of the Trinity constitute "an eternal relation." Thornwell spoke
pithily: "So intimate is the connection between society and personality that in our
humble judgment, the infinite God could neither be holy nor blessed unless there
was a foundation for society in the very essence of the Deity." God as single person "would want that union without which the person would be imperfect." Before
time, "The Father rejoiced in the Son, and the Son rejoiced in the Father. There
was the deepest union and the most ineffable communion, and it was only to reflect
their blessedness and glory that other persons and other societies were formed." If
the unity of God implied a single Person, "It would be hard, perhaps impossible, to
conceive how He could have been a moral being when as yet there existed no object
but Himself on which His affections might be placed." If God were a solitary Being, "How could benevolence, fidelity or love exist in Him, except as susceptibilities
dominant in His nature?" Society constitutes the element of virtue.[61]

Some things never change. Our friend Professor Bo Morgan of Delta State University recently distinguished between today's northern and southern Baptists: "Northern Baptists say, 'There ain't no hell'; southern Baptists say, 'The hell there ain't.'"
   Heaven and hell, like original sin and the Trinity, became a political as well as
doctrinal battleground. Southern divines saw the northern interest in the abolition
of capital punishment primarily as a denial of hell. Calvinists like T. E. Peck led in
the defense of capital punishment, but the Arminian Henry Bascom, rebuking idol-
atrous love of wealth and luxuries as well as impatience with moral restraint, also
saw the promise of immortality as *fearful and momentous, in view of the hazards
it involves.* Bascom described hell as a residence in which no hope remains for
the condemned. Dabney conceded that hell might include bodily pain, but, citing
Turretin, he played down the hellfire while recalling that the God of love metes out
punishments as a "consuming fire." The Reverend William Barr of Abbeville, South
Carolina, wrote Calhoun in 1824: "Nothing but the inculcation of the strict morality
of the Bible with its awful sanctions of future rewards and punishments, can restrain
the passions of men and raise the tone of morals in any community." James Warley
Miles called upon Plato in defending the concept of punishment in the afterlife.[62]

---

[61] Breckenridge, *Knowledge of God,* ch. 15, quotes at 228–9; R. L. Dabney, *Systematic Theology,* 211
and, generally, chs. 16 and 17. Dagg regarded "person" as a poor rendering and preferred "substance":
Manual of Theology, 1:246, 252. In *JHTW* see "The Personality of God" (1:511) and "The Necessity of the Atonement" (2:234–5); also, "The Personality of the Holy Ghost" (2:337–67) – a sermon
delivered in Columbia and Charleston.

[62] Peck, *Miscellanies,* 2:52–4; Bascom, *Sermons from the Pulpit,* 149 and, generally, 141–70; William H.
Barr to John C. Calhoun, June 18, 1824, in *JCCP,* 9:164; Miles, *Philosophic Theology,* pt. 2:ch. 5. For

Explicit rejection of the doctrine of eternal torments appeared in seventeenth-century England and gained momentum in the eighteenth and nineteenth. But for orthodox Christians, the afterlife promised eternal torment to the unrepentant and eternal peace in reconciliation with God to the repentant. "Without fear of purgatory and the hope of the Last Judgment," the eminent legal scholar Harold J. Berman has written, "the Western legal tradition could not have come into being." The earliest colonial statutes and case law in South Carolina acknowledged the right of slaves to religious participation precisely in recognition of their immortal souls. In any case, by the late eighteenth century some were questioning the moral compatibility of eternal punishments with God's goodness. Significantly, while appealing to Scripture, those who upheld the doctrine concentrated on the practical necessity for the maintenance of social order and the suppression of crime and immorality. Richard Baxter's *Saints' Everlasting Rest* (1649) set the tone for the Puritans with its theocentric, otherworldly vision of heaven. A more anthropocentric heaven emerged in the eighteenth century, one clothed in human love and progress, but Baxter remained popular in the South.[63]

Post-Kantian agnosticism, focusing on earthly perfection, undermined belief both in heaven and hell and in angels and devils. James Mill and John Stuart Mill advanced the curious notion that a just God would not consign people to eternal damnation. Nineteenth-century Romanticism strengthened the vision of afterlife as a continuation of earthly life without pain and trifles. But whereas Emerson considered heaven and hell as states of mind, orthodox Christians considered them places, with sophisticated southern theologians no less than rough-hewn country preachers reinforcing fears of hell and the hopes of those separated from loved ones by distance or death. Poignant private letters and diaries demonstrated even more than eloquent sermons the depth and extent of faith in a heaven in which the redeemed forever dwelt with loved ones.[64]

southern concern with the mounting campaign against capital punishment in the North see Plumer, *Law of God*, 421–2; "B.", "The New Social Propositions," *SLM*, 20 (1858), 299; W. A. Cave, *Two Sermons on the Times, Preached in St. John's Church, Tallahassee* (n.p., n.d. but 1860s), 10; *DD*, 852–62.

[63] A. O. Lovejoy, *The Great Chain of Being: A Study in the History of an Idea* (New York, 1960), 24–5; Harold J. Berman, *Law and Revolution: The Formation of the Western Legal Tradition* (Cambridge, MA, 1983), 558; James Lowell Underwood, *The Constitution of South Carolina*, 4 vols. (Columbia, SC, 1992–94), 3:10–11; D. P. Walker, *The Decline of Hell: Seventeenth-Century Discussions of Eternal Torment* (Chicago, 1964), esp. chs. 1 and 2; also, Geoffrey Rowell, *Hell and the Victorians: A Study of Nineteenth-Century Theological Controversies Concerning Eternal Punishment and the Future Life* (Oxford, U.K., 1974), 29–30 and ch. 8. See also Supplementary References: "Baxter."

[64] Lewis Perry observes that there is no way of knowing how many abolitionists doubted the existence of an afterlife, but he suggests considerable influence: Lewis Perry, *Childbirth, Marriage, and Reform: Henry Clarke Wright, 1797–1870* (Chicago, 1980), 155. For the influence of Horace Mann see Martin E. Marty, "Hell Disappeared. No One Noticed. A Civic Argument," *Harvard Theological Review*, 78 (1985), 391–8.

For commentaries on heaven from diverse sources see Susan L. Roberson, *Emerson in His Sermons: A Man-Made Self* (Columbia, MO, 1995), 49–50; Marianne Palmer Gaillard to Thomas Gaillard and John S. Palmer, Feb. 27, 1852, and Elizabeth Palmer Porcher to Esther Simons Palmer, Sept. 7, 1862, in Louis P. Towles, ed., *A World Turned Upside Down: The Palmers of South Santee, 1818–1881*

A great many white Southerners, in contrast to their black slaves, thought of heaven as a place of persisting inequalities. Their aspiration had ample precedent in an old British belief in a three-tiered heaven for the elite, middling estate, and the poor. Medieval Scandinavians, among others, sometimes buried slaves in the graves of their masters, presumably to serve them in the next world. "Is it possible," a plantation mistress asked the Reverend Francis Le Jau in 1711, "that any of my slaves could go to Heaven, & must I see them there?" The idea of class divisions in heaven captured the imagination of some prominent southern ministers. The Reverend Willard Preston, pastor of the Independent Presbyterian Church of Savannah, Georgia, may not have intended to say that heaven recapitulated class society in benign form, but his congregation could hardly be blamed for drawing that conclusion. He spoke glowingly of heaven as a "locality" within which ordinary men and women steadily improved through association with "prophets and apostles, and martyred confessors, and others most favored and distinguished on earth." He asked, "What will it be to sit at their feet and still learn lessons, which they will be capable of teaching!" He allowed "grades in heaven, of different degrees of knowledge, though eternally ascending. For heaven is a world, a state of endless progress."[65]

To what extent country preachers agreed with Preston we cannot say. At this distance and without a full text we cannot interpret the sermon of the Baptist preacher who, extolling the beauties of heaven, brought his subject home: "O my dear honeys, heaven is a Kentucky of a place." Among laymen, John Fletcher – citing Genesis, 25:23, and Romans, 9:12 – asked: "Can the inequality of man be more strongly inculcated? And St. Paul seems to suggest that such inequality will exist hereafter." Fletcher quoted Corinthians, 15:41–42: "There is one glory of the sun, another of the moon, and another glory of the stars; for as one star differeth from another star in glory, so also is the resurrection of the dead." The great object in the creation of the individual is his advance toward "an approximation of being able to see God as he is."[66]

(Columbia, SC, 1996), 175, 342; Samuel Benedict, *"The Blessed Dead Are Waiting for Us": A Sermon* (Macon, GA, 1863), 7; Robert Partin, "Sustaining Faith of an Alabama Soldier," *Civil War History,* 6 (1960), 427, 429; Walter W. Pharr, *Funeral Sermon on Capt. A. K. Simonton, of Statesville, N.C.* (Salisbury, NC, 1862), 11–12; J. M. Pringle to W. P. Miles, July 20, 1842, in Miles Papers, at UNC-SHC. Also, Girardeau, *Sermons,* 33; Anna Matilda King to Thomas Butler King, Nov. 28, 1853, in T. B. King Papers, at UNC-SHC; Sarah E. Watkins to Letitia A. Walton, June 4, 1854, Feb. 6, 1858, July 10, 1860, July 22, 1861, June 27, 1862, in E. Grey Dimond and Herman Hattaway, eds., *Letters from Forest Place: A Plantation Family's Correspondence* (Jackson, MS, 1993), 78, 121, 172, 241, 283; A. L. Broiderick, "Recollection of Thirty Years" (ms.), 8, at LSU; Dickson D. Bruce, Jr., *And They All Sang Hallelujah: Plain-Folk Camp-Meeting Religion, 1800–1845* (Knoxville, TN, 1974), 103.

65 Keith Thomas, *Religion and the Decline of Magic* (London, 1971), 152; Ruth Mazo Karras, *Slavery and Society in Medieval Scandinavia* (New Haven, CT, 1988), 65–6; Frank J. Klingberg, ed., *The Carolina Chronicle of Dr. Francis Le Jau, 1706–1717* (Berkeley, CA, 1956), 102; *Sermons by Willard Preston,* 302–16, quotes at 304, 308, 309.

66 Baptist preacher quoted in Arthur K. Moore, *The Frontier Mind: A Cultural Analysis of the Kentucky Frontiersman* (Lexington, KY, 1957), 24; Fletcher, *Studies on Slavery,* 407–8 (Fletcher added Matt., 25:21, 29, 30). In the Bluegrass the saying goes: "Heaven must be a Bluegrass of a place": R. Gerald

Southern divines did not dwell on a heaven that continued earthy inequality; indeed, many rejected it. However strongly they championed earthly inequality and social stratification, they resisted an extension they probably considered heretical. Citing Job, the Baptist Reverend Thornton Stringfellow, a wealthy slaveholder, held that, at death, "The small and the great are there, and the servant is free from his master." Death, he said, terminates the earthly distress that accompanies inequalities of wealth and power. Thornwell stared down protestors who objected to having a black church in Charleston: "There will be no bondage in heaven." Girardeau reminded parishioners that in this world the ungodly often fare well while the godly suffer. But on Judgment Day every one must stand alone, "patriarchs, kings, masters and dependents, parents and children, blacks and whites." After the War, Dabney, supporting racial segregation, conceded, "The unequal distribution of retributions here on earth, coupled with our confidence in the righteousness of God, compels a belief in a future existence, where all shall be equalized."[67]

Yet Calvinist and Arminian preachers described heaven in a manner that encouraged the notion of stratification. According to Thomas Curtis in *Southern Presbyterian Review,* Joseph Butler's *Analogy of Religion* established the probability of an afterlife "on the great law of nature, and of our human nature in particular – that we continue to be the same individuals in very different stages of existence, from the womb to the grave." Dagg taught that the soul separated from the body retains its mental powers. He viewed the damnation of sinners as everlasting awareness of separation from God's peace. Dagg may not have meant to imply a stratified heaven, but his words comforted those who did. Bishop Bascom described heaven as a "scene of action and display – the theater of Jehovah's immediate majesty" and "a magnificent scene of relationship and intercourse." Heaven housed the resurrected body and the active mind: "There will be intellectual enlargement .... Individuality and difference of character, obtaining among the good and devout of earth, will be perpetuated." As we approach the throne of God, the stronger the Christian character, the nearer we shall stand: "Heaven is a state of society but feebly typed by that of earth."[68]

The idea of a stratified heaven did not sit well with all slaveholders. Methodists might recall Bishop Asbury's infelicitously expressed assurance that in heaven all souls are white. "The grave levels all," wrote the Methodist Reverend H. N. McTyeire. Among laymen, in 1819 Ebenezer Jones of Tennessee advised his sons to treat their slaves kindly, for they will meet them in heaven, where "Christ will not

---

Alvey, *Kentucky Bluegrass Country* (Jackson, MS, 1992), 3. Some Protestants attributed to Catholics a belief in a socially stratified heaven. Bishop England protested vehemently that his Church held no such bizarre idea: in Messmer, ed., *Works of John England*, 3:316.

[67] Thornton Stringfellow, "Bible Argument," in E. N. Elliott, ed., *Cotton Is King and Pro-Slavery Arguments* (New York, 1969 [1860]), 469; "Christian Doctrine of Slavery," *JHTW*, 4:419; Girardeau, "Last Judgment," in *Sermons*, 13–37; Dabney, *Systematic Theology*, 823, also 850.

[68] Thomas Curtis, *SPR*, 7 (1853), 553–4; Dagg, *Manual of Theology*, 1:343–5; Bascom, *Sermons from the Pulpit*, 346–78, quotes at 351, 361, 364, 375. At a memorial for Thornwell, Benjamin Morgan Palmer envisioned Thornwell in heaven in the company of Luther, Calvin, and Beza: see Thornwell Jacobs, *The Life of William Plumer Jacobs* (New York, 1918), 65.

ask if folks are black or white." In 1837 John Walker, a planter in Virginia who had recently survived the attempt of a slave woman to poison him, prayed: "Prepare us oh Lord for a better world than this and eventually receive us both coloured and white to live with Thee for ever in Glory is the humble prayer of one of thine poor earthly worms. Amen." Many years later the young Eliza Frances Andrews cried, "I don't think there ought to be any distinction of classes or races in religion. We all have too little 'gentility' in the sight of God for that. I only wish I stood as well in the recording Angel's book as many a poor negro that I know." Here and there a slaveholder concluded that oppression of slaves in this world would disappear in the next.[69]

A substantial number of southern whites did believe in a stratified heaven. The idea of the absolute equality of souls in heaven encountered stiff resistance from the usually sober. Everard Green Baker – a young, educated, thoughtful planter in Jefferson County, Mississippi – read Boswell's *Samuel Johnson* in 1849: "Boswell said he believed there were, in the future state, different degrees of happiness adopted to our several capacities & that 'a worthy carman will get to Heaven as well as Sir Isaac Newton. Yet though equally good they will not have the same degree of happiness.' Johnson said, 'Probably not.'" Baker mused, "I deem Dr. Johnson as honest & efficient an Authority as any man that ever lived upon any subject he ever examined, gave his views upon." Baker's views provoked an exchange at his own family hearth. He believed in a stratified heaven, his relatives did not. He expected heathens who lived a moral life to enter heaven, whereas his relatives expected only those who professed Christ to enter. The more pious masters felt troubled about the eternal consequences for themselves of their treatment of slaves. Susan Dabney Smedes of Mississippi ended her postwar memoir with a telling incident. When her father died, one of his daughters asked the plantation Mammy, who had been warmly attached to him, if she thought he would be afraid to meet any of his servants in heaven. Miss Susan sighed in relief at Mammy's assurance that he would not.[70]

Slaves had their own ideas about heaven as a place in which the godly, regardless of earthly fortune or condition, dwelt in perpetual peace, and they prayed to meet in heaven the loved ones from whom they had been forcibly parted by sale or the division of an estate. But according to former slaves, no few white preachers

---

[69] Herbert Asbury, *A Methodist Saint: The Life of Bishop Asbury* (New York, 1927), 149; H. N. Mc-Tyeire, *Duties of Christian Masters,* ed. Thomas O. Summers (Nashville, TN, 1859), 214; Jones quoted in Chase C. Mooney, *Slavery in Tennessee* (Bloomington, IN, 1957), 92; John Walker Diary, Dec. 30, 1837, at UNC-SHC (Walker regularly prayed for his slaves); Eliza Frances Andrews, *War-Time Journal of a Georgia Girl* (New York, 1907), 72; Jean Bradley Anderson, *Piedmont Plantation: The Bennehan–Cameron Family and Lands in North Carolina* (Durham, NC, 1985), xxvii. Andrews later became a socialist. Some preachers specifically insisted upon equality in heaven; see e.g. the Methodist Reverend Tobias Gibson in early Mississippi: John D. Jones, *A Complete History of Methodism as Connected with the Mississippi Conference of the Methodist Episcopal Church, South,* 2 vols. (Nashville, TN, 1908), 1:106.

[70] E. G. Baker Diary, Oct. 4, 1849; Susan Dabney Smedes, *Memorials of a Southern Planter,* ed. Fletcher M. Green (New York, 1965 [1887]), 341.

advised them that blacks would continue to serve whites in heaven. When one slave shouted in church, her mistress sneered, "Shout on old 'nig' there is a kitchen in heaven for you to shout in, too." Sarah Fitzpatrick, an ex-slave, had a different notion: In heaven "everyday will be Sunday."[71]

Only a rare slave accepted white hopes or expectations for continued white supremacy in heaven. Adeline Johnson, one such who had been a mammy in South Carolina, expected to see her Savior and meet "all my white folks, just to wait on them and love them and serve them, sorta lak I did in slavery time." Bob Young, an ex-slave, thought that since blacks had been trained to serve, they would do better than whites as servants of God. Such attitudes fed the vanity of whites, who registered every such manifestation. According to one white Virginian, slaves "often" said that seeing their masters and mistresses in heaven would be their greatest pleasure. Other slaves doubted that whites would enter heaven at all. Jackson Whitney wrote his old master, who had reneged on a promise to allow him to buy his wife and children: If God will not punish you in the afterlife "for inflicting such distress on the poorest of His poor, then there is no use for *having any* God or *talking* about one." Black preachers found ways to indict the master's power as a temptation to sin and damnation.[72]

Slaves' attempts to live according to the Decalogue and the Sermon on the Mount may have earned them expectations of salvation, but too many whites saw such slave behavior as confirmation of the justice of slavery and of their own superior virtue.

---

[71] J. S. Buckingham, *The Slave States of America,* 2 vols. (New York, 1968 [1842]), 2:423–4. For black recollections of white preachers on inequality in heaven, see Franklin Moss in Norman R. Yetman, ed., *Life under the "Peculiar Institution"* (New York, 1970), 232; Ophelia Settle Egypt et al., eds., *Unwritten History: Autobiographical Accounts of Ex-Slaves* (Washington, DC, 1968 [1945]), 329; Benjamin A. Botkin, ed., *Lay My Burden Down* (Chicago, 1945), 25–6, 273; Charles Ball, *Fifty Years a Slave; Or, the Life of an American* (New York, 1859), 188–9; Julius Lester, *To Be a Slave* (New York, 1968), 80–2, 86–7; also, Charles L. Perdue, Jr., et al., eds., *Weevils in the Wheat: Interviews with Virginia Ex-Slaves* (Charlottesville, VA, 1976), 184; Fitzpatrick in John W. Blassingame, ed., *Slave Testimony: Two Centuries of Letters, Speeches, Interviews, and Autobiographies* (Baton Rouge, LA, 1977), 655.

[72] George Rawick, ed., *The American Slave: A Composite Autobiography,* 19 vols. (Westport, CT, 1972), South Carolina, 3 (pt. 3), 38–9, 273; Lawrence W. Levine, *Black Culture and Black Consciousness: Afro-American Folk Thought from Slavery to Freedom* (New York, 1977), 34–5; Jackson Whitney to William Riley, Mar. 15, 1859, in Blassingame, ed., *Slave Testimony,* 19, 22, 49–50, 114–15, quote at 115 (Whitney). For the white Virginian see Letitia A. Burwell, *A Girl's Life in Virginia before the War,* 2nd ed. (New York, 1895), 15.

For a brief statement of modern black theological assessment see Nicholas Cooper-Lewter and Henry H. Mitchell, *Soul Theology: The Heart of American Black Culture* (Nashville, TN, 1986), 32–3, 39–42, 95; for role reversals see Albert J. Raboteau, *Slave Religion: The "Invisible Institution" in the American South* (New York, 1978), 291–2, and Hortense Powdermaker, *After Freedom: A Cultural Study in the Deep South* (New York, 1939), 245–6; for the response to the death of hated masters see Egypt et al., eds., *Unwritten History,* 67; Lyle Saxon et al., *Gumbo Ya-Ya: A Collection of Louisiana Folk Tales* (New York, 1945), 447. For superb illustrations of a black preacher's warnings of the damnation of the whites see John G. Williams, *"De Ole Plantation"* (Charleston, SC, 1895), 2–3, 11. See also E. S. Abdy, *Journal of Residence and Tour in the United States of North America,* 3 vols. (New York, 1969 [1835]), 2:292; James Curry in Blassingame, ed., *Slave Testimony,* 135. Some slaves envisioned a stratified heaven in which whites served blacks.

When slaves prayed for the salvation of their masters' souls, they were simultaneously praying for the salvation of their own. An unidentified slave woman: "O Lord, bless my master. When he calls upon thee to damn his soul, do not hear him, but hear me – save him – make him know he is wicked, and he will pray to thee. I am afraid, O Lord, I have wished him bad wishes in my heart – keep me from wishing him bad – though he whips me and beats me sore, tell me of my sins, and make me pray more to thee – make me more glad for what thou hast done for me, a poor negro." Whites, few of whom grasped the meaning of the spirituals, displayed a magnificent capacity to hear only what they wanted to hear and pounced on the occasional testimony of a pious slave who accepted class and racial stratification in this world and the next.[73]

Christians could not readily separate belief in God and heaven from belief in Satan and hell. According to assorted wits, the devil's most brilliant and successful ploy has been to convince people he does not exist. "If the devil does not exist," writes Jeffrey Burton Russell, "then Christianity has been dead wrong on a central point right from the beginning." The devil-as-person lies at the heart of the problem of theodicy – the existence of evil in a world created by an omnipotent, omniscient, all-good God. Southern divines refused to subject the goodness of God to human criteria of goodness. They said with Isaiah, 55:9: "As the heavens are higher than the earth, so are my ways higher than your ways, and my thoughts than your thoughts."[74]

The reaction against the witch craze in the seventeenth century, the horrors of the religious wars, and the dramatic advance of science and secular rationalism undermined the idea of the devil as a person responsible for the evil in the world. As the predestinarianism of Luther and Calvin receded, God became more the embodiment of forgiveness and less of wrath, and the devil became an embarrassment to the sophisticated. With Ben Jonson the devil became a comic figure – an "ass." He emerged in nineteenth-century romantic literature as an attractive rebel against arbitrary authority. By 1800 the devil was well on his way to disappearing from Christian theology. Schleiermacher's retreat from the doctrine of original sin ended

---

[73] "A Slave Woman's Prayer," in Joseph Melvin Washington, ed., *Conversations with God: Two Centuries of Prayers by African Americans* (New York, 1994), 19; also, Byrl Anderson in Perdue et al., eds., *Weevils in the Wheat*, 9. Modern black theologians have stressed that, upon embracing Christianity, the slaves – who had inherited African traditional religion without a concept of hell – had to choose between the God of the hell-and-brimstone preachers, who would make their masters pay for their atrocities, and a God who was responsible for their own oppression.

[74] Jeffrey Burton Russell, *Satan: The Early Christian Tradition* (Ithaca, NY, 1981), 25, and see his perceptive remarks at 229. Russell's five volumes (Ithaca, NY, 1981–86) are indispensable for the history of the devil in Western thought. In *Mephistopheles: The Devil in the Modern World,* Russell traces the movement from a monistic notion of God as simultaneously good and evil to a dualistic conception of a good God and an evil devil to the tension-ridden Christian notion of a good and omnipotent God who suffers the existence of a rebellious evil spirit. On the evolution of the idea of the devil and its theological and social ramifications in the ancient, medieval, and modern worlds see, in addition to *Satan* and *Mephistopheles,* J. B. Russell, *The Devil: Perceptions of Evil from Antiquity to Primitive Christianity* as well as *Lucifer: The Devil in the Middle Ages.* Russell focuses on the problem of radical evil in *The Prince of Darkness: Radical Evil and the Power of Good in History.*

with the denial of the devil-as-person and his reconstruction as a metaphor for human frailty. Neither the Unitarians Herman Melville and Nathaniel Hawthorne, nor even the Trinitarian Edgar Allan Poe, found much use for a devil external to the human self. Orthodox divines were fighting one more rear-guard action.

The witch craze had taken a heavy toll, for the greater the power attributed to the devil and the greater the terror it conjured up, the greater the temptation toward religious skepticism. John Milton probably did not intend his Satan to be the attractive figure Romantics later found in *Paradise Lost*. But the Romantics employed Christian symbols to plumb the problem of good and evil in the human heart while draining those symbols of Christian content. Satan emerged as a heroic warrior against an arbitrary authority – a force for the liberation of the individual from the constraints of an oppressive order. Disbelief in the devil accompanied disbelief in such pillars of orthodoxy as the Trinity. Jeffrey Burton Russell comments on *Paradise Lost*: "The Devil, Sin, and Death are thus a monstrous parody of the Holy Trinity, the *circuminsessio* mutual indwelling of the three Persons of the Trinity disgustingly mirrored by this mutual incest."[75]

Milton, a best seller in such cultural centers as Nashville, received considerable attention in the South. After Shakespeare, Southerners quoted him more often than any other literary figure. Negative reactions were few and far between, most notably from Jefferson Davis, who loved Byron, Cervantes, and Shakespeare but found Milton a bore. More typically, commentators gushed in the manner of the Baptist Reverend J. L. Reynolds of Richmond, who described *Paradise Lost* as "the most sublime creation of human genius," or of Sarah Lois Wadley of Louisiana, who also found it "sublime." Elite ladies like Catherine Edmonston and Mary Moragné and the less affluent as well knew – in addition to *Paradise Lost* – Milton's *Allegro*, *Penserosa*, and *Comus* and read them aloud to other young ladies. Divines from every denomination joined in celebration of Milton and quoted him often. Among the Baptists, the Reverend J. R. Graves, a man hard to please, summoned Milton as an authority on church discipline, and Dagg summoned him on immersion.[76]

---

[75] Russell, *Mephistopheles*, 116. For the transformation of Milton's Satan at the end of the eighteenth century into a "generous outlaw or sublime criminal" see Mario Praz, *The Romantic Agony*, tr. Angus Davidson, 2nd ed. (London, 1970), 59; Abrams, *Natural Supernaturalism*, 12–13, 33. The Gnostics of the first Christian centuries had the devil as the bearer of knowledge, not a deceiver: Andrew Delbanco, *The Death of Satan: How Americans Have Lost the Sense of Evil* (New York, 1995), 25–6.

[76] F. Garvin Davenport, *Cultural Life in Nashville on the Eve of the Civil War* (Chapel Hill, NC, 1941), 174; William C. Davis, *Jefferson Davis: The Man and His Hour* (New York, 1991), 382; J. L. Reynolds, *The Man of Letters* (Richmond, VA, 1849), 13; Sarah Lois Wadley Private Journal, Nov. 3, 1863, at UNC-SHC; June 19, 1862, in Beth G. Crabtree and James W. Patton, eds., *"Journal of a Secesh Lady": The Diary of Catherine Devereux Edmonston, 1860–1866* (Raleigh, NC, 1979), 199; Moragné Journal, Mar. 3, 1838, in Craven, ed., *Neglected Thread*, 77; also, Oct. 9, 1860, in William R. Snell, ed., *Myra Inman: A Diary of the Civil War in East Tennessee* (Macon, GA, 2000), 71–2; Elizabeth Scott Neblett to Will Neblett, May 8, 1864, in Erika L. Murr, ed., *A Rebel Wife in Texas: The Diary and Letters of Elizabeth Scott Neblett, 1852–1864* (Baton Rouge, LA, 2001), 405; J. R. Graves, *The Great Iron Wheel; Or, Republicanism Backwards and Christianity Reversed* (Nashville, TN, 1856), 37, 39; Dagg, *Manual of Theology*, 2:47. The Methodist Bascom had nothing but praise for Milton: *Sermons from the Pulpit*, 70.

Much in Milton's theology and ecclesiology struck the right chord for southern ears, particularly his appeal to the authority of the Church fathers in defense of *sola scriptura*. Writing on the Bible in the 1853 *Southern Presbyterian Review*, D. H. Hill included Milton in his list of great poets who turned to the Bible for truth and inspiration. Presbyterians eagerly made him their own, and Thomas Smyth exploded at the temerity of Unitarian appropriation of him. Typically, Presbyterians celebrated, in the words of the Reverend J. M. Atkinson, Milton's "magnificent plea for the liberty of unlicensed printing," and they quoted "the immortal" Milton frequently and lovingly on theology, philosophy, and politics. After all, Milton defended free speech, scorned Catholicism, brilliantly personified sin in Satan, explained the ways of God to man, and acquitted God of responsibility for evil. Yet although Thornwell lauded Milton as a republican theorist on church polity and secular government, he surely knew that Milton moved away from his early Presbyterianism and derided the Presbyterian clergy. Southerners, like Northerners, read Milton through Joseph Addison's eyes as a Puritan poet and ignored the thinly disguised anti-Trinitarianism in *Paradise Lost*. Thornwell recognized Milton's Arianism but had to swallow hard.[77]

Few Southerners saw Milton's Satan as a praiseworthy symbol of rebelliousness against authority, although he chose to rule in hell rather than to serve in heaven. In 1844 a fascinated but horror-struck writer on the qualities of the statesman in *Southern Quarterly Review* observed that Milton's devil displayed amoral genius. In 1860 R. B. Witter, Jr., speaking in Pineville, Tennessee, playfully cited the attractions of Milton's devil. In Charleston, Mary Chesnut wrote that Milton obliterated all other devils so that only one of Miltonic proportions compelled belief. Even Goethe's Mephistopheles, she added, takes second place and less resembles the devil than his emissary. Southern divines doted on Bacon and Newton but faced a difficulty they did not meet squarely: The Nominalism espoused by Bacon and Newton undermined the idea that the devil had any referent outside of men's minds. Even Bunyan's beloved *Pilgrim's Progress* focused more on the evil within than on the evil spirit without. Southern divines sensed where liberal theology was leading: Abandon the idea of the devil-as-person, reducing the devil to a metaphor, and soon God-as-Person will disappear, also reduced to a metaphor. Thornwell alluded to a particularly dangerous implication for southern social as well as religious

---

77 [D. H. Hill], "The Bible," *SPR*, 7 (1853), 374–90; *TSW*, 9:313, also on Milton's republicanism see 3:42, 10:492; J. M. Atkinson, *God, The Giver of Victory and Peace: A Thanksgiving Sermon* (Raleigh, NC, 1862), 11; "Church-Boards and Presbyterianism," *JHTW*, 4:286. For the "immortal Milton" see *JHTW*, 3:550. For Thornwell's use of Milton see the perceptive remarks of Thomas E. Jenkins, *The Character of God: Recovering the Lost Literary Power of American Protestantism* (New York, 1997), 100 (cf. *JHTW*, 2:257–8). *Paradise Lost* was widely taught, especially at women's schools: Elizabeth Barber Young, *A Study of the Curricula of Seven Selected Women's Colleges of the Southern States* (New York, 1932), 4. On Addison's influence see Christopher Hill, *Some Intellectual Consequences of the English Revolution* (Madison, WI, 1980), 5. On Milton's religious thought and influence see Reventlow, *Authority of the Bible*, 155–66. Some left-wing critics still see Milton's Satan as an attractive rebel against the established order. For a critical assessment see Lydia Dittler Schulman, *Paradise Lost and the Rise of the American Republic* (Boston, 1992), 62–3, also 51–6 and literature cited.

thought. He referred, without specific citation, to "Kurtz's ingenious effort to explain the malice of the Devil." Presumably, Thornwell was referring to John Henry Kurtz's argument that the devil, a fallen angel incapable of repentance and salvation, was a manifestation of "ungodly self-determination." The Reverend Charles Minnigerode spoke more directly when he told his Episcopalian congregants in Richmond that they were a power either for God or for the devil.[78]

Many abolitionists substituted the Spirit for the Word and substituted the spirit or conscience of the individual for the Holy Spirit, understood as the Third Person of the triune God. Despite fierce resistance in northern churches, Southerners saw Northerners as steadily accommodating to the abolitionists' implicit divorce of the Holy Spirit from the Word. In contrast, Southerners stood on the Word as the embodiment of the Spirit. As the abolitionists shifted theologically, they destroyed any remaining chance for a significant conversion of the South to antislavery. Despite much puffery, rationalization of special interests, and demagogy, those proslavery and antislavery divines who preached holy war saw the Kingdom of God arrayed against the Kingdom of Satan. Tragically, honest Christians could not agree on which was which. They assumed that Northerners and Southerners shared the same understanding of conscience and morality – an understanding derived from a commonly held Christian doctrine. They were wrong. Those who upheld and those who denied the divine sanction of slavery disagreed on the essentials of Christian doctrine and on the nature of conscience and moral standards. In consequence, they had incompatible visions of the social relations necessary to sustain Christianity in a sinful world.

---

[78] "Characteristics of a Statesman," *SQR*, 6 (1844), 114; R. B. Witter, Jr., "A Lecture – Not on the Devil," *SLM*, 30 (1860), 452. For another playful treatment of the devil see "R." [of Tennessee], "A Lecture Not on the Devil – But on Whiskers," *SLM*, 33 (1861), 47–55; Chesnut Diary, Jan. 14, 1864, in Woodward, ed., *Mary Chesnut's Civil War*, 543; *JHTW*, 1:299; John Henry Kurtz, *The Bible and Astronomy: An Exposition of the Biblical Cosmology and Its Relations to Natural Science*, tr. T. D. Simonton (Philadelphia, 1857), esp. 215–22, quote at 220; Charles Minnigerode, *Power: A Sermon* (Richmond, VA, 1964), 4; also, Henry W. Miller, *Address Delivered before the Philanthropic and Dialectic Societies of the University of North-Carolina* (Raleigh, NC, 1857), 13.

18

Jerusalem and Athens – Against Paris

What has Athens to do with Jerusalem? What concord is there between the Academy and the Church? what between heretics and Christians?

—Tertullian[1]

There was no disagreement: Young Southerners, in particular the young men slated to steer southern slave society through times of mortal danger, had to be steeped in moral philosophy. Moral philosophy meant core Christian doctrine. Core Christian doctrine had to be defended through reason as well as upheld through faith. Hence, southern college students were treated with heavy doses of "Evidences of Christianity." "Evidences" offered historical accounts for miracles – a major point in William Paley's textbooks on moral philosophy and ethics. A good many southern schools also assigned the work of President Francis Wayland of Brown University. Hampton-Sidney added Bishop Joseph Butler to Paley when it inaugurated its own course in 1825, and LaGrange College in Tennessee and Oglethorpe College in Georgia added Archibald Alexander. The Associate Presbyterians at Erskine College in western South Carolina used Butler; Baptist and Methodist Colleges used Paley. Municipal and state colleges – the College of Charleston, South Carolina College, and the universities of Alabama, Mississippi, and Louisiana – introduced courses in evidences of Christianity. While Mr. Jefferson spun in his grave, even the University of Virginia, the most secular of the southern universities, offered such a course in 1851/52 with lectures by a string of Presbyterian divines.[2]

---

[1] Tertullian, "The Prescription against Heretics," in Alexander Roberts and James Donaldson, eds., rev. by A. Cleveland Coxe, *Ante-Nicene Fathers*, vol. 3, *Latin Christianity: Its Founder, Tertullian* (Peabody, MA, 1995 [1885]), 246. Mrs. Roger Pryor found a special use for Tertullian, quoting his advice on the proper dress and deportment of ladies: Mary A. H. Gay, *Life in Dixie during the War*, 5th ed. (Atlanta, GA, 1979 [1897]), 73.

[2] *DCA*, 71–2; E. Brooks Holifield, *The Gentlemen Theologians: American Theology in Southern Culture, 1795–1860* (Durham, NC, 1978), 95–6. Presbyterians who lectured at Virginia: William S. Plumer, Alexander McGill, James Alexander, Robert Breckenridge, Stuart Robinson, N. L. Rice, and Moses Dury Hoge.

But the divines wondered whether courses in moral philosophy and evidences of Christianity, instead of demonstrating the compatibility of the Bible and science, might inadvertently serve as transmission belts for those on their way from Christian theology to materialism or to some non-Christian ethical theory. In a difficult battle to reconcile science and philosophy with the Bible, the divines sought to distinguish the deified "Reason" of Hume and the French Enlightenment from "right reason." In the South, even more readily than in the North, moral philosophy mounted a counterattack against the radical French Enlightenment and a defense of the conservative features of the Scottish Enlightenment. The Methodist Protestant Reverend Andrew Adgate Lipscomb warned students at the University of Alabama to combat both materialism and subjective idealism: "If there had been no Materialism, there would have been no Transcendentalism." To the Methodist Bishop George Foster Pierce of Georgia, "The reign of reason was the reign of terror, torment, and wickedness," which drove Europeans to prefer popery and military despotism. Calvinist and Arminian professors of moral philosophy agreed on an innate sense of good and evil and on the guidance of Scripture.[3]

For a long time, southern colleges relied on the texts of the widely read Anglican theologian William Paley and on the northern Baptist Francis Wayland. Robert Lewis Dabney, among many others, credited Paley with repelling David Hume's onslaught against the argument from design and applauded his "teleological argument for the being and attributes of a God." But Paley made conservatives uneasy, in part because in 1802 – in his defense of the argument from design in his *Natural Theology* – Paley supported Lyell's evolutionary geology and the theory of gradual operations of natural agencies to explain the order, structure, and function

---

[3] A. A. Lipscomb, *The Morbid Exhibition of the Human Mind* (Tuscaloosa, AL, 1846), 8–9, 19–20, quote at 9. The windy Lipscomb enjoyed a reputation for learning and eloquence even among Baptists: see Rhoda Coleman Ellison, *History of Huntingdon College, 1854–1954* (University, AL, 1954), ch. 2. Atticus G. Haygood, ed., *Bishop Pierce's Sermons and Addresses, with a Few Special Discourses by Dr. [Lovick] Pierce* (Nashville, TN, 1887), 24; also, Jasper Adams, *Elements of Moral Philosophy* (Philadelphia, 1837), ch. 1; R. H. Rivers, *Elements of Moral Philosophy*, ed. Thomas O. Summers, 3rd ed. (Nashville, TN, 1883 [reprint of 1871 edition, which corresponded to the edition of 1860 except for the chapter on slavery]), 9–40. Of the South's twenty leading professors of moral philosophy, only four were laymen: Thomas Roderick Dew, George Tucker, David Swain, and Francis Lieber. Of the sixteen clerical professors, six were Presbyterians, six Methodists, two Baptists, and two Episcopalians. See Holifield, *Gentlemen Theologians*, 127–8 n. 4; also, James Oscar Farmer, Jr., *The Metaphysical Confederacy: James Henley Thornwell and the Synthesis of Southern Values* (Macon, GA, 1986), 161–2.
    The Scots, most notably Thomas Reid, stressed the centrality of self-consciousness in a philosophy dependent on scientific observation. Moral principles are self-evident intuitions not deducible from nonmoral judgments. An egalitarian epistemology assumed a common sense in ordinary men as well as the most learned. "Common sense" meant mankind's "communal sense": see esp. Sydney E. Ahlstrom, "Scottish Philosophy and American Theology," *Church History*, 24 (1855), 261. Moral philosophy, Norman S. Fiering observes, became for Americans a "semi-secular way station" between the era of theological predominance and that of science: "President Samuel Johnson and the Circle of Knowledge," *WMQ*, 3rd ser., 28 (1971), 199–236, quote at 233.

of nature. In Paley's generally optimistic view of human nature, men arrived at a sound morality through reason. As the transcendentalist Ralph Waldo Emerson saw, "Paley's deity and Calvin's deity are plainly two beings."[4]

Southern critics also objected to Paley's tendency to treat Scripture as supplementary rather than primary. In the 1850s John Fletcher (respectfully) and Albert Taylor Bledsoe (not so respectfully) pronounced Paley unsatisfactory. The Episcopalian Reverend Charles Cotesworth Pinckney of Charleston much preferred Jasper Adams's *Moral Philosophy* to Paley's text because it rested on "*the revelation of God's will in Jesus Christ.*" The Presbyterian Reverend S. J. Cassells of Savannah criticized Paley and the infidel Hume alike for denying man an intrinsic moral faculty: "The chief objection to Paley's system is not that it is utilitarian, but that it is *immoral.*" Cassells rebuked Paley for exalting self-love and selfishness and for basing moral obligation on self-interest. A contributor to the secular *Southern Quarterly Review*, in contrast, criticized him for denying an inherent moral faculty but applauded his seminal contributions to moral philosophy, insisting that utilitarianism had a legitimate place notwithstanding its excesses.[5]

Paley's *Moral Philosophy* projected an afterlife of rewards and punishments, pleasing Thornwell and Dabney, but Thornwell wondered "How so good a man as Dr. Paley, and so vigorous a thinker, could have written so bad a book." He deplored Paley's reduction of the problem of truth and lying to contractual relations and political economy. Thornwell recoiled from Paley's denial that conscience was an "original" (innate) sense. Paley, he objected, replaced Scripture with moral philosophy and dwelt on happiness: "This fundamental error, that Happiness is pleasure, pervades society. It is the animating spirit of the eager and restless struggle for wealth, honour, and power. It is the grand delusion of sin." Social leveling ensued: "Let all men be equally rich is the insidious fallacy – equally fed, equally clothed, equally exalted in social and political condition – and, like cattle in the same pasture, they must be all equally happy." Impetuous youth "have yet to learn the emptiness of pleasure, the agonies of power and the vanity of wealth." The liberal Francis Lieber, usually at sword's point with Thornwell, complained that Paley's theory of property invited communism, much as Jean-Jacques Rousseau's

---

[4] Robert L. Dabney, *Systematic Theology* (Carlisle, PA, 1985 [1878]), 13, 110, and Dabney, *The Sensualistic Philosophy of the Nineteenth Century, Considered*, new and enlarged edition (n.p., 1887), 161; Jaroslav Pelikan, *The Christian Tradition: A History of the Development of Doctrine*, 5 vols. (Chicago, 1989), 5:189–90; Emerson, undated, in James Elliot Cabot, *A Memoir of Ralph Waldo Emerson*, 2 vols. (Boston, 1887), 1:106.

[5] John Fletcher, *Studies on Slavery, in Easy Lessons* (Natchez, MS, 1852), 57–67; Albert Taylor Bledsoe, *An Essay on Liberty and Slavery* (Philadelphia, 1856), ch. 1; C. C. Pinckney, "Sermon on the Death of Jasper Adams," in Daniel L. Dreisbach, ed., *Religion and Politics in the Early Republic: Jasper Adams and the Church–State Debate* (Lexington, KY, 1996), 175; [S. J. Cassells], "Conscience – Its Nature and Authority," *SPR*, 6 (1853), 460–1, 436; "The Works of William Paley," *SQR*, n.s. (3rd), 1 (1856), 118–50. Paley's *Evidences* drew fire from Bishop John England: Sebastian G. Messmer, ed., *The Works of the Right Rev. John England, First Bishop of Charleston*, 7 vols. (Cleveland, OH, 1908), 2:272, 278–310, 5:474–514; also, J. W. Miles, *The Ground of Morals: A Discourse Delivered before the Graduating Class of the College of Charleston* (Charleston, SC, 1852), 10.

political theory invited "democratic absolutism." Lieber, accusing Paley of carrying utilitarianism to an "atrocious" point, dismissed him as a driveler and "an old granny" who fudged difficulties.[6]

Jeremy Bentham's pleasure–pain calculus and "the greatest good for the greatest number" kept resurfacing in southern thought despite much opposition, and some proslavery Southerners put utilitarianism to as good use as antislavery Northerners did. But in disparaging "metaphysics" Bentham, like subsequent logical positivists, disparaged theology and any meaningful statements about God, and utilitarianism's morally corrosive spirit upset the Episcopalian Jasper Adams, the Catholic John England, and the Methodist W. M. Wightman, as well as the Presbyterian Thornwell.[7]

The Presbyterian Reverend W. A. Hall, preaching to Confederate troops, denounced Paley's utilitarianism as a philosophy of selfishness akin to the doctrines of French materialism and of German idealism's diminution of the Bible. Utilitarianism, Hall added, led logically to majority rule. Dabney accused New England theologians of implicitly following utilitarianism into marketplace ethics. Alexander Stephens, agreeing that mutual love requires concern for the happiness of others, counterpoised a doctrine of the greatest good for the constituent parts of humanity. Stephens explicated this common southern theme with reference to the greater competence of some relative to others, which translates as justice for all within their capacity and social station. Chancellor William Harper and J. H. Hammond identified utilitarianism with abolitionism and political and social radicalism; Thomas Caute Reynolds derided utiliarianism as "abominable and groveling"; and George Frederick Holmes excoriated "beggarly Benthamism" and delighted in Madame Germaine De Staël's moral critique of utilitarianism. It says a great deal about the importance to Southerners of Paley's critique of Hume that they tolerated his text at all, but until they began to write their own textbooks on moral philosophy, his looked as good as any available.[8]

---

[6] J. H. Thornwell, "Principles of Moral and Political Economy," *SPR*, 7 (1853), 1–52, quote at 33. *JHTW*, 2:458–9, 466, 494, 522–3. See also Holifield, *Gentlemen Theologians*, ch. 4; Francis Lieber, "History and Political Science" (1859), in Daniel C. Gilman, ed., *The Miscellaneous Writings of Francis Lieber*, 2 vols. (Philadelphia, 1881), 362, 385; Frank Friedel, *Francis Lieber; Nineteenth-Century Liberal* (Gloucester, MA, 1968 [1947]), 146; M. LaBorde, *History of South Carolina College* (Charleston, SC, 1874), 358–60.

[7] Adams, *Moral Philosophy*, 14–15, 36; W. M. Wightman, *Inaugural Address Delivered at the Opening of the Southern University, Greensboro, Ala.* (Marion, AL, 1859), 9; B. M. Palmer, *The Life and Letters of James Henley Thornwell* (Richmond, VA, 1875), 92. For a rosier view see Gray Carroll, "Essay on the Utilitarian Spirit of the Present Day as Affecting Our Literature" (M.A. thesis, 1855, typescript at UVA). Alexander B. Meek of Alabama in 1841 and Cassells in 1855 worried about utilitarian influence on the southern campuses: Meek, "Discourse before the Literary Societies of LaGrange College," *Magnolia*, 3 (1841), 429–31; Cassells, "Relation of Justice to Benevolence," *SPR*, 7 (1855), 95–6.

[8] Dabney, *Systematic Theology*, 169, 101, 296–7, 508–10; William A. Hall, *Historic Significance of the Southern Revolution* (Petersburg, VA, 1864). See also John Randolph's strictures on Paley's "great mischief": Randolph to Francis Scott Key, Feb. 7, 1814, in Hugh A. Garland, *The Life of John Randolph of Roanoke*, 2 vols. (New York, 1969 [1859]), 2:31. See also *Plantation Life: The Narratives of Mrs.*

Southerners warmly embraced Francis Wayland's defense of legitimate authority in socially stratified society, but he, too, proved a disappointment. Wake Forest, the University of Mississippi, and other colleges – but not the University of North Carolina – dropped his *Moral Philosophy* because of its antislavery and because of Wayland's support for dissemination of antislavery tracts by the American Tract Society and his opposition to the Kansas–Nebraska Act. John Fletcher opened his *Studies on Slavery* with a critique of Wayland's *Moral Science,* appealing solely to the Bible as the source of moral law and assailing William Ellery Channing and Albert Barnes. Bledsoe, alarmed that *Moral Science* had sold more than fifty thousand copies, got off a ferocious salvo. William A. Smith, in lectures at Randolph-Macon College and in his *Philosophy and Practice of Slavery,* worried that Wayland was leading the young astray by antislavery conclusions drawn from Christian principles. Smith need not have worried so much, for southern students rebelled against the assignment of antislavery propaganda. One teacher who assigned *Moral Science* told his students to ignore the section on slavery, whereupon a young lady wanted to know why, if that section was unreliable, he expected her to trust the rest.[9]

Those who sought support for slavery in moral philosophy proceeded from theology. For Thornwell, the search for truth depended on the idea of creation and, with it, the obligation of God's creatures to each other. Slight that idea, he said, and amoral utilitarian criteria would guide human conduct: "Strike out justice and moral law, and society becomes the mere aggregation of individuals, and not their union by solemn and sacred ties upon the basis of mutual rights and duties; and man ceases to be anything but a higher class of beast." He recalled the Reign of Terror: "He who trifles with the eternal distinctions of right and wrong, not only forgoes the blessedness of the next world, but introduces disorder and confusion in this."[10]

Henry Schoolcraft (New York, 1969 [1860]), 186; Alexander H. Stephens, *A Constitutional View of the Late War between the States,* 2 vols. (New York, 1970 [1868, 1870]), 1:540–1; Chancellor Harper, "Slavery in the Light of Social Ethics," in E. N. Elliott, ed., *Cotton Is King, and Pro-Slavery Arguments* (New York, 1969 [1860]), esp. 552, 556, 562; Drew Gilpin Faust, *James Henry Hammond and the Old South* (Baton Rouge, LA, 1982), 261–2; [T. C. Reynolds], "Mr. Simms as a Political Writer," *SLM,* 9 (1843), 755; George Fredrick Holmes, *Inaugural Address, Delivered at the Occasion of the Opening of the University of the State of Mississippi* (Memphis, TN, 1849), 19; [Holmes], "The Nineteenth Century," *SLM,* 17 (1851), 460; also, J. A. Winslow, "Utilitarianism," *VUM,* 4 (1860), 297–300. For an Episcopalian attack on utilitarianism's disregard of God's moral law, see C. E. Gadsden, *The Times, Morally Considered* (Charleston, SC, 1843): 10. For a Charlestonian's version of Stephens on rights within station see James M. Walker, *The Theory of the Common Law* (Boston, 1852), 59. On southern reactions to the utilitarians' support for majority rule see Charles J. Holden, *In the Great Maelstrom: Conservatives in Post–Civil War South Carolina* (Columbia, SC, 2002), ch. 2; Rivers, *Moral Philosophy,* 47.

9 Fletcher, *Studies on Slavery,* 7–57; Bledsoe, *Liberty and Slavery,* ch. 2; William A. Smith, *Lectures on the Philosophy and Practice of Slavery* (Nashville, TN, 1856), vi–vii; also, Rivers, *Moral Philosophy,* 28–9; Frederick Law Olmsted, *A Journey in the Back Country* (New York, 1970 [1860]), 452–3. Yet, the College of Louisiana adopted Paley's *Evidences* and Wayland's *Moral Philosophy,* finding them in accord with southern interests. See William Hamilton Nelson, *A Burning Torch and a Flaming Fire: The Story of Centenary College of Louisiana* (Nashville, TN, 1931), 92.

10 *JHTW,* 1:504–6.

Elements of Moral Philosophy by the Massachusetts-born Episcopalian Reverend Jasper Adams, president of the College of Charleston, became a popular alternative to British and northern texts. Adams defended the theory of an innate sense of good and evil, and – like Thornwell, who much preferred Adams to Paley – he regarded conscience as a prime human faculty that must be enlightened by knowledge. Of Paley's utilitarianism Adams wrote: "The rule of expediency is a rule of calculation," valuable for external conduct but no substitute for an enlightened and unsophisticated conscience. Scripture must take priority. Adams, a unionist, quoted Elias Horry, who had endowed his chair, "You [Adams] have properly expressed what I understand by Political Philosophy, or Political Law, by the terms 'constitutional and international law,' regarding, however, each State in our Union or confederacy, as a sovereign State or community." Adams credited a divinely sanctioned slavery for freeing planters to cultivate the leisure that social and political leadership required.[11]

The Methodist Reverend R. H. Rivers – professor at Wesleyan University in Florence, Alabama – rejected Paley's text. The Calvinist Adams taught his course through lectures instead until, in 1860, he published his own *Elements of Moral Philosophy* on "Theoretical Ethics" (moral law, agency, obligation, conduct, and governance) and "Practical Ethics" (duties to God, personal and political ethics, and duties of superiors to inferiors). The principal difference between Rivers's book and its Calvinist rivals lay in his forceful defense of freedom of the will; in social and political philosophy it differed little, if at all. Rivers, too, defended slavery, stressed the obligation to care for the poor and unfortunate, and extolled republican government as most closely approximating moral government.[12]

Philosophical quarrels had political implications as well. Baptist colleges assigned Thomas Roderick Dew's *Essay on Slavery*, along with *Elements of Moral Science* by President John Leadley Dagg of Mercer College. The Calvinist Dagg stressed intention for the moral quality of an act. Arminians such as the Methodist Reverend Edward Wadsworth of Alabama agreed. Defending slaveholders against the charge of sinfulness, Dagg denied the existence of an equality of rights independent of social condition. Thomas Smyth, conversant with Scottish and German philosophy, emerged as a leading spokesman for an ethic in which, if morality depends upon purity of motives, then the social order depends upon "relations." A nonslaveholder himself, Smyth saw God's world, natural and moral, as a hierarchy, concluding that slavery constituted a part of God's political economy.[13]

---

[11] Adams, *Moral Philosophy*, 14–15, 113, 134, quoted at 36–7 and Horry quoted at vii. For Thornwell's preference see *JHTW*, 2:554 n. 1. Jasper Adams, a fellow of the American Academy of Arts and Sciences and a cousin of John Quincy Adams, settled gracefully in Charleston and married well.

[12] Rivers, *Moral Philosophy*, xv–xvii, 26–30, 264–5. Rivers spoke without manuscript or notes and required students to take copious notes and prepare abstracts. He acknowledged that his book drew on students' abstracts.

[13] J. L. Dagg, *Manual of Theology: A Treatise on Christian Doctrine and a Treatise on Church Order*, 2 vols. (New York, 1980 [1857–58]), 144; E. Wadsworth, "God and Adam Are Co-Workers," in William T. Smithson, ed., *The Methodist Pulpit South* (Washington, DC, 1858), 103; also, James Porter,

It took George Fitzhugh to ridicule philosophy altogether: "Philosophy can neither account for the past, comprehend the present, nor foresee and provide for the future. 'I'll none of it.'" Fitzhugh probably missed Tertullian's quip, "Philosophers are the patriarchs of heresy," much as he missed Pascal's reply, "Se moquier de la philosophie, c'est vraiment philosopher." Impatient with German idealism, Fitzhugh also lashed out at the *philosophes* for doubting "whether there was any other than a physical world." Dew thought differently: "Philosophy is the ally of the true religion, while ignorance leads on to idolatry and superstition." Thornwell stood with Dew, regarding philosophy as "only a name for the love of truth," but he saw in Johann Gottlieb Fichte a confession that philosophical idealism ended as nothing. In short, implicitly and explicitly, theology lay at the heart of philosophical disputes.[14]

Southern participants in transatlantic philosophical controversies acknowledged the talent of the most formidable of their adversaries – Rousseau, Kant, Hegel, Fichte – but they rarely responded to their philosophies with the care accorded their theologies. Southerners scoffed that German philosophy was conquering New England in a form too superficial for discussion. J. E. Snodgrass of Baltimore – physician, publisher, and good friend of Edgar Allan Poe – defended the Transcendentalists against the accusation of obscurantism and admired their search for truth, but he, too, complained that Yankee imitators rendered the search ridiculous. Southern critics themselves showed little disposition to examine closely the philosophers they thought New Englanders were distorting. George Frederick Holmes, however, called for adequate study and proper measurement of German philosophy's formidable challenges, especially for closer attention to – and refutation of – Hegel. Similarly, a commentator in *Southern Quarterly Review* asked for better balance, as he honored Friedrich von Schelling for rescuing German philosophy

---

Compendium of Methodism (Boston, 1851), 258–60. On the use of Dagg's book see George P. Schmidt, *The Liberal Arts College: A Chapter in American Cultural History* (New Brunswick, NJ, 1957), 49; *DGB*, 1:241; R. G. Gardner, "The Alabama Female Athenaeum and John Leadley Dagg in Alabama," *Alabama Baptist Historian*, 5 (1969), 3–32; Mark E. Dever, "John L. Dagg," in Timothy George and Davis S. Dockery, eds., *Baptist Theologians* (Nashville, TN, 1990), 180. For a fine introduction to Smyth see Holifield, *Gentlemen Theologians*, 149–54.

[14] George Fitzhugh, *Cannibals All!; Or Slaves without Masters* (Cambridge, MA, 1960 [1857]), 56; Tertullian quoted in Francis Turretin, *Institutes of Elenctic Theology*, ed. James T. Dennison, tr. George Musgrave Giger, 3 vols. (Phillipsburg, NJ, 1992–97), 1:47; Pascal quoted in Owen Chadwick, *From Bossuet to Newman: The Idea of Doctrinal Development* (Cambridge, U.K., 1957), 54; Thomas Roderick Dew, *Digest of the Laws, Customs, Manners, and Institutions of the Ancient and Modern Nations* (New York, 1884 [1852]), 61; *JHTW*, 3:150–1, quote at 461.

For attacks on philosophic idealism see "Standard and Nature of Religion in Three Sections," *JHTW*, 3:9–182, also, 4:167–8; *DD*, 1:440–65; *DD**, 4:66; Dabney, *Systematic Theology*, 22–3; T. E. Peck, *Miscellanies,* ed. T. C. Johnson, 3 vols. (Richmond, VA, 1895–97), 2:36–58; W. Rees, *A Sermon on Divine Providence* (Austin, TX, 1863, originally published in *SPR* in 1851), 3, 5. From Heidelberg in 1858, Charles Edward Everett, Jr. – theology student and son of a lowcountry Episcopalian minister – saw German religion as superficial and dishonest: C. E. Everett to Milton Everett, Apr. 13, 1858, in Frances Wallace Taylor et al., eds., *The Everett Letters: Correspondence of a South Carolina Family, 1851–1868* (Columbia, SC, 2000), 60–7.

from Fichte's subjective idealism, Hegel's objective idealism, and Spinoza's pantheism. Schelling, he said, demonstrated that the ultimate philosophy must be "a Philosophy of Theology."[15]

Talented Southerners able to evaluate the work of René Descartes, Samuel Taylor Coleridge, or the most difficult German philosophers felt little need to proceed once they concluded that the theology was unacceptable. The Descartes who divorced philosophy from theology drew criticism, but southern philosophers and theologians largely contented themselves with passing swipes. Holmes waved off Descartes as a purveyor of half-truths. A contributor to *Southern Quarterly Review,* noting Descartes' extraordinary influence, brushed him aside as an overrated philosopher who prepared the way for unbelief. In scattered remarks Thornwell displayed respect and occasional agreement but strong opposition as well: "It is yet a matter of experience that no one has ever, in point of fact, attained to right and worthy conceptions of the nature and character of God by the unassisted light of reason."[16]

A few voices rose to defend Descartes. William Somerville of Virginia in 1822, writing from Paris on revolutionary French politics, declared that he "came like the rosy steeds of Apollo to usher in the glorious morning of science." In the 1850s Professor W. J. Sasnett of Emory College, a prominent figure among southern Methodist intellectuals, took the measure of Descartes' formidable qualities as a philosopher and his extraordinary influence, but while criticizing Descartes' "ideal and subjective" thought he contented himself with a few broad strokes. A fellow Methodist ranked Descartes with Bacon as "profoundly philosophical minds" but offered little substantial criticism. J. P. Tusten, a contributor to *Southern Presbyterian Review,* credited Descartes with demolishing the medieval scholastics' "tottering systems" of the physical sciences, and a contributor to *Southern Literary Messenger* regretted the lack of attention paid to the relation between Descartes' method and that of Socrates and Plato. A contributor to *North Carolina University Magazine* complained: "Few of us have read Descartes, and yet his name is frequently on our lips; nay, we often hear him quoted from the very pulpit." The writer considered "cogito, ergo sum" a scientific starting point for philosophical support to religion, denied that Descartes sought to deduce existence from thought,

---

[15] J. E. Snodgrass, "Transcendentalism: A Miniature Essay," *Magnolia,* 4 (1842), 214–15; [George Frederick Holmes], "Thimm's Book," *SQR,* 11 (1847), 103; 117–67; [Holmes], "Morell's Philosophy of the Nineteenth Century," *SLM,* 16 (1850), 387; "The Philosophy of Schelling," *SQR,* n.s. (3rd), 2 (1857), 371–2, 387, 375–6, quote at 376, also 58, 69. For other calls to respect German achievements see "American Literature – 1," *SQR,* 11 (1847), 153–7, esp. 167; "Goethe's Auto-Biography," *SQR,* 11 (1847), 443. Two Methodists called for respectful treatment of German philosophy, in particular for appreciation of Kant's contributions to philosophy despite his errant theology: "R. C. P.", "The Relation of Christianity to Literature," *QRMECS,* 1 (1847), 189–90; W. J. Sasnett, "German Philosophy," *QRMECS,* 12 (1858), 343–4.

[16] [Holmes], "Vestiges of Civilization," *MMQR,* 4th ser., 5 (1853), 219, and [Holmes], "The Bacon of the Nineteenth Century – Second Paper," *MMQR,* 4th ser., 5 (1853), 493; "History of Philosophy," *SQR,* n.s. (3rd), 2 (1856), 245–250; *JHTW,* 1:59, 66, 74, quote at 74.

and rated *Meditations* "one of the noblest and most solid monuments to philosoph-ical genius." But these were passing remarks.[17]

Coleridge suffered a similar fate. The Calvinist Stuart Robinson of Kentucky and the Arminian R. H. Rivers of Alabama offered no elaboration when they cited Co-leridge favorably on the limits of religious reasoning and on crime and guilt. Nor did William Gilmore Simms when he referred to Coleridge as "one of the most remark-able of the poets and psychologists of the age." It was a common southern refrain that New England Transcendentalists, with a few exceptions like Theodore Parker, did not know the German philosophy they talked about and relied on secondary sources, principally on Coleridge and Thomas Carlyle. Southerners, however, were as culpable as Northerners.[18]

A contributor to *Southern Literary Messenger* (J. H. Bocock?) assured read-ers that Coleridge stirred only schoolboys and a handful of precious intellectuals, and Enoch Pond told readers of *Southern Presbyterian Review* that Coleridge in-fluenced only "a few young ministers" and that "Coleridgeism" had run its course in America. Meanwhile, Pond regretted the contributions of a superior intellect to a spreading pantheism. More plausibly, "R. C. P." wrote in *Quarterly Review of the Methodist Episcopal Church, South*: "No man has left a deeper impression on the inner spiritual life of the present century, than Coleridge."[19]

---

[17] William C. Somerville, *Letters from Paris on the Causes and Consequences of the French Revolu-tion* (Baltimore, 1822), 86; Sasnett, "German Philosophy," 324; "The Conflict of Modern Philoso-phy," *QRMECS*, 15 (1861), 163–5; [J. P. Tusten], "Chivalry and Civilization," *SPR*, 5 (1851), 225; "Descartes and His Method," *SLM*, 30 (1860), 314–15, 318–19. "On the True Meaning of 'Cogito, Ergo Sum,'" *North Carolina University Magazine*, 5 (1856), 66–71.

[18] Stuart Robinson, *Discourses of Redemption* (New York, 1866), 197; Rivers, *Moral Philosophy*, 33; [Simms], "Critical Notices," *SQR*, 9 (1854), 266; Simms had earlier extolled Coleridge in "Critical Notices," *SQR*, n.s., 8 (1853), 537. For southern sneers see e.g. *SQR*, 11 (1847), 146.

[19] "J. H. B." [J. H. Bocock probably, but possibly John H. Bernard], "Ralph Waldo Emerson," *SLM*, 18 (1852), 247; [Enoch Pond], "Coleridge," *SPR*, 2 (1861), 44; "R. C. P.", "Relation of Christianity to Literature," 191–2, quote at 191. Others in *QRMECS* acknowledged Coleridge's genius but re-gretted his hedging on Christian doctrine and his failure to offer a coherent doctrine of his own: see A. B. Stark, "Thomas Carlyle," *QRMECS*, 15 (1861), 195, 198; Sasnett, "German Philosophy," 338. A. B. Meek quoted Coleridge approvingly but called him a "solemn plagiarist": *Romantic Passages in Southwestern History* (New York, 1857), 171. Poe heatedly defended Coleridge as a literary critic: [E. A. Poe], *SLM*, 2 (1836), 451, 453; also, George Herbert Calvert, "German Literature," *SLM*, 2 (1836), 378. Mirabeau Lamar, president of the Republic of Texas and a respected poet, celebrated Coleridge in his own verse: Philip Graham, *The Life and Poems of Mirabeau B. Lamar* (Chapel Hill, NC, 1938), 116. George Frederick Holmes referred to "the high authority of that eminent critic, Samuel Taylor Coleridge": [Holmes], "Life and Writings of Rabelais," *SQR*, 7 (1845), 139. *Southern Presbyterian Review*, hostile to Coleridge's theology, nonetheless acknowledged a "great and origi-nal thinker" of unsurpassed psychological insight: "Critical Notices," *SPR*, 6 (1853), 593–4.
During the 1840s and 1850s, philosophical articles in *Southern Quarterly Review* and other jour-nals censured the idealism of Kant, Fichte, and Schelling – and also Goethe, Herder, and Cousin – as essentially pantheistic: see C. C. S. Farrar, "The Science of History," *DBR*, 5 (1848), 351–5; [Holmes], "Thimm's Book," 102–3; [Enoch Pond], "Philosophy in the Church," *SPR*, 4 (1850), 160–4. George Howe attacked DeWette and Spinoza for denying Moses' authorship of the Pentateuch and linked them to Thomas Paine: Howe, "The Genuineness of the Pentateuch," *SPR*, 4 (1850), 258–60. William

Yet another philosopher-theologian made Southerners uneasy. In 1736 *The Analogy of Religion* by Joseph Butler, bishop of Durham, provided, in Owen Chadwick's words, a "high example of the new theology of the eighteenth century, the effort to repose Christian truth upon an empirical basis of natural observation." Hugh Blair Grigsby reported that *Analogy* was Patrick Henry's "standard book through life." Its great impact came in the nineteenth century, going through many editions in the South as elsewhere in America and Britain.[20]

Perhaps more than any other work, *Analogy* strengthened those who appealed to reason to support revelation and who, like Dabney and Dagg, believed that *Analogy*'s natural religion defeated Deism and rational skepticism on their own ground. The Baptist Reverend Richard Furman of South Carolina saw a great work that dealt Hume a "death blow," and Methodists like D. M. Martindale of Louisiana similarly credited Butler with the best refutation of Hume's attack on the argument from design and also for "having established the probability of a future state" and for treating men "as free moral agents." Butler won plaudits, too, for his methodological contribution to the value and limits of analogy in scientific reasoning. Holmes valued analogy as probability, not proof, and denied that analogues justify positive conclusions. Unless as strict and precise as the data for induction, analogues provided only limited defense against objections. Butler's "immortal work" of "remarkable excellence" confined analogy to its legitimate sphere.[21]

Analogy drew high praise across the South but also induced nervousness – rather in the manner of Walpole's reply to Queen Caroline, who urged him to read it: "My religion is fixed: I do not want to change or improve it." The Baptist Reverend Richard Fuller wondered if *Analogy* did not encourage skepticism by raising more doubts than it allayed. Adherence to Scottish commonsense philosophy, evidences of Christianity, and appeals to reason proceeded in tension with stern Biblicism, and the effects of the tension are still debated. The usually steady Thornwell squirmed over a work he regarded as masterly and imperishable, but as early as 1841 he told R. J. Breckenridge that he intended to bring out a new edition of Butler with a chapter-by-chapter analysis "and a special consideration of the glaring defects in

Porcher Miles defended Spinoza against the "absurd" allegation of atheism and called him a great if underestimated thinker: "Oeuvres de Spinoza," *SQR*, 16 (1849), 76–81, quote at 79; for a qualified defense of Fichte see also *SQR*, 10 (1846), 253–4. Theodore Clapp, however, argued that atheists were in fact pantheists since they dissolved God in nature: "Discourse," New Orleans *Daily Picayune*, Dec. 16, 1849.

20. Chadwick, *Bossuet to Newman*, 77–8, quote at 78; Hugh Blair Grigsby, *The Virginia Convention of 1776* (New York, 1969 [1855]), 145. On the reception of *Analogy* see A. C. McGiffert, *Protestant Thought before Kant* (Gloucester, MA, 1971 [1911]), 239. See also Supplementary References: "Butler's *Analogy*."

21. Glenn T. Miller, *Piety and Intellect: The Aims and Purposes of Ante-Bellum Theological Education* (Atlanta, GA, 1990), 311 (Dagg); *DD**, 4:569; Richard Furman, *Pleasures of Piety and Other Poems* (Charleston, SC, 1859), 201–2; D. Martindale, "Footprints of the Creator," *QRMECS*, 5 (1851), 509; [George Frederick Holmes], "Butler's Analogy," *QRMECS*, 8 (1854), 231–2. For Butler's exemplary use of analogy and recognition of its limits, see "Butler's Analogy," *QRMECS*, 8 (1854), 214–48; "The Doctrine of the Trinity," in William T. Brantly, *Sermons* (Charleston, SC, 1858), 104.

the statement of Christian doctrine, with which the book abounds." Still, on balance Butler looked safe.[22]

The influential French philosopher Victor Cousin proved more troublesome than Butler. To southern applause, Cousin drew heavily on the Scots and resurrected medieval thought while rejecting the clerical authoritarianism attributed to it. Simms touted Cousin as a man who compels thought even if he does not satisfy it, and an array of intellectual luminaries invoked Cousin's views as authoritative support for their own. J. D. B. De Bow, especially addressing lawyers, recommended Cousin's treatise on natural and human law. A favorable review of *Beulah* chided Augusta Jane Evans for trivializing "the great Cousin" as a shallow pantheist. With a good deal of stretching, a contributor to *Southern Quarterly Review* enlisted Cousin in the defense of slavery, and in 1862 *Southern Literary Messenger* published an excerpt from Cousin on war to bolster the South's moral position and inspire its people. During the War, the Reverend John Jefferson DeYampert Renfroe, a leading Alabama Baptist, referred his congregation to Cousin's view that wars and catastrophes may benefit for future generations.[23]

Severity accompanied compliments. John Reuben Thompson of *Southern Literary Messenger* dismissed Cousin's *Philosophy of History* as weak pleading for a pet thesis. Charles Farrar, in *De Bow's Review,* scoffed at Cousin's vain effort to make God entirely comprehensible to the human mind. Thornwell, too, protested Cousin's assertion that reason could attain an absolute comprehension of the Godhead. He dismissed Cousin's psychology as "only another name for the intellectual intuition of Schelling," adding that his speculations "end exactly where those of Hegel begin – AT NOTHING." Still, Thornwell sometimes quoted Cousin favorably *in extenso*.[24]

So too, John Daniel Morell, another philosopher with a substantial transatlantic audience, got a mixed reception. *Southern Quarterly Review* and *Southern Literary Messenger,* which sometimes flirted with theological liberalism, generally approved of Morell's *Speculative Philosophy of Europe in the Nineteenth Century,* as did William Porcher Miles and James Warley Miles. Morell set the teeth of most

---

[22] Walpole quoted in Chadwick, *Bossuet to Newman,* 97; Richard Fuller, "Predestination," in Thomas J. Nettles, ed., *Southern Baptist Sermons on Sovereignty and Responsibility,* 2nd ed. (Harrisonburg, VA, 1995), 107; *JHTW,* 1:242; Thornwell to Breckenridge, Jan. 27, 1841, in Palmer, *Life and Letters of Thornwell,* 224.

[23] [William Gilmore Simms], *SQR,* n.s., 6 (1852), 242–4; [Simms], *SQR,* n.s., 10 (1854), 517–18; *DBR,* 13 (1852), 104–5; J. D. B. De Bow, "Law and Lawyers – No. 1," *DBR,* 19 (1855), 302 n.; "Beulah," *SLM,* 31 (1860), 247–8; "Mr. Smith" [of Virginia], "Character of the American People," *SQR,* n.s. (3rd), 2 (1857), 404–5; Victor Cousin, "War," *SLM,* 34 (1862), 445–50; J. J. D. Renfroe, *"The Battle Is God's": A Sermon Preached before Wilcox's Brigade* (Richmond, VA, 1863), 4, and on Renfroe see B. F. Riley, *History of the Baptists of Alabama from the Time of Their First Occupation of Alabama in 1808, until 1894* (Birmingham, AL, 1895). Also, [George Frederick Holmes], "History of Literature," *SQR,* 2 (1842), 518–40; *SQR,* 11 (1847), 138. See also Supplementary References: "Cousin and Morell."

[24] [J. R. Thompson], *SLM,* 15 (1849), 519; [Thompson], *SLM,* 18 (1852), 319; Farrar, "Science of History," 351–5; *JHTW,* quote at 3:88, see also 1:59, 104–5, 469, 491–2, 469, 3:14, 82, 87–8, 136–7.

orthodox on edge, but, surprisingly, *Southern Presbyterian Review* welcomed his work, acknowledged his learning, praised his substantial intellect, and published Thomas Smyth's paean to the "beautiful thoughts" on intuitive reason in his *Philosophical Tendencies of the Age*. The tune changed when Thornwell and Holmes derided the heterodoxy displayed in Morell's *Philosophy of Religion*. Morell followed Cousin, "his master," in a "shadowy transcendentalism" that leads to repudiation of Christianity. Holmes reproved Morell for maintaining that revelation's credibility depends on fallible human judgment and, in a long essay in *Southern Literary Messenger*, warned of "the dangers to be apprehended from the pernicious heresies to which it [liberalism] tends." Holmes thought Morell's *History of Philosophy* gave aid and comfort to Transcendentalism. A contributor to *Southern Quarterly Review*, associating *Philosophy of Religion* with Cousin's eclecticism, gave it short shrift. The southern response to both Cousin and Morell, having begun positively, ended with distaste for destructive philosophical tendencies and lapses from Christian doctrine.[25]

Southerners shared in the transatlantic admiration for the poetry and wisdom of Johann Wolfgang von Goethe, but, like theologically conservative Northerners, they harbored deep reservations about his religious views. Americans of German origin and descent, especially the well-to-do, had grown up with Goethe and Friedrich Schiller, but most southern intellectuals probably came upon Goethe through Thomas Carlyle. Goethe became a favorite of the ladies, some of whom read him in German, including Mary Chesnut and Emma LeConte. R. Dillon Boylan's 1854 translation of *Novels and Tales of Goethe* became popular in Mary Chesnut's circle during the War. *Sorrows of Werther* attracted the attention of Lucy Wood and of Mrs. Schoolcraft, who found it "excruciating." The Methodist Reverend A. A. Lipscomb, who admired Goethe, considered *Sorrows of Werther* a "forcible exemplification of the effects of morbid science."[26]

---

[25] *SQR*, 16 (1849), 77–8; [B. B. Minor], *SLM*, 13 (1847), 381; [J. R. Thompson], *SLM*, 15 (1849), 375–6; [William Porcher Miles], "Philosophy of Spinoza," *SQR*, 16 (1849); James Warley Miles, *Philosophic Theology; Or, Ultimate Grounds of All Religious Belief Based on Reason* (Charleston, SC, 1849), vi, 224–8; *SPR*, 1 (1847), 162–3; Thomas Smyth, "Assurance," *SPR*, 2 (1848), 103 n., also 105–6; [Holmes], "Morell's Philosophy of the Nineteenth Century," 385–96, and see 385 for Holmes's arraignment of Morell for ignorance of Plato and Aristotle and for substituting "eleemosynary learning and borrowed opinion" for research; also, [Holmes], "Philosophy and Faith," *MMQR*, 4th ser., 3 (1851), 202, 208, 213; "History of Philosophy," *SQR*, n.s. (3rd), 2 (1856), 252–3. See also Basil Manly, Jr., *The Bible Doctrine of Inspiration* (Nashville, TN, 1995 [1888]), 50.

[26] Mary Hübner Walker, *Charles W. Hübner: Poet Laureate of the South* (Atlanta, GA, 1976), 3. Chesnut Diary, May 6, July 18, 21, 1862, Jan. 15, 1864, in C. Vann Woodward, ed., *Mary Chesnut's Civil War* (New Haven, CT, 1981), 333–4, 419; Elisabeth Muhlenfeld, *Mary Boykin Chesnut: A Biography* (Baton Rouge, LA, 1981), 51; Apr. 13, 1864, in Earl Schenck Miers, ed., *When the World Ended: The Diary of Emma LeConte* (New York, 1957), 86–7; Lipscomb, *Morbid Exhibition*, 21. See also Clitherall Diary, Sept. 1853, and Haigh Diary, Jan. 22, 1844, at UNC-SHC; William S. Powell, *When the Past Refused to Die: A History of Caswell County, North Carolina, 1777–1977* (Durham, NC, 1977), 409. The ladies of Middle Georgia read Goethe in translation: Curtis Carroll Davis, *That Ambitious Mr. Legaré: The Life of James M. Legaré of South Carolina, Including a Collected Edition of*

Although Goethe, who admired Spinoza, expressed views distasteful to orthodox Christians, he proved hard to resist. Thomas Holcombe, while pronouncing
Goethe's work morally deficient – wanting religion and patriotism and tending toward pantheism and materialism – paid tribute to Goethe's philosophical genius
and sincere pursuit of truth, citing August von Schlegel's judgment of Goethe as the
German Voltaire. In the 1840s *Southern Literary Messenger* published a number
of translations, and Goethe became something of a rage with the intellectual elite.
Simms extolled him as the greatest modern teacher of aesthetics and "emphatically
the great artist of the age." Joseph LeConte, a favorite of *Southern Presbyterian Review* who sought to reconcile science with Christianity, considered Goethe a great
philosophical poet.[27]

Since Southerners left few specifics, their understanding of *Faust* remains cloudy.
The divines did applaud Goethe's struggle to uphold science and reason while reining in destructive pretensions, but they did not much like the details. Probably, few
knew Goethe's aphorism, "When we do natural science, we are pantheists; when
we do poetry, we are polytheists; when we moralize, we are monotheists." But as
the more discerning read *Faust,* they grew nervous. Thornwell and Dabney had to
be repelled by what they saw as pantheism and apostasy and even by Mephistopheles' characterization of Faust's contempt for science and rationality as a direct road
to sorcery, although they had to be moved by Faust's repentance and ultimate triumph over evil and by Goethe's celebration of the love activated by God's grace.[28]

The philosophical idealism associated primarily with Germany and epitomized
in the North by Emerson, the Transcendentalists, and Horace Bushnell alarmed
southern intellectuals. In 1839 Thornwell told the students of South Carolina College that Transcendentalism was "a monster that should never have seen the light"
and that Immanuel Kant, Johann Gottlieb Fichte, and Friedrich von Schelling were
"miserable tools in the hands of the fiend of darkness." In southern eyes, Transcendentalism purveyed subjectivity and abandonment of the Word. And it was
dangerous, for although it had few adherents even in New England, it wielded
considerable influence among the well educated within and without the churches.

His Poems (Columbia, SC, 1971), 49. Clitherall Diary. Sept. 1853; Haigh Diary, Jan. 22, 1844; L. W.
Wood Diary, Jan. 1, 1863, at UNC-SHC; *Plantation Life: Narratives of Schoolcraft*, 155. Rosena
Lassiter's mother gave her *Wilhelm Meister*, which Simms considered second only to *Faust* among
Goethe's works: Rosena H. Lassiter to Susan E. Southall, Apr. 12, 1864, in L. C. and E. S. Lawrence
Letters, at North Carolina State Archives (Raleigh); see also [William Gilmore Simms], "Critical Notices," *SQR*, n.s., 4 (1851), 248. Basil Lanneau Gildersleeve came across Goethe ("the most important
of all the teachers I ever had") in Carlyle: Ward W. Briggs, Jr., ed., *Soldier and Scholar: Basil Lanneau Gildersleeve and the Civil War* (Charlottesville, VA, 1998), 3, 45, and Briggs, ed., *The Selected
Classical Papers of Basil Lanneau Gildersleeve* (Atlanta, GA, 1992), xix.
[27] Thomas B. Holcombe, "Moral Tendency of Goethe's Writing," *SLM*, 22 (1856), 180–8; for a reference to Goethe's moral teachings on disciplined effort see J. N. D. Graham, *VUM*, 3 (1859), 437;
[William Gilmore Simms?], *SWMR*, 2 (1845), 423–4; Joseph LeConte, "Morphology and Its Connection with Fine Art," *SPR*, 12 (1859), 104–5. See also Supplementary References: "Goethe."
[28] Goethe as quoted in Jaroslav Pelikan, *Faust the Theologian* (New Haven, CT, 1955), 19.

Orthodox Southerners agreed with Charles Hodge that Transcendentalists were "addicted to the speculative method," made the human mind the center of all Revelation, and reduced theology to anthropology. If Channing and Parker thought man perfectible, Emerson made him appear divine, with Jesus reduced to spiritual adviser. Thornwell distrusted all opinions that slighted the individuality of God, confusing Him with His works. "The universe is to be considered as an arbitrary product of will," he wrote T. E. Peck, "Hence to know the universe, *a priori*, is to know God."[29]

Transcendentalists bolstered the spreading denial of a corrupt human nature. Although Emerson – whom the abolitionist Lydia Maria Child saw as "the Plato of America" – did deal with evil in his own way, his tone invited denial. The friendly Henry James, Jr., expressed astonishment at Emerson's "unconsciousness of evil," and the unfriendly John Quincy Adams and Herman Melville seethed. Transcendentalists carried forward the logic of the liberal theology that was creeping through New England. To the disgust of Southerners, the parties in the many-sided theological wars in New England were steadily retreating from the orthodoxies of Calvin and Wesley on original sin and much else.[30]

Here and there a Southerner espoused Transcendentalism. In 1851 Emily Wharton Sinkler reported from the lowcountry, "The Russell Middletons are growing very transcendental," slighting regular church attendance and family prayer. Occasionally, a college professor or student, while criticizing Emerson's religious views,

---

[29] Thornwell quoted in Farmer, *Metaphysical Confederacy*, 133; Charles Hodge, *Systematic Theology*, 3 vols. (Grand Rapids, MI, 1993 [1871]), 1:5–6; Thornwell to T. E. Peck, Apr. 15, 1853, in Palmer, *Life and Letters of Thornwell*, 376. William S. Plumer added that the Transcendentalists had taken on Spinoza's mantle: Plumer, *The Law of God as Contained in the Ten Commandments, Explained and Enforced* (Harrisonburg, VA, 1996 [1864]), ch. 14. See also Claude Welch, *Protestant Thought in the Nineteenth Century*, 2 vols. (New Haven, CT, 1972, 1985), 1:178–87. Hostility to Transcendentalism did not preclude admiration for the intellect of its best representatives. *Southern Quarterly Review* pronounced the Transcendentalist *Dial* the work of men of great ability: *SQR*, 2 (1842), 437–44.

  Southerners read Fichte more readily than Schleiermacher or Hegel – but probably more for politics and ideology than philosophy. The South's few liberal theologians admired Fichte as theologian for his transformation of God into the supreme idea of moral duty. Thornwell, however, warmly applauded Madame Germaine De Staël for exposing Fichte's anthropomorphizing of God, citing her response to Fichte's atrocious announcement that, in a future lecture, "We shall proceed to make God." See Ralph Luker, *A Southern Tradition in Theology and Social Criticism: The Religious Liberalism and Social Conservatism of James Warley Miles, William Porcher DuBose and Edgar Gardner Murphy* (New York, 1984), 107 and ch. 1; "The Personality of God," *JHTW*, 1:502; for Fichte's view of Jesus see Colin Brown, *Jesus in European Protestant Thought, 1778–1860* (Grand Rapids, MI, 1985), ch. 2. Rivers paid Fichte a backhanded compliment, describing him as "the most accomplished" of the philosophers who slight free will: Rivers, *Moral Philosophy*, 79–81, quote at 79.

[30] Lydia Maria Child to Mrs. M. J. C. Mason, Dec. 17, 1859, in *Letters of Lydia Maria Child* (New York, 1969 [1883]), 136; F. O. Matthiessen, *American Renaissance: Art and Expression in the Age of Emerson and Whitman* (New York, 1941), 4 (quoting James), 61 n., 184–6, also 180–1; Anne C. Rose, *Transcendentalism as a Social Movement, 1830–1850* (New Haven, CT, 1981) xi; Henry F. May, *The Enlightenment in America* (New York, 1976), 57–61. No Southerner was harsher on Emerson's Harvard Divinity School Address of 1838 than John Quincy Adams, who viewed the Transcendentalists as enemies of religion. See Paul C. Nagel, *John Quincy Adams: A Public Life, a Private Life* (New York, 1997), 367–8, 377.

hailed his "genius," especially as displayed in *Representative Men*. Emerson's southern friends rejected his views but upheld him personally. Emerson, who spent some
months in 1826–27 in the Lower South and preached at Samuel Gilman's Unitarian
Church in Charleston, later declared the Southerner a "spoiled child" who wasted
his time on "rifles, hunting, and dogs." Still, the influential Robert Woodward Barnwell of South Carolina had struck up a lasting friendship with Emerson when they
were students at Harvard, each admiring the other's intellect and character.[31]

As a young Unitarian, Emerson preached the historical rather than the divine
Jesus as the model for a moral life, but in time he also saw Jesus as, in Susan Roberson's words, "a symbol of the self's authority and eloquence." No wonder Hodge
saw Emerson as "an infidel and an atheist." His religious thought bore strong resemblance to the Quaker's "inner light." Few southern preachers could swallow
Emerson's pronouncement, "In all my lectures I have taught one doctrine, namely
the infinitude of the private man," or his notion that instead of preaching "Christ
and Him crucified" a preacher should express "the moral sentiment in application
to the duties of life." Even less could they swallow his remark in *The Oversoul*:
"The simplest person who, in his integrity, worships God becomes God." In the
1830s Emerson's congregation in Boston appreciated his liberal theology, accepting his resignation from the ministry with regret after he could not bring himself
to conduct communion. But Emerson also came under heavy fire from many New
England Unitarians, as well as from Calvinists, who deprecated his pantheism and
atheism as harshly as Southerners did.[32]

[31] Emily Wharton Sinkler to Mary Wharton, Apr. 11, 1851, in Anne Sinkler Whaley LeClerq, ed., *Between North and South: The Letters of Emily Wharton Sinkler, 1842–1865* (Columbia, SC, 2001),
148; Emerson quoted in Linda T. Prior, "Ralph Waldo Emerson and South Carolina," *South Carolina Historical Magazine*, 79 (1978), 253–4; Rhoda Coleman Ellison, *Early Alabama Publications:
A Study in Literary Interests* (University, AL, 1947), 126–7, 187–9. For praise of Emerson in college
publications see J. N. D. Graham, *VUM*, 3 (1859), 441–2; also, Thomas R. Price, "The Courtship of
Miles Standish," *VUM*, 3 (1859), 427; on Barnwell see Daniel Walker Hollis, "Robert W. Barnwell,"
South Carolina Historical Magazine, 56 (1955), 131–7; Prior, "Emerson and South Carolina," 254–
5; and William M. Mathew, ed., *Agriculture, Geology, and Society in Antebellum South Carolina:
The Private Diary of Edmund Ruffin* (Athens, GA, 1992), "Biographical Supplement," 302. Moncure
Conway as Methodist circuit rider carried Emerson's *Essays* with him: Peter Walker, *Moral Choices:
Memory, Desire, and Imagination in Nineteenth-Century American Abolition* (Baton Rouge, LA,
1978), 52. In 1829 a writer quoted Emerson approvingly: "Education in Germany," *SR*, 4 (1829), 89.
Southern Quarterly Review criticized Emerson in 1846 for his religious and philosophical views but
paid him tribute as a formidable intellectual and a gifted writer: *SQR*, 9 (1846), 538–9. Sisters Jennie and Ann Speer of western North Carolina, well educated at Greensboro Female College and in
the North (respectively), much admired Horace Greeley and Margaret Fuller and were attracted to
Transcendentalism: Allen Paul Speer and Janet Barton Speer, *Sisters of Providence: The Search for
God in the Frontier South (1843–1858)* (Johnson City, TN, 2000), 18–20, 218. Emerson's friendship
with Carlyle may account for some of the respect – and hostility – Southerners accorded him. For an
attack on Carlyle for his influence on Emerson see A. W. Dillard, "Thomas Carlyle – His Philosophy
and Style," *SLM*, 34 (1862), 290–1. For the Emerson–Carlyle friendship and its impact in America
see Mary Cayton Kupiec, "The Making of an American Prophet: Emerson, His Audiences, and the
Rise of the Culture Industry in the United States," *American Historical Review*, 92 (1987), 602–3.
[32] Emerson quoted in Merton M. Sealts, Jr., *Emerson on the Scholar* (Columbia, MO, 1992), 27–8,
49–50, quotes at 115, 117, 125, 140. On Emerson's changing view of Jesus see Susan L. Roberson,

Lydia Sigourney, a Northerner much admired in the South, offered a poem that provided a typical riposte in *Southern Literary Messenger*. To Transcendentalist laments about the hold of the past over the present: "The past she ruleth." Southerners considered the Transcendentalists dangerous obscurantists, not to say drivelers, and politicians made "Transcendentalism" shorthand for abolitionist nihilism. Poe encapsulated their contempt: "Above all, study innuendo. Hint everything – assert nothing. If you feel inclined to say 'bread and butter,' you may hint at buckwheat cake, or you may even go so far as to insinuate oatmeal porridge, but if bread and butter be your real meaning, be cautious, my *dear* Miss Psyche, not on any account to say 'bread and butter.' "[33]

During the 1850s, *Southern Literary Messenger* stepped up its assaults on Emerson. John Reuben Thompson, reviewing a publication devoted to contributions of inmates of an insane asylum, sighed, "In metaphysics it scarcely becomes more comprehensible than Mr. Emerson." Thompson cited the comment of the editor of *Central Presbyterian* that Emerson understood nothing of religion but, presumably, everything about his own transcendental vagaries, which no one else understood. For George William Bagby the pantheism of Parker and Emerson "pervades and pollutes" northern literature and appears with special virulence in the "spasmodic idiocy of Walt Whitman." Emerson's mind reminded Bagby of "a rag-picker's basket – full of all manner of trash." Bagby thought the books of this "moral nuisance" valuable illustrations of "the utter worthlessness of the philosophy of free society." The editors of *Southern Quarterly Review* declared that Emerson worshiped the "Goddess of Rigmarole."[34]

During the War, Emerson became a topic of conversation among well-read women of the southern elite. Some became acquainted with his religious thought indirectly through Augusta Jane Evans's *Macaria*. References to Emerson in *Macaria* led the intellectually impressive Emma Holmes of Charleston to talk with knowledgeable friends about him as a man who knew nothing of human nature. Catherine Edmonston read some Emerson so that she could discuss him with her niece, whose mother had unwisely permitted her "to dabble in his polluted stream." She dismissed Emerson's thought as "a weak tincture of Carlyleism" and could not decide which was worse, his "utter want of principle or depth of folly." She was amused by

---

Emerson in His Sermons: A Man-Made Self (Columbia, MO, 1995), 19–20, quote at 19; Charles Hodge, "Transcendentalism," *BRPR*, 11 (1839), 97; George M. Marsden, *The Evangelical Mind and the New School Experience: A Case Study of Thought and Theology in Nineteenth-Century America* (New Haven, CT, 1970), 108–9.

[33] Lydia H. H. Sigourney, "Memory," *SLM*, 12 (1846), 586; Poe quoted in Matthiessen, *American Renaissance*, 57 n. 4. On the attack on and defense of the past see especially George B. Forgie, *Patricide in the House Divided: A Psychological Interpretation of Lincoln and His Age* (New York, 1979), chs. 3 and 5. Some scholars have attempted to make Poe a Transcendentalist, but he "sought rational proof of spiritual transcendence rather than accepting its existence on intuitive faith": Darlene Harbour Unrue, "Edgar Allan Poe: The Romantic as Classicist," *International Journal of the Classical Tradition*, 1 (1995), 114.

[34] [J. R. Thompson], *SLM*, 21 (1855), 327, and 23 (1856), 314; [G. W. Bagby], *SLM*, 31 (1860), 74, and 32 (1861), 326–7; *SQR*, 11 (1847), 493–6. For rough treatment of Emerson's radical individualism see [John H. Bocock], "Ralph Waldo Emerson," *SLM*, 18 (1852), 249–55.

Emerson's remark on a foolish consistency as the hobgoblin of small minds, since she considered his own writing illogical. Mary Chesnut dismissed his antislavery writing along with that of Horace Greeley and Henry David Thoreau, although on less dangerous subjects she cited or quoted him with respect and occasional agreement.[35]

Horace Bushnell, pressing the logic of liberal theology, envisioned the Gospel as a gift to human imagination. Southern theologians distrusted Kant because they believed he read the Bible essentially as allegory. Now they saw Bushnell embrace the very assumption of the liberal theology he claimed to oppose. In effect, Bushnell allied himself with those who regarded the Bible as too complicated for anyone except experts or the especially endowed to understand. T. E. Peck cast a net broad enough to snag both Emerson and Bushnell, along with the New Divinity. In reviewing Bushnell's *God in Christ,* Peck opened up on its theory of language and insisted that words mean what they say. He related Bushnell's theories to those of Morell and the German philosophical idealists, deriding him for pandering to the Unitarians and for substituting "poetic insight" for logic. Bushnell "furnishes melancholy evidence of the progress of infidel principles." Christian churches challenged by atheism were now challenged from within by liberals who denied the existence of hell.[36]

Bushnell acknowledged that every child comes into the world in bondage to sin, but, along with Unitarians and Universalists, he opposed the doctrine of human depravity. Stressing the socializing function of the family, he questioned a doctrine that considered sin and virtue choices rather than consequences of accumulated social acts. In a way reminiscent of the dangerous Rousseau, he invited the ire of Calvinists by taking Arminian ground, but he did not endear himself to Arminians when he announced that God created "venom": "If we have any conception of goodness that forbids this kind of possibility, then our God plainly enough does not exist, or the God that does exist is not he." Bushnell dismissed Emerson's

---

[35] Aug. 15, 1864, in John F. Marszalek, ed., *The Diary of Miss Emma Holmes* (Baton Rouge, LA, 1979), 370; Apr. 22, May 26, Nov. 24, 1863, in Beth G. Crabtree and James W. Patton, eds., *"Journal of a Secesh Lady": The Diary of Catherine Devereux Edmonston, 1860–1866* (Raleigh, NC, 1979), 382–3, 397, 494; Chesnut Diary, Feb. 10, 19, Apr. 7, June 10, Nov. 27, 1861, in Woodward, ed., *Mary Chesnut's Civil War,* 7, 21, 43, 72, 245. Margaret Fuller was another matter; for her popularity in the South, see Supplementary References: "Fuller."

[36] Peck, *Miscellanies,* 2:36–58, quotes at 2:44 (notes 2 and 3) and 48–9. Peck's friend, the Reverend Stuart Robinson of Kentucky, accused Bushnell of displaying "an almost insane hate for the doctrine of Christ's atonement as expiatory": Robinson, *Discourses of Redemption,* 310 n. Mark Noll demonstrates that Bushnell, Charles Finney, Nathaniel Taylor, and others, "all of whom honored Edwards' memory," eviscerated the essentials of his teaching: Mark A. Noll, *America's God: From Jonathan Edwards to Abraham Lincoln* (New York, 2002), 237. Bushnell's greatest impact came well after the War, but Noll writes that *God in Christ* (1849), specifically its radical discussion of language, signaled the beginning of the end of Calvinist intellectual leadership in America (319, 323).
         Not all references to Bushnell were hostile. *Southern Literary Messenger* respectfully noticed his Phi Beta Kappa lecture on work and play, although it slyly suggested that his claims to originality rested on his ability to mine German scholarship: "Dr. Bushnell's Oration," *SLM,* 14 (1848), 753–4. In 1861 Robert Breckenridge's *Danville Quarterly Review* had good words for Bushnell's *Sermons for the New Life,* finding nothing heretical therein, but it rejected his *The Character of Jesus,* which it found immersed in Coleridge's errors: *DQR,* 1 (1861), 352–5.

projection of an Oversoul as merely a subjective and pantheistic view of the Holy Spirit, yet he followed Coleridge in emphasizing intuition. The orthodox, seeing in Bushnell the view that theology was an art form replete with a language capable of expressing divine mysteries, condemned it as an effort to undermine confidence in the Word. "Christianity," wrote the Baptist Reverend Basil Manly, Jr., "is the religion of the Book." Without faithfulness to the Word, Christianity "would present no authoritative rule for obedience and no ground for confident and everlasting hope. It would contain advice instead of commands, suggestions instead of instructions." The New School Reverend Joseph Stiles defended the "plain meaning of God's words" and called for strict adherence to the Word. The South, he wrote, hewed to orthodoxy while the North was sliding into philosophical speculation. Christianity, a contributor to *Southern Literary Messenger* protested in 1862, is being "diluted into moral speculations."[37]

Southerners abhorred subjectivity in theology, philosophy, constitutional theory, and politics, seeing themselves as staunch supporters of the objective truth of Scripture against the religious heresy and political radicalism spawned by Yankee subjectivity. Holt Wilson advanced the common southern understanding of truth as "objective" and "outside of man." Holmes described as "the grossest of fallacies" the dream of proving the existence of the very mind by which we seek to prove or disprove its existence. The existence of mind and matter are postulates – truths firmly believed but incapable of rational negation since their denial would render all reasoning impossible.[38]

Southern Calvinists and Arminians alike distinguished between subjective perception and empirically verifiable objective reality, the truth of which pointed toward God as ultimate truth. The Reverend H. T. Winkler provided a succinct statement of the prevalent southern distinction between rationalism and reason: "Rationalism denies the Divine in religion: Reason accepts it." Thus Thornwell considered theology the science of religion or "the system of doctrine in its logical connection and dependence, which, when spiritually discerned, produces true piety."[39]

Northerners, too, welcomed Scottish Realism, and liberal theology, contrary to southern claims, had not conquered public opinion in the North. Not quite yet. With a few exceptions, notably at Harvard, colleges remained largely under the influence of men who considered themselves religiously orthodox and had little use

---

[37] Welch, *Protestant Thought*, 1:264–5; Horace Bushnell, *Sermons*, ed. Conrad Cherry (New York, 1985), esp. 56, 63–65, 180; Manly, *Bible Doctrine of Inspiration*, 21, 23; Joseph C. Stiles, *Modern Reform Examined* (Philadelphia, 1857), 73, 111, 140–2; "Christianity versus Philanthropy," *SLM*, 34 (1862), 574; see also *SLM*, 26 (1858), 466. For Hodge on Bushnell see his *Systematic Theology*, 2:569–70.

[38] Holt Wilson, "Socrates and Philosophy," *SLM*, 29 (1859), 21; [Holmes], "Philosophy and Faith," 195–6; [Holmes], "The Positive Religion," *MMQR*, 4th ser., 6 (1854), 333.

[39] H. T. Winkler, "The Pulpit and the Age," *RM*, 2 (1858), 485; "Lectures in Theology," *JHTW*, 1:36. For denunciation of the Sophists' denial of the "reality of objective truth" see [J. L. Reynolds], *SQR*, 5 (1844), 229. For Augustine's insistence on objective existence outside our minds see Meyrich H. Carré, *Realists and Nominalists* (New York, 1946), 26. For one of the more influential relevant texts see Supplementary References: "Turretin."

for political radicalism. New Divinity theologians and New Haven theologians insisted that they were defending the faith by purging its irrationality and superstition. Yet what passed for theological orthodoxy and political conservatism in the North looked anything but in the South – or at Princeton Seminary, for that matter. The South saw northern theologians surrendering, step by step, precious ground to the liberals and opening the floodgates to massive unbelief.[40]

The struggle against French materialism looked easier than the parallel struggle against German idealism, but it, too, was full of traps. Some early critics tried to discredit the Enlightenment by obliterating the differences within it, stamping it all with philosophical materialism and political radicalism. Others like George Tucker rejected the notion that the French Enlightenment brought on the Terror; Tucker considered radicalism not a logical outcome but a perversion of its philosophy. Southern critics could not blithely treat Rousseau as a materialist, but they did view him as the spiritual father of Jacobins, anarchists, socialists, and the worst in the French Revolution. Frederick Porcher described Rousseau as a major contributor to the diseased philosophy of the age, "howling out of his lair of infidelity," and Henry A. Washington called *Contrat Social* the "textbook of revolution." For Holmes, Rousseau's *Confessions* was simply "shameless." David McCord judged Rousseau a "madman" and lumped him with Jeremy Bentham as the father of modern radicalisms. To Dagg, Rousseau was a great infidel who nonetheless respected the Bible.[41]

---

[40] For a clear exposition of the Scots' position on objective truth, see Theodore Dwight Bozeman, *Protestants in an Age of Science: The Baconian Ideal and Antebellum American Religious Thought* (Chapel Hill, NC, 1977), 10–11, 55–63. Following the lead of Jonathan Edwards, Samuel Hopkins and the New Divinity men considered themselves "consistent Calvinists" and determined to create, in the words of Joseph Conforti, "a complete, consistent system of evangelical Calvinism." Conforti acknowledges, however, that Hopkins "Arminianized" Edwards's thought: Joseph A. Conforti, "Samuel Hopkins and the New Divinity: Theology, Ethics, and Social Reform in Eighteenth-Century New England," *WMQ*, 3rd ser., 34 (1977), 572–89. William Breitenbach also defends the New Divinity men's claim to be consistent Calvinists: "The Consistent Calvinism of the New Divinity Movement," *WMQ*, 3rd ser., 41 (1984), 241–64. Whether one views the doctrinal alterations – original sin, the nature of the Atonement – as improvements or apostasy, it is clear that the orthodox, especially in the South, had reason to recoil. For the political conservatism as well as elitist arrogance of the Boston–Cambridge Unitarians, see Harlow W. Scheidley, *Sectional Nationalism: Massachusetts Conservatives and the Transformation of America, 1815–1836* (Boston, 1998), 92–4.

[41] George Tucker, "A Discourse on the Progress and Influence of Philosophy," *SLM*, 1 (1835), 412–14; F. A. Porcher, "Nature and the Claims of Paradox" *RM*, 1 (1857), 466; Henry Augustine Washington, "The Virginia Constitution of 1776," *SLM*, 18 (1852), 672; [George Frederick Holmes], "The Wandering Jew," *SQR*, 9 (1846), 80; [David J. McCord], "Political Elements," *SQR*, n.s., 10 (1854), 383–431, esp. 384, 387–8; [McCord], "Slavery and the Abolitionists," *SQR*, 15 (1849), 210; Dagg, *Manual of Theology*, 1:31, 40.
    Henry May has distinguished four overlapping phases of the Enlightenment: (i) a "moderate" Enlightenment that preached balance, order, and religious compromise; (ii) a "skeptical" Enlightenment that culminated with Hume, Voltaire, and Holbach's materialism; (iii) a "revolutionary" Enlightenment that projected a New Heaven and New Earth – Rousseau and on to Paine and Godwin; and (iv) the "didactic" Enlightenment of the Scots, which triumphed in America between 1800 and 1825 and

Critics had an easy time convincing Southerners that Rousseau's theories were destructive, but not that "the eccentric but kind hearted Rousseau" – as a southern lady called him – was a bad man with nothing to offer. Rousseau, in his *Confessions,* pointed to his uncle Gabriel Bernard as a principal figure in the defense of Charleston against the Indians in the early eighteenth century, and Southerners heard echoes of the connection 150 years later. James Simmons, seeing genius in *Confessions,* wondered how good he might have been if he had come from the right class and acquired proper moral grounding.[42]

George Armstrong, Presbyterian pastor of Norfolk, dismissed the philosophies of Rousseau, Voltaire, and Volney as erroneous and ultimately responsible for the horrors of the Reign of Terror, but he could not help admiring their discrete insights. Railing against the hated doctrines of the *philosophes,* the Methodist Reverend Augustus Baldwin Longstreet let slip a grudging tribute: "A band of intellectual giants had risen up in France, embodying a moral force which must have swept the religion of the Bible off the earth, had it not been of origin divine." Archibald Haralson, reading Rousseau at the University of North Carolina, found him a giant figure among dwarfs. Then too, Rousseau's view of female education pleased conservatives, northern as well as southern. Rousseau wanted women educated primarily to please and be useful to men – trained to encourage men to love and esteem them. Women must tend boys and youths, advise and console men in middle age, and care for them in old age.[43]

Rejection of Rousseau and French materialism led to a southern engagement with Auguste Comte, not well known even in France until the mid-1850s. His emphasis on carefully guided social change to eradicate social antagonisms earned him the appreciation of a good many southern commentators, who tempered their disapproval of his materialism. Joseph Le Conte, notwithstanding his own commitment to a scientific sociology, criticized Comte for applying methods of the organic sciences insufficient to a mankind "spiritual as well as material." In 1856 a friendly

tried to reconcile reason, progress, and firm moral judgment. See May, *Enlightenment in America,* esp. xv–xvi, 153–7. The French Enlightenment had "a critical and skeptical attitude toward religion," but Voltaire proceeded more cautiously than the Encyclopedists who followed him and declared "war openly on religion and its claims to validity and truth": Ernst Cassirer, *The Philosophy of the Enlightenment,* tr. Fritz C. A. Koelin and James P. Pettegrove (Boston, 1951), 134.

42 Quotes from Elizabeth Eve Carmichael's Notebook, 1803, at UNC-SHC; Paul Hamilton Hayne, "Ante-Bellum Charleston," *Southern Bivouac,* 1 (1885), 335; *SLM,* 27 (1858), 194; James Simmons, "Thoughts on Spring," in [William Gilmore Simms], ed., *The Charleston Book: A Miscellany in Prose and Verse* (Spartanburg, SC, 1983 [1845]), 256–7 n. Walker Gilmer of Virginia quoted Rousseau positively and translated long passages from his work: Gilmer, *Sketches, Essays and Translations* (Baltimore, 1828), 49, 154–72.

43 George D. Armstrong, *The Theology of Christian Experience, Organized as an Exposition of the "Common Faith" of the Church of God* (New York, 1858), 163–4; A. B. Longstreet, *Eulogy on the Life and Public Services of the Late Rev. Moses Waddel* (Augusta, GA, 1841), 17; Archibald Haralson to Archibald D. Murphey, Sept. 13, 1811, in William Henry Hoyt, ed., *The Papers of Archibald D. Murphey,* 2 vols. (Raleigh, NC, 1914), 1:54. Here and there during the early nineteenth century, even in Mississippi a planter like Dr. John C. Cox named a son after Rousseau: Terry Alford, *Prince among Slaves* (New York, 1977), 82.

reference to Comte in *Southern Literary Messenger* carried lengthy critiques that charged him with atheism, ridiculed his pretense of having replaced philosophy with science, and brushed off his positivist Religion of Humanity as a contradiction in terms.[44]

Holmes, too, went after Comte, although acknowledging him as "acute" for his contributions to a science of history and society, diagnoses of the many ills of modern society, and "strong and accurate censures" on political morals. By 1854 Holmes was acerbic on Comte's portrayal of progress toward perfection: "This is Humanity, whose place is curiously asserted to have been hitherto usurped by God." Meanwhile, the Reverend Thomas Smyth and the editors of *Southern Quarterly Review* and *Southern Literary Messenger* dissociated themselves from Comte's philosophy but recommended careful study of his work. With this backing-and-filling the slaveholders combined a taste for social corporatism with distaste for the materialism that encouraged collectivism. In the 1850s Holmes, LeConte, George Fitzhugh, and Henry Hughes were offering an alternative proslavery sociology they considered reconcilable with Christian doctrine.[45]

---

[44] For critical but respectful reviews of Comte see *TSW*, 5:439–40; Joseph LeConte, "Relation of Organic Science to Sociology," *SPR*, 13 (1860), 39–77; [William Gilmore Simms], "Critical Notices," *SQR*, n.s., 4 (1851), 255; also, Theodore Dwight Bozeman, "Joseph LeConte: Organic Science and a 'Sociology for the South,'" *JSH*, 39 (1973), 565–82. For Comte's influence on American theological discussion see Charles D. Cashdollar, *The Transformation of Theology, 1830–1890: Positivism and Protestant Thought in Britain and America* (Princeton, NJ, 1989).

[45] [Holmes], "Morell's Philosophy of the Nineteenth Century," 385–96; [Holmes], "Cimon and Pericles," *SQR*, n.s., 3 (1851), 3; [Holmes], "Greeley on Reforms," *SLM*, 17 (1851), 260–1; "The Nineteenth Century," *SLM*, 17 (1851), 461; [Holmes], "The Positive Religion," 343; *TSW*, 5:439–40; *SQR*, n.s., 10 (1854), 240; "Some Thoughts on Social Philosophy," *SLM*, 22 (1856), 308. "Sociology" first appeared in American book titles in 1854 – in the proslavery tracts by Fitzhugh and Hughes.

19

Serpent in the Garden

Liberal Theology in the South

> We have failed to lay the stress of the argument on the right and duty of society to care for all its members, placing all in the positions for which God fitted them, partly because our minds have to some degree been infected by the virus of Red Republican theory which has made the social system at the North rotten to the core.
>
> —W. A. Cave[1]

The southern churches, for all their vaunted orthodoxy, could not wholly resist the rising tide of theological liberalism, as capitalism inexorably transformed the world into one grand marketplace of ideas as well as commodities. No society could insulate itself from marketplace sentiments and ideas, which themselves metamorphosed into commodities. Supposedly, heresies, cults, and isms flourished only in the free states, but they were making troublesome inroads into the slave states. Vigilance emerged as the South's order of the day.

Long-standing theological and ecclesiastical differences within the national Presbyterian Church flared into acrimony in the 1830s, and the split in 1837 between the orthodox Calvinist Old School and the more variegated New School exposed the strength but also the greater weakness of theological liberalism in the South. Beneath ecclesiastical and political issues lay theological ones: faithfulness to the orthodox Westminster Confession and to the formulaic five points of Calvinism or "TULIP" (total depravity, unconditional election, limited atonement, irresistible grace, and perseverance of the saints). The New School arose in the Northeast primarily among men who professed to defend Calvinism against the Unitarians but who made more and more concessions to advocates of free will (Arminians). They repudiated predestination or interpreted it so flexibly as to make Arminians gloat over their surrender.[2]

---

[1] W. A. Cave, *Two Sermons on the Times, Preached in St. John's Church, Tallahassee* (Tallahassee, AL, n.d. but during the War), 14.

[2] Ernest Trice Thompson, *Presbyterians in the South,* 3 vols. (Richmond, VA, 1963), 1:353. More than half the New School members were in New York and New Jersey. For contending interpretations of

A "Plan of Union" brought Presbyterians and Congregationalists into close co-operation, but it provoked deep suspicions of a Trojan horse in the making. Many Congregationalists did not subscribe to the Westminster Confession, and, increasingly, many Presbyterians expressed reservations or offered questionable reinterpretations. The New School Zebulon Crocker of Connecticut charged that the hard-line Old School "makes man responsible for actions not his own, and lays him under obligation to do, what he is acknowledged to have no ability to perform." The Old School, which saw Church polity as scripturally determined, could brook no compromise, whereas the New School opposed what men like Crocker considered debilitating dogmatism and rigidity. In Old School eyes, the Plan of Union opened the way for a dangerously backsliding New Haven theology. The strength of the New School nationally did in fact lie in areas settled by New England Congregationalists, who generally tolerated a wide variety of theological opinions. In 1865 the northern Congregationalist churches, in their "Burial Hill Declaration," omitted all reference to Calvinism. "[Lyman] Beecher's generation," Ronald Walters tersely observes, "softened Calvinism still further and [Charles] Finney, nominally a Presbyterian, overthrew it." Finney – who detested ecclesiastical machinery and the Presbyterian hierarchy – quipped, "There was a jubilee in hell whenever the Presbyterian General Assembly met."[3]

In 1837, Old School and New School split after what amounted to a purge of 28 New School presbyteries, 509 ministers, and 60,000 (almost a fifth) of the Church's communicants on charges of heterodoxy. The New School denied that God counted Adam's sin against all men but agreed that all men were sinners. Simultaneously, it affirmed Christ's substitutionary atonement for the redemption of man and acknowledged that regeneration depended upon the Holy Spirit, not man's initiative. In effect, as New School tried to find a middle way between the Westminster Confession and the liberalization that came to be known as the New England theology, it plunged into internal strife over how far to go. In the 1840s, as a reaction built against the more radical Finney and his supporters, the New School veered toward formulations more theologically conservative but not nearly orthodox enough by the standards of Virginia and South Carolina. In time, the sectional implications of the changes in New England became manifest.[4]

the split of 1837 and the primacy of theology see George M. Marsden, *The Evangelical Mind and the New School Experience: A Case Study of Thought and Theology in Nineteenth-Century America* (New Haven, CT, 1970), esp. ch. 3 and App. 1; see also Morton H. Smith, *Studies in Southern Presbyterian Theology* (Phillipsburg, NJ, 1962), 31–5, 99.

[3] Zebulon Crocker, *The Catastrophe of the Presbyterian Church in 1837, Including a Full View of the Recent Theological Controversies in New England* (New Haven, CT, 1838), 41–2, 71–3, 77–8, 114, 228–9, quote at 77. For Finney's quip see Charles C. Cole, Jr., *The Social Ideas of the Northern Evangelists, 1826–1860* (New York, 1954), 64. On the strength of the New School in Congregationalist areas see Lewis G. Vander Velde, *The Presbyterian Church and the Federal Union, 1861–1869* (Cambridge, MA, 1932), 14; also, *DCA*, 201 (Congregationalists in 1865); Ronald G. Walters, *American Reformers, 1815–1860* (New York, 1978), 27. See also Supplementary References: "New School Presbyterians."

[4] Marsden, *New School Experience*, 63. For a brief account see W. A. Hoffecker, "New School Theology," in Walter A. Elwell, ed., *Evangelical Dictionary of Theology* (Grand Rapids, MI, 1999), 767–8. The New School in the South became steadily more orthodox after 1837: Harold M. Parker, Jr., *The*

Albert Barnes and Lyman Beecher, two of the most prominent of northern Presbyterians, faced trial for heresy before the Church split of 1837, but their acquittals only intensified factional bitterness. Barnes beat back charges of heresy in 1832 and 1835 and received a clean bill of health from the New School–controlled General Assembly of 1836. Beecher never ceased to extol the New School as the soul of orthodoxy while steadfastly refusing to repudiate Nathaniel Taylor of Yale, the controversial and increasingly influential theologian who frankly put Reason on a par with Revelation. Although Beecher, like Taylor, intended to combat Unitarian liberalism, he and a number of other New School Presbyterians who fancied themselves orthodox watered down the Calvinist doctrine of election, original sin, the Atonement, and human agency – conceding so much ground to the Arminians that William Ellery Channing and the Unitarians welcomed what they perceived as a capitulation. Meanwhile, Beecher tirelessly protested that proslavery men stood behind the accusations of heresy.[5]

Southern Methodists gleefully greeted the move toward Arminianism, while southern Calvinists fumed. But even southern Methodists believed that Beecher's theology denigrated the Word and led him to antislavery. They were not surprised when he ended with Horace Bushnell. Meanwhile, Daniel Baker, the great evangelist, reacted to the widening schism with disgust. He deplored what he regarded as endless hairsplitting but, appalled by the Church's failure to disavow Barnes's views, joined the Old School. In retrospect he was glad he did, for the New School opened the way "to certain forms of heresy and wild measures" that were reaching flood-tide proportions.[6]

George Marsden has made a strong case for the New School's Calvinist orthodoxy during the 1840s and well after, but he acknowledges that, from the beginning, it tolerated a broad spectrum of opinion of which much looked flagrantly heterodox to critics. And when the New School – seeking to defend itself against its rival – tightened its doctrine, it drove its more liberal communicants to Congregational or other churches. Marsden's criteria for orthodoxy will not satisfy everyone (he considers Hopkinsianism orthodox), but for our immediate purposes that is not

United Synod of the South: The Southern New School Presbyterian Church (Westport, CT, 1998), 76–7; also, J. R. Wiers, "Henry B. Smith, Theologian of New School Presbyterianism," in Charles G. Dennison and Richard C. Gamble, eds., *Pressing Toward the Mark: Essays Commemorating Fifty Years of the Orthodox Presbyterian Church* (Philadelphia, 1986), ch. 12.

5 Charles Beecher, ed., *Autobiography, Correspondence, Etc. of Lyman Beecher*, 2 vols. (New York, 1871), 1:165, 241–2, 2:30–1, 36–7, 301–2, 358–60, 394–6, 428–9, and, generally, 2:ch. 18; Vincent Harding, *A Certain Magnificence: Lyman Beecher and the Transformation of American Protestantism, 1775–1863* (Brooklyn, NY, 1991), esp. 188–9, 460–1 (Bushnell), and chs. 4, 8, 10, and 11, and for an especially good account of the trials of Barnes and Beecher in the Presbyterian Church see chs. 22–24. On Barnes's trial from an Old School point of view see Samuel J. Baird, *A History of the New School and of the Questions in the Disruption of the Presbyterian Church in 1836* (Philadelphia, 1868), chs. 22 and 23. Harriet Beecher Stowe noted that the trial of Barnes occurred about the same time as James Smylie launched the militant defense of slavery in Mississippi: *A Key to Uncle Tom's Cabin* (Port Washington, NY, 1968 [1853]), 205.

6 Thompson, *Presbyterians in the South*, 1:364–5; William M. Baker, *The Life and Labors of the Rev. Daniel Baker, D.D., Pastor and Evangelist,* 3rd ed. (Philadelphia, n.d.), 205–8.

the main issue. Rather, the struggles in the New School principally highlighted the difficulties of maintaining orthodoxy in the North. The Calvinist orthodoxy of Charles Hodge and the Princetonians, Nathan O. Hatch observes, prevailed only in the South. Shortly after the War, Samuel Baird, an Old School Northerner, stressed the New School's willingness to tolerate theological heterodoxy rather than the heterodoxy of most of its members. Baird zeroed in on the Plan of Union, regretting that an intended temporary tactic had become entrenched. Through it, Congregational ministers spread theological liberalism throughout the Presbyterian Church. Baird thereby captured the southern divines' long-standing critique of the northern churches: Even if most communicants remained orthodox, laxity in church discipline permitted the spread of heresy.[7]

The Presbyterian split of 1837 came when economic panic struck the land and called forth the Church's reaction against a rising political radicalism. In the Northwest, howls went up in religious and lay circles over financial scandals and blatant corruption by state politicians. Although close correlations of political, economic, and religious struggles would be misleading, strains in the one exacerbated strains in others. Within the Old School, southern muttering against northern domination rose. Yet most southern Presbyterians initially paid little attention to the teachings of Samuel Hopkins and the even more offensive Nathaniel Taylor, and most reacted with restraint to the heresy proceedings. During the 1830s, as the New School gained strength in the North, Southerners – resisting a schism – swallowed repeated assurances that the new formulations did not violate the Westminster Confession.

In later years, Baird denied that slavery dictated the course of the South. He maintained that a generally tolerant southern clergy resisted witch-hunting and supported calls for moderation and compromise. Until the explosion of the mid-1830s, Hodge and the Princetonians resisted demands to purge those who questioned the Westminster Confession. Baird protested that, after 1833, the high-handed tactics of New School men and their embrace of new standards alienated moderates in the North and South alike. N. S. S. Beman, a radical abolitionist, emerged as a principal New School leader, and all four of the northern synods that had been expelled passed strong antislavery resolutions.[8]

As Southerners chafed over the mounting abolitionist offensive, they found bold, fresh leaders of their own in Robert Breckenridge and Stuart Robinson in Kentucky, Thomas Peck and Robert Lewis Dabney in Virginia, and James Henley Thornwell and Benjamin Morgan Palmer in South Carolina. Speaking for a growing number of Southerners, Dr. John Witherspoon of Camden, South Carolina, moderator of the General Assembly meeting of 1836, identified abolitionist agitation as a natural

---

[7] Marsden, *New School Experience,* esp. chs. 5 and 6. Nathan O. Hatch, *The Democratization of American Christianity* (New Haven, CT, 1989), 201; Baird, *New School,* 11, 16–17, 163–6.

[8] Baird, *New School,* chs. 23, 24, 31, and 34; W. W. Sweet, *Religion on the Frontier: The Presbyterians, 1783–1840: A Collection of Sources* (New York, 1936), 118; R. Carlyle Buley, *The Old Northwest: Pioneer Period, 1815–1840,* 2 vols. (Bloomington, IN, 1950), 2:440–3. For documents on the constitutional resistance to the exclusions in southern synods, see ch. 19 in Marsden, *New School Experience.* The Church had six theological seminaries, three in each section, but the General Assembly controlled only four; the Synods of Virginia and South Carolina controlled, respectively, Union and Columbia.

outgrowth of New School heresies. Witherspoon wrote Thomas Smyth: "It is said that there are 150 abolitionists on the floor of the Assembly. I can scarcely believe this, and yet I am convinced *they be very many....* I say, Sir, let the *South look well to her interests.*" In Virginia, George Addison Baxter led a reaction against the New School's liberal theological tendencies, and a broad southern phalanx recommitted the church to what it regarded as biblical standards.[9]

New School Southerners declared their intention to restore harmony in the Presbyterian Church by repelling abolitionism. If we may judge by the temper of South Carolina's Presbyterians, the exclusion of the antislavery synods undercut a burgeoning movement to split the church along clearly sectional lines and create a southern Presbyterian Church. At the New School General Assembly in Buffalo in 1853, Reverend Robert McLain infuriated abolitionists by crowing that Presbyterian ministers in Mississippi bought slaves as soon as they could afford them. In 1856, Reverend William E. Hollet of Mississippi told the Assembly that he owned slaves on principle and by choice – an assertion reinforced by Alexander Newton of Jackson in the *Christian Observer,* who wrote, "We are slaveholders from principle." In Alabama the irrepressible Frederick Ross took every opportunity to defend slavery with his cutting wit.[10]

In the mid-1850s Barnes counted only 301 southern Presbyterian churches and 199 ministers out of the 677 churches and 474 ministers in the country. In 1857, 20 of the New School's 26 synods and seven eighths of its communicants lay north of the Mason-Dixon line. The South had 14 of the Old School's 35 synods and well over a third of its 250,000 communicants. At most, no more than a quarter of the southern Presbyterians went with the New School. Some strong southern bases did develop, especially in counties of eastern Tennessee that had become theologically liberal well before 1837. With marvelous irony, the New School proclaimed itself the "Constitutional Assembly," and the Old School proclaimed itself the "Reforming Assembly."[11]

---

[9] Smith, *Southern Presbyterian Theology,* 96–107; Thompson, *Presbyterians in the South,* 1:362–5, 384–5, 511; J. Witherspoon to Smyth, May 26–27, 1836, in Thomas Smyth, *Autobiographical Notes, Letters, and Reflections,* ed. Louisa Cheves Stoney (Charleston, SC, 1914), 157–8; Albert Barnes, *The Church and Slavery* (New York, 1969 [1857]), 147–50; Vander Velde, *Presbyterian Church and Federal Union,* 27; for the small New School group in Texas see *HT,* 2:408. In the 1860s, *Danville Quarterly Review* lumped together "the great defection of Rationalism in Germany, Broad Church Liberalism in Britain, and Arian heresy of New England" as a movement "characterized by a denial of all that is essential in Christian faith": "The New Gospel of Rationalism," *DQR,* 1 (1861), 367. Baird fired at the New Englanders, "Retaining partially the old forms of speech, these theologians utterly rejected the old doctrines of original sin – the atonement and the justification": Baird, *New School,* 172–3.

[10] For the view from South Carolina see William Childs Robinson, *Columbia Theological Seminary and the Southern Presbyterian Church: A Study in Church History, Presbyterian Polity, Missionary Enterprise, and Religious Thought* (Decatur, GA, 1931), 34; Victor B. Howard, *Conscience and Slavery: The Evangelic Calvinist Domestic Missions, 1837–1861* (Kent, OH, 1990), 164–6; Margaret Burr DesChamps, "The Presbyterian Church in South Atlantic States" (Ph.D. diss., Emory University, 1952), 187–8.

[11] On Hopkinsianism and the New School in the Border States, see Supplementary References: "New School Presbyterians."

Many orthodox Southerners, including William Hill, a hard critic of theological backsliding, deemed the exclusion of the four northern synods unconstitutional and a threat to the constitutional defense of southern rights. In Charleston the churches that had emerged from Congregationalism, including the prestigious Circular Church, opted for independency. In Georgia, when two of the three synods supported the Old School, Hopewell Synod split. Some ministers and churches went with the New School or chose an independency they were unable to sustain. In Mississippi and South Alabama, Presbyterians approved the exclusions by only about three to two. In 1846, the historian Robert Howison referred to Virginia's New School Presbyterians as "*Constitutional* Presbyterians."[12]

The New School's intellect (if not its numbers) worried its adversaries. Thomas Smyth fretted over New School sentiment in Charleston in the 1840s. The threat loomed even larger in Virginia: A good many Presbyterians in Richmond defected in the late 1830s; by 1847, Moses Drury Hoge was Richmond's only Old School Presbyterian pastor. In the Confederacy, Dabney worked to reunify the two schools and found himself at loggerheads with Adger and Palmer. Dabney considered the southern New School theologically sound, especially since the War had driven its worst ministers, who had been Yankees, back north. Dabney and Palmer feared the influence of the Reverend Dr. A. H. H. Boyd of Winchester, a pastor who held views they considered heterodox but whose prestige was enhanced by his unwavering defense of slavery as scriptural and his steadfast support for the Confederacy, which earned him imprisonment by Union troops. By uniting the churches, Dabney hoped to head off the establishment of a theological seminary that the New School had been ready to launch when the War came – a seminary Boyd would have controlled. Rumbles from the dissemination of New England theologies recurred down to the War. Thomas Cobb, a devout Presbyterian, subscribed to New Divinity theology, and Louis LeConte, father of Joseph and John, held theologically liberal views. In the 1830s Presbyterian ministers complained of having to combat parishioners who balked at orthodox Calvinism. In 1852, the firmly orthodox Reverend John Adger of South Carolina fumed that some Presbyterians in Charleston were softening their Calvinist view of the Atonement and abandoning the concept of original sin.[13]

---

[12] Smith, *Southern Presbyterian Theology*, 99–100 (Hill); James Stacy, *A History of the Presbyterian Church in Georgia* (Atlanta, GA, 1912), 183–5, 190; Thompson, *Presbyterians in the South*, 1:399–409; Robert R. Howison, *A History of Virginia from Its Discovery and Settlement by Europeans to the Present Time*, 2 vols. (Philadelphia, 1846), 2:484. Benjamin Morgan Palmer much admired the Reverend James Gallagher of Missouri, regarding his adherence to the New School as based on constitutional principles and implying no deviation from theological orthodoxy: see Palmer in William Buell Sprague, *Annals of the American Pulpit*, 9 vols. (New York, 1859–69), 4:537–8. Carlisle Pollock Beman, brother of Nathan S. S. Beman, spent his adult life as a successful teacher and New School pastor in Hancock County, Georgia.

[13] Smyth, *Autobiographical Notes*, 177–9; Peyton Harrison Hoge, *Moses Drury Hoge: Life and Letters* (Richmond, VA, 1899), 73, 96; "Our Position," *DD*, 2:176–83, and Thomas Cary Johnson, *Life and Letters of Robert Lewis Dabney* (Carlisle, PA, 1977), 285–90; Thomas Cary Johnson, *The Life and Letters of Benjamin Morgan Palmer* (Richmond, VA, 1906), 275–6; *DGB*, 1:203 (Cobb) and 2:611

Like eastern Tennessee, western North Carolina in the 1850s saw theologically liberal inroads in the churches. Consider Basil Armstrong Thomasson of the Methodist Protestant Church, a teacher and nonslaveholding farmer. Thomasson read the Bible every day and believed that Christians should read it through at least once a year. "Read Geology, which being understood rightly, and the Bible translated properly, would not disagree." He believed in an afterlife. When he read *Paradise Lost*, he commented at some length on the evils of rebellion against God. Thomasson's quasi-vegetarianism and doubts about the divine sanction of slavery were both out of step, but if he slipped into heterodoxy it was in some quasi-Manichean musings rather than in any apparent concession to liberal theology. Thomasson prided himself on being open to "new ideas" and was pleased when he got a few. As a Methodist who often attended the Baptist Church and Quaker meetings, he defended the doctrines of his church in friendly exchanges with neighbors. Yet Thomasson buckled on a core doctrine. He agreed with one of his favorite preachers, the Reverend Q. Holton, who "preached doctrines new to me and contradicted the preaching of many learned divines.... He says 'We are not sinners by nature.' "[14]

The Protestant Episcopal Church's willingness to give some space to liberal theologians – the openness known as latitudinarianism – aroused largely unjustified suspicions of heterodoxy. *Southern Literary Messenger,* hardly a bastion of orthodoxy, warned in 1857 that latitudinarianism was encouraging infidelity in the Episcopal Church. Bishop Stephen Elliott of Georgia thundered that toleration of theological liberalism was opening the way "through folly and crime, to anarchy and barbarism!" The Episcopal Church, in fact, included two of the South's foremost liberal theologians, James Warley Miles and Albert Taylor Bledsoe. Ensconced in Charleston's intellectual elite, Miles and his fellow Episcopalian William Porcher DuBose ranked among America's ablest nineteenth-century liberal theologians, and later in the century Episcopalians came to regard him as their greatest American theologian. It is a distinction many still accord him. Since these liberals supported slavery and accepted the South's social order, they, no less than religiously orthodox Southerners, got a cold shoulder in the North. Miles, who stood close to the Transcendentalists in his own theology, sought to wed German philosophical theology to a broad Anglican ecclesiology. In Transcendentalist fashion, he envisioned not a transcendent Lord and Master but an immanent Spirit. Thornwell was not amused.[15]

(LeConte); Adger to Thornwell, June 1852, in Thornwell Papers, at Historical Foundation of the Presbyterian and Reformed Churches (Montreat, NC); also, Smith, *Southern Presbyterian Theologians,* 100. On Boyd and others see also Supplementary References: "New School Presbyterians."

[14] Thomasson's Diary entries in Paul D. Escott, ed., *North Carolina Yeoman: The Diary of Basil Armstrong Thomasson, 1853–1862* (Athens, GA, 1996): Oct. 16, 1853 (10), Mar. 21, 1855 (72), Jan. 20, 1856 (119), "Portion of a Lecture or Sermon" delivered at a Sabbath school (352), Nov. 18, 1855 (77), Jan. 27, 1856 (121), Jan. 31 and Feb. 28, 1858 (188, 193), Sept. 23, 1858 (213), quotes at 122 and 213.

[15] *SLM,* 24 (1857), 111; *Sermons by the Rt. Rev. Stephen Elliott, D.D., Late Bishop of Georgia, with a Memoir by Thomas M. Hanckel, Esq.* (New York, 1867), 167; also, C. R. Vaughan, ed., *Selections from the Religious and Literary Writings of John H. Bocock* (Richmond, VA, 1891), 167–8.

After flirting with controversial movements to reinvigorate Anglicanism, Miles spent a half dozen years as a missionary in the Near East. A formidable linguist, he read Arabic, Persian, Sanskrit, Turkish – all in all, more than thirty languages. In 1847 he settled in Charleston as pastor of St. Michael's Church and in 1850 became a professor at the College of Charleston. Miles swung steadily toward theological liberalism – influenced by Kant, Hegel, Schleiermacher, Coleridge, Cousin, and Morell – and took essentially Kantian ground on the relation of man's reason to eternal truth.[16]

The Presbyterian phalanx in South Carolina pounced on Miles's *Philosophic Theology* (1849). *Southern Presbyterian Review* reviewed it impatiently, identifying Miles as a follower of Morell and a fellow traveler of "Boston Pantheists." Miles defended the authenticity of Scripture but irritated the orthodox by slighting the importance of its historically specific accuracy. Miles identified the function of theology as vindication of great religious truths that appeal to the deepest consciousness of man, and he sought to awaken recognition of a personal God who reveals Himself through prophets and apostles. He understood Revelation as a moral and religious power that guides the soul in a holy life. Miles thus simultaneously separated himself from the higher criticism and complained of rigid adherence to the Word, identifying reconciliation through a personal redeemer as the central idea of all religion. He looked conservative by northern standards but radical by southern. Miles felt himself shunned and the object of hostility. In 1851 he whined to his cousin, David James McCord: "The Presbyterians have branded me an infidel, the Baptists as the same, a Romanist reviewer pronounced me little short of an utter Deist, even the Jews have thought me on the brink of infidelity." The cruelest blow: His fellow Episcopalians, both high and low church, pretty much agreed that he was "a heretic of horrid dye."[17]

By 1854 a self-pitying Miles was acting like a broken man, notwithstanding the support of his important southern admirers. J. D. B. De Bow, editor of the influential *De Bow's Review*, hailed him as "one of the most powerfully metaphysical minds in the country," whose every work proved illuminating. Among Charleston's leading men of letters, James Smith Rhett, William Gilmore Simms, and James Johnston Pettigrew lauded him in leading journals. Simms, recommending *Philosophical*

For Miles's relation to Transcendentalism see Ralph Luker, *A Southern Tradition in Theology and Social Criticism: The Religious Liberalism and Social Conservatism of James Warley Miles, William Porcher DuBose and Edgar Gardner Murphy* (New York, 1884), ch. 1. Luker defends Miles against the charge of pantheism, but his own summary (66) suggests that, although Miles explicitly attacked pantheism as a way station to atheism, Thornwell was close to the mark: see Ralph Luker, "God, Man and the World of James Warley Miles, Charleston's Transcendentalist," *Historical Magazine of the Protestant Episcopal Church*, 39 (1970), 101–36, esp. 101, 108–10; and James Warley Miles, *Philosophic Theology; Or, Ultimate Grounds of All Religious Belief Based on Reason* (Charleston, SC, 1849), 6–7, 38–9, 130–5. On W. P. DuBose (1836–1918), see also *DCA*, 367.

[16] Miles, *Philosophic Theology*, 27–8, 39.
[17] "Critical Notices," *SPR*, 5 (1851), 564–9; Miles to McCord, Apr. 24, 1851, in J. H. Easterby, comp., "Letters of James Warley Miles to David James McCord," *South Carolina Historical Magazine*, 44 (1942), 188.

Theology, expressed admiration for a "writer and a gentleman." Rhett accepted Miles's contention that reason constitutes the ultimate ground of all religious belief and that self-consciousness, not the Bible, must be the starting point. Pettigrew carried a copy of his *Philosophic Theology* with him to Germany, where it received a warm reception. The eminent German church historian Johann Wilhelm Neander welcomed it as a major American contribution to theology and arranged to have it translated into German. In Virginia, John Reuben Thompson, editor of *Southern Literary Messenger,* warmly supported Miles's work. Although the impact of support from some important secular intellectuals should not be exaggerated, the orthodox themselves recognized an undercurrent of theological backsliding that challenged them to remain on guard lest the dam break even in the South.[18]

Albert Taylor Bledsoe, known primarily as a political theorist and the author of *Liberty and Slavery,* rooted his proslavery views in theology. A professor of mathematics at the University of Mississippi and (in 1854) the University of Virginia, he had begun his career with a critique of Jonathan Edwards and struggled with the problem of evil, which he apparently thought he had solved a decade later in his widely discussed *Theodicy.* A talented dialectician and polemicist, Bledsoe set out to transcend Arminian and Calvinist views and to refute any notion that made God responsible for sin. Not surprisingly, he provoked the wrath of both camps. By emphasizing God's moral government, he tried to account for the ubiquity of sin while upholding God's goodness. Bledsoe abhorred the doctrines of original sin and predestination. For him, man faced constant temptations that he had the free will to resist. Bledsoe interpreted much of the Bible allegorically and symbolically. Still, Bledsoe's opposition to Calvinism flowed in part from what he perceived as its tendency toward Universalism. In political theory he championed experience as humanity's guide to the future and Christianity as the propeller of human progress. Political radicalism he regarded as a siren call to destruction. He feared that Unitarianism in various guises was expelling the divinity of Christ from the northern mind and that even professedly orthodox churches reduced everything to "the standard of Rationalism, culminating in German theology." Despite his controversial theology, Bledsoe passed muster as a true Southron for his assaults against northern infidelity.[19]

---

[18] [J. D. B. De Bow], *DBR,* 10 (1851), 602, 697; [James Smith Rhett], "Philosophic Theology," *SQR,* n.s., 1 (1850), 123–4, 481–99; [William Gilmore Simms], *SQR,* 9 (1846), 541–3, and *SQR,* n.s., 2 (1850), 258–60; [Simms], "Philosophic Theology," *SQR,* n.s., 1 (1850), 537; Simms also lauded Miles's *Ground of Morals: SQR,* n.s., 6 (1852), 265–6; [John Reuben Thompson], *SLM,* 18 (1852), 636; and on Miles and "his bosom friend" Simms see Paul Hamilton Hayne, "Ante-Bellum Charleston," *Southern Bivouac,* 1 (1885), 268. For Miles's life and thought see Luker, *Southern Tradition in Theology and Social Criticism,* chs. 1–4; also, E. Brooks Holifield, *The Gentlemen Theologians: American Theology in Southern Culture, 1795–1860* (Durham, NC, 1978), 67–70. Among the Southerners who admired Neander see [William Gilmore Simms], "Critical Notices," *SQR,* 9 (1846), 541–3; J. L. Reynolds, *Church Polity: Or, the Kingdom of Christ in Its Internal and External Development,* 2nd ed. (Richmond, VA, 1849), 28, 34, 113, 187–8.

[19] For Bledsoe on good and evil see *A Theodicy; Or, Vindication of the Divine Glory, as Manifested in the Constitution and Government of the Moral World* (New York, 1853), the accounts in Holifield,

God will save all men. A loving God would never damn any of His creatures to eternal hell. During the first half of the nineteenth century, this Universalist doctrine appealed to many in mainstream churches as well as in the radical sects that mushroomed in the North. Spiritualists found the small Universalist Church congenial up to a point but parted company on a special role for Jesus in salvation. Spiritualism, which believed in communication with the spirits of the dead through human mediums, spread from Maine to California and across the Atlantic to Europe. "Americans in astounding numbers," writes R. Lawrence Moore, its historian, "studied the reputation of a growing roster of professional mediums and crowded into the séance rooms of those judged the best." One hundred spiritual mediums held forth in the small New York town of Auburn alone.[20]

Spiritualists held their first convention in 1852. By 1853 they had more than a dozen journals, but they barely circulated in the South. Prominent Transcendalists, utopian socialists, temperance advocates, free-love enthusiasts, and some of the North's most visible antislavery men and women were intrigued by spiritualism. Southerners gave no indication of believing the boast of four to ten million spiritualists in the North, but they saw enough to distress them. Spiritualists were by no means of one mind on marriage and free love, but since free lovers were strongly attracted to spiritualism, spiritualists and other radicals constantly faced such accusations. Spiritualists claimed that they advocated consensual, loving, stable marriages, free of patriarchal oppression and externally imposed norms. Even so, their fierce denunciations of "traditional" marriages and their embrace of Fourier's "passional

Gentlemen Theologians, 199–202, and J. B. Bennett, "Albert Taylor Bledsoe: Transitional Philosopher of the Old South," *Methodist History,* 11 (1972), 3–14. Bledsoe, who became a Methodist minister after the War, took pains to show that both Arminians and Calvinists, despite serious errors, made important contributions to a proper understanding of Christianity; although the Methodists received Theodicy kindly, the Calvinists denounced it. For Calvinist attacks see [J. H. Bocock], "Bledsoe's Theology," *SPR,* 8 (1855), 516–45, and the more contemptuous [Bocock], "Modern Theology: Taylor and Bledsoe," *SPR,* 9 (1856), 492–512; also, Robert L. Dabney, *Systematic Theology* (Carlisle, PA, 1985 [1878]), 79–80, 86, 128–32, 291, 298, 563. William C. Preston described Bledsoe as "a joyous lighthearted bluff gentleman somewhat a ladies man and addictive to joking. You would never guess that he was 'Theodicy'": Preston to Waddy Thompson, Sept. 22, 1857, in Preston Papers, at USC. *Theodicy,* neither bedtime reading nor a candidate for parlor display, sold out quickly and passed through several editions in the next few years: Bledsoe, *Theodicy,* 369, 389. See also Supplementary References: "Universalism."

20 R. Laurence Moore, *In Search of White Crows: Spiritualism, Parapsychology, and American Culture* (New York, 1977), 3; our discussion of spiritualism draws heavily on this able study. Also, John C. Spurlock, *Free Love: Marriage and Middle-Class Radicalism in America, 1825–1860* (New York, 1988), 2, 55, 94–8, 140–4; Arthur Charles Cole, *The Irrepressible Conflict, 1850–1865* (New York, 1934), 252. Relations between the Universalist Church and the Spiritualists were complex, and the Church as such kept its distance. Spiritualism nonetheless made deep inroads especially among the more radical Universalists, some of whom eventually left the Church. See Ann Lee Bressler, *The Universalist Movement in America, 1770–1880* (New York, 2001), ch. 5. On spiritualism's denial of a hell of eternal torments see Geoffrey Rowell, *Hell and the Victorians: A Study of Nineteenth-Century Theological Controversies Concerning Eternal Punishment and the Future Life* (Oxford, U.K., 1974), 10–11. For the complex relation of abolitionism to the occult see Russ Castronovo, "Antislavery Unconscious," *Mississippi Quarterly,* 53 (1999/2000), 41–56.

attraction" struck many as a thinly veiled assault on the family. The spiritualist movement outdid liberal churches in bringing women to prominence, primarily as mediums but also as lecturers. Spiritualists stood out among the ultras of the abolitionist and women's-rights movements, in which women especially asserted – in the words of a sympathetic historian – "the primacy of individual conscience over all other religious authority." Spiritualists scorned organized religion in their own version of "Christianity versus Churchianity," and Southerners knew that séances and spiritualism fed the abolitionist version of higher-law doctrine. Under the banner of "self-sovereignty," theological liberalism's extreme left-wingers dispatched original sin, hell, and judgment day, demonstrating to their own satisfaction that humanity needed no savior. As Henry Clarke Wright put it, every man and woman could be his/her own savior and god.[21]

Much of spiritualism's intellectual attraction came from its repudiation of the occult and its appeal to science. It assimilated the spirit world to the material and, along with phrenology and homeopathic medicine, took its place within the rationalistic currents of the day. A committee of distinguished scientists at Harvard, led by the great paleontologist Louis Agassiz, dismissed spiritualism as unscientific and morally corrupting, but to little effect. Even the exposure of the Fox sisters, America's most celebrated mediums, as frauds did not end its influence.[22]

Spiritualism, Swedenborgism, and other heresies had no foothold in the South. Or so the leaders of Southern opinion said. R. L. Dabney – assailing spiritualism, Mormonism, free love, and communism in one breath – boasted that the South suffered from them not at all. George Sawyer relegated the Fox sisters and other spiritualists to an array of wild-eyed northern fanatics. The Presbyterian Reverend William S. Plumer of Richmond called spiritualism a sin and a black art. But some prominent South Carolinians, nullifiers and unionists alike, caught the spiritualist bug. Both lowcountry and upcountry had more spiritualists than anyone cared to admit. James Henry Hammond turned to spiritualism, apparently as a buffer against his periodic bouts of religious skepticism. Simms consulted mediums in New York City in 1856. While reiterating his Christianity, he wrote Hammond that "Spiritualism as a philosophy is more in complete accordance with my own speculations, felt & pursued for 30 years than any other system." Governor James Hamilton, Jr., of South Carolina, a famed nullifier, visited the Fox sisters and tearfully related to Benjamin Perry how they had called up the spirit of his deceased son.

[21] Anna M. Speicher, *The Religious World of Antislavery Women: Spirituality in the Lives of Five Abolitionist Lecturers* (Syracuse, NY, 2000), 7, quote at 76; Ann Braude, *Radical Spirits: Spiritualism and Women's Rights in Nineteenth-Century America* (Boston, 1989), 36–7, 41, 56–7, 62, 70, and for free love see ch. 5; Lewis Perry, *Childbirth, Marriage, and Reform: Henry Clarke Wright, 1797–1870* (Chicago, 1980), ch. 3 ("Dethroning God"), esp. 99, and for Wright's spiritualism see 156–65. Wright – who promoted the speaking tour of the Grimké sisters in 1838 – abandoned Calvinism, departed the ministry, and preached "self-sufficiency." In the 1840s he joined the spiritualists and conversed with Jesus.

[22] With no discernible effect, William Campbell Preston chided his spiritualist friend Waddy Thompson about the reaction at Harvard, which arrayed science and religion against spiritualism: Preston to Waddy Thompson, July 27, 1857, in Preston Papers.

Waddy Thompson, a Bible-reading Episcopalian, joined Hamilton at the Foxes and became a firm believer. William Campbell Preston seemed incredulous that Thompson, his friend and fellow Whig unionist, was succumbing. Preston's dry wit could not disguise his apprehension: "There have been two great dispensations of Civilization, the Greek and the Christian and now comes the railroad, or the Locomotive, of which I am inclined to think [is] one of the earliest developments in the spiritual rappings. Now the railroads I heartily concur in and am a believer, but as to the Spiritual manifestations I hold myself in a wise & masterly inactivity. I wait to see into what shape the Cub's to be licked." During the War, Mary Chesnut and Louisa McCord shook their heads over the spiritualist inclinations of Thompson and Dr. Daniel Haywood Trezevant.[23]

Interest in spiritualism often accompanied interest in Mesmerism and phrenology, both of which enjoyed something of a vogue in Charleston. Medical scientists and intellectuals, Simms among them, pleaded for unbiased examination of its ideas. In time clerical opposition and abolitionist attraction to spiritualism provoked a negative reaction. Chancellor George Dargan, a respected legal scholar and an ardent nullifier who bragged he had never set foot outside South Carolina, plunged into spiritualism and Mesmerism and claimed to have established contact with the spirit world directly through a black boy. Certified by the unionist Benjamin Perry as incapable of telling a falsehood, Dargan commanded attention for his many such stories. If Simms could be believed, in 1843 every third man in Charleston was a Mesmerist. In 1857 William Lawton, a wealthy and socially prominent merchant, hosted a dinner party in Charleston attended by Edmund Ruffin, Richard Yeadon, editor of the Charleston *Courier,* and Attorney General Isaac Hayne. Ruffin reported that much of the conversation concerned slavery and secession, but "Mesmerism & spiritualism, or rather the physical phenomena (as table-moving, &c) were discussed. Mr. Yeadon is a believer in both – & stated some remarkable examples of apparent miracles in both."[24]

---

[23] Robert L. Dabney, *Defence of Virginia (and Through Her of the South) in Recent and Pending Contests against the Sectional Party* (New York, 1969 [1867]), 285; George S. Sawyer, *Southern Institutes; Or, an Inquiry into the Origin and Early Prevalence of Slavery and the Slave Trade* (New York, 1967 [1858]), 359; William S. Plumer, *The Law of God, as Contained in the Ten Commandments, Explained and Enforced* (Harrisonburg, VA, 1996 [1864]), 156, 440; Mary C. Oliphant et al., eds., *The Letters of William Gilmore Simms,* 6 vols. (Columbia, SC, 1952–82), 3:475–84, 431, 475–83; Stephen Meats and Edwin T. Arnold, eds., *The Writings of Benjamin F. Perry,* 3 vols. (Spartanburg, SC, 1980), 2:324, 3:321–2; *SQR,* n.s., 12 (1855), 502; W. C. Preston to Waddy Thompson, Sept. 7, 1853, and July 22, 1857, in Preston Papers; Chesnut Diary, Apr. 22, 1862, in C. Vann Woodward, ed., *Mary Chesnut's Civil War* (New Haven, CT, 1981), 328; also, Cornish Diary, May 12, 1855, at UNC-SHC. For Hammond see Drew Gilpin Faust, *James Henry Hammond and the Old South* (Baton Rouge, LA, 1982), 262; Carol Bleser, ed., *The Hammonds of Redcliff* (New York, 1981), 24 n. 4; Dec. 13, 1853, in Carol Bleser, ed., *Secret and Sacred: The Diaries of James Henry Hammond, a Southern Slaveholder* (New York, 1988), 262. In the 1840s William Walker, the future filibusterer then studying medicine in Europe, found prominent scientists taken with Spiritualism: Walker to Lindsley, July 15, 1843, in Appendix to John Edwin Windrow, *John Berrien Lindsley: Educator, Physician, Social Philosopher* (Chapel Hill, NC, 1938), 181, 256.

[24] Oliphant et al., eds., *Letters of Simms,* 1:cxxxiii, 347; Meats and Arnold, eds., *Writings of Perry,* 2:157; May 16, 1857, in *ERD,* 1:72; and Peter McCandless, "Mesmerism and Phrenology in Antebellum

A few leading Georgians became spiritualists, including the English-born Godfrey Barnsley, one of Georgia's wealthiest merchant-planters. The ordinarily sensible Thomas Holley Chivers, Georgia's premier poet who spent much time in the Northeast, said he envisioned Allegra Florence – his adored 8-year-old daughter, now dead – eight years before her birth. Sarah Morgan of Baton Rouge fell ill, and a series of doctors proved useless. "Of course I do not actually believe in Spiritualism; but there is certainly something in it one cannot understand; and Mrs. Badger's experience is enough to convert one, alone." An Episcopalian, she kept telling herself that she would not convert to spiritualism.[25]

Spiritualism's modest impact in the South came largely through the influence of Emanuel Swedenborg (Svedberg), the eighteenth-century Swedish philosopher and mystic whose ideas crossed the Atlantic along with Mesmerism in the eighteenth century and were promoted in the nineteenth by Ralph Waldo Emerson, Henry James, Sr., and, more directly, by Andrew Jackson Davis. Swedenborg called for adherence to the Word but in a special sense. He transformed the Trinity from three persons into three principles: love, wisdom, and energy. Insisting that the Trinity appeared with the Incarnation, he called the concept of an eternal Trinity thinly disguised tritheism and compared its Protestant and Catholic devotees to "lascivious harlots and purveyors of death." In his view, the Nicene Council inaugurated the false version perpetuated by a corrupt Catholic Church. He also suggested that the existence of evil undermined the idea of God's omnipotence.[26]

Swedenborg, raised a Lutheran, became a notable geologist before dreams and mystic experiences ("relations") convinced him he had direct communication with

Charleston: 'Enough of the Marvellous,' " *JSH*, 58 (1992), 199–230. William Sims Reynolds was also attracted: see Oliphant's sketch, "The Reynolds Brothers," and Simms to James Lawton, Apr. 6, 1843, in Oliphant et al., eds., *Letters of Simms*, 1:347.

[25] A. D. Amerson, "Historic Barnsley Gardens," in Olin Jackson, ed., *A North Georgia Journal of History*, 2 vols. (Alpharetta, GA, 1992), 2:5–6; *DGB*, 1:59; Charles Henry Watts II, *Thomas Holley Chivers: His Literary Careers and His Poetry* (Athens, GA, 1956), 45–6, 182; Jan. 30 and Feb. 9, 1863, in Charles East, ed., *The Civil War Diary of Sarah Morgan* (Athens, GA, 1991), 415 (quoted), 423. About 1850, "thousands" were attending séances in the North: Braude, *Radical Spirits*, 19. On the interest in Mesmerism, homeopathy, and spiritualism see e.g. the correspondence in Eliza Cope Harrison, ed., *Best Companions: Letters of Eliza Middleton Fisher and Her Mother, Mary Herring Middleton, from Charleston, Philadelphia, and Newport, 1839–1846* (Columbia, SC, 2001); Amelia Akehurst Lines Diary, June 10, 1857, in Thomas Dyer, ed., *To Raise Myself a Little: The Diaries and Letters of a Georgia Teacher, 1851–1886* (Athens, GA, 1982), 54; Jan. 21, 1863, in Kate Mason Rowland and Mrs. Morris S. Croxall, eds., *The Journal of Julia LeGrand: New Orleans, 1862–1863* (Richmond, VA, 1911), 98; Elizabeth Scott Neblett to Will Neblett, May 3, 1864, in Erika L. Murr, ed., *A Rebel Wife in Texas: The Diary and Letters of Elizabeth Scott Neblett, 1852–1864* (Baton Rouge, LA, 2001), 401, and see Editor's Introduction, 15. To the orthodox, phrenology equated the mental and spiritual with the material: Theodore Dwight Bozeman, *Protestants in an Age of Science: The Baconian Ideal and Antebellum American Religious Thought* (Chapel Hill, NC, 1977), 91–3.

[26] Emanuel Swedenborg, *The True Christian Religion: Containing the Universal Theology of the New Church*, tr. "T. G. W." (Philadelphia, 1876), viii, ch. 1; Sydney E. Ahlstrom, *A Religious History of the American People* (New Haven, CT, 1972), 483–8; Jon Butler, *Awash in a Sea of Faith: Christianizing the American People* (Cambridge, MA, 1990), 234. For condemnation of Swedenborg on the Trinity, see "L." [Robert W. Landis?], "The Relation which Reason and Philosophy Sustains in the Theology of Revelation," *DQR*, 1 (1861), 48.

angels and spirits. His doctrine of precise correlation between the phenomenal and the spiritual won adherents in England and America. The British Theosophical Society, formed to study his thought, generated the Church of the New Jerusalem, which appeared in America in 1817. Swedenborg's ideas, notably his Universalism and perfectionism, proceeded in association with homeopathy, spiritualism, Mesmerism, and utopian socialism and influenced many outside the Swedenborgian churches. Adherents sought direct conversation with God, held séances, and believed the millennium had begun. Swedenborgians had 58 churches in the United States. By 1800 every large northern city had a Swedenborgian congregation, each attracting some distinguished citizens over the years. Baltimore housed a small Swedenborgian church. One of its preachers, Robert "Councillor" Carter, freed his slaves when he joined the church and left Virginia. Another, John Hargrove, pastor of the Church of the New Jerusalem, preached a Swedenborgian "Sermon on the Second Coming of Christ" on Christmas Day 1799 to the luminaries of the federal government at the Capitol. In Virginia, J. P. Holcombe and several members of the family of John Hartwell Cocke became Swedenborgians, as did Richard Crallé, Calhoun's friend and the editor of his papers, who solicited support for the church in Washington. Frank Cabell – a planter, scholar, nephew of Joseph Cabell, and Cocke's son-in-law – wrote an able defense of Swedenborg. Hugh Blair Grigsby thought Cabell "in religion rather twisted," but "I sincerely wish that he was my neighbor." According to Bishop O. P. Fitzgerald, Swedenborg, who preached free will and salvation by faith and works, influenced some leading Methodist clergymen among Calhoun's friends and supporters. James R. Gilmore, who wrote as "Edmund Kirke," must have thought that Swedenborg had a southern audience since he assigned a starring role in his *My Southern Friends* to a Swedenborgian planter in North Carolina.[27]

Here and there accounts may have missed small and transient congregations without enough support to establish a church. In Georgia, where we have a good county-by-county survey, a few Swedenborgians and Universalists turned up in Savannah and even in small towns and villages. Swedenborgians included Chivers and Herschel V. Johnson, who ran for vice-president with Stephen Douglas in 1860. Adherents came principally from the intellectual elite, although some spiritualist shipworkers regaled the ladies on Mississippi steamboats. In Texas the Reverend William Baker, son of the great evangelist Daniel Baker, joined some prominent

[27] See Carl J. Guarnieri, *The Utopian Alternative: Fourierism in Nineteenth-Century America* (Ithaca, NY, 1991), 116–17, 168; "The Older Religiousness of the South," in George M. Curtis III and James J. Thompson, Jr., eds., *The Southern Essays of Richard M. Weaver* (Indianapolis, IN, 1987), 139. On the South see Clement Eaton, *The Freedom-of-Thought Struggle in the Old South* (New York, 1964), 316, 387; Henry Howe, *Historical Collections of Virginia* (Charleston, SC, 1845), 499; O. P. Fitzgerald, *Fifty Years: Observations – Opinions – Experience* (Nashville, TN, 1903), 110; "Edmund Kirke" [James R. Gilmore], *My Southern Friends* (New York, 1863), 307; John Hargrove, "A Sermon on the Second Coming of Christ," in Ellis Sandoz, ed., *Political Sermons of the American Founding Era, 1730–1805* (Indianapolis, IN, 1991), 1571–96. For Carter see Robert B. Semple, *A History of the Rise and Progress of the Baptists in Virginia* (Richmond, VA, 1894 [1810]), 178–9. For Swedenborgian church members in Virginia see Mrs. Burton [Constance Cary] Harrison, *Recollections Grave and Gay* (London, 1912), 16. W. Pinkney Starke of Charleston sent Calhoun Swedenborg's work with a glowing recommendation: Starke to Calhoun, Apr. 4, 1849, in *JCCP*, 26:369.

citizens in a small spiritualist circle. South Carolina's contingent included Augustus Requier, a poet who achieved much of his fame in Alabama. Requier, a correspondent for the Charleston *Courier* and a respected man of letters, raised eyebrows when he became identified as a Unitarian and a Swedenborgian. A curious Lucy Breckenridge found Swedenborg's doctrines "certainly very beautiful and attractive" and noted several prominent converts among Episcopalians. Mesmerism and phrenology attracted some prominent men in Alabama for a short while. And in Natchez, William H. Holcombe embraced homeopathy and Swedenborgism as a pure Christianity that rejected such "superstitions" as the resurrection of the body. After the War he wrote several books to propagate the faith.[28]

In 1843 *Southern Quarterly Review* published a favorable fifty-page review-essay on Swedenborg and his thought, probably written by Daniel Whitaker of Charleston, describing him as a "great and good man" and as a powerful thinker of considerable influence in Europe whose ideas were making headway in America. In 1846 a professed Swedenborgian – again probably Whitaker – defended Swedenborg's theology and declared "that extraordinary man ... certainly one of the most gifted geniuses ever to appear on the face of the earth." With noticeable discomfort the editors separated themselves from some important American intellectuals for whom Swedenborg's views had strong appeal. Whitaker's evaluation found a grudging echo in R. J. Breckenridge's *Danville Quarterly Review,* which conceded that Swedenborg was "upright and Intelligent" and "a truly learned, exemplary, and serious man" with "numerous and respectable followers," adding that only "folly and mental imbecility" could fail to recognize the challenge of his thought. The Methodist W. S. Grayson of Mississippi rejected Swedenborg's theology but described him as "this wonderful man." Nancy Robinson of Mississippi captured the fascination of spiritualism to a Christian woman who thought she had found evidence of its validity: "There is strange mystery in it – it is too happy a thought to believe that the spirits of the blest made perfect can watch over us here in our sinful state and be our guardians."[29]

---

[28] J. S. Buckingham, *The Slave States of America,* 2 vols. (New York, 1968 [1842]), 2:273. According to the county-by-county survey in George White, *Statistics of the State of Georgia* (Savannah, GA, 1849), 166, 454, Universalists could be found in at least fifteen counties. William H. Holcombe Diary, June 23, 185?, at UNC-SHC; Michael Allen, *Western Rivermen, 1763–1861: Ohio and Mississippi Boatmen and the Myth of the Alligator Horse* (Baton Rouge, LA, 1990), 192; Camilla Davis Trammel, *Seven Pines: Its Occupants and Their Letters, 1825–1872* (Houston, TX, 1986), 119; Rollin G. Osterweis, *Romanticism and Nationalism in the Old South* (Baton Rouge, LA, 1971), 117; R. F. W. Allston to Adele Petigru Allston, in J. H. Easterby, ed., *The South Carolina Rice Plantation, as Revealed in the Papers of Robert F. W. Allston* (Chicago, 1945), 99; Aug. 13, 1862, in Mary D. Robertson, ed., *Lucy Breckenridge of Grove Hill: The Journal of a Virginia Girl, 1826–1864* (Kent, OH, 1979), 25; R. K. Crallé to A. T. Smith, Nov. 30, 1844, in *JCCP,* 20:404–5; H. B. Grigsby to Henry Stephens Randall, Sept. 3, 1858, in Frank J. Klingberg and Frank W. Klingberg, eds., *The Correspondence between Henry Stephens Randall and Hugh Blair Grigsby, 1856–1861* (Berkeley, CA, 1952), 144; William Garrett, *Reminiscences of Public Men in Alabama for Thirty Years* (Atlanta, GA, 1872), 263; Holcombe Diary, Jan. 21, 1855; Willliam H. Holcombe, *Our Children in Heaven* (Philadelphia, 1869), esp. 34–40. Grisby, for one, much admired Holcombe but regretted his Swedenborgism: [Hugh Blair Grigsby], *SLM,* 30 (1860), 475–6.

[29] In *SQR* see: [D. K. Whitaker?], "The Life and Writings of Swedenborg," 4 (1843), 414–66; "Life of Emanuel Swedenborg," 10 (1846), 306–29, esp. 306 n.; "Critical Notices," 9 (1846), 533–5; "Mesmer

William D. Valentine of North Carolina attended a meeting at the house of his brother George with a 15-year-old white girl and a black girl. (Since Valentine was a prude, we may dismiss speculations about the foursome.) The table actually moved, and the spirits rapped answers to questions. It was all "astonishing." Afterwards, Valentine went back to his Bible and struggled to reconcile his experience with his Christian conscience. William Frierson Cooper of Tennessee described the rise and progress of spiritualism and Mormonism as every bit as "astounding as the career of the Anabaptists or the Dancing mania of the middle ages." "If you have time & think there is no harm," Anna Matilda King of Georgia wrote Thomas Butler King, her politician husband who was in New York in 1856, "I wish you would go to the Fox's & enquire if spirits are permitted to tell us the future in this world." She reported on "some very strange some pleasant communications" and on the direct testimony of some of their lowcountry friends, and she subsequently hoped that Thomas would be not be annoyed by her own "continued communications with the SPIRIT WORLD," for she had once more received "so IMPRESSIVE a message it has opened my eyes to the fatal flaw I am guilty of." Thomas probably could not afford to get annoyed, for Anna was invoking spirits to help her curb her temper with the children.[30]

Despite the conversion of Councillor Carter and a few others to emancipation, southern spiritualists proved solid defenders of slavery, but most Southerners came to associate spiritualism with abolitionism and such political heresies as women's rights. They did in fact have something to fear, since covert materialism and secularization proceeded together with an obsession with the self. Spiritualism gave the abolitionists a chance to ground authority for their higher-law doctrine – in the voice of the dead. Among abolitionist spiritualists, John Murray Spears communicated with Channing, Swedenborg, Rush, Franklin, Seneca, and Lafayette; Henry Wright knew the spirit of the Bible condemned slavery because he communicated personally with Jesus, who told him so. Phrenology had materialist foundations, and George Combe of Edinburgh, its pioneer, wrote *Of the Constitution of Man* in 1828 to promote it along with social reform.[31]

and Swedenborg," 11 (1847), 212–44, esp. 219; [D. K. Whitaker?], "Philosophical Works of Swedenborg," 13 (1848), 427–69; for flattering mention of Swedenborg's intellectual prowess see "Swedenborg's Poems," 8 (1845), 248–51, also 9 (1846), 533–5. "The Claim of Emanuel Swedenborg to Divine Illumination," *DQR,* 1 (1861), 177–229, quotes at 177, 178, 179; W. S. Grayson, "Cromwell and His Religion," *QRMECS,* 5 (1851), 83; Nancy McDougall Robinson Diary, July 17, 1853, at Mississippi Department of Archives and History (Jackson). For brief, friendly sketches of Swedenborg and his doctrines see "N. H.", "Swedenborg," *Baltimore Literary Monument,* 2 (1839), 148–50; "Extracts from the Life of Swedenborg," *Baltimore Phoenix and Budget,* 1 (1841), 238–9.

[30] Valentine Diaries, June 8, 9, 11, 1853, at UNC-SHC; William Frierson Cooper, "Notes on a Trip to Europe, 1862–1863," 178, at Tennessee State Library and Archives (Nashville); Anna Matilda King to Thomas Butler King, June 5 and 8, 1856, at UNC-SHC. Phrenology had little impact in the South, but in the 1840s curiosity drove throngs to lectures on phrenology in the towns and among the tobacco planters of North Carolina. The intellectual elite of Charleston discussed it gravely, inviting luminaries like William Porcher Miles to present their views: see e.g. S. Gilman to W. P. Miles, May 8, 1842, in Miles Papers, at UNC-SHC. On phrenology see Peter J. Bowler, *The Invention of Progress: The Victorians and the Past* (London, 1989), 88–9.

[31] David Brion Davis, *Slavery and Human Progress* (New York, 1984), 149–50; Lewis Perry, *Radical Abolitionism: Antislavery and the Government of God in Antislavery Thought* (Ithaca, NY, 1973),

The South firmly resisted these isms, although they did infiltrate the elite of the lowcountry and the southern cities. Devotees kept a low profile. In Nashville the Reverend Jesse B. Ferguson, a leader of the Disciples of Christ, held his own in some ferocious debates with Alexander Campbell over doctrinal differences until he ruined his reputation by invoking spiritualism; he finished himself off when the spirit of William Ellery Channing warned him to stay away from Campbell and preach spiritualism instead. Following Channing's advice, he wandered through Mississippi, Alabama, and Missouri, shedding influence as he went. Spiritualism attracted significant support from the common people of the North but not of the South. Lewis Macy of Indiana, who spent the winter of 1851/52 in Memphis, commented, "I almost begin to think that the people of the north are more easily humbugged than those of the south .... I believe I have never heard of a 'spiritual manifestation' in the south yet." The small inroads nonetheless signaled trouble in Zion. In 1857 Thomas Smyth constructed a Christian version of the notion that the dead remain in spiritual communion with the living. As late as the end of the century, John Girardeau was saying of spiritualism: "It cannot be laughed away, it cannot be sneered down, it cannot be explained away upon scientific grounds. It is based in a natural craving of the human mind to read the dread secrets of the invisible world, and to hold communion with the dead."[32]

"Watch these religious lunatics," the Methodist Reverend Lovick Pierce of Georgia exhorted his flock as he warned against the intrusions of resurgent Deism in the form of Swedenborgianism and Unitarianism. And without doubt, Unitarianism and Universalism mounted formidable challenges to Christian orthodoxy.[33]

Thomas Jefferson and Edmund Ruffin were only two of the prominent Virginians, from the Revolution to secession, who liked what they heard from the Unitarians.

218–22, 224. Theodore Weld and the Grimké sisters admired George Combe's work and applied his theories, with unfortunate results. Angelina Grimké to Theodore Weld, Jan. 21, 1838, Theodore Weld to Sarah Grimké, Feb. 8, 1838, and Sarah Grimké to Gerrit Smith, Feb. 16, 1838, in Gilbert H. Barnes and Dwight L. Dumond, eds., *Letters of Theodore Dwight Weld, Angelina Grimké and Sarah Grimké, 1822–1844*, 2 vols. (Gloucester, MA, 1965), 2:524, 531, 552, 841 n. 2. *Southern Literary Messenger*, however, published a series of lectures by Combe: "Combe on Phrenology," *SLM*, 5 (1839), 667–70, 725–33, 810–13. See also the friendly article by "Waters", datelined Boston, in "Combe's 'Constitution of Man,' " *SLJ*, n.s., 1 (1837), 252–6. Combe's *Travels* was read and discussed in Charleston in 1830: James Stuart, "Bad Roads, Loose Morals, Sadism, and Racetrack Discipline, 1830," in Thomas D. Clark, ed., *South Carolina: The Grand Tour, 1780–1865* (Columbia, SC, 1973), 196.

32 F. Garvin Davenport, *Cultural Life in Nashville on the Eve of the Civil War* (Chapel Hill, NC, 1941), 106–7; Lewis O. Saum, *The Popular Mood in Pre–Civil War America* (Westport, CT, 1980), 47–9, Macy quoted on 49; "Teachings of the Dead," *TSW*, 10:5–76; "The Signs of the Times – In the World," in George A. Blackburn, ed., *Sermons by John L. Girardeau* (Columbia, SC, 1907), 111. J. S. Lamar linked Swedenborg to George Fox and the Quakers but acknowledged his learning and good character: Lamar, *The Organon of Scripture; Or, the Inductive Method of Biblical Interpretation* (Philadelphia, 1860), 66–70. When, in the 1850s, the editors of *Southern Quarterly Review* lamented the "spread of the absurd superstition of spiritualism," they doubtless knew of the séances in Nashville: see Castronovo, "Antislavery Unconscious," 51–2. Holmes referred testily to a spiritualist colony in Virginia: [George Frederick Holmes], "Revival of the Black Arts," *MMQR*, 4th ser., 6 (1854), 210.

33 Lovick Pierce, "Paul's Commission to Preach," in Atticus G. Haygood, ed., *Bishop Pierce's Sermons and Addresses, with a Few Discourses by Dr. Pierce* (Nashville, TN, 1887), 129.

The Unitarian Church per se did not flourish in the South despite the best efforts of such devoted souls as Winifred Gales, the daughter of John Marshall and a novelist of some reputation, and Joseph Gales, the editor of the popular Raleigh *Register,* and the Reverend Dr. Eliot of St. Louis. Augusta and Mobile had small Unitarian societies in the 1820s and 1830s, but they faded quickly. Only in Charleston and New Orleans did the Unitarian church have strongholds, if they may be called that. Hence, Thornton Stringfellow, on the offensive against the isms that accompanied liberal theology, recalled in the 1850s that the churches of New England had begun as pillars of Christian orthodoxy but now housed "the *astonishing number* of two hundred and two Unitarian and two hundred and eighty-five Universalist churches." In contrast, the Atlantic slave states had one Unitarian and seven Universalist churches. And yet, while the southern Unitarian church fared poorly, Unitarian ideas made strides in the South as well as the Northwest.[34]

Unitarianism and Universalism had elusive appeals that, while not necessarily winning southern converts to their creeds or churches, exposed a sensibility dangerous to those committed to orthodoxy. Edmund Ruffin spoke of theology as "the *science* of misconstruction." He valued the teachings of Jesus but found no justification for a belief in the Trinity or an afterlife of rewards and punishments. Ruffin, believing in one all-wise, all-just, all-merciful, all-benevolent God who created and preserves the universe, expressed his dissident views only to a few close friends and tried not to shock his neighbors. He explained poignantly that he kept his views even from his children because he knew they would fear for his eternal damnation. Ruffin found the deception distasteful, and, shortly before he committed suicide in response to the fall of the Confederacy, he noted in his diary that for the last 25 years he had prayed daily and that he dreaded punishment for his sins – but not for holding unpopular or possibly erroneous religious opinions.[35]

A few Unitarian ministers established themselves as pillars of southern urban communities, enjoyed considerable prestige, and formed cordial, mutually respectful relations with leaders of other churches. In the early 1800s the Reverend Anthony Foster left the Presbyterian Church to lead the Unitarian church, which dated in Charleston from 1772. The defection did not cost him personally, and William McPheeters, the well-known Presbyterian divine with whom he had studied theology, conducted his funeral service back in North Carolina. Samuel Gilman, Foster's successor, moved easily among Charleston's elite. In 1856, *Southern Quarterly Review* published long extracts from Gilman's *Contributions to Literature* and praised him as an intellectual leader of the southern clergy. Charleston's Baptist Reverend W. T. Brantley concurred. John Reuben Thompson, editor of *Southern Literary Messenger,* in a memorial on Gilman's death in 1858 lauded him as the very soul of the New England Society of South Carolina and as a man deeply respected by

---

[34] Although our pages on the Unitarians in the South were in draft before we had the pleasure of seeing the manuscript of John Allen Macaulay's book, we have taken it into account and drawn on it. We thank Dr. Macaulay for letting us see it and warmly recommend his book: *Unitarianism in the Antebelllum South: The Other Invisbible Institution* (Tuscaloosa, AL, 2001). See also Supplementary References: "Unitarianism."

[35] See esp. June 18 and Aug. 9, 1863, as well as Feb. 24 and 25, 1864, in *ERD,* 3:16–17, 106–7, 346–7, 349–51, quote at 17.

all of Charleston. The memorial extended its respect to the Unitarians of Boston for their political and social conservatism. It praised the high intellectual quality and political moderation of their press, noting as late as 1859 that even its antislavery views "are never offensively set forward." In Savannah, Richard D. Arnold, a prominent Unitarian, enjoyed a fine reputation as mayor and as a physician who served as guardian for a number of free blacks. Such cultured gentlemen as Henry Franklin Stearns and Harry Toulmin, former president of Transylvania University, became respected judges in Alabama.[36]

The most serious defection to Unitarianism came in New Orleans in the 1830s, when the redoubtable Presbyterian Reverend Theodore Clapp finally came clean after having denied, long and lamely, any departure from Calvinism. Clapp led much of his congregation, as well as some Episcopalians and others, into the Unitarian Church. His brilliant pulpit style and special appeal across social-class lines filled his church, rivaling the theater in drawing crowds. The New Orleans *Daily Picayune* published many of his sermons, in which he expounded Christianity as, above all, a code of ethics. He ridiculed the notion of a depraved human nature and warmly endorsed Channing's teachings on sin and human goodness. He did agree with the orthodox on the reality of a depraved humanity but objected to the "gloomy notions of" Augustine, Calvin, and Edwards on origins. He denied the sinfulness of newborn infants while acknowledging their entrance into a sinful world of irresistible lures. The *Daily Picayune* devoted much space in 1848 to a controversy between Clapp and several other Protestant ministers in which he staunchly upheld the existence of an afterlife but rejected eternal punishment. His sermons suggest hell as a kind of purgatory through which chastised sinners pass on the road to ultimate redemption. In general, his notion of "our entire and absolute dependence on God" accorded well with Schleiermacher's. Clapp probably could have gotten away with anything, for he was revered for ministering to the laboring classes as well as the elite and for his heroic work among the victims of the epidemics that plagued New Orleans. And he not only defended slavery but took high ground in espousing slavery as the necessary and proper condition of the laboring classes without regard to race.[37]

---

[36] *DNCB*, 2:224; *SLM*, 27 (1858), 156–8, and 28 (1859), 160; *SQR*, n.s. (3rd), 1 (1856), 430–6; W. T. Brantly, "God's Gracious Purpose," in *Sermons* (Charleston, SC, 1858), 50–2; [John R. Thompson], *SLM*, 23 (1856), 160; *DGB*, 36. The Presbyterian Mitchell King was among those who found Gilman's sermons able if not scriptural: Mitchell King Diary, Feb. 1, 1852, at USC. For favorable notice of Gilman's published oration on literature see [D. K. Whitaker], *SLJ*, n.s., 1 (1837), 286. For J. R. Thompson's tribute to Gilman on his death see *SLM*, 26 (1858), 316–18. On Stearns see Benjamin Franklin Riley, *History of Conecuh County, Alabama* (Blue Hill, ME, 1964 [1881]), 121–2, and on Toulmin see Anson West, *A History of Methodism in Alabama* (Spartanburg, SC, 1983 [1893]), 87–8. The proslavery Charles Manson Taggart, Unitarian minister in Nashville and then Charleston, published "The Diversity and Origin of the Human Races" in Simms's *SQR*, n.s., 4 (1851), 392–419. Simms also welcomed Taggart's *Religion a Life, Not a Social Experience*, describing him as a sensible and able exponent of Unitarianism: [William Gilmore Simms], "Critical Notices," *SQR*, n.s., 7 (1853), 524; [Simms], "Critical Notices," *SQR*, n.s., 5 (1852), 254. Simms also paid tribute to Gilman's literary efforts: "Critical Notices," *SQR*, n.s., 1 (1856), 430–6.

[37] In the New Orleans *Daily Picayune* see Theodore Clapp, Dec. 3, 1848, and Mar. 4, 1849 (infants) as well as "Thanksgiving Sermon," Apr. 14; also, Jan. 14, 1849 (absolute dependence); Nov. 10, Feb.

Despite impressive growth in some localities, the Universalist Church, more rural than urban, remained small even in New England, where it influenced artisans and laborers repelled by church hierarchies and establishments. At the beginning of the nineteenth century the Universalists had become fervently evangelical and established bridgeheads in the Mid-Atlantic States and the Old Northwest. In the Burned-Over District of upstate New York, the more orthodox Christians among the antislavery radicals considered the Universalists a greater threat than the hated Catholics. One Union soldier from Indiana who was fighting in Virginia thought an orthodox Presbyterian would consider three quarters of his regiment "infidels," and he was certain that a majority were Universalists. By the 1840s the Universalists counted some 600,000 adherents nationally, which for a time placed them among the top half dozen denominations, and they boasted of their openness to women in the ministry. Theologically, as well as socially and economically, a gulf separated Universalists from Unitarians. Oriented by Hosea Ballou's *A Treatise on Atonement* (1805), the more conservative Universalists rejected Arminianism along with Trinitarianism, held fast to predestination, and sought to "improve" Calvinism. The gulf slowly closed because many Unitarians also believed that God would save all souls in the fullness of time, although class differences inhibited merger of the denominations and their individual churches until the 1960s. The Universalists saw the Unitarians as elitists, and the Unitarians looked down on poorly educated, rural, often socially conservative Universalist ministers prone to appeal to crowds at evangelical rallies. In 1858 the Reverend Hope Bain, itinerant Universalist, asked himself why his church had so few adherents in the South. He replied that many communicants of other churches accepted the universalist doctrine of general salvation but were reluctant to speak up.[38]

Louisa and David McCord, among other Southerners, floated between Deism and Unitarianism, viewing Christianity as ethical standard not as doctrine. In Nashville, William Walker, the professedly Christian filibusterer, moved toward Unitarianism in theological discussions with John Berrien Lindsley, an old college chum who viewed the Bible as primarily a great source of history and literature. In Georgia, U.S. Representative and Judge Robert Raymond Reid professed Unitarianism. Barton Stone and powerful figures in the Christian Church veered toward Unitarianism or Arianism. Alexander Campbell rejected Arianism and Unitarianism but shied away from "Trinity" as unspecified in the New Testament and

---

24, Dec. 22, 1850; and on slavery see Clapp, *Slavery: A Sermon* (New Orleans, 1838). For the debate see the contributions of Clapp (Jan. 14 and Apr. 2, 1848, Feb. 5 and Mar. 4, 1849) and the Reverend Joseph H. Martin, as well as those of the Reverend J. Twichell (Apr. 16, 21, 29, 1848). On the Episcopalian defections to Clapp see Hodding Carter and Betty Werlein Carter, *So Great a God: A History of the Episcopal Church and of Christ Church Cathedral, 1805–1955* (Sewanee, TN, 1955), 27–8, 46.

38 Paul K. Conkin, *The American Originals: Reformed Christianity in Antebellum America* (Chapel Hill, NC, 1995), 101; Eaton, *Freedom-of-Thought Struggle*, 316; "Discourse on Hell" (1858), Bain Papers, at UNC-SHC. Ann Lee Bressler notes that by midcentury the Universalist Church's hopes for large-scale recruiting faded in part because the mainstream Protestant churches were, if not conceding its doctrines, offering little resistance to parishioners who were so inclined: Bressler, *Universalist Movement in America*, 76.

as an invitation to diversionary debates over abstractions. Methodist preachers complained about communicants who harbored anti-Trinitarian and Universalist doctrines, and Lutheran ministers faced arraignment for heresy. The Disciples of Christ took stern criticism for Unitarian and Universalist theological tendencies, which they emphatically denied, but at least some of their·ministers did welcome those who took essentially Unitarian and Universalist ground. In the Northeast, many Disciples defected to the Universalists.[39]

Especially during the eighteenth century, the principal southern churches occasionally suffered minor defections from parishioners attracted by Universalist and anti-Trinitarian ideas. The Reverend Elkanah Tally of the Episcopal Church of Virginia defected late in the eighteenth century, but God punished him – at least according to Bishop Meade, who said that Tally "died the death of the drunkard." Some influence remained, for Richmond and Petersburg had small Universalist churches as late as 1860. Several Episcopalian ministers who espoused Universalist tenets but did not defect retained the respect and affection of their peers. The congenial God of the Universalists, who redeemed even the most atrocious sinner, had strong appeal but also ran into ridicule. In 1840, the Reverend Hosea Holcombe of Alabama regaled fellow Baptists with a story about a Universalist who read the story of Cain and Abel to his little daughter. When she asked about Abel's fate, her father said he had gone to heaven. When she then asked about Cain, he replied with some nervousness that, well, he also went to heaven. Oh, the little one replied, but wouldn't Cain kill Abel again once he got there?[40]

In 1854, Bishop J. H. Otey of Tennessee referred to "a large congregation" that had gathered at the courthouse in Ripley to hear the Universalist Reverend Mr. Quinby. The Reverend John C. Burruss set out to preach in North Carolina with

[39] Richard Lounsbury, "Afterword," in Lounsbury, ed., *Louisa S. McCord: Poems Drama, Biography, Letters* (Charlottesville, VA, 1996), 446–7; Walker to Lindsley, Nov. 14, 1843, in Appendix to Windrow, *J. B. Lindsley*, 183; Stephen F. Miller, *The Bench and Bar of Georgia: Memoirs and Sketches*, 2 vols. (Philadelphia, 1858), 2:217; Conkin, *American Originals,* ch. 1, esp. 7, 14, 22, 29; Paul K. Conkin, *Cane Ridge: America's Pentecost* (Madison, WI, 1990), 133–4; *The Backwoods Preacher: Being the Autobiography of Peter Cartwright* (London, 1870), 29, 98–9; Lutheran Church in America (South Carolina Synod, History of Synod Committee), *A History of the Lutheran Church in South Carolina* (Columbia, SC, 1971), 183; Charles C. Ware, *Barton Warren Stone, Pathfinder of Christian Union: A Story of His Life and Times* (St. Louis, MO, 1932), ch. 18; for charges of Unitarianism against the Disciples see also Glenn T. Miller, *Piety and Intellect: The Aims and Purposes of Ante-Bellum Theological Education* (Atlanta, GA, 1990), 30, and the account of Campbell's views in *Millennial Harbinger*, 2 (Dec. 5, 1831). T. C. Thornton, president of Centenary College in Mississippi, taunted the abolitionists that, among the 100,000 or so blacks he knew, he could find no Universalist or atheist: Thornton, *An Inquiry into the History of Slavery* (Washington, DC, 1841), 108. That the Universalists had women ministers in the North did not improve their chances for proselytizing in the South.

[40] William Meade, *Old Churches, Ministries, and Families of Virginia*, 2 vols. (Berrysville, VA, 1978 [1857]), 1:420; John C. Burruss to Hope Bain, Feb. 10, 1852, in Bain Papers; Emory M. Thomas, *The Confederate State of Richmond: A Biography of the Capital* (Austin, TX, 1971), 30; Frederick Dalcho, *An Historical Account of the Protestant Episcopal Church in South Carolina* (Charleston, SC, 1970 [1820]), 180–3; Hosea Holcombe, *A History of the Rise and Progress of the Baptists in Alabama* (Philadelphia, 1840), 48 n.

high hopes, expecting that "the friends are very much encouraged at the thought of having a regular pastor" and promising to "preach doctrinal & controversial Sermons." He felt buoyed by the "many strangers" who attended his meetings and asked to have the doctrinal differences explained. Universalist preachers turned up here and there even in the rough Southwest, where they drew interested or at least curious audiences. The few Universalist ministers in Alabama caused an occasional stir, publishing short-lived periodicals that attracted the momentary interest of at least a few planters. They had a small church in Montgomery in the mid-1830s and remained active, if feebly so, thereafter. Mary Dean, staunch Presbyterian of Russell County, was aghast when her aged grandparents converted to Universalism. Burruss exulted, "How I love to see Universalism embraced and practiced. There is a vast work to be done in the middle and Southern States."[41]

Hostility toward Universalism ran into the countercurrent of religious toleration and southern hospitality. In 1838 the Universalist Reverend George Rogers, in one of several swings through Louisiana and the Southwest, found no co-religionist ministers in New Orleans but met Clapp, who much impressed him. Rogers preached in New Orleans, Bayou Sara, and elsewhere in Louisiana and in Woodville, Clinton, and Jackson in Mississippi, usually at courthouses, although Methodists, Baptists, and Presbyterians opened their pulpits to him. At Clinton, his preaching got a warm welcome from what seemed to be the entire town population. He did encounter some "bigotry," most notably at Selma, Alabama, where he had to preach in a theater after its ministers refused him their churches, but in Nashville the Disciples and Baptists received him graciously. That he converted anyone may be doubted. Apart from other considerations, as he sadly noted, the South had few Universalist pastors in residence, and heavy expenses kept the number of itinerants to a bare minimum.[42]

A Universalist preacher who walked the line in the South on slavery and race had little trouble. Andrew Johnson publicly praised Reverend W. S. Balch, for one, as a staunch exponent of democracy. The Universalist churches in the South tried to be prudent, but cracks appeared. In the 1850s, when the church in Richmond made a tentative offer to Moncure Conway to become its minister, he declined – perhaps because he had recently converted to antislavery. From 1838 to 1845 Lewis F. W.

---

[41] Otey Diary, May 14, 1854, at UNC-SHC; John C. Burruss to Hope Bain, June 12, 1851, and July 2, 1855, in Bain Papers; also, West, *Methodism in Alabama*, 208–9, 222–3; Marion Elias Lazenby, *History of Methodism in Alabama and West Florida* (Nashville, TN, 1960), 112–13; Thomas McAdory Owens, *History of Alabama and Dictionary of Alabama Biography*, 4 vols. (Spartanburg, SC, 1978 [1921]), 1:536; Rhoda Coleman Ellison, *Early Alabama Publications: A Study in Literary Interests* (University, AL, 1947), 89–90; Mary Dean to James Norman, June 2, 1851, in Susan Lott Clark, ed., *Southern Letters and Life in the Mid 1800s* (Waycross, GA, 1993), 74–5.

[42] George Rogers, *Memoranda of the Experience, Labors, and Travels of a Universalist Preacher, Written by Himself* (Cincinnati, 1845), 250–3, 262, 283, 313, 316. Universalist preachers turned up to debate in Tennessee: Francis Terry Leak Diary, Feb. 16, 1853, at UNC-SHC. In Abbeville, South Carolina, Mary E. Moragné argued with her uncle over Universalism: Moragné Journal, Sept. 19, 1839, in Delle Mullen Craven, ed., *The Neglected Thread: A Journal of the Calhoun Community* (Columbia, SC, 1951), 159; T. C. Anderson, *Life of Reverend George Donnell, First Pastor of the Church in Lebanon, with a Sketch of the Scotch-Irish Race* (Nashville, TN, 1859), 297–9.

Andrews toured the South, preaching Universalism to small groups and launching the *Evangelical Universalist* in Macon, Georgia, which he could not get off the ground. In the 1850s he edited the *Georgia Citizen,* also in Macon, but at a public meeting he found himself threatened with a lynching when he defended free speech for critics of slavery. When Jefferson Davis put Richmond under martial law in 1862, Brigadier General Winder arrested the Universalist Reverend Alden Bosserman for preaching openly on the defeat of "this unholy rebellion." The Unitarian and militantly proslavery John Moncure Daniel, who edited the Richmond *Examiner,* argued that Universalism could be rendered compatible with proslavery beliefs.[43]

Universalist and Unitarian doctrines aroused suspicions, for they ran counter to the widespread identification of orthodox Christianity and to reliance on the Word with proslavery social doctrine. Southern Universalists and Unitarians accepted slavery, but that was not good enough. Fairly or not, Reverend Milo Parker Jewett, president of Judson College and editor of the *Alabama Baptist,* expressed a common feeling when he rebuked Universalists for preaching a "Perfectionism" that reduced the doctrine of salvation to trivia and thereby led straight to abolitionism. The editors of *Southern Quarterly Review* blasted William Ellery Channing and his fellow Unitarians for considering man only a little less than God, and the editors of *Southern Literary Messenger,* notwithstanding their praise of Gilman, rather fancifully had Unitarianism derive from the Puritan corruption of Christianity.[44]

Universalists suffered, too, from a prevailing tendency to view them as propagandists for women's rights. Nor were Southerners delighted to learn that Julia Ward Howe supported the ordination of women and frequently preached in Unitarian pulpits. Some Southerners who might have responded favorably to the theology recoiled from the liberal social practices. In the North, abolitionism reverberated in the Unitarian and Universalist churches. Julia Marsh Patterson of Georgia attended a Universalist service in New York and was impressed by its Christian tone but offended by the minister's oblique criticism of slavery. She seems to have been surprised to learn what most observant Southerners knew – that the Universalists of New England, like the Unitarians, were overwhelmingly antislavery. William Hamilton, a free black, delivered an important antislavery address to the New-York African Society

---

[43] "To the Freemen of the First Congressional District of Tennessee," Oct. 15, 1845, in Leroy P. Graf and Ralph W. Haskins, eds., *The Papers of Andrew Johnson* (Knoxville, TN, 1967–), 1:241; Mary Elizabeth Burtis, *Moncure Conway, 1832–1907* (New Brunswick, NJ, 1952), 47; for Andrews see "Introduction," in Emma Lester Chase and Lois Ferry Parks, eds., *The Complete Works of Thomas Holley Chivers:* vol. 1, *Correspondence* (Providence, RI, 1957 [only volume published]), 1: 291–5; Emory Thomas, *The Confederate Nation, 1861–1865* (New York, 1979), 151 (Bosserman); Eaton, *Freedom-of-Thought Struggle,* 314–15 (Daniel). Daniel, considered something of a misanthrope, offended many people and "was not a respected community leader": Carl R. Osthaus, *Partisans of the Southern Press: Editorial Spokesmen of the Nineteenth Century* (Lexington, KY, 1994), 97–9, quote at 116. The Universalist Church, congregational in form, did not take a stand against slavery, although a great many of its clerics and laymen did: Bressler, *Universalist Movement in America,* 85–8.
[44] "Fruits of Oberlin," *Alabama Baptist,* 2 (Feb. 24, 1844); *SQR,* n.s. (3rd), 2 (1857), 464; "Christianity versus Philanthropy," *SLM,* 34 (1862), 575; Eward Riley Crowther, *Southern Evangelicals and the Coming of the Civil War* (Lewiston, NY, 2000), 66–7.

for Mutual Relief, which met in a Universalist church in 1809. After 1830 or so, notable groups of radical artisans embraced the Universalist program for the total reform of society, which often added abolitionism and socialism to opposition to capital punishment and assorted crusades for human perfection. Among Universalist preachers, Charles Spear aided Lunsford Lane and fugitive slaves in Boston, and Moses Harman carried abolitionism to Missouri in the 1850s. Universalism's insistence that God be loved but not feared comported uneasily with the temperament of the immediatists. In Vermont in the 1840s, a Universalist church barred John Allen, its minister, from preaching against slavery, and he quit to join Brook Farm. Yet about 300 Universalist ministers, roughly half the total, spoke against slavery.[45]

Upon hearing that Harriet Martineau was a Unitarian, an old lady aboard a steamer on the Mississippi remarked, "She had better be done with that; she won't find it go down with us." Mary Moragné observed the Unitarian Church in Augusta, Georgia, in 1838: "It looks like the spirit of desolation had assailed its doors & windows – its shrine is deserted." Thus did the orthodox find solace in the marginality of the Unitarian churches. After all, among 664 Universalist ministers in the United States in 1860 only 20 were in the South. The Unitarian Reverend Samuel Gilman of Charleston firmly believed that Unitarian ideas widely permeated the Trinitarian denominations, but Methodists, Presbyterians, and Baptists accepted challenges to debate Unitarians in the South and seem to have had an easy time bringing backsliding folks back to contemplation of a God of Wrath.[46]

Anti-Trinitarianism nonetheless made quiet inroads in professedly Trinitarian congregations, and Unitarian and Universalist ideas remained under heavy fire throughout the South. Orthodox preachers constantly expressed anxiety over their effect on the minds of the faithful. At the beginning of the nineteenth century Baptist churches in the Southwest expelled Unitarians. In the 1820s the Catholic Bishop John England complained that the Unitarians wielded considerable influence in U.S. intellectual circles and fretted over their inroads in Charleston. During the religious revival of 1826, when Susan Nye Hutchinson of Georgia heard Stephen Olin deliver "one of the most impressive and eloquent sermons" she had ever heard, she noted that he excoriated "the Unitarian heresy among us." In Mississippi in 1829, Bishop Soule held forth to Indian converts on the Trinity and the errors of Unitarianism.[47]

[45] J. M. Patterson Journal, 137 (1850), at UNC-SHC; on Howe see *DCA*, 558; Perry, *Radical Abolitionism*, 135–6; Hamilton excerpted in Herbert Aptheker, ed., *A Documentary History of the Negro People in the United States*, 4 vols. (New York, 1990), 1:52–3; Louis P. Masur, *Rites of Execution: Capital Punishment and the Transformation of American Culture, 1776–1865* (New York, 1989), ch. 6; Spurlock, *Free Love*, 58, 222; Guarnieri, *Utopian Alternative*, 73 (on Allen).

[46] Harriet Martineau, *Retrospect of Western Travel*, 2 vols. (London, 1838), 2:19; Moragné Journal, Feb. 20, 1838, in Craven, ed., *Neglected Thread*, 647; for Gilman see Daniel Walker Howe, "A Massachusetts Yankee in Senator Calhoun's Court," *New England Quarterly*, 44 (1971), 200. On the number of ministers see Holifield, *Gentlemen Theologians*, 199. Unitarianism in and out of the Church attracted a disproportionately high number of intellectuals and reform-minded political activists. As the movement spread westward, it slowly sloughed off its professions of Christianity: Conkin, *American Originals*, ch. 2.

[47] J. B. Lindsley, "Table Talk," Oct. 6, 1861, in John Berrien Lindsley Papers, at Tennessee State Library and Archives (Nashville); [Rev.] John Taylor, *Baptists on the American Frontier: A History of*

In 1847, the New England–reared Daniel Whitaker of *Southern Quarterly Review* warned of the increasing influence of Unitarianism in the United States, and Thomas Smyth of Charleston preached on the Trinity in a manner that suggested the need to continue the struggle against Unitarian notions. Smyth doubtless knew that the citizens of Charleston, inveterate church-hoppers, attended the Unitarian Church along with others. The Baptist Reverend W. T. Brantly believed that Universalism, too, was exercising its pernicious influence much more widely than generally appreciated. Southern Trinitarians took Unitarianism seriously enough to publish pamphlets against it down to the War. Public sentiment overwhelmingly supported the outburst of the Presbyterian Robert Breckenridge, for whom the "madness of Universalism" denied the justice of God and thereby freed the wicked of all terror. The Universalists' denial of hell even got them into trouble at law, for public opinion objected to acceptance of evidence in court from those under oath who did not fear divine retribution.[48]

The tenuous hold of the anti-Trinitarian churches in the South has long encouraged the notion among historians that their ideas lacked resonance. But theological liberalism in fact exerted a subtle and persistent influence even within churches committed to Trinitarianism and to a belief in eternal damnation. Southern preachers, like preachers everywhere, were forever finding evidence of backsliding and never tired in calls for repentance and reformation. They had grounds to fear that their bastion of orthodoxy might not hold against the rising pressures of a transatlantic bourgeois world. Preachers had long been calling for eternal vigilance, and in 1860 – as the South readied itself for a death struggle with a heathen, not to say satanic,

---

Ten Baptist Churches of Which the Author Has Been Alternately a Member, ed. Chester Raymond Young, 3rd ed. (Macon, GA, 1995), Editor's Introduction, 62; Sebastian G. Messmer, ed., *The Works of the Right Rev. John England, First Bishop of Charleston,* 7 vols. (Cleveland, OH, 1908), 2:186, 3:452–518; Susan Nye Hutchinson Journal, Dec. 6, 1856, at UNC-SHC; John D. Jones, *A Complete History of Methodism as Connected with the Mississippi Conference of the Methodist Episcopal Church, South,* 2 vols. (Nashville, TN, 1908), 2:200–1 (Soule). In the 1850s the southern churches faced a spread of the contagion, since the Whigs across the river in Ohio had a reputation for Unitarian tendencies: David Brown, "The Political Culture of the Whig Party in Ohio" (Ph.D. diss., University of Toledo, 1995), 36, 59–60.

[48] D. K. Whitaker, *SQR,* 11 (1847), 172, also 406–41; *TSW,* 10:623–38. Much of volume 9 of *TSW* discusses the Trinity with extended attacks on Unitarianism. In a dozen articles in *SPR* in the 1850s, Smyth defended the concept of the Trinity against Unitarian and especially Jewish criticism. His careful attention to Jewish writers indicated his respect for their scholarship and intellectual quality: see esp. "Objections to the Doctrine of the Trinity," *SPR,* 8 (1855), 305–29, and "Testimony of the Ancient Jews," 10 (1858), 94–105.

See also "God's Gracious Purpose," in Brantly, *Sermons,* 50–2; Robert J. Breckenridge, *The Knowledge of God, Objectively Considered* (New York, 1858), 5; also, *DD,* 1:29–72. On the legal difficulties see Alfred Norman to Willie P. Mangum, Oct. 7, 1858, in Henry Thomas Shanks, ed., *The Papers of Willie P. Mangum,* 5 vols. (Raleigh, NC, 1955–56), 5:355; Eaton, *Freedom-of-Thought Struggle,* 310. In New York's Genesee Conference, the Reverend Benjamin Titus Roberts led protests against the liberalization of Methodist doctrine and the toleration of Unitarian heresy: Roger Finke and Rodney Stark, *The Churching of America, 1776–1890* (New Brunswick, NJ, 1992), 15. In the struggle for Kansas in the 1850s, missionaries deplored the threat of Unitarianism even more than slavery: Gunja SenGupta, *For God and Mammon: Evangelicals and Entrepreneurs, Masters and Slaves in Territorial Kansas, 1854–1860* (Athens, GA, 1996), 71.

North – their voices grew shrill. E. A. Nisbet was satisfied that the South suffered less infidelity and "perverted Christianity" than any other part of the world, but he still thought it suffered from too much. J. S. Lamar of Georgia, a Disciples theologian, suggested that a great many people proclaimed religious faith but displayed persistent skepticism. For the most part the South did stand firm for orthodoxy, but potentially dangerous incursions never ceased to frighten the orthodox. Secular and religious leaders alike worried that theological heterodoxy might yet undermine their hard-won proslavery consensus.[49]

---

[49] [E. A. Nisbet], "Presbyterian Preaching at the South," *SPR*, 13 (1860), 113–14; Lamar, *Organon of Scripture*, Bk. 1. For an indication of continued concern about the inroads of Universalism, see the front-page attack in *Alabama Baptist*, 2 (Feb. 24, 1844). The same issue nonetheless reported friendly debates between Universalists and Orthodox Christians in Marion, Alabama.

20

Theopolitics

Golden Rule, Higher Law, and Slavery

> Is there any way to penetrate to the heart of a document – of any document – except on the assumption that its spirit will speak to our spirit through the actual written words? This does not exclude a criticism of the letter by the spirit, which is, indeed, unavoidable. It is precisely a strict faithfulness which compels us to expand or to abbreviate the text, lest a too rigid attitude to the words should obscure that which is struggling to expression in them and which demands expression.
>
> —Karl Barth[1]

Opponents of slavery, uncomfortable on shaky constitutional ground, maintained that God's higher law had priority over all imperfect human constitutions and political arrangements. Their proslavery antagonists denied that the U.S. Constitution violated the revealed Word of God. Southern scriptural and constitutional arguments were, at least, of a piece. Together and separately, their doctrine of strict construction placed slavery at the center of the sectional quarrel and the split in American national consciousness. They identified slavery as a system of social relations, not merely a congeries of social and economic interests. Ideally, the Constitution united two social systems – the southern based on slavery, the northern on free labor – by a solemn oath of mutual toleration and respect. George Cheever, in biblical exegesis, and Harriet Beecher Stowe, in didactic fiction, agreed that southern slavery did constitute a comprehensive social system – although one they condemned as sinful, immoral, and a corrupting influence on the best of its slaveholding practitioners.[2]

---

[1] Karl Barth, *The Epistle to the Romans,* tr. Edwyn C. Hoskyns (London, 1968), 18–19.

[2] For the close connection between biblical criticism, political struggles, and constitutional interpretation in early modern England, see Henning Graf Reventlow, *The Authority of the Bible and the Rise of the Modern World* (Philadelphia, 1984). Calhoun observed with irritation that everyone, in good faith and bad, claimed that his interpretation conformed strictly to a proper understanding of the letter of the Constitution: Calhoun to Duff Green, Sept. 20, 1834, in *JCCP,* 12:363. The idiosyncratic Methodist Samuel Davies Baldwin claimed that not only the U.S. Constitution but also the corpus of American law accorded with divine law: *Dominion; Or the Unity and Trinity of the Human Race* (Nashville, TN, 1858), 14–15.

When Southerners, intent upon the defense of slavery and their constitutional rights, came to consider secession their only remaining option, they split into intellectually irreconcilable but politically reconcilable positions. The great majority believed a state had a right to secede, but, whereas some appealed to constitutionally sanctioned state rights, others appealed to the doctrine of resistance to tyranny as annunciated in their forefathers' Declaration of Independence.

Within the churches the strongest proslavery suit rested on the demand to confine political questions to the civil arena – to "render unto Caesar that which is Caesar's" (Matt., 22:21). Countless antislavery Christians in North and South also refused to commit their churches *qua* churches since, despite their personal aversion to slavery, they saw no biblical sanction for churches to condemn slavery as sinful in all circumstances (*malum in se*). The spirited Old School Presbyterian Reverend Dr. James Henley Thornwell carried the demand for a radical separation of realms to its furthest point with the doctrine of "the spirituality of the church," opposing the Church's engagement with efforts not required by Scripture: "Her power is solely ministerial and declarative. Her whole duty is to believe and obey .... Whatever is not commanded, expressly or implicitly is unlawful." Thornwell denounced the doctrine that whatever is not forbidden is allowable: "The silence of Scripture is as real a prohibition as a positive injunction to abstain. Where God has not commanded, the Church has no jurisdiction." Thornwell protested the conception of the Church as "a voluntary society, aiming at the promotion of universal good" and "a contrivance for every species of reform" – individual, social, and political.[3]

Thornwell linked the spirituality of the church to Calhoun's constitutional theory: "The Church, like the government of the United States, is a positive institution, with positive grants of power, and whatever is not given is *withheld*." Thornwell's hard line threatened to subvert the uneasy coalition of orthodox southern Presbyterians and their northern allies. When Stalwart Calvinists – notably, Charles Hodge of Princeton and Thomas Smyth of Charleston – supported the creation of church boards to spur missionary work, Thornwell and Robert Breckenridge countered that the Church itself was a missionary society with no right or duty to delegate authority to scripturally unsanctioned boards. The silence of the Bible on "such contrivances as Boards seals their condemnation." Thornwell condemned Hodge's position as "utterly rotten." "Despotism does not depend upon the instruments by which power is exercised, but upon the nature of power itself. The essential idea of despotism is a government of *will*, in contradistinction to a government of *law and right*." The church holds accountable rulers who transcend their commission. "No one is bound to obey them." Church leaders "stand in the same relation to the Church that the rulers of the United States sustain to the people, and if the one government is free, the other cannot be despotic." For Hodge and Smyth, the Church could do many things Scripture did not forbid. Hodge taxed Thornwell

---

[3] "Church-Boards and Presbyterianism," *JHTW*, 4:244, 246, 2:47. For Presbyterian formulations of the spirituality of the Church see also George D. Armstrong, *The Christian Doctrine of Slavery* (New York, 1967 [1857]), 7–8; William S. Plumer, *The Law of God, as Contained in the Ten Commandments, Explained and Enforced* (Harrisonburg, VA, 1996 [1864]), 33.

with "hyper-hyper-hyper High Church Presbyterianism" – pretty much the rebuke New School Presbyterians were laying on Hodge. Hodge prevailed then, but after secession Thornwell prevailed in the southern Presbyterian Church. The same issue troubled other denominations. In 1828 a long smoldering revolt against episcopacy split the Methodist Episcopal Church and led to formation of the Methodist Protestant Church. In later years, the Methodist Episcopal Reverend William A. Smith consistently upheld the southern interpretation of the constitution of his church in harmony with that of the Constitution of the United States. For the Methodist Protestants, the Reverend A. A. Lipscomb, in a fast-day discourse to the Georgia Legislature in 1860, refused to consider secession and slavery political issues: "Were they party-questions, you should not hear my voice."[4]

Then and since, Presbyterian advocates of the spirituality of the church have suffered castigation for their bolt into politics during the secession crisis and the War. Rousing calls to action from southern pulpits led contemporary critics – as well as recent ones – to dismiss Thornwell's doctrine as a proslavery tactical maneuver. We disagree with the assignment of motive, but the proslavery divines opened themselves to attack by having done little to prepare themselves and their parishioners for the *crise de conscience* that came in 1860.[5]

The proper relation of slavery to church and to state remained intractable for both pro- and antislavery Americans. Revivalists concentrated on saving individual souls and maintaining them largely through the establishment of Christian communities of moral rectitude. Southerners who did not view slavery as a narrowly political or civil issue did consider social relations broadly critical to morals. But "Render unto Caesar" meant something different to Northerners and Southerners. The Reverend William A. Hall told Confederate troops that the clergy had rallied to the "Southern Revolution" out of loyalty to God against a wicked and armed infidelity. The Confederate Revolution "aims to conserve the perfection of republican government and therein to vindicate the organic law under which civil government was first constituted by God." Both North and South had come to see slavery, for good or evil, as the warp and woof of the southern social system and attendant worldview.[6]

Because – in proslavery eyes – the North's free-labor system encouraged infidelity, social disorder, and moral degeneracy, its condemnation of slavery transcended

---

[4] "Church-Boards and Presbyterianism," *JHTW*, 4:259, 261–2, quotes at 259, 286; John Nelson Norwood, *The Schism in the Methodist Episcopal Church, 1844: A Study of Slavery and Ecclesiastical Politics* (Alfred, NY, 1923), 100 n. 54; Ernest Trice Thompson, *Presbyterians in the South*, 3 vols. (Richmond, VA, 1963), 1:510–19; Hunter Dickinson Farish, *The Circuit Rider Dismounts: A Social History of Southern Methodism, 1865–1900* (Richmond, VA, 1938), 3–4; Andrew A. Lipscomb, *Substance of a Discourse Delivered before the Legislature of Georgia* (Milledgeville, GA, 1860), 15, also 17. See also Supplementary References: "Spirituality of the Church."

[5] For criticism of Thornwell's apparent *volte face*, see e.g. H. Shelton Smith, "The Church and the Social Order in the Old South as Interpreted by James H. Thornwell," *Church History*, 7 (1938), 124; Jack P. Maddex, Jr., "From Theocracy to Spirituality: The Southern Presbyterian Reversal on Church and State," *JPH*, 14 (1970), 438–57; Maddex, "'The Southern Apostasy' Revisited," *Marxist Perspectives*, 7 (1979), 132–41, and references cited therein.

[6] William A. Hall, *Historic Significance of the Southern Revolution* (Petersburg, VA, 1864), 14, quote at 4.

taste and social preference. In an 1850 *Southern Presbyterian Review* the Reverend Dr. A. A. Porter, while denying any intent to intervene in politics, portrayed slavery as a morally superior – a properly Christian – social order and the "only safeguard and defense" against northern infidelity and the social and political radicalism he described as "an inevitable result of modern civilization where slavery does not exist." The Christian people of the South stood together: "In fact, the Christian people of the South, *are the South*." In Missouri the militantly proslavery Reverend James Shannon of the Disciples of Christ tartly described as "supremely and contemptibly ridiculous" the criticism of a defense of slavery in a slave state as "an act of dabbling in *party politics*." Slavery, as a moral question, had to be appealed to Scripture. The Reverends William A. Smith and William Capers simultaneously espoused a Methodist version of spirituality of the church and supported "southern rights." Most Southerners long defended slavery as both ordained of God and necessary to social order. Their defense had to move from the constitutional and legal ground of southern rights to the ground of the social relations necessary to preserve a Christian community. In their eyes, secession and support for the Confederacy became a clear duty – as long as everyone understood that secession and the War were first and foremost about the maintenance of a God-ordained social order.[7]

In 1860 the Presbyterian Reverend Benjamin Morgan Palmer of New Orleans, a Thornwell protégé, delivered a two-hour pro-secession Fast Day sermon to a packed house of a thousand. Departing from his practice of preaching extemporaneously, Palmer read this sermon carefully and soberly. He went to considerable lengths to explain his apparent plunge into politics. Or rather, he pleaded that the interlocked questions of slavery and secession far transcended politics, for the South faced a struggle against the Antichrist for the very survival of Christian civilization. On the day Palmer held forth in New Orleans, the Reverend Thaddeus McRae, a unionist, preached in Baton Rouge on "the madness of the times." To McRae's grief, his congregation went for secession soon after Palmer's sermon appeared in print. William O. Rogers, a prominent citizen of New Orleans, testified that the eloquent Palmer had propelled waverers, doubters, and the fearful into the secessionist camp. The governor of Mississippi asked Palmer to stump his state and concluded that he was worth more than a thousand troops.[8]

[7] A. A. Porter, "North and South," *SPR*, 3 (1850), 337–80, quotes at 344, 345, 378; James Shannon, *An Address ... on Domestic Slavery* (St. Louis, MO, 1855), vi; Harmon L. Smith, "William Capers and William A. Smith: Neglected Advocates of the Pro-Slavery Moral Argument," *Methodist History*, 3 (1964), 27–9; R. H. Rivers, *The Life of Robert Paine, D.D., Bishop of the Methodist Church, South* (Nashville, TN, 1916), ch. 26. On James Shannon as a secessionist see David Edwin Harrell, Jr., *A Social History of the Disciples of Christ*, vol. 1, *Quest for a Christian America: The Disciples of Christ and American Society to 1866* (Nashville, TN, 1966), 122–6. The Reverend Augustus Baldwin Longstreet, president of South Carolina College, apologized – sort of – to the graduating class for entering into politics. His disunionist speech suggested that the people of the North had arrayed themselves against the South: O. P. Fitzgerald, *Judge Longstreet. A Life Sketch* (Nashville, TN, 1891), 112, 124; for Longstreet's text, see 97–107.

[8] Thomas Cary Johnson, *The Life and Letters of Benjamin Morgan Palmer* (Richmond, VA, 1906), 219 (Rogers), 222–3 (text of sermon on 206–19); Thompson, *Presbyterians in the South*, 2:64–5, 3:77; Margaret Burr DesChamps, "Benjamin Morgan Palmer, Orator-Preacher of the Confederacy," *Southern*

The unionist Judah P. Benjamin tried to keep Louisiana cool after Lincoln's election, but the radical tide swamped him. Louisiana had given Breckenridge 45 percent of its vote in 1860, and unionism ran high among the Whig sugar planters, upcountry yeomen, and numerous immigrants in New Orleans. The New Orleans *Delta* got Benjamin's attention when it reported some 30,000 copies of Palmer's sermon in circulation. The *Delta* printed it on three successive days, and other newspapers throughout the Southwest printed the full text or lengthy excerpts. The New Orleans *Bee* thrilled to its "masterly discourse." The secessionists, who carried New Orleans only with great difficulty, credited Palmer as a principal force in their change of fortunes.[9]

Palmer's sermon sent tremors all the way from the Mississippi Valley to the Atlantic coast. Family reading circles pored over it, as did politicians who assessed the public temper. In Vicksburg, Sarah Lois Wadley found it "magnificent," "temperate," "forceful and eloquent." "Oh! if the South would only unite and not disgrace herself in this hour of common peril by internal bickerings." Palmer's "incontrovertible arguments" especially proved "that slavery is providential and *right*." Palmer was "a talented minister, well known throughout these states"; Wadley reported that her father, who had heard the sermon in New Orleans, expected it to have wide influence as a pamphlet. In Virginia, Fannie Page Hume read Palmer's "splendid sermon" aloud to her aunts Sallie and Hannah. John S. Wise reported that Virginians read and discussed it avidly, and even Edmund Ruffin (for whom almost nothing was ever good enough) pronounced it "admirable & eloquent." The editors of the New Orleans *Delta* saluted Palmer for proclaiming "the true idea of the Church, as a spiritual body" and dismissed the unionist charge that he had exercised a *volta face* and politicized the church. The editors refused to reduce slavery to a political question, saluted Palmer for defining it as a moral question, and noted that the churches had split over the morality of slavery long before the Union split over its politics. In context, Palmer could deny scuttling the doctrine of spirituality and make a respectable case for his course. His rationale remains debatable, but no one effectively elaborated its implications for the divines' long-developing social thought.[10]

Speech Journal, 19 (1953), 15. In 1864 R. J. Breckenridge's antislavery and unionist *Danville Quarterly Review* bitterly recalled Palmer's sermon as effective: "Slavery in the Church Courts," *DQR,* 4 (1864), 526. D. G. Hart makes an important point: "The spirituality doctrine required the church to stay out of politics," and then adds, "strictly defined": Hart, "The Spirituality of the Church, the Westminster Standards, and Nineteenth-Century America Presbyterianism," in John H. Leith, ed., "The Westminster Confession in Current Thought," *Calvinist Studies,* 8 (1996), 115.

9 Robert Douthat Meade, *Judah P. Benjamin: Confederate Statesman* (New York, 1943), 143–4. New Orleans *Bee,* Dec. 5, 1860, in Dwight Lowell Dumond, ed., *Southern Editorials on Secession* (Gloucester, MA, 1964), 305–6; L. N. Powell, in *EC,* 3:952–6, 1137. Palmer was deluged with laudatory mail, and circulation may have risen to 50,000: see James W. Silver, *Confederate Morale and Church Propaganda* (New York, 1957), 17. In New Orleans in 1860, the Reverend Dr. Leacock's unionist sermon provoked a walkout by a number of parishioners: Clyde Lottridge Cummer, ed., *Yankee in Gray: The Civil War Memoirs of Henry E. Handerson, with a Selection of His Wartime Letters* (Cleveland, OH, 1962), 24.

10 Sarah Lois Wadley Private Journal, date unclear but about one week after Palmer had delivered his sermon, and Fannie Page Hume Diary, Dec. 18 and 20, 1860, at UNC-SHC; John S. Wise, *The End of*

Palmer fled when Federal troops occupied New Orleans, but he continued to apply his oratorical gifts to the war effort. At a critical moment he preached to Braxton Bragg's troops in Tennessee, and he urged a fight to the death when Sherman scorched his way through Georgia. Mary Boykin Chesnut burst forth, "What a sermon. There was more exhortation to fight and die than meek Christianity." In trying to convince his people to secede, Palmer had taken on a tough job, but one made easier by their ready assent to his premise that slavery was ordained of God.[11]

The relation of Word to Spirit recurred in doctrinal and political struggles. The abolitionists, knowing that they needed the Bible to sustain their war against slavery, found God's higher law manifested, above all, in the Golden Rule to do unto others as you would have them do unto you and in St. Paul's admonition, "All the law is fulfilled in one word, even in this, thou shalt love thy neighbour as thyself" (Gal., 6:14). In early eighteenth-century Massachusetts, Samuel Sewall, famous for repenting over his role as a judge in the Salem witch trials, appealed to the Golden Rule against slavery in his *The Selling of Joseph*; John Saffin, prominent jurist and merchant, replied that Sewall's exegesis threatened to destroy every authority sanctioned in the Bible. Cotton Mather implicitly supported Saffin in urging Christians to treat slaves in accordance with the Golden Rule. In 1845 the Presbyterian Reverend W. T. Hamilton of Mobile brought the theme up to date: The sins that accompany slavery result from the personal deficiencies of masters who violate the Golden Rule.[12]

Early in the nineteenth century, conservative New Englanders worried that free workers might turn the Golden Rule against employers. "Do unto others" ought to be understood within a hierarchical context. The Reverend R. T. Stanton preached in Connecticut, doubtless to the great relief of his congregation, that, no, the poor cannot confiscate half the goods of the rich. Justice Joseph Story instructed a grand jury that Christians must adhere to the Golden Rule, which condemns slavery, but he brooked no extension of the Rule to the wage-labor system. Antislavery men

an Era (Boston, 1900), 145–6; *ERD*, 1:536–7; Thomas C. Johnson, *The Life and Letters of Benjamin Morgan Palmer* (Richmond, VA, 1906), 193, 220–1. Long after the War, Henry Whitney Cleveland proudly wrote Jefferson Davis from Louisville, Kentucky, that Palmer had given him a copy of "his famous sermon of 1860": Cleveland to Davis, Mar. 3, 1888, in Dunbar Rowland, ed., *Jefferson Davis, Constitutionalist: His Letters, Papers, and Speeches*, 10 vols. (Jackson, MS, 1923), 10:38. For Palmer's immense prestige and influence with the army and civilians in the Mississippi Valley, see Nathaniel Cheairs Hughes, Jr., *The Pride of the Confederate Artillery: The Washington Artillery in the Army of Tennessee* (Baton Rouge, LA, 1997), 50.

[11] Chesnut Diary, Sept. 21, 1864, in C. Vann Woodward, ed., *Mary Chesnut's Civil War* (New Haven, CT, 1981), 644.

[12] In Louis Ruchames, ed., *Racial Thought: America*, vol. 1: *From the Puritans to Abraham Lincoln: A Documentary History* (Amherst, MA, 1969), see Samuel Sewall and John Saffin, 1:53–8, and Cotton Mather, "Negro Christianized," 1:59–70; W. T. Hamilton, *Duties of Masters and Slaves Respectively; Or, Domestic Servitude as Sanctioned by the Bible* (Mobile, AL, 1845), 6, 15–17, 20–1. Richard N. Longenecker writes of the relevant ethical problems: "The Christian doctrine of oneness in Christ, does not mean the end of all social distinctions or the dissolution of every functional distinction among people. That would be anarchy, not reform, and the gospel is just as much opposed to anarchy as it is to slavery": *New Testament Social Ethics for Today* (Grand Rapids, MI, 1984), 69. See also Supplementary References: "Golden Rule."

cited the Golden Rule during the congressional debates over reception of antislavery petitions (the "Gag Rule"), and Francis Wayland hammered Richard Fuller about it in their much-publicized debate over the scriptural basis for slavery. To Wayland, author of a leading textbook in political economy, the Golden Rule meant that both capital and labor must share in the fruits of production – which, he said, slavery denied.[13]

"You would not make yourself a slave," the abolitionist Cheever cried. The Methodist Reverend Charles Elliott of Xenia, Ohio, replying to southern taunts about wage slavery, pointed to freedom as a value in itself, protecting families against forcible separation, promoting literacy, and encouraging religion. Southerners parried that the threat of unemployment and hunger spawned similar evils, and that abolitionist meddling was preventing reform of the slave codes. "A Lady of Georgia" advised Harriet Beecher Stowe to preach the abolitionist version of the Golden Rule to John Jacob Astor and bid capitalists share their wealth with workers. While you are at it, she added, practice it yourself: Spend less on yourself and more on the poor. Mary Henderson Eastman of Virginia, in the preface to her novel *Aunt Phyllis's Cabin,* simply pronounced the abolitionist interpretation "absurd."[14]

In colonial times blacks combined appeals to the Bible with appeals to natural rights, and in Massachusetts blacks petitioned not only for emancipation but, further, for equal rights, appealing to the principle of the rights of Englishmen and of equality before the law. With the coming of the Revolution, blacks turned to the Declaration of Independence as justifying their appeals. In these early days, petitions to legislatures acknowledged the responsibility of all, even the enslaved, to obey the powers that be as ordained of God and to render loyal service. In time, black voices, like white, became bolder. In 1852 Henry Bibb, having fled slavery, labeled Albert Sibley, his former master and a Methodist minister, a hypocrite: "Listen to the language of inspiration ... 'Feed the hungry, and clothe the naked: Break every yoke and let the oppressed go free': 'All things, whatsoever ye would that men should do unto you, do ye even so unto them, for *this* is the law and the prophets.' " James Curry in North Carolina said, "*There is no sin which man can commit, that the slaveholders are not guilty of.*"[15]

[13] R. P. Stanton, *Slavery Viewed in the Light of the Golden Rule* (Norwich, CT, 1860), 3–4; W. W. Story, ed., *The Miscellaneous Writings of Joseph Story,* 2 vols. (Boston, 1852), 140; William Lee Miller, *Arguing about Slavery: The Great Battle in the United States Congress* (New York, 1996), 54–5; Richard Fuller and Francis Wayland, *Domestic Slavery, Considered as a Scriptural Institution in Correspondence,* 5th ed. (New York, 1847), 113–14.

[14] George B. Cheever, *The Guilt of Slavery and the Crime of Slaveholding, Demonstrated from the Hebrew and Greek Scriptures* (New York, 1969 [1860]), 34, and Cheever, *God against Slavery; And the Freedom and Duty of the Pulpit to Rebuke It as a Sin against God* (Cincinnati, 1857), 95–6; Charles Elliott, *Sinfulness of American Slavery: Proved from Its Evil Sources,* 2 vols. (New York, 1968 [1850]), 2:297ff.; and esp. "A Lady of Georgia", "Southern Slavery and Its Assailants," *DBR,* 16 (1854), 61–2; Mary H. Eastman, *Aunt Phyllis's Cabin; Or, Southern Life as It Is* (Philadelphia, 1852), 19. Bishop J. H. Hopkins of Vermont, supporting the southern interpretation, sidestepped criticism of free labor: *A Scriptural, Ecclesiastical, and Historical View of Slavery from the Days of the Patriarch Abraham to the Nineteenth Century* (New York, 1864), ch. 31.

[15] See the petitions of blacks in Massachusetts to the royal governor and then the state government (1773, 1774, 1777) in Herbert Aptheker, ed., *A Documentary History of the Negro People in the*

Proslavery theorists accepted the challenge from the Golden Rule, struck back early, and stayed on course. The Reverend William Graham made the Golden Rule the centerpiece of his defense of slavery in the 1780s and 1790s, and proslavery theorists followed suit. Graham resurrected Saffin's view of the antislavery interpretation as a subversion of all legitimate authority. Thomas Jefferson inadvertently acknowledged the southern version when he wrote Edward Coles in 1814 that, until Virginians freed their slaves, they had a duty "to feed & clothe them well, protect them from all ill usage, require such reasonable labor only as is performed voluntarily by free men, and be led by no repugnancies to abdicate them, and our duties to them."[16]

The years 1836–37 brought forth widely circulated statements from William Drayton of South Carolina, George Baxter of Virginia, and the Reverends Jasper Adams of South Carolina, Theodore Clapp of Louisiana, James Smylie of Mississippi, and George Freeman, rector of Christ Church in Raleigh and afterwards bishop of Texas. Baxter (and subsequently the Reverend George Howe of South Carolina) had fun with the abolitionist version of "do unto others." They wanted to know whether creditors should refuse to collect from debtors, and whether executioners should refuse to hang condemned prisoners. Eschewing ridicule, Adams told slaveholders to treat slaves as they themselves would want to be treated if enslaved. Freeman – in a sermon warmly endorsed by Bishop Levi Silliman Ives and several leading politicians – accused the abolitionist of advancing interpretations of the Golden Rule that struck "at the foundation, not merely of *slavery, but of all distinctions whatsoever among men.* Carry it out in practice, and Society would be immediately reduced to its original elements." Harriet Beecher Stowe was furious at Freeman, at Ives, and at the Protestant Episcopal Society for the Advancement of Christianity in South Carolina, which republished Freeman's sermon and, in effect, endorsed the defense of enslavement of whites as readily as of blacks. Stowe had reason for alarm. In later years George Paschal credited the dissemination of Freeman's pamphlet and the secular defense of slavery by William Harper, Chancellor of South Carolina's Court of Equity, with hardening a proslavery perspective among small farmers.[17]

United States, 4 vols. (New York, 1990), 1:5–12, 36. In 1810 Daniel Coker published an antislavery tract entitled *A Dialogue between a Virginian and an African Minister*: see Theosophus H. Smith, *Conjuring Culture: Biblical Formations of Black America* (New York, 1994), 184–5 (Coker); Henry Bibb to Albert G. Sibley, Sept. 23, 1852, in John W. Blassingame, ed., *Slave Testimony: Two Centuries of Letters, Speeches, Interviews, and Autobiographies* (Baton Rouge, LA, 1977), 50; "Narrative of James Curry," in Blassingame, ed., *Slave Testimony,* 138.

[16] "Lectures on Human Nature Aula Libertatis, Delivered by Wm. Graham: Notes Taken by Joseph Glass, 1796," 161–9, in Graham Philosophic Society Papers, at Washington and Lee University; and on Graham see D. W. Robson, " 'An Important Question Answered': William Graham's Defense of Slavery in Post-Revolutionary Virginia," *WMQ,* 37 (1980), 649–51; Jefferson to Coles, Aug. 25, 1814, quoted in Edwin Morris Betts, ed., *Thomas Jefferson's Farm Book: With Commentary and Relevant Extracts from His Writings* (Charlottesville, VA, 1987), 38; [William Drayton], *The South Vindicated from the Treason and Fanaticism of the Northern Abolitionists* (Philadelphia, 1836), 98–9.

[17] [Drayton], *The South Vindicated,* 98–9; George A. Baxter, *An Essay on the Abolition of Slavery* (Richmond, VA, 1836), 12–13, 21; [George Howe], "The Raid of John Brown, and the Progress of Abolition," *SPR,* 12 (1860), 797; Jasper Adams, *Elements of Moral Philosophy* (Philadelphia, 1837),

In 1850 the Reverend Theodore Clapp struck hard at a vulnerable point. He contested the "utterly fallacious" abolitionist interpretation by asserting that, when God told the Israelites to "love thy neighbor," God also said they might hold slaves. Albert Taylor Bledsoe replied similarly to Wayland that Leviticus commands love of one's neighbor and simultaneously sanctions slavery. "We can conceive that we are poor, helpless, dependent beings, possessing the passions of men and the intellects of children. We can conceive that we are by nature idle, improvident, and utterly unable to take care of ourselves."[18]

Proslavery preachers returned to the theme year after year: Robert Dabney wrote G. Woodson Payne in 1840, "I cannot conceive of any duty arising from the command to love thy neighbor as myself which compels me to inflict a ruinous injury on that neighbor, and such would be immediate freedom to the slave." If blacks were emancipated, Dabney argued, they would surely suffer the fate of the Indians. In 1851 Thornwell, in a document unanimously adopted by the Presbyterian Synod of South Carolina, wrote, "The same line of argument, carried out precisely in the same way, would make havoc with all the institutions of civilized society," for it "would make the master emancipate his servant on the grounds of benevolence, would make the rich man share his estates with his poor neighbours." The abolitionists "will have reason to repent, that they have set in motion an engine which cannot be arrested, until it has crushed and ground to powder the safeguards of life and property among themselves." A decade later, at the behest of the Presbyterian Church of the seceding states, Thornwell described tyranny and oppression as either the unjust usurpation or the unlawful exercise of power, adding: "The master may, indeed, abuse his power, but he oppresses not simply as a master, but as a wicked master." The Golden Rule demands that free men ask themselves what they would consider reasonable and just if they were slaves. Between these two statements Thornwell explained, "We are not bound to render unto them what they might in fact desire. Such a rule would transmute morality into caprice. But we are bound to render unto them what they have a right to desire – that is, we are bound to render unto them that which is 'just and equal.'" And again: "The Saviour requires us to exchange places in order that, free from the benumbing influences which are likely to pervert judgment, we may appreciate what is just and equal, when there is no personal interest in the discussion."[19]

140; George W. Freeman, *The Rights and Duties of Slaveholders* (Raleigh, NC, 1836), 13 n.; Harriet Beecher Stowe, *A Key to Uncle Tom's Cabin* (Port Washington, NY, 1968 [1853]), 196; George W. Paschal, *Ninety-Four Years: Agnes Paschal* (Spartanburg, SC, 1974 [1871]), 279–80. See also James Smylie, *Review of a Letter from the Presbytery of Chillicothe to the Presbytery of Mississippi on the Subject of Slavery* (Woodville, MS, 1836). C. K. Whipple, another abolitionist, added his disgust when the Presbyterians of Charleston endorsed Freeman's sermon: *The Family Relation as Affected by Slavery* (New York, 1858), 10.

[18] Theodore Clapp, "Thanksgiving Sermon," New Orleans *Daily Picayune*, Dec. 22, 1850; also, Clapp, *Slavery: A Sermon* (New Orleans, 1838), 23–4; Albert Taylor Bledsoe, "Liberty and Slavery," in E. N. Elliott, ed., *Cotton Is King and Pro-Slavery Arguments* (New York, 1969 [1860]), 304–7, quote at 307.

[19] R. L. Dabney to G. Woodson Payne, Jan. 22, 1840, in Thomas Cary Johnson, ed., *Life and Letters of Robert Lewis Dabney* (Carlisle, PA, 1977), 68; for Dabney's interpretation of the Golden Rule see his

President John Leadley Dagg of Mercer College in Georgia, the southern Baptists' most formidable theologian, began simply: "God is perfectly just." Dagg distinguished between commutative justice (fair dealing in exchange of goods) and the higher realm of distributive justice (allotment of happiness according to rule): "In the moral government of God, men are regarded as moral and as sentient beings, and the amount of their enjoyments is regulated with reference to their moral character. The precise adaptation of this is province of justice. In the blindness of human depravity, men claim enjoyments as natural right, irrespective of their moral character and conduct." Methodists stood on the Golden Rule as readily as Calvinists. "The Word," the Reverend Thomas Boswell of Tennessee preached, "is the sword of the Spirit." God gives every man according to his ability and assigns attendant responsibilities. Masters must give slaves "that which is just and equal" – security, succor, and everything appropriate to their capacity and station. As the Reverend William A. Smith taught his students at Randolph-Macon College, "The Africans of this country, in common with minors, imbeciles, and uncivilized persons, have a right to be governed and protected, and to such means of physical comfort and moral improvement as are necessary and compatible with their providential condition." By this stricture, anyone who exercises the right to own slaves assumes responsibility to care for them.[20]

Secular theorists and ordinary slaveholders also appealed to the Golden Rule to defend slavery and condemn free labor. The Golden Rule, George Fitzhugh held, cannot readily prevail in a dog-eat-dog free-labor market society, but it flows naturally in a slave society. The master acts like a good Christian because "his whole life is spent in providing for the minutest wants of others." Ownership of labor imposes that responsibility as a matter of fundamental self-interest: " 'Love thy neighbor as thyself.' And this can't be done till he has a property in your services as well as a place in your heart." As expressed by James Henry Greenlee, a planter in McDowell County, North Carolina: "The same feelings & principals [sic] that actuate us in

---

Defence of Virginia (and through Her of the South) in Recent and Pending Contests against the Sectional Party (New York, 1969 [1867]), 192–8. In *JHTW*: "Relation of the Church to Slavery," 4:391, 394; "Address to All Churches of Christ," 4:458; "Sermon on National Sins," 4:544–5. For similar arguments from an Old School and a New School Presbyterian see Ferdinand Jacobs, *The Committing of Our Cause to God* (Charleston, SC, 1850), 9–10, and Frederick A. Ross, *Slavery Ordained of God* (Philadelphia, 1857), 160–85, which specifically (164–7) taunted the abolitionist Barnes by asking how he would apply the Golden Rule to wives. For a northern proslavery tract on the same issue see Samuel Seabury, *American Slavery Distinguished from the Slavery of English Theorists and Justified by the Law of Nature* (New York, 1861), 184–6.

20 J. L. Dagg, *Manual of Theology: A Treatise on Christian Doctrine and a Treatise on Church Order*, 2 vols. (New York, 1980 [1857–58]), 1:84, 85; T. L. Boswell, "Salvation in Its Individual Relations," in William T. Smithson, ed., *The Methodist Pulpit South* (Washington, DC, 1858), 218, 226–7; W. A. Smith, *Lectures on the Philosophy and Practice of Slavery* (Nashville, TN, 1856), 276; also, Joseph C. Stiles, *Modern Reform Examined* (Philadelphia, 1857), 27; H. N. McTyeire, *Duties of Christian Masters*, ed. Thomas O. Summers (Nashville, TN, 1859), 121–32. Other important Baptists stressed the Golden Rule: *Notes of a Sermon Delivered by Rev. Basil Manly, D.D., at Pleasant Grove Church, Fayette Co., Ala.* (Tuscaloosa, AL, 1849), 8–9; Thornton Stringfellow, "Bible Argument," in Elliott, ed., *Cotton Is King*, 479–80.

our own affairs in relation to ourselves and ours should govern us in our course of conduct to our fellow men both as it regards person, property & reputation and if this supreme love to *God* filled our hearts the Task of Loving our neighbors would be easy for it naturally flows from it because it is the command of him whom we love above all else." H. R. Saddler of Georgia, a big planter described by the anti-slavery Henry Benjamin Whipple as a frank, intelligent, manly, and unostentatious gentleman, acknowledged the slaveholders' regime as despotic but thought that the slaves' indolence and degradation made despotism a kindness.[21]

Chancellor Harper asked, "Would you do a benefit to the horse or the ox, by giving him a cultivated understanding or fine feelings?" Harper answered: "So far as the *mere laborer* has the pride, the knowledge, or the aspirations of a free man, he is unfitted for his situation, and must doubly feel its infelicity. If there are sordid, servile, and laborious officers to be performed, is it not better that there should be laborious beings to perform them?" Harper preferred to restrict his remarks to blacks, but he added: "*He who works during the day with his hands,* does not read in the intervals of leisure for his amusement or the improvement of his mind." The proslavery theorist John Fletcher of New Orleans wondered what would happen to the Decalogue under the abolitionists' interpretation of the Golden Rule, facetiously asking what would become of the injunction not to covet a neighbor's house, wife, and servants.[22]

The theologically liberal Episcopalian James Warley Miles took basically the same position as Alexander Stephens and the orthodox theologians in referring to the "so-called slavery" in the South because he regarded true slavery as the subjugation of racial equals. The enslaved southern black "is really in his highest and most favorable condition as a human creature." Louisa McCord did not flinch from the analogy to women. God made every creature for its place and may not have given women the most enviable place: "Let her object, then, be to raise herself *in* that position. *Out* of it, there is only failure and degradation."[23]

A voice in Mobile turned the southern interpretation of the Golden Rule against slavery. The Reverend George Simmons, pastor of a Unitarian Church who made clear his antislavery views, acknowledged that, in the Golden Rule, "equal" means

[21] George Fitzhugh, *Sociology for the South, or, The Failure of Free Society* (New York, 1965 [1852]), 69; Fitzhugh, *Cannibals All!; Or Slaves without Masters* (Cambridge, MA, 1960 [1857]), 28; Greenlee Diary, Feb. 23, 1861, at UNC-SHC; Dec. 2, 1843, in Lester B. Shippee, ed., *Bishop Whipple's Southern Diary, 1843–1844* (New York, 1968), 40; also, "A North Carolinian", *Slavery Considered on General Principles; Or, a Grapple with Abstractionists* (New York, 1861).

[22] William Harper, as quoted by Frederick Law Olmsted, *A Journey in the Seaboard Slave States, with Remarks on Their Economy* (New York, 1968 [1856]), 77, 492. John Fletcher, *Studies on Slavery, in Easy Lessons* (Natchez, MS, 1852), 92–9, 411–15, quote at 415. Fletcher noted that Confucius had advocated an equivalent of the Golden Rule: 411–14. See also Supplementary References: "Golden Rule."

[23] James Warley Miles, *The Discourse on the Occasion of the Funeral of the Hon. John C. Calhoun* (Charleston, SC, 1850), 16; [J. W. Miles], *The Relation between the Races at the South* (Charleston, SC, 1861), quote at 4 n.; Alexander H. Stephens, *A Constitutional View of the Late War between the States*, 2 vols. (New York, 1970 [1868, 1870]), 1:540–1; "Enfranchisement of Woman," in Richard Lounsbury, ed., *Louisa S. McCord: Political and Social Essays* (Charlottesville, VA, 1995), 108.

"equitable" and could not bear the burden the abolitionists placed upon it. "Were we very ignorant and poor, we might desire that some person of wealth, should transfer to us all his property; but that certainly is not to be done by him." Simmons met head-on the familiar case from black incapacity, allowing that the emancipation of men incapable of freedom would be akin to a father's sending young children to fend for themselves in streets. "But the incapacity for freedom is itself an evil to be deplored and removed. It is not natural." He concluded that the Golden Rule required masters to prepare slaves for freedom. The message proved unpopular, and Simmons departed Mobile for the North.[24]

In the widely cited formulation of Senator William E. Seward of New York, a God-ordained natural law overrode any constitutional sanction for slavery. Seward took a big political gamble when, in the words of Michael Holt, he "determined to deliver an antislavery harangue that might make him the preeminent leader of the North's antislavery Whigs." Seward's speech upset his close associate, Thurlow Weed, who sensed a political blunder, and it infuriated President Zachary Taylor. To pursue his national ambitions, Seward simultaneously had to consolidate his antislavery supporters in New York, fight the Fillmore faction for control of the Whig party, and maneuver against the Democrats. Appealing to a higher law, Seward chose to go whole hog against "radically wrong and essentially vicious" legislative compromises that allowed slavery's extension. In Holt's view, Seward did not summon people to put conscience above the Constitution but rather to recognize that God had reserved the annexed territory for the progress of freedom. Seward's distinction remained without a difference. For what exactly guides an understanding of God's will? And that question returns to the relation of Word to Spirit in attempts to understand God's will.[25]

Southern Literary Messenger complained that Seward's higher-law speech of March 11, 1850, "has made a considerable noise in the world." No speech in the last session of Congress "has attracted more attention, or aroused such a variety and virulence of passion." Basil Gildersleeve responded with the popular southern sneer, "What is the Constitution among friends?" Seward had chosen to interpret the Constitution in accordance with the dictates of a presumably godly conscience, and northern and southern conservatives, seeking God's will in the Bible, censured him for arrant subjectivism. The Calvinist Smyth, the Arminian Smith, and the theologically liberal James Warley Miles stood together. The Holy Spirit, Smyth wrote, "does not operate independently of Scripture by an inward light." The Holy Spirit "only testifies to what He has made known in the Word." For Smith, conscience (properly understood) does constitute a higher law but because it embodies God's

---

[24] George Frederick Simmons, *Two Sermons on the Kind Treatment and on the Emancipation of Slaves* (Boston, 1840).

[25] Michael F. Holt, *The Rise and Fall of the American Whig Party: Jacksonian Politics and the Onset of the Civil War* (New York, 1999), 489–94, 512–15. Seward's speech advanced Whig economic ideas against alleged southern aggression and identified economic prosperity as God's cause: see Louis S. Gerteis, *Morality and Utility in American Antislavery Reform* (Chapel Hill, NC, 1987), 57, 107.

Word: "No precept, enforced even by a legal authority, can make that Right which the Natural Law condemns as wrong." An objective standard of right, Miles wrote in *Philosophic Theology* (1849), emanates from a God who embodies right; human conscience registers divine will. Divine law comes through natural law, which reflects reason and conscience, as well as through the revelation of Holy Scripture, but conscience must be understood as the imprint on the mind of the will of God as expressed in Scripture and not as opinion independent of the Word. Miles dismissed as subjectivity the invocation of conscience to establish individual right, making all truth relative and thereby destroying it.[26]

The polemical fireworks of the 1850s gave rise to a persistent misunderstanding that has attributed to southern thought a positivistic defense of man-made law as beyond appeal. A moment's reflection should scotch any such idea. Southerners spoke as Christians and, as such, knew they could not repudiate higher-law doctrine. Henry David Thoreau said it, but a southern divine might have also: "The law will never make men free; it is men who have got to make the law free. They are the lovers of law and order, who observe the law when the government breaks it." In Boston, Theodore Parker said of conscience: "The laws of matter depend for their execution only on the infinite will of God, and so cannot be violated. The laws of man depend for their execution also on the finite will of man, and so may be broken." Southern divines concurred, but they would not swallow George Cheever's extension, which judged anarchy a thousand times preferable to submission to a wicked law.[27]

[26] "The Doctrine of the Higher Law," *SLM*, 17 (1851), 130; Basil Gildersleeve, *Hellas and Hesperia: Or the Vitality of Greek Studies in America* (New York, 1909), 102; [Thomas Smyth], "Assurance," *SPR*, 2 (1848), 118, also 126; James Warley Miles, *The Ground of Morals: A Discourse Delivered before the Graduating Class of the College of Charleston* (Charleston, SC, 1852), 19, and Miles, *Philosophic Theology: Or, Ultimate Grounds of All Religious Belief Based on Reason* (Charleston, SC, 1849), 103, 178–9. For an incisive interpretation of Seward's position see Lawrence Frederick Kohl, *The Politics of Individualism: Parties and the American Character in the Jacksonian Era* (New York, 1989), 175–6. For a southern view of conscience in relation to consciousness and God's will see R. H. Rivers, *Elements of Moral Philosophy* (Nashville, TN, 1859), 49–73. For the relation of higher-law doctrine to the quarrel over the interpretation of Scripture see Eugene D. Genovese, "Religion in the Collapse of the Union," in Randall M. Miller et al., eds., *Religion and the American Civil War* (New York, 1998), ch. 3.

How do we recognize the voice of God? How do we know it is not the voice of the devil? Nancey Murphy answers: through "discernment," "Christian judgment," and the "testing of the spirits." Jonathan Edwards and Ignatius Loyola – no less than the Anabaptists – presupposed that the Holy Spirit works in Christian community. See Nancey Murphy, *Theology in the Age of Scientific Reasoning* (Ithaca, NY, 1990), 15, 132–41, 193; also, D. G. Mathews, "Evangelical America: The Methodist Ideology," in Russell E. Richey and Kenneth E. Rowe, *Rethinking Methodist History: A Bicentennial Historical Consultation* (Nashville, TN, 1985), 98. Since pro- and antislavery communities seem to have received different messages from the Holy Spirit, the problem remains. Among those who wrestled with this problem was Henry Ruffner, "Miracles Considered as an Evidence of Christianity," in *Lectures on the Evidences of Christianity Delivered at the University of Virginia, during the Session of 1850–51* (New York, 1859), 61–107.

[27] "Slavery in Massachusetts," in Henry D[avid] Thoreau, *A Yankee in Canada, with Anti-Slavery and Reform Papers* (New York, 1969 [1892]), 105; George Cheever, *Some Principles According to Which This World Is Managed, Contrasted with the Government of God, and the Principles Exhibited for*

Proslavery men granted that when laws defy the Decalogue, Christians must follow conscience, even at the risk of their lives. Christians must also render unto Caesar that which is Caesar's and resist the temptation to use the Holy Spirit as an excuse to rebel against governments to promote policies their individual consciences prefer. How, then, can men be reasonably sure that their individual experience of the Holy Spirit is not a mere expression of their own will – a particularly dangerous manifestation of the sin of pride, the deadliest of the sins that constitute rebellion against God? The answer can come only through the Church or Christian community, relying upon the Holy Spirit to work through the collective judgment of the faithful, which alone can save the individual from confusing his own moral views with the will of God. Proslavery men appealed primarily to the Word, the abolitionists primarily to the Spirit. For the proslavery leaders of the southern Christian churches, Word and Spirit rose or fell together. If Biblical formalism threatened to transform the Word into a sterile Phariseeism that ignores the Spirit, Antinomianism threatened to transform the Spirit into a higher law of individual conscience that substituted the word of man for the Word of God. William Elliott, South Carolina's intellectual luminary, mocked "that paramount law of conscience" to be found in "the recesses of man's own breast." A dedicated unionist, he cried, "Behold the sublime morality of the present age."[28]

Antislavery constitutional theorists appealed to the Founding Fathers, who – following John Locke – offered resistance to tyranny as a duty to God and natural law. Man has property in himself but not absolute property. He belongs to his Maker and has no right to alienate that which he does not wholly possess or to surrender himself completely to the arbitrary will of any being other than God. If this doctrine applied to colonial Americans who rebelled against a metaphorical "slavery," surely it applied to those physically enslaved. Conservatives read the intentions of the Founding Fathers, the Constitution, and the Bible differently: Jesus came to fulfill God's law by freeing believers from man's law. Jesus' command to "render unto Caesar the things which are Caesar's" meant also to render unto God the things that are God's. No man-made law that contradicted God's law deserved allegiance. In

---

Man's Guidance in the Bible (Boston, 1833), 19, 50–1; Theodore Parker, "The Function of Conscience," in David B. Chesebrough, ed., *"God Ordained This War": Sermons on the Sectional Crisis, 1830–1865* (Columbia, SC, 1991), 36–7; Cheever, *God against Slavery*, 26, 172–3, 192–3, 249–50.

A contributor to *De Bow's Review* came dangerously close to arguing that the injunction to obey the powers that be meant that Christians should carry out laws contrary to the will of God since the sin would fall on those who enacted them: "A Mississippian", "Slavery – The Bible and the 'Three Thousand Parsons,'" *DBR*, 26 (1859), 44. Aristotle, Cicero, and Seneca applied the doctrine of higher law in court cases but rooted it in reason and experience: see Carl J. Richard, *The Founders and the Classics: Greece, Rome, and the American Enlightenment* (Cambridge, MA, 1994), 169–72. R. S. Gladney invoked Vattel to support a proper understanding of higher law in relation to the laws of men: "Relation of State and Church," *SPR*, 16 (1866), 354–5. The liberal Francis Lieber and the conservative Beverley Tucker both rested their arguments for the legitimacy of government on God's higher law: Lieber, *Manual of Political Ethics* (London, 1839), 7, 27, 213–14; Tucker, *A Discourse on the Study of Political Science as a Branch of Academic Education in the United States* (Richmond, VA, 1840), 13, 18–20.

[28] [William Elliott], *The Letters of Agricola* (Greenville, SC, 1851), 11.

G. W. F. Hegel's formulation, morality transcends legality because love transcends the law. Thus Hegel recalled John the Baptist's admonition to the Jews: "It matters not that you have Abraham for your father, for the axe is even now laid to the roots of the trees." Adolphe von Harnack's later formulation: Since Christianity's higher justice conforms to the Christian law of love, the Gospel "frees men from all legality, which, however, at the same time lays upon them the highest moral obligations."[29]

The Presbyterian Reverend Ferdinand Jacobs of Charleston pilloried the Yankee interpretation of the higher law as a broadside against all authority, and he related higher law to the Constitution: "Ours is not a Union held together by the energy of a central power .... Constitutional provisions, knowing no 'higher law,' by an upright and honest and religious people, should be held inviolate." The southern Unitarian Reverends Charles Farley and Charles Taggart assented. Farley preached the southern version in Richmond in 1835, and in 1851 Taggart told his congregation in Nashville that republican government under law becomes a chimera when individual conscience is allowed to prevail.[30]

Secular writers, no less than clerical, accepted higher-law doctrine and repudiated only its perversion. In an 1853 assault on the continued use of northern textbooks in southern schools, the Richmond *Daily Dispatch* declared: "We can't say what your '*northern* Bibles' teach, for we are aware that northern fanatics have enacted a 'higher law' than the Bible or the Constitution." The Bible nevertheless remains "the strongest bulwark any southern man could desire" for slavery "as prescribed and regulated among the Jews" and "recognized by the Savior and the Apostles." God, John Fletcher recalled, proclaimed himself "a jealous God." Since man comprehends God's will only through His revealed Word, the Bible and not individual conscience must govern moral behavior. Fletcher accused the northern abolitionist Reverend Albert Barnes of the most "insidious specimens of abolition

---

[29] See Ellis Sandoz, *A Government of Laws: Political Theory, Religion, and the American Founding* (Baton Rouge, LA, 1990), esp. 89–93. Justice Story adhered to higher-law doctrine in his lifelong opposition to slavery but insisted he would do his duty as a judge and uphold the Constitution: William W. Story, ed., *Life and Letters of Joseph Story*, 2 vols. (Boston, 1851), 2:431; "The Spirit of Christianity and Its Fate," in G. W. F. Hegel, *Early Theological Writings*, tr. T. M. Knox and Richard Kroner (Philadelphia, PA, 1948), 222–3; Adolf Harnack, *Outline of the History of Dogma*, tr. Edwin Knox Mitchell (Boston, 1957), 17. See Supplementary References: "Natural Law and Natural Rights."

[30] Ferdinand Jacobs, *A Sermon for the Times* (n.p., n.d.), 3, and Jacobs, *Committing of Our Cause to God,* 3; Charles A. Farley, *Slavery; A Discourse Delivered in the Unitarian Church, Richmond, Va.* (Richmond, VA, 1835), 13–14; Charles M. Taggart, *Slavery and Law, in the Light of Christianity* (Nashville, TN, 1851), 12. During Reconstruction, Baptist preachers recalled Seward's doctrine as an appeal to a law of conscience above the Bible: Paul Harvey, *Redeeming the South: Religious Cultures and Racial Identities among Southern Baptists, 1865–1925* (Chapel Hill, NC, 1997), 23–4. For northern theologians who "were readier to use conscience to interpret Scripture than either Jonathan Edwards or Samuel Hopkins had been" see Mark A. Noll, *America's God: From Jonathan Edwards to Abraham Lincoln* (New York, 2002), 271. Jacobs elsewhere noted that the Founders of the American nation, Southerners included, ignored God in their Constitution. Southerners were now paying for their error, but they have repented and recognized God in the Confederate Constitution: *Sermon for the Times,* 4–5.

logic" and berated him for transforming conscience into a "distinct mental power" that intuitively and infallibly spread falsehood as truth and qualified man as "fit to govern the universe, and successfully carry on a war against God!" To Fletcher, Christians find the principle that distinguishes good from evil in the Word.[31]

Speaking in New York in 1858, Jefferson Davis contrasted the higher law of the abolitionists with the law of the Bible and placed the Constitution in harmony with the Bible on slavery: "Men who are *traitors* to the compact of their fathers – *men who have perjured the oaths they have themselves taken*" – take for themselves "a higher law than the Bible, the Constitution, and the laws of the land." Alexander Stephens opposed secession but considered the revolutionary right to secede as itself an expression of biblically sanctioned higher law. Louisa McCord, unwilling to let the disputants forget the needs of women, spoke up: "There are male spontaneities and intuitions as well as female ones; the former possessing the indisputable advantage of being backed by physical force, which will secure, as it has always secured, male supremacy, in case of a clash between contending spontaneities. Man's 'higher law' must certainly override woman's."[32]

Southerners recalled that Saint-Just appealed to the inner voice of conscience to exalt the radical egalitarianism of the Reign of Terror. Robert Owen proclaimed socialism the Second Coming of Christ: The first coming of Christ made truth available to the few; the second would enlighten the many. Francis Wayland spoke of many truths unidentified in the Bible but identified by human reason, experience, and observation. Proslavery advocates, clerical and lay, acknowledged as much, but – distrusting man's fallible reason and emotions – they stipulated the preeminence of the Word. "Christian conscience," writes Owen Chadwick, "was the force which began to make Europe 'secular'; that is, to allow many religions or no religion in a state, and repudiate any kind of pressure upon the man who rejected the accepted and inherited axioms of society." The severance of conscience from objective authority rendered it private and reduced it to mere opinion.[33]

---

[31] Richmond *Daily Dispatch*, Dec. 14, 1853, in *DHE*, 5:290–1; see also "The Doctrine of the 'Higher Law': Mr. Seward's Speech," *SLM*, 17 (1851), 140–2; Fletcher, *Studies on Slavery*, 93–5, 180–1, 243–4, quotes at 244, 93. For a defense of higher law against abolitionist distortions that attack all lawful authority see "The Phases of Society," *SPR*, 8 (1855), 217. Paul Tillich implicitly made the antislavery case more clearly than the abolitionists: *Systematic Theology*, 3 vols. (Chicago, 1951–63), 3:232–3.

[32] Davis, as quoted in Jesse T. Carpenter, *The South as a Conscious Minority, 1789–1861: A Study in Political Thought* (New York, 1930), 159–60; Henry Cleveland, *Alexander H. Stephens in Public and Private. With Letters and Speeches before, during, and since the War* (Philadelphia, 1866), 649; Stephens, *Constitutional View*, 1:626; "Woman and Her Needs," in Lounsbury, ed., *Louisa S. McCord: Essays*, 139; also, Charles E. B. Flagg, *Oration Delivered before the '76 Association at the Society of the Cincinnati* (Charleston, SC, 1858), 12–15.

[33] On Wayland and the responses of Fletcher, Grayson, Rivers, and others see William Sumner Jenkins, *Pro-Slavery Thought in the Old South* (Gloucester, MA, 1960), 234–7; Frank E. Manuel and Fritzie P. Manuel, *Utopian Thought in the Western World* (Cambridge, MA, 1979), chs. 23 and 24 (Owen quoted at 589); Owen Chadwick, *The Secularization of the European Mind in the Nineteenth Century* (Cambridge, U.K., 1993), 23. Some southern temperance advocates invoked the higher law against those who justified the manufacture and sale of liquor as legal: Anne C. Loveland, *Southern Evangelicals and the Social Order, 1800–1860* (Baton Rouge, LA, 1980), 153.

During the fierce debates over the Compromise of 1850, northern conservatives, led by the prestigious Moses Stuart of Andover, rallied to Webster's Seventh of March Speech. "Conscience," wrote Stuart, "when misled by rashness and heated party spirit and enthusiasm, can turn into any shape whatever." Abolitionists, he charged, appealed to a wholly subjective conscience that reduced to passions and prejudices. The Reverend Ichabod Spencer of Brooklyn granted a higher law when he called for obedience to the Fugitive Slave Law: "Any violent resistance is positive rebellion against government; and either the resistance must be crushed, or the government be overturned." Christians, he argued, resist only if they deem the government hopelessly lost to sin and have a better government to put in its place. A government's injustices and unrighteousness do not sanction violent resistance if there is a potential peaceful redress of grievances. Spencer challenged abolitionists to confess their readiness "to overthrow any régime they thought incapable of reformation."[34]

Advocacy of a biblically sanctioned individual freedom that set limits to governmental power upheld Jeffersonian tradition, which in this instance corresponded to the slaveholders' jealousy of their own prerogatives. But the most difficult problems remained. Various disputes over constitutional theory, interstate comity, and the proper nature of republican government had a common denominator: They accepted property in man – or, as most Southerners would have it, property in man's labor and services. Behind the endless constitutional wrangling lay a powerful historical defense of a particular theory of property, and, accordingly, the anger that roared from the southern bench over violations of interstate comity and from the politicians over the territorial question proved irrepressible. Northerners saw southern disputation as tedious hairsplitting, logic-chopping, and self-serving oratory. Southerners reproached abolitionists and free-soilers for bad faith – for substituting human judgment for God's law.[35]

---

[34] Moses Stuart, *Conscience and the Constitution* (Boston, 1850), 61; Ichabod Spencer, *The Religious Duty of Obedience to Law* (New York, 1850), 14–16; also, *Oration Delivered by Hon. David A. Bokee, in First Baptist Church, Brooklyn* (Brooklyn, NY, 1851). Moses Stuart had practiced law in Connecticut before he entered the ministry: see William Buell Sprague, *Annals of the American Pulpit,* 9 vols. (New York, 1859–69), 2:476. In Mark Noll's weighty judgment, no American stood higher as a biblical scholar than Stuart: Noll, *America's God,* 303. Stuart, who denied the sinfulness of slavery, supported the Compromise of 1850; however, like Clark he believed that Christianity would lead to the abolition of slavery and therefore opposed immediatism and radical agitation. Thornwell admired Stuart as the ablest man at Andover: James Oscar Farmer, Jr., *The Metaphysical Confederacy: James Henley Thornwell and the Synthesis of Southern Values* (Macon, GA, 1986), 139. De Bow noted with pleasure Stuart's *Conscience and the Constitution,* while indicating serious disagreements: *DBR,* 10 (1851), 698.

[35] For an elaboration of the property question see Elizabeth Fox-Genovese and Eugene D. Genovese, *Fruits of Merchant Capital: Slavery and Bourgeois Property in the Rise and Expansion of Capitalism* (New York, 1983), ch. 12; Christopher M. Curtis, "Jefferson's Chosen People: Legal and Political Conceptions of the Freehold in the Old Dominion from Revolution to Reform" (Ph.D. diss., Emory University, 2002). To maintain credibility and authority, positive law accommodated a doctrine rooted in Aristotelian philosophy and developed in Christian theology. Harold J. Berman illuminates the analogy to American constitutional law: "Any positive law must conform to the constitutional

The Catholic Bishop Augustin Verot stood with Thornwell on natural law's support of slavery. "Natural law," Verot wrote, "does not establish or institute Slavery: no one is by nature, the slave of another; but natural law approves of reasons and causes by which a man may become the slave of another man." It paralleled the division of property: "No land belongs to anybody by the right of nature, but legitimate titles constitute it the property of individuals." Slavery in antiquity was probably "coeval with the division of property." For Thornwell, natural rights "belong to man as man, which spring from his constitution as a social and responsible being, and which consequently attach to all men in the same relations and circumstances." Natural law "coincides with natural jurisprudence as distinguished from the municipal regulation of States and nations."[36]

Southern Christians maintained that Christianity stimulates conscience to restrain rebelliousness. W. T. Brantly, professor of belles lettres and oratory at the University of Georgia, distinguished the South's view of conscience from New England's: "I speak of conscience informed by revelation and submitting itself in all things to the authority of God." Northerners might have protested that they, too, stood on that ground, but Brantly identified revelation with the Word. Conscience, the prestigious Presbyterian Reverend George Howe wrote, "makes us cognizant of a higher law, of a superior tribunal, of an after reckoning." Conscience, in the formulation of President John Leadley Dagg of Mercer College, rewards or punishes actions according to their moral character: "The Bible contains the precepts of God, and is therefore a Rule of Duty. We are bound to obey the commandments of parents and civil rulers, but God has a higher claim on our obedience." God pronounces sentence "by the voice of *conscience* within us, which is to us as the voice of God." Brantly, Howe, and Dagg found nothing in properly administered slavery to assault Christian conscience. Smyth arraigned the abolitionist who acts as if every man "has the liberty to mark out a new track for himself" and who takes as gospel only that which "he has rendered most familiar to his own imagination." Conscience

---

requirements of 'due process,' 'equal protection,' 'freedom,' 'privacy,' and the like, or lose its validity. 'Due process of law' is in fact a fourteenth-century English phrase meaning natural law": Berman, *Law and Revolution: The Formation of the Western Legal Tradition* (Cambridge, MA, 1983), 12.

 Lydia Maria Child acknowledged that conservatives recognized a higher law and denied that all positive laws should be obeyed: L. M. Child, in *National Anti-Slavery Standard,* Aug. 19, 1841. The Garrisonians took a positive-law position on the Constitution, leaving the appeal to higher law to others. John Codman Hurd appealed to Hegel's *Philosophy of Right* to reinforce judicial positivism. In Georgia the Reverends Patrick Mell and Iveson Brookes simply asserted that God's higher law sanctions slave property: [Mell], *Slavery. A Treatise, Showing that Slavery Is Neither a Moral, Political, nor Social Evil* (Pennfield, GA, 1844), 18; Brookes, *A Defence of Slavery against the Attacks of Henry Clay and Alex'r Campbell* (Hamburg, SC, 1851), 12.

36 Augustin Verot, *A Tract for the Times* (Baltimore, 1861), 3; [J. H. Thornwell], "Principles of Moral and Political Economy," *SPR,* 7 (1853), 37. Neither Augustine nor Thomas Aquinas wrote a treatise on slavery or discussed it systematically. Verot was deeply influenced by Francis Patrick Kenrick's *Theologia Moralis.* Augustine considered the submission of woman to man as natural but the submission of slave to master unnatural.

enforces but does not discover truth or duty: "The convictions of conscience presuppose a knowledge of truth or object." For S. J. Cassells, the Word – "the revealed will of God" – must ground an appeal to conscience: "When this course is honestly and faithfully pursued, it is next to impossible that the conscience should be in 'fundamental error.' "[37]

Thornwell cautioned that men deceive themselves as readily as they let others deceive them and hence that the testimony of conscience cannot be final. Apostasy exposes men to the sinful abuse of reason: "We may misjudge where we have the right to judge, but we do it at our risk." Echoing Augustine: "Conscience does not make the right, it only declares it; the right exists independently of it, as the world exists independently of our senses." More boldly: "Conscience fills the mind with prejudices against the nature and character of God," and "Conscience, in the bosom of a sinner, becomes a fruitful source of ignorance and mistake in relation to God." In 1860 Thornwell deplored Union-sundering "sentiment over reason and truth." The assertion of conscience offered an excuse "to violate the faith of treaties, the solemnity of contracts, and the awful sanctity of an oath." Antislavery militants trampled "the plainest obligations of duty." On the struggle for the western territories: "The doctrine of a higher law we are far from repudiating. God is greater than man, and no human covenants can set aside or annul the supreme obligations of His will." If slavery is a sin, then Americans should repudiate the constitutional contract that sustains it. Sounding like William Lloyd Garrison himself, Thornwell called upon those who considered slavery sinful to withdraw from the Union: "To swear to observe the Constitution, when the Constitution binds them to do what they believe to be wicked, is an oath, whether broken or kept, that cannot be taken without dishonor. To break it is to be guilty of perjury. The only escape from this dilemma is not to take it at all."[38]

In December 1861 the General Assembly of the Presbyterian Church of the Confederate States issued an address to all Protestant churches, written by Thornwell and warmly applauded by other southern denominations: "Men have listened to

---

[37] W. T. Brantly, *A Discourse Delivered before the Phi Kappa Society of the University of Georgia* (Athens, GA, 1852), 15; George Howe, "Secondary and Collateral Influences of the Sacred Scriptures," *SPR*, 7 (1853), 103; Dagg, *Manual of Theology*, 1:16–17, 40, 157, 161; [S. J. Cassells], "Conscience – Its Nature, Office, and Authority," *SPR*, 6 (1853), 467–8; also, Nathaniel Beverley Tucker, "Moral and Political Effect of the Relation between the Caucasian and the African Slave," *SLM*, 10 (1844), 742; "A Northerner" [Elias Lyman Magoon], "Christianity and Patriotism," *SLM*, 8 (1842), 602; "The Last Judgment," in George A. Blackburn, ed., *Sermons by John L. Girardeau* (Columbia, SC, 1907), 15; *TSW*, 6:257, 590.

[38] In *JHTW*: "The Call of the Minister," 4:35; "The Office of Reason in Regard to Revelation," 3:213, 215; "The State and Nature of Sin," 1:358, 366, quote at 366; "Man's Natural Ignorance of God," 1:92, 94; "Christian Doctrine of Slavery," 4:401; "Sermon on National Sins," 4:530–1. For the charge of perjury against Seward, see also "The Doctrine of the Higher Law," *SLM*, 17 (1851), 132. The southern response to violations of oath was akin to that of the common people of modern Greece, who consider perjury especially vile since the perjurer makes God "a collaborator in his own sin": J. K. Campbell, "Honour and the Devil," in J. G. Peristiany, ed., *Honour and Shame: The Values of Mediterranean Society* (Chicago, 1966), 154.

what they falsely considered as primitive intuitions, or, as necessary deductions from primitive cognitions, and then have gone to the Bible to confirm the crotchets of their vain philosophy." In consequence they made Scripture rather than interpreting it. Southern Christians, to the contrary, stood firmly on the Word, which leads conscience aright because it expresses the Holy Spirit.[39]

How, Robert Lewis Dabney asked, should a free conscience act in the face of a clearly immoral statute? "I answer, it asserts the higher law by refusing to be an accessory to the sin." An individual must not actively resist; rather, he must refuse to obey and accept the consequences. Even so, Dabney affirmed an oppressed people's right of revolution. A people, that is, not an individual: "If the outraged citizen is moved to resist merely by his own private wrong, he is sinful. If his resistance is disinterested, and the expression of the common breast, it is patriotic and righteous. There is the dividing line." Dabney paid tribute to Thomas Hobbes, "an intellectual giant" who, in his own way, recognized the ubiquity of human depravity, but he shrank from Hobbes the "bad eminence," who carried materialism to its logical and most destructive conclusions. Dabney especially faulted Hobbes's teaching that might makes right – that "there is no supreme uniform standard of moral obligation, and no conscience in man." Fallible conscience commands obedience only when in accordance with God's will as revealed in his Word. Each man may claim his own conscience as true for himself, but then there follow "as many clashing views of duty, as men." What one man believes to be the proper guide of conscience another finds outrageous. Those who have committed the most odious acts in history have claimed to act in good conscience. R. S. Gladney underscored Dabney's point by recalling that, when Saul of Tarsus persecuted Christians, he did so out of ignorance and thus in good conscience.[40]

"We cheerfully acknowledge," *Southern Presbyterian Review* declared, "that there is a higher law than the law of man." Replying to Seward, a contributor to *Southern Literary Messenger* agreed that moral law takes precedence over constitutional law. "No one in his senses can deny or dispute it .... The law of God is unquestionably superior to the enactments of men." The Presbyterian Reverend John Girardeau of South Carolina, a formidable theologian, described conscience as "a moral faculty" that remains, even after the Fall, "the law of God within man." To combat the heterodox appeal to conscience, Southerners appealed to Genesis, 8:21: "For the imagination of man's heart is evil from his youth." And to the words

---

[39] "Address to All Churches of Christ," *JHTW*, 4:456–7. Thornwell argued this way while upholding the right of private judgment: see *JHTW*, 3:129–36, 467–9.

[40] "Civic Ethics," *DD*, 3:115, 118; also, R. L. Dabney, *The Sensualistic Philosophy of the Nineteenth Century, Considered*, new and enlarged edition (n.p., 1887), 7, 11–13 (Hobbes); Robert L. Dabney, *Systematic Theology* (Carlisle, PA, 1985 [1878]), 72–3, 118–19, 137, 139, 299, 560, 872; R. S. Gladney, "Moral Philosophy," *SPR*, 9 (1855), 116. In 1897, near the end of his life, Dabney held fast, defining conscience as "simply the moral reason" and defending slavery as scriptural, especially focusing on abolitionist distortion of the Golden Rule: *The Practical Philosophy, Being the Philosophy of the Feelings, of the Will, and of the Conscience, with the Ascertainment of Particular Rights and Duties* (Harrisonburg, VA, 1984 [1897]), 282, 321–6, 403–19, quote at 282.

of Jesus: "Out of the heart proceed evil thoughts, murders, adulteries, fornications, thefts, false witness, blasphemies" (Matt., 15:19–20). "Trust not your heart," cried the Presbyterian Reverend William S. Plumer of Richmond, "Trust God's word." Plumer warned that "prejudice or passion" is easily mistaken for conscience. David McCord of South Carolina, a legal scholar, blamed the perversion of the doctrine of higher law on Rousseau's celebration of popular will and the replacement of all law with the enthronement of "Judge Lynch." Yankees, these Southerners protested, desecrated higher law. Robert Patrick of Clinton, Louisiana, described Daniel Ruggles, a Confederate officer, as an "old brute": "Being an old army officer and a New Englander, he had no conscience nor mercy on any one." More philosophically, the proslavery theorist George Sawyer of Louisiana deplored the abolitionist view of the higher law for making each individual "a law unto himself" and "an independent sovereignty" that breaks "society into its original elements."[41]

Orestes Brownson, a northern convert to Catholicism, slammed Seward hard: "Mr. Seward had no right, while holding his seat in the Senate under the Constitution, to appeal to the higher law against the Constitution, because that was to deny the very authority by which he held his seat." Seward, having called upon God to witness his assent to the Constitution, had no right to claim God's sanction for blatant disregard for what he had solemnly sworn to uphold. Brownson rubbed Seward's apostasy in the faces of southern Protestants: The abolitionists and free-soilers had summoned the Protestant assertion of private judgment: "No man can ever be justifiable in resisting the civil law under the pretence that it is repugnant to the Divine law, when he has only his private judgment, or, what is the same thing, his private interpretation of the Sacred Scriptures, to tell him what the Divine law is on the point in question, because the principle on which he would act in doing so would be repugnant to the very existence of government, and therefore a contravention of the ordinance, therefore of the law, of God." The Reverend Alfred Watson of North Carolina took up the cudgels for the Episcopalians. Defending the higher law against northern interpretations, he, too, needled Southerners who

---

[41] "Critical Notices," *SPR*, 4 (1851), 445; "The Doctrine of the Higher Law," *SLM*, 17 (1851), 13, 133; John L. Girardeau, *The Will in Its Theological Relations* (Columbia, SC, 1891), 26; Plumer, *Law of God*, 363, 610; [David J. McCord], "Political Elements," *SQR*, n.s., 10 (1854), 392, 413; Diary, 1862, in F. Jay Taylor, ed., *Reluctant Rebel: The Secret Diary of Robert Patrick, 1861–1865* (Baton Rouge, LA, 1996), 37; George S. Sawyer, *Southern Institutes; Or, an Inquiry into the Origin and Early Prevalence of Slavery and the Slave Trade* (New York, 1967 [1858]), 18; see also Robert Toombs, "Slavery – Its Constitutional Status and Influence on Society and on the Colored," *DBR*, 20 (1856), 582; George Fitzhugh, "Black Republicanism in Athens," *DBR*, 23 (1857), 22. The Presbyterian Church sponsored a series of Thanksgiving sermons in 1850 that condemned the abolitionist version of the higher law: Wesley Norton, "The Presbyterian Press and the Compromise of 1850," *JPH*, 40 (1962), 206–7. For implicit defenses of the higher law see B. F. Porter, "An Attempt to Infuse into the English Language Some Thoughts of Heineccius' Elementa Juris Civilis – Part I," *DBR*, 2 (1846), 24–7; John McKrum, "The True Functions of Government," *DBR*, 4 (1847), 95–106. For wartime and postwar reiteration of conscience as objectively based see "Rationalism False and Unreasonable," *SPR*, 16 (1863), 165–6; [S. J. Barnett], "Buckle's History of Civilization," *SPR*, 17 (1866), 193, 197; [H. M. Smith], "What Is Conscience," *SPR*, 18 (1867), 405–32.

rejected tradition for *sola scriptura*. They interpreted Scripture properly as sanctioning slavery, but he wondered what prevented their communicants from deciding upon another interpretation. The Methodists had once denounced slavery. What prevented them from doing so again?[42]

With the onset of the War, B. W. Lacy, in *Virginia University Magazine,* called upon the higher law as the basis for the right of revolution against oppression as exemplified in the American Revolution and the impending secession of the South. The Episcopalian Reverend A. M. Randolph of Fredericksburg, Virginia, denied that patriotism excused violation of God's laws. Appealing to conscience, he attacked those who supported the Union on the false principle of my country right or wrong. Heathen nations, the Presbyterian Reverend J. W. Tucker preached in Fayetteville, North Carolina, have no revelation and are therefore guided only by the light of nature and their own moral and spiritual intuitions. The reason or conscience or passion of man, Bishop Alexander Gregg of Texas said, set itself up as God. America, the Episcopalian Reverend W. A. Cave of Tallahassee protested, is the only country that teaches children to make conscience subservient to money.[43]

In 1864, when the near-victorious Union compelled Southerners to swear allegiance to the United States, the Presbyterian Reverend William H. Ruffner of Virginia reflected on oaths that call God's name in commission of sin and concluded that such oaths ought not to be taken even under penalty of severe repression. Applauding the principled stand of the abolitionist Wendell Phillips, Ruffner excoriated those who took an oath to uphold the Constitution and then refused to abide by the constitutionally sanctioned Fugitive Slave Law.[44]

In 1860 a hopeful George Fitzhugh, echoed by J. T. Wiswall of Alabama, perceived a rising movement against liberalism: "In religion, the admiration for the Catholic Church as a political institution, and the daily adoption of more form, of rule and ceremony, by the Orthodox Protestant Trinitarian churches is a most important point, and symptom, of a salutary reaction." During the War, southern preachers forcefully reiterated a long-standing theme: Atheism, apostasy, and heresy had corrupted northern society, weakening scriptural faith and piety, whereas southern society had resisted such evils and remained untouched. Well, largely untouched.

---

[42] For Brownson see Russell Kirk, *Redeeming the Time* (Wilmington, DE, 1998), 207; Alfred A. Watson, *Sermon Delivered before the Annual Council of the Diocese of North Carolina upon the Festival of the Ascension* (Raleigh, NC, 1863), 7–8, 14–15; Verot, *Tract for the Times,* 5.

[43] B. W. Lacy, "Government a Divine Institution," *VUM,* 4 (1860), 327–8; A. M. Randolph, *Address on the Day of Fasting and Prayer* (Fredericksburg, VA, 1861), 12; J. W. Tucker, *God Sovereign and Man Free* (Fayetteville, NC, 1862); Alexander Gregg, *The Duties Growing Out of It, and the Benefits to Be Expected, from the Present War* (Austin, TX, 1861); W. A. Cave, *Two Sermons on the Times, Preached in St. John's Church, Tallahassee* (n.p., n.d. but War years).

[44] W. H. Ruffner, *The Oath: A Sermon on the Nature and Obligation of the Oath* (Lexington, VA, 1864), 10; also, H. A. Tupper, *A Thanksgiving Discourse* (Macon, GA, 1862), 6. Parson Brownlow, who excoriated the abolitionists for their application of the higher law, coolly applied it himself to denounce the secessionists: William G. Brownlow, *Sketches of the Rise, Progress, and Decline of Secession, with a Narrative of Personal Adventures among the Rebels* (Philadelphia, 1862), 73–4.

Those preachers warned no less forcefully that unless Southerners, too, turned away from sinful practices, the Lord would send Yankee infidels to crush them.[45]

In 1869 Dabney ruefully concluded that the South's long association with the North had gravely impaired its own moral fiber by drawing it into materialist modes of thought and behavior. In 1894, heartsick but unbroken, Dabney renewed his life-long call for militant opposition to Catholicism, recalling that – during the decades from 1830 to 1860 – orthodox Protestants had taken the measure of the threat of "popery" and combated theological backsliding in their own churches. Dabney de-nounced the Protestant churches for yielding to Jacobin doctrines and opening the way for the Catholic Church to emerge as the principal defender of the Word and the bulwark against sociopolitical radicalism. "Democratic Protestantism" had grown "so ignorant, so superficial and willful," that it could no longer resist the rising tide of infidelity and Jacobinism. It had surrendered the ground to the Catholic Church, which "proposes herself as the stable advocate of obedience, order, and permanent authority." With evident disgust he allowed, "To the shame of our damaged Protes-tantism, popery remains, in some essential respects, more faithful to God's truth than its rival." Dabney feared, as Karl Barth feared in later years, that a mod-ern, rationalistic Protestantism was accepting everything and standing for nothing. Catholics might be forgiven for replying: "Thou sayest it."[46]

---

[45] George Fitzhugh, "Disunion within the Union," *DBR*, 28 (1860), 6; J. T. Wiswall, "Causes of Aristoc-racy," *DBR*, 28 (1860), 560; for problems of wartime preaching see Eugene D. Genovese, *A Consuming Fire: The Defeat of the Confederacy in the Mind of the White Christian South* (Athens, GA, 1998); also, Silver, *Confederate Morale and Church Propaganda*, 14; William W. Bennett, *A Narrative of the Great Revival Which Prevailed in the Southern Armies during the Late Civil War between the States of the Federal Union* (Harrisonburg, VA, 1989 [1876]), 23; D. G. Hart, *Defending the Faith: J. Gre-sham Machen and the Crisis of Conservative Protestantism in Modern America* (Baltimore, 1994), 3, 68, 71.

[46] "The Attractions of Popery," *DD*, 3:362–89, quotes at 364, 366; also, *DD**, 4:133. Referring to New England's abandonment of Calvinism for liberalism, Joseph Haroutunian writes, "The Protestant Reformation, compared with the 'rise of modern religious ideas,' was a negligible theological per-formance": Haroutunian, *Piety versus Moralism: The Passing of the New England Theology* (New York, 1932), xxv. Karl Barth ruefully charged that twentieth-century Protestant churches were slip-ping into a cult of interiority and personality while the Catholic Church, which he continued to criticize sharply, was upholding the Word. Hans Urs von Balthasar, the Catholic theologian, was de-lighted to hear it: *The Theology of Karl Barth*, tr. John Drury (New York, 1971), 32–4.

Coda

St. John of Pottawatamie

For they have sown the wind, and they shall reap the whirlwind: it hath no stalk: the bud shall yield no meal: if so be it yield, the strangers shall swallow it up.

—Hosea, 8:7

John Brown invoked private judgment and higher law to justify his slaughter of defenseless proslavery farmers in Kansas in 1856, while the abolitionist Charles Stearns called for the killing of proslavery settlers he described as wild beasts. When in 1859 Brown seized a federal arsenal at Harper's Ferry, Virginia, the Baptist Reverend Thornton Stringfellow, speaking for southern public opinion, declared Brown's bloody course the logical outcome of the abolitionists' understanding of the Golden Rule and higher law. Brown's rampage horrified most antislavery Northerners, who feared that – moral revulsion aside – his fanaticism and brutality discredited their cause. Hatred of slaveholders, nonetheless, mounted in the North, culminating in the glorification of Brown as martyr after Harper's Ferry and the fable that the Slave Power had fabricated the massacre at Pottawatomie.[1]

Southerners themselves had mixed reactions to Harper's Ferry. A great many cried, in effect, that they knew the abolitionists would murder their wives and children, for that is what those thinly disguised infidels understood by the Golden Rule. Yet many were shocked. Perhaps they had not entirely believed their own direst warnings. Constance Cary Harrison of the slaveholding elite was among the many Virginians who "devoured" *Uncle Tom's Cabin,* and she may also have had company in thinking that Brown's raid might be "God's vengeance for the torture of such as Uncle Tom."[2]

---

[1] Thornton Stringfellow, *Slavery: Its Origin, Nature, and History, Considered in the Light of Bible Teachings, Moral Justice, and Political Wisdom* (New York, 1861), 6; Lewis Perry, *Radical Abolitionism: Antislavery and the Government of God in Antislavery Thought* (Ithaca, NY, 1973), 240–1. Merrill D. Peterson says, "The Pottawatomie Massacre was destined to become the blackest blot on John Brown's escutcheon": *John Brown: The Legend Revisited* (Charlottesville, VA, 2002), 6. Brown's apologists claimed that he was retaliating for the murder of six antislavery settlers.

[2] Mrs. Burton [Constance Cary] Harrison, *Recollections Grave and Gay* (London, 1912), 42.

In 1859 Henry Stephens Randall of New York, biographer of Thomas Jefferson, wrote Hugh Blair Grigsby of Virginia: "The body of our people are looking on the John Brown controversy without any particular excitement. But the abolitionists are flaming hot – howling & screeching – undoubtedly anxious to dissolve the Union." A few years before Harper's Ferry, the politically moderate Frederick Grimké of Ohio, brother of South Carolina abolitionists Sarah and Angelina, testified that northern public opinion was reining in the small minority of abolitionists: "But opinions which are even tincture with sinister views ought never to be disregarded on that account. Our enemies always tell us more truth than our friends." The conservative Nathan Appleton of Massachusetts – a leading manufacturer, banker, and politician pleading for peace in 1860 – told Virginians that "sober" Northerners who witnessed Brown's "folly with silent contempt and disgust" were surprised to learn that Southerners construed their silence as approval. Southerners weighed the words of northern friends against such events as the overwhelming victory of John Andrew, an ardent supporter of Brown, in the gubernatorial election in Massachusetts. They appreciated the efforts of northern conservatives, but an exasperated J. W. Morgan insisted in *De Bow's Review* that northern opinion and political power were running the other way. L. Q. C. Lamar of Mississippi, a rising political star destined for a postwar career as senator and justice of the Supreme Court, held the Republican party largely responsible. Northern conservatives assured Virginians that Brown's raid would prove a godsend by opening their people's eyes to the real meaning of "Black Republicanism," but, as E. A. Pollard later remarked, the outpouring of northern sympathy for Brown told a different story.[3]

After Harper's Ferry, Ralph Waldo Emerson declared that most Northerners admired and sympathized with Brown, and Southerners believed him. Why not? Brown embarrassed the Republicans of Illinois, and the Democrats made political hay at their expense. But the very ferocity of the Democrats encouraged Republicans to counterattack with tributes to Brown's idealism and courage. As reports of northern reactions filtered south, protestations of revulsion at Brown's deed increasingly sounded hollow. Of two Iowans who fought with Brown, one hanged and the other escaped back to Iowa. When Governor Henry Wise of Virginia asked for his extradition, Governor Samuel J. Kirkwood of Iowa proceeded in the classic

[3] H. S. Randall to H. B. Grigsby, Dec. 14, 1859, in Frank J. Klingberg and Frank W. Klingberg, eds., *The Correspondence between Henry Stephens Randall and Hugh Blair Grigsby, 1856–1861* (Berkeley, CA, 1952), 172; Frederick Grimke, *The Nature and Tendency of Free Institutions*, ed. John William Ward (Cambridge, MA, 1968 [1848, 1856]), 119–420, quote at 420; Nathan Appleton, *Letter to Hon. Wm. C. Rives, of Virginia, on Slavery and the Union* (Boston, 1860), 11; J. W. Morgan, "The Conservative Men, and the Union Meetings of the North," *DBR*, 28 (1860), 514; E. A. Pollard, *Southern History of the War*, 2 vols. (n.p., 1977 [1866]), 1:32–3; for Lamar see Mary A. H. Gay, *Life in Dixie during the War*, 5th ed. (Atlanta, GA, 1979 [1897]), 93–4. Nathaniel Cabell, corresponding with Randall, expressed disappointment that northern conservatives could not overcome pro-Brown sentiment: see Peterson, *John Brown*, 18–19. Adam Gurowski, a passionate Polish abolitionist who fought for the Union, declared world opinion "unanimous" in awarding Brown "the crown of a martyr who fell in the cause of human liberty": Adam Gurowski, *Slavery in History* (New York, 1860), 256.

manner of a Spanish colonial official: "*Obedesco pero no cumplo*" [I obey but do not comply]. He dawdled until the wily guerrilla escaped to parts unknown.[4]

Secular rationales for supporting Brown's foray at Harper's Ferry angered Southerners, and religious rationales outraged them. The early abolitionist espousal of Christian nonviolence gave way to acquiescence in slave revolt and sedition – indeed, any measures to effect emancipation – and now many abolitionists deified a mass murderer. With Brown's execution, church bells tolled across the North, especially in New England; black drapes hung from stores and public buildings; cannon fire punctuated the mourning. When Brown was hanged, a mass meeting in Cleveland, apparently with no satirical intent, lacerated Governor Wise for violating the laws of Jesus Christ as taught by Thomas Jefferson. Brown's raid horrified many in the American Peace Society, but such longtime advocates of nonviolence as Lydia Maria Child referred to Brown as "an old hero" and "no criminal" – "that brave, generous old man, who so willfully gives his life for God's oppressed poor" – "the noble old veteran." She did not know of a single person who approved of Brown's action. "But I and thousands of others feel a natural impulse of sympathy for the brave and suffering man." Like Garrison, she found his foray thrilling. "If the monster [slavery] had one head, assuredly I should be Charlotte Corday." Several years before Harper's Ferry, Child had reiterated her abhorrence of war, but "I could be better resigned to that great calamity rather then to endure the [slaveholders'] tyranny that has too long trampled on us." Antislavery Northerners – of course! – could not endorse Brown's method, but they had to admire the tenacity with which he faced the challenge of ultimate evil. In 1860, John S. C. Abbott, the antislavery northern popular historian, entered the routine assertion that the North abhorred what Brown did, but he conceded widespread admiration for his courage and idealism and announced that many Northerners were ready to replicate his feat. David Potter has remarked that if the mourning had been meant as a tribute to Brown's courage, the damage might have been contained, but unmistakably it also signified damnation of the slaveholders and assent to insurrection.[5]

---

[4] Arthur C. Cole, *The Era of the Civil War, 1848–1870* (Urbana, IL, 1987 [1919]), 182–3; Robert R. Dykstra, *Bright Radical Star: Black Freedom and White Supremacy in the Hawkeye Frontier* (Cambridge, MA, 1993), 195.

[5] On Cleveland see Armstead L. Robinson, *Bitter Fruits of Bondage: The Demise of Slavery and the Collapse of the Confederacy, 1861–1865* (Charlottesville, VA, 2005). Lydia Maria Child to Mrs. S. B. Shaw, 1856; Child to the Editor of the New York *Tribune*, Nov. 10, 1859; Child to Samuel E. Sewall, Sept. 20, 1860; Child to Henry A. Wise, Oct. 26, 1859 – all in *Letters of Lydia Maria Child* (New York, 1969 [1883]), 79 ("tyranny"), 116 ("brave and generous"), 106 ("natural impulse"), 143 (Corday). David M. Potter, *The Impending Crisis, 1848–1861*, edited and completed by Don E. Fehrenbacher (New York, 1976), 378; John S. C. Abbott, *South and North; Or, Impressions Received during a Trip to Cuba and the South* (New York, 1969 [1860]), 176. During 1859 and 1860, *Liberator* published dissents from intransigent pacifists, but for the most part its pages bestowed encomia. For the turmoil and soul-searching in Garrisonian ranks over Brown's resort to violence see Henry Mayer, *All on Fire: William Lloyd Garrison and the Abolition of Slavery* (New York, 1998), ch. 21. Parker Pillsbury preached total nonviolence but somehow accommodated to Brown and the use of force to free fugitive slaves: see Stacey M. Robertson, *Parker Pillsbury: Radical Abolitionist, Male Feminist* (Ithaca, NY, 2000), 129–30.

Coda: St. John of Pottawatamie 639

With astonishing sangfroid, Brown denied any intention to raise a slave revolt. His admirers believed him – or pretended to. How did the Reverend Nathaniel Hall of Massachusetts know that Brown had no intension of raising a slave revolt? Because Brown, "whose word was truth," said so. Hall attributed to Brown "a heroic nobleness; a moral intrepidity," adding, apparently without appreciating the double entendre, "a religious self-devotion." Yet in 1858 Lysander Spooner, abolitionist and constitutional theorist, had advocated slave revolt and the kidnapping of slaveholders and called upon southern nonslaveholders to join slaves to bring about emancipation. After Brown's capture, Spooner tried to organize an effort to free him. Meanwhile, every account in the European press referred to Brown's raid as a "servile" or "Negro" insurrection. Representative John Hickman of Pennsylvania threatened to replicate Brown's feat by marching 18,000 men South "to whip her into submission to the higher law." Representative Thomas Hindman of Arkansas retorted that Southerners would meet them with "hospitable graves." And Virginians did not take kindly to Wendell Phillips's assertion that it was Wise, not Brown, who deserved to be hanged.[6]

After Brown's execution, thousands of northern blacks turned out to mourn him as a Christian liberator. James Newton Gloucester, a black businessman in Brooklyn, paid tribute to Brown for his actions in Kansas and linked him with Davy Crockett as an authentic American folk hero. Others, forgetting Brown's denial of intending to prompt slave revolt, boldly compared Harper's Ferry to the Nat Turner insurrection. In Pittsburgh a mass meeting sanctified him as "a hero, a patriot, and Christian" who epitomized fidelity to the Golden Rule. In Boston the Reverend J. Sella Martin assured a crowd that he was not using the language of rage when, "in the light of all Christian principle," he approved both Brown's means and ends.[7]

In 1858 Wendell Phillips had announced that no slave who failed to rebel deserved to be considered a man. The intrepid Phillips was not a man to ask of others

---

[6] Nathaniel Hall, *The Man – The Deed – The Event* (Boston, 1859), 26, 30; Perry, *Radical Abolitionism*, 204–7 (on Spooner); Seymour Drescher, "Servile Insurrection and John Brown's Body in Europe," *Journal of American History*, 80 (1993), 499; Hickman and Hindman quoted in Diane Neil and Thomas Kremm, *Lion of the South: General Thomas C. Hindman* (Macon, GA, 1997), 70–1; on Phillips see James Brewer Stewart, *Holy Warriors: The Abolitionists and American Society* (New York, 1976), 174; also, Edward J. Renehan, Jr., *The Secret Six: The True Tale of the Men Who Conspired with John Brown* (Columbia, SC, 1997), 173–6, 194–5.

For Brown as a revolutionary see W. E. B. DuBois, *John Brown* (London, 1997), and Herbert Aptheker, *Abolitionism: A Revolutionary Movement* (Boston, 1989), ch. 9. Having promised, "I will carry the war into Africa," Brown denied incitement to slave revolt and protested that he intended only to permit slaves to defend themselves: see Peterson, *John Brown*, 6, 13, 30, quote at 6. John Brown was a hero to Russian revolutionaries. Nikolai Chernyshevskii, whom Lenin much admired, thought the abolitionists had wrested the initiative from the slaveholders at Harper's Ferry and laid the groundwork for a socialist revolution in the United States: see Hans Rogger, "Russia and the Civil War," in Harold Hyman, *Heard Round the World: The Impact Abroad of the Civil War* (New York, 1969), 196–206, esp. 197.

[7] In Benjamin Quarles, ed., *Blacks on John Brown* (Urbana, IL, 1972), see J. N. Gloucester to John Brown, Feb. 19, 1858 (4) as well as "Meeting in Pittsburgh" and "Speech of Rev. J. S. Martin," 23, 26, also 37–41. On the Reverend Henry Highland Garnett's praise of Brown in New York City see Peterson, *John Brown*, 12.

what he did not ask of himself. When some abolitionists who had befriended Brown feared indictment and ran for cover, Phillips defiantly stood by Brown. Before long his boldness paid off, as even weak-kneed abolitionists rallied to the new cause. William Herndon, Lincoln's law partner, was convinced that Brown would "live amidst the world's gods & heroes through all the ages." Theodore Parker offered a dramatic metaphor: "Virginia is a pirate ship, and John Brown sails a sea as Lord High Admiral of the Almighty with his commission to sink every pirate he meets on God's ocean." Henry Wright taunted the Richmond *Enquirer* that the American sin of slavery "is to be taken away, not by Christ, but by John Brown." Many anti-slavery northern ministers did condemn Brown, but others rallied to him ever more extravagantly. Brown was a Christian martyr, a John the Baptist if not the resurrected Christ. Henry Ward Beecher asked that no one pray that Brown be spared: "Let Virginia make him a martyr." It was bad enough when northern ministers echoed Victor Hugo's identification of Brown as "the liberator, the champion of Christ." It became intolerable when they echoed Hugo's pronouncement, "There is something more terrible than Cain's slaying Abel: It is Washington slaying Spartacus." A bemused Basil Gildersleeve later commented, "What Washington would have done with Spartacus can readily be divined."[8]

Henry David Thoreau honored Brown as "by descent and birth a New England farmer, a man of great common-sense, deliberate and practical." It would be vain to kill this Puritan since "he died lately in the time of Cromwell, but he reappeared here." Thoreau expostulated, "You who pretend to care for Christ crucified, consider what you are about to do to him who offered himself to be the savior of four millions of men." Thoreau foresaw the time when, with slavery abolished, men would be free to weep for John Brown: "Then, and not until then, we will take our revenge." A year later, with Brown martyred, he summoned the Bible in words that would have seemed unseemly, even blasphemous, to most Southerners: The men who rallied to Brown "adhere to the spirit and let go the letter."[9]

[8] Ronald G. Walters, *The Antislavery Appeal: American Abolitionism after 1830* (Baltimore, 1976), 23–5, 28, 31, 258; "Harper's Ferry," in *Speeches, Lectures, and Letters by Wendell Phillips*, 2 vols. (Boston, 1863), 1:274; Herndon quoted by David Herbert Donald, *Lincoln's Herndon: A Biography* (New York, 1948), 134; Parker quoted in C. P. Roland, "The South of the Agrarians," in William C. Havard and Walter Sullivan, eds., *A Band of Prophets: The Vanderbilt Agrarians after Fifty Years* (Baton Rouge, LA, 1982), 36; Beecher quoted in Peterson, *John Brown*, 16. Wright called Brown "the embodiment of principle" and also wrote Governor Wise of Virginia. For a sampling of northern reactions see Victor B. Howard, *Conscience and Slavery: The Evangelic Calvinist Domestic Missions, 1837–1861* (Kent, OH, 1990), 173–5. Victor Hugo, "Letters on Slavery," in Belle Becker Sideman and Lillian Friedman, eds., *Europe Looks at the Civil War, an Anthology* (New York, 1960), 6–7. Hugo designed an engraving for John Brown that included the words "Pro Christo – Sicut Christus, John Brown" [For Christ – like Christ – John Brown]: Drescher, "Servile Insurrection and John Brown's Body in Europe," 499. Giuseppe Garibaldi and other European luminaries joined Hugo in hailing Brown. George B. Cheever praised Brown gingerly: *The Guilt of Slavery and the Crime of Slaveholding, Demonstrated from the Hebrew and Greek Scriptures* (New York, 1969 [1860)]), 455; Basil Lanneau Gildersleeve, *The Creed of the Old South* (Baltimore, 1915), 78.

[9] "A Plea for Captain John Brown," "Last Days of John Brown," "Address to the Citizens of Concord," and "Speech at a Meeting to Aid John Brown's Family," in Henry D[avid] Thoreau, *A Yankee in Canada, with Anti-Slavery and Reform Papers* (New York, 1969 [1892]), 154, 178, 181, 277–86.

Emerson, blending the sacred with the secular, moved smoothly from his higher-law doctrine to a ringing defense of Brown. Emerson scolded Webster for conciliating the South in his Seventh of March Speech in 1850, denounced the courts, and denied all such laws a proper legal foundation. He defended Brown as a man with "a perfect puritan faith" who stood squarely on the Golden Rule and the Declaration of Independence. Emerson demanded to know how Governor Wise of Virginia could praise Brown as a man of integrity and courage and then hang him.[10]

In 1860 James Redpath opened his biography of Brown by depicting "one of the earth's worthiest souls – the last of the Puritans." Redpath lauded Brown for eschewing the "cant of conservatism, of politics, and of non-resistance." Comparing Brown to the biblical Sampson, he called Brown a "warrior-saint" who greatly admired Cromwell as well as Nat Turner and Cinque and who was himself in the mold of Gideon, Joshua, and Moses. Redpath appealed to the Golden Rule and the Declaration of Independence, which he, in effect, equated. At Pottawatomie Brown had killed "ruffians" and executed "summary justice" on evildoers – acts "highly beneficial to the security of the Free State men." The rest of the charges against Brown he dismissed as proslavery mendacity. In 1862 Nathaniel Hawthorne wrote in *Atlantic Monthly*: "I shall not pretend to be an admirer of old John Brown, any farther than sympathy with Whittier's excellent ballad about him may go." He saw Brown as a "blood-stained fanatic," observing, "Nobody was ever more justly hanged." But Hawthorne acknowledged the "natural integrity" of a man who "won his martyrdom fairly, and took it firmly."[11]

Brown won the grudging admiration of a good many Southerners, as well. John Wilkes Booth acknowledged his courage and devotion to his cause, in contrast to the run of dishonest and cowardly abolitionists. The eminent Presbyterian Reverend George Howe of South Carolina remarked, "Like other men who have been

[10] Emerson at Dartmouth quoted in Merton M. Sealts, Jr., *Emerson on the Scholar* (Columbia, MO, 1992), 3; "John Brown" (Jan. 6. 1860), in Len Gougeon and Joel Myerson, eds., *Emerson's Antislavery Writings* (New Haven, CT, 1995), 53–72, 118–19, 123. H. Clay Pate criticized Governor Wise for allowing John Brown to deceive him since the record showed Brown to be a liar when he denied any intention to provoke slave insurrection: H. Clay Pate, *John Brown, as Viewed by H. Clay Pate* (New York, 1859), 5–7, 14–17, 21–2. On southern respect for John Brown as a real man ready to die for his beliefs see Kenneth S. Greenberg, *Honor and Slavery* (Princeton, NJ, 1996), ch. 4. In 1838 Emerson told the literary societies of Dartmouth College, "The capital secret is to convert life into truth." Elsewhere he described conscience as "that man within the breast" – which, Susan L. Roberson remarks, establishes "a further identification between man and God and transferring to man powers of the conscience and, therefore, of God." The equation, she adds, "also promotes Emerson's own bid for empowerment and autonomy": Roberson, *Emerson in His Sermons: A Man-Made Self* (Columbia, MO, 1995), 48–9.

[11] James Redpath, *The Public Life of Capt. John Brown, with an Autobiography of His Childhood* (Boston, 1860), 7–8, 13, 39, 45–6, 105, 190, quotes at 7, 8, 115, 119; on Pottawatamie see ch. 5; Hawthorne in Louis P. Masur, ed., *"The Real War Will Never Get in the Books": Selections from Writers during the Civil War* (New York, 1993), 174. Redpath also referred to David Hunter Strother ("Porte Crayon") as a "fiendish historian of [John Brown's] holy invasion" of Virginia: 263. Redpath responded to secession by calling for "John Brown expeditions" and "simultaneous and extended Negro insurrections." Quoted in Howard C. Perkins, "The Defense of Slavery in the Northern Press on the Eve of the Civil War," *JSH*, 9 (1943), 501.

notorious as robbers and pirates, he was a religious enthusiast." Howe did not disguise a sneaking admiration for "a man of iron will, of great self-reliance, with the courage of a mastiff." The military offered tributes. Robert E. Lee – who captured him at Harper's Ferry – said, "I am glad we did not have to kill him, for I believe he is an honest, conscientious old man." J. T. L. Preston, on military duty at Brown's hanging, said Brown was "intrepid, without being braggart," "a man of strong and bloody hand, of fierce passions, of iron will." Thomas (Stonewall) Jackson testified to Brown's dignity, military bearing, and "unflinching firmness" on the gallows. Jackson prayed that Brown was prepared to meet his Maker but doubted that he was.[12]

The comparison of Brown to Jesus invited charges of blasphemy. An appalled George Howe lashed Emerson and the northern clergy. He quoted J. Q. A. Griffin, a Massachusetts politician, as saying that Pontius Pilate's crucifixion of Jesus "whitened into virtue" when compared with Wise's treatment of John Brown. Southern preachers would not let their congregations forget that the North had transformed Brown into a martyred saint and exposed their own yearning to turn the South into another Saint Domingue. In Columbia, South Carolina, Yankee occupiers outraged Emma LeConte by telling freedmen that John Brown died for them, much as Christ had died for the human race. Abolitionists deified Brown as Republicans later deified Lincoln, interpreting his assassination as atonement for America's sins and lauding Tolstoy's depiction of "a Christ in miniature." A poor black woman thought that she had lost more than her God, for God had made her a slave whereas Lincoln had set her free.[13]

---

[12] See the text of Booth's speech written in Philadelphia in December 1860 but probably never delivered: John Rhodehamel and Louise Taper, eds, *"Right or Wrong, God Judge Me": The Writings of John Wilkes Booth* (Urbana, IL, 1997), 55–64 (reference to Brown on 60); [George Howe], "The Raid of John Brown, and the Progress of Abolition," *SPR*, 12 (1860), 804; Lee quoted in William J. Johnson, *Robert E. Lee the Christian* (Arlington Heights, IL, n.d.), 55; James Preston to Margaret Junkin Preston, Dec. 2, 1859, in Elizabeth Preston Allan, *The Life and Letters of Margaret Junkin Preston* (Boston, 1923), 49, 112–13, full text on 111–17; T. J. Jackson to Mary Anna Jackson, Dec. 2, 1859, in Mary A. Jackson, *The Life and Letters of General Thomas J. Jackson (Stonewall)* (New York, 1892), 130–2, quote at 130.

[13] [Howe], "Raid of John Brown," 811; Merrill D. Peterson, *Lincoln in American Memory* (New York, 1994), 7–8, 219; Gardiner H. Shattuck, Jr., *A Shield and Hiding Place: The Religious Life of the Civil War Armies* (Macon, GA, 1987), 16–17, 114; Paul Finkelman, "John Brown's Raid," in Finkelman, ed., *His Soul Goes Marching On: Responses to John Brown and the Harper's Ferry Raid* (Charlottesville, VA, 1995), 3, 5–6; Apr. 13, 1864, in Earl Schenck Miers, ed., *When the World Ended: The Diary of Emma LeConte* (New York, 1957), 85. For the preachers, see e.g. Henry H. Tucker, *God in the War: A Sermon Delivered before the Legislature of Georgia* (Milledgeville, GA, 1861), 7. For a sober account of northern reactions to Harper's Ferry see Finkelman's "Manufacturing Martyrdom," loc. cit., 41–66. Finkelman sums up well: "Brown wrote brilliant letters that helped to create, in the minds of some Northerners, his image as a Christ-like martyr, who gave his life so that the slaves might be free." For a fierce critique of the invocation of Lincoln as Christ figure see M. E. Bradford, *A Better Guide than Reason: Studies in the American Revolution* (LaSalle, IL, 1979), 29–57, 185–203. During the late nineteenth and the twentieth centuries, liberals continued to compare Brown to Jesus: see Peterson, *John Brown*, 60, 154. Even the ablest southern theologians occasionally slipped into the same mire they accused abolitionists of slipping into. Dabney shocked William Brown, editor of *Central Presbyterian*, by comparing the criminality of the North with the crucifixion of Jesus. Brown

Long after the War, Southerners remembered their horror at Brown's raid and pondered its implications. John Wise, the governor's son, indirectly replied to Emerson's jibe at his father: "Pity, pity, pity it is to see that splendid quality perverted and destroyed by such fatal accompaniments .... It was with a genuine sigh of admiration for this fortitude that, without one doubt about their duty, the Virginians imposed the penalty for his crime upon John Brown." John Wise recorded Virginians' shock at the northern reaction to Brown's raid and to northern women's dubbing Brown "St. John the Just" – perhaps in a cutting allusion to St. Just of the Reign of Terror? Southerners' hostility toward women preachers improved not at all when they learned that Antoinette Brown Blackwell, a Congregationalist (later Unitarian) and the first woman ordained as a minister by a leading denomination, had hailed John Brown as a hero and a martyr while reaffirming her preference for nonviolence. Senator T. M. Norwood of Georgia assailed Brown as a quintessential Puritan fanatic who perfectly represented Yankee sensibilities. W. H. Holcombe of Natchez, writing in the 1890s, still shuddered at his response as a boy to Nat Turner's slave revolt, which conditioned his shock at Brown's raid. Holcombe referred to Turner as "a black John Brown."[14]

William A. Freehling rejects the "fable" that Brown's raid, like the Nat Turner revolt in 1831, terrified the South and plunged it toward secession. Freehling offers a necessary corrective. As he says, secessionism had been building slowly over time and, if Southerners reacted forcefully to acts of violence, they showed no signs of panic. We should not, however, carry the corrective so far as to deny that the northern response to Brown's raid deeply affected southern politics. Throughout the South, even most unionists recognized secession as a right but opposed it as injudicious. Little by little the unionist ranks thinned as one event or another proved the proverbial last straw for this or that individual. For many, Harper's Ferry or its aftermath either proved to be that last straw or put them in a frame of mind to reject Lincoln's election more firmly than they might have done.[15]

feared blasphemy. See Sean Michael Lucas, " 'Hold Fast that Which Is Good': The Public Theology of Robert Lewis Dabney" (Ph.D. diss., Westminster Theological Seminary, 2002), 141.

[14] John S. Wise, *End of an Era* (Boston, 1900), 132–4 and ch. 9, quotes at 132, 134. Thomas Manson Norwood, *A True Vindication of the South: In a Review of American Political History* (Savannah, GA, 1917), 42–3; William H. Holcombe, "Autobiography" (ms.), 66, at UNC-SHC. On the strong anti-abolitionist reaction after John Brown's raid see Renehan, *Secret Six*, 236–7, and Peterson, *John Brown*, 11; on northern women in the forefront of the women's-rights movement who spearheaded the campaign to turn John Brown into a martyr, see W. H. Venet, " 'Cry Aloud and Spare Not,' " in Finkelman, ed., *His Soul Goes Marching On*, 101 and ch. 4; by then Blackwell had become a Unitarian: *DCA*, 165. In 1863 a Pennsylvania-born but prosouthern tutor was still expressing outrage at northern praise of John Brown: Emilie Riley McKinley, June 19, 1863, in Gordon A. Cotton, ed., *From the Pen of a She-Rebel: The Civil War Diary of Emilie Riley McKinley* (Columbia, SC, 2001), 32. Suspicion of and hostility to Northerners was especially severe in Maryland, which reeled under the impact of John Brown's raid. Bart Rhett Talbert, *Maryland: The South's First Casualty* (Berryville, VA, 1995), 13–15. For a contemporary remark on the intense fear of a slave insurrection in Coosa County (Alabama) after John Brown's raid, see Davis Blake Carter, *The Story of Uncle Minyard Told: A Family's 200-Year Migration across the South* (Spartanburg, SC, 1994), 203.

[15] William W. Freehling, *The Road to Disunion* (New York, 1990), 178. Freehling has since suggested that, although Brown's raid did not inflame the South, subsequent northern support for Brown did.

The death of Calhoun in 1850 had created an opportunity for unionists to swing the Democrats of South Carolina toward cooperation with the national party, and they made substantial progress until Brown's raid strengthened the secessionists. The northern response appalled C. G. Memminger, a veteran southern unionist, who saw a strong current of conservatism in the North but was badly shaken by the subsequent elections. In Virginia, William P. J. Pegram's regiment could muster no more than 350 men before Harper's Ferry; the number doubled afterwards. In North Carolina, the northern reaction proved a windfall for Thomas Clingman in his electoral struggle against the unionists. In Alabama, Albert Barry Moore, future war governor, spoke softly as a unionist Democrat until Brown's raid left him feeling betrayed. During the election campaign of 1859 in Texas, unionists Sam Houston and John Reagan had put aside their differences to throw the radical Louis Wigfall on the defensive . Brown's raid catapulted Wigfall into the Senate. Southern students left northern campuses to protest the response to Harper's Ferry. At the University of Mississippi, students beat and branded their black servants and carried guns on campus in defiance of the rules. The agitation over Harper's Ferry coincided with a wave of arson across the South, generally attributed to slaves. No evidence of coordination among slaves or of an abolitionist conspiracy exists. But Southerners had difficulty believing in coincidence. Virginians, in particular, saw a relation between Brown's raid and an ensuing wave of arson: Edmund Ruffin reported from Charleston on that wave, for which he blamed abolitionists. When a rash of fires terrified Texas and then Georgia, whites attributed them to abolitionist-inspired slave arson. In Tennessee, local mobs hanged blacks. In Rapides Parish, Louisiana, ten or more blacks arrested on suspicion were lynched before trial. And yet, in the endless ambiguity of southern life, whites congratulated themselves that, after all, no slave revolt had occurred anywhere, proving – or so the story went – that, despite all provocations, the slaves remained contented and loyal to their masters.[16]

The argument for a powerful impact on southern politics of John Brown's raid is made in Steven A. Channing, *Crisis in Fear: Secession in South Carolina* (New York, 1970); and Clarence L. Mohr, *On the Threshold of Freedom: Masters and Slaves in Civil War Georgia* (Athens, GA, 1986). For typical reactions by unionists who turned sharply in Mississippi see Frank A. Montgomery, "Reminiscences," excerpted in James W. Silver, ed., *Mississippi in the Confederacy: As Seen in Retrospect* (Baton Rouge, LA, 1961), 28; also, George Green Shackelford, *George Wythe Randolph and the Confederate Elite* (Athens, GA, 1988), 43–4, 47–8; Clyde N. Wilson, *Carolina Cavalier: The Life and Mind of James Johnston Pettigrew* (Athens, GA, 1990), 113–14, 130–1. John Brown radicalized the generally unionist students in Virginia: Peter S. Carmichael, *The Last Generation: Young Virginians in Peace, War and Reunion, 1850–1900* (Chapel Hill, NC, 2005), ch. 3.

[16] Roy F. Nichols, *The Disruption of American Democracy* (New York, 1948), 151, 266, 355–6; Henry McGilbert Wagstaff, *States Rights and Political Parties in North Carolina, 1776–1861* (Baltimore, 1906), 104–5; Henry D. Capers, *The Life and Times of C. G. Memminger* (Richmond, VA, 1893), 254–6; Peter S. Carmichael, *Lee's Young Artillerist: William J. Pegram* (Charlottesville, VA, 1995), 20–1; John C. Inscoe, *Mountain Masters: Slavery, and the Sectional Crisis in Western North Carolina* (Knoxville, TN, 1989), 211–23; Ben H. Proctor, *Not without Honor: The Life of John H. Reagan* (Austin, TX, 1962), 112–14; Malcolm C. McMillan, *The Disintegration of a Confederate State: Three Governors and Alabama's Wartime Home Front, 1861–1865* (Macon, GA, 1986), 11 (Moore); Alvy L. King, *Louis T. Wigfall: Southern Fire-eater* (Baton Rouge, LA, 1970), 4, 70–2, 77–8, 99–100; for the students see Arthur Charles Cole, *The Irrepressible Conflict, 1850–1865* (New York, 1934), 45–6,

For a while Northerners had a bad time in the South, as angry mobs tarred and feathered suspected abolitionists. Businessmen, usually shielded from political uproars, returned home after deciding that this latest wave of anti-Yankeeism had turned dangerous. Catherine Cooper Hopley measured the Virginians' bitterness and took pains to let people know that she was English, not Yankee. Slaveholders voiced fears that some Border State yeomen and workingmen harbored antislavery views and secretly sympathized with Brown. James Anderson, a planter in central North Carolina, wrote his son, who would soon marry the daughter of James Henley Thornwell, "I believe we have among us a great many who would not have been distressed if Jno. Brown had succeeded." He recounted the words of an old local magistrate: "He will be talked of as much as Gen. Washington two hundred years hence." Anderson snorted, "He forgets that it is a 'successful treason that makes a hero.'" During the War in coastal North Carolina, a good many artisans, laborers, and small farmers spoke sympathetically of Brown.[17]

The rising voices of pro-Brown clergy in the North strengthened the secessionism of Bishops Stephen Elliott of Georgia and Leonidas Polk of Louisiana. In 1861 the New Orleans *Daily Picayune* published a pro-secession Fast Day sermon by the Methodist Reverend Joseph B. Walker, who thundered: "They have glorified as a martyr and canonized as a saint, a blood-thirsty ruffian and midnight assassin, who more than any other stained his hands with unoffending southern blood, and died as a felon on the gallows." In Tennessee, Franc Carmack of the Disciples of Christ embodied within himself the conflicted reactions of many unionists. On New Year's Day of 1860 he reflected on the upheavals in Europe and the rise of powerful new tyrants. As for the United States, "The excitement and the events of Harper's Ferry are transferred to the Congress of the United States, and 1860 finds the jarring elements of political power in collision at Washington, threatening the dissolution of our once glorious Union. The end is not yet. 1860 may record the last hope of history of the United States, and begin to record – perhaps in letters of blood – the annals of the Disseveral States of America." Columbus Morrison, a small slaveholder in Georgia, spoke for countless laymen when he invoked another version of the Golden Rule in a comment on rumors of an attempt to rescue Brown and his comrades: "It is hoped that none will escape. Philanthropy calls for their blood."

and James Allen Cabaniss, *A History of the University of Mississippi* (University, MS, 1949), 54. Philip J. Schwarz, *Twice Condemned: Slaves and the Criminal Law of Virginia, 1705–1865* (Baton Rouge, LA, 1988), 308–11; Nov. 22, 1850, in *ERD*, 1:359; Ophelia Settle Egypt et al., eds., *Unwritten History of Slavery: Autobiographical Accounts of Ex-Slaves* (Washington, DC, 1968), 59; Terry L. Seip, "Slaves and Free Negroes in Alexandria, 1850–1860," *Louisiana History*, 10 (1969), 147–65; Mohr, *Threshold of Freedom*, chs. 1 and 2.

[17] Catherine Cooper Hopley, *Life in the South from the Commencement of the War*, 2 vols. (New York, 1971 [1863]), 1:8–9. On southern students in the North see Clement Eaton, *The Freedom-of-Thought Struggle in the Old South* (New York, 1964), 230–2; J. O. Breeden, "Rehearsal for Secesssion," in Finkelman, ed., *His Soul Goes Marching On*, 174–210; James Anderson to Robert Burton Anderson, n.d. but obviously 1859, in Anderson–Thornwell Papers, at UNC-SHC; Wayne K. Durrill, *War of Another Kind: A Southern Community in the Great Rebellion* (New York, 1990), 53, 60. In South Carolina, Brown's raid led to considerable agitation to reduce the already frail rights and privileges of free blacks: H. M. Henry, *The Police Control of the Slave in South Carolina* (New York, 1968), 188–9.

Governor John Pettus of Mississippi cited northern applause for John Brown to justify his demand for secession. For a contributor to *Southern Literary Messenger* in
1862, John Brown epitomized anti-Christian northern philanthropy.[18]

"The logical manipulation of concepts in the mind," writes Marion Montgomery, "does not issue in an actual restructuring of the community of being in nature.
What does result, however, is heroic self-righteousness in which a willful alienation from existence is declared virtue rather than sin." On the eve of secession,
Keziah Brevard of South Carolina made that point in her own way. She condemned
"that wretch John Brown," who might have come in the spirit of Jesus and the
apostles to help uplift the slaves but instead brought the threat of a war of extermination. She prayed to God to change the "wicked ways" of "those northern cut
throats" and "selfish & envious sons of Satan" and to give her the strength not to
hate them. But, she wondered, how could Southerners not hate those who wanted
to exterminate them? Slaveholders would get along fine with their slaves if only
those "un-Christian" Yankees would leave them alone. But the fanatical Yankees
believe they are doing God's work. They really believe that "we are sinners as if
they were pure & undefiled." Bertram Wyatt-Brown has remarked that, although
John Brown is usually pictured as a Calvinist, in fact he had a quirky religion of his
own – quirky and Antinomian: "Only Brown actually brought insurrectionary action and antinomian ideas together as a conscious, aggressive, and dynamic part of
the abolitionist movement."[19]

Mary Brown, John Brown's widow, said that religion had always been "the ruling
motive of his life." Southerners did not doubt her, but they found no Christianity
in his religion.[20]

---

[18] New Orleans *Daily Picayune*, June 13, 1861 – a copy was clipped and inserted in the C. C. Carter Pa-
      pers, at Southwestern Louisiana University (Hammond); Franc M. Carmack Diary, Jan. 1, 1860, at
      UNC-SHC; Dunbar Rowland, ed., *Mississippi: Comprising Sketches of Counties, Towns, Events, In-
      stitutions, and Persons, Arranged in Cyclopedic Form*, 4 vols. (Spartanburg, SC, 1976 [1907]), 2:636
      (Pettus); Joseph H. Parks, *General Leonidas Polk, C.S.A.: The Fighting Bishop* (Baton Rouge, LA,
      1962), 153; Columbus Morrison Journal, Nov. 13, 1859, at UNC-SHC; "Christianity versus Philan-
      thropy," *SLM*, 34 (1862), 574–6.
[19] Marion Montgomery, *Possum: And Other Receits [sic] for the Recovery of "Southern" Being* (Ath-
      ens, GA, 1987), 44; Brevard Diary, Oct. 12, 24, 1860, Nov. 2, 1860, Mar. 3, 1861, at UNC-SHC; Bertram
      Wyatt-Brown, *Yankee Saints and Southern Sinners* (Baton Rouge, LA, 1985), 103, 116 (quoted), and
      see ch. 4 for a fine discussion of Brown and the significance of Harper's Ferry.
[20] Mary Brown quoted in Quarles, ed., *Blacks on John Brown*, xiii.

PART FIVE

AT THE RUBICON

Take we the course which the signs of the Gods and the false dealing of our foes point out. The die is cast.

—Julius Caesar, according to Suetonius

21

Between Individualism and Corporatism

From the Reformation to the War for Southern Independence

> We quarrel not with the reformation of Luther and Calvin, but with "the right of private judgment" engrafted on it by infidels and fanatics. It has begotten socialism, infidelity, agrarianism, abolitionism, and radicalism of every hue and shade.
>
> —George Fitzhugh [1]

The centuries between the end of the Middle Ages – roughly the conclusion of the Hundred Years' War – and the American Revolution confronted Southerners with a succession of special and troubling problems. For these were the years during which many of their most cherished values took shape and gained a secure base. Historians have argued about whether the decisive changes originated in the material or ideological realm and whether they were promoted by one or another social group. Did the bourgeoisie "cause" the French Revolution, or, increasingly, was it a "revolution" at all? The debates over the origins of capitalism and individualism show no promise of abating any time soon. What remains beyond debate is that Southerners in general and slaveholders in particular simultaneously embraced and repulsed aspects of the changes that had shaped their own society and worldview but that increasingly threatened their destruction.

The Reformation that spawned Protestant denominations from orthodox to liberal heightened the centrality of individual conscience, the individual's obligation to read and interpret Scripture, and the concept of a priesthood of all believers. It thereby invited a dangerous religious radicalism. Capitalism had brought the acceleration of trade and expansion of markets that gave birth to the slaveholding South and sustained its survival. By the early nineteenth century, capitalism, accelerating the expansion of free labor, transformed much of the labor it "freed" into an exploited and disaffected working class. Southerners held fast to key tenets of individualism, notably absolute property rights, representative government, and the equality of those who qualified to be considered individuals – primarily, propertied free men.

---

[1] George Fitzhugh, "Disunion within the Union," *DBR,* 28 (1860), 6.

The history of the last three centuries posed for nineteenth-century slavehold-ers, as for other Christian traditionalists and political conservatives, the daunting question of how to tame what was beginning to look like a permanent revolution. Many Southerners were reluctant to concede that historical developments they had been taught to admire may have been misguided from the start. No Protestant could repudiate the Reformation, but no few wondered where and how it should be arrested.

The Reformation should have offered southern Protestants an uplifting story of the origins of the very spirit of individual initiative that had led to the founding of their own society. But what the Reformation gave with one hand it took away with the other. George Frederick Holmes identified clearly the main problem: The Reformation's spirit of radical individualism did not comport well with the corpo-ratism inherent in the slaveholders' worldview. Holmes found the root of current political heresy in the damage done by the Reformation to the principle of author-ity. In 1829 *Southern Review,* reviewing the progress of education in Germany, rejected the dichotomy of a progressive Protestantism and reactionary Catholicism. The author maintained that in the sixteenth century Catholics instituted deep, salu-tary reforms and in modern Germany actually matched Protestant efforts to uplift the poor and the laboring classes through education and other social measures. In *Southern Literary Messenger* in 1838, E. A. Lynch wondered if the Reformation had been worth the slaughters of the religious wars and the proliferation of sects that risked every kind of error and outright infidelity. Might it not have been "bet-ter to have purified and remodeled the ancient temple, venerable for its age and coeval with Christianity"? As it happened, Protestants proceeded with "angry and exacerbated feeling," and "The red car of reform rolled in the blood of slaughtered recusants." Admirable, necessary, and healthy reforms proceeded with "licentious indulgence and lax morality." Lynch drew a straight line between the revolt against authority and the emergence of Voltaire and Rousseau.[2]

---

[2] [George Frederick Holmes], "Spencer's Social Statics," *QRMECS,* 10 (1856), 185–219; "Education in Germany," *SR,* 4 (1829), 89–90, 11; E. A. Lynch, "Influence of Morals on the Happiness of Man," *SLM,* 4 (1838), 145–51, 273–80. Teaching at Richmond College in the late 1840s and at the University of Virginia from 1857, Holmes criticized the Reformation ever more firmly and assigned his students reading largely from Catholic authors: Neal C. Gillespie, "The Spiritual Odyssey of George Frederick Holmes: A Study in Religious Conservatism in the Old South," *JSH,* 32 (1966), 299. What Theodore Dwight Bozeman says about the Presbyterians applied to other southern Protestants: "The Old School wished to see in the Reformation nothing less than the foundations of modern learning and enter-prise": Bozeman, *Protestants in an Age of Science: The Baconian Ideal and Antebellum Amercan Religious Thought* (Chapel Hill, NC, 1977), 125.

  We have found nothing about E. A. Lynch other than his identification as a former resident of Pe-tersburg, Virginia. Possibly he was a Catholic, but if so, so much the more significant that *Southern Literary Messenger* published his article. "A Native of Goochland, Virginia" replied to Lynch in the August issue via "Benefits of the Reformation on the Happiness of Man," *SLM,* 4 (1838), 524–8, in which he eloquently recited the standard Protestant account of the Catholic Church's evil deeds. Lynch saw the outburst of freedom of thought as an invitation to confusion and infidelity; his critic saw a triumph of Christian virtue in the expansion of free thought and the encouragement to free institutions. John Blair Dabney defended *sola scriptura* as the foundation of American religious and

Most southern commentators, Arminian and Calvinist, were guided by the eminent historians Johann Lorenz von Mosheim and Jean Henri Merle D'Aubigné in locating the origins of modern individualism in the Reformation and credited it with liberation of the human mind, stimulation of science, and promotion of commerce. The Reverend J. L. Reynolds of Charleston drew on Mosheim to support specific Baptist interpretations of history and doctrine, and the Methodist Protestant Reverend A. A. Lipscomb treasured him as historian of Catholic atrocities. Southerners followed Edward Gibbon in crediting Mosheim with the extrication of church history from theology and admired his not-always-successful effort at scientific objectivity and what Kenneth Scott Latourette has called his "irenic orthodoxy." D'Aubigné's *History of the Reformation in the Sixteenth Century* also became popular in the South, invoked as authoritative by Thomas Roderick Dew, John Fletcher, and other secular as well as clerical writers. Baptists and Presbyterians alike found merit in his work, and the Presbyterian Reverend John Bocock even found in it evidence that Luther and all the great leaders of the Reformation basically espoused Calvinism. The Methodist "J. E. C." of Arkansas, however, criticized D'Aubigné for slighting the impact of free will and imposing predestinarianism on historical events.[3]

Southern divines joined the abolitionist George Cheever in applauding D'Aubigné's defense of religious freedom and separation of church and state. The private papers of educated laymen, too, contain references to D'Aubigné on Catholic persecution of Protestants and the travail of the Huguenots. D'Aubigné's accounts of Protestant martyrs and Catholic barbarism fascinated Elizabeth Ruffin of Virginia and Marianne Palmer Gaillard of Alabama, who, like many other women, devoured

political liberty, and criticism from Anglicans and Catholics generated some ringing reaffirmations of that doctrine. Even the theologically liberal Unitarian Reverend Theodore Clapp of New Orleans claimed to stand on *sola scriptura* as strongly as any Reformed Protestant. John Blair Dabney, "Capt. Marryatt," *SLM,* 7 (1841), 265–6; see also the extensive Editors' Note to "The Annals of the English Bible," *SQR,* 9 (1846), 477–9; Theodore Clapp, Sermons, New Orleans *Daily Picayune,* May 28, 1848, Mar. 4 and 13, 1849. For a defense of Luther as a champion of freedom of thought, see George Herbert Calvert, "German Literature," *SLM,* 2 (1836), 375.

3 J. H. Merle D'Aubigné, *History of the Reformation of the Sixteenth Century,* 5 vols. (Rapidan, VA, reproduction of London edition of 1846), 418; J. L. Reynolds, *Church Polity: Or, the Kingdom of Christ in Its Internal and External Development,* 2nd ed. (Richmond, VA, 1849), 96, 160, 187–9; Andrew A. Lipscomb, *Our Country: Its Danger and Duty* (New York, 1844), 67; [J. H. Bocock], "The Reformation in England," *SPR,* 7 (1858), 163–4; Thomas Roderick Dew, *Digest of the Laws, Customs, Manners, and Institutions of the Ancient and Modern Nations* (New York, 1884 [1852]), 365; John Fletcher, *Studies on Slavery, in Easy Lessons* (Natchez, MS, 1852), 263, 358; Kenneth Scott Latourette, *Christianity in a Revolutionary Age,* 5 vols. (Grand Rapids, MI, 1958), 1:64; "J. E. C.", "Review of Daubigné's Theory of Divine Agency, in the History of the Reformation," *QRMECS,* 2 (1848), 208–27 ("J. E. C." was incensed that the American Tract Society published a work he considered flagrantly sectarian). See also Robert L. Dabney, *Systematic Theology* (Carlisle, PA, 1985 [1878]), Syllabus and 469; Cottrell Diary, Nov. 8, 1855, at UNC-SHC; C. Beatty Diary, Aug. 13, 1843, at UNC-SHC. "H. R.", "The Slow Progress of Mankind," *SLM,* 18 (1852), 404; "Modern Republicanism," *SLM,* 19 (1853), 545–52. For Mosheim on Baptist roots see Hosea Holcombe, *A History of the Rise and Progress of the Baptists in Alabama* (Philadelphia, 1840), 16, 24, 27. See also Supplementary References: "D'Aubigné and Mosheim."

histories of the Reformation and the Inquisition. But in 1843 *Southern Quarterly Review* said that his work had been "magnified into a great literary production by indiscreet and undiscriminating praise." Finding D'Aubigné's account of history and doctrine wanting and biased, it coolly recommended the cheap new edition to "an intelligent but not highly educated family." In an about-face in 1846, it acknowledged D'Aubigné as the towering figure in Reformation history.[4]

Protestant Southerners increasingly wondered aloud: Did the Reformation bear responsibility for the individualism that was now careening out of hand? Criticism began with criticism of Luther, perhaps in part because the Presbyterians, the South's theological luminaries, prized their own descent from Calvin. A contributor to *Southern Literary Messenger,* referring to Luther's "bluntness and impetuosity" and his "incoherence and vanity," quoted his blood-chilling recommendation that the German lords slaughter rebellious peasants, condemned his submission to oppressive German princes, and concluded that he hardly qualified as a champion of secular freedom. The Reformation, he added, bequeathed to Germany a political state no freer than that of Catholic Spain. The Reverend J. R. Graves, the fierce Landmark Baptist, assailed Luther as an enemy of civil and religious liberty who led his church into an "adulterous union" with the state.[5]

Another contributor to *Southern Literary Messenger* complained that if Catholic "superstition" had retarded the arts in the Middle Ages, Protestant "iconoclastism" compounded the error. Dew found "melancholy" the course of Protestants, who began the Reformation by proclaiming freedom of thought and opposing religious

---

4 George B. Cheever, *Wanderings of a Pilgrim in the Shadow of Mont Blanc and the Jungfrau Alp* (Glasgow, 1865), 46–7. According to William Gilmore Simms's friends, the Duyckincks, *Jungfrau* was "favorably received": Evert A. Duyckinck and George L. Duyckinck, *Cyclopaedia of American Literature,* 2 vols. (New York, 1856), 2:454. Simms nonetheless dismissed it as "commonplace declamation without the slightest particle of freshness": Simms to Evert Augustus Duyckinck, Feb. 9, 1846, in Mary C. Oliphant et al., eds., *The Letters of William Gilmore Simms,* 6 vols. (Columbia, SC, 1952–82), 2:143. Elizabeth Ruffin Diary, Feb. 11 and 13, 1827, in Edmund Ruffin Papers, at UNC-SHC. For reminders of Catholic persecution of the Huguenot see also W. Noel Sainsbury, ed., "The French Protestants of the Abbeville District, S.C., 1761–1765," in *Collections of the South-Carolina Historical Society,* 2 vols. (Charleston, SC, 1858), 2:75–103; Marianne Palmer Gaillard to John S. Palmer, Aug. 8, 1844, in Louis P. Towles, ed., *A World Turned Upside Down: The Palmers of South Santee, 1818–1881* (Columbia, SC, 1996), 95, and Harriet R. Palmer Diary, Jan. 8, 1861, loc. cit., 285; also, Philip Schaff, *History of the Christian Church,* 1:45–6. Maria Bryan Connell of Georgia praised D'Aubigné's eloquence and piety: Connell to Julia Ann Bryan Cumming, Apr. 1, 1843, in Carol Bleser, ed., *Tokens of Affection: The Letters of a Planter's Daughter in the Old South* (Athens, GA, 1996), 359–60. *Southern Quarterly Review* declared D'Aubigné well known and much admired: *SQR,* 9 (1846), 544; it also recommended D'Aubigné's "beautiful introduction" to Calvin, which it quoted at length: *SQR,* 6 (1844), 257–8. For the discordant note see *SQR,* 4 (1843), 514, but also "Critical Notices," *SQR,* 9 (1846), 544. For the reading of D'Aubigné see the following manuscripts, at UNC-SHC: McCorkle Diary, Jan. 1 and 4, 1846, Mar. 4, 1847; Garrett Diary, 1849; Carmack Diary, Oct. 16 and 23, 1852; Carmichael Diary, Oct. 16, 1852; Agnew Diary, May 6, 1854, Feb.–Mar. 1863; L. W. Butler Diary, Jan.–May 1863. Also, R. H. Kim in W. A. R. Goodwin, ed., *The History of the Theological Seminary in Virginia and Its Historical Background,* 2 vols. (New York, 1923), 2:187. Also, Bocock's review in C. R. Vaughan, ed., *Selections from the Religious and Literary Writings of John H. Bocock* (Richmond, VA, 1891), 246–7.

5 "Martin Luther, His Character and Times," *SLM,* 4 (1838), 596–602; J. R. Graves, *Trilemma: Or, Death by Three Horns,* 2nd ed. (Texarkana, TX, 1881 [1860]), 103.

persecution – and then persecuted each other. In a discourse lauded by *Southern Quarterly Review,* the Episcopalian Reverend William Baker Stevens, Georgia's notable historian, remarked wryly that Carolina was settled "by Huguenots escaping from Papal bigotry; Maryland, by Papists, retiring before Protestant intolerance." The South's leading theological liberals, Episcopalian James Warley Miles of South Carolina and New School Presbyterian Frederick Ross of Alabama, spoke harshly: Miles about hidebound institutions that petrified the Reformation's principle of freedom and unleashed "licentiousness, folly, and skepticism"; Ross about the transit of liberty advanced by the Reformation into licentiousness. For Ross, inalienable rights adhered not to individuals but to families governed by rules and subordination: "*Mankind is only the congeries of families.*"[6]

J. S. Lamar of the Disciples of Christ groaned that Protestants who professed the right of private judgment rarely practiced it and, instead, transformed their churches into agents of coercion and repression. Edmund Ruffin, who supported Luther on the right of private judgment, excoriated the Protestant churches for generating a veritable "priesthood" of thought control and "fear & terror." The people select their own churches and deceive themselves that they are exercising private judgment, whereas in practice they accept the interpretations of scripture laid down by the clergy or risk giving offense to "all associates – perhaps all friends and kindred – to be denounced by all & to be excommunicated from Christian fellowship & friendly association with all."[7]

John Calvin's burning of Michael Servetus haunted discussions of the Reformation. The caustic J. R. Graves depicted Episcopalianism as "black and bloody with the murders of the martyrs of Jesus" and turned on Calvin, pointing to the fate of

---

[6] Dew condemned as a disgrace Mary's persecution of English Protestants, and with comparable fervor he sternly chronicled the English bloody conquest of Ireland in Cromwell's time: "Influence of the Fine Arts on the National Character," *SLM,* 30 (1860), 204–5; Dew, *Digest,* 456–8; William Baker Stevens, *The Providence of God, in the Settlement and Protection of Georgia* (Athens, GA, 1845), 10; see "Critical Notices," *SQR,* 8 (1845), 525; [James Warley Miles], "The Aggressive Nature of Christianity," *RM,* 1 (1857), 199; Frederick A. Ross, *Slavery Ordained of God* (Philadelphia, 1857), 48, 118–19, quote at 149–50. For a protest against Protestant persecution of Catholics and each other – delivered, significantly, at a high school in South Carolina – see J. W. Tucker [a judge in St. Louis], *Thoughts on Truth as Applied to Practical Christianity* (Mobile, AL, 1864), 13–14.

[7] J. S. Lamar, *The Organon of Scripture; Or, the Inductive Method of Biblical Interpretation* (Philadelphia, 1860), 128–47; Ruffin, June 18 and Aug. 9, 1863, Feb. 24 and 25, 1864, *ERD,* 3:16–17, 346, 349. For an earlier complaint that the Protestant churches have not upheld the Reformation ideal of a right to private judgment, see *Baltimore Monthly Visiter* [*sic*], 1 (1842), 32.

Protestant offenses against religious freedom during the Reformation caused heartburn for American evangelicals of various stripes. The Baptist John Leland of Virginia and Massachusetts, having condemned Constantine for his repression of Arian heretics and pagans, condemned the German Anabaptists for having repeated the error during the Reformation: John Leland, "The Rights of Conscience Inalienable" (1791), in Ellis Sandoz, ed., *Political Sermons of the American Founding Era, 1730–1805* (Indianapolis, IN, 1991), 1083. The abolitionist version of higher-law doctrine posed a challenge to the right of private judgment, touching off considerable soul-searching among southern Protestants, who noticed that the plurality of voices led to widespread disagreements over the truth of the Bible. See e.g. "The Doctrine of the Higher Law," *SLM,* 17 (1851), 130–42; Holt Wilson, "Socrates and Philosophy," *SLM,* 29 (1859), 14–29.

Servetus. Southern Presbyterians, defending Calvin, laid responsibility not on the church but on the state, which considered Servetus' teachings against the Trinity to be politically subversive. The Presbyterian Reverend Stuart Robinson of Kentucky, without mentioning Servetus, regretted that political realities had forced the Reformation to veer toward subservience of church to state (Erastianism). While tut-tutting the execution of Servetus as excessive, apologists took comfort in the fierce reaction of Catholics as well as anti-Calvinist Protestants to his anti-Trinitarian heresies. The Presbyterian Thomas Smyth of Charleston did not tut-tut but warmly embraced Hegel's defense of the execution. The imperatives of order trumped those of freedom. How could any slave master not know that much about the realities of life?[8]

Two seventeenth-century European Catholic writers especially appealed to southern intellectuals and preachers: Jacques-Bénigne Bossuet, a pillar of the Catholic Church and the Dauphin's tutor; and the aristocratic Abbot and Archbishop François de Salignac de la Mothe Fénelon, both (particularly Bossuet) widely admired despite their staunch support for monarchy in subordination to divine law as the most natural form of government. Fénelon excoriated the aristocracy for permitting the wretchedness of the lower classes, and, as southern critics knew well, publicly disavowed Louis XIV's militarism and the sexual laxity of his court. Catholic monarchism of this kind could readily be enlisted in the service of a conservative republicanism. Thus Francis Lieber spoke highly of "the works of the great Bossuet," which exposed the French addiction to the centralization and concentration of power, and the Presbyterian Reverend James Henley Thornwell, who choked on Bossuet's support for the revocation of the Edict of Nantes, acknowledged his stature. Presbyterians and Methodists agreed that the Catholic Church had not yet wholly degenerated and still boasted honest, intellectually and morally gifted men.[9]

---

[8] Graves, *Trilemma*, 104, 140; Stuart Robinson, *The Relations of the Secular and Spiritual Power* (Louisville, KY, 1859), 7; *TSW*, 9:328–9, 337–9. Smyth was in good odor at *Southern Quarterly Review*, which, however, objected to his defense of Calvin for an execution it considered indefensible: "Critical Notices," *SQR*, 3 (1843), 257. A Methodist Protestant minister warned that wherever the church becomes allied with the state, "It will be identified with all the infirmities and passions of men; it will be made eventually a party instrument; it will be enlisted in violent strife and struggle": Lipscomb, *Our Country*, 30.

   For other defenses of Calvin see: [James A. Wallace], "Michael Servetus," *SPR*, 9 (1856), 520–54; John B. Adger, "Calvin and Servetus," *SPR*, 30 (1879), 485–515; and an account of the burning of "this wretched Spaniard" in "The Life of Michael Servetus," *BRPR*, 8 (1836), 74–6, quote at 74. John L. Girardeau effectively put down the Catholic rationale that the state, not the Church, carried out executions, but his argument implicitly applied just as well to Calvin and Servetus: *Discussions of Theological Questions*, ed. George A. Blackburn (Harrisonburg, VA, 1986 [1905, written in 1890s]), 239. In a similar vein some writers, particularly in *Southern Quarterly Review*, excused the persecution of Christians by Marcus Aurelius (among other Roman emperors) as an attempt to defend religious toleration against a sect perceived to be bigoted and unwilling to respect the rights of others: see e.g. "Marcus Aurelius," *SQR*, n.s., 6 (1852), 360–413. A UVA graduate student came close to excusing the Romans in this way: W. B. Meredith, "Religious Intolerance" (M.A. thesis, 1859, typescript at UVA).

[9] Francis Lieber, *On Civil Liberty and Self-Government*, 3rd ed., rev. by Theodore D. Woolsey (Philadelphia, 1874 [1853]), 371; [James H. Thornwell], "Dictionary of Philosophical Sciences," *SQR*, n.s.

The South prided itself on its great orators and preachers, and A. B. Meek, Thomas Cobb, William H. Stiles, and George Dabney, among many Southerners who rejected Bossuet's monarchism, placed him among the world's greatest great orators and thinkers. Cobb called attention to Bossuet's judgment that condemnation of slavery condemned the Holy Spirit, who commanded it by the mouth of St. Paul. In 1857 an irritated contributor to *Southern Quarterly Review* protested that Southerners were lavishing praise, with only few offering criticism. The harshest of those few critics, Charles Farrar, criticized Fénelon's excessive rationalism and also Bossuet's "arrogant theory" of history. Yet, while Farrar condemned the theories of Bossuet and Giambattista Vico as "beneath the dignity of criticism," he acknowledged Bossuet as a foremost intellectual figure. In *Quarterly Review of the Methodist Episcopal Church, South*, "S." of South Carolina described Bossuet and Fénelon as "the greatest men in France." Daniel Whitaker cited Bossuet as an authority on literature, Mitchell King pronounced him a French ornament, and J. Q. Moore called him "sublime." Thomas Smyth enlisted him as an authority against scientific racism. Not necessarily in disagreement, George Frederick Holmes lauded Bossuet's *Discours sur l'histoire universelle* (1681) as a pioneering work in the philosophy of history that – along with those of Montequieu, Voltaire, and Michelet – demonstrated the races' uneven contributions to human development.[10]

Bossuet's *L'histoire universelle* treated Protestantism severely, yet its Augustinianism provided grist for the southern mill, insisting that providential intervention led men to Christianity, that the collective wisdom of communities takes precedence over individual insight, and that fidelity to tradition counts heavily in human affairs. He defended the Bible as authentic history and denied profane history any meaning without sacred history. Dew, an Episcopalian, risked the ire of Reformed Protestants by recalling Bossuet's charge, made "with great power," that Luther's

(3rd), 2 (1857), 346; "Character and Writings of Fénelon," *BRPR*, 24 (1852), 533–64, and 25 (1853), 165–203. Charles Hodge's *Biblical Repertory and Princeton Review* poured encomia over the four-volume *Oeuvres de Bossuet* (1837–44), pronouncing Bossuet worthy of the title "the French Demosthenes" and devoting some thirty pages to excerpts from his great sermons. See also "R. C. P.", "The Relation of Christianity to Literature," *QRMECS*, 1 (1847), 185.

10 A. B. Meek, *Romantic Passages in Southwestern History* (New York, 1857), 13; Thomas R. R. Cobb, *An Inquiry into the Law of Negro Slavery in the United States* (New York, 1968 [1858]), cix–cx n. 6; William H. Stiles, *Connection between Liberty and Eloquence: An Address Delivered before the Phi Kappa and Demosthenean Societies of Franklin College* (Augusta, GA, 1852), 21; and an anonymous writer in the *Southern Literary Messenger*, "The Inefficiency of the Pulpit," *SLM*, 24 (1857), 101. George E. Dabney, "Bossuet and Robert Hall," *SLM*, 11 (1845), 486–91; C. C. S. Farrar, "The Science of History," *DBR*, 5 (1848), 350 (Fénelon), 59, 211–14, 355; "Louis XIV," *SQR*, 11 (1855), 326–7; "S.", "Madame Guyon and Fénelon," *QRMECS*, 4 (1847), 479–509, quote at 499; [Daniel K. Whitaker], "From Our Arm-Chair," *SLJ*, 2 (1836), 235; Mitchell King, *A Discourse on the Qualifications and Duties of an Historian* (Savannah, GA, 1843), 20; J. Q. Moore, "Louis Napoleon and the French," *DBR*, 16 (1854), 384; "Unity of the Human Races," *TSW*, 8:88; George Frederick Holmes, "Schlegel's Philosophy of History," originally published in *SQR* (1843), 203–4, in Michael O'Brien, ed., *All Clever Men, Who Make Their Way: Critical Discourse in the Old South* (Fayetteville, AR, 1982), 182, 191; [G. F. Holmes], "Gibbon's Decline and Fall," *MMQR*, 4th ser., 10 (1856), 330. In opposition to Gibbon, Holmes welcomed Bossuet's Christian "vision" as a model for the reconstruction of Roman history and the rise of Christianity. See Supplementary References: "Bossuet."

Antinomian tendencies opened the floodgates to the radical Anabaptists and the bloody course of Thomas Münzer and John of Leyden.[11]

Bossuet's *History of the Variations of the Protestant Churches* laid the foundation for a critique of the individualism that Protestantism had unleashed. It opens with an account of the endless subdivisions that followed Luther's break with Rome and Protestant attempts to paper them over. It asserts that variations in faith constitute "a certain proof of falsehood" and that heresy is inherently changeable. Thus did Bossuet, in effect, attack all Protestants in the same terms in which orthodox Protestants, including southern, were attacking liberals. *Variations'* account of doctrinal controversies earned the respect of European Protestant theologians. Robert Dabney, whose opinion of the Catholic Church bordered on the unprintable, nevertheless cited *Variations* by "that great papal divine, Bossuet." The Reverend J. L. Reynolds even managed to mine Bossuet for support of the Baptists' doctrine of immersion. The Baptist Reverend J. L. Burrows ranked Bossuet and Fénelon among Christianity's ornaments, much as the Methodist Protestant Reverend Andrew Lipscomb set Thomas à Kempis and Blaise Pascal apart as men whose lives demonstrated the inability of popes to realize fully their aspirations to absolute power.[12]

Orthodox Protestants could swallow Bossuet's formidable assaults on Protestantism because he exposed doctrinal variations as a sign of error and because they valued his optimistic historical vision of progress as the spread of Christianity to people around the world. "As a true Augustinian," writes Owen Chadwick, "Bossuet saw Providence in supreme dominion and transcendent wisdom, guiding and controlling the historical series, hurling down empires and raising them up, delivering to the sword a Rome obdurate in her heathenism and intoxicated with the blood of martyrs, [and] creating a new Rome." The Christian idea of universal history had been manifest at least as early as Augustine and, more recently, in Pascal. Bossuet, defending miracles, held that God guides human affairs through a "providence particulière." Less to southern tastes, he also invoked "providence particulière" to defend absolute monarchy.[13]

---

[11] Dew, *Digest,* 443–4. Southerners, like others, attributed to Augustine the distinction between sacred and profane history, and most found no meaning in history divorced from eschatology.

[12] Jacques Bénigne Bossuet, *The History of the Variations of the Protestant Churches,* 2nd ed., 2 vols. (Dublin, 1836), 1:1, 11, 18–47; *DD,* 1:219; J. L. Reynolds, *Church Polity: Or, the Kingdom of Christ in Its Internal and External Development,* 2nd ed. (Richmond, VA, 1849), 152, 164; J. L. Burrows, *The Christian Scholar and Soldier* (Augusta, GA, 1864), and *Nationality Insured* (Augusta, GA, 1864); Lipscomb, *Our Country,* 16, 102; also, David S. Doggett, *The Destiny of Educated Young Men, Delivered before the Literary Societies of Emory and Henry College* (Richmond, VA, 1848), 23. For Protestants' respect for Bossuet as a fair and worthy opponent see Jaroslav Pelikan, *The Christian Tradition: A History of the Development of Doctrine,* 5 vols. (Chicago, 1989), 5:39.

[13] Owen Chadwick, *From Bossuet to Newman: The Idea of Doctrinal Development* (Cambridge, U.K., 1957), 1, 5–6, 9, 10, 17, 79, quote at 9; Jacques-Bénigne Bossuet, *Politics Drawn from the Very Words of Holy Scripture* (New York, 1999). For the relation of Bossuet's interpretation of history to that of Augustine and Pascal see Etienne Gilson, *The Spirit of Medieval Philosophy,* tr. A. H. C. Downes (New York, 1940), 392, and Herbert Butterfield, "Historiography," *DHI,* 2:488. Bossuet extended

Fénelon's *Télémaque* [*Telemachus*] and *Traité de l'éducation des filles* were popular in America, among women as well as men. Parson Weems reported a great demand in Virginia for *Telemachus* in French and in English. Fénelon's works were well represented in private libraries of colonial South Carolina. They were assigned in schools in North Carolina during the early nineteenth century and also sold well in Maryland. *Princeton Review* and Thomas Smyth of Charleston lauded Fénelon for a Christian love reminiscent of that of the Apostle John, particularly recommending *Traité de l'éducation des filles,* which pleased Protestants as well as Catholics by encouraging conservatively guided female education.[14]

Robert Howison, a New School Presbyterian, admired *Telemachus* and quoted Fénelon in his *History of Virginia*. William Gilmore Simms lauded *Télémaque* as a beautiful moral story especially appropriate for the young. Rereading it, Mary Moragné exulted, "This amiable prose poem is not inferior in dramatic excellence to Homer's 'Iliad,' & is far superior in moral worth"; she declared it "my *text book*." Somehow, it increased her hostility to Robespierre and the Reign of Terror. Benjamin Perry, the leading unionist editor in upcountry South Carolina, speaking at Walhalla Academy (women's) after the War, praised "the wise and good Fénelon, the purest and most eloquent of all the Roman catholic Bishops in France."[15]

Augustine's suggestion that heretics help the Church by compelling it to explain itself: Bossuet, *History of Variations*, 1:1, 11, 18–47. Thus, for John Girardeau, the Church established Christian theology through fierce confrontation with error: Girardeau, *Theological Questions*, 51.

[14] "Character and Writings of Fénelon," *BRPR*, 24 (1852), 533–64, and 25 (1853), 165–203; *TSW*, 5:153–6; also, "Classical Learning," *HLW*, 2:31. Kevin J. Hayes, *A Colonial Woman's Bookshelf* (Knoxville, TN, 1996), 62–4, 102–3; Joseph Tower Wheeler, "Books Owned by Marylanders, 1700–1776," *Maryland Historical Magazine*, 35 (1940), 351; George K. Smart, "Private Libraries in Colonial Virginia," *American Literature*, 10 (1938), 35; Walter B. Edgar, "Some Popular Books in Colonial South Carolina," *South Carolina Historical Magazine*, 72 (1971), 175; Charles J. Johnson, Jr., *Mary Telfair: The Life and Legacy of a Nineteenth-Century Woman* (Savannah, GA, 2002), 316–17; Charles L. Coon, *North Carolina Schools and Academies: A Documentary History, 1790–1840* (Raleigh, NC, 1915), 773, 793. For *Telemachus* at Aberdeen Academy in Richmond see Benjamin Fleet, July 19, 1860, in Betsey Fleet and John D. P. Fuller, *Green Mount: A Virginia Plantation Family during the War* (Charlottesville, VA, 1962), 21. Bossuet's views on education favorably impressed John Berrien Lindsley of Nashville: John Edwin Windrow, *John Berrien Lindsley: Educator, Physician, Social Philosopher* (Chapel Hill, NC, 1938), 90. For the suggestion that Fénelon had virtually a Protestant sensibility see "S.", "Madame Guyon and Fénelon," 479–509. Fénelon's treatise on the education of girls was translated into English in 1707.

[15] Robert R. Howison, *A History of Virginia from Its Discovery and Settlement by Europeans to the Present Time,* 2 vols. (Philadelphia, 1846), 1:126; [William Gilmore Simms], "Critical Notices," *SQR*, n.s., 10 (1854), 256; Mary E. Moragné Journal, Apr. 31 and May 24, 1837, July 13 and 28, 1837, Feb. 17, 1842, in Delle Mullen Craven, ed., *The Neglected Thread: A Journal of the Calhoun Community* (Columbia, SC, 1951), 35, 98, 101, 230. Stephen Meats and Edwin T. Arnold, eds., *The Writings of Benjamin F. Perry,* 3 vols. (Spartanburg, SC, 1980), 1:474. For other women readers see Chesnut Diary, Feb. 19, 1865, in C. Vann Woodward, ed., *Mary Chesnut's Civil War* (New Haven, CT, 1981), 722; Eliza Ripley, *Social Life in Old New Orleans: Being Recollections of My Girlhood* (New York, 1975 [1912]), 10. The story of *Telemachus* parallels that of the *Odyssey* and breathes a classical style: see Gilbert Highet, *The Classical Tradition: Greek and Roman Influence on Western Literature* (New York, 1949), 336–43.

From *Sociology for the South* to *Cannibals All!* and on through many articles, George Fitzhugh left no doubt of his impatience with the right of private judgment. On the eve of secession he described the southern cause as "a *rolling back of the reformation! Of reformation run wild.*" The Episcopalian Fitzhugh carefully bowed to Luther and Calvin for having ended the irrationalities and tyranny of medieval Catholicism, but not to their appeals to private judgment. Mary Chesnut, another Episcopalian, smarted under the tirades of her friend, William Henry Trescot, against Jefferson Davis and the Confederate government. Chesnut insisted that Luther had a right to free himself from the Catholic Church, but where does it all end when people everywhere, "exercising their right of private judgment," seek to free themselves from authority?[16]

Fitzhugh argued that the Protestants of the Reformation could not prevent their protest against a perceived illegitimate authority from passing into a broader distrust of all authority, which eighteenth-century ideologues widened and deepened. By legitimating protest against the Church, the Reformers had, however unintentionally, legitimated protest against themselves as yet another illegitimate authority. For Fitzhugh, such protests always could be – sometimes deserved to be – seen as manifestations of a self-serving will to power that substituted the individual for God. "The process of anti-authoritarian revolt," H. Richard Niebuhr has observed, "cannot be stopped within the person himself." For once an individual sets his own conscience against the God-given law of the church, he "becomes prey to rebellious desires within him." The Protestant churches resisted Antinomianism, but by upholding freedom as a positive affirmation of duty and responsibility they opened the door to internal struggles. Southerners saw the northern churches as sliding toward Antinomianism and their own churches as bastions against it.[17]

The Reformation confronted proslavery Southerners with theological and political embarrassments. The doctrine of *sola scriptura* provided the foundation for the right of private judgment and – in the words of Francis Turretin, a leading authority for southern Calvinists – was the "primary question and almost the only one" in Protestantism's revolt against the Catholic Church. *Sola scriptura* originally meant "no authority above the Bible," but by the eighteenth century it effectively became "the Bible alone." Mark Noll observes: "Even though Luther spoke of his conscience as bound by Scripture, he had introduced, with moving power, a new principle of authority" – a new sense of the self as sovereign in matters religious and secular. In nineteenth-century America, the Second Great Awakening opened the

---

[16] George Fitzhugh, "The Revolutions of 1775 and 1861 Contrasted," *SLM*, 35 (1863), 722–3; Chesnut Diary, July 1861 and Nov. 30, 1864, in Woodward, ed., *Mary Chesnut's Civil War*, 121, 679.

[17] George Fitzhugh, "Reaction and the Administration," *DBR*, 25 (1858), 546; H. Richard Niebuhr, "Protestant Movement and Democracy in the United States," in James Ward Smith and A. Leland Jamison, eds., *The Shaping of American Religion* (Princeton, NJ, 1961), 29; also Hatch, "Sola Scriptura and Novus Ordo Seclorum," in Nathan O. Hatch and Mark A. Nolls, eds., *The Bible in America: Essays in Cultural History* (New York, 1982), 64–5. Niebuhr also carefully criticizes all-too-easy submission to authority. Rather tongue-in-cheek, James Mercer Garnett defined man as "a self-loving, self-destroying animal": "Odds and Ends," *SLM*, 2 (1836), 357.

sluices to a democratization that encouraged theological liberalization, including the right of personal interpretation of Scripture. "The insurgents," Nathan Hatch writes, "considered people's common sense more reliable, even in theology, than the judgment of an educated few. This shift involved new faith in public opinion as an arbiter of truth."[18]

Catholics and Episcopalians, summoning tradition with Scripture, drew blood from their Reformed adversaries, for *sola scriptura* increasingly became the banner of those determined to undermine the structures of church authority. Luther and Calvin, who unfolded the banner, had combated the dangers posed by a radical individualism that bent Scripture to political purposes. They did their best to maintain discipline in the ranks, but the Pandora's box they opened cost nineteenth-century American Calvinists dearly. The Reverend Thomas Peck, speaking for Reformed Protestants, rejected John Henry Newman's *Development of Doctrine* and countered that true religious development came only from improved knowledge of Scripture. Bishops John England and J. H. Otey articulated, respectively, the Catholic and Episcopal positions. England wrote: "Although [the Bible] contains the Words of Truth, those Words are susceptible of contradictory interpretations, and, in fact, are interpreted contradictorily." Without the guidance of an infallible church, "We cannot know Scripture from foolish and blasphemous forgery." England assailed *sola scriptura* as an invitation to the subjectivism that conservative Protestants were fiercely combating. Otey asked, "Who is to be the umpire between us? There is no decision to be had in such a case, without an appeal to the authority of the Church."[19]

Protestantism's inherent tendencies toward radical individualism and democratization posed a direct threat to the South's slaveholding social order. Slave society's organicism rested on the master–slave relation, bourgeois society on the buying and selling of labor power (abstract labor divorced from the person of the laborer). Catholics, while denying the inherent sinfulness of slavery, recognized the Protestant origins of an individualism that should logically have rejected slavery. After the War, Father J. J. O'Connell of South Carolina taunted Protestants who wanted not only the right of private judgment and other Reformation doctrines but also a patriarchal social order and a Christian slave society: "It is only under Catholic

---

[18] Francis Turretin, *Institutes of Elenctic Theology,* ed. James T. Dennison, tr. George Musgrave Giger, 3 vols. (Phillipsburg, NJ, 1992–97), 1:154; Mark Noll, *Turning Points: Decisive Moments in the History of Christianity* (Grand Rapids, MI, 1997), 156, 242; Nathan O. Hatch, *The Democratization of American Christianity* (New Haven, CT, 1989), 162 and ch. 6.

[19] For the resistance of Luther and Calvin to subjective renderings of *sola scriptura* see Willis B. Glover, *Evangelical Nonconformists and Higher Criticism in the Nineteenth Century* (London, 1954), 15–17; "The Sufficiency of Scriptures," in T. E. Peck, *Miscellanies,* ed. T. C. Johnson, 3 vols. (Richmond, VA, 1895–97), 1:296; also, *JHTW,* 4:168; Sebastian G. Messmer, ed., *The Works of the Right Rev. John England, First Bishop of Charleston,* 7 vols. (Cleveland, OH, 1908), quotes at 1:9, 17, and see also 2:171–209; Otey, "The Unity of the Church," in William Mercer Green, *Memoir of the Rt. Rev. James Hervey Otey, D.D., LL.D., the First Bishop of Tennessee* (New York, 1885), 223. For another Episcopalian's view see Christopher E. Gadsden, *The Times, Ecclesiastically Considered* (Charleston, SC, 1861), 12.

governments, where the church can regulate the relative duties between the servant and the master, that slavery can exist as a Christian institution."[20]

The history and legacy of Puritanism challenged, as little else did, the proslavery effort to reconcile Protestant individualism with the corporatism inherent in slavery. Influential Southerners had long found much to admire – and detest – in the Puritans. John Randolph and Nathaniel Macon counterpoised the Puritan plain style to what they saw as the moral and political decadence of early nineteenth-century America. At the University of Alabama, Thomas Newton Wood presented the Puritans as pioneers of English freedom, and in South Carolina the Presbyterian Reverend John Girardeau denounced "unprincipled" Charles I for leading the Church of England from Calvinism to Arminianism.[21]

Thornwell felt a strong bond to Puritan ecclesiology and strict adherence to God's commands. When he and Charles Hodge of Princeton debated church polity, both cited Puritan divines as authorities. *Southern Literary Messenger* published a piece by the Yankee H. T. Tuckerman that extolled the virtues of the New England Puritans and commended their legacy. J. S. Wise of Virginia, complimenting his Philadelphia-born mother for her attentiveness to her slaves, wrote, "She had too much of the old Puritan blood in her to ignore the word duty." In 1860 Lipscomb told the young ladies of Wesleyan Female College in Macon, Georgia, that Puritanism, with all its defects, "was still a grand assertion of Christian manhood." According to a proudly displayed local tradition, Puritan descendants first settled the Midway district of Georgia and subsequently led resistance to the British.[22]

---

[20] J. J. O'Connell, *Catholicity in the Carolinas and Georgia: Leaves of Its History* (Westminster, MD, 1964 [1879]), 72.

[21] On southern admirers of the plain style see Loren Baritz's perceptive Introduction to John Taylor, *An Inquiry into the Principles and Policy of the Government of the United States,* ed. Loren Baritz (Indianapolis, IN, 1919 [1814]), x–xi; Thomas Newton Wood, *An Address Delivered before the Two Literary Societies of the University of Alabama* (Tuscaloosa, AL, 1840), 11–12; George A. Blackburn, ed., *Sermons by John L. Girardeau* (Columbia, SC, 1907), 124. Denunciations of Charles I and his court for moral degeneracy stretched from the eighteenth century to the mid-nineteenth: see e.g. Henry Pattillo, *The Plain Planter's Assistant* (Wilmington, NC, 1887), 8; David Chauncey Knowlton, ed., *The Journal of William H. Crawford* (Northampton, MA, 1925), 13.

[22] *JHTW,* 4:255–7; Morton H. Smith, *Studies in Southern Presbyterian Theology* (Phillipsburg, NJ, 1962), 174–5; H. T. Tuckerman, "Joseph Stevens Buckminister," *SLM,* 24 (1957), 50–7; John S. Wise, *The End of an Era* (Boston, 1900), 34; A. A. Lipscomb, *The Relation of the Anglo-Saxon Race to Christian Womanhood* (Macon, GA, 1860), 19; also, Lipscomb, *Our Country,* 27; Charles C. Jones, Jr., and Salem Dutcher, *Memorial History of Augusta* (Syracuse, NY, 1890), 63; Josephine Bacon Martin, *Midway Georgia in History and Legend, 1852–1869,* 2nd ed. (Darien, GA, 1961), 2–4; George Sheldon, *The Hand of God Recognized: A Discourse* (Charleston, SC, 1846), 10. For the corruption of Charles II and the waning of Puritanism deplored, see Lipscomb, *Anglo-Saxon Race,* 19. Lengthier and even harsher is [John H. Bocock], "Martyrs of Scotland and Sir Walter Scott," *SPR,* 10 (1858), 69–94.

For an arresting account of Bishop Meade as a man in the Puritan tradition, see W. A. R. Goodwin, "Northern Influences in the Life of the Virginia Seminary," in Goodwin, *History of the Theological Seminary in Virginia and Its Historical Background,* 2 vols. (Rochester, NY, 1923), 1:438–9. For a

Simms struggled to balance Puritan virtues and vices as well as southern values and interests. "The immense self-esteem of the English," he wrote a northern friend, "from which they derive all their insolence and arrogance, is, at the same time, the source of their tremendous and self-sustaining strength. That old genius of Puritanism, which dogmatized on all occasions, and would have rebelled in Heaven itself, was still a genius of inflexible principles, laws as fixed as those of the Medes and Persians, severe investigation, and prejudices, which though bitter as the grave, yet sprang out of a truthful consideration of their own and the characteristics of other people." Their bigotry and intolerance arose from "a pride of character and a just consciousness of strength" that recalled the bigotry displayed by the ancient Hebrews who faced similar circumstances and held similar convictions. "The error was easy, and still continues to be so – by which he who felt himself so especially chosen as a law unto him, should fancy an especial right in himself to be a law unto his neighbors." Simms held that this self-righteousness explained New Englanders' constant meddling in southern affairs – "now with our Indians, now with our Slaves" – and their conviction of a mental and moral superiority grace, "which should entitle them fairly to control the other nations."[23]

The identification of Puritanism with fanaticism and bigotry became a staple of southern criticism of the North. From colonial times to secession, Southerners hugely enjoyed *Hudibras* – a satirical three-part poem by the Anglican and royalist Samuel Butler – which ridiculed Puritans and pummeled the Presbyterian Church and portrayed the New Model Army as staffed by selfish, bigoted hypocrites and brutal political fanatics. During the nineteenth century, elite women like Mary Moragné and Mary Chesnut of the Carolinas and the small slaveholding Elizabeth Scott Neblett of Texas were reading *Hudibras*. According to Virginia lore, Chief

---

scathing denunciation of Charles I see W. C. Rives, *Discourse on the Character and Services of John Hampden, and the Great Struggle for Popular and Constitutional Liberty in His Time* (Richmond, VA, 1845), 31–2, 42–3, 57. Charles II also took his lumps. Dew, citing Macaulay, suggested that Charles II "had seen, if ever man saw," both sides of human nature, but remembered only one side. "He had merely learned to distrust his species – to consider integrity in men, and modesty in women, as mere acting": *Digest*, 567.

[23] William Gilmore Simms, *The History of South Carolina* (New York, 1849), 47, 61–73. See 1841 in Oliphant et al., eds., *Letters of Simms*. Michael Tuomey, South Carolina's state geologist, heard Simms speak of the evils of Puritanism's suppression of popular amusements: Michael Tuomey to J. H. Hammond, Feb. 4, 1847, in Lewis S. Dean, ed., *The Papers of Michael Tuomey* (Spartanburg, SC, 2001), 108. Simms got rough with the Puritans when it suited him, and in 1843 *Southern Quarterly Review* complained that he had gone too far against the Puritans in *The Social Principle*. Yet subsequent issues, while acknowledging the Puritans' "manly virtues," spoke harshly of them. Some applauded the Puritans for overthrowing the monarchy but added that they replaced one despotism with another: *SQR*, 4 (1843), 245, and 8 (1845), 518–22; [David F. Jamison], "The National Anniversary," *SQR*, n.s., 2 (1850), 170–1; and, more cautiously, Nelson Mitchell, *Oration Delivered before the Fourth of July Association, on the Fourth of July, 1848* (Charleston, SC, 1849), 12. For respect for Puritan New England and criticism of Virginia as insufficiently puritanical, see "L. M. B.", "The Past and the Present," *VUM*, 4 (1860), 257–8. The early Virginians, in one Calvinist version, were "grave, not stern; sedate, not sour; confident, not arrogant; pervading, not aggressive. In short, they were Presbyterians, not Puritans": "Critical Notices," *SQR*, n.s., 1 (1856), 209.

Justice John Marshall "has 'Hudibras' at his tongue's end." Whether T. R. Price, Jr. (an M.A. candidate at the University of Virginia) knew *Hudibras* is unclear, but he adored Dryden and Pope and welcomed the overthrow of "the gloomy rule of the Puritans," which he said had retarded English literature. Edgar Allan Poe, among many, traced the roots of riots and radicalism to seventeenth-century England and eighteenth-century France. President James Monroe and Governor George M. Troup of Georgia proudly claimed descent from pro-Stuart Scots families, and Mrs. [Mary Howard] Schoolcraft of South Carolina proudly identified with the Cavaliers and ridiculed the Puritans. In Virginia, Walter Monteiro protested the sending of southern students to northern colleges, where they acquired "a puritanical stiffness of demeanor." Even David Hunter Strother ("Porte Crayon"), Virginia's celebrated artist who fought for the Union, contrasted the "prim puritanical" expressions of New Englanders with the "jovial generous" countenances of Southerners.[24]

Although the Puritans had great strengths to match their vices, P. H. Woodward wrote in *Russell's Magazine* that their religion exhibited a fanaticism comparable to "oriental fatalism" and the just cause of their revolution – a spontaneous mass movement against despotism – had passed into bigotry and oppression. Frederick Porcher objected to the Puritan religious intolerance that led to the condemnation of adversaries to hell for honest differences of political opinion. B. R. Carroll inquired in his *Catechism of United States History*, a secondary school text that had gone through twenty printings by 1859, "Who were the Puritans?" and answered, "They became the intolerant persecutors of all who differed with them in religious worship." A number of Southerners denounced modern Puritanism as Manichean – a view some recent scholars have endorsed. We are two different peoples, J. S. Lamar of Georgia wrote, who differ "as radically and as rigidly as Puritanism differs from Christianity or as Abolitionism differs from the Bible."[25]

The positive qualities of the Cavaliers and negative qualities of the Puritans – real and imagined – became a focal point for Southerners' understanding of the roots of northern hostility to the South. "The odor of Puritanism," J. D. B. De Bow wrote in 1851, "surrounds much of the population of the North." He drew a straight line

---

[24] Moragné Journal, in Craven, ed., *Neglected Thread*, xxxiii; Chesnut Diary, Oct. 15, 1861, July 6, 1864, in Woodward, ed., *Mary Chesnut's Civil War*, 216, 620; Mar. 26, 1852, in Erika L. Murr, ed., *A Rebel Wife in Texas: The Diary and Letters of Elizabeth Scott Neblett, 1852–1864* (Baton Rouge, LA, 2001), 48; T. R. Price, Jr., "The Augustan Era of English Literature" (M.A. thesis, 1858, typescript at UVA); Edgar Allen Poe, review of Paulding and Manly on slavery in *SLM*, 2 (1836), 337; Stuart Jerry Brown, ed., *Autobiography of James Monroe* (Syracuse, NY, 1959), 21; Edward J. Harden, *The Life of George M. Troup* (Savannah, GA, 1859), 7–8; *Plantation Life: The Narratives of Mrs. Henry School-craft* (New York, 1969 [1860]), 63; [Walter Monteiro], *Address before the Neotrophian Society of the Hampton Academy* (Richmond, VA, 1857), 10; Cecil D. Eby, Jr., *"Porte Crayon": The Life of David Hunter Strother* (Chapel Hill, NC, 1960), 59. See also Supplementary References: "Hudibras."

[25] [P. H. Woodward], "The Puritan," *RM*, 1 (1857), 419–24; F. A. Porcher, "Bancroft's History," *RM*, 2 (1858), 525, 529; B. R. Carroll, *Catechism of United States History*, 2nd ed., rev. (Charleston, SC, 1859), 29–31. Carroll offered a sop: "As yet the true principles of religious liberty were not yet generally understood" (31); J. S. Lamar, *A Discourse in the Christian Church on Confederate Fast-Day, Nov. 5th, 1861* (Augusta, GA, 1861), 9; also, *VUM*, 3 (1859), 314. See also Henning Graf Reventlow, *The Authority of the Bible and the Rise of the Modern World* (Philadelphia, 1984), 97.

from the English Puritans through Robespierre and the French Terror to the abolitionists. In 1853 De Bow denied intent to file another harsh indictment against the
Puritans but protested the partiality shown the Puritans by American public opinion. He condemned their bigotry, religious fanaticism, and persistent bad influence,
singling out their hanging of Quakers, persecution of Catholics, and rough treatment of Anne Hutchinson and others who challenged their rule. According to A.
Clarkson of Alabama, only the French Jacobins excelled the Puritans in meanness
and hypocrisy. Clarkson praised the Cavaliers as "brave, honorable, social; loyal to
their king, and loyal to the church. Knowing that earth could not be made a paradise, they did not, therefore, seek to turn the fair footstool of God into a gloomy
hell. Failings they had, but dishonor, sordid meanness, and mammon worship they
knew not."[26]

Among the Episcopalians, the Reverend Daniel Dreher of North Carolina located the "secret of all this obstinacy" in "the peculiar character" of New England
descendents from a rebellious and restless people, fond of liberty but intolerable
masters when in power. Those Puritans killed "poor Charles" and, upon arriving
in America, introduced religious persecution. The Reverend A. F. Watson, another
Tarheel, thought the Church of England's hostility to slavery derived in part from
the lingering effects of Puritan radicalism. In 1864 the Catholic Bishop Patrick
Lynch of South Carolina attributed the abolitionists' exaggerations of cruelty to
slaves to the "vivid imagination of Puritan hatred."[27]

Southern laymen and divines differed over whether Puritanism had always been
demonic or had become so in New England. During the Webster–Hayne debate of
1830, John Rowan of Kentucky conceded sarcastically that New Englanders were
"moderately pious." Charlestonians still sang the virtues of the New England Puritans in the mid-1830s, but in 1849 the Virginia-born Elwood Fisher of Cincinnati
accused the North of backsliding in religion while the South held firm. In New
England a stern Puritanism was giving way to Unitarianism, and in the South Episcopalianism was giving way to the sternness of the Baptists: "Thus under the operation of their respective institutions the religion of Massachusetts has receded from
one of the most strict, to one of the most relaxed systems of the Protestant faith,
while Virginia has advanced from one of the most indulgent to one of the stricter
forms of religious discipline."[28]

[26] *DBR*, 10 (1851), 519; "Bancroft's History of the United States," *DBR*, 15 (1853), 178–81; A. Clarkson, "The Basis of Northern Hostility to the South," *DBR*, 28 (1860), 9.

[27] Daniel I. Dreher, *Sermon, June 13, 1861, Day of Humiliation and Prayer* (Salisbury, NC, 1861), 9;
Alfred A. Watson, *Sermon Delivered before the Annual Council of the Diocese of North Carolina
upon the Festival of the Ascension* (Raleigh, NC, 1863), 16–18; Patrick N. Lynch, "A Few Words on
the Domestic Slavery in the Confederate States of America," *Avery Review*, 3 (2000), 103–4.

[28] John Rowan, Feb. 4, 1830, in Herman Belz, ed., *The Webster–Hayne Debate on the Nature of the
Union: Selected Documents* (Indianapolis, IN, 2000), 45, 265; for praise of New England Puritans
in Charleston in 1836 see Daniel K. Whitaker's review of an address by Joshua Barker Whitridge:
[Whitaker], "From Our Arm-Chair," *SLJ*, 2 (1836), 239–40, and "Democracy in America," *SLJ*, 4
(1838), 271; Elwood Fisher, *Lecture on the North and South, Delivered before the Young Men's Mercantile Library of Cincinnati* (Wilmington, NC, 1849), 25.

More often than not, southern critics distinguished the solid piety and civic responsibility of the early New England Puritans from a subsequent degeneration into heresy. The Methodist Reverend William A. Smith told his students at Randolph-Macon College that, once New England found slavery unprofitable, the efforts of "our Puritan fathers" to promote education turned into a medium for antislavery propaganda. The Baptist Reverend Thornton Stringfellow, doubtless mindful that Cromwell's army had been full of Baptists, praised the religious orthodoxy of the Puritans who settled New England. Southern Presbyterians had strong ties to Scotland – where their forebears had fought against Charles I, the Cavaliers, and the established Church – and in 1859 the Presbyterian Reverend Stuart Robinson of Kentucky condemned the New England Puritans for destruction of the proper line between church and state. Even the Scots Presbyterian Thomas Smyth, who staunchly lauded the Puritans of Old and New England for their contributions to republican liberty, deplored the degeneracy into an Antinomianism he saw manifest in recent New England fanaticism. Seventeenth-century English Puritanism and nineteenth-century New England Puritanism, wrote J. H. Bocock, have little in common besides an unfortunate intolerance of opposing views.[29]

In 1860 the Calvinistic Episcopalian Reverend William Prentiss of Charleston, preaching a Fast Day sermon, criticized the early New Englanders for bigotry toward Quakers and Baptists and also criticized their congregationalism for having laid the basis for popular democracy. He fumed at the claims of an infallible congregation to impose its interpretation of God's will. With the Presbyterian Robert Dabney, Prentiss held that the Church sustained the authority and power of God's law, and he denounced the reduction in the power of pastors and the emphasis on voting, which folded the individual will into a shifting collective. Prentiss saw in Puritanism a Socinian precursor to Unitarianism. A year later, Bishop Thomas Atkinson of North Carolina carried the Episcopalian critique further. He found much to admire in New England, but "New England is Puritan, and Puritanism is not reverential; but on the contrary, Puritanism is essentially independency in matters of

---

[29] William A. Smith, *Lectures on the Philosophy and Practice of Slavery* (Nashville, TN, 1856), 15; Thornton Stringfellow, "Statistical View of Slavery," in E. N. Elliott, ed., *Cotton Is King and Pro-Slavery Arguments* (New York, 1969 [1860]), 524; Stuart Robinson, *The Relations of the Secular and Spiritual Power* (Louisville, KY, 1859), 14, 22; *TSW*, 3:8–88, 6:172–3, 299; [Bocock], "Martyrs of Scotland," 93–4. A. B. Meek referred to the Puritans as "stern, clear-headed, faith-abiding": *Americanism in Literature: An Oration before the Phi Kappa and Demosthenian Societies of the University of Georgia* (Tuscaloosa, AL, 1844), 9. George S. Sawyer, among others, skirted Puritanism as such and lamented the decline in the high moral standards of New England: *Southern Institutes; Or, an Inquiry into the Origin and Early Prevalence of Slavery and the Slave Trade* (New York, 1967 [1858]), 15. Bocock notwithstanding, southern Calvinism drew on several sources: Scots and Scots-Irish Presbyterians, English Puritans, and French Huguenots: see Ernest Trice Thompson, *The Spirituality of the Church: A Distinctive Doctrine of the Presbyterian Church in the United States* (Richmond, VA, 1961), 7. Southern denunciations of Puritanism as the root of abolitionist fanaticism increased with the revolutions of 1848: see e.g. Henry B. Goodwin [of Maryland] to Calhoun, Feb. 6, 1849, in *JCCP*, 26:274; Richard K. Crallé to Calhoun, Feb. 2, 1849, in *JCCP*, 26:266. The Reverend George Sheldon of South Carolina quoted Bancroft's opinion that the Puritans deserved credit for making England Protestant: Sheldon, *Hand of God Recognized*, 10 n.

religion. It makes religion to be entirely an individual relation between each particular soul and its Creator," becoming ever more "enthusiastic, self-confident, but
irreverent and destructive, that is, fanatical." If, Atkinson continued, you show such
a man that the Bible sanctions slavery, he will respond by repudiating the Bible.[30]

The War brought southern Presbyterians a problem all their own. They did not
want to be identified with the Puritans, but neither did they want to traduce fellow
Calvinists, especially since most people could not tell the difference. The Presbyterian Reverend Joseph Atkinson of South Carolina, noting the salutary effect of
the publication of Cromwell's speeches, went to some lengths to give the Puritans
their due while rejecting their radicalism. Atkinson held Presbyterianism up as a
moderate and responsible version of orthodox Calvinism. Joseph LeConte, the eminent scientist, agreed with Atkinson that a just estimate of Puritanism was finally
emerging in place of blind hostility and blind admiration. Puritan asceticism in art
as well as politics and social life, he noted, provided a powerful corrective to such
prevalent abuses as sensuousness and frivolity.[31]

The War encouraged a view that arrayed a Puritan North against a Cavalier
South. The Richmond *Examiner* bemused Frederick Law Olmsted with its dogged
adherence to the myth of Cavaliers and Roundheads in the formation of America.
Acerbic contributors, most of whom affirmed the mythical Puritan versus Cavalier origins of North and South, peppered *Southern Literary Messenger* with shots
at the Puritans as the forerunners of Yankee barbarism: "the canting hypocrisy"
of the North's "Puritan Canaan"; "from that religiously fanatic source has arisen
abolitionism, transcendentalism, and 'higher-lawism' "; the "selfish, cold and ambitious" Cromwell qualified as the "Alaric of Ireland"; "Puritanism is the first step
in a corrupt Christianity."[32]

In 1861, the visiting Englishmen J. L. Fremantle and Samuel Phillips Day were
taken aback by southern denunciations of Puritans and Puritanism. Day reported
that the gentlemen of the Confederate officer corps, invoking Cavaliers and Roundheads, called the War a battle between alien races, nationalities, and governments.
Jefferson Davis depicted the War as a struggle between two different peoples who
had descended from opposite sides in the English Civil War. Davis likened the behavior of the Union army in the South to that of Cromwell's Roundheads in Ireland.

---

[30] William O. Prentiss, *A Sermon Preached at St. Peter's Church* (Charleston, SC, 1860), 10–12; Thomas
Atkinson, *On the Cause of Our National Troubles: A Sermon Delivered in St. James Church, Wilm-
ington, N.C.* (Wilmington, NC, 1861), 9. For similar remarks see Robert L. Dabney, *Defence of
Virginia (and through Her of the South) in Recent and Pending Contests against the Sectional Party*
(New York, 1969 [1867]), 131.

[31] [Joseph M. Atkinson], "The Puritans," *SPR*, 15 (1862), 230–55; Joseph LeConte, "On the Nature
and Uses of Art," *SPR*, 15 (1863), 312–13. For Presbyterian moderation against the radicalism of the
English Puritans, see "Puritanism and Presbyterianism," *SPR*, 16 (1866), 309–26.

[32] Frederick Law Olmsted, *A Journey in the Back Country* (New York, 1970 [1860]), 438; "The New
Republic," *SLM*, 32 (1861), 398; "The Difference of Race between the Northern and Southern People," *SLM*, 30 (1860), 404–5; "Christianity versus Philanthropy," *SLM*, 34 (1862), 574. For specific
affirmations of the Cavalier–Puritan split see Frank H. Alfriend, "A Southern Republic and a Northern Democracy," *SLM*, 35 (1863), 283–9. Cromwell got extended and mixed reviews in the South:
see Supplementary References: "Caesarism."

Proslavery writers attributed the origin of northern abolitionism to the "fanaticism" of the New England Puritans and, farther back, to the leveling tendencies of the English Revolution.[33]

Fitzhugh, describing the English Puritans as "these vulgar parvenus, these psalm-singing regicides, these worshippers of mammon," located the birth of all the modern isms in Geneva and the infidel wing of Calvinism. The sarcastic Fitzhugh did have a good word for the New England Puritans' suppression of Quakers and other troublemakers: "Many tokens of their zeal and affection were soon seen pendant from the elms of New England." Augusta Jane Evans, for whom Yankees were "*latter-day Philistines*" and "Puritanic *locusts*," suggested in her novel *Macaria* that the War was the price the South had to pay for the overthrow of "puritanical hypocrisy." Julia LeGrand of Maryland, living in New Orleans, condemned Yankees as Puritans and as "cold, hard, unscrupulous, persevering meddlers."[34]

With the defeat of the Confederacy, ambivalence about the Puritans gave way to a hard negative. For Confederate Brigadier General St. John Richardson Liddell, the fall of the Confederacy marked the victory of "the Puritans." Boiling over the destruction wrought by General Banks, Liddell called him a "wretch of Yankee Puritanical proclivities." A despondent Edmund Ruffin poured out his own wrath: "To all the merit of Puritanism the New Englanders are entitled – & they are welcomed to its exclusive enjoyment." Deriding the " 'Pilgrim Fathers' and their puritanical successors," he noted the transformation of their vices and crimes into badges of honor. The Puritan settlers of Massachusetts, while ready "to encounter danger & to endure suffering & persecution, in defense of their sour & diabolical system of religion," outdid even their European brethren as "fanatics & bigots in religion." Edward Pollard of Virginia wrote, "The characteristic religion of New England, composed of about equal quantities of blasphemy and balderdash, went hand in hand with the war." Josiah Gorgas, genius of the Confederacy's ordnance:

---

[33] Arthur J. L. Fremantle, *Three Months in the Southern States: The 1863 Diary of an English Soldier* (Edinburgh, 1863), 31; Day quoted in Rollin G. Osterweis, *Romanticism and Nationalism in the Old South* (Baton Rouge, LA, 1971), 148; William C. Davis, *Jefferson Davis: The Man and His Hour* (New York, 1991), 486. Also, "Python," *DBR*, 28 (1860), 267–8; [G. Fitzhugh?], "Bonaparte, Cromwell, and Washington," *DBR*, 27 (1860), 143.

[34] George Fitzhugh, *Sociology for the South, or, The Failure of Free Society* (New York, 1965 [1852]), 234, 198; Augusta Jane Evans, *Macaria; Or, Altars of Sacrifice* (Baton Rouge, LA, 1992 [1864]), 335; Augusta Evans to Rachel Lyons, Oct. 3, 1861, in Rebecca Grant Sexton, ed., *A Southern Woman of Letters: The Correspondence of Augusta Jane Evans Wilson* (Columbia, SC, 2002), 37; Feb. 16, 1863, in Kate Mason Rowland and Mrs. Morris S. Croxall, eds., *The Journal of Julia LeGrand: New Orleans, 1862–1863* (Richmond, VA, 1911), 126–7. For a Catholic comment on Cromwell's savagery in Ireland, see Messmer, ed., *Works of John England*, 4:271. In contrast to Fitzhugh, George Sawyer recoiled from the Puritans' hanging of Quakers: *Southern Institutes*, 288. Fitzhugh in effect followed the Puritan line on the execution of the Quakers. Whether the early Quakers in Massachusetts were peaceful preachers or aggressive subversives who threatened state as well as church has long remained a bone of contention among historians: Carla Gardina Pestana, "The Quaker Executions as Myth and History," *Journal of American History*, 80 (1993), 441–69. Fitzhugh, however, professed respect for Quakers' virtues, especially since they had ostensibly abandoned their early radicalism, emerged as pillars of social order, and applied stern discipline to rein in ultra-individualist tendencies: "Mr. Bancroft's History and the Inner Light," *DBR*, 29 (1860), 601–3.

"I cannot believe that there is no future for this country but abject submission to the puritan." Emma Holmes: "We, the free-born descendants of the Cavaliers to submit to the descendants of the witch burning Puritans, whose God is the Almighty Dollar. Never!"[35]

During and after Reconstruction, W. H. Sparks of Georgia and other Southerners pursued the indictment. In 1880 J. F. H. Claiborne of Mississippi, acknowledging that Massachusetts had once been "pious and pragmatical," growled that, as early as the eighteenth century, it had emerged as a "hot-bed of schisms, heresies, and idealisms." Its clergy had become "swayed by passion and prejudice; they shift about with every wind of doctrine, truckle to the judgment of the mob, and court the applause of the world." Years later, Senator Thomas Manson Norwood of Georgia interpreted the lost War as a struggle between two distinct peoples, stressing the Puritan origins of the Yankees. Most of his book, *True Vindication of the South* (1917), is an onslaught against the Puritan tradition from the Reformation forward as a crystallization of bigotry, fanaticism, and greed. Some 65 years later, Andrew Lytle declared the Puritans Satanists and Satan the first Puritan.[36]

Consideration of the Reformation and its aftermath threw into relief the problem of individualism in a slave society that preached Christian–corporate values. In the slaveholders' version, everyman's destiny lay within corporate entities – family, church, communities – which create the framework for a spiritual flourishing that makes individuality attainable. The slaveholders, who envisioned social classes as bound together, condemned secular projections of individual autonomy as both a disorder of the soul and an absurdity. Reuben Davis of Mississippi expressed the folkish version: "Their creed was generally simple. A man ought to fear God, and mind his business. He should be respectful and courteous to all women; he should love his friends and hate his enemies. He should eat when he was hungry, drink when he was thirsty, dance when he was merry, vote for the candidate he liked best, and knock down any man who questioned his right to these privileges."[37]

---

[35] Nathaniel Cheairs Hughes, Jr., *Liddell's Record* (Baton Rouge, LA, 1985), 171, 198; Apr. 3, 1864, in *ERD*, 3:386; E. A. Pollard, *Southern History of the War*, 2 vols. (n.p., 1977 [1866]), 1:439; July 1, 1866, in Sarah Woolfolk Wiggins, ed., *The Journals of Josiah Gorgas, 1857–1878* (Tuscaloosa, AL, 1995), 197, and see xviii; Feb. 14, 1863, in John F. Marszalek, ed., *The Diary of Miss Emma Holmes* (Baton Rouge, LA, 1979), 231.

[36] W. H. Sparks, *Memories of Fifty Years* (Philadelphia, 1872), 15, 138, 202–3, 219–21; J. F. H. Claiborne, *Mississippi as a Province, Territory, and State, with Biographical Notices of Eminent Citizens* (Spartanburg, SC, 1978 [1860]), 168, 291; Thomas Manson Norwood, *True Vindication of the South: In a Review of American Political History* (Savannah, GA, 1917); Andrew Lytle, "Discussion," in William C. Havard and Walter Sullivan, eds., *A Band of Prophets; The Vanderbilt Agrarians after Fifty Years* (Baton Rouge, LA, 1982), 177. Also, George Hill Winfrey to My dear Joseph, Apr. 1, 1903, in Walbrook D. Swank, ed., *Confederate Letters and Diaries, 1861–1865* (Charlottesville, VA, 1988), 152–3; Robert L. Preston, *Southern Miscellanies* (Leesburg, VA, 1919), 23. Counterpoint: Puritans and Cavaliers, wrote a contributor (presumably, a Scots) to *Southern Presbyterian Review*, were both decidedly English and two sides of the same coin: "Puritanism and Presbyterianism," *SPR*, 16 (1866), 309–26.

[37] Reuben Davis, *Recollections of Mississippi and Mississippians* (Oxford, MS, 1889 [1872]), 19. For the radical difference between Christian social-bond individualism and bourgeois atomistic individualism

Led by Thomas Roderick Dew, thoughtful Southerners tempered their enthusiasm for the political ways of the ancient Greeks, who had tied the freedom of the individual to the collective judgment of the community and state. They remained torn between antagonistic tendencies: their fondness for individual freedom, descended from the Greeks and transformed by Christian doctrine; and their approval of a socially cohesive medieval corporatism designed to minimize class antagonisms. Unlike many Continental conservatives, they did not look back wistfully to the Middle Ages and seek to restore a lost corporate world. Slavery made them look forward as well as backward in pursuit of a corporatism that left room for the political and economic freedom of qualified individuals.[38]

Every southern writer of note – Whig or Democrat, religious or secular – agreed that man is born into society and that political and civic freedom is a social creation. "I prefer the collected experience and reasoning of the bulk of society," the Catholic Bishop John England said, "to the results of my own weak efforts, [and] I believe it to be the suggestion of reason, and the duty of an individual, to admit that he is not as wise as is the collective body of his fellowmen." For the Methodist Bishop George Foster Pierce of Georgia, infidelity, speculative unbelief, and false religion denigrate man's nature: "They despoil him of his true glory by their chilling, preposterous theories, even while they affect to magnify him by fulsome eulogy of his intellect and its capacious powers." False notions of personal independence isolate and stagnate man "till the heart grows rank and putrefied in its own corruption." Personal rights and interests notwithstanding, "No choice of his own, no social caste, no civil distinctions, can detach him from it. Linked with the world around him by a law of his nature and the decree of his Maker, every plan of isolation is abortive; and the very effort at separation and exclusiveness brands him a miser, a misanthrope, a selfish, heartless wretch, without natural affection or any redeeming principle."[39]

see Ernst Troeltsch, *The Social Teachings of the Christian Churches,* tr. Olive Wyon, 2 vols. (London, 1950), 2:991; Eric Voegelin, *From Enlightenment to Revolution* (Durham, NC, 1975), 63, 93–5.

[38] For an appraisal of the tendency represented by Coleridge and Scott see M. Morton Auerbach, *The Conservative Illusion* (New York, 1959), 25–6, 66–7. For the complexities of the slaveholders' attachment to freedom as the spur of progress and to slavery as the foundation of freedom, see Eugene D. Genovese, *The Slaveholders' Dilemma: Freedom and Progress in Southern Conservative Thought, 1820–1860* (Columbia, SC, 1991).

[39] Messmer, ed., *Works of John England,* 7:426; G. F. Pierce, "Devotedness to Christ" (1855), in William T. Smithson, ed., *The Methodist Pulpit South* (Washington, DC, 1858), 56–7. (Pierce preached from Romans, 14:7, 8: "For none of us liveth to himself, and no man dieth to himself .... We are the Lord's.") Pierce also said that government must interpose a stern hand when the people become corrupt and defy God's laws: "The Word of God a Nation's Life," in Atticus G. Haygood, ed., *Bishop Pierce's Sermons and Addresses* (Nashville, TN, 1887), 140. The Bible, according to the Methodist Protestant Reverend A. A. Lipscomb, plainly presents "individuality" and no less plainly "social attitude": *The Social Spirit of Christianity, Presented in the Form of Essays* (Philadelphia, 1846), 19.
   "The very idea of a social system," wrote Joseph Caldwell Huske, a college junior, "implies the sacrifice of every feeling like individuality." A "reigning principle" must promote harmony and to hold together the discordant elements of society: "Wherever the general interest reigns paramount to individual claim, then may we look for the perfection of Socialism." Approximation to equality is compatible "with a just consolidation of rank, which does not destroy 'the gradations just & nice

The nature of social relations, specifically the master–slave relation, commanded the attention of both laity and clergy. Ex-president Thomas Cooper of South Carolina College edited Justinian's *Institutes,* which drew a hard line between slavery and freedom and offered no intermediate status. But that line was a legal fiction mocked by social reality. In Roman society, numerous intermediate statuses existed; freedmen stood in a patron–client relation to former masters; much of the peasantry had been transformed into *coloni* and formally bound to the soil by Constantine. Roman jurists had a different understanding of freedom from the one that later emerged with bourgeois liberalism. The doctrine that the Roman slaveholder, as head of household, had absolute power over his slaves, wives, and children gave way to recognition of the moral personality of the slaves and the human rights of all dependents. The extent to which the state should intervene in the master–slave relation was a constant source of dispute from Roman times onward. Slaveholders coveted absolute power over their households but understood that abuse of power invited violent resistance and threatened the social fabric. Hence, Roman Censors established a principle of state intervention in households to check cruelty by masters. Much earlier, Greek society had sought to rein in the destructive tendencies of individual slaveholders and to correct imbalances of power dangerous to slaveholding society. Xenophon, reflecting on the immense fortunes that some citizens made off slave labor in the silver mines, proposed that the state buy and distribute slaves across a wide range to guarantee the broadest possible slaveholding.[40]

Roman comedies belied the stark separation of free from slave in Roman law and revealed to the historically grounded Southerners overlapping statuses. Thomas Cobb described emancipation in Greece and Rome as a kind of apprenticeship in a system of social stratification. Freedmen could achieve "real" freedom only if a free family adopted them. George Frederick Holmes, acknowledging intermediate statuses, saw each as tending either toward slavery or freedom and saw the intermediate statuses in free-labor societies in the context of class divisions that pushed laborers toward a disguised slavery. "Slaveholders," James Hammond wrote Clarkson in 1845, "are responsible to the world for the humane treatment of their fellow-beings whom God has placed in their hands." From the particular to the general: "Every man in independent circumstances, all the world over, and every Government, is to the same extent responsible to the whole human family for the condition of the poor and labouring classes in their own country." Fifteen years later: "Glorious Young America with whom *independence* is all and all, if it is also starvation: or

dependencies' of Society." See Huske, "Speech on the Influence of Christianity Socially and Politically Considered" (May 18, 1841), in Junior Compositions, 1839–1842, at UNC-NCC.

[40] Alan Watson, *Roman Slave Law* (Baltimore, 1987), 7, 42–3, 116–17, 127–8; Keith R. Bradley, "Roman Slavery and Roman Law," *Historical Reflections/Réflexions historiques,* 15 (1988), 494. The lex Aquila (probably late third century) "introduced a fundamental distinction between the free and the nonfree," which became blurred in practice and even at law: Yvon Thebert, "The Slave," in Andrea Giardina, ed., *The Romans,* tr. Lydia G. Cochrane (Chicago, 1993), 151, 167–8. On the Roman comedies see William Fitzgerald, *Slavery and the Roman Literary Imagination* (Cambridge, U.K., 2000), esp. ch. 3. On statuses between chattel and freemen in ancient Greece, see Yvon Garlan, *Slavery in Ancient Greece,* tr. Janet Lloyd (Ithaca, NY, 1982), ch. 2.

rather if it is the most ridiculous fallacy that ever entered the human brain. Who ever was, who ever can be independent?"[41]

Defenders of slavery, committed as they were to the notion of responsibility of masters to those of lower station, accepted self-interest as the guiding principle in human affairs. "The strongest moral propensity of man," wrote John Taylor of Caroline, "is to do good to himself. This begets a propensity to do evil to others." An "unalterable law" makes man guided by self-interest. From this premise, Taylor, like the later nullifiers, reasoned that the self-interest of majorities inexorably leads to the oppression of minorities. "He knows nothing of the human heart," John C. Calhoun told the Senate in 1838, "or the working of a political system extended over so wide a country, who does not see that there must be a constant tendency on the part of the stronger portion to monopolise all the advantages for itself and to transfer all its burthens to the weaker." Maria Henrietta Pinckney, an outstanding voice for the nullifiers, rested sovereignty on the will of civil society, self-constituted as "a moral person" whose will cannot be divided except as an act of self-destruction: "Self-interest is the governing principle of three-fourth of mankind." The unionist Reverend C. C. Jones of Georgia agreed: "The *power* of the principle of *self-interest* is the '*primum mobile*' of human action." Susan Dabney Smedes of Mississippi and Mary Howard Schoolcraft of South Carolina applied Pinckney's words to slaveholding: In the governance of slaves, self-interest combines self-protection with humane treatment of slaves.[42]

In theory, a chivalrous concern for the weak and dependent would reinforce enlightened self-interest to encourage masters to behave like good Christians. On North Carolina's Supreme Court the antislavery William Gaston and the proslavery Thomas Ruffin agreed that the progress of Christianity, combined with a heightened sense of self-interest, was engendering milder treatment of slaves. Fredrika Bremer, visiting the plantation of one of the most respected planters (probably, James Couper) on St. Simon's Island, observed his slave jury system and his encouragement of black self-reliance. She considered him too strict a disciplinarian to qualify as a reformer, thinking that he calculated a measure of benevolence to

---

[41] Cobb, *Law of Negro Slavery*, lxxiii, 283, 312; George Frederick Holmes, "Observations on a Passage in the Politics of Aristotle Relative to Slavery," *SLM*, 16 (Apr. 1850), 193–205; [Clyde N. Wilson], ed., *Selections from the Letters and Speeches of James H. Hammond* (Spartanburg, SC, 1978), 153–4; J. H. Hammond to Marcus C. M. Hammond, June 24, 1859, in Carol Bleser, ed., *The Hammonds of Redcliff* (New York, 1981), 59.

[42] J. Taylor, *Inquiry*, 72, 543; "Remarks on Daniel, Webster's Bill on the Public Deposits," June 28, 1838, in *JCCP*, 14:351; M. H. Pinckney, *The Quintessence of Long Speeches, Arranged as a Political Catechism, by a Lady for Her God-Daughter* (Charleston, SC, 1830), 19, 6; Ralph T. Eubanks, "The Rhetoric of the Nullifiers," in Waldo W. Braden, ed., *Oratory in the South, 1828–1860* (Baton Rouge, LA, 1970), 66–7; C. C. Jones to the graduating class of Columbia Seminary in 1837, quoted in Erskine Clarke, *Wrestlin' Jacob: A Portrait of Religion in the Old South* (Atlanta, GA, 1979), 65; Susan Dabney Smedes, *Memorials of a Southern Planter*, ed. Fletcher M. Green (New York, 1965 [1887]), lvii; "Letters on the Condition of the African Race," in *Plantation Life: Narratives of Schoolcraft*, Appendix, 15, 20. On self-interest considered as a rational function in the early Republic see Daniel W. Howe, "The Political Psychology of The Federalist," *WMQ*, 3rd ser., 4 (1987), 485–509, esp. 490.

serve his interests. Bremer did not understand that slaveholders defended their system precisely as one that blended self-interest with moral demands for humane treatment of labor. Proslavery pronouncements from the courts usually combined appeal to moral sentiment and to self-interest as complementary.[43]

Thomas Cooper loved and George Fitzhugh hated laissez-faire economics, but neither touted self-interest. "The people," Cooper told his students at South Carolina College, "are too often ignorant of, and too often false and traitorous to their own best interests." Although education might reduce the danger, "Neither individuals or bodies of men are generally guided by just considerations of their own good. They act as often from present temptations, from caprice, from prejudice, from flattery, from temporary excitements, from unfounded likings and dislikings." Fitzhugh agreed that self-interest drove men forward but considered Southerners culturally imprisoned by free trade in ideas as well as commodities and blind to their own interests: "No people have more individual pride and self-esteem than Southerners; none are so wholly destitute of national self-respect and appreciation." Fitzhugh reconciled the apparent contradiction between the doctrine of self-interest and the Christian–corporatist doctrine of social order: "Man has a double nature, which is necessary to his happiness and to his very existence. He has centripetal and centrifugal affections, selfishness and anti-selfishness." Slavery, the oldest and most natural form of human association, encouraged mutual affection: "The law of love in this naturally organized society is the law of self-interest." Slavery secured kind and humane treatment to the slave: "All the legislative ingenuity in the world will never enact so efficient a law in behalf of free laborers."[44]

College students got heavy doses of the prevalent version of individualism. Robert L. Dabney of Union Theological Seminary and Albert Taylor Bledsoe of the University of Virginia, although theological adversaries, agreed on the essentials. "Now it is the genius of slavery," Dabney wrote, "to make the family the slave's

---

43 For the typical southern view, see e.g. Iveson L. Brookes, *A Defence of the South against the Reproaches of the North* (Hamburg, SC, 1850), 12; for Gaston and Ruffin see Thomas D. Morris, *Southern Slavery and the Law, 1619–1860* (Chapel Hill, NC, 1996), 191; Fredrika Bremer, *Homes of the New World: Impressions of America,* 2 vols. (New York, 1853), 2:488. For James Hamilton Couper's reputation as a model master of the 1,500 slaves he owned or supervised, see James E. Bagwell, *Rice Gold: James Hamilton Couper and Plantation Life on the Georgia Coast* (Macon, GA, 2000), ch. 9. On the courts see also William E. Wiethoff, *A Peculiar Humanism: The Judicial Advocacy of Slavery in the High Courts of the Old South, 1820–1850* (Athens, GA, 1996), 13, and Mark V. Tushnet, *The American Law of Slavery: Considerations of Humanity and Interest* (Princeton, NJ, 1981). R. S. Gladney of Mississippi accepted the "coincidence" of morality with individual interest but insisted on limits: "Moral Philosophy," *SPR,* 9 (1855), 120–1.

44 Thomas Cooper, *Lectures on Political Economy,* 2nd ed. (Columbia, SC, 1830), 332; George Fitzhugh, "Uniform Postage, Railroads, Telegraphs, Fashions, Etc.," *DBR,* 26 (1859), 662; Fitzhugh, "The Middle Passage; Or, Suffering of Slave and Free Immigrants," *DBR,* 22 (1857), 571; Fitzhugh, *Cannibals All!; Or Slaves without Masters* (Cambridge, MA, 1960 [1857]), 79. Francis Lieber rejected the identification of Manchesterian political economy with utilitarianism: "Leading Truths in Political Economy," *DBR,* 15 (1853), 190. "A South Carolinian" attacked Paley for "making self interest the sole basis for virtue": "Slavery and Political Economy," *DBR,* 21 (1856), 345. But a pro-Manchester student asserted that self-love constituted the mainspring of human action: William D. Thomas, "Connection of Political Economy with Natural Theology" (M.A. thesis, 1854, typescript at UVA).

commonwealth. The master is his magistrate and legislator, in all save certain of the graver criminal relations, in which the commonwealth deals directly and personally with him." The slave became a member of the municipal society only through his master, who represented him with all other dependents: "To the commonwealth, the slave is only a life-long minor under the master's tutelage. Under slavery single families, authoritatively represented by the father and master, not single human beings, constitute society." Therein lies the fundamental difference between "the theory of the Bible, and that of radical democracy."[45]

Bledsoe, supported by George Frederick Holmes, said substantially the same from his own free-will perspective: Man loses his individuality and becomes a cog in a Rousseauan machine when he succumbs to an egalitarian democracy. Democracy he considered a wonderful system for a nation of gods, but not of men. W. J. Sasnett of Emory College depicted America's political freedoms as excessively broad and an invitation to wild social radicalism as more and more people claimed the right to place their subjective opinions above the Constitution and the laws. And William Frierson Cooper of Tennessee, who studied Alexis de Tocqueville carefully, concluded that democracy led to anarchistic "individualizing." Democracy weakened each person, concentrated power in a few hands, and ended with an overly powerful government – if not outright Caesarism.[46]

Fitzhugh, like Bledsoe, thought that even Samuel Johnson and Alexander Pope made dangerous concessions to bourgeois individualism. Bledsoe, Fitzhugh wrote, "justly argues that there is too much *individuality* in modern times. He hits the nail on the head. Individuality means liberty; the absence of government, the 'letting alone' of the individual." Similarly, a contributor of *Southern Quarterly Review* saw the great strength of America in its balance between individuation and the exigencies of social relations, which alone ground the process of individuation. Northern free-labor industrialism transformed healthy individualism into egotism, greed, and "unmanly homage to Mammon."[47]

---

[45] Dabney, *Defence of Virginia*, 229; also, Fletcher, *Studies on Slavery*, 5, 12, 23.

[46] John B. Bennett, "Albert Taylor Bledsoe: Transitional Philosopher of the Old South," *Methodist History*, 11 (1972), 243–5; "Mr. Smith" [of Virginia], "Character of the American People," *SQR*, n.s. (3rd), 2 (1857), 393–405; George Frederick Holmes, "Theory of Political Individualism," *DBR*, 22 (1857), 137–8, 146–7; W. J. Sasnett, "The United States – Her Past and Future," *DBR*, 12 (1852), 625; William Frierson Cooper, "Notes on a Trip to Europe, 1862–1863," 165, in Cooper Papers, at Tennessee State Library and Archives (Nashville). Following Wesley, southern Methodists established considerable doctrinal unity in their church, with minimal room for individual interpretation of Scripture: see Cynthia Lynn Lyerly, *Methodism and the Southern Mind, 1770–1810* (New York, 1998), 28. Two postbellum books on the family, one by a Calvinist and the other by an Arminian, well expressed the long-standing southern attitude toward the place of "servants" in the family and the limits of claims to individual rights: see Benjamin Morgan Palmer, *The Family, in Its Civil and Churchly Relations: An Essay in Two Parts* (Harrisonburg, VA, 1991 [1876]), and James O. Andrew, *Family Government: A Treatise on Conjugal, Parental, Filial and Other Duties* (Nashville, TN, 1882).

[47] George Fitzhugh, "Oliver Goldsmith and Dr. Johnson," *DBR*, 28 (1860), 513. "L.", writing in *Southern Quarterly Review*, prefigured Bledsoe's argument by denying that man surrendered any genuine liberty in the formation of society. "The law of individualism is not the foundation of liberty: the

Northern evangelicals, too, preached both individual liberty and stewardship as they sought to curb the radical individualism that threatened social order. But whereas northern evangelicals focused on reform of the capitalist marketplace, the southern defended an organic slave society. When northern and southern divines proclaimed property rights, they meant different things. For Northerners, property in one's self was the only just foundation for ordered liberty. They, too, spoke of the family as the cornerstone of society and upheld the authority of the male head of household. If the essential elements of bourgeois domesticity, which had emerged in Western Europe and the United States during the late eighteenth century, decisively shaped both northern and southern values, the great difference in outcomes lay in the dominant social and economic systems of the two regions: The slaveholding South remained more rural than the North. More important, the mainspring of economic production remained within slaveholding households rather than, as in the North, within an increasingly separate sphere of the market. Even where large areas of the North remained dominated by farm households, they tended to generate a more egalitarian spirit, primarily because the success of the farm depended upon the labor of all members of the family. Southerners were just as ready to acknowledge the moral personality and human rights of each member of the household, but the presence of slaves ensured that few would challenge the appropriateness of a male head as authoritative representative of slaves, women, and children. Thus, Southerners repudiated even the qualified egalitarianism of conservative northern divines.

Southerners themselves criticized bourgeois individualism and preached individual liberty and responsibility before God in a corporatist context, but they sometimes tripped over each other, displaying a tension brought to the fore by considerations of Catholic Spain. The Reverend Benjamin Morgan Palmer contrasted the thriftiness, industriousness, and enterprise of Protestant countries with the self-indulgence, indolence, and ignorance of Catholic, and he had especially hard words for Spain as cold, bigoted, and stern. Reporting from Spain, James Johnston Pettigrew, an Episcopalian, expressed admiration for the Catholic rites Palmer sneered at. Pettigrew did not so much disagree with Palmer's description as turn it against itself, warmly identifying Spaniards with American Southerners: "Of all the countries of Europe, therefore, Spain seems to me the best fitted for a republic, and the Spaniards to possess most happily the combination of national, local and personal pride, which fits men for living in an organized community, with the advantages of self-government." Expounding his view of the relation of the individual to society, Pettigrew suggested that the "Protestant idea" offered little consolation for

law of society presents it": "Religion in America," *SQR*, 7 (1845), 355. Holmes supported Bledsoe's critique of Blackstone, Burke, et al. on the surrender of liberty, noting Bledsoe's *Theodicy* and qualifications as a theologian: George Frederick Holmes, "Bledsoe on Liberty and Slavery," *DBR*, 21 (1856), 137–9. Stonewall Jackson, embodying the tension, agreed with Robert E. Lee that "duty" is the greatest word in the English language but also said, "You may be whatever you resolve to be": John Bowers, *Stonewall Jackson: Portrait of a Soldier* (New York, 1989), 56, 71.

the disappointed and crushed in spirit, although it "is, perhaps, better fitted for the affairs of this world, as it dwells more upon the fulfillment of our duties toward our fellow-men."[48]

The divines had to unravel a paradox inherent in Christian acceptance of self-love. They especially disparaged Claude Adrien Helvetius, the *philosophe* whose materialism had man act principally, if not solely, out of self-love. Simms, discussing "a tendency at once virtuous and vicious," took aim at Adam Smith's *Theory of Moral Sentiments,* which he understood to say that men act virtuously to secure social standing: "This sacrifice of our passive impressions to our active principles is nothing more than an exchange of commodities – we give up one set of interests merely that we secure another."[49]

In the much-reprinted *An Essay on the Influence of Religion, in Civil Society* (1788), the Presbyterian Reverend Thomas Reese of South Carolina, a schoolmaster, derided self-love as a destructive urge to immediate gratification. In later years, Thomas Peck proceeded more cautiously, telling his students in Richmond that self-love establishes a tendency more toward sin than virtue and passes into selfishness – blind appetite unrestrained by reason. Peck acknowledged self-love as indispensable, since to love your neighbor as yourself is to love yourself. Similarly, a contributor to *Southern Presbyterian Review* described self-love as "innate to man" and necessary to promote concern for others through a sense of dependence upon Jesus. The Reverend C. P. Gadsden, a Calvinistic Episcopalian and Thornwell protégé, cautioned that self-seeking leads away from God: "Self-will is the darling of the soul, which must be placed entire upon the altar, if the service is to be complete." So where does an acceptable form of self-love end and selfishness or self-seeking begin? Thomas Smyth, in two discourses on "Fear as a Christian Motive," endorsed "self-love" as a healthy impulse to do right, lest you suffer eternal punishment for sins. He explicated the Golden Rule: "In absolute literality no man can or ought to love his neighbor as himself, for he may love himself to an extent that is sinful and unjust – nor to do to others just as, in any given case, he might *selfishly* desire them to do to him."[50]

Among the Episcopalians, the theologically liberal James Warley Miles urged a *via media* between the excessive individualism of the right of private judgment and the need for collective stability. Bishop Richard Wilmer of Alabama assailed the Disciples of Christ: "Individualism bursts into full-bloom under their favoring

[48] Benjamin M. Palmer, *Influence of Religious Belief upon National Character: An Oration Delivered before the Demosthean and Phi Beta Kappa Societies of the University of Georgia* (Athens, GA, 1845), 22–3; [James Johnston Pettigrew], *Notes on Spain and the Spaniards in the Summer of 1850, with a Glance at Sardinia* (Charleston, SC, 1861), 77–8, 377.

[49] [William Gilmore Simms?], *SWMR,* 2 (1845), 413.

[50] Thomas Reese, *An Essay on the Influence of Religion, in Civil Society* (Charleston, SC, 1788); Peck, *Miscellanies,* 2:136–56; "The Phases of Society," *SPR,* 8 (1855), 217; James H. Elliott, ed., *Tributes to the Memory of the Rev. C. P. Gadsden, with Thirteen of His Sermons* (Charleston, SC, 1872), 216; *TSW,* 6:277–301, quote at 372; also, Brevard Diary, Aug. 31, 1860, at UNC-SHC. For the commercially oriented J. D. B. De Bow, self-love both causes and remedies social evil: *DBR,* 3 (1847), 168–9.

auspices. Every man can be a preacher, and every woman if she claims the privilege." The Disciples, in turn, filed that very indictment against others. Alexander Campbell, whose revivalist theology turned men inward, firmly stressed the common life of the visible church as witness to the presence of the Holy Spirit. Franc Carmack, a Disciples preacher and college professor, commented in a sermon on the difference between the old and new covenants: "Under the Patriarchal covenant a man might be religious alone – that is religion was rather an individual than a social institution. The family constituted the congregation of worshippers under the supervision of the father or patriarch, hence the name. Under the new covenant men cannot live to themselves, but they are connected together in a social capacity .... The Kingdom of Heaven is eminently a social institution." In accents reminiscent of St. Cyprian's controversial dictum, Carmack announced, "There is no such thing as doing the service of God outside the Church."[51]

Although southern divines resisted the interpretation of society as a collection of atoms, they often slipped into it. Presbyterians resisted by concentrating on the conversion of whole families, but even the Baptists and Methodists, who focused on individuals, recoiled from the consequences of their strategy. Presbyterians campaigned for family prayers more strongly than Methodists, but Methodist "classes" accomplished something of the same purpose. Evangelicals stressed personal sin, guilt, and redemption – but also corporate discipline through the church in a manner compatible with the ideology and politics of slave society.[52]

Just before and also during the War, the southern divines honed their indictment of bourgeois individualism. Episcopalian Bishop Thomas Atkinson of North Carolina, preaching "On the Causes of Our National Troubles" after Lincoln's election, castigated New England's "self-sacrificing, individualism." To its abandonment of Christian teaching and discipline he attributed much of the violence, disrespect for human life, and shameful condition of northern cities: "Our institutions themselves have fostered the spirit of individualism, that sense of the duty and right of each person to judge for himself what he is to do or refuse to do."[53]

The Scottish Enlightenment had taught that the interests of society and of individual coincided. Still, during the eighteenth century, American Protestants generally agreed that the public good might require suppression of minority views, and

[51] James Warley Miles, *Philosophic Theology; Or, Ultimate Grounds of All Religious Belief Based on Reason* (Charleston, SC, 1849), 224–8; Richard Wilmer, *The Recent Past from a Southern Standpoint: Reminiscences of a Grandfather* (New York, 1887), 106–7; on Campbell see W. C. Gilpin, "Communal Theology of the Disciples," in Kenneth Lawrence, ed., *Classic Themes of Disciples Theology: Rethinking the Traditional Affirmations of the Christian Church (Disciples of Christ)* (Fort Worth, TX, 1986), 29–48; Carmack Diary, Nov. 9, 1856.

[52] See esp. Margaret Burr DesChamps, "Presbyterian Church in the South Atlantic States" (Ph.D. diss., Emory University, 1952), 37, 39. The southern churches heavily emphasized the family, not the individual.

[53] W. S. Powell, "Opening Years of Thomas Atkinson's Episcopate," in Lawrence Foushee London and Sarah McCulloh Lemmon, eds., *The Episcopal Church in North Carolina, 1701–1959* (Raleigh, NC, 1987), 240–1.

the early state constitution of South Carolina made political rights subject to the exigencies of community life. Jefferson Davis nonetheless plausibly wrote after the War: "A marked characteristic of the Southern people was individuality." They learned the hard way, Davis thought, that war requires surrender of the individual will. How well Southerners learned that lesson remains moot, but, since almost every southern writer followed Aristotle in insisting upon the social basis of individuality, the characteristic to which Davis alluded appears paradoxical.[54]

The strength of the southern "social bond individualism," as Richard Weaver has called it, arose from the confluence of two socially grounded attitudes that might seem mutually exclusive: a folkish "I'm as good as any man," which existed everywhere yeomen prevailed; and the expectation of deference among those who commanded slaves and saw themselves as masters of all they surveyed. The genius of prewar southern politics lay in its ability to merge these tendencies, although by no means totally, into a conservative republicanism that assured social stability. To exercise hegemony and forge a broad defense of slave property, the slaveholders had to present their anti-egalitarianism in a way that accommodated the sensibilities of proud and tough nonslaveholders who valued nothing so much as their own independence. Southern individualism has always coexisted, if uneasily, with characteristics familiar to folk cultures all over the world: authoritarianism, fatalism, ethnocentrism, and a cultural conservatism that buttresses hierarchy in communities perceived as organic.[55]

"Jeffersonian democracy" and evangelical religion accommodated and contributed to a fundamentally conservative transcendence of opposites. The folk ethic, disciplined by evangelical religion, made the individual responsible for his acts in a fluid and socially mobile society. The fate of everyman in this world, although perhaps not the next, depended upon individual effort as well as on God's providence. It accorded with the persistent spirit of the Celtic clans, which prompted eveyone to rally around local leaders and promote community coherence. These "individualists" did not easily succumb to the lures of Emerson's "age of the first person singular" or to a philosophy that recognized nothing as sacred except the integrity of one's own mind, and they had little patience with Thoreau's dream of an America that freed the individual from social repression and promoted community as an association of free individuals unencumbered by prejudice and tradition.[56]

---

[54] Jefferson Davis, *The Rise and Fall of the Confederate Government*, 2 vols. (New York, 1958), 1:443. The term "individualism" made its way into the English language from the French about 1840 with the translation of Tocqueville and Chevalier. See Barry Alan Shain, *The Myth of American Individualism: The Protestant Origins of American Political Thought* (Princeton, NJ, 1995), 84, 91–2.

[55] Our discussion owes much to the outstanding work of John Shelton Reed on southern folkways and their persistence and on the contradictions those folkways posed for an individualism that in some ways approximated the bourgeois spirit. See especially his succinct argument given in "The Same Old Stand," in "Fifteen Southerners", *Why the South Will Survive* (Athens, GA, 1981), esp. 22–4. Our main criticisms concern his slighting of the slaveholders' worldview and its reconciliation of the antagonistic elements he carefully delineates.

[56] For a sympathetic treatment of Emerson and Thoreau that bares everything that "individualistic" Southerners deplored, see F. O. Matthiessen, *American Renaissance: Art and Expression in the Age of*

Tocqueville, whom Southerners as well as Northerners read with respect, observed that democracy and erosion of class lines made every American a stranger to every other – neither owing nor being owed anything: "Thus not only does democracy make every man forget his ancestors, but it hides the descendants, and separates his contemporaries, from him; it throws him back for ever upon himself alone, and threatens in the end to confine him entirely within the solitude of his own heart." Few Southerners relished such a democracy, no matter how loudly they proclaimed themselves equal to the high and mighty. For slaveholders and yeomen alike, the men who made Calhoun's "constitutional democracy" possible were not isolated individuals but heads of households, morally responsible for all in their charge.[57]

Looking beyond the South, slaveholders and countless other Southerners saw a world that mocked their aspirations and threatened their vision of social order. "Now we witness," Holmes wrote in 1853, "the universal anarchy of the world in all forms of speculation and practice, brought about by the tyranny and exclusive dominion of the intellectual autocracy, which we have entrenched and enthroned and almost canonized." Holmes could not contain himself: "It is the lawless ascendancy, the riotous license of the reason from which we suffer – the want of any moral authority – the disregard and contempt of religion, except so far as it is the plastic creature of our own capricious interpretations. We forge in these days the creeds in which we profess to believe; and we make with our own fancies the idols which we pretend to venerate as gods." In later years he added that the struggle for freedom of thought had gone so far as to recognize no authority except individual reason, and he declared the collectivism of Fourier, Proudhon, Saint-Simon, and Owen discredited and yielding to the extreme political individualism of Herbert Spencer and Stephen Pearle Andrews.[58]

The War brought intensification of southern preaching against radical individualism. The Reverend Richard De Veaux of Alabama called for prostration to God and "renunciation of self-dependence and self-reliance." The Reverend William Wheelwright told troops in Virginia that "self" lay at the heart of Confederate difficulties. While he admired the chivalrous spirit, he warned that it easily passed into boastfulness and led Southerners to forget that "He that exalteth himself shall be abased." Self-reliance is a virtue and an integral part of the heroic character, but only when subjected to knowledge and discipline. The Reverend William Hall identified the fundamental conditions of human history as sin and redemption. The

Emerson and Whitman (New York, 1968) esp. 5–8, 77–9, 106, 194. New England Transcendentalists "came to see the individual as the fount of eternal truths and society as a conspiracy to silence these truths": John C. Spurlock, *Free Love: Marriage and Middle-Class Radicalism in America, 1825–1860* (New York, 1988), 43.

[57] Alexis de Tocqueville, *Democracy in America*, tr. Henry Reeve, 2 vols. (Boston, 1873), 2:121.

[58] [George Frederick Holmes], "Revival of the Black Arts," *MMQR*, 4th ser., 6 (1854), 193; [Holmes], "The Bacon of the Nineteenth Century," *MMQR*, 4th ser., 5 (1853), 352; Holmes, "Theory of Political Individualism," 137–8, 146–7; also, Sasnett, "United States – Past and Future," 625; [Holmes], "Spencer's Social Statics," 185–219. Joseph R. Wilson agreed with Holmes that Fourierism and radicalism were waning: J. R. Wilson, *Mutual Relations of Masters and Slaves, as Taught in the Bible* (Augusta, GA, 1861), 9.

Fall meant that selfishness dethroned the law of love in man's breast, so that man seeks unchecked power over others. "Extreme individualism" assaulted theology and social order. Hall lauded the South for fighting to preserve individual liberty within ordered society. In 1888 Basil Manly, Jr., reiterated: "The priesthood of all believers is exercised within a community of fellow believers-priests who share a precious faith." It "should not be reduced to modern individualism, not used as a cover for theological relativism." Hall and Manly, like Cooper and Hammond before them, problematically assumed that slavery could cure the disease. The militantly proslavery Frederick Porcher approved of slavery's influence in making the slaveholder self-reliant and encouraging him to care for others, but he added ruefully that it also made him "little regardful of the power or the claims of society."[59]

For a long time after the War, southern novelists focused on community and family – in contrast to northern novelists, who focused on the individual. In the twentieth century acute Southerners, whether liberals like Clement Eaton or conservatives like John Gould Fletcher, agreed on the curious blend of individualism and corporatism in southern culture and, more important, on the roots of corporatism in the family. Eaton wrote of the Old South: "Southerners tended to evaluate people not so much as individuals but as belonging to a family, a clan." Fletcher wrote that the people of Arkansas display "the contrasting qualities of social conservatism and individual daring, generosity and narrowness, adaptability to circumstances and freedom from outside influence, matter-of-factness and mysticism, that the English, Scotch, North Irish peasantry also have displayed." Recently, Marion Montgomery has expressed the underlying attitude as succinctly as anyone in the Old South ever did. There can be no such thing as the self-made man, "only the self-unmade man, the first in our long history of unmakings usually spoken of under the name Old Adam. For whatever the nature of man's actions as 'maker,' whatever his calling, he is always operating upon *givens,* with *givens,* and *out* of his own givenness."[60]

---

[59] Richard De Veaux, *Fast-Day Sermon* (Mobile, AL, 1862), 3; William H. Wheelwright, *Discourse Delivered to the Troops Stationed at Gloucester Point* (Richmond, VA, 1862), 10–11; also, Thomas S. Dunaway, *A Sermon Delivered ... before the Coan Baptist Church* (Richmond, VA, 1864), 8; William A. Hall, *Historic Significance of the Southern Revolution* (Petersburg, VA, 1864); Basil Manly, Jr., *The Bible Doctrine of Inspiration* (Nashville, TN, 1995 [1888]), 260–1; F. A. Porcher, "Southern and Northern Civilization Contrasted," *RM,* 1 (1857), 100. See also a Catholic version of this theme: Aug. 22, 1863, in Mary D. Robertson, ed., *A Confederate Lady Comes of Age: The Journal of Pauline DeCaradeuc Heyward, 1863–1888* (Columbia, SC, 1992), 22.

[60] Clement Eaton, *The Mind of the Old South* (Baton Rouge, LA, 1964), 226; John Gould Fletcher, *Arkansas* (Fayetteville, AR, 1989), 262; also, Rollin G. Osterweis, *Romanticism and Nationalism in the Old South* (Baton Rouge, LA, 1971), 19; Marion Montgomery, *Possum: And Other Receits [sic] for the Recovery of "Southern" Being* (Athens, GA, 1987), 40; on the postbellum novelists see Robert A. Lively, *Fiction Fights the Civil War: An Unfinished Chapter in the Literary History of the American People* (Chapel Hill, NC, 1957).

Vilfredo Pareto, a severe critic of radical democracy, ridiculed the ideas of interdependence and "solidarity" that engrossed the European Right as well as Left at the opening of the twentieth century: "Since one individual is dependent on the other individuals, he can realize his own welfare only by working for the welfare of others." The trouble is, Pareto replied, "The wolf realizes its welfare by

Individualism, even in its peculiarly conservative southern form, tends to place the state in hostile relation to society's discrete units, individual and corporate. Herein lies a principal germ of the disintegration of community itself, for a competitive marketplace turns its losers over to the state for the protection and succor that their communities cannot provide. The republican South remained rent by the tension between a preference for laissez-faire economics, hostility to the concentration of political power, adherence to an individualism of heads of families, and a simultaneous preference for the implicit corporatism of the family as the fundamental institution of society.[61]

devouring the sheep, the slave-owner by exploiting the slave." Pareto, *The Mind and Society: A Treatise on General Sociology*, tr. Andrew Bongiorno and Arthur Livingston, 4 vols. (New York, 1963), 3:948.

[61] [William Gilmore Simms], "Critical Notices," *SQR*, n.s., 1 (1856), 554. Simms, conceding that Catholic historians had their own biases, was pleased to report on a recent book by Peter Fredet, a Catholic who held his bias to a minimum and treated his antagonists courteously.

22

Past and Future Caesars

"Extremes necessitate extremes" is axiomatic in the Science of Government. I have been pained and astonished to find how many are now willing to glide unhesitatingly into a dictatorship, a military despotism – even into a state of colonial dependence, with gradual emancipation as a condition for foreign intervention and protection. Hatred of Lincoln, not love of our liberties, principles and institutions now actuates the masses.

—Augusta Jane Evans (1864)[1]

So far as we know, no southern slaveholders read *The Communist Manifesto*. They did not have to: They saw for themselves the specter that was haunting Europe – and the North. "The great sore of modern society," M. R. H. Garnett of Virginia's social and intellectual elite proclaimed, "is the war between capital and labour." That war, according to the Reverend Thornton Stringfellow of Virginia, began in biblical times, often spun out of control, and invited military dictatorship. The proslavery preachers, teachers, editors, and theorists who shaped public opinion pondered the lessons of ancient and modern history, fascinated by the careers of Julius Caesar, Oliver Cromwell, and the two Bonapartes.[2]

A letter to the editor of *Virginia Literary Museum* in 1829 listed the principal destroyers of liberty: Caesar, "listening to the suggestion of unprincipled ambition"; Cromwell, "under the show of asserting the rights of conscience"; and Napoleon, driven by the desire to create "universal and unlimited monarchy." For Judge Joseph Lumpkin of Georgia, Caesar and Cromwell qualified as "scourges and destroyers of our species, and Napoleon resembled Nero, Caligula, Genghis Khan, and Tamerlane – a man whose life taught "the doctrine of man's fall and total depravity." Well and good, but not good enough. Military despots, the Reverend R. H. Rivers

---

[1] Augusta Jane Evans to J. L. M. Curry, Jan. 21, 1864, in Rebecca Grant Sexton, ed., *A Southern Woman of Letters: The Correspondence of Augusta Jane Evans Wilson* (Columbia, SC, 2002), 92.

[2] [M. R. H. Garnett], *The Union, Past and Future: How It Works, and How to Save It*, 4th ed. (Charleston, SC, 1850), 30–1; Thornton Stringfellow, *Slavery: Its Origin, Nature, and History, Considered in the Light of Bible Teachings, Moral Justice, and Political Wisdom* (New York, 1861), 31.

of Alabama remarked, arise in times of anarchy, arrogate to themselves the law of the land, and resort to oppressive iron rule. Yet, in times of "great corruption of morals," military despotism "is certainly better than anarchy." Dedicated republicans though the slaveholders were, they found themselves gripped by the thought that only some form of military dictatorship – Caesarism or Bonapartism, as you prefer – could save Europe and eventually the North from a plunge into proletarian revolution and anarchy.[3]

For Francis Pickens of South Carolina, Julius Caesar's "universal genius seemed to grasp every thing." For Henry Hughes of Mississippi, Caesar united thought and action. For the Reverend William A. Hall of New Orleans, he opened a new historical period by launching "the Roman Empire, the last and grandest of the old-world powers." Southerners admired Caesar as a great general, political leader, prose stylist, and orator. The editors of *Southern Quarterly Review* rated him an orator second only to Cicero and his *Commentaries,* "a model of good composition and literary ability." George Frederick Holmes considered him Cicero's superior as a judge of men and as the finest grammarian of his day. For all that, these and other southern critics agreed with Cicero: "It is in the greatest souls and in the most brilliant geniuses that we usually find ambitions for civil and military authority, for power, and for glory." Plutarch, who sympathized with Caesar's struggle against the aristocratic party, linked him to Alexander and Cyrus as men with an unquenchable and ultimately destructive thirst for empire: Great men have great vices to match great virtues. Weighing pros and cons, Southerners doubtless approved Caesar's lenient treatment of rebellious Jews, much as they cringed at his proverbial bisexual promiscuity. And whatever the reality and complexities of Caesar's life, he appeared in *chansons de geste* – along with Hector, Alexander, and Scipio – as exemplar of the chivalric tradition.[4]

Influenced by Plutarch and Shakespeare, Southerners nonetheless viewed Caesar as embodiment of a danger that standing armies pose to free institutions. Every schoolboy knew Patrick Henry's famous outburst, "Caesar had his Brutus – Charles the first his Cromwell, and George the Third [cries of "treason"] may profit by their

---

[3] M. T. Gabbleton to the Editor, *VLM,* 1 (1829), 164; Joseph Henry Lumpkin, *Address Delivered before Hopewell Presbytery, the Board of Trustees of Oglethorpe College* (Milledgeville, GA, 1837), 7, 8; R. H. Rivers, *Elements of Moral Philosophy* (Nashville, TN, 1859), 262–3, quote at 263.

[4] Francis W. Pickens, *Science and Truth: An Address Delivered before the Literary Societies of Erskine College, S.C.* (Fraziersville, SC, 1849), 7; Douglas Ambrose, *Henry Hughes and Proslavery Thought in the Old South* (Baton Rouge, LA, 1996), 57; William A. Hall, *Historic Significance of the Southern Revolution* (Petersburg, VA, 1864), 6; "American Literature – 1," *SQR,* 11 (1847), 133; *SQR,* n.s. (3rd), 1 (1856), 437; [G. F. Holmes], "History of Literature," *SQR,* 2 (1842), 515; Cicero, *De Officiis,* tr. Walter Miller (LCL), Bk. 1:8, 27; Plutarch, *The Lives of the Noble Grecians and Romans,* tr. John Dryden, ed. and rev. by Arthur Hugh Clough, 2 vols. (New York, 1992), 2:446, quote at 485; Zvi Yavetz, *Julius Caesar and His Public Image* (Ithaca, NY, 1983), 61, 104–8; Robert C. Stacey, "The Age of Chivalry," in Michael Howard et al., eds., *The Laws of War: Constraints on Warfare in the Modern World* (New Haven, CT, 1994), 27. Caesar lowered Judea's taxes. Many planters named their slaves Caesar; some named their sons Julius or Augustus. Georgia had an "Augustus Burrell Julius Nicholas Paschal": George W. Paschal, *Ninety-Four Years: Agnes Paschal* (Spartanburg, SC, 1974 [1871]), 46.

example." When the Whigs sought to discredit Andrew Jackson as an incipient Caesar, Henry Clay echoed Henry: Just as Greece had its Alexander, Rome its Caesar, England its Cromwell, and France its Napoleon, America faced a tyranny fed by popular adulation of a military hero. Suetonius provided a chilling account of the response of Sulla, the Roman dictator, to pleas to pardon Julius: "Have your way and take him. But bear this in mind: the man you are so eager to save will one day be the ruin of the nobles, whose side you have upheld with me; for in this Caesar there is more than one Marius." Respect for the republicanism that Julius' coup trashed led Southerners to his arch-foe, Cato the Younger – William Byrd II's "honest Cato" and Senator Edward Livingston's "stern republican." The Cato of "imperishable renown" comforted Franklin Smith of Canton, Mississippi, much as "the stern and inflexible countenance of a Cato" comforted W. J. Tuck of Memphis.[5]

In modern Europe aristocrats extolled the "mixed government" of the Roman republic and viewed the Empire as a tyranny, but bourgeois doted on the Empire. Southerners, having little use for hereditary aristocrats and less for bourgeois, charted their own course. Thomas Jefferson poured his wrath over Alexander Hamilton for describing Caesar as the greatest man who ever lived. (Apparently Hamilton, whose private and public papers reject Caesar as a tyrant, was teasing the humorless Jefferson, who took him straight.) Frank Alfriend, in *Southern Literary Messenger,* styled Caesar "the most detestable of tyrants, and the worst of men." Holmes portrayed the extinction of the Roman Republic and the onset of the Empire as "the saddest, but the most significant period of secular history." He ironically announced that Julius Caesar stood as "the grandest and the most splendid figure in all profane history" and recalled that Shakespeare had called him "the foremost man of all the world." Holmes ended caustically: "All current civilization does homage at the shrine of Caesar." In a similar vein, Elliott Story of Southampton County, Virginia, concluded that Alexander had triumphed in part because of his "temperance, moderation, and simplicity" but had become a less effective leader when he gave in to "voluptuousness, cruelty and extravagance." Eyeing the nomination of Zachary Taylor in the light of ancient history, Story concluded that societies place themselves at risk when they raise military men to political power.[6]

---

[5] Henry's words were popularized by William Wirt in *Sketches of the Life and Character of Patrick Henry* (Philadelphia, 1817), 68. On the Whigs see Edwin A. Miles, "The Whig Party and the Menace of Caesar," *Tennessee Historical Quarterly,* 27 (1968), 361–79 (the Whigs dropped the theme of ambitious military heroes when they nominated Harrison in 1840); Suetonius, *The Lives of the Twelve Caesars,* tr. Joseph Cavorse (New York, 1931), 3; Kevin Berland et al., eds., *The Commonplace Book of William Byrd II of Westover* (Chapel Hill, NC, 1996), 149 (#261); Edward Livingston, Mar. 9, 1830, in Herman Belz, ed., *The Webster–Hayne Debate on the Nature of the Union: Selected Documents* (Indianapolis, IN, 2000), 435; Franklin Smith to J. C. Calhoun, Dec. 22, 1847, in *JCCP,* 25:35; W. J. Tuck, "The Mind, Its Powers and Results," *SLM,* 10 (1844), 662; also, Thomas Roderick Dew, *Digest of the Laws, Customs, Manners, and Institutions of the Ancient and Modern Nations* (New York, 1884 [1852]), 323–4. See also Supplementary References: "Addison's *Cato.*"

[6] Andrea A. M. Kinneging, *Aristocracy, Antiquity and History: Classicism in Political Thought* (New Brunswick, NJ, 1997), 110–11; Thomas P. Govan, "Alexander Hamilton and Julius Caesar: A Note on Historical Evidence," *WMQ,* 3rd ser., 32 (1975), 475–80; Frank H. Alfriend, "A Southern Republic and a Northern Democracy," *SLM,* 37 (1863), 283–6; [G. F. Holmes], "Recent Histories of

Throughout the nineteenth century, European and American liberals grudgingly conceded and conservatives proclaimed that the record of military strongmen from Caesar to Napoleon showed the ease with which democracy passes into despotism. During Virginia's constitutional debates, both Alexander Campbell, speaking for reformers, and James Monroe, speaking for conservatives, invoked Caesar's rise to power to demonstrate that tyranny inexorably follows the concentration of power in the hands of a few. Chief Justice John Belton O'Neall of South Carolina referred contemptuously to a repressive legal action as "an unfit garb to clothe a republican" and as akin to "putting on the statue of Washington the robe of the Caesars." As O'Neall knew, Romans gave the title "Father of his country" both to Cicero for having saved the Roman Republic and to Caesar for having overthrown it. Before and after the War, Southerners contrasted the patriotic purity of Robert E. Lee with the selfishness of Julius Caesar, who conquered barbarians only to destroy the liberties of his own people. Lee himself classified Caesar with Frederick the Great and Bonaparte as "great tyrants." Still, in 1861 secessionists could not resist recalling the fateful words of Caesar ("the die is cast") at the Rubicon.[7]

In *Southern Quarterly Review*, J. L. Reynolds of South Carolina referred to "the despotism of the Caesars" and its attendant "moral degeneracy." An anonymous author sarcastically painted the historian Jules Michelet as denigrating the early Romans but sparing Caesar, who reminded Michelet of "the great and estimable" Napoleon. Another dubbed Caius Gracchus an inadequate leader: "The Roman people, even at the time of the Gracchi, needed a Julius Caesar." Meanwhile, William J. Grayson, poet and politician of coastal South Carolina, found in Caesar the noble qualities of a true gentleman.[8]

Caesarism compelled consideration of the proper relation of elites to plebeians and of democracy to dictatorship, and it rekindled disgust with demagogic pandering to the masses. The "dregs of Rome," wrote a contributor to *Southern Literary Messenger*, facilitated Caesar's subversion of the republic, much as *sans culottes*

Julius Caesar," *SR* (Baltimore), 1 (1867), 383–4, 412; Elliott Story quoted in Daniel W. Crofts, *Old Southampton: Politics and Society in a Virginia County, 1834–1869* (Charlottesville, VA, 1992), 46–7. Caesar never mentioned the extent of the casualties in his wars, but southern writers did: see e.g. "Observations on the 'Caesars' of De Quincy," *SLM*, 29 (1859), 279. Americans had access to Pliny the Elder's remarks on the human cost of Caesar's victories over his Roman rivals: A slaughter that was "a very great wrong against the human race, even though this had been forced upon him": *Natural History: A Selection*, tr. John F. Healy (London, 1991), Bk. 7:92. Caesar prudently did not publish the relevant details. See also Supplementary References: "Caesarism."

[7] On Campbell and Monroe see Dickson D. Bruce, Jr., "The Conservative Use of History in Early National Virginia," *Southern Studies*, 19 (1980), 132, 135; O'Neall quoted in A. E. Keir Nash, "Negro Rights, Unionism, and the Greatness of the South Carolina Court of Appeals: The Extraordinary Chief Justice John Belton O'Neall," *South Carolina Law Review*, 21 (1969), 152; J. William Jones, *Personal Reminiscences of General Robert E. Lee* (Baton Rouge, LA, 1989 [1875]), 46, 224; also, R. M. T. Hunter's oration at the inauguration of Crawford's equestrian statue of Washington in Richmond in 1858, in *SLM*, 26 (1858), 172–4; Yavetz, *Caesar and His Image*, ch. 1.

[8] [J. L. Reynolds], "Roman Literature," *SQR*, 10 (1846), 369, and 11 (1847), 508; "Caius Gracchus," *SQR*, n.s., 4 (1851), 63; [William J. Grayson], "The Character of the Gentleman," *SQR*, n.s., 7 (1853), 55–6.

facilitated the imposition of despotism in France. But since all Roman emperors pandered to the plebs, bread and circuses alone cannot account for the greater popularity of one emperor over another. Style had much to do with it. Tacitus admitted that Nero and Caligula had significant support among the plebs, in part because of their behavior at circuses. Pompey may have matched Caesar in dispensing largesse, but Pompey did not win the hearts of the plebs as Caesar did. Caesar projected the image of a man of the people; Pompey did not. Nero won a reputation for aversion to the signing of death warrants. Caesar, too, affirmed abhorrence of cruelty, and he often did cushion his ruthlessness with compassion. A lesson: James Walker of Charleston observed that the Roman masses loved Nero because his blows fell not on them but on the privileged classes.[9]

To win the hearts of the people, Roman rulers, like the Greek, made hated oligarchs tremble and showed them a measure of contempt. Yet no ruler could with impunity render property unstable, much less carry out a social revolution. Rome had boisterous, threatening, politically influential crowds, but they rarely carried more than sticks and stones. Men of power, including emperors, understood that the crowds they tried to please and pacify hardly constituted a threat to the social order. When plebs soured on a ruler they yearned for a better one, not for the overthrow of the Principate. "There are no instances in history of the people as whole," writes Zvi Yavetz, "taking part in revolutions or uprisings." Thomas Roderick Dew and J. L. M. Curry read Roman history in precisely that way, concluding that ancient slave societies escaped the modern world's destructive class warfare.[10]

In Dew's view, Caesar had no intention of reestablishing the republic. Guided largely if not solely by "inordinate ambition," he ruled as emperor in everything but name. Yet, Dew the republican, like Oliver Goldsmith the monarchist, considered the assassination of Caesar "a great misfortune for Rome" since the shattered republic was beyond repair anyway. Goldsmith, in a history of Rome recommended by George Fitzhugh and assigned in southern schools, glorified Caesar, passed lightly over his faults, and left little doubt that Rome would have been better off had he not been assassinated. Dew, more partial to the Greeks than to the Romans, ranked Caesar below Alexander in part because Caesar knew much about the establishment of dominion but little about its preservation. Dew reluctantly conceded that Augustus gave Romans the best government they could sustain. Similarly, Dew defended the autocracy of Constantine: "For an empire fallen so low, as the Roman was at this time, despotism was almost the only support that remained."[11]

9 "The Early History of Virginia," *SLM*, 22 (1856), 112; *Tacitus: The Histories,* tr. Clifford H. Moore (LCL), 9; and see Yavetz, *Caesar and His Image,* 55–6; [James M. Walker], *Tract on Government* (Boston, 1853), 26. For reference to Nero's aversion see *Magnolia,* 4 (1842), 120.

10 Zvi Yavetz, *Plebs and Princeps* (Oxford, U.K., 1969), quotes at 14, and see chs. 2 and 3; Yavetz, *Caesar and His Image,* 55–6; Dew, *Digest,* 291; Curry, "Perils and Duty of the South," in Jon L. Wakelyn, ed., *Southern Pamphlets on Secession, Nov. 1860–April 1861* (Chapel Hill, NC, 1996), 8–19. Much of Nero's power and popularity with the masses, Dew said, rested on the dole.

11 Dew, *Digest,* 278, 287, 310, quote at 287; *Oliver Goldsmith's Roman History, for the Use of Schools,* revised and corrected by William Grimshaw (Philadelphia, 1835), chs. 19–21. Dew knew of Edward Gibbon's description of Augustus as at first the enemy and at last the father of the Roman world:

Oliver Cromwell – a modern Caesar to many Southerners – became the center of prolonged, passionate debate in sermons, books, and leading journals. Some condemned Cromwell for his massacre of Irish royalists at Drogheda and for the destruction of English liberties. Others credited him with raising England to new heights of glory and respect. In 1846 *Southern Quarterly Review* devoted more than thirty pages to Thomas Carlyle's edition of Cromwell's *Letters and Speeches,* giving Cromwell a good report while it strove mightily to balance David Hume's hostility against Carlyle's apologetics.[12]

Edmund Randolph of Virginia and Joseph B. Cobb of Mississippi assailed Cromwell as a usurper, a fanatic, and a hypocrite. John Taylor of Caroline wrote: "Cromwell, a fanatick, was stubbornly honest, but authority melted that honesty because human nature cannot resist the moral law which imposes new opinions with new circumstances." W. C. Rives contrasted Hampden's disinterested statesmanship with "the guilty ambition of Cromwell." Fitzhugh peppered a polemic with "coarse and cruel as Cromwell," "the despotism of Cromwell," and the "usurper Cromwell" who seized power "by treason, perjury, and regicide." In South Carolina, John C. Calhoun referred to Cromwell as a "Despot" in the manner of Caesar, Napoleon, "and every other successful usurper of the People's rights."[13]

If detractors abounded, so did admirers. J. C. Thompson, a Nashville businessman, pronounced Cromwell, "a man of valour and loved of the people." An anonymous author had him stand with Hildebrand and Peter the Great among the great empire-builders of northern Europe who sought to do God's work by restoring order and effecting beneficial changes. But, like Hildebrand and Peter, Cromwell began as a reformer and ended as a despot. The Reverend Edward Reed – preaching at Flat Rock, South Carolina – lauded Cromwell, pummeling the Stuarts and decrying the heart of the English people as too sinful to endure Puritanism. Despite the long southern war against Puritans and Puritanism, Confederates repeatedly proclaimed

---

Edward Gibbon, *The History of the Decline and Fall of the Roman Empire,* ed. David Womersley, 3 vols. (London, 1994), 1:96.

[12] J. D. B. De Bow, "Bancroft's History of the United States," *DBR,* 15 (1853), 184; S. F. Glenn, "Sydney and His Compatriots," *DBR,* 15 (1853), 291–6; on Drogheda and the massacres in Ireland see "Ireland in 1834," *SQR,* 6 (1844), 3; "Cromwell's Letters and Speeches," *SQR,* 10 (1846), 257–92, esp. 288. In praise also see "The Study of History," *SQR,* 10 (1846), 142; and for a glowing defense of Cromwell and the Puritans as godly and constructive see Henry D. Inglis, "Oliver Cromwell," *SQR,* 12 (1855), 384–406. For Simms's attempt at balanced judgment see "Headley's Life of Cromwell," *SQR,* 14 (1848), 506–38. The Baptist Reverend Basil Manly even praised Cromwell as an enlightened supporter of progressive agriculture: "An Address on Agriculture," in *Proceedings of the Agricultural Convention of the State of Alabama* (Tuscaloosa, AL, 1842), 12.

[13] Edmund Randolph, *History of Virginia,* ed. Arthur H. Shaffer (Charlottesville, VA, 1970), 106, 149, 153; "J. B. C." [J. B. Cobb], "Macaulay's History of England," *American Whig Review,* 11 (1850), 355; John Taylor, *An Inquiry into the Principles and Policy of the Government of the United States,* ed. Loren Baritz (Indianapolis, IN, 1919 [1814]), 444; W. C. Rives, *Discourse on the Character and Services of John Hampden, and the Great Struggle for Popular and Constitutional Liberty in His Time* (Richmond, VA, 1845), 62; George Fitzhugh, "Frederick the Great by Thomas Carlyle," *DBR,* 29 (1860), 157, 163. Recollections of Cromwell's dictatorship in Virginia fed opposition to standing armies and preference for militia: see Robert K. Brock, *Archibald Cary of Ampthill: Wheelhorse of the Revolution* (Richmond, VA, 1937), 31–2.

their army rightful heir to Cromwell's bible-reading army. Presbyterians especially invoked the inspiring triumphs of the pious Roundheads and sometimes linked Cromwell to George Washington. *Southern Presbyterian Review* limned a slandered Cromwell as a great Christian and a political leader whose death ended England's last hope of a seventeenth-century regeneration. The Reverend D. H. Hall thought Cromwell a good Calvinist and rejoiced that Carlyle, Merle D'Aubigné, and Thomas Babington Macaulay repelled the canard that he was a "cold-blooded canting hypocrite." During the War, Presbyterians in Lexington, Virginia, hung two portraits in their homes: Stonewall Jackson and Oliver Cromwell. Jackson's troops likened him to Cromwell, and Jackson himself was impressed with Macaulay's account of Cromwell's religiously motivated army.[14]

The Reverend Benjamin Morgan Palmer, addressing Louisiana's Crescent Rifles in 1861, quoted Cromwell with approbation, as did Albert Gallatin Brown of Mississippi when he called for resistance to northern aggression – "Pray to God and keep your powder dry." The Reverend J. W. Jones, author of *Christ in the Camp*, ranked Cromwell's army just below the army of Northern Virginia among the most religious armies in world history. As W. W. Bennett, who also chronicled religious life in the Confederate army, wrote: "Whatever some may think of Oliver Cromwell, there is no doubt that he was a devout and earnest Christian, and that there was much sound religion among his invincible 'Ironsides.'" The Reverend Robert Dabney dissented but within limits, hotly noting that, unlike Cromwell, Jackson did not try to usurp the place of the clergy. Jackson, he said, was no fanatic and would never have committed such atrocities as the execution of Charles I or the massacre at Drogheda. To Catherine Cooper Hopley, an English schoolteacher in Virginia, Stonewall Jackson embodied the best of the Puritans and Cavaliers, deeply pious without fanaticism, and with a gentler temperament than Cromwell had. So powerful did the revivals in the Confederate army become that William Corsan, a pro-Confederate English businessman, compared Stonewall Jackson to Cromwell: "It is possible that such Generals may be beaten, if opposed to superior numbers and skill, of course, but what chance equal forces and ability can have against an army led by such a man ... I cannot imagine."[15]

[14] [J. C. Thompson], "Butler's Analogy," *SQR*, n.s., 10 (1854), 208; "Peter the Great," *SQR*, n.s., 12 (1855), 124–6; Edward Reed, *A People Saved by the Lord* (Charleston, SC, 1861), 7; "Letters and Speeches of Oliver Cromwell," *SPR*, 1 (1847), 124–5; D. H. Hall, "The Bible," *SPR*, 7 (1853), 388–9; John S. Wise, *The End of an Era* (Boston, 1900), 240. The highly regarded Merle D'Aubigné upheld the claims of Cromwell – "the great Oliver" – to religious sincerity: "I present him as a Christian – a Christian to Christians – to Protestant Christians": D'Aubigné, *The Protector: A Vindication* (New York, 1847), v–vi, quote at 21. For Cromwell as a great progressive leader see John S. Preston, Jr., "Address at the Laying of the Corner Stone of the University of the South," *University of the South Papers*, ser. A, 1 (Sewanee, TN, 1860), 50. But Basil Manly credited Catherine, not Peter, for having "introduced Russia to notice among the civilized nations": Basil Manly, Sr., "An Address on Agriculture," in *Proceedings of the Agricultural Convention of the State of Alabama* (Tuscaloosa, AL, 1842), 9.

[15] Thomas C. Johnson, *The Life and Letters of Benjamin Morgan Palmer* (Richmond, VA, 1906), 239; Brown in Dunbar Rowland, ed., *Mississippi: Comprising Sketches of Counties, Towns, Events, Institutions, and Persons, Arranged in Cyclopedic Form*, 4 vols. (Spartanburg, SC, 1976 [1907]), 2:494;

Robert Howison, in his *History of Virginia* (1846), slammed as stupid and malicious Robert Beverley's criticism of Cromwell. According to Howison, Cromwell's "sagacious intellect" made him too wise to be harsh, and his Protectorate became "the most glorious period that his country had known." *Quarterly Review of the Methodist Church, South,* proceeding more cautiously, combined respect for Cromwell's contributions as a Christian statesman with measured criticism of his failing. In 1849 it reprinted a short piece from the *Spectator* that sought to be evenhanded while supporting Cromwell's claims to be an honest Christian. Subsequently, W. S. Grayson of Mississippi credited Cromwell with "the exalted hope" of establishing a Christian government, and even credited his "fanaticism" for a regime that respected "spiritual liberty." But Grayson saw a tragic flaw that led Cromwell to become "corrupted by the charm and lust of power." The pro-Irish Methodist James Davis, writing in *Southern Repertory and College Review* of Emory and Henry College, reasoned that such a spirit as Cromwell's, once aroused, must be expected to go to extremes and unleash destructive forces. From an Episcopalian perspective, Bishop Stephen Elliott, in the heady days of June 1861, lauded Cromwell's "genius" but referred to his "usurpation," which after his death "crumbled to the dust." Elliott shifted his tone in 1862 when the War started to go badly, commenting warmly on the piety of Cromwell and his army, which made them irresistible. The teen-aged Eliza Frances Andrews of Georgia looked up to Governor Joseph Brown as a man who would have fit right in with Cromwell's Ironsides, but she associated "prudence" with a puritanical self-seeking at variance with southern gallantry.[16]

Charles Royster, *The Destructive War: William Tecumseh Sherman, Stonewall Jackson, and the Americans* (New York, 1991), 44–5, 268; J. William Jones, *Christ in the Camp; Or, Religion in Lee's Army* (Richmond, VA, 1888), 20; William W. Bennett, *A Narrative of the Great Revival, Which Prevailed in the Southern Armies during the Late Civil War between the States of the Federal Union* (Harrisonburg, VA, 1989 [1876]), 11; R. L. Dabney, *Life and Campaigns of Lt. Gen. T. J. (Stonewall) Jackson* (Harrisonburg, VA, 1983 [1865]), 112–14; Catherine Cooper Hopley, *"Stonewall" Jackson, Late General of the Confederate States Army: A Biographical Sketch, and an Outline of His Virginian Campaigns* (London, 1863), 172–3; W. C. Corsan, *Two Months in the Confederate States: An Englishman's Travels through the South,* ed. Benjamin H. Trask (Baton Rouge, LA, 1996 [1863]), 100–1; also, George Cary Eggleston, *A Rebel's Recollections* (Baton Rouge, LA, 1996 [1871]), 154–5. The execution of Charles I still rankled in Virginia in the 1840s. Students at Hampden-Sidney in Virginia were debating the justice of the execution of Charles I: Marion Harland to Dorinda, Feb. 3, 1843, in [Mary Virginia Hawes Terhune], *Marion Harland's Autobiography: The Story of a Life* (New York, 1910), 90.

For other Presbyterian celebrations of Cromwell's army see T. V. Moore, *God Our Refuge and Strength in This War* (Richmond, VA, 1861), 13; *A Discourse Delivered by the Rev. J. Jones to the Rome Light Guards and Miller Rifles* (Rome, GA, 1861), 13; Alexander Sinclair, *A Thanksgiving Sermon Preached in the Presbyterian Church at Six Mile Creek, Lancaster District, S.C.* (n.p., 1862), 8. Also, Cornelia Peake McDonald, Mar. 10, 1863, in Minrose C. Gwin, ed., *A Woman's Civil War: A Diary, with Reminiscences of the War from March 1862* (Madison, WI, 1992 [1875]), 246. After the War, the Reverend George Junkin, who supported the Union, announced that Cromwell ruled well because he respected the Sabbath: George Junkin, *Sabbatismos: A Discussion and Defence of the Lord's Day of Sacred Rest* (Philadelphia, 1866), 134–5. When *Southern Literary Messenger* needed a space-filler, it sometimes found an item in praise of Cromwell: see e.g. *SLM*, 26 (1858), 61.

[16] Robert R. Howison, *A History of Virginia from Its Discovery and Settlement by Europeans to the Present Time,* 2 vols. (Philadelphia, 1846), 1:303, 308 n. b; "Daubigné's Vindication of Oliver

The extremes to which Cromwell's critics and admirers went betrayed deep-seated uneasiness over Caesarism as a regime both abominable and sometimes necessary. J. D. B. De Bow remarked ruefully, "Caesars, Alexanders, and Napoleons have deluged the world with blood," but he described Cromwell's party as one of the best in history and his Protectorate as one of the most brilliant periods in British history. De Bow commended both Cromwell and Charles II for advancing the cause of commerce, which, under Christian influence, would bring world peace and order to the world. Even Edmund Ruffin, ordinarily the most decisive of men, equivocated a bit. Influenced by Macaulay, he described Cromwell as "the greatest king, if not the greatest man that England has produced – the most virtuous of usurpers, & the most moderate, just, & benign of despots." The exigencies of the War for Southern Independence raised the disagreeable possibility that the modern world might need a Cromwell after all.[17]

Reflections on Caesar, Cromwell, and Caesarism provided a context for evaluations of Napoleon Bonaparte and Napoleon III – Louis Bonaparte or "Napoleon The Little," as Victor Hugo and Karl Marx unfairly called him. Thomas Carlyle and Sir Walter Scott directly influenced perceptions of the first Napoleon. Scott's nine-volume *Life of Napoleon* became the subject of extensive correspondence between Rachel Mordecai Lazarus of Virginia and Scott's friend, Maria Edgeworth, a novelist much admired by Jefferson and Southerners generally. Edgeworth referred to Scott's biography as of "the most useful and moral kind" and as a stern admonition against blind ambition. Lazarus, citing William Ellery Channing, concurred. Southerners also weighed the conflicting judgments of other historians they regarded highly. Jean Charles Léonard Simonde de Sismondi took anti-Napoleonic ground until he witnessed the Bourbon restoration; then he supported Napoleon during the Hundred Days, concluding that, on balance, Napoleon benefited the cause of European liberty. In 1857, the anonymous author of a lead article in *Southern Literary Messenger* carried southern adoration of Madame Germaine De Staël a bit far: "The time may come when the conqueror of Lodi will be remembered only as the Banisher of De Staël." In contrast, Mary Chesnut scoffed at Napoleon's "so-called persecution" of Madame De Staël. Napoleon's chivalry or lack of it added a touch of humor. For the antis, Julia Pardoe, author of works popular in the South,

Cromwell," *QRMECS*, 3 (1849), 190–2; W. S. Grayson, "Cromwell and His Religion," *QRMECS*, 5 (1851), 58–85, quotes at 59, 60, 75; James A. Davis [the editor], "Enthusiasm as an Element of Enterprise and Success," *SRCR*, 2 (1853), 224; Stephen Elliott, *How to Renew Our National Strength* (Richmond, VA, 1862), 15; Stephen Elliott, *God's Presence with the Confederate States* (Savannah, GA, 1861), 11; Eliza Frances Andrews, *War-Time Journal of a Georgia Girl* (New York, 1907), Apr. 18 and June 27. *Quarterly Review of the Methodist Episcopal Church, South* hailed Carlyle's edition of Cromwell as superior to all others: A. B. Stark, "Thomas Carlyle," *QRMECS*, 15 (1861), 192.

17 [J. D. B. De Bow], *DBR*, 1 (1846), 107–8, 209–10; De Bow, *The Industrial Resources, Statistics, &c. of the United States and More Particularly of the Southern and Western States*, 3rd ed., 3 vols. (New York, 1966 [1854]), 1:305–6; Dew, *Digest*, 567–9; Ruffin, Aug. 24, 1862, in *ERD*, 2:429, also Jan. 31, 1863 (2:562). W. C. Rives of Virginia celebrated the merchants as magnificent in the English and American revolutions: *Discourse on the Character and Services of John Hampden, and the Great Struggle for Popular and Constitutional Liberty in His Time* (Richmond, VA, 1845), 35–6 n.

made unflattering comments on his unchivalrous attitude toward women. For the pros, Dr. J. G. M. Ramsey of Tennessee, historian and staunch democrat, had good words for Napoleon, characterizing his campaign in Russia as chivalric in the leniency and humanity shown lords and serfs alike. But then, Ramsey intended less to glorify Napoleon than to indict the barbarism displayed by the Yankees in their occupation of east Tennessee.[18]

For Protestants, Napoleon's conquests significantly reduced Catholic power in Europe despite his concordat with the Vatican. For opponents of bigotry, the southern press congratulated him for liberating the Jews. Women especially reacted against British treatment of Napoleon in exile. Mary Hamilton Campbell decried a "cruel and useless severity very much to their discredit." Like Eleanor Parke Custis and others, she probably read Edward O'Meara's sympathetic *Napoleon in Exile* (1822) and admired Napoleon as a patriot and man of honor. Mary Howard Schoolcraft ranked him with Webster and Calhoun as a genius.[19]

The stance toward Napoleon as a historical figure and toward his immediate political course did not always coincide. Federalists and Republicans alike protested

[18] Rachel Mordecai Lazarus to Maria Edgeworth, Jan. 6, 1827, Maria Edgeworth to Rachel Mordecai Lazarus, Aug. 19 and 20 (quoted), 1827, and Rachel Mordecai Lazarus to Maria Edgeworth, Oct. 1 and Nov. 28, 1827, in E. E. MacDonald, *The Education of the Heart: The Correspondence of Rachel Mordecai and Maria Edgeworth* (Chapel Hill, NC, 1977), 112, 139, 147–8, quote at 139; J. C. L. Sismondi, *A History of the Italian Republics,* ed. Wallace K. Ferguson (Gloucester, MA, 1970), 288–90; "Great Monarchs of France," *SLM,* 25 (1857), 407; Chesnut Diary, Aug. 27, 1861, in C. Vann Woodward, ed., *Mary Chesnut's Civil War* (New Haven, CT, 1981), 167; Miss [Julia] Pardoe, *Episodes of French History during the Consulate and the First Empire,* 2 vols. (London, 1859), 1:185; William B. Hesseltine, ed., *Dr. J. G. M. Ramsey, Autobiography and Letters* (Knoxville, TN, 2002), 130, 168–9. *Southern Review* assayed a balanced estimate of Napoleon's accomplishments and his offenses against liberty, finding Scott's *Napoleon* a brilliant narrative but marred by Tory bias, blanket hostility to the French Revolution, and failure to appreciate Napoleon's genius and such achievements as the Code Napoleon: *SR,* 1 (1828), 159–93, 272–5. J. B. Cobb of Mississippi dismissed Scott's *Napoleon* as inferior work: [Cobb], "Macaulay's History of England," 348. Jasper Adams, however, drew on Scott to stress Napoleon's fear of freedom of the press: Adams, *Elements of Moral Philosophy* (Philadelphia, 1837), 464–5. "A volume should be written," Perry Miller observed, "on the image of Napoleon in democratic America": *The Raven and the Whale: The War of Words and Wits in the Era of Poe and Melville* (New York, 1956), 189. See also Supplementary References: "Napoleon – Southern Assessments" and "De Staël."

[19] Joseph I. Shulim, *The Old Dominion and Napoleon Bonaparte: A Study in American Opinion* (New York, 1952), chs. 1, 4, and 6; Campbell Diary, 1823, at UNC-SHC; Eleanor Parke Custis to Elizabeth Bordley, Jan. 15, 1823, in Patricia Brady, ed., *George Washington's Beautiful Nelly: The Letters of Eleanor Parke Curtis Lewis to Elizabeth Bordley Gibson, 1794–1851* (Columbia, SC, 1991), 131; also, Margaret Galbreath Autobiography, 1825, in Joan E. Cashin, ed., *Our Common Affairs: Texts from Women of the Old South* (Baltimore, 1996), 219; *Plantation Life: The Narratives of Mrs. Henry Schoolcraft* (New York, 1969 [1860]), v. For a complimentary reference to Napoleon's justice for Jews see William C. Somerville, *Letters from Paris on the Causes and Consequences of the French Revolution* (Baltimore, 1822), 200. On Napoleon and the Catholic Church see Kenneth Scott Latourette, *Christianity in a Revolutionary Age,* 5 vols. (Grand Rapids, MI, 1958), 1:143–57. Robert L. Dabney, toward the end of his life, suggested that Napoleon's Concordat with the pope actually reduced the threat of Catholic domination of France and provided new evidence for the necessity of the separation of church and state: Thomas Cary Johnson, *Life and Letters of Robert Lewis Dabney* (Carlisle, PA, 1977), 429.

his coup d'etat, and economic considerations strengthened sentiment for neutrality in the unfolding European war. The Charleston *Courier*'s opening issue in 1803 called him the "Colossus of Europe" and predicted that he would invade America through the Mississippi Valley. Virginians were selling tobacco and wheat to France but much more wheat to Britain. When war came, Federalists supported the coalition while the Republicans adhered to neutrality. In 1822 William Somerville of Virginia derided Napoleon for not knowing when to stop, for collecting sycophants, and for being "a man who considered mankind nothing and himself as everything," but he credited him with restoring order during the first two years of the Consulate. Much as Somerville deplored Napoleon's tyranny and "contempt for human nature," he considered him more humane, generous, and civilized than Alexander, Augustus, and other predecessors. In 1829 a contributor to *Virginia Literary Museum* offered, "Napoleon, with that penetration for which he was so distinguished," and in 1837 Henry Lee recalled Napoleon as a great man and military genius.[20]

Other Virginians challenged the impression left by Parson Weems in his bestselling *Life of Washington,* in which Napoleon appeared as "that wonderful man." In 1811 John Randolph called Napoleon, among other niceties, a "coward," and his opinion worsened over time. Napoleon, according to John Tyler in 1837, had little to show for his effort beyond a torrent of blood. From Paris during the Hundred Days, Representative Thomas B. Robertson sent the Richmond *Enquirer* letters subsequently republished by the *National Intelligencer* and as a book by Matthew Carey in Philadelphia. The pomp and pretense of Napoleon's court stung Robertson's republican soul, and he declared the "magnificent" proceedings fit for infants and the frivolous, although he agreed with Napoleon's sentiment that Americans – facing a continuing threat from Britain – wanted a strong hand in Paris. Robertson defended the "necessary revolution" of 1789 that had destroyed a privileged nobility and priesthood, and he laid into the counterrevolutionaries of 1815: "The royalists exhibit themselves in their true colors. Jacobinism was never so prosperous; and vengeance and blood, and terror are the order of the day." He concluded, with Sismondi, that the good Napoleon probably did overmatch the evil. Robertson's balance sheet included respect for his personal courage and for a "generous and humane" regime replete with immense public works, schools, and hospitals. He drew a hard lesson for Americans. By becoming a despot who depoliticized the people, Napoleon dug his own grave: He destroyed "that patriotism and zeal which his own safety and greatness as well as that of France equally required."[21]

---

[20] Herbert Ravenel Sass, *Outspoken: 150 Years of the News and Courier* (Columbia, SC, 1953), 3–4; Somerville, *Letters from Paris,* 178–9, 186–7, 190–4, 200 (Jews), quotes at 186 and 190; "Obituary: Count Daru," *VLM,* 1 (1829), 428; Henry Lee, *The Life of Napoleon Bonaparte, Down to the Peace of Tolentino and the Close of His First Campaign in Italy* (London, 1837). For earlier apologies for Napoleon see also Richard Beale Davis, *Intellectual Life in Jefferson's Virginia, 1790–1830* (Chapel Hill, NC, 1964), 273. Pro-Napoleon plays and demonstrations in New Orleans and elsewhere especially drew praise from those who boldly defended the chivalric tradition. Southern literary journals published poems about Napoleon, some biting but most with a measure of sympathy: see e.g. William H. Holden, "Napoleon," *Magnolia,* 2 (1836), 181.

[21] Mason Locke Weems, *The Life of Washington. A New Edition with Primary Documents* (Amonk, NY, 1996 [1809]), 131; Randolph, July 15, 1814, in [N. B. Tucker], ed., "Mss. of John Randolph,"

In 1848 a contributor to *Southern Literary Messenger* assailed Napoleon for imposing tyranny over the people's thoughts as well as action. James Johnston Pettigrew then arraigned Napoleon and Metternich for using armed force to repress intellectual freedom. Toward the close of the War for Southern Independence, Edmund Ruffin recalled his youthful reaction to Napoleon's exile to Elba. The War of 1812, he wrote, "had made me a bitter hater of England – & therefore a well-wisher of Napoleon, as the great enemy of England." Ruffin considered his own attitude excusable in time and place, but a reading of Lamartine and other historians made him admire Louis XVIII. Thomas Ritchie, among other Virginians, also regretted the initial defeat of Napoleon and wished him success in his dramatic Hundred Days. Southerners found themselves drawn to and repelled by the great man who promised to humble the British Empire, spread French law and civilization, crush reactionaries and Jacobins alike, and reestablish political and social order. In January 1813, Representative Joseph Pearson of North Carolina, a Federalist, sent John Steele news of Napoleon's defeat in Russia and of his probable death: "I would not deny myself the satisfaction of endeavoring to be the first to communicate this glorious news." But even old Federalists like Richard Furman of Charleston got nervous when Napoleon went down at Waterloo. They wondered if Britain would turn its military buildup against America. And there were men like Ellwood Fisher, who groaned that not even Napoleon's genius could secure continental Europe against the power of British capital. Napoleon had a special appeal in the South, where the Presbyterian Reverend George Armstrong of Norfolk spoke for many educated Southerners in declaring that the French were in need of a strong leader to govern them. R. S. Gladney and Albert Taylor Bledsoe appealed to the testimony of Napoleon, dubbed by Gladney "the hero and statesman of the age," as one who believed France incapable of sustaining free government. Bledsoe – citing Napoleon on the French love for equality and indifference to liberty – observed, "The French are not the only people who care little for liberty, while they are crazy for equality."[22]

SLM, 2 (1836), 570; John Tyler, "Oration at Yorktown," *SLM*, 3 (1837), 750; [Thomas B. Robertson], *Letters from Paris, Written during the Period of the Late Accession and Abdication of Napoleon, by a Representative in the Congress of the United States* (Petersburg, VA, 1816), June 10, 18, 30, 1815 (13–16, quotes at 15, 16), July 8, 1815 (101, 102–3), Aug. 15, 1815 (149).

[22] "Hannibal and Bonaparte," *SLM*, 14 (1848), 421–35; [James Johnston Pettigrew], *Notes on Spain and the Spaniards in the Summer of 1850, with a Glance at Sardinia* (Charleston, SC, 1861), 9; Mar. 12, 1865, in *ERD*, 3:800–1, quote at 800; Joseph Pearson to John Steele, Jan. 24, 1813, in Henry McGilbert Wagstaff, ed., *The Papers of John Steele*, 2 vols. (Raleigh, NC, 1924), 2:700; James A. Rogers, *Richard Furman: Life and Legacy* (Macon, GA, 1985), 160–1; [Ellwood Fisher] et al., *Letter to the Secretary of the Treasury, on the Effect of the Tariff of 1842* (Cincinnati, 1845), 10; George D. Armstrong, "Three Letters to a Conservative – Letter I," *Presbyterian Magazine*, 13 (1858), 12; R. S. Gladney, "Relation of State and Church," *SPR*, 16 (1866), 350; Albert Taylor Bledsoe, *An Essay on Liberty and Slavery* (Philadelphia, 1856), 129. Gladney was right about Napoleon's abiding contempt for the French, especially the Parisians: see Paul Johnson, *Napoleon* (New York, 2002), 41–2, 115–16. On Ritchie see William Glyde Wilkins, ed., *Charles Dickens in America* (New York, 1970), 185; also, Charles Henry Ambler, *Thomas Ritchie: A Study in Virginia Politics* (Richmond, VA, 1914), 60, 62. John Felton Mercer of Virginia – Federalist and later Whig – considered Napoleon's educational system a force for political stability and the overcoming of class warfare. But he, too,

The southern elite never lost its fascination with Napoleon. Abiel Abbot of New England recounted a dinner conversation in Charleston at which Mitchell King judged Napoleon a great man less for his military exploits than for the Code Napoleon, which he deemed unequaled in jurisprudence. Bishop Christopher Gadsden and his brother John Gadsden agreed that the Code Napoleon was a great work but not greater than Blackstone's Commentaries. They twitted King that Napoleon proved a ruthless despot, and besides, France's leading jurists wrote most of the Code Napoleon. King retorted that a great man may be a great villain. In 1829 in *Virginia Literary Museum,* "C. C." reproached Napoleon for having retarded mass education as dangerous to his rule, but the Napoleon he reproached had "masterly genius." Henry W. Miller of North Carolina, referring to Cromwell and Napoleon, derided power-hungry tyrants who justified themselves as enemies of existing tyranny and disorder. But a touch of grudging admiration marked his reference to "the fiery despotism of Napoleon." Benjamin Perry, unionist leader in the South Carolina upcountry, considered Napoleon the greatest of all military conquerors and also a great orator and literary stylist. Dew agreed with Adolphe Thiers's estimate of Napoleon as a man who continued the French Revolution "by seating himself, a plebeian, on a throne."[23]

Napoleon's funeral procession in 1841 stirred a wave of nostalgia, which was fed by reports from Paris written by Virginia's David Hunter Strother ("Porte Crayon"). If Napoleon had not become Europe's great conqueror, A. B. Meek told students at LaGrange College in Alabama, he "would perhaps have been its first philosopher." A contributor to *Southern Literary Messenger* wrote that Napoleon wielded "monstrous" power but displayed a "superhuman intellect" and emerged as "the master intellect of his race." Thomas Cobb, Georgia's outstanding legal scholar, admired the "sagacious wisdom of his master mind," restoring monarchy even as he suppressed the obnoxious pretensions and abuses of the old aristocracy while trying to restore slavery in Haiti. In 1854 even the deeply conservative Robert Dabney credited the Napoleonic Code as an embodiment of the great movement for "securing liberty of conscience and domestic order." Howison commented that the French Revolution's terrible course "was only relieved by the stern rule of the Man of

---

welcomed Napoleon's fall. See Douglas R. Egerton, *Charles Fenton Mercer and the Trial of National Conservatism* (Jackson, MS, 1989), 44, 92. European exiles in America responded variously. In the wake of the Reign of Terror and subsequent wars, they welcomed Napoleon's invitation to return. The Belgian-born Rosalie Stier Calvert of Maryland began with gratitude, grew hostile, became pro-British, and cheered at Napoleon's fall. See e.g. Margaret Law Callcott, ed., *The Mistress of Riversdale: The Plantation Letters of Rosalie Stier Calvert, 1795–1821* (Baltimore, 1991), 29–30, 33, 153–4, 249.

23 John Hammond Moore, ed., "The Abiel Abbot Journals: A Yankee Preaches in Charleston Society, 1818–1827," *South Carolina Historical Magazine,* 68 (1967), 125–6 (Nov. 27, 1818); "C. C.", "Education of the People," *VLM,* 1 (1829), 252; Henry W. Miller, *Address Delivered before the Philanthropic and Dialectic Societies of the University of North-Carolina* (Raleigh, NC, 1857), 13–14, quote at 23; Stephen Meats and Edwin T. Arnold, eds., *The Writings of Benjamin F. Perry,* 3 vols. (Spartanburg, SC, 1980), 1:325, 336; Dew, *Digest,* 656–7. "B. H. B." of LaGrange, Georgia, agreed that Napoleon rescued France from anarchy, but his reading of Thiers led him to an emphasis on the tragic results of Napoleon's despotism: "The Consulate," *QRMECS,* 2 (1848), 447, 451, and "The Empire," *QRMECS,* 2 (1848), 618–25.

Destiny." Jefferson Davis had four busts in his presidential office in Montgomery: Calhoun, Clay, Webster, and Napoleon.[24]

During the War, Confederate Brigadier General St. John Richardson Liddell named Hannibal and Napoleon as the two greatest generals in history. Not even the most politically conservative preachers could resist the lure of the great Napoleon, some regretting that the Confederacy had no such man. Bishop Alexander Gregg of Texas criticized Napoleon but gushed over "that wonderful man, who convulsed Europe and astonished the world." Although the Presbyterian Reverend J. M. Atkinson of Raleigh compared him unfavorably to Washington and Andrew Jackson, he acknowledged "the incarnate genius of the great Revolution," whose "brilliant endowments" and "indefatigable power of bodily endurance" accompanied "insatiable thirst of military glory and supreme indifference to human life." In Virginia Charles Minnigerode, professor of classics and an Episcopal priest, spelled out the tragic consequences of the complex nature and historical significance of a Napoleon "doomed in his living death to see the world fall back a hundred years, which his ambition thought to overleap on the wings of his victorious eagles." Thus men, while wallowing in sin, may aim to benefit the human race by employing deplorable methods. "When a nation has filled up the measure of its iniquities," Reverend S. H. Higgins told the state legislature of Georgia in 1863, "and is ripe for the sickle of divine vengeance, God may put a rod into the hands of a Bonaparte." Recalling that God often uses a Nebuchadnezzar, an Alexander, a Caesar, a Napoleon to scourge sinful peoples, he picked up an old theme expressed by (among others) C. A. Woodruff of Tuskegee, Alabama, in 1851: God used Napoleon to inflict retribution for French infidelity. Neither suggested that Bonaparte had God's favor. Rather, God used him much as He had used heathens to smite His rebellious Chosen People.[25]

Notwithstanding the backing and filling, a majority view emerged: A strongman, however detestable, is preferable to the democratic excesses that generate anarchy, the tyranny of the lower classes, and a Jacobin reign of terror. In an open letter to Governor Edmund Randolph of Virginia in 1787, the anti-Federalist Richard Henry Lee ridiculed the widespread desire for a bad government to overcome anarchy, which he translated "as really saying that we must kill ourselves for fear of dying."

[24] Cecil D. Eby, Jr., *"Porte Crayon": The Life of David Hunter Strother* (Chapel Hill, NC, 1960), 35; Gary Philip Zola, *Isaac Harby of Charleston, 1788–1828: Jewish Reformer and Intellectual* (Tuscaloosa, AL, 1994), 65–6; A. B. Meek, *Romantic Passages in Southwestern History* (New York, 1857), 171; "Destiny of Russia," *SLM,* 19 (1853), 43; Thomas R. R. Cobb, *An Inquiry into the Law of Negro Slavery in the United States* (New York, 1968 [1858]), cxvi, clxxxiii; *DD,* 2:16; Howison, *History of Virginia,* 2:343; William C. Davis, *Jefferson Davis: The Man and His Hour* (New York, 1991), 314. For tortured remarks akin to those of Howison see J. B. Ferguson, *Address on the History, Authority, and Influence of Slavery* (Nashville, TN, 1850), 19.

[25] Nathaniel Cheairs Hughes, Jr., ed., *Liddell's Record: St. John Richardson Liddell* (Baton Rouge, LA, 1997), 28; Alexander Gregg, *A Sermon Preached in St. David's Church, Austin* (Austin, TX, 1862), 4; Joseph M. Atkinson, *God, the Giver of Victory and Peace* (Raleigh, NC, 1862), 9; Charles Minnigerode, *Power: A Sermon Preached at St. Paul's Church* (Richmond, VA, 1864), 10; S. H. Higgins, *The Mountains Moved; Or David upon the Cause of Public Calamity: Sermon ... at the Request of the General Assembly of Georgia* (Milledgeville, GA, 1863), 6; [C. A. Woodruff], "Islamism," *SQR,* 4 (1851), 179.

His polemic did not fare well in later years. George Fitzhugh attributed to Napoleon a conviction that liberation of the West Indian blacks meant the enslavement of European whites. Edmund Ruffin considered Napoleon's dictatorship the inevitable outcome of the absurd egalitarian doctrines and radical practices of the French Revolution. James Shannon of the Disciples of Christ demanded to know who doubted "that the military despotism established by Napoleon was infinitely preferable to a lawless mobocracy, which it succeeded." Holmes supported Napoleon's stern suppression of pernicious ideologies and a morally corrupt press. Napoleon, Americus Featherman wrote in *De Bow's Review,* qualified as a "misshapen monster" morally but a "giant" intellectually, a "genius" who restored order but fell prey to tyrannical ambition. William Gilmore Simms credited Napoleon with checking radical democracy. After the fall of the July Monarchy, Simms distinguished Napoleon and Louis Philippe as different sorts of despots. Napoleon "contrived to enslave, without degrading his people, while Louis Philippe degraded the people whom he had not the capacity to enslave." But then, what should one expect from a "selfish and cunning merchant-king"? Nathaniel Beverley Tucker mused that Napoleon had restored order and the world awaited repetition of his example. Yet proslavery theorists knew that Napoleon radicalized even as he conserved. As expressed by Michael Bakunin (the anarchist who challenged Karl Marx for leadership of the revolutionary Left), Napoleon, in spite of himself, advanced in politics the leveling principles advanced in philosophy and social theory by Kant, Fichte, Schelling, and Hegel.[26]

History – or the southern response to history – repeated itself with the emergence of Louis Bonaparte as Napoleon III. Before and after secession Southerners, prominent and obscure, clerical and lay, looked askance at the man and his distasteful regime. Margaret Johnson Erwin of Mississippi admired political strongmen and was presented to him at a ball in Paris; in 1849 she wrote, "Pshaw, what an oaf." Louisa McCord of South Carolina and the Reverend William A. Smith of Virginia denounced his "despotism." J. A. Turner of Georgia, a leading agricultural editor, rebuked him for restoring the pope's temporal power in Italy. Turner, like Smith and others, saw a dark Catholic plot to subjugate the free peoples of Europe. An article in *Jefferson Monument Magazine,* published by the University of Virginia's Jefferson Society, vilified Louis Napoleon's course as infamous, bloody, and reckless. Among prominent South Carolinians, Frederick Porcher denounced

[26] "Letter of Richard Henry Lee to Goveror Edmund Randolph," Dec. 22, 1787, in Bruce Frohnen, ed., *The Anti-Federalists: Selected Writings and Speeches* (Washington, DC, 1999), 364; George Fitzhugh, "The Conservative Principle," *DBR,* 22 (1857), 451–2; Fitzhugh, "The Revolutions of 1775 and 1861 Contrasted," *SLM,* 37 (1863), 721; James Shannon, *The Philosophy of Slavery, as Identified with the Philosophy of Human Happiness* (Frankfort, KY, 1840), 28; [George Frederick Holmes], "The Wandering Jew," *SQR,* 9 (1846), 78; Americus Featherman, "French Revolutionary History," *DBR,* 29 (1860), 679; [William Gilmore Simms], "Democracy in France," *SQR,* 15 (1849), 117–18, 153–4, quotes at 117, 118; [Nathaniel Beverley Tucker], "The Present State of Europe," *SQR,* 16 (1850), 291. For Simms, Napoleon was the "dead lion": see "The Tomb of Napoleon," *SLM,* 3 (1837), 367. For Bakunin see Eric Voegelin, *From Enlightenment to Revolution* (Durham, NC, 1975). President Mirabeau [Buonaparte] Lamar of the Republic of Texas, with some literary reputation, never used his middle name, dissociating himself from the Napoleon his father had admired in the 1790s: Philip Graham, *The Life and Poems of Mirabeau B. Lamar* (Chapel Hill, NC, 1938), 4 and n. 2.

his plebiscitary democracy. Among the obscure, Eliza Clitherall read of the wars that ravaged Europe in 1859 and, perhaps worrying about the impending civil war at home, blamed the "cruel heartless ambition" of Louis Bonaparte, whom she held responsible for the "vast catalogue of crime" and of "savage warfare." During the War, Basil Gildersleeve denigrated Jefferson Davis as following Louis Bonaparte's example, surrounding himself with clerks rather than statesmen.[27]

Yet, as hopes for stable republican regimes faded, southern apprehension over working-class insurrection rose. Louis Bonaparte, despot or no, looked better and better. In contrast to Margaret Johnson Erwin, the celebrated Madame Octavia Walton Le Vert of Mobile, a Clay Whig, offered a good opinion of Louis Bonaparte. In Paris a French countess assured her that the Republic had been horrible and that the arrival of Napoleon's iron hand was God-sent. Although the Reverend Daniel Dreher – alerting the citizens of Salisbury, North Carolina, to Yankee intentions in 1861 – denounced "military despotism" as "the most wretched of all governments," De Bow and Augustus Baldwin accepted Louis Bonaparte as a despot whose regime towered over its predecessors and greatly improved France.[28]

In 1853 William Forrest of Virginia, a local historian, remarked that the exiled Louis Bonaparte, whom Norfolk greeted warmly in 1837, now presided over France with an ability hitherto unsuspected even by his friends. James Johnston Pettigrew, calling Louis Bonaparte a man "really ambitious of advancing humanity," expected trouble from the "democratic element" that had helped raise him to power. Having seen southern Europe firsthand and being conversant with its languages and cultures, Pettigrew drew a bleak picture of Europe in 1850 as "a civilization which reduces men to machines, which sacrifices half that is stalwart and individual in humanity to the false glitter of centralization, and to the luxurious enjoyments of a manufacturing, money age!" Europe needed Louis Bonaparte's "consummate skill as a ruler" and his "hand of iron," for, sad to say, the course of the recent revolution had discredited republicanism. And not just republicanism: The course of the French, Simms wrote in 1856, has been fatal to the cause of democracy. Indeed, Louis Bonaparte's plebiscitary democracy discredited parliamentary government and universal suffrage so thoroughly as to cast reasonable doubt on the future of European liberalism and its social foundations.[29]

---

[27] Margaret Johnson Erwin to Eleanor Ewing, Dec. 14, 1849, in John Seymour Erwin, *Like Some Green Laurel: Letters of Margaret Johnson Erwin, 1821–1863* (Baton Rouge, LA, 1981), 45; Richard Lounsbury, ed., *Louisa S. McCord: Political and Social Essays* (Charlottesville, VA, 1995), 362; William A. Smith, *Lectures on the Philosophy and Practice of Slavery* (Nashville, TN, 1856), 267–8; J. A. Turner, *Letter to Hon. N. G. Foster* (Milledgeville, GA, 1855), 34; *JMM*, 2 (1851), 261; Clitherall Diary, July 19, 1859, at UNC-SHC; Charles J. Holden, *In the Great Maelstrom: Conservatives in Post–Civil War South Carolina* (Columbia, SC, 2002), ch. 2 (Porcher); B. L. Gildersleeve, "Davis (Altered by David)," in Richmond *Enquirer*, Dec. 3, 1863, reprinted in Ward W. Briggs, Jr., ed., *Soldier and Scholar: Basil Lanneau Gildersleeve and the Civil War* (Charlottesville, VA, 1998), 185.

[28] Frances Gibson Satterfield, *Madame Le Vert: A Biography of Octavia Walton Le Vert* (Edisto Island, SC, 1987), 123; Daniel I. Dreher, *A Sermon, June 13, 1861, Day of Humiliation and Prayer* (Salisbury, NC, 1861), 6; De Bow, *Industrial Resources*, 3:402; Augustus Baldwin Longstreet, *Fast-Day Sermon: Delivered in the Washington Street Methodist Episcopal Church* (Columbia, SC, 1861), 6.

[29] William S. Forrest, *Historical and Descriptive Sketches of Norfolk and Vicinity* (Philadelphia, 1853), 208; [Pettigrew], *Spain and the Spaniards*, 7, 8, 15, 16, quotes at 8, see also 51, 378, 381; [William

Southern commentators expressed disdain for Louis Bonaparte as a new despot who combined monarchy, democratic demagogy, and a bastardized socialism, but many simultaneously acknowledged him as the iron-fisted man of order needed to contain the class war between capital and labor. Among literary luminaries, William Elliott, in accord with John Berrien Lindsley, hailed Bonaparte as a "great man" whose strong-arm tactics kept "the discordant elements in the population in subjection." Clergymen who denounced him for restoring the pope to Rome recognized him as the long predicted military dictator needed to restore social order to a deranged continent. In Mississippi the Reverend T. T. Castleman informed students at Oakland College that the blind accumulation of capital in Europe and the North was destroying the values and institutions necessary to sustain civilization while fostering a struggle between capital and labor that must end with a Caesar or a Bonaparte.[30]

Even Southerners critical of Louis Bonaparte's Caesarism gratefully acknowledged him a man who knew how to discipline the bourgeoisie and repel the threat from the lower classes. Howard Caldwell of Charleston, lawyer and poet, scoffed at Victor Hugo for "stupidly railing at Louis Bonaparte." J. Q. Moore, in *De Bow's Review*, welcomed the coup d'état and Bonapartist restoration as the work of a heroic adventurer who saved France from anarchy, recapitulating his uncle's "merciful despotism" and restoring a "healthy, high-toned conservatism." Fitzhugh viewed Louis Bonaparte as a "physician" who was undoing the ravages of the radicalism run wild since 1789 and as a "practical socialist" architect of "a great economy" that taxed the rich to feed the poor, subjected labor to stern control, and reined in capitalist avarice. Holmes succinctly remarked that Louis Bonaparte, having triumphed over General Louis Eugène Cavaignac and his right-wing supporters, "crushed the Socialists and Red Republicans." To defend Louis Bonaparte against vicious detractors, Holmes compared him not with his uncle but with Augustus. Holmes emphasized the ability of both to mobilize the army politically and to win the support of "capitalists." He suggested that in those respects the career and regime of Augustus marked the beginnings of a modern history that was culminating in military despotism. Holmes ended with a muted testimony to Louis Bonaparte as savior of a corrupt and deranged Europe.[31]

Gilmore Simms], "Critical Notices," *SQR*, n.s., 1 (1856), 543. Simms praised *Sketches of Norfolk* in *SQR*, n.s., 10 (1854), 249–50.

30 Elliott quoted in Robert Nicholas Olsberg, "A Government of Class and Race: William H. Trescot and the South Carolina Chivalry, 1860–1865" (Ph.D. diss., University of South Carolina, 1972), 109 n. 39, 169; T. T. Castleman, "Address to the Literary Societies of Oakland College" (1859), 9, typescript at Oakland College; J. B. Lindsley, "Table Talk," June 2, 1862, in John Berrien Lindsley Papers, at Tennessee State Library and Archives (Nashville). See also *ERD*, 1:163, 3:69; Pamela Elwyn Thomas Colbenson, "Millennial Thought among Southern Evangelicals" (Ph.D. diss., Georgia State University, 1980), 70–5. By 1860, conservative opinion was ecstatic over Napoleon III's actions against the papacy: see e.g. "Napoleon III and the Papacy," *BRPR*, 32 (1860), 686–702. Alexandria City Hall and the Baltimore City Hall, as well as the city halls of Boston and Philadelphia, were built in the Second Empire style: John O. Peters and Margaret T. Peters, *Virginia's Historic Courthouses* (Charlottesville, VA, 1995), 133.

31 [Howard H. Caldwell], "Victor Hugo," *RM*, 1 (1857), 259; J. Q. Moore, "Louis Bonaparte and the French," *DBR*, 16 (1854), 382–96, quotes at 388, 392; George Fitzhugh, *Sociology for the South, or,*

Responses to the political career and historical writing of Alphonse de Lamartine exposed the ambiguities in southern attitudes toward Louis Napoleon. As early as 1836, William Drayton of South Carolina, in a proslavery polemic, embraced Lamartine's remarks on "the primitive constitution and the blood" of race as a powerful and immutable historic force. Southerners approved of Lamartine's defense of private property and the family against the radical measures of the French Revolution of 1848. Mary Chesnut found Lamartine an antidote for religious skepticism and was pleased that, in *Génieve*, he portrayed servants of Augustus Caesar's time as loyal to their masters. She reflected on the servants of the era of the French Revolution who, she imagined, also remained loyal unto death. Louisa McCord, however, judged Lamartine well intentioned but airy and enamored of the cant of "Liberty, equality, fraternity." Probably, Lamartine's gross ignorance of American institutions annoyed her as much as it annoyed Francis Lieber, a frequent guest at her table. Edmund Ruffin dismissed Lamartine's history of the Revolution of 1848 as poor and romantic, but found his history of the Restoration "the most interesting historical work I have ever read, except for Macaulay's England." The romance appealed to others like Sarah Lois Wadley of Mississippi, a bright young lady who found Lamartine's *Girondists* as exciting as a novel.[32]

Contributors to southern journals admired Lamartine as a poet, less so as a historian, and not at all as a statesman. Just before the revolutionary outbreak in 1848, William Boulware confidently assured readers of *Southern Literary Messenger* that Lamartine stood as the best known of French authors. The cultured David Jamison of South Carolina treated him with respect but recoiled from the "self-satisfied dogmatism" in "readable and instructive" historical writing marred by an overwrought imagination and poetic fancy: "Save us from his political, religious, moral reflections." In contrast, A. B. Meek told Oddfellows in Alabama that Lamartine uttered the great revolutionary political truths – Liberty, Equality, and Fraternity – with "the tongue of an angel."[33]

Simms, who had little sympathy for Lamartine's politics, pronounced him "honest" and "sincere," describing his books as "able – and may be truthful" while complaining that overweening vanity often ruined his efforts. Even in a pamphlet

The Failure of Free Society (New York, 1965 [1852]), 45–8; Fitzhugh, "Mr. Bancroft's History and the Inner Light," *DBR*, 29 (1860), 604; [Fitzhugh], "The War upon Society – Socialism," *DBR*, 22 (1857), 634; [George Frederick Holmes], "Napoleon III and Augustus Caesar," *SQR*, n.s., 10 (1854), 1–37, esp. 9. Louis Bonaparte's southern critics admired Victor Hugo and Alexandre Dumas for their opposition to him: see e.g. Paul Hamilton Hayne, "Ante-Bellum Charleston," *Southern Bivouac*, 1 (1885), 335; also *SLM*, 27 (1858), 303.

32 [William Drayton], *The South Vindicated from the Treason and Fanaticism of the Northern Abolitionists* (Philadelphia, 1836), 228–9 n.; Chesnut Diary, Oct. 20, 1861, in Woodward, ed., *Mary Chesnut's Civil War*, 220–1; "Right to Labor," in Lounsbury, ed., *Louisa McCord: Essays*, 85; Lieber to Calhoun, Oct. 29, 1848, in *JCCP*, 26:113; *ERD*, Nov. 24, 1857 (1:134), and Mar. 12, 1865 (3:800) – Ruffin also despised Louis Bonaparte, see Mar. 2, 1857 (1:123); Sarah Lois Wadley Private Journal, Sept. 7, 1861, and L. W. Butler Diary, 1863, both at UNC-SHC. For appreciation of Lamartine's attacks on radicalism see "R. E. C." [Cochrane], "The Problem of Free Society," *SLM*, 27 (1858), 6, 9.

33 William Boulware, "Charlotte Corday," *SLM*, 14 (1848), 142; [David F. Jamison], "Histoire des Girondins," *SQR*, 16 (1849), quotes at 57, 75; A. B. Meek, *The Mysteries of Benevolence: An Address before the Grand Lodge of Alabama, I.O.O.F.* (Mobile, AL, 1849), 17.

against atheism Lamartine mostly discussed himself, shedding little light on his subject. Simms was generous, for Lamartine histories became a joke for their abundance of errors, which one European critic took 113 pages to expose. And Lamartine's idealization of Robespierre did not help his reputation outside radical circles. In his eight-volume *Histoire des Girondins* (1847), he demonstrated that his talent as a historian lay almost completely in fertile imagination and poetically brilliant style. Alexandre Dumas, intending a compliment, credited Lamartine with raising the writing of history to the level of the novel. Alexis de Tocqueville, intending no compliment, scowled that he never knew a man with "more contempt for the truth" than Lamartine.[34]

For reasons hard to fathom, Lamartine's *History of the Girondins* enjoyed tremendous success in the English-speaking world, including the South. De Bow crowned it and Lamartine's *Restoration of Monarchy in France* with encomia, but before long he, too, was lashing out at the substitution of romantic gush for sound history. John Reuben Thompson, Virginia's much-respected man of letters, portrayed Lamartine as a man with many admirable qualities but "insufferably vain" and a "dangerous man – this Gallic orator, minstrel, statesman, philosopher and hero." William W. Mann of Virginia, writing from Paris in 1848, described Lamartine as a pompous aristocrat and an opportunist who courted popularity – "the vainest man in Europe." In 1855 a contributor to *Southern Literary Messenger* referred to the "eminently unpractical" Lamartine, who "prayed with Chateaubriand and believed with Rousseau" – an attractive poet and a brilliant propagandist but a failed politician. Lamartine undoubtedly had genius, Nathaniel Beverley Tucker conceded, but only the French could mistake a "fantastic coxcomb" for a great man.[35]

William Hutson of South Carolina gave Lamartine no quarter. Reviewing *History of the Girondists* for *Southern Presbyterian Review,* he needled those who were disappointed by Lamartine's account of 1848. He wanted to know why anyone should have expected better of Lamartine, whose earlier historical work had surely exposed his addled brain. Hutson acknowledged his fine prose style but flayed his wishy-washy liberalism and concessions to democratic radicalism. As for Lamartine's fantasy that the Revolution replaced authority with reasoning: "Stubborn history says the guillotine was substituted for both." In the wake of the June

---

34 [William Gilmore Simms], "Critical Notices," *SQR*, n.s., 2 (1850), 254–5, 539–40, also 5 (1852), 242, and 6 (1852), 272. For Lamartine's reputation and the comments of Dumas and Tocqueville see James Westfall Thompson, *A History of Historical Writing*, 2 vols. (Gloucester, MA, 1967 [1942]), 2:253.

35 *DBR*, 11 (1851), 689. William Gilmore Simms declared the morality displayed in Lamartine's fiction "scarcely any better than that of Georges Sand": "Sentimental Prose Fiction," *SQR*, n.s., 1 (1850), 369; see also "Lamartine," *SQR*, 12 (1855), 52–98, esp. 70–2, 97; [John R. Thompson], *SLM*, 15 (1849), 701–2; [William W. Mann], "The Provisional Government of France," *SLM*, 14 (1848), 301–7 (quote at 307); [Tucker], "The Present State of Europe," 299. Lamartine ranked high as a poet. *Southern Literary Messenger* published translations of his poetry and essays: "Souvenir," *SLM*, 14 (1848), 452–3; "Lamartine's Thoughts on Poetry," *SLM*, 14 (1848), 605–11, 665–71. *Southern Quarterly Review* devoted much space to Lamartine in the 1840s and 1850s and in 1855 offered its readers a lengthy biographical sketch: *SQR*, 12 (1855), 52–98. John R. Thompson (the editor of *SLM*) did not, however, respect much of Lamartine's prose works: *SLM*, 15 (1849), 371–5.

Days, Hutson recalled the first Napoleon and prophesied the coming of the next. He expressed a widely held southern view: "In France, the silly king [Louis XVI], influenced by some silly notions of reform, let the Bourgeoisie know and feel their own strength. They, in turn, with still greater stupidity, suffered the Jacquerie to learn theirs." The outcome was the first Napoleon, who used power more discreetly than his bourgeois predecessors. "Any despotism is better than that of the 'Many headed monster thing.' " Would history now repeat itself? Hutson expected it would.[36]

When the War came, Southerners once again recalled the two Napoleons with mixed emotions. The War brought vain hopes of French intervention, and no few Southerners discovered the sagacity – and cunning – of Louis Bonaparte, who would grasp the advantage of a pro-Confederate course. In 1859 Edmund Ruffin labeled Louis Bonaparte an "iniquitous tyrant and usurper," a mischievous and untrustworthy "villain" who betrayed the Italians. But by 1862 Ruffin credited the tyrant, usurper, and villain with a far-seeing mind that surely would lead him to recognize the Confederacy. An effusive Mary Chesnut hoped for French recognition because Louis Bonaparte "does not stop at trifles," is "thorough," and "never botches his work." In Texas, the politically powerful William Pitt Ballinger expected him to intervene to shore up his frail regime in Mexico.[37]

In a Fast Day sermon in February 1861, Bishop William Meade of Virginia discouraged Southerners from looking for a military savior, since Napoleon, like Alexander and Tamerlane, sought "the gratification of mere ambition." But the Presbyterian Reverend Mr. Armstrong, praising "the brilliant campaign of Napoleon III in Italy," looked for Confederate emulation. From 1861 to 1865 Mary Chesnut and her friends talked of Caesar's writing, oratory, and military prowess, praying for a Caesar or a Napoleon to lead the Confederacy. As the War went badly, Bishop Elliott rallied Confederate troops by calling up Napoleon's military achievements against the odds. After the War, P. G. T. Beauregard, hoping for a counterrevolution against radical Reconstruction, told Lee that the South needed a Washington or a Louis Bonaparte.[38]

---

[36] [W. H. Hutson], "History of the Girondists," *SPR*, 2:387–413 (Dec. 1848), 394, 400, quotes at 396, 394.

[37] Ruffin, Jan. 24, Feb. 24, July 23, July 25, 1859, Dec. 21, 1862, in *ERD*, 1:274, 289, 323, 324, 2:517, quotes at 1:274 and 323; Chesnut Diary, June 16, 1862, in Woodward, ed., *Mary Chesnut's Civil War*, 387; John Anthony Moretta, *William Pitt Ballinger: Texas Lawyer, Southern Statesman, 1825–1888* (Austin, TX, 2000), 152. Louis Napoleon's intervention in Mexico pleased some Southerners, who, like Cornelia Peake McDonald, thought it would help the Confederacy: see McDonald, Jan. 1, 1863, in Gwin, ed., *A Woman's Civil War*, 11.

[38] William Meade, *Address on the Day of Fasting and Prayer* (Richmond, VA, 1861), 4; George D. Armstrong, *"The Good Hand of Our God upon Us": A Thanksgiving Sermon Preached on the Victory at Manassas* (Norfolk, VA, 1861), 6; Chesnut Diary, Feb. 25, 1861, also June 19 and Aug. 26, 1861, Feb. 19, 1865, in Woodward, ed., *Mary Chesnut's Civil War*, 10, 103, 167, 724; Stephen Elliott, *Gideon's Water-Lappers* (Macon, GA, 1864), 11; T. Harry Williams, *P. G. T. Beauregard: Napoleon in Gray* (Baton Rouge, LA, 1955), 267. Relating Washington's greatness to that of various conquerors and despots remained a problem. In 1800 the Baptist Reverend Henry Holcombe of Savannah delivered a famous sermon in which he called Washington greater than the Caesars, Philip of Macedon, and Alexander: "A Sermon Occasioned by the Death of Washington," in Ellis Sandoz, ed., *Political Sermons of the American Founding Era, 1730–1805* (Indianapolis, IN, 1991), 1399, 1401.

While some prominent Southerners longed for a Caesar to replace an inadequate Jefferson Davis, others saw in Davis himself too much of the tyrannical Caesar. Edward Pollard, a leading journalistic critic, cited Edward Gibbon and Edward Bulwer-Lytton to compare Davis, whom he despised, with Cola di Rienzi, the fourteenth-century revolutionary: "The two men are examples of that mixed character, always fated to various and opposite criticism, alike liable to the extremes of censure and of praise." Their vices and the virtues "flourish on an uncertain boundary, and are often intertwined." Grave weaknesses accompanied their admirable accomplishments despite a rarified scholarship and culture that more often than not undermined practical judgment. Pollard assailed their vanity, ambition, arrogance, and tyrannical dispositions, which together forfeited the affections of peoples that had been swayed by their great oratory and refined tastes.[39]

Pollard's remarks on Rienzi and his hostile glances at Davis recalled the debates over the Gracchi, the common censure of the Roman nobility, and the no less common distrust of popular revolutionaries. Fourteenth-century Rome had suffered under the oppression of rapacious nobles and the ravages of lawlessness and turmoil. When Rienzi arose from the poorer plebs to establish a revolutionary government, he enjoyed the support of the upper middle class and lesser nobility. Characterizing Rienzi as "a modern Brutus," Gibbon censured the arrogant nobles for mistaking a dangerous man for a buffoon. Rienzi himself admired Caesar rather than Brutus. Assuming the title of Tribune, he defeated, disgraced, and humiliated the nobles and ruled as dictator. In time he, too, grew arrogant, oppressive, slothful, fat, and careless. His religious heterodoxy alienated the previously sympathetic papacy, and his heavy taxes alienated his propertied supporters. To the applause of a once-adoring populace, his enemies executed him. A commentator in *Southern Quarterly Review* considered Rienzi a good and honorable man doomed to defeat by fickle followers unable to sustain their liberty.[40]

Southern thought featured the conservative constitutional republicanism of St. George Tucker, John C. Calhoun, and Alexander Stephens; monarchism attracted few, notwithstanding repeated efforts by abolitionists and inveterate South-haters to pretend that it did. In 1848 Henry Hilliard of Alabama, a Whig, deplored the radicalism and threat of anarchy in the European revolutions but added, "I solemnly

---

[39] Edward Pollard, *Life of Jefferson Davis* (Philadelphia, 1869), 501–2, and Pollard, *Black Diamonds Gathered in the Darkey Homes of the South* (Philadelphia, 1859), 84–5. Mrs. Chesnut was among the Southerners who read Bulwer's *Rienzi*: Chesnut Diary, Jan. 18, 1864, in Woodward, ed., *Mary Chesnut's Civil War*, 543. In Bulwer-Lytton's generally laudatory account, Rienzi committed no crimes: see esp. Edward Bulwer-Lytton, *Rienzi, the Last of the Roman Tribunes* (New York, 1902 [1835]), Appendix 1:626. Daniel Whitaker pronounced Bulwer's *Rienzi* morally sound: "Rienzi," *SLJ*, 2 (1836), 217–18. See also Supplementary References: "Rienzi."

[40] Gibbon, drawing on Ludovico Antonio Muratori, discussed the fourteenth-century revolutionary Cola di Rienzi at length in *Decline and Fall*, 3:1023–42 (quote at 1025); "History of the Italian Republics," *SQR*, 1 (1842), 160; see also the comments in T. M. Garrett Diary, June 14 and 15, 1849, at UNC-SHC. See John Wright's succinct and perceptive Introduction to *The Life of Cola di Rienzo*, tr. J. Wright (Toronto, 1975). Cola di Rienzo usually appears in Roman dialect as Cola di (or da) Rienzi.

believe that the time has come when kingcraft has lost its hold upon the human mind. The world is waking from its deep slumber, and mankind begin to see that the right to govern belongs not to crowned kings, but to the great masses." During the early days of the Republic and its struggles with the swelling democratic impulses of the middle and lower classes, sympathy for a limited monarchy surfaced in North and South. Even George Washington momentarily wondered whether the United States ought not to take that road, and less steady men found themselves sorely tempted in the wake of Shays's rebellion. The constitutional and subsequent sectional crises brought monarchy back into discussion since it offered an attractive way to establish and maintain stability and order. Slaveholders celebrated their own virtues as the most reliable guardians of conservative republicanism and traditional social values, but not all could avoid flirtations with monarchy. As time went on, the flirtations grew stronger among prominent men, at least as expressed privately or in guarded communications. In 1827 Robert Turnbull, in the Charleston *Mercury* and his book *The Crisis,* stated his preference to live under the Spanish, French, or Dutch monarchy rather than be subjected to Yankee consolidation. A few years later George William Featherstonhaugh of Great Britain attended a dinner party in Columbia, South Carolina, with Thomas Cooper and other leading citizens. To his surprise he heard open denigration of republican government, with side shots at James Madison in "discussions of great ability, the object of which was to show that there never can be a good government if it is not administered by gentlemen." Professor Robert Saunders of the College of William and Mary, whom Dew admired, openly declared his preference for monarchy.[41]

---

[41] Hilliard in the House of Representatives, Apr. 3, 1848: *Speeches and Addresses by Henry W. Hilliard* (New York, 1855), 152, also 362–3. Pettigrew quoted in Clyde N. Wilson, *Carolina Cavalier: The Life and Mind of James Johnston Pettigrew* (Athens, GA, 1990), 43; yet he admired the Hungarian nobles (45). Trevor Colbourn, ed., *Fame and the Founding Fathers: Essays by Douglass Adair* (New York, 1974), 118–19; Forrest McDonald, *Novus Ordo Seclorum: The Intellectual Origins of the Constitution* (Norman, KS, 1985), 179–83; Cathy D. Matson and Peter S. Onuf, *A Union of Interests: Political and Economic Thought in Revolutionary America* (Lawrence, KS, 1990), 87–8; [Robert J. Turnbull], *The Crisis: Or, Essays on the Usurpation of the Federal Government by Brutus* (Charleston, SC, 1827), 148; G. W. Featherstonhaugh, *Excursion through the Slave States* (New York, 1968 [1844]), 157; for Saunders see Ludwell H. Johnson, "Between the Wars," pt. 2 of Susan H. Godson et al., *The College of William & Mary: A History,* 2 vols. (Williamsburg, VA, 1993), 1:263; see also Catherine Cooper Hopley, *Life in the South from the Commencement of the War,* 2 vols. (New York, 1971 [1863]), 1:271.

For Washington's horror at the prospect of an American monarchy, see e.g. Washington to John Jay, Aug. 15, 1786, and Washington to Madison, Mar. 31, 1787, in W. B. Allen, ed., *George Washington: A Collection* (Indianapolis, IN, 1988), 333–5, 360–2. In 1849, William Gilmore Simms protested against the superficial assumption of François Guizot and others that Washington could have made himself a king. To the contrary, the American people were too deeply imbued with republican principles to permit anyone, not even the great and beloved Washington, to impose a monarchy. See [Simms], "Guizot's Democracy in France," *SQR,* 15 (1849), 136–8. Edmund Randolph and other southern Founders feared the concentration of executive power in a single hand as an invitation to monarchy: James Madison, *Notes of the Debates in the Federal Convention of 1787* (Athens, OH, 1966), 46, 58–9, 67. The first newspaper published in Edgefield District, South Carolina, was duly christened the *Anti-Monarchist* in 1811: H. L. Watson, "Early Newspapers of the Abbeville District," *Proceedings*

Few Southerners wanted to hear anything about monarchy at home, but no few cast an appreciative eye on monarchies abroad – especially on the Brazilian monarchy, which sustained a slaveholding regime. William Henry Trescot, while no monarchist, combated the bias against the European monarchies, crediting them with the establishment of international law and seeing them as potential allies of an independent South within a concert of nations. Trescot believed that Europe and America had come to understand that a just balance of power rested on mutual respect for different forms of government, including the monarchical.[42]

According to "L. M. B." in *Virginia University Magazine* in 1860, Americans, with marginal exceptions, had enjoyed their most cherished principles of liberty and law under the British Crown. He was "bold to add" that most of the political evils that threatened the Union derived from "too wide a divergence from the more stable principles of the government of Great Britain, a country which we are every day more and more inclined to regard as the freest and best governed on the globe." In 1861 William Howard Russell, a British observer, found South Carolinians privately voicing monarchist sentiments. Elsewhere, Sarah Morgan and St. John Richardson Liddell, among others, allowed that they would rather live under British or French monarchies than under the Yankees. That the eccentric, antislavery, wildly negrophobic John Jacob Flournoy of Georgia declared for monarchy called forth mirth or yawns: He was, after all, a nut. No one thought John Esten Cooke, Virginia's literary leading light, a nut. Cooke wrote to Simms: "I am a Virginian, a monarchist, what is called a cavalier by blood and strain and feeling, and I believe that any merit of my writings has been, and will be found in the fact that I am Virginian and Cavalier." In 1858 a contributor to *De Bow's Review* who viewed the American government as a failure gingerly asked whether a monarchy might not be superior. Another provided a good old republican reply, but he, too, lamented the straits through which an excessively democratic America was passing. The collapsing fortunes of the Confederacy brought Edmund Ruffin to some grim thoughts. He cheered Governor Henry Watkins Allen's declaration that Louisiana would join any European power rather than be ruled by the North and – applauding a recent American advocate of monarchy – ruminated that, if the southern colonies had remained in the Empire, they could have blocked West Indian emancipation.[43]

---

of the South Carolina Historical Society (Columbia, SC, 1940), 18. As Southerners knew, Aeschylus and Herodotus (among other Greek writers) considered those who willingly submitted to a king to be slaves: Paul A. Rahe, *Republics, Ancient and Modern: Classical Republicanism and the American Revolution* (Chapel Hill, NC, 1992), 37.

42   William H. Trescot, *The Diplomacy of the Revolution: An Historical Study* (New York, 1852), 51, 154–5. Lexington, Virginia, boasted the celebrated Franklin debating club, which drew on Virginia Military Institute, Washington College, etc. In the late 1850s it debated, "Would a separation of the states be preferable to a limited Monarchy?" – Negative won by one vote: Mary Price Coulling, *Margaret Junkin Preston: A Biography* (Winston-Salem, NC, 1993), 106.

43   "L. M. B.", "The Past and the Present," *VUM*, 4 (1860), 256; W. H. Russell to John T. Delane, July 16, 1861, in Martin Crawford, ed., *William Howard Russell's Civil War: Private Diary and Letters, 1861–1862* (Athens, GA, 1992), 89; William H. Pease and Jane H. Pease, *James Louis Petigru: Southern Conservative, Southern Dissenter* (Athens, GA, 1995), 7; June 29, 1862, in Charles East, ed., *The*

The passionately republican Presbyterians irritated Methodists, most notably Parson William Brownlow of Tennessee, who believed Presbyterian church government incompatible with republicanism in civil life. Presbyterians were aghast at the accusation. Thomas Smyth pleaded that Presbyterianism, ecclesiastically, was neither monarchy nor democracy but republicanism. He denied that the Bible called for a particular form of secular government. Christian doctrines "breathe the spirit of republicanism" and the Presbyterian Church qualified as a "spiritual republic."[44]

Republicans or no, Presbyterian spokesmen considered much of the antimonarchical rhetoric dangerous. In 1843 the Presbyterian Reverend Samuel Jones Cassells of Norfolk bewailed the spread of French influence: "Not only have the oppressions of monarchy been denounced, but monarchy itself. Not only have the evils of government been resisted, but government itself in some cases decried as an evil! The parental relation, too, has by some been assailed; the relation between husband and wife spoken against; and in short every relation but that of equality, and every duty incompatible with perfect personal liberty have been denied!" In the immediate aftermath of the revolutions of 1848, William Hutson wrote, "The government even

---

Civil War Diary of Sarah Morgan (Athens, GA, 1991), 141; Hughes, ed., *Liddell's Record*, 29–30; Flournoy to R. F. W. Allston, Dec. 1858, in J. H. Easterby, ed., *The South Carolina Rice Plantation, as Revealed in the Papers of Robert F. W. Allston* (Chicago, 1945), 146–7; on Cooke see Mary C. Oliphant et al., eds., *The Letters of William Gilmore Simms*, 6 vols. (Columbia, SC, 1952–82), Editor's Introduction, 1:xcix–c; "R. C. H.", "Progress of Federal Disorganization," *DBR*, (1848), 136–46; "H. R. G.", "Monarchy vs. Democracy," *DBR*, (1858), 312–20; in *ERD*, vol. 3, see: Mar. 3, 1864 (358), Nov. 1, 1864 (633–4), Nov. 4, 1864 (637–40).

[44] *TSW*, 3:5–8, 1–216, 4:369, quotes at 3:2, 18; and [Thomas Smyth], "National Righteousness," *SPR*, 12 (1859), 26–7. See also George J. Stevenson, *An Increase in Excellence: A History of Emory and Henry College* (New York, 1963), 20; Herbert Alexander White, *Southern Presbyterian Leaders* (New York, 1911), 265. William G. Brownlow attacked the Presbyterians as monarchists throughout *The Great Iron Wheel Examined; Or, Its False Spokes Extracted* (Nashville, TN, 1856) and other works. For a sober if gingerly Methodist discussion of types of governments with a suggestion that republics most closely approximate the Christian, see Rivers, *Elements of Moral Philosophy*, 264–5.

The divines had a problem since most agreed that the Bible did not sanction any particular form of government (see Chapter 7). James Madison, in a prayer delivered at the chapel of the College of William and Mary, referred to heaven as a republic: Davis, *Intellectual Life in Jefferson's Virginia*, 53. In response to disunionist sentiments in the early Republic, Mason Locke Weems, in ch. 16 of his widely read *Life of Washington*, declared Jesus Christ the founder of the American Republic and suggested that preservation of the national Union was a holy task. Sanctification of the American Republic was by no means only southern. Presbyterians generally claimed for their church a government that most closely captured the spirit of the American Republic: see Mark A. Noll, *America's God: From Jonathan Edwards to Abraham Lincoln* (New York, 2002), 240.

Thornwell, preaching in Columbia in 1860, declared the day of small states over and that the federal principle alone guaranteed freedom to extensive territories. It "must constitute the hope of the human race." Thornwell feared that representative democracy was being sacrificed to a tyrannical "pure democracy." See "Sermon on National Sins," *JHTW*, 4:529, 536. In Richmond the Presbyterian Reverend William S. Plumer and the Episcopalian Reverend Philip Slaughter stressed that nothing in scripture commanded any particular form of government: Plumer, *The Law of God, as Contained in the Ten Commandments, Explained and Enforced* (Harrisonburg, VA, 1996 [1864]), 378; Slaughter, *Coercion and Conciliation: A Sermon Preached in Camp, at Centreville, Virginia* (Richmond, VA, 1861). Nathaniel Beverley Tucker agreed: *A Discourse on the Importance of the Study of Political Science, as a Branch of Academic Education in the United States* (Richmond, VA, 1840), 13.

of a king is not repugnant to any of God's laws, or opposed to correct views of human liberty." Hutson preferred a republic but doubted its survival if democracy continued to expand and corrupt political life. According to the Reverend Iveson Brookes of Georgia in 1850, only slavery can keep societies from ending in monarchy and tyranny and can provide the foundation for stable republics. Without slavery, he added, Mexico was tottering and France was facing disaster. Civil government, the Reverend Thomas Peck reiterated after the War, must be accommodated "to the character, genius, civilization of a people." A Bishop of the Protestant Episcopal Church might more readily be expected to have such inclinations, especially an old Federalist and veteran Jefferson–Jackson hater like Stephen Elliott. Although the Bible does not dictate forms of government, he agreed, and makes no case for monarchy, nonetheless, a monarchy with an aristocracy and established church in tow would be, for Christians, infinitely preferable to anarchy, licentiousness, and all such popular excesses. Elliott lamely added that Americans did not need a monarchy because their republic served as well.[45]

Before secession and after the start of the War, charges of monarchism filled the air. Those who wished to discredit political opponents readily accused them of harboring pro-monarchist views. Thus, the young William Plumer Jacobs assumed in 1860 that Robert Barnwell Rhett sought to transform an independent South Carolina into a monarchy. Francis Lieber thought South Carolinians pro-English because they admired England's aristocratic government. He murmured about having heard C. G. Memminger say he would prefer a return to the British monarchy to submission to the Yankees. In the North, stories spread about the monarchist inclinations of Varina Howell (Mrs. Jefferson) Davis and about pro-monarchist delegates to the founding convention of the Confederacy.[46]

On the eve of the War, George Fitzhugh imagined that Virginians "thought, and still think, that monarchy is the proper form of government for old countries, democracy for infant colonies, and republicanism for young states or nations." Fitzhugh saluted Carlyle as "the great mind of England, and the only man in England who dares openly sustain royalty." Fitzhugh discreetly described monarchy as inappropriate for the United States, but an anonymous critic fumed that Fitzhugh and northern abolitionists plotted to establish rival American monarchies. An article in *De Bow's Review*, probably by Fitzhugh, argued that rejection of the divine right of kings constituted the worst of the political heresies of the Reformation: "If

---

[45] [Samuel J. Cassells], *Servitude and the Duty of Masters to Their Servants* (Norfolk, VA, 1843), 4; [Hutson], "History of the Girondists," 404; Iveson L. Brookes, *A Defence of the South against the Reproaches of the North* (Hamburg, SC, 1850), 46; Iveson L. Brookes, *A Defence of Slavery against the Attacks of Henry Clay and Alex'r Campbell* (Hamburg, SC, 1851), 44–5; Thomas E. Peck, *Miscellanies*, ed. Thomas Cary Johnson, 3 vols. (Richmond, VA, 1895), 2:162–3; Stephen Elliott, "*New Wine Not to Be Put in Old Bottles": A Sermon Preached at Christ Church* (Savannah, GA, 1862).

[46] Dec. 6, 1860, in Thornwell Jacobs, ed., *Diary of William Plumer Jacobs, 1842–1917* (Atlanta, GA, 1937), 67; Lieber to George S. Hilliard, Apr. 1853, in Thomas Sergeant Perry, ed., *The Life and Letters of Francis Lieber* (Boston, 1882), 259–61; Vernon L. Parrington, *Main Currents in American Thought*, 3 vols. (New York, 1954), 2:60–1.

kings have no natural right to their thrones and their kingdoms, Southern planters have far less natural right to their dominion and their subjects. They are but little kings, with farms for kingdoms and slaves for subjects." In Georgia, the unionist Augusta *Chronicle and Sentinel* got little support for its editorial stand in February 1861, but stand it did. Furious with the collapse of American democracy, it proposed a constitutional monarchy for the new southern Confederacy.[47]

Republicanism ran deep, and true monarchists appeared only here and there. But doubts grew about America's ability to sustain its great republican experiment. The republic was rapidly becoming a democracy and, if the cancer spread much further, drastic measures would be necessary. Jefferson and John Taylor of Caroline had long before identified the British monarchy with the rule of big business. In 1840 the usually restrained Calhoun burst forth that the South would be better off under a monarchy than saddled with a fifty-million-dollar bank in New York or Philadelphia. Calhoun, a republican to his core, pleaded in *Discourse on the Constitution* that if America did not return to the spirit and letter of the Constitution, it would face either disunion or monarchy. In North Carolina, Bartholomew Moore wrote William Graham, recounting a conversation with Thomas Clingman, the powerful political leader in the western counties. Clingman said that if Lincoln were elected, the South should secede. But, replied Moore, secession would spell the end of slavery. Clingman remained unmoved. An incensed Moore remarked: "Now, if our liberty and property are to be trusted to such apes, what man of sense will long hesitate between a perpetual gov't of this kind, and a sober, wise and conservative monarchy?"[48]

The sectional crisis and the War provoked wild talk. Augustus Baldwin Longstreet considered Russia's despotism preferable to Mexico's anarchic republicanism. Confederate officers assured J. L. Fremantle that 90 percent if not 99 percent of their soldiers preferred to live as subjects of Queen Victoria than to return to the Union. Beauregard told Fremantle that he preferred submission to the emperor of China to submission to the Yankees. These hyperbolic outbursts and exaggerated

---

[47] Fitzhugh, "Mr. Bancroft's History and the Inner Light," 598; Fitzhugh, "Frederick the Great by Thomas Carlyle," 167; Fitzhugh, "Popular Institutions," *DBR*, 28 (1860), 524–5; Fitzhugh, "The Revolutions of 1775 and 1861 Contrasted," 724; and (probably Fitzhugh), "Bonaparte, Cromwell, and Washington," *DBR*, 28 (1860), 146, 149–50. See "Editorial Miscellany," *DBR*, 28 (1860), 612–13, for the attack on Fitzhugh; Donald E. Reynolds, *Editors Make War: Southern Newspapers in the Secession Crisis* (Nashville, TN, 1966), 180, 269 n. 41.

[48] Dumas Malone, *Jefferson and His Time*, 6 vols. (Boston, 1962–81), 2:451; J. C. Calhoun to Armstead Burt, Nov. 2, 1840, in *JCCP*, 15:372; J. C. Calhoun, "A Discourse on the Constitution and Government of the United States," in Ross M. Lence, ed., *Union and Liberty: The Political Philosophy of John C. Calhoun* (Indianapolis, IN, 1992), 264–5; B. F. Moore to W. A. Graham, Aug. 12, 1860, in J. G. deRoulhac Hamilton, ed., *The Papers of William Alexander Graham*, 5 vols. (Raleigh, NC, 1957–73), 5:172. In 1858 Grayson revived the old charge that Alexander Hamilton was a monarchist who spoke for the rich and powerful: [Grayson], "Jefferson," *RM*, 2 (1858), 107–29. Jefferson and Madison had been among those who feared that Hamilton was taking a monarchist course: Forrest McDonald, *States' Rights and the Union: Imperium in Imperio, 1776–1876* (Lawrence, KS, 2000), 32.

formulations of intent may not be taken literally, but behind them lay frustration and disgust with popular democracy and every form of social radicalism.[49]

Since Southerners, slaveholders in particular, took enormous pride in their own revolutionary heritage, they strove mightily to see the bright side of any republican revolution. Almost invariably, they grew disillusioned. They denounced the oppression that drove men to revolt but kept a wary eye on ensuing radicalism. Tyranny, according to John Francis Mercer of Maryland in 1788, inescapably follows all unsuccessful popular insurrections. Subsequent generations added: Yes, and most successful ones as well. In Charleston, J. Barrett Cohen, a prominent Jewish lawyer, hit the sour notes in an "Oration Delivered on the First Anniversary of the South Carolina Historical Society" in 1856: "The revolution in England, which put Cromwell at the head of affairs, was stained with cruelty, injustice, and fanaticism" and "violated the fundamental principles of the English constitution." Even England's Glorious Revolution of 1688 appalled him because royal children had turned on their father. Only the American Revolution – "the great one" – met with his approval.[50]

The ambiguity in southern appraisals of the Puritans and of John Brown betrayed grudging respect for the personal qualities of revolutionaries. Dew hated fanaticism but admired the élan displayed by the most radical of revolutionaries. Characterizing seventeenth-century English Puritans as "in many ways ridiculous and unamiable," he conceded them four formidable qualities largely attributable to belief in predestination and a sense of being a chosen people: "zeal, perseverance, courage, and cool judgment." He loathed the brutality of the Jacobins but admired them for a vigor that gave France "the most hard-working, energetic, decisive government of which history gives any account."[51]

The politically moderate Dew concealed neither his admiration for the élan of revolutionaries nor his disdain for many of his fellow moderates. His heart quarreled with his head when he contrasted Desiderius Erasmus with Louis Antoine de Saint-Just. Dew found "rather discreditable" Erasmus' tepid response to the struggles of the Reformation, judging him "one of those men who outrun the world in thought, and lag behind in action." Discussing the French Revolution, Dew remarked that in great crises moderates forfeit respect and followers since too many

[49] Longstreet, *Fast-Day Sermon*, 6; Diary, May 21 and June 14, 1863, in A. J. L. Fremantle, *Three Months in the Southern States: The 1863 Diary of an English Soldier, April–June 1863* (London, 1863), 120–1, 199. For Frederick Douglass, "Monarchical freedom is better than republican slavery": Philip Foner, ed., *The Life and Writings of Frederick Douglass*, 5 vols. (New York, 1950), 1:172.

[50] [John Francis Mercer?], "Essays by a [Maryland] Farmer" (originally published in the *Maryland Gazette* in 1788), in Frohnen, ed., *Anti-Federalists*, 567; J. Barrett Cohen, "Oration Delivered on the First Anniversary of the South Carolina Historical Society" (June 28, 1856), in *Collections of the South-Carolina Historical Society*, 2 vols. (Charleston, SC, 1858), 2:108–10.

[51] Dew, *Digest*, 522–3 (Puritans), 620, 628–38; also, "Demosthenes," *HLW*, 1:471. For similar praise for the French revolutionary army see Joel R. Poinsett, "Our Army in Mexico," *DBR*, 2 (1846), 428. Dew's respect for Jacobin vigor in economic policy is all the more impressive since he regarded the *maxima* and similar policies as theoretically blind and eventually disastrous: *Digest*, 635.

reveal themselves to be "trimmers and cowards." His tone changed signally when he turned to Saint-Just, whom Southerners abhorred as a mass murderer. Saint-Just "was in earnest" – and that compelled respect. Saint-Just "was the very incarnation of the metaphysical, abstract spirit of democracy, and hence he was the most terrible of all the actors in the reign of terror, because he never relented and never felt remorse. Like the Israelite of old, he slew his enemy hip and thigh, and really believed that he was hastening the reign of virtue – such was his political fanaticism."[52]

Southerners' respect for the élan of revolutionaries accompanied contempt for abolitionists and others they viewed as poseurs. Dew saw the *philosophes* as armchair theorists with no influence on the people. The ancien régime gave them a wide swath to run their mouths about abstract principles of liberty, equality, and anything else but would have made short work of them had they insulted the king or posed a political threat. The repressive rigidity of the régime left little room for criticism except for idle dabbling in the aristocratic and grand bourgeois salons: "When, therefore, the French revolution came, and the evils of government were at last to be corrected, unfortunately for France, there was nothing but this utopian philosophy to shed light on the path of the revolution." Dew recalled Carlyle's bon mot that when a national assembly of some 1,200 individuals spoke in the name of 25,000,000 Frenchmen, it had nothing in its pocket but "the gospel of Jean Jacques Rousseau."[53]

No proslavery theorist credited the revolutionary lower classes, white or black, with the capacity to retain power, much less sustain freedom. In 1836 President George Addison Baxter of Hampden-Sydney College warned that the abolitionist agitation threatened to provoke slave revolts and their bloody suppression. He could not imagine a slave revolt that did not end with the extermination of one side or the other. Baxter, a moderate who looked to eventual emancipation, saw no chance for a slave revolt to succeed in the face of white preponderance in numbers, arms, and military skill. Slaveholders read most revolutions as Aristotelian tragedies in which the lower classes destroyed indispensable social structures along with oppressive ones only to usher in worse regimes.[54]

Dew designed his generalizations for the political instruction of Southerners. He paid tribute to Pericles for raising the educational and social level of the lower classes to ensure rough equality with the affluent, for a free state without a strong middle class must expect frequent convulsions and insurrections. "The danger of innovation is most to be feared where the exercise of rights have been unknown to the people." Governments are much more easily overthrown in small states than large, for government constitutes the "organized power" in society. Since armies are more efficacious in the suppression of revolutions in large states, southern whites have little to fear from blacks. "Change and revolution are the besetting sins of small democratical states."[55]

---

[52] Dew, *Digest*, 452, 626, 650 n.
[53] Ibid., 587.
[54] George A. Baxter, *An Essay on the Abolition of Slavery* (Richmond, VA, 1836), 3–4, 19.
[55] Dew, *Digest*, 61–2, 84, 198, 268, 563.

Dew, a student of the great insurrectionary movements, had registered the impact of the Sicilian slave revolt on events in the time of the Gracchi, and he paid tribute to the exceptional talent of Spartacus in the servile war of 73–71 B.C. As Spartacus swept the Compagna, "Outraged beings sought to revenge their wrongs," but with the road to the Alps open his hordes, greedy for loot, demanded a sack of Rome that led to his defeat. Dew interpreted the French Revolution as a great uprising of affluent middle classes shut out of political power. The Revolution did not come from the propertyless but from the propertied and increasingly rich Third Estate. The affluent propertied classes wished to moderate the Revolution, but "they were pushed onwards by the classes behind them." Property drove the great modern revolutions. The English and French revolutions, despite appearances, ranged privileged property against unprivileged property. They also demonstrated that anarchy, terror, and despotism follow appeals for intervention of the propertyless and abstract appeals to the rights of man. Dew prized the French Revolution as an unprecedented experiment that taught "the true value and the true danger of the popular element."[56]

The writings of Dew, Thomas Cobb, George Sawyer, and other proslavery theorists informed Southerners of the rebellions of the peasants and urban poor in medieval and early modern Europe. Chancellor William Harper of South Carolina expressed a common view: "It is fearful to see with what avidity the worst and most dangerous characters of society seize on the occasion of obtaining the countenance of better men, for the purposes of throwing off the restraints of law." Men "without reputation, or principle, or stake in society" find their natural element in disorder. Lacking "all moral principle and moral feeling," they "are eager to avenge themselves upon society." The anarchy that ensues from their quest of power is "not so much the absence of government, as the government of the worst, a state of things, which to the honor of our nature, has seldom obtained among men, and which perhaps was only fully exemplified during the worst times of the French Revolution, when that horrid hell burnt with its most lurid flame." Harper's salvo came, appropriately, in his discussion of "Slavery in the Light of Social Ethics." On the eve of secession, E. N. Elliott republished Harper's essay of the 1830s in *Cotton Is King and Pro-Slavery Arguments*. By the 1850s the argument that social order and political virtue must be grounded in slavery – the slavery of whites, should blacks not be available – was no longer startling.[57]

Dew gently criticized the revered Madame De Staël for her unwary acceptance of the intervention of the Parisian mobs in the politics of the French Revolution. He loathed "the fatal precedent established of placing the cause of freedom under the protection of mobs." Dew surely agreed with Nathaniel Beverley Tucker that, if ruling classes refused to tax themselves to take care of the poor, they would provoke insurrections. For Tucker the mounting evidence of the oppression of the laboring classes presaged what was to come. Implicitly, Tucker provided an addendum to

---

[56] Dew, *Digest*, 258, 269–70, 564–8, 582–3, 605, 661, quotes at 605 and 661.
[57] Harper, "Slavery in the Light of Social Ethics," in E. N. Elliott, ed., *Cotton Is King and Pro-Slavery Arguments* (New York, 1969 [1860]), 610.

Simms's articulation of a belief widespread among southerners: Stability depends upon political, social, and cultural progress – not vice versa – and therefore revolution occurs when society tries to maintain stability at the expense of progress. Tucker would not have disagreed; but, noting that the British press was (with reason) comparing the radical wave on the continent to the Jacquerie and Wat Tyler, he saw something new. Property lies at the heart of great social struggles. Previously, men fought to establish their own claims to it. Now, powerful "communist" forces were assaulting the very idea of private property rights. The French Revolution taught that the demand for political rights can quickly pass into a demand for vast social rights that provokes military repression. Holmes added that – throughout history – commerce, war, militarism, and land greed provoked fierce rebellions by the oppressed and suffering but also engendered wildly dangerous agrarian, leveling, and egalitarian revolutionary theories. Culture and intelligence, constitutions and laws, material prosperity, and pretension to moral and political enlightenment constitute no safeguards against revolutionary tumults and atrocities.[58]

Southerners concerned with the trajectory of transatlantic capitalism hoped that the United States had a constitutional system strong enough to resist the radicalism that threatened Europe. But they feared that, as America filled up with people and recapitulated European socioeconomic development, it too would succumb to murderous class warfare and a reenactment of the Reign of Terror. Meanwhile, Dew expressed their common anticipation: "We may with confidence assert that there can be no texture of society better calculated to ward [off radicalism] than that which exists under the much reviled, much slandered institutions of the South."[59]

---

[58] Dew, *Digest,* 601; Nathaniel Beverley Tucker, "Moral and Political Effect of the Relation between the Caucasian and the African Slave," *SLM,* 10 (1844), 472–3; [Tucker], "Present State of Europe," 284–91; George Frederick Holmes, "Theory of Political Individualism," *DBR,* 22 (1857), 134, 146; [Holmes], "Recent Histories of Julius Caesar," 391; David Moltke-Hansen, "Ordered Progress: The Historical Philosophy of William Gilmore Simms," in John Caldwell Guilds, ed., *"Long Years of Neglect": The Work and Reputation of William Gilmore Simms* (Fayetteville, NC, 1988), 126. In decadent periods, Polybius taught, the masses flatter themselves as bearers of "Liberty and Democracy" and fall prey to those ready to impose the "despotism of the crowd": Polybius, *The Histories,* tr. W. R. Paton, 6 vols. (LCL), Bk. 6:ch. 57.

[59] Dew, *Digest,* 659. Dew died in 1846, his life sadly cut short at age 44. He did not live to witness the storms of 1848, which he had, in effect, predicted. Nor did he live to have his confidence in slavery shattered at Appomattox.

Epilogue

King Solomon's Dilemma

God hath numbered thy kingdom and finished it .... Thou art weighed in the balances, and art found wanting.

—Daniel, 5:26

Think too how difficult it would be, even if you were fighting feeble opponents, to preserve the purity of your religion, and how you will be forced to transgress the very laws which furnish your chief hope of making God your ally, and so will alienate Him.... But if in the war you transgress your ancestral Law, I don't see what you have left to fight for, since your one desire is that none of your ancestral customs should be broken. How then will you be able to call the Deity to your aid, if you deliberately deny Him the service that is His due?

—King Agrippa II, according to Josephus[1]

With the outbreak of the War, white Southerners staked their all on the consolidation of their slaveholding society into an independent nation. The slaveholding states had flourished within the Union, and, when eleven seceded, four chose to remain. Of the Southerners who favored secession, few seriously underestimated the magnitude of the step they were taking, although opinions varied on their prospects. For the great majority, their vision of the best possible slaveholding society included state rights – an attachment to the state as their first and most enduring home place. In this inclination, they followed the sentiments of their beloved Roman republicans, who, like Cicero, wrote eloquently about life on one's own rural estate.

That substantial slaveholders believed slavery essential to their rural independence is hardly surprising, but many nonslaveholders and the smallest of slaveholders agreed, primarily because they, too, valued rural independence – including the light hand and limited intrusion of the government, federal or state. Slavery

---

[1] Josephus, *The Jewish War*, tr. G. A. Williamson, ed. E. Mary Smallwood (New York, 1970), 161. For Josephus, Jewish law proceeded from Moses without alteration: see Jehoshua Amir, "Josephus on the 'Mosaic Constitution,'" in Henning Graf Reventlow et al., eds., *Politics and Theopolitics in the Bible and Biblical Literature* (Sheffield, U.K., 1994), 13–27.

guaranteed much of what they cared most about, notably a clear delineation between men and women's roles, a low rate of urban and industrial growth, and a
vision of social order. No one would deny that, to a significant extent, the material
interests of slaveholders and also the comfort of many of the less affluent whites
derived from racial stratification. But neither consideration, by itself, justified the
momentous step of secession. That step required a distinct worldview, with slavery its cornerstone, and even then could be taken only with prayers as well as with
courage and daring.

As thoughtful Southerners weighed their prospects, many turned again to the
history they had long looked to for guidance and reassurance. Their reading had
impressed on them the inexorability of historical cycles, although it never smoth-
ered hopes that the cycles could be broken. The commitment to the formation of
a new nation moved them to a higher level of danger. For nation-building represented a break with the simple defense of rural tranquility, even if ostensibly done
in its service. This lesson blazed from the pages of the very source to which they
had most frequently turned for their defense of slavery: the Bible.

For more than half a century, Southerners had shared a government with the
free society of the North. Those years had seen a steadily widening rift between
southern and northern goals, but both sides persisted in loyalty to the Union even
as each sought to impose its vision on the whole. With secession, the die was cast.
The South now faced the daunting challenge of creating something genuinely new
under the sun: a modern slaveholding republic. Southerners' immersion in the study
of ancient Greece and Rome and medieval Europe did not blind them to their own
modernity. The magnitude of their undertaking made a sound reading of the lessons
of history all the more pressing, but history could take them only so far, since its
most applicable lessons were less than promising. The building of a Confederate
nation required that the slaveholding South do what no society or nation had ever
done: break the historical cycle of glory, decadence, and collapse. Slaveholders, if
anything more strongly than nonslaveholders, understood that realization of their
dream required the slave society they were building to be truly Christian. God's
sanction, according to their own reading of Scriptures, rested on the slaveholders'
intent and capacity to make the master–slave relation of the modern South accord
with that of the Abramic household and the teachings of the Gospels.

Overwhelmingly, Southerners – Presbyterians, Methodists, Baptists, Episcopalians, Disciples, Unitarians, Catholics, Jews – had understood the Bible not as a
collection of metaphors but as sacred history. "P. A. M." of Georgetown, South
Carolina, called the Bible "a book of facts," and the Unitarian Theodore Clapp of
New Orleans stressed that biblical truth was grounded in the Fall and the Incarnation. The distinguished naval scientist Matthew Fontaine Maury of Virginia proclaimed, "The Bible *is* authority for everything it touches." Thomas Roderick Dew,
who rarely plunged into theology or church doctrine, began his impressive history
of Western civilization with "Cosmogony or the Creation of the World" in order
to show that history, science, and theology were not at odds. Implicitly dismissing
David Hume, he wrote: "*Why the belief in an intelligent cause? Order, harmony,
and design, in the physical world prove its existence.*" The Mosaic accounts of

creation could be interpreted either as six days or an extended period of time. He also saw the Fall and the deluge as consistent with Hindu and other religious accounts. "Geology and tradition, then, must test the Noachian flood; and with that test the Mosaic account must stand or fall." The evidence from geology and linguistics, Dew declared, established the validity of the Bible as history.[2]

Biblical history abounded with cautionary tales as well as models of excellence. But the "Hebrew Theocracy" especially fascinated both divines and secular theorists. In 1822, Edwin Holland of South Carolina told of God's direct rule through a Theocracy that presided over a slaveholding Jewish people. In later years the Reverend William Buck of Kentucky, editor of *Baptist Banner,* called that Theocracy "a *Republic of Fathers* – ruled by those appropriately termed 'Elders of Israel.'" When the South seceded, the Jackson (Alabama) *Republican* proclaimed, "Looming up from the golden portals of the east, the sun throws his broad beams upon the landscapes of the very Eden of the South – the Palestine of the new Republic." The Atlanta *Gate-City Guardian* prophesied: "We will in a half century show to the world such a people and such a Government as has not existed since the days of Theocracy." To B. W. Lacy of the University of Virginia, the Theocracy was as a model of a patriarchal system. To the Presbyterian Reverend Thomas Vernon Moore of Richmond, Virginia, "the Hebrew commonwealth" was "a Theocracy in relation to God" and "a republic in its relation to man."[3]

---

[2] "P. A. M.", "The Bible," *SLM,* 11 (1845), 620; Theodore Clapp, "Sermon," New Orleans *Daily Picayune,* Mar. 18, 1849; Frances Leigh Williams, *Matthew Fontaine Maury: Scientist of the Sea* (New Brunswick, NJ, 1963), 339–49, quote at 340; Thomas Roderick Dew, *Digest of the Laws, Customs, Manners, and Institutions of the Ancient and Modern Nations* (New York, 1884 [1852]), 1–9, quote at 7. For the Old Testament as history, see J. L. Reynolds, *The Man of Letters: An Address Delivered before the Literary Societies of Wake Forest College* (Richmond, VA, 1849), 21; Thomas O. Summers, ed., *Sermons by the Late Rev. David Seth Doggett* (Nashville, TN, 1882), 232–3; "D. M.", "Bishop Butler," *QRMECS,* 2 (1848), 235; Sermons for 1858, in Otey Papers, at UNC-SHC; J. L. Dagg, *Manual of Theology: A Treatise on Christian Doctrine and a Treatise on Church Order,* 2 vols. (New York, 1980 [1857, 1858]), 1:144; *JHTW,* 3:221–76; [Thomas Smyth], "Nature and Origin of the Pagan Doctrine of Triads," *SPR,* 8 (1855), 560–80. Also, Morton H. Smith, *Studies in Southern Presbyterian Theology* (Phillipsburg, NJ, 1962), 148–9, 300, and James Oscar Farmer, Jr., *The Metaphysical Confederacy: James Henley Thornwell and the Synthesis of Southern Values* (Macon, GA, 1986), 136.

During the eighteenth century, a shift took place from a literal reading of the Bible as history – historical referents for biblical stories – to a textual reading that offers the most plausible explanation as evidence of an accurate report of past occurrences: see Hans W. Frei, *The Eclipse of Biblical Narrative: A Study in Eighteenth and Nineteenth Century Hermeneutics* (New Haven, CT, 1974). At the time of the Founding, Americans generally accepted the Bible as historically accurate: Forrest McDonald, *The American Presidency: An Intellectual Portrait* (Lawrence, KS, 1994), 68–72. For a strong defense of the centrality of biblical history to the foundations of Christianity see Mark Noll, *Turning Points: Decisive Moments in the History of Christianity* (Grand Rapids, MI, 1997), 14–16.

[3] [Edwin C. Holland], *A Refutation of the Calumnies Circulated against the Southern and Western States, Respecting the Institution and Existence of Slavery among Them* (Charleston, SC, 1822), 40–1; William C. Buck, *The Slavery Question* (Louisville, KY, 1849), 7 (pamphlet version of articles from the *Baptist Banner*); also, Dew, *Digest,* 11–13, 357–8. On the press see Donald E. Reynolds, *Editors Make War: Southern Newspapers in the Secession Crisis* (Nashville, TN, 1966), 177; Jackson *Republican,* Jan. 17, 1861, and Atlanta *Gate-City Guardian,* Feb. 12, 1861. B. W. Lacy, "Government a Divine Institution," *VUM,* 4 (1860), 327; Thomas Vernon Moore, *The Christian Lawyer, or The Claims of*

For the most radical of the proslavery theorists, the Theocracy provided valuable support for their doctrine of "slavery in the abstract," according to which personal servitude was the natural and socially safe condition of all labor regardless of race. The widely influential Baptist Reverend Thornton Stringfellow of Virginia interpreted the post-Theocratic compulsory mobilization of free labor by Saul and Solomon as the beginning of "bitter hostility and deadly strife" between capital and labor. Going further, George Frederick Holmes, reinforced by George Fitzhugh of Virginia and Henry Hughes of Mississippi, interpreted the laws of the Theocracy as inconsistent with the practices of the modern free-labor system.[4]

The Baptist Reverend Iveson Brookes pointedly mentioned that God authorized the Hebrew Theocracy to institute slavery, which existed in every society that God favored. But even admirers of the Theocracy did not advocate it as a model for the modern world. A "Lady of Georgia" reflected the sentiments of many in pronouncing the Hebrew Theocracy proper for its time and place but an inadequate government for the United States. The Methodist Bishop George Foster Pierce told the Georgia General Assembly that the Hebrew "patriarchal supremacy" had served its purposes in time and place but would not suit a more complex society. The Theocracy, he explained, provided not a model for government but an indication of its proper spirit. The divines saw nothing innately sinful in the passage from patriarchal to monarchical government.[5]

Problems, nevertheless, arose with the transformation of the Theocracy into a kingdom under Saul and, more pertinently, its consolidation and expansion under David and Solomon. Exuberant proslavery Southerners faced a political and theological conundrum when they tried to evaluate Solomon's reign. Solomon had relied upon forced labor, taxation, and control of trade to strengthen his kingdom and build the Temple. Although Southerners embraced the evidence that Solomon relied heavily on foreign slave labor to supplement an Israelite corvée, they were troubled that he and David exploited the mines and built the Temple with state-slaves, who were unprotected by the humane laws that shielded privately owned "domestic" slaves from appalling brutality. Israelites took slavery for granted, but most Israelite slaves worked on small units in a diversified economy. In troubling contrast,

Christianity on the Legal Profession (Richmond, VA, 1857), 13. Reverend W. T. Hamilton of Mobile did not refer to the Theocracy but he did credit Moses with the establishment of a "commonwealth" – a confederacy of republics that prefigured the government of the United States: "Character of Moses," *SPR,* 18 (1852), 523. Josephus coined the term "Theocracy."

4 Thornton Stringfellow, *Slavery: Its Origin, Nature, and History, Considered in the Light of Bible Teachings, Moral Justice, and Political Wisdom* (New York, 1861), 30–1, quote at 31; [George Frederick Holmes], "Slavery and Freedom," *SQR,* 3rd ser., 1 (1856), 70; for Fitzhugh see Eugene D. Genovese, *The World the Slaveholders Made: Two Essays in Interpretation,* new ed. (Middletown, CT, 1988), 188–9; Henry Hughes, *Treatise on Sociology, Theoretical and Applied* (New York, 1968 [1854]), 82–3.

5 Iveson L. Brookes, *A Defence of the South against the Reproaches of the North* (Hamburg, SC, 1850), 9, 45; "A Lady of Georgia", "Southern Slavery and Its Assailants," *DBR,* 16 (1854), 59; *Sermons of Bishop Pierce and Rev. B. M. Palmer, Delivered before the General Assembly at Milledgeville, Ga., on Fast Day, March 27, 1863* (Milledgeville, GA, 1863), 10. Also, A. W. Dillard, "The Jewish Nation and Its History," *SLM,* 35 (1863), 694; *SPR,* 1 (1847), 36.

David and Solomon's military–bureaucratic measures, replete with imported chariots and horses, created the state centralization most Southerners loathed.[6]

Disagreements arose in the Old South over Solomon's reign, but since he ranked as an Old Testament hero, critics had to tread carefully. Calhoun, nonetheless, having applauded the twelve tribes of Israel for their strong and decentralized confederation, deplored Solomon's imposition of burdensome taxes to support the "profuse expenditures" of his centralized "magnificent reign." James Johnston Pettigrew, in a critique of modern political and economic centralization, looked back with evident repugnance on Solomon's taste for luxuries. William Gilmore Simms let fly at Solomon as the most subtle and selfish of biblical kings, the "Augustus Caesar of his nation" who achieved great things but left his successors to face disaster. To Simms, Solomon qualified as "the first Sultan," who destroyed the confederacy by concentrating power in Jerusalem and grinding the tribes with taxation. And indeed, Solomon's military–bureaucratic measures created what Max Weber described as a virtual oriental despotism in the manner of Pharaoh, which dangerously exacerbated social antagonisms.[7]

Paul's warning that God demands perfect obedience from imperfect men (Rom., 7:22) weighed heavily on those who dreamt of a Confederacy that would break the historical cycle and pioneer in the establishment of a grand new slaveholding world order. The Confederacy recapitulated Solomon's dilemma. Had Solomon not taken the path of state-building – militarization, bureaucratization, and all – then powerful enemies would have crushed Israel. But by taking that path, Israel

---

[6] On labor conditions see E. E. Urbach, "The Laws Regarding Slavery, as a Source for Social History of the Period of the Second Temple, the Mishnah and Talmud," in J. G. Weiss, ed., *Papers of the Institute of Jewish Studies, London,* 2 vols. (Jerusalem, 1964), 1:12, 84; Roland de Vaux, *Ancient Israel,* 2 vols. (New York, 1965), 1:80–5, 88–90; Isaac Mendelsohn, *Slavery in the Ancient Near East* (New York, 1949), 95–7, 101–2, 117–18, 189. For forced labor and the appalling conditions of state slaves under David and Solomon, see also Gösta Ahlström, *The History of Palestine* (Minneapolis, MN, 1993), 508–9; Isaac Mendelsohn, "State Slavery in Ancient Palestine," *Bulletin of the American Schools of Oriental Research,* 85 (1942), 14. State slavery did not exist under the Judges; it came and went with kingship (13).

On the Egyptian model for Solomon's administration and the extent of the use of chariots, see Edwin Yamauchi, "Solomon," in Edward M. Blailock and R. K. Harrison, eds., *The New International Dictionary of Biblical Archeology* (Grand Rapids, MI, 1983), 419, and Yamauchi, "Political Background of the Old Testament," in David S. Dockery et al., eds., *Foundations for Biblical Interpretation: A Complete Library of Tools and Resources* (Nashville, TN, 1994), 316. For Solomon's bureaucracy see Ahlström, *History of Palestine,* 455–542. Chariot warfare and defense proved extraordinarily costly and required heavy taxation: Gunther Wittenberg, " 'Let Canaan Be His Slave' (Gen. 9:26): Is Ham Also Cursed?" *Journal of Theology for Southern Africa,* 74 (1991), 450. For a concise analysis of the centralization of power, the development of a professional organization, and labor conditions under David and Solomon see Harry M. Orlinsky, *Ancient Israel,* 2nd ed. (Ithaca, NY, 1960), 64–6, 74–6, 81–2, 99.

[7] "Speech on the Force Bill," in *JCCP,* 12:80; [James Johnston Pettigrew], *Notes on Spain and the Spaniards in the Summer of 1850, with a Glance at Sardinia* (Charleston, SC, 1861), 131; Max Weber, *Ancient Judaism,* tr. and ed. Hans H. Gerth and Don Martingale (Glencoe, IL, 1952), xviii, 99–100. For Simms see [William Gilmore Simms], "Critical Notices," *SQR,* n.s., 3 (1851), 294–5, quote at 295; Simms to William Porcher Miles, Feb. 26, 1860, in Mary C. Oliphant et al., eds., *The Letters of William Gilmore Simms,* 6 vols. (Columbia, SC, 1952–82), 4:199. For Simms's hostility toward Solomon see also his passing remarks in [Simms], "Democracy in France," *SQR,* 15 (1849), 118.

could not live in accordance with the laws of God: could not employ the measures
necessary to secure national security while remaining faithful to the Decalogue. No
more possible was the Confederacy's dream, projected with special power in Henry
Timrod's poem, *Ethnogenesis,* of combining the global spread of Christianity with
the establishment of a slaveholding world order.[8]

Yet God eventually came down hard on Solomon for reasons other than those
Calhoun, Dew, and Simms might have wished. Neither Solomon's state-building
militarization, bureaucratization, or forced labor accounted for the fall of the kingdom. Solomon incurred God's wrath not by political overreaching but by infidelity:
In defiance of Mosaic law, he opened his regime (to say nothing of his bed) to Baal
worshipers. And nowhere does Kings say that forced labor had anything to do with
the miseries that befell Solomon's successors; Rehoboam had an Ammonite mother
and tolerated paganism.[9]

For Southerners like Dew, centralization per se was not the problem. Dew acknowledged David's militarism but praised him for restoring order and guiding Israel to prosperity. He described Solomon more gingerly as a man "fond of magnificence and show," who taxed his people heavily, imposed severe corvées, and thereby
provoked the revolt against his son Rehoboam and the secession of Judah from
Israel. Judge J. H. Lumpkin of Georgia countered that, under David and Solomon,
the ancient Jews achieved "great splendor" and took their place among nations "as
a rich and powerful and heroic people." Neither Dew nor Lumpkin nor the divines
allayed the political fears of Solomon's southern critics, because the sacred and secular history to which Solomon's critics and defenders both appealed called into
question the grand dream of a cycle-breaking southern slaveholding republic.[10]

---

[8] For the contradictions in Solomon's reign and their consequences for Judaism and Christianity, see
Eric Voegelin, *Order and History,* 5 vols. (Baton Rouge, LA, 1956–87), 1:243, 258–9, and for an extended evaluation of the problem of kingship see vol. 4. See also Abraham J. Heschel, *The Prophets,*
2 vols. (Peabody, MA, 2000), 2:257–8, 1:161.

[9] Of Solomon's 700 wives and 300 concubines, a good many were Moabites, Ammonites, Edomites,
Sidonians, and Hittites: Yamauchi, "Political Background of the Old Testament," in Dockery et al.,
eds., *Foundations for Biblical Interpretation,* 317. On the influence of Solomon's wives in promoting apostasy see Edwin Yamauchi, "Solomon," in Blailock and Harrison, eds., *New International
Dictionary of Biblical Archeology,* 421. Some of Solomon's successors allowed Baal worship, others
suppressed it. God judged the kings precisely by this action (2 Chron., and Neh., 13:26). Flavius Josephus stressed that Solomon's tolerance of pagan religions was propelled by wives and mistresses:
Antiquities (LCL), 1:295. In 1 Kings (5:12–18), forced labor appears positively and receives no rebuke. On Rehoboam see Richard D. Nelson, *First and Second Kings* (Atlanta, GA, 1987), 42, 64,
72, 77, 101. According to Basil Armstrong Thomasson, a small farmer and teacher in western North
Carolina, "Solomon was a great and good man," superior to all others "in happiness, riches, and
wisdom," but none of his innumerable wives was "a good woman." They deluded an old man, leading him from "the worship of God as taught in the Law of Moses, to the worship of idols." See Oct.
5, 1861, in Paul D. Escott, ed., *North Carolina Yeoman: The Diary of Basil Armstrong Thomasson,
1853–1862* (Athens, GA, 1996), 316.

[10] Dew, *Digest,* 11–13, 357–8; Joseph Henry Lumpkin, *Address Delivered before Hopewell Presbytery,
the Board of Trustees of Oglethorpe College* (Milledgeville, GA, 1837), 21. Among others, "L. S."
in *Southern Quarterly Review* condemned Rehoboam's decision to continue his father's stern rule:
"Mississippi Affairs," *SQR,* 8 (1845), 364. The divines' enthusiasm for the wealth and magnificence

Less wedded to slavery than to the independent rural life it afforded, other Southerners were ever more resentful of the effects of centralization: conscription, mounting taxation, and the increasing intrusion of a "modern" nation into the lives of its
citizens. The problem was not, as many like to claim, preeminently one of hostility
to slavery as a social system or even to the slaveholders as a ruling class. Elements
of that hostility festered, ever ready to flare up when the pressures upon nonslaveholding whites accumulated. As the Confederate leaders rapidly discovered, it was
impossible to build a nation and wage a modern war without contravening many of
the principles that had justified their nation's existence in the first place. Nor could
they or their foes foresee that the war upon which they were embarking would become the first modern war and would leave neither side – nor the world at large –
unchanged.

Historians have documented the extent to which the exigencies of war compelled
the Confederacy to risk replication of the government consolidation and repression
it had often complained about. Southerners of all political stripes had often warned
of the consolidationist consequences of secession. In 1828 James Monroe had written Calhoun that disunion would mean wars in which "our free system of Government would be overwhelmed." In subsequent decades Henry St. George Tucker and
Abel Upshur in Virginia, Frederick Nash in North Carolina, and Henry W. Hilliard
in Alabama, among others, predicted that secession would result in militarized, nationally consolidated rival states. Indeed, in South Carolina that prospect worried
Robert Barnwell Rhett, the fiery secessionist, as well as unionists and moderates
like the Reverends Ferdinand Jacobs and James Henley Thornwell. Disunionist no
less than unionist newspapers worried that postsecession northern hostility would
compel the South to institute a repressive and expensive government, a standing
army, and even military dictatorship.[11]

For those who sought to create a cycle-breaking South, the challenge far transcended such considerations, important as they were. Realization of the dream depended on the Christian character of the slave society they were intent on building.

---

generated by the economic policies of David and Solomon sometimes rivaled that of such commercially minded secular writers as De Bow and S. J. Barnett: J. D. B. De Bow, *The Industrial Resources,
Statistics, &c. of the United States and More Particularly of the Southern and Western States,* 3rd
ed., 3 vols. (New York, 1966 [1854]), 1:302, and *DBR,* 1 (1846), 100, 112; see also the hints in *DBR,*
15 (1853), 543; [Barnett], "Buckle's History of Civilization," *SPR,* 17 (1866), 209.

[11] Monroe to Calhoun, Aug. 4, 1828, in *JCCP,* 10:409; Henry St. George Tucker, *Lectures on Government* (Charlottesville, VA, 1844), 58–9, 62, 172, 181, 191, 203, 212, 57; Claude H. Hall, *Abel Parker
Upshur: Conservative Virginian, 1790–1844* (Madison, WI, 1963), 92; Frederick Nash to Willie P.
Mangum, Jan. 23, 1833, in Henry Thomas Shanks, ed., *The Papers of Willie P. Mangum,* 5 vols.
(Raleigh, NC, 1955–56), 2:11–12; "Slavery and the Union" (Dec. 12, 1849) and "Boundary of Texas
and New Mexico" (Aug. 28, 1850), in H. W. Hilliard, *Speeches and Addresses* (New York, 1855), 228,
313–14; Laura A. White, *Robert Barnwell Rhett: Father of Secession* (Gloucester, MA, 1965 [1931]),
88; Ferdinand Jacobs, *The Committing of Our Cause to God* (Charleston, SC, 1850), 4, 22. In B. M.
Palmer, *The Life and Letters of James Henley Thornwell* (Richmond, VA, 1875), see Thornwell to
Breckenridge, Mar. 28, 1851 (477), Thornwell to Rev. Dr. Hooper, Mar. 8, 1850 (478), and Thornwell, "Our Danger and Our Duty" (Appendix 2:582). Dwight L. Dumond, ed., *Southern Editorials
on Secession* (Gloucester, MA, 1964), 157, 212, 286, 446–7; Reynolds, *Editors Make War,* 167, 204.

Accordingly, before and after secession, the churches preached against a broad variety of sins: from the overarching sins of pride and envy to such specifics as Sabbath breaking, violation of family norms, and "extortion" (wartime price gouging) – and the abuses attendant upon slaveholding. For while all but a handful of preachers firmly endorsed slavery as God-ordained, they warned against its abuse at the hands of irresponsible and cruel masters. They warned that if Southerners did not live up to Christian standards in their daily lives and, in particular, did not bring slavery up to Abramic standards, then a wrathful God would use the heathen Yankees, as He had used heathens of yore, to smite his Chosen People. For southern Christians, then, the war of 1861–65 was a test of their faithfulness to God – a test they failed.[12]

In the wake of Appomattox, Southerners, surveying the ruin of their world, faced the question with agonizing immediacy. Even the most somber of historical examples had not prepared them. It was one thing to reflect upon the defeat of others as evidence of God's judgment or upon the inexorable recurrence of historical cycles. It was another to choke on the ashes of their own defeat and the destruction of their world. What freedmen experienced as a crossing of the Red Sea, their former masters experienced as the Babylonian captivity, replete with bitter tears and much gnashing of teeth. History offered little consolation. The object of God's judgment rather than His instrument, Southerners plunged into a radically altered world unlikely to bring out the best in them. Those whom William Faulkner would call "the unvanquished" could not write the authoritative history of the world their forebears had attempted to build and defend. For as Jefferson Davis, Alexander Stephens, and no few other Confederates understood, it would fall to the side that won the War to write the history of the old regime and its struggle unto death.

[12] For an elaboration see Eugene D. Genovese, *A Consuming Fire: The Fall of the Confederacy in the Mind of the White Christian South* (Athens, GA, 1998).

Supplementary References

Addison's *Cato*: Addison's *Cato* triumphed in theaters in eighteenth- and early nineteenth-century America, including in Richmond and Charleston and on college campuses. Its immediate political impact seems to have rested primarily on its encouragement of rising anti-British feeling, but its picture of Caesar as usurper and tyrant had lasting effect. It had an additional attraction to southern planters as well as northern conservatives: The unabashedly pro-aristocracy Cato served with distinction in the campaign against Spartacus. See Frederic M. Litto, "Addison's Cato in the Colonies," *WMQ*, 3rd ser., 23 (1966), 431–49. For performances of *Cato* in Williamsburg and Charleston in the 1730s see James D. Hart, *The Popular Book: A History of America's Literary Taste* (New York, 1950), 28–9. Addison's *Cato* was performed at Moses Waddel's famous Willington Academy with William H. Crawford in the lead role: "J. B. C." [of Longwood, MS], "William H. Crawford," *American Whig Review*, 7 (1851), 195. For student presentations at the University of Georgia see Paul DeForest Hicks, *Joseph Henry Lumpkin: Georgia's First Chief Justice* (Athens, GA, 2002), 15. William Lowndes was among the students who performed in Addison's *Cato* in Charleston in the early 1800s: Carl J. Vipperman, *William Lowndes and the Transition of Southern Politics, 1782–1822* (Chapel Hill, NC, 1989), 9. Jasper Adams, who considered Caesar (as well as Alexander) a power-hungry despot, also quoted Addison's *Cato* on belief in God as necessary for morality: Adams, *Elements of Moral Philosophy* (Philadelphia, 1837), 46, 56. For the glorification of Marcius Porcius Cato and the severing of Washington from Caesar see Garry Wills, *Cincinnatus: George Washington and the Enlightenment* (New York, 1984), 135–8; M. N. S. Sellers, *American Republicanism: Roman Ideology in the United States Constitution* (New York, 1994), 153–5; Eran Shalev, "Ancient Masks, American Fathers: Classical Pseudonyms during the American Revolution and Early Republic," *JER*, 23 (2003), 155. Recall that, according to Plutarch, the Romans admired Cato the Younger but few followed him: *The Lives of the Noble Grecians and Romans*, tr. John Dryden, ed. and rev. by Arthur Hugh Clough, 2 vols. (New York, 1992), 1:729.

American Revolution in the South: For southern complaints about underappreciation see also Robert R. Howison, *A History of Virginia from Its Discovery and Settlement by Europeans to the Present Time*, 2 vols. (Philadelphia, 1846), 2:213; [Benjamin F. Perry], "The Revolutionary History of South Carolina," *SQR*, 11 (1847), 468–85; Joseph Johnson, *Traditions and Reminiscences of the American Revolution in the South* (Spartanburg, SC, 1972 [1851]), v, 555–7. Robert Y. Hayne, in his debate with Webster, proudly reminded the Senate of South Carolina's contributions to the American Revolution: Hayne, in *Congressional*

Globe: Senate, Jan. 25, 1830 (424). M. R. H. Garnett of Virginia stressed that the slave states sent troops north during the Revolution but the North did not reciprocate: [Garnett], *The Union, Past and Future: How It Works, and How to Save It*, 4th ed. (Charleston, SC, 1850), 9. For the bold assertion that Southerners carried the American Revolution see also Samuel Cartwright, *Essays in a Series of Letters to Rev. William Winans* (Natchez, MS, 1843), 46, 59; [George Atkinson], "Civil Warfare in the Carolinas and Georgia," *SLM*, 12 (1846), 257–8; W. H. Holcombe Diary, Note, 1850, at UNC-SHC; Henry W. Miller, *Address Delivered before the Philanthropic and Dialectic Societies of the University of North-Carolina* (Raleigh, NC, 1857), 19. Bertram Wyatt-Brown has suggested that Charles Sumner provoked Preston Brooks's caning in part by an affront to southern honor that accused South Carolinians of cowardice during the Revolution: *Yankee Saints and Southern Sinners* (Baton Rouge, LA, 1985), 198.

For the war in South Carolina see Lawrence S. Rowland et al., *The History of Beaufort County, South Carolina*, 2 vols. (Columbia, SC, 1996), 1:ch. 13; Edward McCrady, *South Carolina in the Revolution, 1775–1780* (New York, 1902), 296–8, esp. ch. 14; for a fine modern assessment, see John S. Pancake, *This Destructive War: The British Campaign in the Carolinas, 1780–1782* (Tuscaloosa, AL, 1985), esp. ch. 5. W. H. Sparks, C. C. Jones, Jr., and other notable writers kept alive southern memories of "barbarous cruelties" of the British, the atrocities, and the Whig–Tory struggle in the Carolinas. See Sparks, *The Memories of Fifty Years* (Philadelphia, 1872), 16–18; Charles C. Jones, Jr., and Salem Dutcher, *Memorial History of Augusta* (Syracuse, NY, 1890), ch. 10. Yet, even some who recalled Tory atrocities acknowledged cruelty on both sides and divided the Tories into good if misguided people and rogues: see e.g. David L. Swain, *British Invasion of North Carolina in 1776* (n.p., 1853), 16, 21.

Ancient Egypt: For Egyptian culture and Greece's debt to it, see "B.", *SLM*, 20 (1854), 294–5; Isaac W. Stuart, *On the Classical Tongues and the Advantages of their Study* (Columbia, SC, 1836), 4; [Conway Robinson], "Philosophy of Antiquity," *SLM*, 2 (1836), 740, and 3 (1837), 32; W. N. Pendleton, *Science: A Witness for the Bible* (Philadelphia, 1860), 34; William B. Shepherd, *An Address Delivered before the Two Literary Societies of the University of North Carolina* (Raleigh, NC, 1838), 15; [George Frederick Holmes], "History of Literature," *SQR*, 2 (1842), 479–80. Ancient Egypt and Persia, reported J. D. B. De Bow, elevated concepts and practices of law: "Law and Lawyers," *SQR*, 6 (1844), 377–8; also, De Bow, "Law and Lawyers – No. 1," *DBR*, 19 (1855), 305. For student awareness of the profound effect of Egyptian culture on Greek see Edwin Taliaferro, "The Poetry of Greece" (M.A. thesis, 1855, typescript at UVA).

Southerners invoked Arnold Heeren to refute the thesis that Egyptians were black: "Relations of the Ancient World," *SQR*, 5 (1844), 164–5. Benjamin Blake Minor had the Egyptian – and Ethiopian – ruling classes white and the servile classes black: "Progress of Archeological Science in America," *SLM*, 11 (1845), 427. Southerners relied heavily on Herodotus, who did not demean Egypt: Stephanie West, "Cultural Antitheses: Reflections on Herodotus 2.35–36," *International Journal of the Classical Tradition*, 5 (1998), 5. Herodotus, among other ancients, suggested that the further south one went in Africa, the greater the sexual promiscuity and the more monstrous the human beings. William Wells Brown and Frederick Douglass interpreted Herodotus as claiming that Egyptians were black Africans: see David S. Weisen, "Herodotus and the Modern Debate over Race and Slavery," *Ancient World*, 3 (1980), 15–16.

Anti-abolitionist Bible Arguments in the North: In 1846 John C. Calhoun complimented the Reverend George Junkin, who became notorious in Pennsylvania and Ohio for his staunch defense of slavery: "I have read several able discussions on the subject, but in none of them have the various passages of the Bible in reference to the subject of slavery been presented in so clear & systematick a manner, and discussed with such a thorough knowledge of it, under all its aspects. You have left no loophole for the most subtle & sophisticated opponent to escape." In 1848 Junkin became president of Washington College in Virginia, but as an intransigent and unconditional unionist he left the South when the War came. Calhoun to George Junkin, Sept. 17, 1846, in *JCCP*, 23:450; Junkin, *The Integrity of Our National Union vs. Abolitionism: An Argument from the Bible* (Cincinnati, 1843). Junkin was also a colonizationist and a supporter of manifest destiny: see Ollinger Crenshaw, *General Lee's College: The Rise and Growth of Washington and Lee University* (New York, 1969), 112–17. Junkin believed the Union holy and an expression of God's will. He defended slavery as scripturally sanctioned, but the mere suggestion of secession sent him into a rage: Mary Price Coulling, *Margaret Junkin Preston: A Biography* (Winston-Salem, NC, 1993), 109, 113.

Among conservative Northerners, Nathan Lord, president of Dartmouth College, "confessed" that he leaned toward the view of slavery as ordained of God, and he asked Calhoun to recommend authorities who had soundly established it: Nathan Lord to Calhoun, Apr. 19, 1848, in *JCCP*, 25:332–3. Fitzhugh hailed Lord and Samuel Nott as conservative voices of sanity in the North: George Fitzhugh, "Mr. Bancroft's History and the Inner Light," *DBR*, 29 (1860), 608. Samuel How, pastor of the First Reformed Dutch Church of New Brunswick, New Jersey, also denied the sinfulness of slavery in his pamphlet *Slavery Not Sinful* (New Brunswick, NJ, 1855): see the praise offered in *SPR*, "Critical Notices," 9 (1856), 471. Moses Stuart, another important moderate, referring to Tacitus' account of the execution of 400 slaves for the killing of a master, questioned whether a system that gave some men ownership of others could possibly prevent atrocities well beyond those inherent in all hierarchical institutions: *Conscience and the Constitution* (Boston, 1850), 37.

Antislavery Southern Ministers: For David Barrow, Jacob Gruber, and other early antislavery ministers who eventually departed for the North, where they made significant contributions to the rise of abolitionism, see Herbert Aptheker, *Abolitionism: A Revolutionary Movement* (Boston, 1989), chs. 1 and 8; also, Daniel W. Crofts, *Old Southampton: Politics and Society in a Virginia County, 1834–1869* (Charlottesville, VA, 1992), 92–3; Jean Libby, ed., *From Slavery to Salvation: The Autobiography of Rev. Thomas W. Henry of the A. M. E. Church* (Jackson, MS, 1994 [1872]), 16, 32. In 1841, Ezekiel Birdseye, a Connecticut Yankee who settled in eastern Tennessee, reported that 600 antislavery men had removed to Indiana: Ezekiel Birdseye to Gerrit Smith, Jan. 25 and Nov. 27, 1841, in W. Freeman Galpin, ed., "Letters of an East Tennessee Abolitionist," *East Tennessee Society Historical Publications*, 3 (1931), 144–9. Reverend Harvey Woods reported from Kentucky that the best antislavery men were departing. W. W. Sweet, *Religion on the Frontier: The Presbyterians, 1783–1840: A Collection of Sources* (New York, 1936), Woods quoted at 279 n. 36. Samuel M. Janney, an outspoken Quaker, John Hampden Pleasants, editor of the Richmond *Whig*, and C. C. McIntyre, editor of the Leesburg *Washingtonian*, preached moderate antislavery doctrine in Virginia through the 1840s. Even in the lower South, some churches continued to debate slavery into the 1840s. The principal outcome seems to have been the departure of the antislavery men to the North. See Patricia Hickin, "Gentle Agitator: Samuel M. Janney and the Antislavery Movement in Virginia, 1842–1851," *JSH*, 37 (1971), 159–90.

Arabian Nights: Southerners apparently saw a chivalric message in *Arabian Nights* (*A Thousand and One Nights*). Read primarily as a moral tract, it reinforced social norms, defending family honor and calling for vengeance against slights to women. See B. L. Gildersleeve,

"Small Favours," Richmond (VA) *Examiner,* June 4, 1864, in Ward W. Briggs, Jr., ed., *Soldier and Scholar: Basil Laneau Gildersleeve and the Civil War* (Charlottesville, VA, 1998), 323; [John R. Thompson], *SLM,* 14 (1848), 334. On the values of *Arabian Nights* see Marshall G. S. Hodgson, *The Venture of Islam: Conscience and History in a World Civilization,* 3 vols. (London, 1974), 1:141. Considered light but instructive reading, *Arabian Nights* became a favorite of the lowcountry elite and also among the less well-to-do of the upcountry from the mid-eighteenth century; it remained so thereafter. Gildersleeve referred to its incidents in newspaper editorials in a manner that assumed reader familiarity. John R. Thompson condescendingly recommended *Arabian Nights* for family reading aimed primarily at the children. Henri Garidel of New Orleans also considered it fit for children, but he kept reading it anyway, as did a woman who worked in his wartime office in Richmond: Oct. 3, 5, 7, in Michael Bedout Chesson and Leslie Jean Roberts, eds., *Exile in Richmond: The Confederate Journal of Henri Garidel* (Charlottesville, VA, 2001), 229, 231. For the reading of *Arabian Nights* see Richard Beale Davis, *Intellectual Life in the Colonial South, 1515–1763,* 3 vols. (Knoxville, TN, 1978), 2:533, 577; Hennig Cohen, *The South Carolina Gazette, 1732–1775* (Columbia, SC, 1953), 138, 152; Hugh A. Garland, *The Life of John Randolph of Roanoke,* 2 vols. (New York, 1969 [1859]), 1:14–15, 2:173; Lawrence S. Rowland et al., *The History of Beaufort County, South Carolina,* 2 vols. (Columbia, SC, 1996), 168; Chesnut Diary, Mar. 12, 1865, in C. Vann Woodward, ed., *Mary Chesnut's Civil War* (New Haven, CT, 1981), 761 (Chesnut and perhaps others read it in French); Maria Bryan to Julia Ann Bryan Cumming, Nov. 13, 1830, in Carol Bleser, ed., *Tokens of Affection: The Letters of a Planter's Daughter in the Old South* (Athens, GA, 1996), 123. For small slaveholders in Texas and east Tennessee see (respectively) Elizabeth Scott Neblett to Will Neblett, Oct. 15, 1863, in Erika I. Murr, ed. *A Rebel Wife in Texas: The Diary and Letters of Elizabeth Scott Neblett, 1852–1864* (Baton Rouge, LA, 2001), 169, and Feb. 14, 1863, in William R. Snell, ed., *Myra Inman: A Diary of the Civil War in East Tennessee* (Macon, GA, 2000), 186. For the popularity of *Arabian Nights* as children's entertainment see Frank Luther Mott, *Golden Multitudes: The Story of Best Sellers in the United States* (New York, 1947), 34, 305.

Art and Freedom: The patronage of despots, wrote Hugh Legaré, never matched the creativity unleashed in free republics: Legaré, in Benjamin F. Griffin, *The Southern Orator, Consisting of Elements of Elocution, and Selections Suitable for Declamation and Recitation from Eminent Southern Orators and Writers* (Macon, GA, and Charleston, SC, 1851), 159. Ancient Egypt, wrote Professor Isaac Stuart, provides "the history of gigantic art born of superstition." Yet he acknowledged its great accomplishments: I. W. Stuart, *On the Classical Tongues and the Advantages of their Study* (Columbia, SC, 1836), 4. "J. R. D." argued that Greco-Roman experience shows that free institutions nourish talent: "General Superiority of the Ancients to the Moderns," *Southern Ladies' Book,* 2 (1840), 79. For republics as the best government to develop a peoples' genius, see Walter Monteiro, *Address before the Neotrophian Society of the Hampton Academy* (Richmond, VA, 1857), 12–13. But for praise of Augustus for his encouragement of literature see Joseph B. Cobb [of Mississippi], "Roman Literature," *QRMECS,* 12 (1853), 74. Representative William B. Shepherd of North Carolina paid lip service to the autocracy of Louis XIV as a "brilliant era" but disparaged it for merely aping the classics and denigrating religion. Frederick Porcher saw Louis XIV as promoter of an "era of intellectual activity," but S. J. Barnett snorted that, in fact, he suffocated it. See Shepherd, *An Address Delivered before the Two Literary Societies of the University of North Carolina* (Raleigh, NC, 1838), 14; Porcher, "Nature and the Claims of Paradox" *RM,* 1 (1857), 484; [Barnett], "Buckle's History of Civilization," *SPR,* 17 (1866), 190–1.

Ballads: During the 1850s, *Southern Literary Messenger* published articles on British ballads, noting their origins in or relation to the common people. Tasso, Dante, and Spenser drew notice for their mining of folk culture to produce "marvelous" works. For ballads as historical evidence and for literary value see, in *SLM*: "History and Constitution of the Early Roman Commonwealth,"14 (1848), 265–78; "National Ballads," 15 (1849), 10–15; "English Ballads," 15 (1849), 356–62; for the 1850s see (among many) "The Ancient Ballads of Percy and Douglas and Chevy Chase," 28 (1859), 195–200, which rebuked Samuel Johnson for pouring contempt on the "old ballads" and "inflicting a wound upon the literature and the glory of his country" (195). *Southern Literary Messenger* also regularly published material on Indian legends and folklore. On Gillies and William Mitford see Frank M. Turner, *The Greek Heritage in Victorian Britain* (New Haven, CT, 1981), 84; [James Johnston Pettigrew], *Notes on Spain and the Spaniards in the Summer of 1850, with a Glance at Sardinia* (Charleston, SC, 1861), 135–6; Neal C. Gillespie, *The Collapse of Orthodoxy: The Intellectual Ordeal of George Frederick Holmes* (Charlottesville, VA, 1972), 68–9.

Balzac: Although Honoré de Balzac's novels should have been to southern tastes, references appeared sparingly – most notably in the diary of Mary Chesnut, who read them avidly. George Frederick Holmes linked Balzac with Sand and Sue as a purveyor of decadent literature, but Simms, praising *Père Goriot*, declared that the only thing to be held against Balzac morally was his "very consideration of subjects which trespass upon the delicacy of the marital tie." C. Vann Woodward, ed., *Mary Chesnut's Civil War* (New Haven, CT, 1981), 191, 225, 282, 288, 336, 393, 413, 468, 804; [George Frederick Holmes], "The Wandering Jew," *SQR*, 9 (1846), 79; [William Gilmore Simms?], "Editor's Note," *SWMR*, 1 (1845), 150. The editors of *SLM* regretted that Balzac's "genius" was not better known in America, and in 1859–60 they published an unusually long appreciation by H. T. Tuckerman, a Northerner, and another by George William Bagby of Virginia. In *SLM* see Tuckerman, "Balzac," 28 (1859), 81–99; [Bagby], 31 (1860), 157–8; [Editors], 28 (1859), 149.

Bancroft: In 1823 Bancroft translated Arnold Heeren's history of ancient Greece, which opened with the causes of Europe's world hegemony and emphasized the inferior performance of black peoples relative to other nonwhites: *Ancient Greece. From the German of Arnold H. L. Heeren, by George Bancroft*, 2nd ed. (New York, 1842 [1823]), 1–11, esp. 5. At UVA, Bancroft's translation was denounced as worthy of a schoolboy – inelegant, full of unintelligible Germanisms, and unfit for students. In contrast, his translation of a German book on Latin grammar was praised: "Xy," "Bancroft's Translation of Heeren on Antient [*sic*] History," *VLM*, 1 (1829), 247–9; "G.", "Antient [*sic*] Languages," *VLM*, 1 (1829), 256. In the 1850s Bancroft, perceiving a slave-power conspiracy, grew increasingly hostile to slavery and to the South. He condemned secession as a conspiracy of slaveholders to shore up an economically faltering system. See esp. Lillian Handlin, *George Bancroft: The Intellectual as Democrat* (New York, 1986), 172–3, and ch. 11; also, Harlow W. Scheidley, *Sectional Nationalism: Massachusetts Conservatives and the Transformation of America, 1815–1836* (Boston, 1998), 108–12.

Bancroft had family connections in Louisiana, and when his sister died there he sold her slaves to guarantee a competence for her children: Handlin, *George Bancroft*, 173. The Tyler administration continued Bancroft in his position of Collector of the Port of Boston, and Simms was pleased by the friendliness with which Bancroft had received him in New York: Simms to Israel Keech Teeft, Oct. 27, 1843, in Mary C. Oliphant et al., eds., *The Letters of William Gilmore Simms*, 6 vols. (Columbia, SC, 1952–82), 1:30. Bancroft's southern readers extended from leading intellectuals to obscure planters, ministers, and college students. See, at UNC-SHC: E. G. Baker Diary, Sept. 27, 1849; Metcalfe Diary, June 4, 1843; W. H. Haigh, Diary, 1840s; Samuel Agnew Diary, May 12, 1862. Also, L. M. W. Fletcher Diary, Summer 1842, at Duke University; Douglas Ambrose, *Henry Hughes and Proslavery Thought in the Old South* (Baton Rouge, LA, 1996), 191; Sally McDowell to John Miller, Oct. 19, 1855, in Thomas E. Buckley, ed. *"If You Love That Lady Don't Marry Her": The Courtship Letters of Sally McDowell and John Miller, 1854–56* (Columbia, MO, 2000), 408; Mary Jones Taylor to Mary Mallard, Sept. 14, 1858, in Robert Manson Myers, ed., *The Children of Pride: A True Story of the Children of the Civil War* (New Haven, CT, 1972), 443.

Baxter: For Richard Baxter's popularity in colonial America see Kevin J. Hayes, *A Colonial Woman's Bookshelf* (Knoxville, TN, 1996), 7. For the popularity of Baxter's writings throughout the United States see David Paul Nord, "Religious Reading and Readers in Antebellum America," *JER*, 15 (1995), 260–1; William L. Joyce et al., eds., *Printing and Society in Early America* (Worcester, MA, 1983), 30. On the reading of Baxter see also Richard Furman, *The Pleasures of Piety and Other Poems* (Charleston, SC, 1859), 71, 206–7; Susan Nye Hutchinson Journal, Oct. 1, 1826 (read aloud), at UNC-SHC; Maria Bryan to Julia Ann Bryan Cumming, May 7, 1828, and Maria Bryan Connell to Julia Ann Bryan Cumming, July 25, 1842, in Carol Bleser, ed., *Tokens of Affection: The Letters of a Planter's Daughter in the Old South* (Athens, GA, 1996), 73–4, 347; Richard J. Purcell, "Judge William Gaston: Georgetown University's First Student," *Georgetown Law Journal*, 27 (1939), 865; Sarah Lois Wadley Private Journal, Aug. 13, 1863, at UNC-SHC. On Baxter see Donald G. Mathews, *Religion in the Old South* (Chicago, 1977), 15, 63; Dickson D. Bruce, Jr., *And They All Sang Hallelujah: Plain-Folk Camp-Meeting Religion, 1800–1845* (Knoxville, TN, 1974), 8; William W. Bennett, *A Narrative of the Great Revival Which Prevailed in the Southern Armies during the Late Civil War between the States of the Federal Union* (Harrisonburg, VA, 1989 [1876]), 80–1. For *Saints' Everlasting Rest* see also Anne Floyd Upshur and Ralph T. Whitelaw, eds., "Library of the Rev. Thomas Teackle," *WMQ*, 2nd ser., 23 (1943), 305. Thornwell considered Baxter basically Arminian: *JHTW*, 2:387.

Bible Criticism: Modern Bible criticism began in England and flourished in nineteenth-century Germany. Henning Graf Reventlow traces it to the stirrings of English Deism in the seventeenth century: *The Authority of the Bible and the Rise of the Modern World* (Philadelphia, 1984), esp. pt. 2, ch. 2. For the response of Christians in Europe see Willis B. Glover, *Biblical Origins of Secular Culture: An Essay in the Interpretation of Western History* (Macon, GA, 1984), 25–30. James Warley Miles criticized Strauss respectfully but stressed that his method would invalidate all historical study: *Philosophic Theology: Or, Ultimate Grounds of All Religious Belief Based on Reason* (Charleston, SC, 1849), 69. Holmes found a strong tie between Strauss and Comte's positivism, both of which he attacked vigorously. [George Frederick Holmes], "Morell's Philosophy of the Nineteenth Century," *SLM*, 16 (1850), 392; [Holmes], "Grote's History of Greece," *SQR*, n.s. (3rd), 2 (1856), 98–100. For a strong attack on Strauss see "The New Gospel of Rationalism," *DQR*, 1 (1861), 365–89, esp. 379. We are puzzled by John Patrick Daly's assertion that Southerners were "paranoid" in relating Strauss and Christian Bauer with an insurgent abolitionism: Daly, *When Slavery Was Called Freedom: Evangelicalism, Proslavery, and the Causes of the Civil War* (Lexington, KY, 2002), 60. For twentieth-century debates relevant to the southern tradition see D. G. Hart, *Defending the Faith: J. Gresham Machen and the Crisis of Conservative Protestantism in Modern America* (Baltimore, 1994), 88–90.

Southerners drew on H. H. Milman, the eminent British clergyman, for empirical refutation of Strauss's contention that Jesus' life belongs to myth: Milman, *The History of*

Christianity from the Birth of Christ to the Abolition of Paganism in the Roman Empire (New York, 1844), esp. iii, 59–63. *Southern Quarterly Review* recommended Milman's eight chapters on the life of Christ above all others: "Milman's History of Christianity," *SQR*, 4 (1843), 261–92. Presbyterian Reverend Thomas Vernon Moore of Richmond, Virginia, quoted Milman on the historical impact of the Mosaic law: Thomas Vernon Moore, *The Christian Lawyer, or The Claims of Christianity on the Legal Profession* (Richmond, VA, 1857), 10. Thornwell also cited Milman approvingly: *JHTW*, 2:55–6, and see Owen Chadwick, *From Bossuet to Newman: The Idea of Doctrinal Development* (Cambridge, U.K., 1957), 100. A liberal, Milman acknowledged that the early Christians accepted slavery as part of the social order: *History of Christianity*, 438–9. Southerners overlooked his earlier indiscretion, which aroused a storm in transatlantic church circles, of describing (in his previous history of the Jews) the biblical Patriarchs as sheikhs. For the controversy see James Westfall Thompson, *A History of Historical Writing*, 2 vols. (Gloucester, MA, 1967 [1942]), 2:571. George Frederick Holmes dismissed Milman as "not a scholar of sufficient depth, accuracy, or variety": [Holmes], "Gibbon's Decline and Fall," *MMQR*, 4th ser., 10 (1856), 322.

Boethius and Thomas à Kempis: George Wymberley-Jones quoted Boethius in his defense of the compatibility of psychology with Christian doctrine in *Theory Concerning the Nature of Insanity* (Wormsley, GA, 1847), esp. 8–11, 33–8; see also William Harris Bragg, *De Renne: Three Generations of a Georgia Family* (Athens, GA, 1999), 62; James Porter, *Compendium of Methodism* (Boston, 1851), 18; Frank Lambert, *"Peddler in Divinity": George Whitefield and the Transatlantic Revivals, 1737–1770* (Princeton, NJ, 1994), 144. Boethius, wrote George Frederick Holmes, "furnished the instruments for the renewal of philosophical pursuits in the middle ages": [Holmes], "The Bacon of the Nineteenth Century," *MMQR*, 4th ser., 5 (1853), 345.

On Boethius see Philip Schaff, *History of the Christian Church*, 5th ed., rev., 8 vols. (Grand Rapids, MI, 1944), 6:284–5; Jaroslav Pelikan, *The Christian Tradition: A History of the Development of Doctrine*, 5 vols. (Chicago, 1989), 4:3, 37, 5:154. Howard Rollin Patch writes of Boethius: "His religion was far more than mere ethics; and the theme of God's love runs through the *Consolation*, in no sentimental fashion but with the fervor of sound reasoning." See Patch, *The Tradition of Boethius: A Study of His Importance in Medieval Culture* (New York, 1935), 12, and 18–19 on Boethius' Christianity; see also Josef Pieper, *Scholasticism: Personalities and Problems of Medieval Philosophy* (New York, 1960), 25–32. Jack Lindsay, among others, interprets *Consolation* as non-Christian, but Lindsay's own account could easily be turned against him: *Song of a Falling World: Culture during the Break-up of the Roman Empire (A.D. 350–600)* (London, 1948), 234–6. Christopher Dawson sees it as "a masterpiece which, in spite of its deliberate reticence, is a perfect expression of the union of the Christian spirit with the classical tradition": *The Making of Europe: An Introduction to the History of European Unity* (New York, 1956), 70. Also, Pelikan, *Christian Tradition*, 1:224, 349–51, 3:61, 265; Schaff, *Christian Church*, 4:607; Gian Biaggio Conte, *Latin Literature: A History*, tr. Joseph B. Solodow, rev. by Don Fowler and Glenn W. Most (Baltimore, 1994), 714–18; Elizabeth Fox-Genovese, "Faith, Reason, and the Liberal Arts," *Cresset*, 65 (2001), 7–14.

Born to artisan parents in 1379 or 1380 at Kempen in the Diocese of Cologne, at age 13 he began to study at the schools of Deventer in Holland, where he absorbed the principles of the "Brothers and Sisters of the Common Life." These religious men and women took no vows, living lives of poverty, chastity, and obedience, seeking to imitate the lives of the early Christians – especially in the love of God and neighbor and in cultivating their virtues of simplicity, humility, and devotion. Charles Hodge wrote that *Imitation of Christ* had "diffused itself like incense through all the aisles and alcoves of the Universal Church": Hodge, *Systematic Theology*, 3 vols. (Grand Rapids, MI, 1993 [1871]), 1:79. Much of *Imitation of Christ* preached meekness as the great Christian virtue in a manner readily assimilated to the chivalric tradition as understood in the South: "No man is safe above but he that is glad to be beneath. No man commandeth safely but he that hath learned to obey. No man rejoicheth safely but he that hath the witness of a good conscience." And again: "If thou couldst at all times abide meek and little in thyself and measure and rule thy spirit, then wouldst thou not fall so soon into peril and into offence." See Thomas à Kempis, "Imitation of Christ," in Irwin Edman, ed., *Consolation of Philosophy* (New York, 1943), 153, 203.

Pelikan suggests that *Imitation of Christ* is "probably the most widely circulated book in Christian history except the Bible": *The Melody of Theology: A Philosophical Dictionary* (Cambridge, MA, 1988), 173. The influence of *Imitation of Christ* spread during the eighteenth and nineteenth centuries in part through the influence of John Wesley, who translated it into English. Charleston's book dealers were selling Thomas à Kempis at least as early as the 1750s: Hennig Cohen, *The South Carolina Gazette, 1732–1775* (Columbia, SC, 1953), 138, 142, 148. For attention to him in the colonial South see Richard Beale Davis, *Intellectual Life in the Colonial South, 1515–1763*, 3 vols. (Knoxville, TN, 1978), 2:541–2, 573. Protestants' discomfort with Thomas à Kempis's reference to Mary as "the expiator of all the sins I have committed" did not impede their appreciation of his devotion to the pursuit of holiness. Patch notes that for Boethius, like Dante after him, nobility is a moral characteristic, not an extension of family or wealth – a stance Southerners would be prone to approve of: *Tradition of Boethius*, 43.

Borrow: George Borrow, a writer immensely popular in the 1840s, attracted the attention of Benjamin Perry, R. Q. Mallard, and J. D. B. De Bow, among others, for his accounts of the customs and folklore of the Spaniards and Gypsies and of the forced conversion of Jews. His best-selling *The Bible in Spain* (London, 1930 [1842]) was translated into several languages and had three early American editions; his largely autobiographical *Lavengro* and other works did well. See R. A. J. Walling, *George Borrow: The Man and His Work* (London, 1808), 117–18, 157 (*Uncle Tom*). Simms, who admired Borrow's earlier work but found *Lavengro* disappointing, noted (without passing judgment) that *Bible in Spain* was under attack for inaccuracies, and he expressed irritation with Borrow's hostility to Catholics and to Protestant dissenters. See [Simms], "Critical Notices," *SQR*, n.s., 3 (1851), 546–8. *Bible in Spain* drew favorable comment from the laity as well as the clergy, although it remains unclear whether Southerners knew that Borrow dismissed *Uncle Tom's Cabin* as "tomfoolery." When Maria Bryan Connell read excerpts from *Bible in Spain* in Albion, she could not wait to read the book: Maria Bryan Connell to Julia Ann Bryan Cumming, Apr. 1, 1834, in Carol Bleser, ed., *Tokens of Affection: The Letters of a Planter's Daughter in the Old South* (Athens, GA, 1996), 361. De Bow praised Borrow's *Lavengro*, and J. R. Thompson, noting Borrow's *Romany Rye: A Sequel to Laverngro*, affectionately referred to him as "the very prince of vagabonds." Thompson liked Borrow's work on the Gypsies but not his political prejudices and ill treatment of Sir Walter Scott. See *DBR*, 10 (1851), 599; [John R. Thompson], *SLM*, 25 (1857), 157. Edd Winfield Parks has provided a lengthy, loving, but critical appraisal of Borrow in *Segments of Southern Thought* (Athens, GA, 1938), ch. 17.

Bossuet: Joseph B. Cobb, author of *Mississippi Scenes* (1851), tried to dismiss Bossuet as "bitter and bigoted": "J. B. C." [Cobb], "Macaulay's History of England," *American Whig Review*, 11 (1850), 351. James Woodrow, criticizing Bossuet on science and religion, referred to "the eloquent Bossuet": [Woodrow], "Geology and Its Assailants," *SPR*, 15 (1863), 564. The Methodist Reverend John E. Edwards of Virginia applauded Bossuet's history but warned against "his papal standpoint": "Christ in History," *QRMECS*, 8 (1854), 249. On Fénelon's reception in America see James D. Hart, *The Popular Book: A History of America's Literary Taste* (New York, 1950), 33. For the context of Bossuet's denial of slavery's inconsistency with natural law see Régine Pernoud, *Those Terrible Middle Ages: Debunking the Myths,* tr. Anne Englund Nash (San Francisco, 2000), 86. For praise of Bossuet see also Alva Woods, *Valedictory Address, Delivered Dec. 6, 1837, at the Close of the Seventh Collegiate Year of the University of the State of Alabama* (Tuscaloosa, AL, 1837), 14; "Oeuvres de Massilon," *SQR*, 3 (1843), 18, 24, 34, 37; [William H. Stiles], *Connection between Liberty and Eloquence: An Address Delivered before the Phi Kappa and Demosthenean Societies of Franklin College (University of Georgia)* (Augusta, GA, 1852), 21; R. M. T. Hunter, Jr., "Advantages of Historical Study," *VUM*, 3 (1859), 66. For Bossuet's readership in the South see G. W. Grace Warren Landrum, "Sir Walter Scott and His Literary Rivals in the Old South," *American Literature,* 2 (1930), 63; also, Thomas Haughton to Ebenezer Pettigrew, Apr. 4, 1804, in Sarah McCulloh Lemmon, ed., *The Pettigrew Papers,* 2 vols. (Raleigh, NC, 1971, 1988), 1:341; R. M. T. Hunter, Jr., "Advantages of Historical Study," *VUM*, 3 (1859), 66. For Bossuet's influence among southern Catholics see A. J. X. Hart, *The Mind and Its Creations: An Essay on Mental Philosophy* (New York, 1853), iii, iv.

Bulwer: Among those outside the political fray, Edward George Bulwer-Lytton's novels "delighted" Mary H. Legge, but their moral effect worried Rachel Mordecai Lazarus: Mary H. Legge to Harriet R. Palmer, July 7, 1861, in Louis P. Towles, ed., *A World Turned Upside Down: The Palmers of South Santee, 1818–1881* (Columbia, SC, 1996), 311; Rachel Mordecai Lazarus to Maria Edgeworth, Mar. 10, 1832, in Edgar E. MacDonald, *The Education of the Heart: The Correspondence of Rachel Mordecai Lazarus and Maria Edgeworth* (Chapel Hill, NC, 1977), 228. Bulwer's "noble and generous sentiments" caught Eliza Middleton Fisher by surprise: Eliza Middleton Fisher to Mary Herring Middleton, Oct. 4, 1839, in Eliza Cope Harrison, ed., *Best Companions: Letters of Eliza Middleton Fisher and Her Mother, Mary Herring Middleton, from Charleston, Philadelphia, and Newport, 1839–1846* (Columbia, SC, 2001), 74.

For Bulwer's enormous success in the United States, especially in the 1830s, see James D. Hart, *The Popular Book: A History of America's Literary Taste* (New York, 1950), 78, 101. For the brisk sales of *Rienzi* in the 1830s see Frank Luther Mott, *Golden Multitudes: The Story of Best Sellers in the United States* (New York, 1947), 305. On the rage for Bulwer in Charleston in 1830 see James Stuart, "Bad Roads, Loose Morals, Sadism, and Racetrack Discipline, 1830," in Thomas D. Clark, ed., *South Carolina: The Grand Tour, 1780–1865* (Columbia, SC, 1973), 196; and for the rage in Washington in the 1850s, see Mary A. H. Gay, *Life in Dixie during the War,* 5th ed. (Atlanta, GA, 1979 [1897]), 83. On the scandals see Mary Herring Middleton to Eliza Middleton Fisher, Jan. 18, 1841, in Harrison, ed., *Best Companions,* 176–7; Maria Bryan Harford to Julia Ann Bryan Cumming, Mar. 17, 1834, in Carol Bleser, ed., *Tokens of Affection: The Letters of a Planter's Daughter in the Old South* (Athens, GA, 1996), 176; Mrs. [E. M.] Houstoun, *Texas and the Gulf of Mexico; Or, Yachting in the Gulf of Mexico* (Austin, TX, 1968 [1845]), 173; Basil Lanneau Gildersleeve, *The Creed of the Old South* (Baltimore, 1915), 84–5; Caldwell Delaney, *A Mobile Sextet* (Mobile, AL, 1981), 141; L. W. Butler Diary, Jan.–May 1863 (Charlottesville, VA), at UNC-SHC. *Southern Literary Messenger* published Bulwer's drama, "Cromwell," *SLM*, 2 (1836), 605–11, but another harsh attack on Bulwer as playwright followed: Nathaniel Beverley Tucker, "Bulwer's New Play," *SLM*, 3 (1837), 90–5.

John R. Thompson wrote a poem in praise of Bulwer and *Caxtons*: [Thompson], "To Bulwer," *SLM*, 17 (1851), 667. *Southern Literary Messenger* published Bulwer's "Richelieu," praising Bulwer as a man of enormous talent and the best qualified to plumb the depths of Richelieu's soul: "Notice of 'Richelieu,' " *SLM*, 5 (1839), 509–12, 532–3. John Wilkes Booth often appeared in Bulwer-Lytton's play *Richelieu*: John Rhodehamel and Louise Taper, eds., *"Right or Wrong, God Judge Me": The Writings of John Wilkes Booth* (Urbana, IL, 1997), 67 n. 19. *The Last Days of Pompeii* ranked as Bulwer's most popular work among southern readers, but *Rienzi* also enjoyed a great success: Mott, *Golden Multitudes*, 90; also, [Daniel Whitaker], "Rienzi," *SLJ*, 2 (1836), 217–18; *Magnolia*, 4 (1842), 320.

Burke: In 1863 Edmund Ruffin read Burke's *Reflections on the Revolution in France* for the third time: May 14, 1863, in *ERD*, 2:656. Burke also drew heavy fire. William C. Somerville even suggested that Burke may have enraged Parisian mobs and brought on the "sanguinary excesses" he predicted and "so eloquently described": *Letters from Paris on the Causes and Consequences of the French Revolution* (Baltimore, 1822), 111, 272–4, quote at 111. In 1843 a contributor to *Southern Quarterly Review* gently slapped Burke for concluding from his just abhorrence of the Terror that the Revolution was intrinsically bad. To the contrary, the Terror marred a great and necessary social transformation: "Democracy in America," *SQR*, 4 (1843), 64. The antislavery Henry Winter Davis of Maryland considered the French Revolution the foundation of everything worthwhile in modern Europe and smarted at Burke and Scott: see Bernard C. Steiner, *Life of Henry Winter Davis* (Baltimore, 1916), 30.

For some invocations of Burke's compliment to American slaveholders, see Peter Carr to John C. Calhoun, Aug. 20, 1844, in *JCCP*, 19:615; "A Few Thoughts on Slavery," *SLM*, 20 (1854), 199; John Price, Jr., *An Address Delivered before the Adelphic and Belles-Lettres Societies of Oakland College, April 6, 1853 on the Duty of Drawing from the History and Theory of Our Government, Just Views of Individual and National Life* (Port Gibson, MS, 1853), 17–18; David J. McCord in J. D. B. De Bow, *The Industrial Resources, Statistics, &c. of the United States and More Particularly of the Southern and Western States*, 3rd ed., 3 vols. (New York, 1966 [1854]), 3:63; George S. Sawyer, *Southern Institutes; Or, an Inquiry into the Origin and Early Prevalence of Slavery and the Slave Trade* (New York, 1967 [1858]), 373; F. W. Pickens, *An Address Delivered before the State Agricultural Society of South Carolina* (Columbia, SC, 1849), 14; Stephen Elliott, "Ezra's Dilemma," Aug. 23, 1863, in David B. Chesebrough, ed., *"God Ordained This War": Sermons on the Sectional Crisis, 1830–1865* (Columbia, SC, 1991), 252.

Burr: On Aaron Burr see e.g. E. G. Baker Diary, Aug. 21, 1859, and Carney Diary, June 4, 1861, both at UNC-SHC. J. D. B. De Bow and Daniel K. Whitaker acknowledged Burr's grievous faults and unlawful acts but denied his treasonous intent: De Bow, *The Industrial Resources, Statistics, &c. of the United States and More Particularly of the Southern and Western States*, 3rd ed., 3 vols. (New York, 1966 [1854]), 1:401; [Whitaker], "Editor's Portfolio" and "Life and Character of Aaron Burr," *SLJ*, n.s., 3 (1838), 233–4, 364–77. W. J. Grayson defended Burr as a man who acted honorably in his duel with Hamilton as in all else: [Grayson], "Jefferson," *RM*, 3 (1858), 127–9. A contributor to *Southern Literary Messenger* captured the core southern attitude, attributing Burr's fall from grace less to his duel with Hamilton than to the callousness and "utter insensibility" he displayed afterwards: *SLM*, 26 (1858), 325.

Butler's *Analogy*: Bishop Joseph Butler's *Analogy of Religion* turned up in the better personal libraries of Virginians in the early national period and was especially popular with the orthodox: Richard Beale Davis, *Intellectual Life in Jefferson's Virginia, 1790–1830* (Chapel Hill,

NC, 1964), 83, 100; Joseph Tower Wheeler, "Books Owned by Marylanders, 1700–1776," *Maryland Historical Magazine*, 35 (1940), 343. For its subsequent influence in the South, see John Patrick Daly, *When Slavery Was Called Freedom: Evangelicalism, Proslavery, and the Causes of the Civil War* (Lexington, KY, 2002), ch. 2. Among Butler's nineteenth-century admirers see Jasper Adams, *Elements of Moral Philosophy* (Philadelphia, 1837), 5–6; R. H. Rivers, *Elements of Moral Philosophy* (Nashville, TN, 1859), 63–4; [Thomas Curtis], *SPR*, 7 (1853), 552 ("the best work extant on the philosophy of religion"); J. L. Reynolds, *The Man of Letters* (Richmond, VA, 1849), 10; Basil Manly, Jr., *The Bible Doctrine of Inspiration* (Nashville, TN, 1995 [1888]), 150; also, Robert Lewis Dabney, *The Sensualistic Philosophy of the Nineteenth Century, Considered*, new and enlarged edition (n.p., 1887), 161. One critic complained that few actually read the *Analogy* they frequently cited and praised: "Butler's Analogy," *QRMECS*, 8 (1854), 214–48.

Thornwell's writings are full of quotations from, references to, and discussions of Butler's *Analogy*. Morton Smith suggests that Butler's *Analogy* and Paley's *Evidences,* which "set the pattern of thought" for many orthodox Christians, strengthened anti-Christian rationalism. Smith, conceding that Thornwell and Dabney yielded too much to rationalism, insists that they always ended with the Bible: Smith, *Studies in Southern Presbyterian Theology* (Phillipsburg, NJ, 1962), 203–5, and 117–18 on Butler. James Walker of Charleston added, without direct reference to Butler, "Those who regard reason as the true test of God's will, easily arrive at conclusions which justify disobedience of all human laws": Walker, *The Theory of the Common Law* (Boston, 1852), 78. For the tension over rationalism in Thornwell and Dabney see Luder G. Whitlock, Jr., "James Henley Thornwell," in David F. Wells, ed., *Southern Reformed Theology* (Grand Rapids, MI, 1989), 69–70.

Caesarism: The prevalent southern view foreshadowed Oswald Spengler's, in which Caesarism constituted a threat to "the money power" and was the only force capable of using the requisite "primitive methods of bloody violence when the politics of money becomes intolerable": Spengler, *The Decline of the West,* tr. Charles Francis Atkinson, 2 vols. (New York, 1926–28), 2:406, 427 n. 5, 431, 433, 464. Spengler on the enthusiasm for Brutus in the Jacobin Clubs: "That millionaire extortioner Brutus, who, in the name of oligarchical doctrine and with the approval of the patrician senate, murdered the Man of Democracy" (loc. cit., 1:5).

According to Zvi Yavetz, the term "Caesarism" first appeared with François Romieu, an enthusiastic Bonapartist, in 1850: Zvi Yavetz, *Julius Caesar and His Public Image* (Ithaca, NY, 1983), 16. The work of Theodor Mommsen, which presented Caesar as the strongman who saved the Roman people from a corrupt and predatory aristocracy, received virtually no attention in the South. In 1867 Holmes, commenting respectfully, judged his work severely biased: [George Frederick Holmes], "Recent Histories of Julius Caesar," *SR* (Baltimore), 1 (1867), 402–5. Some Southerners, casting Lincoln as a tyrannical Caesar, hailed John Wilkes Booth as "Brutus." Merrill D. Peterson, *Lincoln in American Memory* (New York, 1994), 45. Brutus, among other prominent Romans, was a usurer and charged up to 48 percent interest: P. A. Brunt, *Social Conflicts in the Roman Republic* (London, 1971), 21; and see the biting remarks of Christopher Dawson, *Medieval Essays* (Garden City, NY, 1959), 31. Conservatives and liberals alike worried about the tendencies in American politics. Calhoun feared that the idolatry attached to Caesar affected the American view of the presidency and threatened republican virtue: Calhoun, "Remarks on the Motion to Expunge the Senate's Censure of Andrew Jackson," Jan. 13, 1837, in *JCCP*, 13:363. Francis Lieber approvingly cited the criticism of Louis Bonaparte's abuse of power leveled by Senator Andrew Pickens Butler of South Carolina: Lieber, *On Civil Liberty and Self-Government,* 3rd ed., rev. and ed. by Theodore D. Woolsey (Philadelphia, 1874 [1853]), 415–16. William Byrd II referred to the designation of Cicero as father of his country [*Pater Patriae*] as "the greatest title that was given man": Kevin Berland et al., eds., *The Commonplace Book of William Byrd II of Westover* (Chapel Hill, NC, 1996), 155. The term "father of his country" was also used for other Romans. "A Virginian" noted that the ambition of Marius, "the father of his country," led to his becoming a usurper, in contrast to Washington: "Ambition," *SLM*, 7 (1841), 50, 52.

Chateaubriand: François-René de Chateaubriand had influential boosters in the South. E. A. Lynch admired his "moral courage": "Influence of Morals on the Happiness of Man," *SLM*, 4 (1838), 419–21. Thomas R. R. Cobb drew on *Essai historique* for his discussion of the influence of Christianity in softening ancient slavery: *An Inquiry into the Law of Negro Slavery in the United States* (New York, 1968 [1858]), xcvii. De Bow was pleased to announce an English translation of *Genius of Christianity* – *DBR*, 21 (1856), 639 – which the Baptist Reverend E. T. Winkler said elucidated the Christian basis of science and learning in European institutions: *Anniversary Address Delivered on the Second Commencement of the Theological Seminary, at Greenville, S.C., May 27, 1861* (Charleston, SC, 1861), 6. Among readers of Chauteaubriand see T. M. Garrett Diary, 1849, at UNC-SHC; Mary E. Moragné Journal, Apr. 8, 1839, in Delle Mullen Craven, ed., *The Neglected Thread: A Journal of the Calhoun Community* (Columbia, SC, 1951), 119. For the popularity of Chateaubriand with the Maryland elite see Rosalie Steir Calvert to Charles J. Stier, Nov. 7, 1816, in Margaret Law Callcott, ed., *The Mistress of Riversdale: The Plantation Letters of Rosalie Stier Calvert, 1795–1821* (Baltimore, 1991), 108.

Christianization – Slave Trade and Slavery: William A. Smith wrote that the African slave trade had performed a civilizing function despite excesses of rapacious individuals: *Lectures on the Philosophy and Practice of Slavery* (Nashville, TN, 1856), 170–5. Robert R. Howison recalled bitterly that the Pope was condemning the slave trade while the Protestant Elizabeth was promoting it: *A History of Virginia from Its Discovery and Settlement by Europeans to the Present Time*, 2 vols. (Philadelphia, 1846), 1:221. Robert H. Smith insisted that slavery was not what it had been seventy years earlier, since great progress had been made in Christianizing and civilizing African slaves: *An Address to the Citizens of Alabama, on the Constitution and Laws of the Confederate States of America* (Mobile, AL, 1861), 18. [J. A. Lyon], "Slavery and the Duties Growing Out of the Relation: Report to the General Assembly of the Presbyterian Church," *SPR*, 16 (July 1863), 1–37. The Committee included such prestigious Presbyterians as J. A. Lyon, J. Leighton Wilson, and Benjamin M. Palmer. Frederick Porcher opposed the trade as inexpedient but denounced the effort to declare it sinful: Alton Taylor Loftus, "A Study of Russell's Magazine: Ante-Bellum Charleston's Last Literary Periodical" (Ph.D. diss., Duke University, 1973), 251. Even many southern colonizationists who accepted the Noahic curse insisted that slavery in America was bringing blacks up to a high standard of civilization: see e.g. Philip Slaughter, *The Virginian History of African Colonization* (Richmond, VA, 1855), Introduction. The Episcopal Reverend W. N. Pendleton of Lexington, Virginia, finessed a difficult problem for white supremacists, insisting that Christianization was raising blacks but questioning how far they could rise: W. N. Pendleton, *Science: A Witness for the Bible* (Philadelphia, 1860), 116–20.

Church Membership: The best estimates put full membership in Protestant churches at about 15 percent of the American population in 1840, more than twice that of 1800. The ratio of churchgoers to church members has been variously estimated, and in different regions of the South contemporary estimates varied from 2 : 1 to 10 : 1. Statistics for church membership remain tricky, but a substantial portion of the populace heard preaching often. See Thomas

Crowder, Jr., to Thomas Ruffin, July 7, 1823, in J. G. deRoulhac Hamilton, ed., *The Papers of Thomas Ruffin*, 4 vols. (Raleigh, NC, 1918), 1:278; "Description of Key West," in Eugene L. Schwaab and Jacqueline Bull, eds., *Travels in the Old South: Selections from Periodicals of the Times*, 2 vols. (Lexington, KY, 1973), 2:456; Walter C. Whitaker, *History of the Protestant Episcopal Church in Alabama* (Birmingham, AL, 1898), 133. Between 1830 and the mid-1850s, Methodists, Baptists, and Presbyterians doubled their membership in the eastern slave states, and by the War somewhere between 22 percent and 37 percent of Americans were "churched" – it depends upon the manner of counting: Anne C. Loveland, *Southern Evangelicals and the Social Order, 1800–1860* (Baton Rouge, LA, 1980), 89–90; Roger Finke and Rodney Stark, *The Churching of America, 1776–1890* (New Brunswick, NJ, 1992), 15; Kenneth Scott Latourette, *Christianity in a Revolutionary Age*, 5 vols. (Grand Rapids, MI, 1958), 3:81. For the United States in general see T. Scott Miyakawa, *Protestants and Pioneers: Individualism and Conformity on the American Frontier* (Chicago, 1964); Richard J. Carwardine, *Evangelicals and Politics in Antebellum America* (New Haven, CT, 1993), ch. 1; Lewis O. Saum, *The Popular Mood of America, 1860–1890* (Lincoln, NE, 1990), 3–104; Paul K. Conkin, *The Uneasy Center: Reformed Christianity in Antebellum America* (Chapel Hill, NC, 1995), 118, 130. With total church membership in the United States at about 3.5 million (or one eighth of the total population) in 1850, C. C. Goen estimates that three to four times that number regularly attended preaching: *Broken Churches, Broken Nation: Denominational Schisms and the Coming of the American Civil War* (Macon, GA, 1985), 55. The Catholic Church included all who had been baptized, no matter how far they had strayed, whereas the Episcopalians held to a strict code before the War and counted as members only those who actually took communion.

Among prominent men who never joined a church was Alexander Stephens, who came to a strong belief after years as a skeptic: see Thomas E. Schott, *Alexander H. Stephens of Georgia: A Biography* (Baton Rouge, LA, 1988), chs. 1 and 11. David Crockett came from a pious family and felt himself a believer, but he did not join a church or invoke religion in more than a passing way: James A. Shackford and Stanley J. Folmsbee, eds., *A Narrative of the Life of David Crockett of the State of Tennessee* (Knoxville, TN, 1976 [1834]). The Reverend A. F. Dickson praised the religious spirit of D. F. Jamison, who never joined a church because he felt he could not carry the responsibilities of membership: [Dickson], "Life and Times of Bertrand de Guesclin," *SPR*, 16 (1866), 377. The father of Jacob Thompson, prominent Mississippi politician, left ample evidence of strong Christian commitment but never joined a church: P. W. Rainwater, "Letters to and from Jacob Thompson," *JSH*, 6 (1940), 95–111.

S. S. Prentiss, a powerful Mississippi politician and brother of a minister, strongly professed his Christianity but protested against endless theological disputes. He may have also wondered if any church would accept a man who drank and gambled ferociously: Dallas C. Dickey, *Seargent S. Prentiss: Whig Orator of the Old South* (Baton Rouge, LA, 1945), 382. George McDuffie regularly attended but did not join the Presbyterian Church. He liked to dance and challenged critics to show a scriptural basis for the ban: Edwin L. Green, *George McDuffie* (Columbia, SC, 1936), 173. Robert Toombs entered the Methodist Church late in life. Although a good family man who read the Bible and attended church, he, too, had a serious drinking problem: Pleasant A. Stovall, *Robert Toombs: Statesman, Speaker, Soldier, Sage* (New York, 1892), 10–11, 373. So did Governor John Sevier of Tennessee; Hugh Campbell and Jonathan Worth of North Carolina; Chancellor George W. Dargon, Wade Hampton II, and J. L. Petigru of South Carolina; and Charles Sherman West, justice of the Texas Supreme Court. The Bible-reading George Wythe Randolph finally did join – at age 46 and after decades of faithful participation. John K. Baldwin of Bladen County, North Carolina, a poor boy raised by devout parents who considered himself "toerible religious" and as having "a great inclination to serve God," did not join the Baptist Church until after he returned from the War: J. K. Baldwin Diary, Jan. 1, 1867, Apr. 30, 1878, at UNC-SHC. For biographical information see Nancy Wooten Walker, *Out of a Clear Blue Sky: Tennessee's First Ladies and Their Husbands* (Cleveland, TN, 1971), 38 (Sevier); Hugh Campbell to Thomas Ruffin, Mar. 18, 1832, in Hamilton, ed., *Papers of Thomas Ruffin*, 2:58; John Belton O'Neall, *Biographical Sketches of the Bench and Bar of South Carolina*, 2 vols. (Charleston, SC, 1859), 1:300–1 (Dargon); Charles E. Cauthen, ed., *Family Letters of the Three Wade Hamptons, 1782–1901* (Columbia, SC, 1953), xiv; Stephen Meats and Edwin T. Arnold, eds., *The Writings of Benjamin F. Perry*, 3 vols. (Spartanburg, SC, 1980), 3:162 (Petigru); J. G. deRoulhac Hamilton, ed., *The Correspondence of Jonathan Worth*, 2 vols. (Raleigh, NC, 1909), 1:x; James Daniel Lynch, *Bench and Bar of Texas* (St. Louis, MO, 1885), 327 (West); George Green Shackelford, *George Wythe Randolph and the Confederate Elite* (Athens, GA, 1988), 41.

Classical Education: Strong emphasis on the classics revealed itself in student papers and speeches: see e.g. "Speeches of Graduates," 1851–1858, at UNC-NCC. Warren DuPre to John S. Palmer, Aug. 14, 1843, in Louis P. Towles, ed., *A World Turned Upside Down: The Palmers of South Santee, 1818–1881* (Columbia, SC, 1996), 82–3; *Proceedings of the Centennial Celebration of South Carolina College, 1805–1905* (Columbia, SC, 1905), 16; also, George Washington Paschal, *History of Wake Forest College*, 2 vols. (Wake Forest, NC, 1935), 1:359–60; Mitchell King Diary, Oct. 30, 1854, and Oct. 13, 1855, at USC. See also Francis Taylor Diary, May 14, 1788 (Virginia), Bills Diary, June 20, 1845, Jan. 21 and Oct. 7, 1846, June 17, 1856, June 28, 1858 (Tennessee), Franc M. Carmack Diary, June 3, 1853 (Tennessee), and James Henry Greenlee Diary, June 3 and Aug. 6, 1858 (North Carolina) – all at UNC-SHC. M. W. Philips Diary, Aug. 1, 1857, in Franklin L. Riley, ed., "Diary of a Mississippi Planter," in *Publications of the Mississippi Historical Society*, 10 (1909), 459; Davis Blake Carter, *The Story of Uncle Minyard Told: A Family's 200-Year Migration across the South* (Spartanburg, SC, 1994), 44–5 (Alabama); Charles L. Coon, ed., *North Carolina Schools and Academies: A Documentary History, 1790–1840* (Raleigh, NC, 1915), xxxvii; Greensboro (Methodist) *Weekly Message,* July 15, 1852; Nora Campbell Chaffin, *Trinity College, 1839–1892: The Beginnings of Duke University* (Durham, NC, 1950), 72–3; Dorothy Orr, *A History of Education in Georgia* (Chapel Hill, NC, 1950), 46. See also "Greek Writers" (*Longinus*) and "Roman Writers" (*Lucretius*).

Cousin and Morell: For appreciation of Victor Cousin's work on the Middle Ages, see Thomas Roderick Dew, *Digest of the Laws, Customs, Manners, and Institutions of the Ancient and Modern Nations* (New York, 1884 [1852]), 206–7; "Irving's Life of Columbus," *SLM*, 6 (1840), 569; L. I. Gogerty, "Scholasticism – Abelard," *QRMECS*, 12 (1858), 49, 54; also, Gladys Bryson, *Man and Society: The Scottish Inquiry of the Eighteenth Century* (New York, 1968), 3. For invocations of Cousin, see R. H. Rivers, *Elements of Moral Philosophy* (Nashville, TN, 1859), 34; William A. Smith, *Lectures on the Philosophy and Practice of Slavery* (Nashville, TN, 1856), 84; Francis Lieber, *A Manual of Political Ethics* (London, 1839), 162; [J. W. Miles], "Philosophy of the Beautiful," *SQR*, 16 (1849), 115–38; A. J. X. Hart, *The Mind and Its Creations: An Essay on Mental Philosophy* (New York, 1853), 27; W. S. Grayson, "Natural Equality of Man," *DBR*, 26 (1859), 32; [George Frederick Holmes], "History of Literature," *SQR*, 2 (1842), 518–40, and 11 (1847), 138. Robert Lewis Dabney recalled Cousin as a great man who combated French materialism and helped reintroduce the spiritual dimension into philosophy. Yet with mounting severity after the War, he disparaged Cousin's psychology of motivation and the will. See Dabney, *The Sensualistic Philosophy of the Nineteenth Century, Considered*, new and enlarged edition (n.p., 1887), 1–2; Dabney,

The Practical Philosophy, Being the Philosophy of the Feelings, of the Will, and of the Conscience, with the Ascertainment of Particular Rights and Duties (Harrisonburg, VA, 1984 [1897]), 152–3.

Thornwell admired Cousin's exposition of philosophical currents, complimenting him for having "beautifully expanded" a good argument from Descartes. A writer in *North Carolina University Magazine* quoted at length Cousin's "plainly and forcefully written" work on Cartesianism: "On the True Meaning of 'Cogito, Ergo Sum,'" 5 (1856), 67–8. But for Cousin's encouragement of subjective idealism and pantheism in Germany, see Enoch Pond, "Philosophy and the Church," *SPR*, 4 (1850), 164, and "Objections to the German Transcendental Philosophy," *SPR*, 4 (1851), 333–4.

At first, Southerners responded positively to J. D. Morell. Theodore Dwight Bozeman, describing Morell as an articulate Transcendentalist and mediator of the theology of Schleiermacher, refers to his "snarling abuse" of Baconian induction: Bozeman, *Protestants in an Age of Science: The Baconian Ideal and Antebellum American Religious Thought* (Chapel Hill, NC, 1977), 144. Still, Reynolds cited Morell positively to distinguish healthy American practicality and concern for usefulness from narrow Utilitarianism: J. L. Reynolds, *The Man of Letters* (Richmond, VA, 1849), 6–8, and R. J. Breckenridge's journal described Morell as "learned and candid," in "The Claim of Emanuel Swedenborg to Divine Illumination," *DQR*, 1 (1861), 179, quote at 211; in the 1890s, John L. Girardeau spoke of the "attractive, though mischievous" Morell as a dangerous opponent: *Discussions of Theological Questions*, ed. George A. Blackburn (Harrisonburg, VA, 1986 [1905, written in 1890s]), 84, 277, quote at 84.

Dante: Emphasis on Dante's criticism of the papacy and characterization of him as a proto-Protestant resonated in the South: see J. H. Merle D'Aubigné, *History of the Reformation of the Sixteenth Century*, 5 vols. (Rapidan, VA, n.d., reproduction of London edition of 1846), 35. Jeffrey Burton Russell movingly demonstrates the Catholicity of Dante's view of heaven: *A History of Heaven* (Princeton, NJ, 1997). Edmund Ruffin read Dante lightly during the War but apparently saw little more than a politics not to his taste: Mar. 20, 1863, in *ERD*, 2:596. J. N. D. Graham stood in awe of Dante's genius: *VUM*, 3 (1859), 442, also on *Divine Comedy* see *VUM*, 3 (1859), 176. Dante's "genius" cleared away much medieval trash, "E. P. H." declared in a review of a translation largely concerned with the problems of translating Italian into English and a complaint that few people outside Italy know the language. One critic bizarrely ranked Dante among poets with "morbid temperament," who "never realize their feelings unless they are embodied." Milton was "inferior to Dante in power to particularize" and in some other respects, yet Dante was "superior in all the highest qualities of intellect, and especially in the co-working of reason, imagination, and spiritual passion": "Milton and His Critics," *QRMECS*, 14 (1860), 326–7. "E. P. H." included one of several sketches of Dante's life to appear in southern publications: "Dante," *SLM*, 12 (1846), 545–54. A review essay for *Southern Literary Messenger* by William Gordon McCabe of Virginia provided a sketch of Dante's life and work, including *La Vita Nuova* and other writings. For McCabe, as for Karl Marx, Dante was "the great Florentine" and a towering figure in world literature: McCabe, "Dante," *SLM*, 34 (1862), 136–48, quote at 136. *Southern Literary Messenger* translated snippets of Dante: see Richard Furman, "Francesca di Ravenna," *SLM*, 29 (1859), 54–5.

D'Aubigné and Mosheim: For Baptist reactions to D'Aubigné see Richard Furman, *The Pleasures of Piety and Other Poems* (Charleston, SC, 1859), 199; Benjamin Griffin, *A History of the Primitive Baptists of Mississippi, from the First Settlement by the Americans up to* *the Middle of the XIXth Century* (Jackson, MS, 1853), ch. 2; and J. L. Dagg, *Manual of Theology: A Treatise on Christian Doctrine and a Treatise on Church Order,* 2 vols. (New York, 1980 [1857–58]), 2:201; Basil Manly, Jr., *The Bible Doctrine of Inspiration* (Nashville, TN, 1995 [1888]), 72. D'Aubigné's *History* sold much more widely in Britain and America than in his native France. T. C. Anderson drew on D'Aubigné for his *Life of Rev. George Donnell, First Pastor of the Church in Lebanon, with a Sketch of the Scotch-Irish Race* (Nashville, TN, 1859). Basil Manly, Jr., extolled D'Aubigné's exposé of "Papist" misdeeds.

On Mosheim see Jaroslav Pelikan, *The Christian Tradition: A History of the Development of Doctrine,* 5 vols. (Chicago, 1989), 4:374; Philip Schaff, *History of the Christian Church,* 5th ed., rev., 8 vols. (Grand Rapids, MI, 1944), 1:393. Thornwell was unusually gentle in his criticism of Mosheim on miracles: "Miracles," in *JHTW,* 3:245; Maurice Keen, *Chivalry* (New Haven, CT, 1984). Edward Gibbon, while critical, hailed "the learned and candid Mosheim" for his "full, rational, correct, and moderate" work on the Christian Church: Gibbon, *The History of the Decline and Fall of the Roman Empire,* ed. David Womersley, 3 vols. (London, 1994), 1:483 n. 104; 2:933 n. 1; also, 3:424 n. 1, 646 n. 87. For criticism of Mosheim for taking his subjects' words out of context, see "The Study of History," *SQR,* 10 (1846), 132. Even professors who found much in Mosheim and D'Aubigné to criticize assigned them as standard college texts. Ladies in Virginia read D'Aubigné's *Reformation* as soon as it appeared in the 1840s: [Mary Virginia Hawes Terhune], *Marion Harland's Autobiography: The Story of a Life* (New York, 1910), 99. For Mosheim as guide to ancient Christian history see "Credibility of the Statements," *QRMECS,* 9 (1855), 489. Dagg at Mercer College and Dabney at Union Theological Seminary assigned Mosheim's *Ecclesiastical History* to their students: Glenn T. Miller, *Piety and Intellect: The Aims and Purposes of Ante-Bellum Theological Education* (Atlanta, GA, 1990), 311; Sean Michael Lucas, *Robert Lewis Dabney: A Southern Presbyterian Life* (Phillipsburg, PA, 2005), 70. *Biblical Repertory and Princeton Review* also praised D'Aubigné: see e.g. *BRPR,* 14 (1842), 119–29.

Deism: For Deism in the South see Richard Beale Davis, *Intellectual Life in the Colonial South, 1515–1763,* 3 vols. (Knoxville, TN, 1978), 2:698–9; R. B. Davis, *Intellectual Life in Jefferson's Virginia, 1790–1830* (Chapel Hill, NC, 1964), 121–3; George J. Stevenson, *Increase in Excellence: A History of Emory and Henry College* (New York, 1963), 12; Arthur H. Shaffer, *To Be an American: David Ramsay and the Making of the American Consciousness* (Columbia, SC, 1991), 152 (Ramsay named as Deists Charles Cotesworth Pinckney, Francis Kinlock, and Thomas Tudor Tucker). Allen's book probably sold some 200 copies: see Henry F. May, *The Enlightenment in America* (New York, 1976), 123.

Deism was much weaker in the South than in the North, and throughout America it primarily attracted the elite, presenting Jesus as the first great Deist preacher. See Herbert M. Morais, *Deism in Eighteenth-Century America* (New York, 1960), esp. 15–16, 82–3, 110–11, 165–6; James Turner, *Without God, Without Creed: The Origin of Unbelief in America* (Baltimore, 1985), 53. In North Carolina, Deism cropped up in the sermons of some Episcopalian ministers in the 1770s, and Paine's short-lived popularity had ministers frothing at the mouth after the turn of the century: in Sarah McCulloh Lemmon, ed., *The Pettigrew Papers,* 2 vols. (Raleigh, NC, 1971, 1988), see Henry Patillo to Charles Pettigrew, Dec. 13, 1788 (1:60–1); Nathaniel Blount to Charles Pettigrew, Jan. 23 (1:278) and May 4, 1802 (1:283), May 9, 1803 (1:300–2). From the 1790s Deism sparked intense dispute in Charleston, South Carolina, but as time went on, the negative prevailed over the positive. Thomas Paine's books disappeared from bookstores: James Raven, *London Booksellers and American Customers: Transatlantic Literary Community and the Charleston Library Society, 1748–1811* (Columbia, SC, 2002), 192, 212, 214. Yet, in the 1840s and 1850s, southern Calvinists and Arminians alike continued to publish full-scale replies to Paine, whose continuing influence they feared: David Seth Doggett, *The Responsibility of Talent: An Address Delivered before the Franklin Literary Society of Randolph-Macon College* (Richmond, VA, 1844), 9; Thomas Curtis, "Life of Thomas Paine," *SPR*, 5:228–49; T. O. Summers, "Theological Works of Thomas Paine," *QRMECS*, 8 (1854), 481–513. A. L. Brent to William Cabell, Sept. 1, 1857, in Cabell–Ellet Papers, at UVA. On the waning of Deism in the Valley of Virginia see H. M. White, ed., *Rev. William S. White, D.D., and His Times (1800–1873): An Autobiography* (Richmond, VA, 1891), 105–6. With only slight exaggeration James D. Hart remarks, "The Reign of Terror numbered American deism among its victims": *The Popular Book: A History of America's Literary Taste* (New York, 1950), 38; also, *DHUNC*, 2:113–14. In Louisville, German turners found themselves roundly condemned in 1855 for parading in honor of Thomas Paine. The Louisville *Courier* excoriated *Age of Reason* and reminded readers that America had been built on Christian foundations. By the 1850s, only scattered individuals openly embraced Deism, among them Augustin Clayton of Georgia, a nullifier who ranked among the upcountry's most prominent politicians, and Stephen Austin of Texas, a Deist of sorts who had been born and raised in New England and attended the liberal Transylvania University in Lexington, Kentucky. Ernest C. Hynds, *Antebellum Athens and Clarke County, Georgia* (Athens, GA, 1974), 34 (on Clayton); Gregg Cantrell, *Stephen F. Austin: Empressario of Texas* (New Haven, CT, 1999), 23, 35–6; also, Herman A. Norton, *Religion in Tennessee, 1777–1945* (Knoxville, TN, 1981), 18; David T. Bailey, *Shadow on the Church: Southwestern Evangelical Religion and the Issue of Slavery, 1783–1860* (Ithaca, NY, 1985), 26–7; Clement Eaton, *The Mind of the Old South* (Baton Rouge, LA, 1964), 200–1.

De Staël: Madame Germaine De Staël enjoyed a large, respectable, and enthusiastic following in the South. The Female College attached to Wofford College in South Carolina boasted a De Staël Society, in which women lectured on such subjects as "Home" and "Woman's Influence": see Mary H. Legge to Harriet R. Palmer, July 17, 1861, and July 3, 1863, in Louis P. Towles, ed., *A World Turned Upside Down: The Palmers of South Santee, 1818–1881* (Columbia, SC, 1996), 306, 370. For De Staël's continuing popularity among educated Southerners, especially the women, see Rosalie Stier Calvert to Charles J. Stier, Dec. 10, 1808, and Rosalie Stier Calvert to Isabelle van Havre, Oct. 25, 1816, in Margaret Law Callcott, ed., *The Mistress of Riversdale: The Plantation Letters of Rosalie Stier Calvert, 1795–1821* (Baltimore, 1991), 196, 304–5; Elizabeth Scott Neblett (wife of small slaveholder in Texas), Diary, Mar. 20, 1852, in Erika I. Murr, ed. *A Rebel Wife in Texas: The Diary and Letters of Elizabeth Scott Neblett, 1852–1864* (Baton Rouge, LA, 2001), 25; L. M. W. Fletcher Diary, 1841–1842, Summer 1844 (biography), at Duke University; Sarah Lois Wadley Private Journal, Nov. 26, 1863, at UNC-SHC; Maria Bryan Harford to Julia Ann Bryan Cumming, Dec. 23, 1839, in Carol Bleser, ed., *Tokens of Affection: The Letters of a Planter's Daughter in the Old South* (Athens, GA, 1996), 276; James Norcom to Mary Harvey, Mar. 4, 1848, in James Norcom Papers, at North Carolina State Archives (Raleigh). Among the southern women who read De Staël were Catherine Edmonston: July 25, 1860, in Beth G. Crabtree and James Welch Patton, eds., *"Journal of a Secesh Lady": The Diary of Catherine Devereux Edmonston, 1860–1866* (Raleigh, NC, 1979), 7; Emma LeConte read *De la literature*, Feb. 23, 1865, in Earl Schenck Miers, ed., *When the World Ended: The Diary of Emma LeConte* (New York, 1957), 64; Eliza Middleton Fisher to Mary Herring Middleton, Nov. 23, 1844, in Eliza Cope Harrison, ed., *Best Companions: Letters of Eliza Middleton Fisher and Her Mother, Mary Herring Middleton, from Charleston, Philadelphia, and Newport, 1839–1846* (Columbia, SC, 2001), 406; Charles J. Johnson, Jr., *Mary Telfair: The Life and Legacy of a Nineteenth-Century Woman* (Savannah, GA, 2002), 81, 117, 245–6; Caroline E. Merrick, *Old Times in Dixie Land: A*

Southern Matron's Memories (New York, 1901), 16. An English translation of De Staël's *Corinne* was published in New York in 1857. De Staël's novels include *Sophie* (1786) and *Jane Gray* (1787). Her first philosophical work was *Letters on Jean-Jacques Rousseau* (1788). J. Fred Rippy, *Joel R. Poinsett, Versatile American* (New York, 1968), 14–15; *Plantation Life: The Narratives of Mrs. Henry Schoolcraft* (New York, 1969 [1860]), 377; Junkin, "The Reconcilement of the Real and the Ideal," in Margaret Junkin Preston Papers, at Washington and Lee University; "Mutual Influence of National Literatures," *SQR*, 12 (1847), 319; *SQR*, 1 (1842), 498; Jane T. Lomax Worthington, "Madame de Staël," *SLM*, 8 (1842), 231–3, and Worthington, "Madame de Genlis," *SLM*, 8 (1842), 591; "Senex", "The Corinne, or Italy, of Madame de Staël," *SLM*, 15 (1849), 377–84. For the relations of John Izard Middleton and other Southerners with Madame De Staël in Europe, see Maurie D. McInnis in collaboration with Angela D. Mack, *In Pursuit of Refinement: Charlestonians Abroad, 1740–1860* (Columbia, SC, 1999), 65–72, 77, 82–5, 160, and Charles R. Mack, ed., *The Roman Remains: John Izard Middleton's Visual Souvenirs of 1820–1823* (Columbia, SC, 1997), 5–6. William C. Somerville cited De Staël on French political character: *Letters from Paris on the Causes and Consequences of the French Revolution* (Baltimore, 1822), 151–2, 184. Dew credited her with restoring polish and elegance to the Parisian salons under the Directory: Thomas Roderick Dew, *Digest of the Laws, Customs, Manners, and Institutions of the Ancient and Modern Nations* (New York, 1884 [1852]), 654. Joseph Le Conte found "admirable" her introduction of German culture into France but thought her too French to do the German spirit justice, judging her criticism superficial: "On the Nature and Uses of Art," *SPR*, 15 (1863), 342.

Dew's *Digest*: Thomas Roderick Dew's *Digest of the Laws, Customs, Manners, and Institutions of the Ancient and Modern Nations* had been circulated long before its publication, since Dew made his lectures available to his students who, in his judgment, had no adequate textbook: see Preface. According to John Reuben Thompson, Henry A. Washington – "one of the finest scholars in the country" – edited the *Digest* and arranged for its publication: *SLM*, 19 (1853), 256. *Digest* went through three antebellum printings: 1854, 1856, 1858, also 1891 and 1893.

Dickens: Joining the chorus against Charles Dickens were Wayne Gridley, whose article in *Southern Review* was republished as a pamphlet, and J. A. Turner of Georgia, the prominent agricultural editor: Wayne Gridley, *Slavery in the South: A Review of Hammond's and Fuller's Letters, and Chancellor Harper's Memoir* (Charleston, SC, 1845), 9; J. A. Turner, *A Letter to Hon. N. G. Foster, Candidate for Congress* (Milledgeville, GA, 1855), 14. For citations of Dickens as an authority on poverty and crime in England, see e.g. *University Literary Magazine*, 1 (1857), 197; [George Fitzhugh], "Southern Thought Again," *DBR*, 23 (1857), 454. For the southern reception of Dickens see William Glyde Wilkins, ed., *Charles Dickens in America* (New York, 1970), 5; John S. Wise, *The End of an Era* (Boston, 1900), 70; J. H. Ingraham, *Sunny South; Or, the Southerner at Home* (New York, 1968 [1860]), 172–3 (Nashville); Bertram Holland Flanders, *Early Georgia Magazines: Literary Periodicals to 1865* (Athens, GA, 1944), 77 (Richards). See the exchange of letters between Eliza Middleton Fisher and Mary Herring Middleton, Feb. 10–11, 1845, in Eliza Cope Harrison, ed., *Best Companions: Letters of Eliza Middleton Fisher and Her Mother, Mary Herring Middleton, from Charleston, Philadelphia, and Newport, 1839–1846* (Columbia, SC, 2001), 301, 427–8. Also, Emily Wharton Sinkler's correspondence in Anne Sinkler Whaley LeClerq, ed., *Between North and South: The Letters of Emily Wharton Sinkler, 1842–1865* (Columbia, SC, 2001), 69, 75, 91, 131.

Even those furious with Dickens for *American Notes* and *Martin Chuzzlewit* found *A Christmas Carol* entrancing, and in the South as elsewhere it provided an occasion for family reading and for young gentlemen to read aloud to young ladies – even unseasonably during the spring. See also the review of *American Notes* in *Orion*, 2 (1843), 175–6; Haigh Diary, May 15, 1844, at UNC-SHC; Sarah Lois Wadley Private Journal, 1864, at UNC-SHC; Elizabeth Silverthorne, *Plantation Life in Texas* (College Station, TX, 1986), 181; Tryphena Fox to Anna Rose Holder, Dec. 27, 1861, in Wilma King, ed., *A Northern Woman in the Plantation South: Letters of Tryphena Blanche Holder Fox, 1856–1876* (Columbia, SC, 1993), 132; Clyde Lottridge Cummer, ed., *Yankee in Gray: The Civil War Memoirs of Henry E. Handerson, with a Selection of His Wartime Letters* (Cleveland, OH, 1962), 112. For a sampling of Dickens's enthusiasts see Harriett Newell Espy to Zebulon Vance, May 22, 1852, in Elizabeth Roberts Cannon, ed., *My Beloved Zebulon: The Correspondence of Zebulon Vance and Harriett Newell Espy* (Chapel Hill, NC, 1971), 91; Camilla Hardin to William Hardin, Nov. 3, 1863, in Camilla Davis Trammel, *Seven Pines: Its Occupants and Their Letters* (Houston, TX, 1986), 173; Hume Diary, Jan 2, 4, 6, 1860, Sept. 4, 1861, at UNC-SHC; Lily Logan Morrill, ed., *My Confederate Girlhood: The Memoirs of Kate Virginia Cox Logan* (New York, 1980), 15–16; Maria Bryan Harford to Julia Ann Bryan Cumming, Jan. 12, 1839, in Carol Bleser, ed., *Tokens of Affection: The Letters of a Planter's Daughter in the Old South* (Athens, GA, 1996), 233; Mahalia Roach Diary, Feb. 3–4, 1853, in Roach–Eggleston Papers, at UNC-SHC; Mary Herring Middleton to Eliza Middleton Fisher, Jan 21, 1843, in Harrison, ed., *Best Companions*, 301; Scott Neblett to Will Neblett, Oct. 15, 1863, in Erika I. Murr, ed., *A Rebel Wife in Texas: The Diary and Letters of Elizabeth Scott Neblett, 1852–1864* (Baton Rouge, LA, 2001), 177; Chesnut Diary, Aug. 17, 1861, in C. Vann Woodward, ed., *Mary Chesnut's Civil War* (New Haven, CT, 1981), 149. On the popularity of *A Christmas Carol* see Penne L. Restad, *Christmas in America: A History* (New York, 1995), 136–7. Mary Chesnut frequently quoted or referred to *Nicholas Nickelby* in her diary; see also Charles J. Johnson, Jr., *Mary Telfair: The Life and Legacy of a Nineteenth-Century Woman* (Savannah, GA, 2002), 235. Southerners read *David Copperfield* and *Great Expectations* in serial form in *Harper's* and elsewhere before their publication as books, and Daniel E. Sutherland has suggested that Wilkens Micawber, the procrastinator who waited for "something to turn up," became a model for many who had to adjust to the defeat of the Confederacy: *The Confederate Carpetbaggers* (Baton Rouge, LA, 1998), 6–7. For references to Dickens's characters to describe men that Stephenson (a Presbyterian) met in the Confederate army, see Nathaniel Cheairs Hughes, ed., *The Civil War Memoir of Philip Dangerfield Stephenson, D.D.* (Baton Rouge, LA, 1995), 42–3, 51, 90, 97.

Dionysius: Many Southerners picked up Dionysius of Halicarnassus' "teaching by example" from Bolingbroke. J. S. Lamar of Georgia said at the beginning of the War: "If history in general is 'philosophy,' the history of the Jews in particular is Providence 'teaching by example' ": *A Discourse Delivered in the Christian Church on the Confederate Fast-Day, Friday, Nov. 5th, 1861* (Augusta, GA, 1861), 4. For two writers who agreed on Dionysius' principle but not on the specific conclusions, see Mitchell King, *A Discourse on the Qualifications and Duties of an Historian* (Savannah, GA, 1843), 13, and *DBR*, 10 (1851), 8, 266; and William Carey Crane, "History of Mississippi," *SLM*, 30 (1860), 81, 1. Among the disparate citations of Dionysius on history as example: Joseph Henry Lumpkin, *An Address on Natural History, Delivered before the Phi Delta and Ciceronian Societies, on the 1st Day of July, 1836, at the Mercer Institute* (Washington, GA, 1836), 3; A. B. Meek, *Americanism in Literature: An Oration before the Phi Kappa and Demosthenian Societies of the University of Georgia* (Tuscaloosa, AL, 1844), 17; for C. C. Jones, Jr., see R. Q. Mallard, *Maybank: Some*

Memoirs of a Southern Christian Household in the Olden Time; Or, the Family of the Rev. Charles Colcock Jones, D.D. of Liberty County, Ga. (Richmond, VA, 1898), 5.

Disciples of Christ: The Baptists suffered a decline of some 20 percent in the wake of their struggle with the "Campbellites" in 1830. The struggle badly split the Baptists in the Mississippi Valley. In North Carolina in early days, the Methodists denied the Disciples of Christ access to their pulpits. See [Rev.] J. Taylor, *Baptists on the American Frontier: A History of Ten Baptist Churches of Which the Author Has Been Alternately a Member,* ed. Chester Raymond Young, 3rd ed. (Macon, GA, 1995), 74; Robert A. Baker, *The Southern Baptist Convention and Its People, 1607–1972* (Nashville, TN, 1974), 142; Walter Brownlow Posey, *Frontier Mission: A History of Religion West of the Southern Appalachians to 1861* (Lexington, KY, 1966), 62–3; Jesse C. Fletcher, *The Southern Baptist Convention: A Sesquicentennial History* (Nashville, TN, 1994), 61; Charles Crossfield Ware, *North Carolina Disciples of Christ: A History of Their Rise and Progress and of Their Contribution to Their General Brotherhood* (St. Louis, MO, 1927), 49 and ch. 7; Thomas A. Langford, ed., *Wesleyan Theology: A Sourcebook* (Durham, NC, 1984), 118.

English Revolutions: Dew's respect for Henry VIII was grudging, his portrait of Charles I uncomplimentary and of James I scathing. On the English revolutions of the seventeenth century Dew recommended Mrs. Hutcheson's *Memoirs* as the best book to take the side of the Roundheads. He found May's *History of Parliament* good up to a point, Ludlow's history "foolish and violent." Oldmixon and Catherine Macaulay, who treated the French Revolution as a case of providential intervention in history, had more zeal than candor or skill. The best books on the other side were Clarendon's and Hume's. See Thomas Roderick Dew, *Digest of the Laws, Customs, Manners, and Institutions of the Ancient and Modern Nations* (New York, 1884 [1852]), 558–9. Clarendon's later admirers included Edgar Allan Poe: "The Classics," *SLM*, 2 (1836), 229. W. C. Rives praised the royalist Clarendon as fair-minded: *Discourse on the Character and Services of John Hampden, and the Great Struggle for Popular and Constitutional Liberty in His Time* (Richmond, VA, 1845), 26–7. Clarendon was popular in colonial Virginia and Maryland: see George K. Smart, "Private Libraries in Colonial Virginia," *American Literature,* 10 (1938), 40; Louis B. Wright, "The 'Gentleman's Library' in Early Virginia: The Literary Interests of the First Carters," *Huntington Library Quarterly,* 1 (1937/38), 27; Joseph Tower Wheeler, "Books Owned by Marylanders, 1700–1776," *Maryland Historical Magazine,* 35 (1940), 347.

Eusebius: Thomas Roderick Dew and J. D. B. De Bow cited Eusebius, the ancient historian, as an authority on both Christian and secular history. In 1870 Dabney, arguing for national recognition of the Sabbath, referred to Eusebius as "the most valuable, because the most learned" ancient witness, but a year later, defending the Trinity, Dabney denounced him as a semi-Arian, a "tricky and time serving" politician, Constantine's "truckling sycophant," and a corrupter of sacred manuscripts: T. R. Dew, *Digest of the Laws, Customs, Manners, and Institutions of the Ancient and Modern Nations* (New York, 1884 [1852]), 359, 363; J. D. B. De Bow, *The Industrial Resources, Statistics, &c. of the United States and More Particularly of the Southern and Western States,* 3rd ed., 3 vols. (New York, 1966 [1854]), 2:344; *DD,* 1:537, 387. For reliance on Eusebius for early history of Christianity by a Methodist, Presbyterian, and Episcopalian see *QRMECS,* 9 (1855), 503–5, 512–13, and 10 (1856), 3; "The Claim of Emanuel Swedenborg to Divine Illumination," *DQR,* 1 (1861), 204; W. N. Pendleton, *Science: A Witness for the Bible* (Philadelphia, 1860), 340. For Eusebius in private libraries in the colonial period see Philip Alexander Bruce, *Institutional History of Virginia in the Seventeenth*

Century, 2 vols. (Gloucester, MA, 1964 [1910]), 413, 425; Stephen B. Weeks, *Libraries and Literature in North Carolina in the Eighteenth Century* (Washington, DC, 1896: "Annual Report of the American Historical Association for the Year 1895"), 190. For a defense of Eusebius against the frequent charge that he was an "erudite trimmer" see R. L. P. Milburn, *Early Christian Interpretations of History* (New York, 1954), 59, and ch. 5. For criticisms of Eusebius see "Milman's History of Christianity," *SQR*, 4 (1843), 289, and "T. C.", "On Historical Authenticity," *SLJ*, 2 (1836), 192. For use of Eusebius on history and church doctrine see *SLM*, 20 (1854), 448; J. L. Reynolds, *Church Polity: Or, the Kingdom of Christ in Its Internal and External Development*, 2nd ed. (Richmond, VA, 1849), 161, also 32 n.; *JHTW*, 3:632, 684.

French Incapacity for Freedom: Among the many Southerners who stressed the inability of the French to sustain a free government and republican liberty were John Taylor, *Arator: Being a Series of Agricultural Essays, Practical and Political: In Sixty-Four Numbers* (Indianapolis, IN, 1977 [1818]), 178; Herschel Gower and Jack Allan, *Pen and Sword: The Life and Journals of Randal W. McGavock* (Nashville, TN, 1959), ch. 13; Ignatius E. Shumate, "The Victim of Passion," *SRCR*, 4 (1856), 218; *VUM*, 2 (1858), 68; J. F. H. Claiborne, *Mississippi as a Province, Territory, and State, with Biographical Notices of Eminent Citizens* (Spartanburg, SC, 1978 [1860]), 252–3; [David F. Jamison], "Histoire des Girondins," *SQR*, 16 (1849), 57–8; E. L. Green, ed., *Two Speeches of George McDuffie* (Columbia, SC, 1905), 60–1; Joseph Glover Baldwin, *Party Leaders: Sketches* (New York, 1868), 74; *SLM*, 24 (1857), 248. Hugh Legaré suggested that only Anglo-Saxons could support a government of laws and that the French were incapable of self-government: Legaré to I. E. Holmes, 1832, and Legaré to Louis McLane, July 2, 1833, in *HLW*, 1:172, 204–5. To John Peyton Little, history afforded no example of a people born into slavery capable of maintaining a free government: [Little], "History of Richmond," *SLM*, 17 (1851), 607.

Southerners also called upon their favorite European writers to support their disdain for the capacity of the French to sustain liberty: see e.g. James Boswell, *The Life of Samuel Johnson, LL.D.* (New York, n.d.), 561; Miss [Julia] Pardoe, *Episodes of French History during the Consulate and the First Empire*, 2 vols. (London, 1859), 1:132. The denigration of France was hardly restricted to the South. See e.g. Iñes Murat, *Napoleon and the American Dream*, tr. Frances Frenaye (Baton Rouge, LA, 1981), 209; [James Kirk Paulding], *Letters from the South*, 2 vols. (New York, 1819), 1:182. Judge James Gould of the Litchfield Law School in Connecticut quipped, "Tell Mr. Beecher I am improving in [Calvinist] orthodoxy. I have got so far as this, that I believe in the total depravity of the whole French nation": quoted in Charles Beecher, ed., *Autobiography, Correspondence, Etc. of Lyman Beecher*, 2 vols. (New York, 1871), 1:225.

Froissart: Five English editions of Froissart appeared between 1801 and 1813, and several other editions appeared in London and New York during the 1840s, supplemented by books on Froissart. Three English editions of Malory's *Morte d'Arthur* appeared between 1815 and 1820. Froissart was a favorite in the ladies' social circles not only in cities like Charleston but in Middle Georgia: Curtis Carroll Davis, *That Ambitious Mr. Legaré: The Life of James M. Legaré of South Carolina, Including a Collected Edition of His Poems* (Columbia, SC, 1971), 49. A. M. Keiley of Virginia, Confederate prisoner of war and later politician and diplomat, opened his memoir by citing Froissart on medieval oratory: *In Vinculis; Or, the Prisoner of War. Being the Experience of a Rebel in Two Federal Pens* (New York, 1866), 13. For the significance of the delineation of great men see Johann Huizinga, *The Waning of the Middle Ages: A Study in the Forms of Life, Thought and Art in France and the*

Netherlands in the XIVth and XVth Centuries (London, 1963 [1924]), 57. Froissart's unacknowledged reliance upon the unpublished work of Jehan de Bel was not exposed until 1861: James Westfall Thompson, *A History of Historical Writing*, 2 vols. (Gloucester, MA, 1967 [1942]), 1:364–70.

John Esten Cooke opened an essay on "Chronicles of the Valley of Virginia" with a quotation from Froissart that declared his intention to tell the unvarnished truth: "Pen Ingleton" [Cooke], "Chronicles of the Valley of Virginia," *SLM*, 18 (1852), 459. Philip Pendleton Cooke, brother of John Esten Cooke and cousin of John Pendleton Kennedy, practiced law and contributed to *Southern Literary Messenger*. His romantic poetry, notably *Froissart's Ballads and Other Poems* (1847), drew on Froissart and Scott as well as Chaucer and Spenser and breathed the chivalric spirit. Cooke (d. 1850 at age 33) was regarded as the most brilliant member of the celebrated Cooke family. *Knickerbocker Magazine* published his early poems. Poe greatly admired him, and J. R. Thompson described him as "the finest poet who ever lived in Virginia." Lowell, among other critics, regarded his "Florence Vane" as a masterpiece, and it was translated into many languages. David Kelly Jackson, "Philip Pendleton Cooke," in Jackson, ed., *American Studies in Honor of William Kenneth Boyd* (Durham, NC, 1940), 282–326, Thompson quoted at 283; *SBN*, 11:228 (Lowell); John O. Beatty, *John Esten Cooke, Virginian* (New York, 1922), 7–8.

Fuller: Margaret Fuller, who commanded surprising respect in the South, wrote from Rome: "I listen to the same arguments against the emancipation of Italy that are used against the emancipation of our blacks; the same arguments against the spoilation of Poland as for the conquest of Mexico." She thought of the abolitionists: "I could never endure to be with them at home, they were so tedious, often so narrow, always so rabid and exaggerated in their tone. But after all they had a high motive, something eternal in their desire and life; and if it was not the only thing worth thinking of, it was really something worth living and dying for to free a great nation from such a terrible blot, such a threatening plague. God strengthen them, and make them wise to achieve their purpose!" Margaret Fuller, "The Roman Revolution: Three Letters," in Philip Rahv, ed., *Discovery of Europe: The Story of American Experience in the Old World* (Cambridge, MA, 1947), 170; on the June Days see M. Fuller, *"These Sad But Glorious Days": Dispatches from Europe, 1846–1850* (New Haven, CT, 1991), 23. For Fuller's reputation in the South see Chapter 18.

Contributors to leading southern journals who brushed off Margaret Fuller's antislavery did admire her strong intellect and "true heart," although Simms caviled at her "antislavery cant": [William Gilmore Simms], "Critical Notices," *SQR*, 12 (1855), 271–2, quote at 272. The more hostile Edgar Allan Poe called her "grossly dishonest": Poe to George W. Evelyth, Jan. 4, 1848, in John Ward Ostrum, ed., *The Letters of Edgar Allan Poe*, 2 vols. (Cambridge, MA, 1948), 2:355. Fuller, wrote a contributor to *Southern Literary Messenger*, was "eminently womanly by natural impulse, but a man by training and philosophy," by "the acuteness of her critical faculty," and by "her courage in the face of life's trials, her good spirit": "Memoirs of Margaret Fuller Ossoli," *SLM*, 20 (1854), 29–40 (quotes at 29, 37, 40). Although a truly "remarkable character," the Christianity that might have led her to realize her best had not enlightened her. A commentator in *Russell's Magazine* regarded Fuller as a superior intellect "justly ranked among the most remarkable women of the century." Pronouncing her gifted and well worth reading, he acquitted her of hypocrisy in her opposition to slavery. See "Margaret Fuller Ossoli," *RM*, 7 (1857), 229–32.

But the southern gentlemen who admired Fuller did not convince all the ladies who read their tributes. Mary Chesnut, for one, tried to read an essay on Fuller "but could not." Catherine Edmonston linked Fuller and Emerson as advocates of the philosophy responsible for the savagery of Yankee invaders. Yet the chivalric gentlemen who let Fuller off lightly for her attacks on slavery and her Unitarianism did not hesitate to take on other northern women; they admired Fuller for her exceptional mind and the firmness of her moral commitments: Chesnut Diary, Feb. 10, 19, Apr. 7, June 10, Nov. 27, 1861, in C. Vann Woodward, ed., *Mary Chesnut's Civil War* (New Haven, CT, 1981), 7, 21, 43, 72, 245; Apr. 22, May 26, Nov. 24, 1863, in Beth G. Crabtree and James Welch Patton, eds., *"Journal of a Secesh Lady": The Diary of Catherine Devereux Edmonston, 1860–1866* (Raleigh, NC, 1979), 382, 397, 494. Caroline E. Merrick of Louisiana, however, thought Margaret Fuller "a large souled-woman": *Old Times in Dixie Land: A Southern Matron's Memories* (New York, 1901), 16.

Goethe: *Southern Literary Messenger*'s translations of Goethe: Nathaniel Beverley Tucker, "Iphigenia at Taurus," 10 (1844), 2–6, 65–70, 129–31, 265–8; "C. L. L.", "The Wanderer," 14 (1848), 420–1; " 'Erl King' and 'Fisher,' " 18 (1852), 352; "The Trial of the Fox," 20 (1854), 466–9. See also Apr. 13, 1864, in Earl Schenck Miers, ed., *When the World Ended: The Diary of Emma LeConte* (New York, 1959), 86–7; Clitherall Diary, Sept. 1853, and Haigh Diary, Jan. 22, 1844, at UNC-SHC; William S. Powell, *When the Past Refused to Die: A History of Carswell County, North Carolina, 1777–1977* (Durham, NC, 1977), 409 (Grasty). For a review datelined Philadelphia see "Goethe's Wilhelm Meister," *SLM,* 17 (1851), 431–43. Henry Charles Lea thought that "Wilhelm Meister presents a perfect picture" of some features of German life: "The Rural and Domestic Life of Germany," *SLM,* 10 (1844), 569. For Goethe's search for truth see "The Auto-Biography of Goethe," *SQR,* 11 (1847), 441–67; Edwin De Leon, "The Vision of Wagner, Pupil of Faust," *SLM,* 11 (1845), 118–27. Whether Southerners knew of Goethe's white-supremacist comments remains unclear: M. E. Musgrave, "Literary Justifications of Slavery," in Reinhold Grimm and Jost Hermand, eds., *Blacks and German Culture* (Madison, WI, 1986), 20 n. 63. George Henry Calvert, who met Goethe in 1825, offered Americans their first translation of his work – "Hymn of the Archangels," from *Faust* – in a small magazine in Baltimore. Calvert, Goethe's first American biographer, also published the first translation of the Goethe–Schiller correspondence and the first translation of a drama by Schiller: Ida Gertrude Everson, *George Henry Calvert: American Literary Pioneer* (New York, 1944), ix. Goethe remains a powerful influence on theologians: see Colin Brown, *Jesus in European Protestant Thought, 1778–1860* (Grand Rapids, MI, 1985), ch. 2; Jaroslav Pelikan, *The Christian Tradition: A History of the Development of Doctrine,* 5 vols. (Chicago, 1989), 5:2–4, and Pelikan, *Faust the Theologian* (New Haven, CT, 1995), upon which we have drawn freely.

Golden Rule: In the early nineteenth-century South, antislavery Methodists invoked the Golden Rule while relying heavily on the Declaration of Independence and secular political doctrines: Lynn Lyerly, *Methodism and the Southern Mind, 1770–1810* (New York, 1998), 129, 137–8. For abolitionist interpretations of the Golden Rule see also William Henry Brisbane, *Slaveholding Examined in the Light of the Holy Bible* (New York, 1847), ch. 10; Mary Stoughton Locke, *Anti-Slavery in America: From the Introduction of African Slaves to the Prohibition of the Slave Trade (1619–1808)* (Gloucester, MA, 1965 [1901]), 176–7. Southerners concerned with enlisting yeomen support for slavery invoked the Golden Rule: see e.g. [Gabriel Capers], *Bondage a Moral Institution, Sanctioned by the Scriptures of the Old and New Testaments, and the Preaching and Practice of the Saviour. By a Southern Farmer* (Macon, GA, 1837), 39–40.

For the argument that the Golden Rule forbids the expropriation of property as theft, see Robert L. Dabney, *Systematic Theology* (Carlisle, PA, 1985 [1878]), 414–15. For secular theorists see Thomas R. R. Cobb, *An Inquiry into the Law of Negro Slavery in the United*

States (New York, 1968 [1858]), 61–3; J. G. M. Ramsey to L. W. Spratt, Apr. 1858, in William B. Hesseltine, ed., *J. G. M. Ramsey, Autobiography and Letters* (Nashville, TN, 1954), 92; George S. Sawyer, *Southern Institutes; Or, an Inquiry into the Origin and Early Prevalence of Slavery and the Slave Trade* (New York, 1967 [1858]), 147–200, 237; George Fitzhugh, "Making Home Attractive," *DBR*, 28 (1860), 634; on Nathaniel Beverley Tucker see Drew Gilpin Faust, *A Sacred Circle: The Dilemma of the Intellectual in the Old South, 1840–1860* (Baltimore, 1977), 120. For acute observations on the attitude of Fitzhugh and others see Gerald David Jaynes, *Branches without Roots: Genesis of the Black Working Class in the American South, 1862–1882* (New York, 1986), 77–8.

For the Golden Rule as according protection to slaves, see [E. T. Baird], "The Religious Instruction of Our Colored Population," *SPR*, 12 (1859), 350–1. The Reverend George Junkin, while living in Ohio, appealed to the Golden Rule to demand to know how anyone could seek emancipation of southern slaves to suffer the fate of free Negroes in the North: Junkin, *The Integrity of Our National Union vs. Abolitionism: An Argument from the Bible* (Cincinnati, 1843), 77–8. During the War, Southerners still fumed over the abolitionist version of the Golden Rule: see e.g. Americus Featherman, "Our Position and That of Our Enemies," *DBR*, 31 (1861), 22–3. J. F. H. Claiborne of Mississippi, looking back on the dispute after the War, summed up the prevalent southern view of the Golden Rule: "Christ was thoroughly conservative; not at all radical": *Mississippi as a Province, Territory, and State, with Biographical Notices of Eminent Citizens* (Spartanburg, SC, 1978 [1860]), 148.

Moderate antislavery men as well as abolitionists made the Golden Rule the centerpiece of antislavery. See e.g. John Hersey, *An Appeal to Christians on the Subject of Slavery*, 2nd ed. (Baltimore, 1833), 57–8; John S. C. Abbott, *South and North; Or, Impressions Received during a Trip to Cuba and the South* (New York, 1969 [1860]), 95–6. The chief texts to which opponents of slavery appealed were Luke, 10:27, and John, 13:34: see e.g. Nathaniel Hall, *The Iniquity: A Sermon Preached in the Free Church, Dorchester* (Boston, 1859); Theodore Parker, *The New Crime against Humanity* (Boston, 1854), 68. B. F. Porter called upon the Stoic principle – render to everyone his right – to bolster the southern argument from Scripture: "An Attempt to Infuse into the English Language Some Thoughts of Heineccius' Elementa Juris Civilis – Part I," *DBR*, 2 (1846), 24. For the influence of the classics on higher-law doctrine in eighteenth-century America, see Meyer Reinhold, *Classica Americana: The Greek and Roman Heritage in the United States* (Detroit, 1984), 97. For a critique of Wayland and Channing on the Golden Rule see A. J. Roane, "Reply to Abolitionist Objections to Slavery," *DBR*, 20 (1856), 650–1.

Goldsmith was ranked as a favorite from Virginia and Georgia to Texas. Intellectual and political luminaries – George Fitzhugh, William Gilmore Simms, Francis W. Pickens – joined planters like Thomas Dabney and such fastidious Presbyterian reverends as Moses Hoge and John Girardeau in celebrating Goldsmith, who was a particular favorite of the ladies. See George Fitzhugh, "Oliver Goldsmith and Dr. Johnson," *DBR*, 28 (1860), 508; Paul Hamilton Hayne, "Ante-Bellum Charleston, S.C.," *Southern Bivouac*, 1 (1885), 262 (Simms); Susan Dabney Smedes, *Memorials of a Southern Planter,* ed. Fletcher M. Green (New York, 1965 [1887]), 81; George A. Blackburn, ed., *Sermons by John L. Girardeau* (Columbia, SC, 1907), 241; Peyton Harrison Hoge, *Moses Drury Hoge: Life and Letters* (Richmond, VA, 1899), 37. For the ladies see *Plantation Life: The Narratives of Mrs. Henry Schoolcraft* (New York, 1969 [1860]), 186 n., 250; Sallie Bird to Saida Bird, Mar. 2, 1862, in John Rozier, ed., *The Granite Farm Letters: The Civil War Correspondence of Edgeworth and Sallie Bird* (Athens, GA, 1988), 68; Camilla Hardin to William Hardin, Nov. 3, 1862, in Camilla Davis Trammel, *Seven Pines: Its Occupants and Their Letters* (Houston, TX, 1986), 174; Elizabeth Silverthorne,

Plantation Life in Texas (College Station, TX, 1986), 181; Mary E. Moragné Journal, June 29, 1839, in Delle Mullen Craven, ed., *The Neglected Thread: A Journal of the Calhoun Community* (Columbia, SC, 1951), 138; Apr. 2, 1864, in Eleanor P. Cross and Charles B. Cross, Jr., eds., *Glencoe Diary: The War-Time Journal of Elizabeth Curtis Wallace* (Chesapeake, VA, 1968), 102; Rachel Mordecai to Maria Edgeworth, June 24, 1827, in Edgar E. MacDonald, *The Education of the Heart: The Correspondence of Rachel Mordecai Lazarus and Maria Edgeworth* (Chapel Hill, NC, 1977), 129.

On Goldsmith's social criticism see Howard J. Bell, Jr., "The Deserted Village and Goldsmith's Social Doctrines," *Publications of the Modern Languages Association,* 60 (1944), 747–72. Goldsmith got a lift from those who read Goethe's *Autobiography* (English tr. 1824), which praised him and especially the *Vicar of Wakefield*: Samuel H. Woods, Jr., *Oliver Goldsmith: A Reference Guide* (Boston, 1982), 26–7, 108. Washington Irving, a southern favorite, also did much to popularize Goldsmith in America: see Woods, *Oliver Goldsmith,* 28, 40. Dr. James Norcom of Edenton, North Carolina – Harriet Jacobs's model for Dr. Flint in *Incidents in the Life of a Slave Girl* – found most novels distasteful but approved of *Vicar of Wakefield*: James Norcom to Mary Harvey, Mar. 4, 1848, in James Norcom Papers, at North Carolina State Archives (Raleigh). On the popularity of *Vicar of Wakefield* in Virginia see James D. Hart, *The Popular Book: A History of America's Literary Taste* (New York, 1950), 61, and Frank Luther Mott, *Golden Multitudes: The Story of Best Sellers in the United States* (New York, 1947), 304; Frances Norton Mason, *My Dearest Polly: Letters of Chief Justice John Marshall to His Wife, with Their Background, Political and Domestic, 1779–1831* (Richmond, VA, 1961), 8.

Gracchi: Under the peculiarities of changing Roman practice, Tiberius' origins were both noble and plebeian, and his noble pedigree could hardly have been more impressive. His mother was the daughter of the great Publius Cornelius Scipio Africanus, and Tiberius was brother-in-law of Scipio Aemilianus, adopted son of Scipio Africanus. For a splendid account of Scipio Africanus see Polybius, *Histories,* esp. 4:Bk. 10:2–20, 31–40; Bk. 14 (2), 1–10. Cornelia's ambitious sons had a strong model in Scipio, whom Polybius described as "beneficent and magnanimous" but also "shrewd and discreet with a mind always concentrated on the object he had in view." Land redistribution and cancellation of debts arose early in Greece as a revolutionary slogan: Paul A. Rahe, *Republics, Ancient and Modern: Classical Republicanism and the American Revolution* (Chapel Hill, NC, 1992), 62–3. On the relevance of slave revolts see: E. Badian, *Publicans and Sinners: Private Enterprise in the Service of the Roman Republic* (Ithaca, NY, 1972), 54; Alvin H. Bernstein, *Tiberius Sempronius Gracchus: Tradition and Apostasy* (Ithaca, NY, 1978), 72–3; and the earlier appraisal of Oswald Spengler, *The Decline of the West,* tr. Charles Francis Atkinson, 2 vols. (New York, 1926–28), 1:138; also, Plutarch, *Lives,* 2:335–7. For a sympathetic account of the rebels see Arnold Toynbee, *Hannibal's Legacy: The Hannibalic War's Effects on Roman Life,* 2 vols. (London, 1965), 2:324–31. M. I. Finley dates the revolt from 139 and accepts the estimate of 60,000–70,000 as the most plausible: *A History of Sicily: Ancient Sicily to the Arab Conquest* (New York, 1968), 139–44. Tiberius Gracchus protested the presence of masses of slaves in the Roman countryside, not out of concern for the condition of the slaves but in the interest of the dispossessed small landholders: see M. I. Finley, *The Ancient Economy* (Berkeley, CA, 1973), 80, 101. D. C. Earl challenges the assumption that the slave revolts bore a direct relation to the latifundia: *Tiberius Gracchus: A Study in Politics* (Bruxelles-Bercheim, 1963), 29; for Tiberius' support from a ruling-class faction see 14–15, and for the enthusiasm of plebs and proletarians for agrarian reform see 40–1. On the posthumous popularity of the Gracchi with the Roman plebs see Zvi Yavetz, *Plebs and Princeps* (Oxford, U.K., 1969), ch. 3.

Southerners, who took pains to teach their children the art of letter-writing, pointed to Cornelia as a superior example who trained her sons accordingly. Quintilian, who with Cicero shaped the teaching of rhetoric in the Old South, attributed much of the Gracchi's celebrated oratorical power to the enduring influence of Cornelia, "whose letters testify to the cultivation of her style." Quintilian, *Institutio Oratoria*, 1:Bk. I:6; Plutarch, *Lives*, 2:355–6. Also, Susan Dixon, *The Roman Mother* (Norman, OK, 1987), 109–11, 172, 193. For the criticism of Michelet see *SQR*, 11 (1847), 508. Ronald Syme, *The Roman Revolution* (New York, 1960 [1931]), 445; Abram Burwell Brown in Dr. and Mrs. William E. Hatcher, *Sketch of the Life and Writings of A. B. Brown* (Baltimore, 1886), 208; On ancient writers and women's passions see Roger Just, "Freedom, Slavery and the Female Psyche," in P. A. Cartledge and F. D. Harvey, eds., *Crux: Essays in Greek History Presented to F. F. M. de St. Croix on His 75th Birthday* (London, 1985), 182, and Pierre Grimal, *Love in Ancient Rome*, tr. Arthur Treen, Jr. (Norman, OK, 1980), 141, 251–2.

Greek Writers – *Aristophanes*: For praise of Aristophanes see Charles Minnigerode, "Greek Dramatists," *SLM*, 9 (1843), 99–101; *SQR*, 5 (1844), 250. On *Wasps* as illustrative of the physical violence in master–slave relations see Gregory Crane, "Oikos and Agora: Mapping the Polis in Aristophanes' Wasps," in Gregory W. Dobrov, ed., *The City as Comedy: Society and Representation in Athenian Drama* (Chapel Hill, NC, 1997), 210. *Frogs* led to Plautus and others who inverted the master–slave relation: Erich Segal, *Roman Laughter: The Comedy of Plautus* (Cambridge, MA, 1968), ch. 4. Aristophanes' comedies, David Konstan argues, contain "a profoundly egalitarian or utopian impulse" that imagines emancipation, women's rights, and abolition of private property, but no Southerner read them that way: Konstan, *Greek Comedy and Ideology* (New York, 1995), 8. For Aristophanes as critic of democratic and egalitarian utopias see Thomas K. Hubbard, "Utopianism and the Sophistic City in Aristophanes," in Dobrov, ed., *City as Comedy*, 23–40; Meyer Reinhold, *Studies in Classical History and Society* (New York, 2002), 13–14; and, more cautiously, Albin Lesky, *A History of Greek Literature*, tr. James Willis and Cornelius de Heer, 2nd ed. (Indianapolis, IN, 1963), 425. For Aristophanes' farmers see Victor Davis Hanson, *The Other Greeks: The Family Farm and the Agrarian Roots of Western Civilization* (New York, 1995), 216.

Longinus: *On the Sublime,* long if inaccurately attributed to Longinus, was available in southern bookstores during the eighteenth and early nineteenth centuries and was taught in some schools: see James Raven, *London Booksellers and American Customers: Transatlantic Literary Community and the Charleston Library Society, 1748–1811* (Columbia, SC, 2002), 154; Joseph Tower Wheeler, "Books Owned by Marylanders, 1700–1776," *Maryland Historical Magazine*, 35 (1940), 349; "Libraries in Colonial Virginia," *WMQ*, 2 (1894), 172–3; Charles L. Coon, ed., *North Carolina Schools and Academies: A Documentary History, 1790–1840* (Raleigh, NC, 1915), 785; Philip Slaughter, *A Memorial of the Rev. George Archibald Smith, A.M.* (New York, 1890), 16; William Martin Reynolds, "Deliberative Speaking in Ante-Bellum South Carolina: The Idiom of a Culture" (Ph.D. diss., University of Florida, 1960), 41–2. For Longinus as "a celebrated Grecian philosopher and critic" and as having hints of Revelation see "Conflicts of Revelation and Science," *DQR*, 3 (1864), 351. William H. Stiles quoted Longinus as insisting that arts and science can flourish only under free governments: *Connection between Liberty and Eloquence* (Augusta, GA, 1852), 26; and in praise of Longinus on the republican foundations of great rhetoric see H. S. Legaré, in Benjamin F. Griffin, *The Southern Orator, Consisting of Elements of Elocution, and Selections Suitable for Declamation and Recitation from Eminent Southern Orators and Writers* (Macon, GA, and Charleston, SC, 1851), 159. Other writers, most notably Euripides and Sophocles, were taught in the better academies and at Furman, the University of North

Carolina, and the University of Mississippi. Students at the University of Virginia were required to translate from Euripides: [R. S. Brockenbrough?], "Examination in the School of Antient [*sic*] Language," *VLM*, 1 (1829), 127; "G.", "Antient [*sic*] Languages," *VLM*, 1 (1829), 255. See also Aug. 19 and 27, 1863, in John F. Marszalek, ed., *The Diary of Miss Emma Holmes* (Baton Rouge, LA, 1979), 296, 297–8; also, John S. Barbour to Calhoun, Dec. 12, 1844, in *JCCP*, 20:527.

Tyrtaeus: On Tyrtaeus as a poet of war and heroism sanctified by the gods see Paul A. Rahe, *Republics, Ancient and Modern: Classical Republicanism and the American Revolution* (Chapel Hill, NC, 1992), 142 (Plato quoted), 146, 150; also, Eric Voegelin, *Order and History*, 5 vols. (Baton Rouge, LA, 1956), 2:188–94. Rahe observes that, on this matter, Athens generally, "owed more to the Lacedaemonian example than Pericles ever admitted" (200). Plato, who admired Tyrtaeus, regretted that he praised bravery in battle as the only virtue: John Edwin Sandys, *A History of Classical Scholarship*, 3 vols. (Cambridge, U.K.: vol. 1, 3rd ed., 1921; vols. 2 and 3, 2nd ed., 1908), 1:15. *Southern Literary Messenger* published a two-page translation from Tyrtaeus: *SLM*, 6 (1840), 410–11, and see "I. E. H." [Holmes], tr., "Martial Songs of Tyrtaeus," *Baltimore Repertory of Papers on Literary and Other Topics*, 1 (1811), 252–4. The Baptist Reverend J. L. Reynolds of Richmond cited Tyrtaeus as a patriot-poet in his *The Man of Letters* (Richmond, VA, 1849), 6–8. For an appreciation of Greek and especially Spartan contributions to chivalry see George Frederick Holmes, "Greece and Its History," *QRMECS*, 9 (1855), 49.

Xenophon: Xenophon, who influenced southern opinion on Sparta, was reviled by pro-Athenians. Thomas Ewing thought *Cyroepaedia* history at its best: "Ancient Literature," *SQR*, 4 (1838), 409–15. But Charles Minngerode scorned "the superficial panegyrist of Sparta": "The Greek Dramatists," *SLM*, 9 (1843), 98. Isaac Stuart and "T. C." treated much of Xenophon as historical romance: Isaac W. Stuart, *On the Classical Tongues and the Advantages of their Study* (Columbia, SC, 1836), 13; and "T. C.", "On Historical Authenticity and the Value of Human Testimony as to Facts," *SLJ*, 2 (1836), 183. Holmes thought Xenophon's history largely useless, although he cited Xenophon as an authority when it suited him: [Holmes], "Cimon and Pericles," *SQR*, n.s., 3 (1851), 341, 366; [Holmes], "The Bacon of the Nineteenth Century," *MMQR*, 4th ser., 5 (1853), 339. The editor of *Southern Literary Messenger* assumed that everyone distinguished between Xenophon's autobiographical *Anabasis* and the untrustworthy *Cyroepedia*: [John R. Thompson], *SLM*, 14 (1848), 190. The editor of *Southern Quarterly Review* referred to *Cyropedia* "a mere historical romance": "Critical Notices," *SQR*, 12 (1847), 524; and Simms followed with a reference to "the twaddle of that silly old political novel": [William Gilmore Simms], *SQR*, n.s., 8 (1853), 286–7. J. L. Reynolds referred to "Xenophon, the elegant historian of that perilous retreat of the ten thousand, in which he himself was the leader": *Man of Letters*, 15–16. Much in Xenophon's and Plutarch's accounts of Sparta has proven reliable: see Paul Cartledge, *Spartan Reflections* (Berkeley, CA, 2001), 26. For a defense of Xenophon against the charge of pro-Spartan bias see Simon Hornblower, "Introduction," in Hornblower, ed., *Greek Historiography* (Oxford, U.K., 1994), 30. Leo Strauss interpreted Xenophon on Sparta as disguised satire: "The Spirit of Sparta or the Taste of Xenophon," *Social Research*, 6 (1939), 501–36.

Although colleges initially assigned Xenophon's *Cyropaedia* and the College of South Carolina continued to do so at least until the 1830s, it fell into disfavor, whereas students had to know *Anabasis* when they entered the University of Virginia and, probably, other colleges. Both church-related colleges (e.g., Mercer, Furman, Emory) and such state universities as those of Alabama and North and South Carolina taught *Anabasis* and *Memorabilia*. For the teaching of Xenophon's *Memorabilia*, *Cyropaedia*, and *Anabasis*, see Dale Glenwood Robinson, *The Academies of Virginia, 1776–1861* (n.p., 1977), 14; Phillip Alexander Bruce,

History of the University of Virginia, 1819–1919: The Lengthening Shadow of One Man, 5 vols. (New York, 1920–22), 2:84–5. Xenophon fared better with his *Memorabilia.* Professor Maximilian LaBorde of South Carolina College charged Plato with gross distortions that attributed "absurd doctrines" to Socrates: [LaBorde], "Characteristics of a Statesman," *SQR,* 6 (1844), 114. On Socrates, Holt Wilson drew upon Xenophon rather than Plato, as did some other prominent Southerners: Wilson, "Socrates and Philosophy," *SLM,* 29 (1859), 14–29; [J. Thomas Ewing], "Ancient Literature," *SLM,* 4 (1838), 409–15; *SQR,* 12 (1847), 523–4; William Porcher DuBose, *Turning Points in My Life* (New York, 1912), 40–1. [L. Martin], "The Women of France," *SLM,* 5 (1839), 297; *SQR,* 5 (1844), 223–4, 248–9; Stephen Meats and Edwin T. Arnold, eds., *The Writings of Benjamin F. Perry,* 3 vols. (Spartanburg, SC, 1980), 1:335; James P. Boyce, discussed in William A. Mueller, *A History of Southern Baptist Seminary* (Nashville, TN, 1959), 54–5. William Gilmore Simms, no fan of Xenophon the historian, took pleasure in a new, well-edited American edition of *Memorabilia* of Socrates for students: [Simms], *SQR,* n.s., 11 (1855), 533. For a strong defense of Xenophon's contributions see Leo Strauss, *Xenophon's Socrates* (Ithaca, NY, 1972). Cobb and Sawyer also called upon Xenophon's *Memorabilia* and *Oeconomicus* to flesh out their accounts of social conditions in ancient slave societies: Thomas R. R. Cobb, "Historical Sketch of Slavery," in Cobb, *An Inquiry into the Law of Negro Slavery in the United States* (New York, 1968 [1858]), esp. ch. 5; George S. Sawyer, *Southern Institutes; Or, an Inquiry into the Origin and Early Prevalence of Slavery and the Slave Trade* (New York, 1967 [1858]), Essay III. Joseph H. Lumpkin recommended *Oeconomicus* especially for its account of husbandry: *An Address Delivered before the South-Carolina Institute at Its Second Annual Fair* (Charleston, SC, 1851), 37.

Haiti: Federalists viewed, if uneasily, an independent Haiti as a weapon against French power in the Caribbean. The reaction against provocations of Citizen Genet and the massacre of whites in Saint Domingue in 1793 substantially altered southern opinion. Word spread that Genet had connections with the *Amis des Noirs.* Wealthy, conservative French planters arrived in South Carolina before the black explosion, having preferred exile to the regime imposed by the revolutionaries in France: see Mary D. Robertson, ed., *A Confederate Lady Comes of Age: The Journal of Pauline DeCaradeux Heyward, 1863–1888* (Columbia, SC, 1992), 2–3. Jefferson's anti-Haitian policy flowed in part from worries that American slaves would be drawn into the insurrectionary orbit, as well as upon doubts that a black republic could remain viable. He followed a zigzag course that had pro-Haitian moments designed to establish a favorable balance of power in the Caribbean: see Tim Matthewson, "Jefferson and Haiti," *JSH,* 61 (1995), 209–48. To the intense discomfiture of white Virginians, news of Haiti did in fact spread to their slaves: see James Sidbury, "Saint Domingue in Virginia: Ideology, Local Meanings, and Resistance to Slavery, 1790–1800," *JSH,* 63 (1997), 532–4. For the diplomatic complexities of the response to Haiti, especially in relation to Cuba, see Robert L. Paquette, "The Everett–Del Monte Connection: A Study in the International Politics of Slavery," *Diplomatic History,* 11 (1987), 1–21.

In Savannah in 1824 the Reverend Nathan Welby Fiske, who became a professor of intellectual and moral history at Amherst College, reported the testimony of a pitiable refugee woman from Saint Domingue on the tortures and savage murders – including of infants – of whites by blacks in Saint Domingue. Fiske to [?], Mar. 1, 1824, in Nathan Welby Fiske Papers, Newberry Library (Chicago). In Washington in 1860, Chief Justice Roger B. Taney recalled the horrors of Saint Domingue with a shudder, praying that the South would not experience a replay: Roger B. Taney to J. Mason Campbell, Oct. 10, 1860, in Benjamin C. Howard Papers, at Maryland Historical Society. Robert L. Paquette, who graciously provided us with these letters, has attested that such descriptions appeared repeatedly.

Cobb referred to Toussaint as a full-blooded Negro. Cobb leaned heavily on the authority of the antislavery Victor Schoelcher for his account of Toussaint, Haiti, and the politics of
colonialism in France. In contrast, Kate Stone of Louisiana, refugeeing in Texas, was appalled
by Harriet Martineau's "disgusting" paean to Toussaint L'Ouverture and her insistence that
he was a greater man than Napoleon: John Q. Anderson, ed., *Brokenburn: The Journal of
Kate Stone, 1861–1868* (Baton Rouge, LA, 1955), June 29, 1865 (313–14); see also Alfred
N. Hunt, *Haiti's Influence on Antebellum America: Slumbering Volcano in the Caribbean*
(Baton Rouge, LA, 1988), 85–91. In early nineteenth-century Charleston – before Denmark
Vesey – bookstores carried a biography of Toussaint L'Ouverture, John Stedman's account
of the black rebellion in Surinam, and Clarkson's history of the slave trade. See James Raven,
*London Booksellers and American Customers: Transatlantic Literary Community and the
Charleston Library Society, 1748–1811* (Columbia, SC, 2002), 215.

Britain's Tory press praised the order and stability of Haiti in 1819 under President Jean-
Pierre Boyer. The population rose significantly under a new system of disguised coercion.
But the export sector did not revive, and Wilberforce and the British emancipationists increasingly dissociated themselves from an economic decline that the introduction of free
labor was supposed to prevent. Despite criticism of sloth and inefficiency, Haiti paid a substantial compensation for the revolutionary expropriations to gain French recognition in the
1820s. See Seymour Drescher, *The Mighty Experiment: Free Labor versus Slavery in British
Emancipation* (New York, 2002), 101–5. The proslavery but antiracist Zephaniah Kingsley
of Florida bucked southern public opinion by complimenting the economic and political
performance of the Haitians, and he promoted resettlement of emancipated slaves in Haiti.
Kingsley had to combat the prevalent view of Haiti as an economic disaster. [Z. Kingsley],
*The Rural Code of Haiti, Literally Translated from a Publication by the Government Press.
By a Southerner* (Middltown, NJ, 1837); also, Daniel L. Shafer, *Anna Kingsley* (St. Augustine, FL, 1994), ch. 6. Thomas Cooper, for one, cited the failure of Haiti and contrasted it
with slaveholding Spanish Santo Domingo: [Cooper], "Slavery," *SLJ*, 1 (1835), 193.

Hallam: Hallam's admirers included Thomas Cobb, J. D. B. De Bow, Lucian Minor, Edward Brown, the Reverends George Addison Baxter, Edwin Hubbell Chapin, Alexander Mc-
Caine, and J. S. Lamar. See Thomas R. R. Cobb, "Historical Sketch of Slavery," in Cobb,
An Inquiry into the Law of Negro Slavery in the United States (New York, 1968 [1858]),
ch. 7; [Lucian Minor], review of Hallam, *SLM*, 4 (1838), 111–13; Edward Brown, *Notes
on the Origin and Necessity of Slavery* (Charleston, SC, 1826), 6, 9; George A. Baxter,
An Essay on the Abolition of Slavery (Richmond, VA, 1836), 8; Edwin Hubbell Chapin,
"Anniversary Address Delivered before the Richmond Lyceum," *SLM*, 5 (1839), 727; Alexander McCaine, *Slavery Defended against the Attacks of the Abolitionists* (Baltimore, 1842),
7; J. S. Lamar, *The Organon of Scripture; Or, the Inductive Method of Biblical Interpreta-
tion* (Philadelphia, 1860), 118; also, "Rise of Despotism in Europe," *SLM*, 21 (1855), 614;
SLM, 7 (1841), 591; *DBR*, 11 (1851), 343; "Ireland in 1834," *SQR*, 6 (1844), 7. For tributes
to Hallam's fair-mindedness see also *RM*, 4 (1859), 563; A. B. Stark, "Thomas Carlyle,"
QRMECS, 15 (1861), 199. For praise for Hallam as superior to Macaulay as a historian, see
"J. B. C." [Joseph B. Cobb of Longwood, MS], "Macaulay's History of England," *American
Whig Review*, 11 (1850), 348–51, 362. When Hallam died in 1859, *Southern Literary Messen-
ger* warmly praised him. Since proslavery writers enlisted Hallam, if without his consent, we
can only regret that the antislavery Jennie Speer of western North Carolina, who read him,
did not share her thoughts: Jennie Speer Diary, Dec. 31, 1850, in Allen Paul Speer and Janet
Barton Speer, *Sisters of Providence: The Search for God in the Frontier South (1843–1858)*
(Johnson City, TN, 2000), 67.

Hallam pilloried the Church for its corruption and abuse of power, but he stressed the limits of his critique in an effort to combat bigotry and promote fairness and accuracy: see Henry Hallam, *History of Europe in the Middle Ages,* rev. ed. (New York, 1899 [1818]), 2:183 and, generally, 2:Bk. 6 (49–71); Hallam, *Introduction to the Literature of Europe in the Fifteenth, Sixteenth, and Seventeenth Centuries,* 2 vols. (New York, 1842), 1:196–7, 200–1, 2:29. Thornwell, who favored the Nominalists, was surely annoyed by Hallam's criticism of them: Hallam, *Introduction,* 1:33, 110–11. [George Frederick Holmes], "Writings of Hugh Swinton Legaré," *SQR,* 9 (1846), 355; "Cromwell's Letters and Speeches," *SQR,* 10 (1846), 269; [Holmes], "Blunders of Hallam's 'Middle Ages,'" *SQR,* 11 (1855), 46–87; [Holmes], "Slavery and Freedom," *SQR,* n.s. (3rd), 1 (1856), 82; [Holmes], "Gibbon's Decline and Fall," *MMQR,* 4th ser., 10 (1856), 324; [Holmes], "Life and Writings of Rabelais," *SQR,* 7 (1845), 130 n. After the War, Holmes added that Hallam's commentary on the historical significance of Roman law was flippant and ignorant: "Recent Histories of Julius Caesar," *SR* (Baltimore), 1 (1867), 397. The pitting of Guizot against Hallam contained a certain irony, since Guizot admired and translated Hallam's *Constitutional History.* Also, the Macaulay who so pleased Southerners admired Hallam's *Constitutional History*: James Westfall Thompson, *A History of Historical Writing,* 2 vols. (Gloucester, MA, 1967 [1942]), 2:285–6. In 1836 the South Carolina Female Institute specifically recommended Hallam's *Middle Ages* to its students: see *DHE,* 5:411, 416.

Hebrew: Hampden-Sydney, Randolph-Macon, East Tennessee College, Trinity College, and the universities of Tennessee, Alabama, and Mississippi all offered Hebrew. See Frederick Rudolph, *The American College and University: A History* (Atlanta, GA, 1990), 25; Philip Alexander Bruce, *History of the University of Virginia, 1819–1919: The Lengthening Shadow of One Man,* 5 vols. (New York, 1920–22), 1:50–1; "Memoirs of Francis S. Sampson," *DD,* 3:431, 433; William B. Hesseltine, ed., *Dr. J. G. M. Ramsey, Autobiography and Letters* (Knoxville, TN, 2002), 53; James Jackson, "Life and Character of Rev. Dr. A. B. Longstreet," in William T. Smithson, ed., *In Memoriam* (New York, 1871), 29; James Riley Montgomery et al., eds., *To Foster Knowledge: A History of the University of Tennessee, 1794–1970* (Knoxville, TN, 1984), 36; Henry Alexander White, *Southern Presbyterian Leaders* (New York, 1911), 59–60; W. A. R. Goodwin, ed., *The History of the Theological Seminary in Virginia and Its Historical Background,* 2 vols. (New York, 1923), 1:153–4, 345, 490, 581, 643–4; Samuel A. Agnew Diary, Apr. 20 and 26, 1854, at UNC-SHC; "Genealogy," in Box 3 of Ramsey Family Papers, at UNC-Greensboro. Some of the better academies offered Hebrew before 1830, few afterwards. Although Jews operated a number of fine southern academies, none seems to have offered Hebrew: Charles L. Coon, ed., *North Carolina Schools and Academies: A Documentary History, 1790–1840* (Raleigh, NC, 1915), 187, 350, 527; James William Hagy, *This Happy Land: The Jews of Colonial and Antebellum Charleston* (Tuscaloosa, AL, 1993), 174–5.

Hegel: Neither Hegel nor Schleiermacher quite repudiated the doctrine of original sin, but their formulations encouraged radical departures: see B. M. G. Reardon, *Religion in the Age of Romanticism: Studies in Early Nineteenth Century Thought* (Cambridge, U.K., 1985), chs. 2 and 3; Claude Welch, *Protestant Thought in the Nineteenth Century,* 2 vols. (New Haven, CT, 1972, 1985), 81–2. Enoch Pond accused Hegel and some of his followers of turning history into "the pretended science of sociology," of peddling fatalism, and of superimposing a "purely a priori process": Pond, "The Philosophy of History," *Christian Review,* 24 (1859), 528–43, quotes at 529. For an interesting and knowledgeable campus invocation of Hegel, see "On the True Meaning of 'Cogito, Ergo Sum,'" *North Carolina University Magazine,*

5 (1856), 67; for an unenlightening reference to Hegel's philosophy of history see *VUM,* 3 (1858), 50. Almost all Southerners who criticized Hegel expressed respect for his intellectual power: see e.g. *SQR,* 11 (1847), 165. Thornwell's admiration for Hegel's intellectual power may be gleaned from his rejection – "with indignation" – of Hegel's argument on the relation of God to evil and from his praise of Hegel's reasoning as "unassailable": *JHTW,* 1:114. For an attack on the "Hegelian conceit" that identifies subject with object, see "History of Philosophy," *SQR,* n.s. (3rd), 2 (1856), 217, 259–60, quote at 217. Stuart Robinson pummeled Hegel for Erastianism: *The Relations of the Secular and Spiritual Power* (Louisville, KY, 1859), 9.

Hildreth: Richard Hildreth got mixed reviews in the South. J. R. Thompson of *Southern Literary Messenger* welcomed Hildreth's *History of the United States* as a fine piece of work, but De Bow and the editors of *Southern Quarterly Review,* acknowledging Hildreth as a superior scholar, condemned the later volumes as irresponsibly biased against the South: [Thompson], *SLM,* 15 (1849), 639; *DBR,* 8 (1850), 206; 10 (1851), 599; 11 (1851), 690. Simms commented charily on the early volumes of Hildreth's *History* in *SQR,* writing that, although Hildreth tried to be just, he could not because he was no philosopher. In subsequent years Simms swatted Hildreth's political philosophy as egalitarian drivel and grumbled about his incorrigible Yankee bias. See [Simms], "Critical Notices," *SQR,* 16 (1849), 258; Simms to Nathaniel Beverley Tucker, Dec. 17, 1849, in Mary C. Oliphant et al., eds., *The Letters of William Gilmore Simms,* 6 vols. (Columbia, SC, 1952–82), 2:573–4; [Simms], "Critical Notices," *SQR,* n.s., 9 (1854), 246–7; 6 (1852), 525; 11 (1855), 269; n.s., 2 (1857), 459.

Historical Cycle Theorists: On Polybius see Arnold Momigliano, *Essays in Ancient and Modern Historiography* (Middletown, CT, 1977), chs. 5, 11, and 12. We here bypass Momigliano's reading of Polybius, for clearly Southerners interpreted Polybius as a cyclical theorist. Momigliano attacks the idea that Greeks generally espoused a cyclical theory. For Polybius as cyclical theorist see F. W. Walbank, *A Historical Commentary on Polybius,* 3 vols. (Oxford, U.K., 1975), 1:642–64, 727–8, 743–5, and Walbank, *Polybius* (Berkeley, CA, 1972), chs. 5 and 6, esp. pp. 133–4, 145–6. The Greeks, Ivan Hannaford suggests, did find a cyclical pattern in history, but they distinguished between barbarians who accepted it fatalistically and civilized people who sought to break the cycle. Hannaford accepts Polybius as a cyclical theorist: *Race: The History of an Idea in the West* (Washington, DC, 1996), 21, 65.

Giambattista Vico drew only passing comment in the South, but after all he was largely unknown outside of Italy until Michelet brought out his two-volume *Oeuvres choisies de Vico* in 1835. George Frederick Holmes said that Vico deserved to be considered "Father of the Philosophy of History": "Schlegel's Philosophy of History," in Michael O'Brien, ed., *All Clever Men, Who Make Their Way: Critical Discourse in the Old South* (Fayetteville, AR, 1982), 203–4. James M. Walker of Charleston referred to the "learned Vico whose merits as a philosophical historian are universally recognized": *The Theory of the Common Law* (Boston, 1852), 13–14 n.

Historical Societies in the South: *Russell's Magazine* cheered the publications of the South Carolina Historical Society, stressing the need to preserve "many precious documents" that were in danger of being lost: *RM,* 3 (1858), 84. In 1846 De Bow praised the advancing culture of New Orleans, citing especially the large nightly audiences for lectures sponsored by the new Historical Society and other organizations. In 1847 he published Charles Gayarré's lecture at the Peoples Lyceum on the early history of Louisiana: *DBR,* 2 (1846), 351; 3 (1847), 449–62. The South-Carolina Historical Society was led by a distinguished group that included William J. Rivers, William H. Trescot, and B. R. Carroll, among historians, as well as such prominent men as J. L. Petigru. B. L. C. Wailes of Washington, Mississippi, founded the Mississippi Historical Society after the publication of his *Report of the Agriculture and Geology of Mississippi* (1854), in which his historical section qualified as the state's first, based on archives. Although the Society found little support and passed away in a few years, it did invaluable work in the collection and preservation of manuscripts. See Charles S. Sydnor, "Historical Activities in Mississippi in the Nineteenth Century," *JSH,* 3 (1937), 142–4, 152–3. The attempt to establish a state historical society in Tennessee at the beginning of the 1850s proved abortive: J. G. M. Ramsey to Lyman Draper, Sept. 18, 1851, in William B. Hesseltine, ed., *J. G. M. Ramsey, Autobiography and Letters* (Knoxville, TN, 2002), 63. *Russell's Magazine* welcomed contributions to the collection of source materials: [Editor's Table], *RM,* 2 (1857/58), 178.

Hudibras: On *Hudibras* (which was modeled on *Don Quixote*) in the southern colonies, see Richard Beale Davis, *Intellectual Life in the Colonial South, 1515–1763,* 3 vols. (Knoxville, TN, 1978), 2:523, 529, 534, 537, 550, 570–4; Bernard C. Steiner, "Rev. Thomas Bray and His American Libraries," *American Historical Review,* 2 (1896), 72; Louis B. Wright, "Richard Lee II, a Belated Elizabethan in Virginia," *Huntington Library Quarterly,* 2 (1938), 15, 33; "Libraries in Colonial Virginia," *WMQ,* 2 (1894), 172, 174; George K. Smart, "Private Libraries in Colonial Virginia," *American Literature,* 10 (1938), 35. For *Hudibras* in the South, see Charles L. Coon, *North Carolina Schools and Academies: A Documentary History, 1790–1840* (Raleigh, NC, 1915), 785; [Mary Virginia Hawes Terhune], *Marion Harland's Autobiography: The Story of a Life* (New York, 1910), 169; *Baccalaureate Address of the Hon. W. B. Reese, LL.D., President of East Tennessee University, Delivered at the Commencement, August 6, 1851* (Knoxville, TN, 1851), 13. The attraction of *Hudibras* may have arisen from other than political affinities. Samuel Johnson – a prime authority for Southerners – spoke of "the great author of Hudibras," which stood as "one of those compositions of which a nation may justly be proud": *The Lives of the Most Eminent English Poets with Observations on Their Work,* 4 vols. (London, 1781), 1:271–95, quotes at 271, 280. Butler opposed established literary ideals and conventions, displayed little respect for philosophers, and was skeptical not so much toward Christianity as toward the clergy and rigid theologies: see John Wilders, "Introduction to Samuel Butler," in *Hudibras* (Oxford, U.K., 1967 [1663–64, 1678]), xiii–xliii, esp. xxiii–xxxii.

Hume: Hume's interpretation of history posited certain constants in human nature that made possible the retrogression of any people toward savagery: Christopher J. Berry, "Hume on Rationality in History and Social Life," *History and Theory,* 21 (1983), 234–47. For an indication of the range of southern readers of Hume see Eliza Harriet Johnston to Elizabeth Mackay, July 18, 1828, in Joan E. Cashin, ed., *Our Common Affairs: Texts from Women of the Old South* (Baltimore, 1996), 93; T. M. Garrett Diary, 1849, at UNC-SHC; Aug. 28, 1862, in Charles East, ed., *The Civil War Diary of Sarah Morgan* (Athens, GA, 1991), 239. James Chesnut, Sr., took the name "Hume" when he joined the Cliosophic Society at Princeton in 1789: J. Jefferson Looney and Ruth L. Woodward, eds., *Princetonians, 1791–1994* (Princeton, NJ, 1991), 150. Mrs. Schoolcraft interpreted Hume's *Essays* as saying that nothing is beautiful or deformed, "but these attributes arise from the peculiar constitution and fabric of human sentiment and affection": *Plantation Life: The Narratives of Mrs. Henry Schoolcraft* (New York, 1969 [1860]), 152. Probably few Southerners knew that Hume ardently supported American independence until his death in 1776 – taking a more radical position than Burke or Fox, who wanted the colonies to remain within the Empire. Hume, in his essay entitled "Idea of a Perfect Commonwealth," also dismissed the prevalent notion that republics could survive only in a small country. See Donald Livingston, "David Hume and American Liberty," *Chronicles: A Magazine of American Culture,* 19 (1995), 20–3.

For Hume's view of state power and its resonance in America see Forrest McDonald, *Novus Ordo Seclorum: The Intellectual Origins of the Constitution* (Lawrence, KS, 1985), 7, 37, and Forrest McDonald, *The American Presidency: An Intellectual History* (Lawrence, KS, 1994), 30, 58–9. On Hume's conservative legacy see Henry F. May, *The Enlightenment in America* (New York, 1976), 112, 119–21; for a critique of Hume's claims against the scientific pretensions of political economy see Joseph A. Schumpeter, *History of Economic Analysis,* ed. Elizabeth Boody Schumpeter (New York, 1954), 124–9, and W. W. Rostow's "Foreword" in Robert Loring Allen, *Opening Doors: The Life and Work of Joseph Schumpeter,* 2 vols. (New Brunswick, NJ, 1990), 1:xiii.

William Blackford, perhaps deceiving himself, believed that Hume's reputation as a historian was sinking as his factual errors and biases became exposed: [William M. Blackford], "Ingersoll's History of the Last War," *SLM,* 12 (1846), 44–5. Park Benjamin declared Hume "often dry," as well as politically one-sided and religiously skeptical: [Benjamin], "Letters from New York," *SLM,* 15 (1849), 187. In contrast, the 1849 publication of Macaulay's *History of England* sparked a new and cheap edition of Hume, which J. R. Thompson of *Southern Literary Messenger* recommended as "the only work of permanent value" on England before the reign of James II: [Thompson], *SLM,* 16 (1850), 64. In 1858 William J. Grayson recalled that Jefferson kept Hume's *History* close by and continued to reread it despite his hostility: [Grayson], "Jefferson," *RM,* 3 (1858), 49, 59–60. Hume's style won the admiration even of the generally hostile Presbyterians: see e.g. Joseph M. Atkinson's acknowledgment of its "vivacity," "pungency," "narrative art," and "graphic force": [Atkinson], "The Puritans," *SPR,* 15 (1862), 230.

Iberian Literature: For the popularity of *Don Quixote* in the eighteenth century see Joseph Tower Wheeler, "Books Owned by Marylanders, 1700–1776," *Maryland Historical Magazine,* 35 (1940), 350; "Libraries in Colonial Virginia," *WMQ,* 2 (1894), 174; Hennig Cohen, *The South Carolina Gazette, 1732–1775* (Columbia, SC, 1953), 137, 143. Cervantes and Lesage circulated in the colonial South and were well represented in private libraries: Richard Beale Davis, *Intellectual Life in the Colonial South, 1515–1763,* 3 vols. (Knoxville, TN, 1978), 2:533; Walter B. Edgar, "Some Popular Books in Colonial South Carolina," *South Carolina Historical Magazine,* 72 (1971), 175. In the early nineteenth century, *Don Quixote* sold well in Spanish and English in Richmond and Charleston: Richard Beale Davis, *Intellectual Life in Jefferson's Virginia, 1790–1830* (Chapel Hill, NC, 1964), 80, 102–3; Frank Luther Mott, *Golden Multitudes: The Story of Best Sellers in the United States* (New York, 1947), 245.

For responses to *Don Quixote* from different parts of the South, see Alfred Mordecai in Jacob Rader Marcus, ed., *Memoirs of American Jews,* 3 vols. (Philadelphia, 1955), 1:248; T. M. Garrett Diary, June 29, 1849, at UNC-SHC (North Carolina); W. H. Holcombe Diary, Jan. 24, 1855, at UNC-SHC (Mississippi); Tally Simpson to Anna Simpson, Aug. 19, 1862, in Guy R. Everson and Edward W. Simpson, eds., *"Far, Far from Home": The Wartime Letters of Dick and Tally Simpson, Third South Carolina Volunteers* (New York, 1994), 141. Myra Inman, of a small slaveholding family in east Tennessee, read *Don Quixote,* but she may not have heard of it until a friend lent it to her: Mar. 20 and 31, 1863, in William R. Snell, ed., *Myra Inman: A Diary of the Civil War in East Tennessee* (Macon, GA, 2000), 191–2. William Elliott, in *Carolina Sports,* alluded to Don Quixote in his ironical portrayals of "knights" and feudal trappings: see Jacob F. Rivers III, "Cultural Values in the Southern Sporting Narratives" (Ph.D. diss., University of South Carolina, 1999), 26. Ollinger Crenshaw, *General*

Lee's College: The Rise and Growth of Washington and Lee University (New York, 1969), 11; Ferdinand Jacobs, *The Committing of Our Cause to God: A Sermon* (Charleston, SC, 1850), 9; Sept. 28, 1853, in Richard L. Troutman, ed., *The Heavens Are Weeping: The Diaries of Richard Browder, 1852–1856* (Grand Rapids, MI, 1987), 69; Henry Alexander White, *Southern Presbyterian Leaders* (New York, 1911), 291.

J. D. B. De Bow, drawing on Ticknor, provided a brief account of Cervantes's life and work and of the greatness of Lope de Vega and Calderon: [De Bow], "Literature of Spain," *DBR*, 9 (1850), 66–85, also *DBR*, 8 (1850), 311 (long, glowing review of Ticknor). Ticknor's *History* drew effusive praise from J. R. Thompson, *SLM*, 16 (1850), 64. Madame Le Vert of Mobile read the Spanish poets (in Spanish) in her youth and then read Ticknor: Frances Gibson Satterfield, *Madame Le Vert: A Biography of Octavia Walton Le Vert* (Edisto Island, SC, 1987), 100. A member of the same noble family as Vasco da Gama, Camõens based his epic, which appeared in its most authoritative version in 1572, on da Gama's voyage of discovery and took the entire Lusitanian people as its hero. J. E. Penn of Virginia extolled Camõens, who had "a counterpart in no land or tongue," for raising Portuguese poetry "from ditties and Troubadour songs to a comparison with the best of other countries." For the "illustrious Camõens" see President William Carey Crane of Mississippi (women's) College: *Literary Discourses* (New York, 1853), 53. G. Norman Lieber noted in *Russell's Magazine* that some critics rated *The Lusiads* above even Torquato Tasso's *Jerusalem Delivered* as "a representation of historical incidents." Lieber suggested that Tasso feared Camõens as his only rival for recognition as the greatest poet in Europe. *Southern Literary Messenger* published Richard Henry Wilde's translation of a sonnet by Camõens and Henrietta Shuck's celebratory "Cave of Camõens." Catherine Edmonston was among the ladies in knowing *The Lusiads*, which she probably read in translation; J. E. Penn, "The Fate of the Gifted," *VUM*, 5 (1860), 508; G. Norman Lieber, "The Portuguese and their Poet," *RM*, 4 (1858), 253, 255; for Wilde's translation see *SLM*, 1 (1834), 187; Henrietta Shuck, "Cave of Camõens," *SLM*, 6 (1840), 822–5; Sept. 11, 1862, and June 6, 1863, in Beth G. Crabtree and James W. Patton, eds., *"Journal of a Secesh Lady": The Diary of Catherine Devereux Edmonston, 1860–1866* (Raleigh, NC, 1979), 253, 339. Edmonston also read Dante, Tasso, Goldoni, Lope de Vega, Calderon de la Barca, and Cervantes. J. A. Leo Lemay, ed., *Robert Bolling Woos Anne Miller: Love and Courtship in Colonial Virginia, 1760* (Charlottesville, VA, 1990), 2, also, 23–6, 46, 63, 74–6; *VUM*, 3 (1859), 313, and 5 (1860), 506.

Indians – Southern Attitudes: Henry R. Craft of South Carolina attracted widespread interest with his studies of Indian life, although Edmund Ruffin (among others) pronounced his work pedantic, dull, and uninspired: Jan. 12, 1865, in *ERD*, 3:715–16. Simms properly rebuked historian William J. Rivers for his incomprehensible claim, in *Topics of South Carolina History,* that previous writers had ignored the Indians: [William Gilmore Simms], "Critical Notices," *SQR*, 9 (1854), 230–1. Simms, a student of Indian life, described Craft as a reliable authority who spent more than thirty years among the Indians. Craft, Simms noted, "married an Indian woman of great intelligence and beauty, and was thus placed in a position to see her people, if we may so phrase it, without disguise. He was admitted to their privacy, and informed of their traditions and character": "Literature and Art among the American Aborigines," in Simms, *Views and Reviews in American Literature, History, and Fiction,* ed. Hugh C. Holman (Cambridge, MA, 1962 [1846]), 147. Contrary attitudes nonetheless existed side by side. John Bachman, Charleston's respected scientist and Lutheran pastor, upheld the unity of the human race against the scientific racists and rejected polygenesis as an invitation to genocide. But he hardly disguised his contempt for Indians: Jay Schuler, *Had I the Wings: The Friendship of Bachman and Audubon* (Athens, GA, 1995), 199, 212.

For the combination of attitudes see e.g. *SQR*, 5 (1844), 118–56. Calhoun encouraged Schoolcraft's work on the Indians: Mrs. Schoolcraft, in *JCCP*, Apr. 25, 1850 (26:62); [Maximillian LaBorde], "Rivers' History of South Carolina," *SQR*, n.s. (3rd), 2 (1857), 264–5; William J. Rivers, "The Carolinas," in Justin Windsor, ed., *Narrative and Critical History of America* (Cambridge, MA, 1889), 295–8, 333. Rivers, a professor of Greek literature, doubled as a historian of South Carolina and a founder of the state historical society. As a historian, he was usually careful by the standards of his day, separating evidence from "old wives' tales": A. S. Salley, Jr., *A Sketch to Commemorate the Presentation of a Portrait of Professor Rivers to the Charleston Library Society* (Columbia, SC, 1906). See Rivers, *A Sketch of the History of South Carolina to the Close of the Proprietary Government by the Revolution of 1719* (Charleston, SC, 1856), which Salley called a "superior work." Pickett acknowledged his intention to treat Alexander McGillivray as a hero: Michael Leonard Woods, "Personal Reminiscences of Colonel Albert James Pickett," *Transactions of the Alabama Historical Society, 1899–1903* (Montgomery, AL, 1904), 609–10. B. F. Carroll, *Catechism of United States History,* 2nd ed., rev. (Charleston, SC, copyright 1859 but clearly published after the War), 51–6; this title went through twenty printings by 1859: *DBR*, 26 (1859), 119. Carroll followed the lead of Alexander Hewitt, who objected to the "unreasonable prejudice" against Indians and tried to write without racial bias. Simms recommended Hewitt: William Gilmore Simms to Robert Pleasant Hall, Feb. 24, 1852, in Marcy C. Oliphant et al., eds., *The Letters of William Gilmore Simms,* 6 vols. (Columbia, SC, 1952–82), 3:165. But J. L. Petigru dismissed Hewitt as more pleasing in style than content: "Oration Delivered on the Third Anniversary of the South-Carolina Historical Society," in *Collections of the South-Carolina Historical Society,* 2 vols. (Charleston, SC, 1858), 2:13.

William Byrd's *History of the Dividing Line* stressed the warfare and atrocities of Indian tribes against each other: Louis B. Wright, ed., *The Prose Works of William Byrd of Westover: Narrative of a Colonial Virginian* (Cambridge, MA, 1966), 302–3, 309. Memories of the Indian wars faded only slowly. Louisa McCord, writing in 1876 of her father, Langdon Cheves, recalled, "His aunt was murdered and scalped by Indians the night of his birth" in 1776: Richard C. Lounsbury, ed., *Louisa S. McCord: Poems, Drama, Biography, Letters* (Charlottesville, VA, 1996), 247; also, Richard Yeadon, *An Address Delivered before the Euphemian and Philomethean Literary Societies of Erskine College, at the Annual Commencement, August 8th, 1855* (Due West, SC, 1855), 5–7. In Florida in 1849, William Cullen Bryant noted the vivid memories of Indian atrocities held by the inhabitants of St. Augustine: William Cullen Bryant, *Letters of a Traveller; Or, Notes of Things Seen in Europe and America* (New York, 1850), 99–100. Yet the emergence of scientific racism in the 1840s and 1850s came as a shock to many, for until about 1830s most American scientists considered Indians as having the potential to achieve equality with whites: Charlotte M. Porter, *The Eagle's Nest: Natural History and American Ideas, 1812–1842* (Tuscaloosa, AL, 1986), 70–1, 153. European fascination with the Indians in the seventeenth century led to comparisons of the Brazilian Indians with the Homeric Greeks. Notably, Europeans perceived licentiousness among Brazilian Indians: see Peter Mason, "Classical Ethnography and Its Influence on the European Perceptions of the Peoples of the New World," in Wolfgang Haase and Meyer Reinhold, eds., *The Classical Tradition in the Americas,* 1st vol. (New York, 1994), 1, 135–72.

Interdenominational Cooperation: Bishop Otey preached in the Methodist and Cumberland Presbyterian churches: Otey Diary, May 23 and June 2, 1852, at UNC-SHC. Not only did congregations appreciate and encourage the exchange of pulpits, they sometimes chose their pastor from another denomination. The Baptist Reverend Henry Holcombe served as pastor for a Presbyterian church in South Carolina for awhile: Bertram Holland Flanders, *Early*

Georgia Magazines: Literary Periodicals to 1865 (Athens, GA, 1944), 7. But then, the Presbyterians and Baptists shared a Calvinist theology. More surprising, the Episcopalian John Hamilton Cornish, eyebrows raised, related that the Presbyterian Church in a village near Charleston chose a Methodist pastor over a Presbyterian candidate: Cornish Diary, Dec. 3, 1852, at UNC-SHC.

A few samples of common modes of interaction: Presbyterians entertained Methodists who gathered for a quarterly meeting; see Maria Bryan Connell to Julia Ann Bryan Cumming, Nov. 23, 1843, in Carol Bleser, ed., *Tokens of Affection: The Letters of a Planter's Daughter in the Old South* (Athens, GA, 1996), 372. James F. Clark attended different churches in North Carolina, apparently to hear particular preachers: James F. Clark Plantation Book, Sept. 1855, at UNC-SHC. Edward Bourne of Tennessee thought the Baptist and Methodist churches fit only for Negroes, but then he really had little contact with them. In time, he came to observe Baptist rituals and ended by joining the Baptist Church: Edward Bourne in *TCWVQ*, 1:354-5. For some time before the arrival of John Bachman, the Lutherans of Charleston had no pastor and depended upon ministers of other denominations: Lester D. Stephens, *Science, Race, and Religion in the American South: John Bachman and the Charleston Naturalists, 1845–1895* (Chapel Hill, NC, 2000), 14. After the establishment of a church at Willington, the Presbyterians used Liberty Church much less often, making it available to the Baptists and Methodists: Della Mullen Craven, ed., *The Neglected Thread: A Journal of the Calhoun Community* (Columbia, SC, 1951), 11 n. 36.

Warring ministers and prominent laymen often cooperated in community affairs. An occurrence repeated often throughout the history of the Old South: In 1750 in Savannah, gentlemen organized the St. George Club to aid orphans – Peter Tondee, a Catholic; Mordecai Sheftall, a Jew; and Richard Milledge, an Episcopalian. See Thomas L. Stokes, *The Savannah* (Athens, GA, 1979), 128. Ministers supported each other's educational pursuits by joining the board of trustees of the college of a denomination other than their own: see e.g. Thomas H. Pope, *The History of Newberry County, South Carolina*, 2 vols. (Columbia, SC, 1973), 1:188.

For illustrations of cross-attendance at churches, see the following (all mss. at UNC-SHC). Virginia: Early Diary, Nov. 12, 1807; John Walker Diary, Aug. 11, 1838. North Carolina: Massenburg Farm Journal, 1836–1838, Jan. 1, 1843. South Carolina: Cornish Diary, May 27, 1855, and Dec. 11, 1859; Archie Vernon Huff, Jr., *Langdon Cheves of South Carolina* (Columbia, SC, 1977), 183; John Belton O'Neall, *Biographical Sketches of the Bench and Bar of South Carolina*, 2 vols. (Charleston, SC, 1859), 2:523–4. Georgia: Charles Hartridge, ed., *The Letters of Robert Mackay to His Wife: Written from Ports in America and England, 1795–1816* (Athens, GA, 1949), 280–1 n. 88; Anna Matilda Page to her mother, Feb. 26 and Mar. 10, 1823, in Thomas Butler King Papers; M. R. Jackson Diary, Oct. 14, 1833. Alabama: Columbus Morrison Journal, Aug. 9, 1846. Mississippi: Ferdinand Lawrence Steele Diaries, Nov. 25, 1843; Ervin Diary, 1846–1848; Southall Diary, Nov. 22 and Dec. 9, 1855; correspondence in E. Grey Dimond and Herman Hattaway, eds., *Letters from Forest Place: A Plantation Family's Correspondence* (Jackson, MS, 1993). Tennessee: Carney Diary, Apr. 10, 1859; Sophia Hunt to Jeanne and Lizzie Hunt, Aug. 12, 1860. In six months of 1837, Susan Nye Hutchinson, a Presbyterian, attended Episcopal and Methodist services and took communion with the Lutherans: Hutchinson Journal, Apr. 16, July 23, Oct. 15, 18, 22, 1837.

Islam and Muhammad: The literature of the Muslim Near East attracted attention among the literati, who made an effort to appreciate its achievements. Southerners who wrote on the Middle Ages noted the extensive contributions of the Muslims to the rekindling of European civilization. See "Arabian Literature," *SLM*, 6 (1840), 457–60, 760–2, and 7 (1841), 113–16, as well as in subsequent volumes. For the "gallant Saladin" see Philip Slaughter [of

Virginia], "John Caldwell Calhoun," *American Whig Review,* 11 (1850), 169; for Saladin as knight see Emily Wharton Sinkler to Thomas Isaac Wharton, Apr. 25, 1851, in Anne Sinkler Whaley LeClerq, ed., *Between North and South: The Letters of Emily Wharton Sinkler, 1842–1865* (Columbia, SC, 2001), 153. For a respectful account of the Muslims in Tripoli in the eighteenth and early nineteenth century, see the five-part article by [Robert Greenhow], "Sketches of the History and Present Condition of Tripoli," *SLM* (1834–35). For commentary on Tasso's treatment of the Muslims see Bernard Knox, "Liberating a Masterpiece," *New York Review of Books* (May 17, 2001), 58. Muslim and Christian chroniclers of the Crusades dreadfully caricatured each other's religion: see Francesco Gabrieli, ed., *Arab Historians of the Crusades,* tr. by Gabrieli from the Arabic and retranslated from the Italian by E. J. Costello (Berkeley, CA, 1984), xvii.

For Islamic contributions to the development of European chivalry and the softening of a violent European society, see Herbert Butterfield, *Christianity in European History* (London, 1952), 31–2. Even in the twelfth century, William of Tyre wrote a history of the Crusades that paid tribute to Muslim valor and to Saladin and others: see Herbert Butterfield, "Historiography," *DHI,* 2:474. Frequently, writers dismissed Muhammad as a fraud: see e.g. "Rationalism False and Unreasonable," *SPR,* 16 (1863), 179. Islam made no converts among white Southerners we know of, but John Randolph confessed to having flirted with the doctrines of Islam as a young man: [N. B. Tucker], ed., "Mss. of John Randolph," *SLM,* 2 (1836), 463.

Voltaire, Gibbon, and other Enlightenment anticlericals presented Muhammad in a generally favorable light – primarily to denigrate Christianity. For a brief review of the shifting image of Muhammad in the Christian West see Gabriel Said Reynolds, "Muhammad through Christian Eyes," *Books and Culture: A Christian Review,* 8 (Jan./Feb. 2002), 6–8. Gibbon pricked southern consciences by noting that Muhammad forbade the separation of slave children from their mothers: see William Henry Milburn, *Ten Years of Preacher-Life: Chapters from an Autobiography* (New York, 1859), 350; Edward Gibbon, *The History of the Decline and Fall of the Roman Empire,* ed. David Womersley, 3 vols. (London, 1994), 3:214. John Fletcher cited Gibbon on Muhammad, although he read Arabic and consulted the Koran and other works for his lengthy remarks on Islam in his *Studies on Slavery, in Easy Lessons* (Natchez, MS, 1852), esp. 388. Emma LeConte, among others, read about Muhammad in Gibbon and also dipped into the Koran: June 27, 1864, in Earl Schenck Miers, ed., *When the World Ended: The Diary of Emma LeConte* (New York, 1957), 109. Charles Mills, whose books on chivalry and the Crusades were assigned in some southern schools, also lauded Saladin despite his opening description of "a compound of dignity and baseness." Mills followed with a "skilful general and a valiant soldier," who had a superior mind and was "simple in manners and unostentatious in deportment": *The History of the Crusades for the Recovery and Possession of the Holy Land* (Philadelphia, 1844), 169–70.

Israelite Servitude: On the ubiquity of slavery in Israel see also the liberal Theodore Clapp, *Slavery: A Sermon* (New Orleans, 1838), 8–14. For the abolitionists, see e.g. Charles Elliott, *Sinfulness of American Slavery: Proved from Its Evil Sources,* 2 vols. (New York, 1968 [1850]), repeatedly in both volumes, but see esp. 1:110; Albert Barnes, *An Inquiry into the Scriptural Views of Slavery* (Philadelphia, 1857), chs. 3 and 6; [George Bourne], *A Condensed Anti-Slavery Bible Argument; By a Citizen of Virginia* (New York, 1845), 39–41, 49–53. For temporary and permanent Israelite slaves in proslavery polemics, see Charles A. Farley, *Slavery; A Discourse Delivered in the Unitarian Church, Richmond, Va.* (Richmond, VA, 1835), 9; [William Hobby], *Remarks upon Slavery, Occasioned by Attempts Made to Circulate Improper Publications in the Southern States. By a Citizen of Georgia,* 2nd ed. (Augusta,

GA, 1835), 9; Alexander McCaine, *Slavery Defended against the Attacks of the Abolition-ists* (Baltimore, 1842), 9; [Patrick Mell], *Slavery. A Treatise Showing that Slavery Is Neither a Moral, Political, nor Social Evil* (Pennfield, GA, 1844), 9–10; [Rev.] George Junkin, *The Integrity of Our National Union vs. Abolitionism: An Argument from the Bible* (Cincinnati, 1843), 30–6; Thornton Stringfellow, "Bible Argument," in E. N. Elliott, ed., *Cotton Is King, and Pro-Slavery Arguments* (New York, 1969 [1860]), 468–9; Thomas R. R. Cobb, *An In-quiry into the Law of Negro Slavery in the United States* (New York, 1968 [1858]), xxx, viii, xl; [Samuel J. Cassells], *Servitude and the Duty of Masters to Their Servants* (Norfolk, VA, 1843), 2; T. C. Thornton, *An Inquiry into the History of Slavery* (Washington, DC, 1841), 55–6; Samuel Davies Baldwin, *Dominion; Or, the Unity and Trinity of the Human Race* (Nashville, TN, 1858), 57; Sebastian G. Messmer, ed., *The Works of the Right Rev. John England, First Bishop of Charleston,* 7 vols. (Cleveland, OH, 1908), 5:198–200; J. H. Gibbon, "The Institution of Slavery in Accordance with the Moral Law," *DBR,* 17 (1854), 410–11; R. S. Breck, "Duties of Masters," *SPR,* 8 (1855), 271; "Slavery," *SPR,* 9 (1856), 345–55; [Maurice Mayer], "Slave Laws of the Jews," *RM,* 5 (1859), 98–9; George S. Sawyer, *Southern Institutes; Or, an Inquiry into the Origin and Early Prevalence of Slavery and the Slave Trade* (New York, 1967 [1858]), 29–42, 67. On free labor in the Near East see Muham-mad A. Dandamaev, *Slavery in Babylonia, from Nabopolassar to Alexander,* tr. Victorian Powell, rev. ed. (DeKalb, IL, 1984), 112–13.

The antislavery George M. Stroud acknowledged two types of servitude in *A Sketch of the Laws Relating to Slavery in the Several States of the United States of America,* 2nd ed. (New York, 1966 [1856; 1st ed., 1827]), 42. For the recognition of the two types of servitude in Is-rael by anti-abolitionist Northerners, see Nehemiah Adams, *South-Side View of Slavery; Or, Three Months at the South in 1854* (New York, 1969 [1854]), 190–1; John Henry Hopkins, *A Scriptural, Ecclesiastical, and Historical View of Slavery from the Days of the Patriarch Abra-ham to the Nineteenth Century* (New York, 1864), 74–5, 136; Samuel Seabury, *American Slavery Distinguished from the Slavery of English Theorists and Justified by the Law of Na-ture* (New York, 1861), ch. 14; N. L. Rice in J. Blanchard and N. L. Rice, *A Debate on Slavery* (New York, 1969 [1846]), 266. For a brief, balanced, modern review see W. N. Kerr, "Slav-ery," in Walter A. Elwell, ed., *Evangelical Dictionary of Theology* (Grand Rapids, MI, 1999), 1021–2. On the difference between indentured Israelites and foreign slaves see Isaac Mendel-sohn, *Slavery in the Ancient Near East* (New York, 1949), 87–91; Paul Flesher, *Oxen, Women, or Citizens: Slaves in the System of the Mishnah* (Atlanta, GA, 1988); Max Weber, *Ancient Judaism,* tr. and ed. Hans H. Gerth and Don Martingale (Glencoe, IL, 1952), xviii, 6, 18, 27, 31, 63–7, 111; John Van Seters, "The Law of the Hebrew Slave," *Zeitschrift für die alttesta-mentliche Wissenschaft,* 108 (1996), 534–46. See the strong summary discussion in Richard N. Longenecker, *New Testament Social Ethics for Today* (Grand Rapids, MI, 1984), 48–51.

Edwin Yamauchi remarks that one of the three men who endured the fiery furnace in Daniel was Abednego ("slave of Nego"): "Slaves of God," *Bulletin of the Evangelical The-ological Society,* 9 (1966), 32–3, 38–40. Yamauchi also suggests that the rendering of *ebed* and *doulos* in the King James version of the Bible as "servants" and the suppression of the word "slave" probably reflected the distaste for slavery among Englishmen (31–49). See also Walter C. Kaiser, "Ebed, Slave, Servant," in R. Laird Harris et al., eds., *Theological Word-book of the Old Testament* (Chicago, 1980), 2:1553; Eugene Carpenter, "Ebed," in Willem A. Van Gemeren, ed., *New International Dictionary of Old Testament Theology and Exege-sis* (Grand Rapids, MI, 1997), 3:62–9.

Jacobinism: Carolinians were not troubled when J. B. Thrasher found the origins of abo-litionism in the Jacobin Clubs of France and "the bloody reign of Robespierre." Thrasher raged: "The very dregs of society got possession of the government, and administered it, not only for the destruction of royalty, but of aristocracy, morality and religion." Thrasher, *Slavery: A Divine Institution* (Port Gibson, MS, 1861), 4. George S. Sawyer threw Infidels, Socialists, Non-Resistants, and Free-Thinkers into one undifferentiated group, labeling them "our Jacobins and Montagnards": *Southern Institutes; Or, an Inquiry into the Origin and Early Prevalence of Slavery and the Slave Trade* (New York, 1967 [1858]), 384. The secrecy of the Know-Nothings gave the Democrats an opportunity to refer to them as "Jacobins": W. Darrell Overdyke, *The Know-Nothing Party in the South* (Baton Rouge, LA, 1950), 78.

Josephus: Flavius Josephus' works, first published in English translation in 1737, went through numerous editions. During the eighteenth century, Josephus was a standard in private libraries and was available in bookstores: Richard Beale Davis, *Intellectual Life in the Colonial South, 1515–1763*, 3 vols. (Knoxville, TN, 1978), 2:506; Louis B. Wright, "The 'Gentleman's Library' in Early Virginia: The Literary Interests of the First Carters," *Huntington Library Quarterly*, 1 (1937/38), 15, 26; Henry Boley, *Lexington in Old Virginia* (Richmond, VA, 1936), 26; Walter B. Edgar, "Some Popular Books in Colonial South Carolina," *South Carolina Historical Magazine*, 72 (1971), 178; Stephen B. Weeks, *Libraries and Literature in North Carolina in the Eighteenth Century* (Washington, DC, 1896: "Annual Report of the American Historical Association for the Year 1895"), 221; Charles L. Coon, ed., *North Carolina Schools and Academies: A Documentary History, 1790–1840* (Raleigh, NC, 1915), 785; Frank Luther Mott, *Golden Multitudes: The Story of Best Sellers in the United States* (New York, 1947), 59, 305; for sales of Josephus in Charleston see Hennig Cohen, *The South Carolina Gazette, 1732–1775* (Columbia, SC, 1953), 136, 137, 143; also, Joseph Tower Wheeler, "Books Owned by Marylanders, 1700–1776," *Maryland Historical Magazine*, 35 (1940), 349; "Library of Edmund Berkeley, Esq.," *WMQ*, 2 (1894), 250; "Libraries in Colonial Virginia," *WMQ*, 2 (1894), 171. Two thousand copies of Josephus were published in Cincinnati in 1838: "Cincinnati Book Trade," *Baltimore Literary Monument*, 2 (1839), 188.

Among scattered nineteenth-century yeomen references to Josephus see Feb. 12, 1862, and Feb. 1, 1863, in William R. Snell, ed., *Myra Inman: A Diary of the Civil War in East Tennessee* (Macon, GA, 2000), 138, 184; Oct. 5, 1861, in Paul D. Escott, ed., *North Carolina Yeoman: The Diary of Basil Armstrong Thomasson, 1853–1862* (Athens, GA, 1996), 316. For Josephus' influence on southern discussions of Noah's curse see Stephen R. Haynes, *Noah's Curse: The Biblical Justification of American Slavery* (New York, 2002), 94–7, and Benjamin Braude, "The Sons of Noah and the Construction of Ethnic and Geographical Identities in the Medieval and Early Modern Periods," *WMQ*, 3rd ser., 54 (1997), 112. Josephus coined "Theokratia," the term most southern commentators accepted: Jehoshua Amir, "Josephus on the 'Mosaic Constitution,'" in Henning Graf Reventlow et al., eds., *Politics and Theopolitics in the Bible and Biblical Literature* (Sheffield, U.K., 1994), 13–27.

For positive citations of Josephus see Jasper Adams, *Elements of Moral Philosophy* (Philadelphia, 1837), 265; J. L. Reynolds, *Church Polity: Or, the Kingdom of Christ in Its Internal and External Development,* 2nd ed. (Richmond, VA, 1849), 25, 171; *DBR*, 16 (1854), 132; Theodore Clapp, "Sermon," New Orleans *Daily Picayune*, Aug. 5, 1849; W. T. Hamilton, "The Character of Moses," *SPR*, 18 (1852), 506–7; Mitchell King, *The History and Culture of the Olive* (Charleston, SC, 1846), 14; "Beta", "Cartwright on Negroes," *SQR*, n.s., 6 (1852), 60; Isaac Denton, "Egyptian Archeology," *QRMECS*, 6 (1852), 52; A. J. Roane, "Reply to Abolitionist Objections to Slavery," *DBR*, 20 (1856), 649; Thomas R. R. Cobb, *An Inquiry into the Law of Negro Slavery in the United States* (New York, 1968 [1858]), xl–xli, lxxviii; W. N. Pendleton, *Science: A Witness for the Bible* (Philadelphia, 1860), 118; Thomas Atkinson, *On the Cause of Our National Troubles: A Sermon Delivered in St. James*

Church, Wilmington, N.C. (Wilmington, NC, 1861), 7; Mary E. Moragné Journal, Mar. 24, 1839, in Delle Mullen Craven, ed., *The Neglected Thread: A Journal of the Calhoun Community* (Columbia, SC, 1951), 115; Samuel Agnew Diary, Nov. 8, 1863, at UNC-SHC. Stuart Robinson, *Slavery, as Recognized in the Mosaic Civil Law* (Toronto, 1865), 31. A master in Virginia named a slave Josephus: Dabney Herndon Maury, *Recollections of a Virginian in the Mexican, Indian, and Civil Wars,* electronic edition (Chapel Hill, NC, 1998 [1894]), 4.

One writer accused Josephus and Philo of sacrificing Hebrew nationality to Greek culture in "Mutual Influence of National Literatures," *SQR,* 12 (1847), 311, and Benjamin Morgan Palmer referred to him as a "time-serving politician": [Palmer], "Import of Hebrew History," *SPR,* 9 (1856), 583. Thomas DeQuincy's assault on Josephus' character got a hearing in [Editor's Table], *RM,* 2 (1857/58), 179–80. But for appreciation of Josephus' accommodation to Rome as the only sensible policy left to the Jews, see R. Kemp, "The Destruction of Jerusalem," *Baltimore Literary Monument,* 2 (1839), 205–7. For use and abuse of Josephus by Christian and Jewish writers, see Steve Mason, *Josephus and the New Testament* (Peabody, MA, 1992), ch. 1. For Josephus' apologia see *The Jewish War,* tr. G. A. Williamson, ed. E. Mary Smallwood (New York, 1970), ch. 12.

Kossuth: The editors of *Southern Quarterly Review* pronounced Kossuth a wonderful speaker who captivated his audiences: *SQR,* n.s., 10 (1854), 272. President Junkin of Washington College praised "the noble Kossuth": George Junkin, *Progress of the Age: An Address Delivered before the Literary Societies of Washington College* (Philadelphia, 1851), 19. *Southern Literary Messenger* published a poem that hailed Kossuth as a "valiant leader of the brave": *SLM,* 16 (1850), 61. John Esten Cooke of Virginia wrote a review essay on Hungary, tracing its history and its struggle for what he considered national rights and defending the liberal character of the revolution of 1848. In addition he contributed a poem, "To Kossuth," that celebrated Kossuth as a hero: [Cooke], "Hungary," *SLM,* 17 (1851), 505–16; see also, "C. J. S.", "Austrian Politics," *SLM,* 18 (1852), 544, and John O. Beatty, *John Esten Cooke, Virginian* (New York, 1922), 24.

William Gilmore Simms, citing Smith's *Kossuth and His Mission,* remarked, "The Hungarians humbugged the Americans, and the Americans humbugged the Hungarians." The European radicals, he suggested, were seeking to spread revolution everywhere, but Kossuth's vanity prevented his seeing that Americans were having none of it. Yet even Simms paid tribute to the oratorical abilities of a remarkable man: [Simms], "Critical Notices," *SQR,* n.s., 5 (1852), 256; 8 (1853), 531; 10 (1854), 272. Kossuth's speeches were still being read in Virginia in the mid-1850s: see Diary, Dec. 16, 1854, in Charles W. Turner, *Captain Greenlee Davidson, C.S.A.: Diary and Letters, 1851–1863* (Verona, VA, 1975), 13.

Protestant leaders of the Northwest did not disguise their approval of Kossuth's anti-Catholicism, but they became increasingly wary of what they perceived as his Deism: Wesley Norton, *Religious Newspapers in the Old Northwest to 1861: A History, Bibliography, and Record of Opinion* (Athens, OH, 1977), 106. For northern Protestant reactions and Kossuth's anti-Catholicism, see also Mark Y. Hanley, *Beyond a Christian Commonwealth: The Protestant Quarrel with the American Republic, 1830–1860* (Chapel Hill, NC, 1994), 69–70. The virulent anti-Catholicism of the abolitionists had an indirect effect, for national Catholic spokesmen and organizations were denouncing Kossuth while Horace Greeley was praising him: see W. Darrell Overdyke, *The Know-Nothing Party in the South* (Baton Rouge, LA, 1950), 211–12.

Lesage and Rabelais: For circulation of Lesage see Joseph Tower Wheeler, "Books Owned by Marylanders, 1700–1776," *Maryland Historical Magazine,* 35 (1940), 350; "Minutes of the

Board of Trustees," in R. D. W. Connor et al., eds., *A Documentary History of the University of North Carolina, 1776–1799*, 2 vols. (Chapel Hill, NC, 1953), 2:431; George K. Smart, "Private Libraries in Colonial Virginia," *American Literature*, 10 (1938), 35; Charles L. Coon, ed., *North Carolina Schools and Academies: A Documentary History, 1790–1840* (Raleigh, NC, 1915), 765, 772; Philip Alexander Bruce, *History of the University of Virginia, 1819–1919: The Lengthening Shadow of One Man*, 5 vols. (New York, 1920–22), 1:343; Henry Boley, *Lexington in Old Virginia* (Richmond, VA, 1936), 159; [Nathaniel Beverley Tucker], "The Present State of Europe," *SQR*, 16 (1850), 289; B. L. Gildersleeve, "Devil on Two Sticks," Richmond *Examiner*, Nov. 26, 1863, and "Foreign Commerce," Richmond *Examiner*, Feb. 19, 1864, in Ward W. Briggs, Jr., ed., *Soldier and Scholar: Basil Laneau Gildersleeve and the Civil War* (Charlottesville, VA, 1998), 167, 252; [James Johnston Pettigrew], *Notes on Spain and the Spaniards in the Summer of 1850, with a Glance at Sardinia* (Charleston, SC, 1861), 96, 234 (on *Gil Blas*); on Mitchell King see John Belton O'Neall, *Biographical Sketches of the Bench and Bar of South Carolina*, 2 vols. (Charleston, SC, 1859), 1, 374; Tryphena Fox to Anna Rose Holder, Aug. 16, 1858, and Sept. 5, 1858, in Wilma King, ed., *A Northern Woman in the Plantation South: Letters of Tryphena Blanche Holder Fox, 1856–1876* (Columbia, SC, 1993), 80; *SQR*, n.s., 3 (1851), 73. Albert Sidney Johnston read carefully but not extensively; *Gil Blas* made his list along with Shakespeare and Dickens: William Preston Johnston, *The Life of General Albert Sidney Johnston* (New York, 1997 [1879]), 152. For Lesage's *Devil upon Two Sticks* see also [Editor's Table], *RM*, 2 (1857/58), 177. J. Hampden Chamberlayn lauded Lesage's style as quintessentially French, much as Gibbon's was English: "Essay on American Literature" (M.A. thesis, 1858, typescript at UVA). Rosalie Roos, on her travels in the 1850s, reported that a lowcountry planter's library included *Gil Blas* as well as Dante in the original languages: Rosalie Roos to Ulrika Roos, Dec. 2, 1853, in Roos, *Travels in America, 1851–1855*, tr. Carl L. Anderson (Carbondale, IL, 1982), 99. Also reading *Gil Blas* was Julia March Patterson of Crawford County, Georgia: J. M. Patterson Journal, 1850, at UNC-SHC. Randolph, Wirt, and Munford – among the best educated men in early national Virginia – read *Gil Blas*, which became especially popular in America toward the end of the eighteenth century: see Richard Beale Davis, *Intellectual Life in Jefferson's Virginia, 1790–1830* (Chapel Hill, NC, 1964), 111–12, and Frank Luther Mott, *Golden Multitudes: The Story of Best Sellers in the United States* (New York, 1947), 41, 24, 56.

Rabelais' southern fans said little beyond testimonies to the great fun he provided. Rabelais was selling in Charleston during 1730–70: Hennig Cohen, *The South Carolina Gazette, 1732–1775* (Columbia, SC, 1953), ch. 11. James Warley Miles and the McCords read Rabelais, Miles with high praise and the McCords probably in agreement. See also William Harris Bragg, *De Renne: Three Generations of a Georgia Family* (Athens, GA, 1999), 22. Basil Gildersleeve contributed an admiring reference to "the playful perseverance of a Rabelais": Gildersleeve, "Devil on Two Sticks," loc. cit., 167. George Frederick Holmes complained that he was little known, and he treated Rabelais – as Wilde treated Tasso, and other Southerners treated Dante – as a quasi-Protestant: [Holmes], "Life and Writings of Rabelais," *SQR*, 7 (1845), 124–52. Holmes also invoked Rabelais in a satirical remark on the pretensions of science and German idealist philosophy that Miles lovingly approved. See Miles to McCord, June 16 and 24, 1851, in J. H. Easterby, comp., "Letters of James Warley Miles to David James McCord," *South Carolina Historical and Genealogical Magazine*, 44 (1942), 192; [George Frederick Holmes], "Philosophy and Faith," *MMQR*, 4th ser., 3 (1851), 214. On Tasso as quasi-Protestant, see the nominally Catholic Richard Henry Wilde, *Conjectures and Researches Concerning the Love, Madness, and Imprisonment of Torquato Tasso*, 2 vols. (New York, 1842), 2:ch. 3.

Macaulay: Macaulay's prestige and following would be hard to exaggerate; among English-language historical works, his *History* became the all-time best seller: James Westfall Thompson, *A History of Historical Writing*, 2 vols. (Gloucester, MA, 1967 [1942]), 2:298. For praise of Macaulay and Carlyle see "Carlyle and Macaulay," *SLM*, 14 (1848), 476; *SLM*, 15 (1849), 187. Edmund Ruffin referred to Macaulay as "this most attractive writer within my knowledge," who made charming and instructive what others made dry and repulsive: Oct. 22, 1861, in *ERD*, 2:150–1. Richard K. Crallé admired Macaulay's willingness to give offense by speaking his mind: Crallé to Calhoun, July 25, 1849, in *JCCP*, 26:520. Macaulay was Sarah Morgan's "favorite of all writers, ancient and modern": Dec. 12, 1862, in Charles East, ed., *The Civil War Diary of Sarah Morgan* (Athens, GA, 1991), 367. Catherine Edmonston's family read his *History*, and she found his review of a biography of Warren Hastings "masterly": July 25, 1862, and June 14, 1863, in Beth G. Crabtree and James Welch Patton, eds., *"Journal of a Secesh Lady": The Diary of Catherine Devereux Edmonston, 1860–1866* (Raleigh, NC, 1979), 223, 432; Everard Green Baker, a planter, read the "impartial" Macaulay aloud to his wife Laura: E. G. Baker Diary, Sept. 27, 1849, at UNC-SHC. Among others who read Macaulay's history and essays with great interest were Henry Hughes and James Chesnut: see Douglas Ambrose, *Henry Hughes and Proslavery Thought in the Old South* (Baton Rouge, LA, 1996), 192. William Browne, who moved in the Chesnut circle in wartime Richmond, knew Macaulay well enough to catch Charles Sumner in messing up quotations from him: Chesnut Diary, Mar. 1861 and June 12, 1865, in C. Vann Woodward, ed., *Mary Chesnut's Civil War* (New Haven, CT, 1981), 26, 826. See also Mitchell King Diary, 1852, at USC; Samuel Agnew Diary, May 30, 1863, at UNC-SHC; C. C. Jones, Jr., to C. C. Jones, June 8, 1850, in Robert Manson Myers, ed., *A Georgian at Princeton* (New York, 1976), 94; for the Reverend John S. Grasty see W. S. Powell, *When the Past Refused to Die: A History of Carwell County, North Carolina, 1777–1977* (Durham, NC, 1977), 409; Emily Wharton Sinkler to Henry Wharton, Feb. 28, 1848, in Anne Sinkler Whaley LeClerq, ed., *Between North and South: The Letters of Emily Wharton Sinkler, 1842–1865* (Columbia, SC, 2001), 100; June 3–4, 1863, in Cynthia DeHaven Pitcock and Bill J. Hurley, eds., *I Acted from Principle: The Civil War Diary of Dr. William M. McPheeters, Confederate Surgeon in the Trans-Mississippi* (Fayetteville, AR, 2002), 23–4. Macaulay and Caesar influenced William Wells Brown's views on the ancient Egyptians and ancient Britons: Wilson J. Moses, *Afrotopia: The Roots of African American Popular History* (Cambridge, MA, 1998), 63–4.

For a restrained defense of Macaulay on Bacon see "R. H. C.", "Thomas Babington Macaulay," *QRMECS*, 15 (1861), 210. Macaulay downplayed Bacon's contribution to the inductive method, ascribing it to a common sense applied in all ages. He also gave offense by dwelling upon the seamier side of Bacon's career: see Theodore Dwight Bozeman, *Protestants in an Age of Science: The Baconian Ideal and Antebellum American Religious Thought* (Chapel Hill, NC, 1977), 27, 73. Another critic rebuked Macaulay for his ill treatment of Socrates: *SQR*, 5 (1844), 251–2. Macaulay attacked Hume as a biased historian, but Joseph B. Cobb of Longwood, Mississippi, hurled that very charge at Macaulay: "J. B. C." [Cobb], "Macaulay's History of England," *American Whig Review*, 11 (1850), 347–69. When Daniel K. Whitaker accused British historians of being driven by political bias, he probably had Macaulay as well as Hume in mind. It was Macaulay who declared facts "the dross of history" and proclaimed the historian an advocate, not a judge: see [Whitaker], "English Views of the Literature and Literary Men, and of the Political and Domestic Character of the People of Ancient Greece and Rome," *SLJ*, 1 (1836), 418.

"Marseilles": *Southern Literary Messenger* published a translation – J. E. Leigh [of Memphis, TN], "The Marseilles Hymn: A Translation," *SLM*, 15 (1849), 634–5 – and their Paris correspondent declared it the first good English translation: [William W. Mann], "From Our Paris Correspondent," *SLM*, 16 (1850), 293. In 1850 *De Bow's Review* published a new – and wretched – translation of the "Marseilles": "Z.", "The Marseilles Hymn," *DBR*, 9 (1850), 346–7. During the slave insurrection panic that swept Mississippi in 1835, emergency measures included "committees of safety": Dunbar Rowland, ed. *Mississippi: Comprising Sketches of Counties, Towns, Events, Institutions, and Persons, Arranged in Cyclopedic Form*, 4 vols. (Spartanburg, SC, 1976 [1907]), 2:372–3.

Medieval Studies: Paul Tillich lamented the failure of Romanticism's organicism to take hold in America as it did in Europe, but like so many others he ignored the experience of the Old South: *A History of Christian Thought, from Its Judaic and Hellenistic Origins to Existentialism*, ed. Carl E. Braaten (New York, 1972), 380–4, 443. Nineteenth-century Romantics constructed a medieval Golden Age to support a utopian vision, and in so doing they elaborated a specifically political critique of the present. A spate of medieval romances and the work of Bishop Richard Hurd, among others, revived interest in medieval history and literature. The medieval romances fed antirepublican biases and inspired a romantic poetry that turned in both conservative and radical directions. See John M. Ganim, "Myth of Medieval Romance," in R. Howard Bloch and Stephen G. Nichols, ed., *Medievalism and the Modernist Temper* (Baltimore, 1995), 148–66. The very idea of "Middle Ages" did not appear until the fourteenth-century Renaissance, and it became an ideological football thereafter: Toby Burrows, "Unmaking 'The Middle Ages,' " *Journal of Medieval History*, 7 (1981), 127–34; Fred C. Robinson, "Medieval, the Middle Ages," *Speculum*, 59 (1984), 745–6. For British attitudes see James Westfall Thompson, *A History of Historical Writing*, 2 vols. (Gloucester, MA, 1967 [1942]), 2:280. These ideas were even reflected in the papers of southern college students: Bernard M. G. Reardon, *Religion in the Age of Romanticism: Studies in Early Nineteenth Century Thought* (Cambridge, U.K., 1985), 11–12. For an example of student papers see William Allen, "Progress of Literature," *VUM*, 3 (1859), 133. Medieval history as well as theology and philosophy had an especially prominent place in the curricula of the theological seminaries. In teaching church history, for example, Robert L. Dabney lectured on the development of "Popery," the Crusades, and the relation of feudalism to the church. See Thomas Cary Johnson, ed. *Life and Letters of Robert Lewis Dabney* (Carlisle, PA, 1977), 141.

Meek: Alexander Beaufort Meek (1814–1865), born in South Carolina, achieved a reputation as a legal scholar; was appointed assistant secretary of the Treasury by Polk; edited the Mobile *Register*; and served in the Alabama legislature in the 1850s. Simms celebrated Meek and his *Red Eagle* in *Magnolia*, 4 (1843), 399, and in "The Red Eagle of Muscoghee," *SWMR*, 2 (1845), 119–20. The most polished circles in Mobile read aloud Meek's *Songs and Poems of the South*, and President Mirabeau B. Lamar of the Republic of Texas, himself referred to as "the Poet Laureate of the Southwest," much admired Meek's *Red Eagle*. See Frances Gibson Satterfield, *Madame Le Vert: A Biography of Octavia Walton Le Vert* (Edisto Island, SC, 1987), 53; Philip Graham, *The Life and Poems of Mirabeau B. Lamar* (Chapel Hill, NC, 1938), 82, 88. In 1845 *Southern Quarterly Review* referred to Meek's "admirable" address to the student societies at Franklin College, alluding to his considerable influence in the South: review of A. B. Meek's *Americanism in Literature* in *SQR*, 7 (1845), 257–8. Meek's appraisal of the Indian experience as historical tragedy attracted the attention of Daniel K. Whitaker, who excerpted Meek's lecture: "From Our Arm-Chair," *SLJ*, n.s., 1 (1837), 185. Mary Henderson Eastman of Virginia – primarily known for *Aunt Phyllis's Cabin*, a reply to *Uncle Tom's Cabin* – wrote several novels about Indians and the frontier in which she portrayed the Indians as a worthy people at bay.

Michelet and Thiers: Southerners had mixed feelings about Michelet. They appreciated his conscious effort to portray the feelings of the people and his campaign for acceptance of oral tradition as an essential historical source. Benjamin Faneuil Porter of Alabama, as well as Cobb, drew upon Michelet for slavery and serfdom in French history: Porter, *The Past and the Present* (Tuscaloosa, AL, 1845), 25–6; Thomas R. R. Cobb, "Historical Sketch of Slavery," in Cobb, *An Inquiry into the Law of Negro Slavery in the United States* (New York, 1968 [1858]), ch. 7. *Southern Quarterly Review,* raving over Michelet's originality and profundity, regretted that his work on Luther was not always impartial and just and dismissed his history of the Roman Republic as largely fanciful and naive in its use of sources: [D. F. Jamison?], "Critical Notices," *SQR,* 7 (1845), 525; 10 (1846), 254; 11 (1847), 504–8. In 1843, George Frederick Holmes placed Michelet astride the nineteenth century: "Schlegel's Philosophy of History," in Michael O'Brien, ed., *All Clever Men, Who Make Their Way: Critical Discourse in the Old South* (Fayetteville, AR, 1982), 182, 191. William Gilmore Simms extolled Michelet as a fine philosophical historian who knew the difference between fact and fiction: [Simms], "Prescott's Conquest of Peru," *SQR,* 13 (1848), 138; see also David Moltke-Hansen, "Ordered Progress: The Historical Philosophy of William Gilmore Simms," in John Caldwell Guilds, ed., *"Long Years of Neglect": The Work and Reputation of William Gilmore Simms* (Fayetteville, AR, 1988). Among those who read Michelet's *Histoire de France* was Emma LeConte: June 27, 1864, in Earl Schenck Miers, ed., *When the World Ended: The Diary of Emma LeConte* (New York, 1957), 109. E. D. E. De Leon and John Reuben Thompson found Michelet an "original thinker" and "brilliant": [De Leon], *SQR,* 8 (1845), 525; [Thompson], *SLM,* 29 (1859), 79. Edmund Ruffin dissented: Mar. 25, 1865, in *ERD,* 3:818.

Before Thiers emerged as a prominent politician under the July Monarchy, he wrote a history of the Revolution, which he called "une arme de guerre" against the Bourbon Restoration. He may have been pleased with his polemic, but critics pummeled him for factual inaccuracies. Thiers took greater pains in his multivolume *Histoire du Consulat et de l'Empire,* the work generally cited by Southerners. See James Westfall Thompson, *History of Historical Writing* (Gloucester, MA, 1967 [1942]), 2:247–8; *SQR,* 1 (1842), 294; W. C. Rives, *Discourse on the Use and Importance of History* (Richmond, VA, 1847), 52–3. Among Thiers's readers was Petigru: see James Petigru Carson, *Life, Letters and Speeches of James Louis Petigru: Union Man of South Carolina* (Washington, DC, 1920), 250; "B. H. B." [of LaGrange, GA], "The Consulate," *QRMECS,* 2 (1848), 442–51; E. Grey Dimond and Herman Hattaway, eds., *Letters from Forest Place: A Plantation Family's Correspondence, 1846–1881* (Jackson, MS, 1993), 3–4.

Modern Historians of the Ancient World – *Gillies*: On Gillies see Frank M. Turner, *The Greek Heritage in Victorian Britain* (New Haven, CT, 1981), 189, 192; Dickson D. Bruce, Jr., "The Conservative Use of History in Early National Virginia," *Southern Studies,* 19 (1980), 134; J. Jefferson Looney and Ruth L. Woodward, eds., *Princetonians, 1791–1994* (Princeton, NJ, 1991), 57–8; George S. Sawyer, *Southern Institutes; Or, an Inquiry into the Origin and Early Prevalence of Slavery and the Slave Trade* (New York, 1967 [1858]), Essay III; also, "Autobiography of Wiley P. Harris," in Dunbar Rowland, *Courts, Judges, and Lawyers of Mississippi, 1798–1935* (Jackson, MS, 1935), 278. For Gillies on the superiority of Greek religion to its pre-Christian competitors, see [D. K. Whitaker], "English Views of Literature and Literary Men," *SLJ,* 1 (1836), 420.

Grote: Students also got Grote's views indirectly as popularized in William Smith's textbook, *A History of Greece from the Earliest Times to the Roman Conquest,* revised and edited by George W. Greene (New York, 1859 [1854]): see [Holmes], "Greece and Its History," *QRMECS,* 9 (1855), 39, 43. Holmes considered Bishop C. C. Thirlwall's work the first "singularly accurate and learned History of Greece": [Holmes], "Cimon and Pericles," *SQR*, n.s., 3 (1851), 341. Holmes respected Thirlwall for painstaking research that prepared the way for Grote, but he criticized Thirlwall as dull, tedious, and inadequate work: see "Greece and Its History," 40–3, quote at 40, and "Grote's History of Greece," *SQR*, n.s. (3rd), 2 (1856), 89–92.

Merivale: Among popular histories of Rome accessible to the general public, Holmes recommended Thomas Arnold's, which also had Simms's endorsement in "Critical Notices," *SQR*, 5 (1852), 224–7. Holmes dismissed Charles Merivale's ancient history as the "pains-taking, tedious and unsatisfactory production of an incompetent man." After the War, Holmes took a softer view but did not alter his basic judgment that Merivale's work had limited value. Holmes probably recoiled from Merivale's smugness; he certainly recoiled from his adulation of Julius Caesar: see [Holmes], "Napoleon III and Augustus Caesar," *SQR*, n.s., 10 (1854), 2; [Holmes], "Recent Histories of Julius Caesar," *SR* (Baltimore), 1 (1867), 397.

Niebuhr: In 1855 George Cornewall Lewis's *Inquiry into the Credibility of the Early Roman History* severely criticized Niebuhr's treatment of early Roman history, but this criticism had little impact in the South before the War. Joseph B. Cobb of Mississippi pronounced Livy "the prince of Roman historians" but conceded that Niebuhr and others had shown that his books were riddled with errors: "Roman Literature," *QRMECS*, 12 (1853), 95–6, quote at 95. For praise of Niebuhr's work on social classes and the need for a large, stable class of small and middling propertyholders, see "Constitution of France," *SQR*, 16 (1850), 518–19.

Holmes respectfully dissented from Niebuhr on the early period: [Holmes], "Ante-Roman Races of Italy," *SQR*, 7 (1845), 265–84. See the account of Niebuhr in Daniel C. Gilman, ed., *The Miscellaneous Writings of Francis Lieber*, 2 vols. (Philadelphia, 1881), 1:47–148. On Niebuhr's racial views see Ivan Hannaford, *Race: The History of an Idea in the West* (Washington, DC, 1996), 59, 62, 81, 235, and, generally, ch. 8. Among Niebuhr's other uses: the Baptist Reverend Sylvanus Landrum of Savannah, outraged by Yankee atrocities, invoked him on the brutality of war in *The Battle Is God's* (Savannah, GA, 1863), 9–10. Niebuhr's *History of Rome* was popular throughout the United States: George H. Calcott, *History in the United States, 1800–1860: Its Practice and Purpose* (Baltimore, 1970), 10. For Niebuhr's attitude toward the agrarian laws see Niebuhr, *History of Rome*, vol. 2 (esp. 80–6). Holmes especially credited Niebuhr with erasing the confusion that had surrounded the agrarian laws in relation to the public domain: [Holmes], "Niebuhr," *MMQR*, 4th ser., 7 (1855), 544. Niebuhr's emphasis on the redistribution of public, rather than private, land was duly noted in defenses of the Gracchi: George Tucker, "A Discourse on the Progress and Influence of Philosophy," *SLM*, 1 (1835), 418; "Progress of Civilization," *SQR*, 3 (1843), 12–13 and note.

The collapsing war effort in 1864 sent several women back to the reading of ancient history: Sarah Lois Wadley Private Journal, Jan. 14, 1864, at UNC-SHC; Mar. 20, 1864, in Beth G. Crabtree and James Welch Patton, eds., *"Journal of a Secesh Lady": The Diary of Catherine Devereux Edmonston, 1860–1866* (Raleigh, NC, 1979), 540; Mar. 8 and June 27, 1864, in Earl Schenck Miers, ed., *When the World Ended: The Diary of Emma LeConte* (Lincoln, NE, 1987), 75, 109–10. Sarah Morgan reread Niebuhr after finishing Plutarch: "Relish my pabulum so much that I propose to review Gillies and even Gibbon, so much for getting interested in a thing": Mar. 20, 1864, in Charles East, ed., *The Civil War Diary of Sarah Morgan* (Athens, GA, 1991), 540. But when Mary Chesnut listened with delight to a gentleman discuss Herodotus and Livy, she confessed that they did not know the texts well enough to evaluate all they heard: Chesnut Diary, Aug. 22, 1864, in C. Vann Woodward, ed., *Mary Chesnut's Civil War* (New Haven, CT, 1981), 314.

Rollin: For Rollin in women's schools see James Monroe Taylor, *Before Vassar Opened: A Contribution to the History of the Higher Education of Women in America* (Freeport, NY, 1972), 25. For other harsh comments on Rollin see "American Literature – 1," *SQR*, 11 (1847), 132–3; Henry Winter Davis [of Maryland] in Bernard C. Steiner, *Life of Henry Winter Davis* (Baltimore, 1916), 29; Thomas Tisdale, *A Lady of the High Hills: Natalie Delage Sumter* (Columbia, SC, 2001), 2. Franklin Smith drew on Rollin for his own account: Smith, "Origin of the American Indians," *DBR*, 3 (1847), 570. For Rollin's considerable impact in America see William Gribbin, "Rollin's Histories and American Republicanism," *WMQ*, 3rd ser., 29 (1972), 611–22, esp. 612–14; Meyer Reinhold, *Classica Americana: The Greek and Roman Heritage in the United States* (Detroit, 1984), 253. But Reinhold criticized Gribbin's excessive claims for Rollin: Reinhold, "Survey of the Scholarship on Classical Traditions in Early America," in John W. Eadie, ed., *Classical Traditions in Early America* (Ann Arbor, MI, 1976), 36; Herbert O. Pappas, "Enlightenment," *DHI*, 2:94. For Rollin see also "American Literature," *SQR*, 11 (1847), 117–67; H. Clay Pate, "Patriotic Discourse on Local and General History," *SRCR*, 2 (1852), 135–43; Darlene Harbour Unrue, "Edgar Allan Poe: The Romantic as Classicist," *International Journal of the Classical Tradition*, 1 (1995), 115. For Rollin and Goldsmith in Charleston bookstores, including abridgements, see Hennig Cohen, *The South Carolina Gazette, 1732–1775* (Columbia, SC, 1953), 133, 140, 155. On Rollin's early popularity see George K. Smart, "Private Libraries in Colonial Virginia," *American Literature*, 10 (1938), 39; Walter B. Edgar, "Some Popular Books in Colonial South Carolina," *South Carolina Historical Magazine*, 72 (1971), 177–8; Harry Clemons, *The Home Library of the Garnetts of "Elmwood"* (Charlottesville, VA, 1957), 7; Stephen B. Weeks, *Libraries and Literature in North Carolina in the Eighteenth Century* (Washington, DC, 1896: "Annual Report of the American Historical Association for the Year 1895"), 201–2, 221; Charles L. Coon, ed., *North Carolina Schools and Academies: A Documentary History, 1790–1840* (Raleigh, NC, 1915), 776–7, 795; Frank Luther Mott, *Golden Multitudes: The Story of Best Sellers in the United States* (New York, 1947), 59; Richard Beale Davis, *Intellectual Life in Jefferson's Virginia, 1790–1830* (Chapel Hill, NC, 1964), 78–83, 105, 112.

Mormons: The Mormons had a hard time in Missouri and Texas in part because they were unfairly accused of abolitionism. See Harrison Anthony Trexler, *Slavery in Missouri, 1804–1865* (Baltimore, 1914), 122–4; Lyle Wesley Dorsett, "Slaveholding in Jackson County, Missouri," *Missouri Historical Society Bulletin*, 20 (1963), 25–51; Michael Scot van Wagenen, *The Texas Republic and the Mormon Kingdom of God* (College Station, TX, 2002); also, Betty L. Fladeland, "Compensated Emancipation: A Rejected Alternative," *JSH*, 62 (1976), 183. On balance, Southerners condemned Mormonism as heresy while expressing admiration for the Mormons' heroic qualities and condemning efforts to crush them by force. For an indictment of Mormonism that also criticizes those who persecuted Mormons see [Edwin De Leon], "Rise and Progress of the Mormon Faith," *SLM*, 10 (1844), 526–38. See also *Weekly Messenger* (Greensborough, NC), June 29 and Feb. 19, 1852; Alexander MacKay, *The Western World; Or, Travels in the United States in 1846–1847*, 3 vols. (New York, 1968 [1849]), 2:151–2; E. G. Baker Diary, Sept. 25, 1855, at UNC-SHC; Aug. 15, 1862, in John F. Marszalek, ed., *The Diary of Miss Emma Holmes* (Baton Rouge, LA, 1979), 190; Elizabeth Silverthorne, *Ashbel Smith of Texas: Pioneer, Patriot, Statesman, 1805–1886* (College Station, TX, 1982), 69; Dismukes in Speeches of Graduates, 1853, at UNC-NCC; "Vindex", "Utah and the Mormons," *Oakland College Magazine*, 2 (1857), 1–8; F. C. Barber, "Mormonism in the United States," *DBR*, 16 (1854), 368–82. But for a sample of rough attacks see "The History of Mormonism," *SQR*, 1 (1842), 398–413; T. T. Castleman, "Address to the Literary Societies of Oakland College"(1859), 9, typescript at Oakland College; *The*

Backwoods Preacher: Being the Autobiography of Peter Cartwright (London, 1870), 168–74. Albert Sydney Johnston, who served in Utah, regarded Mormonism as a manifestation of the radicalism of the "dangerous classes": William Preston Johnston, *The Life of General Albert Sidney Johnston* (New York, 1997 [1879]), 195. To the applause of fellow bishops, Bishop Otey insisted that the United States was a Christian nation on which infidels and Mormons had no claims: "Proceedings of a Convention of the Trustees of a Proposed University of the Southern States," in Telfair Hodgson, ed., *Reprints of the Documents and Proceedings of the Board of Trustees of the University of the South Prior to 1860* (Sewanee, TN, 1888), 45, also report by J. F. Young, 24–5. John S. Preston of South Carolina, addressing Episcopalian bishops, referred to "the beastliness of Mormonism": "Address at the Laying of the Corner Stone," *University of the South Papers* (Sewanee, TN), ser. A, 1 (1860), 54. For a gratuitous attack on Mormon "ignoramuses" and moral degenerates in a generally well-reasoned article on women's education see A. H. Sands, "Intellectual Culture of Woman," *SLM*, 28 (1859), 326.

The Mormons borrowed their principal biblical argument from Martin Madan's late eighteenth-century *Thelypthora,* which denied that Jesus condemned polygamy. It was evident to them that polygamy manifested God's will in history and government, since the world's most long-lived societies had practiced it – a record of revealed truth offered a social law to guide mankind to good health. Mormons recalled that the radical Anabaptists practiced it at Münster and that the Nuremberg resolutions of 1650 saw it as a means of replenishing the population of Europe after the Thirty Years' War; see esp. B. Carmon Hardy, *Solemn Covenant* (Urbana, IL, 1992). Orson Pratt led the Mormon apologists for polygamy with writings that combined historical and biblical arguments: see Philip L. Barlow, *Mormons and the Bible: The Place of the Latter-Day Saints in American Religion* (New York, 1991), 84–5.

Napoleon – Southern Assessments: "All Americans," announced J. L. Fremantle, an Englishman with the Confederate army, "have an intense admiration for Napoleon; they seldom scruple to express their regret that he was beaten at Waterloo": May 21, 1863, in A. J. L. Fremantle, *Three Months in the Southern States: The 1863 Diary of an English Soldier, April–June 1863* (London, 1863), 121. Napoleon has been the subject of more books than anyone except Jesus: Paul Johnson, *Napoleon* (New York, 2002), 4. *Harper's Monthly* attracted much attention in the South with its serialization of J. S. C. Abbott's *History of Napoleon Bonaparte,* which De Bow warmly praised. *Southern Quarterly Review* published a number of citations to Abbott and offered an extended review in which the author dismissed it as "miscellaneous" and "not history at all" yet pronounced it the best book on its subject – rather more a censure of Scott and Alison than an accolade for Abbott: *DBR*, 19 (1855), 118; see also, Cecil D. Eby, Jr., *"Porte Crayon": The Life of David Hunter Strother* (Chapel Hill, NC, 1960), 69; "The History of Napoleon Bonaparte," *SQR*, 12 (1855), 291–324. Benjamin Blake Minor approved the work of Joel Tyler Headley (1813–1897), especially his two-volume *Napoleon and His Marshals,* which appeared in a third edition in 1846 and had a tremendous sale during the Mexican War and again in 1861. In 1846 the editors of *Southern Presbyterian Review* declared with much annoyance that it had achieved extraordinary popularity despite its containing nothing new and constituting a panegyric that disguised Napoleon's lack of moral principles, and *Southern Quarterly Review* trashed Headley for falsifications and self-promotion. See [Benjamin Blake Minor], *SLM*, 12 (1846), 455; *SPR*, 1 (1847), 133–6; *SQR*, 12 (1847), 509–14. Headley of New York and New England knew Edgar Allan Poe, Simms, and other literary Southerners. Poe referred to Headley as "the aristocrat of all quacks." Simms admired much of his work, published him in *Southern and Western Magazine and*

Review, and considered him a friend. Whereas Simms praised *Napoleon and His Marshals,* he condemned Headley's *Washington and His Generals* – a subject Simms knew much more about – as "wretched" as history and art. In Mary C. Oliphant et al., eds., *The Letters of William Gilmore Simms,* 6 vols. (Columbia, SC, 1952–82), see 1:cxiii (Poe); Simms to Evert Augustus Ducyckink, Nov. 18, 1844 (1:440), and Feb. 9, 1846 (1:545–6); Simms to Carey and Hart, Dec. 13, 1847 (2:381). Headley irritated Simms by traducing South Carolina in his account of the nullification struggle: [Simms], "Critical Notices," *SQR,* n.s., 7 (1853), 267–71. On the popularity of *Napoleon and His Marshalls* see James D. Hart, *The Popular Book: A History of America's Literary Taste* (New York, 1950), 116.

Natural Law and Natural Rights: Antislavery and proslavery men recapitulated a debate from the Revolution, when the Reverend John Zubly of Savannah, among others, objected to the revolutionaries' introduction of natural law in a subjective manner that departed from Christian standards. See "The Law of Liberty" (1775) and the "Helvetius Essays," reprinted in Randall M. Miller, ed., *"A Warm & Zealous Spirit": John J. Zubly and the American Revolution, A Selection of His Writings* (Macon, GA, 1982), 124–61, 170–99; also, Jim Schmidt, "The Reverend John Joachim Zubly's 'Law of Liberty' Sermon: Calvinist Opposition to the American Revolution," *Georgia Historical Quarterly,* 82 (1998), 348–68. Zubly, a Tory, spoke of "a law of liberty" to defend American claims against Britain and deny that Americans had cause to resort to arms against duly constituted authority. Most prominent Americans justified the Revolution by speaking of the rights of Englishmen, but a few, notably James Otis and Patrick Henry, chose the higher law: Forrest McDonald, *States' Rights and the Union: Imperium in Imperio, 1776–1876* (Lawrence, KS, 2000), 3.

Theologically sensitive defenders of slavery confronted the tension between a commitment to the sovereignty of the people and a commitment to natural rights. The Middle Ages simultaneously displayed theories of popular consent and of natural rights, grounding both in a consensus on social values that transcended class and interest group. The working out of a coherent theory, difficult under the best of circumstances, became daunting when the underlying consensus collapsed. Calvin, like the medieval schoolmen, did not acknowledge the right of individuals to resist duly constituted authority; he acknowledged their right to join lesser magistrates in remonstrance and appeals to representative assemblies. See Paul Tillich, *A History of Christian Thought, from Its Judaic and Hellenistic Origins to Existentialism,* ed. Carl E. Braaten (New York, 1972), 274; Paul K. Conkin, *Self-Evident Truths: Being a Discourse on the Origins and Development of the First Principle of American Government – Popular Sovereignty, Natural Rights, and Balance and Separation of Powers* (Bloomington, IN, 1974), esp. 110–11 and ch. 1.

New School Presbyterians: The strained relation of the New School to the liberal Congregationalists broke down in the 1840s: Ernest Trice Thompson, *Presbyterians in the South,* 3 vols. (Richmond, VA, 1963), chs. 5 and 6. For the departure of liberals from New School Presbyterianism to Congregationalism, see Vincent Harding, *A Certain Magnificence: Lyman Beecher and the Transformation of American Protestantism, 1775–1863* (Brooklyn, NY, 1991), ch. 26. In Kentucky, the unionist *Danville Quarterly Review* traced the roots of "the doctrinal deterioration of Presbyterianism" in the 1830s to the Plan of Union and the Congregationalists' liberal theology, the "terrible fruits" of which it held largely responsible for the spread of anti-Trinitarianism: "The Relative Doctrinal Tendencies of Presbyterianism and Congregationalism in America," *DQR,* 1 (1861), 1, 4, 5, 15–18, quotes at 4 and 5.

In 1850, the New School had fourteen synods and more than 125,000 members in the free states but only six synods and fewer than 15,000 members in the slave states, about half of them in Tennessee and only one in the Lower South (Mississippi): see Wesley Norton, "The Presbyterian Press and the Compromise of 1850," *JPH*, 40 (1962), 190; Lewis G. Vander Velde, *The Presbyterian Church and the Federal Union, 1861–1869* (Cambridge, MA, 1932), 1:353; Paul K. Conkin, *The Uneasy Center: Reformed Christianity in Antebellum America* (Chapel Hill, NC, 1995), 260; Walter Brownlow Posey, *The Presbyterian Church of Old Southwest, 1778–1838* (Richmond, VA, 1952), 119; William M. Baker, *The Life and Labors of the Rev. Daniel Baker, D.D., Pastor and Evangelist*, 3rd ed. (Philadelphia, n.d.), 316–17.

During the 1790s, Hopkinsianism won some support in the Border States, most notably Tennessee. Theological liberalism in Tennessee owed much to the Hopkinsian preaching of Hezekiah Balch, a local power by the time of his death in 1810, who had stood trial for denying original sin. *Southern Literary Messenger* published a favorable account of him: "A Citizen of Jefferson Co., Va.", "Sketch of the Rev. Stephen D. Balch," *SLM*, 7 (1841), 860–3. On Balch see also Samuel J. Baird, *A History of the New School and of the Questions in the Disruption of the Presbyterian Church in 1836* (Philadelphia, 1868), 131–3, 294–5; James Park, *The History of the First Presbyterian Church in Knoxville, Tennessee: A Discourse* (Knoxville, TN, 1876), 13. Gideon Blackburn, a Balch disciple, touted antislavery and New School doctrines at Danville College until he was forced to resign the presidency and move to Illinois. But Isaac Anderson trained 150 ministers who gave the New School Presbyterians a base in Tennessee. In 1843 Daniel Baker found the New School stronger than the Old in east Tennessee. For Hopkinsianism in east Tennessee see Harold M. Parker, Jr., *The United Synod of the South: The Southern New School Presbyterian Church* (Westport, CT, 1998), 31–6.

The Reverend Abram David Pollock, born and educated in Pennsylvania, settled in Virginia to preach in 1832 and joined the New School: A. D. Pollock, "Discourses and Papers" (ms.), 2, 149, at UNC-SHC. For Andrew Hunter Holmes Boyd see Joseph C. Stiles, *Address on the Life and Death of Rev. A. H. H. Boyd, D.D., of Winchester, Va.* (Richmond, VA, 1866); Parker, *United Synod of the South*, 201–2, 236, and for Boyd's proslavery see 26. For contemporary accounts of Boyd's activities during the War see Mrs. Cornelia McDonald, *A Diary with Reminiscences of the War and Refugee Life in the Shenandoah Valley, 1860–1865*, annotated and supplemented by Hunter McDonald (Nashville, TN, 1934 [1875]), Nov. 29, 1862 (109), Jan. 13, 1863 (130), May 15, 1863 (163–4), Sept. 1864 (227–8). The New School was about to establish a seminary in 1861 and had elected Boyd professor of theology: see J. E. Norris, ed., *History of the Lower Shenandoah Valley Counties of Frederick, Berkeley, Jefferson and Clarke* (Chicago, 1890), 583.

Nominalism and Realism: Thornwell hated Realism and applauded the Nominalism he associated with Baconian induction. Some of Thornwell's staunchest Presbyterian admirers perceived tension in his effort to square a conservative social corporatism with a Protestant, quasi-bourgeois individualism. During the War, the Reverend Benjamin Morgan Palmer declared, "We must renounce the shallow Nominalism which would make such a word as 'nation' a dead abstraction, signifying only the aggregation of individuals. It is an incorporated society, and possesses a unity of life resembling the individuality of a single being": B. M. Palmer, *A Discourse before the General Assembly of South Carolina on December 10, 1863* (Columbia, SC, 1864), 3. The Reverend T. E. Peck saw a contradiction between Thornwell's anti-Realism and his assertions of the organic nature of society and the reality of national characteristics. See T. E. Peck, "Thornwell's Writings," *SPR*, 29 (1878), 421. Ironically, in 1863 Peck had said that Thornwell's demand that the Confederacy commit itself to Christ sounded like the "old realism of the schools, which asserted for abstract ideas a substantive existence, different from and independent of the concrete things in which they were manifested and exemplified": Peck, "Church and State," *SPR,* 16 (1863), 142. For other attacks on Nominalism see Robert L. Dabney, *The Sensualistic Philosophy of the Nineteenth Century Considered,* rev. ed. (New York, 1887), 19, 31, 59, 208; James Warley Miles, *The Ground of Morals: A Discourse Delivered before the Graduating Class of the College of Charleston* (Charleston, SC, 1852), 9.

Thornwell, implicitly supported by John Girardeau, associated Realism, if problematically, with the idea that the individual is nothing and humanity everything – a doctrine he attributed to socialists. See "Consistency of Prayer with Natural Law" (1865), in George A. Blackburn, ed., *Sermons by John L. Girardeau* (Columbia, SC, 1907), 321. Thornwell feared a totalitarian tendency in medieval Scholasticism, which some nineteenth-century corporatists embraced. But he relied on a Christian corporatism to ground his defense of slavery and critique of free-labor societies. Twentieth-century southern conservatives renewed the attack on Nominalism: see Herbert Marshall McLuhan, "The Southern Quality," in Allen Tate, ed., *A Southern Vanguard: The John Peale Burke Memorial Volume* (New York, 1947), 111–12; Richard M. Weaver, *Ideas Have Consequences* (Chicago, 1948), 3–4; Marion Montgomery, "Ideas Have Consequences Fifty Years Later," in Ted Smith, ed., *Steps toward Restoration: The Consequences of Richard Weaver's Ideas* (Wilmington, DE, 1998), 185.

Philemon: For the abolitionist argument see, e.g., George B. Cheever, *God against Slavery; And the Freedom and Duty of the Pulpit to Rebuke It as a Sin against God* (Cincinnati, 1857), 143–4; [George Bourne], *A Condensed Anti-Slavery Bible Argument; By a Citizen of Virginia* (New York, 1845); Albert Barnes, *An Inquiry into the Scriptural Views of Slavery* (Philadelphia, 1857), 318–31. Some abolitionists went to extraordinary lengths to save the antislavery version of Philemon: thus, in Connecticut the Congregationalist Reverend James Pennington, an ex-slave, declared Philemon's slave a free worker. For Pennington see David E. Swift, *Black Prophets of Justice: Activist Clergy before the Civil War* (Baton Rouge, LA, 1989), 95. Mark A. Noll, sympathetically reviewing black contributions to the scriptural debate, concludes that they, too, lacked a convincing theological justification for antislavery: "The Bible and Slavery," in Randall M. Miller et al., eds., *Religion and the American Civil War* (New York, 1998), 53–5.

For typical expressions of the southern interpretation of Philemon see *SQR,* 8 (1845), 527, which praised Longstreet's pamphlet; "Tract #10 Reviewed," *SWMR,* 2 (1845), 293; George A. Baxter, *An Essay on the Abolition of Slavery* (Richmond, VA, 1836), 14; [Rev.] George Junkin, *The Integrity of Our National Union vs. Abolitionism: An Argument from the Bible* (Cincinnati, 1843), 55–62; Theodore Clapp, "Sermon," New Orleans *Daily Picayune,* Apr. 2, 1848; Clapp, "Thanksgiving Sermon," New Orleans *Daily Picayune,* Dec. 22, 1850; E. W. Warren, *Nellie Norton; Or, Southern Slavery and the Bible. A Scriptural Refutation of the Principal Arguments upon Which Abolitionists Rely. A Vindication of Southern Slavery from the Old and the New Testaments* (Macon, GA, 1864), 40–1; Augustin Verot, *A Tract for the Times: Slavery and Abolitionism* (Baltimore, 1861), 6; Thornton Stringfellow, *Slavery: Its Origin, Nature, and History, Considered in the Light of Bible Teachings, Moral Justice, and Political Wisdom* (New York, 1861), 54–6; Stuart Robinson, *Slavery, as Recognized in the Mosaic Civil Law, Recognized Also and Allowed, in the Abrahamic, Mosaic, and Christian Church* (Toronto, 1865), 48–56. See also June 15, 1861, in Elliott Ashkenazi, ed., *The War Diary of Clara Solomon: Growing Up in New Orleans, 1861–1862* (Baton Rouge, LA, 1995), 17, and, generally, K. M. Startup, *The Root of All Evil: The Protestant Clergy and the Economic Mind of the Old South* (Athens, GA, 1997), 9. For a northern interpretation of Philemon that paralleled the southern, see Leander Ker, *Slavery Consistent with Christianity,* 3rd ed. (Weston, MO, 1853), 20–1.

Poland: In South Carolina a frustrated Emma Holmes remarked, "The insurrection in Poland ... will engage the time and attention of all the great European powers – to our exclusion": Mar. 10, 1863, in John F. Marszalek, ed., *The Diary of Miss Emma Holmes* (Baton Rouge, LA, 1979), 237. In 1863 Edmund Ruffin groaned that the revolt in Poland probably ended any chance of French intervention in America: Mar. 14 and 31, 1863, in *ERD*, 2:517, 611. In Georgia a shocked Eliza Frances Andrews learned that Poles were fighting in the Union Army. They, of all people, ought to appreciate the South's struggle for national independence: Jan. 25, 1865, in Eliza Frances Andrews, *War-Time Journal of a Georgia Girl* (New York, 1907), 78. Adam Gurowski – a pro-Union, antislavery Pole – answered, "Old as I am, I feel a more rending pain now than I felt thirty years ago when Poland was entombed. Here are at stake the highest interests of humanity, of progress, of civilization": Sept. 1862, in Adam G. de Gurowski, *Diary*, 2 vols. (Boston, 1862–65), 259. Gurowski argued passionately if poorly that throughout history slavery had caused the decline of civilizations and nations: Gurowski, *Slavery in History* (New York, 1860). In contrast, Dr. G. Tochman, a former major in the Polish army, wrote from Nashville to Polish friends in support of the Confederacy's struggle to uphold Polish principles of resistance to tyranny by standing with the white race against black barbarians: "Dr. Tohman's Letter to the Polish Democratic Societies," *SLM*, 34 (1862), 321–7.

Preaching: For preaching outdoors see Anne Newport Royall, *Letters from Alabama, 1817–1822* (University, AL, 1969), 203–4; Rhoda Coleman Ellison, *Bibb County, Alabama: The First Hundred Years, 1818–1918* (University, AL, 1984), 60, Ferdinand Lawrence Steele Diaries, 1838–1842, at UNC-SHC; *ESB*, 1:17–20; *The Backwoods Preacher: Being the Autobiography of Peter Cartwright* (London, 1870), 4; Rene Ravenel Diary, Nov. 16, 1860, in Nathaniel Cheairs Hughes, Jr., ed., *Liddell's Record: St. John Richardson Liddell* (Baton Rouge, LA, 1997). In stores see Thomas Frederick Davis, *History of Early Jacksonville, Florida* (Jacksonville, FL, 1911), 79–80. In taverns see William Mercer Green, *Memoir of the Rt. Rev. James Hervey Otey, D.D., LL.D., the First Bishop of Tennessee* (New York, 1885), 55; William Edward Wadsworth Yerby, *History of Greensboro, Alabama from Its Earliest Settlement,* ed. Mabel Yerby Lawson (Northport, AL, 1963), 104; Charles D. Bates, *The Archives Tell a Story of the Government Street Presbyterian Church, Mobile, Alabama* (Mobile, AL, 1959), 13; Ellison, *Bibb County, Alabama,* 64; also, Anson West, *A History of Methodism in Alabama* (Spartanburg, SC, 1983 [1893]), 356–7 (on inns), 341 (stores). The Methodist preachers in early Mississippi and Louisiana preached almost exclusively in private homes: John D. Jones, *A Complete History of Methodism as Connected with the Mississippi Conference of the Methodist Episcopal Church, South,* 2 vols. (Nashville, TN, 1908), 1:153, 229–30.

Proslavery Religious Tracts: Edmund Ruffin kept up with the religious tracts, mentioning those of Samuel Nott, George Armstrong, and Parson Brownlow. He rarely thought them good enough and even criticized Stringfellow's for poor organization: *ERD*, 1:154, 327, 338. Ruffin faulted both the proslavery Reverend W. G. Brownlow and the abolitionist Reverend A. Pryne for their performances in a celebrated debate. Complaining that each ignored the other's strongest argument, he thought they had prepared their remarks in advance without leaving themselves room to adjust to any fresh arguments they might hear. See Sept. 7, 1859, *ERD*, 1:339; W. G. Brownlow and A. Pryne, *Ought American Slavery to Be Perpetuated: A Debate* (Miami, 1969 [1858]). The editor of *Southern Literary Messenger* remarked in 1856 that Stringfellow's essays on slavery were too well known to require a review of the latest edition: [John R. Thompson], *SLM*, 23 (1856), 320. On Dagg see Timothy George, "The

Revival of Baptist Theology," in Timothy George and Davis S. Dockery, eds., *Baptist Theologians* (Nashville, TN, 1990), 18. Also popular was Reverend Howell Cobb [of Houston County, Georgia], *A Scriptural Examination of the Institution of Slavery in the United States* (1856), which argued that slavery, having been established by God, must be considered permanent. His writings were often erroneously credited to another Howell Cobb, a kinsman who was a political power in Georgia: see Horace Montgomery, "The Two Howell Cobbs: A Case of Mistaken Identity," *JSH*, 28 (1962), 348–55. For a similar argument for perpetuity see J. C. Mitchell, *A Bible Defence of Slavery and the Unity of Mankind* (Mobile, AL, 1861), 10–11, 13.

Speaking at Oakland College in Mississippi, John Price said that Thornwell's defense of slavery "should be read by every Slaveholder": *The Duty of Drawing from the History and Theory of Our Government Just Views of Individual and National Life* (Port Gibson, MS, 1853), 19. On the circulation of the most popular of such efforts see William Sumner Jenkins, *Pro-Slavery Thought in the Old South* (Gloucester, MA, 1960), 213 n. 21. In 1850, the Alabama Baptist Convention offered a prize for the best essay on "Duties of Christian Masters to Servants" and divided it between C. E. Sturgis of Greensboro and H. N. McTyeire of New Orleans: see Julia Murfree Lovelace, *A History of Siloam Baptist Church, Marion, Alabama* (Birmingham, AL, 1943), 90; also, J. R. Wilson, *Mutual Relation of Masters and Slaves as Taught by the Bible* (Augusta, GA, 1861), 19–21. Newspapers and leading journals often printed religious as well as secular defenses of slavery. For example, see *DBR*, 10 (1851), 485–7, for Thornwell's 1851 proslavery sermon in Charleston, South Carolina, and Whitefoord Smith's essay on religion of the slaves, as well as secular pieces. In 1851 *Southern Quarterly Review* praised the published sermons of Whitefoord Smith (*God, the Refuge of His People*) and Thomas O. Summers (*Christian Patriotism*) as calls for South Carolina to resist oppression: *SQR*, n.s., 3 (1851), 355.

Responses to the French Revolution: Northern Federalists, not at all tongue-in-cheek, denounced southern slaveholders as "Jacobins." See e.g. John Quincy Adams to Thomas Boyston Adams, Dec. 3, 1800, and John Adams to William Vans Murray, Dec. 16, 1800, in Worthington Chauncey Ford, ed., *Writings of John Quincy Adams,* 7 vols. (New York, 1913–17), 2:484–6. Fisher Ames and Rufus King assaulted Virginia as the center of the democratic excess and moral degeneracy that Southerners accused New England of epitomizing. William Lloyd Garrison and other abolitionists built on their polemics. See Marc M. Arkin, "The Federalist Trope: Power and Passion in Abolitionist Rhetoric," *Journal of American History,* 88 (2002), 75–83. The "Old Republicans" who opposed Jeffersonian backsliding fed Federalist suspicions. They did not openly criticize France until 1806, when Napoleon scared them. See Norman K. Risjord, *The Old Republicans: Southern Conservatism in the Age of Jefferson* (New York, 1965), 3, 56, 130–2. Robert R. Howison, a contemporary Virginia historian, considered the slaughters of the French Revolution partly responsible for the Alien and Sedition Acts: *A History of Virginia from Its Discovery and Settlement by Europeans to the Present Time,* 2 vols. (Philadelphia, 1846), 2:349.

For muttering in the 1840s and 1850s over the execution of Louis XVI and Marie Antoinette see Alva Woods, *Valedictory Address, Delivered Dec. 6, 1837, at the Close of the Seventh Collegiate Year of the University of the State of Alabama* (Tuscaloosa, AL, 1837), 31; Andrew A. Lipscomb, *Our Country: Its Danger and Duty* (New York, 1844), 30, 42; Albert James Pickett, *History of Alabama and Incidentally of Georgia and Mississippi from the Earliest Period* (Sheffield, AL, 1896 [1851]), 438, 627. For a tribute to the courage of Marie Antoinette see Robert M. Charlton, *The Romance of Life: A Historical Lecture, Delivered before the Georgia Historical Society* (Savannah, GA, 1845), 9–10. A contributor to *Southern*

Literary Messenger disagreed: Republican liberty, he wrote, came with blood. He declared necessary the executions of Mary Queen of Scots, Charles I, and Louis XVI: "Modern Republicanism," *SLM*, 19 (1853), 497–509, 545–52, 605–13.

In 1860, Hugh Blair Grigsby recalled that not only Randolph but Cabell, L. W. Tazewell, and future governor and senator James Barbour "hailed in rapture" the French Revolution only to be disheartened by its savagery: Grigsby, *Discourse on the Life and Character of the Hon. Littleton Waller Tazewell* (Norfolk, 1860), 34–5. Randolph knew that liberals and radicals in the intellectual and judicial elite of the Old Régime increasingly invoked the image of the African slave to criticize excesses of royal authority. Rousseau, in the famous opening lines of *Social Contract,* conjured up "slavery" as a symbol of political domination: Sue Peabody, *"There Are No Slaves in France": The Political Culture of Race and Slavery in the Ancién Régime* (New York, 1966), 10, 96.

Revivals: For Georgia see James C. Bonner, *Milledgeville: Georgia's Antebellum Capital* (Athens, GA, 1978), 85; James C. Bonner, *Georgia's Last Frontier: The Development of Carroll County* (Athens, GA, 1971), 56; E. Merton Coulter, *Old Petersburg and the Broad River Valley of Georgia: Their Rise and Decline* (Athens, GA, 1965), 164; *The Life and Times of Judge Junius Hillyer: From His Memoirs* (Tignall, GA, 1989); George Gillman Smith, *The Story of Georgia and the Georgia People,* 2 vols. (Macon, GA, 1900), 355; Vincent H. Cassidy and Amos E. Simpson, *Henry Watson Allen* (Baton Rouge, LA, 1964), 31; James Stacy, *A History of the Presbyterian Church in Georgia* (Atlanta, GA, 1912), 100–1; see also Joseph Jones to C. C. Jones, May 12 and Sept. 16, 1858, in Joseph Jones Collection, at Tulane University. For Baptist revivals and church expansion in Georgia see Spright Dowell, *A History of Mercer University, 1833–1953* (Macon, GA, 1958), 32; Wade Crawford Barclay, *History of Methodist Missions: Early American Methodism, 1769–1844,* 2 vols. (New York, 1949), 2:330–1.

For a similar trajectory see Robert B. Semple, *A History of the Rise and Progress of the Baptists in Virginia* (Richmond, VA, 1894 [1810]), 27–8. On the Valley of Virginia and upland North Carolina see, in Eugene L. Schwaab and Jacqueline Bull, eds., *Travels in the Old South: Selections from Periodicals of the Times,* 2 vols. (Lexington, KY, 1973): T. H. Palmer, "Observations of Virginia," 1:107, and J. H. Rice, "Journey about Virginia," 1:195; also, George Washington Paschal, *History of Wake Forest College,* 3 vols. (Wake Forest, NC, 1935–43), 1:3–4 n. 2. For Tennessee see John Witherspoon to Charles Pettigrew, Aug. 5, 1802, in Sarah McCulloh Lemmon, ed., *The Pettigrew Papers,* 2 vols. (Raleigh, NC, 1971, 1988), 1:290; Thomas Perkins Abernethy, *From Frontier to Plantation in Tennessee: A Study in Frontier Democracy* (Chapel Hill, NC, 1932), 159–62, 210. Also, B. F. Riley, *A History of the Baptists in Southern States East of the Mississippi* (Philadelphia, 1898), 222–3; W. C. Rogers, *Recollections of Men of Faith* (St. Louis, MO, 1889), 138. For Alabama see Holland N. McTyeire, *A History of Methodism* (Nashville, TN, 1886), 437; W. H. Barr, H. Hubbard, and J. L. Sloss, "Mission to Alabama," in Schwaab and Bull, eds., *Travels in the Old South,* 1:197–202; also, Mary Welsh, "Reminiscences of Old St. Stephens," *Transactions of the Alabama Historical Society, 1898–99* (Tuscaloosa, AL, 1919), 210–11; Ernest Trice Thompson, *Presbyterians in the South,* 3 vols. (Richmond, VA, 1963), 1:174; William Edward Wadsworth Yerby, *History of Greensboro, Alabama from Its Earliest Settlement,* ed. Mabel Yerby Lawson (Northport, AL, 1963), 3–4.

For the revivals of the 1840s see Haralson Diary, Sept. 18, 1842, Sept. 25–27, 1843, and notations for 1845–1846, at UNC-SHC (Heywood County, TN); Ervin Journal, Oct. 5, 1839, Sept. 1, Oct. 17, 1841, July 27, 1848, at UNC-SHC (Lowndes County, MS); see also Edgar Jones Cheatham, "Washington County, Mississippi: Its Antebellum Generation"

(M.A. thesis, Tulane University, 1950), 94. On the early revivals, see esp. Paul K. Conkin, *Cane Ridge: America's Pentecost* (Madison, WI, 1990), and Dickson D. Bruce, Jr., *And They All Sang Hallelujah: Plain-Folk Camp-Meeting Religion, 1800–1845* (Knoxville, TN, 1974); also, Abernethy, *From Frontier to Plantation in Tennessee*, 214–15. Especially in the Southwest, camp meetings brought together brethren from a wide area, creating lasting friendships, and joining churches in closer Christian fellowship. See [Joseph Holt Ingraham], *The South-West. By a Yankee*, 2 vols. (n.p., 1966 [1835]), 2:166; Roger W. Shugg, *Origins of Class Struggle in Louisiana: A Social History of White Farmers and Laborers during Slavery and After* (Baton Rouge, LA, 1939), 65; Margaret Burr DesChamps, "The Presbyterian Church in the South Atlantic States, 1801–1861" (Ph.D. diss., Emory University, 1952), 93–5. In South Carolina the Guignards, devout Episcopalians, attended camp meetings at least as early as 1814 and continued to do so thereafter: James S. Guignard to John G. Guignard, Aug. 25, 1838, in Arney R. Childs, ed., *Planters and Businessmen: The Guignard Family of South Carolina, 1795–1930* (Columbia, SC, 1957), 27, also 10, 19, 38, 48, 63. Episcopalians in North Carolina attended despite the disapproval of Bishop John Stark Ravenscroft: H. S. Lewis, "Foundation of the Diocese," in Lawrence Foushee London and Sarah McCulloh Lemmon, eds., *The Episcopal Church in North Carolina, 1701–1959* (Raleigh, NC, 1987), 142. For a contemptuous appraisal of the camp meetings by a prominent southern geologist and an Episcopalian, see Michael Tuomey to M. A. Curtis, June 10, 1842, in Lewis S. Dean, ed., *The Papers of Michael Tuomey* (Spartanburg, SC, 2001), 22–3.

For the later revivals' contribution to the overcoming of class antagonisms in Georgia and Alabama see Garnett Andrews, *Reminiscences of an Old Georgia Lawyer* (Atlanta, GA, 1970); Bonner, *Milledgeville*, 89; Chattahoochee Valley Historical Society, *War Was the Place: A Centennial Collection of Confederate Soldier Letters and Old Oakbowery, Chambers County, Alabama* (Bulletin #5, 1961), 126–7. The revivals produced schisms and threatened entrenched church elites, but what Jon Butler says for colonial America held true for antebellum: "Revivals also raised, rather than lowered, the status of the ordained ministry and did little to increase lay authority within either local congregations or their denominational institutions": Butler, *Awash in a Sea of Faith: Christianizing the American People* (Cambridge, MA, 1990), 180. In the wake of the 1831 revival, prominent law firms in South Carolina lost promising young men to the ministry – most notably, Richard Fuller, Thomas Fuller, Jr., Stephen Elliott (later bishop), Charles Cotesworth Pinckney, William H. Barnwell, and James Elliot: see Stephen B. Barnwell, *The Story of an American Family* (Marquette, WI, 1969), 65.

Rienzi: A reviewer of Bulwer-Lytton in *Southern Literary Journal* credited Rienzi with the talent of a Napoleon or a Cromwell but with stronger principles and a more open and ingenuous nature. Unlike most leaders of popular movements, Rienzi sought the common good and eschewed self-aggrandizement. See [Daniel K. Whitaker?], "Rienzi," *SLJ*, 2 (1836), 216. Gildersleeve referred to the Rienzi episode as an attempt to restore the Roman Republic: "Theodora Agrippa D'Aubigné," *QRMECS*, 10 (1856), 79. John Preston Sheffey invoked Rienzi as great figure for South: Sheffey to Josephine Spiller, May 30, 1861, in James I. Robertson, ed., *Soldier of Southwestern Virginia: The Civil War Letters of Captain John Preston Sheffey* (Baton Rouge, LA, 2004), 221. Southern Protestants, repulsed by Cola di Rienzi's revolutionary politics, were open to parts of his religious message. Protestants gasped at his displacement of Jesus by the Holy Ghost, but they surely approved his call for a direct, personal relation to God that undercut the priesthood. Rienzi's alienation of the Papacy did not bother John S. Preston, Jr., of South Carolina, who – in a speech to the hierarchy of the Episcopal Church – referred to "the great heart of Cola di Rienzi": Preston, "Address at the

Laying of the Corner Stone of the University of the South," *University of the South Papers,* (Sewanee, TN), ser. A, 1 (1860), 4.

A reading of Bulwer-Lytton's *Rienzi: The Last of the Tribunes* (1835) persuaded Richard Wagner to write his opera, which was first produced in 1842 and scored a signal success. Its politically radical implications did not go unnoticed and, when Franz Liszt tried to have it performed in Paris in the wake of the uprising of 1848, he thought it in tune with the revolutionary atmosphere there. Wagner ardently supported the German revolutionaries of 1848. See Ernest Newman, *The Life of Richard Wagner,* 4 vols. (New York, 1946), 1:221, 365–6, 374, 2:11, 35, 118.

Roman Writers – *Appian*: Curiously, southern commentators largely ignored Appian, who – in the words of Daniel J. Gargola – arguably provided "the single most detailed and coherent account" of the Gracchan reforms: "Appian and the Aftermath of the Gracchan Reform," *American Journal of Philology,* 118 (1997), esp. 555, 564, 576–7, quote at 555. Appian stressed the oppression of smallholders and increasing reliance on large slaveholdings, but he also described Tiberius' protest against an increase in slaves, which he saw as a serious weakness in time of war – a notion not at all to southern taste. See Appian, *Roman History,* tr. Horace White, 4 vols. (LCL), x, 4:Bk.1.7, 10.

Cicero: From colonial times Cicero's *Orations* and *De Officiis* served as grammar-school texts: M. N. S. Sellers, *American Republicanism: Roman Ideology in the United States Constitution* (New York, 1994), 94; in addition to college catalogs see Nov. 2, 1861, in Thornwell Jacobs, ed. *Diary of William Plumer Jacobs* (Atlanta, GA, 1937), 85. For Cicero's standing in elite circles see e.g. Archibald D. Murphey to Thomas Ruffin, June 10, 1823, in J. G. deRoulhac Hamilton, ed., *The Papers of Thomas Ruffin,* 4 vols. (Raleigh, NC, 1918), 1:276; James E. Bagwell, *Rice Gold: James Hamilton Couper and Plantation Life on the Georgia Coast* (Macon, GA, 2000), xi, 141; Philip Slaughter, *A Brief Sketch of the Life of William Green, LL.D., Jurist and Scholar* (Richmond, VA, 1883), 17, 57. For lavish praise of Cicero – "the immortal Tully" – see also Henry W. Miller, *Address Delivered before the Philanthropic and Dialectic Societies of the University of North-Carolina* (Raleigh, NC, 1857), 14; E. A. Lynch, "Influence of Morals on the Happiness of Man," *SLM,* 4 (1838), 273; J. L. Reynolds, *The Man of Letters* (Richmond, VA, 1849), 16; W. C. Rives, *Discourse on the Use and Importance of History* (Richmond, VA, 1847), 11; J. L. Petigru, "Oration," in *Collections of the South-Carolina Historical Society,* 2 vols. (Charleston, SC, 1857–58), 2:13; [John R. Thompson], *SLM,* 19 (1853), 251; [William Gilmore Simms?], *SWMR,* 2 (1845), 416; [Simms], *SQR,* n.s., 10 (1854), 244; for Boyce see William A. Mueller, *A History of Southern Baptist Seminary* (Nashville, TN, 1959), 54–5; William Gordon McCabe, "Political Corruption," *SLM,* 34 (1862), 82–3. Lucian Minor, professor of law at William and Mary and a classical scholar, translated Cicero on old age and on Cato the Elder for *SLM,* 18 (1852), 732–45. See also [Cicero], "The Dream of Scipio," *SLM,* 18 (1852), 349–52, and 20 (1854), 189. Cicero and Livy directly influenced the early histories of Virginia by Hugh Jones and Robert Beverley: M. E. Bradford, *Generations of the Faithful Heart: On the Literature of the South* (LaSalle, IL, 1983), 17–28.

Horace: For the early circulation of Horace's work see Walter B. Edgar, "Some Popular Books in Colonial South Carolina," *South Carolina Historical Magazine,* 72 (1971), 177. The father of Patrick Henry was more deeply read in Horace than in his Bible: M. E. Bradford, *A Better Guide than Reason: Studies in the American Revolution* (LaSalle, IL, 1979), 15. W. J. Grayson touted Horace's *Ars Poetica*'s definitive aesthetic theory: see Edd Winfield Parks, *Segments of Southern Thought* (Athens, GA, 1938), 170. On *Ars Poetica* as a southern staple see "The University and Its Wants," *SLM,* 22 (1856), 440; "G.", "Antient [*sic*]

Languages," *VLM*, 1 (1829), 255; William Harris Bragg, *De Renne: Three Generations of a Georgia Family* (Athens, GA, 1999), 23; Robert M. Calhoon, *Evangelicals and Conservatives in the Early South, 1740–1861* (Columbia, SC, 1988), 87–8; Forrest McDonald, *The American Presidency: An Intellectual History* (Lawrence, KS, 1994), 157; Ronald Hoffman, *Princes of England, Planters of Maryland: A Carroll Saga, 1500–1782* (Chapel Hill, NC, 2000), 323; Benjamin Johnson Barbour, "Address Delivered before the Literary Societies of the Virginia Military Institute," *SLM*, 20 (1854), 518; Apr. 16, 1864, in Beth G. Crabtree and James Welch Patton, eds., *"Journal of a Secesh Lady": The Diary of Catherine Devereux Edmonston, 1860–1866* (Raleigh, NC, 1979), 603. Clyde Lottridge Cummer, ed., *Yankee in Gray: The Civil War Memoirs of Henry E. Handerson, with a Selection of His Wartime Letters* (Cleveland, OH, 1962), 39; Chesnut Diary, Feb. 25, 1865, in C. Vann Woodward, ed., *Mary Chesnut's Civil War* (New Haven, CT, 1981), 730; also, Charles Edward Leverett, Jr., to Milton Leverett, July 11, 1852, in Frances Wallace Taylor et al., eds., *The Leverett Letters: Correspondence of a South Carolina Family, 1851–1868* (Columbia, SC, 2000), 10–11. For invocations of "sweet to die" see George P. Elliott, *An Oration, Delivered before the Artillery Company at Beaufort, South Carolina, July 5, 1852* (Charleston, SC, 1852), 16–17; Ujanirtus Allen to Susan Fuller Allen, Oct. 9, 1861, in Randall Allen and Keith S. Bohannon, eds., *Campaigning with "Old Stonewall": Confederate Captain Ujanirtus Allen's Letters to His Wife* (Baton Rouge, LA, 1998), 53 (Allen slightly misquoted); Tally Simpson to Caroline Miller, June 3, 1863, in Guy R. Everson and Edward W. Simpson, Jr., eds., *"Far, Far from Home": The Wartime Letters of Dick and Tully Simpson, Third South Carolina Volunteers* (New York, 1994), 241.

Lucretius, Lucian: Lucretius had southern admirers who ranked him a "great thinker" and complained of his being unjustly neglected: see e.g. [George Frederick Holmes], "History of Literature," *SQR*, 2 (1842), 509; "Bulwer," *SLM*, 14 (1848), 234. Thomas Smyth cited Lucretius on sinfulness and moral crisis (*TSW*, 7:211–12, 10:12), but generally Lucretius was distrusted as an atheist and a materialist: "Domestic Slavery," *SLM*, 11 (1845), 514; "The World before the Flood," *SLM*, 16 (1850), 464–5. Lucian was taught at Hampden-Sydney, the University of Tennessee, and other schools, receiving salutes as an enemy of cant: John Luster Brinkley, *On This Hill: A Narrative History of Hampden-Sydney College, 1774–1994* (Hampden-Sydney, VA, 1994), 54; James Riley Montgomery et al., eds., *To Foster Knowledge: A History of the University of Tennessee, 1794–1970* (Knoxville, TN, 1984), 11; "American Literature – 1," *SQR*, 11 (1847), 152; "M." [Frederick A. Porcher], "Philosophy of Spinoza," *SQR*, 16 (1849), 79.

Nepos: Southern academies and colleges assigned Cornelius Nepos in the early nineteenth, less so thereafter. We cannot account for the fading of "the much underestimated Cornelius Nepos," as Fergus Millar calls him: for an appreciation of Nepos see his *Rome, the Greek World, and the East;* vol. 1: *The Roman Republic and the Augustan Revolution* (Chapel Hill, NC, 2002), ch. 7, quote at 321. Nepos' *De Virus Illustribus [On Famous Men]* nicely combined loyalty to tradition, accommodation to modern values, and Roman patriotism with respect for the personal qualities of foreigners and enemies. For Nepos' availability see James Raven, *London Booksellers and American Customers: Transatlantic Literary Community and the Charleston Library Society, 1748–1811* (Columbia, SC, 2002), 105, 189; Charles L. Coon, ed., *North Carolina Schools and Academies: A Documentary History, 1790–1840* (Raleigh, NC, 1915), 767, 77.

Ovid: For Ovid on masters' fears of dependence see William Fitzgerald, *Slavery and the Roman Literary Imagination* (Cambridge, U.K., 2000), 74–5. Women's schools taught Ovid in translation: [George William Bagby], *SLM*, 31 (1860), 160, 320. Ovid may have been the most popular ancient author in colonial Virginia: George K. Smart, "Private Libraries in

Colonial Virginia," *American Literature,* 10 (1938), 37. For recommendations of Ovid see [William Wirt, et al.], *The Old Bachelor* (New York, 1985 [1814]), 47–8; "Brooks' Classics," *SQR,* 14 (1848), 378–89; Franc M. Carmack Diary, Oct. 17 and 23, 1852, Feb. 23, 1852, at UNC-SHC. Virginia boasted of George Sandys's translation of *Metamorphosis* (1626), respected by Pope and Dryden. New York's celebrated publishers called it the first American literary production of note: Evert A. Duyckinck and George L. Duyckinck, *Cyclopedia of American Literature,* 2 vols. (New York, 1856), 1:1; also, and for expurgation of early textbook editions, see Mark Morford, "Early American School Editions of Ovid," *Classical Journal,* 78 (1983), 150–8. In the 1840s, W. C. Rives and Robert R. Howison took pride in Sandys's translation and claimed him as a Virginian: Rives, *Discourse on the Character and Services of John Hampden* (Richmond, VA, 1845), 15; Howison, *A History of Virginia from Its Discovery and Settlement by Europeans to the Present Time,* 2 vols. (Philadelphia, 1846), 2:465–6. For the warm reception accorded Sandys's translation see Richard Beale Davis, *Intellectual Life in the Colonial South, 1515–1763,* 3 vols. (Knoxville, TN, 1978), 3:1341–4; also, Calhoon, *Evangelicals and Conservatives,* 35–6; F. V. N. Painter, *Poets of Virginia* (Richmond, VA, 1907), 14–17. For Ovid through the centuries see Gian Biaggio Conte, *Latin Literature: A History,* tr. Joseph B. Solodow, rev. by Don Fowler and Glenn W. Most (Baltimore, 1994), 258–64, and John Edwin Sandys, *A History of Classical Scholarship,* 3 vols. (Cambridge, U.K.: vol. 1, 3rd ed., 1921; vols. 2 and 3, 2nd ed., 1908), 1:638–46. For women's reading *Metamorphosis* see Philip Alexander Bruce, *Institutional History of Virginia in the Seventeenth Century,* 2 vols. (Gloucester, MA, 1964 [1910]), 1:414; Caroline Gilman, ed., *Letters of Eliza Wilkinson* (New York, 1969 [1839]), 56, 60–2. For Ovid's defense of his writing on sexuality see his autobiographical *Sorrows of an Exile: Tristia,* tr. A. D. Melville (Oxford, U.K., 1992); Sara Mack, *Ovid* (New Haven, CT, 1988), 3–5, 21–2, 62–3.

Pliny: Pliny may have exaggerated the extent of the latifundia and ignored other sources of the oppression of the rural lower classes: see D. C. Earl, *Tiberius Gracchus: A Study in Politics* (Bruxelles-Bercheim, 1963), esp. 40–5, and Alvin H. Bernstein, *Tiberius Sempronius Gracchus: Tradition and Apostasy* (Ithaca, NY, 1978), ch. 3, esp. 82–5. In an effort to separate rhetoric from substance – myth from reality – Earl has challenged the notion of an agrarian crisis and judged Tiberius' measures close to worthless as agricultural reform. Tiberius and a powerful faction of the ruling class supported the law as a measure to permit heretofore excluded classes to shore up a military depleted by wars: "What the Tribunate of Ti. Gracchus is about is not economics, not agriculture, not sociology, but politics, and politics in Roman terms – political support – clientela." The land question alone cannot account for the opposition that Tiberius provoked. Rather, his violation of political norms threatened every faction other than his own. When he tried to monopolize the proletariat as his personal client, he went to the brink; when he tried to add foreign clientele as well, he plunged over it. Southern slaveholders did not have the advantage of the analyses provided by Earl, Brunt, and Bernstein, but they probably would have felt comfortable with them because they sought to secure their own slave society by guaranteeing the prosperity and power of a solid slaveholding yeomanry: Earl, *Tiberius Gracchus,* esp. 30–47, 78, 94.

Terence: Terence had been much more familiar than Plautus in the early Middle Ages: Sandys, *History of Classical Scholarship,* 1:630. Terence was widely read and taught in eighteenth-century America, less so afterwards. Meyer Reinhold, *Classica Americana: The Greek and Roman Heritage in the United States* (Detroit, 1984), 26, 28, 150. See Walter B. Edgar, "Some Popular Books in Colonial South Carolina," *South Carolina Historical Magazine,* 72 (1971), 177; Dale Glenwood Robinson, *The Academies of Virginia, 1776–1861* (n.p., 1977), 14. Terence took a back seat to Plautus in the South. Erich Segal writes suggestively that Terence represents "drama for an aristocratic coterie," whereas Plautus found a popular audience: Segal, *Roman Laughter: The Comedy of Plautus* (Cambridge, MA, 1968), 7. Yet, in the judgment of the president of Mississippi College (for women), Terence grasped "the true spirit of the sublime Christian philosophy": William Carey Crane, *Literary Discourses* (New York, 1853), 9. Hugh Legaré treated the work of Plautus and Terence as stylistically derivative from the Greek but did not attack its content: "Roman Literature," *HLW*, 2:56, 69–70, 76–7, 82. For use of Terence on Roman slavery see Thomas R. R. Cobb, *An Inquiry into the Law of Negro Slavery in the United States* (New York, 1968 [1858]), lxxx; James M. Walker [of Charleston], *The Theory of the Common Law* (Boston, 1852), 50.

Varro: On Varro see Conte, *Latin Literature*, 218–20; Sandys, *Classical Scholarship*, 1:177; Ronald Syme, *Sallust* (Berkeley, CA, 1964), 233. Varro pleased Augustine for encouraging monotheism: Saint Augustine, *The City of God*, tr. Marcus Dods (New York, 1950), Bk. 4:31. On Varro's philosophy through Augustine see "L." [Robert W. Landis?], "The Relation which Reason and Philosophy Sustains in the Theology of Revelation," *DQR*, 1 (1861), 26. For Varro on slave life see K. D. White, *Roman Farming* (Ithaca, NY, 1970), 358–61, and Fitzgerald, *Slavery and Roman Literary Imagination*, 3. Holmes criticized Cato and Varro for wildly distorting the history of the early peoples of Italy: [Holmes], "Ante-Roman Races of Italy," *SQR*, 7 (1845), 265–84. For Mitchell King, Columella produced the best ancient work on husbandry: *The History and Culture of the Olive* (Charleston, SC, 1846), 4. Cobb noted that Columella did not exhibit Cato's ruthlessness to slaves: *Law of Negro Slavery*, lxxviii.

Russia and the Crimean War: Curiosity about Russian society, culture, intentions, and prospects intensified with the Crimean War. Southerners gleaned much of their information about Russia from travelogues of uneven merit. Noteworthy was John S. Maxwell's *The Czar, His Court and People: Including a Tour in Norway and Sweden* (1848), which was recommended in *SLM*, 14 (1848), 262–3. *Southern Presbyterian Review* commended it as pleasant and useful, noting its picture of the haughty Czar Nicholas and his efforts to civilize a semi-barbarous country: *SPR*, 2 (1848), 300–1; also, Harriett Newell Espy to Zebulon Vance, July 6, 1852, in Elizabeth Roberts Cannon, ed., *My Beloved Zebulon: The Correspondence of Zebulon Vance and Harriett Newell Espy* (Chapel Hill, NC, 1971), 103. *Southern Literary Messenger* also praised *Russia as It Is* by Adam Gurowski, "a thoughtful and accurately informed man": [J. R. Thompson], *SLM*, 20 (1854), 319. Southerners believed that Russians treated their serfs barbarously: see "Slavery in England," *RM*, 5 (1859), 20; R. S. Breck, "Duties of Masters," *SPR*, 8 (1855), 271.

For a contemporary statement of southern sympathy for Russia in the Crimean War see "Preston Souther", "Miss Murray's Travels," *SLM*, 22 (1856), 460. In 1855, Francis Lieber railed at ostensibly republican South Carolinians who supported Czarist Russia against England: Lieber to G. S. Hilliard, Jan. 21, 1855, in Thomas Sergeant Perry, ed., *The Life and Letters of Francis Lieber* (Boston, 1882), 278. On the Crimean War see also *SQR*, n.s., 11 (1855), 382–9, and 12 (1855), 37–51. Southern poetry, notably that of A. B. Meek of Alabama and James Barron Hope of Virginia, sang of British gallantry and heroism. Hope scored a signal success in the 1850s, especially with "The Charge of Balaclava" in *Southern Literary Messenger*. The Crimean War was generally considered the poetic property of Lord Tennyson, but Queen Victoria admired Hope's poem. Hope's *A Collection of Poems* drew critical raves from De Bow, who also praised Meek's poetry: A. B. Meek, "Balaklava," *Songs and Poems of the South*, 4th ed. (Montgomery, AL, 1914 [1855]), 89–93; "Editorial Miscellany," *DBR*, 26 (1859), 714–15. Also, Rollin G. Osterweis, *Romanticism and Nationalism in the Old South* (Baton Rouge, LA, 1971), 63, 77.

George Frederick Holmes and James Johnston Pettigrew treated the Crimean War as a blunder and welcomed the pro-Russian swing in public opinion, although Holmes referred to "the rapacity of the present Czar": [Holmes], "The Sibylline Oracles," *MMQR,* 4th ser., 6 (1854), 509; [James Johnston Pettigrew], *Notes on Spain and the Spaniards in the Summer of 1850, with a Glance at Sardinia* (Charleston, SC, 1861), 427. J. H. Hayne also argued that Turkey would long ago have disintegrated if not for the conflicting interests of European powers: [Hayne], *RM,* 3 (1858), 352. Still, Trescot probably agreed with the contributor to *Russell's Magazine* who declared that, if hostile powers threatened England, Americans would recall their common Anglo-Saxon blood and shared liberal tradition and rally to her: "A Letter from Europe," *RM,* 4 (1859), 326.

Schleiermacher: For a defense of Schleiermacher against the charge of surrendering theology to philosophy see Hans W. Frei, *The Eclipse of Biblical Narrative: A Study in Eighteenth and Nineteenth Century Hermeneutics* (New Haven, CT, 1974), 34–8, 67. For W. J. Sasnett, Schleiermacher was infected by narrowly rationalistic German philosophy: Sasnett, "German Philosophy," *QRMECS,* 12 (1858), 336–7, 341–2. John Girardeau saw Schleiermacher's subjectivist theology of feeling as a path to a mysticism that relied on reason over revelation. Girardeau also attacked Schleiermacher's anti-Trinitarianism: *Discussions of Theological Questions,* ed. George A. Blackburn (Harrisonburg, VA, 1986 [1905, written in 1890s]), 84, 134, 403–4. Thornwell credited Schleiermacher with suggesting the arrangement of Plato's Dialogues: [James Henley Thornwell], "Plato's Phaedon," *SQR,* n.s. (3rd), 1 (1856), 415, much as Wilhelm Dilthey later found Schleiermacher's methods much stronger in his critique of Plato than of the synoptic Gospels: Frei, *Eclipse of Biblical Narrative,* 311.

Scott: William Elliott, who considered Walter Scott "the first of Novelists," described his "historical romances" as "in truth, mere vehicles for illustrating the manners, superstitions, and antiquities of various lands and peoples": [Elliott], "Anne of Geierstein; Or the Maiden of the Mist," *SR,* 4 (1829), quotes at 499, 518. Robert Potter of North Carolina, a champion of public education, hailed Scott for educating the world about the true history of Scotland: Charles L. Coon, *The Beginnings of Public Education in North Carolina,* 2 vols. (Raleigh, NC, 1908), 1:325. Edward Brown noted that *Ivanhoe* gives a picture of the suffering of laborers during the Middle Ages: *Notes on the Origin and Necessity of Slavery* (Charleston, SC, 1826), 35. For Scott's popularity in the Southwest as measured by newspaper notices, reviews, and sales, see Rhoda Coleman Ellison, *Early Alabama Publications: A Study in Literary Interests* (University, AL, 1947), 63–5, 117; F. Garvin Davenport, *Cultural Life in Nashville on the Eve of the Civil War* (Chapel Hill, NC, 1941), 174–6. For Scott as a historian whose novels bring the Middle Ages alive, see [Simms], "Epochs and Events of American History," *SWMR,* 1 (1845), 120.

Perhaps nothing so impressed Southerners as Scott's loving attention to families and local communities. A biography of Scott led Susan Nye Hutchinson "to mourn particularly the neglect I have for a long time seemed to exhibit toward my very dear relations": Hutchinson Diary, May 20, 1827, at UNC-SHC. Charleston was agog when the *Courier* published "Marmion": Herbert Ravenel Sass, *Outspoken: 150 Years of the News and Courier* (Columbia, SC, 1953), 22.

Southerners of all classes joined travelers in reporting that even the more modest private libraries contained the *Waverley* novels. Frederick Douglass took his name Douglass from *Lady of the Lake*: William S. McFeely, *Frederick Douglass* (New York, 1991), 78. James Henley Thornwell, son of an overseer, named his plantation Drybush Abbey: James Oscar Farmer, Jr., *The Metaphysical Confederacy: James Henley Thornwell and the Synthesis of*

Southern Values (Macon, GA, 1986), 228–9. Frederick Ross, of the Virginia gentry, named his plantation Rotherwood and his daughter Rowena. See Grace Warren Landrum, "Sir Walter Scott and His Literary Rivals in the Old South," *American Literature*, 2 (1930), 258; Paul Hamilton Hayne, "Ante-Bellum Charleston, S.C.," *Southern Bivouac*, 1 (1885), 264, 355. George Tucker, to the horror of his professorial colleagues in Virginia, turned to the writing of novels under Scott's influence: see "The Autobiography of George Tucker," *Bermuda Historical Quarterly*, 180 (1961), 82–159. Louisiana especially had plantations with names drawn from Scott's work: Woodstock, Rob Roy, Melrose, Ivanhoe, Kenilworth. Between 1820 and 1832 the theater in New Orleans featured nine plays based on Scott's novels and poems. Southern newspapers draped the announcement of his death in black borders. See Lyle Saxon et al., *Gumbo Ya-Ya: A Collection of Louisiana Folk Tales* (New York, 1945), 223; John Hope Franklin, *The Militant South, 1800–1861* (Boston, 1956), 195; M. E. Bradford, *The Reactionary Imperative: Essays, Literary and Political* (Peru, IL, 1990), 152–5.

Secession – Clerical Support and Opposition: Most Methodist and Baptist preachers in Virginia, two thirds of whom were nonslaveholders, opposed secession as late as 1861: Beth Barton Schweiger, *The Gospel Working Up: Progress and the Pulpit in Nineteenth-Century Virginia* (New York, 2000), 78–9, 93. On John Brown's impact see Joseph H. Parks, *General Leonidas Polk, C.S.A.: The Fighting Bishop* (Baton Rouge, LA, 1962), 153. On the change of course after secession see Robert A. Brent, "The Episcopal Church in the Lower South during the Antebelllum Period," in Lucius F. Ellsworth, ed., *The Americanization of the Gulf Coast, 1803–1850* (Pensacola, FL, 1972), 50. Bishop Cobbs was among Alabama's most prominent opponents of secession.

Of the 23 prominent Catholic politicians in the South, 21 supported secession: see R. M. Miller, "A Church in Cultural Captivity: Speculations on Catholic Identity," in Randall M. Miller and Jon L. Wakelyn, *Catholics in the Old South: Essays on Church and Culture* (Macon, GA, 1983), 16. The Church, however, proceeded carefully and, if anything, encouraged unionism: see e.g. James J. Pillar, *The Catholic Church in Mississippi, 1837–65* (New Orleans, 1964), ch. 7. Most Lutheran ministers were unionists who appealed for peace and reconciliation even after Sumter: *EC*, 3:961; and for the Lutheran Church's caution on the slavery issue see Robert Fortenbaugh, "American Lutheran Synods and Slavery, 1830–1860," *Journal of Religion*, 13 (1933), 72–92. In contrast, Cumberland Presbyterian communicants in Kentucky and Tennessee, where the Church was especially strong, enthusiastically supported secession: H. Shelton Smith, *In His Image ... But: Racism in Southern Religion* (Durham, NC, 1972), 190.

By 1861, *Southern Presbyterian Review* had become sufficiently secessionist to provoke some unionists to cancel subscriptions: David Henry Overy, "Robert Lewis Dabney: Apostle of the Old South" (Ph.D. diss., University of Wisconsin, 1967), 97. When Moses Hoge declared for secession, his friend R. L. Dabney advised him against a plunge into the unknown. Cyrus McCormick, the influential layman of reaper fame, spoke for many Presbyterians when he depicted his Church and the Democratic party as the twin pillars of the Union: Lewis G. Vander Velde, *The Presbyterian Church and the Federal Union, 1861–1869* (Cambridge, MA, 1932), 21. In 1863 the Assembly of the northern Presbyterian Church, in a paper prepared by Robert J. Breckenridge of Kentucky, declared that the people of the South had committed a "great crime" by placing themselves outside the pale of religion and morality and by taking up arms against the Union. Having thus revealed themselves as heathens and enemies of God, they deserved to be crushed. Quite a mouthful from Breckenridge, who, as Benjamin Morgan Palmer reminded him, had long denied the sinfulness of slavery. For Breckenridge see Henry Alexander White, *Southern Presbyterian Leaders* (New York, 1911),

349–50; [B. M. Palmer], "A Vindication of Secession and the South," *SPR*, 14 (1861), 136–7. Palmer also chided Breckenridge for spreading fear in Kentucky that the Confederacy would reopen the slave trade and import "millions more of cannibals."

Slavery, Ancient and Modern Compared: In his scriptural critique of slavery, Gerrit Smith of New York stressed the differences between ancient and modern slavery: *Letter of Gerrit Smith to Rev. James Smylie of the State of Mississippi* (New York, 1837), 3–4, 9, and see 27–30 for a summary of the abolitionist position on Jesus' and the Apostles' avoidance of a direct attack on slavery. More cautiously, George M. Stroud suggested that the laws indicate that American slavery was no more humane, and perhaps less, than Roman slavery: *A Sketch of the Laws Relating to Slavery in the Several States of the United States of America,* 2nd ed. (New York, 1966 [1856; 1st ed., 1827]), 10. For characterizations of Roman slavery as much harsher than southern see [William Hobby], *Remarks upon Slavery, Occasioned by Attempts Made to Circulate Improper Publications in the Southern States. By a Citizen of Georgia,* 2nd ed. (Augusta, GA, 1835), 12; "Domestic Slavery," *SLM,* 11 (1845), 516, 523; Alexander McCaine, *Slavery Defended against the Attacks of the Abolitionists* (Baltimore, 1842), 10; [Patrick H. Mell], *Slavery. A Treatise Showing that Slavery Is Neither a Moral, Political, nor Social Evil* (Pennfield, GA, 1844), 10; [Rev.] George Junkin, *The Integrity of Our National Union vs. Abolitionism: An Argument from the Bible* (Cincinnati, 1843), 48; Thornton Stringfellow, *Slavery: Its Origin, Nature, and History, Considered in the Light of Bible Teachings, Moral Justice, and Political Wisdom* (New York, 1861), 48; Joseph R. Wilson, *Mutual Relations of Masters and Slaves as Taught by the Bible* (Augusta, GA, 1861), 11–13; also, "Dr. J. A. W.", "De Servitude," *SLM,* 20 (1854), 427–8; "A Mississippian", "Slavery – The Bible and the 'Three Thousand Parsons,'" *DBR,* 26 (1859), 46; *SPR,* 16 (1863), 154–5. Alexander Campbell, who had little taste for slavery, observed that Roman slavery was "certainly no better than American slavery": [Campbell], "Our Position on American Slavery," *Millennial Harbinger,* 16 (1845), 232; also, George A. Baxter, *An Essay on the Abolition of Slavery* (Richmond, VA, 1836), 13–14. The Reverend George Howe ridiculed abolitionists who cited trivia to declare slavery in biblical times radically different from slavery in the Old South: [Howe], "The Raid of John Brown, and the Progress of Abolition," *SPR,* 12 (1860), 796. For anti-abolitionist northern views, see "Slavery. By William E. Channing," *BRPR,* 8 (1836), 283; Van Renssalaer, "Three Letters," *BRPR,* 8 (1858), 15; John Henry Hopkins, *A Scriptural, Ecclesiastical, and Historical View of Slavery from the Days of the Patriarch Abraham to the Nineteenth Century* (New York, 1864), 91. The antislavery Leonard Bacon conceded that students of history recognized Roman slavery as about as bad as southern, and he used Tacitus' story of the 400 slaves to expose abolitionist exaggerations: Bacon, *Slavery Discussed in Occasional Essays from 1833 to 1846* (New York, 1846), 40–1.

Slavery Commanded: The argument that God commanded Israelite slavery and could not command men to sin recurred frequently. See e.g. A. J. Roane, "Reply to Abolitionist Objections to Slavery," *DBR,* 20 (1856), 647–8; Robert Nuckols Watkins, Jr., "The Forming of the Southern Presbyterian Minister: From Calvin to the Civil War" (Ph.D. diss., Vanderbilt University, 1969), 446; Victor B. Howard, *Conscience and Slavery: The Evangelic Calvinist Domestic Missions, 1837–1861* (Kent, OH, 1990), 26–7, 38; Walter Brownlow Posey, *Presbyterian Church in the Southwest, 1778–1838* (Richmond, VA, 1952), 76–82, 89–90; Joseph C. Stiles, *Modern Reform Examined* (Philadelphia, 1857), 23; Thomas R. R. Cobb, *An Inquiry into the Law of Negro Slavery in the United States* (New York, 1968 [1858]), 55–7; [Samuel J. Cassells], *Servitude and the Duty of Masters to Their Servants* (Norfolk, VA, 1843), 8; R. H.

Rivers, *Elements of Moral Philosophy* (Nashville, TN, 1859), 331–2, 350; J. D. B. De Bow, "Origins, Progress and Prospects of Slavery," *DBR*, 9 (1850), 15–16; Thornton Stringfellow, "Bible Argument," in E. N. Elliott, ed., *Cotton Is King, and Pro-Slavery Arguments* (New York, 1969 [1860]), 474–5, 510–11, 513–15; "Slavery and the Bible," *DBR*, 9 (1850), 282–6; Henry J. Van Dyke [of Brooklyn], "The Character and Influence of Abolitionism" (Dec. 9, 1860), in *Fast Day Sermons: Or the Pulpit on the State of the Country* (New York, 1861), 140–3.

Sparta: On the instability brought about by Spartan dual kingship see Donald Kagan, *The Outbreak of the Peloponnesian War* (Ithaca, NY, 1991), 27–32. On the preference for Sparta in the generation of the Founding Fathers see Meyer Reinhold, "Eighteenth-Century American Political Thought," in R. R. Bolgar, ed., *Classical Influences on Western Thought A.D. 1650–1870* (Cambridge, U.K., 1979), 228; Meyer Reinhold, *Classica Americana: The Greek and Roman Heritage in the United States* (Detroit, 1984), 97–8, 156–7, 253, 258; Carl J. Richard, *Founders and the Classics: Greece, Rome, and the American Enlightenment* (Cambridge, MA, 1994), 73–5, 98–9, 123–5; Paul A. Rahe, *Republics, Ancient and Modern: Classical Republicanism and the American Revolution* (Chapel Hill, NC, 1992), 185–8 (on Key see 185). Southerners welcomed the pro-Sparta histories of John Gillies, William Mitford, and Oliver Goldmith, which denigrated Athenian democracy as an invitation to anarchy and tyranny. Mitford's antirepublicanism, however, irritated "Aristeus", "On Agriculture – As an Occupation," *Magnolia*, 3 (1841/42), 403. On British historiography see Frank M. Turner, *The Greek Heritage in Victorian Britain* (New Haven, CT, 1981), 189–97. For Machiavelli, Guicciardini, Rousseau, and Paine see Jennifer Tolbert Roberts, *Athens on Trial: The Antidemocratic Tradition in Western Thought* (Princeton, NJ, 1994), ch. 8. On Sparta's reputation generally see Elizabeth Rawson, *The Spartan Tradition in European Thought* (Oxford, U.K., 1991), Introduction and ch. 2, and Rahe, *Republics,* ix–x, 136–7. As pro-Athenian scholarship advanced, so did the dubious claim that Athenian slavery was milder than Spartan helotry and milder than slavery in other societies: Glenn R. Morrow, *Plato's Law of Slavery in Its Relation to Greek Law* (Urbana, IL, 1939), chs. 2 and 3, and pp. 68–9, and Roberts, *Athens on Trial,* 262, 365 n. 27. For Athenian slavery as mild and Spartan and Carthaginian harsh, see [William Drayton], *The South Vindicated from the Treason and Fanaticism of the Northern Abolitionists* (Philadelphia, 1836), 29–30. See also "Greek Writers" (*Xenophon*).

For praise of Spartan virtues see also Joseph B. Cobb, "Italian Literature," *QRMECS*, 9 (1855), 577; E. T. Winkler, *An Address Delivered before the Philosophian and Adelphian Societies of Furman University* (Greenville, SC, 1853), 10; Winkler, *The Citizen Soldier* (Charleston, SC, 1858), 7; Rufas H. Barrier to Mathias Barrier, Jan. 19, 1865, in Beverley Barrier Troxler and Billy Dawn Barrier Auciello, eds., *"Dear Father": Confederate Letters Never Before Published* (n.p., 1989), 43. Citizens of Spartanburg, South Carolina, were referred to, positively, as "Spartans": Clemmentina G. Legge to Harriet R. Palmer, Nov. 15, 1860, in Louis P. Towles, ed., *A World Turned Upside Down: The Palmers of South Santee, 1818–1881* (Columbia, SC, 1996), 271. Charles Campbell wrote that the Indians "submitted with Spartan fortitude to cruel tortures imposed by their idolatry": *History of the Colony and Ancient Dominion of Virginia* (Philadelphia, 1860), 89. But William Vans Murray followed Montesquieu, protesting that Sparta's egalitarian military discipline produced social and economic backwardness: *Political Sketches Inscribed to His Exellency John Adams* (London, 1787), 39–41. We here bypass the controversy over the existence of Lycurgus or the confusion of two separate figures. Southerners assumed his existence and credited him with the laws attributed to him. Thomas Roderick Dew mentioned the controversy in *Digest of the Laws, Customs, Manners, and Institutions of the Ancient and Modern Nations* (New York, 1884 [1852]), 72.

On Spartan education see also Rahe, *Republics,* 139, 155, and Paul Cartledge, *Spartan Reflections* (Berkeley, CA, 2001), 26, 84, 97; [Charles E. B. Flagg], "Condition of Women in Ancient Greece," *SQR,* 16 (1850), 328; Mason Locke Weems, *The Life of Washington. A New Edition with Primary Documents* (Amonk, NY, 1996 [1809]), 149; Joseph Henry Lumpkin, *An Address Delivered before the South-Carolina Institute at Its Second Annual Fair* (Charleston, SC, 1851), 31; also, *DBR,* 3 (1847), 355; Richard Yeadon, *An Address Delivered before the Euphemian and Philomethean Literary Societies of Erskine College, at the Annual Commencement, August 8th, 1855* (Due West, SC, 1855), 16. Plutarch led Southerners – and others – astray in his account of Spartan child raising and much else in what Cynthia B. Patterson calls "the fabled 'liberation' of Spartan women": *The Family in Greek History* (Cambridge, U.K., 1998), 73–9. For controversies about the condition of women in Sparta see also Roger Just, "Freedom, Slavery and the Female Psyche," in P. A. Cartledge and F. D. Harvey, eds., *Crux: Essays in Greek History Presented to F. F. M. de St. Croix on His 75th Birthday* (London, 1985), 170–1, 180–2; Ellen Millender, "The Athenian Ideology and the Empowered Spartan Woman," in Stephen Hodkinson and Anton Powell, eds., *Sparta: New Perspectives* (London, 1999), 328; Cartledge, *Spartan Reflections,* ch. 9, esp. 110.

Spirit of Christianity: Gerrit Smith of New York spoke for much of the abolitionist movement when he proclaimed, "The whole genius and spirit of Christianity are opposed to slavery": *Letter of Gerrit Smith to Rev. James Smylie of the State of Mississippi* (New York, 1837), 29. George Frederick Holmes and Daniel Whitaker denied that slavery violated the spirit of Christianity, reiterating that the Spirit cannot contradict the Word and the Law, and added that enslavement of blacks arose from different racial capacities. See [G. F. Holmes], "Some Observations on a Passage from Aristotle," *SLM,* 16 (1850), 197; [D. K. Whitaker], "Channing's Duty of the Free States," *SQR,* 2 (1842), 147–8. George Cheever conceded, "If the letter of Christianity is not against slavery, then its spirit is not": *The Guilt of Slavery and the Crime of Slaveholding, Demonstrated from the Hebrew and Greek Scriptures* (New York, 1969 [1860]), 466. Thomas Roderick Dew and John Reuben Thompson did acknowledge that slavery contradicted the spirit of Christianity, but they described all such social arrangements as consequences of man's sinful nature. See "Professor Dew on Slavery," in *The Pro-Slavery Argument, as Maintained by the Most Distinguished Writers of the Southern States* (Philadelphia, 1853), 451; [J. R. Thompson], *SLM,* 14 (1848), 700–2. During the War, the *Times* of London (Jan. 6, 1863) expressed this view as well as any slaveholder had: "Slavery is indeed contrary to the spirit of the New Testament, but so also are sumptuous fare, purple and fine linen, wealth, ecclesiastical titles, unmarried clergy, good clerical income and many other things": in Belle Becker Sideman and Lillian Freidman, eds., *Europe Looks at the Civil War: An Anthology* (New York, 1960), 207; also, [Patrick H. Mell], *Slavery. A Treatise Showing that Slavery Is Neither a Moral, Political, nor Social Evil* (Pennfield, GA, 1844), 16; Larry Tise, *Proslavery: A History of the Defense of Slavery in America, 1701–1840* (Athens, GA, 1988), 317–18. Augustine linked "famine, war, disease, captivity, or the inconceivable horrors of slavery": Saint Augustine, *The City of God,* tr. Marcus Dods (New York, 1950), Bk. 19:8.

Spirituality of the Church: Preston Graham argues that the movement for depoliticization of the Church – for its "Spirituality" – had roots in Scotland, manifested itself in America as early as the Revolutionary era, and subsequently had its greatest strength in the Border States. The doctrine of the Spirituality of the Church may be considered southern but it had northern supporters, including the prominent Reverend Henry J. Van Dyke of New York. See Preston Graham, Jr., *A Kingdom Not of This World: Stuart Robinson's Struggle to Distinguish the Sacred from the Secular during the Civil War* (Macon, GA, 2002), on the Scots, 7,

27, 170, and esp. ch. 4, and on northern supporters see 129 n. 110. Stuart Robinson, professor of theology at Danville Seminary in Kentucky, deserves much credit for the spirituality doctrine: see D. G. Hart, "The Spirituality of the Church, the Westminster Standards, and Nineteenth-Century American Presbyterianism," in John H. Leith, ed. "Westminster Confession in Current Thought," *Calvinist Studies*, 8 (1996), 113. But Robinson and T. E. Peck acknowledged Thornwell's influence – see Graham, *Kingdom Not of This World*, 28, and for texts see the Appendices: "Our Ideas" (1855), 193–9, and "Two Theories" (1862), 223–30. For Robinson's texts see also his *The Church of God as an Essential Element of the Gospels* (Philadelphia, 1858) and *Discourses of Redemption* (New York, 1866). For another critique of the view of Spirituality of the Church as primarily a political adjustment or "protective gesture" in the slavery controversy, see Sean Michael Lucas, " 'Hold Fast that Which Is Good': The Public Theology of Robert Lewis Dabney" (Ph.D. diss., Westminster Theological Seminary, 2002), 99–101.

A quarrel over the role of the presiding elders also wracked the Old School and pitted Thornwell, R. J. Breckenridge, and most Southerners against Hodge and most Northerners: *TSW*, 6:381–419; G. R. Brackett, "Christian Warrior Crowned," *TSW*, 10:773. Episcopalian Bishop Christopher Edwards Gadsden of South Carolina held to a doctrine similar to that of Hodge and Smyth: Gadsden, *The Times, Ecclesiastically Considered* (Charleston, SC, 1861), 25. During the War, the unionist *Danville Quarterly Review* of Kentucky described Spirituality of the Church as a "monstrosity" and Thornwell as its "father": "Slavery in the Church Courts," *DQR*, 4 (1864), 520, also 526. For the Spirituality doctrine among Methodists and Baptists see Beth Barton Schweiger, *The Gospel Working Up: Progress and the Pulpit in Nineteenth-Century Virginia* (New York, 2000), 89–95. Ironically, Hodge invoked a version in an attempt to block the Spring Resolutions, which in effect read the Southerners out of the church: see Hart, "Spirituality of the Church," 109–110; also, Ernest Trice Thompson, *The Spirituality of the Church: A Distinctive Doctrine of the Presbyterian Church in the United States* (Richmond, VA, 1961).

Tasso: *Southern Literary Messenger* welcomed an 1854 translation of Tasso's *Jerusalem Delivered*: *SLM*, 20 (1854), 445. Tasso and Ariosto were available – in Italian as well as English – in Richmond bookstores. Admirers included Francis Walker Gilmer, *Sketches, Essays and Translations* (Baltimore, 1828), 46. The Methodist *QRMECS* published articles that referred to "Ludovico Ariosto, the prince-poet of chivalry" and declared Ariosto and Tasso sixteenth-century Italy's great literary figures: Joseph B. Cobb, "Italian Literature," *QRMECS*, 9 (1855), 567; "R. C. P.", "The Relation of Christianity to Literature," *QRMECS*, 1 (1847), 183. See also Richard Beale Davis, *Intellectual Life in Jefferson's Virginia, 1790–1830* (Chapel Hill, NC, 1964), 86, 102; H. J. Groesbeck; "National Ballads," *SLM*, 15 (1849), 13; "Classical Learning," *SLM*, 34 (1862), 370 (Michelangelo); "T. W. M.", "Les Miserables," *SLM*, 35 (1863), 438 (sublimities); G. P. R. James, *The History of Chivalry* (New York, 1833), 90, 99–100; Henry Lee, *The Life of Napoleon Bonaparte, Down to the Peace of Tolentino and the Close of His First Campaign in Italy* (London, 1837), 12; "Mutual Influence of National Literatures," *SQR*, 12 (1847), 317. William J. Rivers spoke glowingly and at length on Tasso in an address to the student societies at South Carolina College: "Connection of Epic Poetry with the History and Times in Which They Were Written," in *Addresses and Other Occasional Pieces* (Baltimore, 1893), 1–2, 7, 20–2. Tasso's admirers included Isaac Harby, Hugh Legaré, Richard Furman, Augusta Jane Evans, A. B. Meek, Washington Allston, and the Reverend Albert A. Muller of Alabama, who began his prize-winning poem "Sunset and Rome" with a quotation from Tasso in Italian: see William R. Smith, *Reminiscences of a Long Life; Historical, Political, Personal and Literary*, 2 vols. (Washington, DC, 1889), 162.

Richard Henry Wilde, author of the immensely popular "My Life Is Like a Summer Rose," acquired a reputation in Europe and New York as a scholar of Tasso and Dante both, and his *Conjectures and Researches Concerning the Love, Madness, and Imprisonment of Torquato Tasso,* 2 vols. (New York, 1842), contains Wilde's extensive translations of Tasso's letters and documents. On Wilde see Charles C. Jones, Jr., and Salem Dutcher, *Memorial History of Augusta* (Syracuse, NY, 1890), 237. A. B. Meek, "The Death of Richard Henry Wilde," in *Songs and Poems of the South,* 4th ed. (Montgomery, AL, 1914 [1855]), 107, also, Meek, *Americanism in Literature: An Oration before the Phi Kappa and Demosthenian Societies of the University of Georgia* (Tuscaloosa, AL, 1844), 7–8; H. J. Groesbeck, "American Social Elevation," *SLM,* 2 (1836), 384. Washington Allston read Tasso while a youth in South Carolina, and *Jerusalem Delivered* influenced his painting as well as his writing: Nathalia Wright, ed., *The Correspondence of Washington Allston* (Lexington, KY, 1993), 25–6, 48, 240, 321–2 n. 3, 612. For "the genius of Tasso, the Christian poet – par excellence," see, *SR,* 5 (1830), 65; for the "immortal works" of Camõens and Tasso see "Literature of Virginia," *SLM,* 4 (1838), 684–9. For poems on Tasso by southern women see Jane Taylor Lomax Worthington, "Tasso and Leonora," *SLM,* 5 (1839), 293, and Elizabeth Jessup Eames, "Tasso," *SLM,* 6 (1840), 468. Casual, familiar references to Tasso circulated among the lawyers of Norfolk in 1860: Hugh Blair Grigsby, *Discourse on the Life and Character of the Hon. Littleton Waller Tazewell* (Norfolk, VA, 1860), 25.

For Wilde's reputation in New York as a Tasso scholar see Evert A. Duyckinck and George L. Duyckinck, *Cyclopaedia of American Literature,* 2 vols. (New York, 1856), 2:106–8. Wilde explored the problem of Tasso's imprisonment and defended him against allegations of madness: *Conjectures and Researches,* esp. 2:ch. 4; also, Edward L. Tucker, *Richard Henry Wilde: His Life and Selected Poems* (Athens, GA, 1996), esp. ch. 4. On Wilde as a Dante scholar see Theodore W. Koch, *Dante in America: A Historical and Bibliographical Study* (Boston, 1896), 23–36; Koch also discusses Simms, who knew Dante well and produced an able translation of the fifth Canto of *The Inferno* (24), and Philip Pendleton Cooke, who translated lines from *The Inferno* for his *Froissart and Other Poems* (85). Margaret Junkin contributed a poem, "Dante in Exile," to *SLM,* 16 (1850), 691. Octavia Le Vert read Italian and knew Dante well: Frances Gibson Satterfield, *Madame Le Vert: A Biography of Octavia Walton Le Vert* (Edisto Island, SC, 1987), viii.

Tasso and Ariosto were discussed in the pages of Charleston's *South Carolina Gazette* in the 1770s: Hennig Cohen, *The South Carolina Gazette, 1732–1775* (Columbia, SC, 1953), 113. In later years some Southerners may have been introduced to Tasso by Goethe's *Torquato Tasso,* which *Southern Literary Messenger* touted. In 1836 George Herbert Calvert declared it "a drama of the most exquisite grace and refinement," and a year later the editor, deeming it one of Goethe's finest works, published a long excerpt: George Herbert Calvert, "German Literature," *SLM,* 2 (1836), 380; "A Scene from Torquato Tasso," *SLM,* 3 (1837), 475–7.

It is tempting to speculate on the extent to which Southerners saw Tasso's era and the era he was writing about as precedents for their own experiences. Tasso set *Jerusalem Delivered* in the First Crusade, which ended in 1099, when Christian armies were recruited from every part of Western Europe. Tasso wrote late in the sixteenth century, when Christendom was rent by the Reformation and when, despite the great Christian victory at Lepanto, the Turks were overrunning the Balkans and menacing the heart of Europe. For an intriguing discussion of Tasso and the two eras see Bernard Knox, "Liberating a Masterpiece," *New York Review of Books* (May 17, 2001), 57–9.

Thackeray: Margaret Junkin Preston of Virginia admired Thackeray's portrayals of unsavory characters and his "merciless exhibition of the badness of human nature": Journal, Sept. 24,

1865, in Elizabeth Preston Allan, *The Life and Letters of Margaret Junkin Preston* (Boston, 1903), 204. Julia LeGrand of New Orleans declared *The Virginians* "a splendid page from colonial history." She explained her preference for Wilkie Collins's *No Name* over his *Woman in White*: "I care not for startling incidents, but only for the gradual development of social life and a good delineation of character." She considered Thackeray's works, especially *Vanity Fair,* "magnificent protests against the social life of England," and noted that Thackeray was "no favorite" in New Orleans. "He is not popular because he exposes too much about people, including his respectable readers": Feb. 26, 1863, in Kate Mason Rowland and Mrs. Morris S. Croxall, eds., *The Journal of Julia LeGrand: New Orleans, 1862–1863* (Richmond, VA, 1911), 153–4.

For Thackeray's lectures and poetry readings see also Virginia Clay-Clopton, *A Belle of the Fifties: Memoirs of Mrs. Clay of Alabama* (New York, 1905), 104. Savannah was proud of Thackeray's visit and claimed that he wrote *The Virginians* while a house guest there: Caroline Couper Lovell, *The Light of Other Days* (Macon, GA, 1995), 33. Sally Baxter Hampton knew Thackeray well from her days in New York and later from his visits to South Carolina. He seems to have been smitten with her and made her the model for Ethel Newcombe, the heroine of *Henry Esmond*: Ann Fripp Hampton, ed., *A Divided Heart: Letters of Sally Baxter Hampton, 1853–1862* (Spartanburg, SC, 1980), xii, and the correspondence between Thackeray and Sally Baxter Hampton in this volume. For the popularity of Thackeray's *Virginians* in Louisiana see Aug. 13, 1862, in James I. Robertson, ed., *A Confederate Girl's Diary: Sarah Morgan Dawson* (Westport, CT, 1960), 176. On the rage for *The Virginians* in Washington see Margaret Leech, *Reveille in Washington,* 2nd ed. (New York, 1991), 22; [J. R. Thompson], *SLM,* 19 (1853), 251. Then too, Thackeray came in for a good deal of criticism from the ladies along with much praise, for most did not take well to his portrayals of women. Lucy Breckenridge enjoyed *The Bertrams* as well as *Rebecca and Rowena* – "I enjoy his kind of wit so much, though he is very hard on women." Susan Archer Talley spoke for many in chiding him for creating an aura of unreality and therefore of an incapacity to interest his readers deeply. See Mar. 30, 1864, in Mary D. Robertson, ed., *Lucy Breckenridge of Grove Hill: The Journal of a Virginia Girl, 1826–1864* (Kent, OH, 1979), 174; also, Kate Carney Diary, May 30, 1861, at UNC-SHC.

Tories: Southern Tories, especially in South Carolina, feared slave uprisings or desertions if war came: Robert A. Olwell, " 'Domestick Enemies': Slavery and Independence in South Carolina, May 1775–March 1776," *JSH,* 55 (1989), 21–48. For the Clarks and Troups see Edward J. Harden, *The Life of George M. Troup* (Savannah, 1859), 397. The Mercers of Virginia also split between Whigs and Tories during the Revolution: Douglas R. Egerton, *Charles Fenton Mercer and the Trial of National Conservatism* (Jackson, MS, 1989), 6. The Natchez District of Mississippi had a large contingent of Tories, including many from the wealthiest and most respected families, which contributed sons to both sides. Dunbar Rowland, ed., *Mississippi: Comprising Sketches of Counties, Towns, Events, Institutions, and Persons, Arranged in Cyclopedic Form,* 4 vols. (Spartanburg, SC, 1976 [1907]), 2:307. The experience of New England was not much different. J. F. Jameson estimated that in Connecticut and Massachusetts probably more than half of the wealthy supported the British, and that subsequently the Federalists and Unitarians drew heavily on old Tories. See "The Origin of Political Parties in the United States," in Morey Rothberg and Jacqueline Goggin, eds., *John Franklin Jameson and the Development of Humanistic Scholarship in America,* vol. 1, *Selected Essays* (Athens, GA, 1993), 53–7.

With a softening of the attitude toward Tories went a softening toward the Federalists. John Belton O'Neall, a revered jurist, considered both to be generally good men worthy of respect: *Biographical Sketches of the Bench and Bar of South Carolina,* 2 vols. (Charleston, SC, 1859), passim but e.g. 1:244. For a call for fairness to the Tories see [E. Kennedy], "Scenes and Incidents in the Old Dominion," *SLM,* 18 (1852), 278–85. For a complaint about the expressions of sympathy for the Patriots see [George Atkinson], "Civil Warfare in the Carolinas and Georgia," *SLM,* 12 (1846), 261–2, 332. For extended attacks on Lorenzo Sabine and other northern writers see "South-Carolina in the Revolution," *SQR,* 14 (1848), 37–77, 261–337. Sabine's *Biographical Sketches of Loyalists of the American Revolution* (1847) especially denigrated South Carolina. Sabine, a Maine politician, clearly aimed to discredit Calhoun and the nullifiers: see David B. Van Tassel, *Recording America's Past: An Interpretation of the Development of Historical Studies in America, 1607–1884* (Chicago, 1960), 135. The British reestablished their power in Georgia as nowhere else, and Georgia had a higher percentage of Tories than any other colony. For Tory self-justifications see Charlene Johnson Kozy, "Tories Transplanted: The Caribbean Exile and Plantation Settlement of Southern Patriots," *JSH,* 75 (1991), 18–42; Robert S. Davis, ed., "A Georgia Patriot's Perspective on the American Revolution: The Letters of Dr. Thomas Taylor," *Georgia Historical Review,* 81 (1997), 118–38. For continued hostility to Tories but also for its warnings see Margaret E. Horsnell, *Spencer Roane: Judicial Advocate of Jeffersonian Principles* (New York, 1986), 14–15.

Zubly achieved exceptional popularity, as he preached to French and German immigrants in their own languages: George Howe, *History of the Presbyterian Church in South Carolina,* 2 vols. (Columbia, SC, 1870, 1873), 2:152–3. For Zubly's text see Randall M. Miller, ed., *"A Warm and Zealous Spirit": John J. Zubly and the American Revolution, A Selection of His Writings* (Macon, GA, 1982), esp. Editor's Introduction; also, Jim Schmidt, "The Reverend John Joachim Zubly's 'The Law of Liberty' Sermon: Calvinist Opposition to the American Revolution," *Georgia Historical Quarterly,* 82 (1990), 348–68. On Zubly's preaching and charitable work see Edward J. Cashin, *Beloved Bethesda: A History of George Whitefield's Home for Boys, 1749–2000* (Macon, GA, 2000), 57, 96.

Translations: For availability and reading of translations of Greek and Latin works, see Louis B. Wright, *The Cultural Life of the American Colonies, 1607–1763* (New York, 1957), 131; Joe W. Kraus, "Private Libraries in Colonial America," *Journal of Library History,* 9 (1974), 32; William S. Simpson, Jr., "A Comparison of the Libraries of Seven Colonial Virginians, 1754–1789," *Journal of Library History,* 9 (1974), 55, 57, 61; George K. Smart, "Private Libraries in Colonial Virginia," *American Literature,* 10 (1938), 32, 37–9; Louis B. Wright, "The 'Gentleman's Library' in Early Virginia: The Literary Interests of the First Carters," *Huntington Library Quarterly,* 1 (1937/38), 26; Edgar Legare Pennington, "The Beginnings of the Library in Charles Town, South Carolina," *Proceedings of the American Antiquarian Society,* n.s., 44 (1934), 163; James Raven, *London Booksellers and American Customers: Transatlantic Literary Community and the Charleston Library Society, 1748–1811* (Columbia, SC, 2002), 106, 189. For books in Greek and Latin and translations in Virginia private libraries, see e.g. Louis B. Wright, "Richard Lee II, a Belated Elizabethan in Virginia," *Huntington Library Quarterly,* 2 (1938), 11.

Trinitarianism: Anti-Trinitarians generally appeal to the spirit of early Christian communities against supposed deformations introduced by "elitist" Greek philosophy and Hellenism. Yet, arguably, the intellectuals most removed from popular sentiments were those who rejected Trinitarianism on patently Hellenistic grounds, while the victorious Trinitarians appealed to the faith of the common people as a sign of the presence of the Holy Spirit – baptizing in the name of the Father, the Son, and the Holy Ghost. "The doctrine of the Trinity," Jaroslav Pelikan writes, "was not as such a teaching of the New Testament, but it emerged from the life and worship, the reflection and controversy, of the church as, in the judgment of Christian orthodoxy, the only way the church could be faithful to the teaching of the New Testament." As John Henry Newman put it, the victory of Trinitarianism consti- tuted the victory of the faithful's orthodoxy over the speculations of the theologians. At the Council of Nicea (325 A.D.) the Church decreed as dogma that which had become embodied in church tradition in the wake of vigorous debates among the common people, not merely the elite. From the Arians to the Unitarians, those who have rejected the Trinity have resisted doctrinal appeals to tradition. We write "arguably" because, while the strength of the Trini- tarians and Arians among the common people remains a subject of controversy, the evidence favors the claims of the Trinitarians: see Philip Schaff, *History of the Christian Church,* 5th ed., rev., 8 vols. (Grand Rapids, MI, 1944), 3:618–98; Charles Hodge, *Systematic Theology,* 3 vols. (Grand Rapids, MI, 1993 [1871]), 1:343; also, Edward Gibbon, *The History of the De- cline and Fall of the Roman Empire,* ed. David Womersley, 3 vols. (London, 1994), 1:ch. 25.

Some latter-day left-wing theologians, striving to save the Trinity from Socinian liberals, have discovered "the total mutuality that characterizes the immanent Trinity as a relationship of Father, Son, and Holy Spirit" and have attributed this startling insight to postmodernism. Thus, to be a person means to be in a relationship. Yet Augustine projected human beings as created in the image of all persons of the Trinity, with Father, Son, and Holy Spirit mutually dependent and bound by the communal bond of mutual love. Augustine began his discourse on the Trinity with the assumption of man made in the image of the triune God of Revela- tion, not in the image of the God of natural religion. He therefore proceeded to discover a Trinitarian analogue in all features of man's mental constitution: Love, unlike knowledge, is not a product of the mind; the mind with knowledge and love of itself is the image of the Trin- ity. "These three things," writes Ted Peters, "are marvelously inseparable from each other, and yet each of them is severally a substance, and all together are one substance or essence, whilst they are mutually predicated relatively": Ted Peters, *God as Trinity: Relationality and Temporality in Divine Life* (Louisville, KY, 1993), 180, quote at 15. Karl Barth took "neo- orthodoxy" in a theologically responsible if politically radical left-wing direction, objecting to the word "persons" because of the common tendency to misunderstand it as analogous to the bourgeois concept of human individuality. Other radicals have nonetheless embraced the Left–Hegelian politicization of the Trinitarian dogma. See Augustine, "On the Trinity," in Philip Schaff, ed., *Post-Nicene Fathers,* 14 vols. (Peabody, MA, 1995), esp. 3:Bk. 9 and p. 129; for Barth on "persons" as a bourgeois construct see Jaroslav Pelikan, *The Christian Tradition: A History of the Development of Doctrine,* 5 vols. (Chicago, 1989), 5:204; Moltmann quoted by Peters, *God as Trinity,* 39, and 39–42 for Peters's critique. Probably, few Southerners read Augustine's "Trinity," but many knew the summary in his *Confessions,* tr. Henry Chadwick (New York, 1991), 279–80. For Augustine on relationality of the Trinity see Jaroslav Pelikan, *The Mystery of Continuity: Time and History, Memory and Eternity in the Thought of Saint Augustine* (Charlottesville, VA, 1986), ch. 4, esp. 60. For the Trinity as mutual love see Au- gustine, "On the Trinity," in Schaff, ed., *Post-Nicene Fathers,* 3:Bk. 9, ch. 12, sec. 18.

The transformation of Jesus into a preacher of ethics, with its implicit and explicit repu- diation of the Trinity, appeared forcefully in the radical left wing of the Reformation and in the revival of Stoic influence during the Renaissance. See Henning Graf Reventlow, *The Au- thority of the Bible and the Rise of the Modern World* (Philadelphia, 1984), pt. 1, ch. 3. On the vigorous debates in ancient times among the common people over the Trinity and other theological questions, see esp. Christopher Dawson, *The Making of Europe: An Introduc- tion to the History of European Unity* (New York, 1956), 63, 108–9. Thornwell argued for his own time: The people feel the doctrine in their hearts and from their own experience, even when they cannot grasp it intellectually. "The Personality of the Holy Ghost," *JHTW,* 2:343.

Delio Cantimori has demonstrated the anti-Trinitarian tendencies in the radical movements of the Reformation: *Per la storia degli Eretici Italiani nel seculo XVI in Europa* (1937) and *Eretici Italiani del Cinquecento* (1943); Christopher Hill emphasized the anti-Trinitarianism of Gerrard Winstanley, the Digger: *The World Turned Upside Down: Radical Ideas during the English Revolution* (London, 1975); see also M. H. Abrams, *Natural Supernaturalism: Tradition and Revolution in Romantic Literature* (New York, 1971), 51–7.

Medieval theology understood persona as faces (countenances) of God. Not until the nineteenth century did persona come to mean "person" in a more literal sense. Paul Tillich, *A History of Christian Thought, from Its Judaic and Hellenistic Origins to Existentialism*, ed. Carl E. Braaten (New York, 1972), 190. For a defense of the concept "personality" against the substitution of "modes" and other concepts see Michael O'Carroll, *Trinitas: A Theological Encyclopedia of the Holy Trinity* (Collegeville, MN, 1987), 179–81; also, Hans Urs von Balthasar, *My Work: In Retrospect* (San Francisco, 1993), 118. Jaroslav Pelikan credits Karl Barth with having rescued the Trinity from the obscurity into which it had fallen since Schleiermacher: see Pelikan, *The Melody of Theology: A Philosophical Dictionary* (Cambridge, MA, 1988), 259.

Turretin: Francis Turretin, *Institutes of Elenctic Theology*, tr. George Musgrave Geiger, ed. James T. Dennison, Jr., 3 vols. (Phillipsburg, NJ, 1992–97), 3:503, served as a text in reformed circles: Glenn T. Miller, *Piety and Intellect: The Aims and Purposes of Ante-Bellum Theological Education* (Atlanta, GA, 1990), 111. Like Thornwell, Dabney long assigned the Latin text of *Elenctic Theology*, among other works, to his theology students: "A Thoroughly Educated Ministry" (1883), in *DD*, 2:656–77, also 3:52; Morton Smith, *Studies in Southern Presbyterian Theology* (Phillipsburg, NJ, 1962), 190. Southern theology students at Princeton carried Turretin back south as a textbook for the schools at which they taught. See James T. Dennison, Jr., "The Twilight of Scholasticism: Francis Turretin at the Dawn of the Enlightenment," in Carl R. Trueman and R. Scott Clark, eds., *Protestant Scholasticism: Essays in Reassessment* (Carlisle, U.K., 1999), 244–55; Smith, *Southern Presbyterian Theology*, 69, 70, 184, 190; also, John Miller to Sally McDowell, Aug. 24, 1856, in Thomas E. Buckley, ed., *"If You Love That Lady Don't Marry Her": The Courtship Letters of Sally McDowell and John Miller, 1854–56* (Columbia, MO, 2000), 736–7. Dabney structured his *Systematic Theology* in accordance with Turretin: see Sean Michael Lucas, *Robert Lewis Dabney: A Southern Presbyterian Life* (Phillipsburg, NJ, 2005), 86–8. *Elenctic Theology* distinguished between that which is incomprehensible because "far surpassing the comprehension of reason" and that which is incomprehensible because "opposed to reason." Jack B. Rogers and Donald K. McKim deny that Turretin followed Calvin properly and insist that Hodge and others who taught him made nineteenth-century American Calvinism unnecessarily rigid: *The Authority and Interpretation of the Bible: An Historical Approach* (San Francisco, 1979), esp. ch. 2.

Unitarianism: As a matter of principle Unitarians protested intolerance and harshness in polemics between Protestants and Catholics and between Protestant denominations. Protestants and Catholics alike questioned whether Unitarians had a right to speak as Christians. As a beleaguered minority, Unitarians – like Jews and Catholics – also had a vested interest in maximum toleration; see e.g. Charles Manson Taggart, *Sermons. With a Memoir by John H. Haywood* (Boston, 1856), 334–6. On Jefferson, Ruffin, and Unitarianism see George Tucker, *The Life of Thomas Jefferson*, 2 vols. (London, 1837), 2:563; Sept. 29, 1859, in *ERD*, 1:344. Thornton Stringfellow, "Statistical View of Slavery," in E. N. Elliott, ed., *Cotton Is King, and Pro-Slavery Arguments* (New York, 1969 [1860]), 527–8; R. Carlyle Buley, *The*

Old Northwest: Pioneer Period, 1815–1840, 2 vols. (Bloomington, IN, 1950), 2:486; _DNCB,_ 2:267, 270; for St. Louis see Edward King, _The Great South: A Record of Journeys,_ 2 vols. (New York, 1969 [1875]), 229; Charles C. Jones, Jr., and Salem Dutcher, _Memorial History of Augusta_ (Syracuse, NY, 1890), 385. Although the Unitarians' well-financed church in Mobile waned, the influence of Unitarian ideas remained a problem. See Harriet Elizabeth Amos, "Social Life in an Antebellum Cotton Port: Mobile, Alabama, 1820–1860" (Ph.D. diss., University of Alabama, 1976), 226, 243–4. Frederick A. Ross provoked Methodists and Baptists by lumping them with Unitarians and Universalists as propagators of false doctrine: _Slavery Ordained of God_ (Philadelphia, 1857), 59. The Unitarians did not formally organize as a church until 1825, but they had long controlled particular Congregational churches. The Unitarian Reverend Abiel Abbot of New England, first president of Bowdoin College, made two long trips to Charleston for his health before 1830 and was well received by Benjamin Morgan Palmer and other Calvinists: John Hammond Moore, ed., "The Abiel Abbot Journals: A Yankee Preaches in Charleston Society, 1818–1827," _South Carolina Historical Magazine,_ 68 (1967), 51–5, 70.

Boston emerged as the foremost center of Unitarianism. By 1833 the Unitarians held almost a hundred Congregational churches in and around Boston. The wisecrack: Unitarianism is limited to the fatherhood of God, the brotherhood of man, and the neighborhood of Boston: Sydney E. Ahlstrom, "Scottish Philosophy and American Theology," _Church History,_ 24 (1855), 263. For the Spread of Unitarian ideas in New England well beyond the Unitarian church see Joseph Haroutunian, _Piety versus Moralism: The Passing of the New England Theology_ (New York, 1932), ch. 8. Haroutunian observes that American liberalism was a humanitarian, not a theological movement: "Boston was liberal before it became Unitarian, and its Unitarianism was primarily ethical and social" (179–80). On the social and political conservatism of the religiously liberal elite in New England see Harlow W. Sheidley, _Sectional Nationalism: Massachusetts Conservative Leaders and the Transformation of America, 1815–1836_ (Boston, 1988), esp. 92–4.

The Unitarians had only three churches in South, but at the beginning of the nineteenth century they posed a problem for Baptist churches in the Southwest, some of which resorted to expulsions. Later, southern churches feared contagion since the Whigs across the river in Ohio had a reputation for Unitarian sympathies: see [Rev.] John Taylor, _Baptists on the American Frontier: A History of Ten Baptist Churches of Which the Author Has Been Alternately a Member,_ ed. Chester Raymond Young, 3rd ed. (Macon, GA, 1995), 62; David Brown, "The Political Culture of the Whig Party in Ohio" (Ph.D. diss., University of Toledo, 1995), 36, 59–60; Clement Eaton, _The Freedom-of-Thought Struggle in the Old South_ (New York, 1964), 316. For continuing Methodist difficulties with Unitarianism see William Hamilton Nelson, _A Burning Torch and a Flaming Fire: The Story of Centenary College of Louisiana_ (Nashville, TN, 1931), 136–7.

For southern critiques of Unitarianism see [Thomas Curtis], "John the Baptist, the Unitarian Jesus," _SPR,_ 2 (1848), 250–300. Also, Mary E. Moragné Journal, Feb. 23, 1838, in Delle Mullen Craven, ed., _The Neglected Thread: A Journal of the Calhoun Community_ (Columbia, SC, 1951), 68; _DNCB,_ 5:14. In 1846, "W." reviewed Mrs. S. B. Dana's "Letters to Relatives and Friends" for _Southern Quarterly Review_ and suggested that it portended a revival of a declining Unitarianism: [D. K. Whitaker?], "Mrs. Dana's Letters," _SQR,_ 11 (1847), 168–98. Theodore Clapp remained optimistic, boasting in 1849 that fifty years before a corporal's guard adhered to Unitarian doctrines, but now some 4,000 churches throughout the United States in five separate denominations did so. Clapp devoted much of his energy in the pulpit to refutations of misrepresentations of Unitarianism: see e.g. "Sermons," New Orleans _Daily Picayune,_ Mar. 28 and May 13, 1849.

Universal Histories: Other attempts at universal or comparative history received mixed receptions in the South. Charles Campbell considered Sir Walter Raleigh's *A Historie of the World* a great work, and it circulated in the South both in abridged and complete versions during the eighteenth century. But we find almost no comment on it: Campbell, *History of the Colony and Ancient Dominion of Virginia* (Philadelphia, 1860), 135; Richard Beale Davis, *Intellectual Life in the Colonial South, 1515–1763*, 3 vols. (Knoxville, TN, 1978), 2:511, 537, 547, 577. *Southern Review* noted Raleigh's *History of the World* but only for illustrative purposes: *SR*, 3 (1829), 2–26. Walter Edgar found copies of Raleigh's *Historie* in six private libraries in South Carolina: "Some Popular Books in Colonial South Carolina," *South Carolina Historical Magazine*, 72 (1971), 178. Edmund Randolph, in a history of Virginia he left in manuscript, defended Raleigh and his historical work against charges of Deism – but then, he himself took Voltaire and Hume for models: see Edmund Randolph, *History of Virginia*, ed. Arthur H. Shaffer (Charlottesville, VA, 1970), xxix, 84–5. Howison devoted considerable space to Raleigh but did not mention *Historie* in his *A History of Virginia from Its Discovery and Settlement by Europeans to the Present Time*, 2 vols. (Philadelphia, 1846), 1:45–68.

Constantine François Volney, *The Ruins; Or, Meditations on the Revolutions of Empires,* attributed the loss of empires to natural religion and thereby became especially popular with Deists in early America: see Frank Luther Mott, *Golden Multitudes: The Story of Best Sellers in the United States* (New York, 1947), 63, 305. Eleanor Parke Custis, George Washington's adopted daughter, would have happily hanged Volney along with Talleyrand "without the smallest remorse": Eleanor Parke Custis to Elizabeth Bordley, July 1, 1798, in Patricia Brady, ed., *George Washington's Beautiful Nelly: The Letters of Eleanor Parke Custis Lewis to Elizabeth Bordley Gibson, 1794–1851* (Columbia, SC, 1991), 131. Howison acknowledged Volney's contributions to the introduction of world history and credited him with humane intentions, but saw his project as essentially an attack on Christianity: *History of Virginia*, 2:357. Benjamin M. Palmer lumped Volney with Voltaire as a historian concerned to denigrate Christianity: *Influence of Religious Belief upon National Character: An Oration Delivered before the Demosthean and Phi Beta Kappa Societies of the University of Georgia* (Athens, GA, 1845), 6. Volney doubtless irritated Southerners for another reason. He ascribed to black Africa the origins of civilization and followed Herodotus in viewing the Egyptians as black: David S. Weisen, "Herodotus and the Modern Debate over Race and Slavery," *Ancient World,* 3 (1980), 3–16. Although Michelet was well read in the South, his *Introduction a l'histoire universelle* attracted little attention. A reviewer for *Southern Literary Messenger* found it superficial and governed by an inadequate attempt to establish parallels between Western and Eastern civilizations: "Schediasmata Critica," *SLM*, 16 (1850), 353–4. Joseph Priestly's *A Comparison of the Institutions of Moses with Those of the Hindoos and Other Ancient Nations* had no discernible impact on the South, notwithstanding its defense of the superiority of Christianity and its criticism of Voltaire, Paine, and Volney.

Universalism: Universalism – the idea that all men will be saved – was promoted by Origen, spread during the fourth and fifth centuries, and passed into various Christian sects. Friedrich Schleiermacher, Karl Barth, Emil Brunner, and Hans Urs von Balthassar have considered universal salvation a possibility. For a brief informative survey see Richard J. Bauckman, "Universalism: A Historical Survey," *Themelios*, 4 (1979), 48–53. For a critique of modern attempts to make Christianity a doctrine of universal salvation see Jerry L. Walls, *Hell: The Logic of Damnation* (Notre Dame, IN, 1992), ch. 1.

For the penetration of Universalism even among the professed Calvinists of New England see Joseph Haroutunian, *Piety versus Moralism: The Passing of the New England Theology* (New York, 1932), ch. 6. For a southern Baptist's firm rejection of the association of

Calvinism with Universalism, see P. H. Mell, _Predestination and the Saints' Perseverance,_
Stated and Defended from the Objections of the Arminians (Charleston, SC, 1858 [1850]),
77–8. For a recent discussion of the Universalist tendency in Calvinism see Walls, _Hell,_ 80–1.

Voltaire: For examples of the favorable quoting and citing of Voltaire see "N.", "Review
of Professor Dew's Address," _SLM,_ 3 (1837), 134; "War: Its Causes and Horrors," _SLM,_ 7
(1841), 324. On book-burning see "P. K. W." [Whitney], "The South Defended," _Oakland_
College Magazine, 3 (Dec. 1857), 11; J. D. B. De Bow, _The Industrial Resources, Statistics,_
&c. of the United States and More Particularly of the Southern and Western States, 3rd ed., 3
vols. (New York, 1966 [1854]), 1:70, 332; Christopher Edwards Gadsden, _The Times, Morally_
Considered (Charleston, SC, 1843), 9, and for Gadsden see James H. Elliott, ed., _Tributes_
to the Memory of the Rev. C. P. Gadsden, with Thirteen of His Sermons (Charleston, SC,
1872), 5, 6, 17, 35; Ernest Trice Thompson, _Presbyterians in the South,_ 3 vols. (Richmond, VA,
1963), 1:494. In the 1840s, Judson College for young ladies in Alabama assigned Voltaire's
Charles XII.
    Without apologies, _Southern Literary Messenger,_ in its first issue (1834) under the editor-
ship of Edgar Allan Poe, offered Lucian Minor's translation, "Time, the Consoler: A Story
from Voltaire, Translated," _SLM,_ 1 (1834), 10–11. "T. C." embraced Voltaire as an accurate and reliable historian: "On Historical Authenticity and the Value of Human Testimony
as to Facts," _SLJ,_ 2 (1836), 183. A Virginian approved Voltaire's judgment of the superiority of Machiavelli's _Mandragola_ to anything written by Aristophanes: [Hugh R. Pleasants],
"Machiavelli – The Prince," _SLM,_ 12 (1846), 647. See also Elizabeth Barber Young, _A Study_
of the Curricula of Seven Selected Women's Colleges of the Southern States (New York,
1932), 25, and the unabashed praise for Voltaire from President William Carey Crane of Mississippi (women's) College in his _Literary Discourses_ (New York, 1853), 58, 86. For Voltaire's
good spirit see T. M. Garrett Diary, June 29, 1849, at UNC-SHC.

Wayland: The wide southern readership of Francis Wayland's _Elements of Moral Science_
(1835) was ruefully acknowledged by the Baptist Reverend Patrick Mell, who paid tribute
to Wayland while opposing his arguments: [Mell], _Slavery. A Treatise Showing that Slav-_
ery Is Neither a Moral, Political, nor Social Evil (Pennfield, GA, 1844), 25 n. The Presbyterian Reverend Thomas Smyth of Charleston acclaimed Wayland "a man of genius, as a
profound scholar, an able professor, an author of world-wide celebrity, and a Christian of
deep-toned piety and tender charity": _TSW,_ 9:475–91, quote at 491. The Baptist Reverend
John A. Broadus of Virginia described Wayland as "the most distinguished of all American educators": quoted in Robert B. Selph, _Southern Baptists and the Doctrine of Election_
(Harrisonburg, VA, 1992), 32. For the Methodists, the Reverends William A. Smith of Virginia
and R. H. Rivers devoted no small part of their respective books, _Philosophy and Practice of_
Slavery and _Elements of Moral Philosophy,_ to refutations of Wayland's _Moral Science_ – but
then, so did John Fletcher: _Studies on Slavery, in Easy Lessons_ (Natchez, MS, 1852).
    Having pleased the abolitionists, Wayland then displeased them with _Limitations of Hu-_
man Responsibility (1838), which urged moral suasion and denied the right of Northerners to
try to force their views upon the South. Wayland distinguished between two senses of "moral
evil": a transgression of the moral law of God; and the personal guilt of those who knowingly
transgress. In this way, the moderate Wayland separated himself from the abolitionists, who
conflated the two and thereby treated all slaveholders as wanton sinners. To be held responsible, masters must know that slavery is always a sin. Reviews of the Fuller–Wayland debate in
Southern Literary Messenger complimented both men on the calm way in which they worked
through an explosive question and thereby offered a model of Christian disputation: "Better

men could hardly have been selected." And note the name of the Reverend Dunaway Wayland Fuller, who wrote *Reminiscences of a Rebel* (New York, 1913). Alexander Campbell,
leader of the Disciples of Christ, expressing displeasure at the lack of civility in North and
South in the debate over slavery, commented, "Mssrs Wayland and Fuller are discussing this
matter with great calmness, kindness, and dignity." Alexander Campbell, who considered
slavery a regressive but not a sinful institution, devoted almost all of the space in an article on the slavery question to a quotation *in extenso* from Fuller's response to Wayland. See
[Campbell], "Our Position on American Slavery," Millennial Harbinger, 16 (1845), 146–9.
Even "Publicola" (of Madison County, MS), who saw Wayland as an ally of the radical abolitionists, did not question his intentions: "Domestic Slavery," *SLM*, 11 (1845), 513–28; see
also "Slavery as a Moral Relation," *SLM*, 17 (1851), 393–410; "Publicola", "The Present
Aspect of Abolitionism," *SLM*, 13 (1847), 432. The Reverend George Addison Baxter, president of Hampden-Sydney College in Virginia, treated Wayland gently in his lengthy rebuttal,
Essay on the Abolition of Slavery. Yet proslavery theologians, despite the effort to soften
the rhetoric and credit the sincerity of antislavery adversaries, could not easily avoid filing
a charge of evil intent against the abolitionists. See Robert Bruce Mullin, "Bible Critics and
the Battle over Slavery," *JPH*, 61 (1983), 221.

White and Abbott: James White displayed more affection for the French than did most Englishmen, and Southerners read his popular histories of France more readily than works by
weightier historians. See e.g. "L.", *SLM*, 29 (1859), 234–5; for excerpts from White's work
see *SLM*, 29 (1859), 220–7, 234–5. Simms liked John S. C. Abbott's pleasant biographies
of Madame Roland and Josephine, but he slammed Abbott for the gratuitous intrusion of
antislavery claptrap: [William Gilmore Simms], "Critical Notices," *SQR*, n.s., 3 (1851), 292,
and 5 (1852), 243–4. Abbott's 1860 travelogue had much more antislavery opinion than reportage, and despite protestations of evenhandedness it was often acerbic: *South and North;
Or, Impressions Received during a Trip to Cuba and the South* (New York, 1969 [1860]).
Southern Literary Messenger and other publications received Abbott's many works cheerfully as popularizations. The Prestons of Lexington, Virginia, had "a whole shelf of Abbott's
little red-volume histories," apparently largely for the children: Janet Allan Bryan, ed., *A
March Past: Reminiscences of Elizabeth Randolph Preston Allan* (Richmond, VA, 1938), 96.

Women and the Classics: Virginia's elite ladies read a good deal in the Greek and Roman
classics, mostly in translation: [Mary Virginia Hawes Terhune], *Marion Harland's Autobiography: The Story of a Life* (New York, 1910), 99; Anne Floyd Upshur and Ralph T. Whitelaw,
eds., "Library of the Rev. Thomas Teackle," *WMQ*, 2nd ser., 23 (1943), 298–308. The Baptists' Richmond Female Institute and Margaret Burwell's school for young ladies offered Latin
and Greek. In Georgia, the popular classical department at coeducational Newman Seminary
assigned Xenophon, Pliny, Virgil, Caesar, Cicero, and Livy, and the female Fletcher Institute
in Thomasville taught Plato, Sophocles, Sallust, Cicero's *Orations,* Virgil, Horace, and Juvenal. See Elbert W. G. Boogher, *Secondary Education in Georgia, 1732–1858* (Philadelphia,
1933), 188–9. For Greek at Abbeville Female Academy and Judson, see Elizabeth Barber
Young, *A Study of the Curricula of Seven Selected Women's Colleges of the Southern States*
(New York, 1932), 128; for Miss Mercer's Academy, see the advertisement in Southall and
Bowen Papers. For Latin at other female seminaries see Henry Thomas Shanks, ed., *The
Papers of Willie P. Mangum,* 5 vols. (Raleigh, NC, 1955–56), 5:153–4; Hennig Cohen, *A
Barhamville Miscellany: Notes and Documents Concerning the South Carolina Female Col-
legiate Institute, 1826–1865* (Columbia, SC, 1956), 37; *DHE,* 4:441–2 (Spartanburg Female
College); Henry Thompson Malone, *The Episcopal Church in Georgia, 1733–1957* (Atlanta,

GA, 1960), 71–3; "Andrew College Historical Papers and Events," Georgia Department of
Archives and History (Andrew Female College). In Mississippi, Latin was taught at Elizabeth
Female Academy (*DHE,* 5:393–4) and at Brandon College and Brandon Female Academy
(catalogue in Quitman Papers, at UNC-SHC); for Columbus Female Institute see Suzanne L.
Bunkers, *The Diary of Caroline Seabury, 1854–1863* (Madison, WI, 1991), 126 n. 11. Charles
L. Coon, ed., *North Carolina Schools and Academies: A Documentary History, 1790–1840*
(Raleigh, NC, 1915), 183–4; Samuel Bryant Turrentine, *A Romance of Education: A Narrative Including Recollections and Other Facts Connected with Greensboro College* (Greensboro, NC, 1946), 37. On ancient history in translation at coeducational academies see Coon,
ed., *North Carolina Schools,* 65–6, 96–8; also, R. D. Arnold to Ellen Arnold, Nov. 5, 1849,
in Richard H. Shryock, ed., *Letters of Richard D. Arnold, M.D., 1808–1876* (Durham, NC,
1929), 34; Keziah Brevard Diary, Dec. 9, 1860, at UNC-SHC; Arthur H. Shaffer, *To Be an
American: David Ramsay and the Making of the American Consciousness* (Columbia, SC,
1991), 208–9.

For women with Greek see W. D. Matter, "Cornelia Phillips Spencer," *EC,* 5:1518; Mary
Price Coulling, *Margaret Junkin Preston: A Biography* (Winston-Salem, NC, 1993), 10, 14,
62; also, Coulling, "The Well-Used Library of a Nineteenth Century Southern Litterateur,"
paper presented at the Third Southern Conference on Women's History" (Rice University),
June 1994; James I. Robertson, ed., *A Confederate Girl's Diary: Sarah Morgan Dawson*
(Westport, CT, 1960). In the early 1850s Rosalie Roos of Sweden found South Carolina's
women's schools, notably Limestone Springs Female High School, impressive in teaching
classics and liberal arts: Diary, Oct. 28, 1851, in Roos, *Travels in America, 1851–1855,* tr.
Carl L. Anderson (Carbondale, IL, 1982), 31–2, 36, 51. Christie Farnham, *The Education
of the Southern Belle: Higher Education and Student Socialization in the Antebellum South*
(New York, 1994), suggests that the South did better than the North in teaching girls Greek
and Latin. The matter remains in dispute: Caroline Winterer, *The Culture of Classicism: Ancient Greece and Rome in American Intellectual Life, 1780–1910* (Baltimore, 2002), 23–4.

Index

Abbey, R., 485

Abbott, Rev. Abiel, 692, 788

Abbott, John S. C., 102n30, 411n6, 520, 638, 742, 765, 791

Abelard, 306

Abernathy, Thomas Perkins, 771, 772

abolitionism and abolitionists: and anti-Catholicism, 758; and churches in South, 484–90, 721; on cruelty in treatment of slaves, 379–80, 381–2; and debates on Bible and slavery, 499–504, 507, 508–10, 512–21, 526–7, 540, 541, 545, 565, 720–1, 768, 779; and European revolutions of 1830s and 1840s, 43; Harper's Ferry and John Brown controversy, 636–46; intellectual freedom and suppression of, 229–40; and Kossuth on slavery, 58; and liberal theology in South, 590–1, 602, 609–10; and New England Puritans, 666; and peace movement, 163; and racism, 524; and religious literature, 438; and religious subjectivism, 535; southern response to rise of, 76; and spirit of Christianity, 781; theology and politics of slavery, 618, 742; and Wayland on slavery, 790; and women in southern politics, 391. *See also* antislavery societies; slavery

Abrams, M. H., 16n10, 539n24, 563n75, 787

Academy of Sciences (New Orleans), 186

Acton, Lord, 320

Adair, Douglass, 99n24

Adams, C. F., 103, 253n10

Adams, Gov. James H., 512

Adams, Rev. Jasper, 6, 107, 136, 162, 228, 230, 278, 282, 316, 568, 571, 620, 689n18, 719, 729, 757

Adams, John, 263

Adams, John Quincy, 236, 253, 391, 488, 579, 770

Adams, Nehemiah, 756

Adams, Samuel, 289

Adams–Onis treaty of 1819, 80

Addison, Joseph, 564, 719

Adet, Pierre, 14

Adger, Rev. John B., 22, 147, 206, 212, 228, 242, 358, 495, 498, 592

Affleck's Cotton Plantation Record and Account Book, 369

Africa: history of, 188; and responses of slaves to aristocracy in South, 117; and traditional religions, 562n73

Agassiz, Louis, 597

Age of Reason (Paine), 410

Agnew, Rev. Samuel, 414, 426–7, 452, 453, 465, 466

agnosticism, and debates on Protestant Christianity in North and South, 444, 530, 557

agrarianism, and classical history, 296–7

agriculture, Roman writing on, 280. *See also* pastoralism; rural life

Aiken, David Wyatt, 469

Alabama: local and regional histories of, 183; and state historical societies, 185

Alabama Baptist, 525, 612n49

Alabama Historical Society, 185

Albert, Dr. W., 278

Albertus Magnus, 325

Alexander, Archibald, 566

Alexander, Gen. Edward Porter, 112

Alexander, Sarah, 423

Alfriend, Frank H., 665n32, 682

Algeria, French conquest of, 217

Alien and Sedition Acts, 15

Alison, Sir Archibald, 19–20

Allen, Ethan, 410

Allen, John, 610

Allen, Ujanirtus, 57, 212, 278, 350